# JIM MURRAY'S
# WHISKEY BIBLE
# 2020

This 2020 edition is dedicated to
the memory of
**Neelakanta Rao Jagdale**

This edition first published 2019 by Dram Good Books Ltd

10 9 8 7 6 5 4 3 2 1

The "Jim Murray's" logo and the "Whiskey Bible" logo are trade marks of Jim Murray.

Text, tasting notes & rankings, artwork, Jim Murray's logo and the Whiskey Bible logo copyright © Jim Murray 2019

Design copyright © Dram Good Books Ltd 2019

For information regarding using tasting notes from Jim Murray's Whiskey Bible contact: Dram Good Books Ltd, Unit 2, Barnstones Business Park, Litchborough, U.K., NN12 8JJ Tel: 44 (0)117 317 9777. Or contact us via www.whiskybible.com

A CIP catalogue record for this book is available from the British Library

ISBN: 978-0-9932986-5-3

Printed in Belgium by Graphius Group.

Written by: Jim Murray
Edited by: Peter Mayne and David Rankin
Design: Jim Murray, Vincent Flint-Hill and James Murray
Maps: James Murray, Rob-indesign and Vincent Flint-Hill
Production: Vincent Flint-Hill
Chief Researcher: Vincent Flint-Hill
Eggs on Burnt Toast: Jane Garnett
Sample Research: Vincent Flint-Hill, Ally Telfer, Julia Nourney, Kelly May
Sales: info@whiskybible.com
European Dictionary: Julie Nourney, Tom Wyss, Mariette Duhr-Merges, Stefan Baumgart, Erik Molenaar, Jürgen Vromans, Henric Molin and Kalle Valkonen.

Author's Note
I have used the spelling "whiskey" or "whisky" depending on how the individual distillers prefer. All Scotch is "whisky". So is Canadian. All Irish, these days, is "whiskey", though that was not always the case. In Kentucky, bourbon and rye are spelt "whiskey", with the exception of the produce of the early Times/Old Forester Distillery and Maker's Mark which they bottle as "whisky". In Tennessee, it is a 50-50 split: Dickel is "whisky", while Daniel's is "whiskey".

# JIM MURRAY'S
# **WHISKEY**
# **B I B L E**
## 2020

DRAM GOOD BOOKS

# Contents

# Introduction

**W**hen you celebrate tasting your 20,000th whisky for one book – as I did a couple of weeks ago while writing this fittingly 2020 and latest edition of Jim Murray's Whisky Bible – you take time afterwards to reflect.

For the last 16 years, painstakingly updated edition after updated edition, this book has proudly introduced its readers to a whole new world of whisky. And with the whiskies often come a back story. Though few, I admit, quite as remarkable as the one I am to tell you now.

I think we all know the tale of the ugly duckling. And in Kentucky, in terms of distilleries they came no uglier than the Barton Distillery, Bardstown.

For years, not only was it ugly but in terms of its relationship with its drinkers...well, it was pretty unfriendly, too.

It didn't want to know about distillery tours. Their job was to make whiskey. End of. And none of your fine, late night bourbons: theirs was designed for the lower end of the market place. Even the whisky museum it once housed was moved off the premises and into town, not least do pesky people didn't come snooping around.

Not for them the telling of tales of how bourbon making began in 1879 with the Tom Moore Distillery, before being taken over by Oscar Getz of the eponymous museum fame. Covering 200 acres just off downtown Bardstown, in effect it represents its own division within the city. It didn't pretend to be a beautiful old distillery operating in stunning Kentucky countryside beside a fast running stream where golden orioles would glide among the trees and blue herons statuesquely fish if the snapping turtles let them.

No, this, when I first visited the place over 25 years ago, was a no-nonsense liquor factory operating in early post 2nd World War utilitarian architecture, the blueprints of which contained not a single line of romance, nor a contour to assuage the soul. It was an unapologetically stark whiskey factory.

Some of the whisky then, like its Colonel Lee brand, was a mirror image of the building itself being actually quite unpleasant: young, raw and brash to the taste buds. This was one Kentucky Colonel that never took any prisoners. But, as I was to discover, not all their whiskeys were so fashioned, though the grand majority were no more than four years old and would assault my palate with little mercy. Barton Distillery, unquestionably, then bottled the worst whiskey in all Kentucky.

Two brands in particular, however, had a slight air of potential greatness about them. Never, not once, did I ever turn down their Very Old Barton, originally a 6-year-old, when I stayed in the Old Talbot Tavern nearby. Not least because it was Barton's oldest whiskey – yes, at just six years! – and because there were satisfying hints of richness to the apparently high rye content bourbon. Their other very decent effort was Tom Moore, a little younger but bouncing with small grain complexity. Both had a particular style different to any other Kentucky bourbon.

To find out anything about them was far from easy. I was always a very welcome visitor to the distillery – and I visited quite a few times back in the '90s; indeed, almost on a near regular basis. And there I would meet Jerry Dalton and he and I would play a never-ending game where I would ask questions and he refused to answer them. Not so much about the making, because he kindly took me around the plant quite a few times. But when it came to the mash bill, the yeasts or why they refused to bottle a whiskey older than six years he would clam up and say that was confidential company information. Other than confirming they had no plans whatsoever to mature their whiskeys to anything older than their VOB.

I remember telling their then distiller, Bill Friel, that it was a shame they didn't let his "Willy's whiskey" age further, as its potential, looking at the evidence of the the 6-year-old VOB, seemed great. With a wistful sigh it was obvious Bill didn't disagree.

Some 21 years on from then, the Barton Distillery has come of age. The circle has been completed. For this year's Jim Murray Whisky Bible their 1792 Barton Full Proof is World Whiskey of the Year. Of all the winners of this title, this perhaps presents the greatest surprise even to me...

For when I began the Whisky Bible in 2003, they were still churning out a bourbon that was very much worth missing, VOB apart. The thought they would ever reach such dizzy heights seemed fanciful at best. However, ten years ago the distillery was bought by Sazerac, owners of Buffalo Trace....and things changed. Drastically. And fast.

And now for Jim Murray's Whisky Bible 2020 it has been crowned as the producer of the World Best Whiskey.

So if anyone tries to convince you the romance of whiskey is dead and gone or has all been confected, then don't you believe them. For where else could such an ugly duckling become so beautiful a swan....?

Jim Murray
Willow Cottage
Somewhere in rural Northamptonshire
September 2019

# How to Read
# The Bible

**T**he whole point of this book is for the whisky lover – be he or she an experienced connoisseur or, better fun still, simply starting out on the long and joyous path of discovery – to have ready access to easy-to-understand information about as many whiskies as possible. And I mean a lot. Thousands.

This book does not quite include every whisky on the market... just by far and away the vast majority. And those that have been missed this time round – either through accident, logistics or design – will appear in later editions once we can source a sample.

## WHISKY SCORING

The marking for this book is tailored to the consumer and scores run out just a little higher than I use for my own personal references. But such is the way it has been devised that it has not affected my order of preference.

Each whisky is given a rating out of 100. Twenty-five marks are given to each of four factors: nose (**n**), taste (**t**), finish (**f**), balance and overall complexity (**b**). That means that 50% of the marks are given for flavour alone and 25% for the nose, often an overlooked part of the whisky equation. The area of balance and complexity covers all three previous factors and a usually hidden one besides:

**Nose:** this is simply the aroma. Often requires more than one inspection as hidden aromas can sometimes reveal themselves after time in the glass, increased contact with air and changes in temperature. The nose very often tells much about a whisky, but – as we shall see – equally can be quite misleading.

**Taste:** this is the immediate arrival on the palate and involves the flavour profile up to, and including, the time it reaches maximum intensity and complexity.

**Finish:** often the least understood part of a tasting. This is the tail and flourish of the whisky's signature, often revealing the effects of ageing. The better whiskies tend to finish well and linger without too much oak excess. It is on the finish, also, that certain notes which are detrimental to the whisky may be observed. For instance, a sulphur-tarnished cask may be fully revealed for what it is by a dry, bitter residue on the palate which is hard to shake off. It is often worth waiting a few minutes to get the full picture of the finish before having a second taste of a whisky.

**Balance:** This is the part it takes a little experience to appreciate but it can be mastered by anyone. For a whisky to work well on the nose and palate, it should not be too one-sided in its character. If you are looking for an older whisky, it should have evidence of oak, but not so much that all other flavours and aromas are drowned out. Likewise, a whisky matured or finished in a sherry butt must offer a lot more than just wine alone and the greatest Islay malts, for instance, revel in depth and complexity beyond the smoky effects of peat.

Each whisky has been analysed by me without adding water or ice. I have taken each whisky as it was poured from the bottle and used no more than warming in an identical glass to extract and discover the character of the whisky. To have added water would have been pointless: it would have been an inconsistent factor as people, when pouring water, add different amounts at varying temperatures. The only constant with the whisky you and I taste will be when it has been poured directly from the bottle.

Even if you and I taste the same whiskies at the same temperature and from identical glasses – and even share the same values in whisky – our scores may still be different. Because a factor that is built into my evaluation is drawn from expectation and experience. When I sample a whisky from a certain distillery at such-and-such an age or from this type of barrel or that, I would expect it to offer me certain qualities. It has taken me 30 years to acquire this knowledge (which I try to add to day by day!) and an enthusiast cannot be expected to learn it overnight. But, hopefully, Jim Murray's Whisky Bible will help...!

## SCORE CHART

Within the parentheses () is the overall score out of 100.

**0–50.5** Nothing short of absolutely diabolical.

**51–64.5** Nasty and well worth avoiding.

**65–69.5** Very unimpressive indeed.

**70–74.5** Usually drinkable but don't expect the earth to move.

**75–79.5** Average and usually pleasant though sometimes flawed.

**80–84.5** Good whisky worth trying.

**85–89.5** Very good to excellent whiskies definitely worth buying.

**90–93.5** Brilliant.

**94–97.5** Superstar whiskies that give us all a reason to live.

**98–100** Better than anything I've ever tasted!

## KEY TO ABBREVIATIONS & SYMBOLS

**%** Percentage strength of whisky measured as alcohol by volume. **b** Overall balance and complexity. **bott** Date of bottling. **nbc** No bottling code. **db** Distillery bottling. In other words, an expression brought out by the owners of the distillery. **dist** Date of distillation or spirit first put into cask. **f** Finish. **n** Nose. **nc** Non-coloured. **ncf** Non-chill-filtered. **sc** Single cask. **t** Taste. ◇ New entry for 2020. ⊙ Retasted – no change. ⊙⊙ Retasted and re-evaluated. **v** Variant WB20-001 Code for Whisky Club bottling.

## Finding Your Whisky

**Worldwide Malts:** Whiskies are listed alphabetically throughout the book. In the case of single malts, the distilleries run A–Z style with distillery bottlings appearing at the top of the list in order of age, starting with youngest first. After age comes vintage. After all the "official" distillery bottlings are listed, next come other bottlings, again in alphabetical order. Single malts without a distillery named (or perhaps named after a dead one) are given their own section, as are vatted malts.

**Worldwide Blends:** These are simply listed alphabetically, irrespective of which company produces them. So "Black Bottle" appears ahead of "White Horse" and Japanese blends begin with "Ajiwai Kakubin" and end with "Za". In the case of brands being named after companies or individuals the first letter of the brand will dictate where it is listed. So William Grant, for instance, will be found under "W" for William rather "G" for Grant.

**Bourbon/Rye:** One of the most confusing types of whiskey to list because often the name of the brand bears no relation to the name of the distillery that made it. Also, brands may be sold from one company to another, or shortfalls in stock may see companies buying bourbons from another. For that reason all the brands have been listed alphabetically with the name of the bottling distiller being added at the end.

**Irish Whiskey:** There are four types of Irish whiskey: (i) pure pot still; (ii) single malt; (iii) single grain and (iv) blended. Some whiskies may have "pure pot still" on the label, but are actually single malts. So check both sections.

## Bottle Information

As no labels are included in this book I have tried to include all the relevant information you will find on the label to make identification of the brand straightforward. Where known I have included date of distillation and bottling. Also the cask number for further recognition. At the end of the tasting notes I have included the strength and, if known, number of bottles (sometimes abbreviated to btls) released and in which markets.

## PRICE OF WHISKY

You will notice that Jim Murray's Whisky Bible very rarely refers to the cost of a whisky. This is because the book is a guide to quality and character rather than the price tag attached. Also, the same whiskies are sold in different countries at varying prices due to market forces and variations of tax, so there is a relevance factor to be considered. Equally, much depends on the size of an individual's pocket. What may appear a cheap whisky to one could be an expensive outlay to another. With this in mind prices are rarely given in the Whisky Bible.

# How to Taste Whisky

I t is of little use buying a great whisky, spending a comparative fortune in doing so, if you don't get the most out of it.

So when giving whisky tastings, no matter how knowledgeable the audience may be I take them through a brief training schedule in how to nose and taste as I do for each sample included in the Whisky Bible.

I am aware that many aspects are contrary to what is being taught by distilleries' whisky ambassadors. And for that we should be truly thankful. However, at the end of the day we all find our own way of doing things. If your old tried and trusted technique suits you best, that's fine by me. But I do ask you try out the instructions below at least once to see if you find your whisky is talking to you with a far broader vocabulary and clearer voice than it once did. I strongly suspect you will be pleasantly surprised – amazed, even - by the results.

Amusingly, someone tried to teach me my own tasting technique some years back in an hotel bar. He was not aware who I was and I didn't let on. It transpired that a friend of his had been to one of my tastings a few years earlier and had passed on my words of "wisdom". I'd be lying if I said I didn't smile when he informed me it was called "The Murray Method." It was the first time I had heard the phrase... though certainly not the last!

## "THE MURRAY METHOD"

**1.** Drink a black, unsweetened, coffee or chew on 90% minimum cocoa chocolate to cleanse the palate, especially of sugars.

**2.** Find a room free from distracting noises as well as the aromas of cooking, polish, flowers and other things which will affect your understanding and appreciation of the whisky.

**3.** Make sure you have not recently washed your hands using heavily scented soap or are wearing a strong aftershave or perfume.

**4.** Use a tulip shaped glass with a stem. This helps contain the alcohols at the bottom yet allows the more delicate whisky aromas you are searching for to escape.

**5.** Never add ice. This tightens the molecules and prevents flavours and aromas from being released. It also makes your whisky taste bitter. There is no better way to get the least from your whisky than by freezing it.

**6.** Likewise, ignore any advice given to put the bottle in the fridge before drinking.

**7.** Don't add water! Whatever anyone tells you. It releases aromas but can mean the whisky falls below 40%... so it is no longer whisky. Also, its ability to release flavours and aromas diminishes quite quickly. Never add ridiculous "whisky rocks" or other supposed tasting aids.

**8.** Warm the undiluted whisky in the glass to body temperature before nosing or tasting. Hence the stem, so you can cradle in your hand the curve of the thin base. This excites the molecules and unravels the whisky in your glass, maximising its sweetness and complexity.

**9.** Keep an un-perfumed hand over the glass to keep the aromas in while you warm. Only a minute or two after condensation appears at the top of your glass should you extend your arms, lift your covering hand and slowly bring the glass to your nose, so the alcoholic vapours have been released before the glass reaches your face.

**10.** Never stick your nose in the glass. Or breathe in deeply. Allow glass to gently touch your top lip, leaving a small space below the nose. Move from nostril to nostril, breathing normally. This allows the aromas to break up in the air, helping you find the more complex notes.

**11.** Take no notice of your first mouthful. This is a marker for your palate.

**12.** On second, bigger mouthful, close your eyes to concentrate on the flavour and chew the whisky - moving it continuously around the palate. Keep your mouth slightly open to let air in and alcohol out. It helps if your head is tilted back very slightly.

**13.** Occasionally spit – if you have the willpower! This helps your senses to remain sharp for the longest period of time.

**14.** Look for the balance of the whisky. That is, which flavours counter others so none is too dominant. Also, watch carefully how the flavours and aromas change in the glass over time.

**15.** Assess the "shape" and mouth feel of the whisky, its weight and how long its finish. And don't forget to concentrate on the first flavours as intensely as you do the last. Look out for the way the sugars, spices and other characteristics form.

**16.** Never make your final assessment until you have tasted it a third or fourth time.

**17.** Be honest with your assessment: don't like a whisky because someone (yes, even me!), or the label, has tried to convince you how good it is.

**18.** When you cannot discriminate between one whisky and another, stop immediately.

# Bible Thumping
# A Whisky in Barrel
# Cannot Be Hid...

**The image of the gentleman is still indelibly etched into my mind...**

He stands there clutching a freshly signed copy of Jim Murray's Whisky Bible 2019 and stares at me with a degree of disbelief, wondering if I had given him a straight answer or was teasing him.

His question had seemed innocent enough. It ran something like this: "Jim, I'm pretty new to whiskies outside of Scotch. So I wondered if you could tell me what Irish whiskey tastes like and what flavours make it different from any other."

Without missing a beat I replied: "I'm not sure I can remember these days. Your guess is as good as mine."

Now, I had already clocked that before buying the book he had turned to the Irish section where he would have noticed there were quite a few new entries, 53 to be exact. So, to him, my response didn't make any sense at all. Did it mean that I cheated: that I didn't taste those whiskeys and had made up the notes? Or that I got someone else to taste them for me? In other words, I was a self-confessed fraud.

He looked at me, his face not just a portrait of surprise, but one also riddled with confusion. When he spoke, his impeccable English was coloured by a Germanic accent that had just a little air of desperation: "But last year, in the 2018 Edition, you made an Irish Whiskey number two in the world. That is why I have decided to start trying them out. But now you say you don't know what Irish whiskey tastes like...!"

I put the poor chap out of his misery and admitted I was being somewhat facetious and a little cynical to boot. And maybe with good reason.

Having been bang in the middle of evaluating the 1,250 new whiskies for this edition of The Whisky Bible, I had broken off for a few days to tour Germany and give a series of tastings. It was a welcome relief to have come face to face with people again, after weeks of intimacy with hundreds of whiskies, not all of them as good company as the kind people in the room with me. But just before I left I had given the many hundreds of whiskies still to taste a quick visual check through. And I can't say I was too happy with everything I saw, especially in the Irish section. I had already tasted some pretty unusual bottlings and I could see there were more to come.

And this is what I explained to the poor, perplexed gentleman before me. Over the last couple of years, among the many Irish whiskeys I had tasted, only a handful allowed me to actually taste the malt – or malt and barley – in all its most intricate and dazzling detail. Instead, my taste buds were picking their way through this fruit and that, rich textures and confusing clashes, some jarring, others ending in a sulphurous void.

For Irish whiskey is now plagued by a wine and spirit cask maturation outbreak that has hit epidemic proportions.

"The problem is," I told him "these days you are no longer allowed to taste the distillery style or the grain. It is all about the wood – and that usually means all about the fruit. The taste of Irish whiskey itself is rapidly vanishing under an avalanche of grape."

The gentleman immediately understood my meaning, blinked into the Irish pages of the Bible, which he still had open, and after a few moments said he could see what I meant. This year, he will see even more clearly. While last year I tasted 53 new Irish whiskies, this year I have managed one more at 54. And, sadly, only a handful were exclusively matured in used bourbon barrels. They are easy to spot in the Whisky Bible: they tend to score more highly.

Distillers and bottlers in Ireland appear to have been drawn into some collective hysteria, each one trying to outdo the other in the most exotic casks they can find, to lead whiskey enthusiasts off the Irish highways and into remote byways. Sadly, many are simply a dead end. Others head into an un-navigable swamp; or even sulphur pits of no return.

You think I exaggerate?

Here is an A-Z of the extraordinary number of wine 1 types used in just those 50-odd samples I encountered this year:

Acacia Wood
All Sherry Casks
American Oak from Kentucky and French Cognac Cask
Armagnac Finish
Barleywine Finished
Bodega Sherry Casks
Bourbon and Oloroso
Bourbon, Oloroso and Irish Virgin Oak
Bourbon Sherry and Marsala
Calvados XO Cask Finish
Caribbean Rum Finish
Ex-Rum Barrel
Four Cask Finish (Bourbon, Oloroso, Port and Madeira)
Grand Cru Burgundy Finish
Hybrid Cask (Portuguese, American, French, Hungarian and Chestnut)
Japanese Mizunara
Marsala Cask Finish
Oloroso Cask Finish
Pedro Ximenez Butt
Plantation Rum Finish
Refill Sherry
Rhum Agricole
Rum Cask
Sherry Cask
Sherry Cask Finish
Tequila and Mescal
Triple Casked
Virgin American Oak Finish
White Burgundy Finish

And that's not even including those that have added caramel, which for too many years has played a way too important part in the framing of some Irish whiskey.

So, it begs the question: why do the Irish give the impression of being so ashamed of seeing their own whiskey naked? Or is it just some mad rush to be different, but by doing so they all just become the same...?

Yes, of course I understand the need to create new markets. Whiskey companies must make money, so they pout and add a little rouge and catch the eye. I get all that.

The trouble is, too many of these whiskeys are simply just OK or decent and not reaching the levels of excellence I suspect they might otherwise be capable of. And this worries me, because in the next few years quite a number of new Irish distilleries will either be coming on stream or putting their whiskey in the marketplace. But just how many of them will bother to see what their whiskey is capable of; how good it is as a stand-alone malt or pot still? Or how many will simply follow the trend and hide their whiskeys under the guise of some exotic cask or other?

It is a depressing thought and puts me in mind of the historic inn where I woke up a year or so back to see in my 60th birthday. I am Surrey born, so began my new decade staying in that county's most wonderful hostelry, one where for many years I have drunk and dined. Yet for 200 years, travellers on their way from Godalming to Petworth in Sussex and beyond, or on the return journey, would have driven or been ridden past it blissfully unaware of its extraordinary charms....unless they had ventured inside.

For the outside gave only limited insight into the beauty of this structure because in around the 1750s slates had been nailed to the exterior all the way to near ground level, probably to preserve the oak and keep the residents and guests inside a little warmer. But it was also the architectural fashion of the time and a couple of hours' exploration of the stunning Surrey/Sussex border will reveal a number of old buildings so attired.

It was only as relatively recently as 1951, when urgent repairs were needed and the owners gained permission from the Ministry of Works to see what was under the tiles, that the extent of the magnificence of the building become fully apparent. It turned out that here in aspic was a mediaeval facade dating back to the 14th century. For some 200 years people, it transpired, had been robbed of the stunning visual beauty the Crown Inn in Chiddingfold could have afforded them. Once it became apparent just how architecturally important the building was, permission was granted for the tiles to be removed...and stay removed.

Of course, inside, all the clues were there to be seen, as they still are. But no-one bothered to look and took for granted the building was, from the outside, just, well, pretty. Rather than what it actually was: stunning...

Indeed, how many of you reading this have, as I have done, bought an old house and found hidden away, under layers of 1960's and 70's kitsch, original fireplaces or wallpaper or painting or floor tiles, resplendent in their surroundings, but which fashion and a universal lack of good taste deemed undesirable or surplus to requirement?

So, it is beginning to feel with some whiskeys. Certainly Irish but not exclusively them. The same can be pointed at within Scotland and now even Kentucky where beautiful bourbons have been lost beneath layers of grotesque fruit.

Whiskeys being gaudily painted in grape, or guest spirit or foreign tannins appear to be the fashion. And though I admire the hard work in the name of innovation – and don't for a moment underestimate the amount of money spent on such projects – I have also to hope that soon those carrying out this tile cladding of their whiskies will quietly reflect on where they are going with this.

With the loss of my dear old friend Barry Walsh, I speak as probably the last person working on a daily basis in the industry who had a slight hand in Ireland's first dedicated cask finish.

Barry was the outstanding blender for Irish Distillers at a time when they were responsible for the all the Irish whiskey distilled and matured in Ireland, bar Cooley. Some quarter of a century ago he had been given the project of coming up with a 15-year-old Bushmills that was a bit different from anything else seen in Irish whiskey before. So his plan was to put a mixture of ex-bourbon and ex-sherry casks into Port casks and finish them, having read my exclusive in my Sunday Telegraph column which told how Glenmorangie had come up with the first-ever cask finished whisky...in Port. Barry was intrigued.

So he set off on his journey creating this special whiskey threesome – thankfully at a time when the 1970s distilled whiskey he was working with would be free from any sulphur intrusion. But he simply couldn't get the balance right. Not least because he insisted on all aspects of its personality, the two types of grape, the varied tannins and even barley to each have a say which would ensure a degree of balance. Which is why, for a year, I regularly tasted the maturing whiskey as it went through its transfiguration and discussed with him where it was working and where it wasn't. At one stage, it was so out of sync' I genuinely thought he would not be able to find the balance he was looking for; by contrast he was confident that a mixture of patience and tweaking would do the trick. It did.

His masterpiece is still going strong today, (though sometimes damaged by sulphur that wasn't around in his time), but it is a 16-year-old and not 15 because it took Barry far longer than he thought it would take. And it was a 16-year-old spirit he finished with.

Whether whisky companies are using this degree of diligence and patience to get it right is open to debate. It is possible some are, but I suspect most aren't. For a start, very few have that degree of experience with Irish. But Barry also loved whiskey that matured in ex-bourbon barrel and we spent many happy an hour together going through various samples of that greatest of all prizes from Midleton distillery - pot still whiskey - analysing the different intonations from the grain with bourbon barrel and differing degrees of usage.

And also looking at the results of blending different percentages of different Pot Still types with 1st, 2nd or 3rd fill bourbon casks – and which percentage of those casks worked best when mixed with Pot Still maturing in sherry. And of course the differing results from sherry butts, again of 1st 2nd 3rd and, if I remember correctly, sometimes 4th fill. What I do clearly remember, as if it were yesterday, was the stark difference between the Pot Still coming from 3rd fill sherry and those which had matured in new sherry butts. And how, if you wanted the Pot Still to make its mark and maximize flavour, then you certainly kept maturing whiskey from the fresh sherry butts at a minimum.

So when, as a consultant blender, I created a couple of Irish whiskey brands I always, whenever possible, used bourbon casks and carefully selected a specified variety of 1st, 2nd and 3rd fill casks in order to create maximum complexity and balance, rather than a 'one-trick pony' single style.

Over the forthcoming years will this next generation of Irish distillers be ensuring they set enough whiskey back in the warehouse to make this possible? Or will they simply just round their maturing spirit in increasingly exotic wine and foreign spirit casks looking for flavour max over balance and complexity max?

If it is not something they have yet thought about, they had better do so soon. Because wouldn't it just be fantastic if there were 30 different Irish whiskey distilleries and we could tell them all apart, as we once did quite easily with Cooley, Bushmills and Midleton simply by being able to recognize the clear signature of their malt or Pot Still. Rather than every single bottling being from different distilleries yet, curiously, all being exactly the same thanks to the fruit.

There has always been an old saying in blending, and I remember Barry Walsh saying it once to me: "less can often give you more". It may be a piece of advice that some people creating whiskey today in Kentucky, Scotland and, of course, Ireland, may benefit from remembering...

# Immortal Drams:
# The Whiskey Bible Winners 2004-2019

| | World Whisky of the Year | Second Finest Whisky of the Year | Third Finest Whisky of the Year |
|---|---|---|---|
| 2004 | George T Stagg | N/A | N/A |
| 2005 | George T Stagg | N/A | N/A |
| 2006 | George T Stagg | Glen Moray 1986 Cask 4696 | N/A |
| 2007 | Old Parr Superior 18 Years Old | Buffalo Trace Twice Barreled | N/A |
| 2008 | Ardbeg 10 Years Old | The Ileach Single Islay Malt Cask Strength | N/A |
| 2009 | Ardbeg Uigedail | Nikka Whisky Single Coffey Malt 12 Years | N/A |
| 2010 | Sazerac Rye 18 Years Old (bottled Fall 2008) | Ardbeg Supernova | Amrut Fusion |
| 2011 | Ballantine's 17 Years Old | Thomas H Handy Sazerac Rye (129 proof) | Wiliam Larue Weller (134.8 proof) |
| 2012 | Old Pulteney Aged 21 Years | George T Stagg | Parker's Heritage Collection Aged 10 Years |
| 2013 | Thomas H Handy Sazerac Rye (128.6 proof) | William Larue Weller (133.5 proof) | Ballantine's 17 Years Old |
| 2014 | Glenmorangie Ealanta 1993 | William Larue Weller (123.4 proof) | Thomas Handy Sazerac Rye (132.4 proof) |
| 2015 | Yamazaki Single Malt Sherry 2013 | William Larue Weller (68.1 abv) | Sazerac Rye 18 Years Old (bottled Fall 2013) |
| 2016 | Crown Royal Northern Harvest Rye | Pikesville 110 Proof Straight Rye | Midleton Dair Ghaelach |
| 2017 | Booker's Rye 13 Years, 1 Month, 12 Days | Glen Grant 18 Year Old | William Larue Weller (134.6 proof) |
| 2018 | Colonel E.H. Taylor 4 Grain Aged 10 Years | Redbreast Aged 21 Years | Glen Grant 18 Year Old |
| 2019 | William Larue Weller (128.2 proof) | Glen Grant Aged 18 Years | Thomas Handy Sazerac Rye (127.2 proof) |

**Who has won this year? You are one page away...**

# Jim Murray's Whiskey Bible Awards 2020

**W**ell, don't say Jim Murray's Whisky Bible is not full of surprises. And this year there have been a couple that have taken even my breath away.

True, many of the usual suspects are there, no matter how hard I look for challengers to them. The Buffalo Trace Antique Collection, The Glen Grant family of Scotch single malts, The Ballantine's blends. Still they keep the bar raised and their standards impeccably high. And surely, one day others will either match or supercede them. But, for now, they continue to be the whiskies the others must catch.

Now, one has trumped them all... and, to the doubtless joy of the Sazerac Company, it was a bourbon from a stable outside Frankfort that provided the thoroughbred winner: 1792 Barton. Their lifting of the World Whisky of the Year title meant that not only did all the top three places go to Kentucky distillers, with two bourbons and a rye, but they were all won by the same company.

Curiously, the battle for third place was between two different ryes: Thomas Handy (of Kentucky) and Crown Royal Northern Harvest Rye (of Canada), both a former World Whisky of the Year. I had been wondering if that victory the latter achieved in 2016 was a freak: the bottling that won was a worthy winner without question, but all subsequent samples I had tasted since, though excellent, were never close to World Whisky of the Year standard. This year's sample, however, proved it was not a one off after all: it took the enormous Handy right to the wire.

However, The 1792 Full Proof was on a slightly different plane to any other of the 1,252 whiskies I tasted this year, including last year's World Champion and serial award winner that wheated beast, the William Larue Weller. For reasons fully explained in the introduction, this victory took me aback somewhat: it was only a little over 20 years ago I considered it the worst distillery in Kentucky...

Twenty years ago neither the Annandale distillery in the Lowlands of Scotland nor Nantou whisky from Taiwan even existed. Yet both this year offered bottlings which not only won major awards in the year's Whisky Bible (Nantou even walked off with single cask of the year and reached the final six in my World Whisky of the Year taste off, a breathtaking achievement!) but revealed these two newcomers to the whisky world have the potential to be go onto to even greater things. It did, of course, require ex-bourbon casks for them to reveal the intricacy of their maturing spirit and this they did, with obvious pride.

Elsewhere, The Last Drop kept up their incredibly high standards with their age-defying 56-year-old blend and then backed up their pedigree with a second award with Scotch Grain of the Year with their 1977 from Dumbarton. Indeed, this has been a great year from greybeard whiskies, with Gordon and MacPhail coming out with their usual plethora of astonishing ancients, the pick of the bunch being their 1949 China Special Edition (hardly an unimportant year in that country's history) and even Glen Scotia getting in on the act with their 45-year-old.

## 2020 World Whiskey of the Year
## 1792 Full Proof Kentucky Straight Bourbon

### Second Finest Whiskey in the World
### William Larue Weller 125.7 Proof

### Third Finest Whiskey in the World
### Thomas Handy Sazerac Rye 128.8 Proof

### Single Cask of the Year
### Nantou Distillery Omar Cask Strength Bourbon Cask

## SCOTCH

**Scotch Whisky of the Year**
Glen Grant Aged 18 Years Rare Edition
**Single Malt of the Year (Multiple Casks)**
**Glen Grant Aged 18 Years Rare Edition**
**Single Malt of the Year (Single Cask)**
The Macphail 1949 China Special Edition 1
**Scotch Blend of the Year**
Ballantine's 17 Years Old
**Scotch Grain of the Year**
The Last Drop Dumbarton 1977
**Scotch Vatted Malt of the Year**
Glen Castle Blended Malt 1990

## Single Malt Scotch

**No Age Statement**
Glen Grant Rothes Chronicles Cask Haven
**10 Years & Under (Multiple Casks)**
Glen Grant Aged 10 Years
**10 Years & Under (Single Cask)**
Annandale Man O' Sword
**11-15 Years (Multiple Casks)**
**Glen Grant Aged 15 Years Batch Strength**
**11-15 Years (Single Cask)**
Signatory Vintage Edradour Ballechin 12 Year Old
**16-21 Years (Multiple Casks)**
**Glen Grant Aged 18 Years Rare Edition**
**16-21 Years (Single Cask)**
Whisky Castle Glen Spey Aged 21 Years
**22-27 Years (Multiple Casks)**
**Glenmorangie Grand Vintage 1996**
**22-27 Years (Single Cask)**
The Whisky Shop Glendronach Aged 26 Years
**28-34 Years (Multiple Casks)**
Ben Nevis 32 Years Old 1966
**28-34 Years (Single Cask)**
**Gordon & MacPhail Inverleven 1985**
**35-40 Years (Multiple Casks)**
**Port Ellen 39 Years Old**
**35-40 Years (Single Cask)**
Glenfarclas The Family Casks 1978 W18
**41 Years & Over (Multiple Casks)**
Glen Scotia 45 Year Old
**41 Years & Over (Single Cask)**
**The Macphail 1949 China Special Edition 1**

## BLENDED SCOTCH

**No Age Statement (Standard)**
Ballantine's Finest
**No Age Statement (Premium)**
**Johnnie Walker Blue Label Ghost & Rare**
**5-12 Years**
Johnnie Walker Black Label 12 Years Old
**13-18 Years**
Ballantine's 17 Years Old
**19 - 25 Years**
Dewar's Aged 25 Years The Signature
**26 - 50 Years**
The Last Drop 56 Year Old Blend

## IRISH WHISKEY

**Irish Whiskey of the Year**
Redbreast Aged 12 Years Cask Strength
**Irish Pot Still Whiskey of the Year**
Redbreast Aged 12 Years Cask Strength

**Irish Single Malt of the Year**
Bushmills Aged 21 Years
**Irish Blend of the Year**
Jameson
**Irish Single Cask of the Year**
Kinahan's Special Release Project 11 Year Old

## AMERICAN WHISKEY

**Bourbon of the Year**
**1792 Full Proof Kentucky Straight Bourbon**
**Rye of the Year**
Thomas H. Handy Sazerac 128.8 Proof
**US Micro Whisky of the Year**
Garrison Brothers Balmorhea
**US Micro Whisky of the Year (Runner Up)**
291 Barrel Proof Colorado Whiskey Aged 2 Years

## BOURBON

**No Age Statement (Multiple Barrels)**
**1792 Full Proof Kentucky Straight Bourbon**
**No Age Statement (Single Barrel)**
Colonel E H Taylor Single Barrel Bottled In Bond
**9 Years & Under**
Russel's Reserve Single Barrel
**10 - 12 Years**
Elijah Craig Barrel Proof Aged 12 Years
**11 - 15 Years**
Pappy Van Winkle 15 Years Old
**16 - 20 Years**
Michter's 20 Year Old Kentucky Straight Bourbon
**21 Years & Over**
Pappy Van Winkle 23 Years Old

## RYE

**No Age Statement**
**Thomas H. Handy Sazerac 128.8 Proof**
**Up to 10 Years**
Knob Creek Cask Strength
**11-15 Years**
Van Winkle Family Reserve 13 Years Old
**Over 15 Years**
Sazerac 18 Years Old
**Single Cask**
Knob Creek Single Barrel Select

## CANADIAN WHISKY

**Canadian Whisky of the Year**
Crown Royal Northern Harvest Rye

## JAPANESE WHISKY

**Japanese Whisky of the Year**
**Nikka Taketsuru Pure Malt**
**Single Malt of the Year (MB)**
The Matsui Mizunara Cask

## EUROPEAN WHISKY

**European Whisky of the Year (Multiple)**
**Thy Whisky No. 9 Bøg Single Malt (Denmark)**
**European Whisky of the Year (Single)**
**Penderyn Single Cask no. M75-32 (Wales)**

## WORLD WHISKIES

**Asian Whisky of the Year**
**Nantou Distillery Omar Bourbon Cask no. 11140804 (Taiwan)**
**Southern Hemisphere Whisky of the Year**
Bakery Hill Peated Malt Cask Strength (Australia)

*\*Overall age category and/or section winners are presented in **bold**.*

# The Whiskey Bible Liquid Gold Awards (97.5-94)

Jim Murray's Whisky Bible is delighted to again make a point of celebrating the very finest whiskies you can find in the world. So we salute the distillers who have maintained or even furthered the finest traditions of whisky making and taken their craft to the very highest levels. And the bottlers who have brought some of them to us.

After all, there are over 4,700 different brands and expressions listed in this guide and from every corner of the planet. Those which score 94 and upwards represents only a very small fraction of them. These whiskies are, in my view, the élite: the finest you can currently find on the whisky shelves of the world. Rare and precious, they are Liquid Gold.

So it is our pleasure to announce that all those scoring 94 and upwards automatically qualify for the Jim Murray's Whisky Bible Liquid Gold Award. Congratulations!

## 97.5
**Scottish Single Malt**
Glenmorangie Ealanta 1993 Vintage
Old Pulteney Aged 21 Years
**Scottish Blends**
Ballantine's 17 Years Old
**Irish Pure Pot Still**
Midleton Dair Ghaelach Grinsell's Wood Ballaghtobin Estate
**Bourbon**
1792 Full Proof Kentucky Straight Bourbon
Colonel E.H. Taylor Four Grain Bottled in Bond Aged 12 Years
William Larue Weller 64.1%
William Larue Weller 62.85%
**American Straight Rye**
Booker's Rye 13 Years, 1 Month, 12 Days
Pikesville Straight Rye Whiskey Aged at Least 6 Years
Thomas H. Handy Sazerac Straight Rye
**Canadian Blended**
Crown Royal Northern Harvest Rye bott code L5085 N3
**Japanese Single Malt**
The Yamazaki Single Malt Whisky Sherry Cask

## 97
**Scottish Single Malt**
Ardbeg 10 Years Old
Bowmore Aged 19 Years The Feis Ile Collection
Glenfiddich 50 Years Old
Glen Grant Aged 18 Years Rare Edition
Glen Grant Aged 18 Years Rare Edition bott code: LRO/EE04
Glen Grant Aged 18 Years Rare Edition bott code: LRO/EE03
The Macphail 1949 China 70th Anniversary Special Edition 1
The Last Drop Glenrothes 1970
**Scottish Grain**
Cambus Aged 40 Years
The Last Drop Dumbarton 1977
**Scottish Blends**
Compass Box The Double Single
Johnnie Walker Blue Label The Casks Edition
The Last Drop 1971 Blended Scotch Whisky 45 Years Old
The Last Drop 50 Year Old
Old Parr Superior 18 Years Old
**Irish Pure Pot Still**
Redbreast Aged 12 Years Cask Strength
Redbreast Aged 21 Years
Midleton Dair Ghaelach
**Bourbon**
George T. Stagg 72.05%
George T. Stagg 64.6%
Parker's Heritage Collection Wheated Mash Bill Bourbon Aged 10 Years
Sazerac 18 Years Old
Thomas H. Handy Sazerac 63.6%
Thomas H. Handy Sazerac 64.4%
**American Straight Rye**
Colonel E.H. Taylor Straight Rye

**Canadian Blended**
Canadian Club Chronicles: Issue No. 1 Water of Windsor Aged 41 Years
Crown Royal Northern Harvest Rye bott code: L8 353 N5
**Japanese Single Malt**
Nikka Whisky Single Coffey Malt 12 Years
The Yamazaki Single Malt Whisky Mizunara

## 96.5
**Scottish Single Malt**
Annandale Man O' Sword
Ardbeg 20 Something
Ardbeg 21 Years Old
Ardbeg Corryvreckan
Berry Bros & Rudd Ardmore 9 Years Old
Balblair 1965
Bowmore Black 50 Year Old
Brora Aged 38 Years
Octomore Edition 7.1 Aged 5 years
Dramfool Port Charlotte 2002 16 Years Old
Caol Ila 30 Year Old
Convalmore 32 Year Old
Glencadam Aged 18 Years
Glen Grant Aged 15 Years Batch Strength 1st Edition bott code: LRO/FG 19
The Macphail 1949 China 70th Anniversary Special Edition 1
Scotch Malt Whisky Society Cask 9.128 24 Year Old
The Glenlivet Cipher
Old Particular Glen Moray 25 Years Old
The Last Drop Glenrothes 1968
Whisky Castle Glen Spey Aged 21 Years
Whisky Illuminati Glentauchers 20 Year Old
Highland Park 50 Years Old
The Perfect Fifth Highland Park 1987
Gordon & MacPhail Private Collection Inverleven 1985
Berry Bros & Rudd Arran 21 Years Old
Kilchoman Private Cask Release
AnCnoc Cutter
AnCnoc Rutter
Laphroaig Aged 27 Years
Loch Lomond Organic Aged 17 Years
The Cooper's Choice Lochside Aged 44 Years
Cadenhead's Rum Cask Mortlach 14 Years Old
Port Ellen 39 Years Old
Gleann Mór Port Ellen Aged Over 33 Years
Talisker Aged 25 Years
Tomatin 36 Year Old
Tullibardine 1970
Port Askaig 100 Proof
Alos Sansibar Whisky Speyside Region 1975
Arcanum Spirits TR2UNITY Aged Over 21 Years
Glen Castle Aged 28 Years
**Scottish Vatted Malt**
Collectivum XXVIII
Compass Box Flaming Heart Fifteenth Anniversary
**Scottish Grain**
Berry Bros & Rudd Cambus 26 Years Old

The Whisky Barrel Dumbarton 30 Year Old

**Scottish Blends**
The Antiquary Aged 35 Years
Dewar's Aged 18 Years The Vintage
Dewar's Double Double Aged 27 Years
Blended Scotch Whisky
The Last Drop 1965
The Last Drop 56 Year Old Blended Scotch
Whisky
Royal Salute 32 Years Old Union of the Crowns
Teacher's Aged 25 Years

**Irish Pure Pot Still**
Powers Aged 12 Years John's Lane Release
Redbreast Aged 32 Years Dream Cask

**Bourbon**
1792 Bottled In Bond Kentucky Straight Bourbon
Blanton's Gold Edition Single Barrel
Blanton's Gold Original Single Barrel
Blanton's Uncut/Unfiltered
Colonel E.H. Taylor Single Barrel BiB
Colonel E H Taylor Single Barrel Bottled In Bond
George T. Stagg 69.05%
George T. Stagg 71.4%
Michter's 20 Year Old Kentucky Straight Bourbon
Virgin Bourbon 7 Years Old

**American Straight Rye**
Knob Creek Cask Strength
Thomas H. Handy Sazerac

**American Microdistilleries**
Garrison Brothers Balmorhea Texas Straight
Bourbon Whiskey 2018
Garrison Brothers Balmorhea Texas Straight
Bourbon Whiskey 2019
The Notch Aged 12 Years

**Japanese Single Malt**
The Hakushu Single Malt Whisky Sherry Cask
Yamazaki Single Malt Sherry Cask 2016 Edition

**English Single Malt**
Cotswolds Single Malt Whisky World
Whisky Forum 2018
The Norfolk Farmers Single Grain Whisky
The Norfolk Single Grain Parched

**Welsh Single Malt**
Penderyn Icons of Wales No 5/50 Bryn Terfel
Penderyn Single Cask Ex-Madeira no. M75-32

**Australian Single Malt**
Belgrove Distillery Peated Rye Whisky
Limeburners Single Malt Whisky Darkest Winter

**Belgian Single Malt**
Belgian Owl Single Malt The Private Angels
60 Months

**Danish Single Malt**
Thy Whisky No. 9 Bøg Single Malt

**Indian Single Malt**
Paul John Edited

**Taiwanese Single Malt**
Nantou Distillery Omar Cask Strength
Bourbon Cask

**96**

**Scottish Single Malt**
Gordon & MacPhail Connoisseurs Choice
Aberfeldy 1993
Aberlour A'Bunadh Batch No. 54
Ardbeg 1977
Ardbeg Provenance 1974
Golden Cask Ardmore Aged 17 Years
Old Malt Cask Ardmore Aged 21 Years
Old Particular Ardmore 21 Years Old
Octomore 5 Years Old
Bruichladdich Octomore 7.1 5 Years Old
Gordon & MacPhail Cask Strength
Bunnahabhain 2009
Liquid Treasures Entomology
Bunnahabhain Over 28 Years Old
Caol Ila 18 Year Old
Glenwill Caol Ila 1990
Hidden Spirits Clynelish 1992
The Dalmore Candela Aged 50 Years

Signatory Vintage Edradour Ballechin 12 Year Old
Gordon & MacPhail Glen Albyn 1976
The Whisky Shop Glendronach Aged 26 Years
Glenfarclas The Family Casks 1988 W18
Glenfarclas The Family Casks 1995 W18
Glen Grant Aged 10 Years
Glen Grant Rothes Chronicles Cask Haven
First Fill Casks
The Macphail 1949 China 70th Anniversary
Special Edition 2
Glenmorangie Grand Vintage 1996
The Last Drop Glenrothes 1969
Glen Scotia 45 Year Old
Cadenhead's Glentauchers Aged 41 Years
The Glenturret Fly's 16 Masters Edition
Highland Park Loki Aged 15 Years
Highland Park Aged 25 Years
Highland Park 2002
Highland Park Sigurd
Kilchoman 10 Years Old
Lagavulin Aged 12 Years
Lagavulin 12 Year Old
Laphroaig Lore
Laphroaig PX Cask
Laphroaig Quarter Cask
Gordon & MacPhail Connoisseurs Choice
Macduff 2004
Old Pulteney Aged 25 Years
Rosebank 25 Years Old
The Perfect Fifth Springbank 1993
Gordon & MacPhail Strathisla 1960
The First Editions Teaninich Aged 18 Years
Ledaig Dùsgadh 42 Aged 42 Years
Ben Bracken Islay Single Malt 22 Years Old
Glen Castle Islay Single Malt 1989 Vintage
Cask 29 Years Old
Whiskey Bottle Company Cigar Malt Lover
Aged 21 Years
Lotus Lord 28 Year Old 1988
SaarWhisky Gruwehewwel Edition 3

**Scottish Vatted Malt**
Compass Box 3 Year Old Deluxe
Glen Castle Blended Malt 1992 Sherry Cask
Matured
Glen Castle Blended Malt 1990 Sherry Cask
Matured 28 Years Old

**Scottish Grain**
Xtra Old Particular Carsebridge 40 Years Old
Scotch Malt Whisky Society Cask G14.5 31
Year Old
Single Cask Collection Dumbarton 30 Years Old
The Cooper's Choice Garnheath 48 Year Old
Port Dundas 52 Year Old
The Sovereign Blended Grain 28 Years Old

**Scottish Blends**
Ballantine's Aged 30 Years
Ballantine's Finest
Ballantine's Limited release no. A27380
Dewar's Aged 25 Years The Signature
Grant's Aged 12 Years
Islay Mist Aged 17 Years
Johnnie Walker Blue Label Ghost & Rare
Oishii Wisukii Aged 36 Years
Royal Salute 21 Years Old
That Boutique-y Whisky Company
Blended Whisky No. 1 50 Year Old

**Irish Pure Pot Still**
Powers Aged 12 Years John's Lane Release
Redbreast Aged 12 Years Cask Strength
batch B1/11
Redbreast Aged 12 Years Cask Strength
batch no. B1/18
Redbreast Aged 21 Years

**Irish Single Malt**
Acla Special Selection No. 6 County of
Antrim 24 Years Old
Glendalough 13 Year Old Irish Single Malt
Mizunara Finish
Teeling Whiskey Single Malt Aged 26 Years

**Irish Blends**
Powers Gold Label
**Bourbon**
1792 High Rye Kentucky Straight Bourbon
Ancient Ancient Age 10 Years Old
Buffalo Trace Single Oak Project Barrel #101
Colonel E.H. Taylor Barrel Proof
George T. Stagg
Mayor Pingree Aged 9 Years
Michter's Single Barrel 10 Year Old Kentucky Straight Bourbon
Old Grand-Dad Bonded 100 Proof
Old Weller Antique 107
Pappy Van Winkle Family Reserve 15 Years Old
Pappy Van Winkle Family Reserve Kentucky Straight Bourbon Whiskey 15 Years Old
Stagg Jr
Very Old Barton 100 Proof
William Larue Weller
**American Straight Rye**
Bulleit 95 Rye
Colonel E.H. Taylor Straight Rye BiB
John David Albert's Taos Lightning Straight Rye Whiskey
Sazarac Rye
Sazerac 18 Years Old Summer 2017
Sazerac 18 Years Old Summer 2018
Van Winkle Family Reserve Kentucky Straight Rye Whiskey 13 Years Old No. 99A
**American Microdistilleries**
Balcones Peated Texas Single Malt Aged 26 Months in American Oak
291 Barrel Proof Aged 2 Years
Garrison Brothers Cowboy Bourbon Barrel Proof Aged Four Years
Rock Town Single Barrel Rye Whiskey Aged 32 Months
**American/Kentucky Whiskey Blends**
High West Double Rye
**Canadian Blended**
Crown Royal Noble Collection 13 Year Old Bourbon Mash
Crown Royal Special Reserve
J. P. Wiser's 35 Year Old
Lot No. 40 Rye Whisky
**Japanese Single Malt**
The Hakushu Paul Rusch
Nikka Coffey Malt Whisky
ePower Komagatake
The Yamazaki Single Malt Aged 18 Years
**English Single Malt**
Hicks & Healey Cornish Whiskey 2004
The English Single Malt Triple Distilled
**Welsh Single Malt**
Penderyn Single Cask Ex-Bordeaux Grand Cru
Penderyn Single Cask Tawny Portwood cask no. PT261/1
**Australian Single Malt**
Heartwood @*$% · &*
Heartwood Shade of the Night Single Malt
Redlands Distillery Single Malt
**Austrian Single Malt**
J.H. 13 Years Old Single Malt
**Belgian Single Malt**
Belgian Owl Single Malt Intense 41 Months
**Czech Republic Single Malt**
Gold Cock Single Malt Whisky 2008 Virgin Oak
**Danish Single Malt**
Stauning Rye
**French Single Malt**
Kornog Saint Erwan 2017
**German Single Malt**
Blaue Maus New Make
**Swedish Single Malt**
Smögen Svensk Single Malt Single Cask 18
**Swiss Single Malt**
Langatun Old Woodpecker Organic
**Indian Single Malts**
Amrut Greedy Angels 8 Years Old

Paul John Kanya
Paul John Tula 100%
Paul John Select Cask Peated
**Taiwanese Single Malt**
Kavalan Solist Single Cask Strength Manzanilla Sherry Cask

**95.5**
**Scottish Single Malt**
Ardbeg An Oa
Ardbeg Grooves Committee Release
Aultmore Aged 21 Years
Balblair 2000 2nd Release
Gordon & MacPhail Discovery Range Balblair Aged 12 Years
The Single Malts of Scotland Balblair 19 Years Old 1997
Ben Nevis 32 Years Old 1966
The BenRiach Aged 12 Years Matured In Sherry Wood
Benromach 30 Years Old
Benromach Organic 2010
Bowmore 20 Years Old 1997
Dramfool 13 Port Charlotte 2001 Aged 15 Years
Caol Ila Aged 15 Years
Caol Ila Aged 25 Years
Fadandel.dk Treasure of Islay Caol Ila Aged 10 Years
Gordon & MacPhail Connoisseurs Choice Caol Ila 1990
Kingsbury Gold Caol Ila 21 Years Old
The Dalmore Visitor Centre Exclusive
Glenfarclas The Family Casks 1978 W18
Glenfarclas The Family Casks 1979 W18
The Glenfiddich Unique Solera Reserve Aged 15 Years
Glengoyne 25 Year Old
Gordon & MacPhail Glen Grant 1948
The Glenlivet Archive 21 Years of Age batch no. 0513M
Cadenhead's Single Cask International Glenlossie 23 Years Old
Glenmorangie 25 Years Old
Glenmorangie Grand Vintage 1993
Glenmorangie Private Edition 9 Spios
The Singleton of Glen Ord 14 Year Old
The Last Drop Glenrothes 1968
The Last Drop Glenrothes 1969
The Last Drop Glenrothes 1970
Glen Scotia Distillery Edition No. 6 19 Years Old
Gordon & MacPhail Rare Old Glenury Royal 1984
Highland Park Aged 18 Years
Acla Special Selection No. 4 Highland Park 24 Years Old
Fadandel.dk Orkney Aged 14 Years
AnCnoc 1999
Lagavulin Aged 8 Years
The Whisky Barrel Isle of Islay 10 Year Old
Loch Lomond The Open Special Edition Distiller's Cut
The Macallan Fine Oak 12 Years Old
The Macallan Oscuro
Spirit of Caledonia Macduff 9 Years Old
Old Pulteney Aged 15 Years
Gordon & MacPhail Connoisseurs Choice Pulteney Aged 19 Years
Rosebank 21 Year Old
The Golden Cask Speyside 1992
Tomatin Warehouse 6 Collection 1975
Elements of Islay OC5
The Whisky Agency Speyside Region Single Malt 1973
**Scottish Vatted Malt**
Compass Box The Lost Blend
Compass Box The Spice Tree
Glen Castle Blended Malt 1992 Sherry Cask
Malts Spice King Batch 001
**Scottish Grain**
Glen Fahrn Airline No. 17 Cambus 1991

The Whisky Cask Company Cambus 27 Years Old
The Pearls of Scotland North of Scotland 1971
**Scottish Blends**
The Chivas 18 Ultimate Cask Collection First
Fill American Oak
Chivas Regal Aged 25 Years
Glenalba Aged 34 Years Sherry Cask Finish
Johnnie Walker Black Label 12 Years Old
Royal Salute 21 Year Old The Lost Blend
Royal Salute 62 Gun Salute
**Irish Single Malt**
The Tyrconnell Single Cask 11 Year Old
Bushmills Distillery Reserve Aged 12 Years
Bushmills Aged 21 Years
The Irishman Aged 17 Years
J. J. Corry The Flintlock No. 1 16 Year Old
Kinahan's Special Release Project 11 Year Old
Teeling Whiskey Single Malt Aged 24 Years
**Bourbon**
Abraham Bowman Viriginia Sweet XVI
Blade and Bow 22 Year Old
Blanton's Single Barrel
Buffalo Trace Single Oak Project Barrel #27
Buffalo Trace Single Oak Project Barrel #30
Buffalo Trace Single Oak Project Barrel #63
Buffalo Trace Single Oak Project Barrel #183
Charter 101
Eagle Rare Aged 10 Years
Elijah Craig Barrel Proof Bourbon 12 Years
Elijah Craig Barrel Proof Kentucky Straight
Bourbon Aged 12 Years
Elmer T Lee Single Barrel Kentucky Straight
Bourbon Whiskey
Frankfort Bourbon Society Elijah Craig
Small Batch Serial No 4718833
Knob Creek Aged 9 Years
Michter's Single Barrel 10 Year Old Kentucky
Straight Bourbon
Old Forester 1920 Prohibition Style
Pappy Van Winkle Family Reserve Kentucky
Straight Bourbon Whiskey 23 Years Old
Parker's Heritage Collection 24 Year Old
Bottled in Bond Bourbon
Rock Hill Farms Single Barrel Bourbon
Russel's Reserve Single Barrel
Weller Antique 107
Weller C.YPB Wheated Kentucky Straight Bourbon
Wild Turkey Rare Breed Barrel Proof
**Tennessee Whiskey**
George Dickel Rye
**American Straight Rye**
Knob Creek Rye Single Barrel Select
Michter's No. 1 Straight Rye
Sazerac 18 Years Old
Thomas H. Handy Sazerac 49.5%
Thomas H. Handy Sazerac 64.6%
Wild Turkey 101 Kentucky Straight Rye
**American Straight Wheat**
Parker's Heritage Collection Original Batch
Kentucky Straight Wheat Whiskey Aged 13 Years
**American Microdistilleries**
Garrison Brothers Cowboy Bourbon Barrel
Proof Aged Five Years
Hillrock Single Malt Whiskey
Rock Town Single Barrel Barley Bourbon
Whiskey Aged 26 Months
Rock Town Single Barrel Bourbon Whiskey
Aged 20 Months
Rock Town Single Barrel Four Grain Sour
Mash Bourbon Whiskey Aged 26 Months
Stranahan's Snowflake Cab Franc
High West Campfire
**American White Dog**
Buffalo Trace White Dog Rye Mash
**Canadian Single Malt**
Lohin McKinnon Peated Single Malt Whisky
Forty Creek Port Wood Reserve
**Canadian Blended**
Alberta Premium

Crown Royal Northern Harvest Rye bott
code: 095 B1 0247
Gibson's Finest Rare Aged 18 Years
**Japanese Single Malt**
Ichiro's Malt Aged 20 Years
**Japanese Vatted Malt**
Nikka Taketsuru Pure Malt
**English Single Malt**
Bimber Single Malt New-Make Test Batch
Sample batch no. 25
**Welsh Single Malt**
Penderyn Legend bott code 72965
Penderyn Legend bott code 83045
Penderyn Single Cask no. M729
**Australian Single Malt**
Bakery Hill Peated Malt Cask Strength
Belgrove Distillery Rye Whisky
Heartwood Night Thief
**Austrian Single Malt**
Peter Affenzeller Single Malt 7 Years Old
**Corsican Single Malt**
P & M Aged 13 Years Corsican Single Malt
**Danish Single Malt**
Stauning Peat
Stauning Rye The Master Distiller
**French Single Malt**
Kornog En E Bezh 10 Year Old
Kornog Saint Erwan 2018
**German Single Malt**
New Make Barley Malt Peated
The Glen Els Claret Aged 5 Years
**Slovakian Single Malt**
Nestville Master Blender 8 Years Old
**Swedish Single Malt**
Gute Single Malt Whisky
High Coast Distillery Visitor Center Cask
Mackmyra Brukswhisky
Mackmyra Svensk Rök
**Swiss Single Malt**
Langatun 10 Year Old Chardonnay
Langatun Cardeira Cask Finish
Langatun Old Deer Cask Strength
Langatun Sherry Cask Finish
**Indian Single Malt**
Amrut Peated Port Pipe Single Cask
Paul John Christmas Edition 2018
**Taiwanese Single Malt**
Kavalan Solist Single Cask Strength
Amontillado Sherry Cask

**95 (New Entries Only)**
**Scottish Single Malt**
Glenwill Ben Nevis 1992
Bladnoch 27 Year Old
Gordon & MacPhail Connoisseurs Choice
Caol Ila 1984 Aged 33 Years
Master of Malt Dalmore 14 Year Old
Glenfarclas The Family Casks 1997 W18
SMWS Cask 123.31 10 Year Old
Gordon & MacPhail Glenlivet 1954
Demijohn Glen Moray 10 Years Old
The Glenrothes Whisky Maker's Cut
The Last Drop Glenrothes 1970
Gordon & MacPhail Connoisseurs Choice
Glentauchers Aged 27 Years
Carn Mor Laphroaig 8 Year Old 2010
Loch Lomond 25 Year Old Three Wood
Matured Colin Montgomerie
The First Editions Macduff Aged 21 Years
Sansibar Whisky Springbank 2000
Finlaggan Feis Ile 2018 Vintage 2009 Islay
Port Askaig 33 Years Old Single Cask
Dramfool 22 Elderly Elvis Tilting 25 Years Old
Liquid Treasures Snakes Speyside 26 Year Old
**Scottish Vatted Malt**
Compass Box Juveniles
Old Perth Blended Malt 23 Years Old
**Scottish Blend**
The Half Century Blend

**Irish Single Malt**
Glendalough Single Malt Irish Whiskey Aged 25 Years Tree #2 Jack's Wood
**Bourbon**
Bomberger's Declaration Kentucky Straight Bourbon 2018 Release
Buffalo Trace Experimental Collection Seasoned Staves - 48 Months
Clyde May's Straight Bourbon
Eagle Rare 17 Years Old bott Summer 2018
Four Roses Small Batch
Frankfort Bourbon Society Knob Creek Single Barrel Reserve Aged 9 Years Old
Fitzgerald Bottled-in-Bond Aged 13 Years Spring 2019 Edition
Old Grand-Dad Bonded 100 Proof
Widow Jane Straight Bourbon Whiskey
**American Straight Rye**
Knob Creek Cask Strength Rye
Sagamore Spirit Straight Rye Cask Strength
**American Microdistilleries**
Balcones Texas Rye Cask Strength Aged at Least 27 Months in Oak
Balcones Texas Single Malt Single Barrel Aged at Least 65 Months in Oak
291 Bad Guy Colorado Bourbon Whiskey Aged 291 Days
FEW Bourbon Whiskey batch no. 18K14
Garrison Brothers Texas Straight Bourbon Whiskey 2019
Hillrock Single Malt 7 Under 4 Years Old
Westland Distillery Peat Week Fifth Annual Edition
**Japanese Single Malt**
The Matsui Mizunara Cask
**English Single Malt**
Bimber Single Malt Test Batch Sample re-charred cask
Cotswolds Single Malt Whisky 2014 Odyssey Barley Batch No. 07/2018
Spirit of Yorkshire Maturing Malt Distillery Projects 003
The English Single Malt Smokey Oak
The English Single Malt Virgin Oak
**Welsh Single Malt**
Penderyn Celt
Penderyn Peated Single Cask cask no. P277
Penderyn Single Cask Rich Madeira cask no. M334
Penderyn Single Cask Vintage 2006 Ex-Bourbon Cask
**Australian Single Malt**
Heartwood Shot in the Dark
Iniquity Gold Label Single Malt Batch 004
**Danish Single Malt**
Stauning Peat Festival 2018
**Finnish Single Malt**
Teerenpeli Juhlaviski 13 Year Old
**French Single Malt**
Kornog Saint Ivy 2019
**German Single Malt**
Saillt Mór Single Cask Malt Whisky
Elch Torf vom Dorf
St. Kilian Turf Dog Cask Strength
The Spirit of St. Kilian Batch No. 5 27 Months
**Italian Single Malt**
PUNI Alba Italian Single Malt
**Swedish Single Malt**
High Coast Archipelago Baltic Sea 2019
Mackmyra Moment Prestige
Mackmyra Svensk Ek
**Taiwanese Single Malt**
Kavalan Single Malt Whisky 10th Anniversary Bordeaux Margaux Wine Cask
Kavalan Solist Port Cask

**94.5 (New Entries Only)**
**Scottish Single Malt**
Gordon & MacPhail Connoisseurs Choice Aberfeldy Aged 25 Years

SMWS Cask 54.75 16 Year Old
Ardbeg Traigh Bhan
The First Editions Ardmore Aged 20 Years
Aultmore of the Foggie Moss Aged 18 Years
Benromach Sherry Cask Matured Peat Smoke
The Golden Cask Bowmore 2002
Old Malt Cask Bowmore Aged 21 Years
The First Editions Craigellachie Aged 12 Years
The GlenDronach 25 Years Old
Glenfarclas The Family Casks 1983 W18
Glenfarclas The Family Casks 1996 W18
Glenfarclas The Family Casks 2003 W18
Glen Grant Aged 12 Years bott code: LRO/GC19
Glenmorangie Global Travel Retail 16 Year Old
Glenmorangie Nectar D'Or
Glen Scotia Campbeltown Malts Festival 2019
Fadandel.dk Orkney Aged 12 Years
Master of Malt Littlemill 27 Year Old
The Whisky Shop Loch Lomond Aged 15 Years
The Deveron Aged 12 Years
Lady of the Glen Mannochmore 2007
The Whisky Shop Old Pulteney Aged 12 Years
Master of Malt Springbank 20 Year Old
The First Editions Strathmill Aged 21 Years
Hidden Spirits Teaninich 2006
W.W. Club MCL.2 Speyside Aged 25 Years
**Scottish Grain**
World of Orchids Cameron Brig 1991 26 Years Old
**Irish Single Malt**
The Whisky Cask Company Bushmills Capall 26 Years Old
The Dublin Liberties Copper Alley 10 Year Old Single Malt
The Irishman Aged 17 Years
Sansibar Irish Single Malt 1989 Japonism
Teeling Whiskey Aged 30 Years Single Malt
**Bourbon**
Blanton's Single Barrel Bourbon
Blanton's Straight From the Barrel Bourbon
Boone County Eighteen 33 Straight Bourbon Aged 12 Years
Elijah Craig Barrel Proof Bourbon
John J Bowman Single Barrel Virginia Straight Bourbon
Rebel Yell Small Batch Reserve Kentucky Straight Bourbon Whiskey
Van Winkle Special Reserve 12 Years Old Lot "B" Batch Bourbon Whiskey
The Whisky Shop Maker's Mark
**Tennessee Whiskey**
Uncle Nearest 1820 Premium Whiskey Aged 11 Years Nearest Green Single Barrel
**American Straight Rye**
Michter's Barrel Strength Kentucky Rye
**American Microdistilleries**
Boldt Cereal Killer Straight Rye Whiskey Aged 2 Years
Balcones Texas Single Malt Single Barrel Aged at Least 60 Months in Oak
Glenns Creek OCD#5
Iron Smoke Casket Strength Straight Bourbon Whiskey Aged A Minimum of Two Years
A.D. Law Four Grain Straight Bourbon Whiskey Aged 6 Years 1 Month Cask Strength
Reservoir Distillery Bourbon Whiskey
Rock Town Arkansas Rye Aged 23 Months
**American/Kentucky Whiskey Blends**
Whisky Jewbilee Straight Rye 5 Years and Straight Bourbon 12 Years
**American White Dog**
Buffalo Trace White Dog Wheated Mash
**Canadian Single Malt**
Shelter Point Artisanal Single Malt Whisky Distiller's Select
**Japanese Single Malt**
Meiyo Single Grain Whisky Aged 17 Years
**English Single Malt**
Bimber Test Batch Sample Bourbon

Bimber Test Batch Sample ex-sherry
Cotswolds Single Malt Whisky Founder's Choice Batch No. 01/2018
**Welsh Single Malt**
Penderyn Myth bott code 82262
Penderyn Peated bott code 82141
**Australian Single Malt**
Belgrove Distillery Rye Whisky Wholly Shit Sheep Dung Smoke
Fannys Bay Tasmanian Single Malt
Killara Distillery KD02
Nant Distillery Single Malt White Oak Cask
Overeem Single Malt Whisky Port Cask
Southern Coast Single Malt Batch 007
Sullivans Cove French Oak
Upshot Australian Whiskey Cask Strength
**German Single Malt**
New Make Barley Malt
Stork Club 100% Rye Still Young Aged 2 Years
**Swedish Single Malt**
High Coast Distillery Small Batch No. 09
Smögen Svensk Single Malt Single Cask 7 Year Old Rum Finish
Spirit of Hven Seven Stars No. 7 Alkaid Single Malt Whisky
**Swiss Single Malt**
Langatun Old Woodpecker
Seven Seals Peated Double Wood Finish
**Indian Single Malt**
Paul John Classic Select Cask
**Taiwanese Single Malt**
Kavalan Solist Fino Sherry Cask
Kavalan Vinho Barrique Cask
**Cross-country vatted whiskies**
Mister Sam Tribute Whiskey

## 94 (New Entries Only)
**Scottish Single Malt**
Annandale Man O' Words
Balblair Aged 17 Years
Hidden Spirits Balmenach 2004
Benromach 1972
Gordon & MacPhail Connoisseurs Choice Clynelish Aged 28 Years
Craigellachie Aged 17 Years
Glenfardas The Family Casks 1993 W18 Release
Glen Grant Aged 12 Years
Gordon & MacPhail Connoisseurs Choice Glenlivet Aged 15 Years
Glenwill Glen Moray 1990
The Perfect Fifth Glen Scotia 1992
Loch Lomond Cristie Kerr Vintage 2002
The Deveron Aged 10 Years
The First Editions Macduff Aged 21 Years 1997
Old Malt Cask Miltonduff Aged 23 Years
Gordon & MacPhail Connoisseurs Choice Scapa Aged 30 Years
Wolfburn Langskip
Glen Turner Heritage Double Cask Port Cask
A.D. Rattray Cask Orkney 18 Year Old
Port Askaig 34 Years Old Single Cask
**Scottish Vatted Malt**
St. Ola 8 Year Old 2010 Orcadian Blended Malt
**Scottish Grain**
The Sovereign Cambus 30 Years Old
Berry Bros & Rudd Girvan 12 Years Old
**Irish Single Malt**
The Whisky Cask Company Bushmills Madra 26 Years Old
Liquid Treasures Irish Malt 29 Year Old
**Bourbon**
1792 Small Batch Kentucky Straight Bourbon
Ancient Age 10 Star Bourbon
Blanton's The Original Single Barrel Bourbon Whiskey
Buffalo Trace Kentucky Straight Bourbon
Frankfort Bourbon Society Weller Antique 107 Single Barrel Select Serial

Weller Special Reserve Kentucky Straight Bourbon
**Tennessee Whiskey**
Heaven's Door Tennessee Bourbon Whiskey Aged for a Minimum of 7 Years
Jack Daniel's Single Barrel Select
**American Straight Rye**
Michter's Barrel Strength Straight Rye
Russell's Reserve Straight Rye 6 Years Old
**American Microdistilleries**
Boldt Cereal Killer Straight Triticale Whiskey Aged 2 Years
FEW Rye Whiskey batch no. 18E30
Glenns Creek Café Olé Kentucky Bourbon Barrel No 1 Aged At Least 1 Year
Westland Distillery cask no. 4274
Yellow Rose Outlaw Batch Bourbon
**American/Kentucky Whiskey Blends**
Widow Jane Aged 10 Years
**American White Dog**
Buffalo Trace White Dog Mash #1
**Canadian Single Malt**
Forty Creek Confederation Oak Reserve
Shelter Point Double Barreled Single Malt
**Canadian Straight Rye**
Masterson's 10 Year Old Straight Rye Whiskey
**Japanese Single Malt**
The Akkeshi New Born 2018 Foundations 2 Single Malt Spirit Peated
**English Single Malt**
Bimber Single Malt Test Batch Sample
Fortnum & Mason English Single Malt cask 532
**Welsh Single Malt**
Penderyn Celt
Penderyn Madeira Finish bott code 81927
Penderyn Madeira Finish bott code 83213
Penderyn Rich Oak
Penderyn Sherrywood
Feingeist Ex-Moscatel Finish Single Cask Single Malt Welsh Whisky 2013
**Australian**
Bakery Hill Classic Malt Cask Strength Single Malt Whisky
Hobart Whisky Tasmanian Single Malt Batch 19-002
Killara Distillery KD01 Cask Strength
Lark Single Malt Whisky Cask Strength
Launceston Distillery Tasmanian Single Malt Whisky Cask Strength
Nant Distillery Single Malt Whisky Port Cask
Spring Bay The Rheban Cask Strength Tasmanian Single Malt Whisky Port Cask
**Austrian Single Malt**
Bodding Lokn Single Cask Classic
**Belgian Single Malt**
Belgian Owl Single Malt The Private Angels 60 Months
**French Single Malt**
Kornog Roc'h Hir 2019
**German Single Malt**
Valerie Single Malt
**Italian Single Malt**
PUNI Vina 5 Year Old Italian Single Malt
**The Netherlands Single Malt**
Millstone Dutch Single Rye 92 Rye Whisky
**Indian Single Malt**
Amrut Greedy Angels Peated Sherry Finish Chairman's Reserve 10 Years Old
Paul John Nirvana Unpeated Single Malt
**Taiwanese Single Malt**
Kavalan Solist ex-Bourbon Cask
Nantou Distillery Omar Cask Strength Lychee Liqueur Barrel Finished
**Cross-country vatted whiskies**
The One British Blended Whisky Sherry Expression

21

# American Whiskey

**D**uring the early Spring of this year I took a very long drive. It was from Texas to Kentucky, taking me on a route which cut through the Ozark Mountains in both Arkansas and Missouri, where I dropped in on a forest in which oaks had been felled for the making of bourbon barrels. And then stood beside the stumps of departed trees holding in my hands the last acorns they had ever deposited.

I stopped at quite a few liquor stores en-route, also. And found something possibly even more astonishing. Where, once, the whisk(e)y shelves had contained an ever-increasing number of single malt Scotch whiskies, now they contained bourbon.

Kentucky bourbon, Colorado bourbon, Texas bourbon. They were all there. Alongside ryes and Tennessee and various types of whiskeys from the micro-distilleries. It seemed that in mid-America at least bourbon and rye had Scotch whisky on the run: a nation had fallen back in love with its national whiskey.

And that can hardly be surprising when this year, for the third consecutive time running, it was a bourbon whiskey which scooped the Jim Murray Whisky Bible World Whisky of the Year. Three years ago, E H Taylor. Last year the William Larue Weller. And this year, for the first time ever, a bourbon from the once unloved Barton of Bardstown, these days, under the relatively new ownership of the golden-fingered Sazerac, now known as the much admired 1792 Barton. And with Booker's Rye winning in 2017, that means American whiskey has scooped the top award for four years running.

Even by their own very high standards, this year American whiskey has excelled: for the first time ever it came home in the top three positions in the Whisky Bible Awards – so the top three brands all came from the USA. Phenomenal.

In Texas, so high is the standard of the whiskeys there, I was able to travel to the State to carry out a whiskey shootout between 11 of their distilleries there to see which, through blind tasting, the assembled crowd appreciated most. It was Garrison Brothers. Their enormous Balmorhea was the Whisky Bible 2019 Microdistillery Whisky of the Year and, after their success at the Longview tasting, it went and won it again for the 2020 Bible.

A quarter of a century ago the liquor store owners from New York to San Francisco were telling me that bourbon and rye would soon be a thing of the past as single malts moved in. Bourbon is back and truly back. And, as the top awards of Jim Murray's Whisky Bible underlines, with very good reason.

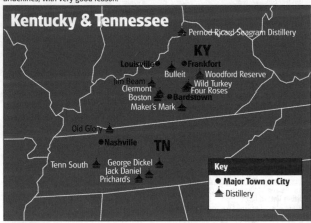

**Kentucky & Tennessee**

Pernod Ricard Seagram Distillery

KY

Louisville ●

● Frankfort

Bulleit ▲ Woodford Reserve

Jim Beam ▲ Wild Turkey

Clermont ▲ Four Roses ▲

Boston ▲ ● Bardstown

Maker's Mark ▲

Old Glory ▲

● Nashville TN

Tenn South ▲ George Dickel ▲

Jack Daniel ▲

Prichard's ▲

**Key**

● Major Town or City

▲ Distillery

**Bardstown**
Heaven Hill
Tom Moore

**Frankfort**
Buffalo Trace
Woodford Reserve

**Louisville**
Bernheim
Early Times
Rabbit Hole
Stitzel Weller

## Bourbon Distilleries

Bourbon confuses people. Often they don't even realise it is a whiskey, a situation not helped by leading British pub chains, such as Wetherspoon, whose bar menus list "whiskey" and "bourbon" in separate sections. And if I see the liqueur Southern Comfort listed as a bourbon one more time I may not be responsible for my actions.

Bourbon is a whiskey. It is made from grain and matured in oak, so really it can't be much else. To be legally called bourbon it must have been made with a minimum of 51% corn and matured in virgin oak casks for at least two years. Oh, and no colouring can be added other than that which comes naturally from the barrel.

Where it does differ, from, say Scotch, is that the straight whiskey from the distillery may be called by something other than that distillery name. Indeed, the distillery may change its name which has happened to two this year already and two others in the last three or four. So, to make things easy and reference as quick as possible, I shall list the Kentucky-based distilleries first and then their products in alphabetical order along with their owners and operational status.

# BUFFALO TRACE Leestown, Frankfort. Sazerac. Operating.

# BROWN-FORMAN Shively, Louisville. Brown-Forman. Operating.

# FOUR ROSES Lawrenceburg. Kirin. Operating

# HEAVEN HILL BERNHEIM DISTILLERY Louisville. Heaven Hill. Operating.

# JIM BEAM Boston and Clermont. Beam Suntory. Operating.

# MAKER'S MARK Loretto. Beam Suntory. Operating.

# WILD TURKEY Lawrenceburg. Campari Group. Operating.

# WOODFORD RESERVE Near Millville. Brown-Forman. Operating.

## Jim Murray's Whisky Bible American Whiskey Award Winners

|      | Overall Winner | Bourbon | Rye | Microdistilleries |
|------|----------------|---------|-----|-------------------|
| 2004 | George T. Stagg | George T. Stagg | Sazerac Rye 18 Years Old | McCarthy's Oregon Single Malt |
| 2005 | George T. Stagg | George T. Stagg | Sazerac Rye 18 Years Old | McCarthy's Oregon Single Malt |
| 2006 | George T. Stagg | George T. Stagg | Sazerac Rye 18 Years Old | McCarthy's Oregon Single Malt |
| 2007 | Buffalo Trace Experimental | Buffalo Trace Experimental | Rittenhouse Rye 21 Barrel No.28 | McCarthy's Oregon Single Malt |
| 2008 | George T. Stagg 70.3% | George T. Stagg 70.3% | Old Potrero Hotaling's 11 Essay | Old Potrero Hotaling's 11 Essay |
| 2009 | George T. Stagg (144.8 Proof) | George T. Stagg (144.8 Proof) | Rittenhouse Rye 23 Barrel No.8 | Stranahan's Colorado 5 Batch 11 |
| 2010 | Sazerac Rye 18 (Fall 2008) | George T. Stagg (144.8 Proof) | Sazerac Rye 18 (Fall 2008) | N/A |
| 2011 | Thomas H. Handy Rye (129 Proof) | William Larue Weller (134.8 Proof) | Thomas H. Handy Rye (129 Proof) | N/A |
| 2012 | George T. Stagg (143 Proof) | George T. Stagg (143 Proof) | Thomas H. Handy Rye (126.9 Proof) | N/A |
| 2013 | Thomas H. Handy Rye (128.6 Proof) | William Larue Weller (133.5 Proof) | Thomas H. Handy Rye (128.6 Proof) | Balcones Brimstone |
| 2014 | William Larue Weller (123.4 Proof) | William Larue Weller (123.4 Proof) | Thomas H. Handy Rye (132.4 Proof) | Cowboy Bourbon Whiskey |
| 2015 | William Larue Weller | William Larue Weller | Sazerac Rye 18 (Fall 2013) | Arkansas Single Barrel Reserve #190 |
| 2016 | Pikesville Straight Rye (110 Proof) | William Larue Weller | Pikesville Straight Rye (110 Proof) | Notch 12 Year Old |
| 2017 | Booker's Rye 13 Years 1 Mo 12 Days | William Larue Weller (134.6 Proof) | Booker's Rye 13 Years 1 Mo 12 Days | Garrison Brothers Cowboy 2009 |
| 2018 | Colonel E.H. Taylor Four Grain | Colonel E.H. Taylor Four Grain | Thomas H. Handy Rye (126.2 Proof) | Balcones Texas Blue Corn |
| 2019 | William Larue Weller (128.2 Proof) | William Larue Weller (128.2 Proof) | Thomas H. Handy Rye (127.2 Proof) | Garrison Brothers Balmorhea |
| 2020 | 1792 Full Proof Bourbon | 1792 Full Proof Bourbon | Thomas H. Handy Rye (128.8 Proof) | Garrison Brothers Balmorhea |

# Bourbon

**1792 Bottled In Bond** bott code: L172731504:465 db **(93) n23 t23.5 f23 b23.5** An unusually salty resonance to this which fractures from the nose to the very last moments of the finish. Certainly does a job in sharpening up the flavour profile! *50% (100 proof).*

◈ **1792 Bottled In Bond Kentucky Straight Bourbon** bott code: L183471505565 **(96.5) n24** one of the most complex noses of the year, with the distillery small grains style (appreciated by literally two or three of us in the know 25 years ago–and that includes then employees!) now going into orbit. A unique salt and pepper complexity to this for a Kentucky whiskey, with the rye element chipping away at the associated sugars and even a delicate maltiness evident. Slightly overaged banana and nibbling tannin intensity also making a subtle but vital contribution. Fabulous! **t24** if it is complex on the nose, then the bittiness on delivery is now becoming the stuff of legend. The rye really does steal the show, turning up in varying guises, both fruity and ultra- crunchy sugars. But the corn oils are strong and melt with the Manuka and ulmo honey blend. Hickory and molasses take up the middle ground and...; **f24** ...move us into the farewell throes. The fade is all about a silky, brooding, husky liquorice and salty honey...; **b24.5** well, it's only gone and improved, hasn't it..!!! I just wish this distillery would give a whiskey I could seriously pan..! Just so damn, indecently beautiful...! *50% (100 proof).*

◈ **1792 Full Proof Kentucky Straight Bourbon** bott code: L181351513:425 **(97.5) n24** spectacularly rich: almost a kaleidoscopic effect on the nose with honey coming at you from every angle and in a multitude of intensities. Orange blossom honey leads the way like a Kentucky locomotive pulling its long freight haul of red and black liquorice and so many layers of tannins – vanilla in at least three different intensities. It needs spice for that third dimension – and gets it in near perfect proportions; **t24.5** you can only sit, eyes closed, in awe. This is a delivery of perfection: intense, seemingly no prisoners. Yet, actually, you find it has the grace to allow every character to make a speech of great erudition, ultimately a discourse of how so many facets can be singular yet together make for such glorious integration. But the intensity of the chocolate on the middle is a show-stopper in its own right...; **f24** long with spices, corn oil and cocoa fading out in unfaltering fashion; **b25** sings on the nose and palate like a wood thrush in a Kentucky forest: melodious, mysterious and slightly exotic. On this evidence Buffalo Trace has a threat to its world supremacy – from a rival distillery...they own! This is a whiskey of stand out, almost stand-alone beauty. Finding fault is not easy with something this intense and magnificently rich. If this is not World Whisky of the Year for 2020, then its master will be something to marvel at. *62.5% (125 proof).*

**1792 High Rye Kentucky Straight Bourbon** db **(96) n23.5 t24.5 f23.5 b24.5** My word! What an exhibition of controlled and sometimes disguised big flavours...! Stupendous! 47.15% .

◈ **1792 Single Barrel Kentucky Straight Bourbon** nbc **(90.5) n22.5** a lovely hickory-liquorice mix with spices in healthy mode; **t22** a creamy and peppery start, the corn oils high on the early flavour profile. The toffees and vanillas take their time to make a mark but get there at their own pace; **f23** more complex now as the tannins and vanillas appear more harmonised and the sugars now deliciously integrated; **b23** typical of a single cask, offering some of what you expect from a distillery though not necessarily all. Delicious and more mouth-filling as it progresses. *44% (88 proof). sc.*

**1792 Small Batch** bott code: L173111514:395 **(94) n23 t24 f23.5 b23.5** Yet again a 1792 expression pulls off Whisky Bible Liquid Gold status. Astonishing. *46.85% (93.7 proof).*

◈ **1792 Small Batch Kentucky Straight Bourbon** bott code: L190461512595 **(94) n23.5** a noticeably lighter nose than the last I encountered with a much more ethereal, nutty presence and a slow build of waxy, liquorice and vanilla notes; **t24** really clever delivery, missing the punch you'd expect but instead a big vanilla surge is rounded by heather honey and delicate spices: so genteel...; **f23** much drier, toasty even, with the chalkiness offering both vanilla and light citrus; **b23.5** on the lighter side of the 1782 spectrum, though definitely within the distillery's new orbit. Where there is often a rich wave of soft tannins, here it concentrates on the defter vanillas, at times delicate to the point of fragility, though the trademark weight and gravitas is not far behind... *46.85% (93.7 proof).*

**1792 Sweet Wheat Kentucky Straight Bourbon** db **(94.5) n23.5 t24 f23 b24** Barton had long been one of the wasted distilleries of the world, its product once bottled and sold way before its intricate, busy bourbon was able to sing to its fullest potential. Under the new management of Sazerac, we are now consistently seeing the greatness from this distillery that for decades was found only in its 6-year-old. This is a wheated, honeyed stunner. *45.6% (91.2 proof)*

**Abraham Bowman Limited Edition Virginia Sweet XVI Bourbon** dist 4-26-02, bott 4-26-18 **(95.5) n23.5 t24.5 f23.5 b24** Probably the most outrageously complex and full-flavoured Virginia whiskey I have ever encountered in bottled form...Just amazin'! *58% (116 proof). Release No. 17.*

◌ **American Rockies Small Batch Bourbon Whiskey** (76) n19 t22 f17 b18 Sweet, soft, fruity and rounded. But very dull. With an unattractive furry finish to boot. Just not sure what all these fruit notes are doing in a bourbon. 44% (88 proof).

**Ancient Age** bott code: 03072163212:09F (94) n24 t23.5 f22.5 b24 Though at times a little youthful and proudly possessing a little nip on the delivery, this still exudes Buffalo Trace character and class and a lot more inner oomph than when I first encountered this brand decades ago – indeed, when the distillery was still called Ancient Age. Enough oak to make a comfortable foil for the busy small grain. Salivating, complex and deeply satisfying, especially when the burnt honey begins to make itself heard .A classic name and my word, this bottling shows it in a classic light. 40% (80 proof)

◌ **Ancient Age Kentucky Straight Bourbon** bott code: L190240120:254 (93) n23 t23 f23.5 b23.5 Very similar to the bottling code above One very slight difference here is just a slight downturn in the intensity of the honey while the spices, perhaps with a fraction less to counter it, have a marginally louder voice. Perhaps not quite the same balance, but the finish goes on so much longer. 40% (80 proof).

**Ancient Age Bonded** (92) n23 t24 f23 b23. Unmistakably Buffalo Trace... with balls. 50%

**Ancient Age 10 Star** bott code: B1704707:294 (86) n21 t22.5 f21 b21.5 Plenty of action but struggles to find a rhythm and balance while the finish is just plain dull. The spiced chocolate and liquorice surge is the highlight but slightly disappointing for an Ancient Age. 45% (90 proof)

**Ancient Ancient Age 10 Years Old** (96) n23.5 t24 f24 b24.5. This whiskey is like shifting sands: same score as last time out, but the shape is quite different again. Somehow underlines the genius of the distillery that a world class whiskey can reach the same point of greatness, but by taking two different routes...However, in this case the bourbon actually finds something a little extra to move it on to a point very few whiskeys very rarely reach... 43%

**Ancient Ancient Age 10 Star** (94.5) n23 t24 f23.5 b24. A bourbon which has slipped effortlessly through the gears over the last decade. It is now cruising and offers so many nuggets of pure joy this is now a must have for the serious bourbon devotee. Now a truly great bourbon which positively revels in its newfound complexity: a new 10 Star is born... 45%

◌ **Ancient Age 10 Star Kentucky Straight Bourbon** bott code: L182010116 (94) n22.5 strangely lacklustre and half cooked on one level, with none of the sugars, vanillas or fruit notes seeming able to harmonise as you might expect, then on another there is an intense and intriguing subplot which promises much; t23.5 ah...that's so much better. What doesn't work on the nose has no such problems on the palate and the delivery struts its ultra corn-rich stuff from the get go, slowly absorbing the growing dark sugars as it goes; f24 now we enter full cocoa mode, which in turn moves towards a full-ish roast coffee, a kind of Java/Gesha Arabica blend; the tannin and muscovado background works so well...; b24 a bourbon which had lost its way slightly in recent years. And though it still splutters about a bit for identity and rhythm on the nose, there is no doubting it is right back on track with some taste-bud catching moments. It is at times, monumental. 45% (90 proof).

**Ancient Age 90** bott code: 03072173209:38W (88.5) n22 t22 f22.5 b22 An emboldened bourbon showing little of genteel complexity of the standard Ancient Age. Delicious, though! 45% (90 proof)

◌ **Ancient Age 90 Kentucky Straight Bourbon Whiskey** bott code: B1310606 (93.5) n23 t23 f23.5 b24 More of the same as above, though now is a lot more vibrant. A little more stark tannin on the nose to this one and an infinitely more lush and bold delivery. If the layering was good before, then now it is excellent with not just an extra layer or two of strata to negotiate but much more Manuka honey coming through at the death. How can two whiskeys be outwardly so similar, yet so different? A bit like having a polished Jaguar XK against a slightly dusty one. 45% (90 proof).

◌ **Barrel Bourbon Cask Strength Aged 9.5 Years** batch 015 (88) n22 firm, with softening butterscotch, lime and liquorice; t23 attractive corn-rich delivery, then quite a pungent oiliness carrying with it maple syrup and treacle; lovely praline throughout; f21 a tad bitter and out of sorts; b22 an interesting bottling which fits cosily together in places and falls apart slightly in others. Overall, though, enjoyable. 53.8% (107.6 proof). Distilled in Tennessee and Kentucky.

◌ **Barrel Whiskey Infinite Barrel Project Cask Strength** bott June 1 2018 (85.5) n21 t22.5 f20.5 b21.5 A strange, thin Tennessee whiskey with a mysterious sub-plot of gin-like botanicals. Which will doubtless appeal to some. 59.3% (118.6 proof). Distilled in Tennessee. 1,497 bottles

**Baker's Aged 7 Years Kentucky Straight Bourbon Whiskey** batch no. B-90-001 (95) n24 t23.5 f23.5 b24 One of those uncompromisingly delicious bourbons which makes spitting as I have to do with each sample tasted, a very unnatural act... 53.5% (107 proof).

**Basil Hayden's Kentucky Straight Bourbon Whiskey** bott code L5222 (87) n22.5 t22 f21 b21.5. Bigs up the bitter marmalade but a relatively thin bourbon with not enough depth to entirely manage the flattening and slightly unflattering vanilla. The usual rye-based backbone has gone missing. *40% (80 proof)*

  ⬦ **Bib and Tucker Aged Six Years Small Batch Bourbon** batch no 018 **(88.5)** n22 lots of toffee present here; t22 soft and soothing with a big sugar presence. A light touch of lime blossom honey mixes in with the natural caramels; f22.5 a growth in the vanillas begins to create some very attractive layering; b22 bit of a straight up and downer, with the complexity at last formulating towards the finale. About as easy-going and even as it gets. *46% (92 proof).*

**Big Bottom Straight Bourbon 91 (95)** n23 t24 f24 b24 Stupendous bourbon. *45.5% (91 proof) ncf.*

**Big Bottom Straight Bourbon 111 (85.5)** n21.5 t20.5 f22.5 b21. An aggressive bourbon and that has nothing to do with the strength. The delivery is tart and lopsided. The sharpness recedes towards the middle and, finally, the lights shine as the praline and mocha enter the fray on the spicy finish. *55.5% (111 proof) ncf.*

**Blade & Bow** batch SW-B1 **(84)** n21.5 t21.5 f20 b21. A simple, if at times massively sweet, offering which minimises on complexity. *45.5%*

**Blade and Bow 22 Year Old (95.5)** n24 t24 f23.5 b24 This may not be the oldest bourbon brand on the market, but it creaks along as though it is. Every aspect says "Old Timer". But like many an old 'un, has a good story to tell... in this case, exceptional. *46% (92 proof)*

**Blade & Bow DeLuxe** batch WLCFSS-2 **(88.5)** n22.5 t22.5 f21 b22.5 A steady ship which, initially, is heavy on the honey. *46%*

**Blanton's (92)** n21.5 t24 f23 b23.5. If it were not for the sluggish nose this would be a Whisky Bible Liquid Gold award winner for sure. On the palate it shows just why little can touch Buffalo Trace for quality at the moment... *40%*

**Blanton's Gold Original Single Barrel (96.5)** n24 t24.5 f24 b24. It is improbable that a whiskey this enormous and with so many star turns can glide so effortlessly over the palate. One of the best Blanton's in years, this is true Gold standard... *46.5% (93 Proof)*

**Blanton's Gold Edition Single Barrel** barrel no 40 dumped 3-6-17 Warehouse H Rick 79 **(96.5)** n24.5 t24.5 f23.5 b24 It does not seem possible that so much beauty, such incomprehensible complexity could be tied up in a single barrel. As astonishing as it is beautiful. *40% (80 proof)*

  ⬦ **Blanton's Gold Edition Bourbon Whiskey** dumped 15 Jan 19, barrel no 131, Warehouse H, Rick 15 **(90)** n22 relatively flat for a Blanton's, with major dependency on a mono-toned caramel note; t23 for a moment it appears some ulmo honey is about to make a joint speech with the fruity rye. But then a buttery note intervenes and becomes stronger. The corn remains dominant throughout; f22 surprisingly thin as the oils wear off, a little acacia honey clinging on to the staves; b23 the last time I tasted a Blanton's Gold, I was stopped in my tracks and knew I had, in my glass, some kind of major Whisky Bible award winner. And so it proved. This time the key honey notes crucial to greatness are thin on the ground. And, lovely whiskey though it may be, this one is no award winner..! *51.5% (103 proof). sc.*

  ⬦ **Blanton's The Original Single Barrel Bourbon Whiskey** dumped 7 March 19, barrel no 199, Warehouse H Rick 11 **(94)** n24 fruity and firm: orange peel and rye form a magnificent bond; t23.5 a multitude of sugar notes – mainly from the acacia honey style, rather than the toastier, heftier variety – make for a comfortable introduction. Even the vanilla is bathed in these sugars while the spices barely both to put up a fight; f23 corn oil and acacia honey all the way, despite a late jolt of tannin; b23.5 not sure bourbon gets any friendlier and sweeter than this without losing shape. Superb! *46.5% (93 proof). sc.*

**Blanton's Single Barrel** barrel no 44 dumped 8-31-17 warehouse H Rick 1. **(95.5)** n24 t24 f23.5 b24 If you can find a bourbon with more sublime mocha notes this year, let me know about it. As gentle as a bluegrass rolling field... *46.5% (93 proof)*

**Blanton's Single Barrel** barrel no 224 dumped 5-12-17 warehouse H Rick 51 **(94.5)** n23.5 t24 f23.5 b23.5 For the odd moment you think the tannin has gone too far. Then you realise there is a choreographed movement of oaks which ensures the sugars to get a fair hearing. Massive is perhaps a bit of an understatement... *66.6% (133.2 proof)*

**Blanton's Single Barrel** barrel no 1943 dumped 10-17-17 Warehouse H Rick 48 **(95)** n23.5 t23.5 f24 b24 Just a random bottling of the many they do of this single cask. Yet it somehow seems to summarise Buffalo Trace's high pedigree and complexity with effortless aplomb. Another thoroughbred and odds on favourite. *46.5% (93 proof)*

  ⬦ **Blanton's Single Barrel Kentucky Straight Bourbon** dumped 30th April 18, barrel no 126, Warehouse H Rick 52 **(94.5)** n23.5 an intriguing small grain busy-ness: some nip and nibble amid the almost malty marzipan and cocoa; t24 mouth-filling, mouth-caressing, palate hugging...yet succulently soft. The corn oils lull you into a false sense of security before a rattling attack of spice plus a crunchy liquorice and Demerara sub-strata send your senses reeling; f23 lots of toffee and cream, but the spices pulse alongside the hickory; b24 a very long journey from beginning to end: intriguing as you are never sure what will be happening next. *46.5% (93 proof). sc.*

◈ **Blanton's Straight From the Barrel Bourbon** dumped 22 March 18, barrel no 29, Warehouse H, Rick 46 **(94.5) n24** alright, this is huge. A five pipe puzzle to ponder over, working out just how much input the oak from aging has made, or because it has not been cut so the oils are unmolested. The light hint of pine, beyond the oaky tannin, suggests decent age and there is a rye and cocoa amalgamation, also, which adds to the startling weight; **t23** the eye-watering tannins at first seem recklessly indulgent. Then a wave of corn oil and mocha dampens the oaky onslaught. Wonderful layers of hickory and liquorice soften the impact further and allows the spices a dignified entry; **f23.5** ridiculously calm after the early splintery storm with light Manuka honey mingling with the deep vanilla; **b24** it doesn't matter their strength, age, natural colour, grain to tannin impact, fruitiness or otherwise or just general style. What is so remarkable about Blanton's as a brand – right across the board – is the consistency of their excellence. In this case it looked, early on, that it had lost out to the oak...how wrong I was..! *65.7% (131.4 proof). sc.*

**Blanton's Takara (91.5) n24.5 t23 f22 b22.** Not quite how many people might envisage a bourbon: certainly not butch enough to keep the wild west gunslingers happy. No this is a bourbon which searches for your feminine side. And being so light, leaves itself open for any off key bitter notes which might just happen along the way. *49% (98 proof)*

**Blanton's Uncut/Unfiltered (96.5) n25 t24 f23.5 b24.** Uncut. Unfiltered. Unbelievable. *65.9%*

◈ **Bomberger's Declaration Kentucky Straight Bourbon 2018 Release** batch no. 18C317, bott code: A18096317 **(95) n23.5** rivetingly rich: orange blossom honey melds with freshly polished leather...and thick corn oil; **t24** my word! What a sumptuous whiskey! The corn oil on the nose is confirmed here with interest. While the honey has given way to a much more fulsome maple syrup and molasses mix...with spices building with confidence and pace; **f23.5** so much honey and chocolate, even late on; becomes increasingly toasty as the sugars melt away; **b24** a breath-taking whiskey which, despite its seemingly soft and inclusive nature, is huge in personality. *54% (108 proof). 1,658 bottles. Bottled by Michter's Distillery.*

◈ **Bondi Bourbon Whiskey Aged 4 Years (85) n20.5 t21.5 f21.5 b21.5** Rammed full of varied honey notes, the feintiness on both the nose and delivery can't be entirely ignored. Still. Chewy and attractive late on. *40% (80 proof).*

**Booker's Bourbon 6 Years, 11 Months, 0 Days** batch no. 2016-01 db **(92.5) n24 t23.5 f22 b23** An usually fast tail off barely detracts from another beguiling bourbon. *63.95% (127.9 proof)*

**Booker's 7 Years 5 Months** batch no. C2014-05 db **(95) n24 t24 f23 b24** Not for the simpering or squeamish. There's an oaky ambush to deal with. And if you ain't man (or woman) enough, then best to mosey on over to the sarsaparilla counter... *63.95%*

**Booker's Big Man, Small Batch 7 Years 2 Months 16 Days** batch no. 2015-01 db **(89.5) n22 t23 f22 b22.5** The driest Booker's I've happened across for a good while: probably ever. Matured for seven years in a warehouse located somewhere near the centre of the sun, one assumes... *64.35% (128.7 Proof)*

◈ **Boone County Eighteen 33 Straight Bourbon Aged 12 Years** nbc **(94.5) n23.5** a relatively lightweight aroma, despite the age and peppery heather honey: so, so sexy! **t24** sensuous on delivery, the corn oils massage in the golden syrup and tannin; for a while the spices buzz like demented bees; **f23** ridiculously long, with still the honey in the ascendancy; **b24** sits as beautifully on the plate as it does in the glass. Gorgeous! *45.4% (90.8 proof). Distilled at DSP-IN-1 (MGP, Indiana, presumably.).*

◈ **Bowman Brothers Small Batch Virginia Straight Bourbon** bott code: L183540513 **(93) n23.5** I'm sure there were delicate Arabica beans all over the nose this last I time I encountered it, and here they are again in tandem with a separate praline note: so lovely and gentle; **t23** a graceful delivery with the corn oils present but not all consuming, aided with a mix of Demerara and icing sugars; vanilla tinged with Jamaican Blue Mountain fills the mid-ground; **f23** its just more of the same: long and drowsy like a summer's day reinforced with light hickory – more Camp coffee now, perhaps; **b23.5** a significant improvement on the last Small Batch I encountered with much more confidence and depth on the finish. The coffee note hangs around wonderfully... *45% (90 proof).*

**Bowman Brother's Virginia Straight Bourbon (90) n21 t23 f23 b23.** Quietly confident and complex: a bit of a gem waiting to be discovered. *45% (90 proof)*

**Bowman Brothers Virginia Straight Bourbon Small Batch** bott code: 71600080ASB08:22 **(88.5) n22** a little Arabica coffee at play here with firm tannin and spiced dates; **t23** a firm, no-nonsense delivery which is full of salivating promise. The tannins do appear a little uncompromising but the starchy sugars counter with liquorice and Java coffee; **f21.5** a little too firm as the vanilla digs deep; **b22** a lovely bourbon, though the sugars are thinly spread. *45% (90 proof)*

**Buffalo Trace (92.5) n23 t23 f23.5 b23.** Easily one of the lightest BTs I have tasted in a very long while. The rye has not just taken a back seat, but has fallen off the bus. *45%*

❖ **Buffalo Trace Kentucky Straight Bourbon** bott code: L190400220 **(94)** n23.5 continuing with its more delicate style, I see. Everything so relaxed, from the dusting of sandalwood to the red and black liquorice mix diluted with deft Manuka honey. Effortless and gentle; **t23.5** like the nose, we have a lot of understatement. But also great complexity, which slowly unfurls mainly on the pulsing dual intensity of the tannin, as well as a glorious two-toned molasses and Demerara sweetness; **f23** long, as the corn oils are projected and allow the spices to gather in pace and intensity; the banana-vanilla-molasses fade is just so well structured; **b24** a huge whiskey dressed up as something altogether more modest. But get the temperature right on this and watch it open up like a petal in sunlight. A true anywhere, anytime bourbon with hidden sophistication. *45% (90 proof).*

**Buffalo Trace Single Oak Barrel #132** (r1yKA1 *see key below*) db **(95)** n24 t23.5 f23.5 b24. This sample struck me for possessing, among the first batch of bottlings, the classic Buffalo Trace personality. Afterwards they revealed that it was of a profile which perhaps most closely matches their standard 8-year-old BT. Therefore it is this one I shall use as the tasting template. *45% (90 Proof)*

## Key to Buffalo Trace Single Oak Project Codes

**Mash bill type:** r = rye; w = wheat
**Tree grain:** 1 = course; 2 = average; 3 = tight
**Tree cut:** x = top half; y = bottom half
**Warehouse type:** K = rick; L = concrete

**Entry strength:** A = 125; B = 105
**Seasoning:** 1 = 6 Months; 2 = 12 Months
**Char:** All #4 except * = #3

**Buffalo Trace Single Oak Project Barrel #1** (r3xKA1*) db **(90.5)** n22 t23 f23 b22.5. Soft corn oil aroma, buttery, big sugars building, silky texture, long. *45% (90 Proof)*

**Buffalo Trace Single Oak Project Barrel #2** (r3yKA1*) db **(91.5)** n23 t23 f22.5 b23. Bright rye on nose and delivery. Juicy red liquorice and soft corn oil to chew on... *45%*

**Buffalo Trace Single Oak Project Barrel #3** (r2xKA1) db **(90.5)** n22.5 t23 f22.5 b22.5. Nutty, dry aroma; apple fruitiness and brown sugars. *45% (90 Proof)*

**Buffalo Trace Single Oak Project Barrel #4** (r2yKA1) db **(92)** n23 t23 f23 b23. Exceptionally crisp; sharp rye, honeycomb, big liquorice. *45% (90 Proof)*

**Buffalo Trace Single Oak Project Barrel #5** (r2xLA1*) db **(89)** n23 t22.5 f21.5 b22. Dullish after a rye-intense and busy nose. Early muscovado followed by vanilla and spice. *45%*

**Buffalo Trace Single Oak Project Barrel #6** (r3yLA1*) db **(90)** n22.5 t22 f23 b22.5. Toast with salted butter and maple syrup. Prickly, mildly aggressive spice throughout. *45%*

**Buffalo Trace Single Oak Project Barrel #7** (r3xLA1) db **(90.5)** n23 t22.5 f22.5 b22.5. Prominent rye on nose and delivery; tannin rich, toasty with big liquorice fade. *45%*

**Buffalo Trace Single Oak Project Barrel #8** (r3yLA1) db **(92.5)** n23 t23 f23.5 b23. Crisp rye aroma. Fruity, firm, salivating. Spiced toffee and muscovado; toasty.*45% (90 Proof)*

**Buffalo Trace Single Oak Project Barrel #9** (r3xKA2*) db **(90)** n22 t22.5 f23 b22.5. Marmalade on singed toast. Soft oils: slow release of natural caramels and mocha. *45%*

**Buffalo Trace Single Oak Project Barrel #10** (r3yKA2*) db **(93)** n23.5 t23.5 f22.5 b23.5. Rich, delicate rye. Complex, busy body; rye oils, tannins; slow sugar build. Bitters. *45%*

**Buffalo Trace Single Oak Project Barrel #11** (r3xKA2) db **(94.5)** n23 t24 f23.5 b24. Pronounced accent on rye, especially on delivery. Oak nose upfront; good muscovado fade. *45%.*

**Buffalo Trace Single Oak Project Barrel #12** (r3yKA2) db **(92)** n24 t23 f22.5 b22.5. The floral, supremely balanced nose isn't matched on the palate in weight or complexity. *45%*

**Buffalo Trace Single Oak Project Barrel #13** (r3xLA2*) db **(89.5)** n22 t23 f22 b22.5. Soft, yielding tactile. Early juicy, rye stance, slow build of duller light vanilla. Late spice. *45%.*

**Buffalo Trace Single Oak Project Barrel #14** (r3yLA2*) db **(95)** n24 t24 f23 b24. Chocolate rye nose and body; silky texture; brown sugar and vanilla; rye-rich sweet finish. *45%.*

**Buffalo Trace Single Oak Project Barrel #15** (r3xLA2) db **(90.5)** n22.5 t23 f22 b23. Mouth feel concentrates on sugars and spices, which grow well. Fruity on nose and finish. *45%.*

**Buffalo Trace Single Oak Project Barrel #16** (r3yLA2) db **(91.5)** n22.5 t23.5 f22.5 b23. Explosive delivery: big spices, juicy, firm rye. Silky middle butterscotch & ulmo honey finish. *45%.*

**Buffalo Trace Single Oak Project Barrel #17** (r3xKB1*)db **(88.5)** n21.5 t22.5 f22.5 b22. Liquorice nose; oily body sweetens; big vanilla, caramel; dull spice. *45% (90 Proof)*

**Buffalo Trace Single Oak Project Barrel #18** (r3yKB1*) db **(92.5)** n23 t23 f23.5 b23. Full bodied from nose to finish. Cocoa mingles with rye and rich corn oil. Deep, intense, even. *45%*

**Buffalo Trace Single Oak Project Barrel #19** (r3xKB1) db **(93)** n23 t23.5 f23 b23.5. Solid, crisp rye hallmark on nose, delivery. Sugars firm and fractured. Precise whiskey. Salivating. *45%*

**Buffalo Trace Single Oak Project Barrel #20** (r3yKB1) db **(95)** n23.5 t24 f23 b23.5. Buttery nose; profound rye kick on delivery; ulmo honey body; complex toasty fade. *45%*

**Buffalo Trace Single Oak Project Barrel #21** (r3xLB1*) db **(92)** n23 t23 f23 b23. Estery, clipped rye nose; salivating delivery, dark sugars, moderate spice. 45%

**Buffalo Trace Single Oak Project Barrel #22** (r3yLB1*) db **(91)** n22 t23.5 f22.5 b23. Corn/rye mix nose with manuka honey; silky corn oil throughout. Sweet, soft.45%.

**Buffalo Trace Single Oak Project Barrel #23** (r3xLB1) db **(89)** n21 t22.5 f22.5 b23. Massive spices throughout; juicy, rye-dominated middle. Soft corn oil and rounded. 45%.

**Buffalo Trace Single Oak Project Barrel #24** (r3xLB1) db **(90)** n22 t23 f22.5 b22.5. Big liquorice nose and delivery; toffee raisin; big corn oil; medium spice; even ulmo honey. 45%

**Buffalo Trace Single Oak Project Barrel #25** (r3xKB2*) db **(90.5)** n22.5 t23 f22.5 b22.5. Much more accent on the rye and a slow revealing of rich caramels and Demerara. 45%

**Buffalo Trace Single Oak Project Barrel #26** (r3yKB2*) db **(89.5)** n22 t23.5 f22 b22. A sugary volley follows a shy nose. Quietens quickly; small grains add complexity. 45%

**Buffalo Trace Single Oak Project Barrel #27** (r3xKB2) db **(95.5)** n23 t24 f24.5 b24. Bold timber on nose and delivery; hickory and liquorice evident; a big spiced honey finale. 45%

**Buffalo Trace Single Oak Project Barrel #28** (w3yKB2) db **(94.5)** n23 t24 f23.5 b24. Sublime balance between sugars and grains on body. Controlled spice; layered cocoa. 45%

**Buffalo Trace Single Oak Project Barrel #29** (r3xLB2*) db **(91)** n23 t22.5 f23 b22.5. Crisp rye nose; more precise grain. Excellent spices. 45% (90 Proof)

**Buffalo Trace Single Oak Project Barrel #30** (r3yLB2*) db **(95.5)** n23.5 t24 f24 b24. One of the most delicate yet: crisp rye and sugars, minty forthright oak. Clean yet deep. 45%

**Buffalo Trace Single Oak Project Barrel #31** (r3xLB2) db **(87.5)** n22 t22 f21.5 b22. Dull, rumbling and herbal; oily caramel and sugars. Soft. 45% (90 Proof)

**Buffalo Trace Single Oak Project Barrel #32** (r3yLB2) db **(90.5)** n23.5 t23 f21.5 b22.5. Soft corn oils dominate. Buttery, molten muscovado. Late hickory. Bitterish finish. 45%

**Buffalo Trace Single Oak Project Barrel #33** (w3xKA1*) db **(94.5)** n24 t23.5 f23 b24. Huge, busy baking spiced cake; muscovado sugar delivery; remains sweet, silky and spicy; 45%

**Buffalo Trace Single Oak Project Barrel #34** (w3yKA1*) db **(90)** n21.5 t23.5 f22.5 b22.5. Lazy nose but big succulent spiced molasses on delivery, with a mint cocoa finale. 45%

**Buffalo Trace Single Oak Project Barrel #35** (w3xKA1) db **(89.5)** n22 t22 f23 b22.5. Soft mint, yeasty; soft toffee delivery, builds in spice. 45% (90 Proof)

**Buffalo Trace Single Oak Project Barrel #36** (w3yKA1) db **(91.5)** n23 t23 f22.5 b23. Vague rum and toffee; bold, salivating, slow spice. 45% (90 Proof)

**Buffalo Trace Single Oak Project Barrel #37** (w3xLA1*) db **(90)** n21 t23 f22 b22. Typical big spice beast. Complex, doughy middle with accent on butterscotch and citrus. 45% (90 Proof)

**Buffalo Trace Single Oak Project Barrel #38** (w3yLA1*) db **(87.5)** n22 t23.5 f20.5 b21.5. Fizzy, busy nose matched by massive spice attack on delivery. Bitter, thin finish. 45% (90 Proof)

**Buffalo Trace Single Oak Project Barrel #39** (w3xLA1) db **(87)** n21.5 t22 f21.5 b22. Oak dominated: a degree of bitterness runs from nose to finish. Spices build slowly. 45%

**Buffalo Trace Single Oak Project Barrel #40** (w3xLA1) db **(93)** n23 t23 f23.5 b23.5. Soft, spiced cake, big citrus; silky, oily, bananas and golden syrup; late spice, balancing bitters. 45%

**Buffalo Trace Single Oak Project Barrel #41** (w3xKA2*) db **(92.5)** n22 t23 f23.5 b24. Less spice than expected. Docile start, builds in intensity. Buttery, big sugars. Balanced. 45%

**Buffalo Trace Single Oak Project Barrel #42** (w3yKA2*) db **(85.5)** n22 t21.5 f21 b21. Tight nose opens slowly; sultana pudding with maple syrup. Sweet, late bitterness. 45%

**Buffalo Trace Single Oak Project Barrel #43** (w3xKA2) db **(89)** n22 t23 f22 b22. Dates & plum nose; succulent fruit with broad maple syrup & molasses flourish. Big late spice. 45%.

**Buffalo Trace Single Oak Project Barrel #44** (w3yKA2) db **(89)** n23 t23 f21 b22. Spice rack nose; superb warm liquorice eruption on palate but dull finale. 45%

**Buffalo Trace Single Oak Project Barrel #45** (w3xLA2*) db **(87)** n23 t22 f21 b21. Ginger and allspice nose; body thick corn oil and toffee. Short finish.45%.

**Buffalo Trace Single Oak Project Barrel #46** (w3yLA2*) db **(88)** n21.5 t22 f22.5 b22 Doughy aroma. Big corn oils and sugars. Late spice growth. Big vanilla. Quietly complex. 45%

**Buffalo Trace Single Oak Project Barrel #47** (w3xLA2) db **(88.5)** n22.5 t22 f22 b22. Floral, waxy aroma; sugars dominate on palate with vanilla-butterscotch-ulmo theme. 45%.

**Buffalo Trace Single Oak Project Barrel #48** (w3yLA2) db **(90.5)** n22 t23 f22.5 b23. Sound, rounded from first to last. Greater accent on sugar intensity and vanilla inclusion. 45%.

**Buffalo Trace Single Oak Project Barrel #49** (w3xKB1) db **(93)** n24 t23 f23 b23. Chocolate spice, apples, oaky aroma; treacle pudding, soft oils; banana and custard; bitters. 45%

**Buffalo Trace Single Oak Project Barrel #50** (w3yKB1) db **(88)** n21.5 t23 f21.5 b22. Flat nose. Muscovado delivery. Slow spices. Late liquorice. Even. Limited depth. 45% (90 Proof)

**Buffalo Trace Single Oak Project Barrel #51** (w3xKB1) db **(89.5)** n23 t23 f21.5 b22. Firm and well spiced from start. Oils play bigger role as sugar develops. 45%.

**Buffalo Trace Single Oak Project Barrel #52** (w3yKB1) db **(87.5)** n21.5 t22 f22 b22. Yeasty nose; blend of molasses and toffee on delivery then slow spice increase.45%

**Buffalo Trace Single Oak Project Barrel #53** (w3xLB1*) db **(91)** n22 t23 f23 b23. Full bodied on nose and palate. Toasty, big liquorice and molasses. Even and elegant. 45%

**Buffalo Trace Single Oak Project Barrel #54** (w3yLB1*) db **(89)** n22 t23 f22.5 b22.5. Crisp sugars and coconut nose; big molassed delivery, nutty and gentle oil. Late vanilla. 45%

**Buffalo Trace Single Oak Project Barrel #55** (w3xLB1) db **(89)** n22 t22 f23 b22. Mocha nose with sturdy tannin and vanilla early on delivery. Red liquorice and vanilla late on. 45%

**Buffalo Trace Single Oak Project Barrel #56** (w3yLB1) db **(91)** n24 t22.5 f22 b22.5. Chocolate vanilla and tannins; soft, slow build up of spice, oily; bitters. 45% (90 Proof)

**Buffalo Trace Single Oak Project Barrel #57** (w3xKB2*) db **(94)** n23 t23.5 f23.5 b24. Immediate spice kick on nose and delivery. Caramels and marmalade. Busy, balanced. 45%

**Buffalo Trace Single Oak Project Barrel #58** (w3yKB2*) db **(90.5)** n22.5 t23 f22.5 b22.5. Liquorice and Fisherman's Friend nose; molassed middle and big spice finish. 45%

**Buffalo Trace Single Oak Project Barrel #59** (w3xKB2) db **(87.5)** n22 t23.5 f23 b23.5. Lighter Fisherman's Friend; roasted fudge; busy small grains attack. Mega complex. 45%

**Buffalo Trace Single Oak Project Barrel #60** (w3yKB2) db **(85)** n22.5 t22.5 f21 b21.5. Aggression to spice nose; tame delivery and body. Soft corn oil and muscovado. 46%

**Buffalo Trace Single Oak Project Barrel #61** (w3xLB2*) db **(94.5)** n24 t23 f23.5 b24. Classic spiced wheat; Demerara sugars and spices abound. Big. 45% (90 Proof)

**Buffalo Trace Single Oak Project Barrel #62** (w3yLB2*) db **(88)** n22 t22.5 f21.5 b22. Caramel is leading theme; soft, big wheated spice. Oily. 45% (90 Proof)

**Buffalo Trace Single Oak Project Barrel #63** (w3xLB2) db **(95.5)** n24 t23 f24 b24.5. Subtle dates, spice, cocoa; gentle, oily, perfect spice build. Ultra complex. 45% (90 Proof)

**Buffalo Trace Single Oak Project Barrel #64** (w3yLB2) db **(91)** n22.5 t23.5 f22.5 b23. Citrus nose. Big oak and spice delivery; treacle tart and liquorice. Softens into caramel. 45%

**Buffalo Trace Single Oak Project Barrel #65** (r2xKA1) db **(91)** n23.5 t22 f23 b22.5. Small grain nose; crunchy muscovado, corn oil; liquorice, vanilla; late spice. Complex. 45%

**Buffalo Trace Single Oak Project Barrel #66** (r2yKA1*) db **(88.5)** n22.5 t22.5 f21.5 b22. Dry tannin dominates on nose and palate; good spice kick and treacle. Short finish. 45%

**Buffalo Trace Single Oak Project Barrel #67** (r2xKA1) db **(89.5)** n22 t23 f22 b22.5. Blandish nose; tart, tight, sharp, some toffee raisin. 45% (90 Proof)

**Buffalo Trace Single Oak Project Barrel #68** (r2yKA1) db **(92)** n22.5 t23 f23.5 b23. Rye depth; deeper, warmer spices, liquorice and light molasses. 45% (90 Proof)

**Buffalo Trace Single Oak Project Barrel #69** (r2xLA1*) db **(94.5)** n23 t24 f23.5 b24. Crisp, sharp rye on nose and delivery. Jagged muscovado and spice. Goes down a treat... 45%

**Buffalo Trace Single Oak Project Barrel #70** (r2yLA1*) db **(91.5)** n22.5 t23 f23 b23. Yielding caramel and vanilla. Rye and hot spice breaks up the sleepy theme. 45% (90 Proof)

**Buffalo Trace Single Oak Project Barrel #71** (r2xLA1) db **(92)** n22.5 t23 f23.5 b23. Busy, small grain and citrus nose; rye backbone then darker sugars and tannin. 45%

**Buffalo Trace Single Oak Project Barrel #72** (r2yLA1) db **(89)** n22.5 t22 f21.5 b22. Floral nose; juicy, tangy, citrus. Liquorice, sugary vanilla. Bitter marmalade finish. 45%

**Buffalo Trace Single Oak Project Barrel #73** (r2xKA2*) db **(87.5)** n21.5 t22 f22 b22. Tight, unyielding nose. Initially crisp rye then thick vanilla and baked apple blanket. 45%

**Buffalo Trace Single Oak Project Barrel #74** (r2yKA2*) db **(88)** n22 t22 f22 b22. Corny nose; more corn oil early on; syrup, huge rye sure on finish; bitters slightly. 45% (90 Proof)

**Buffalo Trace Single Oak Project Barrel #75** (r2xKA2) db **(91.5)** n23 t22.5 f23 b23. Clean with accent firmly on grain throughout. Spiced minty mocha middle and fade. 45%.

**Buffalo Trace Single Oak Project Barrel #76** (r2yKA2) db **(89)** n22.5 t22.5 f22 b22. Bristling rye on nose and delivery; fruity edge then dullish spiced fudge and mocha. 45%

**Buffalo Trace Single Oak Project Barrel #77** (r2xLA2*) db **(88)** n22 t23 f21 b22. Busy, bitty nose; sugary blast on delivery; spice follow through then vanilla overload. 45%

**Buffalo Trace Single Oak Project Barrel #78** (r2yLA2*) db **(89)** n22.5 t22 f22.5 b22. Small grain busy nose; light spice to oils; light rye, late sugars; chewy caramels. 45% (90 Proof)

**Buffalo Trace Single Oak Project Barrel #79** (r2xLA2) db **(93)** n23 t23.5 f23 b23.5. Juicy crisp sugars. Toasty with slow liquorice burn. Creamed spiced hickory fade. Complex. 45%.

**Buffalo Trace Single Oak Project Barrel #80** (r2yLA2) db **(91.5)** n23 t22.5 f23 b23. Broad oily strokes on nose, delivery. Simple vanilla tannins and ulmo honey. 45%.

**Buffalo Trace Single Oak Project Barrel #81** (r2yKB1*) db **(94)** n23 t23 f24 b24. Candy shop fruitiness; delicate oils and flavour development; big yet subdued brown sugars. 45%

**Buffalo Trace Single Oak Project Barrel #82** (r2yKB1*) db **(91.5)** n22.5 t23.5 f22.5 b23. Liquorice, manuka honey; lurid rye bite and lychee fruitiness; mocha and Demerara. 45%

**Buffalo Trace Single Oak Project Barrel #83** (r2xKB1) db **(92)** n22.5 t23 f23.5 b23. Sharp, angular grain, rye dominant. Softer salty praline fade. 45%.

**Buffalo Trace Single Oak Project Barrel #84** (r2yKB1) db **(94)** n23.5 t24 f23 b23.5. Hefty nose mixing tannin, rye and hickory. Huge sugar and corn oil theme. 45%

**Buffalo Trace Single Oak Project Barrel #85** (r2xLB1*) db **(88.5)** n21.5 t22.5 f22 b22.5. Shy nose of soft vanilla; firm body with more vanilla and butterscotch; low level sugar. 45%

**Buffalo Trace Single Oak Project Barrel #86** (r2yLB1*) db **(90)** n22.5 t22 f23 b22.5. Salty, sweaty nose; sharp delivery with rye, red liquorice dominant; spiced mocha finish. 45%

**Buffalo Trace Single Oak Project Barrel #87** (r2xLB1) db **(93.5)** n22.5 t23.5 f23.5 b24. Citrus-led nose; slow, corn oil start then explosive grain; rye, liquorice & honey to the fore. 45%

**Buffalo Trace Single Oak Project Barrel #88** (r2yLB1) db **(89)** n23.5 t22 f21.5 b22. Hickory, rye nose; liquorice delivery big caramel surge; bitters on finish. 45% (90 Proof)

**Buffalo Trace Single Oak Project Barrel #89** (r2xKB2*) db **(89.5)** n22 t22.5 f22 b22.5. Rye radiates on nose and delivery. Big spice surge to the middle. Late mocha, liquorice. 45%

**Buffalo Trace Single Oak Project Barrel #90** (r2yKB2*) db **(94)** n23.5 t24 f23 b23.5. Big tannin, cocoa and caramel throughout. Major peppery spice. Complex. 45% (90 Proof)

**Buffalo Trace Single Oak Project Barrel #91** (r2xKB2) db **(86.5)** n21.5 t22 f21.5 b21.5. Half-cooked: dull caramel throughout. Short spice peak. Sweet, oily, lacking complexity. 45%

**Buffalo Trace Single Oak Project Barrel #92** (r2yKB2) db **(91)** n22 t23 f23 b23. Silky texture. Big corn oil but intense tannin thinned by beech honey. Hickory and maple syrup. 45%

**Buffalo Trace Single Oak Project Barrel #93** (r2xLB2*) db **(89)** n22.5 t22 f22 b22.5. Soft rye and sugars; juicy grain, tangy citrus, muscovado. 45% (90 Proof)

**Buffalo Trace Single Oak Project Barrel #94** (r2yLB2*) db **(92.5)** n22.5 t24 f23 b23. Rich, hefty. Slightly salty, crisp rye. Light caramel, hint of Guyanese rum. Delicate spice. 45%

**Buffalo Trace Single Oak Project Barrel #95** (r2xLB2) db **(94)** n23 t23.5 f23.5 b24. Citrus, banana; soft vanilla, profound rye sharpness, spices. Big. 45% (90 Proof)

**Buffalo Trace Single Oak Project Barrel #96** (r2yLB2) db **(89)** n22 t22.5 f21.5 b22. Bright, grainy delivery in contrast to oily nose and finish. Heavy, dry molasses at the death.45%

**Buffalo Trace Single Oak Project Barrel #97** (w2xKA1*) db **(87)** n22.5 t22 f21.5 b21.5. Toffee apple nose; heavy corn oil, light muscovado sugar, bitters out; 45% (90 Proof)

**Buffalo Trace Single Oak Project Barrel #98** (w2yKA1*) db **(93)** n23 t23.5 f23 b23.5. Peppers on at full blast on nose and delivery; big oily liquorice and treacle counter. 45%

**Buffalo Trace Single Oak Project Barrel #99** (w2xKA1) db **(86.5)** n22 t22 f21 b21.5. Malty, vanilla; thin maple syrup, caramel. Dull. 45% (90 Proof)

**Buffalo Trace Single Oak Project Barrel #100** (w2yKA1) db **(94)** n23 t23.5 f23.5 b24. Busy, green, fresh; big juicy, vanilla, muscovado, spices. 45% (90 Proof)

**Buffalo Trace Single Oak Project Barrel #101** (w2xLA1) db **(96)** n23.5 t24 f23.5 b25. Unerring chocolate and mint aided by even muscovado, vanilla and spice. Hugely complex. 45%

**Buffalo Trace Single Oak Project Barrel #102** (w2yLA1*) db **(88.5)** n22 t22 f22.5 b22. Insane tannin on nose; overcooked caramel. Massive sugar-spice mix. 45% (90 Proof)

**Buffalo Trace Single Oak Project Barrel #103** (w2xLA1) db **(89)** n22.5 t22 f22 b22.5. Early spice on nose; prominent brown sugars on deliver; corn oil follow through. 45%

**Buffalo Trace Single Oak Project Barrel #104** (w2xLA1) db **(91)** n23 t23 f22.5 b22.5. Apple, cinnamon; light spice; corn oil; vanilla and ulmo honey; spices, bitters out. 45%

**Buffalo Trace Single Oak Project Barrel #105** (w2xKA2*) db **(89)** n22.5 t22 f22.5 b22. Spiced, lively nose; hot cross buns; oils and sugars build slowly; spices intensify at end. 45%

**Buffalo Trace Single Oak Project Barrel #106** (w2yKA2*) db **(92.5)** n24 t23 f23 b23.5. Mega complex nose: busy sugars and spices; silky texture; nougat, caramel. 45%

**Buffalo Trace Single Oak Project Barrel #107** (w2xKA2) db **(93.5)** n23.5 t23 f23 b24. Bold, rich nose; pepper bite; thick body: maple syrup, molasses, cocoa. Classic wheat recipe. 45%

**Buffalo Trace Single Oak Project Barrel #108** (w2yKA2) db **(94)** n22.5 t24 f23.5 b24. Soft, delicate. Ulmo honey leads the sugars; corn oil but complex liquorice and lavender. 45%

**Buffalo Trace Single Oak Project Barrel #109** (w2xLA2*) db **(87.5)** n21.5 t23.5 f21 b21.5. Dull nose and finish. Delivery lush, souped-up spiced caramel-toffee fudge. 45%.

**Buffalo Trace Single Oak Project Barrel #110** (w2yLA2*) db **(90)** n22 t22.5 f22.5 b23. Intense caramel; liquorice and toffee middle, citrus and salt; caramel finish. 45% (90 Proof)

**Buffalo Trace Single Oak Project Barrel #111** (w2xLA2) db **(89)** n22.5 t22.5 f22 b22. Intriguing sugar operatic. Varies from castor to muscovado. Countering spices make it work. 45%

**Buffalo Trace Single Oak Project Barrel #112** (w2yLA2) db **(90)** n21.5 t23 f22.5 b23. Caramel fudge lead. Usual whited spice before heavier, liquorice development. 45%.

**Buffalo Trace Single Oak Project Barrel #113** (w2xKB1*) db **(88)** n22.5 t22 f22 b21.5. Big vanilla nose; minor spice, oily, buttery vanilla. Simple. 45% (90 Proof)

**Buffalo Trace Single Oak Project Barrel #114** (w2yKB1*) db **(90)** n22 t23 f22 b23. Elements of citrus. Oily corn. Controlled spice. Earthy and sweet. 45% (90 Proof)

**Buffalo Trace Single Oak Project Barrel #115** (w2xKB1) db **(88.5) n22 t22.5 f22 b22.** An even mix of corn oil and persistent light sugars. Low level spice until finish. A tad dull. 45%

**Buffalo Trace Single Oak Project Barrel #116** (w2yKB1) db **(90.5) n22 t22 f23.5 b23.** Caramelised biscuit nose; polite, corny start; finish rich with hickory, manuka honey. 45%

**Buffalo Trace Single Oak Project Barrel #117** (w2xLB1*) db **(82.5) n20 t20.5 f22 b20.** Weird pineapple nose; fruity delivery with spices trying to escape. Entirely different. 45%

**Buffalo Trace Single Oak Project Barrel #118** (w2yLB1*) db **(86) n20.5 t21.5 f22 b22.** Fruity (less than 117); big toffee body, busy spice, developing ulmo honey. Soft. 45%

**Buffalo Trace Single Oak Project Barrel #119** (w2xLB1) db **(93.5) n22.5 t24 f23.5 b23.5.** Spices from nose to fade, accompanied by chewy burnt fudge. French toast finale. Big. 45%

**Buffalo Trace Single Oak Project Barrel #120** (w2xLB1) db **(89.5) n23 t22 f22.5 b22.** Controlled oak throughout. Intermittent dry vanilla. Delicate sugars. 45% (90 Proof)

**Buffalo Trace Single Oak Project Barrel #121** (w2xKB2*) db **(89) n22.5 t23 f21.5 b22.** Citrusy corn oil apparent and dominates. Sugars rampant, spices shy. Rather flat finale. 45%

**Buffalo Trace Single Oak Project Barrel #122** (w2yKB2*) db **(93) n22 t23.5 f23.5 b24.** Serious wheat-spice with cocoa back up. Demerara sugars evenly spread. Complex. 45%

**Buffalo Trace Single Oak Project Barrel #123** (w2xKB2) db **(85.5) n21 t22 f21 b21.5.** One of the dullest yet: limited sparkle despite light spice. Big caramel. 45% (90 Proof)

**Buffalo Trace Single Oak Project Barrel #124** (w2yKB2) db **(90.5) n22.5 t23 f22.5 b22.5.** The startling, extra sugars over #123 impact hugely. Juicy; oak (liquorice) support.45%

**Buffalo Trace Single Oak Project Barrel #125** (w2xLB2*) db **(93) n24 t22 f22.5 b22.5.** Heavy oak, spices; firm, juicy. Softer caramel fade. 45% (90 Proof)

**Buffalo Trace Single Oak Project Barrel #126** (w2yLB2*) db **(90) n22 t23 f22.5 b22.5.** Floral nose (primroses); elaborate delivery of spice and creamed mocha plus molasses. 45%

**Buffalo Trace Single Oak Project Barrel #127** (w2xLB2) db **(85.5) n21.5 t22 f21 b21.** Off balance, citrus; juicy at first, bitters later. 45% (90 Proof)

**Buffalo Trace Single Oak Project Barrel #128** (w2yLB2) db **(89) n21.5 t22 f22.5 b22.5.** Conservative nose, OTT spice on delivery. Molassed dates and walnut. 45% (90 Proof)

**Buffalo Trace Single Oak Project Barrel #129** (r1xKA1*) db **(88) n22.5 t22 f22 b22.** Firm grainy, tannin nose; nougat, nutty, corn oil; clean but dim vanilla fade. 45% (90 Proof)

**Buffalo Trace Single Oak Project Barrel #130** (r1yKA1*) db **(92.5) n22 t23.5 f23 b24.** Macho: cloaked in oak. Kumquats on nose, oily, punchy tannins on sharp, silky delivery. 45%

**Buffalo Trace Single Oak Project Barrel #131** (r1xKA1) db **(92.5) n23 t23 f23.5 b23.** Relaxed vanilla, light tannin; corn oily, icing sugars, marzipan. 45% (90 Proof)

**Buffalo Trace Single Oak Project Barrel #132** See above.

**Buffalo Trace Single Oak Project Barrel #133** (r1xLA1*) db **(89) n22.5 t23 f21 b22.5.** Small grain busyness does the business: rye leads the dark sugar procession. Bitters out. 45%

**Buffalo Trace Single Oak Project Barrel #134** (r1yLA1*) db **(91.5) n22 t23.5 f23 b23.** Velvet delivery: big spice cushioned by muscovado and butterscotch. Mixed honey finale. 45%

**Buffalo Trace Single Oak Project Barrel #135** (r1xLA1) db **(92.5) n23 t23 f23.5 b23.** Chocolatey theme, except on firm, grainy nose. Silky oils, intense flavours, rye rigidity. 45%

**Buffalo Trace Single Oak Project Barrel #136** (r1yLA1) db **(92) n23.5 t22.5 f23 b23.** Liquorice on nose and delivery. Spicy. Richer oils. Demerara. Spice. 45% (90 Proof)

**Buffalo Trace Single Oak Project Barrel #137** (r1xKA2*) db **(90.5) n22 t23.5 f22 b23.** Fruity opening with a hardening rye presence and emphasis on muscovado. Late cocoa. 45%

**Buffalo Trace Single Oak Project Barrel #138** (r1yKA2*) db **(87) n22.5 t21.5 f21.5 b21.5.** Marzipan, citrus nose; dull delivery, slow build of muscovado and vanilla. Soft. 45%

**Buffalo Trace Single Oak Project Barrel #139** (r1xKA2) db **(88) n22.5 t22 f21.5 b22.** More or less flatlines throughout. Big corn oil with limited spice and cocoa. 45%.

**Buffalo Trace Single Oak Project Barrel #140** (r1yKA2) db **(93) n23 t24 f23 b23.** Classic bourbon: citrus-rich nose, thumping spicy molassed liquorice-hickory delivery. 45%

**Buffalo Trace Single Oak Project Barrel #141** (r1xLA2*) db **(90) n23.5 t22 f22.5 b22.** Busy nose & finish. Corn dominates the mid ground. Sugar, spice growth. Complex finale. 45%

**Buffalo Trace Single Oak Project Barrel #142** (r1yLA2*) db **(89.5) n22.5 t22.5 f22 b22.5.** Light tannin nose; oils, liquorice, spice bite. More corn oil. Sugars, spicy vanilla. 45%

**Buffalo Trace Single Oak Project Barrel #143** (r1xLA2) db **(88.5) n22.5 t22.5 f21.5 b22.** Hickory drifts in and out of narrative. Light rye & tannin. Very soft – overly gentle. 45%.

**Buffalo Trace Single Oak Project Barrel #144** (r1yLA2) db **(91) n23 t23 f22.5 b22.5.** Tannin led. Bristling dark sugars. Oily with comforting vanilla.45%.

**Buffalo Trace Single Oak Project Barrel #145** (r1xKB1*) db **(91) n22.5 t22 f23.5 b23.** Nougat, cocoa; busy small grains; oily corn; spiced chocolate. 45% (90 Proof)

**Buffalo Trace Single Oak Project Barrel #146** (r1yKB1*) db **(93) n23 t24 f22 b24.** Rye dominates with clarity and aplomb. Crystal clean nose and delivery: Dundee cake. 45%

**Buffalo Trace Single Oak Project Barrel #147** (r1xKB1) db (93) n23.5 t23 f23.5 b23. Macho rye & tannins. Toasty & dry delivery; liquorice, sugars, soft spice gain ascendency.45%.

**Buffalo Trace Single Oak Project Barrel #148** (r1yKB1) db (94) n22.5 t24 f23.5 b24. Quiet aroma but intense delivery. Big sugar up front, liquorice and manuka honey fade. 45%

**Buffalo Trace Single Oak Project Barrel #149** (r1xLB1*) db (92) n22.5 t23.5 f23 b23. Massive tannin influence. Heavy nose; heavier body with toasty liquorice and cocoa.45%

**Buffalo Trace Single Oak Project Barrel #150** (r1yLB1*) db (93) n23 t23.5 f23 b23.5. Huge tannin softened by big dark sugars, hickory, sharp rye notes. Long, chewy finish. 45%

**Buffalo Trace Single Oak Project Barrel #151** (r1xLB1) db (91.5) n22 t23 f23.5 b23. Diced citrus; light body with busy grains. Powerful dark sugars gain upper hand. 45%.

**Buffalo Trace Single Oak Project Barrel #152** (r1yLB1) db (81.5) n21 t20.5 f20 b20.5. Vaguely butyric; harsh, hot fat corn, light rye; bitters out. 45% (90 Proof)

**Buffalo Trace Single Oak Project Barrel #153** (r1xKB2*) db (94) n23.5 t23.5 f23 b24. Complex nose, delivery. Big spice with crisp, juicy rye. Praline, delicate oils. Big but elegant. 45%

**Buffalo Trace Single Oak Project Barrel #154** (r1yKB2*) db (92) n22.5 t23 f23 b23.5. Rye dominates. Hard on palate; yet burnt raisin, lychee and muscovado soften. 45% (90 Proof)

**Buffalo Trace Single Oak Project Barrel #155** (r1xKB2) db (93) n23 t24 f22.5 b23.5. Fierce spice. Dynamic rye shapes all directions. Hickory and manuka honey combine. 45%

**Buffalo Trace Single Oak Project Barrel #156** (r1yKB2) db (85.5) n22 t21 f21.5 b21. Doesn't work. Spices too hot. Caramels and oils negate development. 45% (90 Proof)

**Buffalo Trace Single Oak Project Barrel #157** (r1xLB2*) db (84.5) n21 t21.5 f20.5 b21. Vague butyric; sharp, juicy corn with slow rye build. Bitter. 45% (90 Proof)

**Buffalo Trace Single Oak Project Barrel #158** (r1yLB2*) db (88) n22 t22 f22 b22. Another brawny, corn-oily, oaky effort. Excellent cocoa, citrus and spice development. 45%

**Buffalo Trace Single Oak Project Barrel #159** (r1xLB2) db (88) n20.5 t22.5 f22 b22.5. Vague butyric; firm sugars then watery, confident spices, soft honey. Complex. 45% (90 Proof)

**Buffalo Trace Single Oak Project Barrel #160** (r1yLB2) db (92.5) n23.5 t23 f22 b23. A salty style with fruity, crisp rye right behind. Steady and firm. 45% (90 Proof)

**Buffalo Trace Single Oak Project Barrel #161** (w1xKA1*)db (87) n21 t22 f22 b22. Cream caramel candy; juicy corn, oily; more caramel, Light spice. 45% (90 Proof)

**Buffalo Trace Single Oak Project Barrel #162** (w1yKA1*) db (88.5) n22 t22 f22.5 b22. Cream soda and minty fudge. Early treacle kick then settles for simple life. 45%

**Buffalo Trace Single Oak Project Barrel #163** (w1xKA1) db (90) n23 t22.5 f22 b22.5. Citrus, bubble gum; spiced muscovado sugars at first, bitters. 45% (90 Proof)

**Buffalo Trace Single Oak Project Barrel #164** (w1yKA1) db (94.5) n23.5 t23 f24 b24. Citrus and vanilla; massive spice, building. Demerara. Warm and complex. 45% (90 Proof)

**Buffalo Trace Single oak Project Barrel #165** (w1xLA1*) db (91.5) n22.5 t23 f23 b23. Lively, spice dominated. Ulmo honey offers superb back up.45% (90 Proof)

**Buffalo Trace Single Oak Project Barrel #166** (w1yLA1*) db (91) n22 t23 f23 b23. Heady, leathery. Sublime spice middle; molasses and liquorice enrich the tail.45% (90 Proof)

**Buffalo Trace Single Oak Project Barrel #167** (w1yLB1) db (94) n23.5 t23.5 f23 b24. Demerara, rummy; intense liquorice, hickory; dark sugars and big spice. 45% (90 Proof)

**Buffalo Trace Single Oak Project Barrel #168** (w1xLA1) db (89.5) n22 t23 f22 b22.5. Clean, spiced nose; juicy grains with toffee and raisin. Mocha and liquorice on finish. 45%

**Buffalo Trace Single Oak Project Barrel #169** (w1xKA2*) db (94) n23.5 t23.5 f23 b24. Spice, lavender & leather on delivery; spicy nose. Honey & corn oil follow through. 45% (90 proof)

**Buffalo Trace Single Oak Project Barrel #170** (w1yKA2*) db (92.5) n22.5 t23 f23.5 b23.5. Sweet, spiced nose; firm, spicy delivery; Demerara and ulmo honey. 45% (90 Proof)

**Buffalo Trace Single Oak Project Barrel #171** (w1xKA2) db (88.5) n22 t23 f21.5 b22. Friendly corn oils dominate. Estery. Dry finish after sugar and spice crescendo. 45%.

**Buffalo Trace Single Oak Project Barrel #172** (w1yKA2) db (90.5) n22.5 t23 f22.5 b22.5. Tannins prevalent on nose and spiced delivery. Good bite, esters and oils. Late mocha. 45%

**Buffalo Trace Single Oak Project Barrel #173** (w1xLA2*) db (91) n23.5 t23 f22 b22.5. Bold nose & delivery: honeycomb, tannins. Liquorice & vanilla middle; good spice balance. 45%.

**Buffalo Trace Single Oak Project Barrel #174** (w1yLA2*) db (89) n22 t22.5 f22.5 b22. Delicate oak; juicy corn, liquorice, light spices, hickory corn. Bitter marmalade. 45%

**Buffalo Trace Single Oak Project Barrel #175** (w1xLA2) db (91.5) n21.5 t23 f24 b23. Lazy nose, juicy delivery. Big vanilla profile. Buttery caramel; light honey & spice. Long. 45%.

**Buffalo Trace Single Oak Project Barrel #176** (w1yLA2) db (89) n21.5 t22.5 f22.5 b22.5. Light caramel aroma; sharp, juicy (rye-esque) delivery with mocha & butter toffee finale. 45%.

**Buffalo Trace Single Oak Project Barrel #177** (w1xKB1*)db (87) n21.5 t22 f22 b21.5. Vaguely spiced corn oil; soft, nutty, marzipan sweetness, citrus. Late mocha. 45% (90 Proof)

**Buffalo Trace Single Oak Project Barrel #178** (w1yKB1*) db (88.5) n22.5 t23 f21.5 b21.5. Complex marzipan and Demerara nose and delivery; runs out of things to say. 45%.

**Buffalo Trace Single Oak Project Barrel #179** (w1xKB1) db (88) n21 t22 f22.5 b22.5 Dull caramel nose. Toffee caramel continues on palate. Late fudge sweetness. Growing spice. 45%.

**Buffalo Trace Single Oak Project Barrel #180** (w1yKB1) db (92) n22 t23.5 f23 b23.5. Molasses/cough sweet nose; scrambled grains and citrus; thickens with corn at end. 45%

**Buffalo Trace Single Oak Project Barrel #181** (w1xLB1*) db (94.5) n22.5 t24.5 f23 b23.5. Silky chocolate fudge delivery with perfect spice. Nose more austere, finish intense. 45%

**Buffalo Trace Single Oak Project Barrel #182** (w1yLB1*) db (86) n21.5 t21.5 f22 b21. Nose over fruity; profound sugars but tart, thin body. Vanilla and mocha on finish. 45%

**Buffalo Trace Single Oak Project Barrel #183** (w1xLB1) db (95.5) n24 t24 f23.5 b24. Intense. Brilliant fudge/honey/molasses delivery; cocoa finish; perfect spices: mini Weller! 45%

**Buffalo Trace Single Oak Project Barrel #184** (w1yLA1) db (93) n23.5 t23 f23 b23.5. Tannins, walnut oil; nutty, corn oils. Light spice, firm Demerara. Late fruity spice. Complex. 45%

**Buffalo Trace Single Oak Project Barrel #185** (w1xKB2*) db (92.5) n23 t23.5 f23 b23. Dry, riveting nose; liquorice dominates the palate. Cocoa, hickory enlivened by sugars. 45%

**Buffalo Trace Single Oak Project Barrel #186** (w1yKB2*) db (90) n23 t22.5 f22 b22.5. Rampant spice from delivery onwards. Burnt fudge and toasted raisin. 45% (90 Proof)

**Buffalo Trace Single Oak Project Barrel #187** (w1xKB2) db (88) n22 t22 f22 b22. Exceptionally even and caramel rich. Unbalanced tannin and lack of spice. 45% (90 Proof)

**Buffalo Trace Single Oak Project Barrel #188** (w1yKB2) db (90) n21.5 t23.5 f22.5 b22.5. Lazy nose. Bright delivery; citrusy corn oil and muscovado. Late mocha and liquorice. 45%

**Buffalo Trace Single Oak Project Barrel #189** (w1xLB2*) db (88.5) n24 t22 f21 b21.5. Complex citrus, delicate yet big; tart, sweet, fresh, strangely off balance. 45% (90 Proof)

**Buffalo Trace Single Oak Project Barrel #190** (w1yLB2*) db (94) n23.5 t24 f23 b23.5. Ulmo/manuka honey mix on nose and delivery; silky corn oil; spiced mocha. Complex. 45%

**Buffalo Trace Single Oak Project Barrel #191** (w1xLB2) db (94.5) n23 t23.5 f24 b24. Big, spicy, classic; firm wheaty spiciness, juicy, thick caramels. Complex. 45% (90 Proof)

**Buffalo Trace Single Oak Project Barrel #192** (w1yLB2) db (94.5) n23 t24 f23.5 b24. Demerara rum nose; heavy, dry liquorice body; late spice; molassed butterscotch finish. 45%

◇ **Buffalo Trace Experimental Collection Seasoned Staves - 36 Months** dist 10-26-09, barrelled 10-27-09, bott 11/26/2018, still proof: 130, entry proof: 125, warehouse/ floor: K/7, rick/row/slot: 7/1/1-4, charred white oak, age at bottling: 9 years, evaporation: 28.1% db (92.5) n23 t23.5 f23 b23 A really fascinating experiment, comparing this with the 48 month seasoned staves. Here the whisky is burnished gold; the 48 month is deep amber. From tip to toe this is all about subtlety with all the leading notes, from the red liquorice and corn oils in pastel shades and no particularly firm form. Only the delivery offers something firm and crystalline as the demerara sugars make a crisp entry. The remainder is all super-soft and vanilla rich. 45% (90 proof).

◇ **Buffalo Trace Experimental Collection Seasoned Staves - 48 Months** dist 10-26-09, barrelled 10-27-09, bott 11/26/2018, still proof: 130, entry proof: 125, warehouse/ floor: K/7, rick/row/slot: 7/1/1-4, charred white oak, age at bottling: 9 years, evaporation: 29.7% db (95) n23.5 t24 f23.5 b24 As the richer colour suggests, there is more going on here and the extra intervention of the oak brings about a sturdier bourbon. There is still the meaningful Demerara, but now it is backed by liquorice-edged tannin both on nose and delivery and greater weight all round. It is even juicier and more salivating! The spices have certainly upped their game and have make their mark two thirds the way in. This is a better-balanced and more confident bourbon shewing a lot more of everything...and in perfect balance and equal measures, too... Fascinating! 45% (90 proof).

**Bulleit Bourbon** (87) n21.5 t22 f21.5 b22. Vanilla-fashioned on both nose and flavour development. If it was looking to be big and brash, it's missed the target. If it wanted to be genteel and understated with a slightly undercooked feel yet always friendly, then bullseye... 45% (90 seeyo)

**Bulleit Bourbon 10 Year Old** (90) n23 t22.5 f22 b22.5 Not remotely spectacular. But does the simple things deliciously. 45.6% (91.2 proof)

**Bulleit Bourbon Barrel Strength** (91.5) n22.5 t22.5 f23.5 b23 The extra oils at full strength make such a huge difference in seeing the fuller picture. 59.6% (119.2 proof)

**Calhoun Bros Straight Bourbon** (84.5) n20.5 t22 f21 b21. Very different! A much wider cut than the norm on straight bourbon whisky results in an oily fellow which you can chew until your jaws ache. Massively toasty, vanilla gorged and intense. 43% (86 proof)

**Charter 101** (95.5) n23.5 t24.5 f23.5 b24. Now here is a whiskey which has changed tack dramatically. In many ways it's like the Charter 101 of a year back. But this bottling suggests they have turned a warehouse into a giant beehive. Because few whiskeys offer this degree of honey. You can imagine that after all these years, rarely does a whiskey genuinely surprise me: this one has. No wonder there is such a buzz in the bourbon industry right now... *50.5%*

**Clarke's Old Kentucky Straight Sour Mash Whisky Bourbon (88.5)** n22.5 t22 f22 b22. Honest and hugely impressive bourbon. The rich colour – and remember straight bourbon cannot be falsely coloured – tells its own tale. *40%. Aldi.*

◈ **Clyde May's Straight Bourbon** batch CR 079 recipe no 2. **(95)** n23.5 everything you want from a bourbon nose: roast chestnut puree, dried dates, hickory, waxy liquorice, controlled pepper...; **t24** just so silky on delivery. The Manuka honey and molasses mix is in just-so proportions. The vanilla crashes in dramatically, but is immediately held in place by the bulging corn oils; the mid ground is not short of mocha and spice; the layering is breathtaking; **f23.5** lingering and tapered, the more intense notes take their good time to pack their bags and leave; **b24** though from a Florida company, this busy Kentucky bourbon sings pure Bluegrass. Love it! *46% (92 proof). ncf. Distilled in Kentucky*

**Colonel E.H. Taylor Barrel Proof** bott code: B1319909:44M **(93)** n23 t23.5 f23 b23.5 It is as though every last trace of natural caramel has been sucked from the barrel... *67.7% (135.4 proof).*

◈ **Colonel E.H. Taylor Barrel Proof** bott code: L81313910:20M db **(96)** n24.5 if Sherlock Holmes were here now, I think even he would be unable to solve the conundrum as to how a bourbon of such colossal strength can offer on the nose an aroma with almost as many pieces as a jigsaw...and with none missing. The small grains burble and mutter; the tannin-rich liquorice and hickory fade in and out at random intervals; the molasses pulses in intensity. It is a constantly moving, organic experience...just wonderful...; **t24** forget the 67.7% strength. Using the Murray Method this simply kisses the palate with the same tenderness you might kiss your new-born baby. The corn oil acts as the suspension, allowing the firmer tannins to arrive with virtually no violence whatsoever. The liquorice is at the fore, then a wonderful sweetened toastiness, all the time, the taste buds are salivating on ridiculous levels, set off by the sharpness of the grains...; **f23.5** despite the light spices, settles down for a gentle toasted vanilla finish...; **b24** this, amazingly, is the 19,999th whiskey I have tasted for the Jim Murray's Whisky Bible since it first began in 2003. I chose E H Taylor as I have had (very happy) memories going back over 25 years of trying to piece together and discover where his distillery was. And really, if you are going to taste a special bourbon, then it really should be at a strength nature intended. And as for the whiskey itself...? Just another exhibition from this distillery of truly astonishing bourbon making. *67.7% (135.4 proof).*

**Colonel E H Taylor Cured Oak (93.5)** n23 t24 f23 b23.5 Not sure about the oak being cured: coming from Buffalo Trace, I doubt if there was anything wrong with it in the first place...In many ways a much quieter than normal and delicate bourbon with the tannins harnessed and led to a path quite different from the normal toasty/liquorice style. *50%. (100 Proof)*

**Colonel E.H. Taylor Four Grain Bottled in Bond Aged 12 Years** db **(97.5)** n24.5 t24.5 f24 b24.5 Unquestionably one of the greatest whiskeys bottled worldwide in the last 12 months, simply because of the unfathomable depths of its complexity. Every aspect of great whiskey making clears its respective hurdle with yards to spare: brewing, distilling, maturation...the nose and taste confirms that a team of people knew exactly what they were doing...and achieved with rare distinction what they set out to do. Forget about the sheer, undiluted beauty of this bourbon: for me, it is simply a true honour – and thrill - to taste. *50% (100 proof).*

**Colonel E. H. Taylor Old Fashioned Sour Mash (94)** n24 t23.5 f23 b23.5. When they say "old fashioned" they really aren't joking. This is a style which takes me back to my first bourbon tasting days of the mid 1970s. And, at the moment, it is hard to name another bourbon offering this unique, technically brilliant style. Outstanding! *50% (100 Proof)*

**Colonel E.H. Taylor Seasoned Wood** db **(93.5)** n25 t24 f21.5 b23 I am sitting in my garden in near darkness tasting and writing this, the near-thousand-year-old church just 75 yards or so behind me clanging out that it is ten of the clock. Although mid-July, it is the first day warm enough in this apology of a British summer where I have been able to work outside. Oddly, it reminded me when I used to write my books and chapters on bourbon in the grounds of Buffalo Trace in the 1990s, the sun also set and a warm breeze kissing my face. No possums here for company, although the bats are already circling me, kindly protecting me from midges. And as I can't read the label of the whiskey, it makes my senses all the more alive. A whiskey, though not perfect, for when the sun sets but your day is really about to begin... *50% (100 Proof)*

**Colonel E.H. Taylor Single Barrel Bottled in Bond** bott code: L172190110:45K **(96.5)** n24 t24.5 f24 b24 A single barrel has no right to be this incredibly good: how can so much complexity yet balance be stored in one cask alone? Simply mind-blowingly mesmerising.... *50% (100 proof).*

◈ **Colonel E H Taylor Single Barrel Bottled In Bond** bott code: L190740114 **(96.5)** n24 this is just too good...so many layers of orange and cocoa, all of varying sweetnesses and intensity; as well as toffee apple and spices. But the rye notes, conjuring fruit and firmness, stars by adding the backbone required to make this a substantial BIB and one of near faultless elegance; **t24** what a delivery: no bourbon could be this firm and yielding at the very same moment, surely, but it achieves it, with the corn and rye appearing to understand the other's countering demands perfectly. So salivating and spicy, a wonderful chocolate fudge note pulses in its degree of roastiness; **f24** butterscotch and vanilla offer a traditional trail off, though now ulmo honey and light molasses filter through; the spices continue on warming way... **b24.5** absolutely no single cask whiskey, of any type, has the right to be this good. How on earth does it achieve this balance? So many nuances, yet each in league or sympathetic to another? A world single cask of the year contender for certain. Breathtaking. *50% (100 proof). sc.*

**Colonel E.H. Taylor Small Batch Bottled in Bond** (no bottling number) **(94.5) n23.5** a dreamy, soft butterscotch tart on a nose; a little ulmo honey mixes in with the gentle, half-heartedly toasted oak-vanilla. But for a BIB, this really is a real softie...; **t23.5** again the caramels rule the roost. A mix of ulmo and Manuka honey make a thin strike for sweetness before a surge of roasty tannins: toasted fudge and lightly burnt mallow; **f23.5** more caramels with the corn oils finally petering out to give the toastiness a much drier feel at the death; **b24** just balances out so beautifully. *50% (100 proof).*

◈ **Colonel E.H. Taylor Small Batch Bottled in Bond** bott code: L190980115:45D **(90) n23** a real bit of fizz around the nose here in most un-Colonel E H Taylor fashion. The oaks are really nipping while the corn oils look on quietly; **t23** wow! The caramel cascades down in thick, creamy torrents, ulmo honey sweetening it as it goes. But then met by a rigid, almost abrasive oakiness offering a bite that matches the nip of the nose. There is a moment's glimpse of some liquorice-clad, but it soon vanishes; **f22** so much happening on the finish. Still the vanillas soothe, but that oak is fighting like a dog with a bone. Hot and slightly bitter...; **b22** well, I'd not have recognised this as a Colonel Taylor offering unless I had opened the bottle and poured it myself. Not a patch on the exquisite single barrel and, for all its caramel softness and other riches, still one for a dirty glass... *50% (100 proof).*

**Cougar Bourbon Aged 5 Years (95) n25 t24 f23 b23.** If Karl Kennedy of Neighbours really is the whisky buff he reckons he is, I want to see a bottle of this in his home next to Dahl. By the way: where is Dahl these days...? (And by the way, Karl, the guy who married you and Susan in London is a fan of mine. So you had better listen up...!) *37% (74 proof). Foster's Group, Australia.*

**Daniel Stewart 8 Years Old (92.5) n22 t23 f23.5 b24.** Stellar sophistication. Real complexity here, and, as 8-year-olds go, probably among the most complex of them all. A deep notch up on the previous bottling I encountered. *45%*

**Eagle Rare Aged 10 Years** bott code: L172800119:194 **(95.5) n23.5 t24 f24 b24** To the British and Europeans Eagle Rare means Crystal Palace not losing a game...very rare indeed. In the US it will probably mean a lot more to those who once hankered after Ancient Age 10, as this is not the Single Barrel incarnation. And while Crystal Palace may be pointless, literally, this striking whiskey most certainly isn't... That's one soaring, beautiful eagle... *45% (90 proof)*

**Eagle Rare Aged 10 Years Single Barrel (89) n21.5 t23 f22 b22.5.** A surprising trip, this, with some dramatic changes en route. *45%*

**Eagle Rare 17 Years Old** bott Spring 2016 db **(95) n24 t23 f24 b24** An eagle with a slightly different plumage, this one really determined to display its tannin – though never at the cost of compromising its excellent complexity. *45% (90 proof).*

**Eagle Rare 17 Years Old** bott Summer 2017 db **(94.5) n24 t23.5 f23 b24** Just goes a fraction easier on both the sugars and cocoa here. But the toastiness always remains in control and impressively underscores the big age. *45% (90 proof).*

◈ **Eagle Rare 17 Years Old** bott Summer 2018 db **(95) n24** superb aroma of busy spices and liquorice but overloaded by cream caramel. Thick, intense and the molasses ensures with just that right degree of sweetness; **t24** the taste buds are given a bear hug by the most muscular and intense liquorice-caramel duo you can imagine. So firm, yet so ridiculously soft...!! How does it do that....? **f23** toasty fudge with a drying molasses and spice tit to the gathering tannins; **b24** this version goes into cream toffee overload. But, it does it so well... *50.5% (101 proof).*

**Early Times Bottled-in-Bond Straight Bourbon** bott code: A146171040 3131550 **(94) n23 t23.5 f23.5 b24** They call this "Old Style", and it really is. A blast from the past bourbon, oozing personality. A bit of a stunner. *50% (100 proof).*

**Elijah Craig Barrel Proof Kentucky Straight Bourbon** batch no. A117 db **(94.5) n23.5 t23.5 f24 b23.5** An old-fashioned bourbon full of joy. *63.5% (127 proof).*

**Elijah Craig Barrel Proof Kentucky Straight Bourbon** batch no. B517 db **(91) n23.5 t23 f22 b22.5** Not exactly the most complex EC, but really makes the most of the big liquorice intervention. *62.1% (124.2 proof).*

**Elijah Craig Barrel Proof Kentucky Straight Bourbon** batch no. C917 db **(95) n23.5 t24 f23.5 b24** A bourbon which is winner just for much for its rich texture as it is the subtle complexities of its nose and delivery. A real honey – in every sense! *65.5% (131 proof).*

**Elijah Craig Barrel Proof Bourbon 12 Years of Aging** db **(95.5) n23.5 t24 f24 b24** Not sure when I saw a darker bourbon at 12 years commercially available. Remember that in straight bourbon colour represents interaction between spirit and barrel. So expect big oak presence and you will not be disappointed! A bourbon for bourbon lovers with very hairy chests – male or female.. *67.1% (134.2 proof) ncf.*

◆ **Elijah Craig Barrel Proof Kentucky Straight Bourbon** batch no. C918 db **(94.5) n23.5 t24 f23 b24** Just classic stuff! All the usual cast members of red liquorice and Manuka honey are trotted out to make their bow, but there is a slight saltiness to this bottling also...something that isn't usually in the script. Intense, yet at the same time restrained; the burnt toast and marmalade towards the finish works rather well and fits the narrative. *65.7% (131.4 proof).*

◆ **Elijah Craig Barrel Proof Kentucky Straight Bourbon Aged 12 Years** batch no. A119 db **(96) n24 t24.5 f23.5 b24** When you get this degree of toastiness from a bourbon, either there has been one hell of an average temperature rise over the last dozen years in Kentucky. Or this has been plucked from near the top of a warehouse, where it has been cooking happily for over a decade. The result is bourbon that takes no prisoners. It is also a fascinating bourbon, not just because of the intensity of the blood oranges on the nose or the prickle of the splinters on the palate. But it is because it shews an inordinate degree of copper in the flavour profile, the mid-point to the finish in particular. It is as though something was just done to the still, maybe some repair work, just prior to this being distilled. And that to the blindingly busy small grain input and the result is a bourbon of cor blimey richness! *676% (135.2 proof).*

◆ **Elijah Craig Barrel Proof Kentucky Straight Bourbon Aged 12 Years** batch no. B519 db **(90.5) n22.5 t23 f22 b23** One of those quietly delicious bourbons which is saturated in caramel and goes for mouth feel effect over complexity. Mouth-puckering on delivery, this is sticky whiskey on the palate so thick is that corn oil. But the growth of cocoa and spice is nothing to quibble about. *61.1% (122.2 proof).*

**Elijah Craig Small Batch Kentucky Straight Bourbon** db **(89.5) n22.5 t22.5 f22 b22.5** About as quiet and understated as Elijah Craig ever gets. *47% (94 proof).*

**Elmer T Lee Single Barrel (91) n22 t23.5 f(22.5) b23.** A sturdy, dense bourbon with above average sweetness. So effortless, it is hard to immediately realise that greatness has entered your glass. *45%*

**Elmer T Lee Single Barrel** bott code B162282138K **(89.5) n23 t22.5 f22 b22.5** One of the more caramel dominant of the Elmers. *45%*

**Elmer T Lee Single Barrel** bott code: L172400121:26K **(94.5) n24 t23.5 f23.5 b24** If my dear old friend Elmer was still with us and visited my tasting room today, I think he'd be going home with cap tightly on head and the bottle this sample came from held even more firmly under his arm.... *45% (90 proof)*

◆ **Elmer T Lee Single Barrel Kentucky Straight Bourbon Whiskey** bott code: L18199011025K **(95.5) n24** this was the kind of nose Elmer would purr over: rammed full with natural caramels, instead of being boring and one-dimensional it teases the nostrils with so many variances of spicy tannin and blood orange fruit, it is hard to know quite where to begin...; **t24** ohhhh! Let me taste that again...was it really that soft and sexily yielding....? Gosh, it actually was: a quicksand of sweet caramels sucking any heavier notes inside and then caressing them. Just the slightest hint of hickory and cough sweet melds with molasses and Manuka honey. But none of these bigger notes are allowed to get above their station as the rich, creamy caramels and muscovado sugars hold sway. For all its softness, this remains, always a juicy, mouth-watering experience; **f23.5** simplifies down towards the spicier finish as the tannins take a polite but firmer grip; **b24** a peach of a single cask. The great man would have celebrated this one... *45% (90 proof). sc.*

**Evan Williams 23 Years Old (94) n22 t23.5 f24.5 b24.** Struts his stuff, refusing to allow age to slow him or dim the shine from his glowing grains. Now oak has taken its toll. This seems older than its 23 years... Or so I first thought. Then a light shone in my soul and it occurred to me: hang on...I have wines going back to the last century. For the older ones, do I not allow them to breathe? So I let the whiskey breathe. And, behold, it rose from the dead. This Methuselah of a whiskey had come alive once more...and how!! *53.5%*

◆ **Ezra Brooks Bourbon Whiskey** bott code: A193180914 **(90) n22.5** delicate citrus melds effortlessly with the light liquorice and Fisherman's Friend cough sweet; **t22.5** superb oils coat the palate and intensify both the delivery and follow through. An elegant Demerara sugar is supported by the that vaguely phenolic and oak base, the tannins quavering on the palate; **f22** long, but thinning out as the dry vanilla takes hold; **b23** a truly classic young to medium bourbon which celebrates the beautiful arrangement come to between the corn and tannin. An absolutely classic old style of bourbon that the grandfather of whoever distilled this would instantly recognise. *40% (80 proof).*

◆ **Four Roses Bourbon** bott code: 2018/11/20 db **(88) n24** qualifies as perhaps the most understated but complex nose of all the standard bourbons. There is a rose petal floral touch to accompany the mix of lime and diced kumquat. It is almost perfumey, but a vague saltiness suggests a fagged perfume at the end of the day; **t22.5** a small posse of honey-style sugars form on delivery, but dissolve quickly. Thins towards red liquorice rapidly; **f20** little backbone and just a hint of butterscotch on a very abrupt finish; **b21.5** after a few years with a little extra weight behind it, the standard Four Roses has reverted back to a light and flimsy style recognisable to those of us who encountered it between the 1970s and late 1990s. One of the most fragile Kentucky bourbons in the market place, but profiting from a sublime nose. *40%.*

⟡ **Four Roses Single Barrel** warehouse No. LE, barrel no. 4-25, bott code: 1400 05218 0655 db **(91) n23** busy, nippy spices add an extra dimension to an already intense, vaguely heady aroma. Polished leather and maple syrup form the more intense core; **t23** all kinds of sticky toffee pudding, but those spices on the nose erupt early on. The corn oils slowly surface to offer a sugary sheen to the mouth feel; **f22** lightens in the usual Four Roses style, though the glossy sugars last the course as it dries; **b23** a very distinctive style of bourbon: crisp caramelised shell around the house light corn and vanilla. *50%.*

⟡ **Four Roses Small Batch** bott code: 1316 14318 1363 db **(95) n23.5** a halfway house between an assertive confidence on the nose and its trademark appealing, understated fruitiness. All spruced up with a little salt and pepper...and pine; **t24** a beautiful delivery with some real age shewing from the very first moment. The oils are, as near as damn it, perfect, adding just the right weight to further enrich the crackling, spiced-up caramelized sugars and add lustre to the hugely intense, almost concentrated corn sub-stratum; **f23.5** long and luxurious. The spices are like a dog with a bone, refusing to let go. But the vanilla is of epic proportions and rich enough to easily contain the light liquorice notes which flicker late on; **b24** a hugely satisfying, high quality bourbon. Undisputed class. *45%.*

⟡ **Frankfort Bourbon Society Buffalo Trace Single Barrel Select (86) n21.5 t22 f21. b21.5** A spluttering bourbon in part, haunted by a lactic note visible on both the nose and finish. At least the denser, sugar-spiced high points are truly majestic. *45% (90 proof).*

⟡ **Frankfort Bourbon Society Elijah Craig Small Batch Serial No 4718833** bott Fall 2018 **(95.5) n24** toasty and nutty, dried orange peel adds to the stirring undercurrent of complexity to be found writhing below the broader tannin notes; **t24** two-toned caramels rage, one soft and toffee chewy, the other a little more along the burnt chocolate line. But all the time the spices gang together, like embers of the char. The sugars break out to ensure a toasty juiciness; **f23.5** much more liquorice coming into play, again joining forces with the caramels. But the spiced Demerara sugars star, pulsing out their warming message but the rich honey intensifies by the second; **b24**. This gem of a barrel was hand-picked by members of the Frankfort Bourbon Society and I suspect that had they had a hundred stabs at the stocks, they would not have come away with something more alluring and complex than this. *47% (94 proof).*

⟡ **Frankfort Bourbon Society Knob Creek Single Barrel Reserve Aged 9 Years Barrel No 6225** bott Spring 2018 **(95) n23.5** pine and eucalyptus suggest that this barrel was dragged down from one of the highest storeys of the warehouse as the tannin injection is profound. Lots of coffee mixing it with the roasty molasses; **t24** kind of outlines Knob Creek in its bruising yet complex style, the oak influence leading the way proudly but the rye within the mash bill ensuing a sharpness to puncture the natural caramels; all the time there is a glorious juiciness which underscores the lighter, balancing element; **f23.5** busy, spicy and still more spicy tannin; **b24** unusual for a single barrel to so comprehensively typify an entire brand. Bold, bracing and brilliant! *60% (120 proof).*

⟡ **Frankfort Bourbon Society Weller Antique 107 Single Barrel Select Serial (94) n23** firm, almost harsh, grains show excellent sugar and peppers but little yield; **t23.5** chewy and salivating, the toasty tannins are at odds with the lighter, slightly undercooked sugars. Busy and almost tripping over itself to thrust the sharper edges of its personality onto the palate; **f23.5** warming now but it is the toasted honeycomb which closes your eyes as you swoon...; **b24** despite the relative youth of this bourbon, the effect of the wheat is astonishing, radiating its spicy intent from the very first moment. But only when the honey catches up and mingles with an exquisite feel for balance do things become truly special. Tasting this on a day when Frankfort, Ky, dropped to around minus 15 degrees — one of the coldest days here in many a year — those warming spices came in most welcome...even though the bourbon was not swallowed! *53.5% (107 proof).*

**George T. Stagg (96.5) n24.5 t24 f24 b24** The alcohol by volume of one of the sexiest whiskeys on the planet is 69... and it goes down a treat. Much harder to spit than swallow...*69.05% Buffalo Trace Antique Collection.*

**George T. Stagg Limited Edition (96.5) n24 t24.5 f24 b24** As spectacular as a sunset from the hilltop village of Coldharbour in my beloved Surrey *71.4% (142.8 proof). ncf.*

**George T. Stagg** db **(96.5) n24 t24 f24 b24.5** It is impossible not to finish a mouthful of George T without letting out a long, contented, slightly awe-felt and entirely fulfilled sigh, just as one might make after listening to the final strains of Vaughan Williams' London Symphony or Strauss' Tod und Verklarung. Most of the usual traits to be had in abundance, plus one or two slight differences as the pot was stirred for another dip into one of world's whisky's deepest caverns.... *69.1% (138.2 proof)*

**George T. Stagg** db **(97) n24 t24.5 f24 b24.5** Amazing consistency: this is the fourth year running it has been given a score of 96.5 or above - a Stagg-ering achievement. *72.05% (144.1 proof).*

**George T. Stagg** db **(97) n24 t24.5 f24 b24.5** Funny: I nosed this and I thought: "T-bone steak."Huge whiskey deserving to be the warm-up act for a meal at either RingSide Steakhouse, Portland or Barberian's Steak House in Toronto or even some outdoor parrilla in Uruguay. It is the kind of whiskey that demands something very special: it just refuses, point-blanc, to do ordinary... *64.6% (129.2 proof)*

◈ **George T. Stagg** db **(96) n24** most intriguing is the heather and Manuka honey mix tied up with the searing spices; below that comes another mix, this time of red and black liquorice.... this is big...; **t24.5** the rye grains in this burst out into a volley of crisp, juicy bitter-sweet bullets strikingly randomly at the taste buds. Much more deft caramels act too late as the silencer, but still creates a delightful essay of bitter-sweet bourbon tones, allowing both the tannins and the molasses a ride on its yielding back; **f23.5** the spices, which had been running quietly and parallel to the main theme, have a slightly more prominent role now. The tannins have a vaguely bitter but unquestionably toasty countenance; **b24.5** as a George T Stagg goes, this is a bit of a wimp: some 20 proof weaker than some of its incarnations. So for those of you of a delicate disposition, you might be able to tackle this tamed monster for once. *62.45% (124.9 proof).*

◈ **H. Deringer Bourbon Whiskey (88) n21.5** soft vanilla and weightier nougat; **t22** early spice prickle, but has little to fight against to get to the fore. A little hickory on the tannin while delicate Demerara ensures a sweeter side; **f22** very gentle toffees; **b22.5** despite the huge, weighty bottle, this is the lighter side of bourbon whiskey with vanilla and sugars in quiet agreement. *40%. Aiko Importers, Inc.*

**Hancock's President's Reserve Single Barrel** bott code: B1710117:26K **(90.5) n22.5 t23 f22.5 b22.5** A joyous Bourbon that gives the impression that it is performing well within itself. *44.45% (88.9 proof)*

**Hancock's Reserve Single Barrel (92) n25 t23 f21.5 b22.5.** A slightly quieter example of this consistently fine brand. The nose, though, is the stuff of wet whiskey dreams... *44.45%*

◈ **Hartfield & Co Whisky** batch 2.5 month **(81.5) n20 t21 f20 b20.5** So here it is: the first whiskey legally produced from Bourbon County, Kentucky (which gave the unique whiskey its name) since before prohibition arrived in Kentucky in 1919. A nutty, sweet, largely off-key whiskey, this probably isn't the best made you can find in the State, and hopefully future bottlings will have a cleaner cut and far more copper interaction. But it is enjoyable for what it is, a nutty chewy whisky full of caramel and thinned honey which some of the 26 distillers closed down in Bourbon County exactly a century ago might have looked upon with a degree of awe... And certainly the bottle will be a collectors' item... *50% (100 proof). Distilled from Corn, rye and barley.*

**Hogs 3 Bourbon Aged Over 3 Years (86.5) n22.5 t21.5 f21 b21.5** A bang on standard mid-towards upper warehouse Kentucky 3-year-old with plenty of juicy but ungainly vanilla, Demerara sugar and citrus.... and absolutely no frills. *40% (80 proof). Quality Spirits International.*

**I.W. Harper Kentucky Straight Bourbon (87.5) n22 t22 f21.5 b22.** The puckeringly dry delivery and finish forms the toast for the well spiced light sugar sandwich. *41% (82 Proof)*

**I.W. Harper Kentucky Straight Bourbon 15 Year Old (94.5) n23.5 t23.5 f24 b23.5** Class in a glass. *43% (86 Proof)*

◈ **James E. Pepper 1776 Straight Bourbon Whiskey Aged Over 3 Years (91.5) n23** a lovely hickory, liquorice and molasses lead: classic! **t23** fizzing cola on delivery, which darkens and deepens as the oak starts to saunter into the picture. The spices keep up their assault while a little orange blossom honey lightens things slightly; **f22.5** settles for a light liquorice and caramel fade; **b23** beautiful old school bourbon. *50% (100 proof). ncf.*

**Jim Beam Black Double Age Aged 8 Years (93) n23 t24 f22.5 b23.5.** Rather than the big, noisy, thrill-seeking JB Black, here it is in quiet, reflective, sophisticated mode. Quite a shift. But no less enjoyable. *43% (86 proof)*

**Jim Beam Bonded 100 Proof** db **(92.5) n22.5 t23.5 f23 b23.5** Takes its time to get going. But when it does, it just won't shut up.... Complex and compelling, the toastiness takes time to make itself felt but does so with panache. *50%*

**Jim Beam Signature Craft Aged 12 Years** db **(92.5) n23** gorgeous roasted coffee and liquorice. The rye pokes through gamely; **t23.5** soft delivery with a toasted fudge quality. Takes time for the rye to arrive but it does as the spices mount; **f23** softly spiced with plenty of creamy mocha; **b23** classic Beam: big rye and massive fruit. Quite lovely. *43%.*

**John B. Stetson Straight Bourbon Whiskey (92) n23.5 t23.5 f22 b23.** Absolutely love it! Quality: I take my hat off to you...*42%*

**Jim Beam Repeal Batch Bourbon** bott code: L8226FFE222730700 db **(89) n22** though the colour in the glass is light, the tannins make more noise than you'd think, sitting prettily with layers of lime and pepper; **t22.5** a soft, sweet, yielding delivery but the spices soon swing into action. The early, almost gristy, sugars serve for the duration, though weakening as the spices up their game; **f22** perhaps thins a little too enthusiastically, leaving chalky deposits though those spices keep things interesting...; **b22.5** good, honest, unspectacular, understated but unerringly delicious and charming bourbon bottled to celebrate the 85th Anniversary of the repeal of Prohibition. On this evidence, I think they should equally celebrate the 86th anniversary... 43% (86 proof). ncf

**Jim Beam Signature Craft Brown Rice 11 Year Old** db 45% **(78) n20.5 t21 f18 b18.5.** A whiskey I nosed and tasted before looking to see what it was. And immediately alarm bells rang and I was reaching to inspect the bottle in a state of panic and shock. RICE!!! Well that explains the unsatisfying simplicity to the finish where, really, only oak can be heard....apart from the wallpaper paste, that is. And the fact the whiskey never quite gets off the ground despite an attractive cocoa thread. Or was that actually real cocoa...? Sorry, but in the great name of Jim Beam, this is one that should have just stayed in the lab. (90 Proof)

**Jim Beam Signature Craft Soft Red Wheat 11 Year Old** db **(92) n22 t23.5 f23 b23.5** A beautifully weighted bourbon making a big deal of the sugar-spice interplay. Hugely enjoyable and at times fascinating. 45% (90 Proof)

**Jim Beam Signature Craft Small Batch Quarter Cask Finished 3rd Release** db **(92) n23.5 23.5 f22 b23** Quarter casks are not normally associated with deftness and poise. This one certainly is. Elegant, if a little lightweight at the end. 43% (86 Proof)

**John E. Fitzgerald Larceny (94) n23 t23.5 f23.5 b24.** If this doesn't win a few converts to wheated bourbon, nothing will. A high quality, stunningly adorable whiskey, pulsing with elegance and personality. Every drinks cabinet should have this wonderful new addition to the bourbon lexicon. 46%

**John E. Fitzgerald Very Special Reserve Aged 20 Years (93) n22.5 t24 f23 b23.5** A bourbon lover's bourbon! 45% (90 proof)

**John J Bowman Virginia Straight Bourbon Single Barrel** bott code: L172010507:28B **(93) n23 t23.5 f23 b23.5** This is very high quality bourbon making the most of both its big toastiness and its more intrinsic honey tones. Simple...yet devastatingly complex... 50% (100 proof)

**John J Bowman Single Barrel Virginia Straight Bourbon** bott code: L190070510 **(94.5) n23** firm on the rye front and a brisk Demerara introduction; vague fruit, too; **t24** fabulous waxy delivery. The honey and tannin appear to be gripped in an arm lock from the first moment and we are a good ten to fifteen seconds in before the light Manuka honey and muscovado sugars begin to take command...; **f23.5** now the tannins hold sway as the bourbon dries up. Some concentrated liquorice fills out a finish which suggests either great age, or a well-cooked barrel taken from high in the warehouse; **b24** a very different animal to the Small Batch with a greater emphasis on the sugars and just more all round drama and muscularity. Stunning. 50% (100 proof). sc.

**Johnny Drum (Black Label) (89.5) n22 t23 f21.5 b23.** How often does that happen? The same whiskey, different strength, virtually same quality (though this has a little more depth) but gets there by a slightly different route. 43%

**Johnny Drum (Green Label) (89) n22.5 t23 f21 b22.5.** Much more honey these days. Worth making a bee-line for. 40%

**Johnny Drum Private Stock (90.5) n22.5 t22.5 f23 b22.5.** One of those bourbons where a single glass is never quite enough. Great stuff! 50.5% (101 proof)

**Kentucky Owl Kentucky Straight Bourbon Whiskey** batch no. 2 **(91) n22.5 t23.5 f22.5 b22.5** A big, corn-led bourbon but with some extra oaky depth. 58.6% (117.2 proof). 1,380 bottles.

**Kentucky Owl Confiscated** bott code: 3158860834 **(80) n19 t22 f19 b20** From the moment the boiled cabbage nose hits you, this is one very disappointing whiskey. Stands up to scrutiny on delivery, where the intense caramels and vanillas combine rather well. But the dirty, buzzy finale is also a let down. Not a bourbon, in this form, I could give two hoots about, to be honest. 48.2% (96.4 proof).

**Kentucky Tavern Straight Kentucky Bourbon** bott code: L190081510 **(92) n22.5** banana skins and liquorice; **t23** big corn dominance on delivery, then a fabulous – and unexpected – wave of ulmo honey, moving into a maple syrup and molasses mix; **f23** attractively long with the vanilla enjoying a delicate tinge of liquorice and raspberry jam: wow! **b23.5** what a great improvement on when I last tasted this several years back. Much more depth, balance and chewability. One of the biggest – and most pleasant - surprises of my tasting day. Delicious! 40% (80 proof).

**Kentucky Vintage** batch 08-72 **(94.5) n23.5 t24.5 f23 b23.5** Staggered! I really didn't quite expect that. Previous bottlings I have enjoyed of this have had hair attached to the muscle.

This is a very different Vintage, one that reaches for the feminine side of a macho whiskey. If you want to spend an hour just getting to know how sensitive your taste buds can be, hunt down this batch... *45%*

**Knob Creek Aged 9 Year**s bott code L6154 **(95.5)** n23.5 t24 f23.5 b24.5 Seems like more barrels have been included from the lower echelons of the warehouse. Lighter, sweeter and more feminine. One of the most complex Knob Creeks I have ever encountered: a true Kentucky belle! *50% (100 proof)*

**Knob Creek Aged 9 Years (94.5)** n23.5 t24 f23.5 b23.5 No whiskey in the world has a more macho name, and this is not for the faint-hearted. Big, hard in character and expansive, it drives home its point with gusto, celebrating its explosive finish. *50%*

**Knob Creek Single Barrel Reserve Aged 9 Years** bott no L6133 **(95)** n23 t24 f24 b24 A macho bourbon of a wonderfully high standard. Just a degree juicier than you normally find with a Knob Creek. *60% (120 proof)*

**Knob Creek 25th Anniversary Single Barrel** barrelled 2/25/2004 db **(93)** n23 t24 f23 b23 A caramel-rich critter, yes-siree! But let it hang around the glass a bit and a rich liquorice edginess will develop... *62% (124 proof). sc.*

**Maker's 46 (95)** n23.5 t24.5 f23 b24 Some people have a problem with oak staves. I don't; whisky, after all, is about the interaction of a grain spirit and oak. This guy is all about the nose and, especially, the delivery. With so much controlled honey on show, it cannot be anything other than a show-stopper. Frankly, magnificent. I think I've met my Maker's... *47% (94 proof)*

**Maker's 46** barrel finished with oak staves, bott code: L6155MMB 00651 1233 **(89)** n22.5 t22.5 f22 b22 Maker's at its most surprisingly genteel. *47% (94 proof).*

**Maker's Mark (Red Seal) (91)** n22.5 t23.5 f22 b23. The big honey injection has done no harm whatsoever. This sample came from a litre bottle and the whiskey was darker than normal. What you seem to have is the usual steady Maker's with a helping hand of extra weight. In fact this reminds me of the old Maker's Gold wax. *45%*

**Mayor Pingree Aged 9 Years Straight Bourbon Whiskey** batch no. 16-314 **(96)** n23.5 t24 f24 b24.5 This is my second darling Valentine from Indiana... *58.6% (117.2 proof). ncf.*

**Mayor Pingree Aged 10 Years Straight Bourbon Whiskey Single Barrel** barrel no. 2-1 **(89)** n22.5 t22.5 f22 b22 Compare this to the 9-years-old to see what happens when the oak and grains are just very slightly off beat... *52.7% (105.4 proof). ncf. 159 bottles.*

**McAffee's Benchmark Old No 8 Brand** bott code: 03072193223:04W **(89)** n22.5 t23 f21.5 b22 Above average standard bourbon full of chewy riches but which can't quite keep up with its exceptional nose and delivery. *40% (80 proof)*

**McAffee's Benchmark Old No 8 Brand Kentucky Straight Bourbon** bott code: L190260113 **(87.5)** n22 t22 f21.5 b22 A good, honest, unspectacular bourbon which ticks all the boxes without for a moment trying to go into superdrive. Lays on the natural caramels thickly, then some low voltage spice to stir things up. The sugars are on a slow build, but get there. *40% (80 proof).*

**Michter's 10 Years Old Single Barrel** barrel no. 174/1135 **(93)** n23.5 t23.5 f23 b23 Like the rye, has a slight metallic persona which adds a degree of lustre to both the nose and taste. *47.2% (94.4 proof). sc.*

**Michter's No. 1 Bourbon (87)** n23 t22.5 f20 b21.5. This one is mainly a nose job: all kinds of heavy liquorice and diced kumquat. But there is also a brooding tannin menace lurking in the shadows, which reveal themselves more fully – and with a tad of bitterness – on delivery and finish. *45.7%*

**Michter's 20 Year Old Kentucky Straight Bourbon** batch no. 18I1370, bott code: A182681370 **(96.5)** n24 toasty, without a hint of scorching; fruity, yet dry; sweet, yet always spicy; weighty, but so many ethereal notes; ancient, yet always active and busy...; t24 the degree of salivation on delivery defies logic and belief. Yet there it is: lush corn oils and molten muscovado. The oak is charred and brimming with Camp coffee. Yet the balance not for a moment threatened; f24 the mix of hickory and molasses here deserves a medal struck. It is a just-so amount to ensure the bourbon remains on course and is uncompromised to the end, even when the darker cocoa notes mount. Amazing...; b24.5 when people ask me why I think that bourbon has the edge over Scotch at the moment, perhaps I should point them in the direction of a bottling like this to give them some understanding as to why... One of the best 20+ year-old bourbons I have ever encountered. *57.1% (114.2 proof). 463 bottles.*

**Michter's Single Barrel 10 Year Old Kentucky Straight Bourbon** barrel no. 19D625, bott code: A19095625 **(95.5)** n24.5 one of the most sensuous noses from anywhere in the world this year: a triumph of small grains over the corn and oak, making for a breathtakingly complex experience. The constant murmur of grain is like a buzz of excitement to the nose, no particular personality trait in control, but so many things happening, harmoniously at the same time. A fascinating light saltiness, too, which seems to sharpen the orangey citrus and hickory elements. But with cocoa on display, as well, anyone with a penchant for Terry's

Chocolate Orange will be well and truly hooked...; **t3.5** the corn oil reveals its host plant, but the oil is delightfully adroit and does all it can to further the cause of the light molasses and mocha which shapes the early to mid-part of this whiskey. The oak is confident, too, and pulses out a regular spicy beat while liquorice fills in the gaps so the flavour waves just keep on lapping; **f23.5** the molasses and spice quieten, though refuse to disappear entirely, while a proud nutty toastiness gathers momentum...; **b24** an incredibly beautiful whiskey. A contender for the single barrel of the year, for sure... 47.2% (94.4 proof). sc.

◇ **Michter's Single Barrel 10 Year Old Kentucky Straight Bourbon** barrel no. 19D662, bott code: A19099662 **(96) n24** truly classic bourbon nose: thick liquorice and blood orange heads the heavyweight section; molasses rumbles at a lower, sweeter level; **t24** you are placed on immediate full kumquat alert as the powerful citrus notes bore down on the taste buds. The corn oils are exceptional and offer body without dominating in flavour. Soft red liquorice and molasses ensures the sweeter side of things stay pristine; **f23.5** a long, drying fade with a light butterscotch and latte edge to the oak; **b24.5** a classic top quarter of warehouse 10-year-old (barrel 625, above, was much nearer midpoint) which has seen some heat action and ensures maximum depth and entertainment for its age. Beautifully made, too...! 47.2% (94.4 proof). sc.

◇ **Michter's Small Batch Kentucky Straight Bourbon** batch no. L18F873, bott code: A8172873 **(87.5) n22 t22.5 f21 b22** An attractive, slightly minty and ungainly offering with extra bitterness to the toastiness, especially at the death. Some subtle orange blossom honey aids the sweetness. 45.7% (91.4 proof).

◇ **Michter's Small Batch Original Sour Mash** batch no. L18V1608, bott code: A183041608 **(92) n23.5** so much Demerara sugar and orange peel on display here...! **t23** full fruitiness on delivery with both the grain and the oak contributing to a reprise of the citrus no prevalent on the nose. Initially salivating with gorgeous muscovado sugar lead with a light hickory undertone; **f22.5** the lower strength means the corn oils have left us earlier to allow a much freer hand to the chalky vanilla; **b23** one of the weaker Michter's by strength, but lacks nothing in subtlety. 43% (86 proof).

◇ **New Riff Kentucky Straight Bourbon Aged At Least 4 Years** dist Fall 2014, bott Fall 2018 nbc **(92.5) n22** the sugars appear to be hiding slightly behind the weightier earthy theme; **t23.5** wow! I have seen many bees lately in Kentucky: they must be escapees from this distillery as the honey content on the delivery is as startling as it is delicious. Ulmo leads the way with heather and Manuka close behind. Red liquorice breaks out all over the place and if it wasn't salivating enough, the spices arrive late but with purpose to add even further to the complexity. An under-theme of crisp fruit and Demerara sugars appears to be the high rye content in action; **f22.5** a long fade with the vanilla really now taking hold; **b23.5** I will have to get to Newport, on the opposite banks of the Ohio to Cincinnati, to see this excellent new Kentucky distillery in action. This is as big and impressive as the river that flows astride the two towns. 50% (100 proof). 65% corn, 30% rye 5% malted barley.

**Old Charter 8** bott code: B170871 10:094 **(91) n22.5 t23 f22.5 b23** A wonderfully oily affair which sticks to the palate like a limpet. From taste alone, appears no longer to be an 8-year-old but has retained the number 8. Probably a mix of years as the layering and complexity is significant. 40% (80 proof)

◇ **Old Charter 8 Kentucky Straight Bourbon** bott code: L183420122 **(92) n22.5 t23.5 f22.5 b23.5** Very similar to the bottling above, except here the sugars, up in attack earlier, gleam and sparkle while the later spices bristle a little more aggressively: slightly more polarisation, but more polish, too. Such great stuff! 44% (88 proof).

◇ **Old Charter Oak Mongolian Oak Kentucky Straight Bourbon (92) n22** well, this is different! Much more of a herbal quality to this, vaguely like a cleaning fluid but without the astringency and softened by citrus. Certainly an acquired nose, but the Murray Method does help you find the sweeter traces, especially the crisp candy sugars; **t3.5** and, for a bourbon, that is quite different again. The tannins and corn combine for a recognisable early bourbon signature, full of sweet liquorice promise. Then it moves off on a tangent, towards that semi-menthol and citrus tone detected on the nose. We are venturing into uncharted whisky land here as old and very new whisky styles merge...; **f23** an amazingly dry finish, with a big effort put in by the vanillas which become chalky in a way far more usually associated with Scotch single malt; **b23.5** how strange that just two or three weeks ago I was in London, being booked up for a whisky tasting next year in Mongolia. And now here I am in Kentucky tasting a bourbon matured in Mongolian oak, the first such whiskey I have ever heard of. Talk about whisky being an international spirit these days... This is very different to any bourbon I have tasted before: positively schizoid. Starts off, unmistakably, as a bourbon, though offering a unique profile, and finishes something much closer in style to Speyside single malt but taking a previously uncharted route between the two empires: less Murray Method than Marco Polo. Not exactly a silk road of a bourbon but as intriguing as it is delicious. 45% (90 proof).

⁂ **Old Carter Straight Bourbon Barrel Strength Batch 1 (91.5) n22** a very simple array of vanillas and light honey. It should offer more complexity, but the spices kick in instead to stir interest; **t23.5** ah, much more like it! Fabulous delivery with a maple syrup and pepper flourish, followed by a breezy orange blossom honey and liquorice follow through; intensifies with aplomb, especially the liquorice; **f23** remains impressively juicy even into the fade, when the vanillas and butterscotch notes begin to build deliciously; **b23** the nose may be slightly cumbersome and plodding, like the horse on the label, but as soon as it hits the palate you know you are backing a winner. *54.45% (108.8 proof). 1567 bottles.*

**Old Forester** bott code: A083151035 db **(94.5) n23.5 t23.5 f23.5 b24** Solid as a rock: a classic and criminally under-rated bourbon which is wonderfully true to the distillery. *43%.*

⁂ **Old Forester 1897 Bottled in Bond** bott code: L297811823 **(92.5) n22.5** takes time for the layering to harmonise, but given patience and warmth it gets there. Ultimately weighty with toasted yams and walnuts; **t23.5** sonorously rich on delivery, the corn oils really making a full impact from the first. Burnt fudge and toasty tannin sticks like a limpet to the roof of the mouth; **f23** so chewy and deep, hefty molasses clinging to the overdone toast as perfected by my wonderful PA, Jane; **b23.5** the toast starts to slowly smoulder in a gorgeous bourbon that creeps up and mugs you. Surprisingly rich and just so lush. *50% (100 proof).*

⁂ **Old Forester 1910 Old Fine Whisky** nbc **(92) n23** a lilting crescendo of subtle Demerara sugar, figs and spices in firm but happy harmony; **t23.5** a typically lush encounter at first with the corn oils prominent and soft. The more business-like tannins circle then dive in, distributing heavy liquorice, prominent spice and Manuka honey riches; **f22.5** fades a little too enthusiastically in intensity but the burnt toffee sticks to the long-running corn oils; **b23** the kind of dark, hefty bourbon this distillery has long championed. Substantial and satisfying. *46.5% (93 proof).*

⁂ **Old Forester 1920 Prohibition Style** nbc **(95.5) n23.5** deep rumbling like a barely audible cello, a salty edge gives extra life to the seemingly moribund tannin and slowly, the complexity levels rise as floral and treacle notes rise and then merge; **t24** exemplary mouth feel: silky soft but daggers of spice pierce the cosiness. The sugars are profound yet controlled, all of the darker style, especially molasses; **f24** still spicy and busy with a mix of Manuka and heather honeys dovetailing and mingling sublimely with the varied toasty oaks; **b24** just oozes with classic Old Forester depth and oomph! A classic of its style. *57.5% (115 proof).*

⁂ **Old Fitzgerald Bottled-in-Bond Aged 9 Years Fall 2018 Edition** made: Fall 2008, bott 05/23/2018 db **(93.5) n23.5** the spices explode from the glass despite the best attention of the Demerara sugars; **t23.5** superb, salivating delivery: the corn oils are muted, allowing he smaller grains the stage. Again spices abound but now, after a period of light maple syrup, it is the oaky vanillas which keep them in check; **f23** just a little bitterness and the oak fades with a butterscotch and red liquorice theme; **b24** middle aged wheated bourbon at its deliciously complex best. *50% (100 proof).*

⁂ **Old Fitzgerald Bottled-in-Bond Aged 13 Years Spring 2019 Edition** made: Fall 2005, bott 01/30/2019 db **(95) n23.5** a real toastiness to this one: the spices are a bit higher pitched and busier. Marmalade on burnt toast; **t24** so mouth-filling! The corn oils here have taken a semi-syrupy feel with the maize itself high on the flavour wheel. Pounding tannin and molasses herald in the striking spices from the wheat. A chocolate liquorice middle melts into the corn; **f23.5** long, chewy, but the spices become more pointed and busy. Lots of natural caramels at play, too; the wheat returns in bready fashion; **b24** a very different animal to their 9-year-old offering, which is tighter and with a more precise game plan. By contrast, this drifts and is less attentive to the wheat...though you never lose sight of it. *50% (100 proof).*

**Old Forester Statesman** bott code: L2337123:49 db **(92.5) n23 t23.5 f23 b23.5** A very laid back and relaxed Forester. *47.5% (95 proof).*

**Old Fitzgerald Very Special 12 Years Old (93) n24 t23.5 f22.5 b23.** There is always something that makes the heart sing when you come across a whiskey which appears so relaxed in its excellence. At the moment my heart is in the shower merrily lathering itself... *45%*

**Old Grand-Dad (90.5) n22 t23 f23 b23.5.** This one's all about the small grains. A busy, lively bourbon, this offers little to remind me of the original Old Grand-Dad whiskey made out at Frankfort. That said, this is a whisk(e)y-lover's whiskey: in other words the excellence of the structure and complexity outweighs any historical misgivings. Enormously improved and now very much at home with its own busy style. *43%*

⁂ **Old Grand-Dad 80 Proof** bott code: L7119FFB140640030 **(87) n21.5 t22.5 f21 b22** Steady and pretty light weight. Doesn't have quite the same backbone as the 43%. But who cannot fall for the charm of delicate citrus and chalky vanillas? Just enough liquorice and rye juiciness to lift it into the easy drinking category. *40% (80 proof).*

**Old Grand-Dad Bonded 100 Proof (94.5)** n22.5 t24 f23.5 b24.5 Obviously Old Grand-dad knows a thing or two about classy whiskey: this is a magnificent version, even by its own high standards. It was always a winner and one you could bet your shirt on for showing how the small grains can impact upon complexity. But this appears to go a stage further. The base line is a touch deeper, so there is more ground to cover on the palate. It has been a whiskey-lover's whiskey for a little while and after a few barren years, has been inching itself back to its great Frankfort days. The fact that Beam's quality has risen over the last decade has played no insignificant part in that. *50% (100 proof)*

⟐ **Old Grand-Dad Bonded 100 Proof (95)** n23 a sublime combination of corn oil and sharper rye notes stimulate the nose buds onto full alert. The odd aniseed and African violet note offers a flowery effect to soften the crispness of the Demerara sugars; t24.5 a sweet, mouth-filling delivery which makes you let out a gasp of satisfaction on arrival! As on the nose, the demerara sugars make a significant, crunchy mark – the hardness amplified by the unmissable rye notes which both crisp and fruit up the experience. Corn oils return for a major chewy middle with the small grains peppering away at the taste buds to add complexity to the overall joy; f23.5 only medium length: any longer and we might have an award winner here. But the corn oils do a good job while just so amounts of liquorice, Manuka honey and spice buzz around contentedly; b24 a brilliant bourbon built for the Bottled in Bond category, the extra oils ramping up the rye to significant and disarming effect. Classically beautiful, a bourbon that appears to be just getting better and better. *50% (100 proof).*

⟐ **Old Grand-Dad Bonded 100 Proof** bott code 258/17 **(96)** n23 this may be a bourbon, but the rye within the mash bill can be heard, clearly and clean, above all else. Something of the Kentucky tobacco barn to this, also; t24.5 the rye is cut glass, almost crystalised in its crunchy sharpness. Salivating, phenomenally spiced, but with the most acute of edges; f24 long, a smattering of mocha and vanilla here and there, as well as toffee caramels dripping from the oak. But it is the Demerara sugars and spices which are to be remembered best of all; b24.5 for a bourbon, I have tasted rye less rye-like than this. A bourbon standing erect, proud pretty much top of its game wallowing in its faultless distillation and maturation; indeed, probably the best Grand-Dad Bonded I have yet encountered, which really is saying something over so many years! Glorious. *50% (100 proof).*

⟐ **Old Pepper Straight Bourbon Whiskey Aged 10 Years** new white oak barrel, barrel no. L18U **(90.5)** n23 incredibly, the first thing to cross my mind was ground white pepper even before I was aware what it was I was nosing...; the secondary dressing is a gorgeous ulmo honey sweetness; t23.5 fat, chewy with the most complex array of light honey tones – ranging from ulmo, though lime-blossom to Manuka – all mixed with a yielding natural caramel, and punctuated by those percolating peppers; f21.5 just a little on the oily and bitter side; b22.5 Pepper by name, pepper by nature...! *56.9% (113.8 proof). sc.*

**Old Rip Van Winkle 10 Years Old (93)** n24 t23 f23 b23. A much sharper cookie than it once was. And possibly a Maryland Cookie, too, what with the nuts and chocolate evident. As graceful as it is entertaining. *45% (90 Proof). Buffalo Trace.*

**Old Rip Van Winkle Aged 10 Years** bott code: B17053113:497 **(91.5)** n23 t23.5 f22 b23 Those who know the Weller Antique 107 will find this enjoyable, but just a little lacking in body by comparison. *53.5% (107 proof)*

⟐ **Old Rip Van Winkle Aged 10 Years** bott code: B1705307:267 db **(93.5)** n24 one of the most intricate bourbon noses in the marketplace. Traces of toasted hazelnut, marzipan and ulmo honey inlock beautifully with the understated liquorice and acacia honey A three pipe nose if ever there was one...; t23 belies its strength by bringing the corn right into the forefront of the delivery. This makes for an oily delivery and follow-through, allowing the muscovado sugars to indulge quietly; f23 a slight spice buzz, the vanillas, sugars and corn oil take their time to leave the stage; b23.5 there is something of the old Ancient Age 10 in this, you know... *53.5% (107 proof).*

**Old Taylor 6 (89.5)** n22.5 t23 f21.5 b22.5 A relaxed, stylish and surprisingly complex bourbon with a distinctly fruity edge. *40% (80 proof).*

⟐ **Old Taylor 6 Kentucky Straight Bourbon** bott code: B1631608446 **(90)** n22.5 t23 f22 b22.5 Exactly as above. Except we now see a little more corn oil and rye glisten on the finish. What a lovely old-fashioned kind of bourbon this is, especially for Old Timers like me...! *40% (80 proof).*

⟐ **Old Virginia Kentucky Straight Bourbon Aged 6 Years** bott code: L833901B **(91.5)** n23 peppered hickory and leather: perfect bitter-sweet balance; t22.5 crisp and salivating, the sugars brittle and determined to impact. Slow liquorice and Manuka honey; f23 gorgeous sweetened spice; b23 the kind of old-fashioned style bourbon I fell in love with over 40 years ago... *40%. La Martiniquaise.*

**Old Weller Antique 107 (96)** n24.5 t24 f23.5 b24 This almost blew me off my chair. Always thought this was pleasant, if a little underwhelming, in the past. However, this bottling has had a few thousands volts passed through it as it now comes alive on the palate with a glorious blending of freshness and debonair aging. One of the surprise packages of 2012. *53.5% (107 proof)*

**Orphan Barrel Forged Oak (87)** n22 t22 f21 b22. Decent bourbon, but a little stiff and mechanical in its development. The finish has a tad too much toast for its own good. Still, a good chewing bourbon. *45.25%*

⟐ **Orphan Barrel Forged Oak Kentucky Straight Bourbon Aged 15 Years** bott code: L6019K1001 **(87.5)** n22 t23 f20.5 b22 Not sure if this is from the same batch as the last one I tasted, but still fails to really carry through as you hope a 15-year-old might. Seems extremely corn centric for a bourbon – almost showing the traits of a corn whiskey, though without the usual fun and sweetness. The finish remains distant and mechanical, but there appears more polish to the delivery, with a bees-waxy feel to the delightful but all too brief kumquat, black cherry and liquorice explosion. *45.25% (90.5 proof).*

**Orphan Barrel Rhetoric 21 Year Old** batch 0109-67 **(94.5)** n23.5 t24 f23 b24 A bourbon drinker's bourbon. How's that for rhetoric...? *45%*

**Orphan Barrel Rhetoric 22 Year Old** batch no. L6063J3 **(87)** n20.5 t23.5 f21 b22. Certainly has a few proud war wounds to show for 22 searing hot Kentucky summers. Some outstanding tannins and roasty sugars at play on delivery, and a few grapefruit notes for good measure. But some bitterness, also, as the oak gives up a degree of its less impressive qualities. Very hard to call it right on whiskeys this age. This comes home just the right side of very good, but another summer might have done some fair damage. *45.2% (90.4 proof)*

**Orphan Barrel Rhetoric Aged 24 Years** bott code: L8059K1002 **(95)** n24 t24 f23.5 b23.5 An unusual bourbon for this kind of great age. Usually they head down a heavy duty tannin route. Instead this one almost drowns in natural creamy caramels. Almost as meek as Theresa May when facing the EU bully boys though, of course, nothing on the planet is that pathetic. *45.4% (90.8 proof).*

**Pappy Van Winkle Family Reserve 15 Years Old** bott code: L172520110:237 **(96)** n24 t23.5 f24 b24.5 Weller Antique fans will possibly find a closer match here structure-wise than the 10-year-old. While those in pursuit of excellent bourbon should just linger here awhile. Anyone other than true bourbon lovers need not sample. But there again... *53.5%*

⟐ **Pappy Van Winkle Family Reserve Kentucky Straight Bourbon Whiskey 15 Years Old** bott code: L181340105:017 db **(96)** n24 polished leather and Lubeck marzipan. Add to that orange blossom honey and liquorice...and now you're talking! t24.5 remember what I said about the nose...now put that into liquid form...! A dream-like bourbon coating the mouth so perfectly proportioned intensity; f23.5 butterscotch and more orange blossom honey/ liquorice. Just a little bitterness from the oak late on; b24 usually I spit everything I taste. I accidentally found myself swallowing a drop of this without thinking. A bourbon-lover's bourbon... *53.5% (107 proof).*

**Pappy Van Winkle's Family Reserve 20 Years Old** bott code: L172640108:18N **(95)** n24 t22.5 f24.5 b24 An ancient bourbon, so should be a flavour powerhouse. But this is all about understatement and complexity. *45.2% (90.4 proof).*

⟐ **Pappy Van Winkle Family Reserve Kentucky Straight Bourbon Whiskey 20 Years Old** bott code: L18233C10723N db **(85.5)** n21 t22.5 f21 b21 Some profound vanilla and citrus moments on delivery. But the nose tells you things aren't as they should be and the finale confirms it. One or two casks used here that has gone through the top, bringing out some pretty tired notes from the oak. Just never comfortable in its own skin. *45.2% (90.4 proof).*

**Pappy Van Winkle's Family Reserve 23 Years Old** bott code: L1707013:20N **(94.5)** n24.5 t23 f23.5 b23.5 I well remember the first Pappy boasting this kind of age: it was horrifically over-oaked and lacked any form of meaningful structure. Well, this also has the odd moment where the tannins are slightly out of control, especially just after delivery. But the structure to this is sound, the complexity a joy. And as for the nose....wow! *47.8% (95.6 proof).*

⟐ **Pappy Van Winkle Family Reserve Kentucky Straight Bourbon Whiskey 23 Years Old** bott code: L180590111:08N db **(95.5)** n24 scorched honeycomb and a similar orange blossom honey note found on the 15-year-old! The tannins shape-shift as well offer a variance of weight; t24 the corn oils kiss and caress, the tannins barge and batter in a good cop/bad cop delivery; slowly molasses gathers with enough intensity to matter; f23.5 slightly burnt butterscotch tart; b24 one of the holy grails of bourbon is to produce consistently a 23- to 25-year-old which is still sweet and not tannin dominated: no easy ask. This has certainly moved a little way towards that, shewing some of the character of the last bottling I tasted, although this is unquestionably drier. At least on the nose a decisive sweetness I detected and there are still sugars enough to give some fabulous moments on the palate. The tannins do, though, still have the biggest say. But remember: this whiskey has matured for a very long time. In the glass it takes well over an hour to get the best out of it: the secrets of such an ancient bourbon are always revealed tantalisingly slowly... *47.8% (95.6 proof).*

**Parker's Heritage Collection 11 Year Old Single Barrel Bourbon** barrel no. 5027255, OED: 4/10/2006, rickhouse : DD, Floor: 6, Rick: 39 db **(84.5)** n19.5 t23 f20.5 b21.5 Now there's a rarity: a cask kink apparent with the milkiness on the nose and bitterness at the death. But at least the middle is a joy with cream toffee perked up by moderate spices and the obligatory molasses as well as a little cocoa butter and liquorice. *61% (122 proof). sc.*

**Parker's Heritage Collection 24 Year Old Bottled in Bond Bourbon** dist Fall 90 **(95.5)** n24 t24 f23.5 b24 For my 999th whisky for the 2018 Bible, thought I'd take on the oldest commercially bottled Kentucky bourbon I can ever remember seeing. Had no idea how this one would go, as the heat of the Midwest means there is little room for the whiskey to manoeuvre. What we actually have is a bourbon in previously unchartered territory and clearly experiencing new, sometimes mildly bewildering, sensations, having proudly gone where no bourbon has gone before... *50%.*

**Parker's Heritage Collection Wheated Mash Bill Bourbon Aged 10 Years (97)** n24 t24 f24.5 b24.5. Hard to find the words that can do justice. I know Parker will be immensely proud of this. And with every good reason: I am working exceptionally hard to find a fault with this either from a technical distillation viewpoint or a maturation one. Or just for its sheer whiskeyness...A potential World Whisky of the Year. *62.1% (124.2 Proof). ncf*

◈ **Quarter Horse Kentucky Bourbon Whiskey Aged a Minimum of 1 Year in New Oak (87)** n21.5 t23 f21.5 b21.5 An intriguing whiskey which simultaneously shews its youth and the spirit and maturity from the cask. The creamy toffee notes on delivery and follow through are superb. For a Quarter Horse it's not half bad... *46% (92.*

◈ **Rebel Yell Kentucky Straight Bourbon Whiskey** bott code: A305181406 **(88)** n22.5 an attractive, clean ulmo honey and light liquorice mix; **t22** it's hickory all the way with only the lightest brush of oil to elongate the molasses; **f21** straightforward vanilla and spice; **b22** When, back in 1992 I had set off on my uncertain future as the world's first full time whisky writer, the London underground was festooned with adverts for Rebel Yell, complete with Confederate flag, if memory serves over the passing quarter of a century. It was United Distillers' (now Diageo) great hope of conquering the world with bourbon. They didn't and the company, with their fingers scorched, turned their backs on not only what was actually a very good bourbon, but the entire genre. They had gone in all guns blazing, when in fact bourbon needed – after so many decades of decline - was a softly softly approach. This doesn't have quite the richness of that defeated Rebel Yell from a previous era, but the delicate nature of the sweetness is very attractive. *40% (80 proof).*

◈ **Rebel Yell Small Batch Reserve Kentucky Straight Bourbon Whiskey (94.5)** n23.5 confident, intense and punchy spices suggests wheat at work here, as does the delightful doughy bready and tannin mix **t24** a near faultless delivery. The oils and spices work hand-in-hand to ensure the most velvety kick-delivery you could imagine...and always pitch perfect. The mid-ground is rich in mocha and toffee, a little molasses moving into the middle; **f23** the sugars remain reserved while the spices are nothing like so and punch out the message from both grain and oak with gusto; **b23.5** a full on, toasty bourbon making the most of the ample spices on hand. *45.3% (90.6 proof).*

**Redemption High Rye Bourbon (74.5)** n19 t20 f17.5 b18. Hugely disappointing bottling. Vaguely butyric, and its failure to reach any high point of quality is really driven home by the car-crash finish, complete with less than pleasant tang. Seriously needs to redeem itself next time round. *46%*

**Ridgemont Reserve 1792 Aged 8 Years (94.5)** n23.5 t24 f23.5 b23.5 Now here is a whiskey which appears to have come to terms with its own strengths and, as with all bourbons and malts, limitations. Rarely did whiskey from Barton reach this level of maturity, so harnessing its charms always involves a bit of a learning curve. Each time I taste this it appears a little better than the last...and this sample is no exception to the rule. Excellent. *46.85% (93.7 Proof)*

**Rock Hill Farms Single Barrel Bourbon** bott code: B1717118:40K **(95)** n24 t24 f23.5 b24 Almost impossible to find fault with this. Anyone who loves whisky, bourbon in particular, will simply groan in pleasure in the same way your leg might jolt out when the knee is tapped. The only fly in the ointment is that I cannot tell you the barrel or bottling, because it isn't marked on the bottle. This really is bourbon at it sexiest. *50% (100 proof)*

◈ **Rock Hill Farms Single Barrel Bourbon** bott code: L18102010829K **(95.5)** n24 Natural Caramel is the favourite in this horsey-themed bourbon...with Crisp, Semi-Fruity and Demerara Sugars, each looking good here in the ring, all strongly fancied outsiders...; **t24** well, they're off, and it's Toasty Sugars leading the way with Big Spice right behind and Intense Tannin keeping right up with the front runners. Sitting comfortably is Manuka Honey and Hickory Middle as we come into the home straight; **f23.5** it's an exciting finish with Chewy Liquorice coming up on the rails while Natural Caramel is nowhere to be seen. Subtle Spice has overtaken Big Spice and Vanilla Impact is finishing strongly. But it's a photo finish between Intense Tannin, Lusty

Liquorice, Subtle Spices and possibly Toasty Sugars...; **b24** take a bet on this and you are likely to be a winner. A true bourbon connoisseur's favourite... *50% (100 proof).*

◇◇ **Russell's Reserve Kentucky Straight Bourbon 10 Years Old** bott code: LL/GI210755 db **(92.5) n23** good Lord! My nose feels that it has just landed in a caramel and vanilla-flavoured blancmange. A softer landing than a head in a brand new feathered pillow – Turkey feathers, of course...; **t23** a velvety landing on the palate: the corn oils are pronounced, but the ulmo honey attached to the vanilla is astounding. In contrast, the oak builds in strength through an ever-increasing degree of spice; **f23** much later than normal the traditional bourbon values of liquorice and hickory arrive, but so subtly you barely realise they are there...; **b23.5** one of the softest decade-old bourbons I have tasted in a very, very long time. *45% (90 proof).*

**Russell's Reserve Single Barrel (94) n23.5 t24 f23 b23.5.** Old-fashioned, thick as treacle bourbon. Delicious. *55%. ncf. Wild Turkey.*

◇◇ **Russell's Reserve Single Barrel no 17-0208** Rickhouse B Floor 6 17 2 **(95.5) n23.5** floral with matching bees. Heather honey with golden syrup attaching to the gentle tannins; **t24** perfectly oiled with an equally correct degree of honey. The spices are clearly set in motion by the breast-beating oak. But once more the intricate but salivating sugars are a match. The corn oils formulate unusually early and make for a chewy mouthfeel; **f23.5** the spices buzz like those early bees; **b24.5** so understated, this bourbon communicates in gentle whispers. Comes across sweet as honey but thickens into a gentle giant - yet all the time the balance is never threatened, only continually enhanced. Sublime. *55% (110 proof). Selected by the Frankfort Bourbon Society*

◇◇ **Seven Devils Straight Bourbon Whiskey (82.5) n20 t21.5 f20.5 b20.5** Nutty, caramel-laden and sweet, there is a buzz on the palate to this which suggests the distillate has not been quite as well made as it could be. Doesn't sit right, despite (or maybe because of) the praline. *45% (90 proof). Bottled by Koenig Distillery*

◇◇ **Shenk's Homestead Kentucky Sour Mash 2018 Release** batch no. 18C322, bott code: A18094322 **(89) n22.5** peppery and busy, there is quite a nip to this. A little red liquorice and trace Demerara sugar perform the balancing act; **t22.5** a very curious delivery. Immediately the lack of corn oil is apparent and those squabbling spices on the nose appear in double-quick time The thin mid-ground is very unusual in a Kentucky bourbon, so the vanillas fill in the gaps; **f22** incredibly light with a faint hickory note ensuring some bourbon clout to accompany the spices; **b22** a pleasant, non-taxing, small grain dominated bourbon, but with a curious lack of body. *45.6% (91.2 proof). 2,691 bottles. Bottled by Michter's Distillery.*

**Stagg Jr (91.5) n22.5 t24 f22.5 b22.5.** A whiskey of staggering brinkmanship. Who will blink first? The massive oak or the taste buds. To be honest, this is the kind of bourbon that sorts out the men from the boys, the women from the girls. Doesn't have quite enough covering sweetness of varying type and intensity to match the complexity found in the original Stagg. One that needs a very long time to get to the bottom of. *67.2% (134.4 proof)*

◇◇ **Stagg Jr** bott code: B1707310457 **(96) n24 t24.5 f23.5 b24** I well remember the first Stagg Junior I encountered. Which though truly excellent, skimped a little too much on the sugars and struggled to find its balance and, thus, full potential. Certainly no such worries with this bottling: indeed, the honey is remarkable for its abundance. Staggering... *64.75% (129.5 proof)*

◇◇ **Ten High Kentucky Bourbon** bott code: L172211518053 **(72) n19 t19 f16 b18** Docile, unusually sweet early on but the finish never quite feels right, the flavours jarring badly. Bitter at the death. This is a bourbon...? *40% (80 proof).*

**Trails End Bourbon 8 Year Old (87) n21.5 t22.5 f21.5 b21.5.** A light bourbon, where the end of the trail begins early. The citrus outpoints the tannins all too easily. *45% (90 Proof). Hood River Distillers, Inc.*

◇◇ **Treaty Oak Distilling Red Handed Bourbon Whiskey** db **(90) n22** the corn oils are profound here and gel attractively with the muscly tannin; **t23** a tad feinty perhaps, but the small grains are so intense here, the oils so gushing, the spices so warm it is easy to forgive. A lovely honey thread ensures balance; **f22.5** those toasty tannins bite deep; **b22.5** as thick cut as a Texas steak....and no less juicy! *47.5% (95 proof).*

**Van Winkle Special Reserve 12 Years Old Lot "B"** bott code: L172550110:147 **(93.5) n23 t23 f24 b23.5** Those looking for comparisons between certain Weller products and Van Winkle's might find this particular bottling a little better weighted, less forthright and more complex. *45% (90 proof)*

◇◇ **Van Winkle Special Reserve 12 Years Old Lot "B" Batch Bourbon Whiskey** bott code: L181300112 **(94.5) n23.5 t23.5 f23 b23.5** Roughly consistent in quality to the bottling above, but better here and takes a slightly different route - by putting its foot on the toastiness and steering by some very impressive waxy Manuka honey. For those who like their bourbon hairy, bristling with spice, honey and big oak interaction. *45.2% (90.4 proof).*

**Very Old Barton** bott code: L17/60111:104 **(87.5) n22 t22 f21.5 b22** Attractive, brittle and with a delicious slow burn of first delicate, then broader hickory tones. The small grains fizz and dazzle in typical VOB style. If anything, slightly undercooked at this strength, and missing the extra oils, too. *40% (80 proof)*

**Very Old Barton 6** bott code: 907:104 **(93) n22 t24 f23.5 b23.5** The VOB 6, when the number stood for the years, has for the last quarter of a century been one of my bourbons of choice: an understated classic. This version has toned down on the nose very slightly and the palate underlines a far less definite oak-to-grain parry and counter-thrust. That said, still a bourbon which mesmerises you with its innate complexity and almost perfect weight and pace on the palate. One that has you instinctively pouring a second glass. *45% (90 proof)*

**Very Old Barton 86** Proof bott code: B1635619:024 **(89) n21.5 t22.5 f22.5 b22.5** It is not the three percent extra alcohol which makes the difference here: simply the marriage of barrels. These ones have allowed the rye tones within the small grain to positively shine...; *43% (86 proof)*

**Very Old Barton 90 Proof (94) n23 t24 f23.5 b23.5.** One of the most dangerously drinkable whiskeys in the world... *45% (90 proof)*

⬦ **Very Old Barton 90 Proof Kentucky Straight Bourbon** bott code: L181370113 **(92) n22.5** a little thin, allowing the accent to fall on the light, oaky vanillas; **t23.5** the usual busy delivery from this distillery, but content for the smaller grains to whizz around seemingly without control any great direction being taken; a tad salty and a highly satisfying chocolate and hickory blend fills the mid-ground; **f23** long with soft oils, a gentle maple syrup breeze and crispier rye tones; **b23** gorgeous whiskey, though not perhaps the tour de force of previous bottlings. *45% (90 proof).*

**Very Old Barton 100 Proof** bott code: L17/640102:074 **(96) n23.5 t24.5 f23.5 b24.5** Here's a challenge for you: find fault with this whiskey... Brilliant bourbon of the intense yet sophisticated variety. *50% (100 proof)*

⬦ **Very Old Barton Kentucky Straight Bourbon** bott code: 3820123 **(87.5) n22 t22 f21.5 b22** A consistent bourbon (just noticed I have marked it identically to the last bottling!) giving a limited but delightful account of the VIB brand, ensuring the busy small grains keeps on scrambling around the palate and just enough liquorice and hickory meets the onrushing caramel and praline. Deceptively delicious. *40% (80 proof).*

**Virgin Bourbon 7 Years Old (96.5) n24 t24.5 f24 b24** This takes me back nearly 40 years to when I first began my love affair with bourbon and was still a bit of a whisky virgin. This was the very style that blew me away: big, uncompromising, rugged...yet with a heart of honeyed gold. It is the type of huge, box-ticking, honest bourbon that makes you get on your hands and knees and kiss Kentucky soil. *50.5% (101 proof)*

**Virgin Bourbon 15 Years Old (92.5) n23.5 t23 f23.5 b23.** The kind of bourbon you want to be left in a room with. *50.5% (101 proof)*

**Virginia Gentleman (90.5) n22 t23 f23 b23.5.** A Gentleman in every sense: and a pretty sophisticated one at that. *40% (80 Proof)*

**Weller Aged 12 Years** bott code: B17081 20:56 **(91) n22.5** the oak takes few hostages but has a tender, sweeter side to it also: a kind of spiced Manuka an acacia honey, liquorice mix; **t23** chewy, then a little crunchy and the oils firm up slightly. Big hickory and even a slight teasing of camp coffee. Curling oils help pile on the sugars; **f22.5** long with the honey staying its ground, though the oak now drifts into drier, vaguely sawdusty territory; **b23** firm, crunchy, sweet bourbon and very warming... *45% (90 proof)*

⬦ **Weller Aged 12 Years Kentucky Straight Bourbon Whiskey** bott code: L190790117 **(91.5) n22.5 t23.5 f22.5 b23** Spookily similar to the bottling above, the only noticeable difference being the degree of waxy honey on delivery. *45% (90 proof).*

**Weller Antique 107** bott code: B17044 17:374 **(95.5) n23.5 t24.5 f23.5 b24** The higher strength has helped bring the best from the great whiskey as the oils are left unchecked and allowed to help the other elements cast their magic spells. To add water to this, especially, would be sacrilege. *53.5% (107 proof)*

⬦ **Weller Antique 107 Kentucky Straight Bourbon** bott code: L190170117 **(88) n22** a testy aroma, barking out tannin and spice, the waxy orange-blossom honey coming through intermittently; **t23** a bold, salivating impact: unusually firm despite the molasses taking a decisive, chewy hold; **f21** an odd finish with a slight bitterness outflanking the previously rich sugars; **b22** enjoyable, but nothing like the Antique 107 I have become used to swooning over. Attractive, but some antiques are more desired than others. *53.5% (107 proof).*

⬦ **Weller C.Y.P.B Wheated Kentucky Straight Bourbon** bott code: L18163011042N **(95.5) n24** it is almost impossible not to fall into a trance of sheer delight here: the mesmeric honey, a kind of blend of Manuka on steroids and ulmo at its most becalming, punctuated by a succession of spice waves. Add to that the audible tannin, a squeeze of kumquat and even a hint of roast yam, and it is borderline impossible to find fault with this nose...; **t24** maybe the delivery isn't quite so complex as that nose, but there is no escaping the gorgeous glossiness to this, a waxiness which holds together a crisper. Also, the softness of the dark sugar suck you down into the inner elements of this bourbon: dark, lyrical and mysterious; the oils come into their fore at just gone the halfway mark and provide the means to help the spices on the distance; **f23.5** and don't those spices just rumble on...; **b24** has all the chutzpah of a wheated bourbon that knows it's damn good and goes out to shock. Enjoy the myriad little favour and spice explosions. And the deceptive depth.... 47.5% (95 proof).

**Weller Special Reserve** bott code: L172080115:014 **(93) n23** a warm, nutty mocha lead heads slowly towards liquorice; a light Demerara background; **t23.5** salivating and surprisingly firm for a wheated bourbon. The spices are intact, though, and acts as fanfare to the more muscular oak notes; **f23** dry and toasty with **b23.5** imperiously excellent, yet somehow given to understatement. 45% (90 proof)

◆ **Weller Special Reserve Kentucky Straight Bourbon** bott code: L19018 0118 **(94) n23** despite the peppery bombardment, a nutty, liquorice harmony melts into the soothing corn oils; **t23.5** one of the softest bourbon deliveries I have tasted this year, those oils – just as on the nose – soothing palate and wrapping the ulmo honey around every taste bud; **f24** now goes into spicy, wheated overdrive...; **b24** almost too soft and easy to drink. A thousand kisses in a glass.. 45% (90 proof).

**Western Gold 6 Year Old Bourbon Whiskey (91.5) n22 t23 f22.5 b23** Taken from barrels sitting high in the warehouse, that's for sure. You get a lot for your six years... 40%.

◆ **The Whisky Shop Maker's Mark** batch no. 002, oak staves with barrel finish **(94.5) n23.5** oh, the subtlety of the interplay between the red and black liquorice...wow! **t24** gin on delivery that mix of red and black liquorice, but sweetened with molasses and manuka honey...in an imperiously elegant manner. And then comes the spice...; **f23** and yet more spice, though the vanilla caramel levels are rising to meet it; **b24** so rare to find Maker's Mark at this strength. The kind of whisky that give wheated bourbon lovers a little stiffy... 54.95%.

**Whiskey Thief Straight Bourbon (87) n22 t22 f21.5 b21.5.** Straight as a die, unwavering bourbon which sticks to an uncomplicated, intense vanilla theme. Very pleasant. 40%

◆ **Widow Jane Straight Bourbon Whiskey Aged 10 Years** barrel no. 1785, bott 2018 **(95) n23.5** great age spews from the glass, bubbling over with all kinds of burnt toast and honey moments; the element are stripped bare and naked while the vanilla, orange blossom honey and peppers tease...; **t23.5** the softest corn oils kiss, the spices bite playfully while the Manuka honey and liquorice caresses; **f24** a beautifully dark, toasty afterglow with salt and honey still on the lips...; **b24** this is one very passionate Widow.. 45.5% (91 proof). sc.

◆ **Wilcox Bourbon Whiskey (73.5) n19 t19 f17.5 b18** When you buy a bourbon whiskey, you have in your mind a clean, complex Kentuckian. Not sure who made this, but far too feinty for its own good with none of the liquorice and honey notes you should rightfully expect. A very poor representation of bourbon, and not remotely in the true Kentucky style. 40% (80 proof). BBC Spirits.

◆ **Wild Turkey 81 Proof** bott code: LL/DF291109 db **(91.5) n23** impressively elegant: light ulmo honey mixes beautifully with the buttery vanillas and soft red liquorice; **t23** ridiculously soft on the palate: one of the gentlest landing of all the main bourbon brands. Again, it is the honey which shapes the bourbon, this time a slightly weightier heather honey; only a third the way in does the tannin begin to really unfold with some delightful hickory moments; **f22.5** gentle yet spicy; **b23** a much sweeter, more relaxed bottling than the old 40% version, gathering up honey notes like a wild turkey hoovering up summer berries. 40.5% (81 proof).

◆ **Wild Turkey 101** Proof bott code: LL/GE170523 db **(93) n23** weightier than the 81, as you might expect, but the honey is lost at the expense of the natural caramels. So heftier, but a tad duller, though spices here where on the 81 there are none; **t23.5** beautifully fat, the corn oil has its fingerprints over every aspect of this bourbon. The honey missing on the nose is evident here, though laid back – a halfway house between thin Manuka and light molasses. A beautiful chocolate-liquorice middle as it thickens and spices up; **f23** still corn oily but here the vanilla develops alongside a gentle citrus; **b23.5** perhaps now the most corn-rich of all the major Kentucky bourbons. 50.5% (101 proof).

**Wild Turkey American Spirit Aged 15 Years (92) n24 t22.5 f22.5 b23.** A delightful Wild Turkey that appears under par for a 100 proofer but offers much when you search those nooks and crannies of your palate. 50.0% (100 proof)

◆ **Wild Turkey Kentucky Spirit Single Barrel** barrel no. 0401, warehouse A, rick no. 6, bott 01/14/19, bott code: LL/HA152135 db **(89) n22.5** a cream toffee, anyone...? **t23** the natural caramels were pretty major on the nose: here they are borderline overwhelming. So delicious, though – and perked up by the spices; **f21.5** a strangely bitter finale; **b22** a real enjoyable softie if, perhaps, a tad one dimensional. 50.5% (101 proof). sc.

⟨⟨⟨ **Wild Turkey Longbranch** oak and Texas mesquite charcoal refined bott code: LL/ GI180207 db **(91.5) n23** something of the Maryland cookie about this: a little bit of moist syrup and chocolate plus a nutty edge, all patted on the back by a light but busy spice; **t23** caramel and honey lead the way in a typically soft Wild Turkey delivery; stunningly juicy with the corn oil rich in demerara sugars and soft citrus; **f22.5** now the spice holds court with a delicate vanilla background; **b23** Mesquite must be America's answer to peat: here there is a just a light touch, barely noticeable until the finish, and emphasised by the very late warmness to the finale itself. *43% (86 proof).*

**Wild Turkey Rare Breed** bott code L0049FH **(94) n22.5 t24.5 f23 b24.** It is hard to credit that this is the same brand I have been tasting at regular intervals for quite a long while. Certainly nothing like this style has been around for a decade and it is massively far removed from two years ago. The nose threatens a whiskey limited in direction. But the delivery is as profound as it is entertaining. Even on this bottling's singular though fabulous style, not perhaps quite overall the gargantuan whiskey of recent years. But, seeing as it's only the nose which pegs it back a point or two, still one that would leave a big hole in your whiskey experience if you don't get around to trying. *54.1%*

⟨⟨⟨ **Wild Turkey Rare Breed Barrel Proof** bott code: LL/GD020831 db **(95.5) n23.5** exemplary layering of acacia honey, polished leather, red liquorice and toasty tannin: elegant, mainly gentle but always with a threat of spice; **t24** immediate salivation of delivery with a gloriously lithe mouthfeel, though the corn builds up the fats to a near perfect degree; as the middle spices up, do molasses come through any more elegantly than this...? **f24** long, graceful with the delicate sweetness now more of a heather honey style and vanillas sloping off, again of varying hues and intensities; **b24** a clever glass bottle, its roundness reinforcing the mouthfeel and character of the bourbon itself: one of the most rounded in all Kentucky. In some ways this whiskey is the blueprint for bourbon: its characteristics embrace what we mentally define as bourbon. *58.4% (116.8 proof).*

⟨⟨⟨ **Wilderness Trail Single Barrel Kentucky Straight Bourbon BIB Sweet Mash** barrel no 14E23 **(83.5) n20.5 t21.5 f21 b20.5** A hot, aggressive bourbon with more bite than spice. The corn element ticks the right boxes and does a great job, but this bourbon struggles to find its rhythm despite an attractive mocha finale. *50% (100 proof). ncf. 245 bottles. 64% corn, 24% wheat 12% malted barley. sc.*

**William Larue Weller** db **(96) n24 t24.5 f23.5 b24** the most relaxed and lightly spiced Weller since its first launch. May lack its inherent oomph, but the deft, complex notes are still one of life's great pleasures... *67.7% (135.4 proof).*

**William Larue Weller** db **(97.5) n24 t25 f24 b24** ...The most delicious lesson in whiskey structure imaginable. This was my 1,263rd and final new whiskey for the Jim Murray Whisky Bible 2019. Did I leave the very best until last....? *64.1% (128.2 proof).*

⟨⟨⟨ **William Larue Weller** db **(97.5) n25** I think my work for the day has ended. How can I put this down; how can I stop myself from nosing true perfection? I don't quite know where to start, not least because some things in life are beyond words. And this nose is one of them. It does its own talking, singing. For a start, I have picked out three types of honey in play: Corsican bruyere, ulmo and Manuka – a blend found in only the finest whiskeys. There is a wonderful char to the hickory, also, giving it a slightly acidic note while spices nibble politely. On top of this liquorice and molasses for a heavy sub-culture of controlled sweetness; **t24.5** as ever...just wow! A monumental delivery where you wonder if you can survive the enormity of the delivery, only to find that the flavours recede quickly and quietly, but only enough to allow you to understand what is going on. Some red liquorice has been added to the incredible team of all talents that is seducing your taste buds, its black cousin at the vanguard; **f23.5** vanillas and caramels roll in like a sea fog from the barrels, just calming things down and allowing those sweeter elements to reform and join the light corn oils...; **b24.5** I have before me a glass of whiskey. It is pure amber in colour and has won more top honours, including World Whisky of the Year, in Jim Murray's Whisky Bible than any other brand. For that reason the sample before me is, as I nose and taste it on the evening of 26th August 2019, the 20,000th whisky I have specifically tasted for this book since it was first published in 2003. There really could be no other I could possibly bestow this personal honour upon. It is a landmark whiskey in every sense... Oh, once again, I have not been let down. I will have to wait to see if this is World Whisky of the Year once more: on the evidence before me it will be close. But I do know no whiskey will better its truly perfect nose... *62.85% (125.7 proof).*

⟨⟨⟨ **Winchester Bourbon Whiskey Aged a Minimum of 6 Months in New Oak** bott code: L219A090024564 **(85.5) n21.5 t22 f21 b21** That is one very curious bourbon with an arrangement of tobacco and leather on the nose and thick corn oil and orange blossom honey on delivery. A little chunky and feinty towards the close, but the spices do a good job. Complex and decidedly idiosyncratic. *45% (90 proof*

**Woodford Reserve Distiller's Select Batch 296** bott code: L197611812 db **(88.5) n22** a little praline, lime and spice barely lays a glove on the thick caramels; **t22.5** the nose certainly forewarns what's coming next: caramel! A little spice tries to liven things up a bit, but the creamy oak-rich procession stays the course; the of hazelnut note pops in and out to balance with the light cocoa; **f22** slightly toastier, but the natural caramels persist; **b22** soft, nutty and not keen to change gears too often. *43.2% (86.4 proof).*

**Woodford Reserve Double Oaked (95)** n24.5 t23.5 f23 b24 The old Labrot and Graham Distillery has just entered a new phase of excellence since its reopening. Well done blender on creating a bourbon not just of beauty but of great significance. *43.2% WB16/052*

◈ **Yellowstone Select Kentucky Straight Bourbon Whiskey (90.5) n22.5** bursting at the seams with molasses and fruity rye; toned and leathery – something the old Yellowstone never was...; **t22.5** classic liquorice and hickory delivery with a Manuka honey background; **f22.5** excellent vanilla and spice, still with that honey offering a weak but welcome pulse; **b23** a good, solid Kentucky bourbon, shewing more body and balance than the Yellowstone of yesteryear. *46.5% (93 proof).*

## Tennessee Whiskey

◈ **Heaven's Door Tennessee Bourbon Whiskey 10 Year Old** bott code: 10/25/18 **(85) n21.5 t22.5 f20 b21** I'm knock-knock-knocking this Heaven's Door: far too heavy, I'm afraid. But, wow! What a delivery...!!! *50% (100 proof).*

◈ **Heaven's Door Tennessee Bourbon Whiskey Aged for a Minimum of 7 Years** bott code: 2019/04/120555 **(94) n23** outwardly clean but on another level vaguely earthy, too; abounding in delicate molasses notes; **t24** beautifully well manicured hickory and maple syrup; top dollar oils caress the palate as a gorgeous, slightly nutty mocha note fills the middle; **f23.5** excellent spice attack as the oils grow; the mocha stays the course; **b23.5** another bewildering whiskey type to contend with in the USA. Now it is Tennessee Bourbon. I presume that is a bourbon whiskey made in Tennessee but without deploying the charcoal mellowing process. Whatever, it is quite Heavenly.... *45% (90 proof).*

◈ **Uncle Nearest 1820 Premium Whiskey Aged 11 Years Nearest Green Single Barrel** barrel no. US-1 **(94.5) n23** very clever nose: equally light (thanks to the vanilla-caramel) and intense (bravo the liquorice and treacle); **t24** less inclined towards delicacy here! The tannins are straining at the leash, the toast is slightly burnt and the liquorice is on maximum liquoriceness....; **f23.5** mmm, such a sexy climb down, as the caramels and manuka honey combine for a chewy finale; **b24** a real roller coaster of a ride. Let's get back on again... *57.6% (115.1 proof).* 164 bottles.

◈ **Uncle Nearest 1820 Premium Whiskey Aged 11 Years Nearest Green Single Barrel** barrel no. US-2 **(92.5) n23** soft liquorice and hickory in a vanilla bubble; **t23** toasty delivery with burnt toffee and deeper tannins. Creamy, buttery and intense; **f23** elegant creamy finale with light spices adding the extra dimension; **b23.5** have to applaud the delicate nature of this whiskey and its superior layering. Just too easy to enjoy. *55.1% (110.2 proof).* 146 bottles.

◈ **Uncle Nearest 1856 Premium Whiskey (89.5) n22** a light blending of chicory and kumquats; **t22.5** molasses and maple syrup integrate into the delicate vanillas with ease; **f22.5** dry vanilla sponge cake; **b22.5** no bells and whistles. Just a slow radiating of gentle sugar and tannin tones. Easy sipping. *50% (100 proof).*

## BENJAMIN PRICHARD

**Benjamin Prichard's Tennessee Whiskey (83)** n21.5 t21 f20 b20.5. Majestic fruity rye notes trill from the glass. Curiously yeasty as well; bounding with all kinds of freshly crushed brown sugar crystals. Pleasant enough, but doesn't gel like Prichard's bourbon. *40%*

## GEORGE DICKEL

**George Dickel Aged 17 Years** bott code: L6154K1001 db **(94) n24 t24 22.5 b23.5** The oldest George Dickel I have ever encountered has held its own well over the years. A defiant crispness to the piece makes for memorable drinking, though it is the accommodating and comfortable nose which wins the greatest plaudits... *43.5% (87 proof).*

**George Dickel Barrel Select (90.5)** n21 t23 f23.5 b23 The limited nose makes the heart sink. What happens once it hits the palate is another story entirely. Wonderful! *43%*

**George Dickel Distillery Reserve Collection 17 Year Old (91.5)** n23.5 t23.5 f21.5 b23 Outside of a warehouse, I'm not sure I've encountered a Tennessee whiskey of this antiquity before. I remember one I tasted some while back, possibly about a year older or two older than this, was black and like tasting eucalyptus concentrate. This is the opposite, showing extraordinary restraint for its age, an almost feminine charm. *43.5%*

**George Dickel No. 12** bott code: L7034R60011402 db **(89) n21.5 t23.5 f22 b22** In a way, a classic GD where you feel there is much more still in the tank... *45% (90 proof).*

**George Dickel Rye (95.5) n24 t23.5 f24 b24** Dare I say it? On this evidence, they do rye probably a fraction better than they produce straight Tennessee. This is a belter! *45%*

**George Dickel Superior No 12 Brand Whisky (90.5) n22.5 t23 f22.5 b22.5.** A different story told by George from the last one I heard. But certainly no less fascinating. *45%*

# JACK DANIEL

**Jack Daniel's 120th Anniversary of the White Rabbit Saloon (91) n22.5 t23.5 f22 b23** On its best-behaved form. After the delivery, the oils are down a little, so not the usual bombastic offering from JD. Nonetheless, this is pure class and the clever use of sugars simply make you drool... *43%. Brown-Forman.*

◈ **Jack Daniel's Gentleman Jack** bott code: 141734518B db **(90.5) n22.5** probably one of the most delicate noses in American whiskey, an even nuttiness mingling gently with light hickory and soft corn oils; **t22.5** "double mellowed", as it described itself, doesn't quite cover it. The tannins have made a statement, but they can barely be heard...; **f22.5** residual oils help gather the heftier notes and spices together for a warming and pleasantly complex finale; **b23** a Jack that can vary slightly in style. A couple of months back I included one in a tasting which was much fuller bodied and dripping in maple syrup. This one is infinitely more laid back. *40% (80 proof).*

**Jack Daniel's Old No.7 Brand (Black Label) (92) n23 t23 f22.5 b23.5.** Actually taken aback by this guy. The heavier oils have been stripped and the points here are for complexity...that should shock a few old Hell's Angels I know. *40%*

**Jack Daniel's No. 27 Gold Double Barrelled** extra matured in maple barrels **(82) n21 t21.5 f19 b20.5.** Pleasant enough. But it appears the peculiar tannins from the maple barrels have just done slightly too good a job of flattening out the higher, more complex notes from the grains themselves. Slightly bitters towards the finish also. Tennessee Gold with precious little sparkle at all... *40%*

**Jack Daniel's Master Distiller Series No 1** db **(90.5) n24** wonderful dose of extra tangy kumquat over the normal JD signature; something of the fruity cough sweet about this one; **t22** a massive, pleasantly oiled mix of molassed fudge and liquorice; **f22** drier, toastier hickory; **b22.5** no mistaking the JD pedigree. Just a few telling extra degrees of fruit. *43%*

**Jack Daniel's Rested Tennessee Rye** batch 2 **(88.5) n22 t23 f21 b22.5** Possibly the most intriguing whiskey of the year: America's most flavour-enhancing stills take on the world's most flavoursome grain. The result is surprisingly well mannered, though the oils from both the stills and grain do help obliterate any meaningful complexity. Probably the only world whiskey type I have never tasted in a warehouse at full strength (though I now intend to correct that). Instinct tells me a trick has been missed by not making this a 101...Oh, and one important thing. Normally I suggest you take your whiskey at body temperature. This is one whiskey which needs to be tasted at normal room temperature to keep the oils to a minimum and allow the rye maximum airtime. *40% WB16/022*

◈ **Jack Daniel's Single Barrel Select** barrel no. 18-7604, rick no. R-18, bott 10 18 18 db **(94) n23** a liquorice-honey blend backed by spiced Manuka honey; **t23.5** beautiful delivery. A magnificent marriage of earthy tannins and gentle oils with spices popping up all over the palate. The mid-point even includes some extra eucalyptus to ride alongside the liquorice; the sugars meanwhile are represented by a blend of ulmo and Manuka honey; **f23.5** softens towards spiced hickory and vanilla; **b24** outwardly very similar to a standard Jack, only with a few extra waves of honey and a little less fat around the edges. More subtle but incontrovertible evidence that JD is a far better distillery than most connoisseurs give it credit for. *45% (90 proof). sc.*

◈ **Jack Daniel's Straight Rye Whiskey** bott code: L184601033 db **(87.5) n21.5 t23 f21.5 b21.5** For some reason the rye refuses to take pole position and is lost behind a series of pretty ordinary corn and oak-vanilla notes, though the cool mintiness is a classy touch. Pleasant and plodding without being in any way - well, except minty moments - exciting or stimulating...as a good rye should always be! *45% (90 proof).*

# Corn Whiskey

**Dixie Dew (95) n22.5 t24 f24 b24.5** I have kept in my previous tasting notes for this whiskey as they serve a valuable purpose. The three matured corn whiskeys I have before me are made by the same distillers. But, this time round, they could not be more different. From Mellow Corn to Dixie we have three whiskeys with very differing hues. This, quite frankly, is the darkest corn whiskey I have ever seen and one of world class stature with characteristics I have never found before in any whiskey. Any true connoisseur of whisk(e)y will make deals with Lucifer to experience this freak whiskey. There is no age statement... but this one has gray hairs attached to the cob... *70%*

**J. W. Corn (92.5) n23 t23.5 f23 b23.** In another life this could be bourbon. The corn holds the power, for sure. But the complexity and levels are so far advanced that this – again!

– qualifies as very high grade whiskey. Wonderful that the normal high standard is being maintained for what is considered by many, quite wrongly, as an inferior spirit. *50%*

**Mellow Corn** (83) n19 t21 f22 b21. Dull and oily on the nose, though the palate compensates with a scintillating array of sweet and spicy notes. *50%*

## Single Malt Rye
## ANCHOR DISTILLERY

**Old Potrero Single Malt Straight Rye Whiskey Essay 10-SRW-ARM-E** (94) n24 t23 f24 b23 The whiskey from this distillery never fails to amaze. With the distillery now under new management it will be fascinating to see what lands in my tasting lab. Even at 75% quality we will still be blessed with astonishing whiskeys. *45% (90 proof)*

## Straight Rye

**Basil Hayden's Rye Whiskey 2017 Release** re-barreled in charred oak quarter casks, bott code: L7129CLA 153330822 (88.5) n23 t22 f21.5 b22 You can have too much of a good thing and it appears here the quarter casks have managed to over dose this rye with a surfeit of caramel. *40% (80 proof).*

**Benjamin Prichard's Tennessee Rye Whiskey** (86) n20 t21.5 f23 b21.5. Bit of a scruffy nose, but polishes up pleasantly. The rye itself is not of the sharp variety and at times is hard to identify. But the ulmo honey and lush butterscotch offer the gloss at the finish. *43%*

**Booker's Rye 13 Years, 1 Month, 12 Days** batch no. 2016-LE db (97.5) n25 t24 f24 b24.5 This was a rye made in the last days of when Jim Beam's Yellow Label was at its very peak. Then, it was the best rye commercially available. Today, it is simply a staggering example of a magnificent rye showing exactly what genius in terms of whiskey actually means. If this is not World Whisky of the Year for 2017, it will be only fragments of molecules away... *68.1% (136.2 proof)*

**Bulleit 95 Rye** (96) n25 t24.5 f22.5 B23.5 This is a style of rye, indeed whiskey, which is unique. Buffalo Trace makes an ultra high-quality rye which lasts the course longer. But nothing compares in nose and delivery to this...in fact few whiskies in the world get even close... *45%. Straight 95% rye mash whiskey.*

**Bulleit 95 Rye** bott code: L6344R60010848 (83) n20.5 t22 f20 b20.5 In some 30 years of tasting rye from the great Lawrenceburg, Indiana, distillery, this has to be the weirdest batch I have yet encountered. The highly unusual and mildly disturbing tobacco note on the nose appears to be a theme throughout the tasting experience. A rye which rallies briefly on delivery but ultimately falls flat on its face. *45% (90 proof).*

**Colonel E.H. Taylor Straight Rye** (97) n24 t24.5 f24 b24.5 reminds me of the younger ryes when Sazerac Handy first hit the shelves, with the emphasis on the clarity of the grain and the fallout of oak and spice. Really, a bottle which should never be left on a liquor store shelf. *50%*

**Colonel E.H. Taylor Straight Rye Bottled in Bond** bott code: L1728501 (94.5) n23.5 t24 f23.5 b23.5 Nothing like the big rye lift I found on the previous E. H. Taylor rye: this is happier to play the subtle game with a slow build rather than a naked graininess. A genuine surprise package. *50% (100 proof).*

⟐ **Colonel E.H. Taylor Straight Rye Bottled in Bond** bott code: L182130113.007 (96) n24 rye crisp enough that you chisel a statue of Colonel Taylor from...; t24 so clean and salivating. The rye appears as though in concentrated form, but sweetened by perfect proportions of demerara sugar; f24 the tannins roll up in fine fettle, offering a mix of vanilla and hickory as well as mocha. But the rye just keeps on pulsing...; b24 those were the very simplified notes of a long and beautiful story... *50% (100 proof).*

**Cougar Rye** (95) n25 t24 f23 b23. The Lawrenceburg, Indiana Distillery makes the finest rye I have ever tasted - and that is saying something. Here is a magnificent example of their astonishing capabilities. Good luck hunting the Cougar. *37%. Foster's Group, Australia.*

⟐ **Frankfort Bourbon Society Knob Creek Single Barrel Select Rye Barrel No 7540** bott Fall 2018 (88.5) n22 minty and soft, light vanilla leaks into the mix; spices push drift and poke; t23 surging spices are tempered with a mix of Calabrian honey and custard; the grain's fruitier edge finally alights; f21.5 a strange, vaguely phenolic note intertwines with the probing vanilla; a tad dry and bitter late on; b22 one of the spicier rye whiskeys you are likely to encounter. Pleasant, but the inert nature of the vanilla and the rapid loss of sugars make this a bit of an also ran in Knob Creek terms. *57.5% (115 proof).*

**Governor's Reserve Taos Lightning Straight Rye Whiskey** (94.5) n24 t24 f23 b23.5 Now this is rye, believe me!!! Those who love the Lawrenceburg, Indiana, type rye (and who doesn't?!?) will adore this... *45% (90 proof). sc. Bottled by KGB Spirits LLC.*

⟐ **Highspire Whiskey 100% Rye Grain Aged 4 Months** oak, finished with oak staves, batch no 3 (73.5) n18.5 t19 f18 b18 Youthful and a rather feinty. Both the rye and tannin are there in spades, but with little integration; some hefty flavours, especially on the oak side which somehow over-dominates the grain. An interesting young whiskey, but the oak seems forced and at no times forms an attractive allegiance with the rye. I think they need to go a little gentler on this one. *40% (80 proof). Distilled by Kindred Distilled Spirits Crestwood, Ky.*

**High West Whiskey Rendezvous Rye Batch 12431** db **(94.5) n23.5 t24 f23 b24** After a few disappointing batches, this one appears to have found that vital spark. It could be a whole new set of whiskeys, a change of one barrel, or even the same whiskey re-stirred before bottling. It doesn't matter: something has clicked. *46%. ncf. WB15/176*

⬥ **James E. Pepper 1776 Straight Rye Whiskey (88.5) n22** good staunch, fruity rye; peppers on some light cabbage; **t22.5** you expect from the nose for the rye grain to go into orbit...it doesn't disappoint. Has to fight through a fair bit of oil; **f21.5** the dull throb of the oily wide cut; **b22.5** not technically quite on the ball, but the intensity of the rye deserves a standing ovation. *50% (100 proof). ncf.*

⬥ **James E. Pepper 1776 Straight Rye Whiskey Barrel Proof (87.5) n22 t22 f21.5 b22** On the nose, delivery and finish there is evidence of a wider than normal cut here, giving the whisky a slightly murky feel. Great rye contribution and spices. But the oils are a bit OTT. *57.8% (115.6 proof). ncf.*

**Jim Beam Pre-Prohibition Style Rye** db **(95) n23 t24.5 f23.5 b24** Very similar to how Jim Bean Yellow Label was over 20 years ago. In other words: simply superb! *45% (90 Proof)*

**John David Albert's Taos Lightning Straight Rye Whiskey** batch no. A1 **(96) n24 t24.5 f23.5 24** Some decent age to this has really ensured enormous complexity. And astonishing beauty. *45% (90 proof). sc. Bottled by KGB Spirits LLC.*

⬥ **Kentucky Owl Aged 10 Years Kentucky Straight Rye Whiskey** bott Nov 18 **(90.5) n22.5** charming crisp grains offer a lovely eucalyptus lilt to the rye itself; on another level, intriguingly green and fresh, also...; **t23.5** heather honey softens the intensity of the salivating rye grain blast, so a two-toned soft and hard mouthfeel perfectly fits the flavour profile. The spices are up early and quartering; with vanilla, light liquorice and ulmo honey; the grain ensures a firm backbone; **f21.5** a tad oily and tangy; the peppers buzz to the very end; **b23** unlike their pretty poor bourbon offering, this rye is more Owl than Ow! *57% (114 proof).*

**Knob Creek Cask Strength** warehouse A, barreled 2009, 2018 release, bott code: L8106CLA **(96.5) n24** anyone who drank Jim Beam Yellow Label Rye two decades ago will immediately recognise the incisor-like sharpness. But there is much more: the deeper resonance within fruitiness of the grain is not entirely dissimilar to the freshly plucked corked of a better Bordeaux; **t24** you could almost punch the air with delight as the highly concentrated rye explodes upon impact, sending shards of oak-toughened grain to every corner of the palate. Yet, simultaneously, the crisper element of rye produced maximum salivation, liquid Demerara sugar and rye swamping the taste buds and thinning out the red liquorice tannin; **f24** so much dark chocolate. And what goes better together than rye mixed into dark chocolate mousse...? **b24.5** Knob Creek rye has always been excellent, but having tasted Jim Beam's rye output for some 40 years I always thought it delivered within itself. Now this one is much closer to what I had been expecting. Brilliant! And the first rye to give the great rye of Buffalo Trace a serious run for their money. Indeed; this is going for a head to head... *59.8% (119.6 proof).*

⬥ **Knob Creek Cask Strength Rye** db **(95) n24 t24 f3.5 b23.5** Another unforgettable rye from Knob Creek, not least for the amount of hairs you'll find on your chest the next day. This is uncompromising in every sense of the word, but scores a little lower than last year's award winner as the tannin just seems a little tighter and less willing to give the grain full scope. The delivery, though...just rye-t on...!!! *63.1% (126.2 proof).*

⬥ **Knob Creek Rye Single Barrel Select** barrel no. 7809 **(95.5) n23.5** graceful yet crisp rye...impeccably polite vanilla...shy molasses...does one need more...? **t24** if the layering on this became any more dynamic, my jaws would drop off. The Demerara sugars arrive clean and crunchy in the truest rye tradition, they salivate, they explode but all is done within context. So, even on delivery we are met by a rare egalitarian feel between huge, sugary rye and no less enormous oak. The result is an understated minor masterpiece of nip and tuck, give and take which, layer upon layer, builds into the mid-ground; and, from the very first moment, so salivating, also...; **f23.5** oh, those trembling, nibbling spices; the toastiness to remind you of decent age...; somehow, though, the finish is soft and silky, nudging towards vanilla; **b24.5** a cleverly selected bottle by Kelly May, who appears to have eschewed the usual pile-driver Knob Creek style for a nuanced and satisfying rye where both the barrel and grain appear to have an equal say. Stunning stuff! Just hope you can get to their bar before this little classic runs out! Certainly one of my favourite ryes for 2019 and unquestionably one of the most enigmatic... *57.5% (115 proof). Selected by Kelly May of Bourbon on Main, Frankfort, Ky. sc.*

**Knob Creek Straight Rye Whiskey (92.5) n23.5 t23.5 f22.5 b23** a slightly more genteel rye than I expected, if you compare standard Knob Creek to their usual bourbon. *50% (100 proof).*

**Knob Creek Straight Rye Whiskey** batch L5349CLA **(92.5) n23.5 t23.5 f22.5 b23** Curious: just checked: I scored a batch from last year at 92.5 also. Can't say this isn't consistent quality...! *50%*

**Michter's 10 Years Old Single Barrel Straight Rye** barrel no. 16A113 **(88) n22.5 t23 f20.5 b22** Michter's and rye go together like all the great names of America and success: like David Beckham and football, Christopher Nolan and Hollywood directing, Hugh Laurie and Hollywood acting, my old Fleet Street colleague Piers Morgan and chat shows, my girlfriend's old chum Simon Cowell and talent shows. This, though, isn't quite in the same league as the bottle I tasted from them last year, which was in a Saville Row suit compared to the dowdy hand-me-down here. Enjoyable, but by Michter's high standards... *46.4% (92.8 proof).*

⟶ **Michter's Barrel Strength Kentucky Straight Rye** barrel no. 19C467, bott code: A19071467 **(94.5) n23.**5 pretty classic stuff; the rye is three dimensional while the toastiness makes a subtle but probably equal impact; **t24** razor-sharp delivery with the rye cutting through the tannins to deal a deliciously precise, salivating account of itself. The spices keep a low profile but carry a vague eucalyptus oakiness which fits in with the grain perfectly; **f23** dry and vanilla rich. But the rye keeps on coming...; **b24** one or two moments here are pure textbook rye. Just savour that amazing sharpness and clarity on delivery! *56% (112 proof). sc.*

**Michter's No. 1 Straight Rye (95.5) n23.5 t24 f24 b24** Truly classic rye whiskey. The stuff which makes one write swoonerisms... *42.4%*

⟶ **Michter's Barrel Strength Kentucky Straight Rye** barrel no. 19C386, bott code: A19066388 **(94) n24** impressed! Presses all the right buttons, especially when it comes to the intense rye and accompanying eucalyptus and spearmint; **t23.5** oddly, the delivery carries a huge wave of caramel from the oak. The grain turns up a flavour wave or two later, Demerara sugars and spices biting in not long after. The complex rumble at the mid-point is great fun; **f23** settles slightly thought the spices still nip and oak takes a tastier tone; **b23.5** a full-bloodied rye that isn't for the squeamish. *55% (110 proof). sc.*

⟶ **Michter's Single Barrel Kentucky Straight Rye** barrel no. L18F881, bott code: 8173881 **(88.5) n22** sweet with muscovado and Demerara sugars mixing in with the rye. Quite an interesting vanilla back note; **t22** wow! That vanilla really is ahead of the game: almost like a rye-flavoured ice cream...; **f22** spices at last...working hard to rouse that docile vanilla. The rye flickers, but half-heartedly; **b22.5** a pretty low voltage rye. *42.4% (84.8 proof). sc.*

⟶ **Old Forester Straight Rye 100** proof bott code A016 191607 **(93) n23** there is a double rye tone drifting across the glass: a defensive, closed shop one and a firmer, juicier, more active style; **t23.5** big delivery, fat, chewy and salivating all in a moment, the lighter sugars up early, juicy and active. Next comes the battle between the dark sugars and tannins, and here the spices intervene; **f23** until now, things had been rocky and mildly aggressive. Now the oak and rye join forces with the softer spices for a simple glide home; **b23.5** beautifully made, beautifully devised...and a beautiful, slightly rugged, experience. *50% (100 proof). 65% rye, 20% malted barley 15% corn*

⟶ **Old Pepper Straight Rye Whiskey Aged Over 2 Years** barrel no. G18Q **(88.5) n21.5** a sharp green tobacco note on the equally sharp rye; **t23.5** a fabulous delivery with an explosion of concentrated rye notes, in all its Demerara sugared finery, brittle and bold, gelling with the spiced maple syrup and green apple. Tannins flood the mid-ground, leading, almost inevitably towards cocoa and hickory; **f21** a long fade on the oils, perhaps with that odd note of tobacco spotted on the nose and a slightly grimy bittering out at the very death; **b22.5** perhaps technically not quite perfect, but the flavour profile on delivery warrants a standing ovation. *55.35% (110.7 proof). sc.*

⟶ **Peerless Straight Rye Aged 3 Years** batch 150812105 **(84.5) n22 t21 f20.5 b21** A new whiskey distilled in Louisville. Peerless might not be quite the way to describe it. A tad feinty, alas, *54.55% (109.1 proof).*

**Pikesville Straight Rye Whiskey Aged at Least 6 Years (97.5) n24.5 t24.5 f24 b24.5** The most stunning of ryes and the best from Heaven Hill for some time. *55% (110 Proof)*

⟶ **Rebel Yell Small Batch Rye Aged 24 Months** bott code: A075181421 **(83.5) n21.5 t21.5 f21.5 b19** Normally ryes coming out of Indiana score highly, as they should because with Buffalo Trace the output from there represents, on their day, the best rye in the world. However, this is a classic example of when a whiskey is undercooked; it is way too young in that the grain and tannin are barely on speaking terms. Negligible balance, though the light liquorice note early on in delivery and late spices do salvage something. *45% (90 proof).*

**Redemption Riverboat Rye (78) n19 t21 f19 b19.** Dry, weirdly off key and oily – and holed below the water line. *40%*

**Redemption Rye (85.5) n22 t22.5 f20 b21.** The tobacco nose is a bit of a poser: how did that get there? Or the spearmint, which helps as you try to chew things over in your mind. The big rye wave on delivery is supported by mixed dark sugars yet something ashy about the finish. *46%*

⟶ **Russell's Reserve Kentucky Straight Rye 6 Years Old** bott code: LL/GD240744 db **(94) n23.5** beautiful, clean diced apples go perfectly with the crisp rye and Demerara sugars;

good toasty tannin to the background; **t23.5** salivating – much lighter than the nose suggests. Sweeter, too, with those Demerara sugars really leading the way. Naturally, the rye makes its own distinguished fruity offering; **f23** just a gentle vanilla fade...with the rye and Demerara, of course. The expected spices fail to materialise; **b24** all incredibly charming and understated – a bit like Jimmy Russell himself... 45% (90 proof).

⫸ **Sagamore Spirit Straight Rye Whiskey** batch no. 7C **(90.5) n23.5** a superb eucalyptus note mingles tantalisingly with the crisper grain; **t23** any softer and you could turn this into a pillow! Unlike most ryes, this has no backbone at all on delivery, the natural caramel and vanillas ensuring the softest rye delivery I have probably ever encountered; the mid-ground perks up with some sharpness to the Demerara sugars; **f21.5** just falls apart a little as a tangy oak residue appears; **b22.5** very attractive rye, but seems underpowered and slightly lacking in the oils required for the expected rich finish. 41.5% (83 proof).

⫸ **Sagamore Spirit Straight Rye Whiskey Cask Strength** batch no. 4A **(95) n24** the clarity of the toastiness is met perfectly by the depth of the honey attached to the rye: the gorgeous blend of heather and Manuka honey underlines some good age here; **t24** taste bud-tingling delivery. The spices fizz along with the initial Demerara sugar brusqueness of the grain; **f23.5** slightly burnt toast lends to a dry finale; the spices and Manuka honey compensate; **b23.5** wow! What a way to start another Whisky Bible tasting day...!!! 56.1% (112.2 proof).

⫸ **Sagamore Spirit Straight Rye Whiskey Double Oak** batch no. 2C **(91) n24** the rye remains ramrod straight, as it should, despite the best efforts of the hickory-led tannins. Profound...; **t23** crisp with lots of treacle to add to the light fruity note; **f21.5** annoyingly bitters slightly as the oak goes just a shade too gung-ho, even testing the patience of the lingering sugar and late spices; **b22.5** beautiful in part but a little too intense with the oak late on. 48.3% (96.6 proof).

**Sazerac Rye** bott code: L172540108: 414 ref 1A 5C VT 15C **(96) n24 t24.5 f23.5 b24** The nose and delivery are just about as good as it gets. Anyone thinking of making a clean and succulent rye whiskey should plant this on a dais and bow to it every morning before heading into the stillroom... 45% (90 proof).

**Sazerac 18 Years Old** bott Spring 2015 db **(97) n25 t24 f24 b24** It is as though all excess oils have been drained from this whiskey in the last year or two and we are seeing something stark, naked and even more desirable than before. Technically sublime. 45% (90 proof).

**Sazerac 18 Years Old** bott Spring 2016 db **(95.5) n24 t24 f23.5 b24** Simply a classic, gilt-edged rye. 45% (90 proof).

**Sazerac 18 Years Old** bott Summer 2017 db **(96) n24 t24.5 f23.5 b24** Brilliant! What else do you expect from a Sazerac 18...? 45% (90 proof).

⫸ **Sazerac 18 Years Old** bott Summer 2018 db **(96) n24.5** diced apple, complete with the vaguest cinnamon, meets orange blossom honey and pink grapefruit. Fruity, but also beautifully firm with the grain adding Demerara sugars into the mix; **t24.5** pretty much the perfect rye delivery: the grains are handsomely crisp and sleek, the sugars ensuring a mouth-watering dimension of distinction. The spices arrive fast to turn up the heat. Just fantastically busy and every new flavour explosion is a delicious one; **f23** tapers down slightly as the complexity just decreases alongside the reduction of oils. Spicy still with a slight bitter edge to the drying oak; **b24** I have chosen this as my 1,250th whisky for the Whisky Bible 2020 (and 20,026th whiskey sample tasted for the book) because, many years ago, I (with my blending hat on) played a part in the development of this whisky – for which I was given the priceless very first bottle off the production line as a token of thanks. Sadly, it was stolen just a few days later in New York at a Whiskey Festival there. But I can still remember vividly as Elmer T Lee and I pieced this whiskey together how it might taste and feel in the mouth. And, you know, some 15 years or so on it really hasn't altered that much, other than in this case the finish perhaps... But someone, somewhere - hopefully with a guilty conscience - might be able to be able to tell me differently... 45% (90 proof).

**Smooth Ambler Old Scout Straight Rye Aged 7 Years** batch 17, bott 9 Nov 13 **(82) n21 t22 f19 b20.** Now this is odd. What do you get when you combine the characteristics of rye and gin? Something, probably, like this. Never been to these guys in West Virginia, though I'll try and make a point of paying a visit when next in that stunning state. No idea if they are involved with gin. But something about the botanical feel to the nose and finish in particular suggests they might be. Perhaps a bottling problem for this single batch? Intrigued. 49.5% WB15/373

**Thomas H. Handy Sazerac** db **(95.5) n23.5 t24.5 f23.5 b24** With each bottling, the style of the Thomas Handy moves away from the Sazerac 18 in style 63.45% (126.9 proof).

**Thomas H. Handy Sazerac Straight Rye Whiskey** **(97.5) n24 t24.5 f24.5 b24.5** This was World Whisky of the Year last year and anyone buying this on the strength of that will not be disappointed. Huge whiskey with not even the glimmer of a hint of an off note. Magnificent: an honour to taste and rye smiles all round... 66.2%. ncf.

**Thomas H. Handy Sazerac Straight Rye** (95.5) n24 t24 f23.5 b24 Perhaps because this has become something of a softie, without all those usual jagged and crisp rye notes, it doesn't quite hit the spot with quite the same delicious drama. Still a beauty, though. *64.6%*

**Thomas H. Handy Sazerac** db (96.5) n24 t25 f23.5 b24 When Thomas Handy hits the very height of its powers, which for a significant period it does here, very few whiskeys can match its gregariousness and sheer force of nature. A whiskey to be as much worshipped as savoured... *63.1% (126.2 proof).*

**Thomas H. Handy Sazerac** db (97) n24 t24.5 f24 b24.5 Just one of those must have whiskeys. Dramatic. And dreamy. All in one. *63.6% (127.2 proof).*

**Thomas H. Handy Sazerac** db (97) n24 a slightly different phraseology to the nose from the normal Handy: here there's more caramel which slightly lessens the trademark ultra-crisp rye aroma and instead bathes it in a much softer light; t24.5 the power conflict between the rye and caramel is less pronounced here: the rye, at least in the opening stages, comes out in full Demerara sugar fragility and grasps the taste buds firmly and shakes them into submission. This is a rye-watering experience - both salivating and bring a tear to the eye - as the grain drives home deep, like a Norman warlord taking the virtue of the village maiden... and only then does the caramels begin to make an entry, a soothing one in full cream toffee mode; f24 still the rye comes, relentless, unquenchable in its thirst dominance. The spices are subordinate but slowly delightful mocha joins forces with the caramels to ensure a complex, yielding finish; b24.5 rye whiskey par excellence. How can one grain do so much to the taste buds? As bewildering as it is beautiful. *64.4% (128.8 proof).*

**Treaty Oak Distilling Red Handed Rye Whiskey Aged 10 Years** db (91) n22 not your normal rye nose: everything is low wattage, from the gentle rye to the banana-tinged vanilla; some docile lime-blossom honey, too; t23 salivating, offering first a non-committal sweetness, then a serious build-up of rye. Some chocolate forms in the midground as the oak at last wakes up; f22.5 some wonderful mocha and hazelnut; b23.5 a very odd rye, where the tannins appear half-hearted and happy to allow the grain a bigger say than normal. Different, but delicious. *50% (100 proof).*

**Turley Mill Straight Rye Western Whiskey** aged 6 years, batch no. 12 (94) n23.5 t24 f23 b23.5 So, with this from KGB Spirits, here's my Cold War: don't add ice to this superb rye under any circumstances...*58% (118 proof). sc. Bottled by KGB Spirits LLC.*

**Van Winkle Family Reserve Rye 13 Years Old** batch Z2221 (90) n22.5 a two-toned nose: the usual crisp fruit edge as expected but also a slightly yeasty softness, also; t23.5 that hard edge on the nose hardens further on delivery: granite like entry with a massive degree of salivation; this is all about the grain with the oak tones there, but side-lined; f22 bitters out slightly both on the tannin side and the chocolate; spices gather slowly then stick around; b22 a hard-as-nails, uncompromising rye with a slightly tangy finale. A whiskey to break your teeth on... *47.8% (95.6 proof)*

**Van Winkle Family Reserve Kentucky Straight Rye Whiskey 13 Years Old No. 99A** bott code: L180400107:23N db (96) n24.5 what a wonderful example of crystal clear, cut-glass rye. The demerara sugars are of BT-style mega-crispness; a touch of the Murray Method and you'll find some spearmint and menthol, too...; t24 just so amazing. Genuine Thomas H Handy feel to this one, with the clarity of the rye beyond measure. Salivating with the rye in super-juicy mode, yet there is a darker feel to this, too as the tannins begin to grow into the picture, while the spices, though there, hang back...; f23.5 soft oils project the distinct rye flavour a very long way; buttery vanillas begin to congregate; b24 quite simply, textbook rye whiskey... *47.8% (95.6 proof).*

**WhistlePig Old World 12 Year Old** European casks (87) n23 t23.5 f20 b20. What a tragedy! The spirit itself is magnificent. The grain positively glistens on both nose and delivery and is on a par with Kentucky's finest. Sadly, a pretty rough finish thanks to the cask...which is always the danger when dealing with European wine barrels. *45% (90 Proof)*

**Wild Turkey Rye** bott code: 194712P22:59 db (91.5) n23 decent tannin and hickory. The rye blends into the mix quietly; t23 again, a busy delivery with lovely oak to the fore. Good, delicate spice and then the rye turns up almost as an afterthought; f22.5 gentle spice and vanilla; b23 a perfectly graceful, well-made rye. But at this strength a bit like Rolls Royce powered by a lawnmower engine. *40.5% (81 proof).*

**Wild Turkey 101 Kentucky Straight Rye** bott code: LL/GH130429 db (95.5) n23.5 full, rich and with the rye shewing sharp enough to cut the glass in two...; t24 stunning delivery. This is a mouth-filler, at first you think lots of natural caramel and vanilla. But as the dust settles you realise the rye is at the very heart of the mêlée, ram-rod hard, mouth-puckeringly sharp and radiating a sumptuous fruitiness. Elsewhere the spices dazzle and the tannins rumble; f23.5 long, thanks to the fabulous oils that keep both the spices and the grain on song; b24.5 simply magnificent. The kind of whiskey, when you spot in the bar, it is almost impossible not to order. *50.5% (101 proof).*

## Straight Wheat Whiskey

**Bernheim Original (91.5) n22 t23 f23 b23.5.** By far the driest of the Bernheims I have encountered showing greater age and perhaps substance. Unique and spellbinding. *45%*

**Parker's Heritage Collection Original Batch Kentucky Straight Wheat Whiskey Aged 13 Years** db **(95.5) n23.5 t24 f23.5 b24.5** Not sure if they get Bassett's Liquorice Allsorts in the US. But, if they did, they would immediately recognise the brown ones in this...though in an insanely beautiful mutated form. So, so delicious....! *63.7%. ncf.*

## American Microdistilleries
### Alabama
### JOHN EMERALD DISTILLING COMPANY Opelika, Alabama.

**John's Alabama Single Malt Whiskey Aged Less Than 4 Years** batch no. 59 db **(87.5) n22 t22 f21.5 b22** Interesting they have a horse on their label as this pleasant offering never quite reaches a trot. The natural caramels offer only an outline of the pecan and peach smoke. Instead it is the mix of barley and toffee which dominate...slowly and drowsily. *43% (86 proof).*

**John's Alabama Single Malt Whiskey Aged Less Than 4 Years** batch no. 63 db **(86) n21 t21 f22.5 b21.5** Far more oil abroad here, unmistakably from the distillation. That pays off on the finish which is longer and more intense than normal, and very comfortable, too. Again, no great complexity to speak of, just an enjoyable degree of malt and toffee at large with the smoke stirring up light spices. *43% (86 proof).*

**John's Alabama Single Malt Whiskey Aged Less Than 4 Years** batch no. 65 db **(89.5) n23 t22 f22 b22.5** The extra surge of smoke has added a degree of dynamism to the charming house simplicity. *43% (86 proof).*

◇ **John's Alabama Single Malt Whiskey Aged Less Than 4 Years** batch no. 102 db **(86) n21.5 t22 f21 b21.5** This distillery has the propensity towards going for a wider cut during distillation, ramping up the oils and spices in the process. Makes for an uneven affair, though very much to type the caramels are lush and chewy. *43% (86 proof).*

◇ **John's Alabama Single Malt Whiskey Aged Less Than 4 Years** batch no. 103 db **(89) n22.5** a gentle breeze of smoke softens the nippy spices and nuttiness; a little orange blossom honey sweetens; **t22.5** soft and succulent on delivery, the house oils cling limpet-like to the roof of the mouth ensuring the dark sugars sticks around; toasty and warming through the middle; **f22** a slight tang from the generous cut, but the smoke returns for a warming finale; **b22** a little extra thrust from the delicate smoke makes a huge difference. *43% (86 proof).*

◇ **John's Alabama Single Malt Whiskey Aged Less Than 4 Years** batch no. 104 db **(88) n22** agreeably toasty: stave-loads of oak in play here softened only by a smoky sub-text; **t23** luxurious both thanks to the big barley kick and the usual house oils . The mid-ground goes into cocoa mode as the chocolate and spices point towards the surging oak; **f21** despite the prominent tannin, undone slightly by a gathering of feints; **b22** presumably the horse on the label of this whisky was presented to Troy... *43% (86 proof).*

### Alaska
### ALASKA DISTILLERY Wasilla, Alaska.

**Alaska Proof Bourbon** db **(86) n22 t22.5 f20 b21.5.** It must be Alaska and the lack of pollution or something. But how do these guys make their whiskey quite so clean....? For a rugged, wild land, it appears to concentrate on producing a bourbon which is borderline ethereal and all about sugary subtlety. The downside is that such lightness allows any weakness in the wood or distillation to be flagged up, though with nobody saluting. *40% (80 proof)*

### Arizona
### ARIZONA DISTILLING Tempe, Arizona.

**Desert Durum Wheat Whiskey Batch no. 2** db **(87.5) n21.5 t23 f21.5 b21.5.** Another hairy-chested gung-ho whiskey which pins you back in your chair. And my notes for the first edition fits this one equally as well. Except here it loses out slightly by having a slightly too wide cut, meaning the feints bite on the nose and finish. But still about as macho as a whiskey gets. And as chocolatey, too. *46%.*

### HAMILTON DISTILLERS Tuscon, Arizona.

**Whiskey Del Bac Classic Unsmoked Single Malt** batch US15-16, bott 19 Aug 15 db **(91) n23 t23 f22 b23** These guys know how to make mighty fine whiskey. Literally, a cut above... *42%*

**Whiskey Del Bac Clear Mesquite Smoked Single Malt** batch MC15-4, bott 2 Dec 15 db **(91) n21.5 t23 f23.5 b23.** I was in Arizona recently, but sadly didn't make it to this distillery. Shame: I would have loved to have seen how the smoking is carried out for one of the sweetest and most surprisingly soft, idiosyncratic and attractive white dogs currently barking. *45% (90 proof)*

**Whiskey Del Bac Dorado Mesquite Smoked Single Malt** batch MC16-1, bott 29 Feb 16 db **(94)** n23 t23.5 f24b23.5 Dang! I'd sure like to see a bottle of this come sliding up to me next time I'm-a-drinkin' in the Crystal Palace Saloon Bar in Tombstone, yesiree! And I'd take my own dirty glass – one smoked with mesquite!! *45% (90 proof). ncf.*

# Arkansas
## ROCK TOWN DISTILLERY Little Rock, Arkansas.

⟐ **Rock Town 8th Anniversary Arkansas Rye Whiskey 4 Years Old Bottled in Bond** db **(92)** n23.5 such intense grain at work here: crisp Demerara but jutting through a cloud of liquorice and caramel; t23 a thick layer of rye crashes head-first into the taste buds; the oils are cool and soothing, slightly minty even; f22.5 a long rye sigh amid the light spices; b23 a very pure rye for the rye purists... *50%. ncf. 475 bottles.*

**Rock Town Arkansas Straight Bourbon Whiskey Aged 3 Years** db **(85)** n21.5 t22 f21 b21 Has its butterscotch and molasses moments, but too much mysterious bitterness intervenes here. *46%.*

**Rock Town Arkansas Four Grain Sour Mash Bourbon Whiskey Aged 20 Months** batch no. 5 db **(91.5)** n23 t23 f22.5 b23 A satisfyingly intricate and impressively complex whiskey. *46%.*

**Rock Town Arkansas Bourbon Whiskey Aged 19 Months** batch no. 49 db **(94)** n22.5 t24 f23.5 b23 I really do love this distillery... *46%.*

⟐ **Rock Town Arkansas Bourbon Whiskey Aged 19 Months** batch no. 62 db **(91.5)** n23 some classical bourbon vibes, especially the polished leather and honey mix; t23 a lovely corn spread to this, and the molasses aren't too bad, either; f22.5 impressive spice and liquorice fade; b23 an undemonstrative exhibition of quality. *46%.*

**Rock Town Arkansas Bourbon Whiskey Flavour Grain Series Golden Promise Aged 12 Months** db **(88.5)** n22 t22 f22 b22.5 An intense feller, and certainly golden. *46%.*

**Rock Town Arkansas Bourbon Whiskey Flavour Grain Series Peated Malt Aged 12 Months** db **(92)** n22.5 t23 f22.5 b23 A complex, almost disorganised bourbon, which tries to send you on several different routes simultaneously. Fully worth the effort of getting to understand. *46%.*

**Rock Town Arkansas Rye Whiskey Aged 18 Months** batch no. 19 db **(94)** n23.5 t23.5 f23 b24 Arkansas is slowly becoming a major rye destination: this is excellent! Better, in fact, than some ryes made by the established distilleries of Kentucky. *46%.*

⟐ **Rock Town Arkansas Rye Whiskey Aged 23 Months** batch no. 23 db **(94.5)** n24 the grains sing so crisply...! Of choral quality; t23.5 Rock by name, rock by nature: supremely salivating with the grain calling the shots from the first moment with a breath-taking firmness: not sure rye gets any cleaner or more brittle than this; f23 returns to a more mocha friendly mode; b24 sharper than a Harvard graduate. And worth a whole lot more... *46%.*

⟐ **Rock Town Arkansas Single Malt Aged 3 Years** finished in Cognac casks db **(90)** n22.5 malty with a lime and greengage twist; t23 typically of a Cognac cask, the delivery is a little warm, but the malts still dazzle; lots of juicy freshness; f22 a little untidy as the drying process is accelerated a shade too fast; a touch too tangy though the sugars are impressive; b22.5 a pathetic 90 for their Single malt. What are you thinking of? I thought you had turned your back on excellent and gone for a grade or two higher. *46%.*

⟐ **Rock Town Four Grain Sour Mash Bourbon Whiskey Aged 20 Months** batch no. 7 db **(86.5)** n22 t22 f21 b21.5 A much drier, slightly bitter version with as much oil from the distillation as the corn. *46%.*

⟐ **Rock Town Single Barrel Barley Bourbon Whiskey Aged 26 Months** cask no. 7 db **(95.5)** n23.5 Liquorice Allsorts, especially the chocolate one...; t24.5 just magnificent: had this been a Kentucky bourbon I would not have told the difference. So many strains of cocoa it is hard to keep track; between them sits Manuka and Bruyerre honey, as a well as maple syrup and red liquorice; the vaguest hint of hickory fills the mid-ground; f23.5 much drier now and some Jamaican Blue Mountain coffee mingles with the vanilla; b24 they should call themselves Choc Town after this stunner...One of the non-Kentucky bourbons of the year. And the best thing I have yet encountered from this outstanding distillery...*56%. sc.*

**Rock Town Single Barrel Bourbon Whiskey Aged 18 Months** cask no. 422 db **(94)** n23.5 t23.5 f23 b24 This bourbon Rocks...! *57.9%. sc.*

**Rock Town Single Barrel Bourbon Whiskey Aged 18 Months** cask no. 430 db **(87)** n22 t22 f21.5 b21.5 Plenty happening: sugars crashing like dodgems around the palate, tannins blindly bumping around the place not sure where they are going, spices with no rhythm or consistent intensity or a game plan. Enjoyable whiskey in so many ways. But confusing and frustrating, too. *55.3%. sc.*

⟐ **Rock Town Single Barrel Bourbon Whiskey Aged 20 Months** cask no. 661 db **(95.5)** n24 bloody hell, guys. Give me a break...not just any old 'old', but one bursting at the seams with a small grain intensity matched only by the old leather oakiness embraced by the corn oil. A ten-minute nosing, and not a moment less...; **t23.5** big corn oils again, plus a sublime mix of Manuka and heather honey; **f24** long, impossibly long...and still so salivating and fresh; **b24** Rock Town have upped their game a few notches, and in so doing have taken the micros into a whole new ball park... *59.39%. sc.*

**Rock Town Single Barrel Bourbon Whiskey Aged 22 Months** cask no. 494 db **(90) n22.5** **t23 f22 b22.5** An oily but entirely delicious bourbon. *57.8%. sc.*

◈ **Rock Town Single Barrel Bourbon Whiskey Aged 24 Months** cask no. 614 db **(91.5)** **n23** superb corn and molasses; **t23.5** the corn oils have amassed a huge amount of molasses in the bank, and here some maple syrup is added also; **f22** vanilla with a red liquorice edge; **b23** thank God! Just an ordinary excellent whiskey from Rock Town instead of outrageously brilliant! I was getting worn out... *56.83%. sc.*

◈ **Rock Town Single Barrel Four Grain Sour Mash Bourbon Whiskey Aged 26 Months** cask no. 41 db **(95.5) n24** such busy small grains at work here: the nose is positively twitching as it tries to keep track. The corn oils appear to add only sweetness while the tannins and grains work an improbably complex magic; **t24** you know what I said about the nose: well, apply exactly the same here. None of the heftiness or intensity of their cask 7. Just dashing grains enchanting you with their every move; **f23.5** soft mocha and custard; **b24** a few months ago I was in Little Rock, but my insane schedule – plus some ill luck with the car I had hired – meant I had no time to visit the distillery. Next time I shall somehow engineer a day or two. Because what they are achieving at this distillery deserves all the publicity it can get. This is another classic and actually eclipses the brilliant Cask No 7... *58.8%. sc.*

◈ **Rock Town Single Barrel Peach Wood Smoked Bourbon Whiskey Aged 23 Months** cask no. 2 db **(88) n22.5** a pleasing extra, softening depth to the oak; **t22.5** explosive corn and oaky spice deliver followed by maple syrup; the tannins and sugars seems to take turns in elevating their status; **f21** bitters out somewhat; **b22** anyone who has driven the back roads from Rock Town to the Ozark mountains will have experienced the extraordinary undulating character of the highway, with one blind peak following another. Up, down, up, down...for miles. And so it is with this bourbon, the smokiness playing hide and seek with the sweeter elements. *56%. sc.*

**Rock Town Single Barrel Rye Whiskey Aged 23 Months** cask no. 90 db **(91) n23.5 t23.5** **f21.5 b22.5** Probably one of the truest and most impressive ryes made outside Kentucky and Indiana. The high spots are very high, indeed. *59.01%. sc.*

◈ **Rock Town Single Barrel Rye Whiskey Aged 32 Months** cask no. 109 db **(96) n23.5** the big grains are off from the start, though a little caramel from the oak blunts a little of the usual sharpness; **t24** mouth-hugging, the rye, infused with a little spice, follows every contour on the palate, bombing the taste buds with the most salivating and precise grain intensity imaginable. It's just...wow!!! **f24.5** no whiskey has a right to have a finish of this length. Wave after wave after wave of fruity rye, always slightly different in its intensity of sweetness or fruitiness; **b24** I'm not sure any micro distillery makes their cuts any cleaner than these guys. Just put them into the Premier class... *59.88%. sc.*

**Rock Town Whiskey from Wheat Mash** sherry cask finish db **(94) n22 t24.5 f23.5 b24** Yay...!!! No sulphur!! This mention of sherry cask gets me worried, but without cause here.... and, beyond the nose, it plays only a bit part anyway. A strange fish, this, but one which grows on you until you are fatally in its thrall. *50%.*

## California
### ALCHEMY DISTILLERY Arcata, California.

**Boldt Blue Corn Whiskey** batch no. 27 db **(89.5) n23 t23.5 f21 b22** Cleanly made, mega intense, sweet as a nut white dog corn whiskey which hits you like a Boldt from the Blue... Shade more copper on the finish will enrich it even further. *62.5% (125 proof).*

◈ **Boldt Cereal Killer Straight Rye Whiskey Aged 2 Years** batch no. 8 **(94.5) n23.5** the grain comes at you three dimensionally and from all directions: as crisp and sharp as you can reasonably expect it to be, despite the oils; **t24** OK, if I'm going to be a technical Detective Inspector, there are some incriminating traces of feints apparent. But so gloriously sharp and entertaining is the concentrated rye, frankly, I couldn't give a damn! **f23** some lovely chocolate raisin notes to accompany the granite-like and increasingly spicy grain; **b24** don't know about cereal killer: more the Rye Ripper! *62% (124 proof). nc nc.*

◈ **Boldt Cereal Killer Straight Triticale Whiskey Aged 2 Years** batch no. 10 **(94) n23.5** now that is one very different nose. It is similar to others...but not. Although the tannins are poking through enthusiastically, they are being beaten back by an exceptionally sharp grain note, that reaches towards sweetness but never quite makes it. Big spices – as is the house style – but as intriguing as it is attractive; **t24** one of the best deliveries of the year so far, The mouthfeel is almost perfect: rounded, weighty, slightly oily but not even remotely overpowering. The house feints style is also in operation, but it soon vanishes under the onslaught of salivating grassy notes, as well as a non-specific sultana note; **f23** spice, tannin and a vague feinty oiliness; **b23.5** in the 20,000 whiskies I have tasted for the Whisky Bible since 2003 this may be the first time I have tasted mash made from Triticale. This is one big-arsed killer and I can see this being a massive whiskey favourite among Star Trek fans... and Tribbles. *62.5% (125 proof). nc sc.*

◈ **Boldt Cereal Killer Straight Wheat Whiskey Aged 2 Years** batch no. 4 **(92) n22.5** moist, freshly baked brown bread –but with a spice and molasses kick; the oak makes no effort to hold back; **t23.5** a few imperfections apparent, but no doubting the depth to the grain or tannins. Rich, toasty and bathed in molasses; **f23** dries as those tannins really take hold. But those spices....wow! **b23** sticking very much to the wheat whiskey style, this is some spicy cuss.. *61.5% (123 proof). nc sc.*

## CHARBAY DISTILLERY Napa Valley, California.

**Charbay Hop Flavoured Whiskey** release II, barrels 3-7 **(91) n22 t22 f23 b24.** Being distilled from beer which includes hops, it can – and will - be argued that this is not beer at all. However, what cannot be disputed is that this is a rich, full-on spirit that has set out to make a statement and has delivered it. Loudspeaker and all. *55%*

**Charbay 1999 Pilsner Whiskey Release III Double Alambic Charentais Pot Distilled Whiskey** aged 6 years in new American white oak barrels and 8 additional years in stainless steel tanks db **(84.5) n21 t22 f21.5 b20** Just a point: you can't age for 8 years in stainless steel tanks. The moment it leaves the barrel the aging process stops: the term makes no sense. Lots of sugars at play and a distinctive fruity and spicy edge, though harmonisation is at a premium. *66.2%.*

**Charbay Lot S 211A Hop Flavored Whiskey Aged 29 Months** French oak barrels, distilled from Bear Republic Black Bear Stout db **(74) n18 t20 f18 b18** Hop, but no glory. *49.5% (99 proof).*

**Charbay R5 Lot No. 4 Hop Flavored Aged 28 Months** French oak barrels, distilled from Bear Republic Racer 5 IPA db **(72) n17 t19 f18 b18** I'm sure Charbay once did a distillation from a hopped beer which worked agreeably well: I remember it, as it is an unusual occurrence. Most hopped whiskeys (if, indeed they are whiskeys, which I dispute) really don't work. This is one such failure, though there is a pleasant round of chocolate on the delivery. *49.5% (99 proof).*

## GRIFFO DISTILLERY Petaluma, California.

◈ **Belgian Hen Single Malt Whiskey** db **(83.5) n21 t21.5 f20 b21** Well, that was different. Less single malt. More lightly spiced soft centred orange liqueur chocolate. *46% (92 proof).*

◈ **Stony Point Whiskey** db **(85) n20 t22 f21.5 b21.5** Makes up for the tobacco feinty tones with a rush of muscovado sugars. Good texture and chewability and spice. *47% (94 proof).*

◈ **Stout Barreled Whiskey** db **(84.5) n21 t22 f20 b21.5** Robust, sweet and full bodied. But I must say I have a problem with hops in whisky. Sorry. *45% (90 proof).*

## LOST SPIRITS DISTILLERY Monterey County, California.

**Abomination The Crying of the Puma Heavily Peated Malt (93) n23.5 t24 f22.5 b23** An utterly battling experience. This is, for all intents and purposes a Scotch whisky: at least in personality. If this was distilled in the US, then they have cracked it. The thing I particularly couldn't work out was an unrecognisable fruit edge. And after tasting I dug out the bottle and read the small print (so small, the detail was left off the heading by my researchers) that Riesling seasoned oak staves had been used. From the bizarre label and even brand name to the battle on your palate this is a bewildering and nonsensical whisky – if it is whisky at all, as the term is never used. But wholly delicious if raw...and boasting an impact that blows the taste buds' doors down... *54%. nc ncf.*

**Abomination The Sayers of the Law Heavily Peated Malt (94) n23 t23.5 f24 b23.5** More of the same as The Crying of the Puma. Except, despite the identical strength, this has a softer all-round feel and a much more Caol Ila-style oiliness to sooth and maximise the length of the sugars and lighten the smoky load. The fruit here is negligible other than muscovado sugar mixing in with the liquorice and ulmo honey. Feels older than the Puma and the spices are far more accentuated yet controlled, especially towards the complex coffee-stained finale. *54%. nc ncf.*

## MOYLAN'S DISTILLING COMPANY Petaluma, California.

**Moylan's American Cask Strength Single Malt Whisky Aged 4 Years** finished in orange brandy, stout & French oak chardonnay barrels db **(80) n19 t23 f19 b19.** Ladies and Gentlemen of Moylan. I cannot fault you for your kaleidoscopic delivery which enthrals and entertains with a wild and delicious a cross section of fruity riches as you are likely to find. But remember: it is about balance. So don't lose sight of what a wide cut and hops from the stout can do... *58.7% (1174 proof)*

## SONOMA DISTILLING COMPANY Rohnert Park, California.

◈ **Sonoma Bourbon Whiskey** nbc, db **(87.5) n21.5 t23 f21 b22** Big and flavoursome, they just need to get that cut reduced slightly so all the oils belong to the corn and are not from elsewhere. The small grains pile out a lot of coffee-rich vitality and there are fabulous molasses in midstream. But the finish is slightly undone by the feints. *46% (92 proof). 70% corn (CA & Midwest), 25% wheat (CA & Canada) & 5% Malted Barley (Wyoming).*

◈ **Sonoma Cherrywood Rye Whiskey** lot: CRO1AC db **(91) n22.5** ultra-crunchy grain with a Demerara bit;...; **t23.5** the mouth-watering grain busts through the oaky caramels and sugars like Superman ripping off his clothes to reveal his identity; **f22** just a little oily and flat; **b23** when the rye pops through, it rips... *478% (95.6 proof). 80% rye (California & Canada), 10% wheat (California) & 10% cherrywood smoked malted barley.*

◈ **Sonoma Rye Whiskey** nbc, db **(89.5) n22.5** delightful two-toned rye pierce the restricting oils; **t23** mouth-filling grain becomes increasingly more lurid in its sharpness by the second. If the nose left you wondering if this was a rye, there are no doubts now! Fabulous...; **f21.5** chocolate and nagging oils; **b22.5** a rye that could do with a polish when distilling, but the sheer enormity of the rye wins through in the glass...and your heart. *46.5% (93 proof). 80% rye (California & Canada) & 20% malted rye (United Kingdom).*

## ST GEORGE SPIRITS Alameda, California.

◈ **Baller Single Malt Whiskey Aged 3 Years** batch no. BW-5 db **(87) n22.5 t22 f21 b21.5** The nose made me laugh out loud: only one distillery on the planet could produce something that outrageously apple strewn...Elsewhere, though, I'm not so sure. After the initial big malt delivery, it then zips of into European style malt, the type where hops are at play. Certainly there is an imbalance to the marauding light bitterness which undermines what should be, one feels, a fragile and juicy malt. *47% (94 proof).*

◈ **Breaking & Entering American Whiskey Aged no less than 2.5 Years** batch no. 06302018 **(92) n23** freshly bitten into apple – only two distilleries in the world offer such a nose, and only one in the USA....; a slightly wide-ish cut by St George's standards, but the grainy spice bites playfully; **t24** not sure any whisky can come more mouth-watering than this: there is a sherbet fizz to the crisp rye, which crackles over the palate with sugary crunchiness. For a good 15 seconds we are in supernova whiskey land...; **f22** mostly dry vanilla and cocoa; a few feints turn up very late on; **b23** the crisp apple aroma wafted through long before I realised this was from St George. Not only breaking and entering, but St George has left his fingerprints everywhere... *47% (94 proof).*

◈ **St. George Single Malt Whiskey** batch no. SM018 db **(88) n22.5** an unusual hint of moist ginger cake adds a fresh spiciness to the nutty barley background; **t22** that ginger, it seems, comes from a light feintiness which in turn gives way to a chewy pudding middle; lashings of vanilla at the midpoint; **f21.5** eye-wateringly dry; **b22** definitely shewing signs of a wider cut these days. Gets away with it, but a return to a cleaner style might be the way forward. Characterful, nonetheless. *43% (86 proof).*

## Colorado
## 10TH MOUNTAIN WHISKEY & SPIRIT COMPANY Vail, Colorado.

**10th Mountain Rocky Mountain Bourbon Whiskey Aged 6 Months** db **(92) n22 t23 f23.5 b23.5** The youth of the spirit is apparent on the nose where slightly more hostile tannins have not yet had a chance to say howdy to the corn. But once on the palate the entire story changes as the maple syrup and molasses – and, amazingly, even liquorice already – makes a far better attempt to find a happy medium with the grain. Beautifully made and a really sumptuous and spice-ridden offering. *46% (92 proof).*

**10th Mountain Rye Whiskey Aged 6 Months** batch 10, bott 11.28.16 db **(94.5) n23.5 t24 f23.5 b23.5** The grain is crisp, allowing its friable, fruity personality to star from nose to finish. It also infiltrates the sexy and sultry oily sub-plot in which most of the ulmo honey stars. But what makes this a star turn is the roasty, cocoa aspect to this which works so well with the rye-laden crispness. What a treat this is... Now, good people of 10th Mountain, you are holding out on us: the barrel strength version, if you please... *43% (86 proof).*

**Colorado Clear Mountain Moonshine 100% Corn Whiskey** db **(92.5) n23 t23.5 f23 b23** Whenever I pick up a pickle jar full of clear corn moonshine, it is near impossible to wipe the smile off my face...yesiree! So many happy moments over the last 30 years in some wilderness spots of the US where the local hooch has been handed to me in near identical receptacles...and by so many wonderful people. At a mere 80 proof, this weighs in at about the friendliest of them all – and possible the cleanest and sweetest. But the corn comes through as it should and it is hard not to pour yourself a refill...even in a tasting lab 3,500 miles from where I should be. *40% (80 proof).*

## AXE AND THE OAK Colorado Springs, Colorado.

**Axe and the Oak Bourbon Whiskey** batch no. 20 db **(86.5) n20.5 t22.5 f21.5 b22** Although this is batch number 20, you still get the feeling this is a work in progress. The nose at times displays some most unbourbon-like traits with far more of the still and/or fermentation room than opened cask. But the whiskey recovers with admirable calm: on the palate the corn oils establish themselves and the rye present kicks in with a firm sweetness while the tannins crank up the light liquorice and spice. The soft chocolate mousse on the finish works well with the molasses. Promising. 46% (92 proof).

**Axe and the Oak Cask Strength Bourbon Whiskey** batch no. 1 db **(87.5) n21 t23 f21.5 b22** Big, bustling, no-prisoners whiskey which reveals quite a wide cut. That adds extra weight for sure, but a tanginess interrupts the flow of the excellent liquorice and molasses tones which had made the delivery and immediate aftermath something genuinely to savour. Get the cut right on the run and this will be one hell of a bourbon. 64.4% (128.8 proof).

## BRECKENRIDGE DISTILLERY Breckenridge, Colorado.

⬧ **Breckenridge Bourbon Whiskey** db **(84.5) n21 t21.5 f21 b21** Definitely on the flat side, with a dusty, dry character. 43% (86 proof).

⬧ **Breckenridge Colorado Bourbon Whiskey Single Barrel** barrel no. 12H 31-1db **(88.5) n22** the blood orange house style remains, though the sweetness is suppressed by the chalky vanilla; **t22.5** at last the shackles are off and we enter honey mode, the distinct corn oils helping to propagate a delicate sweetness in corners of the palate where the drier vanillas have already landed; slightly juicy with a red liquorice thread that leads to light spice; **f22** thin Manuka honey, a spicy beat and milky vanilla; **b22** this distillery has certainly created a style all its own. 46% (92 proof). sc.

⬧ **Breckenridge Colorado Whiskey Powder Hound** batch no. 1 db **(91) n22** a bitter-sweet aroma veering between lime peel and drier butterscotch and vanilla: intriguingly different...; **t23.5** the usual sumptuous house style on delivery. But, unusually it is neither flat out sweet and unashamedly dry for this distillery: hits a delightful mid-ground with demerara sugars melting into a corn oil, the layering supplied by both vanilla and cocoa in just about equal measures; **f22** long, gently spiced with a gorgeous praline and citrus fade; a tad furry towards the finish; **b23.5** despite a slight blemish at the death, this is probably the most complex and well balanced whiskey I have yet seen from this distillery. 45% (90 proof).

⬧ **Breckenridge Colorado Whiskey PX Cask Finish Aged a Minimum of at least Three Years** batch no. 2 db **(84.5) n22 t22 f20.5 b20** Some enjoyable early spice amid the fruity, prune-rich soup. But, ultimately, flat as a witch's tit. 45% (90 proof).

⬧ **Breckenridge Colorado Whiskey Sauternes Finish Aged a Minimum of at least Three Years** batch no.1 db **(82.5) n22 t21.5 f20 b19** Very clean grape with no shortage of over-ripe greengages on display. But it is hard to follow the narrative, as the grape and grain appear to largely cancel the other out. A little furriness at the death? 45% (90 proof).

⬧ **Breckenridge Dark Arts** batch no. 5 db **(87.5) n20 t24 f21 b22.5** I appear to have missed out on batch 4 (apologies) but this appears to have started when batch 3 ended. Some of the sensations on delivery are borderline orgasmic, the golden syrup, praline and barley melding together with the spices with uncanny intuition and balance. But, once more, the very wide cut has a negative effect on both nose and finish. As for the delivery and aftershocks, though: world class! 46% (92 proof). Whiskey distilled from malt mash.

⬧ **Breckenridge High Proof Blend Aged a Minimum of at least Two Years** db **(90) n22.5** oily and happy to take the liquorice route; **t23.5** powering flavours for the first moment. The explosion of heather honey and molasses on delivery is exceptionally beautiful. Goes through the hickory, spice and caramel gears with ease; **f21.5** just a little on the bitter and oily side; **b22.5** maybe not technically perfect, but some of those honey tones are pure 24 carat... 52.5% (105 proof). A blend of straight bourbon whiskeys.

## COLORADO GOLD DISTILLERY Cedaredge, Colorado.

**Colorado Gold Rye** charred oak barrel no. 23, bott 31 Oct 15 db **(80) n20 t21 f19.5 b19.5.** Insane sugars – Manuka honey concentrate – still can't fully overcome the tobacco bitterness. A certain dirtiness when a rye should sparkle. 45% (90 proof). sc.

**Colorado Gold Straight Bourbon** aged 3 years, new oak barrel no. 43, bott 1 Dec 15 db **(91) n22.5 t23 f23 b22.5** If you have a sweet tooth, buy a case...!! 45% (90 proof). sc.

## DEERHAMMER DISTILLING COMPANY Buena Vista, Colorado.

**Deerhammer American Single Malt Whiskey** virgin oak barrel #2 char, batch no. 32 db **(87.5) n21.5 t23.5 f20.5 b22** This, like most Colorado whiskeys, is huge. Had the cut been a little less generous, the oils a little less gripping and tangy, this would have scored exceptionally highly. For there is no doubting the deliciousness of the big toasted malt, the kumquat citrus element, the moreishness of the heavyweight dark fudge and the magnificent Java coffee. All these make a delivery and follow through to remember. I look forward to the next bottling where hopefully the cut is a little more careful: a very significant score awaits as this is borderline brilliant... 46% (92 proof). 870 bottles.

## DISTILLERY 291 Colorado Springs, Colorado.

**291 Bad Guy Colorado Bourbon Whiskey Aged 311 Days** distilled from a bourbon mash, American oak barrel, aspen stave finished, batch no. 3 db **(92) n23.5 t23.5 f22 b23.5** Gorgeous, as usual! 60.4% (120.7 proof). 785 bottles.

 **291 Bad Guy Colorado Bourbon Whiskey Aged 291 Days** distilled from a bourbon mash, American oak barrel, aspen stave finished, batch no. 4 db **(95) n24.5** one of the most complex noses from any Micro this year, the corn oils complementing the maple syrup and treacle. The subtlest kumquat imaginable with even more delicate Chinese gooseberry and even kiwifruit. All from oak and small grains...remarkable! **t24** super-salivation levels are reached quicker than a F-type Jag can get from 0-60. Crisp, seemingly rye-shaped sugars go into overdrive; **f23** slows and settles as the caramels come out to play, **b23.5** this distillery was always very good. Now it is hitting genius status on a regular basis. 60.6% (121.1 proof). 598 bottles.

**291 Barrel Proof Colorado Whiskey Aged Less Than 2 Years** distilled from a rye malt mash, American oak barrel, aspen stave finished, barrel no. 255 db **(92.5) n23 t23.5 f22.5 b23.5** Their rye mash is getting noticeably better. This bristles with the grain. 63% (126 proof). sc. 49 bottles.

**291 Barrel Proof Colorado Whiskey Aged Less Than 2 Years** distilled from a rye malt mash, American oak barrel, aspen stave finished, barrel no. 195 db **(95) n24 t24 f23.5 b24** You know these boys will come up with a blockbuster among their latest releases...this is it! 63.1% (126.1 proof). sc. 45 bottles.

 **291 Barrel Proof Colorado Whiskey Aged Less Than 2 Years** distilled from a rye malt mash, American oak barrel, aspen stave finished, barrel no. 378 db **(87.5) n21.5 t23.5 f21 b21.5** Never quite the star turn of the Distillery 291 range, though I feel it should be. Always big on the rye but intensity is never matched by clarity with the finish offering touch a bit too much oil. But that delivery...? Wow! 64.6% (129.3 proof). sc. 47 bottles.

 **291 Barrel Proof Colorado Whiskey Aged 2 Years** distilled from a bourbon mash, American oak barrel, aspen stave finished, barrel no. 398 db **(96) n24** possibly the ultimate hickory and liquorice mix for 2020...! Incredible...; **t24.5** although 65%abv, there is (when using the Murray Method) no burn whatsoever. Instead we are treated to Camp Coffee with chicory and red liquorice merging into the high propane Manuka honey and crisper Demerara sugars; **f23.5** an oily fade with tannins now working towards a drier, vanilla rich fade. But still enough sugars about to balance things; **b24** I have just had to abandon tasting a batch of Scotch single malts for the Bible as 40% of them had been sulphur tarnished and my tortured taste buds were on the point of catastrophic failure. So I found this cask specially to bring back some life into my palate - as well as a will to live - where before there had been nearly none. And if you want to add restorative to the adjectives for this whiskey, go right ahead. You wouldn't be wrong! 65.3% (130.6 proof). sc. 57 bottles.

 **291 Barrel Proof Colorado Whiskey Aged 2 Years** distilled from a bourbon mash, American oak barrel, aspen stave finished, barrel no. 383 db **(93.5) n23** big small grain presence here, and that magnificent brittleness to the Demerara sugars leaves you in no doubt which grain is leading the pack; **t23.5** mouth-puckering and eye-watering. Any sharper and this bourbon will cut the glass in half when being poured into it. So much flavour, they probably need a license...; **f23.5** enough corn oil to stretch the toasty cocoa, liquorice and hickory to seemingly impossible lengths. Taste this when you have time on your hands – it just refuses to finish...; **b23.5** no doubt in my mind that Distillery 291 are getting their bourbons pretty much on the money and they are consistently better than both their malt and rye. Surely this will be their main thrust forward... 64.8% (1296 proof). sc. 42 bottles.

**291 Single Barrel Colorado Bourbon Whiskey Aged Less Than 2 Years** distilled from a bourbon mash, American oak barrel, aspen stave finished, barrel no. 196 db **(88) n22.5 t22 f21.5 b22** Perhaps a little too much oil from the still for greatness, but not too much to spoil it. 50% (100 proof). sc. 53 bottles.

**291 Single Barrel Colorado Rye Whiskey Aged Less Than 2 Years** distilled from a bourbon mash, American oak barrel, aspen stave finished, barrel no. 231 db **(92) n22 t23.5 f23 b23.5** Would gladly down one of these after a T Bone steak...or if I fancied a decent rum and there wasn't one around. 50.8% (101.7 proof). sc. 60 bottles.

**291 Single Barrel Colorado Rye Whiskey Aged Less Than 2 Years** distilled from a bourbon mash, American oak barrel, aspen stave finished, barrel no. 261 db **(77) n18 t22 f18 b19** Well, didn't expect that! On the palate the rye is profound: crisp, sweet and as juicy as it comes. But the nose displays a degree of a butyric-style aroma – exceptionally unusual for this on the money distillery. The finish is, as expected, less than up to scratch, either. *50.8% (101.7 proof). sc. 55 bottles.*

**291 E Colorado Whiskey Single Malt Whiskey Aged 479 Days** American oak barrel, aspen stave finished, batch no. 4 db **(88.5) n22** profound grape must, the skins in particular; **t23** silky and enveloping, again a big fruit note dominates, giving this distillery bottling an unusual thinness of texture. Waves of spice hit, while heather honey arrives late to add some sweeter depth; **f21.5** dry and a little out of tune; **b22** well, it may have been matured in an American oak barrel but this is dripping with fruit... *61.1% (122.2 proof). 281 bottles.*

**291 E Colorado Whiskey Single Malt Whiskey Aged 479 Days** American oak barrel, aspen stave finished, batch no. 5 db **(92) n23** salty as well as malty. A light scrape of bruyerre honey sweetens; **t23.5** mouth-tingling and malty. Love the praline middle, though that saltiness on the nose really kicks of some serious salivation on the palate; **f22.5** toasty, mildly oily and deep. The spices up a gear; **b23** how it all began, with their single malt. This is much cleaner distilled than in those early day and less oak in play. What a beauty! *62% (124.1 proof). 362 bottles.*

## DOWNSLOPE DISTILLING Centennial, Colorado.

**Double Diamond Whiskey** cask no. WR-283 db **(86) n21 t22 f21.5 b21.5** The aroma of new-baled hay suggests a whiskey a long way from stating its original intentions. Some lovely light and citrusy sugars at play, nonetheless. *40% (80 proof). sc.*

**Double Diamond Whiskey Aged 4 Years Cognac Finish** cask no. WR-290 db **(93) n23 t23 f23.5 b23.** An old British advert from the 1960s for a beer warbled: "A Double Diamond Works Wonders, Works Wonders. A Double Diamond Works Wonders. So drink some today..." It could equally apply to this hugely different whiskey! *41% (82 proof). sc.*

**Downslope Malt Whiskey Aged 3 Years Sherry Finish** cask no. WR-184 db **(87) n20 t21 f24 b22** Doesn't really gel until towards the finish when the most brilliant chocolate mousse kicks in. Then, out of nowhere, it suddenly becomes something rather special... *50% (100 proof). sc.*

**Downslope Rye Whiskey** cask no. WR-235 db **(90.5) n23.5 t22 f22.5 b22.5** OK, not quite technically on the money but the flavour profile is a delight. *46% (92 proof). sc.*

## LAWS WHISKEY HOUSE Denver, Colorado.

**A.D. Law Four Grain Straight Bourbon Whiskey Aged 5.2 Years** batch no. 174, 53 gallon white American oak char 3 barrels db **(90) n23 t23 f21.5 b22.5** Very good aged oakiness to the big bourbon. *59.3% (118.6 proof).*

**A.D. Law Four Grain Straight Bourbon Whiskey Aged 6 Years Bottled in Bond** batch no. A-19 db **(93.5) n23.5** liquorice and black cherry; polished leather. Very attractive; **t23.5** excellent integrity on the delivery: a firmness to the corn oils while the toasty oak and small grains work busily in tandem; **f23** dry, with a little late chocolate caramel; **b23.5** high class bourbon. Love it! *50% (100 proof).*

**A.D. Law Four Grain Straight Bourbon Whiskey Aged Over 3 Years** batch no. 18 db **(82) n21 t21 f20 b20** The cuts are all wrong here leaving the feints far too much say. *47.5% (90 proof).*

**A.D. Law Four Grain Straight Bourbon Whiskey Bottled in Bond Aged Over 4 Years** batch no. B-17-S, 53 gallon white American oak char 3 barrels db **(94) n22.5 t24 f23.5 b24** Really impressive and complex whiskey. *50% (100 proof). Summer Season.*

**A.D. Law Four Grain Straight Bourbon Whiskey Aged 6 Years 1 Month Cask Strength** barrel no. 342 db **(94.5) n23.5** the most complex nose I have tasted today: those four grains a doing their job! **t24** just brilliant! The delivery has just the softest oil so the impact of the grain itself is in no way hampered. The result is a slightly biting, complex essay of varied notes. There had been a slight eucalyptus note to the honey on the nose and here it plays out with a sharpness to the tannin, the fires met squarely by the salivating quality of the grains and most extinguished. Presumably rye is among those grains, as it shimmers on the palate; **f23.5** long, still those grains teasing and tormenting even as a nutty mocha arrives; **b23.5** this is one of those brands where you are never quite sure what you are going to get from the bottle quality-wise. Well, three cherries on this one... *56.4% (112.8 proof). sc.*

**A.D. Law Secale Straight Rye Whiskey Aged 4.5 Years** batch no. 172, 53 gallon white American oak char 3 barrels db **(95) n23.5 t24 f23.5 b24** A mixture of indigenous oils and The Murray Method makes this the easiest 70+% abv whiskey you'll ever taste. Talk about a gentle giant...! By far the best rye I've seen from A D Law and deserves to stand proudly beside America's finest. This is, truly, a Law unto itself... *71.5% (143 proof).*

**A.D. Law Secale Straight Rye Whiskey Bottled in Bond Aged Over 4 Years** batch no. C-17-F, 53 gallon white American oak char 3 barrels db **(86) n20.5 t23 f20.5 b22** A more usual Law rye: technically not quite the full shilling, but for sheer, unadulterated ryeness it has few peers. *50% (100 proof). Fall Season.*

⟐ **A.D. Law Straight Rye Whiskey Aged Over 3 Years** batch no. 1 db **(77.5)** n18.5 t21 f19 b19 I think the distillery went through a little period when they really weren't getting all their feints out of their middle cut. A shame. *50% (100 proof).*

⟐ **A.D. Law Straight Rye Whiskey Aged 6 Years Bottled in Bond** batch no. A-19 db **(87)** n22 t22.5 f21 b21.5 There are times you can tell from the sheer élan of the early Demerara reminds you that this distillery is capable of making stupendous rye. But there is a slight dulling buzz note to this especially towards the finish that shews that the cut was just a shade too generous for greatness. Much to enjoy, though. *50% (100 proof).*

⟐ **A.D. Law Straight Rye Whiskey Aged 6 Years 5 Months Cask Strength** barrel no. 46 db **(92.5)** n23 clean, crisp, unambiguous rye; t23.5 tooth cracklingly hard and salivating – as it should be. Toasty with a light Blue Mountain Jamaican coffee tone alongside the Demerara sugars...; f22.5 liquorice and mocha; b23.5 when this distillery get their cuts right, they make a formidable rye whiskey. *58.4% (116.8 proof).*

**A.D. Law Triticom Straight Wheat Whiskey Aged Over 3 Years** batch no. 2, 53 gallon white American oak char 3 barrels db **(92.5)** n22 t24 f23 b23.5 Fans of Wheat Whiskey will be delighted with this deliciously bold and memorable offering. *50% (100 proof).*

## LEOPOLD BROS Denver, Colorado.

⟐ **Leopold Bros Maryland-Style Rye Whiskey** barrel no. 174 db **(77.5)** n20.5 t19 f19 b19 Because of the vast over generosity of the cut, their bourbon shows more rye character than this actual rye does. Very much in the German mould of whisky making with those feints offering a distinct nougat style. Badly needs a far more disciplined approach to their cut points. Their bourbon shews they have much more to offer than this. *43%. sc. American Small Batch Whiskey Series.*

⟐ **Leopold Bros Straight Bourbon Cask Select** barrel no. 135, bott 11 Mar 19 db **(87.5)** n22 t22.5 f21 b22 Really interesting here how the rye plays such a significant role in the flavour personality of this bourbon. The given mash bill reveals 17% malted barley as 15% rye, yet it is that latter grain that can be found in all the highlights. Especially on the nose and eye-watering delivery. Good spice, but just need to get the feints down a little to make the most of the growing honey tones. Seriously promising. *50%. sc.*

## SPIRIT HOUND DISTILLERS Lyons, Colorado.

⟐ **Spirit Hound Distillers Bottled in Bond Straight Malt Whiskey 4 Years Old** barrel no. 13 db **(85.5)** n21 t22 f21 b21.5 The chocolatey nutty nougat reveals that this is an early example of the distillery's work, before the distiller had worked out the better cut points (as exhibited in the later barrel 93 below). Despite some faults, including perhaps not quite enough copper at play, there are enough ulmo honey spots to make for some attractive moments. *50% (100 proof). sc. 212 bottles.*

⟐ **Spirit Hound Distillers Cask Strength Straight Malt Whiskey 2 Years Old** barrel no. 93 db **(93)** n23 both the dark sugars and the barley pile on the sweetness and weight: so attractive! t23.5 a huge delivery, almost a nuclear explosion of natural oak caramels sweetened with maple syrup; the mouthfeel is nearly as amazing as the delivery: this is mega-chewy and the late arriving spices spring a surprise but welcome package; f23 though now much calmer, the oils persist with bewildering succulence. Excellent firm barley matched by equally firm but non-aggressive tannins; b23.5 the balance on the delivery is pretty close to perfect. A fantastic exhibition of controlled sugars. A three course meal of a malt. *63% (126 proof). sc. 72 bottles.*

⟐ **Spirit Hound Distillers Straight Malt Whiskey 2 Years Old** barrel no. 66 db **(88.5)** n21.5 slightly copper starved but the barley is entertaining; t22.5 silky soft and luxurious a soft marzipan note ends a nuttiness to the quiet sugars; the vanilla builds gently but with intent; f22 quite a dry finish: vanilla dominant and elegant; a late barley flourish works well; b22.5 not sure this distillery benefits from lower strengths, which allows the drier notes to dominate. But there is a big malt theme if you can tune into it. *45% (90 proof). sc. 286 bottles.*

## STRANAHAN DISTILLERY Denver, Colorado.

**Stranahan's Colorado Whiskey Batch #110 (91.5)** n22 t23 f23 b23.5 Lovely interplay between crispy grain and even crispier sugars. Two-toned . Juicy and gorgeously spiced.*47%.*

**Stranahan's Snowflake Cab Franc (95.5)** n24 t24.5 f23 b24. A celebration of great whiskey, and a profound statement of what the small distilleries of the USA are capable of. *47%. sc.*

## VAPOR DISTILLERY Boulder, Colorado.

⟐ **Boulder Spirits American Single Malt Whiskey Peated Aged for 2 Years** 53 gallon white oak barrels db **(91.5)** n23 how elegant is that? The tannins serve up a lovely heather honey and molasses mix, but the phenols gently rise above it all...; t23 soft on arrival, unusually clean with the tannins and gristy sugars merging immediately. As on the nose, the smoke drifts gently above it all; **f22.5** really lovely oak involvement plus a vaguely smoked butterscotch tart; **b23** an impressive malt which eschews the chance to go OTT with the peat. Good call, as the subtlety of this malt is its making...that and the very high quality distillate. 46% (92 proof).

⫸ **Boulder Spirits Straight Bourbon Whiskey Aged for 2 Years** 53 gallon white oak barrels db **(88.5) n22** an avalanche of tannin; **t23** sweet delivery followed by a scree of peppers; corn-rich but a solid rye-rich backbone; **f21.5** just a little on the bitter side as the oils gather; **b22** pretty well made and matured. Doubtless the perfect whiskey to get stoned on. 42% (84 proof).

# WOOD'S HIGH MOUNTAIN DISTILLERY Salida, Colorado.
**Wood's Alpine Rye Whiskey Aged 2 Years** batch no. 9 db **(88) n21.5 t23.5 f21 b22** A knife and fork whiskey. But has nailed the rye quite beautifully. 49% (98 proof).

# Florida
## FISH HAWK SPIRITS Gainesville, Florida.
**Sui Generis Conquistador 1513** batch no. 6 db **(68) n21 t20 f12 b15** I had learned the hard way, from tasting their other two whiskies first, to wait until the finish kicked in before even beginning to form a view. And, again, the awful finish makes what goes on before almost irrelevant. 40% (80 proof).

**Sui Generis Silver Queen** batch no. 2 db **(70) n17 t18 f17 b18** There are no words. Perhaps other than "fish".... 40% (80 proof).

**Sui Generis Siren Song** batch no. 6 db **(78) n21 t22 f17 b18** Where the Silver Queen was dethroned (and hopefully guillotined), at least this Siren Song has some allure. The big salty nose and big sweet delivery make some kind of sense. But this song goes horribly out of tune as the fade beckons. 40% (80 proof).

# FLORIDA FARM DISTILLERS Umatilla, Florida.
**Palm Ridge Reserve Handmade Micro Batch Florida Whiskey** orange and oak wood Less the 1 Year Old batch 29 **(94.5) n23 t24 f23.5 b24** I can see why everyone heads to Florida in the winter: obviously to try and grab one of the meager 6,000 bottles of this on offer each year. This is beautifully crafted, truly adorable whiskey where fruit appears to constantly have its hand on the tiller. And rather than blast in like a Hurricane from the sea, it breezes gently around the glass and palate with an easy elegance. I have relatives in Florida: about time I gave them another visit... 45% (90 proof)

# KOZUBA & SONS DISTILLERY INC. St. Petersburg, Florida.
**Mr. Rye Straight Rye Malt Whisky** virgin American oak barrels db **(91) n23 t23.5 f22 b22.5** Okay, the cut has been maximised, but forgivably so. The quality of the rye malt is very high. 45%. ncf.

# Kentucky
## ALLTECH Lexington, Kentucky.
**Pearse Lyons Reserve (85) n22 t21 f21 b21.** A fruity, grainy, pleasant whisky with the higher notes citrus dominant. Never quite finds a place to land or quite tells its story. Attractive but incomplete. 40% (80 proof)

**Town Branch Kentucky Straight Bourbon (88.5) n22.5 t21.5 f23 b22** A delicious Kentucky bourbon of considerable depth and charm. I think they have found their niche: bourbon. In Kentucky. Go for it, guys! 40% (80 proof)

# GLENNS CREEK DISTILLERY Frankfort, Kentucky.
⫸ **Glenns Creek Café Olé Kentucky Bourbon Barrel No 1 Aged At Least 1 Year (94) n23** this is high octane stuff: not so much the strength but the uncompromising depth of the characters involved. It is like superheroes in action and though seemingly earthy, close inspection reveals a mocha and minty depth; **t23.5** just sublime...The delivery shews a surprising degree of early toast, with a little kumquat marmalade for good measure. But the tannins are always on hand, melding beautifully with the acacia honey; **f23.5** once the busy bourbon stuff is through, the mocha promised arrives in spades...; **b24** the thing about big David Meier the distiller is that he like to make whiskies more enormous than himself. And, my word...has he succeeded here! Stupendous whisky! 57% (114 proof). sc.

**Millville Malt barrel 1** db **(91.5) n23 t23.5 f21.5 b23.5** A distillery located just a mile or two from my house on Glenn's Creek has come up with a malt that defies belief. Massive attention to detail on the cuts has paid dividends and has ensured a clean yet majestically rich addition to the malt whisky lexicon. 57.1% (114.2 proof)

⫸ **Glenns Creek OCD#5 (94.5) n23** the house style earthiness is to the fore while the spices and manuka honey make a polite dance of courtship; **t24** here we go: absolutely unreconstructed full on, knife and fork bourbon as thick as a red-neck's...err neck. The delivery is almost concentrated corn oil in which various dark honey and sugar notes are suspended. Wonderful juicy date and molasses make a joy of the mid-ground; **f23.5** those oils linger... while at first elegant spices, though eventually building to peperami levels, add a third dimension to the muscly tannin; **b24** this is one quirky distillery. But, by thunder, it knows how to make truly great bourbon. *57.8 % (115.6 proof).*

**Ryskey** barrel 4 single barrel double oaked db **(92.5) n23.5 t23.5 f22 b23** The usual excellence from the Lawrenceburg, Indiana, distillery but given a curious twist but the stirring in of some muscular tannin. Attractive and intriguing. *59.3% (118.6 proof) distilled Indiana – oak staves added at Glenns Creek.*

**Stave + Barrel Bourbon** single barrel, double aged db **(88.5) n22 t23 f21.5 b22** Full flavoured and salivating, but as well balanced as their Ryskey. *57.9% (115.8 proof) distilled Indiana. Toasted staves added at Glenns Creek.*

## O. Z. TYLER Owensboro, Kentucky.

⁂ **O.Z. Tyler Kentucky Bourbon Aged a Year and a Day Minimum (83) n20 t21 f21 b21** A tight, nutty bourbon shewing good late chocolate and molasses. But the youth of the whiskey means it has little ability to relax, although decent oils allow the sugars to distribute evenly. No off notes: just green and undercooked. Would love to see this at four or five times this age...; *45% (90 poof).*

# Illinois
## BLAUM BROS Galena, Illinois.

**Blaum Bros Bourbon Aged 3 Years** db **(81) n19.5 t22 f19 b20.5** A curious bourbon, this. Has the complex spice make up of a cake mix. Exceptionally sweet and leaves the tongue buzzing... *50% (100 proof).*

**Blaum Bros Fever River Rye Aged 2 Years** new American oak, finished in Port and Madeira barrels db **(86.5) n21.5 t21.5 f22 b21.5** Less bizarre spices at play here, the wine casks making for a friendlier, after experience with an attractive complexity that now makes sense. *40% (80 proof).*

⁂ **Blaum Bros Light Whiskey Algena Reserve 2 Years Old** db **(87) n22 t22 f21.5 b22** Sweet, soft and toffee rich. Lovely liquorice on the nose and spice intervention later. *45% (90 proof).*

⁂ **Blaum Bros Straight Bourbon Whiskey 4 Years Old** db **(86) n21 t22 f21.5 b21.5** Lots of Victory V/Fisherman's Friend cough sweet hickory to this. A touch of the Bowmores... *50% (100 proof).*

⁂ **Blaum Bros Straight Rye Whiskey 4 Years Old** db **(90.5) n23** beautiful, sharp rye notes at the fruity end of the scale; **t23** follows on from the nose in suitably explosive fashion, all cut glass salivating Demerara and spice; **f22** just dulls a little as it bitters out; **b22.5** a sturdy and steady rye with just the right degree of brittleness. *50% (100 proof).*

## FEW SPIRITS DISTILLERY Evanston, Illinois.

⁂ **FEW American Whiskey Aged at Least 1 Year** batch no. 18H30, bott code: FS 18297 333 db **(90) n22** nutty; **t23** sweet, oily and nutty; **f22.5** spicy and nuttier still; **b22.5** they've cracked it...! *46.5% (93 proof).*

⁂ **FEW Bourbon Whiskey** batch no. 17J20 db **(89.5) n22 t23 f22 b22.5** FEW can definitely vary in its quality. This bourbon is very comfortable and though rich, seems to operate well within itself. *46.5% (93 proof).*

⁂ **FEW Bourbon Whiskey** batch no. 18H16 db **(91.5) n23** almost a halfway house between a bourbon and rye nose...with the sharper accent definitely on the rye...; **t24** silky and absorbing, the mix of spice, muscovado sugars and mocha-inspired vanilla is borderline genius; **f21.5** ah...the extra oils from the cut gang up just a little too enthusiastically; **b23** you don't have to check out the mash bill of this bourbon: the rye can be heard loud and clear...! Ridiculously delicious! *46.5% (93 proof).*

⁂ **FEW Bourbon Whiskey** batch no. 18K14, bott code: 318 347 1555 db **(95) n23.5** cleaner than the previous bottling, thus allowing the rye to really go out on a limb; **t24** huge, yet so brilliantly controlled. A flavour explosion contained and orchestrated. Like their rye bottling the generous oils are happy to turn up in the most luxurious mocha form imaginable, even now with a hint of praline; but here the background rye plays a different role, but providing a crisp fruitiness blending perfectly with the spice; **f23.5** chocolate wafer...; **b24** this distillery has moved a long way in a relatively short space of time. A real force for quality now on the US whiskey scene. *46.5% (93 proof).*

⁂ **FEW Rye Whiskey** batch no. 17K30 db **(81) n17 t22 f21.5 b20.5** Sweet chocolate pudding and oily but a bit gruel-like on the flavour front. Back to their cabbage water style again, alas. It was the last of the FEW. *46.5% (93 proof).*

◇ **FEW Rye Whiskey** batch no. 18E30 db **(94) n23.5** exemplary. The mint and shards of rye make for delightful bedfellows; **t24** just so salivating: the rye effect is on full volume early on ensuring the grain is wonderfully intense before a deeper, more chocolate-rich note fills every possible space; light acacia honey adds balance and softness; **f23** long, as there are still plenty of oils from the cut to play with; vanilla; **b23.5** the cleanest FEW whisky I have tasted to date, the grain positively sparkles. And the way this whiskey has panned out... regrets? Too FEW to mention...... 46.5% (93 proof).

## KOVAL DISTILLERY Chicago, Illinois.

◇ **Koval Bourbon Single Barrel Whiskey** barrel no. 3060 db **(93) n23.5** pulsating liquorice with a heavy slap of corn oil; a vaguely wide cut but that helps the spices and honey tones develop to the full; **t23.5** wow...that is some delivery! Viscous and mouth-watering, there is a chewy corn meal delivery, quickly backed by molasses, Manuka honey and explosive spice; the mid-ground reveals a fudge and cocoa depth, **f22** the oils from that wide cut begin to gather with a vaguely phenolic tang to add to the tannins; **b23** although small batch bourbon makers, these guys really are the real deal. Not entirely technically flawless, but enough beauty and brilliance in the glass to forgive easily. 47%. Sc.

◇ **Koval Four Grain Single Barrel Whiskey** barrel no. WB5K42 db **(87.5) n21 t23 f21.5 b22** A busy, bitty and entertaining whiskey with one of the most intrinsic and captivating deliveries of the year. Fabulous layering with the busy-ness of those grains working to startling effect, especially when the soft bruyere honey kicks in. But just a little too wide a cut for true greatness, though the late spiced chocolate notes do make some amends. 55%. sc.

◇ **Koval Rye Single Barrel Whiskey** barrel no. FB3M79 db **(87) n21.5 t22.5 f21 b22** A little on the heavy-handed side. Full flavoured but a touch dull where there should be sparkle. 40%. sc.

◇ **Koval Wheat Single Barrel Whiskey** charred barrel, barrel no. FE8X10 db **(93.5) n23.5** ever been in a bakery first thing in the morning when they have just completed making their spiced buns...? **t23.5** fizzing, tongue-tingling spices are first through the door before a multitude of rich, toast and honey notes barge their way in with few manners; the midpoint is chewy with chocolate fudge at the core; **f23** the very slightly wide cut means another big and layered finish with mocha, delicate maple syrup and tannin interweaving rather prettily; **b23.5** wheat whiskey can be a little spicy....and this is very spicy. You don't need to check the label to confirm the grain. 55%. sc.

## Iowa
## CEDAR RIDGE DISTILLERY Swisher, Iowa.

**Twelve Five Rye** recipe: rye, corn & malted barley, batch no. 131304-A db **(87.5) n23 t22.5 f20.5 b21.5.** Some seriously big rye at work here and the nose is something to enjoy if not marvel at. Once the distillers can just narrow the middle cut, this will be a rye of serious magnitude. As it is, the feints just take the edge off an otherwise impressive rye. 47.5%

## Maryland
## OLD LINE SPIRITS Baltimore, Maryland.

**Old Line Single Malt American Whiskey Aged at Least One Year** **(87.5) n22 t22 f21.5 b22** A beautifully calm and majestic malt whisky which suffers a little from being a touch too round and elegant. Beautifully distilled, the thinned Manuka honey and natural caramels appear to fill every gap, other than a slight bitterness at the death. At times, though, spends a little too much time in the doldrums. 43% (86 proof). Distilled at Middle West Spirits.

**Old Line Single Malt American Whiskey Cask Strength Aged at Least One Year** batch no. 1M **(92) n22.5 t23.5 f23 b23** An altogether more impressive sailing than their 43% version. Not least because the oils, destroyed at the weaker strength, are able to encourage the richer segments of the malt to work full speed ahead. Excellent. 60% (120 proof). Distilled at Middle West Spirits.

## Massachusetts
## BERKSHIRE MOUNTAIN DISTILLERS Great Barrington, Massachusetts.

**Berkshire Bourbon Whiskey (91.5) n23 t23.5 f23 b23.** A bourbon bursting with character: I am hooked! Another micro-gem. 43%

## TRIPLE EIGHT DISTILLERY Nantucket, Massachusetts.

**The Notch Aged 12 Years** cask no. 026-055 dist 2002, bott 2014 db **(96.5) n24 t24.5 f23.5 b24.5** Interesting to see this great whisky cope, as we all must do, with the passing of time. The quiet understatement and elegance of the 10-y-o has given way to a more brash and assertive, oak-stained version. Not that that is a criticism, as it does it with the usual Triple

Eight panache. On the 8<sup>th</sup> of August 2008 (just two days after I had completed the 2009 Whisky Bible) I gave a speech at the distillery predicting that, from the samples I had tasted in their warehouses, this new venture was on course to be one of the great malt whisky distilleries of the world. I am heartened that, for once in my life, I got something right... **48%**

# Michigan
## JOURNEYMAN DISTILLERY Three Oaks, Michigan.

**Journeyman Buggy Whip Wheat Whiskey** batch 38 db **(94.5) n24 t23.5 f23 b24** I'll climb aboard this buggy any day. What a beautiful wheat whiskey this is...cracking, in fact...! *45% (90 proof).*

⬦ **Journeyman Corsets, Whips and Canes 100% Wheat Whiskey** batch no. 7 db **(89.5) n22** spiced dark cherry and tannin; **t23** silky at first with big oils starting off alongside a muscovado sugar effect and even bigger spices; **f22** dries as the huge tannins bite; **b22.5** one mouthful of this and I thought: "Oh, yes! The cough syrup distillery!" And sure enough this was one the one whose whiskey, a year or two back, reminded me of pleasant medication I had taken as a child. *64.5% (129 proof).*

**Journeyman Featherbone Bourbon Whiskey** batch 72 db **(84) n21 t21.5 f20 b21.5** The first mouthful of this flung me back 50 years to when I was a kid tucked up in bed and having to swallow a couple of spoons-worth of cherry-flavoured cough syrup. I can picture their salesmen getting people to gather round and peddling this as Dr Journeyman's Elixir for Coughs and Colds. In truth, though, a forceful corn-rich, oily, muscovado-sugared bag of tricks. *45% (90 proof).*

**Journeyman Last Feather Rye Whiskey** batch 72 db **(91) n22.5 t23.5 f22 b23** Truly a unique rye whiskey profile and one, that despite the odd fault, literally carries you on a delicious journey. *45% (90 proof).*

**Journeyman Silver Cross Whiskey** batch 61 db **(86) n22 t22 f20.5 b21.5** I am a fan of this fascinating distillery, that's for sure, and wondering what they are up to next. Not sure if this was designed to ward off vampires, but to be on the safe side I tasted this long after the sun set. A serious mish-mash of a whiskey which celebrated a rich ulmo-honey sweetness, but is ultimately undone by a bitterness which, sadly, no amount of sugar can keep fully under control and gets you in the neck in the end... *45% (90 proof).*

## NEW HOLLAND BREWING COMPANY Holland, Michigan.

⬦ **New Holland Beer Barrel Bourbon** bott code: 192201 db **(80.5) n22 t21.5 f18 b19** It was doing so well until that heavy hop kicked in on the finish: the bourbon notes on this are as good as anything I've encountered from this distillery. I want my hops with my beer, not whisky. I just don't even begin to understand the concept of this style of whisk(e)y. Sorry. *40% (80 proof).*

**New Holland Beer Barrel Rye** American white oak db **(80) n21 t21 f19 b19** Were this from Speyside, I dare-say it would be called hopscotch... The hoppiest whisk(e)y I have tasted anywhere in the world. Apart from a brief chocolate intervention, this is seriously not my kind of thing. I mean: I love whisky and I love beer. But just not together. Less befuddled by it than befuggled... *40% (80 proof).*

**New Holland Zeppelin Bend Reserve American Single Malt** sherry cask finish db **(87) n22 t21.5 f22 b21.5** My Panama off to the chaps at Zep Bend for finding some outstanding sherry casks to help infuse the most wonderful, succulent grape note to this mouth-filling malt and slow-burning cocoa. Rich fruit cake at its most moist and spicy, though a slight, off-key hop note somewhat paddles against the style and grain. Otherwise, close to being a stunner. *45% (90 proof).*

**Pitchfork Wheat Michigan-Grown Wheat Whiskey** aged 14 months, American oak barrels db **(93) n22.5 t23.5 f23.5 b23.5** So love it! Like a digestive biscuit you want to dunk in your coffee...By far and away the best thing I have ever seen from this distillery: this really is top drawer microdistillery whiskey just brimming with flavours and personality. Genuinely impressed. *45% (90 proof).*

**Zeppelin Bend Straight Malt Whiskey** American oak barrels db **(84.5) n21 t21.5 f21 b21** The Zep is back!! Not seen it for a while and this is a new model. Actually, in some ways barely recognise it from the last one I saw about five years ago. Much more effervescent than before, though that curious hop note I remember not only persists but appears to have been upped slightly. *45% (90 proof).*

## VALENTINE DISTILLING CO. Ferndale, Michigan.

**Mayor Pingree Small Batch Bourbon Whiskey** batch no. 39 db **(89.5) n23.5 t22.5 f21.5 b22** A very different animal, or mayor, and obviously distilled in different stills from their 9- and 10-year-old Mayor Pingree brands. A little confusing for the punter but a very attractive but under-stated micro-bourbon without doubt. *45% (90 proof).*

## Montana
### MONTGOMERY DISTILLERY Missoula, Montana.

Montgomery American Single Malt Whiskey Aged 5 Years American white oak barrels, dist 2013 db **(84) n20.5 t22.5 f20.5 b20.5** That's a pretty hefty middle cut there and the resulting oils make for a lot of chewing. A toffee-nougat nose sets the scene but the delivery of intense bruyere honey is exceptionally beautiful. Sadly, those feints kick in with a vengeance further down the line. *45% (90 proof). 1,750 bottles. Third Release.*

Sudden Wisdom Straight Rye Whiskey Aged 2 Years American white oak casks db **(89.5) n22.5** no doubting the rye and this is a sweet version, with a little muscovado sugar mixing in with a pinch of spearmint; a little feinty, but some cocoa, too; **t23** the rye is first, second and third out of the blocks, giving both a crisp, precise delivery and a far more juicy one, too; dark sugars about, crunching about the palate with rye-fuelled gusto; **f21.5** those feints just detectable on the nose are much more prevalent here; **b22.5** in the three years that passed from making their malt to making this rye, it appears they have learned how to tone down (though not entirely eradicate) the feints. So less Sudden Wisdom, as hard learned. Where the grain wasn't visible in the malt bottling, here it certainly is. Must say, though, that I'm intrigued by the label's description of this whiskey giving notes of "autumn leather" Intriguing, as I have no idea what that is: must be a Montana thing. I need to get there and investigate... *45% (90 proof).*

## Nevada
### LAS VEGAS DISTILLERY Las Vegas, Nevada.

Nevada 150 Bourbon Whiskey American white oak barrels, aged 2 years, 4 months db **(92) n24 t22.5 f22.5 b23.5** Who would have thought that the loudest, brashest city in the world could conjure the most delicate, intricate and shy bourbon for many a year? Don't let this whisky fool you: it has much to say...but all in whispers...*45% (90 proof). 2,014 bottles.*

## New England
### SONS OF LIBERTY Rhode Island, New England.

Battle Cry American Single Malt Whiskey db **(77.5) n19 t21 f18 b19.5** A sweet, nutty whisky weakened by the butyric-like off notes. *46% (92 proof).*

Battle Cry American Single Malt Whiskey finished in Sauternes wine barrels db **(71) n18 t19 f16 b18** When even something as magical as a Sauternes cask fails to deal with the fire on the throat and the persistent weaknesses of the spirit, you know it's back to the drawing board. Less Battle Cry: more hara kiri... *46% (92 proof).*

Battle Cry American Single Malt Whiskey finished in oloroso sherry barrels, batch no. 2 db **(80) n20 t21 f19 b20** An acceptable malt which does little to entertain other than allow the richer notes of the oloroso to show a sweet, fruit cake intensity. Still a bit of flame-thrower late on, though. *46% (92 proof). 625 bottles.*

Uprising American Single Malt Whiskey finished in Pedro Ximenez sherry barrels, batch no. 4 db **(83.5) n21.5 t21 f20 b21** A hot, mildly aggressive whisky where for once the PX is a force for good by sculpting an intensely rich, sugary grapeyness to fill in the plot holes of the malt itself. *46% (92 proof). 900 bottles.*

## New Mexico
### SANTA FE SPIRITS Santa Fe, New Mexico.

Colkegan Single Malt Whiskey American white oak barrels, batch no. 9 db **(90) n23 t23.5 f21 b22.5** They have learned to control the Mesquite...! Much better! *46% (90 proof).*

Colkegan Single Malt Whiskey American white oak barrels, batch no. 10 db **(91) n23 t23.5 f22 b22.5** Yep! Toning down the smoke has been a good move, but that finish still needs some attention...That said...superb! *46% (90 proof).*

## New York
### BREUCKELEN DISTILLING Brooklyn, New York.

77 Whiskey Bonded Rye Aged 4 Years American oak barrels db **(86.5) n21.5 t22 f21.5 b21.5** Big flavoured and butch, but a few too many nougat and tobacco notes point an accusing finger towards the cut. Plenty to enjoy, but perhaps not up to Breuckelen's usual very high standards. *50% (100 proof).*

77 Whiskey Bonded Rye & Corn Aged 4 Years American oak barrels db **(95) n23.5 t24 f23.5 b24** There you go: Breuckleyn back on track with a spot edition of their signature brand. Sings from the glass like a barber-shop quartet. *50% (100 proof).*

77 Whiskey Local Corn 700 Days Old db **(92) n23 t23.5 f22.5 b23** It is as if very single atom of sugar has been sucked out of the oak though, thankfully, baser tannins give balance. Remarkable and delicious! *45% (90 proof).*

**77 Whiskey Local Rye & Corn 538 Days Old** American oak barrels db **(92.5)** n22.5 t23.5 f23 b23.5 The 377th whisky tasted for my Bible 2018 just had to be this. I remember last year tasting a younger version of this which was quite astonishing. Here the rye, which was so prominent last time, has been overtaken by the corn which has clipped its brittle wings. Still an astounding experience, nonetheless... *45% (90 proof).*

**77 Whiskey New York Wheat 622 Days Old** American oak barrels db **(89.5)** n22 t23 f22 b22.5 A very busy whiskey which never quite decides which direction it wishes to take. Still, there's something to say for a mystery tour... *45%*

**Project No 1: Wheated Straight Bourbon Bottled in Bond Aged 4 Years** dist 2013 db **(88)** n22 a hefty nose: corn appears to dominate but the nip from the wheat is unmistakable; t22.5 salivating delivery. Tannins have a slight upper hand in the first few waves, before that attractive corn oil and wheat spice combine again to fill in the middle; f21.5 a few feints kick in late on, but there is vanilla and spice enough to compensate; b22 a bit heavy on the oils, but the wheat and associated spices make their mark. *50% (100 proof).*

**Project No 2: Single Malt Whiskey Bottled in Bond Aged 4 Years** dist 23 Mar 13, bott 26 Feb 18 db **(84.5)** n21 t21 f21.5 b21 Sweet and widely cut. A project still in development, I suspect... *50% (100 proof).*

## COOPERSTOWN DISTILLERY Cooperstown, New York.

**Cooper's Classic American Whiskey** bourbon mash finished in French oak barrels, bott code. 148 10 db **(90.5)** n22.5 t22.5 f23 b22.5 Plugs into the sugars and takes full voltage. *45%.*

**Cooper's Legacy Bourbon Whiskey Grant's Recipe** bott code. 147 02 db **(95)** n23.5 t24 f23.5 b24 I'd like, with this exceptional bourbon, to raise a toast to my son, James', new (indeed, first) dog: Cooper. Named, naturally, after Dale Cooper of Twin Peaks fame. Dale whippet. Dale bourbon. *50% (100 proof).*

**Cooper's Ransom Rye Whiskey** db **(86.5)** n21 t22 f21.5 b22 If they could just keep the cut points a little more tight, they'd really have some rye here. Despite the light feints the rye does at times sparkle with commendable crispness. *51% (102 proof).*

## FINGER LAKES DISTILLING Burdett, New York.

**McKenzie Wheated Bourbon Whiskey Bottled in Bond Aged a Minimum of 4 Years** American oak db **(93)** n23 rich and fluting, a distinct chocolate-liquorice nose takes hold; t23.5 despite the best attention of some early spice, the corn oils rule the roost, making for a succulent body on which muscly tannin is evident; f23 back to that chocolate liquorice again, the bourbon turns full circle from the nose; b23.5 rich, full flavoured and well powered. Not a bourbon for the faint of heart. Beautifully constructed and structured. *50% (100 proof). ncf.*

**McKenzie Straight Rye Whiskey Aged a Minimum of 3 Years** American oak db **(90)** n23 how proud is that rye! The grain is angular and crisp and reaches from the glass to meet you with its clean fruity bite before the spices and tannins can make an impression; t23.5 immediate rye impact: firm despite the surrounding oils; f21 some residual feints among the vanilla; b22.5 just adore the intermittent crispness of the grain. Great stuff. *45.5% (91 proof). ncf.*

## HILLROCK ESTATE DISTILLERY Hudson Valley, New York.

**Hillrock Double Cask Rye Whiskey** American oak barrels, barrel no. Port-4, aged under 4 years db **(88)** n22.5 t21.5 f22 b22 A rare case of a Port finish working amid bourbon or rye, mainly because it eliminates the more aggressive vegetable notes and allows the attractive rye a relatively free hand. *45%*

**Hillrock Double Cask Rye Whiskey Under 4 Years Old** barrel no. 91 db **(86)** n21.5 t22.5 f21 b21 It is a dangerous game mixing rye or bourbon with wine casks. Rare precision is required to ensure that the grain still has the loudest say, or half at least. Yes, a great spice attack and a few rich chocolate notes poke through. And were this a single malt it would doubtless score more highly, and I would enjoy it more, as this style is far more acceptable; the lushness of the fruit par for the course. But this is a rye, a unique style to be cherished and protected, and as such I'm looking for the fruitiness to be broadcast from the grain, not the barrel. Enjoyable, for sure. And yes, about four waves in there is a rye-rich burst. But it is too little amid a fruity, oily cacophony. *60% (120 proof). sc.*

**Hillrock Single Malt Whiskey** American oak barrels, finished in sherry casks, barrel no. HS-1, aged under 4 years db **(95.5)** n23.5 t24 f24 b24 Smoke and fruit rarely make happy bedfellows from a balancing viewpoint. Here they do, doubtless helped by the fact that, for once, the sherry butt does not possess a sulphur-stained edge. You won't get it until about the fifth mouthful: then is all clicks. The classiest of class acts. *48.2%*

**Hillrock Single Malt Whiskey Under 4 Years Old** sherry cask finish, barrel no. OPX-22 db **(95)** n23.5 thumping, earthy peat: high in phenols and a little fire with that smoke....; a sub strata of grape is trod underfoot; **t24** lush in typical Hillrock style, the fruit having the lion's share of the early exchanges. As the smoke infiltrates, a lime-blossom honey sweetness develops and with it a beautiful juiciness. Tannin now forms a further degree of weight to join the phenols; **f23.5** long, the smoke clinging to the now substantial oils; soft fruits, but half a mark lost for a little furry tang on the finale; **b24** spectacularly beautiful. When I first met distiller Dave Pickerell in deepest, darkest Kentucky mining absolutely classic bourbon I doubt either of us thought that 25 years on he would be responsible for one of North America's finest single malts... 48.2% (96.4 proof). sc.

**Hillrock Solera Aged Bourbon Whiskey** American oak barrels, finished in sherry casks, barrel no. 48 db **(89)** n22.5 t23 f21.5 b22 A rare case of the wine finish working with a bourbon, but probably because the grape remains subtle. 48.2%

⬩ **Hillrock Solera Aged Bourbon Whiskey** sherry cask finish, barrel no. NAPA CAB-18 db **(82.5)** n21 t22.5 f19 b20 Starts brightly but dulls and bitters significantly...and quickly. 46.3% (92.6 proof). sc.

# IRON SMOKE WHISKEY Fairport, New York.

**Iron Smoke Apple Wood Smoked Whiskey** batch no. 11, bott 3/28/17 db **(93.5)** n23 t23 f23.5 b24 Quite a step down in terms of weight and intensity to their last batch, as though this is a little younger. But most rewarding to see two different styles, yet both of the highest standard. Congratulations to these guys for really taking care with their whiskey. 40% (80 proof).

⬩ **Iron Smoke Casket Strength Straight Bourbon Whiskey Aged A Minimum of Two Years** batch no. 1, bott 12/27/18 db **(94.5)** n23.5 hickory and liquorice comfortably with the walnut oil; **t23.5** gorgeous delivery: huge bodied, corn oil lapping all over the palate and the liquorice intense and purposeful; **f23.5** long with a return of the nuttiness, and a little Manuka honey, too, rubbed into the tannin; **b24** after having tasted the latest Apple Wood version, normal service is resumed with this superbly distilled and beautifully functioning bourbon. 60% (120 proof).

**Iron Smoke Four Grain Bourbon With Apple Wood Smoked Wheat Aged A Minimum of Two Years** barrel no. 196, bott 4/11/18 db **(94)** n23.5 t23.5 f23 b24 Just all fits together like a hand-made shoe and no less comfortable. 45% (90 proof). sc. Bottled for DW Select.

⬩ **Iron Smoke Four Grain Bourbon With Apple Wood Smoked Wheat Aged A Minimum of Two Years** batch no. 24, bott 5/7/19 db **(91.5)** n22.5 the apple wood smoke rumbles over every aspect of this slightly feinty nose, though a little hickory underlines its bourbony credentials; **t23** mouth-filling and elegantly sweet with extra fat corn oil; **f22.5** now it's all about the tannins and smoke...what a battle! **b23.5** considering it was only the wheat that was smoked, this is one big ass Kentuckian. And they have pulled it off beautifully by, somehow, getting the balance near enough spot on, despite the cut being wider than usual. Superb. 40% (80 proof).

⬩ **Iron Smoke Special Reserve Single Barrel Straight Bourbon Whiskey Aged A Minimum of Two Years** batch no. 380, bott 12/18/18 db **(93)** n22.5 a sharp fruitiness contrasts well with the weightier smoke; **t23.5** an initial Demerara sugar blast is gradually worn down by a mix of vanilla and natural caramel; the smoke begins a drying process, though only after a little mocha interlude; **f23** smoke dried vanilla and caramel...and so delicious! **b23.5** a thoroughly lip-smacking, though ultimately dry version. 45% (90 proof). Bottled exclusively for Whole Foods.

# KINGS COUNTY DISTILLERY Brooklyn, New York.

**Kings County Distillery Bottled-in-Bond Straight Bourbon Whiskey Four Years Old** batch no. 3 db **(94)** n24 t23 f23.5 b23.5 Easy to mistake as a fine old Kentucky bourbon: there is no higher praise than that...!! 50%.

**Kings County Distillery Peated Bourbon Whiskey** aged one year or more, batch no. p4 db **(94)** n23.5 t24 f23 b23.5 No problem with this. You can use peat-smoked grain and still produce bourbon, which is how I assume this was produced. Just not a bourbon finished in a peated cask. That ain't bourbon. Whatever this is – and it appears to be the former – it is quite stunningly lovely. 45%

**Kings County Distillery Straight Bourbon Whiskey Aged Two Years or More** batch no. 142 db **(89)** n22 demerara sugars on liquorice; **t23** this distillery knows how to kick off with a Kentucky style liquorice and hickory volley. Lovely treacle and caramel follow up; **f22.5** a real lingering bourbony liquorice stamp as the tannins keep their shape; **b22.5** keeps it simple and satisfying. 45% (90 proof).

**Kings County Distillery Straight Rye Whiskey Aged Two Years or More** batch no. 1 db **(88)** n22.5 the crispness of the rye is matched only by the spice; **t23** superb delivery, soft oils balancing the crunchiness of the grain. Fruity muscovado sugars drift and meet a warm pepperiness; **f20.5** a shade too bitter; **b22** KC's first entry into rye is a success: the grain is profound and every bit as salivating as it should be. Room for improvement, but some great moments. *51% (101 proof).*

### TACONIC DISTILLERY Stanfordville, New York.

**Taconic Dutchess Private Reserve Straight Bourbon Whiskey** db (86) n21.5 t22 f21 b21.5. A pretty bourbon, with the sugars sitting in the right place, if sometimes over enthusiastically. Good spice balance, roastiness and generous oils. Also, some decent rye in that mash bill it seems. *45%*

**Taconic Straight Bourbon Whiskey** db (92.5) n23 t23.5 f23 b23 I well remember their bourbon from last year: this appears to have upped a gear...not only in strength but in far better usage of the sugars. *57.5% (115 proof).*

**Taconic Straight Rye Whiskey** db (91.5) n22.5 t23.5 f22.5 b23 If memory serves, this is the same distillery which came up with a resounding rye last year. This, though, has a different feel with the oak enclosing in on the grain like a python gets all up close and personal to a lamb. *57.5% (115 proof).*

### TOMMYROTTER DISTILLERY Buffalo, New York.

**Tommyrotter Triple Barrel American Whiskey** batch no. 3 French oak Finish (88.5) n22 hardly surprisingly, gentle tannin makes its mark playing anchor, no end of vanilla takes up a lighter role; t22.5 sweet and silky delivery the malt and vanilla appear joined at the hip. The oaky spices certainly aren't; f22 the spices form a jagged edge to the gentle caramels; b22 despite using three barrels, it as though the caramel has merged many of the facets to create a continuous flavour stream. Not as a complex as I hoped for, but not a whiskey to turn down a second glass to. *46% (92 proof). nc ncf.*

### TUTHILLTOWN SPIRITS Gardiner, New York.

**Hudson Baby Bourbon Year 13 Batch E1** (86) n21 t21.5 f22 b21.5. A big, heavy duty bourbon. Feinty, though nothing like as oily as some previous bottlings I've encountered from these guys over the years. Enough toasted honeycomb and liquorice for this to make a few lovely noises. *46%. WB15/174*

### VAN BRUNT STILLHOUSE Brooklyn, New York.

**Van Brunt Stillhouse Bourbon** db (81.5) n19 t21 f21 b20.5. For a bourbon, this has a peculiarly malty kick to it. Distinct whiff of the hay ricks about this, before the fledgling liquorice becomes involved. *42%*

**Van Brunt Stillhouse Rye** db (86) n20.5 t22 f22 b21.5. Technically wins few awards. But something, seemingly instinctual, seems to have dragged out the very best from this distillery with its rye. The oils are a bit of a problem, yet the grain rises above it enough to tap out a delightfully fruity and spicy message, and even confident enough to, late on, stray into mocha land.... *42%*

### WIDOW JANE DISTILLERY Brooklyn, New York.

**Baby Jane Bourbon Whiskey** batch no.1 db (85.5) n21 t22 f21 b21.5 Jane is a chubby little thing, displaying plenty of baby fat. Sweet, though, with an enjoyable molasses and nougat theme. *45.5% (91 proof).*

**Widow Jane Straight Bourbon Whiskey Aged 10 Years** barrel no. 1609, bott 2017 db (90.5) n23 t23 f22 b22.5 Good, honest, rock solid if oily, old-fashioned bourbon. *45.5% (91 proof). sc.*

**Widow Jane Whiskey Distilled From A Rye Mash Oak & Apple Wood Aged** batch no. 13 db (86) n22 t21.5 f21 b21.5 Sweet, firm, has a few teeth that aren't afraid to nip – and a slight tobacco note on the nose. Plenty to chew on, for sure. *45.5% (91 proof).*

## North Carolina
### BLUE RIDGE DISTILLING CO. Golden Valley, North Carolina.

◈ **Defiant American Single Malt** 100% malted barley, bott code: 307/18 04:43 L32 db (81.5) n18 t22.5 t20.5 b20.5 Wow! I see they have done nothing to reduce the cut since I last tasted this, resulting in a challengingly feinty nose. Must say, though, that the malty, ulmo honey on delivery is a delicious surprise! *41% (81 proof).*

◈ **Defiant Rye Whisky** bott code: 066/18 05:26 L32 db (86.5) n21.5 t22 f21.5 b21.5 With the exception of slightly more honey on delivery, the tasting notes (and quality of rye) remains absolutely identical to the last time I tasted this! *46% (92 proof).*

## Ohio
### CLEVELAND WHISKEY Cleveland, Ohio.

**Cleveland Underground Bourbon Whiskey Finished with Black Cherry Wood** batch no. 05 db (88) n22.5 t22.5 f21 b22 In the blurb on the back of this bottle they claim their methods of maturation are regarded as sacrilegious to some. But these methods "adds a series of flavours and aromas never before experienced in traditional whiskies." Well, let's take the first claim for a start: there is nothing in this whiskey I have never tasted hundreds, indeed, thousands of times before. Sorry about that. Only one whisky of this year's intake of over 1,000 whiskies gave me something I had never encountered before: and it wasn't this. I have no idea what these maturation techniques might be, and I am really keen to find out: I am truly fascinated. But I don't regard any whiskey finished (as well as started and middled) in anything other than virgin oak to be bourbon. Sorry. Back to the whiskey: pleasant with an intriguing layering structure to the nose which certainly points to something other than a species of Quercus. However, these notes have, over the last 25 years, cropped up many times elsewhere in the USA and around the globe. More importantly, the finish, so vital in any whiskey, needs some serious attention as it is bitter and unbalanced and undoes a lot of good work. *47% (94 proof). Uncommon Barrel Collection.*

### MIDDLE WEST SPIRITS Columbus, Ohio

**OYO Michelone Reserve Bourbon Whiskey** db **(86) n22.5 t22 f20 b21.5** A mainly attractive, restrained bourbon showing limited age and therefore depth. Lovely small grains to the busy nose and the sugars rise early before the buttery spices begin, but runs out of steam quite soon after. Not too happy with the tangy finish. *45% (90 proof).*

**OYO Oloroso Wheat Whiskey** db **(88) n23.5 t22.5 f20 22** As any good wheat whiskey should, this radiates spices with abandon. The fruit helps paper over some cracks in the distillate, especially towards the weak finish. *51% (102 proof).*

### TOM'S FOOLERY Chargin Falls, Ohio.

**Tom's Foolery Ohio Straight Bourbon Whiskey** aged 3 Years, batch 6, dist 2012 db **(83) n19 t22 f21 b21.** Not sure if Tom's fooling or feinted. Superb arrival on palate with some pretty smart spices, well backed up by maple syrup. But the cut needs to be narrowed considerably. *45% (90 proof)*

### WOODSTONE CREEK DISTILLERY Cincinnati, Ohio.

**Woodstone Creek 10 Year Old Peated Malt (92) 24 23 22 23.** Just read the previous tasting notes. There is nothing I can either add or subtract. Quite, quite wonderful... *46.25%*

## Oregon
### CLEAR CREEK DISTILLERY Portland, Oregon.

**McCarthy's Oregon Single Malt Aged 3 Years** batch W16-01, bott 6 May 16 db **(88.5) n22 t23 f21.5 b22** For the first time since I tasted their first bottlings – in the days when my beard was still black – this whiskey has changed. Appears to have far less copper in the system to give the normal all-round richness; this is quite apparent on the nose and finish in particular. But they appear to have upped the peat ratio to good effect. *42.5% (85 proof)*

### RANSOM SPIRITS Sheridan, Oregon.

**Ransom The Emerald 1865** batch no. 005 db **(86.5) n21 t23 f21 b21.5** "This whiskey rings a bell", thought I. Brilliant delivery, magnificently complex grains at play, but OTT feints. I've tasted this one before, I concluded. And, on checking in a previous Bible, I see I had a couple of years back, though an earlier bottling and then not called The Emerald. Brilliant Irish style mix of malted and unmalted barley. But just need to sort that cut out. *43.8%.*

**Ransom Rye, Barley, Wheat Whiskey Aged a Minimum of 2 Years** batch no. 003 db **(85.5) n21 t22 f21 b21.5** A little too much earthiness to this for its own good, meaning the wheat has to fight hard to get its sweet and spicy message out there. Needs a tad more copper in the system to get the most out of this whiskey, as a metallic spark appears missing. Just love this distillery's labels, by the way: real class. *63.4%.*

### ROGUE SPIRITS Newport, Oregon.

**Rogue Dead Guy Whiskey** ocean aged in oak barrels at least 1 year db **(86) n22.5 t22 f20.5 b21.** Ah, I remember this guy from a year or two back: I had a bone to pick with him about his finish. Well, not the preferred drink of the Grim Reaper now, and makes good use of its malty, peppery structure. The finish is still a bit tangy and salty. But a big improvement. *40% (80 proof)*

## Pennsylvania
### DAD'S HAT RYE DISTILLERY Bristol, Pennsylvania.

**Dad's Hat Pennsylvania Straight Rye Whiskey Aged Minimum 3 Years** db **(91.5) n23 t23.5 f22** That persistent vague bitterness does gather momentum towards the end; **b23** the truest rye I have seen from you yet: I take my hat off to you guys...quite literally...! *47.5% (95 proof).*

# South Carolina
## PALMETTO DISTILLERY Anderson, South Carolina.

**Palmetto Moonshine Bootlegger Proof Corn Whiskey** db **(92)** n23.5 t23 f22.5 b23 As one might expect, this is along the same lines as their Lightning white dog (see below) except the oils are more intact ensure greater length and a cocoa powder finish demanded of new make of this strength. Beautifully made, the corn gets every opportunity to shine. *65% (130 proof).*

**Palmetto Moonshine White Lightning Corn Whiskey** db **(91)** n23 t23.5 f22 b22.5 Apart from a slight thinning of the copper effect on the finish, this is near flawless white dog. Sweet and exceptionally well distilled the corn profits by the cleanness of the cut. *52.5% (105 proof).*

**Palmetto Whiskey** new French oak db **(84)** n20.5 t22.5 f21 b20 Despite the high rye content this simply overdoses on chocolate caramel. Has been bottled at a time when the balance isn't quite right. *44.65% (89.3 proof).*

# Tennessee
## BENJAMIN PRICHARD'S DISTILLERY Kelso, Tennessee.

**Benjamin Prichard's Lincoln County Lightning Tennessee Corn Whiskey (89)** n24 t22.5 f21 b22. Another white whiskey. This one is very well made and though surprisingly lacking oils and weight has more than enough charm and riches. *45%*

## NELSON'S GREEN BRIER DISTILLERY Nashville, Tennessee.

**Belle Meade Aged 9 Years Sherry Bourbon** finished in Oloroso sherry casks, batch no. 3 **(87)** n22 t22 f21 b22 A far better sherry bottling than I tasted before from these guys. The actual bourbon itself is able to poke through the smothering fruit with far greater energy. The fruit is clean and clear enough to offer a second dimension, though still not too keen on that soupy flavour profile. *45.2% (90.4 proof). Bottled by Nelson's Green Brier Distillery.*

**Belle Meade Cognac Bourbon** finished in XO Cognac casks, batch no. 2 **(78.5)** n21 t20 f18.5 b19 Very frustrating. This distillery makes a very high class bourbon which is a joy to experience, and here it is being muzzled by the restrictive limitations of a poor Cognac cask. Seriously and untidily bitter from the midpoint onwards. *45.2% (90.4 proof).*

**Belle Meade Madeira Bourbon** finished in Malmsey Madeira casks, batch no. 6 **(89)** n23 t22 f21.5 b22.5 Give me a straight bourbon over a cask finished job any day. But this works as well as they come and even offers a degree of sophistication. *45.2% (90.4 proof). Bottled by Nelson's Green Brier Distillery.*

# Texas
## BALCONES DISTILLERY Waco, Texas.

◈ **Balcones 1 Texas Single Malt Aged at Least 26 Months in Oak** batch no. SM19-1, bott 3.12.19 db **(84.5)** n22 t21.5 f20 b21 Nowhere near Balcone's normal high standard with the cut as wide as a Texas rib eye, even more fatty and thick but with nothing like the taste. Some big natural caramel and lighter molasses...but it isn't enough. This weekend of 20-21 July 2019 I am tasting all my remaining Texas whiskeys for this forthcoming Bible. Because it was 50 years ago this weekend that man first walked on the Moon, an event I remember vividly as a child watching in thrilled awe on our black and white television with my now departed parents. And Texas played a key part in that amazing event, something that will never be forgotten by those who witnessed it. Houston: this whiskey has a slight problem... *53%. nc ncf.*

**Balcones Brimstone Texas Scrub Oak Smoked Whisky Aged At Least 1 Day In Oak** batch no. BRM18-1, bott 1-23-18 db **(93)** n23.5 t23.5 f22.5 b23.5 I can neither add nor subtract from my tasting notes to the previous bottling. Actually, upon reflection, I can. An extra half point for some clever extra spices on delivery... *53% (106 proof). nc ncf.*

**Balcones Brimstone Redux Aged 33 Months in American Oak** barrel no. 4880 db **(94)** n23.5 t24 f22.5 b24 Welcome to Texas's very own Tannin Fest...in a bottle... Phew...! One of a kind, for sure. *64.9% (129.8 proof). sc.*

**Balcones FR.OAK Texas Single Malt Whisky Pot Distilled Aged At Least 35 Months In Oak** batch no. FROAK18-1, bott 4-27-18 db **(92.5)** n21.5 t24 f23.5 b23.5 Discernible barley gets lost in a forest of sweet tannin. *59.9% (119.8 proof). nc ncf. Tenth Anniversary.*

**Balcones Peated Texas Single Malt Aged 26 Months in American Oak** barrel no. 10472 db **(96)** n24 t24 f24 b24 There's no smoke without fire...and this has both. Enormous and really cleanly and beautifully made. Rarely has peated malt and new oak been so happily married. One of the greatest malt whiskeys ever produced in the USA. *63% (126 proof). sc.*

◈ **Balcones Texas Rye 100 Proof Aged at Least 15 Months in Oak** batch no. RYE0019-1 db **(85.5)** n20 t22.5 f21.5 b21.5 Another strange rye offering from Balcones who definitely have some room for improvement with consistency with this style of whiskey. The nose is definitely broken, but once passed the oils on delivery, the grain really zeros into the taste buds and hits its target unerringly. Too short lived though as the fade shews a little attractive rye sweetness. *50%. nc ncf.*

**Balcones Texas Rye 100 Proof Pot Distilled 100% Straight Rye Whiskey Aged At Least 15 Months** batch no. RYE10018-1, bott 2-28-18 db **(85) n20 t21 f22.5 b21.5** By Balcones astonishingly high standards, this is an underwhelming rye. Neither the nose nor delivery get off the ground, or feel particularly comfortable. Only once the big cocoa finish hoves into view do we get some idea of the distillery's usual excellence, though the very last off key notes of the fade tell a story *50% (100 proof). nc ncf.*

⟪ **Balcones Texas Rye Cask Strength Aged at Least 27 Months in Oak** batch no. RCS19-1, bott 1.29.19 db **(95) n23** the grain glows unambiguously, brightly and crisply on one level but much earthier and sharp on another; **t24** brilliant...just brilliant! Toasted Manuka honey crystalises the rye like an ant trapped in amber. Huge, controlled and resounding; **f23.5** long, soft spiced with the toasted honey and sugars melting...; **b24.5** every bit as beautiful and on the money as their 15-month old rye was lacklustre. It is this type of excellence I normally associate with this distillery. *63.3%. nc ncf.*

**Balcones Texas Single Malt Whisky Classic Edition Aged At Least 19 Months In Oak** batch no. SM18-2, bott 2-8-18 db **(93) n22.5 t23.5 f23.5 b23.5** A deceptive Balcones: it is like coming out of the dark into the light, being blinded and then slowly adjusting to what is around you. Easy to underestimate in its excellence. *53% (108 proof). nc ncf.*

**Balcones Texas Single Malt Whisky Pot Distilled Rum Cask Finished Aged At Least 32 Months** batch no. SMR18-1, bott 4-6-18 db **(92) n23.5 t23.5 f22 b23** Not even a rum cask, capable of clipping some bigger whiskies' wings, can get a look in here, perhaps until the final fade. Typically enormous. *55% (110 proof). nc ncf. Tenth Anniversary.*

⟪ **Balcones Texas Single Malt Rum Cask Finished Aged at Least 27 Months in Oak** batch no. SMR19-1, bott 1.15.19 db **(91.5) n22.5** the tannins act like an oaky fence around the malt; incredibly firm going; **t23.5** another cream toffee Balcones, but this one really has a mouth-watering hardness to its chewability, plus some delightful liquorice and mocha; the spices just can't help themselves from being busy, biting and entertaining; **f22.5** long and back with the tannins; **b23** rum cask whiskeys have a tendency to be hard as nails. This is one very big nail... *63.5%. nc ncf.*

⟪ **Balcones Texas Single Malt Single Barrel Aged at Least 24 Months in Oak** cask no. 17222, American oak cask, dist 5.3.17, bott 6.13.19 db **(88) n22.5** maybe not technically a zinger, still has just the right firm honey; **t22** a stirring delivery offering massive salivation and molasses. Loads of toffee fudge becomes increasingly toasty and burnt; **f21.5** toasty and just a little tangy; **b22** enjoyable and another that is not quite up the distillery's usual brilliant standard. *64%. nc ncf sc.*

⟪ **Balcones Texas Single Malt Single Barrel Aged at Least 65 Months in Oak** cask no. 2642, American oak cask, dist 1.8.14, bott 6.11.19 db **(95) n23.5** the cut has been stretched as wide as possible without causing damage, so the oils are slick and the liquorice/hickory tones fierce but so attractive; **t24** such a rich mouth feel. A mercurial cough sweet, molasses and black pepper delivery far more bourbon on style than a single malt; **f23.5** long, lush, metallic and still pushing all the right buttons...; **b24** so thick and dense, probably has more gravitational pull than that Moon these Texans went out and lassoed 50 years ago. *66.4%. nc ncf sc.*

⟪ **Balcones Texas Single Malt Single Barrel Aged at Least 60 Months in Oak** cask no. 2504, American oak cask, dist 2.17.14, bott 2.20.19 db **(94.5) n23.5** so buttery and rich. Butterscotch, too; **t24** immediately, it's the copper which strikes home: metallic, flinty and with sublime molasses and red liquorice. The spices are patient and subdued, especially as the vanillas start to leak into the mix; **f23** a wonderful gurgle of fading mixed sugars and honey. The vanilla is a constant; **b24** a wonderfully honeyed and metallic malt from when the stills were younger and at times upping the richness dramatically. A five-year-old with an attractive aloofness. *64.8%. nc ncf sc.*

**Balcones True Blue Straight 100 Proof Corn Whisky Aged At Least 24 Months** batch no. TB10018-1, bott 3-26-18 db **(94.5) n23.5 t23.5 f23.5 b24** The type of whiskey which just makes you sigh with contentment. *50% (100 proof). nc ncf.*

# DALLAS DISTILLERIES Garland, Texas.

⟪ **Herman Marshall Texas Bourbon** batch 18/12 **(90.5) n22.5** attractively nutty and soft, a succession of malty caresses balanced by a light spicy stabbing; **t23** an avalanche of natural caramel notes cascade over the palate, leaving deposits of muscovado sugar and cocoa; **f22.5** a little more bitter but the liquorice is now building up a head of steam; **b22.5** a very confident and beautifully-made Texan which never sits still. *46% (92 proof).*

## DEVILS RIVER WHISKEY San Antonio, Texas.

◇ **Devils River Barrel Strength Texas Bourbon** batch SW8325 **(87.5) n22 t21.5 f22 b22** A light, delicate Texan with the emphasis on a vanilla and almost cream soda theme. Busy spices up the salivation levels to a considerable degree, while the light oils from the uncut spirit stretch the icing sugar almost to breaking point. Nothing like so hefty as your average Texas bourbon despite the strength. And as the bottle suggests: "sin responsibly". *48.5% (117 proof).*

## FIRESTONE AND ROBERTSON DISTILLING CO LTD Fort Worth, Texas.

◇ **TX Texas Straight Bourbon** bott code: 20181214B **(91) n22.5** crisp from the grain, but tannins still make an imprint; **t23** no less crunchy on impact, the grain ensuring a steel rod of a spice. The sugars are distinctly brown and increase with dusky intensity to make quite a thick middle once the tannins have settled. Really good oils ensure an excellent chewy quality...; **f22.5** ...and length as some chocolate makes a late entrance...; **b23** a well-made, satisfying whiskey. Once you get past its unusual firmness on both nose and palate, it becomes pretty easy to start picking out the impressive layering and balance. Another quality bourbon from Texas. *45% (90 proof). Firestone and Robertson Distilling Co Ltd.*

## GARRISON BROTHERS Hye, Texas.

**Garrison Brothers Balmorhea Texas Straight Bourbon Whiskey** db **(96.5) n24 t24.5 f24; b24** The quality of their whiskey is simply ridiculous. The smaller independent distilleries from outside Kentucky are just not supposed to be this good.... If it doesn't win some kind of Whisky Bible gong, then the standard this year must be extraordinary... *57.5% (115 poof).*

◇ **Garrison Brothers Balmorhea Texas Straight Bourbon Whiskey** #1 panhandle white corn, corn harvest 2013, dist 2014, bott 2019 db **(96.5) n24** a Sea of Tranquillity as a small step of crisp grain becomes a giant step for Texas bourbon kind...; **t24** with raging spices, corn and ultra-toasty tannins, delivered at an uncompromising 115 proof, the arrival is an Ocean of Storms. Oaky liquorice and thick natural caramel. Soon a Sea of Nectar swells as the astonishing blend of corn oils, heather honey and Manuka honeys converge and intertwangle; **f24** at last settles into a Sea of Serenity as the tannins calm to the honey's soothing tune...; **b24.5** tasting this just about 50 years ago to the very minute of the first man setting foot on the Moon. He had started his journey in Texas...of course... And the whiskey? Out of this world class... *57.5% (115 poof).*

**Garrison Brothers Cowboy Bourbon Barrel Proof Aged Four Years** #1 panhandle white corn, corn harvest 2011, dist 2012, bott 2017 db **(96) n24 t24 f24 b24** These guys have proved once again that they do a mighty mean four-year-old... another improbably spectacular bourbon from Garrison Brothers. *68.5% (137 poof).*

◇ **Garrison Brothers Cowboy Bourbon Barrel Proof Aged Five Years** #1 panhandle white corn, corn harvest 2011, dist 2012 db **(95.5) n24** this liquorice and honey festooned nose has been branded with the Garrison Bothers mark...; **t24** as huge as it may be, this is so stunningly controlled. The liquorice looks as though it about to stampede when the rich caramels lasso it back under control. The heather honey and tannin mix really is something...; **f23.5** after the bucking bronco of a delivery, this settles for a quiet finale to die for caramel and vanillas...just so well weighted...; **b24** a macho bourbon at first but shows a far softer side when needed. The epitome of a balanced whiskey. *66.95% (133.9 poof).*

**Garrison Brothers Texas Straight Bourbon Whiskey Single Barrel Aged Three Years** #1 panhandle white corn, corn harvest 2011, cask no. 3433, dist 2012 db **(93.5) n23 t23.5 f23.5 b23.5** Delicious, but Garrison's whiskey at this strength always seems a fraction under par. *47% (94 poof). sc.*

◇ **Garrison Brothers Texas Straight Bourbon Whiskey Single Barrel** #1 panhandle white corn, corn harvest 2013, dist 2014, barrel no. 6103 db **(93.5) n23.5** the corn really does make a statement here. Melted honey sweetens it, but this is another softie...; **t24** wow! The controlled explosion really gets those sugars up and running! But again the corn plays a huge part here, first dampening the impact of the of the warming spices and then toning down the liquorice; **f22.5** so much vanilla, but a little bitter, too; **b23.5** delicious, yet a surprisingly muted Garrison Brothers bourbon. *47% (94 poof). sc. 63 bottles.*

**Garrison Brothers Texas Straight Bourbon Whiskey Aged Three Years** #1 panhandle white corn, corn harvest 2011, dist 2012, bott 2016 db **(88.5) n22 t22.5 f22 b22** This is the first time any whiskey by Garrison has shown the remotest hint of a wide cut. So not quite the usual brilliance, but still plenty to be getting on with... *47% (94 poof).*

◇ **Garrison Brothers Texas Straight Bourbon Whiskey 2019** #1 panhandle white corn, corn harvest 2013, dist 2014 db **(95) n23.5** a teasing aroma with plenty of room for the citrus notes to show their worth; **t24** none of the usual GB launching into space...and spice! This is all about craft and tact. The corn is evident early on the oils, but the sugars roll up in force at the same moment. Their contribution is gentle but pleasing, with light molasses leading the way before earthier, more liquorice-rich tannins make their entrance; **f23.5** so much molasses and caramel...; **b24** Garrison Bros going all soft and touchy-feely. A rare example of their bourbon offering nothing other than subtlety. 47% (94 poof).

# IRONROOT REPUBLIC DISTILLING Denison, Texas.

◈ **Ironroot Republic Harbinger Bourbon 199 Edition Aged 30 Months** db **(91) n23** such an enticing nose: soft dates with a blend of red and black liquorice. Some apple jam and acacia honey add the balance; not technically perfect, but still pushes many of the right buttons...; **t23.5** the nose...in liquid, concentrated form. Just...wow!!! **f21.5** that little technical snag on the nose resurfaces as the sugars fade. But there is enough liquorice to see us through the end; **b23** more like Iron Boot, such is the kick to this one...absolutely delicious Texas bourbon. 60.1% (120.2 proof).

◈ **Ironroot Republic Harbinger XC Straight Bourbon 2018 Edition Aged 24 Months** db **(88) n21.5** Just a slight feint present, a certain tobacco note, but the old fruit cake richness slowly seeps through; **t22.5** excellent mouth feel and oil presence. The sugars are wonderfully structured, of varying intensity, always allowing the tannins to have their drier say; salivating and with good spicy depth; **f21.5** the slight blip on the nose can be detected again. But no real damage done as the sugars and spice still have much to say; **b22.5** though the nose gets this one off to a wobbly start, its improvement is immediate and impressive. 45% (90 proof).

# KIEPERSOL DISTILLERY Tyler, Texas.

◈ **Jimmy's 100 Texas Straight Bourbon** db **(86) n21.5 t22 f22 b20.5** It is not the extra strength of alcohol that is the problem here, but the unforgiving nature of the oak. To carry this amount of tannin in a bourbon there must be balancing sugars, and most have been spent here. That said, for those looking at pure oomph and eye-watering wood, you may have found your perfect mate. 50% (100 proof).

◈ **Jimmy's Through Heroes Eyes Texas Straight Bourbon** db **(91) n22** quite a gripping encounter with the oak: the tannins drive the aroma with a lack of subtlety but to impressive effect; **t23** a deliciously fruity edge to this, almost like a peach jam and marzipan confection suddenly zapped by an explosion of spice; lovely mocha layering as it moves towards the middle; **f22.5** just more of the same with the fade moving towards a chalky vanilla, though the spices refuse to let go; **b22.5** a clean, well-made bourbon with a big spicy depth. From a distance, Jimmy's Second World War goggles look like a pair of peaches on the label...and ironically there is a delicate hint of peach in the whiskey. 45% (90 proof).

# RANGER CREEK DISTILLING, San Antonio, Texas.

◈ **Ranger Creek .36 Straight Texas Bourbon Aged For a Minimum of 2 Years** db **(91) n23** does nothing to hide a fruity, zesty kick. The tannins offer broad sweeps and depth but those lighter, gently honeyed tones cannot be silenced; a further sub-strata of ulmo honey does no harm at all; **t23** such a satisfying delivery: there are impressive oils present from the first moment coating the palate with a luscious mix of muscovado sugars and liquorice; **f22** just the vaguest tangs to the finale, though the liquorice – and a little nougat – make for a deliciously chewy depth; **b22.5** not technically perfect, but the nose and taste profile cannot be faulted, nor the subtle range of honeys at play. 48% (96 proof).

**Ranger Creek Rimfire Mesquite Smoked Texas Single Malt** batch 1 **(85) n21.5 t22 f20.5 b21.** As I have never tasted anything smoked with mesquite before – especially whiskey – I will have to guess that it is the tree of the semi-desert which is imparting a strange, mildly bitter tang on the finish. Whether it is also responsible for the enormous degree of creamed toffee, I am also not sure. Enjoyable, fascinating even...but something the ol' taste buds need a bit of acclimatising to. 43% (86 proof)

# TAHWAHKARO DISTILLERY Grapevine, Texas.

◈ **Tahwahkaro TAH Four Grain Bourbon Whiskey Aged Not Less Than 1 Year** batch 1 **(79) n19 t21 f19 b20** A very first effort from a new Texas distillery. Shows some lovely toffee apple touches and certainly not short on sugars and character. But appears to need a little extra copper contact to clean up the nose and finish as well as a slightly more precise cut off the stills. 48% (96 proof).

# TREATY OAK DISTILLING Ranch Drippings Springs, Texas.

◈ **Treaty Oak Distilling Ghost Hill Texas Bourbon Whiskey** db **(87) n22 t21 f22 b22** The good folk of Treaty Oak actually let us into the make-up of their mash bill: 57% Texas corn, 32% Texas wheat, 11% American barley (are we to infer that Texas is a separate country from

America..?) No doubt some Texans will raise a glass of this to toast that notion...They will enjoy this whiskey, but that is providing they forgive the very slight indiscretions in the distilling itself which results in a sometimes sharp, often jarring but always full-favoured bourbon. Some real cough sweet hickory depth to this, too. *47.5% (95 proof).*

## YELLOW ROSE DISTILLING Houston, Texas.

**Yellow Rose Outlaw Bourbon Whiskey Over 6 Months** batch 24 db **(87)** n20 t22.5 f23.5 **b21.** The closest whiskey in style found to this anywhere in the world is European, where chestnut casks have been deployed for finishing (at least!). A tannin-dominated whiskey, where the normal liquorice and honey tones don't really apply, though close relatives may be found. Delicious when it settles down towards the end but, overall, little balance to be had. Very different...and like a yellow rose, grows on you. *46%*

⋙ **Yellow Rose Outlaw Batch Bourbon** batch 16-33, made from 100% corn db **(94)** n24 truly glorious, subtly understated nose with a variety of impressive honey notes, ranging from heavier Manuka to a flightier lime blossom. Indeed, it is this shifting between weights and intensity of sweetness which helps this whisky stand out. The tannins look as though might threaten some serious weight, but get caught up in the sweeter nature side of things, a little maple syrup spilling into the liquorice. I could nose this all day...; t23.5 the sweetness, tempered by the layers of drying, toasty tannins, impresses with its many nuances. The lime blossom nose is underscored by a gentle fruit sub note; the corn oils ensure a delicate softness; f23 much drier with a varied degree of vanilla; some late red liquorice ensures a surprising juiciness; b23.5 Outlaw? This should be made both legal and compulsory. Really high grade corn whiskey, even if they do call it, outlawishly, bourbon. *46% (92 proof).*

## Utah
## HIGH WEST DISTILLERY Park City, Utah.

**High West Silver Oat (86)** n20 t22 f22 b22. A white whiskey which at times struggles to find all the copper it needs. But so delicious is that sweet oat – a style that has enjoyed similar success in Austria – that some of the technical aberrations are forgiven. Soft and friendly. *40%*

## Virginia
## CATOCTIN CREEK DISTILLERY Loudoun County, Virginia.

**Braddock Oak Single Barrel Rye Whisky** batch B17K1 db **(90)** n22.5 t23 f22 b22.5 It is heart-warming to see a distillery dedicated to making rye. Still the odd technical off-note but I am sure this will be corrected with time and experience. Plenty here to savour. *46% sc.*

**Catoctin Creek Cask Proof Roundstone Rye Whisky** batch B17A2, charred new oak barrels db **(88)** n21.5 t22.5 f22 b22 So much flavour. But needs to get those cuts cleaner to maximise the rye profile. *57.8% (115.6 proof). ncf.*

⋙ **Catoctin Creek Roundstone Cask Proof Edition Rye Whiskey** batch no. 18919 db **(87)** n20.5 t23.5 f21 b22 Presumably German stills at work here as that unmistakable light feint note just chips the top off the peak of the higher rye notes. Masses of charm and flavour on delivery, and buckets of spice, too. With a little cleaning up, this could be such a substantial and classy whiskey. *58% (116 proof). ncf sc. 125 bottles.*

⋙ **Catoctin Creek Roundstone Distillers Edition Rye Whiskey** batch no. 18621 db **(87.5)** n21 t22.5 f22 b22 This is cleaner than Cask Proof above. But it just its lacks muscular rye complexity and is much more happy for a dithering grain note to merge with the tannins and lingering oils to form a slightly nutty chocolate theme. *46% (92 proof). ncf sc.*

**Catoctin Creek Roundstone Rye Whisky** batch B17G1, charred new oak barrels db **(88)** n21.5 t23.5 f21 b22 The brighter end of the distillery's narrow spectrum: the rye here really is deliciously on song! *46% (92 proof). ncf.*

⋙ **Catoctin Creek Roundstone Single Barrel Virginia Rye Whiskey** batch no. 19A01 db **(88)** n19.5 those damned light feints...grrrr! t23 ah! Much more like it! A stunning mouthfeel with the oils combining beautifully with the sharper grains and softening bruyere honey harmonising with the praline...; f22.5 still that chocolate honey plays on...; b23 again, the wide cut acts as a bit of a ball and chain around this whiskey. But when it gets rolling, the salivating qualities of the crisp rye and then chocolate and honey notes are really impressive. Most enjoyable. *40% (80 proof). ncf sc.*

## COPPER FOX DISTILLERY Sperryville, Virginia.

**Copper Fox Rye Whisky Aged 21 Months** bott 18 Jan 17 db **(94.5)** n23.5 t24 f23 b24 Had this bottle on my tasting lab table ready to explore when I decided I needed to break off, rest my palate for a while and get some exercise. So, I went for a walk, and just as I reached the highest point of the remote countryside around me, I espied a fox crossing a field heading straight for me. Darker than usual, like unburnished copper. It stopped and stared at me as I stared at it, just a few yards separating us. It slunk off downhill in no great hurry and stopped with only its head showing above a hollow: again we regarded each other eye to eye for a few precious minutes. If only I had had this fabulous bottle with me.... 47.5% (95 proof).

**Wasmund's Single Malt Whisky 24 Months Old** batch no. 135 db **(89) n22 t22.5 f22 b22.5** Quite a different style from Rick Wasmund this time. 48% (96 proof). ncf.

# RESERVOIR DISTILLERY Richmond, Virginia.

**Reservoir Distillery Bourbon Whiskey** batch no. 2, bott 2017 db **(92.5) n23 t23 f23 b23.5** No shrinking violet. But nothing like so muscular as the last batch, making the most of the natural caramels. 50% (100 proof).

◇◇ **Reservoir Distillery Bourbon Whiskey** year 18, batch no. 1 db **(94.5) n23.5** huge liquorice, molasses and fig presence, all with a perfect inflection of spice....Just...wow!!! **t23.5** brilliant corn oil base, so incredibly chewy. Then those liquorice and molasses notes come flying in for an eye-watering juicy experience; still a little fruity; **f23.5** long, drying towards hickory and spice with the butterscotch and vanilla peddling in tandem; buttery finale; **b24** they have excelled: a Reservoir that is so damned good... 50% (100 proof).

**Reservoir Distillery Bourbon Whiskey 100% Corn** batch no. 18, bott 2017 db **(88.5) n22.5 t23 f21 b22** OK, this is my 595th whiskey for Bible 2019 and either I am getting punch drunk or physically drunk, though the latter – seeing as I spit every whiskey – is highly unlikely. But how can a bourbon be 100% corn? By definition that is Corn Whisky, surely.... 50% (100 proof).

**Reservoir Distillery Reserve Rye Whiskey 100% Rye** batch no. 4, bott 2017 db **(91) n23** no mistakin' this grain... any more crisp and it'll smash into a 1,000 fruity pieces...; **t23.5** the beautifully crafted fruity rye hits the palate as it does the nose: sure-footed and ridiculously crisp; **f22** the tannins and oils make matters a tad more soft and vanilla-rich, though the rye fights on proudly; **b22.5** an incorrigible rye with the grain leaking out of every pore. 50% (100 proof).

◇◇ **Reservoir Distillery Rye Whiskey** year 18, batch no. 1 db **(89) n22.5** rye rarely comes to the nose more vibrantly than this; blood orange and spices. A little underlying bitterness, too; **t23** fabulous deliver: you can sharpen your teeth on the crunchiness of this grain; the sugars are sharp as the Demerara strikes, and softer too with a lovely ulmo honey sub plot; some mysterious bitters, too; **f21** dries though more molasses. The bitterness fades slightly, but not enough; **b22** an annoying bitter note just takes the edge off what would have been a superb rye. Grrrr! 50% (100 proof).

◇◇ **Reservoir Distillery Wheat Whiskey** year 18, batch no. 1 db **(93) n24** just look at the way the golden syrup and bready spices converge, look at the oils; look at the pulsing, underlying tannins....mind blowing! **t24** a delivery to bring tears to the eyes! Magnificent weight to the oaky layering and the molasses and liquorice that is tightly interwoven; spiced just how a whisky demands to be; **f22** just a little hop-like bitterness creeps inwards the death; **b23** a top (reservoir) dog wheat whiskey. A 50% (100 proof).

**Reservoir Distillery Wheat Whiskey 100% Wheat** batch no. 2, bott 2018 db **(92) n24 t23.5 f21.5 b23** Some of the better moments are as good as a micro-distillery gets. 50% (100 proof).

# VIRGINIA DISTILLERY CO. Lovinston, Virginia.

◇◇ **Virginia Distillery Co. Courage & Conviction Prelude American Single Malt Whisky** db **(88) n22 t22.5 f21.5 b22** Everything about this youthful single malt screams "new distillery!". And what a gorgeous distillery this is, located in the stunning highlands of Virginia, close to the Blue Ridge Mountains. Even if the Scotch Whisky Association arrogantly believe that only Scotland possess such things as highlands and litigiously and ridiculously claim otherwise should any distillery in the world dare mention the fact. Virginia has them also. There's a little feint on the early nose, but this soon burns off with a little Murray Method handling, then an overriding degree of copper and light vanilla. But the nose is ostensibly buttered up new make – and from new stills. The flavour profile is rich from the wide cut but then increasingly, and deliciously, malty. Fascinating! I have seen some of what is coming further down the line. It is ,technically better than this, as you would expect from a fledgling copper pot still distillery, And promising some glorious days ahead. 46% (92 proof).

**Virginia Highland Malt Whisky Port Finished** batch no. 03 **(87) n22 t22.5 f21 b21.5** A vibrant malt, youthful and sharp in places. Exceptionally crisp and clean but sporting an unusually thin body also which means that there is a slight jarring on the grain-fruit transmission. Displays an attractive consistent sweetness until the death when a vague bitterness develops. 46% (92 proof).

American Microdistilleries

## Washington
### BAINBRIDGE ORGANIC DISTILLERS Bainbridge Island, Washington.

**Bainbridge Battle Point Organic Wheat Whiskey** db **(87.5) n21.5 t23 f21 b22** A charming if single-paced wheat whiskey with only a modest degree of the usual spice one associates with this grain type. The delivery, with its mix of silky tannins, lightened molasses and caramel is its high point by a distance; the finish has a slightly bitter edge at the death. Very well distilled without doubt. *43% (86 proof).*

**Bainbridge Battle Point Two Islands Organic Wheat Whiskey** Islay cask db **(95) n23.5 t24 f23.5 b24** Now the Japanese cask (below) may not work quite as had been hoped, but this certainly does! Has to be one of the surprise packages of the year. An exercise in poise and balance: just so effortlessly and gracefully beautiful. *43% (86 proof).*

**Bainbridge Yama American Single Grain Barley Whiskey** Mizunara Japanese oak cask db **(87) n21 t23 f21 b22** Before tasting this, in my mind's eye I tried to picture what was to come. I settled on a sweet and spicy number bursting out all over the palate. Well, it wasn't quite like that: the sugars light and profound early on and the spices peak modestly and then buzz lightly. Elsewhere, though, it is if the grain and the tannin have cancelled each other out a little. *45% (90 proof).*

### CADÉE DISTILLERY Clinton, Washington.

**Cadée Distillery Cascadia Rye Whiskey** finished in Port barrels db **(87) n21.5 t23 f21 b21.5.** Works quite well. A vaguely wide cut does ramp up the oils. But the rye has enough crystalline firmness to cut through the fruit. Think this pretty high quality rye actually deserves better than being masked by the Port which, though clean and juicy, has a flattening effect. *43.5% (87 proof)*

**Cadée Distillery Deceptivus Bourbon Whiskey** finished in Port barrels db **(87) n21 t22 f22.5 b22.** The sweet corn and the fruit combine to form a formidable chewiness. Attractive with some lovely ulmo honey also. The spiced chocolate fruit and vague nougat really does ensure an entertaining finale. *42.5% (85 proof).*

**Cadée Distillery Medusa** db **(71) n18 t18 f17 b18** Stone me! A seriously hair-raising experience. Curiously flat and what notes it does offer are not particularly attractive. *40%.*

**Cadée Distillery Rye Whiskey (93) n23.5** classic intense rye, full of ginger and Demerara sugars. Light spice touches the vanilla and the grainy fruity crispness; **t23** such an attractive mix of crisp rye and vanilla wafer; **f23.5** brilliant spice explosion and a long, juicy grain fade; **b23** have to admit, when I tasted this a rye type crossed my mind: then I looked at the label and spotted where it was actually made.... *42% (84 proof).*

### CHAMBERS BAY DISTILLERY University Place, Washington.

**Greenhorn Bourbon** aged for a minimum of 1 year, batch 1, bott 13 Dec 15 db **(74.5) n18.5 t21 f17 b18.** A sharp, eye-watering experience where an interesting fermentation has given the distiller little room for manoeuvre. *44% (88 proof)*

### COPPERWORKS Seattle, Washington.

**Copperworks American Single Malt Whiskey Release No. 001 Aged 30 Months** new American oak casks db **(91) n23 t22.5 f22.5 b23** Congratulations! An impressive first bottling for a new distillery in Seattle. Going along the lines of Stranahan Distillery, they are maturing their single malt in virgin American oak. This is a lighter, far less in-your-face version. Instead elegance appears to be the goal. Well, it has been achieved. *52% (104 proof). 1,530 bottles.*

**Copperworks American Single Malt Whiskey Release No. 002 Aged 30 Months** new American oak casks db **(95) n24 t23.5 f23 b24** A higher part of the warehouse? More summer months within the 30? Somehow Copperwork has raised the game considerably with much broader and enveloping malt which has flourished in the extra oak. A three course single malt if ever there was one...! *53% (106 proof). 1,753 bottles.*

**Copperworks American Single Malt Whiskey Release No. 003 Aged 34 Months** new American oak casks db **(92.5) n24 t23.5 f22 b23** The closest style to a rye I have ever found a single malt barley. Phenomenal...! *52% (104 proof). 1,559 bottles.*

**Copperworks American Single Malt Whiskey Release No. 004 Aged 31 Months** cask no. 44, new American oak cask db **(88.5) n22 t22 f22.5 b22** A very gin-like feel to this which casts a heavy shadow over the whiskey character. May be wrong, but suspect some gin was bottled not long before this whiskey was using some of the same equipment. *61.75% (123.5 proof). 219 bottles.*

**Copperworks American Single Malt Whiskey Release No. 005 Aged 33 Months** new American oak casks, pale malt recipe db **(90.5) n22.5** intense malt and so beautifully clean. Gentle Brazilian biscuit flour, then a light oaky and apple-y undercurrent; **t22** busy and fizzing malt with plenty of grist and sappy sugars intertwangling; **f23** spices at play as the toastiness increases: classic crossover between malt and bourbon styles with late burnt fudge; **b22.5** some clever sugars at play here. *50% (100 proof). 1,563 bottles.*

**Copperworks American Single Malt Whiskey Release No. 006 Aged 24 Months** new American oak & oloroso sherry casks, five malt recipe db **(89) n23 t22 f22 b22** A surprisingly bitter fellow. I know they don't have hops here, but there is a certain hint of hop throughout. Very curious. *47.5% (95 proof). 2,037 bottles.*

**Copperworks American Single Malt Whiskey Release No. 007 Aged 35 Months** new American oak cask, cask no. 53, five malt recipe db **(89) n22.5 t23 f21.5 b22** Could this be the world's first chewing gum whiskey? It is certainly the mintiest! *59% (118 proof). sc. 210 bottles.*

**Copperworks American Single Malt Whiskey Release No. 008 Aged 35 Months** new American oak cask, cask no. 59, five malt recipe db **(89.5) n23 t23 f21 b22.5** No doubts about this being a malt whiskey: good grief...! *58.85% (117.7 proof). sc. 215 bottles.*

**Copperworks American Single Malt Whiskey Release No. 009 Aged 40 Months** new American oak cask, cask no. 43, five malt recipe db **(86.5) n21 t23.5 f20.5 b21.5** It has been a few years since I last rode, but this is like being on a horse determined to make the jumps: you grip on tight (with knees and everything else) and let it enjoy the course. The highest hurdle is in delivery with a plethora of dark sugars. But a few hurdles are dislodged with that house hop-like bitterness which seems starker still against the sugars. *62.5% (125 proof). sc. 122 bottles.*

**Copperworks American Single Malt Whiskey Release No. 010 Aged 39 Months** new American oak casks, five malt & pale malt recipe db **(88) n21.5 t23 f21.5 b22** So, so odd. The house style appears to have a fruity, languid hop note. But hops aren't used. I am bewildered... *52.5% (105 proof). 1,380 bottles.*

**Copperworks American Single Malt Whiskey Release No. 011 Aged 32 Months** new American oak & sherry oloroso casks, five malt & pale malt recipe db **(87) n21 t22.5 f21.5 b21.5** The lush fruit dulls the majority of that irritating bitterness, but not all. Also, the sugars are welcome but need toning down. A malt that keeps threatening to hit the high notes, but then goes off key. *49% (98 proof). 1,460 bottles.*

◇ **Copperworks American Single Malt Whiskey Release No. 012 Aged 33 Months** new American oak, five malt & pale malt recipe db **(86.5) n21.5 t22 f21.5 b21.5** I really didn't have to look at the distillery to know who it was: Copperworks! I still get this curious cascade hop note on both on nose and delivery. Not big, more a shadow, but there; even though I was told there are no hops in use. So, so strange! Combine that with the sweet cream toffee on delivery and you have the unique fingerprint of Copperworks. *48% (96 proof). 1,410 bottles.*

◇ **Copperworks American Single Malt Whiskey Release No. 013 Aged 30 Months** new American oak, five malt & pale malt recipe db **(87.5) n22 t22 f21.5 b22** Soft and sensual from nose to tail, again the accent is on toffee. Still that mystery bitterness creeps around. But this is a very relaxed malt. *51% (102 proof). 1,740 bottles.*

◇ **Copperworks American Single Malt Whiskey Release No. 014 Aged 38 Months Wine Barrel Select** new American oak, cask no. 102, five malt recipe db **(91.5) n22.5** a firm, clean, confident grapeyness fills the glass, with a measured sweetness balancing out the sharper fruit; **t23.5** delightfully succulent on delivery! That sharpness on the nose is multiplied several times here, like under-ripe gooseberries, though it battles through the house toffee style to make its mark; **f22.5** impressive, warming spice; **b23** what a treat that was! The mystery house bitterness is all but eradicated; while there a fruit pastille quality to the sweetness. *57.1% (114.2 proof). sc. 224 bottles.*

◇ **Copperworks American Single Malt Whiskey Release No. 015 Aged 36 Months** new American oak, cask no. 115, five malt recipe db **(86.5) n22 t21.5 f21.5 b21.5** Far less fruit influence that Release 14, so the toffee and house bitterness make a much bigger stand. Chewy and well-weighted. *57.7% (115.4 proof). sc. 222 bottles.*

◇ **Copperworks American Single Malt Whiskey Release No. 016 Aged 38 Months** new French oak, cask no. 97, five malt recipe db **(92) n23** macho tannins round up some superb orange peel notes, too. The Demerara sugars add an extra edge and crunchiness; **t23.5** big, beautifully succulent and chewy with the toffee now having a toasty feel; a little molasses seeps into the mix. The house hoppy-style bitterness wanders into focus at the midpoint, but is immediately overshadowed by milky chocolate; **f22.5** the cocoa tones get broader and intensify; **b23** they have now added a chocolate note to their repertoire, and it suits them well. Love whiskey. *58.9% (117.8 proof). sc. 200 bottles.*

# DRY FLY DISTILLING Spokane, Washington.

**Dry Fly Bourbon 101 (88) n21.5 t23 f21.5 b22.** A well made bourbon which, with a bit of extra complexity, would stand above some of its Kentucky colleagues. *50.5%*

**Dry Fly Cask Strength Straight Wheat Whiskey (94.5) n23 t24 f23.5 b24** Quite beautiful whiskey. One every whisky lover should experience to further their understanding of this multi-faceted spirit. *60%*

**Dry Fly Port Finish Wheat Whiskey (89) n22 t23 f22 b22.** If you mixed whiskey and jam you might end up with this little charmer. *50% (100 proof)*

**Dry Fly Straight Triticale Rye Wheat Hybrid (86) n22 t22 f21 b21.** Pleasant and easy going. But very surprising degree of natural caramels fill in the gaps and shaves off the higher notes expected from the rye. *44% (88 proof)*

**Dry Fly Washington Wheat Whiskey (89) n22 t22 f22.5 b22.5.** Hugely impressive, well weighted and balanced and a much better use of wheat than bread, for instance... *40%*

# WESTLAND DISTILLERY Seattle, Washington.

**Westland American Single Malt Garryana 2/1** bott 2017 db **(89.5) n23 t22 f22 b22** This second bottling proves Westland have created a universally unique whisky style, though the cut from the still is a little generous. *50% nc ncf.*

**Westland American Single Malt Peat Week** db **(92) n23 t23.5 f22.5 b23** A distillery which does understated smoky whiskey rather well... *50% nc ncf.*

**Westland American Single Malt Winter 2016** db **(88) n22 t22.5 f21.5 b22** A straight up and down maltfest. *50% nc ncf.*

⬦ **Westland Distillery** cask no. 922 db **(93) n22.5 t24 f23 b23.5** A must grape style sharpness to this on the nose and a much sweeter grist and muscovado sugar on delivery, with everything delivered in stark and concentrated form. Balances out beautifully and helped, like most Westland whiskeys, with a rich textured mouth feel to die for. *61.2% (122.4 proof). sc*

⬦ **Westland Distillery** cask no. 4274 db **(94) n23 t24 f23 b24** Breathtaking use of tannin here. The oak has been pulled and stretched into different shapes, weights and flavours. But it is the praline depth which wins your heart, accompanied by lychee. The last of the four Westlands I tasted for the 2020 Bible and if an American micro has sent me four better and more varied whiskeys on average, then they have escaped my mind. *49.5% (99 proof). sc*

**Westland Peat Week 4th Year** db **(94) n23** impressive for the evenness of the smoke: it doesn't try to be dramatically peaty, instead allowing just as much hickory to take centre stage as peat; **t24** fabulously soft, the light oils spread the smoke far and wide. A brilliant, melt-in-the-mouth gristy, sugary quality which underlines just how clean the distillate was; **f23** long, now with a touch of liquorice and toasted treacle to keep the sweetness going as the drier, biscuity vanillins arrive; **b24** one of the best smoke signals to come out of Washington State for a very long time...and surely destined for consumption at The Old Highland Stillhouse in Oregon City! *54.4% (108.8 proof).*

⬦ **Westland Distillery Peat Week Fifth Annual Edition** db **(95) n23.5 t24 f23.5 b24** My tasting notes are just about identical to their Fourth Annual Edition. Except this has just a little more stand-alone phenol; and some extra citrus and even raspberry jam has got into the mix. Bravo! *50% (100 proof). nc ncf.*

⬦ **Westland Distillery Reverie fig. 1** db **(91) n22.5 t23.5 f22 b23** A beautifully made malt that has no second thoughts about fully embracing the fruitier side of life. Some lovely maple syrup and spice fills the gaps. Salivating and with a top-notch mouth feel throughout. *50% (100 proof). nc ncf. Distillery Exclusive.*

# WOODINVILLE WHISKEY CO. Woodinville, Washington.

**Woodinville Straight 100% Rye Whiskey** db **(95) n24 t23.5 f23.5 b24** /rye distilling and maturation to a very high standard, especially for a micro distillery. *45% (90 proof).*

**Woodinville Straight Bourbon Whiskey** db **(93) n24 t23.5 f22.5 b23** A few years back I highlighted this then fledgling distillery as one to watch. This latest, magnificent bottling alongside its sister rye shows you exactly why. What a joy! *45% (90 proof).*

# Wyoming
# WYOMING WHISKEY Kirby, Wyoming.

**Wyoming Whiskey Double Cask Straight Bourbon Whiskey** finished in sherry casks db **(87.5) n23 t22 f21 b21.5** Kind of leaves me scratching my head, this. Yes, the grape infusion is clean and profound, suffering not an atom of the sulphur pollution which wrecks so much scotch. But this is bourbon – which needs unsullied virgin oak. And here we get virtually no meaningful bourbon contribution but masses of delicious grape. Yes, some glorious fruit notes, but this needs more balance so the bourbon has a telling say. *50% (100 proof).*

**Wyoming Whiskey Single Barrel** barrel no. 1840 db **(87) n22 t22 f21 b22** If you like your whiskey to have a big cream caramel and ulmo honey charge, then this guy is for you. Doesn't quite gel towards the end, though. *44% (88 proof).*

**Wyoming Whiskey Small Batch** batch no. 42 db **(86.5) n22 t22.5 f20.5 b21.5** Another Wyoming which has so much going for it but (annoyingly!) falters at the final step towards the finale. Here the accent is on the vanilla and a rich, spicy fruity suet pudding middle. Hard not to like. *44% (88 proof).*

**Wyoming Whiskey Outryder** db **(88.5)** n22.5 t22.5 f21.5 b22 Perhaps should be called Easy Rider, as this is as gentle as it gets... *50% (100 proof).*

# American/Kentucky Whiskey Blends

**Ancient Age Preferred** (73) n16.5 t19 f19.5 b18. A marginal improvement thanks mainly to a re-worked ripe corn-sweet delivery and the cocoa-rich finish. But still preferred, one assumes, by those who probably don't care how good this distillery's whisky can be... *40%*

⟐ **Ancient Age Preferred Blended Whiskey** bott code: L181271517082 **(70)** n18 t19 f16 b17 Remains thin gruel for those looking for the richness of an Ancient Age bourbon. But this is a blend, and a very ordinary one at that. The nose has improved a tad, but the finish falls apart more than it once did. 40% (80 proof).

**Beam's Eight Star** (69.5) n17 t18 f17 b17.5. If you don't expect too much it won't let you down. *40%*

**Bellows** (67) n17 t17.5 f16 b16.5 Just too thin. *40%*

**Calvert's Extra** (79) n19 t20 f20 b20. Sweet and mega-toffeed. Just creaking with caramel but extra marks for the late spice. *40%*

**Carstair's White Seal** (72) n16.5 t18.5 f19.5 b17.5 Possibly the cleanest blend about even offering a cocoa tang on the finale. Pleasant. *40%*

⟐ **Heaven's Door Double Whiskey** bott code: 2018/05/121045 **(90)** n23.5 an attractive vibrancy to the busy small grains; classic light liquorice, too; t22.5 sugars are visible on delivery but politely gagged by the vanilla rich tannin; f22 spiced custard powder; b22 does all the right things and with minimum fuss! *50% (100 proof).*

**High West American Prairie Bourbon** batch no. 17F02 **(92.5)** n23 though blended, this brand does favour that sweet hickory note in its make-up and it comes though like a train here; t23 a camp coffee and liquorice delivery, with spices kicking in with intent; the sugars, dark, buttery and toasty, hang suspended in the oils; f23 long with a serious vanilla and butterscotch thread; the tannins have no intention of letting go; b23.5 this is big and sweet with massive chewability. *46% (92 proof). nc ncf. Blend of straight bourbon whiskies.*

**High West Campfire** batch no. 17F29 **(95.5)** n24 a Fisherman's Friend cough sweet-Bowmore-style smokiness envelops the leading, crisp rye notes. Liquorice and hickory link to a buttery saltiness; t24 you'll find yourself chewing this until your jaw aches... Seriously fat in part, but the star turn is the myriad sugar tones ranging from delicate ulmo honey to an earthier molasses depth; the smoke looks down serenely, filling in any gaps when required; f23.5 that buttery saltiness returns as the rye and smoke linger; b24 like something straight out of my blending lab! Beautifully and skilfully constructed...! And proves that the USA and Britain can work together despite Britain's feeble Prime Minister May's duplicity over Europe. *46% (92 proof). nc ncf. Straight rye whiskey, straight bourbon whiskey, blended malt Scotch whiskey.*

**High West Double Rye** batch no. 18A11 **(96)** n24 just adore that intensity to the grain: as fruity and muscovado-rich as it gets. The cutglass crispness of the rye feels as though it could shatter at any moment; t24 this is big...very big...!! A blend of ulmo honey, butter and molten muscovado soon explodes into glorious rye concentrate; f23.5 so much happening here: the fade allows the cinnamon and mint easier access while the spices show commendable restraint, despite their obvious power; b24.5 complex and bang on the money: one of the most intense and true ryes on the market. *46% (92 proof). nc ncf. Blend of straight rye whiskies.*

**High West Rendezvous Rye** batch no. 17F16 **(93)** n24 a sublime nose: complex with the rye pitching it at different degrees of sharpness and intensity, seemingly a mix of malted and unmalted, the latter magnifying the the sharper edges. Fruity with distinct cinnamon and orange peel, mint and lavender; t23 delightfully two-toned: excellent oils mixing it with the flintier aspects of the grain; f23 the oak bites in at last to deliver a slight bitterness but the muscovado and demerara sugars counter perfectly. Late hickory and cinnamon; b23 a rye-lovers dream. *46% (92 pro of). nc ncf. Blend of straight rye whiskies.*

**Kentucky Dale** (64) n16 t17 f15 b16. Thin and spineless, though soft and decently sweet on delivery. The grain spirit completely dominates. *40%*

**Kessler** (84.5) n20 t21 f22 b21.5. "Smooth As Silk" claims the label. And the boast is supported by what is in the bottle: a real toffee-mocha charmer with a chewy, spicy depth. *40%*

⟐ **Lewis & Clark American Whiskey** bott 30 Aug 18, bott code: L1656 003075 **(85.5)** n21 t21 f22 b21.5 A silky Toffee Fest. Thoroughly attractive and enjoyable in its own way, but don't expect any great complexity. *40% (80 proof). BBC Spirits.*

**Little Book Blended Straight Whiskey** (87.5) n22 t22.5 f21 b22 A silky, sweet whiskey with a small grain sharpness that keeps the taste buds salivating. Even at this strength, easy, semi-complex and very pleasant drinking with the accent on a maple syrup sweetness. Whiskey snobs will turn their noses up at this at their peril. *60.24% (120.48 proof).*

**Little Book Chapter 02: Noe Simple Task Blended Straight Whiskey** (91) n22.5 t23 f22.5 b23 Very distinctive Beam-like elements which is taking blended American whiskey into higher, more rarified atmosphere. *60.55% (121.1 proof).*

⚜ **Louisville Kentucky Style Blended Bourbon** bott code: 1L25080625 **(87) n**21 **t**22 **f**22 **b**22 Pleasant, sweet, enticing and exceptionally soft. Lots of Demerara sugars working in tandem with the liquorice and spice. Simple but very attractive. *40%. Selected for Asda.*

⚜ **Mulholland Distilling American Whiskey** (87.5) **n**21.5 **t**22.5 **f**21.5 **b**22 Fat, exceptionally sweet and a little monotone. That said, has a kick in the right place and a lovely chewing whiskey. Just needs a tidy up at the finish, a change in flavour stance, a bit of complexity... And, dare I say it? A little drive... *50% (100 proof).*

**Sunny Brook** (79.5) **n**20 **t**21 **f**19 **b**19.5. An entirely agreeable blend with toffee and lightly oiled nuts. Plus a sunny disposition... *40%*

⚜ **Whisky Jewbilee Straight Rye 5 Years and Straight Bourbon 12 Years** (94.5) **n**23.5 truly fabulous. The rye is crisp and punchy, just seething with the grain's fruit and spice double whammy; a subplot of even honey appears to represent good aged bourbon; **t**23.5 as on the nose, the spices help shape the whisky from the first moment but for every busy nip there is also a upping of the juiciness. Rye dominant – and what rye! – but again mirroring the nose, the bourbon element creates its own honeyed depth, balancing matters brilliantly; **f**23.5 outstanding oils make sure this one runs and runs, the dark sugars forming along with a little chocolate and ever-intensifying spices; so unusual to have both a crisp yet yielding finale; **b**24 both whiskies comes from the Midwest Grain's fabled Lawrenceburg Indiana distillery which makes the only rye in the US able to stand proud against Buffalo Trace. A rye intense but very unusual whisky which cannot be faulted in any way...well, so few bottles being available apart...; *53% (106 proof). Jewish Whisky Company. 280 Bottles*

⚜ **Widow Jane Aged 10 Years** batch no. 60, bott 2018 db **(94) n**23 firm, crusty grain: sharp, busy, spicy and with a gentle swirl of heather honey; **t**24 just as salivating on delivery as the nose hinted at: a plethora of dark, warming sugars with molaWWses leading the way. Sublime mouth feel, the oils just sticky enough for the chocolate to embrace the natural burnt toffees; **f**23.5 long, with spices buzzing contentedly into the drier tannin; **b**23.5 this is one widow that has been married beautifully..... *45.5% (91 proof). ncf. Blend of straight bourbon whiskies.*

## Straight Malt Whiskey

**Parker's Heritage Collection Kentucky Straight Malt Whiskey Aged 8 Years** db **(93) n**23 **t**23.5 **f**23 **b**23.5 From the distillery which brought you wheat whisky, now comes malt – Kentucky style. As delicious as it is fascinating. *54% (108 proof)*

## Whiskey Distilled From Bourbon Mash

**Angels Envy Bourbon Finished in Port Barrels** (84) **n**20 **t**22 **f**21 **b**21. Almost like a chocolate raisin candy and fruitcake. Silky textured and juicy. *43.3% (86.6 proof)*

## Whiskey Distilled From Rye Mash

**Angels Envy Rye Finished in Caribbean Rum Casks** (78) **n**18.5 **t**20.5 **f**20 **b**19 Frankly, I was hardly expecting to have any teeth left after this sample. The hardest, most crisp of all whiskeys is rye. And if you want to give any whisk(e)y an extra degree of exoskeleton, then just finish it in a rum cask. And here we have the two together : yikes! Some twenty years ago I gave then Jack Daniel's blender Lincoln Henderson his first-ever taste of peated whisky: a Laphroaig. He hated it! I think he's waited a long time to return the compliment by showing me a style I did not know could exist. Beyond fascinating. Weird, even - hence the full tasting notes. One for the ladies with this liqueur-style smoothie. *50%.*

## White Dog

**Buffalo Trace White Dog Mash #1** (94) **n**23 **t**24 **f**23 **b**24 This is the DNA of Buffalo Trace and it is not difficult to see why it goes on to make a bourbon that challenges al the world's whiskeys. You cannot be a shrinking violet to withstand the onslaught of virgin oak, and here the full muscular framework is exposed. Oddly enough, there is a little less copper now than when I first tasted the new spirit – the White Dog – some 25 years ago. But the sublime balance of the grains themselves – offering a sweetness as vague as da Vinci smile – sits beautifully with the late chocolate mousse finale. *62.5% (125 proof).*

⚜ **Buffalo Trace White Dog Mash #1** bott code: L181550112 **(94) n**23 **t**24 **f**23 **b**24 Almost exactly as above: no change, other than being slightly more salivating. But talk about consistent...! *57% (114 proof).*

⚜ **Buffalo Trace White Dog Rye Mash** bott code: L180080113 **(95.5) n**23 **t**24.5 **f**24 **b**24 Just so consistent by comparison to the last bottling, though half a mark off for a slight drop in copper contact. If I was ever to be converted to regularly imbibing white spirits, I would drink this – and, for the odd utopian experience, blend of this and the new make from Glen Grant in Scotland. Get those proportions right and this little gin revolution will be a thing of the past...

Which reminds me: blending the different Buffalo Trace White Dogs can be a thing of endless fun, and occasional surprises, too...(and something I concocted from those here has already outscored the individual bottlings...!) *57% (114 proof).*

**Buffalo Trace White Dog Rye Mash (96) n23.5 t24.5 f24 b24** When the Russians and Finns created their version of whisky back in the day, they distilled from rye...but just never got round to putting it in a barrel. They called it vodka. Find a time machine on ebay and head back into the past – then offer those same people this. Doubtless you will be treated to the finest cut of elk. For the rye almost three dimensional in its crisp, ever-building enormity. Absolutely faultless white dog. Or should that be Siberian Husky....? *62.5% (125 proof).*

**Buffalo Trace White Dog Wheated Mash (94.5) n23 t24 f23.5 b24** Wheated bourbon tends to have a spicier kick than rye mash bourbon...and this sticks to the script. Rich, borderline lush and chewy. Every box ticked and a few more thrown in for good measure. *57% (114 proof).*

✥ **Buffalo Trace White Dog Wheated Mash** bott 9065011647M **(94.5) n22.5 t24 f24 b24** An earthier, oilier version with the spices taking their time to arrive but do so at exactly the same moment the sugars begin to open up. A little more chocolate than before, also. *57% (114 proof).*

# Other American Whiskey

**Basil Hayden's Two by Two Rye (95) n23.5 t23.5 f24 b24** A beautiful blend. I remember some 20 years ago or so asking the good people of Jim Beam why they didn't produce a blend of their fabulous ryes and bourbon and their answer was three fold: they didn't have enough rye, it wasn't a traditional or acceptable whiskey category. And they didn't think anyone would drink it. Well, having upped rye production they now can do this. And so beautiful is it, people would be mugs to turn their back on this massively flavoured whiskey as something inferior. *40% (80 proof). Kentucky Straight Rye whiskies blended with Kentucky Straight Bourbon whiskies.*

**Cascade Blonde American Whiskey** bott code: L8081ZX222 1458 **(85.5) n22 t22 f20.5 b21** An exceptionally easy ride, soft and avoiding any big flavours without ever lacking character. The thin finish apart, abounds with tannin and roasty promise. *40% (80 proof).*

**Early Times Kentucky Whisky** bott code: A027161143 3125362 **(89) n22.5 t22.5 f21.5 b22.5** The fact they are using what they term on the label as "reused cooperage" means this is Kentucky Whisky as opposed to Kentucky Bourbon, which requires virgin oak (and before you ask, YES, bourbon is a whisky...!). So, while may not be a mighty fine Kentucky bourbon, brimming as it is with all kinds of liquorice and molasses this is still mighty fine Kentucky whisky...!! *40% (80 proof).*

✥ **Heaven's Door Straight Rye Whiskey** finished in Vosges oak barrels, bott code: 2019/19/11172 **(87.5) n22 t23 f21 b21.5** Not entirely sure what the point was of using these secondary barrels for maturation. The visible rye seems very high class. But there is dumbing down on both nose and palate with more seemingly taken away than added late on. Even so, some attractive moments, especially when the rye goes into super-fruity mode. *46% (92 proof)*

**Isaac Bowman Straight Bourbon Whiskey Port Barrel Finished** bott code: L173050513:42B 168 db **(81) n21 t21 f20 b20** Pleasant in its own way, I s'pose. But, after the sweet fruit, flatter than your average witch's tit. If God had really wanted this kind of whiskey he would have planted Virginia in Portugal. *46% (92 proof).*

✥ **Isaac Bowman Straight Bourbon Finished in Port Barrels** bott code: L190390513 db **(90) n22.5** hefty and fruity there is a distinctive sugar candy feel to this; **t23** the silky mouthfeel is backed by a salivating delivery of plummy notes, punctuated a little by a rye-style sharpness to the sugars. Then all falls silent as a huge dollop of vanilla ice cream with fruit sauce arrives...; **f22** anyone remember sherry trifles from the 1970s...? **b22.5** interesting that when Scotch, for instance, is finished in Port, there is a definite pinkish tinge to the final whisky. Not here, though: just an extra degree of richness to the gold. An attractive whisky, amazingly sensual and soft throughout, which loses its bourbon character from the very first sniff. The fact the wine cask is clean as a nut helps enormously. *46% (92 proof).*

**James E. Pepper 1776 Straight Rye Whiskey PX Sherry Finish** batch no. PX3 **(72.5) n18.5 t19 f17 b18** Fails on so many levels, hard to know where to begin. Flat and overly sweet in part, overly bitter in others. When will this PX finish insanity end? At least it was sulphur free.... *50% (100 proof). ncf.*

✥ **Jim Beam Bourbon Finished in PX Sherry Casks Distiller's Masterpiece** db **(66.5) n21.5 t19 f12 b14** An uncompromising dullard of a whiskey with virtually no personality once we get past the one third mark: I'm not sure this even makes it as far as half way. A serious waste of good bourbon, as Jim Beam makes some of the finest in the world without question. But why they should ruin it by putting it in a PX cask is entirely beyond me. Do they not understand that the quality of Scotch whisky has often been compromised by the use of an intensely sweet sherry barrel which allows the OTT sugars to neutralise the complexity of a spirit by gaudily filling in the gaps? It does the same nullifying job here, alas. Certainly it gives it a fruity, plummy, spicy lift on the nose that is limited but not at all unpleasant.

And the initial arrival mirrors this big spice and fruit thrust, and even maybe a little rye may come into play. Then after that...tumbleweed. Just a flat line of a whiskey: it is dead. Bereft of life. It is an ex-bourbon. The Scots have been shooting themselves in the foot using these casks for a while, giving bourbon a significant advantage over them. Why Kentuckians would want to emulate their failures defeats me, especially when they have their rivals on the back foot. And, to cap it all...there is a distinct, uncomfortable, frankly unpleasant, dirty buzz of sulphur on the finish...another often fatal weakness of sherry-matured Scotch. A dreadful, flawed finish that haunts you for a long time afterwards, A special award for the most self-defeating nonsensical Kentucky whiskey of the year, surely. And please, may this be an end of this sherry finish nonsense, the glutinous, whiskey-killing PX in particular. NB: Over an hour after having tasted this my taste buds have still not sufficiently recovered to carry on working, so my day's tasting has come to an end. If only the industry could pull itself away from the worthless, navel-gazing hype. And think, instead, what past generations of lifetime bourbon distillers would have done: the Beams, the Lees, the Blantons, the Taylors: they saw greatness in American whiskey with virgin oak. Suddenly, the transitory marketing people in their world of hype and instant experts know better. Yeah. Right... *50% (100 proof).*

**Jim Beam Double Oak** db **(86) n22 t22.5 f20.5 b21.** Attractive, caramel-soaked whiskey with a little too much fade after a big spice and liquorice delivery. *43%*

**Knob Creek Smoked Maple (35) n10 t10 f10 b5.** How can this be called a " Kentucky straight bourbon"? What is straight about this? Am I missing something here? About 98% closer to maple syrup than bourbon, this would make a pleasant spread on your breakfast toast. It may be whiskey, Jim (Beam), but not as we know it. *45% (90 proof)*

◈ **Legent Kentucky Straight Bourbon Partially Finished in Wine and Sherry Casks (88.5) n23** have you ever poured high grade bourbon into a rich fruitcake, left it overnight and smelt it the next morning? I have. And this is the closest whiskey I have ever encountered which matches: very close indeed! A moist aroma, much flatter than you will find in a top bourbon but the ulmo honey and muscovado sugars do a damn fine job here...; **t23.5** an immediately soft and sensuous landing: the taste buds are kissed on impact rather than confronted. The grains only start to make an impression about the sixth or seventh flavour wave in, but when they do there is a busying around the fruit, a million little strikes...then caresses; **f20** ah...so often with sherry/wine finishes: the weak point. Just a little bit too much stray bitterness undoes the elegance of before. It is a nagging, disappointing note...; **b22** "east is east and west is west and never the twain shall meet"...well, so wrote my former fellow Savilian, Rudyard Kipling. And I think in the same poem he gave us "a gift for a gift". Well here there has been a gift for a gift and the twain have met, for this is a joint creation by Fred Noe of Jim Beam and Shinji Fukuyo, chief blender at Suntory, Japan. A highly attractive piece, let down very slightly by a finishing note you will never find at Suntory, but no stranger to sherry or wine casks. It certainly isn't bourbon, but who cares? There are some moments even Kipling might have struggled to find the words for... *47% (94 proof).*

**Michter's No. 1 American Whiskey (84.5) n21 t21.5 f21 b21.** Sugar-coated, oily and easy going. About as friendly as any whiskey you'll find this year *41.7%*

**Michter's No. 1 Sour Mash (86) n22 t22 f21 b21.** A pleasant, clean, light whiskey: perhaps too clean at times. Good mocha throughout, with the accent on the coffee. *43%*

◈ **Michter's Toasted Barrel Finish Kentucky Straight Bourbon** batch no. 18H1191 **(89) n22** a mix of red liquorice and caramel; **t22.5** lovely sugary delivery with plenty of Demerara ensuring a degree of crisp juiciness; the vanillas move towards a toasted toffee note; **f22** beautiful cream toffee; **b22.5** as is so often the case, the extra toasting has resulted in a massive dollop of natural caramels which levels slightly the peaks and troughs. Attractive, but quite restrained. *45.7% (91.4 proof).*

◈ **Micther's Toasted Barrel Finish Kentucky Straight Bourbon** batch no. 18H1193, bott code: A182751193 **(92.5) n23** a serious oaky presence. The tannins are somewhere between being sappy and decidedly charcoal grilled; **t23.5** full on corn oil, but laced with maple syrup and molasses; **f23** fabulous spices hit the spot, then layers of caramel and toasty molasses; **b23** a much perkier and altogether more entertaining bottling than 1191, making far better use of both corn and sugars. *45.7% (91.4 proof).*

◈ **Micther's Toasted Barrel Finish Kentucky Straight Rye batch** no. 18H1329, bott code: A182471329 **(89.5) n22** so much molasses...! **t23** toasty sugars explode all over the palate, along with the peppery spices. The rye passes by like a bystander... Prepare to wipe a tear from the eye... this is eye-watering fayre...! **f22** still spicy with a little marzipan and vanilla. The rye has vanished...; **b22.5** toasted barrel often equates to greater sugar. And that's what we have here – seemingly to the detriment of the rye. Pleasant but, for rye, a little on the dull side. *54.7% (1094 proof).*

◈ **Minor Case Straight Rye Whiskey Aged 24 Months** sherry cask finished **(84.5) n22 t23.5 f19 b20** A confusing label: this is not straight rye, as the sherry finish puts paid to that notion. What a great whiskey this would have been in bourbon cask: why anyone wants to hide its beauty away behind a sherry cask absolutely defeats me. The rye itself is world class for a brief moment on delivery. The tangy, flat finale is a bit of a tragedy. *40% (80 proof). Bottled by Limestone Branch Distilling Co.*

◇◇ **Parker's Heritage Collection 12th Edition Aged 7 Years** bourbon finished in orange Curacao barrels db **(72)** n18 t19 f17 b18 Oh, dear. It's whisky, Jim; but not as we know it... *55% (110 proof).*

◇◇ **Sagamore Spirit Cognac Finish** batch no. 1A **(86.5)** n22.5 t22 f21 b21 The stupendous marzipan on the nose and heather honey delivery apart, too much on the hard, bitter and unyielding side. *52.5% (105 proof).*

◇◇ **Sagamore Spirit Sagamore Reserve Moscatel Barrel Finished Whiskey** batch no. 1A **(91.5)** n23 a slight softening ulmo honey note on the otherwise tight, spicy vanilla and grain; t23.5 clean delivery which immediately lifts off into full salivating mode. Some charming liquorice and vanilla coats the palate, but merely as an undercoat before the fruit us applied as a gloss; f22 long fade of boiled fruit candy; b23 pretty well balanced with no flavour cul-de-sacs. *50.6% (101.2 proof).*

◇◇ **Sagamore Spirit Port Finish** batch no. 1C **(90.5)** n23.5 the rye acts as a very crisp skeleton on which the meatier fruit tones build themselves round; the most subtle of spices and heather honey, too; t23.5 quite superb delivery with the mouth filling first with ultra-crisp demerara-sweetened rye, then a softer series of plummy notes; a little date and walnut through the middle, too; f21 vanilla and spice, but dries with a little too much enthusiasm; b22.5 though not the greatest fan of wine finished American whiskies, this one has got it absolutely spot on. And, thankfully, it doesn't call itself a rye, though that is the base spirit. *50.5% (101 proof).*

◇ **Sagamore Spirit Sagamore Reserve Vintner's Finish** batch no. 1A **(85.5)** n22 t22 f20.5 b21 A cumbersome whisky where the fruit strangles the grain but leaves a little too much bitterness hanging around after the super-soft and salivating delivery. *49.2% (98.4 proof).*

**Ten High Bourbon With Natural Flavors (61)** n18 t18 f10 b15 Not sure what those natural flavours are (though a grotesque vanilla note keeps coming to mind), but seeing as they are not as natural as good old fashioned bourbon, don't see the point of them. Or it. Not exactly pleasant and the finish is almost Herculean in its grimness. *40% (80 proof).*

**Trail's End Batch No 002 Kentucky Bourbon finished in Oregon Oak (92)** n23.5 t23 f22.5 b23 So, here we are: at the Trail's End. This is my final official day of tasting, having spent the last few months working six days a week to bring you Jim Murray's Whisky Bible 2018 in on time. The romantic in me meant that this had to be my last whisk(e)y: what else would fit the bill? Especially as both Kentucky and Oregon are my two adopted states in the US. For the record, it is the 1,199th new whisky for Bible 2018, though there had been a couple of dozen additional re-tastes. And as I write the front of the Bible and we edit and finally put this book to bed, the odd straggler will come in to take the total over 1,200. But for me this, officially, is it...the Trail's End for another year.... *45% (90 proof).*

**WhistlePig Old World 12 Year Madeira Finish** European casks **(88)** n21.5 t23.5 f21 b22 Not sure how this can be called a straight rye. But as a whiskey experience, certainly has its merits. *45%. (90 proof)*

◇◇ **WhistlePig Old World Cask Finish Rye Whiskey Aged 12 Years** 100% Oloroso sherry cask finish, bott code: 20190214ADLWT38 **(77.5)** n23.5 t22 f15 b17 The back label claims this to be a straight rye whiskey. How can it be if it has spent time in a non-virgin oak cask, ie. Sherry...? This is beginning to grate on me seriously now. And to make matters worse, we have a spoiled whiskey. Initially, the nose is stunning, just twitching with cut glass rye. The delivery is a natural follow on of delicious crisp juiciness and then about halfway in it all starts crumbling. The fabulous rye begins to get lost behind a non-specific cloud, then a tingling bitterness creeps in, the tongue going numb. A problem more associated with Scotch or Irish. Not rye. So you have top class rye, probably the best whiskey style in the world...and you then put this liquid gold into the very worst, most ruinous casks on the planet. I really don't understand what is going on. *43% (86 proof). Bottled for Master of Malt.*

◇◇ **Widow Jane Whiskey Distilled From A Rye Mash** batch no. 14 db **(81.5)** n20 t21.5 f20 b20 Never a happy Widow, this. Except the muscovado sugars on delivery, all else fails to find a rhythm, the tobacco nose and slightly dirty finish offering a few clues as to why. Those feints have to be cut out. *45.5% (91 proof).*

◇◇ **Wild Turkey Master's Keep Revival Aged 12 to 15 Years** batch 001, oloroso sherry cask finish, bott code: LL\GD130911 db **(86.5)** n22 t23 f20 b21.5 A boxer's nose: flat. And offers no punch whatsoever. That said, not normally a great fan of this whiskey style. However, this is better than most and the delivery itself offers ten seconds of beauty as a demerara/rye sharpness is caressed by the fruit. But it is too brief and the weakness in the oloroso is visible late on. *50.5% (101 proof).*

# Canadian Whisky

**T**he vastness of Canada is legendary. As is the remoteness of much of its land. But anyone who has not yet visited a distillery which sits serenely on the shores of Lake Manitoba more or less bang in the middle of the country and, in early Spring, ventures a few miles out into the wilderness, has really missed a trick.

Because there, just a dozen miles from the remotest distillery of them all, Gimli, you can stand and listen to the ice crack with a clean, primeval crispness unlike any other thing you will have experienced; a sound once heard by the very first hunters who ventured into these uncharted wastes. And hear a distant loon call its lonely, undulating, haunting song, its notes scudding for miles along the ice and vanishing into the snow which surrounds you. Of all the places on the planet, it is the one where you will feel a sensation as close to nature - and your insignificance - as you are likely to find.

It was also a place where I felt that, surely, great whisky should be made. But in the early days of the Gimli distillery there was a feeling of frustration by the blenders who used it. Because they were simply unable to recreate the depth and complexity of the legendary Crown Royal brand it had been built to produce in place of the old, now closed, distilleries to the east. When, in their lab, they tasted the new Crown Royal against the old there were furrowed brows, a slight shaking of heads and an unspoken but unmistakable feeling of hopeless resignation.

To understand why, we have to dispense with the nonsense which appears to have been trotted out by some supposed expert in Canadian whisky or other

Yukon

BRITISH COLUMBIA

ALBERTA

MANITOBA

Shelter Point    Okanagan    🔺 Alberta
                             🔺 Highwood
            ● Vancouver    Calgary

                        🔺 Palliser        Gimli 🔺

**Key**

● Major Town or City
🔺 Distillery

who has, I have been advised by quite a few people I meet at my tastings, been writing somewhere that Canada has no history of blending from different distilleries. Certainly that is now the perceived view of many in the country. And it is just plain wrong: only a maniac would write such garbage as fact and completely undersell the provenance of Canadian whisky. Crown Royal, when in its pomp, was a meticulous blending of a number of different whiskies from the Seagram empire and by far the most complex whisky Canada had to offer.

The creases in the furrowed brows deepened as the end of the last century approached. Because the key distilleries of LaSalle, Beupre and Waterloo were yielding the very last of their stocks, especially top quality pure rye, and although the much lighter make of Gimli was of a high standard, they had not yet been able to recreate the all round complexity as when adding the fruits of so many great distilleries together. The amount of experimentation with yeasts and distilling speeds and cutting times was a wonder to behold. But the race was on: could they, before the final stocks ran dry, produce the diversity of flavours to match the old, classic distilleries which were now not just closed but in some cases demolished?

When I had sat in the LaSalle blending lab for several days in the 1990s and worked my way through the near extinct whiskies in stock I recognised in Beupre a distillery which, had it survived, probably might have been capable of producing something as good, if not better, than anything else on this planet. And it was clear just what a vital contribution it made to Crown Royal's all round magnificence.

So I have monitored the Crown Royal brand with interest, especially since Gimli and the brand was acquired by Diageo some 15 years ago. And anyone doubting that this really was a truly great whisky should have accompanied me when I visited the home of my dear and now sadly lost friend Mike Smith and worked our way through his astonishing Crown Royal collection which showed how the brand's taste profile had evolved through the ages.

And, at last, it appears all that hard work, all those early days of experimentation and fine tuning at Gimli have paid off. For while the standard Crown Royal brand doesn't yet quite live up to its starry past, they have unleashed upon us a whisky which dazzles, startles and engulfs you in its natural beauty like an early spring morning on Lake Manitoba. The whisky is called Crown Royal Northern Harvest Rye. It is not only the best Canadian to be found in the market, it was Jim Murray's World Whisky of the Year 2016: batch L5085 N3 had redefined a nation's whisky

The fact it should have achieved this at a time when Canadian whisky is at a nadir, with far too many brands dependent on adding too many unacceptable things as accepted flavouring agents, is providential. It shows that keeping the grains at a maximum and allowing them to be the flavouring agents - like Alberta Premium - is not just keeping true to the old Canadian traditions, but the way to go to drag it back onto the world's stage and give it a leading role. Walter Jonke and the other old Canadian blenders I knew understood this. Let this be a lesson to the present generation. And so many so-callled whisky experts.

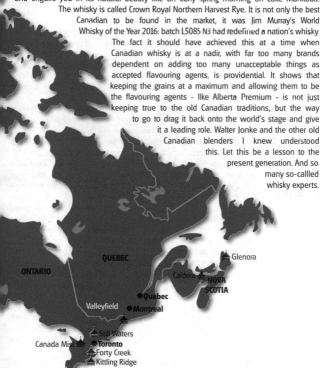

QUEBEC                                      ▲ Glenora

ONTARIO                              Caldera ▲ NOVA
                                              SCOTIA
                                    ●Quebec
              Valleyfield  ●Montreal

                        ▲ Still Waters
Canada Mist ▲   ● Toronto
                ▲ Forty Creek
                ▲ Kittling Ridge
    ▲ Walkerville

| Jim Murray's Whisky Bible Canadian Whisky of the Year Winners | |
|---|---|
| 2004 | Seagram's VO |
| 2005 | Seagram's VO |
| 2006 | Alberta Premium |
| 2007 | Alberta Premium 25 Years Old |
| 2008 | Alberta Premium 25 Years Old |
| 2009 | Alberta Premium |
| 2010 | Wiser's Red Letter |
| 2011 | Crown Royal Special Reserve |
| 2012 | Crown Royal Special Reserve |
| 2013 | Masterson's 10 Year Old Straight Rye |
| 2014 | Masterson's 10 Year Old Straight Rye |
| 2015 | Masterson's 10 Year Old Straight Rye |
| 2016 | Crown Royal Northern Harvest Rye |
| 2017 | Crown Royal Northern Harvest Rye |
| 2018 | Crown Royal Northern Harvest Rye |
| 2019 | Canadian Club Chronicles: Issue No. 1 41 Year Old |
| 2020 | Crown Royal Northern Harvest Rye |

## Canadian Single Malts
### CENTRAL CITY BREWERS & DISTILLERS LTD. Surrey, British Columbia.
**Lohin McKinnon Chocolate Malt Single Malt Whisky** Sauternes barrels db **(80)** n19 t23 f17 b21 Chocolate malt and Sauternes Barrels...? Sound like something straight out of the Glenmorangie blending lab. To taste, this is truly amazing: the closest thing to liquid Jaffa Cake biscuits I have ever encountered. So orangey...so chocolatey... Sadly, the nose and finish tell their own tale: if you are going to use wine casks from Europe, make sure they have not been sulphur treated first. 43%.

**Lohin McKinnon Lightly Peated Single Malt Whisky** oloroso sherry barrels db **(69.5)** n17.5 t19 f16 b17 A polite tip to any micro distillery planning on using European wine casks. Just don't. Or you might end up with a sulphur-ruined disaster like this. 43%.

⋙ **Lohin McKinnon Muscat Wine Barrel Single Malt Whisky** db **(78.5)** n19 t21.5 f19 b19 A reminder, were it needed, that disappointing wine casks are not just restricted to Spain. 43%.

⋙ **Lohin McKinnon Niagara Wine Barrel Single Malt Whisky** db **(87)** n21.5 t22.5 f21 b22 If memory serves, it was these poor chaps who ended up with malt shewing the dangers of maturing whisky in sherry butts. They have wisely gone closer to home for their wine cask this time: Niagara. And this wasn't a barrel that fell over the Falls (well, I don't think so, anyway) but from one of the local vineyards. The result is a full-flavoured but eye-watering experience, certainly sulphur free, but with enough under-ripe gooseberry to keep your eyes watered for quite a while. Just needed an extra year or two in cask maybe for a more meaningful relationship between fruit and oak. Tart but very tasty. 43%.

**Lohin McKinnon Peated Single Malt Whisky** db **(95.5)** n23.5 t24 f23.5 b24.5 I think they have found their forte. This is genuinely top rate, outstandingly distilled and matured peated whisky 43%.

⋙ **Lohin McKinnon Tequila Barrel Finished Single Malt Whisky** db **(92)** n23 not an aroma you come across every day. Or any day, really...until now. Yes, the tequila is there, just latching onto the coat-tails of the malt...but there...; t23 surprisingly, there is a dominant fruit note to this. Non-specific – maybe it's the tequila – I have no previous reference points to be sure. But the mid-ground is busy and tart: not in the manner of their Niagara wine barrel, but much more inclusive of the grist and oaky vanilla; f22.5 medium length with the barley escaping its Mexican captor; b23.5 highly unusual but deeply desirable. A fascinating and salivating addition to the whisky lexicon. 43%.

**Lohin McKinnon Wine Barrel Finished Single Malt Whisky** finished in B.C. VQA Okanagan Valley Back Sage Vineyard Pipe wine barrels db **(90.5 )** n22 blackberries and black pepper; t23 the silky disposition, helps the fruit to wallow around the palate relaxed enough to show no opposition to the gathering spice and mocha; **f22.5** spiced fruit chocolate with a late surge of friendly vanilla; **b23** impressive balance here with the fruit doing enough but not too much. *43%.*

# DEVINE SPIRITS Saanichton, British Columbia.

**Glensaanich Single Malt** batch no. 2 db **(86) n21.5 t22 f21 b21.5** An unexpected tobacco note on the nose mixes it with the malt. The oil wades in to soften, releasing an attractive degree of bruyere honey which covers the slightly more bitter notes with aplomb. *45%.*

◇◇◇ **Glensaanich Single Malt Whisky** batch no. 4 db **(88) n22.5** an unusually attractive vegetable note – fruit, too, if you count cucumbers. Also love the light sugars attached to the black pepper; a lovely barley sugar note ensures balance; **t23** superb gathering of malt on delivery. Indeed, the rotund nature of the mouth feel makes for an elegant fit between the malt and vanilla; **f20.5** bitters out just a tad too enthusiastically; **b22** as the first bottling I encountered this was superb and the second not so, I was curious to see what a pour from the bottle would bring forth this time. Well, something that sits somewhere between the two but with a character all its own. *45%.*

**Glensaanich Quarter Cask Ancient Grains** batch no. 1 db **(91.5) n23 t23 f22 b23.5** A beautiful little essay in complexity. The varied grains spelt, emmer, einkorn, khorosan and, of course, locally grown organic BC barley have been put together to delicious and fascinating effect. A real entertainer, especially when warmed for a while. *45%.*

# FORTY CREEK Grimsby, Ontario.

**Forty Creek Barrel Select (86.5) n21.5 t22 f21 b21.5.** Thank goodness that the sulphur taint I had found on this in recent years has now vanished. A lush, enjoyable easy-goer, this juices up attractively at the start and ends with an almost sophisticated dry pithiness. *40%*

**Forty Creek Confederation Oak Reserve** lot 1867-B **(94.5) n23.5 t24 f23.5 b23.5.** Those who tasted the first batch of this will be intrigued by this follow up. The shape and intensity profile has been re-carved and all now fits together like a jigsaw. *40%*

◇◇◇ **Forty Creek Confederation Oak Reserve** lot no. 1867-I, finished in Canadian wine barrels **(94) n23** pungent and peppery on the nose, quite a slightly different dash than the last Confed' Oak I enjoyed. Some real bristle among the oaky shavings; **t23.5** softly, softly on delivery. Alluring and slightly salivating gentle grains moves towards a warmer light fruitiness, but again it is that buzzing spice which arrests the attention; **f23.5** complex diced kumquat peel and chocolate is invigorated by that persistent spice. The caramels which build slowly reach a head at the finale; **b24** Forty Creek feel relaxed with this brand and seem to know how to pull the strings for near maximum effect. Very clean, too. *40%.*

**Forty Creek Copper Pot Reserve (91.5) n23 t23.5 f22 b23.** One of the beauties of John Hall's whiskies at Forty Creek is that they follow no set pattern in the whisky world. they offer flavour profiles really quite different from anything else. That is why they are worth that bit of extra time for your palate to acclimatise. Here you are exceptionally well rewarded... *43%*

◇◇◇ **Forty Creek Copper Pot Reserve** bott code: DGIHC12074 **(89.5) n22.5** big fruity ignition; **t23** the house style lushness goes into overdrive, though here the spices arrive a lot earlier and there are far more meaningful laying to the bitter-sweet fruit; **f21** just a little tangy and untidy; **b23** they have remained very true to style since this brand first hit the shelves. The finish could do with a clean-up, though. *43%.*

**Forty Creek Double Barrel Reserve** lot 247 **(86) n21.5 t22.5 f20.5 b21.5.** Juicy ride with plenty to savour early on. But something is slightly off balance about the finish. *40%*

◇◇◇ **Forty Creek Double Barrel Reserve** lot no. 267, finished in once used American bourbon barrels **(87) n21.5 t22.5 f21 b22** Incredibly lush, but perhaps a tad too incredibly lush. Those caramel notes dominate with too much of a velvet fist, though it does briefly open out for some enjoyable oaky interplay, though all a little muffled. The finish is somewhat off key, alas. *40%.*

◇◇◇ **Forty Creek Premium Barrel Select** bott code: DGIHC14075 **(81) n21.5 t22 f18.5 b19** Massively thick on delivery, fruity but, sadly, the sulphur has returned. Decent spice, though. *40%.*

**Forty Creek Port Wood Reserve** lot 61 **(95.5) n24.5 t24 f23 b24** John P Hall has got his ducks in a row. Magnificent! *45%*

**Forty Creek Three Grain (76) n19 t20 f18 b19.** Not quite as well assembled as some Three Grains I have come across over the last few years. There is a lopsidedness to this one: we know the fruit dominates (and I still haven't a clue why, when surely this of all whiskies, just has to be about the grains!) but the bitterness interferes throughout. If there have been sherry casks used here, I would really have a close look at them. *40%*

# GLENORA Glenville, Nova Scotia.

**Glen Breton Rare Aged 10 Years** bott 10 db **(89.5) n22 t23 f22 b22.5.** An impressive whisky: one of the best bottlings of this age for some while and showing the malt at full throttle. *43%*

# HIGHWOOD DISTILLERS High River, Alberta.

**Highwood Distillers Centennial Whisky** db (84.5) n21.5 t22 f20 b21 Toffee and raisin. Tangy, though the finish dries significantly. *40%.*

**Highwood Distillers Ninety 5 Year Old Whisky** db (86.5) n21.5 t22 f21.5 b21.5 A sweet, simplistic whisky which ramps up some very attractive spices. *45%.*

**Highwood Distillers Ninety 20 Year Old Whisky** db (90) n23.5 t22.5 f22 b22 This is a grand old man of Canadian whisky yet sprightly and full of very simple Canadian tales... *45%.*

**Canadian Rockies 10 Year Old** (84.5) n21.5 t22 f20.5 b20.5. Resplendent in all its chewy one-dimensional caramel. *40%. Taiwan Exclusive.*

**Canadian Rockies Aged 17 Years** bott code: 8127 (92) n23 typical light and gentle aroma with the accent on lightly sweetened vanilla; t23.5 gorgeous mouth feel: again, light and fragile but enough oils to soften the impact. A mix of light ulmo honey and vanilla, before soft natural caramels and spices fill the mid-ground; f22. Delicate even on the finale with the vanillas showing just a little extra tannin; b23.5 so true to Highwood's style, this could be their signature whisky. Elegant. *50%.*

**Canadian Rockies 21 Year Old** (88) n22 so light, with a mix of apple crumble and vanilla ice cream; t22 soft and simple as you like: vanilla and docile spice; f22 more of the same...; b22 not sure you can find a straighter, simpler whisky... *40%. Taiwan Exclusive.*

⟫ **Canadian Rockies Aged 21 Years** bott code 8127 (92.5) n23 uniquely Highwood, so sexily delicate, almost feeble, is the nose. A kind of apple and rhubarb crumble, as though steaming in the next room with Demerara sugars melting on top; t23 and those sugars do, indeed, melt in the mouth, too! The lightest oil seems to embolden the lightest spices and vanillas as the whisky continues on its tip-toeing way; f23 just more of the same...going on longer than might seem possible...; b23.5 you get the feeling they have got the hang of this whisky now. Has become a classic of its sort in its own right. *46%.*

**Canadian Rockies 34 Year Old** (92.5) n23 t23 f23.5 b23 The most fun I've had with a 34-year-old Canadian for quite a few years now...though that was a little hotter than this... *79.3%. Taiwan Exclusive.*

# OKANAGAN SPIRITS CRAFT DISTILLERY Vernon, British Columbia.

**Laird of Fintry Single Malt Whisky** French & American oak. db (84) n21 t22 f20 b21. A tangy, aromatic whisky where the oak appears to have a disproportionate say. Interesting marmalade depth. *40%. First Batch. 264 bottles.*

# PEMBERTON DISTILLERY Pemberton, British Columbia.

**Pemberton Organic Single Malt Whisky 2013** ex-bourbon cask, cask no. 1, dist 11 Apr 13, bott May 17 db (85.5) n21 t21.5 f22 b21 I was thinking: "peat and nougat...I've encountered this before". And checking the Bible, I see I have...from Pemberton, with their 2011 bottling! Lots of sweet charm from the grist, but this is a malt which struggles to go to the next step of integration. *44%. nc ncf sc.*

# SHELTER POINT DISTILLERY Campbell River, British Columbia.

**Shelter Point Distillery Artisanal Cask Strength Whisky** American oak, finished in French oak db (91) n22.5 t23.5 f22 b23 Looks as though the law in Canada now says you even have to have the barrels from both English and French language... A beautifully complex and intense malt. *54.8%. 1,200 bottles.*

⟫ **Shelter Point Artisanal Single Malt Whisky Distiller's Select** db (94.5) n23 yes, there are some background spices fizzing about. Yes, there is a little dab of kumquat here and there. But this is, essentially, all about the barley...and what barley...! t24 rarely does a malt whisky come with a texture so well balanced as this: oily, gooey weight but not for a moment interfering with or overpowering the intrinsic character of the malt itself. The sugars – mainly provided by a thin dilution of ulmo and bruyere honey – also never for a moment wavers. Everything is on a knife-edge, poised and ready to tip this way or that....; f23.5 ...but it never does and as the vanillas build then make way for a lightly spiced butterscotch finale; b24 when I initially tasted this distillery's very first maturing cask quite a little while ago now, the evidence provided by the lightly yellowing spirit left me fully confident that they would, with great care, be capable of producing a very high class malt. They have not let me down. This is truly beautiful. *46%. nc ncf.*

⟫ **Shelter Point Double Barreled Single Malt Whisky** French oak finish, bott Jul 18 db (94) n23.5 the toastiness is the star of the show. Perhaps, though, it is the controlled spice which really has top billing...; t23.5 the texture is just fabulous. An unusual degree of oil on this, buttery yet sweet as the ulmo honey comes into focus. Meanwhile, the oak veers off in a distinctly chocolatey direction; f23.5 long, drier, lightly spiced and robust...yet always elegant...; **b24** the label kindly informs us that this has spent no less than 1993 hours being finished in French oak. Now, in case you are wondering, that is 83 days: roughly 2 months and 22 days. And if you think they have not been quite specific enough, that is 119,580 minutes. Or, to put it another way, 7,174,800 seconds. Maybe had it been 7,174,801 that might just have done the trick to get those extra points for Canadian whisky of the year.... *50%. nc ncf. 1,131 bottles (That's 28,275 standard 3cl Canadian measures by the way...).*

◊ **Shelter Point Montfort District Lot 141** batch 2018 db (**92**) **n22** the odd new make moment can't detract from the unerring intensity of the barley, or from how well this has been made. But there is oak enough to offer a little spice nibble; **t23.5** my word! That barley comes into play bang on delivery and holds its ground with pride. A light, salivating mocha and Turkish delight sweetness plays a complex game; spices tingle; **f23** a slight reminder of the whisky's comparative youth but the vanilla of the oak more than compensates; **b23.5** still a little young at crucial moments. But, my word, this whisky from the Oyster River is sexy stuff, indeed... *46%. nc ncf. 1,224 bottles.*

# SHERINGHAM DISTILLERY Sooke, British Columbia.

◊ **Sheringham Whisky Red Fife** grain: Red Fife/barley, ex-bourbon cask, bott 2019 db (**86**) **n21.5 t22 f21 b21.5** Not technically a perfect whisky, but the initial produce of new distilleries very seldom are. The usual light feint at work here which adds on the extra oils and slight bitterness on the finish. But provides, also, an attractive chewability to the abundant sweet caramels extracted from an excellent ex-bourbon cask. A work in progress, for sure. But enough good points not to forsake this distillery from Sooke. *45%.*

◊ **Sheringham Whisky Woodhaven** grain: corn/Red Fife/barley, new American oak cask, bott 2019 db (**91**) **n23** such lovely oak tones! Both confident yet gentle at the same time, allowing a light cedar note to enrich the usual red liquorice and sweeter tannins; **t23** Demerara sugars ping around the teeth as if it were a pinball machine. A little liquorice and chocolate attaches itself to the genteel, super-soft nougat; **f22.5** haughtier tannin now shewing a robust age we know it cannot possess; just a little strand of barley among the sawdust; **b22.5** a much better made spirit than the bourbon cask bottling, while the virgin oak does no harm whatsoever. A mouth-filling joy of a malt. *45%.*

# SPIRIT OF YORK Toronto, Ontario.

◊ **Spirit of York 100% Rye** db (**93.5**) **n24.5** a nose that is as beautiful as it is astonishing: cut glass rye at its most crisp and deep but with a softening mintiness to balance the Demerara-sweet grain; classic rye fruitiness both drifts and crashes about the nose.; a little eucalyptus develops for depth. A rye-lover's nose...; **t23.5** instantly salivating and two-toned: fat and chewy as oils, not particularly apparent on the nose, come into play and also a semi-crispness of unadulterated rye. Teasing spice starts on the tongue and fans out in all directions; balancing this the mint and eucalyptus has a slightly cooling effect; **f22** ah, perhaps the one weak spot despite its saltiness. Finishes quite quickly despite the oils and the buzz hints, very gently, of a light degree of feints, but it is negligible. Still, though, the rye echoes...; **b23.5** whoever engineered this, their first-ever whisky bottling, must have been using the Lawrenceburg, Indiana, rye as its blueprint, including virgin oak casks. Matches its intensity and clarity in so many ways, though perhaps not at the death. For a first whisky from Toronto's famous and historic distilling district, the distillers from the Spirit of York should take a bow: this is memorable and authentic stuff distilled, romantically, in part of the old Gooderham and Worts Building...! Toronto is well and truly back on the whisky distilling map... *46% (92 proof).*

# STILLWATERS DISTILLERY Concord, Ontario.

◊ **Stalk & Barrel 100% Rye Single Cask Whisky** (**82.5**) **n18 t21.5 f22 b21** An ashy, dry rye not helped by the feints. But certainly not short on character, the grain full on and commanding and a layer of heather honey sorting out the required sweetness. Even some wonderful chocolate tones towards the finish. *46%. sc.*

◊ **Stalk & Barrel 100% Rye Single Cask Whisky** (**86.5**) **n20 t23 f21.5 b22** Despite the light feintiness, this really does rack up some big rye notes. Rock hard from nose to finish – save for the oils from the wide cut – the delivery and afterglow offer a stupendous degree of grain and spice. Technically not perfect, but worth discovering just for the uncompromising ride. *60.2%. sc.*

◊ **Stalk & Barrel Single Malt Whisky** (**78**) **n19 t22 f18 b19** Well, it's malty: you can say that about it. But the feints as well as giving a nougat feel to this, does very little that is positive to the tangy finish. *46%. sc.*

◊ **Stalk & Barrel Single Malt Whisky** (**84**) **n19 t22.5 f21.5 b21** Full on malty, chocolate-laden spiced toffee nougat. Once past the so-so nose, becomes pretty enjoyable. *60.2%. sc.*

## VICTORIA CALEDONIAN DISTILLERY Victoria, British Columbia

**Mac na Braiche Single Malt Spirit** db (79) n18 t22 f20 b19 From my home from home town, Victoria, in BC. Would like to talk it up, but not that easy with the flavours and balance being all over the place. Some redeeming chocolate on delivery but the rest is very hard work. Wobbles about the palate like a satisfied customer leaving the Garrick's Head...Has the basis for something very good. But some hard work needed to get there. *50%. nc ncf.*

**Victoria Caledonian Mac Na Braiche Single Malt Spirit** Moscatel white wine 225l barrique made with European oak, nbc, db (88.5) n21.5 t22 f22.5 b22.5 A lip-smackingly fulsome malt. The nose suggests a slight untidiness to the distillate, which is pretty normal for a new distillery. But the mix of icing sugar and sultana really makes for a lovely experience once on the palate. *50%. nc ncf sc.*

**Victoria Caledonian Mac Na Braiche Single Malt Spirit** port wine 225l barrique made with white American oak, nbc, db (86.5) n21 t22.5 f22 b21 A pretty clumsy maturing spirit where the profound grapey notes is too big for the malt and oaky body in which it is housed. Trips over itself a bit along the way, though given time this should settle into something substantial. *50%. nc ncf sc.*

**Victoria Caledonian Mac Na Braiche Single Malt Spirit** shaved, toasted and re-charred red wine 225l barrique made with white American oak, nbc, db (93) n22.5 t23 f24 b23.5 Technically, this is too young to be called whisky. The reality in the glass is that whisky is exactly what this is, whether it conforms to the manufactured rigidity of law not. Put it another way: there has been many a technical whisky I have tasted this year and last which, from its performance on the nose and palate, is stretching realms of credulity to its maximum limits. This, however, not only ticks all the boxes required in terms of desirability but adds a few extra on for good measure. There is, it must be said, just a vaguest technical flaw, in that some of the cut here was a bit wider than perfectly desired. But that minor blemish falls by the wayside once the barley begins to kick in and the maple syrup sweetness of the cask merges with the grist. Actually, that extra cut forges the oils which gives that lovely marriage extra body to chew on. The light cocoa and heather honey finale creates a long and delightful send off. A distillery that will need careful nurturing. But on this evidence, it will be worth it. *50%. nc ncf sc.*

## YUKON BREWING Whitehorse, Yukon.

**Two Brewers Yukon Single Malt Release 06 Classic** db (86.5) n22.5 t22 f20.5 b21.5 Soft and understated, the accent falls on the barley which, when in tandem with the light tannin, offers a custard tart sweetness. The finish, though, is undone by some rogue bitter oak. *43%. 1,050 bottles.*

**Two Brewers Yukon Single Malt Release 07 Peated** db (94) n23.5 t23.5 f23 b24 Elegant and making the most of restrained smoke – cleverly showing just how less can mean more. What a massive leap in quality since the last peated malt of their I tasted. Two previous planned trips to this part of Canada to give whisky tastings had been snowed off over the years. I really have to get to the Yukon now... *43%. 1,740 bottles.*

**Two Brewers Yukon Single Malt Release 08 Innovative** db (84.5) n21.5 t21 f21 b21 Sweet, slightly oily and with a citrusy hop character. Reminds me of Marston's New World bitter: an attractive style for a beer, but not so much for a whisky. *43%. 920 bottles.*

**Two Brewers Yukon Single Malt Release 09 Special Finishes** db (87.5) n22 t22 f21.5 b22 You don't really associate The Yukon with softness, silkiness and all things rather twee. A bit like Michael Palin's lumberjack, surely it should be all masculine and...butch. Well, not this girlie. As sweet and fruity as a bride on her wedding night. *46%. 1,340 bottles.*

**Two Brewers Yukon Single Malt Release 10 Classic** db (92) n22.5 t23.5 f23 b23.5 An explosion of flavours on delivery gives lie to the gentle, non-committal, though, clean, nose. Just brilliantly toasty with a breathtaking blend of ulmo honey and molasses. Chewy, salivating and no quarter given as the light liquorice and tannins go in for the kill. *58%. 1,000 bottles.*

**Two Brewers Yukon Single Malt Release 14 Innovative** db (89.5) n22.5 t22.5 f22 b22.5 Despite the volley of spices on both nose and delivery, this is still a real soft cutie. The texture is devoid of any gnarled edges, but all kinds of coffee notes percolate through. Like a whisky distilled at the campfire of the Klondike gold rush prospectors. Oh, and they obviously had a sweet tooth, as well. *46%.*

## UNSPECIFIED SINGLE MALT

**Bearface Aged 7 Years Triple Oak Canadian Single Grain** ex-bourbon barrels, finished in French oak red wine barrels & Hungarian oak, bott no. H1418W1MH (88.5) n22 so light and gentle you really need the Murray Method at full blast to get any tune at all. Eventually, caramel apart, you locate so warming spice attached to the varied oak weight;

t22.5 the silky delivery was a foregone conclusion after that nose, as was the big caramel secondary wave and midpoint mocha moment; f22 light spices...and caramel; b22 about as soft as whisky gets. If they could find a way of tuning out some of the caramel, they'd definitely have a more satisfying whisky. 45.5%.

# Canadian Blended Whisky

**Alberta Premium (95.5) n24 t25 f22.5 b24** It has just gone 8am and the Vancouver Island sky is one of clear blue. My windows are open to allow in some chilly, early Spring air and, though only the first week of March, an American robin sits in the arbutus tree, resplendent in its now two-toned leaves, calling for a mate, as it has done since 5.15 this morning, his song blending with the lively trill of the house finches and the doleful, maritime anthem of the gull. It seems the natural environment of Alberta Premium, back here to its rye-studded best after a couple I tasted socially in Canada last year appeared comparatively dull and restrained. I am tasting this from Bottle Lott No L93300197 and it is classic, generating all I expect and now demand. A national treasure. 40%

**Alberta Premium Dark Horse (84) n18 t22 f22 b22.** The nose is not great: it really does seem as though fruit cordial has been given the lead role. But the taste really does challenge, and I have to say there are many aspects I enjoy. It is as though some peated malt has been added to the mix as the finish does have distinctive smokiness. And the balance has been expertly worked to ensure the sugars don't dominate while the spices are persistent. But if it falls down anywhere, the over reliance on the fruit apart, it is the fact that Alberta makes the best spirit in Canada by a very great distance....yet someone has forgotten to ensure that fact is made clear in the taste and the nose especially. 45%

**Alberta Rye Whisky Dark Batch Blended Rye (86) n19 t23 f22 b22.** A veritable fruitcake of a whisky – and about as moist and sultana-laden as you'll ever find. Not sure about that bitter-tobacco most un-Canadian nose, though. 45% (90 Proof)

**Alberta Springs Aged 10 Years (83) n21 t21 f20 b20.** Really appears to have had a bit of a flavourectomy. Sweet but all traces of complexity have vanished. 40%.

**Bowman's Canadian Whisky (90.5) n22 t22 f23.5 b23.** A delicious blend for chocoholics. 40%

**Black Velvet (78) n18 t20 f20 b20.** A distinctly off-key nose is compensated for by a rich corn and vanilla kick on the palate. But that famous spice flourish is a distant memory. Another big caramel number. 40%

**Caldera Distilling Hurricane 5 Whisky** batch no. 0001 **(87.5) n21.5 t22 f22 b22.** Silky, soft. But lashings of toffee and sugars. Decent spices balance things up a little. 40% (80 proof)

**Campbell & Cooper Aged a Minimum of 36 Months (84.5) n21.5 t22 f20 b21.** Huge flavour profile. An orchard of oranges on the nose and profound vanilla on delivery. 40%

**Canadian Club 100 Proof (89) n21 t23 f22 b23.** If you are expecting this to be a high-octane version of the standard CC Premium, you'll be in for a shock. This is a much fruitier dram with an oilier body to absorb the extra strength. An entertaining blend. 50%.

**Canadian Club 100% Rye (92) n23 t23.5 f22.5 b23** Will be interesting to see how this brand develops over the years. Rye is not the easiest grain to get right when blending differing ages and casks with varied histories: it is an art which takes time to perfect. This is a very attractive early bottling, though my money is on it becoming sharper in future vattings as the ability to show the grain above all else becomes more easily understood. Just so wonderful to see another excellent addition to the Canadian whisky lexicon. 40% (80 proof)

**Canadian Club Chairman's Select 100% Rye (81.5) n21 t21.5 f20 b19.** A bemusing whisky. The label proudly announces that here we have a whisky made from 100% rye. Great news: a Canadian eagerly anticipated. But the colour – a deep orange – looks a bit suspicious. And those fears prove well founded when the taste buds, as well as the nose, go looking for the rye influence in vain. Instead we have a massive toffee effect, offset by some busy spice. Colouring has ruined many a great whisky...and here we have a painful example. What a waste of good rye... 40%

**Canadian Club Chronicles: Issue No. 1 Water of Windsor Aged 41 Years (97) n24.5 t24 f24 b24.5** Have I had this much fun with a sexy 41-year-old Canadian before? Well, yes I have. But it was a few years back now and it wasn't a whisky. Was the fun we had better? Probably not. It is hard to imagine what could be, as this whisky simply seduces you with the lightness and knowledgeable meaning of its touch, butterfly kissing your taste buds, finding time after time your whisky erogenous zone or g spots ... and then surrendering itself with tender and total submission. 45% (90 proof).

**Canadian Club Premium (92) n23 t22.5 f23 b23.5.** A greatly improved whisky which now finds the fruit fitting into the mix with far more panache than of old. Once a niggardly whisky, often seemingly hell-bent on refusing to enter into any form of complexity: but not now! Great spices in particular. I'm impressed. 40%

**Canadian Five Star Rye Whisky** (83) n21 t22 f20 b20. An entirely tame, well behaved Canadian which celebrates the inherent sweetness of the species. That said, the immediate impact on the palate is pretty delicious with a quick, flash explosion of something spicy. But it is the deft, satin-soft mouthfeel which may impress most. *40%*

**Canadian Hunter** (85.5) n20.5 t21 f22 b22. Remains truly Canadian in style. The toffee has diminished, allowing far more coffee and cocoa to ensure a delightful middle and finish. *40%*

**Canadian Mist** (78) n19 t20.5 f18.5 b20. Much livelier than previous incarnations despite the inherent, lightly fruited softness. *40%*

**Canadian Mist At Least 36 Months Old** bott code: L 171007 3133317 (87.5) n21.5 t22.5 f21.5 b22 An old-fashioned style of Canadian which is big on the grain and softens out further with the moderate intervention of fruit and caramel. Doesn't stint on the late spice, either. A lovely every day kind of Canadian. *40% (80 proof)*.

**Canadian Pure Gold** (82) n21.5 t20.5 f20 b20. Full-bodied and still a notably lush whisky. The pure gold may have more to do with the caramel than the years in cask but the meat of this whisky still gives you plenty to chew over. I especially enjoy the gradual building of spices. *40%*

**Canadian Spirit** (78) n20 t20 f19 b19. A real toffee-fest with a touch of hard grain around the edges. *40%. Carrington Distillers (Alberta Distillers)*.

**Centennial 10 Year Limited Edition** (88.5) n21.5 t23 f22 b22. Retains its usual honey-flavoured breakfast cereal style, but the complexity has increased. Busy and charming. *40%*

**Century Reserve 8 Years Old Premium** (82) n20 t21 f20 b21. Clean vanilla caramel. *40%*

**Century Reserve Custom Blend 15 Years Plus** (88.5) n21.5 t22 f23 b22. After two days of being ambushed in every direction, or completely steamrollered by Canadian caramel, my tastebuds are in total shock. Caramel kept to an absolute minimum so that it hardly registers at all. Charming and refined drinking. *40%*

**Century Reserve 21 Years Old** (91.5) n23.5 t23 f23 b22. Quite beautiful, but a spirit that is as likely to appeal to rum lovers as whisky ones. *40%*

**Century Reserve Custom Blend** lot no. 1525 (87) n21.5 t22 f21.5 b22. An enjoyable whisky which doesn't quite reach its full potential. *40%*

**Corby's Canadian 36 Months Old** (85) n20 t21 f22 b22. Attractive with a fine bitter-sweet balance and I love the late spice kick-back. *40%. Barton*

**Crown Royal** (86) n22 t23.5 f19.5 b21. The Crown has spoken and it has been decreed that this once ultra grainy old whisky is taking its massive move to a silky fruitiness as far as it can go. It was certainly looking that way last time out; on this re-taste (and a few I have unofficially tasted) there is now no room for doubt. If you like grape, especially the sweeter variety, you'll love this. The highpoint is the sublime delivery and starburst of spice. The low point? The buzzy, unhappy finale. The Grain Is Dead. Long Live The Grape! *40%*

**Crown Royal** bott code: 318 B4 2111 (87.5) n22 t23 f21 b21.5 Carries on in the same style as above. But at least the finish is a lot happier now with welcome ulmo honey extending further and the spices also working overtime. Still a little residual bitterness shows more work is required but, unquestionably, keep on this course and they'll soon be getting there. *40%*

**Crown Royal Black** (85) n22 t23 f18.5 b21.5. Not for the squeamish: a Canadian which goes for it with bold strokes from the off which makes it a whisky worth discovering. The finish needs a rethink, though. *45%*

⋙ **Crown Royal Blender's Select Bourbon Whiskey** db (91) n22 hefty on the caramel front, though some attractive praline back-up; t23.5 so much livelier than the nose: vivid, even. Clean, salivating Demerara sugars at the front is quickly followed up by an agreeable, intensifying oak buzz; f22.5 back to the toffee and vanilla, but attractive length; a little mocha develops towards the end; b23 a pretty classic Canadian very much in the Crown Royal mould. *44% (88 proof)*.

**Crown Royal Bourbon Mash Bill** bott code: L8 N04 N7 db (94.5) n23.5 t23.5 f23.5 b24 Whiskies like this do so much to up the standing of Canadian whisky. *40% (80 proof)*.

**Crown Royal Cornerstone Blend** (85.5) n21 t22 f21 b21.5. Something of a mish-mash, where a bold spiciness appears to try to come to terms with an, at times, random fruity note. One of the most curious aspects of this quite different whisky is the way in which the weight of the body continues to change. Intriguing. *40.3% (80.6 proof)*

**Crown Royal DeLuxe** (91.5) n23.5 t23 f22.5 b22.5 Some serious blending went into this. Complex. *40% (80 proof)*

**Crown Royal Hand Selected Barrel** (94.5) n23.5 t24 f23.5 b23.5 If this is a single barrel, it boasts extraordinary layering and complexity *51.5% (103 proof)*

**Crown Royal Limited Edition** (87) n22 t22.5 f20.5 b22. A much happier and productive blend than before with an attractive degree of complexity but the more bitter elements of the finish have been accentuated. *40%*

**Crown Royal Noble Collection 13 Year Old Bourbon Mash** bott code: L8037 2S 00108:06 db **(96)** n24.5 t24 f23.5 b24 It's Canadian, Jim· but not as we know it... Deliciously going places where no other Canadian has gone before... 45% (90 proof).

**Crown Royal Noble Collection Wine Barrel Finished** lot no. 0100-43-B1245 **(87)** n21 t22.5 f21.5 b22 A friendly, juicy Canadian. Because Canada is allowed to add things into their whisky – and fruit has (sadly) been a popular choice for the last 20 years – it is hard to see how a wine barrel finish will make a notable difference to a blend. So, perhaps the little cleverly diffused spice apart, it is a major ask to tell the difference between this and standard practice. My guess is the spice. Unquestionably pleasant, though. Despite the late bitterness. 40.5%.

**Crown Royal Northern Harvest Rye** bott code L5085 N3 **(97.5)** n25 t24.5 f23.5 b24.5 This is the kind of whisky you dream of dropping into your tasting room. Rye, that most eloquent of grains, not just turning up to charm and enthral but to also take us through a routine which reaches new heights of beauty and complexity. To say this is a masterpiece is barely doing it justice. 45%

**Crown Royal Northern Harvest Rye** bott code: 095 B1 0247 db **(95.5)** n24 t24 f23.5 b24 Not quite the same beguiling intensity as the batch which once won the Whisky Bible's World Whisky of the Year, but what an absolute salivating treat of a whisky this remains...as sprightly and fresh as any NHR I have tasted yet. 45% (90 proof).

◈ **Crown Royal Northern Harvest Rye** bott code: L8 353 N5 **(97)** n25 the spice....my word...that spice...!!! At once peppery yet sharpened on a sweeter plane with granite-hard rye. There are some profound oaky incursions, too, involving liquorice and the very lightest hint of eucalyptus...; **t24** fat and salivating on the palate and, despite the best efforts of the molasses and Demerara sugar-enriched rye, the spices make their presence felt: momentarily searing, then dying down to a throb totally in sync with the pulsing sharpness of the grain; **f23.5** drier as tannins and caramels begin to outflank the grain; but it is a long finish, chewy and increasingly toasty; **b24.5** having spent a little while in Canada over the last year, I have had the pleasure of a few stunning Northern Harvest Ryes in that time. But I admit I did a double-take when this bottling turned up in my lab for the official sample tasting. It was by far the darkest example of this brand I had ever seen – and I admit that I feared the worst, as that can often mean the sharp complexity which is the hallmark of a whisky such as this can be compromised. I need not have worried: the glass is almost shattering from the enormity of vivid delights contained therein. A stunning whisky, as usual, but they will have to ensure that the colour returns to its lighter gold, perhaps with slightly younger casks, to guarantee the fresh style remains, as this could easily have become a dullard. This, though, is anything but. 45% (90 proof).

**Crown Royal Reserve** bott code: 3046A52219 db **(88)** n22 surprisingly crisp: lots of toasty sugars at play; **t23** no less toasty on the medium sweet delivery: only medium weight to the corn thrust, then a vanilla and liquorice middle; **f21** a slightly untidy, tangy and furry finish; **b22** not sure if this is complex or just confusing. The excellent moments are as good as the lesser moments are not. 40% (80 proof).

**Crown Royal Special Reserve (96)** n24 t24 f24 b24 Complex, well weighted and simply radiant: it is like looking at a perfectly shaped, gossamer clad Deb at a ball. The ryes work astonishingly well here (they appear to be of the malted, ultra-fruity variety) and perhaps to best effect after Alberta Premium, though now it is a hard call between the two. 40%

**Crown Royal XR Extra Rare** lot no. L7064 N4 **(93.5)** n24 t23 f23 b23.5. Just about identical to the previous bottle above. The only difference is on the finish where the rye, fortified with spice, decides to hang back and battle it out to the death; the toffee and vanilla make a controlled retreat. Either the same bottling with a slightly different stance after a few years in the bottle, or a different one of extraordinary high consistency. 40%

**Crown Royal XO (87.5)** n22 t21 f22.5 b22. With an XO, one might have hoped for something eXtraOrdinary or at least eXOtic. Instead, we have a Canadian which carried on a little further where their Cask No 16 left off. Always a polite, if rather sweet whisky, it falls into the trap of allowing the Cognac casks a little too much say. Only on the finish, as the spices begin to find channels to flow into, does the character which, for generations, set Crown Royal apart from all other Canadians begin to make itself heard: complexity. 40% WB15/398

**Danfield's Limited Edition Aged 21 Years (95)** n24 t24 f23.5 b23.5. A quite brilliant first-time whisky. The back label claims this to be small batch, but there is no batch number on the bottle, alas. Or even a visible bottling code. But this is a five star performer. 40%

**Danfield's Private Reserve (84.5)** n20 t21.5 f22 b21. A curious, non-committal whisky which improves on the palate as it goes along. An overdose of caramel (yawn!!) has done it no favours, but there is character enough for it to pulse out some pretty tasty spice. Seamless and silky, for all the toffee there underlying corn-rich clarity is a bit of a turn on. 40%

**8 Seconds Small Batch (86)** n20 t22 f22.5 b21.5. Fruity, juicy, luxurious. Perhaps one of the few whiskies on the market anywhere in the world today which could slake a thirst. 40%

**Fremont Mischief Whiskey** batch MPJ-0803, bott 11 (**77**) n19 t20 f19 b19. Though this was from the Mischief distillery in Seattle, USA, the whiskey was produced in Canada. Overly sweet, overly toffeed and bereft of complexity. Like Alberta Springs on a very bad day. 40%

**Gibson's Finest Aged 12 Years** (**77**) n18 t20 f19 b20. Unlike the Sterling, going backwards rather than forwards. This is way too syrupy, fruity and toffee impacted. Despite the very good spice, almost closer to a liqueur than a true whisky style. 40%

**Gibson's Finest Rare Aged 18 Years** (**95.5**) n24 t24.5 f23.5 b23.5 So far ahead of both Sterling and the 12, it is hard to believe they are from the same stable. But make no mistake; this is pure thoroughbred: truly world class. 40%

**Gibson's Finest 100th Grey Cup Special Edition** (**87**) n21 t23 f21 b22. When the label tells you there is a hint of maple, they aren't joking... 40%

**Gibson's Finest Canadian Whisky Bourbon Cask Rare Reserve** (**89**) n23 t21 f23 b22. A much better version than the first bottling, the depth this time being massively greater. 40%

**Gibson's New Oak** (**88**) n22 t21 f23 b22. Distinctly different from any other Canadian doing the rounds: the oak influence makes a wonderful and clever impact. 40%

**Gooderham & Worts Four Grain** blend no. A.A1129 (**94**) n23 t24 f23.5 b23.5 Four there's a jolly good whisky...worts and all...! 44.4%

**Gooderham & Worts 11 Souls** (**94**) n23.5 buzzes with small grain complexity. The rye fizzes and cuts with a slightly fruity edge, but there is more besides. If that isn't wheat in there bigging up the spice, then something is giving a good impression; t23.5 I stand by my assertion on the nose. Beautiful layering of acacia honey and barley, then a real chattering buzz of grain – the rye in particular now a three dimension essay; f23 the vanillas are now left to their own devices, a little butterscotch making up for the spent grain; b24 this wouldn't be named after Frank Saul, who once famously wore the Millwall number 11 shirt, would it...? Absolutely have no idea what this whisky consists of, but the leading element appears to be small grain complexity with rye, barley and perhaps others, especially wheat, causing all kinds of delicious mayhem. Controlled, of course. Love it! And by far the most exciting whisky I've tasted today – and I'm now more than seven hours into my shift! 49%

**Gooderham & Worts Little Trinity Three Grain Blend** (**94**) n23.5 t24 f23 b23.5 Beautifully complex but will still suit those with catholic tastes... 45%. Ultra-Rare Craft Series.

**Hiram Walker Legends Series Guy Lafleur** (**87.5**) n21.5 t22.5 f21.5 b22 A kind of classic present day style Canadian with plenty of fruit muscling in on the corn. Easy going and very drinkable. 40%. Legends Whisky Series.

**Hiram Walker Legends Series Lanny McDonald** (**85**) n21.5 t21.5 f21 b21 Looks like they are taking a maple leaf out of the Welsh Whisky Company's books by launching whiskies in honour of great fellow countrymen. A friend informs me Lanny McDonald was an ice hockey player. So I suspect he had a touch more personality than this rather sweet straight up and downer. 40%. Legends Whisky Series.

**Hiram Walker Legends Series Wendel Clark** (**94**) n23.5 rye drips from the glass. Firm and fruity with a cinnamon edge. Beautifully two-toned it is both soft and rigid...or neither... or both...! Wow! t23.5 and there it goes again: salivating with a spicy spark now. The fruit reverberates around the palate alongside the Demerara sugars; more cinnamon and red liquorice, too; f23 long, very delicately oiled with extra cinnamon on French toast; light butterscotch accompanies the persistent spices b24 being English, don't know about Wendel Clark being a legend...but this whisky certainly is... 41.6%. Legends Whisky Series.

**Hiram Walker Special Old** (**93**) n22.5 t24 f23 b23.5. Even with the extra degree of all-round harmony, this remains the most solid, uncompromising Canadian of them all. And I love it! Not least because this is the way Special old has been for a very long time with obviously no intentions of joining the fruity bandwagon. Honest, first class Canadian. 40%

**Hiram Walker Special Old Rye Whisky** bott code L16123 (**90.5**) n22.5 t23 f22.5 b22.5 Once one of my daily drinking ryes when in Canada, this has changed course a little in recent years, going easier on the classic old rye itself and making up for it with a richer, sweeter, fatter mouth feel. Not the same magic, but still hard not to love... 40%.

**J.P. Wiser's 18 Year Old** db (**94**) n22.5 dusty, fruity, busy. Soft, fruity sawdust to the sugars; t24 excellent early bite, though the oils make their mark early. Salivating and silky despite the spice build and a little cocoa to accompany the fruit; f23.5 comfortable, with a pleasing acceleration of spice; b24 exceptionally creamy but maintains the required sharpness. 40%.

**J.P. Wiser's 18 Years Old** bott code 54SL24 L16341 (**94**) n23 t24 f23 b24 Some great blending here means this is a slight notch up on the bottling above, though the styles are almost identical. Main differences here concern the fruit aspect: more prolific and spicier on the nose and then added moist date on the delivery. Significantly, there is more honey on the longer finish, also. Remains a deliciously rounded and satisfying whisky. 40%.

**J. P. Wiser's 35 Year Old (96)** n23.5 t24 f24 b24.5 Many, many years ago I tasted Canadian older than this in the blending lab. But I have never seen it before at this age as an official bottling. What I had before me on the lab table could not have engineered this style, so this is as fascinating as it is enjoyable. *50%. Ultra-Rare Craft Series.*

**J. P. Wiser's Canada 2018 Commemorative Series** bott code: L18064EW1332 **(94)** n23.5 t23.5 f23 b24 This whisky, as the front label confirms, has been created to mark the 200th anniversary of the 49th Parallel, the line on which much of Canadian border sits. And this would be the perfect drinking whisky, not just to celebrate, in effect, Canada's birthday. But also to watch the brilliant film The 49th Parallel, by the most extraordinary pairing in cinematic history: Michael Powell and Emeric Pressburger. This 1941 film, designed to help persuade the USA to join in the battle against Germany, picked up an Academy Award for Powell; and many a time have I had the honour of sitting next to another of their Oscars when dining at my club, The Savile, of which both Powell and Pressburger were members. Pressburger was a Jew who had escaped Germany before the war and very famously said of this film: "Goebbels considered himself an expert in propaganda; but I thought I'd show him a thing or two." I can imagine Powell and Pressburger toasting their work – and Canada's special anniversary - with a glass or two of this classical Canadian. I already have. Next time I pop in to my Club, I will do it again from there...on their behalf. *43.4%.*

**J.P. Wiser's De Luxe (86)** n20 t22.5 f21.5 b22. Still nothing like the classic, ultra-charming and almost fragile-delicate Wiser's of old. But this present bottling has got its head partly out of the sand by injecting a decently oaked spiciness to the proceedings and one might even fancy detecting shards of fruity- rye brightness beaming through the toffeed clutter. Definitely an impressive turn for the better and the kind of Canadian with a dangerous propensity to grow on you. If they had the nerve to cut the caramel, this could be a cracker... *40%*

**J. P. Wiser's Dissertation (89)** n22 t22 f22 b22.5 A distinctive and quite different style being handsome, a little rugged but always brooding. *46.1%.*

**J.P. Wiser's Double Still Rye (94)** n23.5 the rye is gorgeously crisp, its natural fruity notes augmented by spearmint; t23.5 every bit as salivating and full-flavoured as the nose predicts. Not as crunchy, maybe, until the Demerara sugars ram themselves home. But the spices arrive in the first few moments and continue building until they become quite a force; f23.5 long, oily, with that spice still impacting positively; b23.5 big, superb rye: a genuine triumph from Wiser's. *43.4%*

**J.P. Wiser's Hopped Whisky (77)** n18 t21 f19 b19. Sorry chaps: one has to draw the line somewhere. But, despite my deep love for great beer, as a whisky this really isn't my kind of thing. Oh, and by the way: been tasting this kind of thing from Germany for the last decade... *40%*

**J.P. Wiser's Last Barrels Aged 14 Years (94.5)** n24.5 t23.5 f23.5 b23.5 You don't need to be pulsing with rye to ensure a complex Canadian of distinction. *45%*

**J.P. Wiser's Legacy (95)** n24 t24.5 f22.5 b22.5. When my researcher got this bottle for me to taste, she was told by the Wiser's guy that I would love it, as it had been specially designed along the lines of what I considered essential attributes to Canadian whisky. Whether Mr Wiser was serious or not, such a statement both honoured and rankled slightly and made me entirely determined to find every fault with it I could and knock such impertinence down a peg or two. Instead, I was seduced like a 16-year-old virgin schoolboy in the hands of a 30-year-old vixen. An entirely disarming Canadian which is almost a whisky equivalent to the finest of the great French wines in its rich, unfolding style. Complex beyond belief, spiced almost to supernatural perfection, this is one of the great newcomers to world whisky in the last year. It will take a glass of true magnificence to outdo this for Canadian Whisky of the Year. *45%*

**J. P. Wiser's One Fifty (86)** n22 t21.5 f21.5 b21 The nose gives hope as heather honey and spices stir. But another Canadian too jammed packed with caramel to enjoy to the fullest, though there is an attractive, if slightly bland, golden syrup thread running through the piece. *43.4%. Commemorative Series.*

**J.P. Wiser's Red Letter 2015 Release** Virgin oak finish **(90.5)** n22.5 t22.5 f23 b22.5 Stubbornly refusing to return to its complex grain past, electing instead to stick to the silky route of more recent years. The sugars are kept in control – just. At times, a little touch and go: this style has been taken as safely as it can go... A backbone to this would be worth so many more points... *43.4%. ncf.*

**J.P. Wiser's Reserve (75)** n19 t20 f18 b18. The nose offers curious tobacco while the palate is uneven, with the bitterness out of tandem with the runaway early sweetness. In the confusion the fruit never quite knows which way to turn. A once mighty whisky has fallen. And I now understand it might be the end of the line with the excellent Wiser's Small Batch coming in to replace it. So if you are a reserve fan, buy them up now. *43%*

**J.P. Wiser's Rye (84.5)** n21 t22 f20.5 b21. Sweet, soft and easy going. The delivery is classic Canadian, with an enjoyable corn oil-vanilla oak mix which initially doesn't go easy on the sugars. The finish, though, is more brittle toffee. *40%*

**J. P. Wiser's Rye 15 Year Old (89) n22** the nose owes much more to a rum style than rye: the golden syrup and molasses make their mark; **t22.5** chewy. Very chewy. More golden syrup and toffee with a late spice development; again a rum-type sheen; **f22.5** simple spice and toffee; **b22** doesn't do too much. But what it does do, it does big... 40%.

**J. P. Wiser's Rye Triple Barrel** bott code L16331 54SL24 **(85.5) n22 t21.5 f21 b21** Three types of toffee barrel by the looks of it. Pleasant but lacking complexity. 45%.

**J. P. Wiser's Seasoned Oak Aged 19 Years** seasoned 48 months, bott code L18114EW0814 **(87.5) n22.5 t23 ff20.5 b21.5** Some high-octane tannin trumps all, though some rich fruit – moist dates especially - rounds off the peppery oak. Enjoys a glossy, coppery but unravels somewhat at the death with a furry, off-key finale. Some lovely, lilting moments but the balance seems controlled. 48%. *Rare Cask Series. Exclusive to the LCBO.*

**J.P. Wiser's Special Blend (78) n19 t20 f19 b19.** A plodding, pleasant whisky with no great desire to offer much beyond caramel. 40%

**J.P. Wiser's Spiced Whisky Vanilla** db **(51) n16 t12 f11 b12.** The policy of the Whisky Bible is not to accept any spiced distillate as, by definition, being whisky. Only Canadian can escape that ban, as they are allowed to put up to 9.09% of whatever into their spirit and still call it whisky. That does not mean to say I am going to like it, though. And, believe me when I tell you I really can't stand this cloyingly sweet liqueur-like offering. Indeed, it may have "whisky" on the label, but this is about as much that great spirit as I am the next Hollywood pin up. 43%

**J.P. Wiser's Triple Barrel (85.5) n22 t21.5 f21 b21.** The barrels, whatever their number, appear to be no match for the big caramel theme. 40% (80 proof)

**J. P. Wiser's Triple Barrel Aged 10 Years** bott code: L17258 **(89) n22** the softest nose imaginable: gentle vanilla...a kind of sherry trifle... but without the sherry; **t23** here it excels: the delivery retains an endearing juiciness despite the marriage in heaven between caramel and vanilla; alert spices ensure you don't get too comfortable; **f21.5** slightly bitter and a tad out of balance; **b22.5** the finale apart, this is a celebration of the gentler side of whisky 40%.

**Lot 40 Cask Strength (88.5) n23.5 t24 f20 b22** At last! Lot 40 at full strength! You will not read this anywhere (or anything to do with my many whisky creations over the last 25 years as journalists can sometimes be a pathetically narrow-minded and jealous bunch disinclined to tell the true story if it doesn't suit their own agenda) but when I first created the style for Lot 40 a great many years back the first thing I proposed was that it should be a rye at cask strength. The idea was liked in principle but regarded way too radical for its time and dropped. So I helped come up with a weaker but still excellent rye. This is a different style to what I had in mind as the oak gives a slant I would have avoided. But it gladdens my heart to see it nonetheless. 53%. *Ultra-Rare Craft Series.*

**Lot No. 40 Rye Whisky** bott code 54SL24 L16344 **(96) n24 t24 f23.5 b24.5** Now this is very close to the rye I had in mind when first involved in putting this whisky together the best part of a couple of decades ago. Much more complex and satisfying than the previous re-introduced bottling I encountered...which in itself was magnificent. Here, though, the honey I had originally tried to lasso has been brilliantly recaptured. Happy to admit: this is better than my early efforts. There really is a Lot going on... Classic! 43%.

**Okanagan Spirits Rye (88.5) n23 t22.5 f21 b22.** A crisp, quite beautiful whisky with a youthful strain. Sort the thin finish out and we'd have something to really remember! Not, by the way, a whisky distilled at their new distillery. 40%

**Pendleton 1910 Aged 12 Years Rye (83) n21 t22 f20 b20.** Pleasant enough. But if it wasn't for the small degree of spice pepping up this fruitfest, it would be all rather too predictable. 40%

**Pendleton Midnight (78) n20 t21 f18 b19.** Soft and soothing. But far more rampant fruit than grain. In fact, hard to detect the grain at all... 45% (90 Proof).

**Pike Creek (92) n22 t23.5 f23 b23.5** A whisky that is more effect over substance, for this really has to be the softest, silkiest world whisky of 2015. And if you happen to like your taste buds being pampered and chocolate is your thing, this Canadian has your name written all over it. 40%

**Pike Creek** French, Hungarian & American oak casks **(89) n23** this is all about the varied intensity and rhythm of the tannin: deep, toasty and rich, a malty sweetness helps keep the lid on the oak. Manuka honey and green tea also give this a slightly medicinal quality; **t22.5** the delivery would need an injection of sugars to work...and they duly arrive in the form of toasty molasses. Slight coffee fudge; **f21.5** back to green tea tannins again; **b22** you know you have a great nose on your hands when a fly drowns in your whisky even before you get a chance to taste it... Decent stuff keeping your taste buds at full stretch. 45%.

**Pike Creek 10 Years Old** finished in port barrels **(80) n21.5 t22.5 f17 b19.** The delivery is the highlight of the show by far as the fruit takes off backed by delicate spices and spongy softness. The nose needs some persuading to get going but when fully warmed, gives a preview of the delivery. The furry finish is a big disappointment, though. 40%

**Pike Creek 10 Year Old Rum Barrels Finish** bott code 54SL24 L16174 EW07:30 **(86.5) n22 t22.5 f20 b22** A far happier fellow than the Port finish, for sure – even though the slight furriness on the finale is a bit of a bore. Before reaching that point, though, there is a velvet revolution involving much honey. 42%.

**Pike Creek 21 Year Old Single Malt Cask Finish (87.5) n21 t23.5 f21.5 b21.5** Pleasant and fruity. As silky as you like with a moist date and spiced theme. But, doubtless, through the cask finish, the age and accompanying complexities seems to have been lost in translation somewhere... 45%. *Ultra-Rare Craft Series.*

**Potter's Special Old** a blend of 5 to 11 year old rye whisky **(91) n23.5 t23 f22 b22.5.** More Canadian than a hockey punch-up – and, for all the spice, somewhat more gentle, too. 40%

**Rich and Rare (79) n20 t20 f20 b19.** Simplistic and soft. One for toffee lovers. 40%

**Rich and Rare Reserve (86.5) n19.5 t21 f23.5 b22.5.** Actually does what it says on the tin, certainly as to regard the "Rich" bit. But takes off when the finish spices up and even offers some ginger cake on the finale. Lovely stuff. 40%

**Royal Reserve Gold (94.5) n24 t23.5 f23 b24.** Retains its position as a classy, classy Canadian that is an essay on balance. Don't confuse this with the much duller standard bottling: this has been moulded in recent years into one of the finest – and among its country's consumers - generally most underrated Canadians on the market. 40%

⬩ **Sam Barton Aged 5 Years** bott code: L814502B **(86.5) n21 t22 f21.5 b22** A much improved blend of late with a much studier structure after the clean, now classically Canadian nose. Good spice buzz and lots of easy charm. 40%. *La Martiniquaise.*

**Seagram's Canadian 83 (86.5) n21 t22 f21.5 b22.** A vastly improved blend which has drastically cut the caramel to reveal a melt-in-the-mouth, slightly crisp grain. There are some citrusy edges but the buttery vanilla and pleasing bite all go to make for a chic little number. 40%

**Seagram's VO (91) n22 t23.5 f22.5 b23.** With a heavy heart I have to announce the king of rye-enriched Canadian, VO, is dead. Long live the corn-dominant VO. Over the years I have seen the old traditional character ebb away: now I have let go and have no option other than to embrace this whisky for what it has become: infinitely better than a couple of years back; not in the same league as a decade ago. But just taking it on face value, credit where credit is due. This is an enjoyably playful affair, full of vanilla-led good intention, corn and complexity. There is even assertive spice when needed and the most delicately fruity edge...though not rye-style. Thoughtfully blended and with no little skill, I am impressed. And look forward to seeing how this develops in future years. A treat which needs time to discover. 40%

⬩ **Signal Hill Whisky** bott no. 181560932 **(82) n21.5 t21.5 f19 b20** There is no little irony that a hill which dramatically juts 470 feet out of the sea to present one of Canada's most startling and historical points should be represented by a whisky that is so intransigently flat... 40%. *ncf.*

⬩ **Stalk & Barrel Canadian Whisky Blue Blend (91) n22.5** impressive vanilla layering; lovely lime blossom honey sweetness; **t23** silky and salivating, again the honey thread wins the day, this time acacia to the fore; **f22.5** beautiful oils hug every contour, the thin fingers of honey reaching out still to all four corners; **b23** supremely easy-going Canadian. Such a treat. 40%.

⬩ **Stalk & Barrel Canadian Whisky Red Blend (84.5) n19 t22 f21.5 b22** Hefty and spicy, the caramel and vanillas dominate Quite a lingering finish. 43%.

**Union 52 (90.5) n23 t23 f22.5 b23** A very different type of Canadian which is as busy as it gets. 40%.

**Western Gold Canadian Whisky (91) n23 t23 f22.5 b22.5.** Clean and absolutely classic Canadian: you can't ask for much more, really. 40%

**White Owl (77.5) n19 t19.5 f20 b19.** White whisky: in others words, a whisky the same colour as water. To both nose and taste somewhat reminds me of the long gone Manx whisky which was casks of fully matured scotch re-distilled and bottled. Sweet and pleasant. But I doubt if connoisseurs will give two hoots... 40%

**Windsor (86) n20 t21 f23 b22.** Pleasant but the majority of edges found on the Canadian edition blunted. Some outstanding, almost attritional, spice towards the middle and finale, though. Soft and desirable throughout: a kind of feminine version of the native bottling. 40%.

# Canadian Straight Rye Whisky

⬩ **Masterson's 10 Year Old Straight Rye Whiskey** white oak casks, batch no. 016 **(94) n23** slightly more oak than normal, giving a calmer, more austere feel. You do get the feeling something is fizzing and brighter just below the surface, though; **t23** immediate salivation alert as the rye foes on the offensive and thickens to mind-boggling levels. Intense grain, sweetened further by a light orange blossom honey injection; **f24** at first bitters then goes into cocoa overdrive, aided by a oiliness which accentuates every last dry oaky morsal; **b24** one of the most beautiful finishes to any whisky on the planet this year. 45% (90 proof).

# Scottish Malts

For those of you deciding to take the plunge and head off into the labyrinthine world of Scotch malt whisky, a piece of advice. And that is, be careful who you take your advice from. Because, too often, I hear that you should leave the Islays until you have tackled the featherlight Speysiders and the bolder, weightier Highlanders. This is just complete, patronising nonsense. The only time that rings true is if you are tasting a number of whiskies in one day. Then leave the smoky ones till last, so the lighter chaps get a fair hearing.

I know many people who didn't like whisky until they got a Talisker from Skye inside them, or a Lagavulin to swamp their tastebuds with oily iodine. The fact is, you can take your map of malt whisky, start at any point and head in whichever direction you feel. There are no hard and fast rules. Certainly with over 2,000 tasting notes for Scottish malts here you should have some help in picking where this journey of a lifetime begins.

It is also worth remembering not always to be seduced by age. It is true that many of the highest scores are given to big-aged whiskies. The truth is that the majority of malts, once they have lived beyond 25 years or so, suffer from oak influence rather than benefit. Part of the fun of discovering whiskies is to see how malts from different distilleries perform to age and type of cask. Happy discovering.

i Abhainn Dearg
LEWIS
Isle of Harris

SKYE · Isle o
Talisker
Torabhaig

Ardn
Tobermory · Nc
MULL
Oba

# Islay

Bunnahabhain
Ardnahoe
Caol Ila
Kilchoman
Bruichladdich
Bowmore
Port Ellen · Ardbeg
Laphroaig · Lagavulin

Isle o
ISLAY
Isle
Springbank
Glen Scotia
Glengyle

**ORKNEY ISLANDS**

Highland Park
Scapa

Wolfburn

Pultney

Clynelish
Brora

Dornoch
Balblair
Dalmore
Teaninich
Invergordon
Glenmorangie

Banff
Macduff

Glen Ord
GlenWyris
Inverness
Glen Albyn
Glen Mhor
Millburn

Speyside see page 24

Glenglassaugh

Royal Brackla

Knockdhu

Glendronach
Ardmore

Glenugie

Tomatin

The Speyside Distillery

Glen Garioch

Royal Lochnagar

**Aberdeen**

Dalwhinnie

Glenury Royal
Fettercairn

Blair Athol

Fort William
Ben Nevis
Glenlochy

Edradour
Aberfeldy

Glencadam
North Port
Lochside

Glenesk

Arbikie

Lindores Abbey

**Dundee**

Strathearn
Glenturret
Aberargie
Tullibardine
Deanston

**Perth**

Daftmill
Eden Mill

Kingsbarns

Cameronbridge
InchDairnie

Glengoyne
Rosebank
St. Magdelene

Loch Lomond
Dumbarton
Interleven
Littlemill
Auchentoshan

Starlaw

Glenkinchie

**Edinburgh**

North British

Glasgow
Strathclyde
Port Dundas
Kinclaith

Borders

Girvan
Ailsa Bay
Ladyburn

Annandale

Bladnoch

| Key | |
|---|---|
| ● | **Major Town or City** |
| ⛰ | Single Malt Distillery |
| ⛰ | (*Italics*) Grain Distillery |
| ✝ | Dead Distillery |

# Speyside

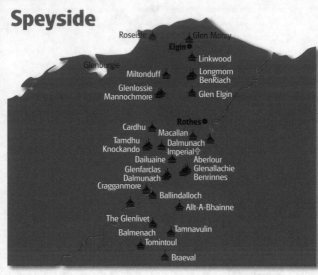

Roseisle
Glen Moray
Elgin
Linkwood
Glenburgie
Miltonduff
Longmorn
BenRiach
Glenlossie
Mannochmore
Glen Elgin
Rothes
Cardhu
Macallan
Tamdhu
Dalmunach
Knockando
Imperial
Dailuaine
Aberlour
Glenfarclas
Glenallachie
Dalmunach
Benrinnes
Cragganmore
Ballindalloch
Allt-A-Bhainne
The Glenlivet
Tamnavulin
Balmenach
Tomintoul
Braeval

| Distilleries by Town | Mortlach | Glenrothes |
|---|---|---|
| **Dufftown** | Dufftown | Glenspey |
| Glenfiddich | Pittyvaich | **Keith** |
| Convalmore | **Rothes** | Aultmore |
| Balvenie | Speyburn | Strathmill |
| Kininvie | Glen Grant | Glen Keith |
| Glendullan | Caperdonich | Strathisla |

## SINGLE MALTS
## ABERFELDY

**Highlands (Perthshire), 1898. Bacardi. Working.**

**Aberfeldy 12 Year Old** db **(81) n21 t21 f19 b20.** A puzzling malt. Aberfeldy makes and matures some of the greatest whisky on this planet, make no mistake. So why this conservative, ultra safe toffee-sultana-fudge offering when their warehouses are crammed with casks which could blow the world away? Pleasant. But so relentlessly dull and disappointing. And 40% abv…? Really…? *40% WB16/031*

⟡ **Aberfeldy Aged 12 Years** bott code: L19032249021553 db **(78.5) n20 t20.5 f19 b19** Reduced to 40% and then rammed with caramel for colouring. And we are talking at this age, when tasted in good bourbon casks, one of Scotland's more delightful and effortlessly complex whiskies. Instead we are still presented with this absolute non-event of a bottling. Bewildering. *40%.*

**Aberfeldy 16 Year Old** db **(89.5) n22.5** Light, leathery and with a citrus freshness; **t23.5** succulent, with a ripe melon sweetness meeting an earthier, almost semi-phenolic, substrata; a beautiful match; **f21.5** should recede in layers. Yet, despite some lingering sugars, fades with a surprising flatness; **b22** finishes far too fast and tamely. But the thrust of the malt is wonderful. *40%*

⟡ **Aberfeldy Aged 16 Years** bott code: L16118ZA805 db **(83.5) n21 t21 f20.5 b21** An astonishingly dull whisky for its age. Sweet and soft for sure, but very little character as it appears to bathe in rich toffee. If you want a safe, pleasant whisky which says very little, here's your dram. *40%.*

**Aberfeldy 21 Year Old** db **(88) n22 t22.5 f21.5 b22** The kind of malt I wish I could be let loose on…this really could be world class. But… *40%*

⟡ **Aberfeldy Aged 21 Years** bott code: L18092ZA803 db **(88) n22** some weak-ish peppery oak has just enough strength to punch its ways through the toffee and sultanas; **t22.5** a thin delivery with the usual big toffee touch. Then a surprising surge of toasty tannin, which soon fizzles out as light fruit engage; **f21.5** glazed cherry and marzipan – and the inevitable caramel – bring us to a gentle conclusion. With perhaps a little unwelcome tang from the sherry butts; **b22** poodles along pleasantly but feels like a Fiat Uno engine in what, for this distillery, should be Jaguar XK… *40%.*

**Aberfeldy Aged 25 Years** db (85) n24 t21 f19 b21. Just doesn't live up to the nose. When Tommy Dewar wrote, "We have a great regard for old age when it is bottled," as quoted on the label, I'm not sure he had as many as 25 years in mind. *40%.*

⬩⬩⬩ **Gordon & MacPhail Connoisseurs Choice Aberfeldy Aged 25 Years** first fill sherry puncheon, cask no. 4054, dist 6 Jun 93, bott 21 Jun 18 (94.5) n23.5 t24 f23 b24 Don't know about Aberfeldy: almost Aberlour a'bunagh-esque in the intensity of its sherry attack. And make no mistake: this is high grape, faultless oloroso at work here. Except, this presents the fruit in a much more clear, untroubled form, making the power of the personality of the distillery, slowly work its way into the picture which it does thanks to its rich, malty chassis. *58.8%. sc. 444 bottles.*

**Gordon & MacPhail Connoisseurs Choice Aberfeldy 1993** first fill sherry puncheon, cask no. 4056, dist 6 Jun 93, bott 21 Feb 18 (96) n24 t24.5 f23.5 b24 A completely untainted sherry puncheon in full, clean richness: not sure whether to run outside and dance naked by the light of the moon. Perhaps after going to quite nearby ancient Rollright Stones. For this is a very rare and special event, these days seemingly prehistoric. *58.7%. nc ncf sc. 589 bottles.*

**Gordon & MacPhail Connoisseurs Choice Aberfeldy 2003** bott 14 Mar 17 (94.5) n23.5 t23.5 f23.5 b24 Just bursting from the bottle with personality. Big, at times muscular, but never coarse... *46%.*

## ABERLOUR
**Speyside, 1826. Chivas Brothers. Working.**

**Aberlour 10 Years Old** db (87.5) n22.5 t22 f21 b22. Remains a lusty fellow though here nothing like as sherry-cask faultless as before, nor displaying its usual honeyed twinkle. *43%*

**Aberlour 10 Years Old Sherry Cask Finish** db (85) n21 t21 f21 b22. Bipolar and bitter-sweet with the firmness of the grain in vivid contrast to the gentle grape. *43%*

**Aberlour 12 Years Old Double Cask** db (89) n22 nutty, but lightened by cherry blossom; t23 salivating with a slow unravelling of ever-intensifying tannin. Quite pithy and chalky on the fruity front; f21.5 dries further towards cocoa powder; a little bitter but the firmness of the malt is impressive; late spice; b22.5 a delicately poised malt which makes as much ado about the two different oak types as it does the fruit-malt balancing act. *40%*

**Aberlour 12 Years Old Double Cask Matured** db (88.5) n22 t22.5 f22 b22. Voluptuous and mouth-watering in some areas, firmer and less expansive in others. Pretty tasty in all of them. *43%*

**Aberlour 12 Years Old Non Chill-Filtered** db (87) n22.5 t22 f21 b21.5. There are many excellent facets to this malt, not least the balance between barley and grape and the politeness of the gristy sugars. But a sulphured butt has crept into this one, taking the edge off the excellence and bringing down the score like a cold front drags down the thermometer. *48%. ncf.*

**Aberlour 12 Years Old Sherry Cask Matured** db (88) n23 t22 f21 b22. Could do with some delicate extra sweetness to take it to the next level. Sophisticated nonetheless. *40%*

**Aberlour 15 Years Cuvee Marie d'Ecosse** db (91) n22 t24 f22 b23. This always was a deceptive lightweight, and it's got lighter still. It is sold primarily in France, and one can assume only that this is God's way of making amends for that pretentious, over-rated, caramel-ridden rubbish called Cognac they've had to endure. *43%*

**Aberlour 15 Year Old Double Cask Matured** db (84) n23 t22 f19 b20. Brilliant nose full of vibrant apples and spiced sultana, but then, after a complex, chewy, malt-enriched kick-off, falls surprisingly flat on its face. *40%*

**Aberlour 15 Year Old Sherry Finish** db (91) n24 t22 f23 b22 Quite unique: freaky, even. Really a whisky to be discovered and ridden. Once you acclimatize, you'll adore it. *43%*

⬩⬩⬩ **Aberlour 16 Years Old Double Cask Matured** traditional oak & sherry oak casks, bott code: L N2 27 2019/05/14 db (88) n22.5 a chalky dryness prevails despite the sharper greengage and Chinese gooseberry notes; t22 soft and mouth-watering on arrival – the expected oily back up doesn't arrive. Soon drifts towards a malty chalkiness not unlike on the nose with only a delicate citrus note lifting the mid-term vanilla; f21.5 more vanilla – and dries further; b22 none of the dreaded S word here, so well done sherry butts. But this is underpowered in this day and age for the kind of malt it could be. The lack of oils are crucial. *40%.*

**Aberlour 18 Years Old** db (91) n22 thick milkshake with various fruits and vanilla; t22 immediate fresh juice which curdles beautifully as the vanilla is added; f24 wonderful fruit-chocolate fudge development: long, and guided by a gentle oiliness; b23 another high performance distillery age-stated bottling. *43%*

**Aberlour 100 Proof** db (91) n23 t23 f22 b23. Stunning, sensational whisky, the most extraordinary Speysider of them all...which it was when I wrote those official notes for the bottling back in '97, I think. Other malts have superseded it now, but on re-tasting I stand by those original notes, though I disassociate myself entirely with the rubbish: "In order to savour Aberlour 100 at its best add 1/3 to 1/2 pure water." *57.1%*

**Aberlour A'Bunadh Batch No. 53** db **(95) n23 t24 f24 b24** A truly beautiful whisky. But, oh! had only Batch 54 been this sulphur free we would have entered a new experience of whisky perfection. *59.7%*

**Aberlour A'Bunadh Batch No. 54** db **(96) n23.5 t25 f23 b24.5** For just the delivery, no whisky will be better this year, or probably next. It had even crossed my mind to give it 25.5! A privilege to experience... *60.7%*

**Aberlour A'Bunadh Batch No. 57** Spanish Oloroso sherry butts db **(81) n20.5 t22.5 f18 b20** Read my notes to batch 47, and we have a similar malt, though here there is not quite so much sparkle on delivery and there may be two rather than one butt at fault. *60.7%. ncf.*

**Aberlour A'Bunadh Batch No. 61** Spanish Oloroso sherry butts db **(95) n23 t24 f23.5 b24.5** Although matured in 100% sherry butts – and clean, sulphur-free ones at that – one of the most remarkable, and delicious, features of this malt is the bourbon-esque quality of the oak notes mixing in with the grape. Wow! *60.8%. ncf.*

⬧ **Aberlour A'Bunadh Batch No. 63** Spanish Oloroso sherry butts db **(93) n23.5** raspberry and cream Swiss Roll; **t24** lush, with ulmo honey in concentrate, before juicy moist date takes control; molasses and mocha moves into midfield. Just the right degree of spices add bite; **f22** a long tannin-grape mixed finale displaying just the lightest trace of bittering sulphur; **b23.5** slightly lighter than some A'Bunadhs, which holds out well and seemingly clean until trace bitterness arrives. But so much to savour here. *61%. ncf.*

**Aberlour Casg Annamh** batch no. 0001 db **(84.5) n21.5 t22.5 f19 b21.5** The nose is at first promising with nutty sherry tones dominating, then dry but with the most subtle countering muscovado and black cherry sweetness. Then comes the threat of the S word...which is confirmed on the rough, furry finish. The delivery starts with those sugars well into their stride, arriving early and mingling with the spice. Dates and figs represent the fruit with panache. *48%. ncf.*

⬧ **Liquid Treasures 10th Anniversary Aberlour 26 Year Old** sherry hogshead, dist 1992, bott 2019 **(86.5) n22.5 t22 f21 b21** A pithy malt in both senses which reaches into its drier, spicier fruitier side, but not much inclined to go any further. *51.9%. sc. 101 bottles.*

⬧ **Scotch Malt Whisky Society Cask 54.75 16 Year Old** 2nd fill toasted hogshead, dist 2 Oct 02 **(94.5) n23.5** the lightness of toast ensures complex interplay between barley and tannin: no shortage of verve; just the faintest hint of mint and lime intervene and move it towards Kentucky inch by inch; **t23.5** huge barley on delivery, as though beating its chest to shew its Speyside credentials. But there is also a lovely salted caramel note, too: subtle and softening which seems to underline the malt rather than obscure it; **f23.5** now goes into mega complexity rather than just fade away with spices, chocolate and even the vaguest hint of Chinese gooseberry to add a sharp sweetness; **b24** it is so good to again find an Aberlour free of sherry, as used to be the case 30 years ago. Here, you can see clearly just how beautiful this whisky is naked. It was my choice as an outside bet for a stunner for my 750th whisky of this 2020 Bible. I have not been let down! *59.8%. sc.*

# ABHAINN DEARG

**Highlands (Outer Hebrides), 2008. Marko Tayburn. Working.**

**Abhainn Dearg New Make** db **(92.5) n23 t23 f23.5 b23.** Exceptionally well made with no feints and no waste, either. Oddly salty – possibly the saltiest new make I have encountered, and can think of no reason why it should be – with excellent weight as some extra copper from the new still takes hold. Given a good cask, no reason this impressive new born son of the Outer Hebrides won't go on to become something significant. *67%*

# AILSA BAY

**Lowland, 2007. William Grant & Sons. Working.**

**Ailsa Bay** db **(92.5) n23.5 t23.5 f22.5 b23** I remember years back being told they wanted to make an occasional peaty malt at this new distillery different in style to Islay's. They have been only marginally successful: only the finish gives the game away. But they have certainly matched the island when it comes to the average high quality. A resounding success of a first effort, though I'd like to see the finish offer a little more than it currently does. Early days, though. *48.9%.*

# ALLT-Á-BHAINNE

**Speyside, 1975. Chivas Brothers. Working.**

**Chapter 7 Allt-A-Bhainne 9 Year Old** 1st fill bourbon finish, cask no. 170, dist 2008 **(78) n18 t19 f21 b20** Hot and tuneless, it takes time for find its rhythm and range and finally settles down for a big malty, if slightly austere finish. Younger than its years, also. *60.7%. sc.*

**The First Editions Allt-A-Bhainne Aged 24 Years 1995** refill bourbon barrel, cask no. 14120, bott 2017 **(93) n22.5 t23 f23 b23.5** A really big oak input here is surprisingly well received by a usually light spirit: a surprise package, indeed! *52.9%. nc ncf sc. 180 bottles.*

**Golden Cask Allt-A-Bhainne Aged 8 Years** cask no. CM230, dist 2008, bott 2016 **(74.5)** **n18 t19 f18.5 b19** The firm, juicy, boisterous maltiness to this is undone by a cask-induced tang to both the nose and finish. A pity. 60.9%. sc. 306 bottles.

**Old Particular Allt-A-Bhainne 21 Years Old** refill hogshead, cask no. 12038, dist Nov 95, bott Aug 17 **(91.5)** **n23 t23 f22.5 b23** Just sings "Speyside" to you. Just so clean and malty: you feel your teeth will sparkle after tasting it... 496%. nc ncf sc. 287 bottles.

**Scotch Malt Whisky Society Cask 108.10 9 Year Old** 1st fill ex-bourbon barrel, dist 12 Mar 08 **(91)** **n22.5 t23 f22.5 b23** Recent bottlings from AAB from this period have been disappointing, to put it mildly. No fear with this one, which makes the most of both the big malt and the high- quality barrel. 61.2%. sc.

⁘ **The Whisky Chamber Allt-A-Bhainne 9 Years Old 2009** Amarone cask **(83)** **n21.5** **t22 f19.5 b20** The trouble with the effects of an all-consuming wine cask which dramatically sweetens up the whisky, is that when there is a bitter, off-key note on the finish, as is the case here, that comes through even more loudly... 60.4%. sc.

# ANNANDALE
**Lowlands, 2014. Annandale Distillery Company Ltd. Working.**
**Annandale Man O' Sword** cask no. 100, dist 2014 db **(92.5)** **n23.5 t23 f21.5 b23.5** The strangest thing...I nosed this and thought: Jim Swan. This delightful style has the late, great whisky consultant's finger prints all over it. A young malt from a brand new distillery already punching way above its weight age-wise and in terms of complexity. Welcome to the whisky world, Annandale. And what a worthy addition you have already become. Now you just have to keep up this standard: no pressure at all... 61.6%. sc. 256 bottles.

⁘ **Annandale Man O' Sword Smoulderingly Smoky** once-used ex bourbon cask, cask no. 470, dist 2014 db **(96.5)** **n24** as it says in the tin, this really is smoulderingly smoky and the peat is helped by having a few rough edges to give it genuine character. A degree of nuttiness here, too; **t24.5** mouth-puckering! For the first time you pick up that this is a relative youngster as a slight new-makey freshness comes across. But, like some 15-year-old making his debut in the Premier League, this precocious malt fears nothing and allows the phenols full reign while turning on the spices and buttery barley at maximum intensity; **f23.5** ah...some tannins make a play, but a little molasses and peat ensure balance remains uncompromised; **b24.5** make no mistake: new distillery or no, this is fabulously and truly faultlessly made and brilliantly matured whisky which allows every last element of the distillery's personality to be seen. What a genuine treat! What an immense start to such a new distillery! 60.2%. sc. 271 bottles.

**Annandale Man O' Words** cask no. 140, dist 2014 db **(89.5)** **n22.5 t22.5 f22 b22.5** A malty delight. Had been meaning to take in Annan Athletic FC and Annandale Distillery over the last four years but my diary just wouldn't allow it. Somehow I have to make it happen. This distillery promises great things. 61.6%. sc. 273 bottles.

⁘ **Annandale Man O' Words** once-used ex bourbon cask, cask no. 149, dist 2014 db **(94)** **n23** young whisky, which means the barley is shewing like it will never shew again...so fresh and sexy; **t23.5** pre-pubescent it may be, but without the phenols you can really see here how this whisky ticks. For a start, this has been brilliantly made: distilled on a slightly slower scale as the malt intensity is almost immeasurable; **f23.5** long, and ultra-malty, with the tannins not yet able to make meaningful headway; **b24** a few months ago I was doing some quality control checks at a warehouse in Scotland and there, much to my surprise, were a whole bunch of newly filled, quietly maturing Annandale casks. You have no idea how much I wanted to take a break from my designated work to sneakily crack open a few of those Lowland barrels to see how they were getting on. I think I should arrange a return visit... Oh, and good people of Annandale, - congratulations and thank you for bottling from ex-bourbon cask. Because we can see the sheer beauty of the malt you are making, something I could not say if it was hidden under (usually faulty) wine casks or obliterated entirely by bloody PX, the scourge of world whisky today. 61%. sc. 268 bottles.

# ARDBEG
**Islay, 1815. Glenmorangie Plc. Working.**
**Ardbeg 10 Years Old** db **(97)** **n24 t24 f24 b25** Like when you usually come across something that goes down so beautifully and with such a nimble touch and disarming allure, just close your eyes and enjoy... 46%

**Ardbeg 10** bottling mark L10 152 db **(95)** **n24.5 t23.5 f23.5 b23.5** A bigger than normal version, but still wonderfully delicate. Fabulous and faultless. 46%. Canadian market bottling in English and French dual language label.

**Ardbeg 17 Years Old** earlier bottlings db **(92)** **n23 t22 f23 b24.** OK, I admit I had a big hand in this, creating it with the help of Glenmorangie Plc's John Smith. It was designed to take the weight off the better vintages of Ardbeg whilst ensuring a constant supply around the world. Certainly one of the more subtle expressions you are likely to find, though criticised by some for not being peaty enough. As the whisky's creator, all I can say is they are missing the point. *40%*

**Ardbeg 17 Years Old** later bottlings db **(90)** n22 t23 f22 b23. The peat has all but vanished and cannot really be compared to the original 17-year-old: it's a bit like tasting a Macallan without the sherry: fascinating to see the naked body underneath, and certainly more of a turn on. Peat or no peat, great whisky by any standards. *40%*

**Ardbeg 19 Years Old** db **(93)** n23 lower than usual phenols drift dream-like away from the glass. Look carefully and you'll find that lightly salted Digestive biscuit tannins enjoy the same foothold and the citrus has its usual seat at the table; t23 that biscuit saltiness acts as a brief spur to ramp up the early juice levels. But is fleeting and the whole dries quickly as the powdery phenols assert themselves; f23.5 the oils have thinned but have enough purchase to ensure the minty chocolate is on an equal footing with the friendly phenols; b23.5 one of the sensuously understated Ardbegs that could be found in style (though with a different peat imprint) from time to time during the 1960s. *46.2%*.

**Ardbeg 20 Something** db **(96.5)** n24 no doubting that a once heavyweight smoke signature has lightened over the years an aged but deft aroma of extraordinary poise: a bit like unearthing the preserved footsteps of a giant dinosaur... The very first hint of exotic fruit also underlines that this is heading towards antique mode...; t24 one suspects from the nose that may be some differing ages in play and the fabulous structure on the palate only confirms this. Despite the peat, nothing heavy, no aggression. Just layering, like one snow fall on top of another, revealing the vanilla and ethereal tannins drifting away. Those little nudges again towards exotic fruit once more remind you of the many passing years; f24 late salivation as the almost sherbet like lemon kicks over the smoky traces; like the 19-year-old a vague minty-chocolate trace fits in effortlessly; b24.5 such mastery over the phenols...such elegance! It is though the whisky was distilled from gossamer... *46%*.

**Ardbeg 21 Years Old** db **(96.5)** n24 it is as though there are three levels of smokiness working in tandem: the layering is ridiculously well-structured. The deepest notes are earthy, rich with even a hint of unpicked tomato; the middle layer is flightier and spiced, seemingly in league with the gristier notes. And a third layer of phenols are sooty and wispy, like thin clouds scudding across on a windy day...amazing....; t24 the delivery by contrast is only two-toned. The malt, sans smoke, is gristy, lemon tinged and juices up with intense barley as the sugars strike home. But it is kept in check by the phenols which hit first with a combined weight, but then scatters about the palate until it reforms later on in liquorice and chocolate vogue; f24 much more ethereal now, though we have moved more towards crystalline sugars only too willing to melt and discreet spices which occasionally nip. To say the finish is long is a little bit of an understatement...; b24.5 tap into Ardbeg with great care, like someone has done here, and there is no describing what beauty can be unleashed. For much of the time, the smoke performs in brilliant fashion somewhere between the ethereal and profound. *46%*

**Ardbeg 23 Year Old** db **(93)** n22.5 takes time for the strongarm oak to get anything less than too firm a grip of proceedings: if there is smoke in there, it has taken cover...; vague citrus pops its head up for a quick look – then quickly down again as it hides with the phenols...; t24 yep, full on tannin....at first. The fragile citrus and more ample barley begins the job of restoring balance, which it does with typical Ardbegian elegance. There is a delicate smokiness which can be found lightly brushed over the milky, vaguely minty mocha which has gathered up enough dark sugars to form the nucleus of the resistance movement; just enough gristy barley lurks about to ensure a degree of defiant salivation, too; f23 those big tannins return to mount a guard, but some lovely chocolate malt and spice manage to get through without being spotted...; b23.5 a malt forever treading on eggshells, trying not to disturb the tannins. As a dram, makes a nervous wreck of you, as you spend the entire time waiting for the shallow truce to be broken and the oak to declare war and come pouring in. Thankfully, it never quite happens. As all whiskies, not be taken with water. But, in this instance, a tranquilliser might not go amiss... *46.3%*.

**Ardbeg 1977** db **(96)** n25 t24 f23 b24. When working through the Ardbeg stocks, I earmarked '77 a special vintage, the sweetest of them all. So it has proved. Only the '74 absorbed that extra oak that gave greater all-round complexity. Either way, the quality of the distillate is beyond measure: simply one of the greatest experiences – whisky or otherwise – of your life. *46%*

**Ardbeg 1978** db **(91)** n23 t24 f22 b22. An Ardbeg on the edge of losing it because of encroaching oak, hence the decision made by John Smith and me to bottle this vintage early alongside the 17-year-old. Nearly ten years on, still looks a pretty decent bottling, though slightly under strength! *43%*

**Ardbeg An Oa** db **(95.5)** n24 t24 f23.5 b24 I'd never say "whoa" if someone poured me an Oa... *46%*.

**Ardbeg Aurivedes** American oak casks with specially toasted cask lids. db **(91.5) n22 t22.5 f24 b23** I have spoken to nobody at Ardbeg about this one but from the slight bourbon character of the nose and the heavy vanilla, this version appears to be about the casks, possibly the char of the barrels. Fascinating, enjoyable...but whatever this is, the usual complexity of the peat feels compromised in the same way a wine cask might. Except here I detect no telling fruit. A real curiosity, whatever it is... 49.9%. Moet Hennessy.

**Ardbeg Blasda** db **(90.5) n23.5 t22.5 f22 b22.5** A beautiful, if slightly underpowered malt, which shows Ardbeg's naked self to glowing effect. Overshadowed by some degree in its class by the SMWS bottling, but still something to genuinely make the heart flutter. 40%

**Ardbeg Corryvreckan** db **(96.5) n23 t24.5 f24 b25** As famous writers – including the occasional genius film director (stand up whoever you are my heroes Powell and Pressburger) – appear to be attracted to Corryvreckan, the third most violent whirlpool found in the world and just off Islay, to boot, - I selected this as my 1,500th whisky tasted for the historic Jim Murray Whisky Bible 2009. I'm so glad I did because many have told me they thought Blasda ahead of this. To me, it's not even a contest. Currently I have only a sample. Soon I shall have a bottle. I doubt if even the feared whirlpool is this deep and perplexing. 57.1%. 5000 bottles.

**Ardbeg Dark Cove** db **(86) n22.5 t22.5 f19.5 b21.5.** For whatever reason, this is a much duller version than the Committee Edition. And strength alone can't explain it, or solely the loss of the essential oils from reduction. There is a slight nagging to this one so perhaps any weakness to the sherry butts has been accentuated by the reduction of oil, if it has been bottled from the same vatting – which I doubt. Otherwise, the tasting notes are along the lines of below, except with just a little less accent on the sugars. 46.5%

**Ardbeg Dark Cove Committee Edition** db **(90.5) n23.5 t23 f21.5 b22.5** Big sherry and bigger peat always struggle somewhere along the line. So once does pretty well until we reach the finale when it unravels slightly. But sulphur-free. And challenging. 55%

&#8618; **Ardbeg Drum** db **(92.5) n23** as gentle and peatily well dispersed an Ardbeg as you'll ever find, the phenols here being flaky and light. Indeed, there is just as much underlying cocoa to be found should you look hard enough. Citrusy, of course, too...; **t23.5** incredibly thin on delivery, little of the usual light oils being present. Again, the smoke is fragmented and allows the vanillas equal room on the podium; only towards the middle does a little ulmo honey begin to sweeten things up; **f22.5** one of the lightest finishes of any Ardbeg I have ever encountered. A delightful mocha and roasted hazelnut rounds things off deftly; **b23.5** well! I wasn't expecting that! It is as if this is from some super-fine cut, with 20% of the usual heart each way being sent back re-distillation. No idea if this is the case, but it is the only way I can think of creating a non-chillfiltered Ardbeg this clean and fragile. Quite extraordinary... 46%.

**Ardbeg Grooves** db **(95) n24 t23.5 f23.5 b24** Groovy. 46%.

**Ardbeg Grooves Committee Release** db **(95.5) n24** as above, except: oilier phenols adding extra depth and weight; **t23.5** as above except: a more rounded gloss to the same traits and development and much greater lustre to the sugars; **f24** as above except: longer finale and now a more apparent spice; **b24** even groovier! 51.6%.

**Ardbeg Guaranteed 30 Years Old** db **(91) n24 t23 f21 b23.** An unusual beast, one of the last ever bottled by Allied. The charm and complexity early on is enormous, but the fade rate is surprising. That said, still a dram of considerable magnificence. 40%

**Ardbeg Kelpie** db **(95) n24 t23.5 f23.5 b24** Beautifully crafted and cleverly – and intriguingly - structured. An understated Ardbeg for true Ardbeg lovers... 46%.

**Ardbeg Kelpie Committee Edition** db **(94) n24 t24 f22.5 b23.5** As Burns might have said: I'se no speer nae to anither helpie o' Kelpie... 51.7%.

**Ardbeg Mor** db **(95) n24 t24 f23 b24** Quite simply... more the merrier... 57.5%

**Ardbeg Perpetuum** db **(94.5) n23.5 t23.5 f23.5 b24** what a beautifully structured malt. There is no escaping the youth of some of the phrases. But you can't help enjoying what it says. 47.4%. ncf.

**Ardbeg Provenance 1974** bott 1999 db **(96) n24 t25 f23 b24.** This is an exercise in subtlety and charisma, the beauty and the beast drawn into one. Until I came across the 25-year-old OMC version during a thunderstorm in Denmark, this was arguably the finest whisky I had ever tasted: I opened this and drank from it to see in the year 2000. When I went through the Ardbeg warehouse stocks in 1997 I earmarked the '74 and '77 vintages as something special. This bottling has done me proud. 55.6%

**Ardbeg Renaissance** db **(92) n22.5 t22.5 f23.5 b23.5.** How fitting that the 1,200th (and almost last) new-to-market whisky I sampled for the 2009 Bible was Renaissance... because that's what I need after tasting that lot...!! This is an Ardbeg that comes on strong, is not afraid to wield a few hefty blows and yet, paradoxically, the heavier it gets the more delicate, sophisticated and better-balanced it becomes. Enigmatically Ardbegian. 55.9%

**Ardbeg Uigeadail** db (89) n25 t22 f20 b22. A curious Ardbeg with a nose to die for. Some tinkering - please guys, as the re-taste is not better - regarding the finish may lift this to being a true classic 54.1%

◇ **Ardbeg Supernova 2019** db (92.5) n23.5 thin lemon blossom honey, but still out arm wrestles the peat which is shy here, especially considering the strength. Clean, delicate and belying its abv in intensity...; t23 the salivating citrus is bang on the money on delivery while the tannins are not far behind and just ahead of the smoke; some gristy sweetness also does the rounds; f23 remains on the theme of being super-delicate. A little smoky coffee walnut towards the finish; b23 a kind of sub-Supernova as it has now lost much of its old explosive oomph. 53.9%.

◇ **Ardbeg Traigh Bhan** db (94.5) n24 typical Islay peat on display: seemingly light and inconsequential...until you realise it is building and building into something very big and special. Also, the growth of the vanillas suggests we are getting some age present here, without it ever going into heavy tannin mode; t23.5 beautiful citrusy sugars show early, but there is also an unusual coppery metallic sharpness to this one, too. Most probably some major work to a still just before it was made. The peat really takes time to get its act together and is happy to manifest itself in spicy form; f23.5 surprisingly short for an Ardbeg and the usual big phenol build-up doesn't quite materialise, though the spices have definitely upped a notch or two... b23.5 ah, Traigh Bhan, the remote Singing Sands beach on Islay, if memory serves. Where back in the very early 1980s, before anyone had heard of Ardbeg – or hardly Islay whisky come to that matter - you could spend a day at the silent, deserted, unknown distillery and then return to Port Ellen. And as the sun thought about setting, but before the midges (teeth freshly sharpened) came out to play, walk past a heard of goats that could win a World Championship for flatulence, and on to the Singing Sands – Traigh Bhan - where I and the lady who was unluckily destined to be, for a short time, Mrs Murray would find a remote spot to try, but only providing we were upwind from the goats, and add to the Murray clan. It as an act that began and ended with a bottle top or two full of Ardbeg 10. Magical.... Maybe I should return to those sands with a bottle of this – which, fittingly, seems, older, softer, less energetic than the elixir Ardbeg I tasted of yore - and see what happens... 46.6%.

# ARDMORE
**Speyside, 1899. Beam Suntory. Working.**

**Ardmore 12 Year Old Port Wood Finish** db (90) n21.5 t23.5 f22 b23 Here we have a lovely fruit-rich malt, but one which has compromised on the very essence of the complexity which sets this distillery apart. Lovely whisky I am delighted to say...but, dammit, by playing to its unique nuances it could have been so much better...I mean absolutely sensational...!46%. ncf.

**Ardmore Aged 20 Years 1996 Vintage** 1st fill ex-bourbon & ex-Islay casks, bott code: L723657A db (89.5) n22 t23 f22 b22.5 Slightly confused by this malt, for all its charm. At 20 years old this distillery projects, through its usual ex-bourbon cask portfolio of varied usages, a quite disarming complexity. To bolster it with extra oak and smoke slightly undermines the inherent subtlety of this malt which sets it apart from all others. Highly enjoyable, nonetheless. 49.3%. ncf.

**Ardmore 25 Years Old** db (89.5) n21 t23.5 f22.5 b22.5 A 25-y-o box of chocolates: coffee creams, fudge, orange cream...they are all in there. The nose may be ordinary: what follows is anything but. 51.4%. ncf.

**Ardmore 30 Years Old Cask Strength** db (94) n23.5 t23.5 f23 b24 I remember when the present owners of Ardmore launched their first ever distillery bottling. Over a lunch with the hierarchy there I told them, with a passion, to ease off with the caramel so the world can see just how complex this whisky can be. This brilliant, technically faultless, bottling is far more eloquent and persuasive than I was that or any other day... 53.7%. nc ncf. 1428 bottles.

**Ardmore 1996** db (87) n22 t22 f21 b22. Very curious Ardmore, showing little of its usual dexterity. Perhaps slightly more heavily peated than the norm, but there is also much more intense heavy caramel extracted from the wood. Soft, very pleasant and easy drinking it is almost obsequious. 43%.

**Ardmore Fully Peated Quarter Casks** db (89) n21 t23 f23 b22. Firstly, Ardmore has rarely been filled in ex-bourbon and that oak type is having an effect on the balance and smoke weight; also they have unwisely added caramel, which has flattened things further. I don't expect the caramel to be in later bottlings and, likewise, I think the bourbon edge might be purposely blunted a little. But for a first attempt this is seriously big whisky that shows enormous promise. When they get this right, it could – and should – be a superstar. Now I await the more traditional vintage bottlings... 46%. ncf.

**Ardmore Legacy** bott code: L713757B db (88) n22.5 t22.5 t23 f20.5 b22 That's much more like it! The initial bottling of this brand was a travesty to the distillery, seemingly making a point omitting all of the personality which makes this potentially one of the great whiskies of the world. No such problem here: a much more sympathetic rendition, though the finish is perhaps a little sharper than ideally desired. So, a massive improvement but still room for further improvement. *40%.*

**Ardmore Traditional Cask** db **(88.5)** n21.5 t22 f23 b22. Not quite what I expected. "Jim. Any ideas on improving the flavour profile?" asked the nice man from Ardmore distillery when they were originally launching the thing. "Yes. Cut out the caramel." "Ah, right..." So what do I find when the next bottling comes along? More caramel. It's good to have influence... Actually, I can't quite tell if this is a result of natural caramelization from the quarter casking or just an extra dollop of the stuff in the bottling hall. The result is pretty similar: some of the finer complexity is lost. My guess, due to an extra fraction of sweetness and spice, is that it is the former. All that said, the overall experience remains quite beautiful. And this remains one of my top ten distilleries in the world. *46%. ncf.*

**Berry Bros & Rudd Ardmore 9 Years Old** cask no. 708628, dist 2008, bott 2018 **(96.5)** n24 t24 f24 b24.5 Confirmation of just what a stupendous distillery this is. For a 9-year-old, the balance defies belief. Few single malts under ten years will match this bottling this year. *52.3%. nc ncf sc.*

⬧ **Berry Bros & Rudd Ardmore 9 Years Old** cask no. 708496, dist 2008, bott 2018 **(89)** n22.5 rumbling, bumbling peat, never too loud, never too soft, spicing up and adding weight to the sweeter barley notes; t23 still a tiny touch of youth attached to this one, the game given away slightly by the exceptional gristy sweetness on hand; the tannins make amends midway through as they form an impressive spine with the light cocoa; f21.5 spicy and tingling; just a little bitterness creeps in; b22 an absolutely straight down the line Ardmore: still youthful but exactly what you should expect at this age from this kind of cask, though the finish does tire a little. *54.6%. nc ncf sc.*

⬧ **The First Editions Ardmore Aged 20 Years 1997** refill hogshead, cask no. 15307, bott 2018 **(94.5)** n23.5 a real countryside aroma: more than a touch of the farmyard byre. A nose to clear the sinuses but always sweet and enticing; t23.5 the sugars hinted at on the nose plant their flag early, but they still have an increasingly smoky mountain to climb. The malt intensifies rather beautifully towards the middle; f23.5 lots of natural caramels merge with the phenols which at last offer a late spicy buzz; b24 a stupendous Ardmore very much on the higher end of their peating spectrum – it is even smokier than a Bowmore sitting in the glass next to it - and this smoke is used to maximum effect without for a moment overpowering and losing balance. A bit of a minor classic. *54.1%. nc ncf sc. 258 bottles.*

**Golden Cask Ardmore Aged 16 Years** cask no. CM231, dist 2000, bott 2016 **(92.5)** n22.5 t23.5 f23 b23.5 One seriously chunky dram. Love this classy act. *55.8%. sc. 80 bottles.*

**Golden Cask Ardmore Aged 17 Years** cask no. CM242, dist 2000, bott 2017 **(96)** n24 t24 f23.5 b24.5 I really admire the quality of Golden Cask's bottlings. Here's one that is a little different for an Ardmore, with the peaty bits seemingly shaved off to ensure the phenols always come across as secondary influence – though, on close inspection, you'll find it is actually the first. One of the most nuanced malts you'll encounter this year. Stunning. *55.3%. sc. 136 bottles.*

⬧ **The John Milroy Selection Ardmore 8 Year Old** refill barrel, cask no. 803059, dist 2010, bott 2019 **(86)** n21.5 t22.5 f20.5 b21.5 Beautiful delivery where the peat, spices and acacia honey are in bon accord. But the ex-bourbon cask does no favours with a distinct tang on both nose and finish. *54.8%. nc ncf sc. Spirit Imports Inc.*

**Le Gus't Selection XIV Ardmore 8 Years Old** bourbon cask, cask no. 705804 **(94)** n23 t23.5 f23.5 b24 Evidence that the eating level at Ardmore may have risen a tad in recent years: much more smoke at work here than in the old days. For its age, outstanding... *60.9%. sc. 242 bottles.*

⬧ **MacAlabur Ardmore Aged 22 Years** hogshead, cask no. 149020, dist 27 Aug 96, bott 15 Oct 18 **(88)** n22 sharp, thin slightly aggressive. The only softness comes from the gentle mintiness defused with the light peat; t22 definitely fire water! More flames than smoke – but have to say that with the malt being this sharp and juicy, there is something strangely exhilarating about it; f22 at last settles with the lazy smoke lands peacefully on the patient vanilla; b22 extremely rare to find a 22-year-old barrel of Scotch malt weighing at over 60% abv. This is a bit of a freak whisky, in more ways than one! And especially enjoyable for masochists. *60.5%. nc ncf sc. 239 bottles.*

**Old Malt Cask Ardmore Aged 20 Years** refill hogshead, cask no. 13770, dist Oct 96, bott Apr 17 **(90.5)** n23 t23 f22 b22.5 Smoke happily plays third fiddle to the fruit and spice. Charming. *50%. nc ncf sc. 278 bottles.*

**Old Malt Cask Ardmore Aged 21 Years** refill hogshead, cask no. 14466, dist Apr 96, bott Nov 17 **(96)** n24 t24 f24 b24 As elegant as it is articulate. An unambiguous, must-find great from this distillery. *50%. nc ncf sc. 167 bottles.*

**Old Particular Ardmore 21 Years Old** refill hogshead, cask no. 12196, dist Oct 96, bott Nov 17 **(96)** n23.5 t24 f24.5 b24 Near faultless. If you want to discover how a relatively low dose of peat can bring a level of balance and complexity to die for, just sample this truly great whisky... *52%. nc ncf sc. 310 bottles.*

**Provenance Ardmore Aged 8 Years** refill barrel, cask no. 11632, dist Jul 08, bott Feb 17 **(91)** n23 t23 f22.5 b22.5 That is some adorable whisky: forget the age, the charm and quality are stupendous. 46%. nc ncf sc. 306 bottles.

**Romantic Rhine Collection Ardmore 9 Year Old** cask no. 1915843, dist 2008, bott 2017 **(89)** n22.5 t21 f23 b22 Takes time to find its feet, but the quality is always there. 52.8%. nc ncf sc.

**Scotch Malt Whisky Society Cask 66.111 8 Year Old** refill ex-bourbon barrel, dist 4 Jun 09 **(89.5)** n23 t22 f22.5 b22 Pretty creamy by Ardmore standards. 58.9%. sc.

**Spirit of Caledonia Ardmore Peated 8 Years Old** cask no. 707029 **(85.5)** n21.5 t22.5 f20 b21.5 Absolutely nothing wrong with the spirit itself, which shows Ardmore in its most salivating and smoky light. However, the contribution of the oak leaves a little to be desired, its vaguely milky weakness particularly noticeable at the death. 61.3%. sc.

**Teacher's Highland Single Malt** quarter cask finish db **(89)** n22.5 t23 f21.5 b22. This is Ardmore at its very peatiest. And had not the colouring levels been heavily tweaked to meet the flawed perceptions of what some markets believe makes a good whisky, this malt would have been better still. As it is: superb. With the potential of achieving greatness if only they have the confidence and courage... 40%. India/Far East Travel Retail exclusive.

◈ **Wilson & Morgan Barrel Selection Ardmore Heavy Peat** dist 2009, bott 2018 **(92)** n23 light smoke drifts across attractive cocoa and vanilla: delicate; t23.5 salivating, with an even degree of peat at work, though giving way to some excellent orange blossom honey development; f22.5 light spices with juicy barley still evident late on; the smoke now is entirely absorbed into the spicy cocoa; b23 heavy peat? I don't think so. Just a normally light peated Ardmore perhaps towards the top of its range but the smokiness amplified by the delicate touch of the oak and barley. Quite lovely. 48%.

# AUCHENTOSHAN
### Lowlands, 1800. Morrison Bowmore. Working.

**Auchentoshan 10 Years Old** db **(81)** n22 t21 f19 b19. Much better, maltier, cleaner nose than before. But after the initial barley surge on the palate it shows a much thinner character. 40%

**Auchentoshan 12 Years Old** db **(91.5)** n22.5 sexy fruit element – citrus and apples in particular – perfectly lightens the rich, oily barley; t23.5 oily and buttery; intense barley carrying delicate marzipan and vanilla; f22.5 simplistic, but the oils keep matters lush and the delicate sugars do the rest; b23 a delicious malt very much happier with itself than it has been for a while. 40%

**Auchentoshan 14 Years Old Cooper's Reserve** db **(83.5)** n20 t21.5 f21 b21. Malty, a little nutty and juicy in part. 46%. ncf.

**Auchentoshan 18 Years Old** db **(78)** n21 t21.5 f17 b19. Although matured for 18 years in ex-bourbon casks, as according to the label, this is a surprisingly tight and closed malt in far too many respects. Some heart-warming sugars early on, but the finish is bitter and severely limited in scope. 43%

**Auchentoshan 21 Years Old** db **(93)** n23.5 t23 f23 b23.5 One of the finest Lowland distillery bottlings of our time. A near faultless masterpiece of astonishing complexity to be cherished and discussed with deserved reverence. So delicate, you fear that sniffing too hard will break the poor thing...! 43%

**Auchentoshan 1975** db **(88)** n22.5 t22.5 f21 b22 Goes heavy on the natural caramels. Does not even remotely show its enormous age for this distillery. I detest the word "smooth". But for those who prefer that kind of malt...well, your dreams have come true...; 45.6%

**Auchentoshan 1979** db **(94)** n23.5 t24 f23 b23.5 It's amazing what a near faultless sherry butt can do. 50.1%

**Auchentoshan 1990 27 Year Old** db **(94)** n23.5 t23 f24 b23.5 The fact this is triple-distilled malt has a major bearing on the structure of this excellent dram. Lighter malty and citrus notes seem able to fly above the more ingrained grape. The result is a two-toned, salivating little charmer which carries its years in a way 'Toshan was never really expected to. The mocha starts creeping in from about the halfway point, laying down a weightiness which is still in keeping with the lighter fruit. Such a delight and elegant experience with the kind of finish blenders can only dream of.... 53.1%. Selected for CWS.

**Auchentoshan 1998 Sherry Cask Matured** fino sherry cask db **(81.5)** n21 t22 f18.5 b20. A genuine shame. Before these casks were treated in Jerez, I imagine they were spectacular. Even with the obvious faults apparent, the nuttiness is profound and milks every last atom of the oils at work to maximum effect. The sugars, also, are delicate and gorgeously weighted. There is still much which is excellent to concentrate on here. 54.6%. ncf. 6000 bottles.

**Auchentoshan American Oak** db **(85.5)** n21.5 t22 f20.5 b21.5. Very curious: reminds me very much of Penderyn Welsh whisky before it hits the Madeira casks. Quite creamy with some toasted honeycomb making a brief cameo appearance. 40%

**Auchentoshan Blood Oak** French red wine & American bourbon casks db **(76.5) n20.5 t19 f18 b19**. That's funny: always thought blood tasted a little sweet. This is unremittingly bitter. 48%. ncf.

**Auchentoshan Classic** db **(80) n19 t20 f21 b20**. Classic what exactly...? Some really decent barley, but goes little further. 40%

**Auchentoshan Noble Oak Aged 24 Years** Oloroso sherry casks & American bourbon hogsheads db **(87.5) n22 t23 f21 b21.5**. Normally a skinny soul on account of its triple distillation, unusual to find a 'Toshan with so much muscle. The fruit from the sherry is piled on high, yet it is a massive toffee effect which takes the firmest grip, presumably tannins from the oak. So the finish is a little flat. But the good news is that this is one fruit cake that is happily sulphur-free. 50.3%. ncf. 2015 Limited Release.

**Auchentoshan Select** db **(85) n20 t21.5 f22 b21.5**. Has changed shape of late, if not quality. Much more emphasis on the enjoyable juicy barley sharpness these days. 40%

**Auchentoshan Solera** db **(88) n23 t22 f22 b21**. Enormous grape input and enjoyable for all its single mindedness. Will benefit when a better balance with the malt is struck. 48%. ncf.

**Auchentoshan The Bartender's Malt** batch 01, bott code: L172749 db **(94.5) n23.5 t24 f23 b24** Seeing as this was assembled by a dozen bartenders from around the world, namely Messrs Alvarado, Billing, Halsius, Heinrich, Jehli, Klus, Magro, Morgan, Schurmann, Shock, Stern and Wareing surely this is the Bartenders' Malt, not Bartender's Malt. Still, I digress. Good job, boys and (presumably) girls. Some might mark this down as a clever marketing ploy (which it may well be...). I'd rather record it as an exceptionally fine Auchentoshan. And by the way, bartenders, you have proved a point I have been making for the last 25 years: the finest cocktail is a blend of whiskies...even if from the same distillery...Now don't you go ruining this by putting ice, water, or anything else in it... 47%.

**Auchentoshan Three Wood** db **(76) n20 t18 f20 b18**. Takes you directly into the rough. Refuses to harmonise, except maybe for some late molassed sugar. 43%

**Auchentoshan Virgin Oak** db **(92) n23.5 t23 f22.5 b23** Not quite how I've seen 'Toshan perform before: but would love to see it again! 46%

◈ **Kingsbury Silver Auchentoshan 14 Year Old** hogshead, cask no. 13706, dist 2003 **(92.5) n23.5** an unusual Ardmore-style light smokiness pulses ahead of the sweet, crystalline barley; **t24** one of the richest, earthiest experiences I have had from this distillery at such an age. Still the smoke is evident, forming a compact richness with the developing cocoa at the chewy mid-point; **f22** thins out slightly as the vanillas gain the upper hand; **b23** until the tiring fade, a Toshan at the top of its game and almost freaky in its smokiness. Superb. 46%. sc. 362 bottles.

**Old Particular Auchentoshan 16 Years Old** refill hogshead, cask no. 11591, dist Sept 00, bott Mar 17 **(89.5) n22.5 t23 f22 b22** After the big, breathtaking barley statement definitely veers on the side of an austere aloofness. 48.4%. nc ncf sc. 319 bottles.

**Old Particular Auchentoshan 18 Years Old** refill hogshead, cask no. 11829, dist Nov 98, bott Jun 17 **(87) n21 t22 f22 b22** Warming, barley-intense and salivating there are some surprisingly good oils on this. A little bit of tired oak tang, also. 47.5%. nc ncf sc. 251 bottles.

**Old Particular Auchentoshan 20 Years Old** refill hogshead, cask no. 12032, dist May 97, bott Aug 17 **(94.5) n24 t23 f23.5 b24** A real sparkling gem of a dram. 51.5%. nc ncf sc. 279 bottles.

**Provenance Auchentoshan Aged 14 Years** refill hogshead, cask no. 11906, dist Oct 02, bott Jun 17 **(84) n21 t22 f20 b21** Well, bless my soul! A vaguely smoky, oily 'Toshan. Now there's a first. Either I have been sent a rogue sample or they went 2D at one stage to try to experiment. Either way, the cask is a bit shot and doesn't add anything positive. 46%. nc ncf sc. 852 bottles.

◈ **Signatory Vintage Un-Chillfiltered Auchentoshan 21 Year Old 1997** refill sherry hogshead, cask no. 2911 **(81) n23 t21 f18 b19** A real strange one this: the nose sets off like a champion, all roasted sultanas and herbs. But after the initial rum-like golden syrup delivery, this bitters out with a vengeance. 52.4%. sc. Exclusive to The Whisky Barrel. 168 bottles.

◈ **Simon Brown Traders Auchentoshan** bourbon cask, dist Feb 98, bott Feb 19 **(90.5) n22** exceptionally clean; a degree of youth on the malty spirit despite the advanced years; **t23** the simple clarity of the nose is amplified here many times over with a delicious castor sugar-gristy sweetness just fizzing with barley; **f22.5** enters into lightly spiced milk chocolate mode; **b23** delightfully delicate. 43%. nc ncf sc.

# AUCHROISK

**Speyside, 1974. Diageo. Working.**

**Auchroisk Aged 10 Years** db **(84) n20 t22 f21 b21**. Tangy orange on the nose, the malt amplified by a curious saltiness on the palate. 43%. Flora and Fauna.

**Auchroisk Aged 25 Years** dist 1990 db **(89) n22 t22.5 f22 b22.5** One of the most rampant Auchroisks I've encountered since the distillery issued its first-ever bottling. The full strength helps galvanise the malt and accentuate the barley sugar. A little rough, but very satisfying. 51.2%. 3,954 bottles. Diageo Special Releases 2016.

**Cadenhead's Wine Cask Auchroisk 16 Years Old** Chateau Lafitte cask, dist 2001 **(84.5)** n21 t22 f21 b20 Lafitte, but not elite. Filling a very average spirit with very limited body into this cask probably didn't much help. Only the fruit shows amid the spices and cocoa. The malt itself vanishes, overwhelmed. *55.4%. sc. 246 bottles.*

❧ **Fadandel.dk Auchroisk Aged 7 Years** 1st fill oloroso sherry cask, cask no. 82, dist 21 Dec 11, bott 20 Nov 18 **(91.5)** n22.5 t23 f23 b23 An audacious bottling which uses a pristine 100% sulphur-free sherry cask to breathe life into one of Speyside's lightest spirits – and, here, a very young one at that. Just admire the chutzpa because the grape makes a blisteringly eye-watering statement, then kindly soothes your battered taste buds by kissing them better with the most gloriously layered sultanas imaginable. A little ulmo honey adds the softest sweetness and harnesses the fruit. *59.3%. sc. 320 bottles.*

**The First Editions Auchroisk Aged 19 Years** refill hogshead, cask no. 14661, bott 2018 **(90.5)** n22.5 t22.5 f23 b22.5 A thoroughly enjoyable bottling showing an unusual degree of complexity for this distillery. *54.2%. nc ncf sc. 290 bottles.*

**The First Editions Auchroisk Aged 22 Years 1994** refill hogshead, cask no. 12429, bott 2016 **(89)** n21.5 t22.5 f22 b23 One of Speyside's lightest malts has put little weight on 22 years. But there is no faulting its delightful elegance. *57.1%. nc ncf sc. 110 bottles.*

❧ **The First Editions Auchroisk Aged 24 Years 1994** refill hogshead, cask no. 15396, bott 2018 **(87.5)** n21 t22.5 f22 b22 I know the first-ever blender to have Auchroisk under his control never thought for a moment that this malt could last to two dozen years in the wood – he felt he had to patch it up even when he released it in its first incarnation at exactly half that age. But although the trademark thinness is evident, equally there is no denying the charm of the juicy barley melding with the delicate vanilla. Elegant, understated and always charming and engagingly delicate. *48.3%. nc ncf sc. 275 bottles.*

**Hepburn's Choice Auchroisk 8 Years Old** red wine cask, dist 2009, bott 2017 **(67)** n16 t18 f16 b17 Can someone tell the wine cask people that sulphur is not a good idea when it comes to whisky. *46%. nc ncf sc. 272 bottles.*

❧ **Hepburn's Choice Auchroisk 9 Years Old** red wine hogshead, dist 2009, bott 2019 **(85.5)** n21.5 t22 f21 b21 Plenty of fruit but never really catches fire. *46%. nc ncf sc. 354 bottles.*

**Old Malt Cask Auchroisk Aged 15 Years** refill hogshead, cask no. 14747, dist Nov 02, bott Feb 18 **(87)** n21 t22 f21.5 b21.5 A malty skeleton on which hangs very little meat. Light, delicately spiced, the occasional snippet of barley sugar. *50%. nc ncf sc. 337 bottles.*

❧ **Simon Brown Traders Auchroisk** bourbon cask & port cask, dist Dec 10, bott Jan 19 **(87)** n21 t22 f22 b22 A soft and even malt which goes some way in making up on the palate what it lacks on the nose. The Port was definitely on rescue mission here as the underlying body seems thin. But the grape does infuse an attractive degree of plum pudding and spice. *43%. nc ncf sc.*

# AULTMORE
### Speyside, 1896. Bacardi. Working.

**Aultmore 12 Year Old** db **(85.5)** n22 t22 f20 b21.5. Not quite firing on all cylinders due to the uncomfortably tangy oak. But relish the creamy malt for the barley is the theme of choice and for its sheer intensity alone, it doesn't disappoint; a little ulmo honey and marzipan doff their cap to the kinder vanillas. *46% WB16/028*

❧ **Aultmore of the Foggie Moss Aged 12 Years** bott code: L18135ZA903 db **(92.5)** n23.5 teasingly complex: the delicate oak notes combine with the barley to form a kind of dry egg nog. The adroit playfulness of the lime is almost worth getting the bottle for alone...! t23.5 the nose suggests a salivating experience awaits...and it does! The barley almost froths in the mouth, accentuated seemingly by the quick arrival of oaky spice; the early barley sugar delights; f22.5 true to style, dries quite quickly, a buzzing tannin having the last word; b23 a whisky purist's delight. So delicate you can see the inner workings of this fine malt. *46%. ncf.*

**Aultmore 18 Year Old** db **(88.5)** n22.5 soft, though with a vague spice nip. Otherwise, a mix of ulmo honey, treacle and cream toffee combine; t22.5 the barley makes the first play on delivery, a grassy volley which slowly vanishes into a mist of caramel; f22 that caramel persists – again of Toffo variety - but at least the spices can be heard; b21.5 charming, but could do with having the toffee blended out... *46%*

❧ **Aultmore of the Foggie Moss Aged 18 Years** batch no. 481, bott code: L15244B100 db **(94.5)** n23.5 though the distillery makes point of their using unpeated malt, a little vaguely spicy smoke drifts across the fragile nose. Gentle vanillas and the lightest dab of heather honey act as the anchor; t24 by far the most honeyed delivery of these three impressive Aultmores, a glossy blend of ulmo and Manuka doing the trick. The sweetness lasts virtually the entire trip, a little cocoa and natural caramels filling into the mid-ground; f23 dry and spicy; b24 it is so satisfying when the sweetness and spices of a malt combine for near perfect harmony. Flattens towards the finish, but this is high grade malt. *46%. ncf.*

◈ **Aultmore Aged 21 Years** refill hogshead, batch no. 00107, bott code: L18281ZA501 db **(95.5) n24** though the tannins emphasise every month of the 71 years of extraction, they are still generous enough to share the platform with a host other personalities, not least orange blossom honey and finest Danish marzipan. A fifteen-minute nosing, this. And even that seems a little short of par; **t24** a classic Speyside old 'un delivery: the barley is still intact and fresh, pulsing out a juicy sweetness. Gristy, even, with a dissolving of vague Manuka honey; a pleasing layering of citrus notes filter through adding both balance and complexity; **f23.5** dries, in time-honoured tradition, but light spices form a pleasing deposit; **b24** when you get a very decent spirit filled into exceptionally good casks, the result – providing the whisky is disgorged neither too early or late – is usually a positive one. The refill hoggies here must have been in fine fettle, for this a bit of a stunner. No, make that a classic! Potential gong material, this. *46%. nc ncf.*

**Aultmore 25 Year Old** db **(92.5) n23 t23.5; f23 b23** Now here's a curiosity: this is the first brand I have ever encountered which on the label lists the seasons the distillery was silent (1917-19, 1943-45, 1970-71) like a football club would once list on the front page of their official programme the years they won the FA Cup! Strange, but rather charming. And as for the whisky: succulent stuff!! *46% WB16/029*

**Aultmore Exceptional Cask Series 21 Years Old 1996** db **(94.5) n24 t23.5 f23.5 b23.5** There is age creaking from every pore of this whisky. The nose is magnificently sensual with its orange blossom honey theme, spicy toasty tannins lurking at every corner. And those tannins carry on their impressive work, yet at the same time allowing a delicious alloy of malt and sultanas to not only thrive but fully fill the palate. Toward the end we are back to those insistent tannins which, if anything display an age greater than its given years. A malt plucked at the very right time from the warehouse: it would never have made half as good a 25-year-old. *54%. Selected for CWS.*

**Cadenhead's Sherry Cask Aultmore 28 Year Old** dist 1989 **(94) n23.5 t23.5 f23 b24** Another sure-footed oldie from Cadenhead. *43.4%. sc.*

**Chapter 7 Aultmore 9 Year Old** Oloroso Finish, cask no. 900160, dist 2008 **(93) n22.5 t24 f22.5 b24** A clean, sulphur-free cask allows the whisky to develop naturally and in a beautifully relaxed manner – something of genuine rarity. Just enough malt gets through to keep the balance happy. *62.2%. sc.*

**Endangered Drams Aultmore 9 Year Old** cask no. 900152, dist Apr 08, bott Jun 17 **(77) n19 t20 f19 b19** Malty. But unlikely to win any gongs at the Speyside Distillers' Technical Distilling Excellence Awards anytime soon... *51.6%. nc ncf sc.*

**Hepburn's Choice Aultmore 6 Years Old** bourbon barrel, dist 2010, bott 2017 **(82.5) n21 t20 f21 b20.5** A curious malt which noses and tastes like a savagely undercooked bourbon. *46%. nc ncf sc. 345 bottles.*

**Hepburn's Choice Aultmore 7 Years Old** refill butt, dist 2010, bott 2017 **(85) n21 t22 f21 b21** Young, decent, no nonsense Speyside with a light banana milkshake sweetness to it. *46%. nc ncf sc. 792 bottles.*

**Hidden Spirits Aultmore 11 Year Old** Amarone cask finish, dist 2006, bott 2018 **(93) n22.5 t24 f23 b23.5** A vague hint of tightness on the nose turns out to be a false warning. Instead we are treated to a malt of rare intensity, a swashbuckling, cut and thrusting dram if ever there was one: Amarone for all, for all for Amarone...! *51.6%.*

**The Whisky Chamber Aultmore 9 Years Old 2008** bourbon hogshead **(92) n23.5 t23 f22.5 b23** An exceptionally fine bourbon cask helps the whisky blossom to a complexity above its years. *61%. sc.*

# BALBLAIR

**Highlands (Northern), 1872. Inver House Distillers. Working.**

**Balblair 10 Years Old** db **(86) n21 t22 f22 b21.** Such an improved dram away from the clutches of caramel. *40%*

◈ **Balblair Aged 12 Years** American oak ex-bourbon & double-fired American oak casks, bott code: L18/357 R18/5536 IB db **(87) n21.5 t22 f21.5 b22** There is no escaping a distinct tired cask tang to this. From the nose to the finale the oak pokes around with a little too much meanness of spirit. But it is the wonderful clarity to the barley – including a delicious citrusy freshness – which keeps the malt on course. I suspect the next bottling will be a whole lot better! *46%. nc ncf.*

◈ **Balblair Aged 15 Years** American oak ex-bourbon casks, followed by first fill Spanish oak butts, bott code: L19 079 R19/5133 IB db **(93) n23** a disarmingly elegant interplay between crisp barley and ripe greengages; **t23.5** such a silky landing! The barley almost glistens on the palate, the sugars are gristy and controlled; the fruit is embroidered into the malt like initials on an elegant night gown; **f23** dries with a soft vanilla fade, plus a very late tang; **b23** ah, after the relative disappointment of the 12-year-old, so good to see we are right back on track here. Twenty years of very bitter experience has taught me to fear the worst and hope for the best so far as the use of sherry butts are concerned. But my hopes are rewarded here: not 100% perfect, but close enough. 46%. nc ncf.

**Balblair Aged 16 Years** db (84) n22 t22 f20 b20. Definitely gone up a notch in the last year. The lime on the nose has been replaced by dim Seville oranges; the once boring finish reveals elements of fruit and spice. It's the barley- rich middle that shines, though, and some more work will belt this up into the high 90s where this great distillery belongs. 40%

**Balblair Aged 17 Years** American oak ex-bourbon casks, followed by first fill Spanish oak butts, bott code: L19/057 R19/5097 IB db (94) n23.5 the late summer aroma of a diced apple among the straw bales; lightly spiced and enticing; t24.5 a triumph on the palate: the barley is Balblair-style salivating while the infused fruit helps raise the heather honey to brilliant depths of intensity; f22.5 a little salty and bitter, though both malt and fruit retain their presence; b23.5 one of the best arrivals on the palate of any Scotch whisky I have tasted this year. 46%. nc ncf. Travel Exclusive.

**Balblair Aged 18 Years** American oak ex-bourbon casks, followed by first fill Spanish oak butts, bott code: L19/121 R19/5220 IB db (83) n22 t23 f18 b20 Balblair's luck has run out on the sherry butts. A heftier expression than the 17-year-old and the sulphur ensures there is nothing like the degree of complexity. 46%. nc ncf.

**Balblair Aged 25 Years** American oak ex-bourbon casks, followed by first fill Spanish oak butts, nbc db (91) n23.5 a rare Balblair nose where the weight of the fruit eclipses that of the barley. This is dripping with moist fruitcake and orange blossom honey; t23.5 beautifully fat delivery. Caramels from the oak help round the shape of this malt, but can't entirely overcome the influence of the grape must; the chocolate fruit and nut in the mid-ground is superb; f21 dries towards toastiness; a little bitter at the death; b23 there has been hard work here to harmonise fruit and oak and allow the barley a say, too. But when sherry is this ripe, not the easiest stunt to pull off. Gets pretty close, though! 46%.

**Balblair 1965** db (96.5) n23 t24.5 f24.5 b24.5 Many malts of this age have the spirit hanging on in there for grim life. This is an exception: the malt is in joint control and never for a moment allows the oak to dominate. It is almost too beautiful for words. 52.3%

**Balblair 1969** db (94.5) n22.5 t23.5 f24 b24.5. A charmer. Don't even think about touching this until it has stood in the glass for ten minutes. And if you are not prepared to give each glass a minimum half hour of your time (and absolutely no water), then don't bother getting it for, to be honest, you don't deserve it... 41.4%

**Balblair 1975** db (94.5) n24.5 t23.5 f23 b23.5. Essential Balblair. 46%

**Balblair 1978** db (94) n24 t24 f23 b23. Just one of those drams that exudes greatness and charm in equal measures. Some malts fall apart when hitting thirty: this one is totally intact and in command. A glorious malt underlining the greatness of this mostly under-appreciated distillery. 46%

**Balblair 1983 Vintage 1st Release** dist 1983, bott 2014 db (95) n23.5 t23 f24.5 b24 the last Balblair 83 I tasted won my heart and undying devotion with its beauty and complexity. This may also be a beautiful and shapely morsel, but the over exuberance of the oak means this is more of a spicy, pleasure-indulging, hedonistic one night-stand than lasting, tender love. Mind you... 46%. nc ncf.

**Balblair 1989** db (91) n23 t23 f22.5 b22.5. Don't expect gymnastics on the palate or the pyrotechnics of the Cadenhead 18: in many ways a simple malt, but one beautifully told. Almost Cardhu-esque in the barley department. 43%

**Balblair 1989** db (88) n21.5 t22 f22.5 b22. A clean, pleasing malt, though hardly one that will induce anyone to plan a night raid on any shop stocking it... 43%

**Balblair 1990** db (92.5) n24 t23.5 f22 b23. Tangy in the great Balblair tradition. Except here this is warts and all with the complexity and greatness of the distillery left in no doubt. 46%

**Balblair 1991 3rd Release** bott 2018, bott code L18/044 R18/5054IB db (94.5) n23.5 t23.5 f23.5 b24 A malt embracing its passing years and has aged, silver temples and all, with great style and panache. 46%. nc ncf.

**Balblair 1997 2nd Release** db (94) n23.5 t23.5 f23 b24 a very relaxed well-made and matured malt, comfortable in its own skin, bursting with complexity and showing an exemplary barley-oak ratio. A minor classic. 46%. nc ncf.

**Balblair 1999 Vintage 2nd Release** dist 1999, bott 2015 db (91.5) n23.5 t22.5 f23 b22.5 Always subtle and sensual. 46%. nc ncf.

**Balblair 2000** db (87.5) n21.5 t22.5 f21.5 b22. No toffee yet still a clever degree of chewy weight for all the apparent lightness. 43%

**Balblair 2000 2nd Release** bott 2017, bott code L17/R121 db (95.5) n24.5 t24 f23 b24 First encountered this malt at a tasting I gave in Corsica earlier in the year. It blew away my audience while equally seducing me. Sampled back in the tasting lab, if anything it is even more stunning. The stock of this under-appreciated distillery rises by the day... 46%. nc ncf.

**Balblair 2001** db **(90.5) n23.5 t23.5 f21.5 b22.5** A typically high quality whisky from this outrageously underestimated distillery. 46%

**Balblair 2003 Vintage 1st Release** dist 2003, bott 2015 db **(89) n21 t23 f22.5 b22.5** just like their 2013 bottling, gets off to an uncertain start on the nose but makes its mark on delivery. 46%. nc ncf.

**Balblair 2005 Vintage 1st Release** dist 2005, bott 2015 db **(86.5) n20 t23 f21.5 b22.** The nose is tight and has problems expanding, while the finish is short and quickly out of puff. But the delivery and follow through are superb with the malt really on maximum volume, and not without a little saline sharpness. Some good citrus, too. 46%. nc ncf.

**Gordon & MacPhail Connoisseurs Choice Balblair 1993** first fill sherry puncheon, cask no. 1965, dist 28 Jun 93, bott 20 Feb 18 **(89) n22.5 t22 f22.5 b22** A decent sherry puncheon, but struggles to find a rhythm. 51.6%. nc ncf sc. 624 bottles.

**Gordon & MacPhail Discovery Range Balblair Aged 12 Years (95.5) n24 t24 f23.5 b24** Balblair is continuing its move to become recognised as one of the world's truly great distilleries. An understated epic whisky. 43%.

**The Single Malts of Scotland Balblair 19 Years Old 1997** cask no. 10117 **(95.5) n23.5 t24.5 f23.5 b24** Every nuance has "Balblair" stamped all over it. A minor classic for this distillery. 56.2%. sc.

# BALMENACH
### Speyside, 1824. Inver House Distillers. Working.

**Balmenach Aged 25 Years Golden Jubilee** db **(89) n21 t23 f22 b23.** What a glorious old charmer this is! An essay in balance despite the bludgeoning nature of the beast early on. Takes a little time to get to know and appreciate: persevere with this belter because it is classic stuff for its age. 58%. Around 800 bottles.

◈ **Deerstalker Balmenach 12 Years Old** Highland Single Malt **(88.5) n22.5** buttered toast and light tannin; **t22** soft, even slightly sensuous but it is all about the mouth feel rather than development of flavours; that said, some good spices evolve for the mid-point; **f22** still a spice buzz as the butterscotch sets in; **b22** attractive, easy going malt, but struggles to get out of second gear. 43%.

**Hepburn's Choice Balmenach 12 Years Old** refill hogshead, dist 2004, bott 2017 **(88) n23 t22.5 f20.5 b22** Drink in that nose...! 46%. nc ncf sc. 396 bottles.

◈ **Hidden Spirits Balmenach 2004** cask no. BL418, bott 2018 **(94) n22.5** coconuts...!!! Anyone for a Nice biscuit...? **t24** salty yet salivating, the barley is out in force. A light oiliness concentrates both the malt and salt which the spices zing about a bit; **f23.5** a fabulous salted chocolate flourish, the barley easily going the distance; some late citrus fits the bill; **b24** coconuts apart, almost the archetypal Speysider! Superb! 51.2%. sc.

◈ **Old Malt Cask Balmenach Aged 13 Years** refill barrel, cask no. 15148, dist Aug 04, bott May 18 **(87.5) n22.5 t22 f21.5 b21.5** A pleasant if regular Speysider with a hint of eggnog on the nose and a well-orchestrated maltiness on delivery. A dry vanilla makes a point of holding the upper hand at the finish. 50%. nc ncf sc. 264 bottles.

◈ **Spirit of Caledonia Balmenach** cask no. 184, dist 7 Mar 07, bott 16 Jul 18 **(87.5) n21 t22.5 f22 b22** Somewhat thin, malty and with a touch of ginger. Superb ten seconds on delivery, though, when the barley goes into mouth-watering overdrive. 58.8%. Mr. Whisky.

# THE BALVENIE
### Speyside, 1892. William Grant & Sons. Working.

**The Balvenie Aged 10 Years Founders Reserve** db **(90) n23 t24 f20 b23** just one of those all-time-great standard 10-year-olds from a great distillery – pity they've decided to kill it off. 40%

**The Balvenie Double Wood Aged 12 Years** db **(80.5) n22 t20.5 f19 b19.** OK. So here's the score: Balvenie is one of my favourite distilleries in the world, I confess. I admit it. The original Balvenie 10 is a whisky I would go to war for. It is what Scotch malt whisky is all about. It invented complexity; or at least properly introduced me to it. But I knew that it was going to die, sacrificed on the altar of ageism. So I have tried to get to love Double Wood. And I have tasted and/or drunk it every month for the last couple of years to get to know it and, hopefully fall in love. But still I find it rather boring company. We may have kissed and canoodled. But still there is no spark. No romance whatsoever. 40%

**The Balvenie 14 Years Old Cuban Selection** db **(86) n20 t22 f22.5 b21.5.** Unusual malt. No great fan of the nose but the roughness of the delivery grows on you; there is a jarring, tongue-drying quality which actually works quite well and the development of the inherent sweetness is almost in slow motion. Some sophistication here, but also the odd note which, on the nose especially, is a little out of tune. 43%

**The Balvenie 14 Years Old Golden Cask** db **(91)** n23.5 t23 f22 b22.5 A confident, elegant malt which doesn't stint one iota on complexity. Worth raiding the Duty Free shops for this little gem alone. 47.5%

**The Balvenie Single Barrel Sherry Cask Aged 15 Years** db cask no 2075 **(58)** n14 t16 f14 b14 Lovely distillery. Shame about this shockingly sulphured cask. 47.8%. sc.

**The Balvenie 16 Year Old Triple Cask** db **(84.5)** n22 t22.5 f19 b21. Well, after their single cask and then double wood, who saw this coming...? There is nothing about this whisky you can possibly dislike: no diminishing off notes (OK, well maybe at the very death) and a decent injection of sugar, especially early on. The trouble is, when you mix together sherry butts (even mainly good ones, like here) and first fill bourbon casks, the intense toffee produced tends to make for a monosyllabic, toffeed, dullish experience. And so it proves here. 40%

**The Balvenie Double Wood Aged 17 Years** db **(84)** n22 t21 f20 b21. Balvenie does like 17 years as an age to show off its malt at its most complex, & understandably so as it is an important stage in its development before its usual premature over maturity: the last years or two when it remains full of zest and vigour. Here, though, the oak from the bourbon cask has offered a little too much of its milkier, older side while the sherry is a fraction overzealous and a shade too tangy. Enjoyable, but like a top of the range Mercedes engine which refuses to run evenly. 43%.

**The Balvenie Double Wood Aged 17 Years** bott 2012 db **(91)** n22.5 t23.5 f22 b23 A far friskier date than the 12-year-old. Here, maturity equals sophistication. Still not as outrageously sexy as a straightforward high grade bourbon cask offering from the distillery. But easily enough to get you hot under the collar. Lip smacking, high quality entertainment. 43%

**The Balvenie Roasted Malt Aged 14 Years** db **(90)** n21 t23 f22 b24. Balvenie very much as you've never seen it before. An absolute, mouth-filling cracker! 47.1%

**The Balvenie Rum Wood Aged 14 Years** db **(88)** n22 t23 f21 b22. Tasted blind I would never have recognized the distillery: I'm not sure if that's a good thing. 47.1%

**Balvenie 17 Years Old Rum Cask** db **(88.5)** n22 t22.5 f22 b22.For all the best attentions of the rum cask at times this feels all its 17 years, and perhaps a few Summers more. Impossible not to love, however. 43%

**Balvenie New Wood Aged 17 Years** db **(85)** n23 t22 f19 b21. A naturally good age for Balvenie; the nose is lucid and exciting, the early delivery is thick with rich malt. This, though, has sucked out lots of caramel from the wood to leave an annoyingly flat finish. 40%

**The Balvenie 17 Year Old Sherry Oak** db **(88)** n23 t22.5 f21 b21.5. Clean as a nut. High-class sherry it may be but the price to pay is a flattening out of the astonishing complexity one normally finds from this distillery. Bitter-sweet in every respect. 43%

**The Balvenie Aged 21 Years Port Wood** db **(94.5)** n24 t24 f23 b23.5 What a magnificently improved malt. Last time out I struggled to detect the fruit. Here, there's no escaping. 40%

**The Balvenie Thirty Aged 30 Years** db **(92)** n24 t23 f22 b23. Rarely have I come across a bottling of a whisky of these advanced years which is so true to previous ones. Amazing. 47.3%

**The Balvenie Tun 1509** Batch 1 db **(89)** n23 t22.5 f21.5 b22 Balvenie is a distillery which struggles with age. And this is hanging on for life by its bloodied claws... 47.1%

**The Balvenie TUN 1509** batch 2 db **(94)** n23.5 t24 f23 b23.5 A far happier and all round better balanced bottling than Batch 1. A big whisky, though you won't at first realise it... 50.3%

# BANFF

### Speyside, 1863–1983. Diageo. Demolished.

**Gleann Mór Banff Aged Over 42 Years** dist 1975 **(91)** n23 t23.5 f22.5 b22 This was distilled in the same year I visited my first distillery in Scotland...and that was a bloody long time ago. Not many casks have made it from then to today, and those that have are in varying states of quality: old age does not always mean an improvement in a whisky's fortunes... often the reverse. This is a classic example of a malt which should have been bottled a little time back. But it is still massively enjoyable, throwing up the odd surprise here and there and keeping to the malty script despite the militant oak. Quite an experience....41.1%.

**Gordon & MacPhail Rare Old Banff 1966** **(90)** n22.5 t23 f22 b22.5 Quite a remarkable tail off in quality from their last bottling – but the age is going now into unknown territory for this lost distillery. Still excellent, though, and so much to enjoy... 46%.

# BEN NEVIS

### Highlands (Western), 1825. Nikka. Working.

**Ben Nevis 10 Years Old** db **(88)** n21 t22 f23 b22. A massive malt that has steadied itself in recent bottlings, but keep those knives and forks to hand! 46%

◈ **Ben Nevis 10 Years Old 2008** batch no. 1, 1st fill bourbon, sherry and wines casks, dist 21 Apr 08, bott Sept 18 db **(86.5)** n21 t22.5 f21 b22 A robust, no holds barred malt which gets you both with the intensity of fruit and oak as well as the sheer power of the spirit itself! The varied wine casks don't perhaps gel as they might (not helped by a small sulphur note), though the intensity of the delivery may bring a pleasurable bead of sweat to the brow. 62.4%.

**Ben Nevis Synergy 13 Years Old** db **(88)** n22 t22 f21.5 b22.5 One of the sweetest Ben Nevises for a long time, but as chewy as ever! A bit of a lady's dram to be honest. 46%

⬦ **Ben Nevis 32 Years Old 1966** dist Jun 66, bott Sept 98 db **(95.5) n24.5** almost too complex to be true: a pith-like dryness to the fruit, as though the grape pips are in concentrate. Perhaps most beguiling is the spice which appears to come in layers – and it is so rare to find that, nipping through with varying pace and intensity. There is a sweet layer of barley, too, but this sits above the chalkier oak tones and even deeper nuttier notes. This is as fascinating as it is entertaining and quietly formidable....; **t23.5** just brilliant: there is a serious bite to this, followed by a light rubbery note not unknown from this distillery during this period. But that hiccup is short-lived and salivating barley gushes from all directions, bringing with it a controlled sweetness. A plum skin note meets up with a strained honey note which struggles to make much of an impact, but does a subtle balancing job; **f24** long with a fabulous oils ensuring the dryness sticks, but the mild sweetness is unable to escape either; **b23.5** way back in 1998 some 1966 Ben Nevis was bottled for the US market as a "101" in 75cl bottles...but for some reason never got there. So for 20 years they slumbered peacefully in a warehouse at the distillery, entirely and blissfully forgotten, about until one day they were rediscovered by chance. That whisky, with a little softening from 20 years in glass, has now been re-consigned to 70cl bottles and at last put up for sale. What we have is a real blast from the past: a window into a Ben Nevis's distilling history, as a 32-year-old whisky bottled now from 1987 stock would certainly have a different feel. This reveals the distillery when it had the type of bite much favoured by blenders and which ensures a single malt with a singular personality. Just magnificent! 50.5%. Forgotten Bottlings Series.

**Acla Selection Ben Nevis 17 Years Old** hogshead, dist 1998, bott 2016 **(94)** n23 t23.5 f23.5 b24 Very fine Ben Nevis, indeed. 48.3%. sc. 89 bottles.

**Acla Selection Ben Nevis 19 Years Old** refill butt, dist 1996, bott 2016 **(87.5)** n22 t22.5 f21 b22 A nutty, slightly salty offering. Expands on delivery with a velvety fruitiness. But elsewhere is just a fraction tight, though there is no faulting the delicate cocoa and spice. 47.3%. sc. 90 bottles.

**Cadenhead's Ben Nevis Rum Cask 18 Years Old** dist 1998 **(89.5)** n22 t22 f23 b22.5 Rum casks can close a whisky slightly due to the sugars, as well as open. For the start, the doors to this malt remain shut, but the slow blossoming is a delight. 50.2%. sc. 210 bottles. 175th Anniversary bottling.

**Cask 88 Ben Nevis 45 Year Old** sherry hogshead, dist 1972 **(88.5)** n22.5 t22 f22 b22 A malt whisky tiring by the minute but gamely hanging on in there. 42%. nc ncf sc. 228 bottles.

⬦ **The Cooper's Choice Ben Nevis 1996 21 Years Old** sherry cask **(79)** n22 t21 f17 b19 As sherry butts go this, at first glance, passes muster so far as overall lack of sulphur is concerned. But there is little joy de vie to this and slowly the dreaded S word begins to gather in intensity, though never entirely dominating. A very pleasant malt I suspect for those who can't pick up sulphur; a bit of a dullard for those who can. 46%. nc ncf sc.

**Fadandel.dk Ben Nevis 21 Years Old** refill sherry cask, cask no. 18/1996, dist 9 Feb 96, bott 31 May 17 **(95.5)** n24 t24 f23.5 b24 That rarest of things: a beautiful clean sherry butt pulling the strings with panache. 51.1%. sc. 487 bottles.

⬦ **Glenwill Ben Nevis 1992** hogshead, cask no. 0076 **(95)** n23.5 rhubarb, ginger and custard; **t24** huge malt presence; heads towards a little saltiness but diverted towards a light chicory tannin dryness; the oils are full, even and carrying a little ulmo honey; excellent spices begin to form; **f23.5** cocoa and spicy vanilla; **b24** anyone who collects distilleries in their very best form should grab a bottle of this: not a bum note to be heard. 48.7%. 217 bottles. Matisse Spirits Company.

⬦ **The Golden Cask Ben Nevis 22 Years Old 1996** cask no. CM252, bott 2018 **(93.5)** n23.5 a little salty and piquant; the barley has almost an extra dimension; **t23.5** the first two or three waves on delivery a little feeble, then it gets its gear together and kicks in with a massive malt and tannin double whammy; a little liquorice and spices go a long way; **f23** levels out, though the spices tingle on; **b23.5** lovely to see a Ben Nevis at this age still capable of keeping you guessing and coming up with surprises. 46.5%. nc ncf sc. 150 bottles.

⬦ **Hepburn's Choice Ben Nevis 7 Years Old** wine cask, dist 2011, bott 2019 **(74.5)** n18 t19 f18.5 b19 With the furry sulphur at large, more of a whine cask... 46%. nc ncf sc. 367 bottles.

**Hidden Spirits Ben Nevis 12 Year Old** heavily peated sherry cask, cask no. BN618, dist 2006, bott 2018 **(76)** n19 t21 f18 b18 The peat may be piled on high, but it can't disguise the failings of the sherry butt. 55.4%. sc.

**Howard Cai Selected Ben Nevis 19 Years** sherry cask no 198 db (**94**) **n23 t23.5 f23.5 b24** Really uplifts the heart when great distillate combines with a faultless sherry butt and have the best art of two decades to work their magic. *50.4%. 260 bottles.*

**Kingsbury Gold Ben Nevis 20 Years Old** butt, cask no. 70, dist 1997 (**94.5**) **n23.5 t23.5 f23.5 b24** So rare to find a Scotch from this period with unspoiled sherry maturation. Superb. And not a bad way to mark my 750th whisky for the 2019 Bible... *57.3%. 247 bottles.*

⬩ **Liquid Treasures Snakes Ben Nevis 20 Year Old** bourbon hogshead, dist 1998, bott 2018 (**88**) **n22.5** firm and, despite the bourbon cask, has a distinct glazed fruit candy aroma; **t22** some early venom in the delivery, spices rising early before slithering back. Likewise the surges then recoil...; **f21.5** slightly flat, with simple vanilla and a late bitterness; **b22** starts off with rattling good pace, then ends as a bit of a boa. *52.1%. sc. 199 bottles.*

**Old Malt Cask Ben Nevis Aged 16 Years** refill hogshead, cask no. 14755, dist Nov 01, bott Feb 18 (**89.5**) **n22.5 t23 f21.5 b22.5** A really good, honest cask showing Ben Nevis is its forthright glory. *50%. nc ncf sc. 280 bottles.*

**Old Malt Cask Ben Nevis Aged 21 Years** refill hogshead, cask no. 14287, dist May 96, bott Sept 17 (**91.5**) **n22 t23 f23 b23.5** Typically and pleasingly chunky and chewy for this distillery: just choc-a-bloc with character. *50%. nc ncf sc. 318 bottles.*

**Old Particular Ben Nevis 21 Years Old** refill butt, cask no. 11767, dist Apr 96, bott Jun 17 (**91**) **n23 t23 f22.5 b22.5** Unusually creamy and sweet for a Nevis: no complaints from me! *51.5%. nc ncf sc. 583 bottles.*

**Saar Whisky N°8** dist 1998, bott 2018 (**79.5**) **n19 t21.5 f19 b20** One of the most oily single malts I have encountered for a while: the barley is huge on this and the spices are inevitable. But also a slightly feinty malt, unusually for a Scotch. *54.2%. ncf sc.*

⬩ **Saar Whisky N°9** ex bourbon barrel, sherry cask finish (01.06.17 - 23.08.18), dist 1998, bott 2018, bott code: LN9E12018 (**86**) **n21.5 t22.5 f21 b21** A clean sherry cask – hurrah! The not so good news is that the malt and grape have not yet come to terms with each other, the result being a vibrant, busy but, ultimately, out of tune effort. *46.5%. ncf sc.*

⬩ **Single & Single Ben Nevis 1996 Aged 21 Years** sherry cask (**81.5**) **n22.5 t24 f16 b20** The nose shows huge fruit and nut from presumably a once dripping oloroso butt. A vague hint of something sinister under the chunky fruit...? The initial delivery is of sopping oloroso which makes for the most moist of sherry trifles. But the finish sees the tannins begin to kick in...as does the drying, off-key sulphur. Looks like someone's let loose a parcel of Ben Nevis sherry butts. This is the first of the batch I have tasted. Imperfect, as the finale reveals. By the standards of sherry butts of that day, it could have been a lot worse. *52.8%. sc.*

**The Single Malts of Scotland Ben Nevis 20 Years Old 1996** cask no. 1528 (**92.5**) **n22.5 t23.5 f23 b23.5** Strap yourself into the chair for this one: it is some ride...! *53.1%. sc.*

⬩ **Single Cask Collection Ben Nevis Aged 22 Years** Fino cask (**90.5**) **n22.5** lively bite with spices peppering the shimmering grape; **t23.5** the lift off is almost pure spice, its rockets searing into the taste buds. A sub plot of muscovado sugar and heather honey wrestles back some sweet control. Eye-poppingly warming still at the mid-point as the oak makes a presence; **f22** the sugars continue on their flight path, but a little bitterness begins to show; **b22.5** sweeter than you might expect a Fino sherry to be and, thankfully, not a trace of an off note. Huge! *57.2%. sc.*

⬩ **Single Cask Collection Ben Nevis Aged 22 Years** olorosso cask (**79.5**) **n20 t21.5 f18.5 b19.5** A bit tangy and tight in the crucial areas. Good sultana thrust to the delivery, though *51.2%. sc.*

**Spirit of Caledonia Ben Nevis 18 Years Old** sherry cask, cask no. 24 (**95**) **n23.5 t24 f23.5 b24** Look what happens when you work with a perfect, unspoiled sherry butt... *51.7%. sc.*

**The Whisky Embassy Ben Nevis Aged 20 Years** cask no. 615, dist May 97, bott Aug 17 (**90.5**) **n22 t22.5 f23 b23** As sweet as a nut. *51.4%. nc ncf sc.*

⬩ **W.W. Club BNV.1 Ben Nevis Aged 20 Years** American oak cask, cask no. 415, dist Sept 96, bott Feb 17 (**93**) **n22.5** salty and a little tight from the oak; **t23.5** relaxes on delivery and the heather honey burst forth with gusto. Quite a powerful vanilla thread and salty too; some very decent cocoa notes build; **f23** dry, almost crunchy late barley. Buzzing, bitty spice and still that mild tang from the oak; a wonderful late hint of chocolate orange...; **b24** the sheer force of the characterful spirit overcomes the oak for an enjoyable encounter. I am also noticing a distinctive salty theme to WW Club whiskies. *51.7%. sc. 235 bottles. William & Co. Spirits.*

# BENRIACH
### Speyside, 1898. Brown-Forman. Working.

**BenRiach 10 Year Old** db (**87.5**) **n20 t23 f22.5 b22.** A much fatter spirit than from any time when I worked those stills. The dry nose never quite decides where it is going. But there's no doubting the creamy yet juicy credentials on the palate. Malty, with graceful fruit sugars chipping in delightfully. *43%*

**The BenRiach Aged 10 Years Curiositas Peated Malt** bourbon, toasted virgin oak & rum casks, bott code: 2018/10/11 LM11452 db **(89.5) n22.5** busy and smoky, there is a hard, semi-metallic note to this where there wasn't before; **t22.5** much softer on arrival with the grist working at full throttle. A curious – or perhaps I should say curiositas - creamy texture, almost like cream soda, froths up the palate; **f22** thins now and bitter-sweet; **b22.5** unrecognisable from the original Curiositas and though the strength is back up to 46% abv, somehow the body has become lighter. Enjoyable but a head scratcher. *46%. nc ncf.*

**The BenRiach Aged 12 Years** db **(82.5) n21 t20 f21 b20.5.** More enjoyable than the 43% I last tasted. But still an entirely inoffensive malt determined to offer minimal complexity. *40%*

**The BenRiach Aged 12 Years Matured In Sherry Wood** db **(95.5) n23.5 t24 f24 b24** Since previously experiencing this the number of instances of sampling a sherry wood whisky and not finding my taste buds caked in sulphur has nosedived dramatically. Therefore, to start my tasting day at 7am with something as honest as this propels one with myriad reasons to continue the day. A celebration of a malt whisky in more ways than you could believe. *46%. nc ncf.*

**The BenRiach Aged 21 Years Classic** bourbon barrels, virgin oak, PX sherry & red wine casks db **(90) n22.5 t23 f22 b22.5** Rich textured and complex, there is a glorious clarity to the sugars and fondant vanillas. Even the spices seem happy to dovetail into the merry mix without creating too many waves. *46%. nc*

**The BenRiach Aged 21 Years Tawny Port Wood Finish** db **(87.5) n22 t21 f22 b21.5** I'm not sure if the cask finish was designed to impart a specific fruitiness profile or simply repair some tired old oak. In either case, it has been a partial success only. The intemperance of the tannin makes its mark in no small measure both on nose and delivery and it is only in the finish that the sugars bond strongly enough together to form a balance with the woody input. *46%.*

**The BenRiach Aged 21 Years Temporis Peated** bourbon barrels, virgin oak, Pedro Ximenez & oloroso sherry casks db **(87.5) n22.5 t22 f21.5 b21.5** Begins nobly with a fanfare of alluring acidic peat, then strange (mainly orangey) fruit notes keeps chipping away at its integrity and ruining the song and balance. And so it also pans out on delivery, though the smoke is soon muzzled. For a flavour wave or two both smoke and fruit are in perfect harmony but it is fleeting and not worth the dull finish which follows. Enjoyable, but kind of irritating, too. *46%. nc ncf.*

**The BenRiach Aged 22 years Moscatel Wood Finish** db **(81) n21 t23 f17 b20** Not sure any wine finish I have tasted this year has thrown up so many huge, one might even say challenging, perfumed notes which score so highly for sheer lip-smacking effect. Had this cask not given the impression of being sulphur treated what an enormous score it would have amassed...! *46%.*

**The BenRiach 25 Years Old** db **(87.5) n21.5 t23 f21 b22.** The tranquillity and excellent balance of the middle is the highlight by far. *50%*

**The BenRiach Aged 25 Years Authenticus** db **(91) n23 t23 f22 b23** Every moment feels as old as a Roman senator...who is eventually stabbed in the back by Oakicus. *46%.*

**BenRiach 35 Year Old** db **(90) n23** juicy dates and plums are tipped into a weighty fruitcake; **t24** sit right back in your armchair (no..? Then go and find one...!!) having dimmed the lights and silenced the room and just let your taste buds run amok: those plums and toasted raisins really do get you salivating, with the spices also whipping up a mid-life storm; **f21.5** angular oak dries and bitters at a rate of knots; **b22** sexy fruit, but has late oaky bite. *42.5%*

**BenRiach Cask Strength** batch 1 db **(93) n22.5 t24 f23 b23.5** If you don't fall in love with this one, you should stick to vodka... *57.2%*

**The BenRiach Curiositas Aged 10 Years Single Peated Malt** db **(90.5) n23 t23 f22 b22.5** "Hmmmm. Why have my research team marked this down as a 'new' whisky" I wondered to myself. Then immediately on nosing and tasting I discovered the reason without having to ask: the pulse was weaker, the smoke more apologetic...it had been watered down from the original 46% to 40%. This is excellent malt. But can we have our truly great whisky back, please? As lovely as it is, this is a bit of an imposter. As Emperor Hadrian might once have said: "ifus itus aintus brokus..." *40%*

**The BenRiach "Heart of Speyside"** db **(85.5) n21.5 t22 f21 b21.** A decent, non-fussy malt where the emphasis is on biscuity barley. At times juicy and sharp. Just a tease of very distant smoke here and there adds weight. *40%*

**The BenRiach Peated Cask Strength** batch 1 db **(95) n24** the gentle, zesty lemon offers a clinically precise degree of lightness to the rolling smoke. A hint of acrid burnt toast in the air but of no greater intensity than the subtle dark sugars which perform a textbook balancing act; **t23** youthful gristiness shows those Demerara sugars up to the max; the smoke is layered though each next one is deeper and with spices mounting...; **f24** as a buttery dimension develops it just gets better and better...; **b24** stunning whisky magnificently distilled and, though relatively young, almost perfectly matured. *56%.*

**BenRiach Peated Quarter Casks** db **(93)** n23.5 there's a lot of peat in them barrels. The citrus is vital...; **t24** a plethora of sugars and caramel leached from the casks make for a safe landing when the smoke and malt – with a slightly new make feel - arrive in intensive form; **f22.5** the caramel continues, now with spice; **b23** though seemingly youthful in some phases, works a treat! 46%

**The BenRiach "Solstice"** db **(94)** n23.5 t24 f23 b23.5. On Midsummer's Day 2011, the summer solstice, I took a rare day off from writing this book. With the maximum light available in my part of the world for the day I set off at daybreak to see how many miles I could walk along remote country paths stopping, naturally, only at a few remote pubs on the way. It was a fraction under 28 miles. Had this spellbinding whisky been waiting for me just a little further down the road, I am sure, despite my troubled left knee and blistered right foot, I would have made it 30... 50%. nc ncf.

**Birnie Moss Intensely Peated** db **(90)** n22 youthful, full of fresh barley and lively, clean smoke; **t23.5** juicy, fabulously smoked, wet-behind the ears gristy sugars; **f22** some vanillas try to enter a degree of complexity; **b22.5** before Birnie Moss started shaving... or even possibly toddling. Young and stunning. 48%. nc ncf.

**Chapter 7 Benriach 9 Year Old** bourbon hogshead, cask no. 133, dist 2008 **(85.5)** n22 t22 f20 b21.5 As bourbon casks go, this is highly unusual. The usual markers have been removed and in their stead is a languid fruitiness, avec tang (which is quite dominant late on), determined to outgun the prolific spice. Those who remember fruit fudge will recognise the main thrust of this – though it never came this warm 59.8%. sc.

**Chapter 7 Benriach 9 Year Old** bourbon hogshead, cask no. 134, dist 2008 **(88.5)** n21.5 t22 f22.5 b22.5 No disguising its comparative tender years. But juicily delicious all the same. 60%. sc.

**Endangered Drams Benriach 9 Year Old** cask no. 61, dist Apr 08, bott Jun 17 **(86.5)** n21.5 t22 f21.5 b21.5 A sparkling, simplistic Speysider. Light, but the barley is out in force with vanilla a generous sidekick. 57.8%. nc ncf sc.

⬥ **The Great Drams Benriach 5 Years Old** 2nd fill oloroso sherry barrel, cask no. 121/2013, dist 7 Nov 13, bott 26 Feb 19 **(75)** n18 t20 f18 b19 A five-year-old malt matured in a lightly sulphured sherry butt does not a great dram make... 46.2%. nc ncf sc.

**Hepburn's Choice Benriach 7 Years Old** refill hogshead, dist 2010, bott 2018 **(84.5)** n20 t23 f20 b21.5 Nothing essentially wrong with this whisky: packed to the gunnels with serious malty intent: indeed, it hits a beautiful spot two or three waves in after the delivery. Yet, like Bambi, its looks cute but is unsteady on its feet and falls flat on its face as often as not. 46%. nc ncf sc. 465 bottles.

⬥ **Hidden Spirits Benriach 2010 Aged 8 Years Heavily Peated** cask no. BH1018, bott 2018 **(91.5)** n22 appears younger than its age but the minty phenols have a pleasant fizz; **t23** a precocious complexity to the peat. The mid-ground minty chocolate merging with the spice, then Demerara sugar and unrestrained smoke is superb; **f23** ridiculously juvenile – so little oak present – yet everything falls into place like a charm; **b23.5** so much personality despite its obvious youth. 50%. sc.

# BENRINNES

**Speyside, 1826. Diageo. Working.**

**Benrinnes Aged 15 Years** db **(70)** n16 t19 f17 b18. What a shame that in the year the independent bottlers at last get it right for Benrinnes, the actual owners of the distillery make such a pig's ear of it. Sulphured and sicklysweet, this bottling has little to do with the very good whisky made there day in day out by its talented team. Depressing. 43%. Flora and Fauna.

**Benrinnes 21 Year Old** ex-sherry European oak casks, dist 1992 db **(83.5)** n21 t22 f19 b21.5. Salty and tangy. Some superb cocoa moments mixing with the muscovado sugars as it peaks. But just a little too furry and bitter at the finish. 56.9%. 2,892 bottles. Diageo Special Releases 2014.

**Acla Selection Benrinnes 18 Years Old** hogshead, cask no. 819, dist 1997, bott 2015 **(89)** n22 t22.5 f22.5 b22 The distillery showing much richer fettle than normal with there being distinct depth to the barley and quite excellent cocoa on the warming fade. May have been bottled a few years back, but still around and worth finding as an above-average version of this distillery. 52.2%. sc. 138 bottles.

⬥ **The First Editions Benrinnes Aged 16 Years 2002** sherry butt, cask no. 15438, bott 2018 **(79)** n18 t21.5 f19.5 b20 A pretty awful nose is compensated for by a boiled-sweet fruitiness and attractive accompanying very un-Benrinnes-like oils on both delivery and finish. Surprisingly assertive at times. 55.1%. nc ncf sc. 270 bottles.

**The First Editions Benrinnes Aged 20 Years** refill hogshead, cask no. 14985, bott 2018 **(78.5)** n19 t21 f19 b19.5 An untidy whisky which never finds its purpose or rhythm. Cloying sweetness and sharp, jagged edges to annoy and ends in a stark bitterness. A first edition hardly worthy of a reprint. 45.4%. nc ncf sc. 94 bottles.

◈ **Gleann Mór Benrinnes Aged Over 24 Years (89.5)** n22.5 t23 f21.5 b22.5 One of the more impressive Benrinnes you'll find in the market place just now. On its days, it can belt out barley with the best of them. But here as well maximising the malt the subtle layering of acacia honey and vanilla sponge ensures that, with an also just-so addition of spice, you are seeing the distillery in its finest fettle. *41.1%.*

**Golden Cask Benrinnes Aged 21 Years** cask no. CM241, dist 1995, bott 2017 **(87)** n22.5 t22 f21 b21.5 Rips into the palate at full throttle but boasts a honey and marzipan padding which absorbs much, though not all, of the warmer moments. *55.8%. sc. 290 bottles.*

◈ **The Golden Cask Benrinnes 1995** cask no. CM248, bott 2018 **(89)** n22 clean, sharp, simplistically malty; t22.5 incredibly tart and fresh, the oak barely laying a glove on the delicious malt; f22 gristy and sweet; b22.5 a Peter Pan of a malt, refusing to grow up and making the most of its juicy vitality. *56%. nc ncf sc. 282 bottles.*

**Hepburn's Choice Benrinnes 8 Years Old** wine cask, dist 2009, bott 2017 **(85.5)** n21 t21.5 f21.5 b21.5 Threatens at times to be a spitfire of a dram but the passive maltiness calms things down for a decent if unexciting ride. The spices can't be tamed late on, though... *46%. nc ncf sc. 300 bottles.*

◈ **Hepburn's Choice Benrinnes 10 Years Old** rum finished cask, dist 2009, bott 2019 **(84.5)** n22 t22 f20 b20.5 A curious choice to put Benrinnes into rum. You start with a malty but limited distillate finding further constraints which rum casks invariably bring. The finish, predictably, does not live up to the earlier charm. *46%. nc ncf sc. 276 bottles.*

◈ **Hepburn's Choice Benrinnes 12 Years Old** sherry butt, dist 2005, bott 2018 **(86.5)** n21.5 t22 f21.5 b22 Benrinnes being shewn in an attractive light here thanks to some very good oak which plays alongside the lightweight malt, rather than trying to overpower it. Delicate and attractively juicy early on. *46%. nc ncf sc. 348 bottles.*

**Kingsbury Gold Benrinnes 20 Years Old** hogshead, cask no. 11711, dist 1996 **(91.5)** n22 t23.5 f22.5 b23.5 Being Benrinnes you'd expect a bit of fire and attitude. But that character trait works well with the honey which has been assembled over the passing 20 years. *56.5%. 225 bottles.*

**Scotch Malt Whisky Society Cask 36.138 19 Year Old** refill ex-bourbon barrel, dist 15 Aug 97 **(86)** n21 t22 f21.5 b21.5 Benrinnes doing what Benrinnes does: a bit thin and hot in parts, but still plenty of attractive barley on the scene to make for a pleasantly mouth-watering dram. Decent oak helps. *60.9%. sc.*

**Scyfion Choice Benrinnes 1997** Artania cask finished, bott 2017 **(86.5)** n22 t21.5 f21.5 b21.5 Not a flavour profile I have often experienced. Mouth-puckering and eye-watering fare where the effects of the cask seem to be above what poor old Benrinnes, hardly the most sturdy of malts, can cope with. Strangely enjoyable, in the same way you might enjoy a spin on the dodgems: expect the occasional very heavy jolt from any angle! *46%. nc ncf. 226 bottles.*

**Stronachie 18 Years Old (83.5)** n21.5 t21 f20 b21. This is so much like the older brother of the Stronachie 12: shows the same hot temper on the palate and even sharper teeth. Also, the same slim-line body. Have to say, though, something strangely irresistible about the intensity of the crisp malt. *46%*

◈ **Whisky Castle Benrinnes Aged 9 Years** rum barrel finish, dist 2009, bott 2018 **(91)** n23 fabulously crisp barley: clean and sugar-coated; t23.5 what a gorgeous delivery: you really couldn't ask more from the grain of the rum influence: a happy and harmonious marriage; f22 the intrusion of the oak appears more bitter than it is due to earlier clean sugars; b22.5 disarmingly orchestrated. A superior Benrinnes. *46%. nc ncf sc. 297 bottles.*

**The Whisky Embassy Benrinnes Aged 20 Years** cask no. 969, dist 1997, bott 2017 **(86.5)** n22 t22.5 f20.5 b21.5 A shame about the tangy fade. Until then the malt had acquitted itself well by keeping its occasional violent tendencies in check and maximising the sweetness of the malt. *48.9%. nc ncf sc.*

◈ **World of Orchids Benrinnes 1997 20 Years Old** bourbon cask, cask no. 821 **(89)** n22 t23 f22 b22 The orchids around here grow in grass. And this is the grassiest malt I have sampled for a while. Delightfully fresh, despite its age. So gristy, too. *48.9%. sc.*

# BENROMACH

**Speyside, 1898. Gordon & MacPhail. Working.**

**Benromach 10 Years Old** matured in hand selected oak casks db **(87.5)** n22 t22 f21.5 b22. For a relatively small still using peat, the experience is a delicately light one. *43%*

**Benromach 15 Year Old** db **(78)** n20 t22 f17 b19. Some charming early moments, especially when the grape escapes its marker and reveals itself in its full juicy and sweet splendour. But it is too short lived as the sulphur, inevitably takes over. *43%*

**Benromach 21 Years Old** db **(91.5)** n22 t23.5 f23 b23 An entirely different, indeed lost, style of malt from the old, now gone, big stills. The result is an airier whisky which has embraced such good age with a touch of panache and grace. *43%*

**Benromach 22 Years Old Finished in Port Pipes** db **(86) n22 t23 f20 b21.** Slightly Jekyll and Hyde. 45%. 3500 bottles.

**Benromach 25 Years Old** db **(92) n24 t22 f23 b23** A classic old-age Speysider, showing all the quality you'd hope for. 43%

**Benromach 30 Years Old** db **(95.5) n23.5 t24 f24 b24** You will struggle to find a 30-year-old with fewer wrinkles than this.. Magnificent: one of the outstanding malts of the year. 43%

**Benromach 39 Year Old 1977 Vintage** db **(94) n23.5** just love that! The oak keeps threatening to go OTT but never quite manages, being pulled back by grapefruit, red liquorice and heather honey; **t24** just love that! The oak keeps threatening to go OTT, but is pulled back by salivating barley, toasty sugars – fudge almost – and now hickory on top of burnt treacle tart; that citrus on the nose dribbles through from time to time; **f23** just love that! A swathe of caramel comforts any tiring oak and blends in beautifully with the intact barley; **b23.5** just love it when a whisky creaks and complains and lets you know just how old it is...but then produces the magic that keeps alive, well and captivatingly complex after all these years. 56%.

◇ **Benromach 1972** cask no. 4471 db **(94) n23** some serious oak at play. But play it does, as it doesn't take itself as seriously as it might, allowing in kumquats and toasted barley; a light walnut oil sheen to this, too; **t23.5** brilliant oils ensure a soft landing for the punchy oak and proud, mocha-riddled barely. A little diced pear sits beautifully with the dates and molasses; **f23.5** long, drying at last with French praline representing the oak splendidly; **b24** has turned completely grey, but this is one sprightly malt. 55.7%. sc.

◇ **Benromach 1977** cask no. 1269 db **(87.5) n22 t21.5 f22 b22** Plucked from the warehouse a little too late with its best days behind it. The oak is overlord here, the tannins aggressive enough to bring water to the eye, as does the grapefruit citrus kick. But by no means is all lost as the malt is proud, robust and rich and puts up a chewy rear-guard action. 49.6%. sc.

**Benromach 100° Proof** db **(94) n23 t23.5 f23.5 b24** For any confused US readers, the strength is based on the old British proof strength, not American! What is not confusing is the undisputed complexity and overall excellence of this malt. 57%

**Benromach 20th Anniversary Bottling** db **(81) n19 t22 f19 b21** Bit of a clumsy whisky never really feeling right on the nose or palate, though has its better moments with a big malt crescendo and a delicate minty-chocolate movement towards the late middle and early finish. 56.2%.

**Benromach 2005 Sassicaia Finish** db **(92.5) n22.5 t24 f23 b23.** A sassy dram! 45%

◇ **Benromach Cask No. 1** dist 1998, bott 2018 db **(89.5) n23** like a bunch of grapes you forgot you had in the bag...; **t22** fat, oily slightly off-key start but corrects itself as a tart but attractive gooseberry notes arrives; **f22** dry powdery mocha; **b22.5** an unusual fingerprint to this and intriguingly haphazard in its development. 60.1%.

**Benromach Cask Strength 1981** db **(91) n21.5 t23 f23.5 b23.** Really unusual with that seaweedy aroma awash with salt: stunningly delicious stuff. 54.2%

**Benromach Cask Strength 2001** db **(89) n21.5 t23 f22 b22.5.** Just fun whisky which has been very well made and matured with total sympathy to the style. Go get. 59.9%

**Benromach Cask Strength 2003** db **(92) n22.5 t23.5 f23 b23.5** Hats off to the most subtle and sophisticated Benromach I have tasted in a while. 59.4%.

◇ **Benromach Cask Strength Batch 1** dist 2008, bott 2019 db **(90.5) n23.5** light praline sits as astride the gentle peat; just the lightest touch of parma violet; **t22.5** like Cask 1, there is a slight wobble on the spirit and for a moment bares some teeth. But soon the gentle smoke returns, alongside a delicate Camp coffee note; **f22** a touch of mint chocolate on the almost apologetic peat; **b22.5** some smoky malts terrify people. This, I suspect, will enjoy the direct opposite effect. As friendly a peated malt as you'll ever find. 57.9%.

**Benromach Heritage 35 Year Old** db **(87) n22 t21.5 f22 b21.5.** A busy exchange of complex tannin notes, some backed by the most faded spice and caramel. All charming and attractive, but the feeling of decay is never far away. 43%

**Benromach Heritage 1974** db **(93) n23.5 t23 f23 b23.5** Made in the year I left school to become a writer, this appears to have survived the years in better nick than I... 49.1%

**Benromach Heritage 1975** db **(89) n22 t22.5 f22 b22.5** A bottling where the malt is hanging on for grim death against the passing of time. But the discreet light honey notes do just the trick. 49.9%.

**Benromach Heritage 1976** db **(86.5) n21.5 t21 f22.5 b21.5** There are times when you can have a little too much tannin and this has crossed the Rubicon. That said, look closely on the nose for some staggering lime and redcurrant notes which escape the onslaught as well as the gorgeous butterscotch on the finish as the sugars fight back at the death in style. Some moments of genius in the oakiest of frames. 53.5%.

**Benromach Madeira Wood** db **(92) n22 t24 f23 b23.** If you want a boring, safe, timid malt, stay well away from this one. Fabulous: you are getting the feeling that the real Benromach is now beginning to stand up. 45%

**Benromach Marsala Wood** db **(86.5) n21.5 t22 f22 b21.** Solid, well made, enjoyable malt, which in some ways is too solid: the imperviousness of both the peat and grape appears not to allow much else get through. Not a dram to say no to, however, and the spices in particular are a delight. *45%*

**Benromach Organic** db **(91) n23 t23 f22 b23.** Young and matured in possibly first fill bourbon or, more likely, European (even Scottish) oak; you cannot do other than sit up and take notice of this guns-blazing big 'un. An absolute treat! *43%. nc ncf.*

**Benromach Organic Special Edition** db **(85.5) n22 t21 f21.5 b21.** The smoky bacon crisp aroma underscores the obvious youth. Also, one of the driest malts of the year. Overall, pretty. But pretty pre-pubescent, too... *43%*

**Benromach Organic 2010** db **(95.5) n24 t24 f23 b24.5** Gentle, refined and exquisitely elegant. *43%*

**Benromach Peat Smoke Batch 3** db **(90.5) n22 t23 f22.5 b23** An excellent malt that has been beautifully made. Had it been bottled at 46 we would have seen it offer an extra degree of richness. *40%*

**Benromach Peat Smoke 2008** db **(85.5) n22 t22 f20.5 b21** Well, that was certainly different! The nose has the oily hallmark of a Caol Ila, though without the phenol intensity. The palate, those oils apart, is a very different tale. A unique flavour profile for sure: a kind of smoked toffee fudge which actually makes your tongue ache while tasting! And there is a bitterness, also. Normally I can spot exactly from where it originates...this one leaves me baffled...though I'd go from the distillation if pushed. *46%.*

⬧ **Benromach Sherry Cask Matured Peat Smoke** dist 2010, bott 2018 db **(94.5) n23.5** the kind of massive sherry and even huger peat noses that some peatophiles I know just lie in bed dreaming about....huge! Oh, and acidic and mildly aggressive, too...; **t24** wow...!! Now that's the kind of delivery I lay in bed and dream about. Perfect, not overly sweet grape, standing toe-to-toe with seriously macho phenol. Neither gives an inch...; **f23** long, with some searing spices to balance the gristy sugars; lovely milky mocha at the death; **b24** these type of whiskies so often fall flat on their face. This, by contrast, is a magnificent beast of a malt... *599%.*

**Benromach Traditional** db **(86) n22 t21 f21.5 b21.5.** Deliciously clean and smoky. But very raw and simplistic, too. *40%*

**Benromach Triple Distilled** db **(88) n23** the firmness to the malt has an almost Irish pot still quality: sharp, yet with a firm, brooding disposition; **t22.5** salivating and ultra-clean. Gristy sugars melt into the mix with vanilla upping the weight; **f21.5** a slight oak-sponsored bitterness from the more antiquated casks makes its mark; **b22** the finish part, a really charming barley character pervades throughout. *50%.*

**Benromach Vintage 1976** db **(89.5) n23 t23.5 f21 b22** hardly complex and shows all the old age attributes to be expected. That said...a very comfortable and satisfying ride. *46%*

**Benromach Wood Finish 2007 Sassicaia** db **(86.5) n22 t22 f21 b21.5.** Now back to the new distillery. Problem with this wood finish is that even when free from any taint, as this is, it is a harsh taskmaster and keeps a firm grip of any malty development – even on a dram so young. A brave cask choice. *45%*

# BLADNOCH

**Lowlands, 1817. David Prior. Working.**

**Bladnoch Aged 6 Years Bourbon Matured** db **(91) n21.5 t22.5 f24 b23** The fun starts with the late middle, where those extra oils congregate and the taste buds are sent rocking. Great to see a Lowlander bottled at an age nearer its natural best and even the smaller cut, in a roundabout way, ensures a mind-blowing dram. *573%*

**Bladnoch Aged 6 Years Lightly Peated** db **(93) n23 t23 f23.5 b23.5** The peat has nothing to do with the overall score here: this is a much better-made whisky with not a single off-note and the cut is spot on. And although it claims to be lightly peated, that is not exactly true: such is the gentle nature of the distillate, the smoke comes through imperiously and on several levels. "Spirit of the Lowlands" drones the label. Since when has outstanding peated malt been associated with that part of the whisky world...?? *58.5%*

**Bladnoch Aged 6 Years Sherry Matured** db **(73.5) n18 t19 f18.5 b18.** A sticky, lop-sided malt where something, or a group of somethings, conjures up a very unattractive overture. Feints on the palate but no excellent bourbon cask to the rescue here. *56.9%*

**Bladnoch Aged 10 Years** db **(94) n23 t24 f23 b24** This is probably the ultimate Bladnoch, certainly the best I have tasted in over 25 years. This Flora and Fauna bottling by then owners United Distillers should be regarded as the must-get-at-all-costs Bladnoch. If the new owner can create something even to hang on to this one's coat-tails then he has excelled himself. For those few of us lucky enough to experience this, this dram is nothing short of a piece of Lowland legend and folklore. *43%.*

⟨⟩ **Bladnoch 10 Year Old** bourbon barrels, bott code: L18/8829 db **(91) n22.5** so tightly knit are the vanillas here there is something of a top-rate Canadian about this. The barley forms the secondary layer, but generating extra sweetness, it does so with aplomb; look carefully and the distillery's old trademark citrus notes can still be spotted...just; **t23** a brilliant delivery where the malts are upfront and in full salivating made and a rich toffee turn follows closely behind. Soon, though, the tannins begin to bite deep, offering little cocoa and just the vaguest hints of a bourbon-style dark liquorice; **f22.5** dry and elegant, the toastier notes move towards a vague molassed sweetness before the spices begin to rumble; **b23** just wonderful to see Bladnoch back in the market place again, and this time obviously receiving the kind of attention in warehouse and tasting lab it deserves. The 10-year-old was for years a Lowland staple before a succession of owners saw it all but vanish off the map. This 10-year-old suggests they have the nucleus of what can again become a much-prized dram. Though a ten-year-old, either some of the casks used in this were a lot older, or there has been heavy usage of first-fill bourbon somewhere along the line, because the tannins have an unusually significant say. The result...rather delicious and you get a hell of a lot for a ten-year-old... 46.7%. ncf.

**Bladnoch Aged 15 Years** db **(91) n22.5 t22.5 f23 b23** Quite outstanding Lowland whisky which, I must admit, is far better than I would have thought possible at this age. 55%

⟨⟩ **Bladnoch 15 Year Old** Adela oloroso sherry casks, bott code: L18/8083 db **(91) n22** heavy and slightly musty, but that appears to be the malt rather than the grape. Toffee and fruitcake abound; **t23** sumptuous and chewy, the more sugary elements of the barley quickly join forces with the plumy fruitiness to ensure a thick and memorable delivery; a little haziness to the second-line flavours suggests maybe a question mark hangs over the quality of the initial spirit. But the oloroso does a great job of papering over the cracks and soon adds an extra layer of spice to create a further, delicious distraction; **f23** long and silky still with the plum jam still mingling with the bolder barley tones; **b23** I still feel a bit like Inspector Clouseau's boss, twitching at the mere thought of a sherry butt. But no need for alarm here: faultless oloroso influence here, indeed coming to the aid perhaps of an initial spirit which may not have been originally up to Bladnoch's excellent name. Surprisingly delightful. 46.7%. ncf.

⟨⟩ **Bladnoch 17 Year Old** Californian red wine finish db **(87.5) n22 t23 f21 b21.5** At its zenith on both nose and delivery, both imparting boiled sweet fruitiness and lustre. After that, as well as spice, a non-sulphured bitterness seeps into the proceedings. 46.7%. ncf.

**Bladnoch 18 Years Old** db **(88.5) n21 t23.5 f22 b22.** The juiciness and clarity to the barley, and especially the big gooseberry kick, early on makes this a dram well worth finding. 55%

⟨⟩ **Bladnoch 27 Year Old** bourbon cask finish db **(95) n24.5** the infusion of rich, clean barley with greengage, lime and vanilla is almost heady in its beauty. A soft saltiness lifts those erudite notes even further and gentle layers of orange blossom as well as Bruyere honey turns an excellent nose into truly great one; **t23.5** the finess and complexity of the spirit on the nose is further amplified by the technically perfect delivery on landing. The barley is crystalised in clarity while the very lightest of oils settle to both at weight and act as a absorbing buffer to the perkier oak tones; **f23** long with a busy, spicy tail to the weightier tannins; **b24** the best nose of a Lowlander I have encountered for a good number of years. A gem of single malt. 43%. ncf

⟨⟩ **Bladnoch Samsara Californian** red wine & bourbon casks, bott code: L18/8081 db **(87) n21.5 t23 f21 b21.5** Wine casks at work and not a sulphur atom in sight. However, there is no escaping a certain unscheduled bitterness or the fact that perhaps some of the malt was technically not the greatest ever distilled in Bladnoch's history. The result is a patchy experience, delicious in part, but bitty and bitter in others. Lush though on delivery and the plusses are big ones. 46.7%. ncf.

⟨⟩ **Cask 88 Bladnoch 27 Year Old** sherry hogshead, sherry quarter cask finish, cask no. 877589 **(84.5) n21.5 t20.5 f21.5 b21** Some whiskies are born great, some achieve greatness and some have greatness thrust upon them. This is the latter. Except more like greatness thrust upon them...but missed. Some almost grotesque grape at work here. 51.3%. nc ncf sc. 88 bottles. Eighty Eight Series.

**Scotch Malt Whisky Society Cask 50.95 27 Year Old** refill ex-bourbon barrel, dist 26 Jan 90 **(94.5) n23.5 t24 f23 b24** Bladnoch revving up a malty intensity massive even for their own scale... Sublime. 59.8%. sc.

**Scotch Malt Whisky Society Cask 50.96 27 Year Old** refill ex-bourbon barrel, dist 26 Jan 90 **(86) n22.5 t21.5 f21 b21** An aggressive delivery with the oak taking few prisoners. Many pointers towards a tired cask: the citrus takes on the sharpness usually reserved for limescale remover, though the malt does its best to hold its ground, especially by launching a defence of concentrated, oily barley. Enjoyable, providing you don't mind the scratches. 53.7%. sc.

# BLAIR ATHOL

**Highlands (Perthshire), 1798. Diageo. Working.**

**Blair Athol Aged 12 Years** db **(77) n18 t19 f21 b19**. Thick, fruity, syrupy and a little sulphury and heavy. The finish has some attractive complexity among the chunkiness. *43%.*

**Blair Athol 23 Year Old** ex-bodega European oak butts db **(90.5) n23 t23.5 f21.5 b22.5** Very often you think: "Aha! Here's an un-sulphur-treated sherry-matured malt!" And then find long into the finish that the taint turns up and sticks with you for another 20 minutes. Is there a slight trace on this late on? Yes. But it is one of the lightest and least concerning I have encountered this year. Which leaves you with plenty of luscious grape to enjoy... *58.4%. 5,514 bottles. Diageo Special Releases 2017.*

**Acla Selection Blair Athol 28 Years Old** hogshead, cask no. 4863, dist 1988, bott 2016 **(91) n23.5 t22.5 f22 b23** A huge malt indicative of the unwieldy new make this would have been 28 years ago but now, in old age, find some charm to match the charisma. *47.3%. sc. 90 bottles.*

**The First Editions Blair Athol Aged 22 Years** sherry butt, cask no. 14656, bott 2018 **(87.5) n21.5 t23 f21.5 b21.5** A superior Blair Athol where the sherry influence is profound – in a juicy, spicy, nutty and all-round positive kind of way. However, the spirit itself is a little uncompromising in its hefty weight, meaning charm and elegance are at a premium. *57.7%. nc ncf sc. 234 bottles.*

 **The First Editions Blair Athol Aged 23 Years 1995** sherry butt, cask no. 15758, bott 2019 **(78) n19 t21.5 f18.5 b19** The fruit flourishes briefly, but the sulphur kicks in quite quickly. *55.7%. nc ncf sc. 289 bottles.*

**Gordon & MacPhail Connoisseurs Choice Blair Athol 1997** refill American hogshead, cask no. 5720, dist 25 Aug 97, bott 21 Feb 18 **(83) n21 t21.5 f20.5 b20** Nothing too wrong with the cask. The spirit, however, is determined to test you. Hops around the palate refusing to find a happy narrative, occasionally happening upon a lick of honey. But too often a dour bitterness. *54.5%. nc ncf sc. 255 bottles.*

**Gordon & MacPhail Connoisseurs Choice Blair Athol 2008** bott 28 Mar 17 **(84) n19 t21 f23 b21** You know how irritating and disappointing Blair Tony is. Yep, at times it's as bad as that. Though, entirely unlike Britain's former Prime Minister, it does actually have something interesting and relevant to say late on that is worth listening to. That spice and honey helped along with some subtle layers of cocoa makes for an elegant, insightful fade before finally shutting up. Mr Blair, grab a bottle and please take note. *46%.*

**Old Malt Cask Blair Athol Aged 21 Years** sherry butt, cask no. 14245, dist Oct 95, bott Sept 17 **(85.5) n21 t22.5 f21 b21** Initially sweet on the tongue, there is also an eye-watering tartness which somehow matches the light mossy note on the nose. *50%. nc ncf sc. 366 bottles.*

**Old Malt Cask Blair Athol Aged 22 Years** sherry butt, cask no. 14455, dist Sept 95, bott Nov 17 **(87.5) n22 t22 f21 b22.5** Elements of walnut brown sherry to this. No off notes, but the original spirit has a Spartan feel, though the malt does surge through in places. Attractively unusual. *50%. nc ncf sc. 328 bottles.*

**Old Malt Cask Blair Athol Aged 22 Years** sherry butt, cask no. 14657, dist Mar 95, bott Feb 18 **(88) n22 t22.5 f21.5 b22** Thick enough on the palate to paint walls with. Enormous presence on the palate with the sugars and fruit flying in every direction. Hardly a sophisticated dram. But, very decent fun all the same. *50%. nc ncf sc. 292 bottles.*

 **Old Malt Cask Blair Athol Aged 23 Years** sherry butt, cask no. 15757, dist Aug 95, bott Feb 19 **(74.5) n18 t20 f18 b18.5** Guess. The clue comes in the bit that comes after "Aged 23 Years"... *50%. nc ncf sc. 321 bottles.*

**Old Particular Blair Athol 15 Years Old** refill hogshead, cask no. 12106, dist Sept 02, bott Sept 17 **(86) n22 t22.5 f20 b21.5** Lively and salivating with the barley sharp, focused and healthy. Just strays towards a certain tautness at the death. *48.4%. nc ncf sc. 357 bottles.*

**Old Particular Blair Athol 21 Years Old** sherry butt, cask no. 11788, dist Nov 95, bott Jun 17 **(86.5) n22 t22.5 f21 b21** By no means a bad sherry butt, offering much on the delivery before the slight awkwardness of the spirit itself begins to form a cloying persona. The tannins are also at times formidable. *51.2%. nc ncf sc. 321 bottles.*

 **World of Orchids Blair Athol 1988 29 Years Old** bourbon cask, cask no. 509 **(87) n21.5 t22.5 f21 b22** You can almost hear this malt panting after such a long journey, for which the spirit was ill-prepared for in a cask like this. The oak has a vice-like grip, which does bring a bit of a tear to the eye, but at least the barley is game enough to put up some sharp, not unattractive, citrusy resistance. *51.3%. sc.*

# BOWMORE

**Islay, 1779. Morrison Bowmore. Working.**

**Bowmore Aged 10 Years** Spanish oak sherry casks & hogsheads, bott code: L172033 db **(92.5) n23.5 t23.5 f22.5 b23** A very happy marriage between some full on peat and decent sherry butts makes for the intense malt promised on the label. *40%.*

**Bowmore Aged 12 Years** db **(91)** n22.5 t23.5 f22.5 b23.5 This new bottling still proudly carries the Fisherman's Friend cough sweet character, but the coastal, saline properties here are a notch or three up: far more representative of Islay and the old distillery style. Easily by far the truest Bowmore I have tasted in a long while with myriad complexity. Even going back more than a quarter of a century, the malt at this age rarely showed such relaxed elegance. Most enjoyable. *40%*

**Bowmore "Enigma" Aged 12 Years** db **(82)** n19 t22 f20 b21. Sweet, molassed and with that tell-tale Fisherman's Friend tang representing the light smoke. This Enigma hasn't quite cracked it, though. *40%. Duty Free.*

**Bowmore Gold Reef** oak casks db **(79)** n19.5 t21 f19 b19.5. Simple, standard (and rather boring and safe) fare for the masses gagged by toffee. *43% WB15/280*

**Bowmore Aged 15 Years** 1st fill bourbon casks, bott code: L172034 031 db **(88)** n23.5 t22 f21 b21.5 This was going swimmingly until the caramel just went nuts. I know first-fill bourbon casks are at work here, but hard to believe that was all natural... *43%.*

**Bowmore Aged 15 Years** sherry cask finish, bott code: L172073 db **(91)** n24 t22.5 f22.5 b23 A sherry influenced whisky outpointing a bourbon cask one....how often will you find that in this book...? *43%.*

**Bowmore Aged 17 Years** db **(77)** n18 t22 f18 b19. For all the attractiveness of the sweet fruit on delivery, the combination of butt and cough sweet makes for pretty hard going. *43%*

**Bowmore Aged 18 Years** db **(79)** n20 t21 f19 b19. Pleasant, drinkable Fisherman's Friend style – like every Bowmore it appears around this age. But why so toffee-dull? *43%*

**Bowmore Aged 18 Years** Oloroso & Pedro Ximénez casks, bott code: L172067 060 db **(82)** n20.5 t22.5 f19 b20 A dirty old nose – and I don't just mean the peat – pre-warns of the furry finish. But there is no denying the sheer joy of the voluptuous grape grappling with the phenols on delivery and in the wonderful moments just after. *43%.*

**Bowmore Aged 19 Years The Feis Ile Collection** first fill sherry puncheon, cask no. 57,dist 13 Jan 98, bott 27 May 17 db **(97)** n24 t24.5 f24 b24.5 If there was an award for the Best Cask Chosen by a Distillery Manager 2019, then it would go to this extraordinary bottling. A problem with sherry butts, even if entirely free from sulphur as this delightfully is, is their propensity to mask the actual distillery from which the whisky comes. Not here: this is as instantly and unmistakably recognisable as a Bowmore as the first three notes are as the signature of 'Goldfinger'. The salt from the No 1 warehouse, the light layering of smoke...well done distillery manager David Turner take a bow for your Bowmore....the finest I have ever tasted...! *54.3%. sc. Distillery Exclusive*

**Bowmore 20 Years Old 1997** sherry cask, bott 2017 db **(95.5)** n24 t24 f23.5 b24 The curtain of thick musky peat which descends on the nose leaves no doubt that we are in for one big sherried, oaky experience. And so it proves, although not quite in the fashion you might expect. For the softness on delivery is at odds with the boldness on the nose though, slowly, rung by rung the oak begins to take an increasingly more powerful hold: it is like experiencing whisky in slow motion. The fruit is a mix of blood orange and concentrated plum, the oak (here taken to its max) and smoke together creating a peaty chocolate spine. A malt of breath-taking enormity and beauty...to be devoured in slow-motion. *54.5%. sc. 231 bottles. Selected for CWS.*

**Bowmore Aged 23 Years Port Matured** db **(86)** n22 t22 f21 b21. Have you ever sucked Fisherman's Friends and fruit pastels at the same time, and thrown in the odd Parma Violet for good measure...? *50.8%*

**Bowmore Aged 25 Years** db **(86)** n21 t22 f21 b22. Not the big, chunky guy of yore: the age would surprise you if tasted blind. *43%*

**Bowmore Aged 25 Years Small Batch Release** db **(85.5)** n21 t22 f21 b21.5. Distilled at the very heart of Bowmore's peculiar and uniquely distinctive Fisherman's Friend cough sweet era. You will never find a more vivid example. *43%*

**Bowmore 29 Years Old 1989** db **(81.5)** n20.5 t21 f20 b20 From that uniquely disjointed: Fisherman's Friend" period of their production history. *44%. 170 bottles. The Whisky Shop Exclusive.*

**Bowmore Aged 30 Years** db **(94)** n23 t24 f23 b24 A Bowmore that no Islay scholar should be without. Shows the distillery at its most intense yet delicate; an essay in balance and how great oak, peat and fruit can combine for those special moments in life. Unquestionably one of the best Bowmores bottled this century. *43%*

**Bowmore Black 50 Year Old** db **(96.5)** n25 t24 f23 b24.5 a little known fact: a long time ago, before the days of the internet and a world of whisky experts who outnumber the stars that puncture the sky on the very darkest of nights, I actually tasted the first Black Bowmore in their very basic blending lab and gave it the required seal of approval before they allowed it to hit the shelves. It wasn't a 50-year-old beast like this one, though. And it proves that though something may have reached half a century, it knows how to give pleasure on at least a par with anything younger ... *41%*

**Bowmore 1985** db (89) n21.5 t24 f22 b21.5. I may have tasted a sweeter Islay. Just not sure when. This whisky is so wrong..it's fantastically right...! 52.6%

**Bowmore 100 Degrees Proof** db (90.5) n22 low key smoke. Anyone who has been to Arbroath looking for where the Smokies are cured and homed in on the spot by nose alone will recognise this aroma...; t23 delicate in all departments, including the peat. The barley is sweet but it is the tenderness of the oils which stars; f22.5 long with a tapering muscovado finale; b23 proof positive! A real charmer. 57.1%. ncf.

**Bowmore Black Rock** oak casks db (87.5) n22.5 t22 f21 b22. A friendly, full bodied dram whose bark is worse than its bite. Smoked toasted fudge is the main theme. But that would not work too well without the aid of a vague backdrop cinnamon and marmalade. If you are looking for a gentle giant, they don't come more wimpish than this. 40% WB15/336

**Bowmore Devil's Casks III** db (92.5) n23 t23 f23.5 b23.5 a whisky created by Charles Williams, surely. So, at last....I'm in league with the devil...! Hawwww-hhaaaa-haaaaaa!!!! 56.7%

**Bowmore Laimrig Aged 15 Years** db (90.5) n22.5 t23.5 f22 b22.5 first things first: absolutely spot on sherry butts at work here with not a hint of an off note. But often it is hard to get smoke and sherry to gel. The exercise here is not without success, but you feel it is straining at every sinew to hit the high spots. 53.7%. 18,000 bottles.

**Bowmore Laimrig III** db (92) n23.5 t23.5 f22.5 b23 I must ask my research team: where the hell are Laimrigs I and II....? 53.7%

**Bowmore Legend** db (88) n22 t22.5 f22 b22.5. Not sure what has happened here, but it has gone through the gears dramatically to offer a substantial dram with both big peat and excellent balancing molasses. Major stuff. 40%

**Bowmore Mizunara Cask Finish** db (90.5) n22.5 t22 f23.5 b22.5 A Bowmore like no other: not always happy in its own skin, but when it relaxes towards the finish, it positively pulses its Islay credentials. 53.9%. 2,000 bottles.

**Bowmore No.1** first fill bourbon casks, bott code: L172026 db (91.5) n23 t23 f22.5 b23 Bowmore was never the most peaty of Islay's malts. But here the phenols are at their shyest. Delicate and all a rather sexy tease... 40%.

**Bowmore Small Batch "Bourbon Cask Matured"** db (86) n22 t22 f21 b21. A big improvement on the underwhelming previous Small Batch from this distillery, then called "Reserve", though there appears to be a naivety to the proceeding which both charm and frustrate. The smoke, hanging on the grist, is very low key. 40%.

**Bowmore Small Batch Reserve** db (80.5) n20 t21 f19 b20.5. With a name like "Small Batch Reserve" I was expecting a marriage between intense Kentucky and Islay. Alas, this falls well short of the mark. 40%

**Bowmore White Sands Aged 17 Years** db (88) n20 t22 f23 b23 A muzzled malt which shouldn't work – but somehow does. 43%

**Cadenhead's Bowmore 16 Years Old** dist 2001 (95) n23.5 t24 f23.5 b24 Mesmerisingly beautiful. 54.8%. 175th Anniversary bottling.

**Cave Aquila The Eagles Collection Islay Single Malt 10 Years Old** batch no. 1 (88.5) n22 t22.5 f22 b22 Errs on the cautious, understated side of things. But tip toes elegantly around. 43%.

**Dramfool 15 Bowmore 21 Years Old** bourbon hogshead, dist 1996 (93.5) n22.5 t23.5 f23.5 b24 Has come of age in every sense: has a beautifully distinguished air. 52.9%. nc ncf. 299 bottles.

**The First Editions Bowmore Aged 21 Years** refill hogshead, cask no. 14868, bott 2018 (90.5) n22.5 t22.5 f22.5 b23 So similar in personality to its sister OMC cask, except here it benefits substantially from better oak. 52.8%. nc ncf sc. 290 bottles.

**Golden Cask Bowmore Aged 16 Years** cask no. CM232, dist 2000, bott 2016 (94) n23.5 t23.5 f23 b24 Very high quality, clean Bowmore, not instantly recognisable thanks to the extra peaty weight. 59.2%. sc. 234 bottles.

◈ **The Golden Cask Bowmore 1995** cask no. CM249, bott 2018 (87) n22 t22.5 f21 b21.5 Probably not from a vintage time for Bowmore. A distinctive Victory V cough sweet nose and delivery. Delicious creaminess and viscosity and some lovely Demerara sugars on the phenols. But all very untidy and bitter from the midpoint onwards. 51.4%. nc ncf sc. 564 bottles.

◈ **The Golden Cask Bowmore 2002** cask no. CM247, bott 2018 (94.5) n23 a classic Bowmore nose for its distillation period, offering a touch of Parma Violets among the airy phenols; t23.5 sweet, with a glorious accentuation on the heather honey and molasses mix; the peat holds its position superbly, adding an anchor, but not unfathomable depth; f24 the oils do their job proudly, allowing the vanillas from a first-class cask to mix languidly with the honey and smoke...so satisfying...and so ridiculously chocolatey...; b24 a chocolate Bowmore...! 58%. nc ncf sc. 234 bottles.

**Old Malt Cask Bowmore Aged 21 Years** refill hogshead, cask no. 14267, dist Sept 96, bott Sept 17 (93.5) n23.5 t23.5 f23 b23.5 A polished malt brimming with quality. 50%. nc ncf sc. 270 bottles.

**Old Malt Cask Bowmore Aged 21 Years** refill hogshead, cask no. 14867, dist Dec 96, bott Mar 18 **(87) n22 t22.5 f21 b21.5** Plenty of sugars at work here, the majority of a muscovado variety, fitting snugly with the spice and coffee-themed smoke. But the oak is a bit on the rough side. *50%. nc ncf sc. 300 bottles.*

**Old Malt Cask Bowmore Aged 21 Years** refill hogshead, cask no. 15033, dist Jun 96, bott Apr 18 **(94.5) n23.5** a genuine elegance to this: a toffee-apple sharpness infiltrates the phenols, even to the point of guiding the style; **t23.5** a gorgeously friendly delivery: silky, malty and deft. Takes time for the peat to make its mark, but this it does by the smoky waves leaving a peaty deposit that slowly builds into a distinguished, spicy Islay; **f23** lightens as a lack of oil means the peat fades and the custardy vanillas take a firmer grip; **b23.5** a magnificent Bowmore that is impossible not to fall a little in love with... *50%. nc ncf sc. 272 bottles.*

**Old Particular Bowmore 15 Years Old** refill hogshead, cask no. 11804, dist Dec 01, bott Jun 17 **(89.5) n22.5 t22.5 f22 b22.5** Unspectacular, but a really attractive and moreish shape to it. *48.4%. nc ncf sc. 321 bottles.*

**Old Particular Bowmore 15 Years Old** refill hogshead, cask no. 12058, dist Sept 02, bott Sept 17 **(86) n21.5 t22 f21 b21.5** Two peas in a pod, but clearly not identical. Compared to the OP cask 11804, this is a little shyer with the smoke and generally more austere, on the finish especially. *48.4%. nc ncf sc. 360 bottles.*

**Sansibar Whisky Bowmore 1998** bott 2018 **(76) n21.5 t21.5 f15 b18** An odd, though at times curiously, almost morbidly, attractive Bowmore – but with something of the grimy factory machine room about it. The finish is aggressively dreadful. *54.1%. Joint bottling with Acla da Fans.*

**The Single Malts of Scotland Bowmore 22 Years Old 1994** cask no. 224 **(89.5) n22.5 t22.5 f22 b22.5** Sturdy and warming very much like in the lost style of its sister distillery Bowmore. *52.8%. sc.*

# BRAEVAL

**Speyside, 1974. Chivas Brothers. Working.**

**Gordon & MacPhail Connoisseurs Choice Braeval 1998** refill American hogshead, dist 1998, bott 22 Feb 18 **(84.5) n21.5 t22 f20 b21** Not the first malt I have tasted this year which has the unmistakable hallmarks of a rushed distillate, where the stills have been fired a little too enthusiastically than is best for the whisky. The thinness to both nose and body coupled with the huge sugary outpouring as the grist and sweeter elements of the oak dominate. Then that flickering, faulting finale....*59%. nc ncf sc. 185 bottles.*

**Howard Cai Selected Braeval (86) n21 t23.5 f21 b20.5** Many Chinese whisky lovers tend to be on the young side: now they have a whisky to match. This is a pre-pubescent Speysider in a stunningly beautiful, entirely blemish-free, clean-as-a-whistle sherry butt. Don't look for balance, as there isn't any of note. But just savour the delivery and first two or three flavour waves which are simply full of the joys of fruity, spicy, juicy young whisky. *46.1%. 1,800 bottles.*

**Kingsbury Gold Braes of Glenlivet 23 Year Old** barrel, cask no. 165588, dist 1994 **(91.5) n23.5** mega complex and refined the heather honey notes augmented by marzipan and sweet polished leather; **t23** the oak makes the expected early entrance, well marshalled by spices and soothed with orange blossom honey; **f22** a slight tangy bitterness from the tannin, as might be expected from a slight whisky of this antiquity. Excellent spice buzz compensates; **b23** you can't expect much more from an ancient Braes than this. *54.1%. sc. 182 bottles.*

**Le Gus't Selection XII Braeval 22 Years Old** bourbon cask, cask no. 165365 **(85) n22 t22 f20.5 b21.5** An extremely malty procession, salivating and spicy at first then slightly wearing and tired towards the end. Not quick enough oomph to see off the slight oak bitterness that creeps in late on. *53.2%. sc. 178 bottles.*

# BRORA

**Highlands (Northern), 1819–1983. Diageo. Closed.**

**Brora 34 Year Old** refill American oak hogsheads db **(88.5) n22.5 t22 f22 b22** The nose kinds of sums things up perfectly: skeletal fingers of age are all over this: citrus offers sinew and a little smoke the flesh...but time is catching up... *51.9%. 3,000 bottles. Diageo Special Releases 2017.*

**Brora Aged 38 Years** dist 1977 db **(96.5) n24 t24 f24 b24.5** Where the 2015 bottling was a battle to keep the braying tannins in harness, this version has managed to link up both the peat and oak in thoroughbred pose. Soul-kissingly beautiful. *48.6%. 2,984 bottles. Diageo Special Releases 2016.*

# BRUICHLADDICH

**Islay, 1881. Rémy Cointreau. Working.**

**Bruichladdich 10 Years Old** db **(90) n22 t23 f23 b22** More oomph than previous bottlings, yet still retaining its fragile personality. Truly great stuff for a standard bottling. *46%*

**Bruichladdich 12 Years Old 2nd Edition** db **(88)** n23 t22 f22 b21. A similar type of wine involvement to "Waves", but this is oilier in the old-fashioned 'Laddie style and lacks a little of the sparkle. The fruit on the finish is outstanding, though, and I don't think you or I would turn down a third glass... 46%

**Bruichladdich 15 Years Old 2nd Edition** db **(86)** n22 t23 f20 b21. Delicious, as usual, but something, possibly fruity, appears to be holding back the show. 46%

**Bruichladdich 16 Years Old** bourbon cask db **(89)** n22.5 t22.5 f22 b22. Plucked from the cask in the nick of time. In this state rather charming, but another Summer or two might have seen the oak take a more sinister turn. 46%

**Bruichladdich XVII Aged 17 Years** bourbon/renegade rum db **(92)** n23 t23.5 f22 b23.5. Always good to see the casks of drier, more complexly structured rums being put to such intelligent use. My sample doesn't tell me which rum casks were used, but I was getting vivid flashbacks here of Ruby-Topaz Hummingbirds flitting from flower to flower in the gardens of the now closed Eigflucht distillery in Guyana in the long gone days when I used to scramble around the warehouses there. That distinctive dryness though is pure Enmore, though some Barbadian rum can offer a similar effect. Something very different and a top quality experience. 46%. nc ncf.

**Bruichladdich 18 Years Old** bourbon/cognac cask db **(84.5)** n23.5 t21 f20 b20. Big oak-spice buzz but thin. Sublime grapey nose, for sure, but pays a certain price, ultimately, for associating with such an inferior spirit... 46%

**Bruichladdich 2004 Islay Barley Valinch** fresh sherry butt db **(89.5)** n22.5 t24 f21 b22. Yet another quite fabulous bottling form Bruichladdich, this one really cranking up the flavours to maximum effect. Having said all that, call me mad if you will...but seeing as this is Islay barley, would it not have been a good idea to shove it into a bourbon barrel, so we could see exactly what it tastes like? Hopefully that is on its way... 57.5%

◈ **Bruichladdich 2005 12 Year Old** fresh sherry hogshead, cask no. 998, dist 20 Jul 05, bott 2018 db **(92.5)** n23.5 the razor-sharp fruit and the plodding peat may not be on speaking terms, but they do make quite a noise together; **t24** the delivery is like Eric Morecambe greeting Ernie Wise...this is one massive slap around the kisser and though there is no harmony between the cantankerous grape and the pugilistic peat, together they have forged an enormous, slightly oily presence..., **f23** surprisingly docile by comparison with an outbreak of molasses to sweeten the phenols up a bit; **b22** there is virtually no balance to this whisky, yet it somehow works. A whisky every home should have: if you receive a bit of a surprise in your life, this will violently shake you back into the world... 60.4%. nc ncf sc. 372 bottles. Bottled for MacAlabur.

**Bruichladdich Bere Barley 2009 7 Years Old** bourbon barrel, cask no. 16/102 db **(94)** n23 t23.5 f23.5 b24 Bruichladdich wearing very different colours. Fabulous. 50%.

**Bruichladdich Infinity Third Edition** refill sherry tempranillo db **(94.5)** n24 t24 f23 b23.5. I dare anybody who says they don't like smoky whisky not to be blown away by this. Go on...I dare you... 50%

**Bruichladdich Islay Barley Aged 5 Years** db **(86)** n21 t22.5 f21.5 b21. The nose suggests a trainee has been let loose at the stills. But it makes amends with an almost debauched degree of barley on delivery which lasts the entirety of the experience. Heavens! This is different. But I have to say: it's bloody fun, too! 50%. nc ncf.

**Bruichladdich Classic Laddie** cask no. 16/175 db **(93)** n22.5 t23.5 f23.5 b23.5 Well, call me an ol' stick in the peat. But I'd regard a Classic Laddie as unsmoked....then, I must be of a certain age now, I suppose. This youthful cracker'll more than do, though... 50%.

**Bruichladdich Islay Barley 2010 7 Years Old** bourbon/French wine cask, cask no. 17/011 db **(87.5)** n21.5 t23.5 f21 b22 There is a rawness to this which brings a tear to the eye. Both the nose and finish are perhaps a little hamstrung, most probably by the French influence. But the delivery is something else! Brilliantly youthful, the peat doesn't even try to integrate, but comes at you full force. The grist still shews a fresh barley side to its nature divorced from the phenols, while a red liquorice and ulmo honey middle reveals a light degree of oak and sticky sweetness. But it is that no-holds-barred delivery which will win your smoky heart. 50%.

**Bruichladdich The Laddie Eight Years Old** American & European oak, cask no. 16/070 db **(83)** n21.5 t22 f19 b20.5 Doesn't chime anything like so well as the Classic Laddie, for instance. The sugars surge and soar in impressive manner, the mid-range smokiness benefitting. But there is a tightness which does very few favours. 50%.

**Bruichladdich Laddie Classic Edition 1** db **(89.5)** n23 t23 f21 b22.5. You probably have to be a certain vintage yourself to fully appreciate this one. Hard to believe, but I can remember the days when the most popular malt among those actually living on Islay was the Laddie 10. That was a staunchly unpeated dram offering a breezy complexity. Not sure of the age on this Retroladdich, but the similarities almost bring a lump to the throat... 46%

**Bruichladdich Scottish Barley The Classic Laddie** db (78.5) n20 t21.5 f18 b19. Not often a Laddie fluffs its lines. But despite some obviously complex and promising moves, the unusual infiltration of some sub-standard casks has undone the good of the local barley. If you manage to tune out of the off-notes, some sublime moments can still be had. *50%. nc ncf sc.*

**Bruichladdich Sherry Classic Fusion: Fernando de Castilla** bourbon/Jerez de la Frontera db **(91)** n23 t23 f22 b23. What a fantastically stylish piece of work! I had an overwhelming urge to sing Noel Coward songs while tasting this: for the Dry Martini drinkers out there who have never thought of moving on to Scotch... *46%*

**Bruichladdich X4** db **(82)** n18 t22 f21 b21. Frankly, like no new make I have ever come across in Scotland before. Thankfully, the taste is sweet, malty and compact: far, far better than the grim, cabbage water nose. Doesn't really have the X-Factor yet, though. *50%*

**The Laddie Ten** American oak db **(94.5)** n24 t23.5 f23 b24 This, I assume, is the 2012 full strength version of an Islay classic which was the preferred choice of the people of Islay throughout the 70s, 80s and early 90s. And I have to say that this is already a classic in its own right.... *46%. nc ncf.*

**The Laddie Sixteen** American oak db **(88)** n22 huge natural caramels dipped in brine; t22.5 very even and gentle with a degree of citrus perking it up; f21.5 reverts to caramels before the tannins strike hard; b22 oak 'n' salt all the way... *46%*

**The Laddie Twenty Two** db **(90.5)** n24 a breakfast plate of three pieces of toast: one with salted butter, another with ulmo honey and the last one with marmalade; light spices, too. Busy yet understated; t23 silky salted butters again on delivery immediately backed by intense barley sugar; f21.5 the oak cranks up significantly; b22 fabulous coastal malt, though the oak is a presence always felt. *46%*

**Octomore 5 Years Old** db **(96)** n23.5 t24.5 f24 b24. Forget about the age. Don't be frightened by the phenol levels. Great whisky is not about numbers. It is about excellent distillation and careful maturation. Here you have a memorable combination of both... *63.5%*

**Octomore Edition 5.1** db **(91.5)** n23 t22.5 f23 b23. A slightly less complex version, probably because of the obvious lack of years. Great fun, though. *59.9%*

**Octomore Edition 6.1 Aged 5 Years** bourbon cask db **(91.5)** n24 t23 f22 b22.5 A slightly different Octomore, a little more tart than usual and wears its youth with pride. *57%*

**Octomore Edition 6.2 Aged 5 Years** Cognac cask db **(90)** n22.5 t23.5 f22 b22 One of the sweetest bottlings from this distillery of all time. Some warming late spice, too; *58.2%*.

**Octomore Edition 7.1 Aged 5 years** (208 ppm) db **(96.5)** n24 t24.5 f24 b24 A gargantuan malt which will make short work of the feint hearted... This, also, was the whisky which Islay whisky maker par excellence Jim McEwen decided to bow out on. Farewell, Jim, my dear old friend of some 35 years. You have been to Scotch whisky what Jock Stein was to Scottish football; what Octomore is to Islay malt.... *59.5%*

**Bruichladdich Octomore 7.1 5 Years Old** ex-bourbon casks, cask no. 16/080 db **(96)** n23.5 t24.5 f24 b24 Fan-bloody-tastic...!! A kid of a whisky which sorts the men from the boys... *57%*.

**Bruichladdich Octomore 7.2 5 Years Old** bourbon & Syrah casks, cask no. 15/058 db **(81.5)** n21 t23 f18 b19.5 I love the fact that the sample bottles I have been sent under "education." Brilliant! An hilarious first. But here, if anything is to be learned by those who for some reason don't already know, is the fact that you don't piss around with perfection. Five-year-old Octomore in bourbon cask is a joy that has just about proved beyond description for me. Pointlessly add wine casks – and the sulphur which so often accompanies them – and you get a whisky very much reduced in quality and stature. Some superb moments on this, especially round the time of the warts-and-all delivery. But as it settles the faults of the Syrah casks slowly become clear. What a shame. And waste of great whisky. An education, indeed! *58.5%*.

**Octomore 10** db **(95)** n24 t24 f23 b24. When I am tasting an Octomore, it means I am in the home straight inside the stadium after running (or should I say nosing and tasting) a marathon. After this, there are barely another 20 more Scotch malts to go and I am closing in on completing my 1,200 new whiskies for the year. So how does this fair? It is Octomore. It is what I expect and demand. It gives me the sustenance and willpower to get to that crossing line. For to tell you guys about a whisky like this is always worth it...whatever the pain and price. Because honesty and doing the right thing is beyond value. Just ask David Archer. *50%.*

**Port Charlotte 2007 CC:01 Aged 8 Years** bourbon/Cognac casks, cask no. 16/072 db **(94.5)** n23.5 t23.5 f23.5 b24 I think today I have tasted no less than seven Cognac/French wine finishes; a record. I had forgotten, but it turns out to be the day the French have elected a new president. Odd that. Here the Cognac can do little to lessen the impact of the huge peat and even offers a comforting, firm sweetness. However, the success of this over the PC 16/002 is the intensity of the phenol rather than the magic of the Cognac cask alone, though it certainly contributes. *57.8%*.

**Port Charlotte Heavily Peated** db **(94.5)** n23 t24 f23.5 b24 Rearrange the following two words: "giant" and "gentle". *50%*

**Dramfool Port Charlotte 2009 8 Years Old** rum barrel **(91)** n22.5 t24 f21.5 b23 A very strange – one might say brave – choice of cask. Rum casks have the propensity to both bottle up the nose, as though putting a sugary straightjacket on, and greatly sweeten a whisky. And if something is already young and gristy... Still, it is enjoyable. And very different.. *62.7%. 218 bottles.*

**Dramfool 8 Bruichladdich 6 Years Old** bloodtub, cask no. 4091 **(86.5)** n23 t22 f20 b21.5 Starts well with the youthfulness of the 'Laddie being played to brilliant, full-flavoured advantage. But after the first initial fruitcake and molasses kick off, descends into an unfortunate bitterness. *56.9%. nc ncf sc. 42 bottles*

**Dramfool 9 Bruichladdich 10 Years Old** bourbon barrel, cask no. 657, dist 25 Apr 07, bott 12 Oct 17 **(89.5)** n21 t23.5 f22.5 b22.5 A beautiful dram, though there is a little hesitancy in the marriage between the barley and oak. *62.7%. nc ncf sc. 258 bottles.*

**Dramfool 13 Port Charlotte 2001 Aged 15 Years** bourbon hogshead, cask no. 847, dist Dec 01, bott Dec 16 **(95.5)** n23.5 t24 f24 b24.5 You know that if there was space for another atom in this improbably thick and fruity dram...it'd be a fruity peaty one... *58.3% nc ncf sc. 195 bottles. Spirit of Speyside 2018 release.*

**Dramfool 14 Octomore 2011 6 Years Old** bourbon barrel **(86)** n22.5 t21 f21.5 b21 Too young for such enormity. Despite the excellent nose, bottled at a point when the peat shouts and screams but struggles to harmonise with any other characters in the play. Enjoyable if it is a peat fix you are after, but disappointing if you are looking for a balanced malt. *58.3%. nc ncf. 253 bottles. Spirit of Speyside 2018 release.*

⟨⟩ **Dramfool 18 Bruichladdich 11 Years Old** bourbon barrel **(92.5)** n23.5 classically fine and malty Laddie, mixing in some Malted Milk biscuit with a salty, grassiness which maximises the freshness. A light citrus sherbet note ramps up the complexity; t23 so salivating and full of malty verve; sherbet again? Because this is lightly fizzing, the grassy juiciness gorgeously weighted by the butterscotch-clad oak; f22.5 settles down to allow a complex and beautifully paced finish. The oak tones alternate between dry and slightly bitter, but the light Lubec marzipan retains the balance; b23.5 an unpeated Laddie of the old school. And that nose is top of the class, too. *57%. nc ncf.*

⟨⟩ **Dramfool 23 Port Charlotte 14 Years Old** dist 24 Sept 04, bott 23 Apr 19 **(86)** n22 t21.5 f21 b21.5 Not what I was expecting...! A real Victory V cough sweet and hickory number once associated with Bowmore. Mouth-watering on delivery, but as a Port Charlotte never hits its straps... *53.4%. nc ncf sc. 2,999 bottles. Fèis Ìle 2019 release.*

⟨⟩ **Dramfool Port Charlotte 2002 16 Years Old** 1st fill bourbon barrel **(96.5)** n24 I'm not one for swooning...but I think I'm going to swoon. Oh, that peat....; t24 ridiculous! All those phenols...and the first thing to hit you on delivery is heather honey! How does it do that...? f24 a lovely gentle fade with butterscotch and mocha mingling with the ever spicier phenols; b24.5 full-on peat. Honey from a first class bourbon cask. Superb distillation. Where do you start...? *60.5%. 221 bottles.*

⟨⟩ **Glen Oak 17 Year Old** ex-bourbon barrels **(92)** n23 exotic fruit abounds while a thin peatiness hides behind the oak; t23 mouth-watering and stunningly malty. Again, a light exotic fruitiness, alongside muscovado sugars play a starring role f22.5 plenty of vanilla as the tannins turn out in force...but quietly...; b23.5 about as delicate as 17-year-old Islay malt gets.... *40%. Branded Spirits USA.*

**Hidden Spirits Lochindaal 10 Year Old** dist 2007, bott 2018 **(94.5)** n23.5 t23.5 f23.5 b24 The one thing not hidden about this spirit is its unambiguous beauty. *53.1%.*

**Hidden Spirits Port Charlotte 14 Year Old** dist 2003, bott 2017 **(64)** n16 t17 f15 b16 And the latest score in during this World Cup summer: Sulphur 6, Peat 0. When even a PC in all its massively peaty glory cannot douse the ugly excesses of a sulphur-treated sherry butt, it shows you the enormity of the problem, however much people try to gloss over it. With my taste buds obliterated, that, I'm afraid, is my tasting day prematurely finished... *55.5%. sc.*

**Old Particular Bruichladdich 12 Years Old** 1st fill bourbon barrel, cask no. 12013, dist May 05, bott Aug 17 **(88)** n22 t22.5 f21.5 b22 Distilled from hazelnuts? *48.4%. nc ncf sc. 253 bottles.*

**Old Particular Bruichladdich 12 Years Old** sherry hogshead, cask no. 12197, dist Jun 05, bott Nov 17 **(74)** n20 t20 f16 b18 The peat and grape find about as much common ground as the Presidents of the USA and Mexico. Bitter, harsh and unforgiving. *48.4%. nc ncf sc. 184 bottles.*

# BUNNAHABHAIN

Islay, 1881. Burn Stewart Distillers. Working.

**Bunnahabhain Aged 12 Years** db **(85.5)** n20 t23 f21 b21.5. Lovers of Cadbury's Fruit and Nut will adore this. There is, incongruously, a big bourbony kick alongside some smoke, too. A lusty fellow who is perhaps a bit too much of a bruiser for his own good. Some outstanding moments, though. But, as before, still a long way removed from the magnificent Bunna 12 of old... *46.3%. nc ncf.*

🔸 **Bunnahabhain 12 Years Old** bott code: 1903372L512-1116327 db **(84)** **n20.5 t23 f19 b21.5** Remains true to the new style of Bunna with its slightly skewed sherry notes on nose and finish compensated for by the fabulously sweet and rich ultra - grapey delivery. The sulphur does stick slightly at the death. Oh, how I would still Wester Home back to the great Bunnas of the early 1980s.... *46.3%. nc ncf.*

**Bunnahabhain Aged 16 Years Manzanilla Sherry Wood Finish** db **(87)** **n20.5 t23 f21.5 b22.** The kind of undisciplined but fun malt which just makes it up as it goes along... *53.2%.*

**Bunnahabhain Aged 18 Years** db **(93.5)** **n24 t24.5 f22 b23** Only an odd cask has dropped this from being a potential award winner to something that is merely magnificent... *46.3%. nc ncf.*

**Bunnahabhain XXV Aged 25 Years** db **(94)** **n23 t24 f23 b24** No major blemishes here at all. Carefully selected sherry butts of the highest quality (well, except maybe one) and a malt with enough personality to still gets its character across after 25 years. Who could ask for more...? *46.3%. nc ncf.*

**Bunnahabhain 46 Year Old** db **(91)** **n24 t23 f21.5 b22.5** Needs a good half hour in the glass to open up and have justice done to it. Perishes towards the end, but the nose and build up to that are remarkably beautiful for a whisky which normally doesn't do age very well... *42.1%.*

**Bunnahabhain Ceòbanach** db **(87.5)** **n21.5 t22.5 f21.5 b22**. An immensely chewable and sweet malt showing little in years but much in character. A charming liquorice and acacia honey lead then a developing, dry smokiness. Great fun. *46.3%*

**Bunnahabhain Darach Ùr Batch no. 4** db **(95)** **n24 t24.5 f23 b23.5** Because of my deep love for this distillery, with my association with it spanning some 30 years, I have been its harshest critic in recent times. This, though, is a stunner.. *46.3%. nc ncf.*

**Bunnahabhain Moine 7 Year Old Oloroso Finish** db **(85)** **n22 t23.5 f18 b21.5** The faults are apparent on both nose and finish especially. But the grape intensity of the delivery is, momentarily, something special. *60.1%.*

🔸 **Bunnahabhain Stiùireadair** bott code: 1910838L514:1919015 db **(83.5)** **n21 t22 f20 b20.5** Although the sherry influence is clear of any sulphur content, the grape never comes across articulately on this, either on the nose or delivery. There are some brief moments on arrival when the malt goes directly into delicious fruitcake mode but it is all too brief. From then on it never sits comfortably. The stiùireadair, the helmsman, has steered the wrong course... *46.3%. nc ncf.*

**Bunnahabhain Toiteach** db **(78)** **n19 t21 f19 b19**. Cloying, sweet, oily, disjointedly smoky. Had you put me in a time capsule at the distillery 30 years ago, whizzed me forward to the present day and given me this, it would have needed some serious convincing for me to believe this to be a Bunna. *46%*

🔸 **Bunnahabhain Toiteach A Dhà** bott code: 1767068L510:0218253 db **(86)** **n22 t22 f21 b21** A heavyweight malt which first thumps you as hard as possible with unreconstructed peat. And after you get up off the floor from that, you are rabbit punched by chunky fruit notes. Eschews subtlety and charm for impact. But have to say it is a great improvement on the earlier Toiteach. Just a slight technical flaw to this, evident on the finish in particular. *46.3%. nc ncf.*

**Bunnahabhain Toiteach Un-Chillfiltered** db **(75.5)** **n18 t21 f17.5 b19**. A big gristy, peaty confrontation on the palate doesn't hide the technical fault lines of the actual whisky. *46%. ncf.*

🔸 **The Cooper's Choice Bunnahabhain 1990 27 Years Old (91)** **n23** an adorable delicacy to the vanilla and barley mix. Seemingly dry but an improbable gristy sweetness is detectable even after all these years; **t23** magically salivating with the tannins leaving no doubt about the age but the malt hanging on gamely, even with a little liquorice being conjured up in the late middle section; takes on silky sheen, too; **f22** hangs onto its malty substance until quite late; excellent restrained spice to underline the age; **b23** Bunna in all its old-fashioned unpeated glory – and in fine fettle, too...! *46%. nc ncf sc.*

🔸 **The Cooper's Choice Bunnahabhain 2001 16 Years Old** sherry cask **(75)** **n18 t20 f18 b19** As Windsor Davies, the actor who died this year and whom I had the pleasure of knowing, might have said from his It Ain't Half Hot Mum days: "Sulphur. Oh dear. How sad. Never mind". *46%. nc ncf sc.*

**Drams by Dramtime Bunnahabhain Staoisha Edition 4 Years Old** dist 2013 **(89)** **n22.5 t23 f21.5 b22** A ridiculously young, outlandish peaty whippersnapper. What fun! *59.5%.*

🔸 **Gleann Mór Bunnahabhain Aged Over 26 Years (91)** **n22 t23 f23 b23** Bunna again in its old-fashioned unpeated form. A wonderful mix of sea salt and molasses see off the excesses of the huge oak, the tannins dominating the nose but just failing to take control of elsewhere. A greybeard older than its years, but so much to enjoy! *49.6%.*

🔸 **The Golden Cask Bunnahabhain 28 Years Old 1989** cask no. CM244, bott 2018 **(88)** **n22** briney with an almost lackadaisical smokiness; **t22** a little too sweet on delivery, the sugars in indecent haste to present themselves, before drifting phenols settle them; **f21.5** quite bitter; **b22.5** an oddball Bunna but with some lovely touches. 45.8% nc ncf sc. 180 bottles.

**Gordon & MacPhail Cask Strength Bunnahabhain 2009** cask nos. 323 & 325, bott 21 Mar 17 **(96) n24.5 t24 f23 b24** A superbly dextrous Bunna, twisting and turning into many shapes and textures on the palate. A new age masterpiece. 60.5%.

**Gordon & MacPhail Cask Strength Bunnahabhain 2009** cask nos. 326, 327 & 329, bott 14 Jun 17 **(86.5) n22.5 t23.5 f19 b21.5** Bunna in bottled form as I have never quite seen it before. Unrecognisable from the "Westering Home" malt of the early 1980s. There is young spirit at work here which ensures the most salivating delivery of any Bunna known to mankind. Saltiness, too. But the overwhelming fruitiness does offer spice but at the cost of balance. 59%.

**Gordon & MacPhail Cask Strength Bunnahabhain 2009** cask nos. 337 & 338, bott 20 Sept 17 **(86.5) n21.5 t21.5 f22 b21.5** This is so far removed from the 12-year-old Bunna I grew up on, it is hard to know exactly where to start! This is very tart and for the start of its life on the palate unsure of its direction. Only when a vaguely salty, malty and distinctively chocolatey persona begins to form does it relax into something distinguished. 59%.

◈ **Gordon & MacPhail Discovery Range Bunnahabhain Aged 11 Years (81) n20.5 t20.5 f20 b20** Dull and very ordinary: had a personality bypass. 43%.

◈ **Hidden Spirits Bunnahabhain 2013 Aged 5 Years** cask no. BU1318, bott 2018 **(87.5) n22 t22 f21.5 b22** A bit raw in part, as you might expect. But sublimely juicy with peat rounded and balanced. The sugars melt in the mouth and the oils live long. Anyone with an age prejudice should set it aside for this little beauty. Technically, a much better made malt than their earlier peated style. 50%. sc.

◈ **Kingsbury Gold Bunnahabhain 13 Year Old** butt, cask no. 3597, dist 2004 **(86) n21.5 t23 f20 b21.5** Quite mercurial and magical before a minor flaw in the sherry butt strikes. But no reason not to enjoy the delivery and afterglow which pits spice against blood orange, with just a little mocha on the side. 61.1%. sc. 587 bottles.

**Kingsbury Gold Bunnahabhain 19 Years Old** rum cask, cask no. 5386, dist 1997 **(87.5) n22 t23 f21 b21.5** Was working rather beautifully and effortlessly until the bitter, unkempt finish arrived. But still plenty of scope to enjoy the docile, seemingly accidental, smokiness pitted against rich vanilla streaked with acacia honey: bliss. 54.3%. 198 bottles.

**Le Gus's Selection XIII Bunnahabhain 6 Years Old** hogshead, cask no. 704139 **(92.5) n23 t23 f23 b23.5** Though the freshness of youth is there to see, this has grown up sufficiently to be regarded as a serious peated whisky of no little sophistication. 59.7%. sc. 278 bottles.

**Liquid Treasures Entomology Bunnahabhain Over 28 Years Old** ex-bourbon cask, dist 1989, bott 2018 **(96) n24.5 t24 f23.5 b24** Old school Bunna. Spectacularly beautiful and one of the malts of the year. 44.9%.

**The Loch Fyne Bunnahabhain 12 Year Old** sherry cask, cask no. 1312, dist Sept 05, bott Oct 17 **(92) n23.5 t23.5 f22 b23** Away above average sherry butt, not something normally associated with Bunna. For a 12-y-o, the delivery and follow-through could hardly be any better. Superb! 46%. sc. 950 bottles.

**The Loch Fyne Bunnahabhain 16 Year Old** sherry cask, cask no. 3687, dist Dec 01, bott May 18 **(86) n22 t24.5 f19.5 b20** Obviously has a bit of a weakness and it is all in the finish (other than the bit on the nose). But until it arrives, just suck on that amazing honey: it is though the sherry butt was filled with English summer flower honey (especially a type specialised in around Hook Norton, Oxfordshire). Worth going through the pain of the finish for the sheer ecstasy of the delivery. 57%. sc. 850 bottles.

**Provenance Bunnahabhain Aged 10 Years** refill hogshead, cask no. 12220, dist Oct 07, bott Dec 17 **(84) n20 t22 f21 b21** Sweet, smoky, young but lacking coastal character and overly simplistic. 46%. nc ncf sc. 658 bottles.

**Provenance Bunnahabhain Aged 12 Years** refill barrel, cask no. 11899, dist May 05, bott Aug 17 **(87) n21 t22 f22 b22** A well-oiled dram revealing delicate peating levels and a high cocoa character. 46%. nc ncf sc. 275 bottles.

**Romantic Rhine Collection Bunnahabhain 9 Year Old** cask no. 3813596, dist 2008, bott 2017 **(78) n19 t19 f20 b20** Poorly made malt filled into a less than brilliant cask: about as romantic as coming home to find your partner in bed with your best friend. 52.3%. nc ncf sc.

**Scotch Malt Whisky Society Cask 10.145 9 Year Old** refill ex-bourbon barrel, dist 07 Feb 08 **(94) n23 t24 f23 b24** Bunna in rip-roaring form...! 61.7%. sc.

**Scotch Malt Whisky Society Cask 10.146 9 Year Old** refill ex-bourbon barrel, dist 07 Feb 08 **(91) n22.5 t23.5 f22 b23** A very charmingly etched peated malt. 60.1%. sc.

◈ **Scyfion Choice Bunnahabhain 2007** Pastoral cask finished, bott 2018 **(91.5) n22.5** gentle smoke encouraged by a dry grape skin fruit note; **t23** much sweeter on the palate than nose, with muscovado sugars and over-ripe plum notes filtering through; a light earthiness offers the base; **f23** still salivating late on, though now even earthier and a little spicy; **b23**

Pastoral cask...? I am sure I can smell the odd member of the clergy in there and as for tasting a Bishop...let's not go there... 46%. nc ncf. 348 bottles.

**The Whisky Embassy Bunnahabhain Aged 9 Years** cask no. 3813649, dist 2008, bott 2017 **(82.5) n21 t21 f20 b20.5** Malty but seriously struggles to find a happy combination despite a big vanilla intervention. 52.5%. nc ncf sc.

⬧ **The Whisky Embassy Bunnahabhain 2014** re-charred hogshead, cask no. 10598, dist 20 Oct 14, bott 24 Jan 19 **(89) n23** huge, unsubtle peat and with something of the PVC mac about it, too...; **t22** peat....; pleasant Demerara sugars formulate; spices, too; **f22** peat...; soot among the vanilla; **b22** probably one of the peatiest Bunnas I have ever encountered. You wait for complexity to kick in, it does, but as simplistic as the peat...probably for phenol maniacs only. 59.9%. nc ncf sc. 212 bottles.

# CAOL ILA
**Islay, 1846. Diageo. Working.**

**Caol Ila Aged 10 Years "Unpeated Style"** bott Aug 09 db **(93.5) n24 t23.5 f23 b23** Always fascinating to see a traditional peaty Islay stripped bare and in full naked form. Shapely and very high class indeed. 65.4%. Only available at the Distillery.

**Caol Ila Aged 12 Years** db **(89) n23 t23 f21 b22.** A telling improvement on the old 12-y-o with much greater expression and width. 43%

**Caol Ila Aged 15 Years** dist 2000 db **(95.5) n24 t24 f23.5 b24** Any smoke detected here is token and a mere reflection of the distillery rather than substance. Instead we have a naked malt lustfully showing its beauty and proving there can be fire without smoke... 61.5%. Diageo Special Releases 2016.

**Caol Ila 17 Year Old** American oak ex-bourbon casks, dist 1997 db **(90) n23 t23.5 f21.5 b22** a charming malt. But not one the serious Peat Heads out there will much appreciate. 55.9%. Diageo Special Releases 2015.

**Caol Ila Aged 18 Years** db **(80) n21 t20 f19 b20.** Another improvement on the last bottling, especially with the comfortable integration of citrus. But still too much oil spoils the dram, particularly at the death. 43%

**Caol Ila 18 Year Old** refill American oak hogsheads db **(96) n23.5** hickory acts as a dais from which the still confident phenol makes its impressive speech; mild mint and eucalyptus adds to the honeyed, oaky depth; **t24.5** so, so beautiful...The peat appears to be absorbed into the oak, which in turns radiates honey and spice until you're reduced to a purring mass...; **f23.5** coconut in golden syrup...with a light smoky lustre; **b24.5** pretty sure there is no colouring or chill-filtration. This is the way Caol Ila should be: so true to the distillery. And whisky. 59.8%. Diageo Special Releases 2017.

**Caol Ila Aged 25 Years** bott code: L71860M000 db **(95.5) n24** quite a beefy, meaty phenol kick, with something of the farmyard for good measure. Unusually for Caol Ila, a little salty, too; **t24** soft and buttery on delivery, the usual oils having taken on a more greasy feel. The sugars start to mount up impressively, while the spices become positively warm **f23.5** the smoke rumbles along with spicy mischief; **b24** even after all these years this malt can not only lay on its Islay credentials with its eyes closed, but does so with an almost haughty air, cocking a smoky snook at the passing quarter of a century... 43%.

**Caol Ila 30 Year Old** refill American oak & European oak casks, dist 1983 db **(96.5) n24 t24.5 f24 b24** Indisputably, one of the most complex, well-rounded and complete Caol Ilas I have tasted since they rebuilt the distillery... 55.1%. 7,638 bottles. Diageo Special Releases 2014.

**Caol Ila Moch** db **(87) n22 t22 f21 b22** I think they mean "Mocha"... 43%.

**Caol Ila Stitchell Reserve "Unpeated Style"** bott 2013 db **(89) n23 t24 f20 b22** Not really a patch on the 2012 bottling, mainly due to inferior sherry butts, any smoke which does appear is like a half-imagined movement in the shadows. The delivery, though, is superb! 59.6% WB15/344

⬧ **Cask 88 Caol Ila 9 Year Old** refill hogshead, sherry quarter cask finish, cask no. 4016778 **(88.5) n23** good grief! Now even the most ardent peat lovers will be blown away with this ultra- dry number. The peat is not so much as intense as in concentrate...; **t22.5** pounding peat on delivery and no relenting with the spice, either; **f21** annoyingly bitters as the oak's influence usurps the peat's; **b22** just sorry I couldn't give them 88 points...a bitter finish takes the edge of a wonderfully intense experience. 58.2%. nc ncf sc. 88 bottles. Eighty Eight Series.

**Cave Aquila The Eagles Collection Islay Single Malt 10 Years Old** batch no. 2 **(90.5) n22.5 t23 f22.5 b22.5** Lovely example of the distillery at this age with everything where it should be except for the heavier oils which appear to be hiding. 43%.

**Dramfool 11 Cola Ali 9 Years Old** 1st fill Oloroso hogshead finish **(88) n22.5 t23.5 f20 b22** Not a perfect butt, but worth experiencing for the delivery alone... 58.4%. nc ncf. 150 bottles.

⬧ **Dramfool 17 Cola Ali Too 10 Years Old** 1st fill Oloroso hogshead finish **(87) n22 t22 f21.5 b21.5** Sometimes you have to be a little careful when pitting peat against grape, even when using a perfectly unspoiled sherry hoggy like this. The fruit has nullified some of the peats complexity, leaving a bit of a slug out between the two twains. Oddly, also, a by product has been to give a it a slightly Bowmore-ish quality. *57.5%. nc ncf. 175 bottles*

◈ **Dramfool 19 Cola Ali Three 10 Years Old** bourbon cask, dist 2008 **(89.5)** n22.5 a measured smokiness to this as the oak appears offer a toffee cushion of its own; t22.5 lots of Demerara sugars up early for this one, the spices hard on their heels. The smoke arrives with the expected oils, then a distinct fudge feel...; f21.5 thins somewhat leaving a toffee and light soot shadow; b22.5 supercharged with natural caramels giving an unusual cream toffee feel to the peat. Different. Someone been fooling around...? *59.8%. nc ncf. 129 bottles.*

**Endangered Drams Caol Ila 9 Year Old** cask no. 4016823, dist 2008, bott 2018 **(90)** n22 t23 f22.5 b22.5 a bottle of this is in danger of being drunk in a matter of hours... *53%. nc ncf sc.*

◈ **Fadandel.dk Caol Ila Aged 7 Years** 1st fill Entre Deux Mers Barrique cask, cask no. 900056, dist 10 May 11, bott 20 Nov 18 **(80.5)** n21.5 t23 f17 b19 It is quite possible that Napoleon had lesser battles than this... *60%. sc. 307 bottles.*

◈ **Fadandel.dk Treasure of Islay Caol Ila Aged 10 Years** refill bourbon cask, cask no. 0007, dist May 08, bott Nov 18 **(95.5)** n24 has this been matured actually in the Sound of Islay itself; has it taken a trip down to the bottom of Corryvreckan. So much peat... and even more rock pool richness...; t24 anything other than an eye-watering delivery would have been a let-down after that nose! Unusually flinty in mouth feel, from a distillery noted for its excess oiliness; f23.5 a little oil does at last form and helps settle the malt back to something like its normal form. But there is still a salty edge to this, though the hickory and phenols combine with the molasses and spice make for the busiest finale imaginable; b24 I can't remember the last time I encountered a Caol Ila so steeped in tidal tendencies as this — either for the Bible or wearing my consultant blender's hat. It is as though barnacles had to be chipped off the cask, or even the glass. A malt for those who rather like being astonished.... *58.4%. sc. 272 bottles.*

◈ **Gleann Mór Caol Ila Aged Over 30 Years (93.5)** n23.5 t23.5 f23 b23.5 Held up over the years with seemingly little effort. The sooty dryness of the nose is like a Caol Ila half its age while it has made the most of the sugars gleaned from 30 years of maturing a cask. Meanwhile a lovely caramel-vanilla mix hangs on the oils. Big, bold, proud and in great shape. *53.6%.*

◈ **Glenwill Caol Ila 1990** hogshead, cask no. 1481 **(96)** n24 clean, oily Caol Ila of a classic style and weight. Still the smoke has currency, though now a little lychee has attached itself to ensure a telling sweetness to the grist; t24 beautiful! This is perfectly distilled malt and the sympathetic cask is adding the vanilla touches to the clean phenols; a little tartness to the barley, almost belying the age; f24 long, with the oils still intact and the smoke now being applied in waves of varying intensity. Not an off note, no tiredness...just a late smoky latte finale; b24 exemplary. *53.9%. 254 bottles. Matisse Spirits Company.*

**Golden Cask Caol Ila Aged 25 Years** cask no. CM238, dist 1991, bott 2017 **(94.5)** n23 t24 f23.5 b24 a real smoky, complex stunner. *51.5%. sc. 121 bottles.*

◈ **Gordon & MacPhail Connoisseurs Choice Caol Ila 1984 Aged 33 Years** refill sherry hogshead, cask no. 6078, dist 11 Dec 84, bott 3 Jul 18 **(95)** n24 t24.5 f22.5 b24 When peated whiskies get to a certain age, the phenol levels drop gradually, so you are normally, on an Islay malt of over 30 years, met by a controlled gentleness: a giant tempered with age. And on the nose you might for moment suspect this to be true here. The delivery, however, soon makes a mockery of that notion as the phenols dig deep, aided and abetted by a near perfect combination of heather honey, salt and pepper all within a glazed mouth feel; that salt, incidentally, giving the nose a particularly maritime feel. Were it not for some bitterness on the finish, the score would have been as huge as the whisky. *52.8%. sc. 216 bottles.*

**Gordon & MacPhail Connoisseurs Choice Caol Ila 1990** refill sherry hogshead, cask no. 1112, dist 31 Jan 90, bott 26 Feb 18 **(86.5)** n22.5 t22 f21 b21 A huge amount going on here; one might say too much. The nose warns that the oak is showing signs of advanced age and is not entirely checked and balanced by the still healthy fruit. Spiced, attractive, but fractionally out of sync. Those who like big oak and smoke will score this more highly. *49.6%. nc ncf sc. 176 bottles.*

**Gordon & MacPhail Connoisseurs Choice Caol Ila 1990** refill sherry hogshead, cask no. 1118, dist 31 Jan 90, bott 26 Feb 18 **(95.5)** n24 t24 f23.5 b24.5 From the days when sherry hogsheads were sherry hogshead and not stink bombs and the oak was seasoned for the good of all. Sheer, unadulterated elegance... *50.7%. nc ncf sc. 191 bottles.*

**Gordon & MacPhail Connoisseurs Choice Caol Ila 2000** first fill bourbon barrel, cask no. 309606, dist 27 Oct 00, bott 26 Feb 18 **(93)** n23 t23 f23.5 b23.5 Elegant and understated from first to last moment. *57.5%. nc ncf sc. 180 bottles.*

**Gordon & MacPhail Connoisseurs Choice Caol Ila 2003** first fill bourbon barrel, cask no. 302260, dist 10 Sept 03, bott 26 Feb 18 **(88)** n22.5 t23 f20.5 b22 A very decent spirit slightly undone by the oak. *57.7%. nc ncf sc. 212 bottles.*

**Gordon & MacPhail Connoisseurs Choice Caol Ila 2004** Hermitage wood finish, dist 2004, bott 13 Mar 18 **(67) n16 t19 f16 b16** Oh dear. The "s" word strikes with a vengeance. *45%. nc ncf. 3,950 bottles.*

**Gordon & MacPhail Cask Strength Caol Ila 2005** cask nos. 301522, 301530 & 301532, bott 30 Jan 17 **(88.5) n22.5 t22 f22 b22** A little tight and ashy with the sugars and oils unusually constrained. *56.8%.*

**Gordon & MacPhail Cask Strength Caol Ila 2006** cask nos. 306183, 306184, 306186 & 306187, bott 30 May 17 **(94.5) n23.5 t23.5 f24 b23.5** Succulent and lively. Ever increasing complexity. *60.2%.*

**Gordon & MacPhail Discovery Range Caol Ila Aged 13 Years** **(87.5) n22 t22 f21.5 b22** This is almost a re-run of their 2005 cask Strength Caol Ila (see above), probably drawn from the same family of casks, though at the reduced strength the breaking down of the oils means the intensity and complexity levels are significantly lowered. *43%.*

**Hepburn's Choice Caol Ila 6 Years Old** refill hogshead, dist 2010, bott 2017 **(87) n23 t22.5 f20 b21.5** A lovely peat-head's nose, brimming with oily phenols and the delivery ticks the right smoky boxes, also. The finish, though, is incomplete. *46%. nc ncf sc. 390 bottles.*

⟐ **Hepburn's Choice Caol Ila 7 Years Old** refill hogshead, dist 2011, bott 2018 **(92) n23** for such a youngster the "new makey" element is kept to a minimum while the peat is sweet and constant without being profound; **t23** every bit as salivating as a 7-year-old should be. The gristy barley is split between the malty and peaty factions, but it is the clarity of the spirit which really strikes home: the distiller was having a very good day...; **f23** medium oils lengthen both the smoke and sweetness while a spice buzz begins to settle. Even an unlikely hint of butterscotch is detectable on the finish; **b23.5** if there's a case for bottling more young Caol Ila, here it is...what a beauty! *46%. nc ncf sc. 362 bottles.*

**Hepburn's Choice Caol Ila 8 Years Old** wine cask, dist 2009, bott 2017 **(89.5) n22.5 t23 f21.5 b22.5** Quite a polarising bottling. Not so much among drinkers, but in its distinct make up of very early sweetness on the palate dramatically set flush against the eye-wateringly dry finale. The peat appears to move on to a slightly different plane, above it all but always on the dry, ashy side. *46%. nc ncf sc. 438 bottles.*

**Hidden Spirits Young Rebels Collection Caol Ila 9 Year Old** dist 2008, bott 2017 **(90.5) n22.5 t23 f22 b23** A straight down the line, no frills, exceptionally clean and technically solid example of a youngish Caol Ila. *52%.*

**Kingsbury Gold Caol Ila 21 Years Old** hogshead, cask no. 791, dist 1996 **(95.5) n24 t24 f23.5 b24** If you could picture a 21-year-old Caol Ila in your mind, it wouldn't be far off this. Truly delightful. *56%. 247 bottles.*

**Kingsbury Gold Caol Ila 35 Years Old** hogshead, cask no. 703, dist 1982 **(87) n21 t22.5 f22 b21.5** The entire experience is shaped by oak which at times offers a degree of tannin that bristles a little too haughtily. Orange peel and gentle smoke offers succour. *46.1%. 80 bottles.*

**Old Malt Cask Caol Ila Aged 9 Years** refill hogshead, cask no. 14413, dist Nov 08, bott Nov 17 **(91) n22.5 t23.5 f22.5 b22.5** If you need proof of how beautifully made Caol Ila is, try this. Limited oak means the oils and peat superb structure is fully exposed. *50%. nc ncf sc. 242 bottles.*

⟐ **Old Malt Cask Caol Ila Aged 9 Years** wine cask, cask no. 15799, dist Sept 09, bott Feb 19 **(85.5) n21.5 t22 f21 b21** Pleasant and moderately peated. But the wine, even bringing with it a sweet, juicy softness, untidies rather than sharpens and defines. *50%. nc ncf sc. 385 bottles.*

**Provenance Caol Ila Aged 6 Years** refill hogshead, cask no. 11746, dist Nov 10, bott May 17 **(86.5) n21.5 t23 f 20.5 b21.5** Distinctly new makey. Not only six years old but filled into casks hardly in the flush of youth. At least the vigorous eat and the salivating barley gets unfettered and delicious access to your taste buds. *46%. nc ncf sc. 387 bottles.*

⟐ **Scotch Malt Whisky Society Cask 53.289 8 Year Old** 2nd fill HMTC hogshead, dist 12 Oct 10 **(93) n23** a ferocious nose with the phenols having spicy teeth; **t23.5** fantastically salivating. An almost three-dimensional relief of the phenols...and at times it gets pretty high! The sugars are jagged and of the most brittle Demerara variety but, and here is the rub, there is also a fabulous gristiness leaving you in no doubt that this is malt whisky...! **f23** a long layering of sugars and phenols; **b23.5** a very different take on a well-known Islay, displaying the whisky at its most angular rather than oily. *61.1%. sc.*

**Whiskyjace Caol Ila 5 Years Old** 1st fill Marsala cask, dist May 11, bott Feb 17 **(76) n19 t21 f18 b18** Sorry, chaps, that I can't be more upbeat about such an unusual bottling: the age and cask type were a bit of a gamble. But from the sweaty armpit nose to the off-key finish it is a battle, though one where the cask treatment wins out in the end. *59%. 20 bottles.*

⟐ **Wilson & Morgan Barrel Selection Caol Ila** dist 2011, bott 2018 **(86.5) n22 t22 f21 b21.5** A very young Caol Ila, proud of its youth and celebrating its profoundly fresh gristiness. Not the most heavily peated from this distillery so a little imbalance does show. *48%.*

## CAPERDONICH
**Speyside, 1898. Chivas Brothers. Closed.**

⬧ **Gleann Mór Caperdonich Aged Over 23 Years (86)** n22 t22 f20.5 b21.5 Some beautiful banana skins on the nose. But before it slips up on the clumsy finish, the malt and spice do have a few moments of unbridled glory. A slight failing on the cask, though, means the development is limited and always borderline tangy. 59.4%.

## CARDHU
**Speyside, 1824. Diageo. Working.**

**Cardhu 12 Years Old** db **(83)** n22 t22 f18 b21. What appears to be a small change in the wood profile has resulted in a big shift in personality. What was once a guaranteed malt love-in is now a drier, oakier, fruitier affair. Sadly, though, with more than a touch of something furry. 40%

**Cardhu Aged 15 Years** bott code: L8070IX000 db **(87)** n22 t23 f20.5 b21.5 Decent and easy going. But hang on: this is Cardhu! It should be offering a lot more than that. Does fine until the finish when the caramel kicks in without mercy, and other off-key moments develop. But love the citrus and pineapple on the nose and the oak layering on the delivery. This is a malt which should be 100% bourbon cask, preferably no colouring and allowing its natural brilliance to dazzle. 40%.

**Cardhu 18 Year Old** db **(88)** n22.5 t23 f20.5 b22 Very attractive at first. But when you consider what a great distillery Cardhu is and how rare stocks of 18 year old must be, have to say that I am disappointed. The fruit masks the more intricate moments one usually experiences on a Cardhu to ensure an acceptable blandness and accounts for a poor finish. Why, though, it is bottled at a pathetic 40% abv instead of an unchillfiltered 46% – the least this magnificent distillery deserves – is a complete mystery to me. 40%

**Cardhu Amber Rock** db **(87.5)** n22 t22 t23 f21 b21.5. Amber is the right colour for this: it appears stuck between green and red, not sure whether to go or not. The delivery, in which the tangerine cream is in full flow reflects the better elements of the nose. But the finish is all about being stuck in neutral. Not helped by the useless 40% abv, you get the feeling that a great whisky is trying to get out. The odd tweak and we'll have a winner. That said, very enjoyable indeed. Just even more frustrating! 40%. Diageo.

**Cardhu Gold Reserve** bott code: L8024IX02 db **(86.5)** n22 t22 f21 b21.5 Once, maybe two decades ago, Cardhu single malt was synonymous with malted barley shining at you from the glass in a lightly golden, gristy complexity, in near perfect harmony with bourbon casks in which it had been stored for a dozen years or so. It was very delicate in colour and even more fragile on the palate, flitting around like some exotic form of whisky sprite. The character of this malt is far removed from those halcyon days: this is dull and box-ticking, rather than its old inspiration self. That said, for a few brief moments, there is a fleeting glimpse into its past style, when a gently honeyed sheen flares and then fades. 40%.

⬧ **Game of Thrones Cardhu Gold Reserve House Targaryen** db **(84)** n20.5 t22 f20.5 b21 Not having a single television set in any of my three abodes dotted around the place, I have never seen Game of Thrones. Not once. I cannot tell you, even roughly, what the story is about. I have had Bibles to write, distilleries to visit, shows to perform, birds to watch. So I can't tell you whether Targaryen is a person, a place or some kind of fictional spice. Which means I cannot compare the whisky to the name to see if they somehow match. Sorry. However, if it means "a little flat with off-key fruit and plenty of toffee to chew on" then, bingo! They've nailed it. 40%.

## CLYNELISH
**Highlands (Northern), 1968. Diageo. Working.**

**Clynelish Aged 14 Years** bott code: L7285CM008 db **(86.5)** n22 some malt nips though with a vaguely salty theme. Where is the usual honey? t22.5 soft, but a degree of caramel running through this might answer a previous question. A salty vanilla coupled with a lively maltiness lifts the mid-ground; f20 much duller with an over reliance on caramel; b21 very strange. This is one of the world's true Super Distilleries, in the top five of the most beautifully complex in Scotland. Yet from this very subdued, relatively character-bypassed bottling it would be hard to tell. 46%.

**Clynelish Aged 15 Years "The Distillers Edition"** double matured in oloroso-seco casks Cl-Br: 169-1f, bott code L6264CM000 03847665, dist 1991, bott 2006 db **(79)** n20 t20 f19 b20. Big in places, distinctly oily in others but the overall feel is of a potentially brilliant whisky matured in unsympathetic barrels. 46%

**Clynelish Select Reserve** ex-bourbon, rejuvenated & refilled American oak, and ex-bodega & refill European oak casks db **(92)** n23 t24 f22 b23 Does anyone do honey as well as Clynelish? The fact they can even pull it off with European oak involvement underlines the distillery's brilliance. 54.9%. 2,964 bottles. Diageo Special Releases 2014.

⬧ **Game of Thrones Clynelish 12 Year Old House Tyrell** db **(89)** n23 some striking blood orange and saline notes; a lovely malty background; t23 superb full bodied malt and fruit explosion of delivery, the sweetness courtesy of the house heather honey Superb spice back-up, too; **f21** a little furry and tight; **b22** undone slightly by the finish, but that delivery...wow! *51.2%.*

◈ **Gordon & MacPhail Connoisseurs Choice Clynelish Aged 28 Years** refill American hogshead, cask no. 8204, dist 15 Nov 89, bott 26 Jun 18 **(94) n22.5 t24.5 f23 b24** The nose suggests a once great whisky now tiring and in decline. The delivery suggests a once great whisky that is still great! The marriage of salt, heather honey and the faintest wisp of peat is reminiscent of Highland Park at its absolute peak. The secret to this malt's greatness is the pace at which the flavours unfold and their translucent quality while somehow retaining great weight. A whisky which shapes with rare beauty on the palate and lives long on the finish... and memory. *49.3%. sc. 221 bottles.*

**Gordon & MacPhail Connoisseurs Choice Clynelish 2005** refill sherry butt, cask no. 308764, dist 14 Jun 05, bott 21 Feb 18 **(94) n24 t25 f21.5 b23.5** Such is the fragile complexity of Clynelish my first choice for bottling would never be a sherry butt, even if in entirely tip-top nick. Well, I would have been wrong. Because had this butt not latterly shown signs of sulphur it would most certainly have picked up a major award in this year's Bible. So, forget the imperfections and, once a week, treat yourself to the ecstasy of a mouthful of this outrageously orgasmic organoleptic odyssey. *55.1%. nc ncf sc. 518 bottles.*

◈ **Hidden Spirits Clynelish 1992** cask no. CY9219, bott 2019 **(96) n24** supremely complex and so clever: the oils and saltiness are always apparent, bringing out the most of the lime blossom and ulmo honeys. This is a nose of a thousand layers, the vanillas varying in weight and intensity in almost dizzying degree; **t24.5** ...and so on to a near perfect delivery. Now it is the layering of the honey which causes you to pause and wonder. More ulmo here, but heather honey also giving a sweet weightiness. The barley flutters or stands sting and sings...; a light saltiness sharpens the tune significantly; **f23.5** the vanilla and ulmo honey combine with the noble barley for a sublime finish; **b24** what a distillery...!!! *50.1%. sc.*

◈ **The Whisky Embassy Clynelish Aged 23 Years** refill sherry butt, cask no. 8674, dist 26 Sept 95, bott 5 Dec 18 **(93) n23 t23.5 f22.5 b24** A near faultless sherry butt ensures this malt has a rare fruity polish, especially on delivery. The combination of Clynelish's natural, beautifully honeyed malt, unquestionably the best in the Highlands, gives even greater depth as the mouth is bathed in delightful marzipan as well as the juiciest fruit pudding imaginable, with extra figs thrown in for god measure. Though spices try to compensate, the finish does dry a little too enthusiastically, perhaps, but the overall performance is one of unquestionable elegance and quality. *54.5%. nc ncf sc.*

**Whisky Illuminati Clynelish 20 Year Old** American oak hogshead, cask no. 6921, dist 1997 **(91) n22.5 t23 f22.5 b23** Goes about producing excellence in a quiet and dignified way. *55.3%. sc. 251 bottles. Candlelight Series.*

**Xtra Old Particular Clynelish 21 Years Old** refill hogshead, cask no. 12014, dist Oct 95, bott Sept 17 **(95.5) n23.5 t24 f23.5 b24** So true to this magnificent distillery in full flow. *54.6%. nc ncf sc. 265 bottles.*

# CONVALMORE
### Speyside, 1894–1985. William Grant & Sons. Closed.

**Convalmore 32 Year Old** refill American oak hogsheads db **(96.5) n24 t24 f24 b24.5** Being 32 years old and bottled in 2017, these must be casks from among the very last production of the distillery before it was closed for the final time in 1985. The new spirit then, from what I remember, was not the greatest: thin and with an occasional tendency to be on the rough house side. Time, though, is a great healer. And forgiver. It has passed the last three decades turning from ugly duckling to the most elegant of swans. A sub-species, though, that is on the brink of extinction... *48.2%. 3,972 bottles. Diageo Special Releases 2017.*

**Gordon & MacPhail Rare Old Convalmore 1975 (94) n23 t24 f23 b24** The rarest of the rare. And in tasting, the flavour map took me back 30 years, to when I used to buy bottles of this from Gordon and MacPhail as a 10-year-old...probably distilled around 1975. The unique personality and DNA is identical on the palate as it was then; except now, of course, there is far more oak to contend with. Like finding an old lover 30 years further on: a little greyer, not quite in the same lithe shape as three decades earlier...but instantly recognisable and still very beautiful... *46%*

# CRAGGANMORE
### Speyside, 1870. Diageo. Working.

**Cragganmore** db **(81) n23 t24 f16 b18** A whisky which asks some major questions: such as should I just sit here and sob, or bang my head repeatedly on my tasting table? This had begun as such a promising and sturdy addition to the Cragganmore lexicon, with the complexity of the early sugars really upping the expectations. But the dreaded "s" word arrived in abundance from, presumably, a sherry butt involvement and things went downhill rapidly after that. Tragic. *55.7%. 4,932 bottles. Diageo Special Releases 2016.*

**Cragganmore Aged 12 Years** db **(81.5) n20 t21 f20 b20.5.** I have a dozen bottles of Cragganmore in my personal cellar dating from the early 90s when the distillery was first bottled as a Classic Malt. Their astonishing dexterity and charm, their naked celebration of all things Speyside, casts a sad shadow over this drinkable but drab and instantly forgettable expression. *40%*

**Acla Selection Cragganmore 12 Years Old** bourbon hogshead, dist 2004, bott 2016 **(88.5) n22 t23 f21.5 b22** A competent bottling shewing the distillery in its malty clarity without bothering too much about complexity. *54.6%. sc. Joint bottling with The Whisky Agency.*

# CRAIGELLACHIE
**Speyside, 1891. Bacardi. Working.**

**Craigellachie 13 Year Old** db **(78.5) n20 t22 f18 b18.5.** Oily and intense, it shovels on the malt for all it is worth. That said, the sulphur notes are its undoing. *46%*

**Craigellachie 17 Year Old** db **(88.5) n22** chocolate Liquorice Allsort! A tad oily and boiled vegetable. But enough malt to make the difference; **t22.5** just love that delivery. Not the cleanest. But a mix of those heavy duty oils and an almost biting vanilla-barley note is attractive in an unkempt kind of way; **f22** almost like an oil slick in a sea of oak-splintered barley; **b22** technically falls flat on its face. Yet the whole is way better than the sum parts...*46%*

⟡ **Craigellachie Aged 17 Years** bott code: L190112A500 db **(94) n23** invigorating barley: a real nip, with sharp sugars and some pointy oak, too...; **t23.5** a resounding Speyside-style delivery with the barley bouncing around the palate on delivery; the spices move in pretty sharpish before some top quality tannins add their delicate hickory depth; the elegance of the oils is both enriching...and a surprise; **f23.5** a glorious mix of malt and milky, spiced cocoa; **b24** this bottling is a great improvement on previous versions I have encountered. What an interesting and delicious dram, shewing the distillery at its best! *46%.*

**Craigellachie 23 Year Old** db **(91.5) n23.5 t23 f22 b23.5** Expected a little house smoke on this (the malt made here in the early 1990s always had delicate phenol), but didn't show. The honey is nothing like so shy. *46% WB16/035*

**Craigellachie Exceptional Cask Series 1994** bott May 18 db **(91.5) n22.5 t23 f23 b23** How fascinating. Yes, a sherry butt and yes: there is sulphur. But this time it is not from the sherry, as the nose reveals a particular character from the condenser which does accentuate a mild sulphur character. Yet the clean wine casks tell a different, at once puckering yet juicy, story. Beautifully structured and a jaw-aching chewing malt with an unusual late salivation point. *54.8%. Bottled for Whisky L! & Fine Spirits Show.*

⟡ **The First Editions Craigellachie Aged 12 Years 2006** sherry butt, cask no. 15087, bott 2019 **(94.5) n23.5** always a pleasure to find a clean, fruitcake nose; **t24** superb delivery, just pulsing with ultra- ripe fruit – greengages and dates in particular – with a back drop of barley sugar; the intensity coupled with the spices is terrific; **f23** delightful sherry trifle; **b24** a magnificent bottling benefiting from a sherry butt with not a single atom of sulphur. *59.6%. nc ncf sc. 248 bottles.*

**The First Editions Craigellachie Aged 21 Years 1995** sherry butt, cask no. 13305, bott 2017 **(73) n18 t20 f17 b18** Yes, some massive, eye-watering grape. But furs up considerably. *59%. nc ncf sc. 282 bottles.*

**The First Editions Craigellachie Aged 22 Years** sherry butt, cask no. 14461, bott 2017 **(85.5) n21.5 t22 f21 b21** Earnest and intense in, first, its malty endeavours then, latterly, on the fruit scene. But a degree of bitterness ensures the desired balance proves elusive. *54.7%. nc ncf sc. 180 bottles.*

**Golden Cask Craigellachie Aged 10 Years** cask no. CM237, dist 2006, bott 2017 **(94) n23 t23.5 f23.5 b24** Another golden cask from Golden Cask...awash with honey and character. *54.2%. sc. 134 bottles.*

**Gordon & MacPhail Connoisseurs Choice Craigellachie 1991** refill American hogshead, cask no. 9465, dist 13 Nov 91, bott 19 Feb 18 **(89.5) n23 t22.5 f22 b22** While the oak tires, the spirit itself appears to want to carry on forever. *56.5%. nc ncf sc. 172 bottles.*

⟡ **The Great Drams Craigellachie 11 Years Old** bourbon cask, oloroso sherry cask finish, cask no. 900668/07A, dist 23 Oct 07, bott 30 Oct 18 **(80.5) n19 t22.5 f19 b20** A very odd whisky. The sherry doesn't quite ring true, alas, as the dirty nose and finish testifies. But few moments of honeyed magic on delivery, but not enough to excuse the sub-standard sherry cask. *46.2%. nc ncf sc.*

**Hepburn's Choice Craigellachie 9 Years Old** wine cask, dist 2008, bott 2017 **(86.5) n20 t22 f22.5 b22** Those who like those bitter and sharp green fruit pastels will most probably appreciate this lively little number. *46%. nc ncf sc. 296 bottles.*

⟡ **Hepburn's Choice Craigellachie 9 Years Old** refill hogshead, dist 2008, bott 2018 **(86.5) n21.5 t22 f21.5 b21.5** Youthful, grassy but a bit flat. *46%. nc ncf sc. 368 bottles.*

⟠ **Hepburn's Choice Craigellachie 10 Years Old** new sherry hogshead, dist 2008, bott 2019 **(86.5) n22 t22 f21.5 b21** The malt and grape harmonise quite well on delivery but elsewhere had a fractious time bonding. Not a bad cask – despite the very dry finish - but has been bottled not quite at a happy time in its development. 46%. nc ncf sc. 259 bottles.

**Hepburn's Choice Craigellachie 11 Years Old** sherry butt, dist 2006, bott 2017 **(92) n22.5 t23.5 f23 b23** An absolute joy of a sherry-influenced whisky. 46%. nc ncf sc. 300 bottles.

**The Loch Fyne Craigellachie 10 Year Old** sherry cask, cask no. 311, dist Sept 07, bott Nov 17 **(81) n18 t21 f20 b20** This is one of the most naturally sulphur-producing distilleries in Scotland without getting a helping hand from the sherry butt. An attractive malt-doused delivery considering. 46%. sc. 1,205 bottles.

⟠ **MacAlabur Craigellachie Aged 12 Years** first-fill bourbon barrel, cask no. 8101210, dist 23 Aug 06, bott 15 Oct 18 **(91) n22.5** how can you not just love that nuttiness?; **t23** amazingly rich and intense for this distillery. The malt is falling over itself to pulse out lush yet spikey message. Almost a hint of Hovis towards the middle; **f22.5** toasted Hovis now as the oak begins to make a distinct mark; but even as the last flavour rays die, they are ones of pure malt...; **b23** there have been too many disappointing bottling of Craigellachie in recent years. Thankfully, this isn't one of them! 54.3%. nc ncf sc. 229 bottles.

**Old Malt Cask Craigellachie Aged 21 Years** sherry butt, cask no. 13740, dist Sept 95, bott Apr 17 **(78.5) n21.5 t21.5 f17.5 b18** A malt which makes a bit of a ham fist at engaging your attention. Lollops along with an essentially malty theme interrupted by some very ordinary sherry-influenced moments, not all of them as fruit rich as you might like. 50%. nc ncf sc. 587 bottles.

**Old Malt Cask Craigellachie Aged 22 Years** sherry butt, cask no. 14405, dist Sept 95, bott Nov 17 **(93.5) n23 t23.5 f23.5 b23.5** Clean sherry...!!! And does it repay the palate in kind...! 50%. nc ncf sc. 122 bottles.

**Old Malt Cask Craigellachie Aged 22 Years** sherry butt, cask no. 14460, dist Sept 95, bott Nov 17 **(90.5) n22 t23.5 f22 b23** Weighty and satisfying. 50%. nc ncf sc. 450 bottles.

**Old Particular Craigellachie 18 Years Old** sherry butt, cask no. 12218, dist Jul 99, bott Dec 17 **(84.5) n20 t22 f21 b21.5** Firm both on nose and delivery with no shortage of heat, either. Juicy, but never quite relaxes a little bit of tightness throughout. 48.4%. nc ncf sc. 295 bottles.

**Old Particular Craigellachie 21 Years Old** sherry butt, cask no. 11769, dist Oct 95, bott Jun 17 **(87.5) n21.5 t22 f21.5 b22.5** Crisp and bitter-sweet. The barley is harnessed tightly by the oak while a little butterscotch, acacia honey and cocoa quietens the spice. 51.5%. nc ncf sc. 390 bottles.

**Provenance Craigellachie Aged 8 Years** refill hogshead, cask no. 12202, dist Feb 09, bott Dec 17 **(78.5) n18 t19 f21.5 b19** The same notes as for the bottling above, except here the sulphur is slightly more pronounced, the barley takes longer to convene while an extra dose of cocoa comes to the rescue. 46%. nc ncf sc. 660 bottles.

**Scotch Malt Whisky Society Cask 44.82 13 Year Old** refill ex-bourbon barrel, dist 27 Jun 03 **(84.5) n21.5 t22 f20 b21** Huge amounts of natural cream toffee to chew on from the cask; at times the sweetness is all-engulfing. But the distillery's usual bite and attitude are not put off that easily. 56.7%. sc.

⟠ **Scyfion Choice Craigellachie 2008** pomegranate wine cask finished, bott 2017 **(73) n18 t19 f18 b18** Will be interesting to taste one of these casks not ruined by the dreaded "S" word... 46%. nc ncf. 268 bottles.

⟠ **Simon Brown Traders Craigellachie** bourbon cask, dist Oct 06, bott Feb 19 **(87) n22.5 t22.5 f20.5 b21.5** The nose shews a degree of charm, but with caveats. Busy coriander and banana make intriguing and spicy bedfellows, but there is a warning about an oak weakness further down the line. Which does eventually arrive with an astringent bitterness. But there is, first, time to enjoy a big malty surge on delivery and a rousing spice and maple syrup follow through. 43%. nc ncf sc.

# DAILUAINE
### Speyside, 1854. Diageo. Working.

**Dailuaine 1997 The Manager's Choice** db **(87.5) n21.5 t23 f21 b22.** One of the most enjoyable (unpeated!!) Dailuaines I've come across in an age. There is the usual distillery biff to this, but not without a honeyed safety net. Great fun. 58.6%

**Dailuaine Aged 16 Years** bott lot no. L4334 db **(79) n19 t21 f20 b19.** Syrupy, almost grotesquely heavy at times; the lighter notes of previous bottlings have been lost under an avalanche of sugary, over-ripe tomatoes. One for those who want a massive dram. 43%

**Berry Bros & Rudd Dailuaine 21 Years Old** cask no. 10608, dist 1996, bott 2018 **(91.5) n23 t22.5 f22.5 b23.5** Not often you come across a Dailuaine that is a real joy, so hearty congratulations to BBR buyer Doug McIvor for spotting this collectors' item. And if you want to know how rare: a highly decent Dailuaine like this comes along about as often as a Charlton victory over Millwall: practically never... 46%. nc ncf sc.

**Gordon & MacPhail Connoisseurs Choice Dailuaine 1998** refill American hogshead, dist 11 Aug 98, bott 14 Mar 18 **(82) n21.5 t21 f19 b20.5** Not even some well above average oak, imparting at times spice and cocoa, can disguise the fact that this is a lesser, unsophisticated whisky: a Trabant engine inside a Jaguar F Type. 46%. nc ncf. 661 bottles.

**Hepburn's Choice Dailuaine 7 Years Old** rum barrel, dist 2009, bott 2017 **(85) n21 t21.5 f21 b21.5** An attractive, mouth-watering and vaguely spicy little cove benefiting from the sugary dusting bestowed upon it by the rum. 46%. nc ncf sc. 138 bottles.

**Hepburn's Choice Dailuaine 10 Years Old** sherry butt, dist 2007, bott 2018 **(77.5) n19 t20 f19 b19.5** Only a quick, passing dose of barley sugar saves us from encountering a Dailuaine in one of its well-known off key and belligerent moods. 46%. nc ncf sc. 789 bottles.

**Old Particular Dailuaine 15 Years Old** sherry butt, cask no. 12016, dist Mar 02, bott Aug 17 **(80) n21 t20 f19 b19** Not even a sympathetic sherry butt can entirely save this fiery malt which is as excellent an example of an overheated spirit still as you are ever likely to find. 48.4%. nc ncf sc. 356 bottles.

**Provenance Dailuaine Aged 8 Years** refill hogshead, cask no. 12037, dist Aug 09, bott Aug 17 **(80.5) n20.5 t20 f20 b20** Not untypically for this distillery, this has to be the bare basics of malt whisky. No faults as such, but beyond the intense, youthful malt itself it goes nowhere – and makes no attempt to. 46%. nc ncf sc. 400 bottles.

# DALLAS DHU
### Speyside, 1899–1983. Closed. Now a museum.

**Gordon & MacPhail Rare Vintage Dallas Dhu 1979 (94.5) n23 t23.5 f23.5 b24** I can hardly recall the last time a bottling from this distillery popped along – depressing to think I am old enough to remember when they were so relatively common they were being sold on special offer! It was always a class act; its closure an act of whisky vandalism, whether it be preserved as a museum or not. This, even after all these years, shows the extraordinary quality we are missing day in, day out. 43%

# DALMORE
### Highlands (Northern), 1839. Whyte and Mackay. Working.

**The Dalmore 12 Years Old** db **(90) n22 t23 f22.5 b22.5** Has changed character of late yet remains underpowered and with a shade too much toffee. But such is the quality of the malt in its own right it can overcome any hurdles placed before it to ensure a real mouth-filling, rumbustious dram. 40%

**The Dalmore 15 Years Old** db **(83.5) n21 t21 f20.5 b21.** Another pleasant Dalmore that coasts along the runway but simply fails to get off the ground. The odd off note here and there, but it's the blood orange which shines brightest. 40%

**The Dalmore 18 Years Old** db **(76.5) n19 t21 f18 b18.5.** Heaps of caramel and the cask choice might have been better. 43%

**The Dalmore 21 Year Old** db **(88.5) n22** date and walnut cake...though light on the walnuts...; **t23** fat, chewy, mouth-watering and complex...though light on the complexity; **f21.5** remains chewy, bitter and sweet...though light on the sweetness; **b22** fat, unsubtle, but enjoyable. 42%

**The Dalmore 25** db **(88) n23.5** hugely attractive with a sherry-trifle signature; **t22.5** a glossy delivery with the accent very much on fruit, plums in particular; an attractive degree of sharpness throughout; **f20** just a little dry with a tell-tale tang towards the end; **b22** the kind of neat and tidy, if imperfect, whisky which, were it in human form, would sport a carefully trimmed and possibly darkened little moustache, a pin-striped suit, matching tie and square and shiny black shoes. 42%. Whyte & Mackay Ltd.

**The Dalmore 30 Year Old** db **(94) n24** the grape drifts across the glass; not quite perfect but enough panache and class to carry an aura of slight wonder...; **t24** so thick, so long, so dripping in fruit....; subtle spice and a slow realisation of aged, confident tannin;**f22.5** undone very slightly by a very late degree of bitterness; **b23.5** a malt, quite literally for the discerning whisky lover. Essays in complexity are rarely so well written in the glass as found here... 45%

**The Dalmore 50 Years Old** db **(88) n21 t19 f25 b23.** Takes a while to warm up, but when it does becomes a genuinely classy and memorable dram befitting one of the world's great and undervalued distilleries. 52%

**The Dalmore 62 Years Old** db **(95) n23 t25 f24 b24** If I am just half as beautiful, elegant and fascinating as this by the time I reach 62, I'll be a happy man. Somehow I doubt it. A once-in-a-lifetime whisky – something that comes around every 62 years, in fact. Forget Dalmore Cigar Malt – even I might be tempted to start smoking just to get a full bottle of this. 40.5%

**The Dalmore 1263 King Alexander III** db **(86) n22 t22.5 f20 b21.5.** Starts brightly with all kinds of barley sugar, fruit and decent age and oak combinations, plus some excellent spice prickle. So far, so good...and obviously thoughtfully and complexly structured. But then vanishes without trace on finish. 40%

**The Dalmore 1980** db (81.5) n19 t21 f20.5 b21. Wonderful barley intensity on delivery does its best to overcome the so-so nose and finale. 40%

**The Dalmore 1981 Amoroso Sherry Finesse** amoroso sherry wood cask db (85.5) n21 t22 f21.5 b21. A very tight, fruity, dram which gives away its secrets with all the enthusiasm of an agent under torture. Enjoyable to a degree... but bloody hard work. 42%

**The Dalmore Astrum Aged 40 Years** db (89) n23.5 t21 f22 b22.5. This guy is all about the nose. The oak is too big for the overall framework and the balance hangs by a thread. Yet somehow the overall effect is impressive. Another summer and you suspect the whole thing would have snapped... 42%

**The Dalmore Aurora Aged 45 Years** db (90.5) n25 t22 f21.5 b22. Sophisticated for sure. But so huge is the oak on the palate, it cannot hope to match the freakish brilliance of the nose. 45%

**The Dalmore Candela Aged 50 Years** db (96) n25 t24 f23.5 b23.5. Just one of those whiskies which you come across only a handful of times in your life. All because a malt makes it to 50 does not mean it will automatically be great. This, however, is a masterpiece, the end of which seemingly has never been written. 50% (bottled at 45%).

**The Dalmore Cabernet Sauvignon** db (79) n22 t19 f19 b19. Too intense for its own good. 45%

**The Dalmore Ceti** db (91.5) n24 a nose for fruitcake lovers everywhere: ripe cherries and blood orange abound and work most attractively with the slightly suety, muscovado enriched body...; t23.5 the nose demands a silky delivery and that's exactly what you get. Rich fruit notes form the principle flavour profile but the backing salivating barley and spice is spot on; the mid ground becomes a little saltier and more coastal...;f21.5 a vague bitterness to the rapidly thinning finale, almost a pithy element, which is slightly out of sync with the joys of before; b22.5 a Ceti which warbles rather well... 44.7%

**The Dalmore Cigar Malt Reserve Limited Edition** db (73.5) n19 t19.5 f17 b18. One assumes this off key sugarfest is for the cigar that explodes in your face... 44%

**The Dalmore Dominium** db (89.5) n22.5 thick, full-on grape; t23 lush delivery which becomes progressively more chewy. A few spiced sultanas in there; f22 big on the caramel; b22 like so many Dalmores, starts brightly but as the caramels gather it just drifts into a soupy lump. Still, no taint to the fruit and though the finish is dull you can say it is never less than very attractive. 43%. Fortuna Meritas Collection

**The Dalmore Luceo** db (87) n22 t22 f21.5 b21.5. Pleasantly malty, exceptionally easy going and perfect for those of you with a toffeed tooth. 40%. Fortuna Meritas Collection

**The Dalmore Valour** db (85.5) n21 t22 f21 b21.5. Not often you get the words "Valour" and "fudge" in the same sentence. 40%. Fortuna Meritas Collection

**The Dalmore Regalis** db (86.5) n22.5 t21.5 f21 b21.5. For a brief moment, grassy and busy. Then dulls, other than the spice. The caramel held in the bottling hall is such a great leveller. 40%. Fortuna Meritas Collection

**The Dalmore Visitor Centre Exclusive** db (95.5) n25 t24 f22.5 b24 Not exactly the easiest distillery to find but a bottle of this is worth the journey alone. I have tasted some sumptuous Dalmores over the last 30-odd years. But this one stands among the very finest. 46%

**The Dalmore Quintessence** db (91) n22 t23.5 f22 b23.5 A late night dram after a hard day. Slump into your favourite chair, dim the lights, pour yourself a glass of this, warm in the hand and then study, quietly, for the next half hour. 45%.

⬦ **Gleann Mór Dalmore Aged Over 13 Years** (83.5) n21 t21.5 f20.5 b20.5 Malt ordinaire. 55.6%.

⬦ **Glenwill Dalmore 1991** hogshead, cask no. 11151 (92.5) n22.5 some grizzled malt nipping away; t23.5 supremely intense and juicy barley; f23 still very simple, but delightfully effective, malt with a charming oaky-vanilla build up; b23.5 mouth-cleansing, beautifully made, high grade blending fodder. But a superb single malt instead. 46.2%. 266 bottles. Matisse Spirits Company.

⬦ **Master of Malt Single Cask Dalmore 14 Year Old** bourbon hogshead, dist 24 Apr 03, bott 20 Mar 18 (95) n23.5 sublime nose with a glorious kiwi fruit and lime interplay sitting comfortably beside the butterscotch and honeydew melon; t24 outstanding mouthfeel, with again the accent on a vaguely exotic fruitiness, though more now a mix of ulmo and Bruyere honeys; f23.5 that lightly waxy honey tone continues right towards the end when the vanillas kick in with their drying effect; b24 well done Master of Malt! For years I have been telling people that Dalmore make a very good malt, though there has been scant evidence of this from the distillery's own caramel submerged bottlings and independent offerings, usually from less than impressive casks. Here, though, we have a naturally full bodied Dalmore I often encounter in the lab but rarely seen in public view. Excellent. Oh, and if only the standard Dalmore was this naturally magnificent. 57.8%. sc.

**The Whisky Chamber Dalmore 10 Years Old 2007** sherry refill hogshead (79) n19 t21 f19 b20 Some serious dollops of honey go a long way to disrupt the tangy influence of the cask. A forthright dram taking no prisoners. 55.9%. sc.

# DALWHINNIE
### Highlands (Central), 1898. Diageo. Working.

**Dalwhinnie 15 Years Old** db (95) n24 t24 f23 b24 A malt it is hard to decide whether to drink or bath in: I suggest you do both. One of the most complete mainland malts of them all. Know anyone who reckons they don't like whisky? Give them a glass of this – that's them cured. Oh, if only the average masterpiece could be this good. 43%

**Dalwhinnie Winter's Gold** db (95) n23.5 for such a remote and inland distillery, the coastal saltiness to this is remarkable... golden syrup and earthy heather-honey also at work here; t24 something of the Johnnie Walker Gold about this: there is a clarity to the malt, the citrus and vanilla which reminds one of the air when looking far away into the mountains on a cool winter's morn; f23.5 earthy to the end with the honey (ulmo, naturally!) Still the dominating theme; just a late hint of bitterness; b24 whichever blender came up with this deserves a pat on the back. 43%

 **Game of Thrones Dalwhinnie Winter's Frost House Stark** db (87.5) n22 t22 f21.5 b22 This is my fourth Game of Thrones whisky I have now sampled. And, having never seen the TV series, I am beginning to get the picture: the programme is about toffee, isn't it! Because, again, caramel is the dominating factor here, somehow flattening out the higher peaks from this mountainside distillery, which happens to be one of the world's best. The delightful burst of juicy barley just after the tame delivery is all too brief. 43%.

# DEANSTON
### Highlands (Perthshire), 1966. Burn Stewart Distillers. Working.

**Deanston 6 Years Old** db (83) n20 t21 f22 b20. Great news for those who remember how good Deanston was a decade or two ago: it's on its way back. A delightfully clean dram with its trademark honey character restored. A little beauty slightly undermined by caramel. 40%

**Deanston 10 Year Old PX Finish** db (83.5) n21 t22.5 f20 b20 Displays the uncompromising sweetness of a whisky liqueur. A must-have malt for those who like their sherry influence to be way over the top. The finish, like the nose, reveals minor a dry, furry element. 57.5%.

**Deanston 12 Years Old** db (74) n18 t19 f18.5 b18.5. It is quite bizarre how you can interchange this with Tobermory in style; or, rather, at least the faults are the same. 46%. ncf.

**Deanston Aged 12 Years** db (75) n18 t21.5 f17.5 b18. The delivery is, for a brief moment, a malty/orangey delight. But the nose is painfully out of sync and finish is full of bitter, undesirable elements. A lot of work still required to get this up to a second grade malt, let alone a top flight one. 46.3%. ncf. Burn Stewart

 **Deanston 12 Years Old** bourbon casks, bott code: 17242991509:5018106 db (84) n21 t22 f20 b21 All the fun is on the impact, where the barley is about as intense as anything else produced in Scotland. However, the weakness on both nose and finish points accusingly at the Deanston character of off-key feintiness. 46.3%. ncf.

**Deanston 18 Year Old** batch 2 db (89.5) n23 celebrates a very healthy degree of ulmo honey: soft and sexy; t22.5 big malt kick early on; soft oils bring on the vanillas; juicy and just a touch of lime to lighten things; f22 a little spicier and deeper toned as the tannin takes charge; b22 a soft treat for the palate... 46.3%. nc ncf.

 **Deanston 18 Years Old** 1st fill bourbon casks, bott code: 1911691L511L:2618334 db (89.5) n22 oozes with malt with a light ulmo honey sweetness tempered by a chalkier vanilla dryness; strictly speaking, not technically correct, but gets away with it; t23.5 it is the lush mouth feel which stars here, the oils forming a malty grip of the palate which it refuses to release; salivating and satisfying with the faintest Demerara sweetness leaking in; f21.5 dries as the tannins make a contribution, and warms, too, as the spices fizz. The barley, though, offers constant background music. A little feinty bitterness creeps in at the death; b22.5 an intense, highly enjoyable dram where the malted barley gangs up and gives the other characteristics only bit parts. 46.3%. ncf.

**Deanston 20 Year Old** db (61) n15 t16 f15 b15 Riddled with sulphur. 55.4%. nc ncf.

**Deanston 40 Year Old PX Finish** db (87.5) n22 t23 f21 b21.5 The PX is doubtless in use here to try and give a sugary wrap around the over-aged malt. Some success, though limited. This type of cask has the unfortunate habit of restricting complexity in a whisky by embracing it too tightly with its wealth of syrupy top notes. The aromas and flavours which do escape often seem brittle and clipped, and this is the case here: the whisky has no chance to tell of its 40 years in the cask – the period that counts most now is the time it has spent in PX. Love the spices, though, and the overall mouth feel. Whatever its limitations, this still does offer a lovely dram. 45.6%.

**Deanston Virgin Oak** db **(90)** n22.5 t23 f22.5 b22 Quirky. Don't expect this to taste anything like Scotch... 46.3%

◈ **Deanston Virgin Oak** virgin oak casks, bott code: 1866939L512:4118241 db **(87.5)** n22.5 t22.5 f21.5 b21 The overall lightness of Deanston's malt is emphasised by the lingering impact of the tannin towards the finish which knocks the early balance off kilter. An attractively complex nose, though, and the acacia honey on the barley concentrate delivery, followed by zonking spice, is to die for. 46.3%. ncf.

◈ **The Golden Cask Deanston 22 Years Old 1996** cask no. CM250, bott 2018 **(87.5)** n21.5 t23 f21 b22 The neighbourhood rough dressed in an ill-fitting suit at his sister's wedding. Some outstanding heather honey moments on delivery, which is worth finding alone. But elsewhere bitter, waspish and looking to give your taste buds a good duffing up. 55.4%. nc ncf sc. 222 bottles.

**The Single Cask Deanston 20 Years Old** cask no. 1982 **(84)** n20 t21.5 f21 b21.5 Not an easy task to find great Deanston. And I have failed again here. But despite its inherent roughness, hotness and wayward personality, I have to say I rather like the intense, malty nuttiness. For a Deanston, not a bad shout at all. 52.7%.

## DUFFTOWN

Speyside, 1898. Diageo. Working.

**Singleton of Dufftown 12 Years Old** db **(71)** n18 t18 f17 b18. A roughhouse malt that's finesse-free. For those who like their tastebuds Dufft up a bit... 40%

◈ **The Singleton of Dufftown Aged 15 Years** bott code: L7149DM000 db **(84.5)** n21.5 t22 f20.5 b20.5 Nutty and rich on delivery. Toffee-weighted, thin and boring elsewhere. 40%.

**The Singleton of Dufftown Aged 18 Years** bott code: L7094DM000 db **(86.5)** n21 t22 f21.5 b22 To be honest, I was expecting a bit of dud here, based on some 30-years-experience of this distillery. And though, for an 18-year-old, it can't be said really to hit the heights, it has – as so many less than brilliant distilleries over the years – mellowed enough with age to show a certain malty gentleness worthy of respect. 40%.

**The Singleton of Dufftown Spey Cascade** db **(80)** n19 t20 f21 b20. A dull whisky, stodgy and a little dirty on the nose. Improves the longer it stays on the palate thanks mainly to sympathetic sugars and an ingratiating oiliness. But if you are looking for quality, prepare to be disappointed. 40%

**The Singleton of Dufftown "Sunray"** db **(77)** n20 t20 f18 b19. One can assume only that the sun has gone in behind a big toffeed cloud. Apparently, according to the label, this is "intense". About as intense as a ham sandwich. Only not as enjoyable. 40%. WB15/121

**The Singleton of Dufftown "Tailfire"** db **(79)** n20 t20 f19 b20. Tailspin, more like. 40%.

**Gordon & MacPhail Connoisseurs Choice Dufftown 1999** first fill bourbon barrel, cask no. 8789, dist 18 Aug 99, bott 19 Feb 18 **(85.5)** n21.5 t22 f21 b21 A typical Dufftown offering, the thick, glutinous sugars riding roughshod over the palate. The odd phase of high intensity barley does offer the occasional fascinating interlude. 54.5%. nc ncf sc. 163 bottles.

**Hepburn's Choice Dufftown 10 Years Old** refill hogshead, dist 2007, bott 2018 **(84.5)** n21 t22.5 f20 b21 Oily barley sugar with an acceptable chewability and simplistic outlook. The finish can't help itself but the journey there is surprisingly pleasant. 46%. nc ncf sc. 409 bottles.

◈ **The Whisky Chamber Dufftown 10 Years Old 2008** bourbon cask **(85)** n21 t22.5 f20.5 b20.5 A punchy, salivating malt which works well when the Demerara sugars and intense barley combines, but found a little tangy and wanting elsewhere. A little spiced chocolate late on tames the worst excesses of the oak. 58.9%. sc.

## EDRADOUR

Highlands (Perthshire), 1837. Signatory Vintage. Working.

**Edradour Aged 10 Years** db **(79)** n18 t20 f22 b19. A dense, fat malt that tries to offer something along the sherry front but succeeds mainly in producing a whisky cloyingly sweet and unfathomable. Some complexity to the finish compensates. 43%

**Edradour 13 Year Old** 1st fill oloroso sherry butt, dist 4 Dec 95, bott 4 May 18 db **(95)** n24 t23.5 f23.5 b24 When this whisky was distilled it was made at, then, Scotland's smallest distillery. Well, that may be so, but there is no denying that this is one absolutely huge whisky. And not only that, one where no degree of understated enormity is out step with any other: it is a giant, but a beautifully proportioned one. The spicy, sherry trifle on steroids nose will entrap you. The staggering complexity of the sturdy tannin and muscular fruit will keep you there, spellbound. The chocolate on the finish is almost an arrogant flourish. This really is Edradour from the old school, where its old manager Puss Mitchell had laid down the law on the type of sherry butt the hefty malt had to be filled into. Were he with us now, he'd be purring... 54.2%. 661 bottles. Bottled for Whisky L! & Fine Spirits Show.

⫸ **Signatory Vintage Edradour Ballechin 12 Year Old 2005** refill sherry hogshead, cask no. 160 **(96)** n24 pungent peat just reeking of Palma violets, liquorice, hickory and moist fruitcake: fabulous! Sweaty armpit saltiness, not unpleasant but a bit like your lover's after an hours' long Ugandan discussions...; t24 the spices attached to the peat go pop from the first entry. A secondary phenol attack comes through with no holds barred – like a an express train in the days of steam hitting a smoky tunnel; the barley is still fresh enough and the fruit vivid to create a sumptuous juiciness which briefly rivals the peat; f23.5 smoky fruit and chocolate...with a sublime spice fade; b24.5 what I would give for all sherry refills to be this faultlessly breathtaking. A potential single cask of the year. *61.5%. sc. Exclusive to The Whisky Barrel. 291 bottles.*

⫸ **Signatory Vintage Un-Chillfiltered Edradour 10 Year Old 2008** 1st fill sherry butt **(92.5)** n23 a real Christmas pudding feel to this, with no shortage of spices and lemon peel in the mix; a little salty, too; t23 succulent and safe. No off notes but the grape is so intense the malt has problems getting any kind of toe hold; f23.5 at last the tannins merge with the barley to make an impact. Remains unusually juicy at this late stage while the salt and peppers remain busy; b23 a huge, clean sherry butt at work there. Its only fault is that it rather obscures the malt for a beautiful distillery, making it a tad one-dimensional. But its overall effect is quite lovely. *58.7%. sc. Exclusive to The Whisky Barrel. 339 bottles.*

# FETTERCAIRN
**Highland (Eastern), 1824. Whyte and Mackay. Working.**
**Fettercairn 12 Year Old** db **(66)** n14 t19 f16 b17. If the nose doesn't get you, what follows probably will...Grim doesn't quite cover it. *40%*

**Fettercairn 40 Years Old** db **(92)** n23 t24 f22 b23 Yes, everyone knows my views on this distillery. But I'll have to call this spade a wonderfully big, old shovel you can't help loving... just like the memory of me tattooed ol' granny... 40%. 463 bottles.

**Fettercairn 1824** db **(69)** n17 t19 f16 b17. By Fettercairn standards, not a bad offering. Relatively free from its inherent sulphury and rubbery qualities, this displays a sweet nutty character not altogether unattractive – though caramel plays a calming role here. Need my arm twisting for a second glass, though. *40%*

**Berry Bros & Rudd Fettercairn 11 Years Old** cask no. 107750, dist 2006, bott 2018 **(80)** n21 t20 f19 b20 Pretty survivable for a Fettercairn. Lots of barley weirdness as you might expect. And that vaguely rubbery, nutty noise you always get in the background, especially at the death. But the oak is good, which helps, and the sugars and spices are in just about equal measure. Way above average. *46%. nc ncf sc.*

**Fadandel.dk Fettercairn Aged 21 Years** hogshead, cask no. 1803, dist 27 Sept 96, bott 26 Feb 18 **(85.5)** n21.5 t22 f21 b21 A sticky, glutinous, cloying, nutty dram though the improbable, salivating qualities of the malt is worth the exploration. As Fettercairns go, not too bad at all. *63.5%. sc. 24 bottles.*

⫸ **The First Editions Fettercairn Aged 13 Years 2005** refill butt, cask no. 15140, bott 2018 **(69)** n17 t19 f16 b17 Lots of niggle and bite. Grim, unbalanced and especially bitter towards the end. So, pretty normal for a Fettercairn, then. *59.7%. nc ncf sc. 336 bottles.*

**Hepburn's Choice Fettercairn 9 Years Old** wine cask, dist 2008, bott 2017 **(63)** n15 t17 f15 b16 Poor spirit and not a great cask. Proof that two negatives don't make a positive. *46%. nc ncf sc. 371 bottles.*

**Hepburn's Choice Fettercairn 10 Years Old** wine cask, dist 2008, bott 2018 **(63)** n15 t17 f15 b16 This may have been bottled in a different year, but the result is exactly the same... *46%. nc ncf sc. 406 bottles.*

⫸ **Old Malt Cask Fettercairn Aged 13 Years** refill hogshead, cask no. 15139, dist Nov 04, bott May 18 **(71)** n18 t20 f16 b17 No matter how many decades I spend doing this job, nosing and tasting Fettercairn doesn't get any easier. Proudly malty, but sharp, rock hard and even more proudly out of kilter. Thank God it was matured in a great cask. *50%. nc ncf sc. 341 bottles.*

**Old Malt Cask Fettercairn Aged 20 Years** refill hogshead, cask no. 13736, dist Jan 97, bott Apr 17 **(81)** n20 t22 f19 b20 A barley-sugared beastie. So similar to Littlemill here in its flat malty projection and cardboard backdrop that, just like that lost distillery, it shows that good age can greatly improve an originally poor spirit. *50%. nc ncf sc. 328 bottles.*

**Provenance Fettercairn Aged 10 Years** refill hogshead, cask no. 11776, dist Feb 07, bott May 17 **(75)** n18 t20.5 f18 b18.5 Big and malt intense but, like so many Fettercairns before, a part of its DNA is just plain wrong... *46%. nc ncf sc. 379 bottles.*

# GLEN ALBYN
**Highlands (Northern) 1846–1983. Diageo. Demolished.**
**Gordon & MacPhail Rare Vintage Glen Albyn 1976 (96)** n22.5 t24.5 f24.5 b24.5 Wow! My eyes nearly popped out of my head when I spotted this in my sample room. Glen Albyns

come round as rarely as a Scotsman winning Wimbledon. Well, almost. When I used to buy this (from Gordon and MacPhail in their early Connoisseur's Choice range, as it happens) when the distillery was still alive (just) I always found it an interesting if occasionally aggressive dram. This masterpiece, though, is something else entirely. And the delivery really does take us to places where only the truly great whiskies go... *43%*

# GLENALLACHIE
### Speyside, 1968. The GlenAllachie Distillers Co Limited. Working.

**The GlenAllachie 10 Years Old Cask Strength** batch 2 db **(87.5) n21.5 t22.5 f21.5 b22** Never thought I'd say this of a Glenallachie: but I quite enjoyed this. Despite its strength, the distillery's old trademark flamethrower character didn't materialise. The malt remains intact throughout but it is the natural caramels and vanilla from the oak which seriously catches the eye. This has spent ten years in some seriously good oak. I'll even go as far as to say that the malt-dripping delivery is rather gorgeous. *54.8%. The GlenAllachie Distillers Company.*

**The GlenAllachie 12 Years Old** db **(86.5) n21.5 t22.5 f20.5 b22** Whoever is putting these whiskies for Glenallachie together has certainly learned how to harness the extraordinary malt intensity of this distillery to its ultimate effect. Still a touch thin, at key moments, though, and the bitterness of the finish is purely down to the casks not the distillation. *46%. The GlenAllachie Distillers Company.*

**The GlenAllachie 18 Years Old** db **(89) n23** a pleasing nose, supremely well weighted between muscovado sugars, nippy spices and butterscotch. Specifically, there is a freshly baked, straight out the oven Dundee cake fruit and nuttiness to this; **t22.5** truly amazing: a soft delivery from a Glenallachie! Well, well, well...! The usual high propane barley, but with a delicate fruit edge; **f20** an off key buzz towards the spicy finish; **b22.5** as friendly as it gets from this distillery. *46%. The GlenAllachie Distillers Company.*

**The GlenAllachie 25 Years Old** db **(91.5) n23** raspberry Swiss roll, beside a glass of freshly mixed Robinson's barley water. Clean, fresh, with a vaguely sweet sub plot. But that grassy barley....; **t23.5** one of the juiciest 25-year-old whiskies in the world: beyond salivating – and there is a real nip and bite so you experience pleasure and pain in almost equal measure. But the barley malt is so intense....and, weirdly, despite the strength very little oil surfaces giving the structure an unusual delicacy; **f22** improbably juicy even at the death, though now the vanillas have ventured in...carefully...; **b23** around about the time this whisky was made, distillery manager Puss Mitchell, who then also had Aberlour and Edradour under his auspices, took me from time to time in his office and poured out samples of new make and maturing Glenallachie. The result, usually was a searing sensation to my mouth and a few yelps and cries from me (much to the amusement of Puss): it was then the most unforgiving – and thin - of all Scotland's malts. Indeed, when I wrote Jim Murray's Complete Book of Whisky in 1997, only one distillery in Scotland was missed out: it was Glenallachie. I had written the piece for it. But it just accidentally fell by the wayside during editing and the whisky was so ordinary I simply didn't notice. "It's a filler, Jim", said Puss as I choked on the samples. "This is for blending. It's too hot and basic for a single malt. This is no Aberlour." How extraordinary then, that the distillery now under new and focused ownership have brought out the whisky from that very time. It is still a little thin, and on arrival it still rips into you. But the passing quarter of a century has mellowed it significantly; astonishingly. So now the sugars from the grist act as balm; the gentle tannins as peacemaker. This is, against all the odds, now a very attractive whisky. Even Puss Mitchell would have been amazed. *48%. The GlenAllachie Distillers Company.*

**Old Particular Glenallachie 25 Years Old** refill barrel, cask no. 11771, dist Feb 92, bott Jun 17 **(83) n21.5 t21 f20 b20.5** Some half a century ago, when I watched my old dad replace my neighbour's window I had sent a cricket ball through earlier in the day (missing their new born baby by only a matter of inches), I remember the indelible smell of the putty that he grumpily applied to the frame as he eased the new glass into place. It was something very much like this. Whether it tasted of strained barley or not, and was this hot, history will never record.... *50.6%. nc ncf sc. 210 bottles.*

**Provenance Glenallachie Aged 7 Years** refill hogshead, cask no. 11187, dist Apr 09, bott May 16 **(69.5) n18 t17 f17 b17.5** Oddly enough, there are no faults with this as such. It is just a very poor quality whisky – though standard for the distillery – matured in a tiring cask. Harsh and thin. *46%. nc ncf sc.*

**Rest & Be Thankful Glenallachie 2004** hogshead sherry, cask no. 900641, dist 05 Oct 04, bott 27 Jul 17 **(90) n23** think of the fruitiest cake you've ever encountered, put it in the oven until it is just on the cusp of burning and there you have this celebration of toasty fruitiness; the barley barely lays a glove...; **t23.5** actually, it is the malt which hits first, in a lopsided, less than impressive way. The big fruit comes to the rescue with a succession of raisins, plum, dates and muscovado notes; **f21.5** dries as the malt tries to reconnect. But the bid is a little pathetic and the toasted raisins carry on their good work; **b22.5** bravo, Rest and Be Thankful people. That is the rarest of sherry casks you have unearthed there. The only blemish comes from the malt itself, which (thankfully) has virtually disappeared under the grape like a village might under the waters of a reservoir. 52.2%. nc ncf sc. 607 bottles.

**Whiskyjace Glenallachie 8 Years Old** 1st fill sherry butt, dist Nov 17, bott Aug 17 **(87) n22.5 t22 f21 b21.5** No problem here with the sherry butt which really punches out the clean grape to sensuous effect, especially on the nose where a hint of cinnamon and ginger adds further to the fruit-spattered spices. But the spirit and cask are not yet in sync, so the usual foibles of the malt are fully exposed. Hopefully the cask has not been entirely emptied as this will improve massively over the forthcoming years. 52.5%. 20 bottles.

# GLENBURGIE
### Speyside, 1810. Chivas Brothers. Working.
**Glenburgie Aged 15 Years** bott code L00/129 db **(84) n22 t23 f19 b20.** Doing so well until the spectacularly flat, bitter finish. Orangey citrus and liquorice had abounded. 46%

**Ballantine's The Glenburgie Aged 15 Years Series No. 001** American oak casks, bott code: I KRM1245 2018/04/03 **(86) n21.5 t22 f21 b21.5** Clunking caramels clog up the nose and finish big time. But there are some interesting tannin-laden spice notes in full swing as well. 40%..

⬧ **Berry Bros & Rudd Glenburgie 29 Years Old** cask no. 14087, dist 1989, bott 2018 **(89) n22.5** huge oak, but so well distributed and weighted you'd never know it. A seam of spice runs through this, as well as muscovado sugars; **t23** the delivery is the high point here with a sublime gathering of intense barley at first, dried by vanilla and then a vague pithy fruitiness. Busy spice, too, but always even and non-confrontational; **f21** bitters out slightly too enthusiastically; **b22.5** an intrinsically dry dram, perfect as your pre-prandial tipple if the vermouth has run out. 46%. nc ncf sc.

**Glenkeir Treasures Glenburgie 7 Year Old** cask filled 26/9/10, bott 20/2/18 **(90) n22.5 t23 f22 b22.5** A beautiful malt that is exactly as expected from this age in (probably) second fill cask. A spot- on blender's dream. % strength not given on bottle. Bizarre!

**Hepburn's Choice Glenburgie 8 Years Old** bourbon barrel, dist 2007, bott 2016 **(86.5) n22 t22 f21 b21.5** What it lacks in complexity it more than makes up for with classic Speyside grassy juiciness. 46%. nc ncf sc. 320 bottles.

⬧ **Hepburn's Choice Glenburgie 10 Years Old** refill hogshead, dist 2007, bott 2018 **(84) n21.5 t22 f20 b21.5** A pretty monosyllabic malt which, thanks to its youth, sticks to a grassy theme and refuses to budge. 46%. nc ncf sc. 340 bottles.

**Old Malt Cask Glenburgie Aged 21 Years** refill hogshead, cask no. 14246, dist Jul 99, bott Sept 17 **(91) n22.5 t23 f22.5 b23** Offers a beautiful lustre and depth and brims with malty confidence. 50%. nc ncf sc. 330 bottles.

**Old Particular Glenburgie 25 Years Old** refill hogshead, cask no. 11772, dist Apr 92, bott Jun 17 **(93) n23.5 t23 f22 b22.5** Barley-dominant Bergie in excelsis...Just wonderful. 51.5%. nc ncf sc. 270 bottles.

**The Whisky Embassy Glenburgie Aged 22 Years** cask no. 6520, dist 15 Jun 95, bott 12 Feb 18 **(90.5) n23 t23 f22 b22.5** Another gorgeous Burgie bottling benefitting from excellent oak. 56.7%. nc ncf sc.

# GLENCADAM
### Highlands (Eastern), 1825. Angus Dundee. Working.
**Glencadam Aged 10 Years** db **(95) n24 t24 f23 b24** Sophisticated, sensual, salivating and seemingly serene, this malt is all about juicy barley and balance. Just bristles with character and about as puckeringly elegant as single malt gets...and even thirst-quenching. My God: the guy who put this one together must be a genius, or something... 46%

**Glencadam Aged 10 Years Special Edition** batch no. 1, bott code: L1702608 CB2 db **(90.5) n22.5 t23.5 f22 b22.5** A weightier, oakier version of the standard Glencadam 10. Fascinating to see this level of oak involvement, though it further underlines what a delicate creature its spirit is... 48.2%. nc ncf. Special edition for The Whisky Shop.

**Glencadam Aged 13 Years** db **(94) n23.5 t24 f23 b23.5** Tasting this within 24 hours of Brechin City, the cheek by jowl neighbours of this distillery winning promotion after a penalty shoot out success in their play off final. This malt, every bit as engrossing and with more twists and turns than their seven-goal-thriller yesterday, is the perfect way to toast their success. 46%. nc ncf. 6,000 bottles.

**Glencadam Aged 15 Years** db **(90.5) n22.5 t23 f22 b23** The spices keep the taste buds on full alert but the richness and depth of the barley defies the years. Another exhibition of Glencadam's understated elegance. Some more genius malt creation... 46%

**Glencadam Aged 17 Years Triple Cask Portwood Finish** db (93.5) n23 t24.5 f22 b24 A 17-year-old whisky truffle. A superb late night or after dinner dram, where even the shadowy sulphur cannot spoil its genius. *46%. nc ncf. 1128 bottles.*

**Glencadam Aged 18 Years** db (96.5) n24.5 t24 f23.5 b24.5 So, here we go again: head down and plough on with the Whisky Bible 2018. This is the first whisky tasted in anger for the new edition and I select Glencadam for the strangest of reasons: it is the closest distillery to a football ground (North British, apart) I can think of, being a drop kick from Brechin City's pretty Glebe Park ground. And why is that relevant? Well today is a Saturday and I should really be at a game but decided to start off a weekend when there are fewest interruptions and I can get back into the swing of things before settling into the rhythm of a six day tasting week. Also, Glencadam, though criminally little known beyond readers of the Whisky Bible, is among the world's greatest distilleries producing one of the most charming whiskies of them all. So, hopefully, it will be a little reward for me. And offering the bourbon cask induced natural, light gold - which perfectly matches the buzzard which has just drifted on the winds into my garden - this enticingly fills the gap between their 17- and 19- years old. Strikes me there is a fraction more first fill cask at play here than usual, ensuring not just a distinctively honeyed, bourbony edge but a drier element also. Distinguished and elegant this is a fabulous, almost unbelievable way to start the new Bible as it has the hallmarks of a malt likely to end up winning some kind of major award. Somehow I think the bar set here, one fashioned from gold, will be far too high for the vast majority that will follow over the next five months... *46%. nc ncf.*

**Glencadam Aged 19 Years Oloroso Sherry Cask Finish** db (84) n21.5 t22 f19.5 b21. Mainly, though not quite, free of sulphur so the whisky after 19 years gets a good chance to speak relatively ungagged, though somewhat muffled. *46%. nc ncf. 6,000 bottles.*

**Glencadam Aged 21 Years "The Exceptional"** bott 2011 db (94) n23.5 t24 f23 b23.5. This distillery is emerging out of the shadows from its bad old Allied days as one of the great Scottish single malt distilleries. So good is some of their whisky, this "exceptional" bottling is almost becoming the norm. *46%. nc ncf.*

**Glencadam Aged 25 Years** db (95) n25 t24 f22 b24 Imagine the best-balanced team Mourinho ever produced for Chelsea. Well, it was never as good as this nose... *46%. nc ncf. 1,600 bottles.*

# GLENCRAIG
### Speyside, 1958. Chivas Brothers. Silent.

**Cadenhead's Single Malt Glencraig 31 Years Old** (92) n22.5 t23.5 f23 b23 Well done Cadenhead in coming up with one of the last surviving Glencraig casks on the planet. The feintiness shows why it was eventually done away with. But this is a malt with great distinction, too. *50.8%*

# GLENDRONACH
### Highlands, 1826. Brown-Forman. Working.

**GlenDronach 8 Year Old The Hielan** db (82) n20 t22 f20 b20. Intense malt. But doesn't quite feel as happy with the oil on show as it might. *43%*

**The GlenDronach 12 Years Old** db (92) n22 t24 f22.5 b23.5 An astonishingly beautiful malt despite the fact that a rogue sherry butt has come in under the radar. But for that, this would have been a mega scorer: potentially an award-winner. Fault or no fault, seriously worth discovering this bottling of this too long undiscovered great distillery *43%*

**The GlenDronach Aged 12 Years "Original"** db (86.5) n21 t22 f22 b21.5. One of the more bizarre moments of the year: thought I'd got this one mixed up with a German malt whisky I had tasted earlier in the day. There is a light drying tobacco feel to this and the exact same corresponding delivery on the palate. That German version is distilled in a different type of still; this is made in probably the most classic stillhouse on mainland Scotland. Good, enjoyable whisky. But I see a long debate with distillery owner Billy Walker on the near horizon, though it was in Allied's hands when this was produced. *43%*

**The GlenDronach Aged 18 Years "Allardice"** db (83.5) n19 t22 f21 b21.5. Huge fruit. But a long-running bitter edge to the toffee and raisin sits awkwardly on the palate. *46%*

**The GlenDronach Aged 18 Years Tawny Port Wood Finish** db (94.5) n23.5 t24 f23 b24 A malt with not just an excellent flavour profile but sits on the palate as comfortably as you might snuggle into an old Jag. *46%.*

**The GlenDronach Aged 21 Years Parliament** db (76) n23 t21.5 f15 b16.5 Red-hued, myopically one dimensional, rambles on and on, sulphur-tongued, bitter and does its best to leave a bad taste in the mouth while misrepresenting its magnificent land. Now, who does that remind me of...? *48%.*

◈ **The GlenDronach 25 Years Old** oloroso cask, cask no. GD#7434, dist 9 Jul 93 db **(94.5)** n23.5 t24 f23 b24 Had I any fireworks I would be setting them off outside now in celebration. I'm currently on my 1,058th whisky for the 2020 Bible and this is the first time I have tasted three sherry casks on the trot under 30-years-old that did not have a sulphur problem....and all Glendronach's. At least I don't think this has, though there is a very late, tantalising niggle. But I can forgive that because this is your archetypal fruitcake single malt, complete with burnt raisins and glazed cherries. Toasty, tingly and just wonderful... *54.2%. sc. Bottled for The Whisky Shop.*

◈ **The GlenDronach 25 Years Old** Pedro Ximénez cask, cask no. GD#5957, dist 21 May 93 db **(88.5)** n22 t22 f22.5 b22 I thought this may have been bottled for the Flat Earth Society. Because the PX, as PX has a very annoying tendency of doing, has made this very flat, indeed. Pleasant, for sure. But the usual peaks and troughs have been obliterated by the unforgiving thick sherry, though the busy spices shews there is still plenty of signs of life. Also some attractive sticky dates at the very finish. Oh, 100% sulphur-free, too! *55.6%. sc. Bottled for The Whisky Shop.*

◈ **The GlenDronach 26 Years Old** oloroso cask, cask no. GD#77, dist 15 May 92 db **(81)** n19 t22.5 f19 b20.5 Strangely musty, dull and, late on, tangy. *50.3%. sc. Bottled for The Whisky Shop.*

**GlenDronach Peated** db **(93.5)** n23.5 t23.5 f23 b23.5 I rarely mark the smoky whisky from a distillery which makes peat as an afterthought higher than its standard distillate. But here it is hard not to give massive marks. Only a failing cask at its death docks a point or so... *46%*

**The Duchess Glendronach 13 Year Old Virgin Oak** cask no. 1751, dist 14 Jan 03, bott May 16 **(94)** n23 t24 f23.5 b23.5 This virgin Duchess is a beauty. *53.9%. sc.*

**Scotch Malt Whisky Society Cask 96.14 11 Year Old** refill ex-bourbon barrel, dist 08 Jun 06 **(87)** n22 t21.5 f22 b21.5 A warming, semi-aggressive 'Dronach high on sharp, juicy malt but low on tact, patience and complexity. *57.1%. sc.*

◈ **The Whisky Shop Glendronach Aged 26 Years** sherry cask, cask no. 64, dist 1992 **(96)** n24 a once common aroma of mega-clean over-ripe, toasty sherry but in recent years rarer than British politicians trying notn to talk their country down...; t24.5 a Boris Johnson of a delivery: charming, highly amusing, full of vigour, determined, and knowing which way it is going... f23.5 ...and in this case it is along the path of sweet, unsullied delicious, spicy fruit; b24 from the creamed coffee school of drenched sherry butts. Not a single off note from this pre-Maastricht Treaty made barrel whatsoever. The kind of whisky that makes you proud to be British. *57.1%. sc. 493 bottles.*

# GLENDULLAN *(see also below)*
### Speyside, 1972. Diageo. Working.

**Glendullan Aged 8 Years** db **(89)** n20 t22 f24 b23. This is just how I like my Speysiders: young fresh and uplifting. A truly charming malt. *40%*

**Singleton of Glendullan 12 Years Old** db **(87)** n22 t22 f21 b22. Much more age than is comfortable for a 12-y-o. *40%*

**The Singleton of Glendullan 15 Years of Age** bott code: L7228DM001 db **(89.5)** n22 a gentle framework of vanilla, malt and toffee; t23 the sweetest delivery of any Glendullan I have tasted in some 40 years. A chink of malty light bursts through, then an explosion of intense molasses and fudge; f22.5 the fudge, once burnt, is now creamier; b22 mixed feelings. Designed for a very specific market, I suspect, and really impossible not to like. But would the real Glendullan with all its intrinsic Speyside characteristics please stand up. *40%.*

**The Singleton of Glendullan 18 Years of Age** bott code: L6186DM000 db **(89)** n23 decent mix of Demerara sugars, dates and walnuts: have a problem locating the malt; t22.5 a soft, sugary ultra-friendly delivery. A mix of red liquorice, light molasses and toffee; some welcome juiciness; f21.5 the big caramel I'm afraid puts the dull in Glendullan...; b22 a very pleasant if safe whisky where the real character of the malt is hard to unearth. *40%.*

**Singleton of Glendullan Liberty** db **(73)** n17 t19 f18 b19. For showing such a really unforgiving off key bitter furriness, it should be clamped in irons... *40% WB16/036*

**Singleton of Glendullan Trinity** db **(92.5)** n24 t23 f22.5 b23 Designed for airports, this complex little beauty deserves to fly off the shelves... *40% WB16/037*

◈ **Game of Thrones The Singleton of Glendullan House of Tully** db **(85.5)** n21 t22 f21 b21.5 Annoyingly, the distillery style is in little evidence here so overbearing is the fudge. Some spices whizz around to inject a degree of interest. But it's an OK but one-dimensional incarnation. *40%.*

**Gordon & MacPhail Connoisseurs Choice Glendullan 1993** refill American hogshead, cask no. 8339, dist 2 Sept 93, bott 22 Feb 18 **(95)** n23.5 t24 f23.5 b24 Nothing remotely dull about this Glendullan: this is a whisky story spanning 25 years brilliantly and vividly told. *56.6%. nc ncf sc. 171 bottles.*

**Simon Brown Traders Glendullan 2010** ex-bourbon cask, dist Oct 10, bott Feb 17 **(92.5)** n23 t23 f23.5 b23 A really gorgeous bottling that shows the shape of a whisky like a diaphanous dress of the early 1930s revealed the shape of the wearer. Just enough oak content to show depth as well as the spirit's integrity. A thin, teasing layer of smoke, too... 43%. nc ncf sc.

## GLEN ELGIN
**Speyside, 1900. Diageo. Working.**

**Glen Elgin Aged 12 Years** db (89) n23 t24 f20 b22. Absolutely murders Cragganmore as Diageo's top dog bottled Speysider. The marks would be several points further north if one didn't get the feeling that some caramel was weaving a derogatory spell. Brilliant stuff nonetheless. States Pot Still on label – not to be confused with Irish Pot Still. This is 100% malt... and it shows! 43%

**Glen Elgin 18 Year Old** ex-bodega European oak butts db (89) n23.5 a bit like honey-covered cornflakes, though with bite, an extra sprinkle of Demerara sugar spotted dog pudding still warm in the oven; t24 the complex, malt-rich sugar positively sparkle. More maple syrup now as the malt shows its gristy side; the fruit is happy to take a back seat; f19 a build-up of imperfect furry bitterness with the succulent malt and vanilla play out the long game; b22.5 before the bitterness kicks in, Speyside at its most subtly rich. 58.4%. 5,352 bottles. Diageo Special Releases 2017.

**Gordon & MacPhail Connoisseurs Choice Glen Elgin 1997** first fill sherry butt, cask no. 4331, dist 14 Oct 97, bott 20 Feb 18 (81.5) n20.5 t21 f19 b21 A pea-souper of a malt but somewhat tight, especially at the end. 55.7%. nc ncf sc. 602 bottles.

## GLENESK
**Highlands (Eastern), 1897–1985. Diageo. Demolished.**

**Gordon & MacPhail Rare Old Glenesk 1980** (95) n23.5 t24 f23.5 b24 What a charmer: better dead than when alive, some might argue. But this has weathered the passing three and half decades with ease and really does have something of an ice cream feel to it from beginning to the end...well I suppose the distillery was located close to the seaside...One of the most understated but beautiful lost distillery bottlings of the year. 46%.

## GLENFARCLAS
**Speyside, 1836. J&G Grant. Working.**

**Glenfarclas 8 Years Old** db (86) n21 t22 f22 b21. Less intense sherry allows the youth of this malt to stand out. Mildly quirky as a Glenfarclas and enormous entertainment. 40%

**Glenfarclas 10 Years Old** db (80) n19 t20 f22 b19. Always an enjoyable malt, but for some reason this version never seems to fire on all cylinders. There is a vague honey sheen which works well with the barley, but struggles for balance and the nose is a bit sweaty. Still has distinctly impressive elements but an odd fish. 40%

**Glenfarclas 12 Years Old** db (94) n23.5 a wonderfully fresh mix of grape and mint; t24 light, youthful, playful, mouthwatering. Less plodding honey, more vibrant Demerara and juiced-up butterscotch; f23 long, with soft almost ice-cream style vanillas with a grapey topping; b23.5 a superb re-working of an always trustworthy malt. This dramatic change in shape works a treat and suits the malt perfectly. What a sensational success!! 43%

**Glenfarclas 15 Years Old** db (85.5) n21.5 t23 f20 b21. One thing is for certain: working with sherry butts these days is a bit like working with ACME dynamite....you are never sure when it is about to blow up in your face. There is only minimal sulphur here, but enough to take the edge off a normally magnificent whisky, at the death. Instead it is now merely, in part, quite lovely. The talent at Glenfarclas is unquestionably among the highest in the industry: I'll be surprised to see the same weaknesses with the next bottling. 46%

**Glenfarclas 17 Years Old** db (93) n23 t23 f23 b24 an excellent age for this distillery, allowing just enough oak in to stir up the complexity. A stupendous addition to the range. 40%

**Glenfarclas 17 Years Old** db (94.5) n23.5 t24 f23 b24 When a malt is this delicate, it is surprising the difference that just 3% can make to the oils and keeping the structure together. A dram for those with a patient disposition. 43%.

**Glenfarclas 18 Years Old** db (84) n21 t22 f20 b21. Tight, nutty and full of crisp muscovado sugar. 43%. Travel Retail Exclusive.

**Glenfarclas 21 Years Old** db (83) n20 t23 f19 b21. A chorus of sweet, honied malt and mildly spiced, teasing fruit on the fabulous mouth arrival and middle compensates for the few blips. 43%

**Glenfarclas 25 Years Old** db (84) n20 t22 f20 b22. A curious old bat: by no means free from imperfect sherry but compensating with some staggering age – seemingly way beyond the 25-year statement. Enjoys the deportment of a doddering old classics master from a family of good means and breeding. 43%

**Glenfarclas 30 Years Old** db (85) n20 t22 f21 b22. Flawed yet juicy. 43%

**Glenfarclas 40 Years Old** db (95) n24.5 t23.5 f23 b24 A few moments ago an RAF plane flew low over my usually quiet cottage, violently shaking the windows, silencing my parrot and turning a great spotted woodpecker feeding in my garden to stone: it was too shocked to know whether to stay or fly. And I thought, immediately: Glenfarclas 40! For when, a long time ago now, John Grant paid me the extraordinary compliment of opening his very first bottle of Glenfarclas 40 so we could taste it together, a pair of RAF fighters chose that exact moment to roar feet above his distillery forcing the opened bottle from John's startled hands and onto the lush carpet...into which the initial measures galloopingly poured, rather than our waiting glasses. And it so happened I had a new sample to hand. So, with this whisky I made a fond toast: to John. And to the RAF. 43%

**Glenfarclas 40 Years Old** db (94) n23 t23 f24 b24 Couldn't help but laugh: this sample was sent by the guys at Glenfarclas after they spotted that I had last year called their disappointing 40-year-old a "freak". I think we have both proved a point... 46%

**Glenfarclas 50 Years Old** db (92) n24 t23 f22 b23 Most whiskies cannot survive such great age. This one really does bloom in the glass and the earthy, peaty aspect makes it all the more memorable. It has taken 50 years to reach this state. Give a glass of this at least an hour's inquisition, as I have. Your patience will be rewarded many times over. 44.4%

**Glenfarclas 50 Years Old** III ex-Oloroso sherry casks db (88.5) n23.5 t21 f22 b22 You can actually hear it wheezing as it has run out of puff. But it is easy to recognise the mark of an old champion... 41.1%. ncf. 937 bottles.

**Glenfarclas 105** db (95.5) n23.5 t24 f24 b24 I doubt if any restorative on the planet works quite as well as this one does. Or if any sherry cask whisky is so clean and full of the joys of Jerez. A classic malt which has upped a gear or two and has become exactly what it is: a whisky of pure brilliance... 60%

**Glenfarclas £511.19s.0d Family Reserve** db (88) n22.5 t22.5 f21 b22 Not the best, but this still ain't no two bob whisky, mister, and make no mistake... 43%

◈ **Glenfarclas The Family Casks 1977 W18 Release** 4th fill hogshead, cask no. 7281 db (92.5) n23 t23 f23 b23.5 Where you get the feeling that a cask like the 1979 is at its zenith, this chap, as delightful as it may be, has set off on its downward path. That said, it still has a long way to go on its descent, for the structure here is still sound and although the tannins perhaps have a little too much vinegar about its personality, the sugars and the intensity of the barley remains unbowed and delicious. Just love that little chocolate wafer finale... 44.6%. sc.

◈ **Glenfarclas The Family Casks 1978 W18 Release** 4th fill hogshead, cask no. 661 db (96) n24 t24.5 f23.5 b24 A malt which needs so much time to get to know and understand. Once you are captivated by the gooseberry nose, you stand no chance. And as bright and entrancing as the aroma may be, that is nothing compared to the complexity which unfolds on the palate. Not just in the flavours, but the textures, too. Insanely soft on delivery with an immediate move into sensual chocolate tones. Usually, that comes later, but not here. The malt for the woman of your life, first to enjoy her to seduce and/or be seduced by, and then to share together... 42.7%. sc.

◈ **Glenfarclas The Family Casks 1979 W18 Release** 4th fill hogshead, cask no. 2088 db (95.5) n23.5 t24 f24 b24 A polished charmer capable of sweeping the most discerning whisky lover off their feet. You know it's game on when the nose doesn't just waft any old exotic fruit at you, but a little extra passion fruit and lychee no less. So not surprises that these melt-in-the-mouth fruits become the main theme, even upping the juiciness as it develops. For a perfect ending you really want a delightful, lightly spiced vanilla and chocolate mix.... and guess what you get....! Superb. 48.4%. sc.

◈ **Glenfarclas The Family Casks 1980 W18 Release** refill hogshead, cask no. 1916 db (87.5) n22.5 t22 f21 b22 Walks with a stiff back and a creaking gait as the tannins strong-arms the malt into subservience. Some buttery barley does some important repair work. 43.3%. sc.

◈ **Glenfarclas The Family Casks 1981 W18 Release** refill hogshead, cask no. 1085 db (89) n22 t23 f21.5 b22.5 The little bit of wear and tear on the nose and delivery is countered by soft fruit and vanillas elsewhere. With having long ago reached the exotic fruit stage of its development, it is borderline salivating. But the tannins are always lapping at the dam wall waiting to find the breach... 43.2%. sc.

◈ **Glenfarclas The Family Casks 1982 W18 Release** 4th fill hogshead, cask no. 632 db (92) n22 t23 f23.5 b23.5 For a moment or two on delivery you wonder if tweezers are required to pick the splinters out of your tongue: certainly the big ancient oaky nose had put on you on full alert. But splendid heather honey comes riding to the rescue and tones down the tannins enough to make them both enjoyable and highly effective with their spices. A lovely praline finish fits well with the style. A malt which teeters on the edge for a moment or two, but there is a happy ending. 47.1%. sc.

⟐ **Glenfarclas The Family Casks 1983 W18 Release** refill hogshead, cask no. 28 db
**(94.5)** n23 t24.5 f23 b24 Someone has poured golden syrup over a hot cross bun. Except the
barley here has managed to escape to make a fleeting appearance before the lush sultanas
return. The odd moment on delivery borders on perfection, especially when the spices make
their short by mercurial play. *48.8%. sc.*

⟐ **Glenfarclas The Family Casks 1985 W18 Release** 4th fill hogshead, cask no. 2784 db
**(92)** n23 Fry's Turkish Delight...with oaky undertones; t23 despite the decent oak presence, it is
the softness of texture which stars here, not least with a big caramel flourish; glazed cherries
offers the fruit a juicy, sweet edge; f22.5 tame vanilla and cocoa; b23.5 a malt which looks more
concerned about holding itself together than providing a sweeping fruit and oak vista; *41.6%. sc.*

⟐ **Glenfarclas The Family Casks 1986 W18 Release** refill sherry butt, cask no. 4335 db
**(92)** n23.5 t24 f22 b22.5 If this is a refill, what was the sherry butt like when new...? This is
huge, putting me in mind of a sticky plum pudding I enjoyed in Fortnum and Mason over 20
years ago which buzzed with dark sugar and spice. A slight buzz of another kind on the late
finish is the only downside. *55%. sc.*

⟐ **Glenfarclas The Family Casks 1987 W18 Release** refill sherry butt, cask no. 3831 db
**(87)** n22 t22 f21.5 b21.5 Some might say silky and tannin-rich. Others might say flat and
overcooked. *46%. sc.*

⟐ **Glenfarclas The Family Casks 1988 W18 Release** refill sherry butt, cask no. 1374 db **(96)**
n24 prickly spice, including the lightest nutmeg, as well as diced walnut. The fruit is a distant
echo; t24.5 ah....where did that sweetness come from...? Dates and figs mix sumptuously with
plums and even a little over-ripe banana – the latter presumably representing a vanilla type
from the oak. The blend of bruyere and ulmo honey is not so much to die for, but actually
kill for...; f23.5 oh, that spice and molasses mix.... b24 One of the slightly drier Glenfarclases
which pops up from time to time, this one almost going off the complexometer. The perfect,
unblemished cask doing extraordinary things...and all of them beautiful. *49.2%. sc.*

⟐ **Glenfarclas The Family Casks 1989 W18 Release** sherry butt, cask no. 13010 db **(95.5)**
n23.5 an astonishing array of tannin notes filter through despite the depth of the fruit. Not just
any old fruit, but the kind of polished grape that makes you gasp in delight. Between the two,
a wonderful tale of good age and high quality sherry butt is written...; t24.5 incredible. Just
ridiculously wonderful. The softness of the mouth feel grabs your attention before the flavours
do. That is because it takes a few moments for the grape and tannin to form their stylish duet.
But once you do, it is impossible to take your eyes off them; a whisky to chew...and chew...and
chew...; f23.5 dries, becomes increasingly toasty and very slightly bitter; b24 not quite a perfect
butt, but it is very shapely and deserves to be bitten into.. *51.4%. sc.*

⟐ **Glenfarclas The Family Casks 1990 W18 Release** sherry butt, cask no. 5117 db **(89)**
n23 t23 f21 b22 I remember quite a few of these sherry butts doing the rounds in the early
1990s, absolutely packed to gunnels with thick, almost opaque grape. Always nosed better
than they tasted, and it is a case in point here with just a little too much bitterness towards
the death despite the late mocha intervention. *51.9%. sc.*

⟐ **Glenfarclas The Family Casks 1991 W18 Release** sherry butt, cask no. 5675 db **(91.5)**
n22 t24 f22.5 b23 If the colour doesn't scare you, then the grape will. Often malts displaying this
kind of one-dimensional nose turn out to be grape-infested bores. Not this bottling. While the
nose is too overwhelming for greatness, the unravelling of the sugars on the palate is as witty,
eloquent and erudite as a speech from the despatch box by Jacob Rees-Mogg. So many strains
of sweetness here, most muscovado-based, but also over-ripe greengages at molasses work.
Entirely sulphur free, this malt could qualify for old-fashioned entertainment tax. *56.6%. sc.*

⟐ **Glenfarclas The Family Casks 1992 W18 Release** 4th fill butt, cask no. 5984 db
**(86.5)** n22 t22 f21 b21.5 A degree of tiredness has crept into this, not normally evident
in Glenfarclas' great armoury. A tightness to the tannins amplifies the lack of development
from the fruit. *53.5%. sc.*

⟐ **Glenfarclas The Family Casks 1993 W18 Release** 4th fill butt, cask no. 4662 db
**(94)** n23.5 t23.5 f23 b24 The first Glenfarclas this year I have found shewing a degree of
bourbon character, especially on the nose where liquorice plays a confident and healthy part
of reminding you of this whisky's good age. However, it is the texture and mouth feel which
really blows you away with this, the barley itself still playing an important role in this context,
as well as the type of sugars which will work. Also in keeping the spices under control, though
they are never less than warming. A superbly paced dram, this, for intriguing little sub plots
and secret oaky passages. *56.8%. sc.*

⟐ **Glenfarclas The Family Casks 1994 W18 Release** refill sherry butt, cask no. 1581 db
**(91.5)** n21 t24 f23 b23.5 I'd be lying if I said I was impressed with the nose. Which makes
what comes next on the palate all the more amazing: the most intense marriage between
sultana and ulmo honey. You know spices are on their way, and they arrive in no great rush,

but build in harmonious intensity. But that honey never leaves the table, making this – to taste at least – an absolute gem of a bottling. 56.1%. sc.

 **Glenfarclas The Family Casks 1995 W18 Release** 4th fill butt, cask no. 9 db **(96)** n24 t24 f23.5 b24.5 A malt brimming with both confidence and grapey intent. The perfumed nose makes a mockery of a fourth use butt, as this is still radiating depth – though now of a distinct grape must kind – and becomes turbo charges in the honey department as a glossy fruitiness fills the mouth. Faultless, with not an atom of sulphur, and brilliantly integrated spicing. 52.1%. sc.

 **Glenfarclas The Family Casks 1996 W18 Release** 4th fill butt, cask no. 24 db **(94.5)** n22 t24.5 f23.5 b24.5 On nosing this you might be forgiven that you have been taken into a Jaguar showroom and shown an Audi: pleasant but a bit square and conventional. Only when you taste do you realise you are sitting in an F Type, all effervescence and power and unbelievable style, gripping your palate like the sports car hugs the road. Belt yourself in for this one...it is one delicious surprise ride... 58.9%. sc.

 **Glenfarclas The Family Casks 1997 W18 Release** refill sherry butt, cask no. 5134 db **(95)** n23.5 floral and deep: lavender on the wind; t24 a contradictory delivery, as though going in two different directions at one, but meet in the middle. The first note is dry, oak-led one. But that is immediately squared up to by an equally toasty molasses sweetness; f23.5 burnt Eccles cakes; b24 sublime. Glenfarclas doing what it does best: taking on an unusual fruity tour but with some fascinating diversions along the way. 57.1%. sc.

 **Glenfarclas The Family Casks 1998 W18 Release** 4th fill hogshead, cask no. 4455 db **(93.5)** n23.5 t23.5 f23 b23.5 A charming, black cherry accentuated bottling where the spices not only come out to play but act as the main focal point to the increasingly juicy body. Indeed, the intensity of the barley itself is quite superb. 54.8%. sc.

 **Glenfarclas The Family Casks 1999 W18 Release** refill butt, cask no. 7060 db **(85.5)** n21 t22 f21 b21.5 On the duller side of the 'Farclas family. But the light sulphur can't entirely see off the spice and minty cocoa. 56%. sc.

 **Glenfarclas The Family Casks 2000 W18 Release** refill sherry hogshead, cask no. 6395 db **(91)** n22.5 t23 f22.5 b23 Clean, rich grape offers a Swiss Roll-type fruity-creaminess. A quiet malt much more interested in subtlety rather than volume. The lingering muscovado sugars work well with the light liquorice finale. 56.1%. sc.

 **Glenfarclas The Family Casks 2001 W18 Release** refill hogshead, cask no. 3297 db **(92.5)** n22.5 t23.5 f23 b23.5 A spiky malt with the tannins not frightened to come out and give the taste buds a bit of a belligerent rap. The main theme, though, is all about glorious blend of malt and natural caramels. Loads of flavour to get your tongue round. 56.9%. sc.

 **Glenfarclas The Family Casks 2002 W18 Release** sherry butt, cask no. 3773 db **(93)** n23 t23.5 f23 b23.5 One of those outrageously booming sherry butts displaying so many esters and so much coffee, it is easy to mistake this for an old Demerara rum. 57.8%. sc.

 **Glenfarclas The Family Casks 2003 W18 Release** 4th fill butt, cask no. 1963 db **(94.5)** n23 t24 f23.5 b24 Not sure if Glenfarclas had a new still in around this time, or major work to an old one, but there appears to be lots of coppery richness in play here giving a further lustre to the already eye-watering barley. The light spice and French praline thread running through this malt also marks it out as something rather special. Not the usual Glenfarclas style, other than in its usual exceptionally high quality. 58.3%. sc.

# GLENFIDDICH
**Speyside, 1887. William Grant & Sons. Working.**

**Glenfiddich 12 Years Old** db **(85.5)** n21 t22 f21 b21.5. A malt now showing a bit of zap and spark. Even displays a flicker of attractive muscovado sugars. Simple, untaxing and safe. 40%

**Glenfiddich 12 Years Old Toasted Oak Reserve** db **(92.5)** n22.5 t23.5 f22.5 b24. Another bottling to confound the critics of Glenfiddich. This is as fine an essay in balance, charm and sophistication as you are likely to find in the whole of Speyside this year. Crack open a bottle... but only when you have a good hour to spend. 40%

**Glenfiddich Caoran Reserve Aged 12 Years** db **(89)** n22.5 t22 f21.5 b23. Has fizzed up a little in the last year or so with some salivating charm from the barley and a touch of cocoa from the oak. A complex little number. 40%

**Glenfiddich Rich Oak Over 14 Years Old** new American & new Spanish oak finish db **(90.5)** n23 t22 f23.5 b22. Delicious, thoughtful whisky and one to tick off on your journey of malt whisky discovery. Though a pity we don't see it at 46% and in full voluptuous nudity: you get the feeling that this would have been something really exceptional to conjure with. 40%.

**Glenfiddich 15 Years Old** db **(94.5)** n23 t23 f24.5 b24 If an award were to be given for the most consistently beautiful dram in Scotland, this would win more often than not. This under-rated distillery has won more friends with this masterpiece than probably any other brand. 40%

**Glenfiddich Aged 15 Years Cask Strength** db (85.5) n20 t23 f21 b21.5. Improved upon the surprisingly bland bottlings of old, especially on the fabulously juicy delivery. Still off the pace due to an annoying toffee-ness towards the middle and at the death. *51%*

**Glenfiddich Distillery Edition 15 Years Old** db (93.5) n24.5 t24 f22 b23. Had this exceptional whisky been able to maintain the pace through to the finish, this would have been a single malt of the year contender - at least. *51%. ncf.*

**The Glenfiddich Unique Solera Reserve Aged 15 Years** bott code: L2B 6562 db (95.5) n24.5 t24 f23 b24 Some aspects of this are as good as it gets in Scotch whisky. The nose and delivery are the stuff of a blender's wet dream. Memorable. *40% (80 proof) imported by Wm Grant & Sons New York.*

**Glenfiddich 18 Years Old** db (95) n23.5 t24.5 f23 b24 At the moment, the ace in the Glenfiddich pack. If this was bottled at 46%, unchillfiltered etc, I dread to think what the score might be... *40%*

**Glenfiddich Age Of Discovery Aged 19 Years Bourbon Cask Reserve** db (92) n23.5t24 f22 b22.5. For my money Glenfiddich turns from something quite workaday to a malt extraordinaire between the ages of 15 and 18. So, depending on the casks chosen, a year the other side of that golden age shouldn't make too much difference. The jury is still out on whether it was helped by being at 40%, which means the natural oils have been broken down somewhat, allowing the intensity and richness only an outside chance of fully forming. *40%*

**Glenfiddich Age Of Discovery Aged 19 Years Madeira Cask Finish** db (88.5) n22.5 t22.5 f21 b22.5. Oddly enough, almost a breakfast malt: it is uncommonly soft and light yet carries a real jam and marmalade character. *40%*

**Glenfiddich 21 Years Old** db (86) n21 t23 f21 b21. A much more uninhibited bottling with loads of fun as the mouth-watering barley comes rolling in. But still falls short on taking the hair-raisingly rich delivery forward and simply peters out. *40%*

**Glenfiddich 30 Years Old** db (93.5) n23 t23.5 f23.5 b23.5 a 'Fiddich which has changed its spots. Much more voluptuous than of old and happy to mine a grapey seam while digging at the sweeter bourbon elements for all it is worth. Just one less than magnificent butt away from near perfection and a certain Bible Award... *40%*

**Glenfiddich Rare Collection 40 Years Old** db (86.5) n22.5 t23 f20 b21. A quite different version to the last with the smoke having all but vanished, allowing the finish to show the full weight of its considerable age. The nose and delivery are superb, though. The barley sheen on arrival really deserves better support. *43.5%*

**Glenfiddich 50 Years Old** db (97) n25 t24 f24 b24 William Grant blender David Stewart, whom I rank above all other blenders on this planet, has known me long and well enough to realise that the surrounding hype, with this being the most expensive whisky ever bottled at £10,000 a go or a sobering £360 a pour, would bounce off me like a pebble from a boulder. "Honestly, David," he told my chief researcher with a timorous insistence, "please tell Jim I really think this isn't too oaky." He offered almost an apology for bringing into the world this 50-year-old babe. Well, as usual David Stewart, doyen of the blending lab and Ayr United season ticket holders, was absolutely spot on. And, as is his wont, he was rather understating his case. For the record, David, next time someone asks you how good this whisky is, just for once do away with the Ayeshire niceness instilled by generations of very nice members of the Stewart family and tell them: "Actually, it's bloody brilliant if I say so myself! And I don't give a rat's bollocks what Murray thinks." *46.1%*

**Glenfiddich Cask Collection Select Cask** db (78.5) n19 t22.5 f18 b19. Bourbon and wine casks may be married together...but they are on course for a messy divorce. The honeymoon on delivery is pretty rich and exotic. But it is all too short-lived as things soon turn pretty bitter. *40%*

**Glenfiddich Cask Collection Reserve Cask** db (83) n20 t22 f20 b21. Soft, chewy, occasionally sparkling but the overdose of toffee and a disappointing degree of late furriness means its speech is distinctly limited in its topic. *40% WB16/040*

**Glenfiddich IPA Experiment Experimental Series No 1** bott code: L34A4972141211 db (86) n21.5 t22.5 f21 b21 IPA and XX...all very Greene King brewery of the early 1980s... An IPA is, by definition, extra hopped in order to preserve the beer on a long journey (to India, originally). I can't say I am picking out hop here, exactly, unless it is responsible for the off-key bitter finale. Something is interfering with the navigation and after an attractive early malty blast on delivery everything goes a little bland. *43%.*

**Glenfiddich Malt Master's Edition** double matured in oak and sherry butts db (84) n21 t22 f20 b21. I would have preferred to have seen this double matured in bourbon barrels and bourbon barrels... The sherry has done this no great favours. *43%*

**Glenfiddich Millennium Vintage** dist 2000, bott 2012 db (83.5) n21.5 t22 f20 b20. Short and not very sweet. Good juicy delivery though, reminiscent of the much missed original old bottling. *40%*

**Glenfiddich Project XX Experimental Series No 2** bott code: L34B4041170207 db **(95.5)** n24 t24 f23.5 b24 "20 minds, one unexpected whisky" goes the blurb on the label. And, in fairness, they have a point. It has been a long time since I have encountered a distillery-produced malt this exceptionally well rounded and balanced. All 20 involved should take a bow: this is Glenfiddich as it should be...xxellent, in fact! 47%.

# GLEN GARIOCH
### Highlands (Eastern), 1798. Morrison Bowmore. Working.

**Glen Garioch 8 Years Old** db **(85.5)** n21 t22 f21 b21.5. A soft, gummy, malt – not something one would often write about a dram of this or any age from Geary! However, this may have something to do with the copious toffee which swamps the light fruits which try to emerge. 40%

**Glen Garioch 10 Years Old** db **(80)** n19 t22 f19 b20. Chunky and charming, this is a malt that once would have ripped your tonsils out. Much more sedate and even a touch of honey to the rich body. Toffeed at the finish. 40%

**Glen Garioch 12 Years Old** db **(88.5)** n22 t22 t23 f21.5 b22.A significant improvement on the complexity front. The return of the smoke after a while away was a surprise and treat. 43%

**Glen Garioch 12 Years Old** db **(88)** n22.5 t22.5 f21.5 b22. Sticks, broadly, to the winning course of the original 43% version, though here there is a fraction more toffee at the expense of the smoke. 48%. ncf.

**Glen Garioch 15 Years Old** db **(86.5)** n20.5 t22 f22 b22. In the a bottling I sampled last year the peat definitely vanished. Now it's back again, though in tiny, if entertaining, amounts. 43%

**Glen Garioch Aged 16 Years The Renaissance 2nd Chapter** bott code: L162292 db **(81)** n21 t23 f18 b19 For a wonderful moment, actually two: once on the nose and then again on the delivery, you think you are heading towards some kind of Sauternes-type magnificence...then it all goes wrong. Yes, there are fleeting moments of borderline perfection. But those dull, bitter notes have by far the bigger and longer say. Perhaps the biggest disappointment of the year... 51.4%.

**Glen Garioch 21 Years Old** db **(91)** n21 a few wood shavings interrupt the toasty barley; t23 really good bitter-sweet balance with honeycomb and butterscotch leading the line; pretty juicy, busy stuff; f24 dries as it should with some vague spices adding to the vanilla and hickory; b23 an entirely re-worked, now smokeless, malt that has little in common with its predecessors. Quite lovely, though. 43%

**Glen Garioch 30 Years Old** No. 503 dist 1987, bott 2017 db **(89)** n22.5 t23 f21.5 b22 This is from the exotic fruit school of ancient whiskies, the oak's tannin now out-manoeuvering the fruit. Perhaps moved on a little too far down a chalky, tannin-rich route though a little smoke does cushion the blow. Ancient, but still very attractive. 47.1%. Selected for CWS.

**Glen Garioch 1797 Founders Reserve** db **(87.5)** n21 t22 f22.5 b22. Impressively fruity and chewy: some serious flavour profiles in there. 48%

**Glen Garioch 1958** db **(90)** n24 t21 f23 b22. The distillery in its old smoky clothes: and quite splendid it looks! 43%. 328 bottles.

**Glen Garioch 1995** db **(86)** n21 t22 f21.5 b21.5. Typically noisy on the palate, even though the malty core is quite thin. Some big natural caramels, though. 55.3%. ncf.

**Glen Garioch 1997** db **(89)** n22 t22.5 f22 b22.5 had you tasted this malt as a 15-year-old back in 1997, you would have tasted something far removed from this, with a peaty bite ripping into the palate. To say this malt has evolved is an understatement. 56.5%. Whisky Shop Exclusive.

**Glen Garioch 1997** db **(89.5)** n22 t23 f22 b22.5. I have to say: I have long been a bit of a voice in the wilderness among whisky professionals as regards this distillery. This not so subtly muscled malt does my case no harm whatsoever. 56.7%. ncf.

**Glen Garioch 1998** db **(89.5)** n21 t23.5 f22.5 b23 with dates this good, a chocolate-loving, non-Islamic Tuareg will adore this one... one of the best flawed whiskies I have tasted in a while... 48% WB16/039

**Glen Garioch 2000 Bourbon Cask** db **(93.5)** n23 t24 f23 b23.5 The distance this malt has travelled from the days when it was lightly peated firewater is almost beyond measure. A bourbony delight of a Highland malt. 57.3%. ncf.

**Whiskyjace Glen Garioch 22 Years Old** sherry cask, dist 1994, bott 2016 **(90.5)** n23 t23 f22.5 b22 Perhaps the most warming single malt you will encounter this year: the searing spices should have a health warning. Be brave....be very brave... 55.4%. 20 bottles.

# GLENGLASSAUGH
### Speyside, 1875. Brown-Forman. Working.

**Glenglassaugh 30 Year Old** db **(87)** n22.5 t23 f20 b21.5. A gentle perambulation around soft fruitcake. Moist and nutty it still has a major job on its hands overcoming the enormity of the oak. The buzzing spices underline the oak involvement. Meek, charming though a touch furry on the finish. 44.8%

❖ **Glenglassaugh 40 Years Old** Pedro Ximénez cask, cask no. GG#3060, dist 8 Dec 78 db **(88.5)** n22.5 t22 f22 b22 Despite the best efforts of the molasses and life-giving PX cask, you can't help getting away from the feeling that here is one pretty exhausted malt. Both the nose and delivery in particular reveal oak tones more associated with a spent whisky. Yet it is still breathing and has energy enough to reveal a delicate complexity and grapey charm unbothered by sulphur. Then the late spices arrive like the 8th cavalry when all seems lost. It has hung on in there. Just! 46%. sc. Bottled for The Whisky Shop.

**Glenglassaugh Evolution** db **(85)** n21 t22 f21 b21. Cumbersome, oily and sweet, this youngster is still evolving. 50%.

**Glenglassaugh Revival** new, refill and Oloroso sherry casks db **(75)** n19 t20 f17 b19. Rule number one: if you are going to spend a lot of money to rebuild a distillery and make great whisky, then ensure you put the spirit into excellent oak. Which is why it is best avoiding present day sherry butts at all costs as the chances of running into sulphur is high. There is some stonkingly good malt included in this bottling, and the fabulous chocolate raisin is there to see. But I look forward to seeing a bottling from 100% ex-bourbon. 46%. nc ncf.

**Glenglassaugh Torfa** db **(90)** n23.5 not stinting on the phenols: the peat appears to have been shovelled into the furnace like a fireman feeding coals to the Flying Scotsman; **t22.5** crisp, sugary delivery with some meaningful smoke layering. Some Parma Violet candy nuzzles alongside the treacle-coconut; **f22** good phenolic grist fade; **b22** appears happy and well suited in its new smoky incarnation. 50%.

# GLENGOYNE

**Highlands (Southwest), 1833. Ian Macleod Distillers. Working.**

**Glengoyne 10 Years Old** db **(90)** n22 t23 f22 b23 Proof that to create balance you do not have to have peat at work. The secret is the intensity of barley intertwangling with oak. Not a single negative note from first to last and now a touch of oil and coffee has upped the intensity further. 40%

**Glengoyne 12 Years Old** db **(91.5)** n22.5 salty, sweet, lightly fruity; **t23** one of the softest deliveries on the market: the fruit, gristy sugars and malt combine to melt in the mouth: there is not a single hint of firmness; **f23** a graduation of spices and vanilla. Delicate and delightful...; **b23** the nose has a curiously intimate feel but the tasting experience is a wonderful surprise. 43%

**Glengoyne 12 Years Old Cask Strength** db **(79)** n18 t22 f19 b20. Not quite the happiest Glengoyne I've ever come across with the better notes compromised. 57.2%. nc ncf.

**Glengoyne 15 Years** sherry casks db **(81)** n19 t20 f21 b21. Brain-numbingly dull and heavily toffeed in style. Just don't get what is trying to be created here. Some late spices remind me I'm awake, but still the perfect dram to have before bed – simply to send you to sleep. Or maybe I just need to see a Doctor... 43%. nc. Ian Macleod Distillers.

**Glengoyne 17 Years Old** db **(86)** n21 t23 f21 b21. Some of the guys at Glengoyne think I'm nuts. They couldn't get their head around the 79 I gave it last time. And they will be shaking my neck not my hand when they see the score here...Vastly improved but there is an off sherry tang which points to a naughty butt or two somewhere. Elsewhere mouth-watering and at times fabulously intense. 43%

**Glengoyne 18 Years** first-fill sherry casks db **(82)** n22 t22 f18 b20. Bunches of lush grape on nose and delivery, where there is no shortage of caramel. But things go downhill once the dreaded "s" word kicks in. 43%. nc. Ian Macleod Distillers.

**Glengoyne 21 Years Old** db **(90)** n21 t22 f24 b23 A vastly improved dram where the caramel has vanished and the tastebuds are constantly assailed and questioned. A malt which builds in pace and passion to delivery a final, wonderful coup-de-grace. Moments of being quite cerebral stuff. 43%

**Glengoyne 21 Years Old Sherry Edition** db **(93)** n22 t24 f23 b24. The nose at first is not overly promising, but it settles as it warms and what follows on the palate is at times glorious. Few whiskies will match this for its bitter-sweet depth which is pure textbook. Glengoyne as few will have seen it before. 43%

**Glengoyne 25 Year Old** db **(95.5)** n24 t24.5 f22.5 b23.5 A beautiful sherry-matured malt from the pre-cock up sulphur days. Not a single off note of note and a reminder of what a sherry cask malt meant to those of us who were involved in whisky a quarter of a century ago... 48%

**Glengoyne 40 Years Old** db **(83)** n23 t21 f19 b20. Thick fruit intermittently pads around the nose and palate but the oak is pretty colossal. Apparent attempts to reinvigorate it appear to have backfired. 45.9%

**Gleann Mór Glengoyne Aged Over 21 Years** dist 1995 **(88)** n21.5 t22.5 f22 b22 The tannin really does have a big say and another year in cask might well have been one too many. But the malt, somehow never loses its structure or goal. Will divide opinion, but I certainly wouldn't turn down a second glass... 53%.

**Old Particular Glengoyne 20 Years Old** refill hogshead, cask no. 11629, dist Dec 96, bott Mar 17 **(90.5) n22.5 t23 f22.5 b22.5** A quiet dram which discusses the 20 passing years gently and with little beating of the chest. 50%. nc ncf sc. 287 bottles.

**Provenance Glengoyne Aged 10 Years** refill hogshead, cask no. 11754, dist Apr 07, bott May 17 **(87.5) n21 t22.5 f22 b22** The new makey nose is, thankfully, not quite matched by the beautiful clean barley which cascades over the taste buds. All kinds of barley sugar and thin honey in delightful evidence. 46%. nc ncf sc. 335 bottles.

**Provenance Glengoyne Aged 10 Years** refill hogshead, cask no. 12104, dist Apr 07, bott Sept 17 **(87) n20.5 t22 f22.5 b22** Very similar to cask 11754 above in its original malty outlook, except here some serious spice assembles from the mid-point onwards. 46%. nc ncf sc. 670 bottles.

⬦ **Scotch Malt Whisky Society Cask 123.31 10 Year Old** 1st fill ex-bourbon barrel, dist 29 Aug 08 **(95) n23 t24.5 f23.5 b24** It was on the basis of outstanding ex-bourbon malt like this that I recommended to the current owners that they should buy the distillery – which they duly went and did. Not the sulphured sherry cask nonsense that the previous owners had also filled. So wonderful to see a cask of Glengoyne as it should be: clean, dripping with intense malt and golden syrup and forming a beautiful shape on the palate with near perfect oils. Also, have to say that I think 10-years is the optimum age for this malt in the right bourbon cask as not only do you still feel the distillery itself, but it has the rare ability to form beautiful patterns with the natural sugars from the oak. A faultless blueprint to how this distillery should taste at the decade mark. 61.8%. sc.

# GLEN GRANT
**Speyside, 1840. Campari. Working.**

**Glen Grant** db **(87) n21.5 t23 f21 b21.5.** This is a collector's malt for the back label alone: truly one of the most bizarre I have ever seen. "James Grant, 'The Major'" it cheerfully chirrups, "was only 25 when he set about achieving his vision of a single malt with a clear colour. The unique flavour and appearance was due to the purifiers and the tall slender stills he designed and the decision to retain its natural colour..." Then underneath is written: "Farven Justeter Med Karamel/Mit Farbstoff'" Doh! Or, as they say in German: "Doh!" Need any more be said about the nonsense, the pure insanity, of adding colouring to whisky. 40%

**Glen Grant 5 Years Old** db **(89) n22.5 t22 f21.5 b23.** Elegant malt which has noticeably grown in stature and complexity of late. 40%

**Glen Grant Aged 10 Years** db **(96) n23.5 t24 f23.5 b24** Unquestionably the best official 10-y-o distillery bottling I have tasted from this distillery. Absolutely nails it! Oh, and had they bottled this at 46% abv and without the trimmings...my word! Might well have been a contender for Scotch of the Year. It won't be long before word finally gets around about just how bloody good this distillery is. 40%

**Glen Grant Aged 10 Years** db **(96) n24.5 t24 f23.5 b24** This is the new bottling purely for the UK market without, alas for a traditionalist like me, the famous, magnificent white label. The bottle design may not be a patch on the beautifully elegant one that had served the distillery with distinction for so long, but the malt effortlessly stands up to all scrutiny. The only difference between this and the original bottling available world-wide is a slight reduction in the work of the sugars, the muscovado ones in particular, and an upping in the green, grassy, sharper barley. Overall, this is a little drier yet slightly tarter, more reserved and stylish. My one and only regret is that it is not yet upped to 46% so the people of Britain could see a whisky, as I have so many times in the private and privileged enclave of my blending lab, as close to perfection as it comes... 40%.

⬦ **Glen Grant Aged 10 Years** bott code: LRO/GE01 db **(95.5) n24.5 t24 f23 b24** Perhaps slightly fatter than one or two other bottlings of GG10. But still bang on course with my previous observations, other than the finish not having quite the same sparkle. One of those whiskies which seems delicate and fragile, but at the same time big and robust. Just how does it do that....? 40%.

**Glen Grant Aged 12 Years** db **(95) n23.5 t24 f23.5 b24** Beautifully distilled, thoughtfully matured and deeply satisfying malt. 43%.

**Glen Grant Aged 12 Years** bott code. LRO/FE 03 db **(95) n24 t24 f23 b24** A slightly different slant to previous 12-year-olds but still within the expected and brilliant spectrum. Fabulous. 43%.

⬦ **Glen Grant Aged 12 Years** bott code: LRO/FK06 db **(94) n24 t23.5 f23 b23.5** Very similar to previous bottling, with no shortage of intensity. The only difference is a little less sweetness through the mid-range between delivery and finish and a slightly bigger caramel note, instead. 43%.

**Glen Grant Aged 12 Years Non Chill-Filtered** db **(91.5)** n23 t23 f22.5 b23 In so many ways speaks volumes about what non-filtration can do to one of the world's truly great distilleries... 48%. Exclusive to travel retail.

⟣ **Glen Grant Aged 12 Years** bott code: LRO/GC19 db **(94.5)** n23.5 light lychee and the most delicate barley grist; **t24** fizzes on delivery as the barley goes into salivation orbit. The vanillas and butterscotch arrive early, but so to the spices to ensure there is so much life! **f23** the spices still rumble, but, as you would expect from GG, the delicate nature of the barley, the mild honey notes and the kissing vanilla just makes you sigh...; **b24** that's much more like it: such balance, such dexterity...! The last time I sampled this, though delightful, it didn't quite yield the complexity I was expecting. This one is nearer expectation! 48%. ncf.

**Glen Grant Aged 15 Years Batch Strength 1st Edition** bott code. LRO/FG 21 db **(94)** n23.5 not sure a 15-year-old malt gets any more endearingly gentle than this: clean, but with a light milk chocolate attachment to the thoroughbred malt giving it an unmistakable Malteser candy effect; **t24** oh-my-word...If you think the nose is gentle, wait until you taste this. This is like a grist just melting on the tongue, spreading icing sugar in all directions, then ulmo honey and malted milk shake. A third the way in the spices arrive and with a plan, too...; **f23** just a fraction of bitterness from the oak, but the malt and ulmo honey soothe and kiss their way to the end; **b23.5** one of the maltiest malts of the year! Just a joy! 50%.

⟣ **Glen Grant Aged 15 Years Batch Strength 1st Edition** bott code: LRO/FG 19 db **(96.5)** n23.5 t24.5 f24 b24.5 When I saw this was also 1st Edition, I thought it was the same whisky as I tasted last time. Except with a different bottling code. However, although the early personality is near identical, it really does change on the finish where the bitterness has now been eradicated. This not only improves the score to the finish, but the overall balance and performance. The entire journey is now faultless; and journeys don't often come better than this. 50%.

**Glen Grant Aged 18 Years Rare Edition** db **(97)** n24.5 the hardest decision to make here: full marks or not. Actually, no: an even harder decision is trying to work out the leading forces behind this extraordinary nose. This is so in tune and well balanced it is impossible to nail exactly what leads and which follows. Instead, one is left mesmerised by the incredible brittleness of the barley, which seems to snap if you sniff slightly too hard; the sugars at once delicate and fruity yet with the crafted sharpness of a newly forged sword. And those tannins, somehow caught up in the overall firmness, the friability of it all. Has to be the essential Speyside nose...; **t24.5** oh, wow! When the barley does arrive this beautifully manicured, not a malty molecule out of place? The sugars are as clipped as a 1940's English actor's enunciation, and probably more precise. From somewhere light oils ooze to the surface to ensure some velvet caresses the sword. The oak builds up some steam, but the tannins never once outpoint the sugars and by the mid-ground, when a little cocoa can be detected, honours are even...; so complex it was on about the fifth go I realised just what a vital role those big early spices play; **f23.5** the firmness here is so complete, that I have only tasted whisky like this in commercially bottled form in pure Irish Pot still and rye, though here without the same intensity of spice you find in either. That said, the spices teasingly impact all the same....; **b24.5** the most crystalline, technically sublime Speysider I have tasted in a very long time... I didn't expect to find a better distillery bottled Glen Grant than their superlative 10-year-old. I was wrong... 43%.

**Glen Grant Aged 18 Years Rare Edition** bott code. LRO/EE04 db **(97)** n24.5 t24.5 f23.5 b24.5 See tasting notes to the Glen Grant 18 above. A different bottling, but not a single alteration in character, other than maybe just a fraction extra spice at the very end. Another Glen Grant knocking on the door of perfection. 43%.

⟣ **Glen Grant Aged 18 Years Rare Edition** bott code: LRO/EE03 db **(97)** n24.5 t24.5 f23.5 b24.5 So, I have chosen this as my 1,200th whisky of the 2020 Bible...which means I have tasted the last 1,000 whiskies on average at 15 samples a day, day in day out – analysing, re-analysing and describing - from morning to late evening virtually every single day without a break. Here I look for faults and weaknesses; changes, shifts of emphasis, a variation of pace as the flavours come through. And can find none. Well, maybe the vaguest hint of bitterness at the death. But this, as usual, is sublime. Though perhaps it does have two new challengers now: the Glen Grant 15 and the Glen Grant Chronicles. Didn't think it possible. But this distillery has just upped its game... 43%.

**Glen Grant 40 Year Old** db **(83.5)** n22.5 t21 f20 b20. Probably about ten summers too many. The nose threatens an oakfest, though there are enough peripheral sugars for balance and hope. Sadly, on the palate the cavalry never quite gets there.40%.

**Glen Grant 170th Anniversary** db **(89)** n23.5 t23.5 f20 b22. The odd mildly sulphured cask has slipped through the net here to reduce what was shaping to be something magnificent. Still enjoyable, though. 46%

**Glen Grant Five Decades** bott 2013 db **(92)** n24 the kind of aroma which leaves you transfixed: the trademark crisp, juicy barley is there in force, but the darker, deeper tones rumble with a spiced orange lead: sublimely complex; **t23.5** the delivery is full of the usual malty zest for life. There is a unique clarity to the barley of Glen Grant and here, on delivery and for a few a few moments after, this goes into overdrive. The mid ground is more muddled with tannin and burnt raisin making their presence felt; **f21.5** tangy marmalade; **b23** a nose and delivery of astonishing complexity. Hardly surprising the fade cannot keep up the pace. 46%

**Glen Grant The Major's Reserve** bott Mar 10 db **(85.5) n21.5 t23 f20 b21.** Forget about the so-so nose and finish. This is one of those drams that demands you melt into your chair on delivery, such is the fresh beauty of the malt and stunning honeycomb threads which tie themselves around every taste bud. Pity about the ultra dry, caramel-rich finish, but apparently nearly all the sherry butts have now been used up at the distillery. Thank gawd for that. 40%

◈ **Glen Grant Rothes Chronicles Cask Haven First Fill Casks** bott code: LRO/FG 26 db **(96) n24** just too delicate for words: lemon peel and malt form the core constituents, but we are talking fragile aromas here, though with body enough to keep the more intense notes of the vanillins at bay. Well, not that they needed much power to do that because the oak, like everything else moves on tip-toes...; **t24** heather honey and grist combine and then just melt...and melt...and melt...Playful spice, but nothing rowdy; **f23.5** still honey, though now with a creamy marzipan: surprising oils form late on to ensure the send-off is long and satisfying. Oh, and just like the nose and arrival....technically perfect with not a hint of an off note; **b24.5.** I think only Glen Grant can these days consistently come up with a nose which is unmistakably theirs, a malt which takes understatement to new levels. But when you look, really explore, then you sit there spellbound as its secrets slowly unfold. To give descriptors can barely do it justice, as the nose and delivery is poetry in itself. But, like a lover stripping, you are teased with one tantalising reveal after another. 46%.

**Fadandel.dk Glen Grant Aged 22 Years** bourbon barrel, cask no. 1802, dist 27 Jul 95, bott 26 Feb 18 **(95) n23.5 t24 f23.5 b24** It is as if every bottling of Glen Grant, even a single barrel, these days is a newly composed phrase by Beethoven.... 51.9%. sc. 24 bottles.

**The First Editions Glen Grant Aged 25 Years 1992** refill hogshead, cask no. 13358, bott 2017 **(92) n23 t23.5 f22.5 b23** Just an astonishing exhibition of flavoursome malt tones. 48.2%. nc ncf sc. 180 bottles.

◈ **Gordon & MacPhail Private Collection Glen Grant 1948** first fill sherry butt, cask no. 2154, dist 11 Jun 48, bott 19 Oct 18 **(95.5) n25 t23.5 f23 b24** There are no words really to describe the nose. It is 70 years old, but shews not the slightest sign of weakness. And because it comes from a time when sherry casks were entirely free from arrogance and stupidity, there was not even the remotest chance of picking up an off sulphur note. So this is a pristine aroma, taking us back to the earliest days after the war when an industry was just picking itself up from six years of hardship and international crisis and just getting back into its pre-war stride. Good oak would have been at a premium. So to find something this intact, and coming from sherry which had a crisp charm would have been a major achievement in itself. But because the cask was so clean, the wine so delicate we can now actually inspect the distillery itself...something that has been lost in the last 70 years, as most sherry casks (even if not riddled with sulphur) are so dense, the influence of the distillery is invisible. Not so here, for apparent is the sexiest degree of peat, which in itself is extraordinary. Because 70 years ago, and long before that, Speyside whisky came with a smoky hue. And here, like an insect preserved in prehistoric amber, we can see so visibly into the past it is as though we are there. To be honest, I don't really care what this whisky tastes like. Its nose alone is one of the most significant visions into the past I have seen in some 45 years of visiting distilleries and in over 20,000 whiskies tasted for the Whisky Bible. It is as though, just from this incredible nose, I have entered a time machine and returned to a long lost whisky world... 48.6%. sc. 210 bottles.

◈ **The Macphail 1949 China 70th Anniversary Glen Grant Special Edition 1** 1st fill sherry butt **(97) n24.5** the sweet nuttiness which immediately caresses the nose leaves you in no doubt: outstanding, old-fashioned sherry butt at work. The delicate underpinning by the oak unsurprisingly doesn't act as an extra weight but, rather, an accomplice as the complexity levels rise steadily and in relaxed fashion. A gentle fruit breeze drifts over the proceedings. As the malt warms, then so a light smokiness develops, and here at last we do have some extra weight, but a teasing sweetness also. Remarkably, truly amazingly given the extraordinary antiquity, this smoke falls directly into step with the fruit and tannin, offering the same tame level of intensity and complexity. Less an aroma: more of a miracle; **t24** the opening gambit is an oaky one, framed almost apologetically by nuanced grape. Not aggressively so, but confident and determined to make a statement. But this dominance is short lived as the smoke soon doubles up, offering both a light, cloudy smokiness which lifts the piece, and an earthier contribution to deepen the dungeon providing bickering spices; perhaps most astonishing (of the many astonishing things here) is a fragility but meaningful effect of the light layer of sugars which form a protective layer against the tannins − breathtaking...; **f24** long, with the remaining oils sporting the smoke and spices proudly, while the fruit quaintly sits astride both sweetness and dryness. Which leaves the tannins, a polite chalk and vanilla marriage, layered and happy to accommodate the other delicate forces at work; **b24.5** an improbable exhibition of elegance of complexity. How is such a whisky at such an age remotely possible....? 41.4%.

❖ **The Macphail 1949 China 70th Anniversary Glen Grant Special Edition 2** cask no. 3184, first fill sherry butt, dist 24 Nov 49, bott 2 Aug 17 **(96) n24** the elegance, purity and subtlety of the smoke is as surprising as it is delightful: an old-fashioned peatiness which drifts and settles with equal aplomb reminding me (at its warmest) of the oldest Taliskers of yesteryear, or (when cooler) even a well peated Speysider of ye olde school; though now softened by the mintiness of aged oak, once sharper edges worn and rounded by time. Slowly the phenols settle and the tannins, showing no sprightly bourbon-style character, celebrate their antiquity with a dry, parched leather aloofness, met by gentle layers of orange blossom honey; there is a secondary persona to this, too: a sultana-rich fellow of a lighter hue and offering a more delicate sweetness. Complex? Ridiculously, wonderfully so; **t24.5** such silk kissing the palate, the oils immediately sticking to the roof with a glossy embrace. Juicy, too, as the barley still chimes clearly here. Playful spices emerge almost immediately – from the tannin? From that layer of peat? Both? So beautifully intertwined is the spice with the unlikely heather-honey sweetness blossoming from deep, it is almost impossible to tell...or care! The tone of the spice changes at the midpoint from pulsing to busy and bitty, flickering around the tongue and roof of the mouth; **f23.5** a little milk chocolate develops in this surprisingly simplistic finale. The age of the drying oak is amplified here, as expected, though that persistent peat acts as a delicious muffler. Late on a hint of bourbon character builds as the tannins gather triumphantly. **b24** this is a full blown, gushing malt cocking-a-snook at its preposterous age, determined to reveal at every turn its lushness and vibrancy. The fruit plays more than a bit part, being the glue which holds this together, which the smoke both shocks and comforts. A real surprise package 41.7%.

**Scotch Malt Whisky Society Cask 9.128 24 Year Old** refill ex-bourbon cask, dist 16 Nov 92 **(96.5) n25 t24.5 f23 b24** Only Glen Grant could be responsible for this... 51.3%. sc.

**Scotch Malt Whisky Society Cask 9.140 24 Year Old** refill ex-bourbon cask, dist 16 Nov 92 **(95) n24 t23.5 f23.5 b24** Talk about peas from the same pod: rarely after 24 years in cask have I seen two casks as similar as SMWS's 9.128 and 9.140. But, just like twins, though they may have the same features and mannerisms, one may be heftier than the other. This is the bigger one. 51.4%. sc.

**The Single Cask Glen Grant 22 Years Old** cask no. 119461 **(92.5) n22.5 t23.5 f23 b23.5** Effortlessly elegant. 52%.

❖ **Wilson & Morgan Barrel Selection Glen Grant 25 Year Old** sherry finish, dist 1993, bott 2018 **(91.5) n23** plumptious plum and grape; **t23** fat on delivery with an immediate spice kick; muscovado sugar and plum jam on the follow through; **f23** we have learnt to expect the worst from sherry finishes as a whisky completes its journey: not such problems here. This is a faultless cask with the spices and boiled fruit candy living on for quite a while; **b22.5** very pleasant, and a spot on sherry cask at work. But perhaps a slight overkill in view of the quality of the malt which has vanished under the fruit... 54.3%.

# GLENGYLE
### Campbeltown, 2004. J&A Mitchell & Co. Working.

**Kilkerran 12 Year Old** db **(90.5) n22.5** very polite phenols offer a surprisingly fresh mintiness to the countenance. Wafer light body, and a wafer light caramel has been extracted from the genteel oak; **t23** despite the dozen years in cask, this still retains a degree of youth about it. But the malts are confident and take advantage of the overall lack of body to spread out and blossom; **f22.5** light, with a chocolate chip mint finale; **b22.5** a malt far more comfortable at this age than some of the previous, younger, bottlings from a few years back. Has a fragile feel to it and the air of a malt which must be treated gently and with respect. 46%

# GLEN KEITH
### Speyside, 1957. Chivas Brothers. Working (re-opened 14th June 2013).

**Glen Keith 10 Years Old** db **(80) n22 t21 f18 b19**. A malty if thin dram that finishes with a whimper after an impressively refreshing, grassy start. 43%

**The First Editions Glen Keith Aged 21 Years** sherry butt, cask no. 14986, bott 2018 **(87.5) n21 t23 f21.5 b22** A spicy guy which makes the most of the big malt and citrus theme. Just a fraction off key, alas, but plenty of storming, juicy moments to enjoy. 57.2%. nc ncf sc. 346 bottles.

❖ **Gordon & MacPhail Connoisseurs Choice Glen Keith Aged 24 Years** refill bourbon barrel, cask no. 111152, dist 21 Sept 93, bott 13 Sept 18 **(85) n21.5 t22 f20.5 b21** A busy malt which stretches its thin sugar reserves far. But the ending is rather too oak dominated. 49.3%. sc. 205 bottles.

⁂ **Kingsbury Gold Glen Keith 22 Year Old** hogshead, cask no. 171282, dist 1995 **(88)** n22 busy marzipan and oak; **t22** a brief barley thrust, even a thin veil of honey, then a slow drying – towards cocoa at first and then spiced vanilla; **f22** the cocoa ups its game; **b22** lives on the edge, but just enough honey to see off the encroaching tannins. Sophisticated. *50%. sc. 254 bottles.*

**Old Particular Glen Keith 21 Years Old** sherry butt, cask no. 12198, dist Aug 96, bott Nov 17 **(85.5)** n22 t21.5 f20 b21.5 Marked down not just because of odd off notes from the butt. But more because of the overall flatness of the personality. *51.5%. nc ncf sc. 261 bottles.*

**Whisky-Fässle Glen Keith 24 Year Old** barrel, dist 1993, bott 2017 **(90.5)** n23 t23 f22 b22.5 A very clean malt which revels in its delicate citrus persona. *476%.*

# GLENKINCHIE
**Lowlands, 1837. Diageo. Working.**

**Glenkinchie 12 Years Old** db **(85)** n19 t22.5 f21.5 b22. The last 'Kinchie 12 I encountered was beyond woeful. This is anything but. Still not firing on all cylinders and can definitely do better. But there is a fabulous vibrancy to this which nearly all the bottlings I have tasted in the last few years have sadly lacked. Impressive. *43%*

**Glenkinchie Aged 15 Years The Distillers Edition** Amontillado finished, dist 1992, bott 2007 db **(94)** n23.5 t24 f23 b23.5. Now this is absolutely top class wine cask finishing. One of my last whiskies of the night, and one to take home with me. Sophisticated, intelligent and classy. *46%*

**Glenkinchie 20 Years Old** db **(85.5)** n21 t22 f21.5 b21. When I sampled this, I thought: "hang on, haven't I tasted this one before?" When I checked with my tasting notes for one or two independents who bottled around this age a year or two ago, I found they were nigh identical to what I was going to say here. Well, you can't say it's not a consistent dram. The battle of the citrus-barley against the welling oak is a rich and entertaining one. *58.4%*

**Glenkinchie Aged 24 Years** dist 1991 db **(95)** n24 t24 f23 b24 The old managers at Glenkinchie a generation ago felt their malt didn't quite have the body to become a big aged malt. At the time – roughly about the time this was made – you could see why from the evidence of the fragile 12-years-old. This, though, reveals the distillery in a new light and I'd love to see those responsible for making this aware of joyous fruits of their labours. *57.2%. 5,928 bottles. Diageo Special Releases 2016.*

**Glenkinchie 1992 The Manager's Choice** db **(78)** n19 t22 f18 b19. Has a lot going for it on delivery with a barley explosion which rocks you back in your chair and has you salivating like a rabies victim. But the rest of it is just too off key. *58.1%. Diageo.*

**Glenkinchie The Distillers Edition** Amontillado cask-wood, dist 2005, bott 2017, bott code: L7222CM000 db **(91.5)** n23 t23.5 f21.5 b23 Now that is one very elegant whisky. *43%.*

# THE GLENLIVET
**Speyside, 1824. Chivas Brothers. Working.**

**The Glenlivet 12 Years of Age** bott 2017/03/30 db **(92.5)** n23 t23 f23 b23.5 Probably the best Glenlivet 12 I have tasted for quite a while...lucky Americans! An extra few percentage points of first fill bourbon cask has gone a long way here. Excellent and satisfying. *40% (80 proof)*

**The Glenlivet Aged 12 Years** db **(79.5)** n22 t21 f18 b18.5. Wonderful nose and very early development but then flattens out towards the kind of caramel finish you just wouldn't traditionally associate with this malt, and further weakened by a bitter, furry finale. *40%*

**The Glenlivet Aged 12 Years Old First Fill Matured** db **(91)** n22.5 t22.5 f23 b23. A quite wonderful whisky, far truer to The Glenlivet than the standard 12 and one which every malt whisky lover should try once in their journey through the amber stuff. Forget the tasting notes on the bottle, which bear little relation to what is inside. A gem of a dram. *40%*

**The Glenlivet Excellence 12 Year Old** db **(87)** n22 t21.5 f22 b21.5. Low key but very clean. The emphasis is on delicate. *40%. Visitor Centre and Asian exclusive.*

**The Glenlivet 15 Years of Age** db **(80)** n19 t21 f20 b20.Undeniable charm to the countless waves of malt and oak. But don't expect much in the way of complexity or charisma. *40%*

**The Glenlivet Aged 18 Years** bott Feb 10 db **(91)** n22 t23.5 f23 b23 A hugely improved bottling seriously worth discovering in this form. Appears to have thrown off its old shackles and offers up an intensity that leaves you giving a little groan of pleasure. *43%*

**The Glenlivet 18 Years of Age** bott code 2017/02/02 LKPL0386 db **(83.5)** n22 t22 f19 b20.5 This is a rather flat version of a usually rich malt. Has the odd honey-charmed moment and the spices aren't hiding, either. But way too much caramel has turned the usual undulations on the palate to something of pancake proportions. A little furry at the death, also. *43%.*

**The Glenlivet Alpha** db **(92)** n23.5 t24 f21.5 b23. You get the feeling some people have worked very hard at creating a multi-toned, complex creature celebrating the distillery's position at the centre of Speyside. They have succeeded. Just a cask selection or two away from a potential major Bible award. Maybe for the next bottling.... 50%

**The Glenlivet Archive 21 Years of Age** batch no. 0513M db **(95.5)** n24 t24 f23.5 b24 Less archive and more achieve. For getting so many honey tones to work together without it getting overly sweet or syrupy really is a major achievement. 43%

**The Glenlivet Captain's Reserve** finished in Cognac casks db **(89.5)** n22 t23 f22 b22.5 A laid-back malt playing games being simultaneously spicy and super-soft. 40%.

**The Glenlivet Cipher** db **(96.5)** n24.5 t24 f23.5 b24.5 It has taken over half an hour to distil these tasting notes into something that will fit the book: we have more new entries than normal and I'm running out of room. This is the last entry this year, however, will compare to this. 78%

**The Glenlivet Conglass 14** db **(92.5)** n22 t23 f23.5 b24 A joyous barley and high quality oak interplay: probably what this distillery does best of all. 59.8% WB16/043

◈ **The Glenlivet Distiller's Reserve** bott code: 2019/04/01 db **(87)** n21.5 t22 f21.5 b22 A soft, rotund malt designed to give minimum offence... and succeeds. Unless you are offended by the overstating of the caramels. 40%.

**The Glenlivet Founder's Reserve** db **(78.5)** n20 t21.5 f18 b19. Really can't believe what a shy and passionless whisky this is (not to mention flawed). The strength gives the game away slightly as to where the malt is positioned. But I had hoped for a little more than malty tokenism. 40%

**The Glenlivet Founder's Reserve** bott code: 2017/04/04 LCPL 0591 db **(88.5)** n23 t22 f21.5 b22 Anyone who can remember the less than impressive start to this brand will be pretty amazed at just how deliciously approachable it is now. 40%.

**The Glenlivet French Oak Reserve 15 Years of Age** Limousin oak casks db **(91)** n22.5 t23 f22.5 b23. I have to say that after tasting nearly 800 cask strength whiskies, to come across something at the ancient 40% is a shock to the system. My taste buds say merci... And, what is more, a bottle of this shall remain in my dining room for guests. Having, a lifetime ago, lived with a wonderful French girl for three years I suspect I know how her country folk will regard that... Oh, and forgive a personal message to a literary friend: Bobby-Ann...keep a bottle of this beside the Ancient Age... 40%

**The Glenlivet 15 Years of Age French Oak Reserve** bott code: 2016/12/19 LCPK 2465 db **(93)** n23.5 t23 f23 b23.5 Many years ago when this first came out it wasn't very good, to be honest. Then it was re-shaped, upped a gear and became a very enjoyable dram, indeed. Now, having apparently been steered on a slightly different course again, it is just excellent... An expression that has evolved slowly but quite beautifully. 40%.

**The Glenlivet The Guardians' Chapter** db **(81.5)** n20 t21 f20 b20.5. Read the chapter – but can make neither head nor tail of it. A brief moment of honeyed enjoyment. But nothing else really adds up. Just doesn't gel. 48.7%. WB15/120

**The Glenlivet The Master Distiller's Reserve** bott code: 2016/10/04 LCPK 1866 db **(86.5)** n22.5 t22 f20.5 b21 It is a shame the malty sparkle on the nose and delivery isn't matched by what follows. A pleasant, safe dram. But too toffee-rich and doesn't develop as this great distillery should. 40%.

**The Glenlivet The Master Distiller's Reserve Small Batch** batch no. 9378/006 db **(93)** n23.5 t24 f22.5 b23.5 By far the best Master Distillers Reserve in Glenlivet's armoury. 40%

**The Glenlivet The Master Distiller's Reserve Solera Vatted** bott code: 2017/03/01 LCPL 0371 db **(89.5)** n22.5 t23 f22 b22 Pretty much in line with the 2015 bottling above, except there is slightly more caramel here shaving the top off the higher notes. 40%.

◈ **The Glenlivet White Oak Reserve** bott code: 2019/03/01 db **(89)** n23 one of the most spicy official Glenlivets I have ever encountered on the nose with the tannins nipping and nibbling to fascinating effect; t23 a delivery of pure velvet with malt and vanilla in total harmony; a little too much toffee at the mid-point, though the spices are still bubbling; f21 a tad too dull as caramel takes command; b22 starts promisingly but fades dramatically on the toffee. 40%.

◈ **Gordon & MacPhail Connoisseurs Choice Glenlivet Aged 15 Years** first fill bourbon barrel, cask no. 800772, dist 5 Nov 02, bott 6 Sept 18 **(94)** n23.5 t23.5 f23 b24 A beautifully structured malt, abounding in oily barley and absorbing the top rate tannins with no difficulty whatsoever. The theme is intense malt all the way, until some gorgeous cocoa tones leach into the story late on. Exemplary. 58.4%. sc. 200 bottles.

◈ **Gordon & MacPhail Private Collection Glenlivet 1954** refill sherry butt, cask no. 1412, dist 15 Apr 54, bott 27 Apr 18 **(95)** n24 t24 f23 b24 Another ancient malt which, despite coming from a sherry butt, has no difficulty proving that Glenlivet whisky was once a whole lot smokier than it is today. Indeed, this cask has withstood the test of time quite magnificently and still possesses crisp malt in its armoury to get the taste buds flowing. 41%. sc. 222 bottles.

**The Whisky Barrel Glenlivet 11 Year Old 2006** 1st fill sherry hogshead, cask no. 900552, dist 30 May 06, bott 25 Aug 17 **(92.5)** n22.5 t23.5 f22.5 b23.5 If you think of Glenlivet as this little gentle old distillery in the heart of Speyside responsible for gentle old malts, then think again. This is a prize bull of a dram. And it's snorting in your glass... 63.5%. nc ncf sc. 316 bottles. Bottled by Signatory Vintage.

# GLENLOCHY
**Highlands (Western), 1898–1983. Diageo. Closed.**

**Gordon & MacPhail Rare Old Glenlochy 1979 (95)** n23.5 t24 f23.5 b24 it has been many years since a bottle from this long lost distillery turned up and that was such a classic, I can remember every nuance of it even now. This shows far greater age, but the way with which the malt takes it in its stride will become the stuff of legend. I held back on tasting this until today, August 2nd 2013, because my lad David this afternoon moved into the first home he has bought, with new wife Rachael and little Abi. It is near Fort William, the remote west coast Highland town in which this whisky was made, and where David will be teaching next year. His first job after moving in, though, will be to continue editing this book, for he worked on the Whisky Bible for a number of editions as researcher and editor over the years. So I can think of no better way of wishing David a happy life in his new home than by toasting him with what turned out to be a stunningly beautiful malt from one of the rarest of all the lost distilleries which, by strange coincidence, was first put up for sale exactly 100 years ago. So, to David, Rachael & little Abigail... your new home! And this time I swallowed..46%. ncf.

# GLENLOSSIE
**Speyside, 1876. Diageo. Working.**

**Cadenhead's Single Cask International Glenlossie 23 Years Old** dist 1993 **(95.5)** n23.5 t24.5 f23 b24.5 Hard to imagine a malt more glassy as it slides effortlessly and seemingly without friction around the palate...Magnificent! 56.8%. sc. 175th Anniversary bottling.

⊰◈⊱ **Gleann Mór Glenlossie Aged Over 24 Years (90.5)** n23 t23.5 f22 b22 The ginger and allspice nose leaves you in no doubt that the oak has gouged its way into this malt. The delivery and follow though confirms it. Yet one of those nick of time bottlings, where another summer or two might have been too much. That said, absolutely nothing wrong with the delivery which takes peppery heather honey to the outer limits. 55.6%.

**Gordon & MacPhail Cask Strength Glenlossie 2008** cask no. 6775, bott 11 Jul 17 **(83.5)** n20 t21.5 f21 b21 At times appears to have all the right attributes. But from the dim nose onwards, things fail to gel. Very hit and miss and un-Lossie-like. 61.7%. sc.

**Hepburn's Choice Glenlossie 9 Years Old** refill hogshead, dist 2007, bott 2017 **(84.5)** n21.5 t21 f21 b21 Grassy, simple but very flat textured. 46%. nc ncf sc. 375 bottles.

**Kingsbury Gold Glenlossie 20 Years Old** hogshead, cask no. 2059, dist 1997 **(93)** n23 t23.5 f23 b23.5 Lossie ladelling out the honey and malt in just about equal dollops. Just lovely! 55.1%. 255 bottles.

**Old Particular Glenlossie 19 Years Old** refill hogshead, cask no. 12017, dist Nov 97, bott Aug 17 **(93.5)** n24 t23.5 f22.5 b23.5 If you ever wondered why I think this is a great distillery, grab a glass of this... 50.9%. nc ncf sc. 140 bottles.

**Scotch Malt Whisky Society Cask 46.55 24 Year Old** refill ex-bourbon barrel, dist 16 Nov 92 **(90.5)** n23 t22 f23 b22.5 Big oak means this malt is hanging on a bit at times but comes through beautifully in the end. 52.7%. sc.

⊰◈⊱ **Scotch Malt Whisky Society Cask 46.72 25 Year Old** refill ex-bourbon hogshead, dist 16 Nov 92 **(93)** n22.5 almost like the first strike in the mash tun, as the barley emerges sweet, sharp and desirable; a little oaky vanilla adds bite; t23.5 a sparkling arrival on the palate with the barley sugar on full salivating mode; a spectacular melt-on-the-mouth silky quality is met by balancing spice; f23 here the age starts to mount: tasty, toasty tannin: drying, spicing up and firm; b24 Glen Glossy would be more apt... 53.8%. sc.

**The Whisky Embassy Glenlossie Aged 20 Years** cask no. 6766, dist 20 Nov 97, bott 24 Nov 17 **(87.5)** n22 t22.5 f21 b22 A little ulmo honey and marzipan counters the muscular, dry oak. Some lovely hickory presence as the odd bourbon note seeps through. 51.7%. nc ncf sc.

# GLEN MHOR
**Highlands (Northern), 1892–1983. Diageo. Demolished.**

**Glen Mhor 1976 Rare Malt** db **(92.5)** n23 t24 f22 b23.5. You just dream of truly great whisky sitting in your glass from time to time. But you don't expect it, especially from such an old cask. This was the best example from this distillery I've tasted in 30 years...until the Glenkeir version was unleashed! If you ever want to see a scotch that has stretched the use of oak as far it will go without detriment, here it is. What a pity the distillery has gone because the Mhor the merrier... 52.2%

# GLENMORANGIE
### Highlands (Northern), 1843. Glenmorangie Plc. Working.

**Glenmorangie 10 Years Old** db (94) n24 t22 f24 b24 You might find the occasional "orange variant", where the extra degree of oak, usually from a few too many first-fill casks, has flattened out the more extreme peaks and toughs of complexity (scores about 89). But these are pretty rare – almost a collector's item – and overall this remains one of the great single malts: a whisky of uncompromising aesthetic beauty from the first enigmatic whiff to the last teasing and tantalising gulp. Complexity at its most complex. *40%*

**Glenmorangie 15 Years Old** db (90.5) n23 chunky and fruity: something distinctly sugar candy about this one; the barley's no slouch, either; and, just to raise the eyebrows, just the faintest waft of something smoky...; t23 silky, a tad sultry, and serious interplay between oak and barley; a real, satisfying juiciness to this one; f22 dries towards the oaky side of things, but just a faint squeeze of liquorice adds extra weight; b22.5 exudes quality. *43%*

**Glenmorangie 15 Years Old Sauternes Wood Finish** db (68) n16 t18 f17 b17. I had hoped – and expected – an improvement on the sulphured version I came across last time. Oh, whisky! Why are you such a cruel mistress...? *46%*

**Glenmorangie 18 Years Old** db (91) n22 pleasant if unconvincing spotted dick; t23 sharp, eye-watering mix of fruit and mainly honeyed barley; nutty and, with the confident vanillas, forming a breakfast cereal completeness; f23 Cocoa Krispies; b23 having thrown off some previous gremlins, now a perfect start to the day whisky... *43%*

**Glenmorangie 19 Year Old** db (94) n24 light fruit ensures an ethereal feel totally making a mockery of nearly two decades in the cask: fresh, subtle and sophisticated; t23.5 the most brittle and vulnerable malt I have experienced from this distillery. Every note is gossamer thin, the grist can fracture any moment; the delicate fruit shatter into millions of pieces if you chew too hard...bitters...? f22.5 yes, a slight bitter notes creeps in briefly. But it creeps out again as the light gooseberry and lighter barley notes play their game of peek-a-boo...; b24 fruity or malty...? I can't decide...but then I don't think for a moment that you're supposed to be able to... *43%*

**Glenmorangie 25 Years Old** db (95.5) n24 t24 f23.5 b24 Every bit as statesmanlike and elegant as a whisky of this age from such a blinding distillery should be. Ticks every single box for a 25-year-old and is Morangie's most improved malt by the distance of Tain to Wellingborough. There is a hint of genius with each unfolding wave of flavours with this one: a whisky that will go in 99/100 whisky lover's top 50 malts of all time. And that includes the Peatheads. *43%*

**Glenmorangie 30 Years Old** db (72) n17 t18 f19 b18. From the evidence in the glass the jury is out on whether it has been spruced up a little in a poor sherry cask – and spruce is the operative word: lots of pine on this wrinkly. *44.1%*

**Glenmorangie Vintage 1975** db (89) n23 t23 f21 b22. A charming, fruity and beautifully spiced oldie. *43%*

**Glenmorangie Allta** db (89) n22.5 t23 f21.5 b22 This is a very different 'Morangie: the Allta, could well be for Alternative. Because while the distillery is rightly famed for its cask innovation, there is no barrel style I can think of on the planet which can shape the malt in this unique way. So either grain or yeast is the deciding factor here – perhaps a mixture of both (and you can rule out water!). My money is on yeast, as the only ever time I've come across something quite like this was in a lab in Kentucky with some experimental stuff. The perfect Glenmorangie to confuse your friends by... *51.2%*.

**Glenmorangie Artisan Casks** db (93) n23 t23.5 f23 b23.5. If whisky could be sexed, this would be a woman. Every time I encounter Morangie Artisan, it pops up with a new look, a different perfume. And mood. It appears not to be able to make up its mind. But does it know how to pout, seduce and win your heart...? Oh yes. *46%*

**Glenmorangie Astar** db (93) n24 t23.5 f22 b23.5 Astar has moved a long way from the first bottling which left me scratching my head. This is one of the maltiest of all their range, though the lightness of touch means that any bitterness can be too easily detected. *52.5%*.

**Glenmorangie Bacalta** db (87) n22 t22.5 f21 b21.5. Unusually for a Glenmorangie the narrative is muffled and indistinct. Has some lovely moments, but a bit sharp and lacking in places. *46%*

**Glenmorangie Cadboll** db (86.5) n21 t23.5 f20.5 b21.5 Every year a challenging new breed of Glenmorangie appears to be thrown into the mix, as though to fully test the taste buds. This is this year's offering: different again, with neither the nose nor finish quite up to par with the outstanding delivery – indeed, the finale is pretty bitter, indeed. But the texture and intensity of the barley on arrival is borderline brilliant, as is the most wonderful caramel which frames it with a buttery sweetness. *43.1%*

**Glenmorangie Cellar 13 Ten Years Old** db (88.5) n22 t22.5 f22 b22 Oh, if only I could lose weight as efficiently as this appears to have done... oh, I have! My love and thanks to Nancy, Nigel and Ann Marie. *43%*

**Glenmorangie Companta** Clos de Tart & Rasteau casks, dist 27 Jan 99, bott 14 Nov 13 db **(74) n17 t20 f18 b19.** "I don't think you'll be a fan of this one, Jim" said the Glenmorangie blender to me, letting me know the sample was on its way. How right he was. Have to say there is some breath-taking fruit to be had before the sulphur does its worst. *46%. ncf.*

**Glenmorangie Dornoch** db **(94) n23.5 t23 f23.5 b24** A rare Glenmorangie which this time does not put the emphasis on fruit or oak influence. But this appears to concentrate on the malt itself, taking it through a routine which reveals as many angles and facets as it can possibly conjure. Even if the casks are from a central warehouse, at times a seascape has been created by a light salty influence – so befitting the whisky's name. A real treat. *43%*

**Glenmorangie Ealanta 1993 Vintage** db **(97.5) n24 t24 f24.5 b25** When is a bourbon not a bourbon? When it is a Scotch single malt...And here we have potentially the World Whisky of the Year. Free from the embarrassing nonsense which passes for today's sherry butt, and undamaged by less than careful after use care of second-hand bourbon casks, we see what happens when the more telling aspects of oak, the business end which gives bourbon that extra edge, blends with the some of the very finest malt made in Scotland. Something approaching one of the best whiskies of my lifetime is the result... *46%*

**Glenmorangie Elegance** db **(92) n22** quite herbal and soothing; **t24** the thinnest layer of icing sugar coats the silk-soft malt; every bit as gentle as the nose suggests, **f22** medium to short with some attractive rolling vanilla; **b24** a surprise package that is not entirely dissimilar to the Golden Rum, only a tad sweeter. *43%*

**Glemorangie Finealta** db **(84.5) n21 t22 f20.5 b21.** Plump and thick, one of the creamiest malts around. For what it lacks in fine detail it makes up for in effect, especially the perky oaky spices. *46%*

◇ **Glenmorangie Global Travel Retail 12 Year Old** db **(89.5) n22** a fat, spicy nose with dates and molasses obliterating the usual delicate barley; **t23** and its full on brown sugars deliver, also. Alost syrupy in its countenance, it slowly quietens towards a toasty fudge and mocha middle; **f22** so much caramel. Dark and weighty with lots of chewability until late into the day; **b22.5** heavy duty Morangie with subtlety and dexterity giving way to full on flavour with a cream toffee mouth feel. *43%*.

◇ **Glenmorangie Global Travel Retail 14 Year Old** db **(84) n22 t22 f19 b21** A pretty straightforward offering by Morangie's normally complex standards but let down by the late furry bitterness on the finish. *43%*.

◇ **Glenmorangie Global Travel Retail 16 Year Old** db **(94.5) n23.5** imagine Glenmorangie with all its malty and orangey qualities. Then add the most subtle, sexy, phenols....and there you go...! **t23.5** the trademark mouth feel of mixed softness and confident rigidity is there in spade-loads, but again that soft phenolic note rumbles through to give extra base and, counter intuitively, sweetness, too; serious spices begin to ghost into the mid-point; **f23.5** the controlled extra dryness as the maltier sweet notes play out as to the sophistication; **b24** I particularly love this as the distillery in question is never in doubt: had "Glenmorangie" running through it like a stick of Blackpool rock. Despite the light phenols... *43%*.

**Glenmorangie Grand Vintage Malt 1989** db **(94) n23.5 t23.5 f23 b24** A stunning, silky blend of a single malt where the flavour profile – and even texture - has obviously been sculpted. As much a work of art as a dram... *43.1%*.

**Glenmorangie Grand Vintage Malt 1990** db **(94) n24 t24 f22.5 b23.5** Grand by name, grand by nature...almost. For a malt this outstandingly good, it really should have been at 46% minimum... *43%*

**Glenmorangie Grand Vintage 1991** db **(94.5) n23.5 t24 f23 b24** Some years back – indeed, at around the time this whisky was distilled - I was reliably informed by the blender at Glenmorangie that his whisky was not designed for this kind of great age, hence it was bottled at 10 and, at a push and with sherried sticking plaster and grapey crutches, at 18. This has passed 25 years with no apparent damage and with seemingly many more years still left on the clock. How times have changed... *43%*.

**Glenmorangie Grand Vintage 1993** db **(95.5) n24 t24 f23.5 b24.5** I have known their blender Bill Lumsden long enough to know that he doesn't like to play safely or by the book: if he can bowl a googly (throw a curve ball to our friends Stateside) he will. I'm not exactly sure what he's done with this, but whatever it was I'll be happy for him to do it again. By the way, Bill, if you are reading this: I'd create this by selecting some 1991 casks that are well passed their sell by date and kicking out some salty tannin and reinvigorating them with others that are still juicy and younger than their years. It's a hard trick to pull off, because you have to get the percentages almost exactly spot on (there may be a 3% give either way to hit the required balance), but Dr. Lumsden is one of only a handful of blenders able to pull off the manoeuvre without crashing. *43%*.

◇ **Glenmorangie Grand Vintage 1995** db (89) n23 shews its age with a light tomato character which slightly thins the otherwise broad oak; t23 a layered delivery. Despite the natural caramels arriving early and in force. The tannins have an early muscovado edge, but soon the vanillas arrive; f21 just a little too tangy; b22 some 40 years ago Glenmorangie was never considered a candidate for whiskies aged 21 and over. Not now. This holds together well...until the dying moments. 43%.

◇ **Glenmorangie Grand Vintage 1996** db (95) n23.5 crunchy, crisp sugars capture the malt fresh and youthful as though in aspic; t24 profoundly salivating. Like malt sets off fermentation, icing sugars sets off the barley-rich juiciness to the maximum level...and the mid-point? Hard to believe, but here you hit malt max...! f23.5 not sure it is possible to get better balance between oak and malt in a Highland whisky. Light mocha and liquorice. But a sub-strata of creamy Horlicks, too...; b24 principally has a firm, glazed feel to this. But he intensity of the malt takes the breath away. Too beautiful... 43%.

**Glenmorangie Lasanta** sherry casks db (68.5) n16 t19 f16 b17.5. The sherry problem has increased dramatically rather than being solved. 46%

**Glenmorangie Lasanta Aged 12 Years** sherry cask finish db (93) n23.5 t24 f22 b23.5 A delightful surprise: every bottling of Lasanta I'd ever tasted had been sulphur ruined. But this new 12-y-o incarnation has got off to a flying start. Although a little bit of a niggle on the finish, I can live with that in the present climate. Here's to a faultless second bottling... 43%

**Glenmorangie Legends The Duthac** db (91.5) n23.5 t23.5 f21.5 b23 Not spoken to their blender, Bill Lumsden, about this one. But he's been busy on this, though not so busy as to get rid of the unwelcome you-know-what from the wine casks. Educated guess: some kind of finish involving virgin oak, or at least first fill bourbon, and sherry, probably PX on account of the intensity of the crisp sugar. 43%. ncf.

**Glenmorangie Madeira Wood Finish** db (78) n19.5 t20.5 f19 b19. One of the real problems with wine finishes is getting the point of balance right when the fruit, barley and oak are in harmony. Here it is on a par with me singing in the shower, though frankly my aroma would be a notch or two up. 43%

**Glenmorangie Margaux Cask Finish** db (88) n22 t22 f22 b22. Even taking every whisky with an open mind, I admit this was better than my subconscious might have considered. Certainly better than the near undrinkable Ch. Margaux '57 I used to bring out for my birthday each year some 20-odd years ago... 46%

**Glenmorangie Milsean** db (94) n23 t23.5 f23.5 b24 A quite beautiful malt which goes out of its way to put the orangey in 'Morangie... 46%

◇ **Glenmorangie Nectar D'Or** db (94.5) n23.5 the soft orange blossom honey merges beautifully with the clean barley; a vague polished leather gives an extra sparkle; t24 the delivery is all about velvety sweetness holding just enough oak to keep the balance true. Heather honey ensures a waxy extra sweetness to the barley; f23 dries elegantly with a delightful chalky oakiness; b24 I was told that this was different to the last Nectar D'or as it has no age statement. To be honest, I was never aware that it had! But it doesn't matter: it is always about the blending of the malt styles from the distillery and the pursuit of balance. And what I have said about this whisky before still perfectly sums it up: an exercise in outrageously good sweet-dry balancing... 46%.

**Glenmorangie Nectar D'or Sauternes Finish** db (94) n23 t24 f23 b24 Great to see French casks that actually complement a whisky – so rare! This has replaced the Madeira finish. But there are some similar sweet-fruit characteristics. An exercise in outrageously good sweet-dry balancing. 46%

**Glenmorangie Private Edition 9 Spios** db (95.5) n23 t24.5 f23.5 b24.5 Glenmorangie displaying countless layers of brilliance. Breathtakingly beautiful. 46%.

◇ **Glenmorangie Quinta Ruban 14 Year Old** db (87) n22 t22 f21 b22 Something of the sweet shop about this with the sugary fruitiness. But doesn't quite develop in structure beyond its simple – though thoroughly attractive – early confines. 46%.

**Glenmorangie Quinta Ruban Port Finish** db (92) n24 t23 f22 b23 This replacement of the original Port finish shows a genuine understanding of the importance of grape-oak balance. Both are portrayed with clarity and confidence. This is a form of cask finishing that has progressed from experimentation to certainty. 46%

**Glenmorangie Sherry Wood Finish** db (84) n23 t21 f20 b20. Stupendous clean sherry nose, then disappoints with a somewhat bland display on the palate. 43%

**Glenmorangie Signet** db (80.5) n20 t21.5 f19 b20. A great whisky holed below the waterline by oak of unsatisfactory quality. Tragic. 46%. Travel Retail Exclusive.

**Glenmorangie Sonnalta PX** db (96.5) n24 t24 f24.5 b24 Remains a giant among the tall stills. A mesmeric whisky... 46%

**Glenmorangie Taghta** db (92) n23 t23 f23 b23 A curious Glenmorangie which, unusually, appears not to be trying to make a statement or force a point. This is an old Sunday afternoon film of a dram: an old-fashioned black and whitie, (home grown and not an Ealing, or Bogie or Edward G Robinson) where, whether we have seen it before or not, we know pretty much what is going to happen, in a reassuring kind of a way... 46%

**Glenmorangie Tarlogan** db (95) n24 t24 f22.5 b23.5 Interesting. I have just tasted three new Dalmore. Identical colour and some very similar toffeed characteristics. I allowed a whisky-loving visitor to taste them, without telling him what they were. He could barely tell them apart. Here, I have three new Glenmorangies. All of a different hue. I may not like them all; we will see. But at least I know there will be remarkable differences between them. This fabulous malt radiates the countryside in a way few drams have done before. As refreshing as an early morning dip in a Scottish pond... 43%

**Glenmorangie Traditional** db (90.5) n22 orange blossom, barley sugar and chalk dust; t23 delicate delivery revelling in gentle complexity: really playful young-ish malt makes for a clean start and middle; f22.5 soft mocha notes play out a quiet finish; b23 an improved dram with much more to say, but does so quietly. 57.1%

**Glenmorangie Tayne** db (87.5) n21 t22.5 f22 b22 Tangy back story. But also a curious early combination between butterscotch and Werther's Original candy. The malt – topped with a splash of double cream - in the centre ground, though, is the star showing. 43%. *Travel Retail Exclusive.*

**Glenmorangie Tùsail Private Edition** db (92) n24.5 t23 f21.5 b23 Doesn't quite live up to the nose. But that would have been a big ask! From the Understated School of Glenmorangie.46%. ncf.

⟐ **Fadandel.dk Westport Glenmorangie Aged 11 Years** refill hogshead, finished in a 1st fill oloroso cask, dist 25 Sept 07, bott 11 Mar 19 (86) n21.5 t22 f21 b21.5 Not one of those sherry casks that can kill a whisky from a thousand paces. But just enough on it to take the sparkle out the nose, follow through and finish. Plenty still to enjoy, even if the fruit and intense barley are not quite in sync. The brief clarity of the malt on delivery, though, is something to celebrate. 56.2%. sc. 272 bottles.

**Scotch Malt Whisky Society Cask 125.74 11 Year Old** 1st fill ex-bourbon barrel, dist 07 Aug 05 (94.5) n23 t23.5 f24 b24 Glenchocolatie. 57.9%. sc.

# GLEN MORAY

**Speyside, 1897. La Martiniquaise. Working.**

**Glen Moray Classic 8 Years Old** db (86) n20 t22 f21 b23. A vast improvement on previous bottlings with the sluggish fatness replaced by a thinner, barley-rich, slightly sweeter and more precise mouthfeel. 40%

**Glen Moray 10 Years Old Chardonnay Matured** db (73.5) n18.5 t19 f18 b18. Tighter than a wine cork. 40%

**Glen Moray 12 Years Old** db (90) n22.5 t22 f23 b22.5 I have always regarded this as the measuring stick by which all other malty and clean Speysiders should be tried and tested. It is still a fabulous whisky, full of malty intricacies. Something has fallen off the edge, perhaps, but minutely so. Still think a trick or two is being missed by bottling this at 40%: the natural timbre of this malt demands 46% and no less.... 40%

**Glen Moray 16 Years Old** db (74) n19 t19 f18 b19. A serious dip in form. Drab. 40%

**Glen Moray 20 Years Old** db (80) n22 t22 f18 b18. With so much natural cream toffee, it is hard to believe that this has so many years on it. After a quick, refreshing start it pans out, if anything, a little dull. 40%

**Glen Moray Aged 25 Years** Port Cask Finish dist 1988 db (88) n23 t22.5 f20.5 b22 Thought I'd celebrate Andy Murray's second Wimbledon victory, which he completed just a few minutes ago, by having another go at a Glen Moray 25-year-old (Moray is pronounced Murray). I remember last time being slightly disappointed with this expression. Well this later bottling is a little better, but nowhere near the brilliance Murray displayed in gaining revenge for Canada last year getting World Whisky of the Year. Curiously, if this is a 25-year-old and was distilled in 1988, then presumably it was bottled in 2013...the first time Murray won Wimbledon!43%

**Glen Moray 25 Year Old Port Cask Finish** batch 2 db (95) n23.5 t23.5 f24 b24 Some quite first rate port pipes are involved here. Absolutely clean as a whistle and without any form of off-note. A distillery I have a very soft spot for showing very unusual depth – and age. Brilliant. 43%. 3295 bottles.

**Glen Moray Aged 25 Years Portwood Finish Rare Vintage Limited Edition** bott code. 3153, dist 1986 db (87.5) n22.5 t22 f21 b22. Just get the feeling that the Port pipe has not quite added what was desired. 43%

**Glen Moray Aged 25 Years Port Cask Finish** dist 1988, bott code L709759A 2017/04/07 db (94) n23 t23.5 f23.5 b24 A lovely intense malt where the Port casks leave big fruity fingerprints at every turn. 43%.

**Glen Moray 30 Years Old** db **(92.5)** n23.5 it's probably the deftness of the old-fashioned Speyside smoke in tandem with the structured fruits that makes this so special; **t23.5** for a light Speysider, the degree of barley to oak is remarkable: soft, oil-gilded barley is met by a wonderful, if brief, spice prickle; **f22.5** deft layering of vanilla and cocoa; a sprinkle of muscovado sugar repels any darker oak notes; **b23** for all its years, this is comfortable malt, untroubled by time. There is no mistaking quality. *43%*

**Glen Moray 1984** db **(83)** n20 t22 f20 b21. Mouthwatering and incredibly refreshing malt for its age. *40%*

**Glen Moray 1989** db **(86)** n23 t22 f20 b21. Doesn't quite live up to the fruit smoothie nose but I'm being a little picky here. *40%*

**Glen Moray Bourbon Cask 1994** cask no. 42/0, bott code. 25/04/17 170635 db **(93.5)** n23.5 **t23.5 f23 b23.5** For most people in England Glen Moray is a highly productive goalscorer for Brighton. But it would be great if the world woke up to just what lovely whisky can come from this much under-rated distillery. *56.4%. sc.*

**Glen Moray Classic** db **(86.5)** n22 t21.5 f21.5 b21.5. The nose is the star with a wonderful, clean barley-fruit tandem, but what follows cannot quite match its sure-footed wit. *40%*

**Glen Moray Classic Port Cask Finish** db **(89.5)** n21 t21.5 f23.5 b23.5 A malt which has to somehow work its way to the exit...and finally does so with supreme confidence and a touch of class along the way... *40%*

**Glen Moray Elgin Classic Chardonnay Cask Finish** db **(73)** n19 t19 f17 b18. Juicy. But sulphur-dulled. *40%*

**Glen Moray Elgin Classic Sherry Cask Finish** db **(85)** n21 t22 f20.5 b21.5. Must be a cream sherry, because this is one exceptionally creamy malt. A bit of a late sulphur tang wipes off a few marks, but the delicious grapey positives outweigh the negatives. *40%*

**Glen Moray Elgin Heritage Aged 15 Years** db **(74)** n19 t20 f17 b18. Dulled by some poor, sulphur-laden sherry butts. Glen Moray is one of the maltiest drams on God's earth and at its most evocative in ex-bourbon. Who needs sherry? *40%*

**Glen Moray Elgin Heritage Aged 18 Years** db **(94)** n23.5 t24 f23 b23.5 Absolutely true to the Glen Moray style. Superb. *47%*

⟡ **Glen Moray Fired Oak Aged 10 Years** db **(90)** n22.5 such an attractive blend of mint humbugs and chocolate limes; **t23** the delivery is an impressive layering of alternating oaky vanilla and simplistic barley tones; juicy yet with a fabulous underlying dryness; **f22** a little feeble as the vanilla takes control a tad too easily. Some faint barley sugar persists alongside gentle spices; **b22.5** very attractive. But missing a trick at 40%: it is needing the extra oils to ramp up intensity and take into another dimension. *40%*.

**Glen Moray Mastery** db **(89.5)** n23.5 t22.5 f21.5 b22 Has an expensive feel to this, to be honest. But, though a huge GM fan, have to say that for all its very clean, attractive, unblemished fruit; for all its juiciness I'm afraid it's just a little bit too one-dimensional. No doubting its charm and elegance, however. *52.3%*.

**Glen Moray Peated Classic** db **(87.5)** n21.5 t22.5 f21.5 b22. Really never thought I'd see this distillery, once the quintessential Speyside unpeated dram, gone all smoky... A little bit of a work in progress. And a minor word to the wise to their blenders: by reducing to 40% you've broken up the oils a shade – but tellingly - too much, which can be crucial in peaty whiskies. Up to 46% next bottling and I think you'll find things fall into place – and not apart... Some minor erotic moments, though, especially on the fourth or fifth beats, when the sugars and smoked vanilla do work well together. Too fleeting, though. *40%*

**Glen Moray Sherry Cask Finish 1994** cask no. 904/57, bott code. 25/04/17 170636 db **(92)** n23.5 t23 f22 b23.5 Old-fashioned, traditional dry oloroso influence in its most resounding form. A must find malt for those looking to broaden their positive whisky experiences.*56.7%. sc.*

⟡ **Demijohn Glen Moray 10 Years Old** **(95)** n23 malted milk biscuit with a light Demerara sugar topping; **t24** succulent, salty barley at home with both spices and heather honey: mouth-watering beyond belief and offering a rare, faultless intensity; **f24** fabulous oils keep both the vibrant spices and honey going but now the vanillas and butterscotch enter the fray. Where before the flavours were sharp and attention seeking, now everything is more pastel-shaded and complex, especially the waxiness to the honey and intricate layering of the oak; **b24** one of those rare whiskies which just gets better as it goes along. What a great cask in action here...! *56.4%*.

**The First Editions Glen Moray Aged 21 Years 1995** refill hogshead, cask no. 12831, bott 2016 **(93)** n23.5 t23 f23 b23.5 An unusual Glen Moray, as this contains its usual big malt character, but everything seems encased in a sugar outer shell. Fabulous. *51.9%. nc ncf sc. 102 bottles.*

⟡ **Glenwill Glen Moray 1990** hogshead, cask no. 7626 **(94)** n23 delicate tannins offer a warming fizz to the rich barley; **t23.5** usually chocolate notes arrive late in the day: here they are first up alongside the hints of heather honey and trimmed, warming tannins; the malt reconfigures to spread out through the mid-ground; **f23.5** the chocolate remains, now intertwangling with the intensifying barley; **b24** always heart-warming when a distillery which long ago thought itself incapable of producing fine, big-aged whiskies does exactly that. A little touch of ermine to a noble dram. *52.4%. 234 bottles. Matisse Spirits Company.*

**Hepburn's Choice Glen Moray 10 Years Old** refill barrel, dist 2007, bott 2018 **(91.5) n22.5 t23 f23 b23** Nails the distillery succinctly. A lovely little treat of a dram. *46%. nc ncf sc. 372 bottles.*

◇ **Liquid Treasures Glen Moray 10 Year Old** sherry hogshead, dist 2008, bott 2019 **(89) n23** a busy, lilting aroma where the fruit comes through as a hint only, but there is quite a nip to the freshly carved oak: unusual; **t23** eye-wateringly sharp on delivery. A major mixture of ulmo honey and tannin which somehow appears to really lift the intensity of the malt in the third and fourth flavour waves; creamy mocha towards the middle; **f21** just goes off piste with a little too much tang; **b22** not quite an entirely flawless hoggy at work. But the delivery is stupendous! *59.2%. sc. 134 bottles.*

**Old Particular Glen Moray 25 Years Old** refill hogshead, cask no. 11831, dist Oct 91, bott Jun 17 **(96.5) n24.5 t24 f23.5 b24.5** A malt which even an old pro like me finds very difficult to spit. Mesmerizingly beautiful. *51.5%. nc ncf sc. 247 bottles.*

◇ **The Whisky Chamber Glen Moray 11 Years Old 2007** bourbon cask **(89.5) n22.5** malt. Barley...; **t23** massive, salivating barley which, improbably, intensifies rather than diminishes; **f22** some token vanilla – amid a slightly spicy sea of barley; **b22** a typical Glen Moray Maltfest! *58.4%. sc.*

**The Whisky Chamber Glen Moray 12 Years Old 2005** sherry refill hogshead **(82.5) n21 t21.5 f19 b21** A shockingly tart malt which puckers the taste buds to previously unknown levels. That said, no particularly offensive sulphur at work (well, maybe not until the very end), so the fruit does get a chance to shine. But not for the feint-hearted. *55.2%. sc.*

# GLEN ORD
### Highlands (Northern), 1838. Diageo. Working.

**Glen Ord Aged 12 Years** db **(81) n20 t23 f18 b20.** Just when you thought it safe to go back...for a while Diageo ditched the sherry-style Ord. It has returned. Better than some years ago, when it was an unhappy shadow of its once-great self, but without the sparkle of the vaguely-smoked bottling of a year or two back. Nothing wrong with the rich arrival, but the finish is a mess. I'll open the next bottling with trepidation... *43%*

**The Singleton of Glen Ord Aged 15 Years** European & American oak casks, bott code: L8038DM003 db **(90.5) n23 t23.5 f21.5 b22.5** The fun of the label on many a bottle of whisky is just how far removed the described tasting notes are to what is actually poured from the bottle. Here, there are no quibbles from me: the promised ginger and chocolate come true! *40%.*

**Glen Ord 25 Years Old** dist 1978 db **(95) n24 t24 f23 b24.** Stupendous vatting here: cask selection at its very highest to display Ord in all its magnificence. *58.3%*

**Glen Ord 28 Years Old** db **(90) n22 t23 f22 b23.** This is mega whisky showing slight traces of sap, especially on the nose, but otherwise a concentrate of many of the qualities I remember from this distillery before it was bottled in a much ruined form. Blisteringly beautiful. *58.3%*

**Glen Ord 30 Years Old** db **(87) n22 t21 f23 b21.** Creaking with oak, but such is the polish to the barley some serious class is on show. *58.8%*

**Singleton of Glen Ord 12 Years Old** db **(89) n22.5 t22.5 f22 b22** A fabulous improvement on the last bottling I encountered. Still possesses blood oranges to die for, but greatly enhanced by some sublime spices and a magnificent juiciness. *40%*

◇ **The Singleton of Glen Ord 14 Year Old** db **(95.5) n23.5** such a clever nose! A bitty one, with flakes of barley, honey and peat flying around like chips off a sculptor's stone...; **t24.5** maximum flavour explosion. Just sit back and take in myriad honey tones – heather honey and ulmo at the lead – sharpened by eye-watering barley and warmed by layers of contrasting spices; the weight of a malt and pace of flavour release just doesn't get better than this masterpiece; **f23.5** long, still with a spice glow, but the honey doesn't flinch and finally gives way to mocha – and a light ember of phenol...; **b24** sheer quality. The distillery revealed in all its astonishing complexity. *576%. Diageo Special Releases 2018.*

**Singleton of Glen Ord 32 Year Old** db **(91) n23.5 t23 f22 b22.5.** Delicious. But if ever a malt has screamed out to be at 46%, this is it. *40%*

**Old Particular Glen Ord 13 Years Old** refill hogshead, cask no. 12060, dist Sept 94, bott Sept 17 **(90) n23 t22.5 f22 b22.5** An obviously well-made malt showing exceptionally fine structure. *48.4%. nc ncf sc. 312 bottles.*

◇ **Scotch Malt Whisky Society Cask 77.47 10 Year Old** second fill fine grain French oak hogshead, dist 7 Aug 07 **(89) n22** salty and stripped oak cupboards; **t23.5** sweetness at last on delivery: a little orange blossom honey melts into the intense barley which in turn goes into full salivating mode as spices kick in; **f21.5** lots of natural caramels calm the fire; **b22** wow! That is one very short whisky: unusual for an Ordie. One minute the dram is raging at you, the next minute it's a fast asleep puppy. *59.2%. sc.*

# GLENROTHES
**Speyside, 1878. Edrington. Working.**

◈◈◈ **The Glenrothes 10 Years Old** sherry seasoned oak casks db **(80.5)** n19 t22.5 f19 b20 Neither a nose or finish I much care for: tight, a little tangy and out of sync. But I certainly approve the delivery which shows no such constraints and celebrates the voluptuousness of its maltiness. *40%. nc. The Soleo Collection.*

◈◈◈ **The Glenrothes 12 Years Old** sherry seasoned oak casks db **(68)** n17 t19 f15 b17 Sulphur addled. *40%. nc. The Soleo Collection.*

◈◈◈ **The Glenrothes 18 Years Old** sherry seasoned oak casks db **(87)** n22 t22.5 f21 b21.5 Nutty and hefty, there is always a slight tang to this which slightly reduces the intricate nature of the barley. The off-key finish confirms not all is well, but this being the truly brilliant distillery it is, an inner depth of barley and ulmo honey ensures there always something to treasure from this dram. *43%. nc. The Soleo Collection.*

◈◈◈ **The Glenrothes 25 Years Old** sherry seasoned oak casks db **(86)** n23 t22 f19.5 b21.5 The nose is the star turn here, shewing some of the complexity you might demand of a 25-year-old malt. The adroitness of the barley ripe Chinese gooseberry is particularly alluring. But after a surprisingly malt delivery and a volley of pleasant sultana, it is the finish (again) which reveals a furry weak link. *43%. nc. The Soleo Collection.*

◈◈◈ **The Glenrothes Whisky Maker's Cut** first fill sherry seasoned oak casks db **(95)** n23.5 a semi-simplistic nose of happy, dry oloroso dominating in fruitiness, but delighted to let in the sharply tannin-rich oak; **t23.5** ah...! No faulting that at all...! A sublime burst of rounded grape, sweetened marginally by the odd busy significant strand of molasses; spices move into position early on; **f24** even late on there is an attractive salivating element to this, but the late sherry trifle, enriched with chocolate source, is deeply attractive; **b24** unspoiled casks at work. An absolute must for sherry cask lovers. *48.8%. nc. The Soleo Collection.*

◈◈◈ **The Cooper's Choice Glenrothes 1997 19 Years Old** Jurancon finish **(91)** n22.5 a vaguely phenolic note fits beautifully with the lightly sweetened Cape Gooseberry; t23 alluringly malt from the get-go. The secondary fruitiness seems to emphasise the juiciness of the malt itself; f22.5 pleasing spice to sex up the vanilla; b23 a faultless cask finish but the intensity of the malt is the star of the show. Excellent! *46%. nc ncf sc.*

**The Duchess Glenrothes Lagertha 20 Year Old** cask no. 10/1996, dist 23 Oct 96, bott 24 Mar 17 **(93)** n23 t23.5 f23 b23.5 Impossible not to enjoy. Oh, and salivating.. *52.8%. sc. The Shieldmaiden Series.*

◈◈◈ **Hepburn's Choice Glenrothes 7 Years Old** refill butt, dist 2011, bott 2019 **(76.5)** n19 t20.5 f18 b19 A dull cove, the dreaded "S" word lurking in all corners. Enjoys a brief bright malty moment on delivery. *46%. nc ncf sc. 921 bottles.*

**Kingsbury Gold Glenrothes 20 Years Old** hogshead, cask no. 48, dist 1996 **(93)** n22.5 t23.5 f23 b24 Understated greatness. Seemingly simple, but don't be taken in. Give it as much time as you can as there so much more... *52.3%. 329 bottles.*

◈◈◈ **Kingsbury Gold Glenrothes 20 Year Old** hogshead, cask no. 51, dist 1996 **(79.5)** n20 t21.5 f18 b20 Sweet and malty in part. But, as so often is the case with this infuriating distillery, far too many out of sync moments to let you just relax and enjoy. *51.9%. sc. 214 bottles.*

**The Last Drop Glenrothes 1968** cask no. 13504 **(96.5)** n24 t24 f24 b24.5 No whisky has any right to be in such command of its faculties after half a century. No over-tiredness, no breakdown in balance or structure. Just incredible whisky of which one glass can fill an hour of anybody's time with malty pleasures and complexity *51.3%. sc. 168 bottles.*

**The Last Drop Glenrothes 1968** cask no. 13508 **(95.5)** n24 t23.5 f24 b24 A wonderful old cask plucked from the back of the warehouse just in time. Another summer might have proved fatal. But here, in this mode, we see an aged malt at its very peak of defiance... *50.2%. sc. 141 bottles.*

**The Last Drop Glenrothes 1969** cask no. 16203 **(95.5)** n24.5 t23.5 f23.5 b24 A malt which appears to have spent nearly 50 years treading on eggshells: certainly here everything is gentle and carefully positioned so there nothing collapses after so many passing year. Brilliant. *45.7%. sc. 160 bottles.*

**The Last Drop Glenrothes 1969** cask no. 16207 **(96)** n24 t24 f24 b24 Just a ridiculous whisky for its years. This should have collapsed in upon itself, so well defined are the older oaks. Yet, somehow, the sugars appear at just the right time and in just-so amounts not just to see off a catastrophe, but help create something rather special. *46.6%. sc. 140 bottles.*

◈◈◈ **The Last Drop Glenrothes 1970** cask no. 10586 **(97)** n24.5 the most complex of the trilogy, this one revealing small glimpses of myriad facets, like shards of stained glass found on an archaeological dig. The barley, even after all this time, resembles strands of freshly-plucked moist grass; the vanillas are rounded and soft – reminiscent of Lyons Maid ice cream – and, for the first time and so clean and clear is this nose, small fragments of peat can be detected, providing the most unexpected base note...; **t24** the nose is delicate and complex: the delivery mirrors this exactly. So delicate, in fact, the spices soon make their way forward, meeting little resistance from elsewhere. The malts are bitter-sweet, incredibly juicy and then...ever so slightly smoky...; **f24** a soft chocolate ice cream finale...again with those teasing shards of peat...; **b24.5** it is fascinating how the three Last Drop Glenrothes come from sister casks. But each is so different in its own way, having decided to take a slightly different course in the intervening 49 years...This one has drifted off in the general direction of perfection... 44.3%. sc.

⋙ **The Last Drop Glenrothes 1970** cask no. 10588 **(95) n24** a delicious and highly unusual mix between eggnog and bourbon. The barley is also in fine song, despite the great age; just the vaguest hint of something a little smoky, too..; **t24** surprisingly salivating on delivery, the malt really being back on track. They we come to the layering process of tannins, of varying intensities; **f23** such thick, gorgeous vanilla...; the tannins return to add some sturdy oak; **b23.5** it creaks a bit here, limps a little there. But still saunters around with the unmistakable air of whisky royalty... 43%. sc.

⋙ **The Last Drop Glenrothes 1970 cask** no. 10589 **(95.5) n24** truly classic exotic fruit top quality ye olde Speyside nose...; **t24** anyone of a certain vintage who remember a British sweet called a "fruit salad" you could buy for a farthing each...well, here it is in whisky format. So silky and salivating, and the good news is that despite the oaky intervention the malt can still be enjoyed to the full...; **f23.5** just bitters slightly as those tannins really get a grip, but some lovely prickly spice does a great recovery job; **b24.5** talk about a whisky to bring back the memories...So beautiful... 44%. Sc.

⋙ **Liquid Treasures 10th Anniversary Glenrothes 21 Year Old** sherry hogshead, dist 1997, bott 2019 **(89) n23** proud, chest-beating grape; over-ripe gooseberries in a freshly baked pie...; **t22.5** pleasurable delivery with the fruit beautifully mixed with malt; creamy-textured with a little salt alongside the lightly sprinkled muscovado sugars; **f21** dries quite assertively. Good vanilla, but just the faintest background furriness; **b22.5** not quite a perfect sherry butt, but for Glenrothes, about as good as it gets. 55.8%. sc. 195 bottles.

**The Loch Fyne Glenrothes 12 Year Old** sherry cask, cask no. 2012, dist Jan 05, bott Sept 17 **(77) n19 t20 f19 b19** Dull. Just so dull, dull, dull and, well....dull! 46%. sc. 1,035 bottles.

**Old Malt Cask Glenrothes Aged 12 Years** sherry butt, cask no. 14095, dist Mar 05, bott Aug 17 **(86) n22 t22.5 f20 b21.5** Not too bad by Glenrothes sherry butt standards. Certainly tightens and gives any sugars present a vigorous working over as it dries. But also possesses early on some really excellent moments to savour on delivery as the malt and fruit appear to be in perfect harmony. 50%. nc ncf sc. 492 bottles.

**Old Particular Glenrothes 12 Years Old** sherry butt, cask no. 11792, dist Mar 05, bott Jun 17 **(81) n20 t22 f19 b20** The odd fruitcake moment both on nose and delivery. Slightly bitter on the finish, but the journey there takes you through a field of spice and stubbornly juicy barley. The sherry influence is a slight distraction. 48.4%. nc ncf sc. 808 bottles.

**The Whisky Chamber Glenrothes 21 Years Old 1996** ex bourbon cask **(94.5) n23.5 t23.5 f23.5 b24** ,mm....ex-bourbon Glenrothes! Why can't they all be like that from this distillery...? All those dreadful, dud sherry butts, when they could have been like this! 53%. sc.

**Whisky-Fässle Glenrothes 20 Year Old** sherry butt, dist 1997, bott 2017 **(58) n14 t15 f14 b15** Massively sulphured in classic Glenrothes mid-1990s style. Just horrible. 47.9%.

**Whisky-Fässle Glenrothes 20 Year Old** sherry butt, dist 1997, bott 2017 **(84.5) n22 t22.5 f19 b21** A collectors' item: a Glenrothes sherry cask under 25 years of age not entirely riddled with sulphur. Have to say that the sherry does rather over fruit the experience and is all over the malt like an oversized raincoat. The flaw is evident at the death, but still much to enjoy otherwise...providing you like very juicy grape... 50.1%.

# GLEN SCOTIA
### Campbeltown, 1832. Loch Lomond Distillers. Working

**Glen Scotia Aged 10 Years** bourbon cask, bott Dec 12 db **(90.5) n22.5 t23.5 f22 b22.5.** Fabulous to see Scotia back in this excellent nick again. 46%. nc ncf.

**Glen Scotia Aged 10 Years Peated** first fill bourbon barrels db **(94.5) n24 t23 f23.5 b24** This entire whisky style is a throwback to the very first peated whiskies I tasted 40 years ago. Indeed, anyone still alive and able to remember Glen Garioch when it was heavily peated through its own kilns will raise an eyebrow of happy recognition... One of the greatest Glen Scotias of all time. 46%. nc ncf.

**Glen Scotia 11 Years Old 2006** cask no. 532, dist Dec 06, bott Apr 18 db **(92.5) n22.5 t23.5 f23 b23.5** Absolutely typical Glen Scotia, proudly displaying its rugged charm. 55.6%. sc. 212 bottles. Bottled for The Whisky Shop.

**Glen Scotia 12 Years Old** db **(73.5) n18 t19 f18 b18.5.** Ooops! I once said you could write a book about this called "Murder by Caramel." Now it would be a short story called "Murder by Flavours Unknown." What is happening here? Well, a dozen years ago Glen Scotia was not quite the place to be for consistent whisky, unlike now. Here, the caramel is the only constant as the constituent parts disintegrate. *40%*

**Glen Scotia Aged 12 Years** bourbon cask, bott Dec 12 db **(89) n22 t22 f23 b22.** Simplistic but delicious. *46%. nc ncf.*

**Glen Scotia 13 Years Old 2005** cask no. 17/412-10, dist Mar 05, bott Apr 18 db **(91.5) n22.5 t23 f23 23** A peaty whisky for sure, but so much else happening, too. What entertainment! *55.6%. sc. 330 bottles. Bottled for Loch Fyne Whiskies.*

**Glen Scotia 14 Year Old Peated** bourbon cask db **(87) n21.5 t22 f21.5 b22.** A very straight bat played by this one: a malty up and downer with few frills others than a slow though ineffective build up of smoke. *50%. nc ncf.*

**Glen Scotia Aged 15 Years** American oak barrels db **(91.5) n22.5 t23 f23 b23** Great to see this rather special little distillery produce something quite so confident and complete. *46%. ncf.*

**Glen Scotia Aged 16 Years** bourbon cask, bott Dec 12 db **(87) n22 t22 f21 b22.** Signs of a less than brilliant distillate which has been ironed out to some good effect in the cask. *46%. nc ncf.*

**Glen Scotia Aged 16 Years** American oak barrels, bott code: L12 087 18 db **(92.5) n23.5 t23.5 f22.5 b23** Doesn't stint on character. *46%. nc ncf.*

**Glen Scotia 18 Year Old** American oak casks & first fill oloroso casks, bott code: L2/221/17 db **(95) n24 t24 f23 b24** ,y Panama is doffed in grateful thanks for the excellent use of un-sulphured clean sherry butts which give this malt a genuine lustre. And as three dimensional as its sister PX bottling is just one... *51.3%. ncf.*

**Glen Scotia Aged 25 Years** American oak barrels, bott 2017, bott code: L8/187/17 db **(94) n23.5 t24 f23 b23.5** So beautiful! Truly adorable – and probably a Scotia as you have never quite seen it before. Incredibly rare to find a Scotch single malt so under the thumb of a bourbon character: this must have been filled into very fresh first-fill bourbon barrels to come up with this highly American effect. Trump that! *48.8%. ncf.*

⟐ **Glen Scotia 45 Year Old** db **(96) n24** one of those remarkable whiskies where the oak, revealing the odd grey hair (or is that revelling in...?), appears to be holding off to ensure the salty, exotic (or do I mean erotic...?) fruits are allowed the clearest run...; **t24** immediate oak impact on delivery now. But a little maple syrup mingles with butterscotch and salted butter to ensure special things happen. Towards the mid-point orange blossom honey lands, and then melts in the mouth...; **f23.5** light walnut cake complete with crème fondant; lots of intact barley and lighter red liquorice; **b24.5** outrageously beautiful for its age with not even the hint of a beginning of a crack. Stupendous. *43.8%.*

⟐ **Glen Scotia 1999** refill bourbon barrel, cask no. 455 db **(89) n22.5** a slight salty, grassy note; toffee apple; **t22.5** eye-wateringly fresh barley, but the midground fills with fudge; **f22** soft, linear caramels **b22.5** really extracts every last caramel molecule out of the cask! *60.5%. sc. Bottled for Glenkeir Whiskies.*

⟐ **Glen Scotia 2008 Second Shop Bottling** db **(84) n22 t21 f21 b20** Too salty and bitter for its own good *56.3%. sc.*

**Glen Scotia Campbeltown 1832** American oak barrels, finished in Pedro Ximenez sherry casks, bott code: L2 087 18 db **(85.5) n22.5 t22 f20 b21** Yes, pleasant enough I suppose...but so dull! As usual there is a bitterness to a PX finish as any foibles in the oak is exaggerated massively by the sweetness of the grape, which in turn fills in all the natural ridge and furrows of the malt and leaves the flattest of whiskies. The sooner distillers and bottlers get over this PX fad the better... *46%. nc ncf.*

⟐ **Glen Scotia Campbeltown Harbour** first fill bourbon casks, bott code: 23 10 2018 db **(87) n22 t22 f21.5 b21.5** The best description of Campbeltown and its harbour was provided by 19th century whisky explorer Alfred Barnard. This malt hardly matches the whiskies you would have found of that time, and it doesn't quite match up to how you picture Campbeltown whiskies today, either. For this is very flat and far too caramel dependent, though the mix of saltiness and gentle sweetness is high attractive. The smoke unfurls at the very finish...but for all its easy attractiveness, it is still all a little too docile and tame. *40%.*

⟐ **Glen Scotia Campbeltown Malts Festival 2019** rum cask finish db **(94) n23.5** though a different nose for a Scotia, it certainly retains the distillery contours; crisp, sharp and salty; **t23.5** fabulously engaging barley: juicy from the get-go with a citrus and salty edge; **f23** a light milk chocolate fade; **b24** too often rum casks can tighten a malt to the point of strangulation. Not here. Lively and outstandingly well balanced. *51.3%.*

**Glen Scotia Double Cask** finished in American oak & Pedro Ximenez sherry casks db **(85.5) n22 t22 f20.5 b21.** When blending, I do not like to get too involved with PX casks, unless I know for certain I can shape the effect to further or enrich the storyline on the palate. The reason is that PX means the complexity of a malt can easily come to a sticky end. That has happened here with both the malt and grape cancelling each other out. Soft and easy drinking with an excellent early delivery spike of intensity. But a dull middle and finish. And dull has never been a word I have associated with this distillery. Ever. 46%. ncf.

◈ **Glen Scotia Distillery Edition No. 6 19 Years Old** first fill bourbon cask, dist Jul 99, bott Aug 18 db **(95.5)** n23.5 lemon drops and roses (whiskers on kittens?...?); **t24** oh....that is unreal....!!! The barley is so vivid it is operating in multiple dimensions...this is so, so vivid! Super-salivating, gingered up with spice and even a curious ultra-clean and malty new make note, despite the good age on this. The oils could not be better weighted, nor could the slow growth of the biscuity malt and tannin mix be more teasing; **f24** long, with the malts stills in control but the fried yams make a memorable sign off; **b24** one of the most charmingly, disarmingly beautiful single cask malts I have tasted this year. 57.9%. sc. 195 bottles.

**Glen Scotia Malts Festival 2018 Ruby Port Finish 2008 Vintage Peated** bott code: L2 127 18 db **(88.5)** n21.5 t23 f22 b22 Interesting: in effect, the Glen Scotia 10 Peated (see above) finished in Port. And the winner is...the standard version by a knockout. Here the Port gets in the way of the charm and classiness of the American cask bottling and thrusts fruit at you with all the gum-chewing, flesh-flashing subtlety a lady of the night might try to seduce a punter. 57.8%. nc ncf.

◈ **Glen Scotia Warehouse Edition 2005 13 Years Old** recharred American oak, first fill oloroso sherry finish, dist Sept 05, bott Aug 18 db **(87.5)** n21.5 t23 f21 b21.5 Another salty offering which peaks on delivery with a huge malt and muscovado sugar burst. Flattens out thereafter and bitters out, too. 56.2%. sc.

**Glen Scotia Victoriana** db **(89.5)** n23 t23 f21.5 b22 An unusual malt for a cask strength. Beyond the nose there is limited layering, instead concentrating on the malt-toffee intertwangling. 51.5%

◈ **The Perfect Fifth Glen Scotia 1992** cask no. 05917, dist 22 Jan 92 **(94)** n23 playful, teasing smoke offers an unlikely sharpness to the already busy barley. For its big age, this malt is alive and kicking; **t23.5** brilliant! Sublime depth to the barley which is at its juiciest and glows as the cocoa notes bring out the best of the light smoke; **f23.5** a bitter-sweet finale with the phenols swirling around and spices a-buzzing. No signs of tiredness at all as the barley still plays a big part while the oak offers both cocoa and a proud skeleton on which all else hangs; **b24** just adore that chocolate and light beat mix. Superb! 45.9%. sc.

**The Whisky Embassy Glen Scotia Aged 10 Years** cask no. 16/558-3, dist Nov 06, bott Aug 17 **(87)** n21 t22 f22 b22 An unusually perfumed malt bulging with barley on the juicy delivery. Quietly satisfying with a pronounced sugar and spice finale. 54.7%. nc ncf sc.

# GLEN SPEY
**Speyside, 1885. Diageo. Working.**

**Glen Spey Aged 12 Years** db **(90)** n23 the kind of firm, busy malt you expect from this distillery plus some lovely spice; **t22** mouthwatering and fresh, a layer of honey makes for an easy three or four minutes; **f22** drier vanilla, but the pulsing oak is controlled and stylish; **b23** very similar to the first Glen Spey I can remember in this range, the one before the over-toffeed effort of two years ago. Great to see it back to its more natural, stunningly beautiful self. 43%

**Gordon & MacPhail Connoisseurs Choice Glen Spey 1995** refill American hogshead, dist 6 Oct 95, bott 14 Mar 18 **(94.5)** n23.5 t24 f23 b24 A truly classic nose and profile well known and revered by creators of older blends. Spellbinding. 46%. nc ncf sc. 615 bottles.

◈ **Whisky Castle Glen Spey Aged 21 Years** hogshead, dist 22 Jul 97, bott 1 Sept 18 **(96.5)** n23.5 we are sent head-first into Brazil for one of their divinely and uniquely aromatic nutty biscuits (no longer living with a Brazilian, I don't have an easy reference to what they are called), as well as diced coconut and unmalted barley; a vague citrus note lightens the load; **t24.5** beyond juicy. Salivating is nowhere near the right adjective. The grist, followed by a secretive spice, keeps the taste buds in ecstatic turmoil; the tannins fill the midpoint with a semi-bourbon degree of liquorice and heather honey; **f24** the spice and chocolate fade is almost indecent in its alluring sexiness; **b24.5** just so wonderful to see this criminally underrated distillery displayed in the most elegant lights. As single casks go, it is as near as damn it perfection. Such beauty could bring a tear to the eye... 55%. nc ncf sc. 185 bottles.

# GLENTAUCHERS
**Speyside, 1898. Chivas Brothers. Working.**

**Ballantine's The Glentauchers Aged 15 Years Series No.003** traditional oak casks, bott code: LKRM0071 2018/02/13 **(86)** n22 t22 f21 b21 Alarm bells ring when confronted by the dull nose with a neutral fruit and caramel edge. When the palate offers something fat and glossy (that's a new one for 'Tauchers) with a dull spice development to accompany the vague fruit and caramel, the heart sinks and flashing lights join the ringing alarm. The big, boring caramel finish drives you to distraction.... If anyone on this planet has championed Glentauchers longer or louder than me, or with more heart-felt gusto, then I would like to meet them. For well over 20 years I have been telling anyone who cares to listen – and many who don't – that this is one of Scotland's finest distilleries worthy of its own proprietory bottling. It finally arrives, and instead of a malt which scores in the mid-90s, as it should (and so often has done with independent bottlings in Whisky Bibles past), we have before us something pleasant, bland and not instantly recognisable as a 'Tauchers. Frankly, it could be from any Scottish distillery as the blueprint for the nose and flavour profile is shared by many: too many. As I say, pleasant whisky. But, knowing just how good this whisky really is (using 100% bourbon cask, no colour, no chill-filtration) what a huge and crushing disappointment. A bit like going to see the Sistine Chapel and finding someone had whitewashed over it.... 40%.

**Cadenhead's Cask Strength Glentauchers Aged 41 Years** dist 1976 **(96)** n23.5 t24.5 f23.5 **b24.5** One of the world's truly great distilleries fittingly honoured in its advanced age. 42%. sc. 126 bottles.

⬧ **The Cooper's Choice Glentauchers 2009 8 Years Old** Madeira finish **(86.5)** n22 t22 f21 **b21.5** Surprisingly flat for a Glentauchers. Starts promisingly with the delivery juicy and gushing in barley. But the finish begins early and ends shortly after... 46%. nc ncf sc.

**Fadandel.dk Glentauchers 19 Years Old** cask no. 3825, dist 16 Jul 97, bott 14 Feb 17 **(95)** n23.5 t24 f23.5 **b24** A 'Tauchers fruit cake...with many added extras. Magnificent. 53.3%. sc.

**Gordon & MacPhail Cask Strength Glentauchers 2003** cask nos. 650 & 652, bott 15 May 17 **(92.5)** n22.5 t23.5 f23 **b23.5** One of the most heavy and uncompromising 'Tauchers I've encountered for a while. When the malt speaks, it's all rather muffled. For those who usually savour and celebrate the distillery's treble will have to be satisfied with the base. 55.6%.

⬧ **Gordon & MacPhail Connoisseurs Choice Glentauchers Aged 27 Years** first fill sherry butt, cask no. 6943, dist 20 Jun 91, bott 6 Sept 18 **(95)** n23.5 t24 f23.5 **b24** A sherry butt in the finest fettle with not a single atom of sulphur to ruin things. From the rich sherry trifle nose you suspect you are in for a treat. And the succulent spiced grape on the mouthfeel confirms it. The lushness feel is an added bonus...but those spices...! Wow! A dry finale with a touch of mocha rounds it off. Oh, and did I mention the saltiness? Beware! An excellent sherry butt at work: the shock might kill you! It is the only one I have had this week... 56.8%. sc. 473 bottles.

⬧ **Kingsbury Gold Glentauchers 20 Year Old** barrel, cask no. 3960, dist 1996 **(92.5)** n23.5 incredibly understated...at first. But close scrutiny reveals that under the seemingly dominating bourbon-style sweetness, a little mint and spice garnishes the vanilla; **t23** sublime mouthfeel with a gorgeous mix of grist and icing sugar forming a crust for the eye-watering barley and tannin mix: again you need to concentrate hard to find its little secrets, as it is too easily passed off as simple spices; **f23** dryer, as it should be, with a powdery vanilla which remains agreeably peppery; **b23** 'Tauchers at its inscrutable best... 52.2%. sc. 195 bottles.

**The Loch Fyne Glentauchers 10 Year Old** sherry cask, cask no. 606, dist Mar 07, bott Nov 17 **(88)** n22 t23 f21 **b22** A relatively clean sherry butt. Hurrah! However, the grape fills in the gaps and robs us of the rare complexity which makes 'Tauchers that little bit special... 46%. sc. 1,184 bottles.

**Scotch Malt Whisky Society Cask 63.46 9 Year Old** refill ex-bourbon barrel, dist 6 Dec 07 **(95)** n23 t24 f24 **b24** This is close to perfection as an example of 'Tauchers in well used first/good nick second fill bourbon barrel. An all too easy to overlook gem: a true benders' dream. 61%. sc.

**Single Cask Collection Glentauchers Aged 10 Years** 1st fill sherry hogshead, cask no. 900302, dist 10 May 07, bott 21 Dec 17 **(87)** n22 t22.5 f21.5 **b21** Bitter from first delivery, making a big, fruity but puckering impression from the off. 'Tauchers is one of the most complex malts in Speyside, but the enormity of the sherry really does overbear all. Not a bad sherry butt by modern day standards, but simply too muscular. 55%. nc ncf sc. 237 bottles.

⬧ **Whisky Castle Glentauchers Aged 10 Years** bourbon cask, dist 2007, bott 2018 **(92)** n22.5 a wonderful, slightly sharp peardrop nose; **t23.5** the distillery's juicy, gristy trademark comes through loud and clear; a vaguely salty edge helps brings out the latent oak; **f23** chalky vanilla, drier through the lack of oils, but some outstandingly well-weighted spices add to the complexity and charm; **b23** suffers a little, especially at the death, from not being cask strength. But, otherwise, superb. 46%. nc ncf sc. 500 bottles.

**The Whisky Embassy Glentauchers Aged 9 Years** cask no. 8515933, dist 2008, bott 2017 **(89)** n22 t22 f22.5 **b22.5** Even when the cask is a little lazy, so good is the spirit of 'Tauchers it carries the ensemble through beautifully. 52.6%. nc ncf sc.

**Whisky Illuminati Glentauchers 20 Year Old** American oak hogshead, cask no. 3844, dist 1997 **(96.5)** n24.5 t24.5 f23.5 **b24** Simple question: why can't the official bottling be this beautiful and so true to the distillery? Or even close...? 50.3%. sc. 150 bottles. Candlelight Series.

# GLENTURRET
Highlands (Perthshire), 1775. Edrington. Working.

**Glenturret Aged 8 Years** db (88) n21 t22 f23 b22. Technically no prizewinner. But the dexterity of the honey is charming, as this distillery has a tendency sometimes to be. 40%

**The Glenturret Aged 10 Years** db (76) n19 t18 f20 b19. Lots of trademark honey but some less than impressive contributions from both cask and the stillman. 40%

**The Glenturret Aged 15 Years** db (87) n21 t22 f22 b22. A beautifully clean, small-still style dram that would have benefitted from being bottled at a fuller strength. A discontinued bottling now: if you see it, it is worth the small investment. 40%

**The Glenturret Fly's 16 Masters Edition** db (96) n24.5 t24 f23.5 b24.5 When I first found Glenturret some 30 years so ago, their whisky was exceptionally rare – on account of their size and having been closed for a very long time – but the few bottlings they produced had a very distinctive, indeed unique, feel. Then it changed as they used more Highland Distillers sherry butts which were, frankly, the kiss of death. Here, though, we appear to have reverted back to exactly how it tasted half a lifetime ago. Rich, kissed with copper and stirred with honey. It is, as is fitting to old Fly, the dog's bollocks... 44%. 1,740 bottles.

**Glenturret 30 Year Old** db (94) n23 my word, this is a tired old malt: the oak has ganged up in its most funereal, sawdusty, chalky manner but has been thwarted in its attempt to bury this whisky thanks to some heroic honey and citrus notes which simply refuse to die. Better still, they rally for a copper-rich orange-blossom honey and lime juice hurrah...! t24 the fabulous honey and maple syrup tones again combine with that coppery sheen to cock a snook at the oak which gathers like vultures just the other side of the lightly-smoked curtain; f23 miraculously, a little malt enters the fray to add some unexpected lightness to the spicy gloom: once more its rabid oak is thwarted; b24 the ultimate exhibition of brinkmanship, surely: hangs on to its integrity by a cat's whisker... 43.4%.

**Glenturret Peated Drummond** db (87) n21 t23.5 f21 b21.5 The wide cut from the small still means the odd feint creeps into this one; the peat is too much on the sparse side to paper over the cracks. However, the delivery is something that has to be experienced. A new make freshness can be found all over the show, but even that gives way as the golden syrup and smoke mingle for one of the briefest yet most beautiful star quality moments of the whisky year. 58.9%.

**The Glenturret Peated Edition** db (86) n20.5 t22 f21.5 b22. Pleasant enough, for sure, even if the nose is a bit rough. But in the grand scheme of things, just another peated malt and one of no special distinction. Surely they should concentrate on being Glenturret: there is only one of those.... 43%

**The Glenturret Sherry Edition** db (78) n19 t21 f19 b19. Not sure if this sherry lark is the best direction for this great distillery to take. 43%

**The Glenturret Triple Wood Edition** db (84) n20 t22.5 f20 b21.5. Not the happiest of whiskies, but recovers from its obvious wounds by concentrating on the juicy grain, rather than the grape. 43%

**Gordon & MacPhail Connoisseurs Choice Glenturret 1999** first fill sherry hogshead, cask no. 690, dist 16 Aug 99, bott 22 Feb 18 (86) n22.5 t23.5 f19 b21 usually, the term "First Fill Sherry" associated with any of the old Highland Distillers distilleries has you running to the fallout shelter. Well, yes, there is sulphur on board, and comes through definitively at the finale. But first you can luxuriate in the stunning, honey-riddled delivery. Toasted honeycomb, cinnamon and maple syrup combine stunningly with the roasted tannins for a brilliant opening salvo. Shame about the late sulphur. 51.6%. nc ncf sc. 265 bottles.

# GLENUGIE
Highlands (Eastern). 1834–1983. Whitbread. Closed.

**Deoch an Doras Glenugie 30 Years Old** dist 1980, bott 2011 db (87) n22 t23.5 f19.5 b22. It is now 2017 and it has been six long years since this arrived in my tasting room - something I didn't expect to see again: a distillery bottling of Glenugie. Well, technically, anyway, as Glenugie was part of the Chivas group when it died in the 1980s. As far as I can remember they only brought it out once, either as a seven- or five-year-old. I think that went to Italy, so when I walked around the old site just after it closed, it was a Gordon and MacPhail bottling I drank from and it tasted nothing like this! Just a shame there is a very slight flaw in the sherry butt, but just great to see it in bottle again. 52.13%. nc ncf.

# GLENURY ROYAL
Highlands (Eastern), 1868–1985. Diageo. Demolished.

**Glenury Royal 36 Years Old** db (89) n21 t23 f22 b23. An undulating dram, hitting highs and lows. The finish, in particular, is impressive: just when it looks on its last legs, it revives delightfully. The whole package, though far from perfect, is pretty astounding. 50.2%

**Glenury Royal 40 Year Old Limited Edition** dist 1970, bott 2011 db **(84)** n20.5 t20 f22 **b21.5**. Glenury is these days so rare I kept this back as a treat to savour as I neared the end of the book. The finale throws up a number of interesting citrus equations. But the oak, for the most part, is too rampant here and makes for a puckering experience. *59.4%. 1,500 bottles.*

**Gordon & MacPhail Rare Old Glenury Royal 1984 (95.5)** n23 t24 f23.5 b25 In the rare instances of the early 1980s I tasted a young Glenury, it was never this good and hardly looked up for 30 years in the cask. But this incredibly rare bottling of the malt, the best I have ever encountered from Glenury and distilled in the final days of its 117 year existence, stands its ground proudly and performs, unforgettably, the Last Post with magical honeyed notes... *46%.*

# HAZELBURN (see Springbank)

# HIGHLAND PARK
### Highlands (Island–Orkney), 1795. Edrington. Working.

**Highland Park 8 Years Old** db **(87)** n22 t22 f22 **b21.** A journey back in time for some of us: this is the original distillery bottling of the 70s and 80s, bottles of which are still doing the rounds in obscure Japanese bars and specialist outlets such as the Whisky Exchange. *40%*

**Highland Park 10 Year Old Ambassador's Choice** db **(74)** n17.5 t20 f17.5 b19. Some of the casks are so badly sulphured, I'm surprised there hasn't been a diplomatic incident...*46%*

**Highland Park Aged 12 Years** db **(78)** n19 t21 f19 b19. Let's just hope that the choice of casks for this bottling was a freak. To be honest, this was one of my favourite whiskies of all time, one of my desert island drams, and I could weep. *40% WB16/048*

**Highland Park Aged 15 Years** db **(85)** n21 t22 f21 b21. Had to re-taste this several times, surprised as I was by just how relatively flat this was. A hill of honey forms the early delivery, but then... *40%*

**Highland Park Earl Magnus Aged 15 Years** 1st edition db **(76.5)** n20 t21 f17.5 b18. Tight and bitter. *52.6%. 5976 bottles.*

**Highland Park Loki Aged 15 Years** db **(96)** n24 t24 f23.5 b24.5 the weirdness of the heather apart, a bit of a trip back in time. A higher smoke ratio than the bottlings of more recent years which new converts to the distillery will be unfamiliar with, but reverting to the levels regularly found in the 1970s and 80s, probably right through to about 1993/94. Which is a very good thing because the secret of the peat at HP was that, as puffed out as it could be in the old days, it never interfered with the overall complexity, other than adding to it. Which is exactly the case here. Beyond excellent! *48.7%. Edrington.*

**Highland Park 16 Years Old** db **(88)** n23 t23 f20 b22. I tasted this the day it first came out at one of the Heathrow whisky shops. I thought it a bit flat and uninspiring. This sample, maybe from another bottling, is more impressive and showing true Highland Park colours, the finish apart. *40%. Exclusively available in Duty Free/Travel Retail.*

**Highland Park Thor Aged 16 Years** db **(87.5)** n22.5 t23.5 f19 b22.5. Now, from what I remember of my Norse gods, Thor was the God of Thunder. Which is a bit spooky seeing as hailstones are crashing down outside as I write this and lightning is striking overhead. Certainly a whisky built on power. Even taking into account the glitch in one or two of the casks, a dram to be savoured on delivery. *52.1%. 23,000 bottles.*

**Highland Park Ice Edition Aged 17 Years** db **(87)** n22 t23 f21 b21. The smoke drifts around until it finds some spices. Frustrating: you expect it to kick on but it stubbornly refuses to. Caramel and vanilla up front, then bitters out. *53.9%.*

**Highland Park Aged 18 Years** db **(95.5)** n23.5 t24 f24 b24 If familiarity breeds contempt, then it has yet to happen between myself and HP 18. This is a must-have dram. I show it to ladies the world over to win their hearts, minds and tastebuds when it comes to whisky. And the more time I spend with it, the more I become aware and appreciative of its extraordinary consistency. The very latest bottlings have been astonishing, possibly because colouring has now been dropped, and wisely so. Why in any way reduce what is one of the world's great whisky experiences? Such has been the staggering consistency of this dram I have thought of late of promoting the distillery into the world's top three: only Ardbeg and Buffalo Trace have been bottling whisk(e)y of such quality over a wide range of ages in such metronomic fashion. Anyway, enough: a glass of something honeyed and dazzling calls... *43%*

**Highland Park Aged 21 Years** db **(82.5)** n20.5 t22 f19 b21. Good news and bad news. The good news is that they appear to have done away with the insane notion of reducing this to 40% abv. The bad news: a sulphured sherry butt has found its way into this bottling. *47.5%*

**Highland Park Aged 25 Years** db **(96)** n24 t24 f24 b24 I am a relieved man: the finest HP 25 for a number of years which displays the distillery's unmistakable fingerprints with a pride bordering on arrogance. One of the most improved bottlings of the year: an emperor of a dram. *48.1%*

**Highland Park Aged 30 Years** db **(90)** n22 t22.5 f23 b22.5 A very dramatic shift from the last bottling I tasted; this has taken a fruitier route. Sheer quality, though. 48.1%

**Highland Park 40 Years Old** db **(90.5)** n20.5 t22.5 f24 b23.5 Picking splinters from my nose with this one. Some of the casks used here have obviously choked on oak, and I feared the worst. But such is the brilliance of the resilience by being on the money with the honey, you can say only that it has pulled off an amazing feat with the peat. Sheer poetry... 48.3%

**Highland Park 50 Years Old** dist Jan 60 db **(96.5)** n24.5 t24 f24 b24 Old whiskies tend to react to unchartered territory as far as time in the oak is concerned in quite different ways. This grey beard has certainly given us a new slant. Nothing unique about the nose. But when one is usually confronted with those characteristics on the nose, what follows on the palate moves towards a reasonably predictable path. Not here. Truly unique – as it should be after all this time. 44.8%. sc. 275 bottles.

**Highland Park 2002** cask no. 3374-HCF064 db **(96)** n23 t24.5 f24 b24.5 I have always through HP peaked at around 18 in mixed casks rather than 25. This is breathtaking to the point of whisky life changing and revels in its refined, complex sweetness to make a mockery of my theory. The nose apart, this has all the things that makes HP one of the world's great distilleries, and piles it on to an extent it has rarely been witnessed before. Such awesome beauty... 58.4%. sc. Bottled for Loch Fyne Whiskies.

**Highland Park 2006** cask no. 2132-HCF067 db **(91)** n22.5 t23 f23 b22.5 You'd be hard pushed to recognise this as an HP unless you were told. Has many of the signature traits, but they don't click into place to create that unique style. An atypical HP, but typically delicious. 67%. sc. Bottled for The W Club.

**Highland Park Dark Origins** db **(80)** n19 t23 f18 b20. Part of that Dark Origin must be cocoa, as there is an abundance of delicious high grade chocolate here. But the other part is not so much dark as yellow, as sulphur is around on the nose and finish in particular - and does plenty of damage. Genuinely disappointing to see one of the world's greatest distilleries refusing to play to its strengths and putting so much of its weight on its Achilles heel. 46.8%. ncf.

**Highland Park Earl Haakon** db **(92)** n22.5 t24 f22.5 b23. A fabulous malt offering some of the best individual moments of the year. But appears to run out of steam about two thirds in. 54.9%. 3,300 bottles.

**Highland Park Einar** db **(90.5)** n23 soft, warmingly smoky, toffee apple; t23 fresh, salivating delivery but bordered by tannin and imbued with spice; vague heather honey; f22 dry with the tannins and spices buzzing to the end; b22.5 a curious style of HP which shows most of its usual traits but possesses an extra sharpness. 40% WB15/328

**Highland Park Freya** 1st fill ex-bourbon casks db **(88.5)** n22 t23 f21.5 b22. The majestic honey on delivery makes up for some of the untidier moments. 52.10%.

**Highland Park Harald** db **(74.5)** n19 t20 f17 b18.5. Warrior Harald has been wounded by sulphur. Fatally. 40% WB15/337

**Highland Park Hjärta** db **(79.5)** n18.5 t22 f19 b20. In part, really does celebrate the honeycomb character of Highland Park to the full. But obviously a major blemish or two in there as well. 58.1%. 3924 bottles.

**Highland Park King Christian** db **(83.5)** n22 t22.5 f18.5 b20.5. A hefty malt with a massive fruit influence. But struggles for balance and to keep full control of the, ultimately, off-key grapey input. Despite the sub-standard finale, there is much to enjoy with the early malt-fruit battles on delivery that offer a weighty and buttery introduction to the diffused molasses and vanilla. But with the spice arrives the Achilles heel... 46.8%

**Highland Park Leif Eriksson** bourbon and American oak db **(86)** n22 t22 f21 b21. The usual distillery traits have gone AWOL while all kinds of caramel notes have usurped them. That said, this has to be one of the softest drams you'll find. 40%. Edrington.

**Highland Park Ragnavald** db **(87.5)** n21.5 t22 f22 b22. Thickset and muscular, this malt offers a slightly different type of earthiness to the usual HP. Even the malt has its moment in the sun. But the overall portrait hangs from the wall at a slight tilt... 45.05%

**Highland Park Sigurd** db **(96)** n23.5 t24.5 f23.5 b24.5 Breathtaking, star-studded and ridiculously complex reminder that this distillery is capable of serving up some of the best whisky the world can enjoy. 43%

**Highland Park Svein** db **(87)** n22 t22 f21.5 b21.5. A soft, friendly dram with good spice pick up. But rather too dependent on a tannin-toffee theme. 40% WB15/318

❖ **Highland Park Viking Soul Cask 13.5 Years Old** 18 month sherry seasoned quarter cask finish, cask no. 700066, bott 2019 db **(88.5)** n22 t23.5 f21 b22 The quarter cask finish is a brave move to make after over 13 years of normality. And the extra oak really does punch through, and not always in a way that feels particularly relaxed or natural. The fruitiness arrives in sugary waves and enjoys a delightful spice flourish. But for an HP, the most rounded of all Scotland's malts, it feels a tad frantic. No faulting the fabulous delivery, though, which appears to have had the cocoa rammed forward with the grape ahead of time... 55.4%. nc ncf sc. 159 bottles. Bottled for MacAlabur.

**Acla Special Selection No. 4 Highland Park 24 Years Old** hogshead, dist 1992, bott 2016 **(95.5) n24 t24 f23.5 b24** It is so wonderful to see a HP of this vintage exactly as it should be: a picture of controlled complexity. A gem to warm the heart and soul. 50%. sc. 82 bottles.

⬧ **Fadandel.dk Orkney Aged 12 Years** bourbon hogshead, cask no. 0001, dist 1 Sept 05, bott 26 May 18 **(94.5) n23.5** delicate smoke appears seemingly an atom at a time...earthy yet sweet: a touch of dank bluebell woods but without the bird song. Oh, and some honey...; **t23.5** just seems so joyous in its relative youth, the malt gambling about without a care. The oak appears in just fragments, but building all the time is that stunning heather honey, tinged by intense barley; **f23.5** long, with a malty lustre. The smoke has grown now, and with it the spices...; **b24** the distillery is kept secret on the label. However, this has the unique DNA of HP all over it! And if you think Heather Honey is a cliché when it comes to this distillery, then try this... 62.4%. sc. 333 bottles.

⬧ **Fadandel.dk Orkney Aged 14 Years** bourbon hogshead, cask no. 0008, dist 18 Aug 03, bott 25 May 18 **(95.5) n23.5** very quiet and shy, the smoke and honey most deeply entrenched in light vanilla; **t24.5** heather honey yes. But ulmo honey and maple syrup all mixed in. The tannins are equally forthright and complex and further up the pecking order to ensure parity with the sweeter elements; the mid-ground begins to get smokier; gloriously juicy throughout; **f23.5** smoked mocha with a spicy flourish; **b24** further proof, were it needed, that the quality of HP whisky (if this is HP, which I have no doubt about) is not in question: it is just their appalling sherry butts which have been causing the problems. It needs a sublime bourbon cask like this to ram home the fact. 55.4%. sc. 342 bottles.

⬧ **Fadandel.dk Orkney Aged 15 Years** butt, dist 17 Sept 02, bott 18 Jan 19 **(91.5) n23 t24 f21.5 b23** Intense heather honey core to this malt, but the more complex notes appear to be flattened a little by the cask type, which itself deposits a slight bitterness to the finish. But the nose and delivery are charming, with extra-intense barley and a near perfect proportion of sweetness to counter the oak. In fact, the delivery itself is truly memorable for the near perfection of its intensity, coupled with the honey's contribution. Good balancing spice, too. 58.6%. sc. 170 bottles.

⬧ **Gordon & MacPhail Connoisseurs Choice Highland Park Aged 29 Years** refill sherry butt, cask no. 1087, dist 7 Mar 89, bott 18 Sept 18 **(91) n23 t24 f21.5 b22.5** A clean sherry butt entirely free of sulphur. The delivery is an eye-watering event, full of salted honeys, sharp fruit tones and huge vanilla. The finish is a more subdued and less well-balanced affair, depending on vanilla and caramel to sort out the encroaching bitterness. 57%. sc. 613 bottles.

**Gordon & MacPhail Connoisseurs Choice Highland Park 1999 Cask No. 4262** first fill bourbon barrel, dist 30 Aug 99, bott 21 Feb 18 **(94.5) n23 t23.5 f24 b24** A lighter HP, but still beautifully hefty for all that with its magical mouth feel. And further proof that, given the right cask, HP remains one of the greatest distilleries in the world. 56%. nc ncf sc. 202 bottles.

**Gordon & MacPhail Connoisseurs Choice Highland Park 1999 Cask No. 4265** first fill bourbon barrel, dist 30 Aug 99, bott 21 Feb 18 **(95) n23.5 t24 f23.5 b24** Sweeping, cascading, beautiful soul-touching chords: if this were a film score it would have been written by John Barry. 55.6%. nc ncf sc. 210 bottles.

**Gordon & MacPhail Connoisseurs Choice Highland Park 2004** first fill sherry butt, cask no. 3812, dist 2004, bott 22 Feb 18 **(94.5) n23 t24 f23.5 b24** Come out from behind your sofas: this sherry butt is 100% free from sulphur. And, my word, does it show...!! 60%. nc ncf sc. 655 bottles.

⬧ **The Perfect Fifth Highland Park 1987** cask no. 1531 **(96.5) n24** pretty near perfect HP for its age, and one of the best examples of the distillery of that era I have nosed for a very long time. Slightly above average peat for a HP, which works perfectly in its favour. The usual heather honey has been skewed slightly by the heady mix of tannins and peat. The saltiness is profound, the oak a rich, spicy backbone. The sweetness is subtle and still honeyed, but more now a blend of Manuka and orange blossom. Truly magnificent! **t24** Scotland's silkiest malt at its most silky. The bold smoke on arrival is caught in the velvet gloves of the lightly oiled barley sugar, a dark liquorice sweetness spreading as the oak makes its mark. The spices are prim, proper and just so, never moving out of their set orbit while the honey starts to make its long-awaited mark, bringing with it the light smoke; a quick surge of exotic fruit underlines the antiquity with aplomb; **f24** long, increasingly smoky with the spices still teasing and forging a beautiful duet with the molassed sugars; the oak beats out an aged pulse but the phenols return to soften as well and entertain; **b24.5** this is a malt whisky coming to the end of its life, like a star becomes a white dwarf before the end of its existence. In density is huge...and I mean gigantic. The oaks are about to explode...but the cask has been bottled in the nick of time where the balance is still near perfect. Fine margins...for a very fine whisky... 47.1%. sc.

⬧ **Sansibar Whisky Highland Park 1999 (93.5) n23** operates well within itself with a genteel heather honey lead, flowed by the creak of well-polished old leather; **t23.5** the smoke mysteriously missing on the nose soon presents itself on delivery as both a subtle weight and a vague background accompaniment. The spices and honey are bang on where they should be; f23 a little chocolate malt biscuit ensures a sweet finale, as does the persistent heather honey **b24** a steady, if unspectacular, HP quietly ticking all the right boxes. *49.1%.*

**The Whisky Embassy Highland Park Aged 14 Years** cask no. 5016993, dist 2003, bott 2017 **(88.5)** n23 t22 f21.5 b22 Bit of a spluttering HP, but still has all the trademark gags... *52.8%. nc ncf sc.*

**The Whisky Embassy Highland Park Aged 14 Years** cask no. 5017013, dist 2003, bott 2017 **(93.5)** n23.5 t23.5 f23 b23.5 Almost identical in style to their 6993 cask, but without all the oaky flaws. The greater intensity and integration results in the smoke dovetailing with a richer, now heather honey, sweetness rather than being aloof. The lack of bitterness allows the story to be told without interruption. *53.8%. nc ncf sc.*

# IMPERIAL
**Speyside, 1897. Chivas Brothers. Silent.**
**Imperial Aged 15 Years "Special Distillery Bottling"** db **(69)** n17 t18 f17 b17. At least one very poor cask, hot spirit and overly sweet. Apart from that it's wonderful. *46%*

**Gordon & MacPhail Distillery Label Imperial 1997** bott 9 Aug 17 **(87.5)** n23 t21 f22 b21.5 A breezy light over-simplistic dram on the palate perhaps due to the wafer thin structure of the body. However, the nose is a different matter altogether and excels by offering a beautifully balanced mix of dates, plums and warming malt which fits gloriously with the lightly splintered, toasty oak. *43%.*

**Kingsbury Gold Imperial 21 Years Old** hogshead, cask no. 50406, dist 1995 **(87)** n22 t22.5 f21 b21.5 Plenty of yap, nip and bite. The big malt has some ulmo honey to assist early on, but the teeth get a little sharper, the structure a tad thinner as things progress. *50.7%. 256 bottles.*

# INCHGOWER
**Speyside, 1872. Diageo. Working.**
◈ **Inchgower 27 Year Old** db **(93)** n22.5 t24 f23 b23.5 Delicious and entertaining. Doesn't try to play the elegant old malt card. Instead gets stuck in with a rip-roaring attack on delivery, the fizzing spices burning deep and making the most of the light liquorice and molasses which has formed a thick-set partnership with the intense malt. The only hint of subtlety arrives towards the death as a little butterscotch tart allows a late juiciness from the barley free reign. Just love it! *43%. 8,544 bottles. Diageo Special Releases 2018.*

**Inchgower 1993 The Manager's Choice** db **(84.5)** n21 t21.5 f21 b21. Like your malts subtle, delicate, clean and sophisticated? Don't bother with this one if you do. This has all the feel of a malt that's been spray painted onto the taste buds: thick, chewy and resilient. Can't help but like that mix of hazelnut and Demerara, though. You can stand a spoon in it. *61.9%.*

**The First Editions Inchgower Aged 20 Years 1997** refill hogshead, cask no. 14219, bott 2017 **(83.5)** n21 t21 f20.5 b21 Not atypical of the period with the malt and oak crushed and confined, sometimes uncomfortably, by the heat of the spirit. The sugars which come to the rescue appear to carry the most distant hint of smoke. *56.1%. nc ncf sc. 154 bottles.*

**Gleann Mór Inchgower Aged Over 14 Years** dist 2003 **(89)** n21 t23 f22.5 b22.5 The light powdering of phenols is a pleasant surprise and does nothing to subtract from this distillery's all-round, though not instantly recognisable, charm. *53.3%.*

**Hepburn's Choice Inchgower 8 Years Old** Oloroso sherry finished butt, dist 2008, bott 2016 **(69)** n17 t18 f17 b17 The sulphur is unremittingly grim. *46%. nc ncf sc. 663 bottles.*

**Old Malt Cask Inchgower Aged 21 Years** sherry butt, cask no. 14253, dist Oct 95, bott Sept 17 **(88)** n22 t22.5 f21.5 b22 Not quite the perfect butt, but character enough to see it through the obvious flaws. *50%. nc ncf sc. 708 bottles.*

**Old Particular Inchgower 18 Years Old** sherry butt, cask no. 12102, dist Sept 98, bott Sept 17 **(89)** n22.5 t22 f22 b22.5 An unruined sherry butt helps offer a light fruity glaze to the malt. *48.4%. nc ncf sc. 365 bottles.*

**Provenance Inchgower Aged 9 Years** refill hogshead, cask no. 12028, dist Feb 08, bott Aug 17 **(85)** n22 t22.5 f20 b20.5 A full-flavoured beast which cranks up the malt early on, even with accompanying Demerara sugars, but dramatically falls flat at the death. *46%. nc ncf sc. 416 bottles.*

◈ **The Whisky Chamber Inchgower 9 Years Old 2009** Amarone cask **(89)** n22 sultanas and prune juice; the vaguest background vanilla; t23 a profound fruitiness locks horns with major spices. Slightly burnt raisins, too. Some waves of sticky treacle before the first hint of barley arrives; f21.5 dries in that burnt raisin style; b22.5 a decent wine cask certainly gives some serious attitude to what can be sometimes a bruising malt anyway. *57.9%. sc.*

# INVERLEVEN

**Lowland, 1938–1991. Demolished.**

**Deoch an Doras Inverleven 36 Years Old** dist 1973 **(94.5) n24 t23.5 f23 b24** As light on the palate as a morning mist. This distillery just wasn't designed to make a malt of this antiquity, yet this is to the manor born. 48.85%. nc ncf. Chivas Brothers. 500 bottles.

❖ **Gordon & MacPhail Private Collection Inverleven 1985** refill bourbon barrel, cask no. 562, bott 2018 **(96.5) n24** delicate malt, pulsing out its gentle but beautiful tune aided and abetted by a lightly spiced oak note which is in perfect harmony; **t24.5** sweet, mouth-watering barley which builds and builds in intensity, following on the gentlest healter honey note to aid its cause; the oak early on moves towards a light marzipan; **f23.5** a buzzing spice well within the limits of tolerance sits beside this still faultless barley...; **b24.5** I am still haunted by the day Inverleven distilled for the very last time, their manager telling me: "That's it, Jim. We're done." It was another shocking event: a great Lowland distillery which made a very consistent, malty, mildly fragile make and was absolutely excellent for blenders at about 5 years in decent second fill bourbons, and even better in firsts; and quite magnificent at about 8 years in both. Of course, the demise of Inverleven was the foretelling of the eventual closure of the unbettered Dumbarton grain distillery in which the malt complex was housed. But these were acts of whisky vandalism by a company, Allied Domecq, which never could get it right with the management of their single malts. This delicate and noble malt is a rare testimony to a distillery lost for all the wrong reasons. There is not a bum note, not a blemish. It is Lowland perfection and a whisky tragedy all rolled into one. 57.4%. 130 bottles.

# ISLE OF ARRAN

**Highlands (Island–Arran), 1995. Isle of Arran Distillers. Working.**

**Isle of Arran Machrie Moor 5ᵗʰ Edition** bott 2014 db **(91.5) n22.5 t24 f22 b23** A few tired old bourbon barrels have taken the score down slightly on last year. But the spirit itself is nothing short of brilliant. 46% WB16/049

**The Arran Malt 10 Year Old** db **(87) n22.5 t22.5 f20 b22.** It has been a while since I last officially tasted this. If they are wiling to accept some friendly advice, I think the blenders should tone down on raising any fruit profile and concentrate on the malt, which is amongst the best in the business. 46%. nc ncf.

**The Arran Malt 12 Years Old** db **(85) n21.5 t22 f20.5 b21** Hmmmm. Surprise one, this. There must be more than one bottling already of this. The first I tasted was perhaps slightly on the oaky side but otherwise intact and salt-honeyed where need be. This one has a bit of a tang: very drinkable, but definitely a less than brilliant cask around. 46%

**The Arran Malt Aged 14 Years** db **(89.5) n22 t23.5 f21.5 b22.5.** A superb whisky, but the evidence that there has been a subtle shift in emphasis, with the oak now taking too keen an interest, is easily attained. 46%. ncf.

**The Arran Malt Aged 17 Years** db **(91.5) n23.5 t23.5 f21.5 b23** "Matured in the finest ex-Sherry casks" trills the back label. And, by and large, they are right. Maybe a single less than finest imparts the light furriness to the finish. But by present day sherry butt standards, a pretty outstanding effort. 46%. nc ncf. 9000 bottles. WB15/152

**The Arran Malt Fino Sherry Cask Finish** db **(82.5) n21 t20 f21 b20.5.** Pretty tight with the bitterness not being properly compensated for. 50%

**Berry Bros & Rudd Arran 21 Years Old** cask no. 370, dist 1996, bott 2018 **(96.5) n24 t24 f24 b24.5.** When my dear old friend Harold Currie built this distillery in the mid-1990s he wanted the spirit to be as close in style to Macallan as he could get it. So, when I selected the very first cuts for the very first distillation, it was Harold's wish I had I mind. This bottling was almost certainly made to the cutting points I chose and my only sadness is that Harold is no longer with us to enjoy his malt whisky coming of age. Though this is probably not from oloroso (or if it was, it was so old that very restrained fruit is imparted) – and that is just as well, as most early oloroso butts from the distillery are poor quality – it certainly matches the profile of Macallan of the same age matured in top end second fill bourbon. This is, unquestionably, one of the single malt bottlings of the year. 46.4%. nc ncf sc.

❖ **Cask 88 Isle of Arran 22 Year Old** dist 1997 **(73) n19 t20 f16 b18** When a whisky turns up this colour (brown with a green tinge) in the lab you usually give it a very suspicious once-over. And here you'd have done it with good reason. 42.4%.

**Golden Cask Arran Aged 21 Years** cask no. CM240, dist 1996, bott 2017 **(94.5) n23.5 t24 f23 b24** Impeccable Arran. 51.6%. sc. 254 bottles.

**Gordon & MacPhail Connoisseurs Choice Arran 1996** refill sherry hogshead, cask no. 37, dist 24 Jan 96, bott 22 Feb 18 **(92) n23.5 t23.5 f22 b23** A sound sherry cask at work means this is a rare view of Arran at this great age at its very fruitiest. 49.2%. nc ncf sc. 283 bottles.

**Gordon & MacPhail Connoisseurs Choice Arran 2009** bott 21 Mar 17 **(92.5)** n22.5 t23.5 f23 b23.5 The initial drop on palate from sweetness to dryness is an unusual cliff edge variety with few warnings close to the precipice. No doubts helps to make this exciting malt from a great distillery. *46%.*

**H*A*S*H Barley Bree Isle of Arran Aged 21 Years** ex-sherry puncheon, cask no. 96/1327, dist 17 Sept 96, bott 16 Nov 17 **(85.5)** n21.5 t22.5 f20 b21.5 A rich though slightly laboured malt which is a bit of a battle between the obvious brilliance of the original whisky and the slight failings of the cask. Plenty of good things at work and early on the fruit has a generous, salty depth. But soon tightens and sharpens making the finale a bit of an uphill struggle. *50.2%. sc. 556 bottles.*

**Single Cask Collection Arran 21 Years Old Platin Edition** sherry edition **(88.5)** n22.5 t22.5 f21.5 b22 A mainly clean sherry butt doles out the fruit. *51%. sc.*

**The Whisky Chamber Arran 17 Years Old 2000** sherry cask 1099 **(87)** n22 t23 f20.5 b21.5 Not the Chamber of Horrors from a sherry butt as I had feared. But still a little tight in places That said, the delivery horrors I had feared conjure up all kinds of spicy tricks, most of them involving some busy, prickly tannins. A real mouthful...with plenty of oak-dried sultanas on show *.52.4%. sc.*

◇ **W.W. Club AR.1 Arran Aged 11 Years** American oak cask, cask no. 19, dist Oct 05, bott Feb 17 **(86.5)** n21.5 t22.5 f21 b21.5 Plenty of rich, creamy honey on delivery. And no little succulent malt, too. But a little too much tang towards the finish, confirming a quaver on the nose. *57.7%. sc. 321 bottles. William & Co. Spirits.*

## ISLE OF JURA

Highlands (Island–Jura), 1810. Whyte and Mackay. Working.

**Isle Of Jura Aged 10 Years** db **(79.5)** n19 t22 f19 b19.5. Perhaps a little livelier than before, but still miles short of where you might hope it to be. *40%*

**Isle Of Jura Aged 16 Years** db **(90.5)** n21.5 t23.5 f23 b23 A massive improvement, this time celebrating its salty, earthy heritage to good effect. The odd strange, less than harmonious note. But by far and away the most improved Jura for a long, long while. *40%*

**Isle of Jura 21 Years Old Cask Strength** db **(92)** n22 t24 f23 b23. Every mouthful exudes class and quality. A must-have for Scottish Island collectors... or those who know how to appreciate a damn fine malt *58.1%*

**Isle of Jura 30 Years Old** db **(89)** n22.5 t22.5 f22 b22. A relaxed dram with the caramel dousing the higher notes just as they started to get very interesting. If there is a way of bringing down these presumably natural caramels – it is a 30 years old, so who in their right mind would add colouring? – this would score very highly, indeed. *40%*

**Isle of Jura 40 Years Old** finished in oloroso wood db **(90)** n23 t22 f22 b23 Throw the Jura textbooks away. This is something very different. Completely out of sync in so many ways, but... *40%*

**Jura Elements "Air"** db **(76)** n19.5 t19 f18.5 b19. Initially, I thought this was earth: there is something strangely dirty and flat about both nose and delivery. Plenty of fruits here and there but just doesn't get the pulse racing at all. *45%*

**Jura Elements "Earth"** db **(09)** n23.5 t22 f21.5 b22. I haven't spoken to blender Richard Paterson about these whiskies yet. No doubt I'll be greeted with a knee on the nuts for declaring two as duds. My guess is that this is the youngest of the quartet by a distance and that is probably why it is the best. The peat profile is very different and challenging. I'd still love to see this in its natural plumage as the caramel really does put the brakes on the complexity and development. Otherwise we could have had an elementary classic. *45%*

**Jura Elements "Fire"** db **(86.5)** n22.5 t21.5 f21 b21.5. Pleasant fare, the highlight coming with the vaguely Canadian-style nose thanks to a classic toffee-oak mix well known east of the Rockies. Some botanicals also there to be sniffed at while a few busy oaky notes pep up the barley-juiced delivery, too. Sadly, just a shade too toffee dependent. *45%*

**Jura Elements "Water"** db **(73.5)** n18.5 t19 f18 b18. Oranges the box-full trying to get out but the mouth is sent into puckering spasm by the same sulphur which spoils the nose. *50%*

**Jura One and All Aged 20 Years** db **(83.5)** n21 t22 f19.5 b21 A metallic tang to this. Nutty with tart, fruity borders but nothing to get excited about. Doesn't quite add up. *51%. nc ncf.*

**Jura One For The Road Aged 22 Years** Pinot Noir finish db **(89)** n23 t23 f21 b22 Enjoyable though ultimately a bit too straight and, just like the single road on Jura, goes nowhere... *47%. nc ncf.*

**Jura One For You** db **(87.5)** n22 t22.5 f21.5 b21.5 A straight up and down maltfest with a vaguely salty edge. Very pleasant in its own limited way, but don't spend too much time looking for complexity. *52.5%. nc ncf.*

**Jura Prophecy** profoundly peated db **(90.5)** n23.5 t23 f22 b22 Youthful, well made and I prophesy this will be one of Jura's top scorers of 2011... *46%*

**Jura Superstition** db **(73.5) n17 t19 f18 b18.5.** I thought this could only improve. I was wrong. One to superstitiously avoid. *43%*

**Jura Tastival 2017** db **(90.5) n22 t23 f22.5 b23** One of the better Juras I've encountered in recent times. *51%. nc ncf.*

**Jura Turas-Mara** db **(82.5) n20.5 t22 f19 b21.** Some irresistible Jaffa Cake moments. But the oils are rather too severe and tangy. *42%. Travel Retail Exclusive.*

◇ **The First Editions Jura Aged 12 Years 2006** sherry butt, cask no. 15182, bott 2018 **(86.5) n21 t23 f21 b21.5** An exceptionally juicy bottling with attractively explosive malt on contact and the full gristy sugars still intact after a dozen years. The finish is thin and lacks any form of development. But the ultra salivating malt is an early treat. *58.9%. nc ncf sc. 267 bottles.*

◇ **Gleann Mór Isle of Jura Aged Over 20 Years (83.5) n20 t22 f20.5 b21** Not sure how a whisky of this kind of age can still be sporting a slight youthful, feinty note. The heat on the spirit also points towards a spirit rushed through the stills slightly. So, technically, not the greatest. But there is no faulting the enormity of the barley, helped slightly by the extra oils from the cut. *56.2%.*

**Hepburn's Choice Jura 10 Years Old** refill hogshead, dist 2007, bott 2017 **(81.5) n20 t21.5 f19 b21** The limitations of this distillery are in evidence here. That said, the odd attractive nutty and spicy thread to this. *46%. nc ncf sc. 420 bottles.*

◇ **Hepburn's Choice Jura 10 Years Old** refill hogshead, dist 2008, bott 2018 **(85) n21 t22 f20.5 b21.5** Clean, malty and simplistic. There is a bit of a tang at the death, but the barley sparkles despite the lack of illumination until that point. *46%. nc ncf sc. 334 bottles.*

◇ **Old Malt Cask Jura Aged 12 Years** sherry butt, cask no. 15181, dist Apr 06, bott May 18 **(87) n21.5 t22 f21.5 b22** A sister cask to the First Editions but, despite the extra dilution, the oils here have a greater say ensuring the finish has slightly more malty flesh. Youthful in part with a gristy spring to each barley-rich step. *50%. nc ncf sc. 312 bottles.*

**Provenance Jura Aged 10 Years** refill hogshead, cask no. 12033, dist Mar 07, bott Aug 17 **(82) n19.5 t21 f20.5 b21** A little bit of extra oil softens the blows. Some decent sweet malt here and there. *46%. nc ncf sc. 375 bottles.*

# KILCHOMAN
## Islay, 2005. Kilchoman Distillery Co. Working.

**Kilchoman 10 Years Old** cask no. 150/2007, dist 20 Jul 07, bott 11 Jun 18 db **(96) n24 t24 f23.5 b24.5** Has controlled the oils beautifully. Class in a glass. *56.5%. sc. 238 bottles. Bottled for The Whisky Shop.*

**Kilchoman 10 Years Old 100% Islay** cask no. 84/2008, dist 6 Mar 08, bott 19 Mar 18 db **(91) n23.5 t23 f22 b22.5** Such is the high class of Kilchomen, even an exceptionally good malt on the whisky stage is not quite up to the distillery's normal performance. Not a bad place to be... *53.2%. sc. 239 bottles. Bottled for Loch Fyne Whiskies.*

**Kilchoman 12 Years Old** bourbon cask, cask no. 36/2006, dist 4 May 06, bott 21 Jun 18 db **(93.5) n23.5 t23.5 f23 b23.5** High grade malt taking a slightly different course from this distillery's normal style. *56.9%. sc. 228 bottles. Bottled for Loch Fyne Whiskies.*

**Kilchoman 100% Islay 7th Edition** db **(88) n22.5 t22.5 f21.5 b21.5** At times a lovely experience, and one showing some older ages than normal. But ultimately unlikely to go down in the annals of Kilchoman as one of their great vintages... Looks like this was taken from the casks right in the middle of the flavours not quite harmonising – it is possible the previous month they had and another two months on they might well have again: an unfortunately timed bottling. *50%.*

**Kilchoman Private Cask Release** bourbon cask, cask no. 431/2007, dist 13 Dec 07, bott 26 Feb 18 db **(96.5) n24.5 t24 f24 b24.5** Someone fell on their feet when they bought this cask: holy crap, this is seriously good whisky! *57.2%. sc. Bottled exclusively for The Whisky Club.*

**Kilchoman PX Finish Cask Vatting** dist 2011/12, bott 20 Sept 17 db **(86.5) n22 t22.5 f21.5 b20.5** A peat and sticky fruit soup. Some people, I know, will probably sell their home for a bottle of this. But to me, pleasant, especially on delivery, but ultimately just too much...of everything. *56.7%. Bottled for the Swedish Whisky Federation.*

**Kilchoman Sanaig** bourbon & sherry casks, bott 2016 db **(89.5) n23 t22 f22 b22.5** Never quite seen a Kilchoman toe the line this way before... *46%. nc ncf.*

# KINCLAITH
## Lowlands, 1957–1975. Closed. Dismantled.

**Mo Ór Collection Kinclaith 1969 41 Years Old** first fill bourbon hogshead, cask no. 301453A, dist 28 May 69, bott 29 Oct 10 **(85.5) n22 t22 f20.5 b21.** Hangs on gamely to the last vestiges of life, though the oak, without being overtly aggressive, is squeezing all the breath of out of it. *46%. nc ncf sc. Release No. 2. The Whisky Talker. 164 bottles.*

# KINGSBARNS

**Lowland, 2014. Wemyss. Working.**

**Kingsbarns 2 Year Old Spirit Drink** 1st fill ex-bourbon barrels db (**94**) n23 t23.5 f24 b23.5 Thought I'd bring up my 1,200th tasting note for the 2019 Whisky Bible with this maturing malt from Kingsbarns. It was an inspired choice. For although the youth is more than apparent – as it should be! – there is a surprising degree of complexity to this and balances out far better than most two year olds. For a start, the distillate was beautifully created with the cut points spot on, seemingly clean enough or the malt to flourish, but with a broadness o allow complexity to develop. Even on the nose a wonderful Cadbury's hazelnut and milk chocolate promises good things ahead and you are not remotely disappointed as the barley strikes up proudly before marzipan and mocha make their mark. Delicious! 62.8%. 1,800 bottles.

# KNOCKANDO

**Speyside, 1898. Diageo. Working.**

**Knockando Aged 12 Years** bott code: L7229CM000 db (**82**) n20 t22.5 f19 b20.5 My dear, late friend and mentor Jim Milne was for a very long time J&B blender and for decades this malt came under his clever jurisdiction. It was Jim who persuaded me, over a quarter of a century ago now, to publish my views on whisky, something I felt I was underqualified to do. He vehemently disagreed, so I took his advice and the rest, as they say, is history. I knew Jim's work intimately, so I know he would not be happy with his beloved Knockando in this incarnation. His Knockando was dry, making the most of the interaction between bourbon cask and delicate malt. This is sweet and, worse still, sulphur tarnished by the sherry: I doubt he would ever let grape get this kind of grip, thus negating the distillery's fragile style. Some lovely moments here for sure. But just too fleeting. 43%.

**Knockando 1990** db (**83**) n21 t22 f20 b20. The most fruity Knockando I've come across with some attractive salty notes. Dry, but a little extra malty sweetness these days. 40%

# KNOCKDHU

**Speyside, 1894. Inver House Distillers. Working.**

**AnCnoc 12 Year Old** db (**94.5**) n24 t23 f23.5 b24.5 A more complete or confident Speyside-style malt you are unlikely to find. Shimmers with everything that is great about Scotch whisky... always a reliable dram, but this is stupendous. 40%

**AnCnoc 16 Years Old** db (**91.5**) n22 sharp, pithy, salty, busy...; t23.5 those salts crash headlong into the taste buds and then give way to massive spice and barley; soft sugars and vanilla follow at a distance; f23 salted mocha and spice; b23 unquestionably the spiciest AnCnoc of all time. Has this distillery been moved to the coast..? 46%

**AnCnoc 18 Years Old** db (**88.5**) n22.5 t23 f21 b22 Cleaner sherry at work here. But again, the contours of the malt have been flattened out badly. 46%. nc ncf

**AnCnoc 22 Year Old** db (**87**) n22 t21.5 f22 b21.5. Often a malt which blossoms before being a teenager, as does the fruits of Knockdhu; struggles to cope comfortably with the inevitable oakiness of old age. Here is such a case. 46%. Inverhouse Distillers.

**AnCnoc 24 Years Old** db (**94**) n23 t24.5 f22.5 b24 Big, broad-shouldered malt which carries a lot of weight but hardly veers away from the massively fruity path. For sherry loving whisky drinkers everywhere... 46%. nc ncf.

**AnCnoc 26 Years Old Highland Selection** db (**89**) n23 t22 f23 b21. There is a little flat moment between the middle and finish for which I have chipped off a point or two. That apart, superb. 48.2%

**AnCnoc 30 Years Old** db (**85**) n21 t23 f19 b22. Seat-of-the-pants whisky that is just on the turn. Still has a twinkle in the eye, though. 49%

**AnCnoc 35 Years Old** db (**86**) n21 t21 f22.5 b21.5. Tries to take the exotic fruit route to antiquity but headed off at the pass by a massive dollop of natural caramels. The slow burn on the spice is an unexpected extra treat, though. 43%

**AnCnoc 35 Years Old** bourbon and sherry casks db (**88**) n22.5t22 f21.5 b22. The usual big barley sheen has dulled with time here. Some attractive cocoa notes do compensate. 44.3%. nc ncf.

**AnCnoc 1975** bott 2014 db (**90**) n23.5 creaking, crumbling oak at every turn. Fortunately there's enough sugar at play – a blend of maple syrup and molasses – to see off any negative points. When some form of equality is established, the rich fruitcake comes out to play...; t23 all kinds of timber notes up front but the fruit gushes in quickly to form a lush cushion. Two year old Melton Hunt Cake with fully burned raisin; f21.5 just a little bit of awkward bitterness – and an odd furriness – joins the fruit; b22.5 if it showed any more signs of age, it'd need its own Zimmer frame. But the deep, fruity sugars are a superb restorative. 44.2%. nc ncf

**AnCnoc 1993** db (89) n22 t21 f24 b22. Quite an odd one this. I have tasted it a couple of times with different samples and there is a variance. This one takes an oakier path and then invites the barley to do its stuff. Delicious, but underscores the deft touch of the standard 12-year-old. *46%*

**AnCnoc 1994** db (88.5) n22.5 t22.5 f21.5 b22. Coasts through effortlessly, showing the odd flash of brilliance here and there. Just get the feeling that it never quite gets out of third gear... *46%. ncf.*

**AnCnoc 1995** db (84.5) n21 t22 f20.5 b21. Very plump for a Knockdhu with caramel notes on a par with the citrus and burgeoning bourbon. Some barley juice escapes on delivery but the finish is peculiarly dry for the distillery. *46%*

**AnCnoc 1999** db (95.5) n24 t24 f23.5 b24 I noticed as I was putting the bottle away that on their back label their description includes "Colour: soft, very aromatic with a hint of honey and lemon in the foreground" and "Nose: amber with a slight yellow hue." Which would make this malt pretty unique. But this is worth getting for far more than just the collectors' item typo: this is brilliant whisky – one of their best vintage malts for a very long time. In fact, one of their best ever bottlings...period.*46%. nc ncf. WB15/160*

**AnCnoc 2002** bott Mar 17, bott code: L17/089 R17/5104 IB db (86) n21.5 t23 f20.5 b21 Overall, it is enjoyable and well spiced, but a mushy, tangy, untidy finish shows up the failings of the odd cask used. This is a distillery whose spirit yearns for ex-bourbon so its stunning naked form can be worshipped, loved and salivated over. *46%.*

**AnCnoc Barrow** 13.5 ppm phenols db (88) n22 t21 f23 b22 A quite peculiar Knockdhu. The usual subtle richness of texture is curiously absent. As are friendly sugars. The strange angles of the phenols fascinate, however. *46%. nc ncf. Exclusive to travel retail.*

**AnCnoc Blas** db (67) n16 t18 f16 b17. Blast! Great chocolate. Shame about the sulphur.... *54%. nc ncf.*

**AnCnoc Black Hill Reserve** db (81) n20 t22 f19 b20. The furriness threatened on the nose and realised at the finish does this great distillery no favours at all. *46%. nc ncf. Exclusive to travel retail.*

**AnCnoc Cutter** 20.5 ppm phenols db (96.5) n24 t24 f24 b24.5 Brilliant! An adjective I am far more used to associating with anCnoc than some of the others I have had to use this year. The most Ardbeg-esque mainland malt I have ever encountered. *46%. nc ncf.*

**AnCnoc Flaughter** 14.8 ppm phenols db (88.5) n23 t22 f21.5 b22 interesting to compare the relative heavy handedness of this against the Rutter. A lovely whisky this may be, but has nothing like the poise or balance. *46%. ncf nc. WB15/345*

**AnCnoc Peatheart** batch no. 1, 40ppm, bott code: L17/301 R17/5394 db (91.5) n22 t23.5 f23 b23 Won't be long before Peatheart becomes the peataholics' sweetheart. Curiously underperforming nose, but makes amends in style on the palate. *46%.*

**AnCnoc Peter Arkle Limited Edition** db (87.5) n22.5 t22.5 f20.5 b22. A floral nose, with lavender and honeysuckle in abundance. Also offers dried orange peel. But the malt doesn't move on from there as one might hope, becoming just a little too sugary and caramel stodgy for the malt to do itself justice. All that said, a great dram to chew on for a few minutes! *46%. ncf nc. WB15/321*

**AnCnoc Rùdhan** bott code: L16/273 R16/5391 db (94.5) n24 t23.5 f23.5 b24 Hard to imagine a mainland Scottish distillery producing a more complex, elegant and wholly ingratiating peated malt... What a gem this is! *46%.*

**AnCnoc Rutter** 11 ppm phenols db (96.5) n24.5 t24.5 f23.5 b24 I remember vividly, at this great distillery's Centenary party exactly 20 years ago this summer, mentioning to the then distillery manager that I thought that the style of the malt produced at Knockdhu was perfectly geared to make a lightly malted peat along the lines of its neighbour, Ardmore. Only for a few weeks of the year I ventured. I'm pretty certain this malt was not a result of that observation, but it is heartening to see that my instincts were right: it's a sensation! *46%. ncf nc. WB15/320*

# LADYBURN
### Lowlands, 1966–2000. William Grant & Sons. Closed.

**Mo Ór Collection Rare Ayrshire 1974 36 Years Old** first fill bourbon barrel, cask no. 2608, dist 10 May 74, bott 1 Nov 11 (89.5) n22 t23.5 f22 b22.5. I had a feeling it'd be this distillery when I saw the title on the label... it couldn't be much else! Fascinating to think that I was in final countdown for my 'O' levels when this was made. It appears to have dealt with the passing years better than I have. Even so, I had not been prepared for this. For years during the very early 1990s Grant's blender David Stewart sent me samples of this stuff and it was, to put it mildly, not great. Some were the oakiest malt I ever tasted in my life. And, to compound matters further, the distillery's own bottling was truly awful. But this cask has re-written history. *46%. nc ncf sc. Release No. 4. The Whisky Talker. 261 bottles.*

# LAGAVULIN
Islay, 1816. Diageo. Working.

**Lagavulin Aged 8 Years** bott code: L7285CM013 db (95.5) n25 t23.5 f23 b24.5 Having gone from the colouring-spoiled Cardhu to this chardonnay-hued Lagavulin in all its bourbon cask nakedness, you have to wonder: why don't they do this for all their whiskies. This was the age I first tasted Lagavulin possibly the best part of 40 years ago. It was love at first flight, and my passions – with the whisky in this beautifully natural form, though not as heavily peated now as then – have not been remotely doused. 48%.

**Lagavulin Aged 12 Years** bott 2017, bott code: L7089CM000 db (94) n23.5 t23.5 f23 b24 When I first tasted Lagavulin at this age, the phenol levels were around the 50ppm mark and not the present day 35. That meant the finish offered just a little extra Islay. Even so, I challenge you not to adore this. 56.5%.

⬦ **Lagavulin Aged 12 Years** bott 2018, bott code: L8072CM008 db (96) n24 stunningly dry and soot-like. The phenols come, wave after wave landing on the nose and building in depth like snow on a frozen field...; t24 a stunning exhibition of light oil helps soften the landing as the phenols breeze in with intent... here, though, the magic occurs because a just-so degree of barley sugars filters into the mix to balance the impact of the drier phenols and tannins which had previously held sway; the spices are textbook in weight and intensity; f23.5 a little cocoa is added to the sooty mix but a late slight bitter-bite from the tannin; b24.5 technically, from a distilling perspective, borderline perfection. From a maturation one, slightly weaker for, although the bourbon casks give you the clearest view possible of the brilliance of the spirit, a very slight late bitterness just breaks the spell. Even so, we are talking Islay at its most truly classic. 57.8%.

**Lagavulin 12 Year Old** refill American oak hogsheads db (96) n24.5 t24 f23.5 b24 I think whisky like this was invented by the whisky gods to be experienced at this full strength. Even people who do not regard themselves as peat lovers are likely to be seduced by this one. Talk about controlled power.... 56.5%. Diageo Special Releases 2017.

**Lagavulin 16 Years Old** db (95) n24 t24 f23 b24 Although I have enjoyed this whisky countless times socially, it is the first time for a while I have dragged it into the Tasting Room for professional analysis for the Bible. If anyone has noticed a slight change in Lagavulin, they would be right. The peat remains profound but much more delicate than before, while the oils appear to have receded. A different shape and weight dispersal for sure. But the sky-high quality remains just the same. 43%

⬦ **Game of Thrones Lagavulin 9 Year Old House Lannister** db (89.5) n22 pretty subdued smoke by Laga standards...; t23.5 an early toffee development before so wonderful peat launches in with spice on its coattails. Rich muscovado sugars at play, too. Butterscotch and playful spice at the midpoint as the smoke goes AWOL...; f21.5 back to some dullish caramels; b22.5 Lagavulin as I have never seen it before, the phenols being kept on a tight leash. 46%.

**Dramfool 10 Avian Gull Too 9 Years Old** 1st fill Oloroso Octave finish (91) n22.5 t23 f22.5 b23 No detectable sulphur (hurrah!) and definitely a better and more measured version of this too often OTT style of malt. I admit: I thoroughly enjoyed this classy malt. 57.9%. nc ncf. 66 bottles.

**The Whisky Barrel Isle of Islay 10 Year Old** refill hogshead, cask no. 200703, dist 17 Oct 07, bott Feb 18 (95.5) n24 t24 f23.5 b24 If this is Lagavulin, then this is how it should be commercially bottled: 100% ex-bourbon at full strength and ten years old. It is like being given the elixir of life... 57.1%. sc. 285 bottles.

# LAPHROAIG
Islay, 1815. Beam Suntory. Working.

**Laphroaig 10 Years Old** db (90) n24 t23 f20.5 b22.5 Has reverted back slightly towards a heavier style in more recent bottling, though I would like to see that old oomph at the very death. Even so, this is, indisputably, a classic whisky. The favourite of Prince Charles apparently: he will make a wise king... 40%

**Laphroaig 10 Year Old** bott code: L80099MB1 db (94) n23.5 t23.5 f23.5 b24 An essay in voluptuousness. The oils speak volumes here, gathering the two-toned phenols and landing them in all corners of the palate and ensuring they stick there. The iodine kick off on the nose is like a salty trademark, the balance between the sootier phenols and juicer Demera notes a joy to experience. The finish is not so much enormous as controlled and long, with a sublime degree of mocha moving in for the last blissful moments. Glorious, still after all these years... 40%.

**Laphroaig 10 Years Old Original Cask Strength** db (92) n22 t24 f23 b23 Caramel apart, this is much truer to form than one or two or more recent bottlings, aided by the fresh, gristy sweetness and explosive spices. Wonderful! 55.7%

**Laphroaig 12 Year Old 2005** bott 2017 db (91.5) n21.5 t23.5 f23 b23.5 Here we go: one of the exceptions in whisky that proves the rule. I have long wailed about the usage of PX cask and peaty malt together. And from the nose, you think your case will be won again, for here is another example of one giant nullifying another: both the smoke and fruit cancelling the other out. Yet, confound it, the delivery shows signs of proving me wrong and the finish continues in the same fashion. For once a PX cask is allowing the peat to breathe and sing. And what's more itself kick up a juicy encore. Beyond the nose a PX and smoky giant that walks tall. Who would have thought...? 55.3%. Selected for CWS.

**Laphroaig Aged 15 Years** db **(79)** n20 t20 f19 b20. A hugely disappointing, lacklustre dram that is oily and woefully short on complexity. Not what one comes to expect either from this distillery or age. 43%

**Laphroaig 18 Years Old** db **(94)** n24 t23.5 f23 b23.5 This is Laphroaig's replacement to the woefully inadequate and gutless 15-year-old. And talk about taking a giant step in the right direction. Absolutely brimming with character and panache, from the first molecules escaping the bottle as you pour to the very final ember dying on the middle of your tongue. 48%

**Laphroaig Aged 25 Years** db **(94)** n23 t24 f23.5 b23.5 Like the 27-y-o, an Islay which doesn't suffer for sherry involvement. Very different from a standard, bourbon barrel-aged Laphroaig with much of the usually complexity reined in, though its development is first class. This one's all about effect - and it works a treat! 40%

**Laphroaig Aged 27 Years** dist Oct 88 to Nov 89, bott Mar 17, bott code: L7062VB1 db **(96.5)** n24.5 t24 f23.5 b24.5 The 27 passing years and the added interference of fresh ex-bourbon barrels and quarter casks has taken its toll on the potency of the peat. Instead of Laphroaig pulsing with its renowned style of sea-soaked phenols, we are now faced with a dram which is more than content to allow age and gentility to be the guiding hand; so now less febrile and more cerebral. Such an honour to taste whiskies of this extraordinary yet understated magnitude. I can think of no other presently available whisky which so eloquently demonstrates that you don't have to stand a spoon up in the peat for the phenols to have such a vital input. 41.7%. ncf.

**Laphroaig Aged 30 Years** db **(94)** n24 t23 f23 b24. The best Laphroaig of all time? Nope, because the 40-y-o is perhaps better still... just. However, Laphroaig of this subtlety and charm gives even the very finest Ardbeg a run for its money. A sheer treat that should be bottled at greater strength. 43%

**Laphroaig Aged 40 Years** db **(94)** n23 t24 f23 b24. Mind-blowing. A malt that defies all logic and theory to be in this kind of shape at such age. The Jane Fonda of Islay whisky. 43%

**Laphroaig The 1815 Legacy Edition** bott code: L7059VB1 2070 db **(92.5)** n24 t24 f21 b23.5 a sherry butt away from one of the best new whiskies of the year. 48%. Travel Retail Exclusive.

**Laphroaig Au Cuan Mòr** db **(95)** n24 t24 f23 b24 You don't need to squint at the back label to be told that first fill bourbon barrels are at work here: this is where Kentucky, Jerez and Islay merges with breath-taking ease and harmony. 48%. Travel retail exclusive.

**Laphroaig Brodir Port Wood Finish** bott code: L6157MB1 db **(91.5)** n24 probably one of the most old-fashioned Islay warehouse aromas I have ever encountered: that incomparable mix of smoke, oak and grape hanging thickly in a moist, salty air...; t22 the usual gristy sugars have been silenced by the intense, moody fruit; f23 much better balance late on as a little liquorice and treacle joins the clouds of phenols to ensure complexity; b22.5 this is a big Laphroaig at its most brooding and taciturn. Not for when you are at your most frivolous. 48%.

**Laphroaig Four Oak** bott code: L6327VB1 2359 db **(88)** n22 t22.5 f21.5 b22 Attractive, but the smoke seems a little in awe of the oak as it is unusually quiet. 40%. Travel Retail Exclusive.

**Laphroaig Lore** db **(94)** n23.5 t24 f23 b23.5 Seeing how much I adore this distillery – and treasure my near 40 years of tasting its exceptional malt and visiting its astonishing home – I left this to become my 750th new whisky for the 2016 Whisky Bible. "Our richest expression ever" the label promised. It isn't. Big, fat and chunky? Tick. Bounding with phenols? Yep. Enjoyable? Aye! Richest expression ever. Nah. Not quite. Still, a friendly beast worth cuddling up with. And, whatever they say on the label, this is a stunner! 48%. ncf.

**Laphroaig Lore** bott code: L7229VB1 db **(96)** n23.5 t24 f24 b24.5 Laphroaig how I've never quite seen it before – and we are talking some 40 years of intimately studying this malt: truly a lore unto itself... 48%.

**Laphroaig PX Cask** bourbon, quarter and Pedro Ximenez casks db **(96)** n23.5 t24.5 f24 b24. I get the feeling that this is a breathtaking success despite the inclusion of Pedro Ximenez casks. This ultra sweet wine is often paired with smoky malt, often with disastrous consequences. Here it has worked, but only because the PX has been controlled itself by absolutely outstanding oak. And the ability of the smoke to take on several roles and personas simultaneously. A quite beautiful whisky and unquestionably one of the great malts of the year...in spite of itself. 48%. Travel Retail exclusive.

**Laphroaig Quarter Cask** db **(96)** n23 t24 f24 b25 A great distillery back to its awesome, if a little sweet, self. Layer upon layer of sexed-up peatiness. The previous bottling just needed a little extra complexity on the nose for this to hit mega malt status. Now it has been achieved... 48%

**Laphroaig Select** db (89) n22 t22 f23 b22 Missed a trick by not being unchillfiltered at 46%. An après-taste squint at the back label revealed some virgin oak casks had been used here, which explains much! 40%. WB15/117

**Laphroaig Triple Wood** ex-bourbon, quarter and European oak casks db (86) n21 t21.5 f21.5 b21. A pleasing and formidable dram. But one where the peat takes perhaps just too much of a back seat. Or, rather, is somewhat neutralised to the point of directional loss. The sugars, driven home by the heavy weight of oak, help give the whisky a gloss almost unrecognisable for this distillery. Even so, an attractive whisky in many ways. 48%. ncf.

Carn Mor Laphroaig 8 Year Old 2010 hogshead (95) n23.5 full blown peated Islay does not come more vibrant than this. Not the usual seaweedy style: gristy and fresh but still salty and punchy with a little bit of hickory getting on in the peaty act...; t24 strap yourself in and wheeeee!!! Off we go on a roller-coaster of a delivery, throwing the taste buds all over the show. Fabulous oils soften some of the impact, thankfully, but the smoke is in dual purpose mode here, both adding impressive and expected weight, but also filling the mouth with a three dimensional degree of phenol. Even so, the freshness of the spirit means it is as juicy as you'll ever see a Laphroaig and the sweetness, sometimes profound, are all of a barley sugar variety...; f23.5 deepens and dries, even to the point of a fabulous sootiness quite at odds with the salivating start; b24 oh, god! How I love this!! Young Laphroaig just being allowed to be itself...! And at a criminally overlooked age for this kind of south east coast Islay. What a classic! 63.4%. sc. Exclusive to The Whisky Barrel. 284 bottles.

**The Exclusive Malts Laphroaig Aged 6 Years** refill sherry hogshead, cask no. 195, dist 05 May 11 (87) n21.5 t22 f22 b21.5 Sherry and peat are seldom comfortable bedfellows and here we can see, despite all the phenolic beating of chests and the thumping alcohol present, why. The complexity is reduced a little by the light fruit and the peat cancelling each other out. There is no denying the brilliance of the spice, though, or the attractiveness of the oils and meandering dark sugars. Enjoyable for sure, but you get the feeling that had the age been doubled so, too, would the complexity. 58.7%. nc ncf sc. 237 bottles. Bottled by the Creative Whisky Co.

The First Editions Laphroaig Aged 13 Years 2005 refill hogshead, cask no. 15534, bott 2018 (90) n22 unusually contrite smoke, almost apologetically peeping out from behind the spice and vanilla; t23 beautiful oils on delivery and with it a pleasing mixture of liquorice, smoke and malted milk biscuit; f22.5 dry, with a little cocoa infiltrating the light smoke and persistent spice; b22.5 charmingly understated, but never loses its distillery identity. 52.5%. nc ncf sc. 332 bottles.

The First Editions Laphroaig Aged 18 Years 2000 refill hogshead, cask no. 15530, bott 2018 (87.5) n22.5 t22 f21 b22 Sports that unmistakable, unique, "Allied Domecq" bitterness at the very death. But doesn't entirely subtract from the bold anthracite and peat nose, nor the Manuka honey on the friendly delivery. 48.8%. nc ncf sc. 204 bottles.

Gleann Mór Laphroaig Aged Over 21 Years (91) n23 t23 f22 b23 A pleasing sweet and dry interplay impresses most in this charming and spicy bottling. Some impressive coal tar on the nose, though since the soot ensures a serious depth to the dryness, both on nose and finish. The spices refuse to act their age as does the excellent Manuka honey strand which doesn't just counter the phenols abut actually cocks a snook at them. Great late night imbibing... 56.3%.

**Old Malt Cask Laphroaig Aged 12 Years** refill hogshead, cask no. 14099, dist Sept 04, bott Aug 17 (93) n24 t23 f22.5 b23.5 Old school Laphroaig: the kind of malt which keeps the Peatheads very happy, indeed...and with very good reason. Impressive. 50%. nc ncf sc. 339 bottles.

**Old Malt Cask Laphroaig Aged 16 Years** refill butt, cask no. 13741, dist Feb 01, bott Apr 17 (89) n23 t22 f22 b22 Big on the peat but closes up just a little too early for greatness. 50%. nc ncf sc. 742 bottles.

**Old Particular Laphroaig 18 Years Old** refill hogshead, cask no. 11634, dist Dec 98, bott Mar 17 (95) n24 t23.5 f23.5 b24 Glorious! 48.4%. nc ncf sc. 262 bottles.

**Scotch Malt Whisky Society Cask 29.232 18 Year Old** refill ex-bourbon barrel, dist 11 Nov 98 (92) n23.5 t23 f22.5 b23 Laphroaig being Laphroaig. 59.1%. sc.

**Scotch Malt Whisky Society Cask 29.237 18 Year Old** refill ex-bourbon barrel, dist 11 Nov 98 (84.5) n22.5 t22 f19 b21 The shyness of the nose does at least give some warning of the fiery phenols to follow. The cask has not done the spirit justice, resulting in a hot and unstructured malt with a very dim finish. 60.9%. sc.

# LINKWOOD
### Speyside, 1820. Diageo. Working.
**Linkwood 12 Years Old** db (94.5) n23.5 t24 f23 b24 Possibly the most improved distillery bottling in recent times. Having gone through a period of dreadful casks, it appears to have come through to the other side very much on top and close to how some of us remember it a quarter of a century ago. Sublime malt: one of the most glittering gems in the Diageo crown. 43%

⬩⬩⬩ **Berry Bros & Rudd Linkwood 12 Years Old** cask no. 102, dist 2006, bott 2018 **(91)** n22.5 clean and malty in the classic distillery style; salted lime; t22.5 busy, intense barley with a touch of lemon puff biscuit; f23 heads now more into custard cream and bourbon biscuit territory, But intense barley is never far away...; b23 crumbs! Plays the austere Speysider with panache. 46%. ncf ncf sc.

**Gordon & MacPhail Private Collection Linkwood 1956** first fill sherry hogshead, cask no. 20, bott 23 Aug 17 **(90.5)** n23.5 t23 f22 b22 Always heart-warming to come across a new bottling of a whisky older than me: once quite a common occurrence but in recent years an increasingly and depressingly rare event. Well this is the only one; and also my 1,250th whisky for the 2019 Bible. And which of us has aged better...? I'll let you decide... 49.4%. sc.

**Hepburn's Choice Linkwood 10 Years Old** refill hogshead, dist 2006, bott 2017 **(89)** n22 t23 f22 b22 Delightfully simple. 46%. nc ncf sc. 372 bottles.

**Kingsbury Gold Linkwood 25 Years Old** sherry hogshead, cask no. 10434, dist 1991 **(94.5)** n23.5 t24 f23 b24 Well played Kingsbury: you have again managed to find a Speyside malt matured in sherry but without a hint of sulphur. That really does take some doing these days. Linkwood in sherry – or should that be cherry? - as it should be. 54.1%. 229 bottles.

**Old Malt Cask Linkwood Aged 20 Years** refill hogshead, cask no. 14098, dist Jun 97, bott Aug 17 **(90)** n22.5 t23 f22 22.5 When working on an 18- or 21-year-old blend, this is the type of malt blenders get pretty excited about: a sample which offers a vivid richness to the malt make up and punching the barley through on both nose and delivery. 50%. nc ncf sc. 297 bottles.

**Old Particular Linkwood 20 Years Old** refill hogshead, cask no. 12036, dist Jun 97, bott Aug 17 **(94)** n23 t23.5 f23.5 b24 Real understated class. 51.5%. nc ncf sc. 326 bottles.

⬩⬩⬩ **Scyfion Choice Linkwood 2001** Madrasa cask finished, bott 2018 **(87)** n21.5 t22 f21.5 b22 A bit hefty on the oak as it appears to be missing the usual malty back up. Instead a wafer thin fruit veneer holds everything in place, except the spices which escape at will. Enjoyable. 46%. nc ncf sc. 294 bottles.

**Scotch Malt Whisky Society Cask 39.166 27 Year Old** **(92.5)** n23 t23.5 f23 b23 From the nose you'd be expecting a spiced up, oaky chap with a little bit of the devil. Instead you get a well-constructed, lush, chewy and beautifully paced malt with little of the spice so evident on the aroma until the very measured end. So much natural caramel at work here, too, sitting very comfortably with the fruit to produce a chewy fruit toffee candy effect. 56.6%. sc. Bottled for Whisky L! & Fine Spirits Show.

⬩⬩⬩ **The Whisky Embassy Linkwood Aged 21 Years** refill sherry hogshead, cask no. 4239, dist 17 Apr 97, bott 5 Dec 18 **(77)** n19 t21 f18 b19 Three guesses. No, make that one. 56.9%. nc ncf sc.

**Whisky Illuminati Linkwood 19 Year Old** American oak hogshead, cask no. 10926, dist 1998 **(88.5)** n21.5 t22.5 f22 b22.5 I could wax lyrical about this Malt Fest. Enjoy! 58.5%. sc. 269 bottles. Candlelight Series.

# LITTLEMILL

### Lowland, 1772. Loch Lomond Distillers. Demolished.

**Littlemill 21 Year Old 2nd Release** bourbon cask db **(87)** n22 t21.5 f21.5 b22. So thin you expect it to fragment into a zillion pieces on the palate. But the improvement on this as a new make almost defies belief. The sugars are crisp enough to shatter on your teeth, the malt is stone hard and fractured and, on the finish, does show some definite charm before showing its less attractive teeth....and its roots... Overall, though, more than enjoyable. 47%. nc ncf.

**Littlemill 25 Year Old** db **(92.5)** n22 t24 f23 b23.5 Another example of a malt which was practically undrinkable in its youth but that is now a reformed, gentle character in older age. 52%

⬩⬩⬩ **Littlemill 40 Year Old Celestial Edition** db **(90.5)** n23.5 t23 f22 b22.5 As we all know, when this was distilled four decades back, the new make sprang from the stills as fire water. And for the first few years in the cask it roared at and incinerated the palate of any blender foolhardy enough to try it. And so, inevitably, the distillery died. In later years it is making up for its violent youth and here offers a serene maltiness about as far removed from its original character as is possible. Enjoy the dying rays of this once vituperative spirit, now so charming in its dotage. 46.8%. 250 bottles.

**Littlemill 1964** db **(82)** n21 t20 f21 b20. A soft-natured, bourbony chap that shows little of the manic tendencies that made this one of Scotland's most-feared malts. Talk about mellowing with age... 40%

**Littlemill 2017 Private Cellar 27 Year Old** db **(93)** n23 t23.5 f23 b23.5 How ironic and sad that the last casks of what were unloved – and unusable - firewater when distilled have now, after nearly three decades, calmed into a malt which is the matured embodiment of grace and finesse. 51.3%.

⬩⬩⬩ **Master of Malt Single Cask Littlemill 27 Year Old** dist 1991 **(94.5)** n23 t24 f23.5 b24 Another old Littlemill shewing genuine elegance in its twilight years. Kind of Malteser candy with benefits from the moment it hits the palate right through to the finale. A little bourbon-style tannin on the nose doesn't quite prepare you for the chocolatey maltfest which follows... Truly delicious. I promise you: no-one, and I mean no-one, could envision it would be this good in the days when it was working.... 47.2%. sc.

# LOCH LOMOND
**Highlands (Southwestern), 1966. Loch Lomond Distillers. Working.**

**Loch Lomond Aged 10 Years Lightly Peated** bott code: 10 01 2019 db **(86) n20.5 t22 f21.5 b22** Maybe I'm wrong, but this strikes me as being a vatting of distillation types (Inchmoan, Croftengea etc.) with their usual designated Loch Lomond straight and clean style. The result is a feinty beast, much heavier than any "Loch Lomond" I have before encountered, but buttressed with some major fudge and phenols: the Loch Lomond Monster... 40%.

**Loch Lomond Aged 12 Years** db **(93.5) n22.5 t23.5 f23.5 b24** Great to see they now have the stocks to allow this malt to really flex its muscles... 46%. ncf.

**Loch Lomond 14 Year Old Peated** bourbon cask db **(83) n21 t21.5 f20.5 b20.** Lomond can do a lot, lot better than this. Huge malts but entirely out of sync and never comfortable with the oils present. This isn't the Loch Lomond I know and love. 46% nc ncf.

**Loch Lomond 15 Year Old** db **(87.5) n21.5 t22 f22 b22** Spends a lot of its time waving its malty flag. But a slight tartness on both nose and on palate means it never quite settles into a comfortable narrative 46%.

**Loch Lomond Aged 18 Years** db **(89.5) n22 t23 f22.5 b22.5** There is always something slightly irresistible when you come across a single malt where the peat beats a gentle rhythm rather than its own chest... 46%. ncf.

**Loch Lomond 21 Years Old** db **(89.5) n22.5 t23 f22 b22.** A little while since I last tasted this, and pretty close to exactly how I remember it. Seems to revel in its own enormity! 43%

**Loch Lomond The Open Special Edition** db **(80) n20 t21 f19 b20** Straight into the rough. 46%.

**Loch Lomond The Open 18 Year Old Course Collection Carnoustie 1999** db **(92) n23 t23.5 f22 b23.5** Decided to wait until the 2018 Open at Carnoustie was in full swing before checking to see if this is up to par. Well, it is beyond that: a true double birdie as rarely is Loch Lomond this clean and malt rich. Would grace any 19th hole... 47.2%.

**Loch Lomond Organic 12 Year Old** bourbon cask db **(83.5) n19 t20 f23 b21.5.** A malty beast. But in some respects has more in common with a German still than a traditional pot. Definite traces of feint. 48%. nc ncf.

**Loch Lomond Organic Aged 17 Years** bott code: L2 120 18 db **(96.5) n24 t24.5 f23.5 b24.5** Organic...? Orgasmic, more like! A dram which will win the hearts, minds and souls of both bourbon and scotch whisky lovers. In fact, if you don't like this, whatever the cut of your jib, you might as well give up now... 54.9%. nc ncf.

**Loch Lomond 25 Year Old Three Wood Matured Colin Montgomerie** db **(95) n24** such a gentle sweetness and subtle weight to this: the tannins are easy to spot, yet the barley still holds sway. Light ulmo honey and Lubeck marzipan intertwine effortlessly: ultra-delicate for a 25-year-old and even the vaguest hint of phenols on the breeze; **t23.5** ahhh! We have hit exotic fruit territory here, a sure sign of both outstanding distillate and cask. Lightly salivating, the barley still retains a certain firmness, but now the oak holds the aces; **f23.5** long with a waxy, lime blossom honey fade; the lightest spices move in with the late minty chocolate; **b24** I have never met Colin Montgomery, though his car and my car once parked simultaneously nose to tail in Mayfair, London, our respective personalised number plates almost touching. Mr Montgomery, I noted, was quite a large individual so was not surprised that he could persuade a small rubber ball to travel a great distance with one well-timed thwack. This whisky, then, being of a delicate and fragile nature is very much, physically, his antitheses. No doubt Colin Montgomery found the rough a few times in his long career; he certainly won't with this. 46.3%.

**Loch Lomond Classic** American oak casks, bott code: 17 12 2018 db **(84.5) n21 t22.5 f20 b21** Though called "Classic", the flat, chewy toffee middle and finish makes this pleasant but very un-Lomond like in character. Fudged in every sense... 40%.

**Loch Lomond Cristie Kerr Vintage 2002** db **(94) n23** the vaguest hint of smoky bacon adds what little weight there is to this gentle celebration of barley; **t23.5** such a beautiful presentation of barley in all its heather-honeyed finery. Salivating, lightly oaked and perfectly spiced; **f23.5** continues in the same form, but late on a little nuttiness appears, which moves towards praline; **b24** Lomond at is malty best and cleanest. Someone in Toronto this year told me he had never found a Loch Lomond he'd ever enjoyed. I hope he discovers this minor classic... 48.1%.

**Loch Lomond The Open Special Edition Distiller's Cut** first fill bourbon and refill American oak casks, bott code: 12 03 2019 db **(95.5) n23.5** such a sexy combination of green apple and slightly under-ripe Asian pear dovetailing with the cleanest barley imaginable; **t25** despite a feeling of youth with this, the blend of acacia honey and intense yet refined barley is borderline perfect. No, dammit! It is perfect....!!! **f23** light with a more orthodox vanilla and butterscotch fade; **b24** one of the finest Loch Lomonds I have ever encountered. No: the finest. The distillery will go up several notches above par for anyone lucky enough to encounter this one.... 46%. ncf. Chosen for Royal Portrush.

**Loch Lomond Portrush Open Course Collection** db **(82) n22 t21.5 f19 b20** Pleasant enough start, though dulled and then damaged by the wine cask influence, with sulphur leaking through at the end. Hard going. Reminded me of when I once played Royal Portrush, on a broiling hot day nearly 20 years ago. And despite being only two inches from a hole in one, it was the most punishing and miserable afternoon of my life. From that day I have never visited another golf club to place ball on tee and decided that if I were to spend a rare afternoon in the fresh air, rather than fruitlessly chasing birdies it would be spent watching birds instead. And that is exactly what I have done since that day forth... 46.3%.

**Loch Lomond Original** bourbon casks db **(81.5) n20 t21 f20 b20.5**. Hmmm. Surprisingly feinty, though the really wide cut does ensure a huge number of flavours. A distinctly German style to this. 40%

**Glengarry 12 Year Old** db **(92.5) n22.5 t23.5 f23 b23.5** Probably the most intense malt on the market today. Astonishing. And stunning.46%. ncf.

**Inchmoan Aged 10 Years Peated** bott code: L2 106 18 db **(83) n20 t21.5 f20.5 b21** Living, as I do, in the country, I know a cattle byre when I nose one. And here it is most certainly on show. This can be achieved sometimes when the cut isn't quite right and reacting with the peated malt. Or can just be from the type of peat itself. Well, here is the former case. 46%. nc ncf. Loch Lomond Island Collection.

**Inchmoan Aged 12 Years Peated** recharred American oak & refill bourbon casks, bott code: L2/188/17 db **(89) n20 t23.5 f22.5 b23.5** That little bit of nougat marks this out as distinctively Inchmoan while the vibrancy of the peat offers a bit of a beast... 46%. ncf.
**Inchmoan 1992 Peated** refill bourbon barrels db **(95) n23 t24.5 f23.5 b24** I do believe I was at Loch Lomond distillery in 1992 while they were producing the Inchmoan strand of their output. So to see it after all this time is astonishing. No less astonishing is the sheer excellence of the malt, which here is almost a cross between a light rye-recipe bourbon and a smoky island scotch. This is a true Loch Lomond classic 48.6%. ncf. Loch Lomond Island Collection.

**Inchmurrin 12 Years Old** db **(86.5) n21.5 t22 f21.5 b21.5**. A significantly improved dram which is a bit of a malt soup. Love the Demerara injection. 40%

**Inchmurrin Aged 15 Years** bourbon cask, bott Dec 12 db **(86) n22 t21.5 f21 b21.5**. Slightly tangy with an edge to the cask which interferes with the usual malty procession. 46%. nc ncf.

**Inchmurrin Aged 18 Years** bourbon cask, bott Dec 12 db **(92.5) n22.5 t23.5 f23.5 b23**. Loch Lomond distillery in its brightest colours. 46%. nc ncf. Glen Catrine Bonded Warehouse Ltd.

**Inchmurrin Aged 21 Years** bourbon cask, bott Dec 12 db **(90) n22 t23 f22.5 b22.5**. This has spent 21 years in a very exceptional cask. Not exactly breathtaking complexity, but what it does is completed with aplomb. 46%. nc ncf. Glen Catrine Bonded Warehouse Ltd.

**Inchmurrin Loch Lomond Island Collection 12 Year Old** db **(87) n21.5 t22 f21.5 b22**. A thick malty offering with a weighty grist and maple syrup infusion. Big and clumsy. 46%. ncf.

**Inchmurrin Island Collection Aged 18 Years** db **(87) n21 t22.5 f21.5 b22**. Wow! That is quite a tangle of flavours and messages. Not quite sure where the "summer grass' on the label comes from. But date and walnut cake...now that would have made sense. Big and rather beautiful in an ugly kind of way... 46%. ncf. Loch Lomond Whiskies

**Inchmurrin Island Collection Madeira Wood Finish** db **(77) n17 t23 f18 b19**. Alas, it wasn't only sherry butts which were sulphur damaged. Mind you, the explosion of golden sultana on delivery is worth the discomfort. 46%. ncf. Loch Lomond Whiskies

**Acla Selection Croftengea 10 Years Old** hogshead, cask no. 495, dist 2006, bott 2016 **(84.5) n20 t22 f21.5 b21** Old school Croftengea – unlike the two 6-year-old offerings below – full of the distillery's myriad idiosyncrasies. Chunky, hefty on the peat, lush on the cocoa and not afraid to reveal a little feinty oiliness. 51.6%. sc. 90 bottles.

**The Cooper's Choice Croftengea 2007 11 Years Old** Madeira finish **(87.5) n21.5 t23 f21.5 b21.5** A typical Croftengea in that the peat is nuclear strength but the quirkiness of the stills gives it an impression of being out of focus. Not even a wine cask finish can correct it. Have to say, though: really fun whisky! 53%. nc ncf sc.

**Endangered Drams Loch Lomond 10 Year Old** bourbon cask, dist Mar 03, bott 2017 **(94) n23.5 t23.5 f23 b24** Endangered smoky Loch Lomond...? I should say, so: I didn't know they did one. Now an Inchmoan or Croftengea, maybe... But, right enough: it is in the clean Loch Lomond style... 58.5%. nc ncf.

**Golden Cask Croftengea Aged 6 Years** cask no. CM233, dist 2010, bott 2016 **(92) n23 t23.5 f22.5 b23** The cleanest, most Islay-style Croftengea I've ever encountered. A real style shock and totally delicious. 58.5%. sc. 319 bottles.

⟨⟨ **Hepburn's Choice Inchfad 13 Years Old** refill hogshead, dist 2005, bott 2018 **(82.5)** n20.5 t22 f19.5 b20.5 A little looseness on the cuts means the oils are a tad off key and overpowering, despite the peaty meatiness. Despite its obvious faults, there is a real charm to the jammy, juicy sweetness of the barley before everything wanders off on a tangent. 46%. nc ncf sc. 345 bottles.

⟨⟨ **Old Malt Cask Croftengea Aged 13 Years** refill hogshead, cask no. 15148, dist Feb 05, bott May 18 **(87.5)** n21.5 t23 f21.5 b21.5 A magnificently imperfect malt, groaning with all kinds of technical weaknesses. But there is no denying that the unique peat profile and those breathtakingly salivating gristy notes make for one genuinely delicious malt. 50%. nc ncf sc. 261 bottles.

**Spirit of Caledonia Croftengea 6 Years Old** cask no. 340 **(91.5)** n22.5 t23.5 f22.5 b23 Like the Golden Cask Croftengea, almost more Islay-like than an Islay... 58.3%. sc.

⟨⟨ **Spirit of Caledonia Inchfad** cask no. 426, dist 24 Feb 05, bott 13 Feb 19 **(86.5)** n21.5 t22 f21.5 b21.5 That uniquely Inchfadian mix of light peat and feints. Inchfad is a pretty rare mark to find from Loch Lomond and this bottling confers on it a distinctly German style, certainly the most German of all Scotland's single malt. The grist is also on maximum sweetness, so no lacking of flavour here. 55.4%. Mr. Whisky.

⟨⟨ **The Whisky Shop Loch Lomond Aged 15 Years** cask no. 15/624-1, dist 2004 **(94.5)** n23.5 a little moist ginger cake sits beautifully with the heather honey; t23.5 a LL mouthfeel you don't often find: almost like the crystalised sugar on the outside of a fruitcake; lovely toasted almonds and ever growing spice; f23.5 more tasted sugars now with butterscotch and some very late malt threads; b24 a distillery in its very finest clothes. 54.4%. sc.

⟨⟨ **World of Orchids Croftengea 2007 11 Years Old** bourbon cask, cask no. 58 **(90.5)** n22 cattle byres...with plenty of cattle...; t22.5 resounding oily, peat: a bit like the Inchfad I tasted earlier today except without all the feints. The sugars are intense and dark: smoked molasses; f23 spicy, toasty malt ...oh, and that grungy peat...; b23 living deep in the country as I do, I think I'm perfectly qualified to call this whisky agricultural... 58.5%. sc.

# LOCHSIDE
### Highlands (Eastern), 1957–1992. Chivas Brothers. Demolished.
**The Cooper's Choice Lochside 1967 Aged 44 Years** cask no. 807 **(96.5)** n24.5 t24.5 f23.5 b24 It is amazing that I had to travel 6,000 miles to find this in British Columbia. But, this is the kind of whisky you would travel four times that kind of distance to experience. Easily one of the top ten single casks I have tasted in the last five years. 41.5%. 354 bottles.

# LONGMORN
### Speyside, 1895. Chivas Brothers. Working.
**Longmorn 15 Years Old** db **(93)** n23 t24 f22 b24 These latest bottlings are the best yet: previous ones had shown just a little too much oak but this has hit a perfect compromise. An all-time Speyside great. 45%

**Longmorn 16 Years Old** db **(84.5)** n20.5 t22 f21 b21. This was one of the disappointments of the 2008 edition, thanks to the lacklustre nose and finish. This time we see a cautious nudge in the right direction: the colour has been dropped fractionally and the nose celebrates with a sharper barley kick with a peppery accompaniment. The non-existent (caramel apart) finale of yore now offers a distinct wave of butterscotch and thinned honey...and still some spice. Only the delivery has dropped a tad...but a price worth paying for the overall improvement. Still a way to go before the real Longmorn 16 shines in our glasses for all to see and fall deeply in love with. Come on lads in the Chivas lab: we know you can do it... 48%

**Longmorn 23 Year Old** db **(93)** n23 t24 f23 b23.5 I can just imagine how this would be such rich top dressing for the finest blend I could concoct: as a single malt it is no less a delight. 48%. ncf.

**Golden Cask Longmorn Aged 9 Years** cask no. CM228, dist 2007, bott 2016 **(94)** n23 t23.5 f23.5 b24 Longmorn at this age is criminally neglected for bottling – not least by the distillery owners. This shows the malt in, first, its most playful then most serious and statesmanlike light. Superb. 594%. sc. 115 bottles.

**Gordon & MacPhail Distillery Label Longmorn 2003** bott 18 May 17 **(94.5)** n23.5 t23.5 f23.5 b24 Anyone out for butterscotch and Werther's Originals had better get their skates on before all this has gone... 43%.

⟨⟨ **Kingsbury Silver Longmorn 13 Year Old** hogshead, cask no. 13696, dist 2003 **(92.5)** n22.5 a buttery, biscuity maltiness with a playful hint of nip and spice; t23 a glorious delivery where the malt is clean, salivating and unmolested, full bodied enough to cling to every contour on the palate; f23.5 oh, those spices....it just shouldn't be allowed...!! b23.5 for years and years blenders have used Longmorn as "top dressing": a malt rich in character, high in quality and abounding in enough personality to shape the blend in the direction they wish to take it. Here you can see exactly why... 46%. sc. 336 bottles.

# THE MACALLAN

Speyside, 1824. Edrington. Working.

**The Macallan 7 Years Old** db **(89) n23 t23 f21 b22.** An outstanding dram that underlines just how good young malts can be. Fun, fabulous and in recent bottlings has upped the clarity of the sherry intensity to profound new heights. 40%

**The Macallan Fine Oak 8 Years Old** db **(82.5) n20.5 t22 f20 b20.** A slight flaw has entered the mix here. Even so, the barley fights to create a distinctive sharpness. However, a rogue sherry butt has put paid to any hopes the honey and spice normally found in this brand. 40%

**The Macallan 10 Years Old** db **(91) n23 t23 f21.5 b23.5** For a great many of us, it is with the Mac 10 our great Speyside odyssey began. It has to be said that in recent years it has been something of a shadow of its former great self. However, this is the best version I have come across for a while. Not perhaps in the same league as those bottlings in the 1970s which made us re-evaluate the possibilities of single malt. But fine enough to show just how great this whisky can be when the butts have not been tainted and, towards the end, the balance between barley and grape is a relatively equal one. 40%

**The Macallan 10 Years Old Cask Strength** db **(85) n20 t22 f22 b21.** Enjoyable and would give chewing gum a run for its money. But over-egged the sherry here and not a patch on the previous bottling. 58.8%. Duty Free.

**The Macallan Fine Oak 10 Years Old** db **(90) n23 t22.5 f21.5 b22** Much more on the ball than the last bottling of this I came across. Malts really come as understated or as clever than this. 40%

**Macallan 12 Year Old** db **(61) n15 t16 f15 b15** An uncompromising and comprehensive essay in the present day sulphured sherry butt problem. 43% US tag CP981113

**The Macallan Sherry Oak 12 Years Old** db **(93) n24 t23.5 f22.5 b23** I have to say that some Macallan 12 I have tasted on the road has let me down in the last year or so. This is virtually faultless. Virtually a time machine back to another era... 40%

**The Macallan 12 Years Old Sherry Oak Elegancia** db **(86) n23 t22 f20 b21.** Promises, but delivers only to an extent. 40%

**The Macallan Fine Oak 12 Years Old** db **(95.5) n24 t24 f23.5 b24** A whisky whose quality has hit the stratosphere since I last tasted it. I encountered a disappointing one early in the year. This has restored my faith to the point of being a disciple... 40%

**Macallan Gran Reserva Aged 12 Years** db **(92) n23 t24 f22 b23** Well, you don't get many of these to the pound. A real throwback. The oloroso threatens to overwhelm but there is enough intrigue to make for a quite lovely dram which, as all good whiskies should, never quite tells the story the same way twice. Not entirely without blemish, but I'm being picky. A Macallan soaked in oloroso which traditionalists will swoon over. 45.6%

**The Macallan Fine Oak 15 Years Old** db **(79.5) n19 t21.5 f19 b20.** As the stock of the Fine oak 12 rises, so its 15-y-o brother, once one of my favourite drams, falls. Plenty to enjoy, but a few sulphur stains remove the gloss. 43%

**The Macallan Fine Oak 17 Years Old** db **(82) n19.5 t22 f19.5 b21.** Where once it couldn't quite make up its mind on just where to sit, it has now gone across to the sherry benches. Sadly, there are a few dissenters. 43%

**The Macallan Sherry Oak 18 Years Old** db **(87) n24 t22 f20 b21.** Underpowered. The body doesn't even come close to matching the nose which builds up the expectancy to enormous levels and, by comparison to the Independents, this at 43% appears weak and unrepresentative. Why this isn't at 46% at the very least and unambiguously uncoloured, I have no idea. 43%

**The Macallan Fine Oak 18 Years Old** db **(94.5) n23.5 t24 f23 b24** Is this the new Fine Oak 15 in terms of complexity? That original bottling thrived on the balance between casks types. This is much more accentuated on a cream sherry persona. But this sample is sulphur-free and quite fabulous. 43%

**The Macallan Fine Oak 21 Years Old** db **(84) n21 t22 f20 b21.** An improvement on the characterless dullard I last encountered. But the peaks aren't quite high enough to counter the sulphur notes and make this a great malt. 43%

**The Macallan 25 Years Old** db **(84.5) n22 t21 f20.5 b21.** Dry with an even drier oloroso residue; blood orange adds to the fruity mix. Something, though, is not entirely right about this and one fears from the bitter tang at the death that a rogue butt has gained entry to what should be the most hallowed of dumping troughs. 43%

**The Macallan Fine Oak 25 Years Old** db **(90) n22 t23.5 f22 b22.5** The first time I tasted this brand a few years back I was knocked off my perch by the peat reek which wafted about with cheerful abandon. Here the smoke is tighter, more shy and of a distinctly more anthracitic quality. Even so, the sweet juiciness of the grape juxtaposes gamely with the obvious age to create a malt of obvious class. *43%*

**The Macallan Fine Oak 25 Years Old** db **(89)** n23 t23 f21 b22. Very similar to the Fine Oak 18. However, the signature smoke has vanished, as I suppose over time it must. Not entirely clean sherry, but much remains to enjoy. *43%*

**The Macallan Fine Oak 30 Years Old** db **(81.5)** n22 t22 f18 b19.5. For all its many riches on delivery, especially those moments of great bourbon-honey glory, it has been comprehensively bowled middle stump by the sherry. Gutted. *43%*

**The Macallan Millennium 50 Years Old (1949)** db **(90)** n23 t22 f22 b23. Magnificent finesse and charm despite some big oak makes this another Macallan to die for. *40%*

**The Macallan Lalique III 57 Years Old** db **(95)** n24.5 t23 f23.5 b24 No experience with this whisky under an hour pays sufficient tribute to what it is all about. Checking my watch, I am writing this just two minutes under two hours after first nosing this malt. The score started at 88.5. With time, warmth, oxidation and understanding that score has risen to 95. It has spent 57 years in the cask; it deserves two hours to be heard. It takes that time, at least, not just to hear what it has to say to interpret it, but to put it into context. And for certain notes, once locked away and forgotten, to be slowly released. The last Lalique was good. But simply not this good. *48.5%*

**The Macallan 1824** db **(88)** n24 t23.5 f19 b21.5. Absolutely magnificent whisky, in part. But there are times my job is depressing...and this is one of them.. *48%*

**The Macallan 1824 Estate Reserve** db **(90.5)** n22 excellent clean grape with an intriguing dusting of mint; t23 almost a Jamaican pot still rum sheen and sweetness; beautiful weight and even some barley present; f22.5 satisfying, gorgeously clean with very good vanilla-grape balance; b23 don't know about Reserve: definitely good enough for the First Team. *45.7%*

**The Macallan 1824 Select Oak** db **(82)** n19 t22 f20 b21. Soft, silky, sometimes sugary... and tangy. Not convinced every oak selected was quite the right one. *40%*

**The Macallan 1851 Inspiration** db **(77)** n19.5 t19.5 f19 b19. Flat and uninspirational in 2008. *41%*

**Macallan Cask Strength** db **(94)** n22 t24 f24 b24. One of those big sherry babies; it's like surfacing a massive wave of barley-sweetened sherry. Go for the ride. *58.6%. USA.*

**The Macallan Estate Reserve** db **(84)** n22 t22 f20 b20. Doh! So much juice lurking about, but so much bitterness, too. ...grrrrr!!!! *45.7%*

**The Macallan Fine Oak Master's Edition** db **(91)** n23 t23 f22 b23 Adorable. *42.8%*

**The Macallan Fine Oak Whisky Maker's Selection** db **(92)** n22 t23 f23 b24. This is a dram of exquisite sophistication. Coy, mildly cocoaed dryness, set against just enough barley and fruit sweetness here and there to see off any hints of austerity. Some great work has gone on in the lab to make this happen: fabulous stuff! *42.8%. Duty Free.*

**The Macallan Gold** sherry oak cask db **(89.5)** n22 t23.5 f21.5 b22.5. No Macallan I have tasted since my first in 1975 has been sculpted to show the distillery in such delicate form. *40%*

**The Macallan Oscuro** db **(95.5)** n24.5 t24 f23 b24. Oh, if all sherried whiskies could be that kind - and taste bud-blowingly fabulous! *46.5%*

**The Macallan Ruby** sherry oak cask db **(92.5)** n23 t24 f22 b23.5. Those longer in the tooth who remember the Macallan 10 of 30 years ago will nod approvingly at this chap. Perhaps one butt away from a gong! *43%*

**The Macallan Sienna** sherry cask db **(94.5)** n23 t24 f23.5 b24. The pre-bottling sample presented to me was much more vibrant than this early on, but lacked the overall easy charm and readily flowing general complexity of the finished article. A huge and pleasing improvement. *43%*

**The Macallan Rare Cask Black** db **(83.5)** n21.5 t22 f19 b21. Pretty rich and some intense, molasses, black cherry and liquorice notes to die for. But some pretty off-key ones, too. Overall, average fare. *48%*

**The Macallan Royal Marriage** db **(89)** n23.5 t22.5 f21 b22. Some amazing moments to remember. *46.8%*

**The Macallan Select Oak** db **(83)** n23 t21 f19 b20. Exceptionally dry and tight; and a little furry despite the early fruitiness. *40%*

**The Macallan Whisky Makers Edition** db **(76)** n19 t20 f18 b19. Distorted and embittered by the horrific "S" element... *42.8%*

**The Macallan Woodlands Limited Edition Estate Bottling** db **(86)** n21 t23 f21 b21. Toffee towards the finish brings a premature halt to a wonderfully mollased early delivery. *40%*

◇ **Cask 88 Macallan 1988** mizunara cask, cask no. 18/0H003 **(93)** n23 pungent, slightly floral, as though a lady has just opened her compact...; t23.5 gripping stuff: the unique Japanese oak grips the taste buds, shakes them for a bit and slowly lets go as a little Demerara sugar creeps in; f23 a little malt settles on the oak dust. A little heather honey handles the spice; **b23.5** powerful, but never overpowering. The Japanese influence is unmistakable and entertaining. *48.4%. sc.*

⟐ **Hard To Find Whisky Macallan Aged 30 Years** sherry cask, cask no. 2824, dist 1989, bott 30 Apr 19 **(93) n23.5 t24 f22.5 b23** This is the style Macallan is rightly famed for. Though finding a pure sherry-matured one with not an atom of sulphur really is a hard to find whisky. This is almost there, but not quite. Even so, it is closer to Macallan of yesteryear than 95% of others you are likely to come across these days and makes a point of luxuriating in the richness of the bitter-sweet fruit. Also, Macallan fans could do worse than picking up a bottle of this and comparing it to the Master of Malt's non-sherry influenced bottling. *44.1%. sc. 98 bottles.*

**Heiko Thieme's 1974 Macallan 65th Birthday Bottling** cask no. 16807 dist 25 Nov 74 bott Jul 08 **(94) n23 t23 f24 b24** This is not whisky because it is 38%abv. It is Scottish spirit. However, this is more of a whisky than a great many samples I have tasted this year. Ageism is outlawed. So is sexism. But alcoholism isn't....!! Try and become a friend of Herr Thieme and grab hold of something a little special. *38% 238 bottles.*

⟐ **Master of Malt Single Cask Macallan 30 Year Old** dist 1988 **(93.5) n22.5 t24 f23 b23.5** The oak has its fingers on all the buttons here. This is a significant age for a Macallan and the malt is at full stretch to keep the tannins at bay. But it remains intact and even conjures up some profound barley-sugar moments to ensure the oak doesn't get all its own way. But to its great credit, even when the oak returns with a vengeance, there is no hint of bitterness, though the spice levels rise significantly. High quality. *52%. sc.*

# MACDUFF
## Speyside, 1963. Bacardi. Working.

⟐ **The Deveron Aged 10 Years** bott code: L17 284ZAB03 2327 db **(94) n23.5** so fresh and gristy: the barley virtually warbles from the glass, such clarity does it possess; **t23.5** just brilliant. I am a complete sucker for this kind of fresh malt with minimum oak interference. A light icing sugar sweetness follows the grist, while the tannins are weightier, yet still possessing a degree of spice to keep things quietly lively; **f23** the spice buzz rumbles on; the malt is indefatigable; **b24** does the heart good to see a distillery bring their malt out as a ten-year- old – when so many think that such an age is beneath them. This shews the distillery at its most vivid and fresh, when the oak has had time to work its magic but not overstay its welcome; when the barley is still king. And, my word, its crown positively glitters gold here... *40%.*

**The Deveron 12 Year Old** db **(87.5) n22 t22 f21.5 b22.** Buttery and pleasant. But feels like driving a Ferrari with a Fiat Uno engine. Woefully underpowered and slightly too flat in too many places where it should be soaring. The trademark honey notes cannot be entirely defied, however. *40%*

⟐ **The Deveron Aged 12 Years** bott code: L172018700 db **(94.5) n23.5** retains its big malt personality, though there is far more citrus about now, the oak is weightier and brings onto play delicate layers of acacia honey...; **t23.5** ...and it is the honey which lays the foundations for the dropped malty intro.. The mouth feel is sexy and succulent, a light butterscotch note representing the oak; again, a citrus note hangs about, mainly lime; **f23** at last a little spice comes into play. But the continued complexity...just, wow! **b24** hi honey! I've homed in...! *40%.*

**The Deveron 18 Year Old** db **(94) n24.5 t23.5 f22.5 b23.5** Each bottle should be stamped" Class: handle with care"... *40%*

⟐ **The Deveron Aged 18 Years** bott code: L181168700 db **(93) n23** an audacious bid by blood-orange led citrus to dominate both the firm barley and firmer tannin; **t24** if there could be an award for the sexiest mouth feel of the year, this would be right up there. Lush barley and heather honey, aided by tingling spice and more citrus. The tannins move in slowly but to toasty effect; elsewhere a little exotic fruit gives a feel of hinted antiquity; **f22.5** lovely spice to inject a change of pace to the experience. But the barley persists, the honey hangs on...and the tannins get toastier and heavier still; just the vaguest dull and slightly bitter fuzziness at the finale; **b23.5** someone has started not to just fully understand this always badly underrated distillery, but put it on the map. *40%.*

**Endangered Drams Macduff 19 Year Old** cask no. 5253, dist Sept 97, bott Jun 17 **(95) n24 t24 f23 b24** There are times I would like to simply kiss this distillery. Its adorably gentle, sweet nature is perfectly captured in this delightful, slightly sexy and entirely seductive dram. *54.9%.*

**Fadandel.dk Macduff Aged 14 Years** refill sherry butt, cask no. 1801, dist 18 Mar 03, bott 27 Feb 18 **(88.5) n22 t22.5 f21.5 b22.5** An almost, though not quite, clean sherry butt, but the actual shape of the malt itself has been obfuscated by the fruit. *60.3%. sc. 24 bottles.*

⟐ **The First Editions Macduff Aged 21 Years 1997** refill hogshead, cask no. 15606, bott 2018 **(95) n23.5** freshly opened spice cupboard; **t24** the spiced-up tannins hit home first making for an unusually dry start despite the salivating third flavour wave. A little muscovado sugar and gristy barley lighten the load but the tannin is soon back in charge – or is it? The battle for supremacy is fought all over your taste buds...; **f23** toasty and you even fancy some paprika has crept in; **b24.5** spice is the variety of this malt. A magnificent little hottie! *51.5%. nc ncf sc. 271 bottles.*

❖ **The First Editions Macduff Aged 21 Years 1997** refill hogshead, cask no. 15366, bott 2018 **(94) n23** ground ginger mashed in with a bourbon-style tannin and grassy barley; **t23.5** explosive spice on delivery, propped up but intertwangling layers of golden syrup; **f23** the oak threatens to rake over but balustrades of barley keeps the sweetness ticking over while spices continue to pound; **b23.5** an outrageous spice bomb of a malt. Sheer, delicious entertainment. *54.4%. nc ncf sc. 288 bottles.*

**Golden Cask Macduff Aged 25 Years** cask no. CM235, dist 1992, bott 2017 **(94) n23 t23.5 f23.5 b24** An absolute gem of a cask. *56%. sc. 248 bottles.*

❖ **The Golden Cask Macduff 26 Years Old 1992** cask no. CM251, bott 2018 **(91.5) n22** hammers out a big, brash oaky message, with an orangey nibble on the side; **t23** full oils intact, thankfully, as that ensures the sweeter elements hang around – and with the oak on the warpath, it is just as well. Love the heather honey and its calming influence; **f23.5** return to an oakier theme, but a little chocolate orange hangs on the oils; **b23** what is a whisky this age doing at a strength like that....? Well, you don't often get the chance to experience a near 30-year-old malt whose abv can fair knock you back into the far recesses of your chair. *64.1%. nc ncf sc. 226 bottles*

**Gordon & MacPhail Connoisseurs Choice Macduff 2004** bott 28 Mar 17 **(96) n23.5 t24 f24 b24.5** This year has been a truly great year for MacDuff bottlings. Another peach of a dram showing the distillery in all its subtly honeyed and understatedly smoky brilliance. Early days, but any whisky which outpoints this for an award must be of the very rarest brilliance. *46%.*

❖ **Hepburn's Choice Macduff 11 Years Old** first fill bourbon barrel, dist 2006, bott 2018 **(88) n22.5** rhubarb and custard; **t22.5** sharp malt on delivery but we are soon back to custard for the mid-ground; **f21** very malty fade with a mix of muscovado sugars and oaky bitterness; **b22** almost a dessert whisky, so much custard to be found.... *46%. nc ncf sc. 231 bottles.*

**Kingsbury Gold Macduff 20 Years Old** hogshead, cask no. 4130, dist 1997 **(88.5) n22.5 t22 f22 b22** Surprisingly aggressive for a MacDuff – the distiller must have been in one hell of a hurry to get home. Plenty of pointers to some hidden excellence, though. *54.9%. 257 bottles.*

**Old Malt Cask Macduff Aged 20 Years** refill barrel, cask no. 14414, dist Oct 97, bott Nov 17 **(94) n23.5 t23.5 f23 b24** So pleasingly complex and gloriously manicured. A real triumph of a dram, not least with the surprise smoke element. *50%. nc ncf sc. 134 bottles.*

❖ **Old Malt Cask Macduff Aged 21 Years** refill hogshead, cask no. 15147, dist May 97, bott May 18 **(78) n20 t20 f18 b20** Sticks out like a sore thumb for the other Macduffs in this family, presumably a poor cask undoing the good of the spirit. A duff Macduff... *50%. nc ncf sc. 287 bottles.*

❖ **Scyfion Choice Macduff 2007** Pinot Noir cask finished, bott 2019 **(90.5) n22.5** sharp fruit almost bristles against the much quieter malt; an interesting floral backdrop; **t23** good grief...! The fruit goes on immediate attack, a grape and Chinese gooseberry mix which is calmed by the barley...; **f22.5** spices up as the oak now gets involved; **b22.5** anyone who loves eye-wateringly sharp boiled sweets should hunt this bottling down now..! *46%. nc ncf sc. 160 bottles.*

**Single Cask Collection Macduff 10 Years Old** bourbon barrel **(91) n22 t23.5 f22.5 b23** Evidence of a new still, or part of, here as there is a distinct sharpness t both the barley and sugars. *56.8%. sc.*

**Spirit of Caledonia Macduff 9 Years Old** cask no. 101732 **(95.5) n23.5 t24.5 f23.5 b24** A distillery which, given half a chance and the right circumstances, loves to show its honeyed edge. And it does so here, beautifully and all the while pulsing pure elegance. As 9-year-olds go, it doesn't get much better... *56.5%. sc.*

❖ **The Whisky Chamber Macduff 12 Years Old 2006** bourbon cask **(89) n22** a curious twitch of Parma violets amid the barley; **t23** intense, clean, energised malt still young enough to be naturally juicy; **f22** light spices on the biscuit barley; **b22** a slightly simplistic, though always attractive, malt. *53.1%. sc.*

**The Whisky Embassy Macduff Aged 20 Years** cask no. 4081, dist 12 Jun 97, bott 16 Nov 17 **(88) n22.5 t22 f21.5 b22** Some tangy oak interference can't entirely distract from the elegance of the malt itself. *55.7%. nc ncf sc.*

❖ **World of Orchids Macduff 2003 15 Years Old** bourbon cask, cask no. 106 **(89) n21** tangy and a little uncomfortable; **t22.5** wow! The barley makes up for the cask in style as it goes in mouth-watering, malty orbit; **f23** late mocha lifts the malt further; **b22.5** a little on the tangy side for a bourbon cask, but the highly intense fresh barley guarantees quality. *57.9%. sc.*

# MANNOCHMORE
### Speyside, 1971. Diageo. Working.
**Mannochmore Aged 12 Years** db **(84) n22 t21 f20 b21.** As usual the mouth arrival fails to live up to the great nose. Quite a greasy dram with sweet malt and bitter oak. *43%.*

**Mannochmore Aged 25 Years** dist 1990 db **(90)** n22 t23.5 f22 b23 Less a whisky for more than a battle, starting on your nose and spreading over onto your palate (a little ironic, seeing as this is whisky number 633 for the year). Will the evil tannins destroy all before them, or can enough sugars be conjured up to keep them at bay? Some may feel the evil forces prevailed, others that it was a victory for the goodies. You decide... *53.4%. 3,954 bottles. Diageo Special Releases 2016.*

**Gordon & MacPhail Connoisseurs Choice Mannochmore 1996** bott 28 Mar 17 **(88.5)** n22 t22 f22.5 b22 Even 20 years in the cask can't douse some of the flames... *46%.*

◇ **Lady of the Glen Mannochmore 2007** cask no. 13208 **(94.5)** n23.5 t24 f23.5 b23.5 Mannochmore has a bit of a split perception among blenders: some adore it, some won't touch it. Well, virtually all would be fighting to get their hands on it if all samples were as spellbindingly rich and sweet as this cask. Beautifully made and benefitting from a decade or so in a top rate bourbon cask. The result is a honey-rich, spicy orgy of malt. Even boasting a cheeky hint of peat. Just brilliant. *59.4%. sc.*

# MILLBURN
**Highlands (Northern), 1807–1985. Diageo. Demolished.**

**Millburn 1969 Rare Malt** db **(77)** n19 t21 f18 b19. Some lovely bourbon-honey touches but sadly over the hill and declining fast. Nothing like as interesting or entertaining as the massage parlour that was firebombed a few yards from my office twenty minutes ago. Or as smoky... *51.3%*

# MILTONDUFF
**Speyside, 1824. Chivas Brothers. Working.**

**Miltonduff Aged 15 Years** bott code L00/123 db **(86)** n23 t22 f20 b21. Some casks beyond their years have crept in and unsettled this one. But some real big salty moments to savour, too. *46%*

**Ballantine's The Miltonduff Aged 15 Years Series No.002** American oak casks, bott code: LKRM1193 2018/03/27 **(88.5)** n23 t22 f21.5 b22 Soft, spicy, attractive but far too much one-dimensional caramel for complexity or greatness. Some decent bourbon notes filter through, though. (The Murray Method brings out the caramels further – best enjoyed at cool bottle temperature). *40%.*

◇ **The Golden Cask Miltonduff 8 Years Old 2009** cask no. CM245, bott 2018 **(93.5)** n23 t23 f24 b23.5 For an 8-year-old, this is in need of a Zimmer frame, as it creaks and shuffles along in the oaky onslaught. There are heather honey and marzipan notes further down the line which open this up beautifully, and the chocolate tones are wonderful; and the finish is stunning. But behaves far closer to an 18-year-old than a malt a decade younger! Absolutely beautiful, though, even if you do have to pick out the odd splinter. *60%. nc ncf sc. 238 bottles.*

◇ **The Golden Cask Miltonduff 2009** cask no. CM254, bott 2019 **(89.5)** n22 light caramels and lighter tannins with a soft lime intrusion; t23 ulmo honey, salivating barely and lemon curd tart smother the growing spicy tannins; f22 reverts back to the nose's interest in caramel; b22.5 decent enough, but just has nothing like the same overall panache as cask 245. *60.1%. nc ncf sc. 228 bottles.*

**Gordon & MacPhail Cask Strength Miltonduff 1997** cask no. 9179, bott 25 Sept 17 **(92)** n23 t23.5 f22.5 b23 This uplifting and upbeat little beauty has some serious attitude... Hit me again..! *58.8%. sc.*

**Gordon & MacPhail Discovery Range Miltonduff Aged 10 Years** **(89.5)** n23 t22 f22 b22.5 Packs in a huge amount for a 10-year-old. *43%.*

**Hepburn's Choice Miltonduff 7 Years Old** sherry finished hogshead, dist 2009, bott 2017 **(81.5)** n21 t21.5 f19 b20 Beautifully made, zesty malt, still smacking of new make tendencies. A bit sulphurous here and there, but nothing too disastrous. *46%. nc ncf sc. 288 bottles.*

◇ **Hepburn's Choice Miltonduff 8 Years Old** first fill bourbon barrel, dist 2009, bott 2018 **(87)** n21.5 t22.5 f21 b22 Very obvious here why this is so prized as a blending malt, even at this age. Despite the eye-watering sharpness to the barley, there is no escaping that there is substance to this malt, too. So chewy and fulfilling early on, though the oak – which has surprisingly little impact for a first fill bourbon barrel - does bitter out slightly at the death. *46%. nc ncf sc. 339 bottles.*

**Liquid Treasures Entomology Miltonduff 22 Years Old** ex-bourbon cask, dist 1995, bott 2017 **(92)** n23 t23.5 f22.5 b23 Well measured and beautifully paced. Impeccable malt. *56.1%.*

**Old Malt Cask Miltonduff Aged 20 Years** refill hogshead, cask no. 11234, dist Feb 95, bott Feb 15 **(91)** n23 t23.5 f22 b22.5 A very satisfying Speysider. *50%. nc ncf sc. 171 bottles.*

◇ **Old Malt Cask Miltonduff Aged 23 Years** refill barrel, cask no. 15138, dist Feb 95, bott May 18 **(94)** n23.5 a complex floral aroma, something of balmy summer's evening about this one, aroma with a rising degree of exotic fruit befitting its age; t23.5 a stupendous delivery making the most of the firmness of the malt. Crisp and juicy, the barley truly sparkles at first. But the oak is chatty and has much to say, its voice getting deeper and louder as time goes on; **f23** excellently weighted spice with a malty depth continuing for much longer than can be reasonably expected; **b24** a very pretty whisky which carries its age effortlessly and with considerable grace. Understatedly superb. 50%. nc ncf sc. 150 bottles.

**Old Particular Miltonduff 23 Years Old** refill hogshead, cask no. 12200, dist Apr 94, bott Nov 17 **(94.5) n24 t24 f23 b23.5** Nimble and sprightly for its age, full of agile malt throughout. Class with every nuance. 50.6%. nc ncf sc. 262 bottles.

**Scotch Malt Whisky Society Cask 72.56 35 Year Old** refill ex-bourbon barrel, dist 11 Jun 82 **(82.5) n24 t21.5 f18 b19** Fabulous nose which warns of the over-oaking to come but retains some serious quality. Butterscotch tart goes without saying, and acts as the background for a succession of faux fruity notes, mostly of a boiled sweet variety. The lightest sliver of acacia honey and marzipan. But there is also a tell-tale warning of an off oak note. And this becomes more than apparent once the initial sweetness on delivery has died. The finish, I warn you, is grim. 49.5%. sc.

**The Whisky Embassy Miltonduff Aged 9 Years** cask no. 8316533, dist 2008, bott 2017 **(86) n21.5 t22 f21 b21.5** Malty, rich but not entirely at home with itself. Delicious in part, bit still some growing to do. 53.6%. nc ncf sc.

# MORTLACH
Speyside, 1824. Diageo. Working.

⟨⟩ **Mortlach Aged 12 Years The Wee Witchie** sherry & bourbon casks, bott code: L8284DM001 db **(92.5) n23** a lovely toffee and raisin theme with the barley lively enough to have a nibble at it; **t23** mouth-watering, fresh and sharp on delivery. Far more life on this than expected from the colour with the plum notes offering both depth and more salivating qualities; **f23.5** a pleasing spiciness amid the drier vanillas; **b23** clean, untainted sherry casks at work: rather lovely. 43.4%.

**Mortlach Aged 16 Years** db **(87) n20 t23 f22 b22.** Once it gets past the bold if very mildly sulphured nose, the rest of the journey is superb. Earlier Mortlachs in this range had a slightly unclean feel to them and the nose here doesn't inspire confidence. But from arrival on the palate onwards, it's sure-footed, fruity and even refreshing... and always delicious. 43%

⟨⟩ **Mortlach Aged 16 Years Distiller's Dram** ex-sherry casks, bott code: L833ODM004 db **(93.5) n23.5** the underpinning oak gives a firm stage on which the kumquats and barley can choreograph their elaborate dance; **t23.5** much lighter on delivery than the nose steadies you for, the fruit juices and demerara sugars gushing against the taste buds. Soon the oak is back in place, the tannins affording grip and delicate spice; **f23** soft vanilla and barley sugars – as well as a dry, pulsing spiciness representing age; **b23.5** after quite a long period in the doldrums, this distillery really does have the wind in its sails once more. Excellent whisky. 43.4%.

**Mortlach 18 Year Old** db **(75) n19 t19 f18 b19.** When I first tasted Mortlach, probably over 30 years ago now, it really wasn't even close to this. Something went very wrong in the late '80s, I can tell you...43.4%. Diageo.

⟨⟩ **Mortlach 20 Year Old Cowie's Blue Seal** db **(87) n22 t22 f21.5 b21.5** Pleasant, but apart from a little oak on the nose never gets round to displaying its age. The odd orange blossom honey money opens it up slightly but a shade too tame and predictable. 43.4%.

**Mortlach 25 Year Old** db **(91.5) n23** just love the lemon grass alongside the liquorice and hickory; **t23.5** thick and palate-encompassing. The sugars are pretty toasty with a light mocha element in play; **f22.5** crisp finale with a return of the citrus, sitting confidently with the late spice; **b22.5** much more like it. The sugars may be pretty full on, but there is enough depth and complexity for a narrative to be told. Very much a better Mortlach on so many levels. 43.4%.

**Mortlach Rare Old** db **(79) n20 t21 f19 b19.** Not rare enough... 43.4%. Diageo.

**Mortlach Special Strength** db **(79.5) n20 t21.5 f19 b19.** Does whisky come any more cloyingly sweet than Mortlach...? Not in my experience.... 49%. Diageo.

**Cadenhead's Rum Cask Mortlach 14 Years Old** Guyana rum cask, dist 2003 **(96.5) n25 t24.5 f23 b24** Mind-blowingly beautiful. This really is what malt whisky should be all about. Thank you Cadenhead! 55%. sc. 240 bottles.

⟨⟩ **Glenwill Mortlach 1991** sherry cask, cask no. 4251 **(89.5) n23 t22.5 f22 b22** Once, there was many a blender for whom the words "Mortlach" and "sherry" in the same sentence would bring a shudder. Certainly not with this cask which, in performance, is a bit like a Jumbo Jet hanger accommodating a Spitfire. The sherry has completely dominated the malt, so there is not even a hint of barley anywhere within the flavour framework. But dripping over-ripe raisins...? This is your boy! Must admit: love the late toastiness. 53.9%. 499 bottles. Matisse Spirits Company.

**Gordon & MacPhail Cask Strength Mortlach 1994** cask no. 8192, bott 19 Apr 17 **(85.5) n21.5 t22 f21 b21** A Mortlach of its time: 23 years ago they were producing an outrageously sweet, bouncy malt lacking shape and depth. Even though matured here in good wood, which is in itself a rarity for this distillery and vintage only so much salvation can be achieved. A loud, unruly spirit which offers a little bit of fun, but will do nothing to win the heart of the whisky purist. 54.2%. sc.

◇ **Gordon & MacPhail Connoisseurs Choice Mortlach Aged 30 Years** refill American hogshead, cask no. 4839, dist 7 Dec 88, bott 11 Dec 18 **(86.5) n21 t21.5 f22 b22** Pretty enjoyable if you can grip tightly onto the arms of your chair as the tannins bite without mercy. Settles only late on as the malt regroups to add a degree of both sweetness and shape. 48.8%. sc. 129 bottles.

◇ **Gordon & MacPhail Connoisseurs Choice Mortlach Aged 31 Years** refill sherry hogshead, cask no. 425, dist 5 Feb 87, bott 3 Jul 18 **(80) n20 t22 f19 b19** About as subtle as being hit around the head by a herring dipped in unctuous sherry. Not one of Mortlach's finer moments. 54%. sc. 200 bottles.

**Hepburn's Choice Mortlach 7 Years Old** refill hogshead, dist 2010, bott 2017 **(87) n22 t22 f21.5 b21.5** An attractive, essentially juicy, entirely agreeable malt with an easy-going, untaxing freshness. 46%. nc ncf sc. 420 bottles.

**Hepburn's Choice Mortlach 8 Years Old** refill hogshead, dist 2010, bott 2018 **(86) n21.5 t22 f21 b21.5** A rotund, sweet whisky but for all its massive gristy, malty front fails to really find a direction. The finish disintegrates slightly. 46%. nc ncf sc. 387 bottles.

◇ **Highland Tiger Mortlach 2006** cask no. 15, red wine finish, dist 3 Oct 06, bott 31 Jan 19 **(87.5) n21 t22.5 f22 b22** Mortlach at its most thick-set and cloying, which is saying something. But this Tiger also has teeth and there is no denying the sheer fun as soon as the super-juicy fruit gets going on the high alcohol strength. If you want something more subtle, try a pie in the face. But in the meantime just enjoy the rounded, sweet, rumbustious outlandishness of this. 55.4%. Mr. Whisky.

**Kingsbury Gold Mortlach 22 Years Old** hogshead, cask no. 4873, dist 1995 **(86.5) n21.5 t22 f21.5 b22** Outwardly a chunky whisky, a little on the nutty side but with a surprising hotness to the thinner core. When the early muddle has settled a highly pleasing ultra-malty blast makes for a satisfying all round finale. 53.2%. 255 bottles.

**Old Malt Cask Mortlach Aged 10 Years** refill hogshead, cask no. 14406, dist Jul 07, bott Nov 17 **(93) n23 t23.5 f23 b23.5** A refined, dignified malt complete with cut grass accent. 50%. nc ncf sc. 317 bottles.

**Old Particular Mortlach 12 Years Old** refill hogshead, cask no. 11797, dist Mar 05, bott Jun 17 **(94) n22.5 t24 f23.5 b24** Same age and strength as cask 12219 below, yet this contains so much more malty whoomph and pzazz and all round brilliance... 48.4%. nc ncf sc. 367 bottles.

**Old Particular Mortlach 12 Years Old** refill hogshead, cask no. 12219, dist Mar 05, bott Dec 17 **(87) n21 t22.5 f21.5 b22** A modest nose but intensity and dash of the rich malt on delivery, with the confident barley controlling the show, reveals when this distillery started turning the corner in again making 48.4%. nc ncf sc. 341 bottles.

**Platinum Old & Rare Mortlach 25 Year Old** sherry butt db **(93) n23 t23.5 f23 b23.5** Yes, it one of those famous old Mortlachs that appears to have been distilled from raisins. Oh, and not an atom of sulphur on the scene. 58.8%. sc. 319 bottles. Bottled for The Whisky Shop.

**Provenance Mortlach Aged 10 Years** refill hogshead, cask no. 11828, dist Nov 06, bott May 17 **(88.5) n21.5** a tad youthful; **t22.5** sticky malt with spice and toffee; **f22** dries towards a spiced cocoa finale; **b22** simplistic but effective 46%. nc ncf sc. 366 bottles.

◇ **Scyfion Choice Mortlach 2005** Troyanda cask finished, bott 2018 **(84.5) n21 t21 f21.5 b21** A strange malt, which feels understrength despite being close to 50% abv. Also has a certain tininess, a thin outer shell which allows little to escape. Nothing technically wrong with it, but if you wait for it to take off, you'll be there a bloody long time. 48.4%. nc ncf sc. 328 bottles.

**Scotch Malt Whisky Society Cask 76.137 35 Year Old** dist 29 Sept 87 **(87) n22 t21.5 f22 b22** A true tsunami of malt on both nose and palate. But the sweetness is a shade too cloying for greatness while the gluey elements shew a countering thinness which is magnified by the thick, sugary onslaught. Enjoyable, providing you have arms to your chair. 50.5%. sc.

**Whisky Illuminati Mortlach 19 Year Old** Spanish oak sherry butt, cask no. 3657, dist 1998 **(85) n22 t21.5 f21.5 b20** Being entirely sulphur free, a whisky I should wax lyrical about. But Mortlach at this time was perhaps not the best spirit distilled in Speyside, tending to be on the fat and unruly side. Add to that a sherry butt that appears to be dripping in grape and you get a rather 'in your face' malt where balance is at a premium and subtlety is nil. Gutters at the death. 56.9%. sc. 476 bottles. Candlelight Series.

## MOSSTOWIE
Speyside, 1964–1981. Chivas Brothers. Closed.

**Rare Old Mosstowie 1979 (84.5) n21.5 t21 f21 b21.** Edging inextricably well beyond its sell by date. But there is a lovely walnut cream cake (topped off with brown sugar and spices) to this which warms the cockles. Bless... 43%. Gordon & MacPhail.

## NORTH PORT
Highlands (Eastern), 1820–1983. Diageo. Demolished.

**Brechin 1977** db **(78) n19 t21 f18 b20.** Fire and brimstone was never an unknown quantity with the whisky from this doomed distillery. Some soothing oils are poured on this troubled – and sometimes attractively honeyed – water of life. 54.2%

## OBAN
Highlands (Western), 1794. Diageo. Working.

**Oban 14 Years Old** db **(79) n19 t22 f18 b20.** Absolutely all over the place. The cask selection sits very uncomfortably with the malt. I look forward to the resumption of normality to this great but ill-served distillery. 43%

**Oban The Distillers Edition** special release OD 162.FX, dist 1998, bott 2013 db **(87.5) n22.5 t22.5 f21 b21.5.** Some attractive kumquat and blood orange makes for a fruity and rich malt, though just a little furry towards the finish. Decent Demerara early on, too. 43%

**Oban Little Bay** db **(87.5) n21 t23 f21.5 b22.** A pleasant, refreshing simple dram. Clean and juicy in part and some wonderful oak-laden spice to stir things up a little. Just a little too much chewy toffee near the end, though. 43%

◇ **Game of Thrones Oban Bay Reserve The Night's Watch** db **(87.5) n22 t23 f21 b21.5** Starts promisingly, even offering a saltiness you tend not to see from this distillery these days. The intense grist on the malt makes for a beautiful delivery. But flattens fast and furiously as the caramels kick in. 43%.

## PITTYVAICH
Speyside, 1975–1993. Diageo. Demolished.

**Pittyvaich Aged 12 Years** db **(64) n16 t18 f15 b15.** It was hard to imagine this whisky getting worse. But somehow it has achieved it. From fire-water to cloying undrinkability. What amazes me is not that this is such bad whisky: we have long known that Pittyvaich can be as grim as it gets. It's the fact they bother bottling it and inflicting it on the public. Vat this with malt from Fettercairn and neighbouring Dufftown and you'll have the perfect dram for masochists. Or those who have entirely lost the will to live. Jesus... 43%. Flora and Fauna.

**Pittyvaich 25 Year Old** refill American oak hogsheads & first fill ex-bourbon barrels, dist 1989 db **(80) n21 t20 f19 b20.** No matter what collar you put on it, once a Rottweiler, always a Rottweiler... 49.9%. 5,922 bottles. Diageo Special Releases 2015.

◇ **Pittyvaich 28 Year Old** db **(86.5) n22.5 t22 f20.5 b21.5** The nose is an attractive bend of malt and hazelnut. The delivery is sweet, gristy and promising. But it thins out fast and dramatically. So limited in scope, but pleasant in the early phases. 52.1%. 4,680 bottles. Diageo Special Releases 2018.

## PORT ELLEN
Islay, 1825–1983. Diageo. Closed.

**Port Ellen 1979** db **(93) n22 t23 f24 b24** Takes so long to get out of the traps, you wonder if anything is going to happen. But when it does, my word...it's glorious! 57.5%

**Port Ellen Aged 37 Years** dist 1978 db **(91) n24.5 t22.5 f22 b22** The bark is far better than the bite: one of the great noses of the year cannot be backed up on the palate as the oak is simply too demanding. An historical experience, but ensure you spend as much time nosing as you do tasting... 55.2%. 2,940 bottles. Diageo Special Releases 2016.

**Port Ellen 37 Year Old** refill American oak hogsheads & refill American oak butts db **(88) n23 t21.5 f22 b21.5** The oak scars the overall beauty of the malt. 51%. 2,988 bottles. Diageo Special Releases 2017.

◇ **Port Ellen 39 Years Old** db **(96.5) n24** you breathe in the sea here: salty rock pools and peat reek from the lums of nearby cottages; **t24** the first whisky this year I have been unable to spit out...I just can't bring myself to do it. A wonderful light liquorice background certainly underlines the age and top quality bourbon cask involvement. The spices pitter-patter and play, the vanillas caress, the peat forms an elegant backbone, except for the notes which combine with the tannin to form the base; **f24** the soft oils have lasted nearly four decades intact and with the whisky sensibly at cask strength, it just carries on and on, seemingly into infinity. Now the caramels, mixed with a little ulmo honey, have control... but that little bit of spice and phenol is never far away...; **b24.5** a malt which defies time and logic, and the short-sighted individuals who closed down this distillery and later, unforgivably, ripped out its innards (despite my one-kneed imploring). Tragically beautiful. 50.9%. 1,500 bottles.

**Gleann Mór Port Ellen Aged Over 33 Years** dist 1983 **(96.5) n25 t24 f23.5 b24** If a whisky can bring a tear to your eye, then this one will. It is too elegant and beautiful for this world... 57%. sc.

**Hunter Laing's Old & Rare Port Ellen Aged 33 Years** sherry butt, dist Mar 83, bott Nov 16 **(94.5)** n23.5 t23.5 f23.5 b24 Very enjoyable malt. But odd to see Port Ellen in sherry: so much of their output was in bourbon. Had to actually pick up and define the character f the distillery itself. That said, a punchy and enjoyable dram. *56.8%. nc ncf sc. 174 bottles.*

# PULTENEY
### Highlands (Northern), 1826. Inver House Distillers. Working.

**Old Pulteney Aged 12 Years** db **(90.5)** n22 t23 f22.5 b23 A cleaner, zestier more joyous composition than the old 43%, though that has less to do with strength than overall construction. A dramatic whisky which, with further care, could get even closer to the truth of this distillery. *40%*

**Old Pulteney Aged 12 Years** bott code L15/030 R15/5046 IB db **(91)** n22.5 t23 f22.5 b23 Remarkably consistent from the bottling above. The salt continues to ensure lustre, though this bottling has a little extra – and welcome – barley gristiness. *40%. ncf.*

**Old Pulteney Aged 12 Years** db **(85)** n22 t23 f19 b21. There are few malts whose finish dies as spectacularly as this. The nose and delivery are spot on with a real buzz and panache. The delivery in particular just bowls you over with its sharp barley integrity: real pulse-racing stuff! Then... toffee...!!! Grrrr!!! If it is caramel causing this, then it can be easily remedied. And in the process we'd have a malt absolutely basking in the low 90s...! *43%*

**Old Pulteney Aged 15 Years** db **(95.5)** n24 t24 f23.5 b24 More than a night cap. One you should definitely take to bed with you... *46%.*

**Old Pulteney Aged 15 Years** db **(91)** n21 t24 f23 b23 Only on about the fourth or fifth mouthful do you start getting the picture here: enormously complex with a genuine coastal edge to this. The complexity is awesome. *54.9%*

**Old Pulteney Aged 17 Years** db **(95)** n22 t25 f24 b24 The nose confirms that some of the casks at work here are not A1. Even so, the whisky performs to the kind of levels some distillers could only dream of. *46%*

**Old Pulteney Aged 17 Years** bott code: L15/329 R15/5530 IB db **(82)** n20.5 t22.5 f19 b20 This is usually one of the greatest whiskies bottled anywhere in the world. But not even something of Pulteney 17's usually unfathomable excellence and charisma can withstand this degree of sulphur. Much greater care has to be taken in the bottling hall to preserve the integrity of what should be one of Scotland's most beautiful offerings to the world. *46%. ncf.*

**Old Pulteney Aged 18 Years** db **(81)** n19 t21.5 f20 b20.5 If you are going to work with sherry butts you have to be very careful. And here we see a whisky that is not careful enough as the sulphur does its usual damage. For those in central Europe without the "sulphur gene", then no problem as the fruit is still intact. *46%.*

**Old Pulteney Aged 21 Years** db **(97.5)** n25 t24 f24 b24.5 By far and away one of the great whiskies of 2012, absolutely exploding from the glass with vitality, charisma and class. One of Scotland's great undiscovered distilleries about to become discovered, I think... and rightly so! *46%*

**Old Pulteney Aged 25 Years** American & Spanish oak casks, bott code: L17/282 R17/5353 IB db **(96)** n25 t23.5 f23.5 b24 A quiet but incredibly complex reminder why this distillery is capable of producing World Whisky of the Year. Age is all around you, but degradation there is none. *46%.*

**Old Pulteney 30 Years Old** db **(92)** n23.5 t23.5 f22 b23 I had to laugh when I tasted this: indeed, it had me scrambling for a copy of the 2009 Bible to check for sure what I had written. And there it was: after bemoaning the over oaking I conjectured, "As Pulteney has the fascinating tendency to radically shift style over not too long a period, I can't wait for the next instalment." And barely a year on, here it is. Pretty far removed from last year's offering and an absolute peach of a dram that laughs in the face of its 30 years... *45%*

**Old Pulteney 35 Year Old** db **(89)** n23 t21.5 f22.5 b22 A malt on the perimeter of its comfort zone. But there are enough gold nuggets included to make this work. Just. *46%.*

**Old Pulteney Aged 40 Years** db **(95)** n23.5 t23.5 f24 b24 This malt still flies as close to the sun as possible. But some extra fruit, honey and spice now grasps the tannins by the throat to ensure a whisky of enormous magnitude and complexity *51.3%*

**Old Pulteney 1990 Vintage** American oak ex bourbon & Spanish oak ex sherry butts. db **(85)** n21 t23 f21 b20. As you know, anything which mentions sherry butts gets me nervous – and for good reason. Even with a World Great distillery like Pulteney. Oddly enough, this bottling is, as near a dammit, free of sulphur. Yee-hah! The bad news, though, is that it is also untroubled by complexity as well. It reminded me of some heavily sherried peaty jobs...and then I learned that ex Islay casks were involved. That may or may not be it. But have to say, beyond the first big, salivating, lightly spiced moments on delivery you wait for the story to unfurl...and it all turns out to be dull rumours. *46%. Inverhouse Distilleries.*

**Old Pulteney 2006 Vintage** first fill ex-bourbon casks, bott 2017, bott code: L17/279 R17/5452 IB db **(93)** n23 t23.5 f23 b23.5 A beautiful, lightly salted ceremony of malt with the glycerine feel of raspberry and cream Swiss rolls. Just so love it! *46%.*

**Old Pulteney Duncansby Head Lighthouse** bourbon and sherry casks db (90.5) n23 t23 f22 b22.5 Beginning to wonder if Pulteney is into making whisky or cakes. And malt straight from the oven. 46% WB15/329

**Old Pulteney Dunnet Head Lighthouse** bourbon & sherry casks db (90.5) n22 t23.5 f22 b23 Loads to chew over with this heavyweight.46%. nc ncf. Exclusive to travel retail.

**Old Pulteney Huddart** db (88.5) n22 t22.5 f22 b22 Hopefully not named after my erstwhile physics teacher of 45 years ago, Ernie Huddart, who, annoyingly, for an entire year insisted on calling me Murphy rather than Murray, despite my constant correcting his mistake. One day he told me off for my not remembering some or other Law of Physics. When he finished berating me quite unpleasantly at high volume before my fellow classmates, I simply said: "Well, sir, that's fine coming from you. You've had a year to learn that my name is Murray and not Murphy, and still you failed!" He was so lost for words at this impudence I got away with it, though if his glare could have killed... Anyway, back to the whisky: this seemingly young, lightly smoked version shows all the hallmarks of being finished in peaty casks, as opposed to being distilled from phenolic malt, hence the slightly mottled and uneven feel to this. Odd, but attractive. Oh, and Huddart...? I think that's actually the name of the nondescript old street on which the distillery sits 46%.

**Old Pulteney Navigator** bourbon & sherry casks db (80) n19 t23 f18 b20. Sherry butts have clearly been added to this. Not sure why, as the sulphur only detracts from the early honey riches. The compass is working when the honey and cocoa notes briefly harmonise in beautiful tandem. But otherwise, badly off course. 46%. nc ncf.

**Old Pulteney Navigator** bourbon & sherry casks, bott code: L15/207 R15/5318 IB db (78) n19 t22 f18 b19 Even further lost in sulphurous territory than before... 46%. ncf.

**Old Pulteney Noss Head Lighthouse** bourbon casks db (84) n22.5 t22 f19 b20.5. If Noss Head was as light as this dram, it'd be gone half way through its first half decent storm. An apparent slight overuse of third and less sturdy second fill casks means the finale bitters out considerably. A shame, as the nose and delivery is about as fine a display of citrus maltiness as you'll find. 46%. Travel retail exclusive. WB15/327

**Old Pulteney Pentland Skerries Lighthouse** db (85) n21 t22 f20.5 b21.5. A chewy dram with an emphasis on the fruit. Sound, evens enjoys the odd chocolate-toffee moment. But a little sulphur, apparent on the nose, creeps in to take the gloss off. 46%. WB15/373

**Cadenhead's Small Batch Old Pulteney 11 Year Old** dist 2006 (84) n21.5 t22 f20 b20.5 An odd mix of salivating salt and citrus but the oak isn't quite up to the standard of the spirit. 55.8%.

**Gordon & MacPhail Connoisseurs Choice Pulteney Aged 19 Years** first fill bourbon barrel, cask no. 1071, dist 26 Aug 98, bott 21 Jun 18 (95.5) n23.5 t24 f24 b24 Malt from one of the world's very finest distilleries matured in a first- class cask. The result is inevitable. The interplay between oak and malt starts on the first molecules to hit the nose and ends only when the story is told. Can't ask any more of the spices, or their interaction with the liquorice and Manuka honey mix. Everything is perfectly paced and weighted, even the natural caramels that could so easily have tipped this towards a blander bottling. Toasty, sublimely complex and breath-taking. 57.5%. sc. 192 bottles.

**Gordon & MacPhail Connoisseurs Choice Pulteney 1998** first fill bourbon barrels, dist 1998, bott 15 Mar 18 (95) n23.5 t24 f24 b24 So many facets to win your heart with this one. Just sit back and let this Pulteney go about its beautiful business.... 46%. nc ncf. 528 bottles.

**Hidden Spirits Pulteney 5 Year Old** dist 2012, bott 2017 (86.5) n21 t23 f21 b21 A young, bright barley thumping malt fest showing one of the world's greatest distilleries more or less at the moment its maturing whisky starts to walk... Don't expect any complexity. 50%.

**The Whisky Shop Old Pulteney Aged 12 Years** Spanish oak hogshead, cask no. 1471, dist 2007 (94.5) n23.5 blinding grape; t23.5 the usual spice buzz of a big sherry cask; the lightest malt and marzipan stratum; f24 gorgeous chocolate raisin; b23.5 there's nothing like a drop of whisky in your sherry... 50.2%. sc.

**The Whisky Shop Old Pulteney 2006** cask no. 1448 (91.5) n22.5 t23 f23 b23 Very relaxed Pulteney happy to rely on the considerable charms of ulmo honey and rich barley in unison. Juicy and sharp on delivery but finishes by whistling with its hands in its pockets. 50.2%. sc.

# ROSEBANK

**Lowlands, 1840–1993. Diageo. Closed- soon to re-open. (The gods have answered!)**

**Rosebank Aged 12 Years** db (95) n24 t24 f23 b24. Infinitely better than the last bottling, this is quite legendary stuff, even better than the old 8-y-o version, though probably a point or two down regarding complexity. The kind of whisky that brings a tear to the eye... for many a reason... 43%. Flora and Fauna.

**Rosebank 21 Year Old** refill American oak casks, dist 1992 db **(95.5) n23.5 t24 f24 b24** Rosebank is at its very best at eight-years-old. Well, that won't happen again, so great to see it has proven successful at 21... *55.3%. 4,530 bottles. Diageo Special Releases 2014.*

**Rosebank 21 Years Old Special Release** db **(94) n24 t23.5 f23 b23.5** Can any Lowland be compared to a fully blossomed Rosebank? This is whisky to both savour and worship for this is nectar in a Rose... *53.8%. ncf.*

**Rosebank 25 Years Old** db **(96) n24.5 t23.5 f24 b24.** I had to sit back, take a deep breath and get my head around this. It was like Highland Park but with a huge injection of sweetened chocolate on the finale and weight – and even smoke – from a Rosebank I had never quite seen before. And believe me, as this distillery's greatest champion, I've tasted a few hundred, possibly thousands, of casks of this stuff over the last 25 years. Is this the greatest of all time? I am beginning to wonder. Is it the most extraordinary since the single malt revolution took off? Certainly. Do I endorse it? My god, yes! *61.4%*

**Scotch Malt Whisky Society Cask 25.70 26 Year Old** refill ex-bourbon barrel, dist 14 Nov 90 **(79.5) n20 t21.5 f19 b19** "A perfumed garden" apparently. Must be the odd dead oak in there. This is a pretty exhausted cask far beyond its sell by date despite the odd defiant note of honey on delivery. *58.3%. sc.*

# ROYAL BRACKLA
### Speyside, 1812. Bacardi. Working.

**Royal Brackla Aged 10 Years** db **(73) n18 t20 f17 b18.** A distinct lowering of the colours since I last tasted this. What on earth is going on? *40%*

**Royal Brackla 12 Year Old** db **(82.5) n21.5 t21 f20 b20.** Just one of those bottlings which is pleasant enough if you are just looking for something to drink without too much thought, but there is a frustrating lack of harmony and purpose in this for those of us looking to be entertained. *40%*

⬧ **Royal Brackla Aged 12 Years** bott code: L18192B700 db **(85) n22 t22 f20 b21** A definite improvement on previous bottlings but, coming from Bacardi's formidable stable, I had expected more. The finish is still dull as ditch water, with nothing other than toffee to find but there is an upping of fresh fruit on both nose and delivery. *40%.*

⬧ **Royal Brackla Aged 16 Years** bott code: L18158B700 db **(88) n22.5** light and zesty, a little spice flickers around the caramel; **t22.5** soft, bordering luxuriant, there is a big malt and caramel hook up. But it is the all too brief, refreshing, zingy delivery which stars; **f21** still a little too much on the dull-ish caramel side; **b22** a very pleasant malt, but you get the feeling it is being driven with the handbrake on... *40%.*

**Royal Brackla 21 Year Old** db **(91) n23.5** wonderful dried lychee kick sets the tone for the sweetness of the malt; **t23** silky malt, with a shade of coastal salt ensuring the full flavours are wrung out; **f22** creamy chocolate ice cream before the spices arrive; **b22.5** now that's much more like it! *40%*

⬧ **Royal Brackla Aged 21 Years** bott code: L18297B701 db **(91.5) n23** maintains its unusual but delightful lychee sweetness, that sweetness now extending to maple syrup and fudge; **t23** delicate and salivating, initially shewing little sign of great age. It takes a while but the toastier tannins finally arrive; **f22.5** salty, with a chocolate fudge finale; **b23** where both the 12- and 16-years olds appear both to be tied to a vat of toffee, this beauty has been given its wings. Also, I remember this for being a malt with a curious lychee note, hence tasting it today. For yesterday I tasted a malt matured in a lychee liqueur barrel. Pleased to report no shortage of lychees here, either. *40%.*

**Hepburn's Choice Royal Brackla 8 Years Old** refill barrel, dist 2009, bott 2018 **(87) n20.5 t22.5 f22 b22** While the nose may be a little youthful and untidy, the same can't be said for the experience in the palate. A disciplined celebration of juicy, lightly oiled maltiness, though if it does have a fault it is that it clings to the barley track without attempting too hard to find a branch line. *46%. nc ncf sc. 356 bottles.*

**Old Malt Cask Royal Brackla Aged 18 Years** refill barrel, cask no. 13429, dist May 98, bott Feb 17 **(92.5) n23 t22.5 f23.5 b23.5** An excellent cask has ensured harmony. Superb! *50%.*

⬧ **Single Cask Collection Royal Brackla Aged 11 Years** **(89) n22 t22 f22.5 b22.5** An oily and nutty offering which makes the most of its cask strength. The malt intensity is simplistic, attractive and even throughout. But it is that light chocolate-nut theme which builds and stars. *54%. sc.*

# ROYAL LOCHNAGAR
### Highlands (Eastern), 1826. Diageo. Working.

**Royal Lochnagar Aged 12 Years** db **(84) n21 t22 f20 b21.** More care has been taken with this than some other bottlings from this wonderful distillery. But I still can't understand why it never quite manages to get out of third gear...or is the caramel on the finish the giveaway...? *40%*

◇ **Game of Thrones Royal Lochnagar 12 Year Old House Baratheon** db **(89)** n22 some lively early malt; toffee apple; **t22.5** powering malt emphasising and emphasized by the small stills in play; **f22** a simplistic vanilla and toffee fade; lightest touch of butterscotch; **b22.5** not sure when I last encountered a Lochnager of such simplicity. Friendly and impossible not to like. *40%*.

## ST. MAGDALENE
Lowlands, 1798–1983. Diageo. Demolished.
**Linlithgow 30 Years Old** dist 1973 db **(70)** n18 t18 f16 b18. A brave but ultimately futile effort from a malt that is way past its sell-by date. *59.6%*

## SCAPA
Highlands (Island–Orkney), 1885. Chivas Brothers. Working.
**Scapa 12 Years Old** db **(88)** n23 t22 f21 b22. Always a joy. *40%*
**Scapa 14 Years Old** db **(88)** n22 t22.5 f21.5 b22. Enormous variation from bottling to bottling. In Canada I have tasted one that I gave 94 to: but don't have notes or sample here. This one is a bit of dis-service due to the over-the-top caramel added which appears to douse the usual honeyed balance. Usually, this is one of the truly great malts of the Chivas empire and a classic islander. *40%*
**Scapa 16 Years Old** db **(81)** n21 t20.5 f19.5 b20. For it to be so tamed and toothless is a crime against a truly great whisky which, handled correctly, would be easily among the finest the world has to offer. *40%*
◇ **Scapa Glansa** peated whisky cask finish, batch no. GL05, bott Jul 18 db **(91)** n22 a slightly toffee-obscured nose, but some well-defined phenols poke through like mountain tops through cloud cover...; **t23.5** a supremely soft and melting-textured delivery where the peat appears to play a bigger part than just cask finishing. The varied pace and input from the spices are as intriguing as they are delightful; after a slight fade into caramel it re-bursts into flame with a gorgeous oak and spice attack at the midpoint; **f22.5** a little burnt fudge on the finale, though the spices carry on buzzing; **b23** a delightful whisky which could be raised several notches in quality if the influence of the caramel is diminished. *40%*.
**Scapa Skiren** db **(89.5)** n22.5 t22.5 f22 b22.5 Chaps who created this: lovely, you really have to power this one up a bit... *40%*
◇ **Gordon & MacPhail Connoisseurs Choice Scapa Aged 30 Years** refill bourbon barrel, cask no. 10585, dist 2 Sept 88, bott 13 Sept 18 **(94)** n22.5 t24 f23.5 b24 One of those exceptionally rare occasions when the threatening tannins on the nose fail to materialise on the palate. Instead we have glorious display of varied honey tones far more usually associated with its neighbouring Orkney distillery. Stunning displays of light saltiness mixes brilliantly with the lime blossom honey before the spices and tannins set. A thing of beauty. *53.8%. sc. 148 bottles.*

## SPEYBURN
Speyside, 1897. Inver House Distillers. Working.
**Speyburn Aged 10 Years** bott code: L16/303 R165434 IB db **(84.5)** n21 t21.5 f21 b21 Appears to celebrate and even emphasises its remarkable thinness of body. As usual, juicy with a dominant toffee character. *40%*.
**Speyburn Aged 10 Years Travel Exclusive** American oak ex-bourbon & ex-sherry casks, bott code L18/055 R18/5069 IB db **(89.5)** n21.5 t22.5 f22.5 b23 Really imaginative use of excellent sherry butts. An understatedly complex and delicious malt. *46%. ncf.*
**Speyburn Aged 15 Years** American oak & Spanish oak casks, bott code L1717/253 R17/5323 IB db **(91)** n22 t23.5 f22 b23.5 Well done: not an off sherry butt in sight, helping to make this an enjoyably rich and fulsome malt. One of the most inventive and sympathetic Speyburns of all time. *46%*.
**Speyburn Aged 18 Years** db **(86)** n22 t22.5 f20 b21.5 Nutty, malty and displaying a cocoa tendency. But the finish is a bit on the bitter side. *46%*.
**Speyburn Aged 25 Years** db **(92)** n22 t24 f23 b23. Either they have re-bottled very quickly or I got the diagnosis dreadfully wrong first time round. Previously I wasn't overly impressed; now I'm taken aback by its beauty. Some change. *46%*
**Speyburn Arranta Casks** first fill ex-bourbon casks bott code: L16/097 R16/5130 IB db **(90)** n22 t23 f22 b23 Speyburn at its most vocal and interesting: rather beautifully constructed. *46%*.
**Speyburn Bradon Orach** bott code: L17/039 R17/5048 IB db **(75)** n19 t19 f18.5 b18.5 Remains one of the most curious distillery bottlings on Speyside and one still unable to find either its balance or a coherent dialogue. *40%*.
**Speyburn Hopkins Reserve Travel Exclusive** bott code R18/5066 IB db **(92)** n23 t23 f22.5 **b23.5** The kind of ultra-simplistic raw, smoky Speysider that the distillery's founder John Hopkins would have recognised – and drooled over - over a century ago... *46%. ncf.*

⟨⟩ **The First Editions Speyburn Aged 12 Years 2006** sherry butt, cask no. 15539, bott 2018 **(89.5) n22** deft apple and grape skin on a gentle vanilla base; **t23** very attractive spices take no time to merge with the fruity delivery; superb juiciness and good oil richness; **f22** settles into a cleaner more malty mode; **b22.5** a clean sherry butt free from faults. Very limited complexity but the overall ride is an enjoyable one. *56.3%. nc ncf sc. 288 bottles.*

**Gordon & MacPhail Connoisseurs Choice Speyburn 1989** refill bourbon barrels, dist 2004, bott 14 Mar 18 **(88) n22 t22.5 f21.5 b22** Speyburn at both its most attractive and full bodied. A pleasant surprise. *46%. nc ncf. 528 bottles.*

⟨⟩ **Hepburn's Choice Speyburn 12 Years Old** sherry butt, dist 2006, bott 2018 **(87) n21.5 t22.5 f21 b22** Dry and constrained to the point of being almost paranoid in its personality. There are some lovely, fleeting sultana moments, balanced excellently by spice. But the tightness of the vanilla restricts the promised development. *46%. nc ncf sc. 708 bottles.*

**Old Malt Cask Speyburn Aged 12 Years** sherry butt, cask no. 14655, dist Oct 05, bott Feb 18 **(87) n21 t22.5 f21.5 b22** Sister cask to the First Editions 12 above. Huge malty signature but thins out much more in the distillery's usual style, More spice at work but less overall complexity. Very pleasant, though. *50%. nc ncf sc. 387 bottles.*

⟨⟩ **Old Malt Cask Speyburn Aged 13 Years** sherry butt, cask no. 15306, dist Nov 04, bott Aug 18 **(87.5) n22 t23 f20.5 b22** A pleasant if ultimately unexciting sherried Speyburn but boasting a real spicy sultana cake fruitiness before the unyielding intensity of the chalk-dry vanilla takes hold. A very decent and attractive malt overall. *50%. nc ncf sc. 483 bottles.*

**Provenance Speyburn Aged 8 Years** refill hogshead, cask no. 11785, dist Sept 08, bott May 17 **(82) n20 t21.5 f20 b20.5** Intense, sweet, feisty, basic Speyside malt at its most raw and unprepossessing. *46%. nc ncf sc. 390 bottles.*

⟨⟩ **Scyfion Choice Speyburn 2008** Muscat Dolce Passione cask finished, bott 2018 **(85.5) n20.5 t22 f21.5 b21.5** Tight and tart, this isn't the kind of malt I can get too passionate about, even if it does bring water to the eyes... *46%. nc ncf sc. 140 bottles.*

# THE SPEYSIDE DISTILLERY
### Speyside, 1990. Speyside Distillers. Working.

⟨⟩ **Spey 10 Year Old** port casks db **(87) n22 t22.5 f20.5 b22** Soft and nutty, there is an attractive easiness to the fruit as it makes its salivating, bitter-sweet way around the palate. Just a little bit of a tang on the finish, though. *46%. nc ncf. 3,000 bottles.*

**Spey 12 Years Old** limited edition, finished in new oak casks db **(85.5) n21.5 t23 f19.5 b21.5.** One of the hardest whiskies I have had to define this year: it is a curious mixture of niggling faults and charming positives which come together to create a truly unique scotch. The crescendo is reached early after the delivery with an amalgamation of acacia honey, barley sugar and butter notes interlocking with something bordering classicism. However, the nose and finish, despite the chalky oak, reveals that something was lacking in the original distillate or, to be more precise, was rather more than it should have been. Still, some hard work has obviously gone into maximising the strengths of a distillery that had hitherto failed to raise the pulse and impresses for that alone. *40%. nc. 8,000 bottles.*

**Spey 18 Years Old** ltd edition, fresh sherry casks db **(82.5) n19 t23.5 f19 b21.** What a shame this malt has been brushed with sulphur. Apparent on nose and finish, it still can't diminish from the joy of the juicy grape on delivery and the excellent weight as the liquorice and treacle add their gentle treasures and pleasures. So close to a true classic. *46%. nc.*

**Spey Chairman's Choice** db **(77) n19 t21 f18 b19.** Their Chairman's Choice, maybe. But not mine... *40%*

**Spey Fumare** db **(90.5) n22** minty phenols. Delicate with a light touch of grated milk chocolate; **t23.5** salivating, for a moment heads towards an oily richness then has second thoughts. Checks back to a more citrusy juiciness with the phenols taking their time to regain their intensity; **f22** a little sparse in part with the peat and sugars thinning out noticeably; **b23** a very different type of peaty malt with some surprising twists and turns. As fascinating as it is quietly delicious. I am looking at Speyside distillery in a new light...*46%. nc ncf.*

⟨⟩ **Spey Fumare Cask Strength** db **(93) n23** there is a cool menthol touch to perfectly match the polite loftiness of the phenol. So well groomed...; **t23.5** sweet, smoky, salivating gristiness helps hide a slight technical flaw, like make-up over an old scar. So attractive, though...; **f23** dries as the vanillas make a definite impact. A little diced macadamia nut fits in well with the vaguely spiced phenol and mocha; **b23.5** unquestionably The Speyside Distillery in its prettiest pose. And this strength ensures perfect lighting... *59.3%. nc ncf. 1,500 bottles.*

**Spey Royal Choice** db **(87) n21 t23 f21 b22.** "I'll have the slightly feinty one, Fortescue." "Of course, Your Highness. Would that be the slightly feinty one which has a surprising softness on the palate, a bit like a moist date and walnut cake? But with a touch too much oil on the finish?" "That's the blighter! No ice, Fortescue!" "Perish the thought, Sir."

Or water, Forters. One must drink according to the Murray Method, don't you know!" "Very wise, Sir." 46%

**Spey Tenné** finished in Tawny Port casks db **(90)** n22.5 t23 f22 **b22.5** Upon pouring, the handsome pink blush tells you one of three things: i) someone has swiped the whisky and filled the bottle with Mateus Rose instead; ii) I have just located where I put the pink paraffin or iii) this whisky has been matured in brand spanking new port casks. Far from a technical paragon of virtue so far as distilling is concerned. But those Tawny Port casks have brought something rather magical to the table. And glass. 46%. nc. 18,000 bottles.

◈ **Spey Tenné Cask Strength** db **(88)** n22.5 the underlying spirit has a nagging weakness but the wine casks sent in to finish the job take no half measures: swimming in ripe plummy fruit...; **t22** ker-pow! Off it goes...high propane plumminess with acacia honey stirred in. Underneath, the spirit nags...; **f21.5** a little off beam; **b22** plenty of weirdness to this – and spicy fun, too! What magnificent (port?) casks they must have used for this....!! 59.5%. nc ncf. 1,500 bottles.

**Spey Trutina** bourbon casks db **(90)** n22.5 t23 f22 **b22.5** The best Speyside Distillery bottling I have encountered for a very long time. Entirely feint free and beautifully made. 46%. nc ncf

◈ **Spey Trutina Cask Strength** db **(93)** n22.5 a little thin, but the malt does have a little polish; **t24** oh...my....word!!! This is Speyside! Wow. Beautifully made with a crystalline clarity and hardness to the barley. The softening oils allows the huge flavours to launch into every crevice on the palate...; so stunningly salivating and fresh...; **f23** still the concentrated barley rings out loud and proud... **b23.5** feint free and fabulous! 59.1%. nc ncf. 1,500 bottles.

**Beinn Dubh** db **(82)** n20 t21 f21 **b20**. Mountains. Dogs. Who can tell the difference...? I suppose to a degree I can, as this has for more rummy undertones and is slightly less inclined to layering than the old Danish version. 43%

**Berry Bros & Rudd Speyside 21 Years Old** cask no. 25, dist 1995, bott 2017 **(94)** n23.5 t24.5 f22.5 **b23.5** I am agog... Usually I end the working tasting day with a sherry-matured malt as 49 times out of 50 my palate will have been addled with sulphur and I have an evening and night to remove the taste. Not so with this bottling: I will have to find another malt. Is it entirely free of brimstone? Not exactly, but the trace sulphur is manageable, My main moan is that I would have preferred to have seen this at a minimum 50% abv... 46%. nc ncf sc.

**Cadenhead's Authentic Collection Speyside 26 Year Old** bourbon cask, dist 1991 **(94)** n23.5 t23.5 f23 **b24** The only time I have ever been stuck in a snow drift came when I was on my way back from the warehouses of Speyside distillery. I had reminded the then owner of the distillery that the very oldest barrels of this maturing spirit was about to hit its third birthday – a date he had completely overlooked. So I, accompanied by my then girlfriend and my three children, drove up to Glasgow to be the first to sample the first casks on the very day they legally became Scotch whisky. And on the drive home the skies turned a whiter shade of grey, the snow begun to fall, the road chilled and for the one and only time in my life I became trapped, alongside my fellow prisoners. Now, at 2am of a balmy summer's night – in the middle of the biggest drought in recent British history - I am tasting the oldest malt from The Speyside distillery I have ever seen. Isn't life strange... 48.9%. sc.

**Dramfool 12 Speyside 1995 22 Years Old** sherry butt **(77.5)** n19 t21 f18.5 **b19** Plenty of grape. And a few other things besides. But, sadly, even that doesn't entirely obliterate the very poor spirit. 55%. nc ncf. 156 bottles. Spirit of Speyside 2018 release.

**The First Editions Speyside Aged 24 Years** refill hogshead, cask no. 15001, bott 2018 **(81)** n21 t18 f22 **b20** Not one of the better distilling days at Speyside in this period – and, in truth, good ones were few and far between. The stillman must have been wanting to get home quick for his tatties and neeps (or maybe just his leg over), as this is hotter than the core of the sun. Whatever his hurry was for, I hope was more enjoyable than this... Anyway, if you survive the radiation burns, the malt comes through pleasantly in the end. 59.4%. nc ncf sc. 123 bottles.

◈ **The Golden Cask Speyside 1992** cask no. CM253, bott 2019 **(95.5)** n24 as many rich golden syrup and liquorice bourbon notes as there are barley ones; almost a touch of Belgium waffle about this...; **t24** mouthfeel...perfect. Delivery, aided by a lush intertwangling of intense barley, molasses and fudge...perfect. Mid-ground, with its lightly spiced, soft hickory bourbon-style feel...near perfect...; **f23.5** fade, with its toasty vanilla and growing butterscotch and light barley backdrop...near perfect; **b24** whisky from Speyside distillery – in a short, Golden, Olden period when they were distilling at a higher quality than in following years – really doesn't get better than this. 57.7%. nc ncf sc. 216 bottles.

**Old Malt Cask Speyside Aged 21 Years** refill hogshead, cask no. 14269, dist Sept 96, bott Sept 17 **(88)** n22 t23 f21 **b22** Enjoyable despite the imperfections. 50%. nc ncf sc. 224 bottles.

**Old Particular Speyside 21 Years Old** refill butt, cask no. 12019, dist Sept 96, bott Sept 17 **(93)** n23.5 t23.5 f22.5 **b23.5** A mostly clean sherry butt sees the distillery in an unusual and truly delicious light. 51.5%. nc ncf sc. 362 bottles.

# SPRINGBANK

**Campbeltown, 1828. J&A Mitchell & Co. Working.**

**Springbank Aged 10 Years** db **(89.5) n22 t23 f22 b22.5.** Although the inherent youthfulness of the 10-y-o has not changed, the depth of body around it has. Keeps the taste buds on full alert. 46%

**Springbank Aged 10 Years (100 Proof)** db **(86) n21.5 t22 f21 b21.5.** Trying to map a Springbank demands all the skills required of a young 19th century British naval officer attempting to record the exact form and shape of a newly discovered land just after his sextant had fallen into the sea. There is no exact point on which you can fix...and so it is here. A shifting dram that never quite tastes the same twice, but one constant, sadly, is the bitterness towards the finale. Elsewhere, it's one hell of a journey...! 57%

**Springbank Aged 15 Years** db **(88.5) n22.5 t22 f22 b22.** Last time I had one of these, sulphur spoiled the party. Not this time. But the combination of oil and caramel does detract from the complexity a little. 46%

**Springbank Aged 18 Years** db **(90.5) n23** busy in the wonderful Springbank way; delicate greengage and date; nippy; **t23** yummy, mouthwatering barley and green banana. Fresh with excellent light acacia honey; **f21.5** fabulous oak layering, including chocolate. A little off-key furriness from a sherry butt late on; **b23** just one so-so butt away from bliss... 46%

**Springbank Aged 21 Years** db **(90) n22 t23 f22.5 b22.5** A few years ago I was at Springbank when they were bottling a very dark, old-fashioned style 21-year-old. I asked if I could take a 10cl sample with me for inclusion in the Bible; they said they would send it on, though I tasted a glass there and then just for enjoyment's sake. They never did send it, which was a shame. For had they, they most probably would have carried off World Whisky of the Year. This, though very good, is not quite in the same class. But just to mark how special this brand has always been to me, I have made this the 500th new single malt scotch and 700th new whisky in all of the 2015 Whisky Bible. 46%. WB15/096

**Hazelburn Aged 8 Years** bourbon cask, bott 2011 db **(94.5) n23 t24 f23.5 b24** A very curious coppery sheen adds extra lustre and does no harm to a very well made spirit filled into top grade oak. For an eight year old malt, something extra special. 46%

**Longrow Aged 10 Years** db **(78) n19 t20 f19 b20.** This has completely bemused me: bereft not only of the usual to-die-for smoke, its warts are exposed badly, as this is way too young. Sweet and malty, perhaps, and technically better than the marks I'm giving it – but this is Longrow, dammit! I am astonished. 46%

**Longrow Aged 10 Years 100 Proof** db **(86) n20 t23 f22 b21.** Still bizarrely smokeless – well, maybe a flicker of smoke as you may find the involuntary twitching of a leg of a dying fly – but the mouthfeel is much better here and although a bit too oily and dense for complexity to get going, a genuinely decent ride heading towards Hazelburn-esque barley intensity. Love it, because this oozes class. But where's the ruddy peat...?! 57%

**Longrow 14 Years Old** refill bourbon and sherry casks db **(89) n24 t23.5 f19 b22.5.** Again, a sherry butt proves the Achilles heel. But until then, a charmer. 46%

**Longrow Aged 18 Years (94.5) n25 t23 f23 b23.5** If you gently peat a blend of ulmo, manuka and heather honey you might end up with something as breathtakingly stunning as this. But you probably won't... 46%. WB15/103

**Endangered Drams Springbank 15 Year Old** cask no. 596, dist 1993, bott 2018 **(90) n22 t23 f22.5 b22.5** Not sure exactly what is endangered about Springbank, one of the world's most complex single malts. That said, this delicious bottling will soon be endangered, as I can see it selling out and being consumed very quickly – even though it is a bit on the young and underdeveloped side for this Campbeltown leviathan. 55.2%. nc ncf sc.

**Hunter Laing's Old & Rare Springbank Aged 20 Years** sherry hogshead, dist Oct 96, bott Nov 16 **(94) n23.5 t24 f23 b23.5** Maybe a sherry hoggy, but any grape is, like us, little more than a dazzled bystander as the salty malt and oak hook p. 58.3%. nc ncf sc. 75 bottles.

**Kingsbury Gold Springbank 26 Years Old** hogshead, cask no. 321, dist 1991 **(93) n24 t23.5 f21.5 b23.5** A beauty but worth finding just for the nose alone! 40.7%. 93 bottles.

**The Loch Fyne Springbank 29 Year Old (94.5) n24 t23.5 f23 b23** This cask didn't really have much longer to live. Another summer and it could have ducked below 40%, and those outrageous oaky tones would have dropped some of the sugars to go it alone. This has to be almost the ultimate example of whisky brinkmanship. 40.07%. sc.

⬦ **The Perfect Fifth Springbank 1993** cask no. 315, dist 28 May 93 **(96) n24** anyone who remembers the old Springbank 25-year-olds of the early 1990s will recognise this aroma as a direct descendent – indeed it is near enough identical in both weight and character. The huge, nuggety oak is faultless (this must have come from a cask which had been seasoned in the old – virtually lost – style). Salt dominates but there are dried apricots and spiced pear, too. Meanwhile the vaguest of peaty notes (and I mean the odd atom here and there!!)

teases away as a barely audible background noise, which automatically becomes louder the moment you spot it...; **t24** a malt on the threshold of perhaps dallying too closely with the oak. But that coastal-style bite makes just the right contact with the salty tannins and cocoa-laden phenol to make a course for more complex and satisfying port. Just enough oil makes the middle rich and promises a long finale; **f24** drier, as is to be expected, as the tannins raise their game. Still salty, but a little barley sugar and lemon juice lightens the intensity, though – happily, by not too much; the residual oils ensure the finish is of extraordinary length; **b24** a real return to the past here with Springbank in its most full-bodied, uncompromising and complex style which those of us who discovered the distillery in the 1980s remember with great affection. *52.3%. sc.*

⬧ **Master of Malt Single Cask Springbank 20 Year Old** dist 1998 **(94.5) n23** saltier than a packet of crisps; maltier than a packet of Maltesers; more citrusy than a packet of citrus; **t24** more puckering than a thing that habitually puckers; more honeyed than an American husband; **f23.5** barleyer than a barley mow; still saltier than a kipper, but not as smoky; come to think of it, less smoky than a fire station; **b24** more Springbanky than a Glen Scotia. *48.1%. sc.*

⬧ **Sansibar Whisky Springbank 2000 (95) n23.5** wonderfully complex with a delicate smokiness married to the firm tannin. Barley waltzes around with a distinctive kumquat note...; **t24** hold on tight...the taste buds are in for a right grilling here! So deep and complex. Heather honey leads the way, but the sweetness is restricted by the chunkiness of the thick vanilla-rich oak; **f23.5** count the rings in the oak and the rungs to the dying flavour waves. Even late on that heather honey is still doing its job...remarkable...; **b24** just runs amok with Springbank's unique everythingness...! So much going on, it almost wears you out! *49.1%.*

**Whisky Foundation Springbank Aged 24 Years** ex-sherry cask **(86.5) n21.5 t22.5 f21 b21.5** Highly unusual to find a Springbank suffering from the ill-effects of old age when less than 25 years into maturation – that is when it is normally just getting into its stride. But there is no denying that this is tannin heavy and creased in all the wrong places. Some excellent maple syrup supplements the big malty middle. But it isn't quite enough to make this the kind of malt one had hoped for....or expected. *47.1%. sc. 244 bottles. Bottled by The Maltman.*

# STRATHISLA
**Speyside, 1786. Chivas Brothers. Working.**

**Strathisla 12 Years Old** db **(85.5) n21.5 t22 f21 b21.** A slight reduction in strength from the old bottling and a significant ramping up of toffee notes means this is a malt which will do little to exert your taste buds. Only a profusion of spice is able to cut through the monotonous style. Always sad to see such a lovely distillery so comprehensively gagged. *40%.*

**Strathisla Distillery Edition 15 Years Old** db **(94) n23 t23 f24 b24** What a belter! The distillery is beautiful enough to visit: to take away a bottle of this as well would just be too good to be true! *53.7%*

**Gordon & MacPhail Rare Vintage Strathisla 1960 (96) n23.5 t24 f24.5 b24** This was a sherry cask style that 20 years ago I would have criticised for being far too heavy and over the top. In the two decades which have now passed such, has become the appalling state of Scottish sherry butt stock, that I now fling my arms around this style of whisky with love, glee and reverence. Yes, of course it is still over the top. But the enormity and lusciousness of the grape has protected the cask for the best part of 60 years now, allowing the tannins to go so far and no further. And, of course, there is not an atom of sulphur to be detected: the blenders of that day simply would never have allowed it. Worth raiding your piggy bank and exploring this now lost style. *43%.*

**Gordon & MacPhail Distillery Label Strathisla 2006** bott 28 Jun 17 **(92.5) n23 t24 f22 b23.5** Some moments of this malt are to be cherished. *43%.*

**Hidden Spirits Strathisla 15 Year Old** dist 2002, bott 2018 **(89) n21.5 t23 f22 b22.5** At times simplistic, at others attractively complex. *51.2%.*

# STRATHMILL
**Speyside, 1891. Diageo. Working.**

**Strathmill 25 Year Old** refill American oak casks, dist 1988 db **(89) n23 t22 f22 b22** A blending malt which reveals the kind of big malty deal it offers older brands. *52.4%. 2,700 bottles. Diageo Special Releases 2014.*

**Cadenhead's Cask Strength Strathmill Aged 22 Years** port cask, dist 1995 **(89) n23 t22.5 f21.5 b22** Nothing like I envisaged. A very different take on the port wood theme. *50.8%. sc. 252 bottles.*

⬧ **The First Editions Strathmill Aged 21 Years 1996** refill hogshead, cask no. 15187, bott 2018 **(94.5) n23** fabulous interplay between malt of various hues of intensity and vaguely salty tannins. The sweetness flits about the nose like a butterfly; **t24** amazing finesse from the very first moment. The malt flutters over the taste buds, inducing an incredible degree of salivation. The layering of the oak defies belief: thin wisps of vanilla and marzipan slowly building into something much more profound as it progresses; **f23.5** ah, the malt...the spice....!!! **b24** pure Speyside...! Beautiful. Such a badly neglected distillery: we should see far more of this around...but in the meantime just worship this! *56.2%. nc ncf sc. 208 bottles.*

**Gordon & MacPhail Connoisseurs Choice Strathmill 2004** bott 29 Mar 17 **(95) n24 t23.5 f23.5 b24** Rather beautiful bottlings like this cannot help but make you wonder why the turn of the 19th century status of this being a relatively widely available malt is not resurrected. *46%.*

**Gordon & MacPhail Connoisseurs Choice Strathmill 2004** refill bourbon barrels, dist 2004, bott 15 Mar 18 **(88) n22 t23 f21 b22** Enjoyable enough, but one expects to see Strathmill in a better light. *46%. nc ncf. 990 bottles.*

# TALISKER
### Highlands (Island–Skye), 1832. Diageo. Working.

**Talisker Aged 10 Years** db **(93) n23 t23 f24 b23** The deadening caramel that had crept into recent bottlings of the 10-y-o has retreated, and although that extraordinary, that wholly unique finale has still to be re-found in its unblemished, explosive entirety, this is much, much closer to the mark and a quite stupendous malt to be enjoyed at any time. But at night especially. *45.8%*

**Talisker 12 Years Old Friends of the Classic Malts** db **(86) n22 t21.5 f21 b21.5.** Decent, sweet, lightly smoked...but the explosion which made this distillery unique - the old kerpow! - appears kaput. *45.8%*

**Talisker Aged 18 Years** bott code: L7201CM000 db **(93.5) n23.5 t23.5 f23 b23.5** After such a good age, you don't expect the roaring Talisker of younger days but might expect a little more than is available here. Delicious, nonetheless. *45.8%.*

**Talisker Aged 20 Years** db **(95) n24 t24 f23 b24.** I have been tasting Talisker for 28 years. This is the best bottling ever. Miss this and your life will be incomplete. *62%*

**Talisker Aged 25 Years** bott 2017, bott code: L7023CM000 db **(96.5) n24 t24 f24 b24.5** A malt of magnificent complexity that generously rewards time and concentration. So for some, it may not be easy to get through the forests of oak early on, but switching your senses on to full alert not only pays dividends, but is no less than this great old malt deserves or demands. *45.8%. 21,498 bottles.*

**Talisker 25 Years Old** db **(88) n22.5t22 f21.5 b22.** Pretty taken aback by this one: it has taken a fancy to being a bit of a Bowmore, complete with a bountiful supply of Fisherman's Friends. *45.8%*

**Talisker 30 Years Old** db **(93.5) n23 t24 f23 b23.5** Much fresher and more infinitely entertaining than the 25 year old...!!! *45.8%*

**Talisker 30 Years Old** db **(84.5) n21 t21.5 f21 b21.** Toffee-rich and pretty one dimensional. Did I ever expect to say that about a Talisker at 30...? *53.1%*

**Talisker 57 Degrees North** db **(95) n24 t24.5 f23 b23.5** A glowing tribute, I hope, for a glowing whisky... *57%*

**Talisker Dark Storm** charred oak db **(92) n22 t23.5 f23 b23.5** Much more like it! Unlike the Storm, which appeared to labour under some indifferent American oak, this is just brimming with vitality and purpose. *45.8%.*

**Talisker Neist Point** bott code: L6067CM000 db **(87) n22 t21.5 f22 b21.5** Not exactly Nil Points, but for people like me who adore Talisker (indeed, it was a visit to this distillery 43 years ago that turned my appreciation of whisky into a passionate love affair), it tastes like the malt has barely got out of second gear. Where is the fizz and bite of the peppery phenols on impact? The journey through myriad styles of smoke? The breath-taking and life-giving oomph? Not to be found in this pleasantly tame and overly sweet version, though the spices do mount to something towards the very end. It is like observing a lion that has had its teeth forcibly removed. *45.8%.*

**Talisker Port Ruighe** db **(88) n22 t22 f22 b22.** Sails into port without changing course *45.8%.*

**Talisker Skye** (85) **n21 t22 f21 b21.** The sweetest, most docile Talisker I can ever remember with the spices working hard in the background but weirdly shackled. More Toffee Sky than Vanilla... *45.8% WB16/051*

**Talisker Storm** db **(85.5) n20 t23 f21 b21.5** The nose didn't exactly go down a storm in my tasting room. There are some deft seashore touches, but the odd poor cask –evident on the finish, also - has undone the good. But it does recover on the palate early on with an even, undemanding and attractively sweet display showing malt to a higher degree than I have seen any Talisker before. *45.8%.*

❧ **The First Editions Talisker Aged 9 Years 2008** sherry butt, cask no. 15639, bott 2018 **(89.5) n22** a seemingly docile aroma where the peat battles to make headway against the soft candy fruit; a bit of Murray Method application and the smoke slowly rises to offer an extra dimension; **t24** beautiful lift off: actually, a stunning one! Such is the first compactness then expanding exuberance of the noble rot sweetness, that for a moment you are too startled for words; slowly intense malt emerges from under the grapey shadow; **f21.5** annoyingly, a little tang at the finish; **b22** right, not a perfect sherry butt. But its good points are breathtaking – and use the Murray Method for maximum results 54.5%. nc ncf sc. 342 bottles.

⬦ **Gleann Mór Talisker Aged Over 24 Years** (93) n23.5 t23 f23.5 b23 A nuttier Talisker than normal with some sweeping natural caramels drowning the noise from the peat and anthracite phenols. However, the smoke cannot be denied either on the nose, or on the mocha-sweetened, teasingly-spiced finale. 48.9%.

# TAMDHU
### Speyside, 1897. Ian Macleod Distillers. Working (re-opened 3rd March 2013).

**Tamdhu** db **(84.5) n20 t22.5 f21 b21.** So-so nose, but there is no disputing the fabulous, stylistic honey on delivery. The silkiest Speyside delivery of them all. 40%

**Tamdhu Aged 10 Years** oak sherry cask db **(69.5) n17 t18.5 f17 b17.** A much better malt when they stick exclusively to ex-bourbon casks, as used to be the case. 40%

**Tamdhu Aged 18 Years** bott code L0602G L12 20/08 db **(74.5) n19 t19 f18 b18.5.** Bitterly disappointing. Literally. 43%.

**Tamdhu 25 Years Old** db **(88) n22 t22 f21 b23.** Radiates quality. 43%

**The First Editions Tamdhu Aged 18 Years** first fill hogshead, cask no. 14732, bott 2018 **(89) n22 t22.5 f22 b22.5** About as complex a Tamdhu you'll ever happen across. 51.5%. nc ncf sc. 134 bottles.

⬦ **The First Editions Tamdhu Aged 20 Years 1997** refill hogshead, cask no. 15369, bott 2018 **(88.5) n22** unusual to find Fisherman's Friend cough sweet on a non-peated malt...but there it is...! **t22.5** almost aggressively malty then an eruption of salivating spices; **f22** back to the Fisherman's Friend again, though the malt hangs on gamely; **b22** well spiced, malty and hugely entertaining. By no means your average Tamdhu. 55.8%. nc ncf sc. 265 bottles.

**Hepburn's Choice Tamdhu 10 Years Old** sherry butt, dist 2007, bott 2018 **(85) n20.5 t22 f21 b21.5** The usual malty story but just a little untidy on both nose and finish. 46%. nc ncf sc. 452 bottles.

**Old Malt Cask Tamdhu Aged 18 Years** refill hogshead, cask no. 14731, dist Apr 99, bott Feb 18 **(87.5) n21 t22.5 f22 b22** Sister cask to the First Edition 18 (above) but this is a little tangier and more spice dependent. Enjoyably malty, but doesn't offer quite the same entertainment of its kin cask. 50%. nc ncf sc. 153 bottles.

⬦ **Old Malt Cask Tamdhu Aged 19 Years** refill hogshead, cask no. 14936, dist Apr 99, bott Apr 18 **(79) n19 t20.5 f19 b20.5** Something of the glazed cherry and jam tart about this. That said, not a malt that hangs together particularly impressively and hints of a little grimy off note here and there. 50%. nc ncf sc. 304 bottles.

**Old Particular Tamdhu 18 Years Old** refill hogshead, cask no. 11764, dist Apr 99, bott Jun 17 **(84.5) n21 t21 f21.5 b21** A little on the dour side with the malts and sugars present but never able to stretch their wings or bring fun to the proceedings. 48.4%. nc ncf sc. 290 bottles.

**Old Particular Tamdhu 18 Years Old** refill hogshead, cask no. 12201, dist May 99, bott Nov 17 **(90.5) n22 t22.5 f23 b23** By no means a representative Tamdhu: some delicate bourbon elements give this a lift. 48.4%. nc ncf sc. 337 bottles.

# TAMNAVULIN
### Speyside. 1966. Whyte and Mackay. Working.

**Tamnavulin 1966 Aged 35 Years** cream sherry butt db **(91) n24 t22 f23 b22.** For those who love great old sherry, this is an absolute. Perhaps too much sherry to ever make it a true great, but there is no denying such quality. 52.6%

**Tamnavulin Double Cask** batch no. 0308 db **(87.5) n22.5 t22.5 f21 b21.5** A bottling which deserves – and perhaps needs – to be at 46% at least. Reduced down to this strength it is levelled to a much chalkier, drier plane than it requires to fully project the oils, sugars and obvious intricacies. Entirely pleasant as it is, with an attractive clean maltiness to the thinned golden syrup as well as well-mannered spicing. But, overall, refuses to open out and develop as you might hope or expect. A 92-plus whisky just waiting to happen... 40%.

**C & S Dram Collection Tamnavulin 7 Years Old** hogshead, cask no. 2391, dist 15 Apr 09, bott 26 Sept 16 **(88) n22 t23 f21.5 b21.5** A substantial malt all the more intense due to its tender years. 57.1%. sc. 310 bottles.

# TEANINICH
### Highlands (Northern), 1817. Diageo. Working.

**Teaninich 17 Year Old** refill American oak hogsheads & refill American oak barrels db **(90) n22 t23 f22 b23** A distillery rarely celebrated in bottle by its owners. Here they have selected an age and cask profile which gets the mix between simple barley and far from taxing oak just about right. Minimalistically elegant. *55.9%. Diageo Special Releases 2017.*

⟐ **The Cooper's Choice Teaninich 2009 8 Years Old** Sauternes finish **(91.5) n23 t23 f22.5 b23** Rarely do Sauternes casks dish out the kind of militant peppers experienced on the nose (reminded me of live crabs being freshly boiled). But settles down to its more fruity role on delivery, though the usual sweetness expected from this grape never quite arrives. *54.5%. nc ncf sc.*

**The First Editions Teaninich Aged 18 Years** refill hogshead, cask no. 14771, bott 2018 **(96) n24 t24 f23.5 b24.5** Just brilliant...!!! An 18-year-old successfully passing itself off as a 25- or 30-year-old top quality malt. *57.2%. nc ncf sc. 120 bottles.*

**Golden Cask Teaninich Aged 9 Years** cask no. CM229, dist 2007, bott 2016 **(89) n22 t22 f23 b22** Stands up exceptionally tall and proud for its age. *62.3%. sc. 301 bottles.*

**Hepburn's Choice Teaninich 9 Years Old** refill butt, dist 2008, bott 2017 **(84.5) n21 t21.5 f21 b21** About as simplistic, untaxing a blending malt you'll ever find. *46%. nc ncf sc. 420 bottles.*

**Hepburn's Choice Teaninich 10 Years Old** refill butt, dist 2007, bott 2018 **(85.5) n22 t22 f21.5 b20** In my professional whisky career stretching over a quarter of a century I have tasted literally thousands of 10-year-old samples. Only a handful, though, would have been lesser troubled by oak than this offering. It is close to alcoholic barley water. The gristy malt dominant in every department from first to last. That said, as a pre-prandial dram on a warm day before a grilled fish supper, rather enchanting. *46%. nc ncf sc. 804 bottles.*

⟐ **Hidden Spirits Teaninich 2006** cask no. TH619, bott 2019 **(94.5) n23** barley squared; **t24.5** the intense malt powers through on the taste buds in astonishing style. The intensity of the barley in the nose is, if anything, even more profound here. The background oak has a wafer quality, with a touch of praline for good measure; **f23** dries with a vanilla injection; **b24** in recent years there have been far too many bottlings that have failed to do this distillery justice. Delighted that here is another which redresses the balance. *51.7%. sc.*

**Old Malt Cask Teaninich Aged 18 Years** refill hogshead, cask no. 14770, dist Jul 99, bott Feb 18 **(90) n23 t22.5 f22 b22.5** Has a real malty swagger about it. *50%. nc ncf sc. 148 bottles.*

# TOBERMORY
### Highlands (Island–Mull), 1795. Burn Stewart Distillers. Working.

**Tobermory 10 Years Old** db **(73.5) n17.5 t19 f18 b19.** The last time I tasted an official Tobermory 10 for the Bible, I was aghast with what I found. So I prodded this sample I had before me of the new 46.3% version with all the confidence Wile E Coyote might have with a failed stick of Acme dynamite. No explosions in the glass or on my palate to report. And though this is still a long way short, and I'm talking light years here, of the technical excellence of the old days, the uncomplicated sweet maltiness has a very basic charm. The nose and finish, though, are still very hard going. *46.3%*

**Tobermory Aged 15 Years** db **(93) n23.5 t23.5 f23 b23** A tang to the oils on both nose and finish suggests an over widened middle. But such is the quality of the sherry butts and the intensity of the salt-stained malt, all is forgiven. *46.3%. nc ncf.*

**Tobermory Aged 15 Years Limited Edition** db **(72.5) n17 t18 f19 b18.5.** Another poorly made whisky: the nose and delivery tells you all you need to know. *46.3%*

**Tobermory 42 Year Old** db **(94.5) n23.5 t23.5 f23.5 b24** A real journey back in time. Wonderful. *47.7%*

**Ledaig Aged 10 Years** db **(85.5) n20 t22.5 f21.5 b21.5.** Almost a Bowmore in disguise, such are its distinctive cough sweet qualities. Massive peat: easily one of the highest phenol Ledaigs of all time. But, as usual, a slight hiccup on the technical front. Hard not to enjoy it, though. *46.3%.*

**Ledaig Aged 10 Years** db **(63) n14 t17 f15 b17.** What the hell is going on? Butyric and peat in a ghoulish harmony on nose and palate that is not for the squeamish. *43%*

**Ledaig Aged 12 Years** db **(90) n23 t23.5 f21.5 b22** It has ever been known that there is the finest of lines between genius and madness. A side-by-side comparison of the Ledaig 10 and 12 will probably be one of whisky's best examples of this of all time... *43%*

**Ledaig 18 Year Old** batch 2 db **(71) n16 t20 f17 b18.** There are many ways to describe this whisky. Well made, alas, is not one of them. The nose sets off many alarms, especially on the feinty front. And though some exceptional oak repairs some of the damage, it cannot quite do enough. Sugary, too – and occasionally cloyingly so. *46.3%. nc ncf.*

**Ledaig 19 Year Old Marsala Finish** db **(92) n23.5 t23 f22.5 b23** Hardly textbook malt but a real gung-ho adventure story on the palate. *51%.*

**Ledaig 42 Year Old** db **(93) n23.5 t24 f22 b23.5** Only on the nose and very finish do we encounter excessive age which is borderline OTT but somehow stays within levels of toleration. For the most part this is a triumph of smoky elegance over advancing years. *46.7%.*

**Ledaig Dùsgadh 42 Aged 42 Years** db **(96) n25 t24.5 f22.5 b24** It has to be about 30 years ago I tasted my first-ever Ledaig – as a 12 year old peated malt. This must be from the same stocks, only this has been housed in exceptional casks. Who would have thought, three decades on, that it would turn into some of the best malt bottled in a very long time. A smoky experience unlikely to be forgotten. *46.3%*

**Ledaig 1996** db **(88) n21** some annoying barrels in there have seen better days and the tang distracts from what would have been a playful smokiness; **t23.5** grip your seat, fling your head back, close your eyes and chew...we are in business. Absolutely sublime mouth feel: dense yet passable, lush yet never boggy. The dark sugars and barley intertwangle quite deliciously with the underplayed smoke...; **f21** long, smoky bacon and still that lovely oil trace. Thins out towards a pasty austerity just when it starts getting really interesting.... damn it...!! **b22.5** a malt you feel is at times reaching for the stars. But has to settle for an, ultimately, barren planet. *46.3%*

**Acla Selection Tobermory 20 Years Old** hogshead, cask no. 0342, dist 1995, bott 2015 **(93) n23.5 t23.5 f23 b23.5** Lively and hugely satisfying. *48.4%. sc. 114 bottles.*

**Cadenhead's Single Cask Ledaig 12 Year Old** dist 2005 **(88.5) n22.5 t22.5 f21.5 b22** Good malt. Obviously very good sherry butt. But the smoke and grape don't always see eye to eye. *61.1%. sc.*

**Fadandel.dk Ledaig 10 Years Old** cask no. 700815-1716FD2, dist 2007, bott 2017 **(71.5) n18.5 t20 f15 b17** This is a massively peated dram which has spent four months under a first fill PX octave influence. Sulphur has got into the system, which certainly catches in the finish. But, as is so often the case when PX and peat meat, it is like setting off a bomb with a sledgehammer. Still, if you are into cloyingly sweet smoke with a sulphur-riddled finish, this is your baby. *55.2%. sc. 72 bottles.*

**Fadandel.dk Ledaig Aged 20 Years** refill sherry barrel, cask no. FAP-1801, dist 24 Mar 97, bott 27 Feb 18 **(86.5) n21.5 t22 f21.5 b21.5** A very interesting Ledaig made at a time when things in the still house were not perhaps as they are now. There is evidence this was not brought slowly to boil as the thinness of the body matches the bite which is further sharpened by the strength. Even after 20 years the grape and smoke have yet to make peace with the other and rather than forging a harmonised, balanced dram, our palate is used as little more than a battleground. Certainly not short on character, though! *60.7%. sc. 24 bottles.*

**The First Editions Tobermory Aged 21 Years** refill hogshead, cask no. 14407, bott 2017 **(84.5) n21.5 t21 f21 b21** Puckeringly sharp and salty. If you don't salivate to this, then you are probably fatally dehydrated. *50.4%. nc ncf sc. 90 bottles.*

**Golden Cask Tobermory Aged 20 Years** cask no. CM227, dist 1995, bott 2016 **(84) n21 t21.5 f20.5 b21** 'Mory at its most characterful. Certainly has a bit of spit and vim about it, aggression one might say, though the thin body and texture does ensure that the juiciness of the barley is accentuated. *57.8%. sc. 243 bottles.*

**Gordon & MacPhail Cask Strength Ledaig 2004** cask nos. 16600503 & 16600506, bott 22 Jun 17 **(91.5) n23 t22.5 f23 b23** The slight aggressiveness here is not the work of the alcohol alone: the oak is keen and fights its corner. *55.5%.*

**Gordon & MacPhail Connoisseurs Choice Ledaig 2004** bott 19 Apr 17 **(90.5) n22 t23 f22.5 b23** Less a dessert whisky and more a desert one... *46%.*

**Gordon & MacPhail Cask Strength Ledaig 2004** cask nos. 16600504 & 16600505, bott 20 Sept 17 **(94.5) n23.5 t23.5 f23.5 b24** A truly superior example of this malt and a serious blast from the past: Ledaig very much in the colours of when it was first launched...a long, long time ago now... *56.6%.*

⬧ **Gordon & MacPhail Discovery Range Ledaig Aged 12 Years (93) n23.5 t24 f22.5 b23** Following a plethora of poor 2008 bottlings, great to come across a G&M back on track with a Ledaig in its truer style: rich, chewy, sweet, rounded and well balanced...and all traces of copper intact. A beautiful leather and chocolate sub-plot to this while the waxy heather honey is on full parade. Delicious. *43%.*

**Gordon & MacPhail Private Collection Ledaig 2005** bott 23 Aug 17 **(67) n17 t18 f16 b16** Sulphur laden. *45%.*

⬧ **Hidden Spirits Ledaig 2007** cask no. LG719, bott 2019 **(88) n21.5** clean, a little out of sync, but the peat is promising...; **t22.5** a dynamic roughhouse of a malt. Plenty of bite and attitude, but the smoke is a bit of a pussy; **f21.5** the unresponsive casks add a little sharpness to the sweet phenols; **b22.5** not exactly the most complex whisky out there. But if you are looking for clean, smoky and sweet then here's your boy....!!! *52.2%. sc.*

⬧ **Liquid Treasures Snakes Ledaig 10 Year Old** bourbon hogshead, dist 2008, bott 2018 **(86) n20.5 t22.5 f21.5 b21.5** Echoes many of the failings of the Whisky Chamber 2008 (see below), though this has a slightly more substantial, gristier and juicer delivery. *59.3%. sc. 267 bottles.*

**Old Malt Cask Tobermory Aged 21 Years** refill hogshead, cask no. 14082, dist Jul 96, bott Aug 17 **(87.5) n21 t23 f21.5 b22** Malty but a little stodgy, too. Some of the tannins ensure a busy spiciness but it is the juicy barley on delivery which stars. *50%. nc ncf sc. 272 bottles.*

**Old Particular Tobermory 21 Years Old** 1st fill bourbon barrel, cask no. 11768, dist Apr 96, bott Jun 17 **(89) n21.5 t22.5 f22 b23** if this has been matured in first fill bourbon, then it has spent the last 21 years in a fridge...The oak contribution is negligible, even for a second fill after 21 years. Rather sexy all the same. *51.5%. nc ncf sc. 290 bottles.*

**Old Particular Tobermory 21 Years Old** refill hogshead, cask no. 11485, dist Apr 95, bott Nov 16 **(87) n21.5 t22.5 f21 b22** Never quite reaches star status, but there is something admirable and enjoyable about the precision in the balance between very basic malt and elementary oak. *51.5%. nc ncf sc. 313 bottles.*

**Provenance Ledaig Aged 9 Years** refill barrel, cask no. 12022, dist May 08, bott Aug 17 **(88.5) n22 t22.5 f22 b22** A simple smoky number but most enjoyable. *46%. nc ncf sc. 313 bottles.*

◇ **The Whisky Chamber Ledaig 10 Years Old 2008** bourbon cask **(85) n21 t22 f21 b21** An incredibly raw whisky, the nose in particular shewing a lack of copper at work, an observation confirmed by the thin finish. The main crutch for this malt is provided by the juicy peat which covers many of the obvious cracks. Not entirely without its merits. *59%. sc.*

◇ **Wilson & Morgan Barrel Selection Ledaig Traditional Oak** dist 2008, bott 2018 **(87.5) n21.5 t22.5 f21.5 b22** One of a curious batch of 2008 distilled Ledaigs currently sweeping the market place. Those of you around to remember the first ever-bottlings to be brought out under the name Ledaig will weep quietly. However, this is probably the best of the bunch as there appears to be greater integrity to the malt and a more widespread richness to the smoky barley sugar; even a degree of saltiness. Not great by historic Ledaig standards, being clearly undercooked, but pretty decent amid today's offerings. *48%.*

# TOMATIN
**Speyside, 1897. Takara, Shuzo and Okura & Co. Working.**

**Tomatin 8 Years Old** bourbon & sherry casks db **(89) n22** polite, though youthful exuberance is easy to spot. So is the fruitiness which displays a distant tang; **t23** fabulous delivery of wet-behind-the ears barley and under-ripe greengages: salivating and a lovely lead into the massive toffee; **f21.5** just a little furriness to the latte coffee; **b22.5** a malt very proud of its youth. *40%. Travel Retail Exclusive.*

**Tomatin 12 Years Old** db **(85.5) n21 t21.5 f22 b21.** Reverted back to a delicately sherried style, or at least shows signs of a touch of fruit, as opposed to the single-minded maltfest it had recently been. So, nudge or two closer to the 18-y-o as a style and shows nothing other than good grace and no shortage of barley, either. *40%*

**Tomatin 12 Year Old** finished in Spanish sherry casks db **(91.5) n23 t23.5 f21.5 b23.5** For a great many years, Tomatin operated under severe financial restrictions. This meant that some of the wood brought to the distillery during this period was hardly of top-notch quality. This has made life difficult for those charged with moulding the stocks into workable expressions. I take my hat off to the creator of this: some great work is evident, despite the finish. *43%*

**Tomatin 14 Year Old** Port Finish db **(92.5) n23** under-ripe greengage shows some nip and spice; **t24** salivating, as a Tomatin delivery so often is. But here we get all juiced up by succulent fruit, helped along by glazed muscovado; **f22.5** the fruit tails off allowing the vanilla and spice an easy ride; **b23** allows the top notch port a clear road. *46%. ncf.*

**Tomatin 15 Years Old** American oak casks db **(89.5) n22.5** grass and hay mixed together; malted breakfast cereal with a sprinkling of muscovado sugar; **t22.5** concentrated malt delivery. Salivating, with a profound ulmo honey and vanilla mix; **f22** remains steadfastly malty, though the oak shows just a little sign of wear and tear as a degree of bitterness emerges; the spices rise to the challenge; **b22.5** a delicious exhibition of malt. *46%. Travel Retail Exclusive.*

**Tomatin Aged 15 Years** ex bourbon cask, bott 2010 db **(86) n21 t22 f21.5 b21.5.** One of the most malty drams on the market today. Perhaps suffers a little from the 43% strength as some of the lesser oak notes get a slightly disruptive foothold. But the intense, juicy barley trademark remains clear and delicious. *43% Tomatin Distillery*

**Tomatin 15 Years Old** bourbon barrels and Spanish Tempranillo wine casks db **(88.5) n22 t23 f21 b22.5.** Not free from the odd problem with the Spanish wine casks but gets away with it as the overall complexity and enjoyment levels are high. *52%*

**Tomatin Aged 18 Years** db **(85) n22 t21 f21 b21.** I have always held a torch for this distillery and it is good to see some of the official older stuff being released. This one has some serious zing to it, leaving your tastebuds to pucker up - especially as the oak hits. *40%*

**Tomatin 18 Years Old** db **(88) n22.5 t22 f21.5 b22.** What a well-mannered malt. As though it grew up in a loving, caring family and behaves itself impeccably from first nose to last whimpering finale; *43%*

**Tomatin 18 Year Old** db (82) n21.5 t22 f19 b20 Sadly some sulphur on the casks which makes the finish just too dry and off key. Underneath are hints of greatness, but the sherry butt doesn't give it a chance. 46%.

**Tomatin 25 Years Old** db (89) n22 t23 f21.5 b22.5. Not a nasty bone in its body: understated but significant. 43%

**Tomatin 30 Years Old** db (91) n22 t23 f23.5 b22.5 Malts of this age rarely maintain such a level of viscosity. Soft oils can often be damaging to a whisky, because they often refuse to allow character to flourish. Yet here we have a whisky that has come to terms with its age with great grace. And no little class. 49.3%

**Tomatin 30 Years Old** European & American oak casks db (85.5) n21 t21 f22.5 b21. Unusually for an ancient malt, the whisky becomes more comfortable as it wears its aged shoes. The delivery is just a bit too enthusiastic on the oaky front, but the natural caramels soften the journey rather delightfully. 46%. ncf.

**Tomatin 30 Years Old** bott 2018 db (93) n23 t22.5 f24 b23.5 Puts me in mind of a 29-year-old Springbank I have tasted for this Bible, which showed similar initial signs of wear and tear. But as the whisky warmed and oxidised, then so it grew in the glass and began to reveal previously hidden brilliance. This is not, perhaps, up to those gargantuan standards but what is achieved here shews the rewards for both patience and the use of the Murray Method. Patience and care are most certainly rewarded 46%.

**Tomatin 36 Year Old American & European oak** db (96.5) n24 t24.5 f23.5 b24.5 The difference between old oak and the newer stuff is brilliantly displayed here. Make no mistake: this is a masterpiece of a malt. 46%

**Tomatin 40 Years Old** db (89.5) n21.5 t22 f23 b23. Not quite sure how it's done it, but somehow it has made it through all those oaky scares to make for one very impressive 40-y-o!! Often it shows the character of a bourbon on a Zimmer. 42.9%

**Tomatin 40 Years Old** Oloroso sherry casks db (87.5) n21.5 t23 f21 b22 One of those malts which offers a graceful peep at the past, when sherry butts were clean and offered nothing to fear. But no matter how good the cask time takes its toll and the intense chalkiness reveals tannins that have got slightly the better of the barley. Thankfully the grape is still intact and brings us a beautiful raisin and date depth before the chalk returns a little more determined than before. 43%. Travel Retail Exclusive.

**Tomatin 1995 Olorosso Sherry** db (82) n21 t22 f19 b20 You can peel the grape off the malt. But one of the sherry butts wasn't quite as spotless as one might hope for. The inevitable tang arrives towards the finish. 46%.

**Tomatin Highland 1988 Vintage** db (86.5) n22 t22 f21 b21.5. Few whiskies in the world shows off thier malty muscle like Tomatin and here, briefly, it goes into overdrive. For the most part, a happy meeting of slightly salty malt and oak. 46%. ncf.

**Tomatin Cabernet Sauvignon 2002 Edition** db (82) n21 t22 f18 b21 Surprising degree of weight to this one. The fruit is not quite flawless with a little bit of a buzz on the nose and finish especially. But the rich mouthfeel and a pleasant, lush Garibaldi biscuit effect does ensure some very satisfying phases. 46%.

**Tomatin Caribbean Rum 2007 Edition** db (89.5) n22 t23 f22 b22.5 Beautifully clean malt though, as is their wont, the rum casks keep everything tight. 46%.

**Tomatin Cask Strength** db (80) n19 t22 f19 b20 Stunning malt climax on delivery. But always undone by a dull, persistent off note from the cask. 57.5%.

**Tomatin Contrast Bourbon Casks** from 1973, 1977, 1988, 2002, 2006 db (94.5) n24 t24 f22.5 b24 This is exceptionally fine malt whisky boasting an advanced degree of structure and complexity. If you don't have half an hour to spare to do it justice, don't even open the bottle... 46%. Packaged with sherry edition.

**Tomatin Contrast Sherry Casks** from 1973, 1977, 1988, 2002, 2006 db (87) n21 t22 f22 b22. Certainly a contrast with the bourbon, not least on the complexity front. No damaging off notes, even if the nose is a little tight. But though the grape makes itself heard, it never spreads its wings and flies in this curiously muted offering. 46%. Packaged with the bourbon edition.

**Tomatin Five Virtues Series Earth Peated Malt** refill hogshead oak casks db (88) n22 t22.5 f21.5 b22 Can honestly say I have never seen Tomatin in this kind of shape before: enjoyable once you acclimatise... 46%.

**Tomatin Five Virtues Series Fire Heavily Charred Oak** de-charred/re-charred oak fired casks db (94) n23.5 t24 f23 b23.5 High class malt with a sweet bourbon drizzle. 46%.

**Tomatin Five Virtues Series Metal Bourbon Barrels** first fill bourbon barrels db (95) n24 t24 f23 b24 There's metal enough in the "Earth" bottling. Was wondering where the metal comes into things here. As these are first fill bourbon casks, wonder if it was the type of warehouse they came from in Kentucky... Anyway, talking metal: this is pure gold... 46%.

**Tomatin Five Virtues Series Water Winter Distillation** sherry butts & bourbon barrels db **(72) n18 t20 f16 b18** A small degree of molassed chocolate escapes the grim sulphured tightness of the sherry. *46%.*

**Tomatin Five Virtues Series Wood Selected Oak Casks** French, American & Hungarian oak casks db **(90) n22.5 t23 f21.5 b23** A Franco-Hungarian truce means the malt and bourbon casks can work their magic...Some truly brilliant and unique phrases here. *46%.*

**Tomatin Highland Grand Select** db **(92.5) n23 t23 f23.5 b23** Measured and elegant. *43%.*

**Tomatin Highland Legacy** db **(88) n22** simplistic, untaxing malt and vanilla **t22.5** best bit of the experience: the big malt and marzipan surge and interweaving of sharp tannins; **f21.5** a light, malty buzz; **b22** clean, nutty malt but beyond that unremarkable. *43%.*

**Tomatin Warehouse 6 Collection 1971** db **(87) n22 t22 f21.5 b21.5.** Just one of those terribly frustrating malts where you just have to say: sorry, chaps, but you allowed this one to wallow in the warehouse a summer or two too long. Some superb vanilla and butterscotch, but the tannins have just a little bit too much of a scowl to their faces...That said, still plenty to savour and a fair bit of spice to show there's still life in the old dog... *45.8%*

**Tomatin Warehouse 6 Collection 1972** db **(92.5) n23.5 t23 f23 b23** I actually remember going through the Tomatin warehouse back in 1993 and tasting from some of the casks they were looking to make a 21-year-old malt from. Exactly 25 years on, could these be from that very same batch? *42.08%.*

🔸 **Tomatin Warehouse 6 Collection 1975** db **(95.5) n24 t23.5 f24 b24** When Jim Milne, one of Scotland's greatest-ever blenders, got back under a distillery's boardroom table after a lifetime at J&B, he chose Tomatin as his next destination. He had always appreciated the stunning consistency of its malt, especially in ex-bourbon cask. But once back in the lab again, he would ring me to tell about some ex-sherry he had located among stocks, or would send me samples and asked what I thought. This bottling reminds me very much of the samples Jim would send, although years back when it was a lot fresher. Jim, sadly, is no longer with us. But some of those casks still are. This one, naturally, shows far more grey hairs than the whiskies Jim eventually created. But it remains entirely sulphur free; and once you realise the oak is doing no harm to the fruit whatsoever other than just giving it a dry, powdery dusting, then you can go on to enjoy the still juicy, boiled sugar candy fruitiness on the palate...and even applaud the gravitas of the lightly spiced oak on its return at the finish. Jim would have approved both the complexity and charm of this malt – and he certainly wouldn't have given it an extra year, either. *46.5%.*

🔸 **Cù Bòcan Creation #1** Black Isle Brewery Imperial Stout & Bacalhôa Moscatel de Setúbal wine casks db **(84.5) n21.5 t22 f20 b21** Hands up here. Not much of a fan of whiskies shewing degrees of hops, and this one certainly does. Not like some out there, though, and the roastiness of the Imperial Stout does what it can to compensate, as does a pleasant creamy texture. But it is still more than some whisky lovers can bear... *46%.*

🔸 **Cù Bòcan Creation #2** Japanese Shochu & European virgin oak casks db **(93.5) n23 t24 f23 b23.5** Not the first time I have encountered whisky matured in shochu casks. But the first time I have tasted one that has also involved European virgin oak. And a light phenol note, just for good measure. Sounds as if it should be too much. Surprisingly, though, it is a delicate malt shewing both a sharpness and much softer Brazilian biscuit feel that gives a unique identity. Only a slight bitterness to the very finish offers any degree of discord. Juicy, youthful and an absolute joy! *46%.*

🔸 **Cù Bòcan Signature** bourbon, oloroso sherry & virgin oak casks db **(82) n21.5 t21 f20 b20.5** A virgin defiled amid brimstone. *46%.*

🔸 **Fadandel.dk Tomatin Aged 10 Years** hogshead, cask no. 1837, dist 2 Apr 09, bott 8 Apr 19 **(91) n22** older than its years with a rattling tannin buzz to this, vaguely Canadian in style; **t23** brilliantly intense barley: the sugars concentrate to the point of explosion while the oaky layering – just like on the nose – belies the years; **f22.5** one of the longest, most lip-smacking malt fades of the year...wow! **b23.5** few distilleries do sweet, intense malt like Tomatin, and here is a superb example. *60.2%. sc. 308 bottles.*

🔸 **The First Editions Tomatin Aged 23 Years 1994** refill hogshead, cask no. 15287, bott 2018 **(86) n21.5 t22 f21 b21.5** A surprising malt for its age which has rigidly refused to grow up. The nose has the gristy grassiness of a malt half its age, while the oak involvement is slow out of the blocks. A slight uneven tang from the tannin late on confirms the cask wasn't helping here. *46.1%. nc ncf sc. 252 bottles.*

**Gordon & MacPhail Cask Strength Tomatin 2007** cask nos. 4920, 4921 & 4922, bott 13 Jun 17 **(86.5) n21.5 t21.5 f22 b21.5** A curious, at times downright strange, Tomatin slightly at an angle from the normal concentrated barley style. Here it appears the tannins are on full throttle and polarised from the spirit which, especially on the delivery, does reveal a surprising degree of new make quality. *58.5%.*

⬩⬩ **Gordon & MacPhail Discovery Range Tomatin 2007 (92) n22 t24 f23 b23** Par for the course, this is all about intense malt – but close inspection shows there is much else besides. The light vanilla and butterscotch layering from the oak has a wonderfully light touch. And as a little cocoa begins to form, a delicious alcohol-rich Malteser candy forms. Impossible not to love. *43%.*

## TOMINTOUL

**Speyside, 1965. Angus Dundee. Working.**

**Tomintoul Aged 10 Years** db **(83.5) n21 t20 f21.5 b21** Has bucked up recently to offer a juicy, salivating barley thrust. Yet still a little on the thin side, despite some late oak. *40%*

**Tomintoul Aged 10 Years** bott code: L16 02149 CB2 db **(84.5) n20.5 t22 f21 b21** A very consistent dram but far too much emphasis of the chocolate toffee rather than the big malt you feel is bursting to break free. *40%.*

**Tomintoul Aged 12 Years Oloroso Sherry Cask Finish** db **(73.5) n18.5 t19 f18 b18.** Tomintoul, with good reason, styles itself as "The Gentle Dram" and you'll hear no argument from me about that one. However, the sherry influence here offers a rough ride. *40%*

**Tomintoul Aged 12 Years Oloroso Sherry Cask Finish** bott code: L17 02772 CB2 db **(74.5) n20 t19 f17.5 b18** A slightly cleaner sherry influence than the last of these I tasted, but the ungentle sulphur makes short work of the "gentle dram". *40%.*

**Tomintoul Aged 14 Years** db **(91) n23.5 t23 f21.5.** This guy has shortened its breath somewhat: with the distinct thinness to the barley and oak arriving a little flustered and half-hearted rather than with a confident stride; b23 remains a beautiful whisky full of vitality and displaying the malt in its most naked and vulnerable state. But I get the feeling that perhaps a few too many third fills, or under-performing seconds, has resulted in the intensity and hair-raising harmony of the truly great previous bottlings just being slightly undercooked. That said, still a worthy and delicious dram! *46%. nc ncf.*

**Tomintoul Aged 15 Years Portwood Finish** db **(94) n23 t23.5 f23.5 b24** So rare to find a wine finish which maximises the fruit to the full without allowing it to dominate. Charming. And so clean. Probably a brilliant whisky to help repair my damaged palate after tasting yet another s******ed sherry butt. I'll keep this one handy...*46%. nc ncf. 5,820 bottles.*

**Tomintoul Aged 15 Years With A Peaty Tang** bott code: L17 02975 CB2 db **(89.5) n23 t23 f21.5 b22** Being a bit older than their original Peaty Tang, the phenols here are less forward. But, then, it calls itself "The Gentle Dram" and on this evidence with good reason. *40%.*

**Tomintoul Aged 16 Years** db **(94.5) n24.5 t23.5 f23 b23.5** Confirms Tomintoul's ability to dice with greatness. *40%*

**Tomintoul Aged 21 Years** db **(94) n24 t24 f22.5 b23.5** Just how good this whisky would have been at cask strength or even at 46 absolutely terrifies me. *40%.*

**Tomintoul Aged 25 Years** db **(95) n25 t24 f23 b23.5** A quiet masterpiece from one of Scotland's criminally under appreciated great distilleries. *43%*

**Tomintoul Aged 40 Years** db **(86) n22 t21 f21.5 b21.5.** Groans every single one of its 40 years. Some lovely malty moments still, as well as butterscotch. But the oak has just jogged on past the sign that said 'Greatness' and carried straight on into the woods... *43.1%. nc ncf.*

**Tomintoul 1976 Vintage** bott 2013 db **(94.5) n25 t22 f23.5 b24** When you get that amount of exotic fruit on the nose, you know there is going to be a massive oaky kickback somewhere. However, this copes brilliantly and even has something fruitier up its sleeve further down the line. This can be taken as one of your five fruits a day... *40%*

**Tomintoul Five Decades** bott Jul 15 db **(94.5) n23.5 t24 f23 b24** Writing this Bible, and the inordinate amount of time it takes, day and night, night and day, week in, month out, means that I have to turn down most invites to attend the opening of distilleries and the celebration of anniversaries. Just can't fit it in. So glad the 50th anniversary of Tomintoul came to me in the shape of this luxurious dram. Another whisky which leaves you scratching your head to wonder why Whyte and Mackay sold this brilliant distillery: as though the manager wanted to get rid of the star player to harmonise the dressing room. Anyway, happy 50th birthday, Tomintoul distillery: you are in loving hands now and able to fulfil your enormous potential. *50%. nc ncf. 5,230 bottles.*

**Tomintoul With A Peaty Tang** db **(94) n23 t24 f23 b24.** A bit more than a tang, believe me! Faultlessly clean distillate that revels in its unaccustomed peaty role. The age is confusing and appears mixed, with both young and older traits being evident. *40%*

**Old Ballantruan** db **(89.5) n23.5 t23 f21 b22** Profound young malt which could easily be taken for an Islay. *50%. ncf.*

**Old Ballantruan Aged 10 Years** bott code 1706.15 db **(94.5) n23.5 t23.5 f23.5 b24** Can't say this is a spectacular peated malt. But everything is brilliantly in proportion and so sublimely balanced. *50%. ncf.*

**Old Ballantruan Aged 15 Years** bott code: CBSC4 02976 db **(95)** n23.5 t24 f23.5 b24 A Tomintoul classic. 50%. ncf.

# TORMORE

Speyside, 1960. Chivas Brothers. Working.

**Tormore 12 Years Old** db **(75)** n19 t19 f19 b18. For those who like whisky in their caramel. 40%

**Tormore Aged 14 Years** batch no. A1308, bott 2013 db **(83.5)** n21 t21.5 f20.5 b20.5. Toffeed, flat and inoffensive. Good dram to have last thing at night: chances are you'll be asleep before you finish the glass... 43% WB15/326

**Tormore Aged 15 Years "Special Distillery Bottling"** db **(71)** n17 t18 f19 b17. Even a supposed pick of choice casks can't save this from its fiery fate. 46%

**Tormore Aged 16 Years** batch no. B1309, bott 09 2013 db **(95)** n23.5 t24 f23.5 b24 Tormore as I have never seen it before. The label talks about the "long and dry" finish. It does the bottling such a disservice: this is magnificently complex with cocoa notes a thing of sheer beauty. A landmark bottling for Tormore. 48%

**Alos Sansibar Whisky Tormore 1988** bott 2016 **(86)** n21.5 t23 f20 b21.5 If you do try this try not to concentrate too much on the tangy finish supplied by an unhappy oak note. Instead concentrate on the delivery which boasts a fabulous boiled fruit and barley sugar candy mix. 50.4%.

**Cadenhead's Authentic Collection Tormore 33 Years Old** dist 1984 **(87)** n23.5 t22 f20 b21.5 Even after 33 years, the sins of the distillers way back in 1984 cannot be entirely forgiven and the fault lines of the original distillate are still evident and ready to rumble. However, these weaknesses are fully compensated on the nose which deserves full study: a wonderful butterscotch and subtlest imaginable coriander spice gives the unlikely feel of ice cream in a busy vegetable-packed kitchen. The delivery, likewise, is full of molten Demerara intent. Seek some delicious entertainment here and ye shall find. 51.7%. sc. 175th Anniversary bottling.

◈ **The First Editions Tormore Aged 29 Years 1988** refill hogshead, cask no. 15351, bott 2018 **(91.5)** n23 t23 f22.5 b23 Tormore in a more soft and intricate form, benefitting latterly from an unusual sharpness to the malt which ensures the grassy barley is at full throttle. A pleasant milky trail to the muscovado sugar and cocoa finale. 44.9%. nc ncf sc. 60 bottles.

**Gordon & MacPhail Cask Strength Tormore 2004** cask nos. 901 & 902, bott 24 Mar 17 **(91.5)** n22.5 t23 f23 b23 For a distillery which for years went out of its way to display little or no character, this bottling seems hell-bent on rewriting history. 59.6%.

◈ **Gordon & MacPhail Connoisseurs Choice Tormore Aged 23 Years** first fill sherry butt, cask no. 5383, dist 14 Jun 95, bott 5 Sept 18 **(84)** n21 t22 f20 b21 One dimensional fruit: pleasant but Tormore just doesn't have the guts to cope with this kind of cask. A little furry, too. 60.1%. sc. 615 bottles.

**Gordon & MacPhail Discovery Range Tormore Aged 13 Years** **(84.5)** n21.5 t21.5 f20.5 b21 What you will discover is a malt pretty true to standard distillery character: malty but limited in scope and with a degree of aggressive bite 43%.

**Old Malt Cask Tormore Aged 28 Years** sherry butt, cask no. 14481, dist Nov 88, bott Nov 17 **(93)** n23.5 t24 f22.5 b23 A way above average sherry butt that does not have to have to see off any major obstacles to display its beauty. 50%. nc ncf sc. 106 bottles.

**The Single Cask Tormore 21 Years Old** cask no. 20313 **(85.5)** n21 t22.5 f21 b21 From a time when Tormore's distillate had less body than your average ghost, this one has picked up a creamier character than most, though the sweetness is more often aligned with chestnut casked spirits. 46.8%.

**The Whisky Cask Company Tormore 21 Year Old** bourbon hogshead, dist Aug 95, bott Feb 17 **(94.5)** n23.5 t24 f23 b24 Not sure I've ever seen a Tormore in a bourbon cask of such high calibre before. Some elements of this almost blow the mind. 56.8%. nc ncf sc. 249 bottles.

◈ **The Whisky Chamber Tormore 23 Years Old 1995** bourbon cask **(87)** n21 t22.5 f21.5 b22 Despite the austerity of the nose, this battles back impressively with a huge if perhaps over-simplistic malt statement which makes for a real juicy cove. Don't expect complexity, but if you love crisp malt concentrate... 51.1%. sc.

# TULLIBARDINE

Highlands (Perthshire), 1949. Tullibardine Ltd. Working.

◈ **Tullibardine 15 Year Old** db **(87.5)** n22 t23 f21 b21.5 Starts quite beautifully but stubbornly refuses to kick on. Just adore the nuttiness on both the nose and delivery, as well as the lilting malt in the early stages which is both juicy and barley intense. There is even a light orange blossom honey note soon after...then just fades under a welter of dulling vanilla and caramel tones. Not far off being a little beauty. 43%.

**Tullibardine Aged 20 Years** db **(92.5) n22.5** busy and can't decide which weight to adopt; ethereal hazelnut and citrus rise above the languid tannins; **t24** no doubting the richness of body and the exceptional weight: first it is scorched yet juicy barley by the cartload, then thudding oak with just enough ulmo honey to oil the wheels. And then rampaging spice; **f22.5** settles for more prosaic butterscotch but the spices continue to bristle; **b23.5** while there are whiskies like this in the world, there is a point to this book...43%

**Tullibardine Aged 25 Years** db **(86.5) n22 t22 f21 b21.5.** There can be too much of a good thing. And although the intricacies of the honey makes you sigh inwardly with pleasure, the overall rigidity and fundamentalism of the oak goes a little too far. 43%

**Tullibardine 1970** db **(96.5) n25 t24.5 f23 b24s** I am a professional wordsmith with a very long time in whisky. Yet words, any words, can barely do justice... 40.5%.

**Tullibardine 225** sauternes cask finish db **(85) n20 t22.5 f21 b21.5.** Hits the heights early on in the delivery when the honey and Lubeck marzipan are at full throttle. 43%

**Tullibardine 228** Burgundy cask finish db **(82) n21 t22 f18 b21.** No shortage of bitter chocolate. Flawed but a wow for those looking for mega dry malt. 43%

**Tullibardine 500** sherry cask finish db **(79.5) n19 t21 f19 b20.5.** The usual problems from Jerez, but the grape ensures maximum chewability. 43%

**Tullibardine Custodians Collection 1962 52 Years Old** db **(87.5) n22 t22 f21.5 b22** This oldie has gallantly fought in the great oak wars of 1987 to 2014 and shows some serious scars. Thankfully a little exotic fruit and citrus makes some impact on the austere tannins on the nose, but they aren't around to reduce the excesses of the finale, though a little chocolate does go a long way. The silky delivery doesn't quite hide the mildly puckering, eye-watering aggression of the tannin but butterscotch does its best to add a limp sweetness, as does the unexpected wave of juicy barley. Some fascinating old timer moments but, ultimately, a tad too ancient for its own good. 40.1%.

**Tullibardine The Murray** dist 2004, bott 2016 db **(94.5) n23.5 t24 f23 b24** Beautiful, fulsome whisky which just pulses with personality. Still, I think my lawyers are twitching at this one: for the avoidance of doubt, this whisky has absolutely nothing to do with me and I make no money from any sales. 56.1%. The Marquess Collection.

**Tullibardine The Murray Châteauneuf-du-Pape Finish** dist 2005, bott 2018 db **(91.5) n21.5 t23.5 f23 b23.5** Not too sure my Trademark lawyer's too happy about this one (yes, my name is Trademarked)... Anyway, just for the record: no, I have no connection with this whisky and I don't make any money from sales or use of the Murray name. As I know I'll be slaughtered by the socially and intellectually challenged conspiracy theorist saddoes on the Internet somewhere along the line, thought I'd better make that crystal clear. Also, if I was to have my name linked to a whisky, a wine cask of any description would be the last thing it had matured in. Even one as good as this... 40.1%. ncf. The Marquess Collection.

◈ **Tullibardine The Murray Marsala Cask Finish** dist 2006, bott 2018, bott code: 18/0167 db **(86) n22 t22 f20.5 b21.5** A dry and heavy dram, very much the opposite of the standard sweet, gristy, malty affair from bourbon cask. Lots of frisky bite and nibble of delivery as the plummy fruit gets into full swing. But the tightness of the cask arrests further meaningful development. 46%. The Marquess Collection.

**Tullibardine Sovereign** bourbon barrel db **(89.5) n22.5 t23 f21.5 b22.5** Beautifully salivating despite the intricate oak notes. 43%

**Berry Bros & Rudd Tullibardine 24 Years Old** cask no. 942, dist 1993, bott 2018 **(81) n21 t21 f19 b20** A decidedly odd cove, one minute wittering about baled hay and some such on the nose, the next hollering about the frightful and grimacing barley sugar on the palate. Never for a moment settles down into a happy chappy and then caps it all by becoming deuced bitter of the finish. A borderline bounder, don't you know. 46%. nc ncf sc.

**The First Editions Tullibardine Aged 25 Years** refill hogshead, cask no. 14449, bott 2017 **(88) n22.5 t23 f20.5 b22** The sharp and unusual decline on the finish may have been due to the oxidisation of the sample sent to me rather than the whisky itself: a full bottle may well be a lot better than this. 46.3%. nc ncf sc. 90 bottles.

**The First Editions Tullibardine Aged 26 Years** refill hogshead, cask no. 14177, bott 2017 **(89) n22 t22.5 f22 b22.5** Not always a distillery which rewards years in the cask, this bottling certainly shines the malt in an attractive light. 44.4%. nc ncf sc. 143 bottles.

◈ **Glen Oak Tullibardine 10 Year Old** ex-bourbon barrels **(91) n22.5** an unusual mix: floral yet some cooked vegetables in the background. Slightly peachy, too; **t23.5** amazing intensity to the malt on delivery. Clean and salivating but with a salted, biscuity sub-plot; the vanillas are angular and slightly on a tangent; **f22** a slightly frazzled cask is evident, but the malt remains true; **b23** a singular single malt full of quirks, nooks and crannies. 40%. Branded Spirits USA.

**Golden Cask Tullibardine Aged 10 Years** cask no. CM243, dist 2007, bott 2017 **(86) n21 t22 f21.5 b21.5** Sharp, sugary and intense. Good malt depth. 57%. sc. 189 bottles.

**Old Malt Cask Tullibardine Aged 25 Years** refill hogshead, cask no. 14450, dist Sept 92, bott Nov 17 **(86.5) n22 t22 f21 b21.5** Initially on the sweet, nutty side of single malt, but dries pugnaciously. 46.1%. nc ncf sc. 147 bottles.

**Old Particular Tullibardine 24 Years Old** refill hogshead, cask no. 12026, dist Mar 93, bott Aug 17 **(93.5) n23.5 t23.5 f23 b23.5** A glass of delights. 51.5%. nc ncf sc. 262 bottles.

⟡ **Single Cask Collection Tullibardine Aged 11 Years (93) n23** sublime sweet citrus sits perfectly with the thick malt and fizzy, lightly spiced oak; **t23.5** the nose perfectly played out on the palate, though the spices are more game than expected; light smoke drifts across to add extra gravitas; **f23** soft oils mingle with the intense barley and spice; **b23.5** Tully at its maltiest and most even. Salivating and bursting with youthful energy, this hits the perfect balance between a clean youth and a more grandiose ageing. Super-delicious! 56%. sc.

# WOLFBURN
Highlands (Thurso), 2012. Aurora Brewing Ltd. Working.

**Wolfburn Aurora** sherry oak casks db **(91.5) n22.5 t24 f22 b23** Early days at a distillery and still finding their feet with the still. The cut on this was wider than on the previous bottling I sampled, but there is no faulting the use of the 100% sulphur-free sherry butt. There is the odd aspect of genius attached to this dram, for sure. For the record: just vatted this with some OTT oak-hit sherry-cask 1954 malt in need of the kiss of life, or like a vampire in need of a virgin's blood: I suspect the first time a Wolfburn has been mixed with a 60-year-old Speysider. Result? One of the most complex and complete experiences of the last couple of months – a would-be award winner, were it commercially available! Stunning! 46%. nc ncf.

⟡ **Wolfburn Langskip** bott 27 May 19 db **(94) n23** thick malt and, though young, quite a telling degree of tannin; **t24** enormous delivery. When I say enormous, I mean eye-watering, head shaking, cor-fuck-me kind of delivery which makes the most of its relative youth to magnify the sharpness of the barley to exalted heights; some lovely cocoa notes drift late on; **f23** the freshness of the youth returns. Warming barley most of the way...; **b24** rich, full bodied, intense, unforgiving. A whisky that doesn't just dip its toe in the outgoing surf... 58%. nc ncf.

**Wolfburn Morven** db **(91.5) n23 t23 f22.5 b23** Confirmation, were it needed, that lightly peated malt is a brilliant way of getting a distillery's whiskies out at a young age without the lack of development becoming too clear. This is a delicious and refined amble on the taste buds. 46%. nc ncf.

**Wolfburn Northland** db **(88.5) n22.5 t22 f22 b22** Limited complexity but maximum charm for one so young. 46%. nc ncf.

**Wolfburn Single Malt Scotch Whisky** db **(91.5) n23 t23 f22.5 b23** This is a very young malt showing an intriguing wispy smokiness, its evenness more in line with having been matured in ex-Islay casks than using low phenol barley. Still, it might have been, and, if so, perhaps reveals a style that would not have been entirely unknown to the people of Thurso when they last drank this during Victorian times. It is probably 30 years ago I was shown to a spot in the town where I was told the original distillery had been. Now it is back, and eclipses Pulteney as the producers of the most northerly mainland Scottish whisky. For all its youth, its excellence of quality glimmers from the glass: a malt as beautifully flighted as a cricket ball delivered by the most crafted of spinners. And offers a delightful turn on the palate, too. The building of a new distillery, no matter how romantic its location or story, does not guarantee good whisky. So I am delighted for those involved in a project as exhausting as this that a very good whisky is exactly what they have on their hands. 46%. nc ncf.

**Wolfburn Small Batch Release No. 128** half-sized first fill ex-bourbon barrels db **(88) n22 t23 f21.5 b21.5** Does very well until the home straight when balance is lost. 46%. nc ncf. 6,000 bottles.

**Wolfburn Small Batch Release No. 270** half-sized first fill ex-bourbon barrels db **(92) n23.5 t22.5 f22.5 b23.5** You'd thrash from the lighter colour to Wolfburn 128 this would be less developed and offering fewer flavour options. Curiously, the reverse is true, the flavours more even, satisfying and elegant. 46%. nc ncf. 6,000 bottles.

⟡ **Wolfburn Small Batch Release No. 375** half-sized first fill ex-bourbon barrels & second fill oloroso sherry hogsheads db **(87.5) n22.5 t23 f20.5 b22** Such a wonderful nose! Fry's Turkish Delight, complete with chocolate. There is a slight niggle on the fruit but the barley is pristine. Sadly, that fruity warning comes true on the slightly furry finish. But that doesn't impair the delivery, which is an essay in honey. This distillery is a long way from anywhere, but this was close to being a minor classic. 46%. nc ncf. 5,500 bottles.

⟡ **The Cyprus Whisky Association Wolfburn Aged 4 Years** quarter cask, cask no. 123/14, dist Jan 14, bott Jan 18 **(92) n22.5** though youthful, this has some attitude with distinct meatiness to the barley; **t23.5** huge arrival which is all over the palate with an unusually clean non-oily, maltiness backed by spiced up tannins. Salivating, chewy with a lovely malt and butterscotch middle; **f23** a real Malteser candy kick to this, complete with light milk chocolate. The lack of oils on the finale is really remarkable, but the vanilla compensates to balance the malt beautifully; **b23** this distillery really doesn't muck about, does it! Huge and makes no attempts to pretend to be otherwise. *59.8%. nc ncf sc. 160 bottles.*

# UNSPECIFIED SINGLE MALTS (CAMPBELTOWN)
**Cadenhead's Campbeltown Malt (92) n22 t24 f23 b23.** On their home turf you'd expect them to get it right... and, my word, so they do!! *59.5%*

# UNSPECIFIED SINGLE MALTS (HIGHLAND)
◈ **Asda Extra Special Highland Single Malt** bott code: L6B 8127 1511 **(84.5) n21.5 t22 f20 b21** Nutty and lush. But the degree of toffee on show makes this almost closer to being a candy liqueur than a Highland malt. Perfect...if you like toffee! *40%.*

**Berry Bros & Rudd Orkney Islands 16 Years Old** cask no. 28, dist 1999, bott 2018 **(79) n21 t20 f19 b19** Twenty years ago this would have been a cask that would be the answer to your whisky prayers. Now we have fire and brimstone. Those unable to pick out the obvious problem might enjoy the big chocolate signature. *53.6%. nc ncf sc.*

**Cave Aquila The Eagles Collection Highland Single Malt 10 Years Old** batch no. 1 **(85.5) n21 t22 f21 b21.5** No amount of cajoling can get this tight and reserved malt to open fully and sing. Tangy towards the finish, but all a little too hefty even before then. *43%.*

**Cave Aquila The Eagles Collection Highland Single Malt 10 Years Old** batch no. 2 **(89.5) n22.5** gently nutty, with subtle citrus sharpening things slightly; **t22.5** gorgeous texture on delivery: pure silk as the malt washes over all corners; a little not unexpected praline fills the middle; **f22** dry toasty fudge; **b22.5** this must be the Silky Nut Eagle... *43%.*

◈ **Glen Marnoch Highland Single Malt** bott code: L12 12 18 **(91) n22** firm. Almost wheat-like in its graininess; toasted Hovis; **t23** a silky delivery with a Swiss Roll creamy, fruity edge. Refreshing, juicy and lively at the mid-point with the barley really now ramping up the amps; **f23** back to the toastiness on the nose, but superb spices to intermingle with the lingering brown sugars; **b23** a beautifully even and satisfying Highlander. No great age, but so much charisma. *40%. Produced for Aldi.*

◈ **Glen Oak 28 Year Old** ex-bourbon barrels **(90) n21.5** oak by name, oak by nature....I'm still picking splinters from my nose...; **t22.5** a rich-textured maltiness comes to the rescue, radiating intense barley to such a degree that the tannins are tamed. Instead they offer up a charming mix of natural caramels and heather honey; **f23** the spices take their time, but get there. Just in time for the cocoa to make its mark; **b23** the nose is a bit scary. The experience on the palate something altogether better balanced and delightful. *40%. sc. Branded Spirits USA.*

◈ **Glen Turner Cask Collection Rum Cask Finish** bott code: L907357A **(90.5) n23** the usual crisp sugar-coated nose; firm tannin punches through as well as delicate, muffled moist ginger cake; **t22** a pleasant malt surge, then softer toffee and spiced sugars; **f23** long, thanks mainly to a continuing murmur of spice; light golden syrup balances the toasty oak; **b22.5** a very well-manicured malt. *40%. La Martiniquaise.*

◈ **Glen Turner Heritage Double Cask Port Cask** Finish bott code: L834657A **(94) n23.5** a spot on port involvement here, free from sulphur, where the spiciness of the fruit nibbles sensuously; **t24** mouth-watering with both the plumptious plums and spices going hammer and tongs; an oaky vanilla fills the mid-ground; a stunning mouth feel is the icing on the cake; **f23** now quieter and more evenly complex. All that has gone before but with little gusto or edge; **b23.5** an impressive piece of cask finishing where the speech by the port is pretty and important, but the microphone has not been turned up too loudly. *40%. La Martiniquaise.*

◈ **Glen Turner Malt Legend Aged 12 Years** bott code: L832557C **(87) n21 t23.5 f21 b21.5** A fat, velvety malt with an attractive, lush fruitiness but just a little too much sharpness out of the oak. Plenty to enjoy. *40%. La Martiniquaise.*

◈ **Glenwill Highland Single Malt** sherry butt finish **(86.5) n22 t21.5 f21.5 b21.5** Perfectly good sherry butt at work here. However, where it has come a little unstuck is that the finishing is incomplete: they decided to bottle when the sherry has rather too over-enthusiastically filled in the peaks and troughs of the malt but not left enough character of its own The result, as is often the case, is pleasant whisky but lacking fingerprints... *40%. Matisse Spirits Company.*

◈ **Glenwill Highland Single Malt** rum cask finish **(88) n22** crisp sugars abound, despite the heavy malt; **t22** fat delivery with decent spice-sugar-malt interplay **f21.5** toasty toffee and spice; **b22.5** an easy malt where the sugary shell of the rum comes into play infrequently. *40%. Matisse Spirits Company.*

**Glenwill RV** rum cask finish **(80) n21 t21 f19 b19** Mainly toffeed, characterless and just zzzzzzzzzz..... *40%. Quality Spirits International.*

**Glenwill S = 1** sherry butt finish **(73) n19 t21.5 f16 b17.5** S = Sulphur. *40%. Quality Spirits International.*

**Grangestone Master's Selection Highland Single Malt** bourbon cask finish **(87) n22.5 t22 f21 b21.5** An attractive interplay between tannin and toffee, though the complexity is limited – especially on the simplistic finish. Good, though brief, molasses lift off on delivery. *40%. Quality Spirits International.*

**Hepburn's Choice Nice 'N Peaty 10 Years Old** refill hogshead, dist 2006, bott 2016 **(81) n20 t21.5 f19 b20.5** Dry and tartly metal deficient in part. Rather flat and lifeless. *46%. nc ncf sc. 38 bottles.*

⟨⟩ **Hepburn's Choice Nice 'N Peaty 11 Years Old** refill hogshead, dist 2006, bott 2018 **(77) n18.5 t21 f19 b19.5** Peaty for sure. But usually feinty, too. *46%. nc ncf sc. 189 bottles.*

**Highland Queen Majesty Classic** bott code L14/8634 09.08.14 **(92) n24, t23 f22 b23** The brilliant nose isn't quite matched by the pragmatism of the overall taste experience but a blend to savour nonetheless. *40%. Tullibardine Ltd.*

**Highland Queen Majesty Aged 12 Years** bott code L15/8538 19/08/15 **(86.5) n22 t22 f21 b21.5** A pleasant but lazy blend considering its age. Lots of explosive malt on delivery, some with a lemon sherbet fizz. But a heavy dependence on caramel quietens the party, though a late spice surge gate-crashes to welcome effect. *40%. Tullibardine Ltd.*

**Highland Queen Majesty Aged 16 Years** bott code L15/8265 06 07 15 **(88) n22.5** the house style of lemon sherbet is in full fizz...; **t22.5** salivating, malty delivery with oaky reinforcements soon arriving; **f21.5** caramel wafers and vanilla ice cream make for a simplistic finale; **b22** enjoyable, yet leaves you with a feeling that it could have offered a little bit more. *40%. Tullibardine Ltd.*

**Master of Malt Highland Single Malt (86.5) n21.5 t22 f21.5 b21.5** Pleasant, absolutely middle of the road malt with a juicy, nutty and toffee-rich character. *40%.*

**Muirhead's Silver Seal Aged 12 Years Highland Single Malt (87.5) n22 t22 f21 b21.5** Satisfyingly salivating. The vanillas arrive with a lemon escort from the first moment, ensuring a semi-ethereal element to this. Lightly oiled and a little nutty, just a tad too much caramel at the times you want the malt to begin to fly. *40%. Tullibardine Ltd.*

**Muirhead's Silver Seal Aged 16 Years Highland Single Malt (86) n21 t23 f20.5 b21.5** A hefty malt with a battling, earthy aroma. Hits its zenith about four or five flavour waves after delivery when it strikes up a stunning spicy walnut cake and date middle. Flags towards the finish, even becoming a little flat and furry, save for the wonderful spices.... *40%. Tullibardine Ltd.*

**Muirhead's Silver Seal Maturity Highland Single Malt (84) n19.5 t22 f21 b21.5** Though called "Maturity" the malt displays a youthful gristiness from time to time. Not technically the greatest nose, the malt recovers brightly on the palate with a volley of varied sugars and spice, including a light smothering of heather honey. *40%. Tullibardine Ltd.*

⟨⟩ **Sansibar Whisky Orkney 2006 (86) n21 t22 f21.5 b21.5** Stuffed solid with intense malt. But a little burn on this one, and I don't just mean from the alcohol. *60.4%.*

**Scotch Universe Kepler-186f 187° U.7.1' 1775.1"** first fill Port pipe, dist 2001, bott 2016 **(89.5) n23 t22.5 f21.5 b22.5** That Port pipe must have been very fresh, indeed... *59%.*

**Simon Brown Traders Bridge of Avon 2012** ex-bourbon cask, dist Mar 12, bott Aug 17 **(83) n20 t21.5 f20.5 b21** A very young, nutty, slightly dense malt. Lots of sugars and oils but no great development beyond that. Will appeal to those who like the Fettercairns of this world. *40%. nc ncf sc.*

**Tesco Finest Aged 12 Years Highland Single Malt** bott code L63353 **(80.5) n20 t21 f19 b20.5** Quite possibly one of the most boring single malts of all time: not recommended as a night cap as you'll doze off by the time you reach the third step on your stairs, and it won't be the effect of the alcohol. Bland barely covers it. With the amount of cream toffee found on the nose and palate not sure if this should be stocked in the Spirits or Sweets aisles. Do I like it? No. Do I dislike it? No. But if I am putting 12-year-old malt into my body, I'd like it to have some semblance of character. I suppose it was designed to offend nobody: a mute hardly can. Trouble is, it is hardly likely to get new drinkers wanting to come back and discover more about single malt, either. Oh well, I suppose that buggers up any chance of getting The Bible stocked and sold by Tesco this year. But I'm afraid they need to hear the truth. *40%.*

**Whisky-Fässle Orkney 13 Year Old** sherry butt, dist 2004, bott 2017 **(93.5) n23 t24 f23 b23.5** Did I expect a sherry butt quite this good? I'll be honest: I really didn't: bitter experience has taught me in recent years to be wary of the words sherry and Orkney in the same sentence. So my emergency palate cleaners were primed, but not needed. *50.5%.*

# UNSPECIFIED SINGLE MALTS (ISLAND)

⟨⟩ **A.D. Rattray Cask Orkney 18 Year Old** dist 1999 **(94) n23.5** acacia honey and marmalade topping on a very malty field; **t24** holds its age sublimely: the honeyed sugars arrive early and in tandem with the concentrated barley. Exceptionally clean on both deliver and follow through, which just a light oiliness capturing the oaky-vanillas and spreading their word. The spices become more profound by the second, **f23** incredibly long spice fade with sharp barley hanging on to its coat tails. The most gentle smoke makes a late but courteous entry; **b23.5** a beautiful and satisfying malt on a great many levels. *46%*

**Master Of Malt Island Single Malt (91.5) n22.5 t23 f22.5 b23.5.** Don't know about Lord of the Isles. More like Lord of the Flies...Fruit flies, that is...! They would be hard pressed to find even an over-ripe mango any juicier than this gorgeous malt... *40%*

# UNSPECIFIED SINGLE MALTS (ISLAY)

⬦ **Asda Extra Special Islay Single Malt** bott code: L6C 7619 1109 **(88.5) n22** peaty...; **t22.5** peaty with warming spices and underlying vanilla; **f22** silky, lingering and smoky; a tad bitter at the death; **b22** does exactly what it says on the tin...except for the alleged fruity tones which never materialise... *40%.*

**Ben Bracken Islay Single Malt 22 Years Old** dist 1993 **(96) n24.5 t24 f23.5 b24** A real old timer showing its oaky scars with pride. A serious late night dram. And with an unspoiled palate, for this will be one of your smoky treats of the year... *40%*

**Cadenhead's Islay 9 Years Old (94) n23 t24.5 f23.5 b23** Only a degree of over simplicity has docked marks here. If it is prefect, clean, beautifully rounded, juicy all-enveloping peat you are after, then you might be tempted to give it a straight 100... *58.9%. sc. 175th Anniversary bottling.*

**Cask Islay (91.5) n22.5 t23 f22.5 b23** Does what it says on the tin. *46%. A.D. Rattray*

**Demijohn 8 Year Old Islay Region (92.5) n23 t23.5 f23 b23** Clean, sweet and highly impressive youngster that has never mixed with undesirable company. *59.8%.*

⬦ **Demijohn 10 Years Old Port Askaig (90) n23** peat softened with lavender; **t22.5** soft and sweet, there is a busy mix between vanilla and a toffee-rich phenol; **f21.5** thin vanillas; **b22** the nose promises a peatiness which doesn't quite arrive on the palate. Underpowered but lovely all the same. *42%.*

**Elling Lim Bessie's Dram (88) n22.5 t22.5 f21 b22** A distinctly Laphroaigian type dram complete with Allied style bitter cask (oh, I have just spotted that this is Laphroaig...!!!), s plenty to enjoy. *51.3%.*

**Elements of Islay AR10 (93) n23.5 t23 f23 b23.5** Not a fault, an off note, a flavour profile out of place, just sheer joy, though always on the lighter, less intense side of the distillery's spectrum. Well, just can't think what this might be... Ardbeg by any chance...? *52.4%.*

**Elements of Islay Cl8 (93) n23 t23.5 f23 b23.5** The natural sugars appears to have been piled in to create a real sweetie. This is a deceptively big dram. *55.2%.*

**Elements of Islay Cl10 (95) n23.5 t24 f23.5 b24** One of those moments where my mind wondered, I nosed instinctively and without thinking said: "ah, Caol Ila!" Simply unmistakable and so true to the distillery. Beautiful. *58.2%.*

⬦ **Elements of Islay CL12 (90) n23 t23 f22 b22** Wonderful iodine kick on the nose, but the oiliness gives a slightly restrictive texture once we are through the phenols and sugars of the delicious initial delivery and fabulous spice follow-through. *57.5%.*

**Elements of Islay Lg7 (94.5) n23.5 t24 f23.5 b23.5** Does everything it says on the tin – and more. Some younger elements appear to be at work here, which means the peat intensity can sometimes fly, deliciously and dramatically, off the scale. *56.8%.*

**Elements of Islay LG8 (91) n22.5 t23.5 f22 b23** Against the back drop of excellence, some oak with attitude has slightly too big a say. *59.5%.*

⬦ **Elements of Islay LP10 (93.5) n23.5 t23.5 f23 b23.5** A huge dose of lychee juice is a surprise package in this otherwise docile Islay. The peat is intermittently big, but easily bossed around by the exotic fruit. Unorthodoxly beautiful. *53.9%.*

⬦ **Elements of Islay MA3 (91) n22 t23 f23 b23** Bit of cough sweet intensity, hickory included, to go with slightly citrusy but ultimately sooty peat *55.2%.*

**Elements of Islay OC5 (95.5) n24 t24.5 f23 b24** Anyone who drinks an overdose of this will have "peated to death" on their autopsy report. *59.8%.*

⬦ **Elements of Islay PL6 (92) n22.5 t23 f23 b23.5** Not often you get elements of bourbon on an Islay, but the nose and finish positively quiver with tannin. Betwixt times though roaring spiciness lifts the phenols onto another plane entirely. A malt to make you sweat a bit... *55.3%.*

⬦ **Finlaggan Cask Strength Islay Single Malt (88) n22.5** rich and solid peat with an acidic pinch and softer smoky halo; **t3** like the nose, has a sharper edge than at first looks possible; salivating with a light apple juice kick to the barley and smoke; **f21.5** a little dishevelled as the tannins refuse to jump into line; **b21** a massive peated malt which that phenolphiles will lap up. But for its all its big Islay muscle, struggles to come together and balance out as even as might be hoped. *58%. The Vintage Malt Whisky Company.*

⁂ **Finlaggan Eilean Mor Islay Single Malt (88.50) n22** moderately smoky and gristy; **t22.5** simplistic oily delivery with medium weight to the phenols; **f22** a light chocolate and spice to accompany the smoke; **b22** oily Islay with a pleasant if limited disposition. *46%. The Vintage Malt Whisky Company.*

⁂ **Finlaggan Feis Ile 2018 Vintage 2009 Islay Single Malt (95) n24** young, but just vibrates under the pulsing peat. A little salt is rubbed in with the lime – a Mexican Islay? Near faultless and exemplary for age; **t24** every bit as rich, sweet and chewy as the nose promises. Certainly young, but celebrates the fact with peaty abandon; **f23** thins out slightly through lack of oak, but the big smoked gristy sweetness keeps on going; **b24** a peated Islay in all its undisputed magnificence. Beautifully made and matured. *50%. sc. The Vintage Malt Whisky Company.*

⁂ **Finlaggan Old Reserve Islay Single Malt (91) n23** an impressive degree of iodine pungency to the smoke; **t23** a big explosion of demerara sugars to match the intensity of the peat; the midpoint of gristy barley on heat; **f22.5** light oils and heavier smoke; impressive cocoa at the death; **b23** no great age I suspect. But the intensity and charm are profound. Unmistakably Islay! *40%. The Vintage Malt Whisky Company.*

⁂ **Finlaggan Port Finish Islay Single Malt (92.5) n23** an outrageous sootiness to the peat, the odd atom of fruit trying to make some form of impact against uncompromising peat; **t23.5** a white-knuckle ride of intense phenols, eye-wateringly dry at first, but then mercifully relenting as the fruit and concentrated barley sugar surge together for a juicy middle; **f23** the sugars hang on to the ground gained and make way only for an almost belligerent spiciness; **b23.5** huge peat at work, dry and almost coal dust-like. But its wings are initially clipped by the port before it takes off once more...to profound effect. *46%. The Vintage Malt Whisky Company.*

⁂ **Finlaggan Sherry Finish Islay Single Malt (86.5) n23.5 t23 f19 b21** Delighted and relieved to report that the early damage of the sherry finish to the whisky is limited to the dampening down of what the nose suggests would have been one hell of a peaty experience, and taking the edge off the finale. Some lovely chocolate from the midpoint on... but some very late sulphur furriness confirms the sherry butt was not entirely faultless. *46%. The Vintage Malt Whisky Company.*

⁂ **Glen Castle Islay Single Malt 1989 Vintage Cask 29 Years Old** dist 1989, bott 2018, bott code: LHB 1477-2018 **(96) n24** stunning! An Islay-lover's Islay on the nose, with the throbbing smoke enriched and amplified by a coastal saltiness. Despite its age, there are no cracks, or letting up in the acidic quality of the smoke; **t24.5** you'd expect a big oaky surge because of the age. But, no! It's the crispy Demerara sugars first, second and third, the phenols growing in intensity flavour wave by flavour crashing wave; **f23.5** long, though the oils are modest and the lingering sheen appears still to be the last glowing remnants of the sugars. Dries to a peated sootiness, though some embers of sugar balance out the gathering spice; **b24** though a single malt, this could almost be a composite of the three big South East coast distilleries, at one time or other displaying a little character trait of them all. What a little classic this is, one of the very best non-distillery bottling Islays you will find this year. And so very unusual to uncork an Islay of some 30 years standing still dishing out this degree of phenol intensity... *51%. nc ncf.*

**Glen Castle Islay Single Malt 1990** dist 1990, bott 2017, bott code: L1 1520-2017 11 **(94.5) n24 t24 f22.5 b24** Had the toffee levels been down a bit, this might have carried off an award. Quite brilliant. *52.5%.*

⁂ **The Ileach Cask Strength Islay Single Malt (89.5) n22 t22.5 f22 b23** A rotund, oily number where significant muscovado sugars – in full fruity mode – link stupendously with the bubbling spices to create a charming balance. The smoke chugs through evenly and unerringly like an old puffer through Hebridean waters. *58%. The Vintage Malt Whisky Company.*

⁂ **Islay Storm Islay Single Malt (87) n21.5 t22 f21.5 b22** Having been caught right slap in the middle of some ferocious, frankly white knuckle, Islay storms myself over the last 40 years, this but a five-minute passing shower. The smoke needs seeking, rather than it coming to you, and the gentle maltiness glides over the palate with all the intensity and threat of a child's rusk. Attractive, but could do with some oomph! *40%. C.S. James & Sons Ltd.*

⁂ **Lady of the Glen Secret Islay 2003** cask no. 1828 **(90.5) n22 t23 f22.5 b23** Well-structured Islay with a reasonable, though not enormous, phenol presence and hefty tannin and boiled fruit candy notes at play. One of the sweeter Islays you'll encounter this year. *56.1%. sc.*

⁂ **Liquid Treasures 10th Anniversary Islay Malt 10 Year Old** bourbon barrel, dist 2008, bott 2019 **(90.5) n22.5** something of the ship's engine room about this: oily and full of fumes; **t23.5** fabulous delivery: a livewire of the malt regularly punctuated by spice, but the full gristy, smoky sweetness turned to full volume; a little hickory towards the middle, and mocha Swiss roll; **f22** just a little touch of the "Allied" bitterness seeps out but the elegance of the smoke remains first rate; **b22.5** a bit of a treat of a dram. *58.7%. sc. 171 bottles.*

**Master of Malt Islay Single Malt (90.5) n22 t23 f22.5 b23** A smoky, gristy must for peat heads. *40%.*

**Peat's Beast** bott code: L 07 08 17 **(92) n22.5 t23 f23.5 b23** Nosing this whizzed me back to the late 1980s and my old office in a national newspaper in Fleet Street where, by night, I was taking my first tentative steps into the then unknown and practically non-existent medium of whisky writing. And I remember opening up a Bowmore 5-years-old bottled by Oddbins. I'm not saying this is a Bowmore, but so many features on display in that landmark bottling 30 years ago are also to be found here... 46%. ncf.

**Peat's Beast Twenty Five** bott code: L1 1409-2017 11 **(88.5) n23 t23 f20 b22.5** There are far more beastly Islay whiskies than this out there – a quarter of a century in the cask means the teeth have been blunted, the claws clipped. And if you must "tame it" further, for God's sake ignore the daft advice on the label about adding water. Please use the Murray Method described on page 9. That will keep the thing alive while making it purr at full decibels... And this is so lovely (well, finish apart), it is worth listening to at full volume...which isn't very loud. 52.2%. ncf.

**Port Askaig 8 Years Old (85) n20 t22 f21.5 b21.5** Thankfully the slightly disappointing and sketchy nose isn't matched by the delivery which shows far greater harmony between the phenols and oaky vanillas. The finish, though, doesn't enjoy quite the same assuredness, despite the spice. 45.8%.

**Port Askaig 14 Year Old Bourbon Cask** dist 2004 **(95) n24 t23.5 f23.5 b24** For those who prefer their peat to caress rather than kick. Elegant and so beautifully sensual. 45.8%.

**Port Askaig 15 Years Old** sherry cask **(87.5) n22.5 t22 f21.5 b21.5** I know, I know: I have a blind spot for this kind of whisky. Rather, not blind, but not an over developed appreciation of the big smoke notes slugging it out with and then being neutralised by equally big, occasionally eye-wateringly sharp, fruit ones. At least the sherry is clean and extra marks for that. But, for me, this is just too much of a tit-for-tat malt leaving a neutral toffee fruitiness to claim the big prize. Pleasant, I grant you. But I want it to be so much more.... 45.8%.

⟨⟨⟨ **Port Askaig 25 Years Old (91) n23** gentle, salty peat plus primroses and bluebells. Dank and earthy; **t23.5** sharp and mouth-watering: a mix of lemon blossom honey and exotic fruit elegantly emphasises the age; **f21** just bitters slightly; **b22.5** bottled at the right time – another year or two would have seen a dramatic slide. But as it is, so much to quietly savour. 45.8%.

⟨⟨⟨ **Port Askaig 28 Years Old (92.5) n23.5** what a superb marriage of clean but intense peat with the most delicate peach blossom note imaginable; **t23.5** likewise the delivery captures the full essence of the phenols, but the sweetness is confined to a shadowy fruitiness, a mere ghost of a flavour; superb mouth feel with a genuine lustre; **f22** the phenols have made their mark, but the vanillas replace the broader sweet notes; **b23.5** a classically understated Islay where elegance outscores muscle. 45.8%.

⟨⟨⟨ **Port Askaig 33 Years Old Single Cask (95) n23.5** that is one massively salty nose, which seasons the fading peat beautifully; a lovely banana and custard background competes with the phenols; **t24.5** what a magnificent shewing of orange blossom honey, erotic fruit, light, aged phenols – all topped off with a briny spice; **f23** remains a little salty as the vanillas gently takes the helm; **b24** Islay at its most coastal. Shews its age with rare elegance. Sublime. 50.3%. sc.

⟨⟨⟨ **Port Askaig 34 Years Old Single Cask (94) n23.5** a citrus smile to this while the smoke quietly broods. Remarkably, though, even after all these years, is the gristiness: I could have been standing by the mill 34 years ago...; **t23.5** that citrus note perseveres while the smoke has to build up momentum at the mid-point to get anything like its original power; light acacia honey supplies the broader sweetness; **f23** it takes time but the tannins now leave you in no doubt that this is no spring chicken; **b24** this charming whisky has decided to get old gracefully. And succeeded. 49.7%. sc.

**Port Askaig 45 Years Old (90.5) n23 t23 f22 b22.5** Even in my scaringly long career, I can probably count the number of peated malts that made it to this kind of age and then into a commercial bottling on one hand. Certainly by the end it is showing every year that has passed, but for an unexpected period the malt hangs together...sometimes surprisingly deliciously. 40.8%.

⟨⟨⟨ **Port Askaig 10th Anniversary Aged 10 Years** refill American-oak hogsheads, first-fill bourbon casks & ex-solera casks, bott code: P/000248 **(87.5) n22 t23 f20.5 b22** Lusty and loud peat gets things off to the smokiest of starts both on the nose and palate. Grumbles a bit and rather uneven on the finish, though. But those first five crashing phenol waves on the palate, with a little orange-blossom honey attached to the smoke, ensure a brilliant opening sequence. 55.85%. nc ncf.

**Port Askaig 100 Proof (96.5) n24 t24 f24 b24.5** Just exemplary, high quality Islay: a must experience malt. If you find a more beautifully paced, weighted and elegant Islay this year, I'd like to hear about it... 57.1%.

⟨⟨⟨ **Port Askaig 110 Proof (91.5) n23** just love that pinch of acid to the smoke; **t23** full bodied yet soft and pleasantly sharp: still young enough for the grist to make a gorgeously sweet contribution; **f22.5** smoky custard tart; **b23** beautifully made and elegantly matured. 55%.

**Romantic Rhine Collection Dun Naomhaig Bay Isle of Islay** bott 2017 (89) n22.5 t23 f21.5 b22 Something a little raw and untamed about this. Which makes it rather fun. *55%. nc ncf.*

**Romantic Rhine Collection Dun Naomhaig Water Isle of Islay** batch no. 5 (87) n22 t22 f21 b22 A seemingly tamer, more sanitised version of their Naomhaig Bay but with more vanilla and caramel to blunt the peaty edges. *40%. nc ncf.*

**Single Cask Collection William & Son Aged 9 Years** bourbon barrel, cask no. 1887, dist 19 May 08, bott 21 Dec 17 (90.5) n22 t23 f22.5 b23 From the sweaty armpit school of salty smokiness. *56.8%. nc ncf sc. 260 bottles.*

**Smokey Joe Islay Malt** (94.5) n23 t24 f23.5 b24 A high quality Islay ticking all the required boxes. *46%*

**Smuggler's Vintage Cask Speyside Mystery 14 Years Old** sherry cask (89.5) n23 t23 f21.5 b22 Virtually no sulphur...! Now there's a mystery... *56%. sc. 156 bottles.*

**That Boutique-y Whisky Company Williamson 6 Year Old** batch 1 (86.5) n22.5 t22 f20.5 b21.5 Smoky, pleasant, easy going, friendly. But also, I'm afraid to say, a little boring, too. *50.2%.*

**The Whisky Chamber Buair An Diabhail Vol. XII** (92.5) n23 t23.5 f23 b23.5 After the initial immense bite – something of Great White Shark proportions – eventually settles down into a much more docile and delicious beast. *58.1%. sc.*

**The Whisky Chamber Buair an Diabhail Vol. VIX** (88.5) n23 t22 f21 b22.5 A busy, full-bodied, no-holds barred Islay. *58.3%. sc.*

# UNSPECIFIED SINGLE MALTS (LOWLAND)

**Tweeddale Single Lowland Malt Scotch Whisky 14 Years** db (89) n21.5 t23.5 f22 b22 busy, bustling, elegant and old-fashioned...like a small borders town. *62%. nc ncf sc.*

# UNSPECIFIED SINGLE MALTS (SPEYSIDE)

◈ **A.D. Rattray Cask Speyside 10 Year Old** (89) n22 gristy with a delicate smattering of phenol; a little lime refreshes the drier vanillas; t22.5 ah...revitalising and refreshing on delivery with the barley bursting out gamely around the palate. Then the darker, smokier tones, always understated, drift in bringing spices along with it...; f22 firm barley sugar tempered with a light spice bristle and oakier, drier finish; b22.5 an elegant and lightly smoked malt which would double as either a pre-prandial dram, or one for the wooden hill... *46%.*

**Alos Sansibar Whisky Speyside Region 1975** bott 2016 (96.5) n24.5 t24 f24 b24 Great malt plus magnificent cask multiplied by time equals an unforgettable whisky experience. Exquisite. *46.9%.*

◈ **Arcanum Spirits TR21INITY Aged Over 21 Years** refill ex-bourbon barrel, dist 16 Jul 97, bott 24 Aug 18 db (96.5) n24.5 absolute class: as complex a nose as you could hope for with lime gelling beautifully with the heather honey. Everything is so subtle...and the gentlest smoke is no less delicate. Truly one of the most beautiful noses of the year and anything less than ten minutes investigating it would be a travesty...; t24 here we go again: just like on the nose, we are talking sublime subtlety. Hints, shadows and nudges. Immediately salivating, meaning the barley is prepped and at full stretch Then that vague smoke drifts in and melts into the mouth. And though the label says Speyside, the senses are telling you "Clynelish" or "Highland Park" as there is a distinctive heather honey being touched by languid phenols: anyone remember the old Lawson's blend...? Yes, THAT subtle and clean...! f23.5 lightly smoked mocha, but it is all happening in slow motion as the honey melts into the vanilla while the spices kiss...; b24.5 TR21 reminds me, touchingly, of a magazine my old dad used to bring home from work for me in the mid 1960s: TV21...never could get enough Daleks or Thunderbirds... Well this is Thunderbird 5: out of this world...and complexity like this, such utter, almost moving beauty, can only ever be achieved with a bourbon cask where all is laid bare. *52.1%. ncf sc. 222 bottles. Whisky Edition No. 3.*

◈ **Asda Extra Special Speyside Single Malt** bott code: L6A 8226 1412 (81) n20 t21.5 f19 b20.5 Pleasant, soft and sweet and briefly delicious on delivery...but entirely linear. As it develops, devoid of character or personality as the big dollop of caramel and tired casks has taken its toll. *40%.*

**Ben Bracken Speyside Single Malt Aged 8 Years** American white oak bourbon barrels (85.5) n21.5 t22.5 f20 b21.5. Juicy and pleasant, with an attractive honey and molasses middle. But the caramel wipes out any meaningful complexity. *40%*

**Ben Bracken Speyside Single Malt 28 Years Old** dist 1987 (84.5) n22 t21 f21.5 b20. The early promise on delivery – where the malt powers through with spice on its coattails – isn't backed up quite as one may wish. Goes through a number of tangy turns, where even after 28 years the tannin appears to be uneasy with the malt, or perhaps the other way round, before it settles down for a light vanilla finish, tinged with the lightest coating of ulmo honey. *40%*

◇ **Dramfool 22 Elderly Elvis Tilting 25 Years Old** bourbon cask **(95) n24** reminds me of the little cupcakes my old mum used to make me with those red and green fruit bits in it, when I was a child. Just before she put it in the oven and I was allowed to lick the bowl...add to that some pear crumble and custard...; **t24** sensational delivery. Near perfect mouthfeel, as the malt glides in, sluicing through the palate and leaving the taste buds at the tender mercy of the alternating crisp and soft barley. Spices also cascade down...; **f23** long, rhythmical beats of intense vanilla... and malt and spice, still...; **b24** a malt which has made the use of every single day of its 25 years to compose a hit. Uh-ha! *51.2%. nc ncf. 109 bottles. Spirit of Speyside 2019 Exclusive.*

◇ **Fadandel.dk Secret Speyside Aged 26 Years** refill bourbon barrel, dist 17 Jun 92, bott 28 Jun 18 **(86.5) n21.5 t22 f21 b22** A bit of a tangy old cask at work here which allows the sharp, rich cerealy, barley free rein. But the balance and complexity doesn't quite fit in so comfortably. Eye-wateringly salty, too. *51.3%. sc. 72 bottles.*

**Glenbrynth Aged 21 Years** bott code L8W6323 2103 **(86.5) n22.5 t22 f21 b21** What starts off as a super-sexy nose with apple tart aplenty, tails off into a more prosaic fudge fest as the caramels get a constrictor-like grip: a bit of a bore at the end... *43%. OTI Africa.*

**Glen Castle Speyside Single Malt Aged 12 Years** bott code: L6 7461-2017 10 05-21.14 **(87) n22 t22 f21.5 b21.5** A really lovely sweet dram with a wonderful match between barley and spice. Ridiculously easy to drink and exceptionally more-ish. The only downside is the heavy toffee aspect which dulls the obvious vivacity of the barley itself. *40%.*

**Glen Castle Speyside Single Malt Aged 20 Years** bott code: L1 1419-2017 11 **(89) n22.5** poached pear with spicy vanilla...yummy! **t22.5** a silky mouth feel stirs up some early busy spices which fade surprisingly quickly. Some excellent oak begins to fill the middle ground, but a build of toffee is becoming a bit heavy on the palate; **f22** Neapolitan ice cream...the chocolate in particular; **b22** enjoyable malt which could be better still if the toffee could be tamed. *46.8%.*

**Glen Castle Aged 20 Years Sherry Cask Finish** dist 1996 **(94) n23.5 t23.5 f23 b24** Lucky Japanese! A really satisfying, high quality single malt. *54.1%. ncf. Quality Spirits International.*

**Glen Castle Aged 28 Years** sherry cask, dist 1996 **(96.5) n24.5 t24 f24 b24** A quality spirit from Quality Spirits: sherry butts from before the sulphur plague. Just look how magnificent this is...! Surely an award winner this year of some type... *59%. ncf. Quality Spirits International.*

◇ **Glen Marnoch Speyside Single Malt** bott code: L12 12 18 **(84.5) n19 t21.5 f22.5 b21.5** A malt which improves with time spent on the palate, allowing the juicy barley and sugars to build to impressive and ultimately attractive effect. The nose and delivery, though, are pretty off key. The description of the whisky on the label is interesting, but bore little resemblance to what I tasted here. *40%. Produced for Aldi.*

**James King Aged 12 Years** bott code L6Y 7422 2810 **(84.5) n21 t22 f21 b20.5** "From one of the most revered distilleries in Scotland," crows the label. Glen Toffee, presumably. Chaps, please turn the caramel down – it is obvious that some stupendous notes are trying to get out and speak: give them – and the drinker - a chance. *43%. Quality Spirits International.*

◇ **Liquid Treasures Snakes Speyside 26 Year Old** bourbon barrel, dist 1992, bott 2018 **(95) n23.5** a superior, complex nose where the salt shakes up the definition of the oak. The malt is almost like a good ol' American maltshake. Combine the two...and it works wonderfully...; **t24** the delivery sets the taste buds aquiver: the degree of salt and pepper is set high, but has to be keep tabs on the even higher levels of concentrated barley juice. The tannins begin to gain ground at the midpoint; **f23.5** a gorgeous milky, malty mocha almost makes you purr...; **b24** an essay in malt 'n' honey. This has been stored in some cask, I can tell you...not a single off note! *51.6%. sc. 270 bottles.*

**Master of Malt 60 Year Old Speyside** **(85) n24.5 t21 f19 b20.5** Such a brave try. The delivery for a moment keeps you hoping there is still enough big malt at play to see off the pencil-shaving tannins...but it is not to be. That doesn't mean that you can't spend a good half hour to an hour simply worshipping the nose: name a fruit and it appears to be there. And as it oxidises, it is there – then gone to be replaced with another fruit. A carousel of citrus and mushy conference pear, a fleeting moment of cherry cake, then fruitcake; molasses comes and goes, as does the liquorice and hickory. Sadly, the taste doesn't have the same life force beyond the first few seconds. But that nose.... Just amazing... *42.2%.*

**Master of Malt Speyside Single Malt** **(88.5) n22** light and gristy with a delicate caramel thread; **t22.5** clean delivery, salivating with the oak slowly becoming a match for the malt; **f22** a relaxed, undemanding spiced toffee finale; **b22** not the most exciting malt you'll find but certainly one of the most relaxed and comfortable. *40%.*

**Scotch Universe Mercury I 106° U.1.1' 1897.2"** first fill American bourbon barrel, dist 2007, bott 2016 **(95) n23.5 t24 f23.5 b24** For those who prefer a little whisky in their honey. Stunning! *52.9%.*

**Scotch Universe Pollux I 97° U.2.2' 1967.2"** Oloroso sherry butt, dist 2008, bott 2016 **(72) n17 t20 f18 b17** Oh dear... OK if you like burnt raisin, but otherwise...oh, dear; oh dear.... *59%.*

**Spey River Aged 12 Years** bourbon oak **(88.5)** n22.5 golden syrup weighed down with intense malt and toffee; **t22.5** silky texture with toffee to the fore, a quick release of spice, but a slow intertwangling of caramel and vanilla; **f21.5** butterscotch and light spice; **b22** attractive. But you get the feeling the toffee notes are holding back a top-rate malt. 40%. *Quality Spirits International.*

**Spey River Double Cask** American oak casks, bourbon cask finish **(76)** n19 t21 f18 b18. I was fascinated to see how this unusual maturation technique panned out: but I was not expecting this, or anything like. Not dissimilar to some American micro distillery malts with a tobacco character attached to the sweet sugars. Seriously odd. 40%. *Quality Spirits International.*

**The Whisky Agency Speyside Region Single Malt 1973 (95.5)** n24 t24.5 f23.5 b24 Those into the exotic fruit school of ye olde Speysiders will be pretty delighted with this: ticks every box....with a quilled flourish. 46.9%.

◇ **Whiskey Bottle Company Cigar Malt Lover Aged 21 Years** 1st fill sherry butt, cask no. 3646, dist 1997, bott 2018 **(96)** n24 if someone told you this had the aroma of a fruitcake, which they might, you'd be hard-pressed to find any such fruitcake with riches such as these. There is a peppery tingle to the fruit, which in itself is pristine and concentrated; **t24.5** those spices on the nose up their game tenfold on delivery and merge with a breath-taking black cherry and molasses. Even then, a vague maltiness can be found just below the surface; **f23.5** the fruit takes a broodier outlook as the oak gets more toasty; **b24** a Glenfarclas-style malt boasting a sherry cask of faultless, unimpeachable character. You don't have to smoke a cigar to enjoy this kind of whisky royalty. Indeed, to mix a malt like this with food, cigars or anything other than another glass of the same whisky must be considered, rightly, an act of treason. 54.4%. nc. 510 bottles.

**Whisky-Fässle Speyside Region 26 Year Old** sherry cask, dist 1991, bott 2017 **(76)** n18 t21 f18 b19 The odd fruit chocolate moment but a sulphurous sherry cask, alas.... 50.6%.

**Whisky-Fässle Speyside Region 43 Year Old** sherry butt, dist 1973, bott 2017 **(87.5)** n21.5 t23 f21 b22 Solid, mouth-watering fruit mixes well with the richer bourbon-style notes liquorice notes. But just too heavy on the tannins late on as the passing 43 summers catch up. 51.3%.

◇ **W.W. Club MCL.1 Speyside Aged 26 Years** American oak cask, cask no. 1408826, dist Jun 92, bott Jun 18 **(93)** n24 a nose of almost exotic complexity. Rare charm and balance interweave herewith the oak definitely holding the aces, Fabulous spices, never aggressive but always busy and powerful, perfectly matched by the mix of Manuka honey, maple syrup and liquorice; **t23** the sugars evident on the nose can't contain the muscularity of the tannin once it hits the palate. This is all about age and oak, though the more vigorous sugars put up an heroic struggle but can't prevent the drying...; the great age has also brought out a saltiness to hypnotic effect; **f22.5** excellent cocoa powder trace; exceptionally dry but clean; **b23.5** this is a Speysider from a distillery which doesn't always hit these heights at such an age. The oak has just slightly tipped over the edge, but not enough to spoil a magnificent nose, or undermine the complex elegance of the palate. 51.8%. sc. 273 bottles. Distilled at a Speyside Distillery founded in 1824. William & Co. Spirits.

◇ **W.W. Club MCL.2 Speyside Aged 25 Years** American oak cask, cask no. 1408825, dist Jun 92, bott Jun 18 **(94.5)** n24 t23.5 f23 b24 As the notes above, save two vital differences. Firstly, the oak hasn't travelled too far here and we are rewarded with extra header honey as a result. And, secondly, the saltiness is subtly more telling throughout, adding an extra piquancy to the proceedings. Small differences from its sister cask...but vital! Superb! 51.5%. sc. 276 bottles. Dist in distillery founded in 1824 William & Co. Spirits.

# UNSPECIFIED SINGLE MALTS (GENERAL)

**Burns Nectar Single Malt** bott code: L17/8183 **(77)** n20 t19 f19 b19 An ode to toffee. 40%.

**The Corriemhor Cigar Reserve** sherry & bourbon casks **(84.5)** n21 t22 f20.5 b21.5. You must forgive me if I judge this as a whisky alone. I have never smoked a cigar in my life; not even taken as much as an unlit cigarette to my lips. Not once. Ever. Some doctors and medical specialists in the field reckon it is why my nose and taste buds are so synchronised and alert. So if this is brilliant with a cigar, Cuban or otherwise, I will take your word for it. As a single malt in its own right, it is nutty, lush and pleasant. But rather lacking in complexity, scope or excitement. Dull, in fact. 46%

**Glen Castle Rum Cask Finish (81.5)** n20 t21.5 f21 b19 It must have been over 25 years ago now that I brought to the world the first ever rum cask matured whisky, which I discovered in a long-forgotten corner of a Campbeltown warehouse. It deservedly gained great notoriety and thereafter I went out of my way to taste as many rum cask matured or finished malts as were out there. This one is unique, but for all the wrong reasons. As the sugars which normally define the crispness of the whisky appear to have been underdone by other sugars in toffee form, thus neutralising the effect. Pleasant enough. But so dull. 40%. QSI.

**Glen Castle Sherry Cask Finish (80)** n21 t21 f19 b19 Clean sherry at work here, it appears, though so intense is the toffee the fruit (like anything else) can barely be heard. A malt neutered by caramel. 40%. Quality Spirits International.

⬦ **Kirkwall & St. Ola 10 Years Old** cask no. 001 **(89)** n21.5 t22 f23 b22.5 Though a 10-year-old, the nose and early delivery points in a much younger direction. Slowly, though, some sumptuous heather honey begins to filter through to the point of domination. Could have done with another two years in cask just for those early gremlins to be straightened and the honey aspect to be upgraded. Ultimately, though, after the bumpy start a delicious malt. 61.3%. sc. Mr. Whisky.

**Lotus Lord 20 Year Old 1996** sherry cask finish **(91.5)** n23.5 t23.5 f21.5 The sherry butts do impart a degree of late sulphur, but by then your heart will have been won. 53.3%. ncf. 12,200 bottles. Quality Spirits International.

**Lotus Lord 24 Year Old 1992** sherry cask finish **(95)** n24 t24 f23 b24 What a delightful and classy malt. 53.3%. ncf. 6,200 bottles. Quality Spirits International.

**Lotus Lord 28 Year Old 1988** sherry casks **(96)** n24.5 t24 f23.5 b24 Some 20 years ago I might have given this malt a bit of a ticking off for being far too sherry dominant. But, my! How times have changed. I am so relieved to find absolutely no sulphur at work here, I am smothering with kisses what seems like a long-lost son... 58.4%. ncf. 5,000 bottles. QSI.

**Master of Malt New-Make Malt Spirit (93)** n22.5 t23.5 f23 b23.5 The light body on the nose gives the lie to the splendour of the thickening malt on delivery. Pretty decent, mouth-filling new make. 63.5%.

**Peat's Beast (88.5)** n22 t22.5 f22 b22 "To tame the beast we recommend a dash of water." I don't. Recommend, instead, you use the Murray Method to warm up to body temp; otherwise you fracture the delicate oils and the sugars which hold this together vanish way too soon. 46%. ncf.

**Raasay While We Wait** finished in Tuscan red wine casks **(77)** n18 t21.5 f18.5 b19. I have always maintained that it is a dangerous tactic to link the name of a planned distillery with a malt which doesn't actually come from it. When in professional advisor mode, I always warn against it. I sincerely hope the distillery is built on Raasay one day by R&B, but to say that certain whiskies from other distilleries will taste like what theirs, not yet even constructed, one day might, is fraught with dangers: the truth is, you never know exactly what you'll get –with as much meticulous planning as you like - until you get it. However their whisky one day turns out, they must ensure they don't ruin it by putting it into wine casks as poor as these. 46%. nc ncf. R&B Distillers.

**SaarWhisky Gruwehewwel Edition 3** dist 2007 bott 2015 **(96)** n24.5 t24 f23 b24.5 No problem giving this truly great whisky the high score and award it deserves. But, as a lifelong Millwall supporter, I just wish they'd drop the West Ham Utd motif... 50.3%.

⬦ **Saar Whisky Jahrgangsabfüllung 2019** Islay barrel, dist 2009, bott 2018, bott code: L2019 **(93.5)** n23.5 delicately smoky and charmingly busy, too. A slight hint of Victory V cough sweet, too...; t23.5 a significant oiliness on delivery guarantees a full delivery, against with that slight cough sweet effect to the smoky. Malty and salivating from an early point while the sugars bustle and bristle, fashioned mainly from Demerara; f23 a long vanilla and smoke fade...with butterscotch and still the cough sweet phenols in play; b23.5 the dram that is perfect for a sore throat... 55.5%. ncf sc.

**Saar Whisky Malzbeisser** ex-bourbon barrel, dist 2009, bott 2018 **(90.5)** n22.5 t23 f22.5 b22.5 If anyone wants to know what a very decent Islay whisky is all about, this will do rather well. 53.7%. ncf sc.

**Saar Whisky Mandelbachtal Edition No. 2** dist 2009, bott 2018 **(88)** n22 t23 f21 b22 So much chocolate, not sure if this should be sold as a bottle or a bar... 53.7%. ncf sc.

**Spirit of Caledonia Cairn Guish 12 Years Old** cask no. 42 **(93)** n23 t23.5 f23 b23.5 A master class in the wearing of a light, smoky cloak, yet retaining your elegance. Beautifully made and matured without a single off note: of its type (a style not entirely dissimilar to Ledaig), exceptional. 61%. sc.

**The Whisky Embassy Green Meadows Aged 10 Years** cask no. 2914535, dist 2008, bott 2007 **(85.5)** n21 t22 f21 b21.5 Despite the decade in cask there is a youthfulness to the malt which guarantees a lively, juicy vibrancy at first. But its integration with a cask slightly over-eager on the late bitterness is limited. 53.1%. nc ncf sc.

# Scottish Vatted Malts
### (also Pure Malts/Blended Malt Scotch)

**100 Pipers Aged 8 Years Blended Malt (74)** n19 t20 f17 b18. A better nose, perhaps, and some spice on arrival. But when you consider the Speysiders at their disposal, all those mouth-wateringly grassy possibilities, it is such a shame to find something as bland as this. 40%

**Abrachan Triple Oak Matured (77) n19 t21 f18 b19**. Some superb sugars on delivery, but a fuzzy, furry bitterness sadly gives the game away. 42%

**Acla Selection Burnside 23 Years Old** bourbon hogshead, dist 1992, bott 2015 **(93) n23.5 t23 f23 b23.5** What a magnificent piece of oak this was given the chance to grow up in. As I taste this in my remote garden, a song thrush is celebrating the setting of the sun in spectacular triple-whistled fashion: between the whisky and the bird, nature's harmony cannot be better represented.50.4%. nc ncf.

**Angels' Nectar (81) n21 t21 f19 b20**. This angel has a bitter tooth... 40%

**Angel's Nectar Blended Malt Rich Peat Edition (90.5) n22.5 t23 f22.5 b22.5** Excellently-made malt: sticks unerringly to the script. 46%

**Ballantine's Pure Malt Aged 12 Years** bott code. LKAC1538 **(88.5) n22.5 t23 f21 b22**. No sign of the peat being reintroduced to major effect, although the orange is a welcome addition. Remains a charmer. 40%. Chivas.

**Bell's Signature Blend Limited Edition (83.5) n19 t22 f21 b21.5**. The front label makes large that this vatted malt has Blair Athol and Inchgower at the heart of it as they are "two fine malts selected for their exceptionally rich character". Kind of like saying you have invited the Kray twins to your knees up as they might liven it up a bit. Well those two distilleries were both part of the original Bell's empire, so fair dos. But to call them both fine malts is perhaps stretching the imagination somewhat. A robust vatting to say the least. And, to be honest, once you get past the nose, good back-slapping fun. 40%. 90,000 bottles.

**Ben Bracken Blended Malt Aged 12 Years (85.5) n22.5 t21 f21 b21**. Quite a tight malt with a predominantly toffee theme. 40%

**Berry Bros & Rudd Islay Blended Malt** bott code: L18/8215 **(90.5) n22 t23 f22.5 b23** An endearing vatting which sums up the island's whiskies without any drama but still highly attractively and with no wrong turns. 44.2%. The Classic Range.

**Berry Bros & Rudd Sherry Cask Matured Blended Malt** bott code: L18/8213 **(74.5) n19 t24.5 f14 b17** With Ronnie Cox's name all over this bottle, one can safely assume that the leading light in this vatting is Glenrothes. And, of course, with Glenrothes sherry butts at work, chances are so, too, will sulphur be. Well, it is – as can be picked out on the nose and the finish especially. But, for once, it is worth undergoing the pain of the massive sulphur simply to experience the delivery which scores absolutely maximum points for the lushest of mouthfeels and the extraordinary beauty of the richness of the fruit marrying some intense barley. Between the faulty sulphur start and end is sandwiched something which, for a few spellbinding, heavenly moments, touches perfection. 44.2%. The Classic Range.

**Berry Bros & Rudd Peated Cask Matured Blended Malt** bott code: L18/8214 **(92) n22 t23 f23.5 b23.5** Gentle and evenly paced. 44.2%. The Classic Range.

**Berry Bros & Rudd Speyside Blended Malt (85) n20 t22.5 f21 b21.5** A lot of malt to get your teeth into. The oak isn't exactly sympathetic but the big wave of vanilla at the midpoint carries some attractive maple syrup. 44.2%. The Classic Range.

**Big Peat Batch 31 (90.5) n23** love it: superb mix of allotment bonfire and peat reek. Some young spirit offering great energy; **t22** gristy sweet delivery pounded by spicy attitude; a blast of hickory and cocoa; **f22.5** the smoke rumbles along, but there is no letting up in intensity of peat or spice; **b23** good to see it has maintained its cheery high standard. Youthful, boisterous and challenging throughout. 46%. nc ncf. Douglas Laing & Co.

**Big Peat Bärlin Edition (91.5) n23 t22.5 f23 b23** I imagine the Peat Heads of Berlin are, rightly, very happy fellows... 50%. ncf. Bottled for Big Market Berlin, 50th Anniversary bottling.

**Black Face 8 Years Old (78.5) n18.5 t22 f19 b19**. A huge malt explosion in the kisser on delivery, but otherwise not that pretty to behold. 46%. The Vintage Malt Whisky Co Ltd.

**Blairmhor Aged 8 Years** bott code L15/058 R15/5083 **(86) n22.5 t22 f20.5 b21** Probably a dram never drunk by people of a certain political persuasion who would have been more impressed had it been called Blairless... An attractive malt which suffers from a surfeit of caramel and a cramped finale, though there is a big juicy, ripe pear and malt surge through the middle. 40%. International Beverage Holdings Ltd.

**Burns Nectar (89.5) n22 t22 f23 b22.5**. A delight of a dram and with all that honey around, "Nectar" is about right. 40%

**Cadenhead's Vatted Islay 25 Year Old (89) n23 t22 f22 b22** May be wrong, but there is a feeling of something a little older than 25 in this: definitely shows its antiquity. 46%. 175th Anniversary bottling.

**Carme 10 Years Old (79) n21.5 t20 f18.5 b19**. On paper Ardmore and Clynelish should work well together. But vatting is not done on paper and here you have two malts cancelling each other out and some less than great wood sticking its oar in. 43%

**Castle Rock Aged 12 Years Blended Malt (87) n22.5 t23 f19.5 b22**. Stupendously refreshing: the finish apart, I just love this style of malt. 40%

**Cave Aquila The Eagles Collection Westport 8 Years Old** first fill sherry cask **(73.5)** n17 t20 f17 b18.5 What the odd blender might call "good sulphur". What this one calls "bad sulphur". Indeed, a Westport in a sulphur storm. A great shame because there is enough richness to the grape to confirm this must have once been a stupendous butt. *61.1%. sc.*

**Cearban (79.5)** n18 t21.5 f20 b19. The label shows a shark. It should be a whale: this is massive. Sweet with the malts not quite on the same wavelength. *40%. Robert Graham Ltd.*

**Chapter 7 Island Blended Malt (91.5)** n22 t23.5 f23 b23 Well done, chaps (or do I mean Chapts?).Vatting unpeated Island malt and getting the balance right is not one of the easier tasks in the whisky world. But this has been carried out wonderfully – the exclusive use of ex-bourbon helped. *49%.*

**Chapter 7 Highland Blended Malt (86)** n21 t22 f22 b21 No serious age to this, which partly explains why the oak is in no-man's land here. It is trying to form enough character to make a positive impact but has strength enough only to disrupt the flow of the juicy barley. That said, the very simple, grassy impact of the malt itself is rather delightful. *46.8%.*

**Chapter 7 Peatside 2009** Barrique cask, Port finish, cask no. 5511 **(94.5)** n23.5 t23.5 f24 b23.5 There is a touch of genius to this... *46%. sc.*

**Chapter 7 Simple Malt** batch no. 1 **(90.5)** n22 t23 f22.5 b23 Delightfully sweet and peated: as simple as that! *46%.*

**Chapter 7 Simple Malt** batch no. 2 **(93)** n23 t23 f23.5 b23.5 Delightfully complex: nothing simple here at all... *48%.*

**Chapter 7 Simple Malt** batch no. 3 **(84)** n20 t22 f21 b21 Very flat with the emphasis on tangy creamy toffee. *48%.*

**Chapter 7 Simple Malt** batch no. 4 **(93.5)** n23.5 t23 f23 b24 Like an old-fashioned Highland Park before the invention of sulphur casks. Fabulous. *46%.*

**Chapter 7 Speyside Blended Malt (82.5)** n21.5 t22 f20 b19 Hardly a page turner. The plot doesn't make sense: mild smoke which does well on delivery but the remainder leads you nowhere. *46%.*

**Chivas Regal Ultis** bott code LPNK1759 2016/09/16 **(89.5)** n22.5 t23 f21.5 b22.5 This vatted malt is the legacy of Chivas' five master blenders. But to pay real respect to them, just remove the caramel from the bottling hall. The whisky will be light coloured, for sure, but I suspect the flavour profile will blow us all away... *40%. Chivas Brothers Ltd.*

⬧ **Cladach** db **(91)** n22 t23 f23 b23 The slightly dull, regulation nose doesn't prepare you for the fireworks ahead. The delivery quivers and shimmies and the malt takes a particularly salty course of action – seashores without the usual phenols. The saline touch allows the beautifully layered malt an extra degree of sharpness. The finish of milk chocolate malted biscuit is a quiet serenade after the earlier vividness of the barley. One hell of a surprise package! *57.1%. Diageo Special Releases 2018.*

**Clan Campbell 8 Years Old Pure Malt (82)** n20 t22 f20 b20. Enjoyable, extremely safe whisky that tries to offend nobody. The star quality is all on the complex delivery, then it's toffee. *40%.*

**Clan Denny** (Bowmore, Bunnahabhain, Caol Ila and Laphroaig) **(94)** n24 t23 f23 b24. A very different take on Islay with heavy peats somehow having a floating quality. Unique. *40%*

**Clan Denny Islay (86.5)** n21.5 t23 f21 b21. A curiously bipolar malt with the sweetness and bitterness at times going to extremes. Some niggardly oak has taken the edge of what might have been a sublime malt as the peat and spices at times positively glistens with honey. *46.5%. nc ncf sc. Douglas Laing & Co.*

**Clan Denny Speyside (87)** n22 t22 f21 b22. A Tamdhu-esque oiliness pervades here and slightly detracts from the complexity. That said, the early freshness is rather lovely. *46%*

**Collectivum XXVIII (96.5)** n24t24.5 f23.5 b24.5 This, with boldness, vivaciousness and blinding sparkle is heading us brilliantly into the direction where blended Scotch needs to go. A Wurlitzer of a whisky...wow!!! *57.3%. Diageo Special Releases 2017.*

**Compass Box 3 Year Old Deluxe** bott Aug 16 **(96)** n24 t24 f24 b24 Quite possibly the oldest three-year-old I have ever tasted. Being Compass Box, I have no doubt the flavour of irony is as powerful as any other here: surely this has to be a bunch of ancient malts with a tiny flash of something three years old, making up just a fraction of the composition. If so (and I strongly suspect it is), then it does much – as I am sure it has been designed – to both flag up and undermine the utterly idiotic rules/laws set out by the appalling Scotch Whisky Association, that does not allow blenders to show what actually makes up their whisky – only the age of the youngest constituent no matter how large or, in this case, minuscule its contribution may have been. The SWA: perhaps the only trade body that has been able to get government backing to confuse the public and ensure they have no idea what they are paying for. So, a brilliant whisky on all counts. *46%. nc ncf. 3,282 bottles.*

**Compass Box Eleuthera Marriage** married for nine months in an American oak Hogshead **(86)** n22 t22 f20 b22. I'm not sure if it's the name that gets me on edge here, but as big and robust as it is I still can't help feeling that the oak has bitten too deep. Any chance of a Compass Box Divorce...? 49.2%. *Compass Box for La Maison du Whisky.*

**Compass Box Enlightenment** bott Apr 16 **(94.5)** n24.5 t24 f22.5 b23.5 After the run of disappointing vatted malts I have tasted today, trust Compass Box to come to the rescue. This is not a whisky to have when in a hurry: the nose alone is worth a good 15 minutes... 46%. nc ncf. 5,922 bottles.

**Compass Box Flaming Heart Fifteenth Anniversary** bott Jul 15 **(96.5)** n24 t24.5 f23.5 b24.5 Really, John? Fifteen years? I mean: 15 years....??? Fucking hell! Oh, by the way, mate. It's a bloody masterpiece... 48.9%. nc ncf. 12,060 bottles.

⬧ **Compass Box Juveniles** bott Sept 18 **(95)** n23.5 t24 f23.5 b24 Malt whisky which, were it a metal, would be 24 carat gold. From the very first sniff right through to the last, slightly spiced pulse of flavour, it is centred on a honey-rich style but always tempered with elegant vanillas. This heather honey note is the single consistent as it changes weight and gears with rare subtlety – meaning anything less than half an hour with the Murray Method on this one would be a travesty to such a beautiful incarnation of a vatted malt. The maltiness - sometimes juicy, sometimes with a slight Horlicks-creamy twist - takes on many guises. But it cannot escape that thread of honey. 46%. nc ncf. 14,894 bottles.

**Compass Box The Lost Blend (95.5)** n23 t23.5 f24.5 b24.5 I may be wrong, but I have a feeling that when the nose and flavour profile was being constructed, a little extra smoke than first planned was added. Seems that way by the manner in which the phenols just pipe up a little louder than it first seems...46%

**Compass Box No Name** bott Sept 17 **(92.5)** n23 t23 f23 b23.5 I'll give it a name: Compass Box Bleedin' Delicious! 48.9%. nc ncf. 15,000 bottles.

⬧ **Compass Box No Name, No. 2** bott Feb 19 **(93.5)** n23 t23.5 f23.5 b23.5 Think a lightly oiled Islay whisky where the peat is powering, but totally in sync with the overall balance of the piece. And where a light heather honey note ensures there is no bitterness and the phenols never get too acrid or sooty. Spot on wood management with this fella. 48.9%. nc ncf. 8,802 bottles.

**Compass Box The Peat Monster Cask Strength (89)** n23.5 t23 f20.5 b22 Plenty of peat between your teeth but deserving of some better oak. 57.3%

**Compass Box The Peat Monster Reserve (92)** n23 t23.5 f22.5 b23. At times a bit of a Sweet Monster...beautiful stuff! 48.9%

**Compass Box The Peat Monster Swedish Whisky Federation (91)** n23 t23 f22 b23 What can you say? Its peaty. And it's a monster...! 46%. 2,000 bottles.

**Compass Box The Peat Monster Tenth Anniversary Release** bott Sept 13 **(95)** n24 t24 f23 b24 here we appear to see a mix, or compromise, between the sweeter bottling of two years ago and last year's searing dryness. And, unlike most compromises, this one works... 48.9%.

**Compass Box Phenomenology** bott Sept 17 **(92.5)** n22 t24.5 f22.5 b23.5 Once upon a time, blenders took so much notice of the blend they actually forgot to really look at what it tasted like. Decades ago more than one blender told me that he didn't taste a whisky at final strength until a sample turned up in his lab from the bottling hall. This one appears to be almost the other way round. The nose is attractive and adequate without being anything special. The delivery and follow through, though: gee what a phenomenon...! 46%. nc ncf. 7,908 bottles.

**Compass Box The Spice Tree** first-fill and refill American oak. Secondary maturation: heavily toasted new French oak **(95.5)** n24.5 t24.5 f23 b23.5. Having initially been chopped down by the SWA, who were indignant that extra staves had been inserted into the casks, The Spice Tree is not only back but in full bloom. Indeed, the blossom on this, created by the use of fresh oak barrel heads, is more intoxicating than its predecessor – mainly because there is a more even and less dramatic personality to this. Not just a great malt, but a serious contender for Jim Murray Whisky Bible 2011 World Whisky of the Year. 46%

**Compass Box Spice Tree Extravaganza** bott Aug 16 **(94.5)** n24 t23.5 f23 b24 Perhaps the most important factor to this whisky, which will be overlooked probably by about 99% of those who taste this, is not so much the taste itself but the mouth feel and balance. In other words, it is not always the words that are said which are most important, but the way they are delivered. That is the secret to this complex beauty. 46%. nc ncf. 12,240 bottles.

⬧ **Compass Box The Story of The Spaniard** 48% aged in Spanish wine casks, bott Jun 18 **(90.5)** n23 dry and circumspect. Seeks quiet elegance and finds it...; t23 very good weight on the mouth feel. A malty sweetness underpins the dryer tannin and, presumably, grape skin; f22 remains on the dry, sophisticated road; b22.5 often Compass Box lets the oak do the talking, occasionally too loudly. Here the tannin has a dry edge, but fits into the scenario perfectly. 43%. nc ncf.

⬧ **Copper Dog** batch no. 16/0673, bott code: L8127IY001 **(89)** n22 something of the hot cross bun about this one, being both fruity and buttery...; t23.5 as velvety as a hotel curtain and teasing in the way light heather honey notes escape like moonbeams from between scudding clouds. The malt is impressively multi-layered and not short of finesse; **f21.5** a little too dry and bitter here, though spices try to act as a diversion; **b22** a whisky which first saw the light of day at the fabulous Craigellachie Hotel in Speyside, where I gave my first whisky lectures over a quarter of a century ago and in the 1990s wrote many chapters of my various books. The number of vatted malts we created from the whiskies in the bar...far too many to mention, though none then capable of shewing this kind of finale. 40%. *The Craigellachie Hotel Scotland.*

**Cutty Sark Blended Malt (92.5) n22 t24 f23 b23.5.** Sheer quality: as if two styles have been placed in the bottle and told to fight it out between them. What a treat! 40%.

**Deerstalker Blended Malt Highland Edition (94) n23.5 t23.5 f23 b24** A quite beautiful whisky by any standards. 43%

**Deerstalker Blended Malt Peated Edition (84.5) n22.5 t22 f19 b21** A slightly strange mixture: on one hand creamy, sweet and friendly, on the other somewhat metallic and harsh. Struggles to find either balance or a comfortable course. The finish is way off key and vaguely furry. 43%.

**Demijohn Islay Blended Malt 6 Year Old** cask no. 5512, bott 10 Sept 15 **(91) n23 t23 f22 b23** A very jolly kind of malt, the delicate fruit offering a chirpiness to the chipper young peats. Thoroughly enjoyable. 42.5%.

**Douglas Laing's Rock Oyster Aged 18 Years (90.5) n23 t22.5 f22 b23** Deserves a slug. 46.8%. nc ncf.

⟐ **Douglas Laing's Rock Oyster Cask Strength** batch no. 2 **(87.5) n22 t21.5 f22 b22** A marriage of well-made whiskies. But so young and underdeveloped should be re-named Rock Sprat as opposed to Rock Oyster. Salty and lively though. 56.1%.

⟐ **Douglas Laing's Scallywag 10 Years Old (85.5) n21 t21 f22 b21.5** Just like its older predecessor, the nose a little thin and functional, and the same can be said for the delivery. But gets into its stride only when the oils come out to play, concentrating the sweeter barley beautifully. 46%.

**Douglas Laing's Scallywag Aged 13 Years (87.5) n21 t23 f21.5 b22** Well, for a bit of a scallywag, this strikes me as a remarkably well- behaved individual. The malt is at the centre of attention, recovering beautifully on the palate after a so-so nose. Salivating where you want it to be, too. 46%.

⟐ **Douglas Laing's Timorous Beastie 12 Years Old (91) n22.5 t23 f22.5 b23** Where the 18-year-old version is attractively sleekit, here there's nothing remotely 'cowrin' as the barley sugars gang together to form a luscious, satisfying depth. Youngish and fair; juicy and only the warming spice giving any form of edge. Thoroughly enjoyable. 54.4%.

**Douglas Laing's Timorous Beastie Aged 18 Years (89) n22.5.5 f21.5 b22.5** Attractively sleekit. 46.8%. nc ncf. 7,258 bottles.

**Eiling Lim Older Than Old Blended Malt Whisky (87.5) n21.5 t22 f22 b22.** Charming malt. Entirely non-taxing with a light Arbroath Smoky element as the main thread and genteel vanilla notes filling most of the gaps. 46.5%

**Elements of Islay Peat (91.5) n23 t24 f22 b22.5** This is rather more than elementary slay, trust me.... 46%

**Elements of Islay Peat Islay Blended Malt (94) n23 t24 f23.5 b23.5** Does everything it says on the tin – and more. Some younger elements appear to be at work here, which means the peat intensity can sometimes fly, deliciously and dramatically, off the scale. 45%.

**Elements of Islay Peat Full Proof (92.5) n23.5 t23.5 f22.5 b23** A distinctly two-toned malt with the phenols seeming to be pitched quite differently. 59.3%.

**ePower Extra Old Blended Malt Whisky (93) n23 t23.5 f23 b23.5** This is beautifully constructed vatted malt and suggests some pretty good age, also. 45.2%.

**The Famous Grouse 10 Years Old Malt (77) n19 t20 f19 b19.** The nose and finish headed south in the last Winter and landed in the sulphur marshes of Jerez. 40%. *Edrington Group.*

**The Famous Grouse 15 Years Old Malt (86) n21 t22 f21.5 b21.5.** Salty and smoky with a real sharp twang. 43%. *Edrington Group.*

**The Famous Grouse 15 Years Old Malt (86) n19 t24 f22 b21.** There had been a hint of the "s" word on the nose, but it got away with it. Now it has crossed that fine – and fatal – line where the petulance of the sulphur has thrown all else slightly out of kilter. All, that is, apart from the delivery which is a pure symphony of fruit and spice deserving a far better introduction and final movement. Some moving, beautiful moments. Flawed genius or what...? 40%

**The Famous Grouse 18 Years Old Malt (82) n19 t21.5 f21 b20.5.** Some highly attractive honey outweighs the odd uncomfortable moment. 43%. *Edrington Group.*

**The Famous Grouse Malt 21 Years Old (91) n22 t24 f22 b23.** A very dangerous dram: the sort where the third or fourth would slip down without noticing. Wonderful scotch! 43%.

**The Famous Grouse 30 Years Old Malt (94) n23.5 t24 f23 b23.5.** Whisky of this sky-high quality is exactly what vatted malt should be all about. Outrageously good. 43%

**Five Lions Burnside 22 Years Old** 2nd fill Oloroso sherry hogshead, dist May 93, bott Nov 15 **(93) n23 t23.5 f23 b23.5** An unimpeachable sherry butt - amazing! 55.5%. nc ncf.

**Five Lions Westport 18 Years Old** 1st fill sherry butt, dist Oct 97, bott Nov 15 **(95) n23.5 t24 f23.5 b24** Brilliant! 59.7%. nc ncf.

**Gleann Mór Islay Blended Malt Aged Over 8 Years (87) n22 t22 f21.5 b21.5** A robust vatted malt which, though only a standard strength bottling, rips at you like a whisky half that abv again. Moderately, sweet, not too highly peated, thin bodied and lacking couth. Fun, though! 40%.

**Gleann Mór Speyside Blended Malt Aged Over 30 Years (93) n23 t23.5 f23 b23.5** After a score years and ten, you would expect the oak to have a major say in the constitution of a whisky. And for those looking for it to have a big but not overpowering influence, then here's a malt ticking all the right boxes. While the oak threatens a little too loudly on the nose, fears that this vatting will have been over-sapped are dispelled by a glittering array of honey tones on delivery, ranging from heather to rape flower honey with a little bourbon-esque liquorice thrown into the mix. Profound and impressive. 49%.

**Gleann Mór Vatted Whisky Over 40 Years Old (92.5) n23.5 t23.5 f22.5 b23** An oldie and a goodie...Mor, please...!!! 47%

**Glenalmond Highland Blended Malt (84) n21 t22 f20.5 b20.5** Chugs along in safe, non-demanding caramel-rich fashion. 40%. The Vintage Malt Whisky Co.

**Glenn (89.5) n22 t23 f22 b22.5** A forceful malt. Seems as though at least two strands of the thread are trying to outdo each other. Enjoyable;erratic towards the end. 50%. Svenska Eldvatten.

**Glenalmond 2001 Vintage (82.5) n22 t21.5 f19 b20.** Glenkumquat, more like: the most citrusy malt I have tasted in a very long time. 40%. The Vintage Malt Whisky Co Ltd.

**Glenalmond "Everyday" (89.5) n21.5 t23.5 f22 b22.5.** They are not joking; this really is an everyday whisky. Glorious malt which is so dangerously easy to drink 40%

**Glen Brynth Aged 12 Years Blended Malt (87) n22.5 t23 f19.5 b22.** Deja vu...! Thought I was going mad: identical to the Castle Rock I tasted this morning, right down to the (very) bitter end ..!!! 40%. Quality Spirits International.

**Glenbrynth Blended Malt 12 Years (87.5) n22.5 t22.5 f21 b21.5.** Heavyweight malt which gets off to a rip-roaring start on the delivery but falls away somewhat from the mid ground onwards. 43%. OTI Africa.

**Glenbrynth Ruby 40 Year Old Limited Edition (94) n23.5 t24 f23 b23.5.** Has all the hallmarks of a completely OTT, far too old sherry butt being brought back to life with the aid of a livelier barrel. A magnificent experience, full of fun and evidence of some top quality vatting at work, too. 43%. OTI Africa.

**Glenbrynth Ruby 40 Year Old** bott code L8V 7439 04/11/11 **(95) n24 t23.5 f23.5 b24** You cannot ask much more from a 40-year-old vatted malt than this. Amazing what a lack of colouring (and sulphured sherry casks) can do – like let the whisky speak for itself and allow you to follow its myriad paths, its highways and byways, without the route being blocked by toffee or a rabid bitterness. Each and every cask included in this great whisky should be applauded, as should the blender. 43%. OTI Africa.

**Glen Castle Blended Malt 1992 Sherry Cask Matured** bott code: L7 9595-2017 12 **(96) n24 t24.5 f23.5 b24** I have no official information into what makes up this vatted malt. But this is almost identical in style to the old fashioned Glendronach 12-year-old Sherry Cask that was on the market a quarter of a century ago and more. Then I was annoyed with its OTT characteristics which swamped everything in sight. Now I hug it affectionately like a long-lost friend back from the dead, because this is sulphur-free sherried whisky – such a delight and rarity. All is forgiven... For those who truly adore big, clean sherried whisky: this will take you to a grapey heaven. 51.8%.

**Glen Castle Blended Malt 1990 Sherry Cask Matured 28 Years Old** bott code: LHB 1479-2018 **(96) n24** how about that!! Big fruitcake and almonds – the fruit being roasty raisins, sultanas and plums. The degree of ancient toastiness is just so, while the spices threaten to sizzle, but settle for simmer...for now at least; **t24** the grape is not shy coming forward arriving in its burnt raisin finest. The spices now dazzle and scream antiquity while the tannins are both toasty and moving into mocha mode; **f24** like the death throes of a long and long overdue, orgasm....proving that us oldies still have it in us and that great whisky wasn't invented by the younger, hipster generation... whatever they think...; **b24** anyone who wants to know the difference between ye olde great, untainted sherry butts and the poor and unacceptable offerings we have been subjected to for the last 25 years should grab a bottle of this. Old school brilliance. And beauty. Just...wow! Old Time sherry at its most accessible... and mind-blowing. 55.2%. nc ncf.

**Glen Castle Blended Malt 1992 Sherry Cask Matured** bott code: L7 9595-2017 12 **(95.5 n24 t24 f23.5 b24** Just brilliant whisky to be savoured and cherished, restoring my faith in sherry – very few butts from this era survived the sulphury onslaught – and the perfect after dinner or very late night dram. *46.8%.*

**Glendower 8 Years Old (84)** n21.5 t21 f20.5 b21 Nutty and spicy. *43%*

**The Glenfohry Aged 8 Years Special Reserve (73)** n19 t19 f17 b18. Some of the malt used here appears to have come from a still where the safe has not so much been broken into, but just broken! Oily and feinty, to say the least. Normally I would glower at anyone who even thought of putting a coke into their malt. Here, I think it might be for the best.. *40%*

**Glen Talloch Blended Malt Aged 8 Years (85.5)** n21 t23 f20.5 b21. An invigorating and engulfing vatting, full of intrinsic barley tones on delivery. But the caramel is too strident for further complexity. *40%*

**Glen Turner Heritage Double Wood** Bourbon & Madeira casks, bott code. L311657A **(85.5)** n21.5 t22 f21 b21. A very curious amalgamation of flavours. The oak appears to be in shock with the way the fruit is coming on to it and offers a bitter backlash. No faulting the crisp delivery with busy sugar and spice for a few moments brightening the palate. *40%.*

**Glen Turner Pure Malt Aged 8 Years** L525956A **(84)** n20 t22 f22 b20. A lush and lively vatting annoyingly over dependent on thick toffee but simply brimming with fabulously mouth-watering barley and over-ripe blood oranges. To those who bottle this, I say: let me into your lab. I can help you bring out something sublime!! *40%*

**Glen Orchy (80.5)** n19.5 t21.5 f19.5 b20. Not exactly the most subtle of vatted malts though when the juicy barley briefly pours through on delivery, enjoyable. *40%. Lidl.*

**Glen Orchy 5 Year Old Blended Malt Scotch Whisky (88.5)** n22 t22.5 f22 b22. Excellent malt plus very decent casks equals light-bodied fun. *40%. Lidl.*

**Glen Orrin (68)** n16.5 t17.5 f17 b17. In its favour, it doesn't appear to be troubled by caramel. Which means the nose and palate are exposed to the full force of this quite dreadful whisky. *40%.*

**Glen Orrin Six Year Old (88)** n22 t23 f21 b22. A vatting that has improved in the short time it has been around, now displaying some lovely orangey notes on the nose and a genuinely lushness to the body and spice on the finish. You can almost forgive the caramel, this being such a well balanced, full-bodied ride. A quality show for the price. *40%*

**Grand Macnish Six Cask Edition** bott code L14/8867 **(85.7)** n21 t23 f19.5 b22 A late night chewathon: this is big, ballsy with little time for prisoners. Not exactly free from the odd flaw. But the delivery and middle have wonderful molten walnut and orange cake quality and a lush mouth feel to match. *40%. MacDuff International Ltd.*

**Hedges and Butler Special Pure Malt (83)** n20 t21 f22 b21. Just so laid back: nosed and tasted blind I'd swear this was a blend (you know, a real blend with grains and stuff) because of the biting lightness and youth. Just love the citrus theme and, err...graininess...!! *40%*

**Highland Harvest Organic Blended Malt 7 Casks** batch 002 **(86.5)** n21.5 t22.5 f21 b21.5 Not even remotely complex. But pleasant enough. *40% WB15/371*

**Highland Journey Blended Malt (94.5)** n23.5 t23.5 f23.5 b24 I have been on some memorable Highland journeys in my life, but few have been quite as comfortable as this one. *46.2%. Hunter Laing & Co.*

⬧ **Hogwash Blended Malt Scotch Whisky Blend No. 08** bott code: LBB 3C 4353 **(85.5)** n21.5 t22 f21 b21. Juicy in part. And if you are looking for a gentle, soft, refined, complex, gentleman of a vatted malt...this isn't it. *40%. Produced for Aldi.*

**J & B Exception Aged 12 Years (80)** n20 t23 f18 b19. Very pleasant in so many ways. A charming sweetness develops quickly, with excellent soft honeycomb. But the nose and finish are just so... so...dull...!! For the last 30 years J&B has meant, to me, (and probably within that old company) exceptionally clean, fresh Speysiders offering a crisp, mouth-watering treat. I feel this is off target. *40%. Diageo/Justerini & Brooks.*

**J & B Nox (89)** n23 t23 f21 b22. A teasing, pleasing little number that is unmistakably from the J&B stable. *40%. Diageo.*

**John Black 8 Years Old Honey (88)** n21 t22.5 f22.5 b22. A charming vatting. *40%*

**John Black 10 Years Old Peaty (91)** n23 salty and peaty; t23 soft and peaty; f22 delicate and peaty; b23 classy and er...peaty. *40%. Tullibardine Distillery.*

**Johnnie Walker Green Label 15 Years Old (95)** n24 t23.5f23.5 b24. God, I love this stuff... this is exactly how a vatted malt should be and one of the best samples I've come across since its launch. *43%. Diageo.*

**Jon, Mark and Robbo's The Rich Spicy One (89)** n22 t23 f22 b22. So much better without the dodgy casks: a real late night dram of distinction though the spices perhaps a little on the subtle side... *40%. Edrington.*

**Jon, Mark and Robbo's The Smoky Peaty One (92)** n23 t22 f23 b24. Genuinely high-class whisky where the peat is full-on yet allows impressive complexity and malt development. A malt for those who appreciate the better, more elegant things in life. *40%. Edrington.*

**Le Gus't Selection X Speyside Blended Malt 39 Years Old** sherry cask, cask no. 4 **(94.5)** **n23.5 t24 f23 b24** Truly Xcellent. 60.4%. sc. 109 bottles.

**Le Gus't Selection XI Speyside Blended Malt** hogshead, cask no. 403 **(91) n22.5 t23** **f22.5 b23** Appears to have good age to this and a little bit of class. 49.7%. sc. 262 bottles.

**Liquid Treasures Entomology Wardhead Over 21 Years Old** ex-bourbon hogshead, dist 1987, bott 2018 **(88.5) n22 t22.5 f21.5 b22.5** All the classic signs of a malt which really struggles with great age: so even at 21 the barley is fracturing to allow the oak an ungainly foothold. Lots to savour, though. 55.5%.

**Liquid Treasures Entomology Williamson Over 6 Years Old** ex-bourbon hogshead, dist 2011, bott 2018 **(87.5) n21.5 t22 f22 b22** A beautifully young and raw whisky which tears at your taste buds like a hawk's talon on its prey. Sound peat mingles with decent Demerara sugars and though a few tannin notes gets through, the malt's youth is never in doubt. 59.6%

**The Loch Fyne The Living Cask 1745 (94.5) n23.5 t23.5 f23.5 b24** One of the best whiskies ever created at quarter to six in the evening... and one quite impossible not to love. 46.3%

**The Loch Fyne The Living Cask** Batch One **(92) n22 t23.5 f23 b23.5** Absolutely charming. 46.3%

**The Loch Fyne The Living Cask Batch Two (78) n18 t21 f19 b20.** A charming coincidence today: the first time I visited the Loch Fyne whisky shop, about 30 years ago, I spotted my first ever Spotted Flycatcher at Inveraray Castle. Just a few minutes before tasting this, a spotted flycatcher visited my garden for the first time this summer – and it is now late July. It must have known... Thirty years ago, though, the sherry-influenced bottlings available were so much better than today...43.6%

**The Loch Fyne The Living Cask Batch Four (88) n21 t22.5 f22 b22.5** Oh well, batch 3 gave us the slip but we caught up with Batch 4 which is a vast improvement on 2. A genuinely oily cove; and astonishingly malty, too... 43.6%

**Loch Fyne Living Cask** batch no. 6 **(88.5) n23 t22.5 f21 b22** Well Batch 6 appears to be living and breathing peat... 43.6%.

**The Lost Distillery Company Stratheden** batch no. 2/II **(86) n22 t21.5 f21 b21.5.** A dry malt boasting sporadic muscovado fruity sweetness and the vaguest of underlying phenols. Pleasant, though by no means perfect. I wish the company well, but have to say that putting today's casks together to recreate a malt last distilled in 1926 (and which no-one living has probably ever tasted) is fanciful, to put it mildly. In those days bourbon casks weren't available so not in use, sherry ones were then of a significantly higher standard and the peat, almost certainly, would have been a little more punchy than here. 46%. nc ncf.

**Macaloney's TWA Cask Series Benrinnes & Glenlossie** ex-bourbon casks, finished in re-toasted red wine barriques **(89) n22.5 t22.5 f22 b22** Not a malt for the faint-hearted: the fruit dominates and makes little effort to integrate, leaving the oak to make a violent, forced entry. 57.2%. ncf. 1,198 bottles.

**Macaloney's TWA Cask Series Blair Athol & Macduff** ex-bourbon casks, finished in re toasted red wine barriques **(88.5) n22.5 t23 f20.5 b22.5** Have to admit that those wine barrels, though not faultless, certainly have a charm and do all they can to accentuate any honey notes lurking. 58%. ncf. 797 bottles.

**Macaloney's TWA Cask Series Caol Ila & Bunnahabhain** ex-bourbon casks, finished in re-toasted red wine barriques **(93) n23 t23.5 f23 b23.5** About as juicy a peated malt as you'll ever find! Something for everyone. 55.6%. ncf. 918 bottles.

**Mackinlay's Rare Old Highland Malt (89) n22 t22 f22 b23.** Possibly the most delicate malt whisky I can remember coming from the labs of Whyte and Mackay. Though it still, on the palate, must rank as heavy medium. This is designed as an approximation of the whisky found at Shackleton's camp in the Antarctic. And as a life-long Mackinlay drinker myself, it is great to find a whisky bearing its name that, on the nose only, briefly reminds me of the defter touches which won my heart over 30 years ago. That was with a blend: this is a vatted malt. And a delicious one. In case you wondered: I did resist the temptation to use ice. 47.3%

⬧ **MacNair's Lum Reek 12 Years Old (89) n22** how often do you find apple blossom on a nose? But here it is, hiding shyly behind the spiced vanilla and thin layer of marzipan; **t22.5** crunchy malt with attitude. Bites hard after delivery, drawing out lots of juicy barley sap. Then, like the nose, becomes quite vanilla oriented; **f22** the juiciness has vanished for a spiced mocha fade – again, with bite; **b22.5** interesting chimneys they have in this part of Scotland, which appears to reek marzipan and apple blossom where you might expect, coal peat or wood...! 46%. The GlenAllachie Distillers Company.

⬧ **MacNair's Lum Reek 21 Years Old (91) n22.5** custard cream being poked in the ribs by a niggardly malt; **t23** fabulous malt overture with some welcome oils which both soften the usual jagged edges but also spreads the subtle sugars further and into a pleasing and very refreshing barley sugar theme; **f22.5** clean, with a slight citrus edge to the decent barley and vanilla fade; **b23** a wild malt tamed it seems to me and certainly not lacking in personality 48%. *The GlenAllachie Distillers Company.*

⟡ **MacNair's Lum Reek Peated (88.5) n22 t22 f22 b22.5** Has the consistency of a nail file wrapped in velvet. Enough edges to this to draw blood. But the modest smoke soothes and kisses better. The salivating maltiness is another surprise. Not quite like any other vatted malt I have before encountered. And have to admit: I kind of begrudgingly like it, though McNair's appear to always include a malt that can pick a fight with itself in a 5cl miniature...! 46%. *The GlenAllachie Distillers Company.*

**Master of Malt Reference Series I (82) n19.5 t23 f19 b20.5.** Not quite the happiest of bunnies at times, as it occasionally struggles to find a balance in the face of big, not entirely desired, oils. That said, nothing to stop you embracing the enormity of the date & sugar-drizzled barley soon after delivery & during the period it has escaped a certain feintiness. 47.5% WB15/349

**Master of Malt Reference Series I.1 (87.5) n21 t23 f21.5 b22.** No enormous age – or at least oak involvement - as confirmed by the nose. But some wonderful moments as the juicy, clean barley hits the palate running. 47.5%

**Master of Malt Reference Series I.2 (93) n23 t23 f23.5 b23.5** A charming marriage between Fisherman's Friend phenols and balletic barley. 47.4%

**Master of Malt Reference Series I.3 (91) n22** dry, oak-steered with a nod towards mocha; **t22.5** a deft, peaceful delivery with no drama but loads of development; **f23.5** lightly sweetened cocoa powder makes for a fabulous ending: reminiscent of Merlin lollies of yesteryear; **b23** it's all about the chocolate... 47.1%

**Master of Malt Reference Series II (84.5) n20 t22 f21.5 b21.** The oils have been toned down for this one, though the sugars have reached shrieking point. Malty, but perhaps a tad too cloying for its own good. 47.5% WB15/350

**Master of Malt Reference Series II.1 (88) n21** nothing wrong with it: just dull and uninspiring; **t23** a rich seam of malt appears to be of an oily disposition; **f22** again, technically sound. Plenty of rich malt and all that plus a hint of spice; **b22** an oily cove... 47.5%

**Master of Malt Reference Series II.2 (87) n22 t22.5 f21 b21.5.** Soft lemon drizzle on chunky malt plus an enjoyable volley of sugary grist early on. 47.4%

**Master of Malt Reference Series II.3 (89) n21.5 f floral** – a dank bluebell wood; **t22.5** mouth-filling malt. Playful oils and a steady ramping up of the malt intensity; **f22.5** something of a malt cereal about the finale; a little butterscotch tart thickens the effect; **b22.5** reminiscent of a Kentucky maltshake. 47.2%

**Master of Malt Reference Series III (88) n22 t23 f21 b22** Still one for the sweet toothed, but you don't need a diagram at the back to tell you some decent age has been added to this vatting. The odd blemish, but great fun. 47.5% WB15/351

**Master of Malt Reference Series III.1 (89.5) n22.5** a squeeze of blood orange and grapefruit set the malt off beautifully; **t23** thrusts malt at the taste buds like a politician rams his party line down your earholes; **f21.5** a little vanilla and spice, though the malt lingers; a tad bitter late on; **b22.5** if you like your malt malty, vote for this. 47.7%

**Master of Malt Reference Series III.2 (92.5) n22.5** earthy, yet enticingly malty. And thick...; **t23** superb Malteser style delivery: massive malt with an attractive milk chocolate element; **f24** good grief!! That malt just doesn't know when to call it a day. A little ulmo honey has joined in to intensify the sweetness slightly; even some late spice adds to the ultra late complexity; **b23** similar to III.1, except without the bitter bits. 47.5%

**Master of Malt Reference Series III.3 (78) n19.5 t21.5 f18 b19.** Fruity, fat, sweet. A tad furry. And somewhat one-dimensional. 47.5%

**Matisse 12 Year Old Blended Malt (93) n23.5 t23 f22.5 b23.** Succulent, clean-as-a-whistle mixture of malts with zero bitterness and not even a whisper of an off note: easily the best form I have ever seen this brand in. Superb. 40%. *Matisse Spirits Co Ltd.*

**Matisse Aged 12 Years (79) n17 t21 f20 b21.** Not sure if some finishing or re-casking has been going on here to liven it up. Has some genuine buzz on the palate, but intriguing weirdness, too. Don't bother nosing this one. 40%. *The Matisse Spirits Co Ltd.*

**Milroy's of Soho Finest Blended Malt (76) n18 t19 f20 b19.** Full flavoured, nutty, malty but hardly textbook. 40%. *Milroy's of Soho.*

**Mo'land (82) n21 t22 f19 b20.** Extra malty but lumbering and on the bitter side. 40%.

**Monkey Shoulder** batch 27 **(79.5) n21 t21.5 f18 b19.** Been a while since I lasted tasted this one. Though this claims to be Batch 27, I assume all bottlings are Batch 27 seeing as they are from 27 casks. This one, whichever it is, has a distinctive fault found especially at the finale, which is disappointing. Even before hitting that point a big toffeed personality makes for a pleasant if limited experience. 40%. *William Grant & Sons.*

**New Town Blends The Advocate's Batch (87.5) n21.5 t22.5 f21.5 b22.** Attractive, pleasant and, though a vatting, simplistic. A youthful catch on the nose suggests development might be limited, but it makes amends by the sheer charm of the light, clean, earnest malt. A lovely dram before lunch, I suggest. *43%. Edinburgh Whisky Ltd.*

⬦ **Old Perth Blended Malt 23 Years Old** dist 1994, bott code: 18/182 **(95)** n24 huge oaky investment takes it to the precipice...but not over it. A mix of coffee and kumquat notes equalises the spices to ensure a delightfully ancient but well-balanced arena; t23.5 like on the nose, the oak is quick to surface. But, again, careful not to take things too far, though; there is a rich malt surge through the middle, despite the big oak and fruity muscovado sugars; f23.5 much drier with a thick paste of vanilla and strained molasses; b24 creakier than a haunted mansion. But full of much more welcoming spirits. This shows its oaky age with the same pride a veteran might display his war wounds. Not even a hint of a single off note: amazing! *44.9%. nc ncf.*

**Old St. Andrews Aged 10 Years Twilight** batch no. L1058 G1048 **(91.5)** n22.5 t23.5 grassy, f22.5 b23 As clean a contact as you ever hope to make and travels a long way. *40%.*

**Old St. Andrews Aged 10 Years Twilight** batch no. L3017 G2716 **(91)** n22 t23.5 f22.5 b23 Takes a different course from the previous batch, eschewing the sharper tones for a more rumbling, deeper and earthier character. Very much above par. *40%.*

**Old St. Andrews Aged 12 Years Fireside** batch no. L2446 G2557 **(89)** n22.5 t22 f22.5 b22 Perfect for those who can't make their mind up between a malt and a G&T in the 19th hole... *40%.*

**Old St. Andrews Aged 12 Years Fireside** batch no. L2927 G2716 **(93)** n23 t23 f23.5 b23.5 Returns to its usual high quality brand which usually makes the cut. *40%.*

**Old St. Andrews Aged 15 Years Nightcap** batch no. L2519 G2557 **(86.5)** n21.5 t22.5 f21 b21.5 A little more fizz on delivery than their last round but then again the finish ends up lost in the long grass. Just too much caramel effect from somewhere. *40%.*

**Old St. Andrews Aged 15 Years Nightcap** batch no. L2976 G2716 **(86)** n22 t21.5 f21 b21.5 Well, this certainly is a nightcap: I fell asleep waiting for something to happen. Pleasant honey at times and chewy toffee but a bit short on the charisma front. *40%.*

**Poit Dhubh 8 Bliadhna (90)** n22.5 t23.5 f21.5 b22.5. Though the smoke which marked this vatting has vanished, it has more than compensated with a complex beefing up of the core barley tones. Cracking whisky. *43%. ncf. Pràban na Linne.*

**Poit Dhubh 12 Bliadhna (77)** n20 t20 f18 b19. Toffee-apples. Without the apples. *43%. ncf. Pràban na Linne.*

**Poit Dhubh 21 Bliadhna (86)** n22 t22.5 f21 b20.5. Over generous toffee has robbed us of what would have been a very classy malt. *43%. ncf. Pràban na Linne.*

**The Pot Still Scotch Vatted Malt Over 8 Years Old (90)** n22 t24 f22 b22. Such sophistication: the Charlotte Rampling of Scotch. *43.5%. ncf. Celtic Whisky Compagnie, France.*

**Prime Blue Pure Malt (83)** n21 t21 f21 b20. Steady, with a real chewy toffee middle. Friendly stuff. *40%*

**Prime Blue 12 Years Old Pure Malt (78)** n20 t20 f19 b19. A touch of fruit but tart. *40%*

**Prime Blue 17 Years Old Pure Malt (88)** n23 t21 f22 b22. Lovely, lively vatting: something to get your teeth into! *40%*

**Prime Blue 21 Years Old Pure Malt (77)** n21 t20 f18 b18. After the teasing, bourbony nose the remainder disappoints with a caramel-rich flatness. The reprise of a style of whisky I thought had vanished about four or five years ago *40%*

**Queens & Kings Kenneth I. MacAlpin (86)** n22 t22 f20.5 b21.5 A brittle, unyielding vatting softened only by delicate smoke and a little but attractive Manuka honey, though the late vanilla is a bit aggressive. *53.7%.*

⬦ **Queens & Kings Mac Bethad mac Findláich (91)** n23 t23 f23 b23.5 Sharp, vivacious, fresh, clean and pulsing. A smoky malt to celebrate here, seemingly making the most of no great age to maximise the salivation levels. Whoever put this together should take a bow, as the taste buds are never given a moment's peace... *54.1%. Mr. Whisky.*

⬦ **Queens & Kings Mary of Guise (87.5)** n22 t22 f21.5 b22 Anyone who has chewed on tart, under-ripe gooseberries in the garden will recognise this whisky's profile. Malty and invigorating, though. *53.4%. Mr. Whisky.*

**Queens & Kings Mary, Queen of Scots (91.5)** n22.5 t23 f23 b23 A very comfortable assembling of malt. Impressed. *55.6%. Mr. Whisky.*

**Queens & Kings Robert The Bruce (88)** n21 t23.5 f21.5 b22 A bit of a wobbly vatting, where the part of the peat and its effects have not been thoroughly thought through. *54%. Mr Whisky*

**Rattray's Selection Blended Malt 19 Years Old Batch 1** Benrinnes sherry hogsheads **(89.5)** n22 t23.5 f21.5 b22.5. Absolutely love it! Offers just the right degree of mouth watering complexity. Not a malt for those looking for the sit-on-the-fence wishy-washy type. *55.8%. Auchentoshan, Bowmore, Balblair & BenRiach. A.D. Rattray Ltd.*

⬦ **Royal Salute 21 Year Old Blended Malt (88.5)** n23 a little brine raises the sharper, more malty edges. Despite the good age, some very young almost green and grassy Speyside notes abounding; **t22** huge, juicy barley sugar arrival followed by a softer caramel middle; **f21.5** more toffee, a little fading malt but a fuzzy finale; **b22** malt and caramel-themed throughout. 40%.

**Saar Whisky Gruwefreund** sherry hogshead, dist 2009, bott 2018 (87) **n22 t22.5 f20.5 b22** Though from a sherry hoggy, it is youthful, salivating malt which dominates, though the bitter-ish out of sync finish doesn't do much for the overall picture. 53.4%. ncf sc. Vatted Malt from the Orkney Distilleries.

**Sansibar Whisky Very Old Vatted (74.5)** **n19 t19 f18 b18.5.** Pretty smoky for a Speyside. But bitter and off key. 45.6%

**Scotch Universe Voyager I 231° U.4.4'F 1886.2"TS** first fill Côte de Beaune wine barrique, dist 1997, bott 2016 (78) **n20 t21 f18 b19** Voyager...that's me! A voyager through the universe of whisky having travelled on for what seems now like lightyears. And despite all the malty planets I have explored, I still don't like whiskies which are either sulphured or over fruity. Or both. 52.9%.

**Scottish Collie (86.5)** **n22 t23 f20.5 b21.** A really young pup of a vatting. Full of life and fun but muzzled by toffee at the death. 40%. Quality Spirits International.

**Scottish Collie 5 Years Old (90.5)** **n22.5 t23 f22 b23.** Fabulous mixing here showing just what malt whisky can do at this brilliant and under-rated age. Lively and complex with the malts wonderfully herded and penned. Without colouring and at 50% abv I bet this would have been given a right wolf-whistle. Perfect for one man and his grog. 40%.

**Scottish Collie 8 Years Old (85.5)** **n22 t21.5 f21 b21.** A good boy. But just wants to sleep rather than play. 40%. Quality Spirits International.

**Scottish Collie 12 Years Old (82)** **n20 t22 f20 b20.** For a malt that's aged 84 in Collie years, it understandably smells a bit funny and refuses to do many tricks. If you want some fun you'll need a younger version. 40%. Quality Spirits International.

**Scottish Leader Imperial Blended Malt (77)** **n20 t20 f18 b19.** Now don't be confused here: this isn't Imperial malt from Speyside. And although it says Blended, it is 100% malt. What is clear, though, is that this is pretty average stuff. 40%. Burn Stewart.

**Scottish Leader Aged 14 Years (80)** **n21 t21 f19 b19.** A cleaner, less peaty version than the no-age statement vatting, but still fails to entirely ignite the tastebuds 40%. Burn Stewart.

**Selkie** batch no. 001, bott code: L13/9097 (94) **n23.5** fingers of salted honey beckon you in. Rare to find oak so blithely doing its job in keeping everything grounded: wonderful harmony; **t23.5** the body of this malt is firm, succulent and demands exploring: the barley is intense and focused and it hard to know exactly where the barley ends and ulmo honey starts; **f23** sexy and spicy as that firm yet yielding body succumbs to a salty finish; **b24** the label keeps abreast of this alluring whisky. I'd happily chew on a nip of this any day... 40%. House of MacDuff.

**Selkie** batch no. 002 (80) **n20 t23 f18 b20** Must be the ugly sister. The nose, finish and overall balance aren't a patch on batch 1. But impossible not to fall in love a little with the mid-point peak, which is rich, alive with creamy mocha and maintains that salty character. Now that bit does get my seal of approval... 50%. House of MacDuff.

**Sheep Dip (84)** **n19 t22 f22 b21.** Young and sprightly like a new-born lamb, this enjoys a fresh, mouthwatering grassy style with a touch of spice. Maligned by some, but to me a clever, accomplished vatting of alluring complexity. 40%

**Sheep Dip 'Old Hebridean' 1990** dist in or before 1990 (94) **n23 t24 f23.5 b23.5.** You honey!! Now, that's what I call a whisky...!! 40%. The Spencerfield Spirit Co.

**Shetland Reel Batch No. 1 (72)** **n18 t22 f15 b17** I am just glad that the sulphur comes from dodgy casks used in this vatting of other distillery's malts and not their own. If this isn't a great lesson for the Shetland lads not to touch sherry butts with a pole that can stretch from Lerwick to Norway, I don't know what is. 47%. 1,800 bottles.

**Shetland Reel Batch No. 2 (90)** **n23.5 t23 f21 b22.5** A rogue sherry butt cannot entirely undo the many excellent qualities of this vatting. 47%. 1,800 bottles.

**Shetland Reel Batch No. 3 (93)** **n23.5 t23.5 f22.5 b23.5.** It has been many a long year since I last visited the Shetlands but the salty bite to this, plus the peat reek on the breeze means someone has created a style well in keeping with the feel of those far off isles. A very satisfying dram. 47%. 1,800 bottles.

**S'Mokey (88)** **n22.5 t22 f21.5 b22.** Delicate, sweet and more lightly smoked than the nose advertises. 40%.

**Smokey Joe Islay Malt (87)** **n21.5 t22 f21.5 b22.** A soft, soporific version of a smoky Islay. No thumping of waves here: the tide is out. 46%. ncf. Angus Dundee Distillers.

⟨⟩ **Smokestack Blended Malt (87)** **n22 t21.5 f22 b21.5** The jolting delivery seems to vividly portray an unusual sharpness on the nose, despite the profound peat. An angular, elbowing malt on nose and arrival but finally relaxes to allow the sugars and oils to combine for a far more attractive, distinguished finale. 46%. The Vintage Malt Whisky Company.

**Son of a Peat** batch no. 01 **(91)** n23.5 t23 f22 b23 Peaty, but not just for peat's sake... *48.3%. nc ncf. Flaviar.*

**Spirit of Caledonia Flaitheanas 18 Years Old (94)** n23.5 t24 f23 b23.5 Now that is a proper vatted malt...!!! *578%. Mr Whisky.*

❖ **St. Ola 8 Year Old 2010 Orcadian Blended Malt (94)** n23 a mere kiddie of a nose, but the delicate smoke dovetails so delightfully with the vaguely nippy spice and the shyest of honey tones; t23.5 just so brilliantly alive and buzzing on delivery with those few atoms of smoke washed by the sheer juiciness of the barley; f23.5 a low smoky groan as the oak stands on tip-toes to make itself as big as possible. And now it is you groaning with approval of the sheer élan of the spice; b24 a young, fresh-faced whisky which just bowls you over with its charm. The high strength ensures the oils remain intact for maximum length and volume. I just wish more whiskies were like this! *66.6%. The Whisky Barrel. 82 bottles.*

**Svenska Eldvatten Blended Malt 1994** ex-sherry butt, dist Aug 94 **(71)** n18 t18 f17 b18. There is nothing I need to say... *54.5%. sc.*

**That Boutique-y Whisky Company Blended Malt No. 2** batch 2 **(84.5)** n21.5 t21 f21.5 b20.5. The sugars are a bit too flash and uncouth. Elsewhere, just a tad too tart and struggles to find a balance. *43.1%. 415 bottles.*

**Treasurer 1874 Reserve Cask (90.5)** n23 t23 f22.5 b22. Some judicious adding has been carried out here in the Robert Graham shop. Amazing for a living cask that I detect no major sulphur faultlines. Excellent! *51%. Live casks available in all Robert Graham shops.*

**Triple Wood Blended Malt Scotch Whisky (77)** n17.5 t22 f18.5 b19. At least one wood too many. Tangy...for all the wrong reasons. *42%. Lidl.*

**Usquaebach Cask Strength 2016 Release (86)** n21.5 t23.5 f20 b21 A curate's egg of a dram. The fruitiness is hit and miss: more miss than hit. But there is also a hugely attractive, shimmering sharpness, also, with the barley sparkling on the palate in fabulous fashion. Sadly, the caramels and then dull tanginess is hardly the progression hoped for. *57.1%. ncf.*

**Vintner's Choice Speyside 10 Years Old (84)** n21.5 t22 f20 b20.5. Pleasant. But with the quality of the Speysiders Grants have to play with, the dullness is a bit hard to fathom. *40%.*

**Waitrose Pure Highland Malt (86.5)** n22 t22 f20.5 b22. Blood orange by the cartload: amazingly tangy and fresh; bitters out at the finish. This is one highly improved malt and great to see a supermarket bottling showing some serious attitude...as well as taste!! Fun, refreshing and enjoyable. *40%*

**Wemyss Family Collection Treacle Chest** 1st fill ex-sherry hogsheads, batch no. 2017/02 **(84.5)** n21.5 t22.5 f20 b20.5 There appears to be mainly clean sherry butts at work here: not perfect but by comparison to most, not too bad. And a mix of date and prune briefly fill the palate on delivery. But after that the lights appear to be switched off and though one can grope around in the dark and enjoy oneself to some extent, there is surprisingly little to stimulate the taste buds after. Just too flat by half. *46%. nc ncf. 6,300 bottles.*

**Wemyss Family Collection Vanilla Burst** 1st fill ex-bourbon barrels, batch no. 2017/01 **(86.5)** n22.5 t22.5 f20 b21.5 A pleasant experience. But you can't help feeling that the casks are slightly neutralising each other rather than adding layers of complexity. The nose does express vanilla and the odd hickory note and the delivery, well, delivers. But by the time we reach the finale there is little in reserve. *46%. nc ncf. 4,800 bottles.*

**Wemyss Malts The Hive (87)** n21.5 t22 f22 b21.5 A lush, easy-drinking dram but one with a surprising lack of high spots: it is as though someone has made the common but fatal mistake of putting together styles that have cancelled each other out – certainly at this strength - rather than bringing the best out of and enhancing the other. No lack of honey and spice, for sure, but also toffee aplenty. *46%. ncf.*

**Wemyss Malts The Hive Batch Strength** batch 001 **(90.5)** n22 t23.5 f22 b23 A lovely malt which is heavily dependent on the honey and spice. And there is nothing wrong with that! *54.5%. ncf. 6,000 bottles.*

**Wemyss Nectar Grove Madeira Wine Cask Finished (88.5)** n22.5 t22.5 f21.5 b22 Soft and beautifully honeyed. *46%. nc ncf.*

**Wemyss Malts Peat Chimney (84.5)** n21.5 t21.5 f21 b20.5 A sharp, muddled malt whose unbalanced kippery nose is a peaty indication of what is to follow. Each avenue explored appears to narrow into a dead end: a tight, restricted, frustrating experience. *46%. ncf.*

**Wemyss Malts Peat Chimney Batch Strength** batch 001 **(87.5)** n22 t23 f21 b21.5 Much more comfortable and happy with itself than the 46% version, mainly thanks to the extra oils allowing the molasses to integrate to greater effect with the smoke. But the tinny, off kilter finale shows that some elements here simply refuse to bond. *57%. ncf. 6,000 bottles.*

**Wemyss Malts Spice King (90)** n23.5 t22.5 f22 b22 A lovely malt, but beyond the nose the spices of note are conspicuous by their absence and not a patch on those found on The Hive... *46%. ncf.*

**Wemyss Malts Spice King Batch Strength Batch 001** (95.5) **n23.5 t24.5 f23.5 b24** Notably different in character and storyline to the 46% version...and here spices are in no shortage whatsoever...! Stunningly gorgeous. *56%. ncf. 6,000 bottles.*

**The Whisky Cask Company Peatside 7 Year Old** PX. sherry cask, bott Feb 17 (84.5) **n22 t21.5 f21 b20** This is my 1,110th new whisky for the 2019 Whisky Bible, and it seems like my 1,000th peat and PX sample. Very few of them particularly excite me. Usually, just too uncouth and showy I'm afraid...a bit like a young person staggering noisily along a Spanish resort in the early hours from one nightclub to another, deliberately wearing very little and no better for alcohol. *60.3%. 317 bottles.*

**Whisky D'arche 5 Ans D'âge** lot no. 250817 (90.5) **n22.5 t23 f22 b23** What a joy of a whisky! Such is the joy of youth! *43% (86 proof).*

**Whisky-Fässle Blended Malt Whisky** very old sherry butt, bott 2016 (87.5) **n23 t23 f20 b21.5** Unquestionably some fruity- and fruit cakey - appeal on the nose with the grape showing both a catholic and zesty personality, and this is matched somewhat in the early moments of the rich delivery. But dulls and bitters out within a short period leaving a lopsided tale being told, all the interesting bits being in the opening chapters. *45.2%.*

**Whisky-Fässle Blended Malt 24 Year Old** sherry hogshead, dist 1993, bott 2018 (94) **n23.5 t23 f23.5 b24** Sherry influence but elegant and clean as a whistle! *54.3%.*

〰 **The Whisky Works King of Trees 10 Year Old Blended Malt** part-finished in native Scottish oak (89.5) **n22 t23 f22 b22.5** A native malt matured in native oak. As neat as the whisky. The fabled tightness of Scottish oak certainly comes out with the punchy tannin on the finish. But the barley itself is crystalline and crisp. *46.5%. nc ncf. 2,157 bottles.*

**Whyte & Mackay Blended Malt Scotch Whisky** (78) **n19 t22 f18 b19.** You know when the engine to your car is sort of misfiring and feels a bit sluggish and rough...? *40%. Waitrose.*

**Wild Scotsman Scotch Malt Whisky (Black Label)** batch no. CBV001 (91) **n23.5 t23.5 f21 b23.** The type of dram you drink from a dirty glass. Formidable and entertaining. *47%*

**Wild Scotsman Aged 15 Years Vatted Malt** (95) **n23 t24 f24 b24.** If anyone wants an object lesson as to why you don't screw your whisky with caramel, here it is. Jeff Topping can feel a justifiable sense of pride in his new whisky: for its age, it is an unreconstituted masterpiece... *46% (92 proof). nc ncf. USA.*

**William Grant & Sons Rare Cask Reserves 25 Years Old Blended Malt Scotch Whisky** (82) **n21 t22 f19 b20.** Mouth-filling, chewy and mildly fruity, doesn't quite grow into the decent start offered and finishes untidily. *47%. Exclusive to The Whisky Shop.*

〰 **World of Orchids Blend of Islay Malt** sherry cask finish, bott 2019 (92) **n23** a pungent, acrid smokiness to this, despite the sherry finish; **t23.5** fresh, clean and salivating. Traces of heather honey mingling with the full-on phenols; **f22.5** chocolate fruit and nut with more than a dab of late smoke, **b23** so often sherry and peat cancel each other out. Here they may not exactly work in tandem, but they certainly ensure some spectacularly intense and juicy moments. One for the thrill-seekers... *53.5%.*

# SCOTTISH RYE
## ARBIKIE
Highlands, 2013. Working.

〰 **Arbikie Highland Rye Aged 3 Years Single Grain Scotch** charred American oak, Pedro Ximenez barrels, cask nos. 9, 11 & 16, dist 2015 db (86.5) **n21 t22 f21.5 b22** And finally...now for something completely different. The final whisky I shall taste for the Jim Murray Whisky Bible 2020, the 1,252st, is Scotland's first commercially bottled rye whisky. It is being sampled here straight after tasting the world's ultimate ryes, Sazerac and Handy from Buffalo Trace, but I was so impressed with this distillery trying something so different, I wanted them to bring the curtain down on this year's Whisky Bible. After tasting 20,027 whiskies for this book since 2003 you would have thought that amongst them would have been the odd Scottish rye or two. But no: no such thing existed. Until now. Is it a classic? No. Is it historic? Most certainly. Is it any good? Well, it isn't bad, but could be a lot better, especially if they got away from this hysteria sweeping the industry in which PX casks have to be used for everything. Had they asked me the very last cask they should use, I would have told them PX...simply because it smothers a distillery's character to death. And here even the rye, the most toothsome grain of them all, vanishes under a welter of moist dates; though a tobacco character (of concern) on the nose is not extinguished. Am I disappointed? No. Because getting rye right is not at all easy and for a new distillery it is even harder. But they would help themselves by ditching the PX and giving the grain a chance to speak. I look forward to visiting them before the 2021 Bible is published and see what they are up to. In the meantime, congratulations. And here's to reaching for the stars... and touching them. *46%. nc ncf. 998 bottles.*

# Scottish Grain

It's a bit weird, really. Many whisky lovers stay clear of blended Scotch, preferring instead single malts. The reason, I am often told, is that the grain included in a blend makes it rough and ready. Yet I wish I had a twenty pound note for each time I have been told in recent years how much someone enjoys a single grain. The ones that the connoisseurs die for are the older versions, usually special independent bottlings displaying great age and more often than not brandishing a lavish Canadian or bourbon style.

Like single malts, grain distilleries produce whisky bearing their own style and signature. And, also, some display characteristics and a richness that can surprise and delight. Most of the grains available in (usually specialist) whisky outlets are pretty elderly. Being made from maize and wheat helps give them either that Canadian or, depending on the freshness of the cask, an unmistakable bourbony style. So older grains display far greater body than is commonly anticipated.

That was certainly underlined in most beautiful and emphatic style by this year's Scotch Grain Whisky of the Year. The Last Drop Dumbarton 1977 had all that you should demand from a magnificent grain and more. Certainly, it was one of only two Scotch whiskies that made it into this year's play offs for World Whisky of the Year.

The fact that it was from Dumbarton was significant. For years, right up until its tragic and unnecessary closure in 2002, this distillery made the core grain for the Ballantine's blends and it was, following the closure of Cambus, without question the producer of the highest quality grain in Scotland. I had worked with it many times in the blending lab and it was as though I had the finest marble to sculpt from. Yet the rare bottlings of it which dripped out into the market place never, or at best rarely, seemed adequately to portray the magnificence of this spirit.

Until this year. For not only did The Last Drop unleash upon us a whisky of staggering beauty, but the Scotch Malt Whisky Society likewise obliged with a 31-year-old 2nd fill ex-bourbon bottling that came in a point behind on 96. I trust the Dumbarton flood gates have now opened....

| Jim Murray's Whisky Bible Scotch Grain of the Year Winners | |
|---|---|
| 2004-07 | N/A |
| 2008 | Duncan Taylor Port Dundas 1973 |
| 2009 | The Clan Denny Dumbarton Aged 43 Years |
| 2010 | Duncan Taylor North British 1978 |
| 2011 | The Clan Denny Dumbarton Aged 40 Years |
| 2012 | The Clan Denny Cambus 47 Years Old |
| 2013 | SMWS G5.3 Aged 18 Years (Invergordon) |
| 2014 | The Clan Denny Dumbarton Aged 48 Years Old |
| 2015 | The Sovereign Single Cask Port Dundas 1978 |
| 2016 | The Clan Deny Cambus 25 Years Old |
| 2017 | Whiskyjace Invergordon 24 Year Old |
| 2018 | Cambus Aged 40 Years |
| 2019 | Berry Bros & Rudd Cambus 26 Years Old |
| 2020 | The Last Drop Dumbarton 1977 |

Caledonian - Cambus

# Single Grain Scotch

## CALEDONIAN Lowland, 1885. Diageo. Demolished.

**The Cally 40 Year Old** refill American oak hogsheads, dist 1974 db **(88.5) n23.5 t23 f20 b22** This poor old sod is tiring before your nose and taste buds. But it hangs on grimly to give the best show it can. Quite touching, really...we are witnessing first hand the slow death of a once great distillery. 53.3%. 5,060 bottles. Diageo Special Releases 2015.

**The Sovereign Caledonian 35 Years Old** refill hogshead, cask no. 14271, dist Feb 82, bott Oct 17 **(87) n22 t22 f21 b22** Caledonian MacBrayn? Caledonian Canal? Caledonian Sea? Amazingly salty and coastal, more so than any grain I have encountered before. It has unique and oddly delicious charm,but runs out of legs well before the finale. 46.9%. nc ncf sc. 154 bottles.

## CAMBUS Lowland, 1836. Diageo. Closed.

**Cambus Aged 40 Years** dist 1975 db **(97) n24.5 t24 f23.5 b25** I chose this as my 600th whisky for Bible 2018: a tragically lost distillery capable of making the finest whisky you might expect to find at 40 years of age. And my hunch was correct: this is flawless. 52.7%. 1,812 bottles Diageo Special Releases 2016.

**Berry Bros & Rudd Cambus 26 Years Old** cask no. 61972, dist 1991, bott 2018 **(96.5) n24 t24 f24 b24.5** Few whiskies this year have displayed so many beguiling twists and turns: a true gem of a grain, though always a bit of a rum do. I can imagine my dear friend of nearly three decades, Doug McIvor, leaping from his seat when he unearthed this sample.... something as rare as any kind of satisfying Charlton Athletic experience... 55.1%. nc ncf sc.

**The Cooper's Choice Cambus 1991** refill sherry butt, cask no. 61982, bott 2018 **(90) n23.5 t24 f20.5 b22** A very good whisky from the Swedish Whisky Fed which will probably make it to the quarter finals of any whisky competition – and then lose to an English malt... 58.5%. sc. Bottled for the Swedish Whisky Federation.

**Glen Fahrn Airline No. 17 Cambus 1991** hogshead, cask no. 79889, bott 2017 **(95.5) n23.5 t24.5 f23.5 b24** My 999th whisky of the 2018 Bible gives up some of the secrets of this sadly lost gem of a distillery 54%. nc ncf sc. 279 bottles.

◈ **The Perfect Fifth Cambus 1976** cask no. 05916, dist 27 Oct 76 **(93) n23.5** classic for the distillery, showing good corn oil and accompanying acacia honey sweetness; the oak offers a delicate Canadian touch; **t24** stunning texture: a rare grain that appears both firm and yielding at the same moment. Also, exceptional crispness to the maple syrup sweetness. Big spices up front balance things beautifully; **f22** begins to show a little age here with a vague bitterness apparent. But the tannins hold their own, as do the remedial sugars; **b23.5** an impressive example of the what then was arguably the finest grain distillery in Scotland. The structure is sound and the Canadian style of whisky is exactly wht should be expected of a fine corn Cambus of this age. There is a slightly nagging bitterness caused by the tiring oak, but the inherent sweetness controls this well. The sugar-spice balance is pretty near perfection. Has the odd fault, but the complexity of the sweet riches outweigh those slightly bitter failings. 57.6%. sc.

◈ **Sansibar Whisky Cambus 1991** bott 2019 **(88) n22** almost rum-like with sweet estery qualities; **t23** incredibly sweet delivery, but spices arrive early to harmonise. No shortage of golden syrup; **f21** bitters out as the cask gives way...; **b22** a rather weak bourbon cask has done this no favours. Some superb moments. 47.7%.

**The Sovereign Cambus 29 Years Old** refill hogshead, cask no. 15010, dist Sept 88, bott Apr 18 **(86) n22 t22.5 f20.5 b21** Lots of fat and bubble gum at play here. Some superb moments on the corn, but never feels entirely at ease with itself, thanks to some stuttering oak. 45.6%. nc ncf sc. 299 bottles.

◈ **The Sovereign Cambus 30 Years Old** refill hogshead, cask no. 14857, dist 1988 **(94) n23.5** such a complex array of cut grass, coconut cake mix and citrus. Neither sweet nor dry; neither light nor heavy...; **t24** such a hard whisky to spit out! The delivery simultaneously moulds to your palate and melts in the mouth. Chocolate lime candy, with its inherent juiciness. You expect spice...you get spice; **f23** just the vaguest bitterness. But those citrus-tinged sugar soon put paid to that...; **b23.5** a good hundred years ago, this grain was bottled and marketed as an equal to a single malt. If the distillery was still alive today a similar campaign would not bring in many complaints. A beauty! 45.2%. nc ncf sc. 313 bottles. Exclusive to The Whisky Barrel.

◈ **The Whisky Cask Company Cambus 27 Years Old** bourbon barrel, cask no. 286, dist 24 Sept 91, bott 29 Nov 18 **(95.5) n24** the complexity levels enter the stratosphere as the extraordinary variance in the oak tones keeps your nose hovering over the grass for a good ten minutes. Teasing mint and chocolate as well as light liquorice and molasses notes gives

245

the vaguest outline of Kentucky to this...; **t24** succulent and sweet on delivery, the corn oils line up abreast of the spicier tannins. A lovely lime fruitiness darts around, plus a sticky date note; **f23.5** muscovado sugars emphasise that underground fruit note; now we are into mocha territory but thickened by the prevailing corn oil and liquorice; **b24** ridiculously beautiful. *57.6%. sc. 286 bottles.*

## CAMERONBRIDGE Lowland, 1824. Diageo. Working.

**Old Particular Cameronbridge 26 Years Old** refill hogshead, cask no. 12233, dist Oct 91, bott Dec 17 **(93) n23** the nuzzling in of the red liquorice, cocoa and Demerara into the corn oils has a distinctive Kentucky burr; **t23.5** as does the delivery which accentuates the oaky positives; ulmo honey and hickory make excellent bedfellows; **f23** a serene butterscotch fade with a hint of light muscovado sugars; **b23.5** a Scotch that wanted to be a bourbon when it grew up... *51.5%. nc ncf sc. 569 bottles.*

**The Sovereign Cameronbridge 26 Years Old** refill butt, cask no. 14752, dist Oct 91, bott Feb 18 **(79) n19 t22 f18 b20** Sweet and fruity but curiously tight on the nose and finish. *56.9%. nc ncf sc. 481 bottles.*

◈ **World of Orchids Cameron Brig 1991 26 Years Old** bourbon cask, cask no. 031 **(94.5) n23.5** heather honey...on a grain!! Distinctly Canadian in style, too; **t23.5** simply fantastic. So soft on delivery, but never overly oily. Salivating with its mix of delicate spices and friendly tannins, then a theme of ulmo honey and butterscotch; **f23.5** glorious milk chocolate, with a light wisp of honey; **b24** truly faultless. Cameron Bridge must have had a hell of a bee invasion back in 1991...! *56.4%. sc.*

## CARSEBRIDGE Lowland, 1799. Diageo. Demolished.

**The Sovereign Carsebridge 44 Years Old** refill hogshead, cask no. 14189, dist May 87, bott Sept 17 **(90) n22.5 t23 f22 b22.5** Very attractive, but about as sweet as you'd like a whisky to go. *50.9%. nc ncf sc. 150 bottles. The Whisky Barrel 10th Anniversary bottling #7.*

**Xtra Old Particular Carsebridge 40 Years Old** refill hogshead, cask no. 11587, dist Oct 76, bott Feb 17 **(96) n24 t24.5 f23.5 b24** Not a bad way to celebrate my 1,001st whisky for the 2018 Bible. Sheer class. *49.9%. nc ncf sc. 148 bottles.*

## DUMBARTON Lowland, 1938. Pernod Ricard. Demolished.

**Fadandel.dk Dumbarton 30 Years Old** cask no. 25241, dist 18 Mar 87, bott 27 Mar 17 **(86) n22 t22.5 f20 b21.5** A clumsy grain festooned with honey and spice, but little ability to bring them happily together. Delicious early on but bitters out as the oak finally cracks. *57.2%. sc. 168 bottles.*

◈ **The Last Drop Dumbarton 1977** cask no. 140000004 **(97) n24.5** almost a cross between a high class bourbon and rye blend, the Demerara sugars magically crisp and clean. Blenders used Dumbarton grain for firmness and backbone. Here, even the nose has a spine to it... vanillas drift around like snow on the wind, the tannins proffering the most understated of spices...; **t24.5** how can a delivery of a whisky over 40 years old be this salivating? This clean? This brittle? Again, it is Demerara to the fore, but now the corn oils coat it with a luxurious softness. Light caramels drift on while, like on the nose, the spice takes its time to make a furtive entry; **f23.5** long, with the vanilla and spice now seeing out the show. The caramels to harden and crisp up in true Dumbarton fashion; **b24.5** Last Drop have been and done it again. They've only gone and found a near faultless barrel from what was once, before it was needlessly destroyed, a near faultless grain distillery. Nothing unusual you'd say, except that this spent 42 years in oak, giving it plenty of time to go wrong. Nothing did, so you have a pristine example of a grain distilled in the year I returned to the UK having hitch-hiked through Africa. And in my flat in Melton Mowbray, which also housed my Press Agency, would always sip a bottle of Chivas Regal...a very different, lighter and more delicate blend than you see today. And this barrel, most likely, was filled to be added to another bottling of Chivas, 12 years on. Instead, it remained in a warehouse seeking perfection...and as near as damn it finding it. *48.7%. sc.*

◈ **Scotch Malt Whisky Society Cask G14.5 31 Year Old** 2nd fill ex-bourbon barrel, dist 1 Oct 86 **(96) n24** brilliant nose: so complex. The oak is beautifully layered and structured. No shouting, no egos, no domination. Custard tart with the lightest shades of Corsican bruyere honey, a speck or two of salt ...;**t24** two-toned. The sugars form a soft moat around the brittle centre of grain and tannin: a truly unique signature and as typical of this distillery as you are likely to find; the slowness of the spice development is almost worthy of legend, as is the chocolate deployment; **f23.5** a slow spice burn and the sexiest praline fade; **b24.5** the confident solidity of this grain stands out like Dumbarton Rock...one of the great whiskies of the year, anywhere in the world. *50.6%. sc.*

**Single Cask Collection Dumbarton 30 Years Old** bourbon barrel **(96) n24 t24.5 f23.5 b24** Taste a whisky like this and you'll fully understand why I regard the destruction of this distillery as one of the greatest criminal acts ever perpetrated against the Scotch whisky industry by the Scotch whisky industry. *52.1%. sc.*

**The Sovereign Dumbarton 30 Years Old** refill barrel, cask no. 14247, dist Mar 87, bott Sept 17 **(92) n23 t23.5 f22.5 b23** Beautiful stuff and those who appreciate Canadian will particularly benefit. But a little tiredness to the oak reminds you of its great age. *55.3%. nc ncf sc. 160 bottles. The Whisky Barrel 10th Anniversary bottling #6.*

**The Sovereign Dumbarton 30 Years Old** refill barrel, cask no. 14327, dist Mar 87, bott Oct 17 **(94) n23.5 t24 f23 b23.5** Practically a re-run of the Single Cask Dumbarton 30, except not all the dots on the sugars are joined. That said, still a whisky work of art. *50.2%. nc ncf sc. 135 bottles.*

◈ **The Sovereign Dumbarton 31 Years Old** refill hogshead, cask no. 15477, dist 1987 **(92) n22.5** a light lavender note introduces a bourbon weightiness; **t23.5** ah....the trademark stiff spine delivery. Rock hard sugars are surrounded by more forgiving corn notes. A slight oiliness to fill the mouth, but the spice-sugar battle is the main attraction through to the finish...; **f23** ....and more of the same...! **b23** Dumbarton's style stood alone among Scotland's grain distilleries: its idiosyncratic style is in full spate here. *50.5%. nc ncf sc. 207 bottles. Exclusive to The Whisky Barrel.*

◈ **The Sovereign Dumbarton 31 Years Old** bourbon barrel, cask no. 15801, dist Mar 87, bott Feb 19 **(86.5) n22 t22.5 f20.5 b21.5** Unusually grassy and fresh for a Dumbarton. The firmness arrives later than normal, though with it an unfortunate bitterness from the cask. *43.5%. nc ncf sc. 186 bottles.*

**The Whisky Barrel Dumbarton 30 Year Old** barrel, cask no. 13436, dist 1987 **(96.5) n24 t24.5 f24 b24** Dumbarton at anything from 21to 30 is about as good as grain whisky gets (hence why Ballantine's can be sensational), providing it has lived in the right cask. And this is the right cask...*56.7%. sc. 197 bottles.*

## GARNHEATH Lowland, 1964. Inver House Distillers. Demolished.

**The Cooper's Choice Garnheath 48 Year Old** dist 1967, bott 2016 **(96) n24 t24 f24 b24** It is an honour to experience a whisky both so rare and gorgeous. Perhaps not the most complex, but what it does do is carried out close to perfection. A must find grain. *41.5%. nc ncf sc. The Vintage Malt Whisky Co.*

## GIRVAN Lowland, 1963. William Grant & Sons. Working.

**The Girvan Patent Still Over 25 Years Old** db **(84.5) n21.5 t21.5 f20.5 b21.** A pretty accurate representation of the character these stills were sometimes quietly known for at this time, complete with some trademark sulphury notes – presumably from the still, not cask, as I do pick up some balancing American white oak character. *42%. nc.*

**The Girvan Patent Still No. 4 Apps** db **(87) n21.5 t22 f21.5 b22.** A first look at probably the lightest of all Scotland grain whiskies. A little cream soda sweetens a soft, rather sweet, but spineless affair. The vanillas get a good, unmolested outing too. *42% WB15/369*

◈ **Berry Bros & Rudd Girvan 12 Years Old** cask no. 532388/9, dist 2006, bott 2018 **(94) n23** a soft aroma with a slightly steely undercarriage. A diluted hickory and butterscotch edge; genteel spice and chalky vanilla; **t24** incredibly soft with the degrees of sweetness going through the gears starting with simple, refined sugars through ulmo honey and settling on a deeper more lingering marzipan. By the mid-point most of the oils have vanished, setting off a degree of countering dryness; **f23** dry vanilla and satisfying spices; light echoes of ulmo honey; **b24** if you wondered why Grant's blends have been so good for so many years, then try out this straight down the line example of their 12-year-old grain. If I were asked in a tasting to describe what I should expect from this distillery at this age, then really this bottling has completely nutshelled it! This is when average equals excellence. *46%. nc ncf sc.*

◈ **Dramfool 20 Girvan 11 Years Old** bourbon cask, dist 2007 **(87) n21.5 t22.5 f21 b22** An old cask has resulted in some major inaction between the oak and the grain. Indeed, we get a very clear look at the spirit itself, which is no bad thing considering how sweet and lush it is. But lacks desired development. *65.1%. nc ncf. 162 bottles.*

◈ **Dramfool 21 Girvan 11 Years Old** bourbon cask, ex-Lagavulin sherry octave, dist 2007 **(92) n23** a far, weightier, earthier grain, the type only ever encountered when an Islay cask is someway involved; **t23.5** in a blend, the delicate smoke notes would be quickly lost. But here, where the oils are rich and buttery, there is a deeply satisfying depth to the delicate phenols. There is a jaw-dropping Manuka honey moment, about a third the way in, brief but stunning; **f22** once they have worn through and the smoke has dispersed, a pleasant vanilla takes hold; **b23.5** the influence of the peat far outweighs any grape notes. Indeed, because of the light character of the spirit, the smoke travels a long way. *64.4%. nc ncf. 64 bottles.*

**The First Editions Girvan Aged 38 Years** refill hogshead, cask no. 14749, bott 2018 **(95) n23.5 t24 f23.5 b24** Wears its age and gravity lightly: this is wonderful grain whisky. *50.3%. nc ncf sc. 302 bottles.*

⚜ **The Great Drams Girvan 11 Years Old** cask no. 300609, dist 27 Jun 07, bott 27 Feb19 **(91.5) n22.5** gentle interplay between unstated vanilla and even more understated spice; **t23.5** fat and sweet on delivery: a flavour and texture, at this age, so very well known by blenders. Icing sugars melts as initially light peppers become more confident; a vanilla blancmange feel to the mid-point; **f22.5** just a little bitterness filters in from the oak, but the warm, pulsing vanilla stills holds sway; **b23** any softer or more shy and this grain would barely escape from your glass. But with some cajoling you end up with a very accurate representation of this distillery for its age. 46.2%. nc ncf sc.

⚜ **Lady of the Glen Girvan 1991** cask no. 54459 **(89.5) n22.5 t23 f22 b22.5** Though seemingly soft and yielding, the sturdy subplot maximises the otherwise limited oak influence. Good spice prickle while late sugars are able to counter the encroaching bitterness. 43.2%. sc.

**Liquid Treasures Entomology Girvan Over 28 Years Old** ex-bourbon barrel, dist 1989, bott 2018 **(86.5) n23 t22 f20.5 b21** A typical pea-souper of a Girvan, thick on the nose with sugary promise and no shortage of oak-encouraged vanilla depth then eye-smartingly sweet delivery with golden syrup mixing in with the oils. A warming sub plot as the spices build but a little disappointing as the oak gives way to bitterness. 52.7%.

**Old Particular Girvan 26 Years Old** refill hogshead, cask no. 11601, dist Dec 89, bott Feb 16 **(88.5) n22 t22.5 f22 b22** Attractive, easy going and ridiculously simplistic. 51.5%. nc ncf sc. 224 bottles.

**Old Particular Girvan 27 Years Old** refill hogshead, cask no. 12191, dist Dec 89, bott Nov 17 **(91) n24 t22.5 f22 b22.5** It's all about the amazing nose, yesiree...! 51.5%. nc ncf sc. 148 bottles.

⚜ **Scyfion Choice Girvan 2006** Islay whisky cask finished, bott 2018 **(92) n23** a Bowmore-style smoky bacon edge to the crystalline sugars; **t23.5** fabulously rotund mouthfeel, the perfect stage for a two-tone peaty attack: one being one the spicy, nippy side, the other a rich, enveloping smokiness; **f22.5** reverts to that Bowmore-style hickory/smoky bacon again...! **b23.5** an intriguing concept brilliantly executed! 46%. nc ncf sc. 90 bottles.

# INVERGORDON Hihghland, 1959. Emperador Distillers Inc. Working.

**Cadenhead's Single Cask International Invergordon 43 Years Old** dist 1973 **(94.5) n23 t24.5 f23.5 b23.5** You are more likely to find a jagged edge on a snooker ball than you are this luscious grain! 51.3%. sc. 175th Anniversary bottling.

**Cave Aquila A Knight's Dram Invergordon 44 Years Old** cask no. 20, dist Dec 72, bott Mar 17 **(95) n24 t24 f23.5 b23.5** You almost want to give the spices a standing ovation... 46.7%. sc.

⚜ **The Cooper's Choice Invergordon 1974 43 Years Old (91) n24 t23 f21.5 b22.5** If the delivery and finish can't quite live up to the nose, that is hardly surprising. This is the aroma of all talents, offering a small grain bourbon type leathery sweetness together with a more genteel vanilla-clad Canadian of high quality. The immediate delivery has a good stab at matching that, and at first succeeds, especially with the depth of the maple syrup and honeycomb. But it understandably fades, then tires late on as the bitterness evolves. 46.5%. nc ncf sc.

**The First Editions Invergordon Aged 45 Years** refill barrel, cask no. 14772, bott 2018 **(94) n23.5 t24 f23 b23.5** Almost a halfway house between ancient grain and a simplistic liqueur. But not so sweet as to be beyond a thing of beauty. 49.6%. nc ncf sc. 230 bottles.

**Old Particular Invergordon 30 Years Old** refill butt, cask no. 12052, dist Aug 87, bott Sept 17 **(83) n21 t23 f19 b20** Some do die for concentrated sultana, but right royally undermined by the dreaded S word... 55%. nc ncf sc. 278 bottles.

**Single Cask Collection Invergordon 26 Years Old** rum barrel finish **(87) n22 t22.5 f21 b21.5** Soft and sweet in the time-honoured Invergordon tradition. But with this amount of sugar at work, it needs to breathe and evolve. Rum casks have a tendency to clip a whisky's wings so, though a very decent and soothing grain, the fun comes to a slightly premature and bitter end. 57.4%. sc.

**The Sovereign Invergordon 30 Years Old** refill hogshead, cask no. 15012, dist May 87, bott Apr 18 **(88) n23** a trip to the candy store...or maybe a bourbon bar...; **t23** the ultra-sweet delivery is predictable, though the muscovado sugars soon have a galaxy of tannin notes to deal with; **f20.5** a tangy bitterness is at odds with the general theme; **b21.5** promises so much, but the oak can't quite match the deal. 51.6%. nc ncf sc. 314 bottles.

# LOCH LOMOND Highland, 1966. Loch Lomond Group. Working.

**Loch Lomond Single Grain** db **(93) n23** crisp sugars are willing to absorb the vanilla; **t23.5** indeed, the sugars on the nose are indicative of a sweet grain, for the delivery centres around the maple syrup lead. The oak is something like most anchors at work: barely visible to invisible; **f23** the oaks do have a say, though you have to wait a while on the long finale. A little spice arrives, too; **b23.5** elegant grain; keeps the sweetness controlled. 46%

**LOCHSIDE** Highland, 1957. Pernod Ricard. Demolished.

**The Cooper's Choice Lochside 44 Year Old** dist 1964, bott 2015 **(92.5)** n23.5 not unlike a bourbon-Canadian blend (yes, I have encountered such a thing) where a muscular coconut-honey candy theme dominates the subservient vanilla; t24 salivating and soft, corn oils drift among the obliging sugars without a care in the world; you can hear the tannins knocking, but only the spices gain entry; f22 back to a coconut toffee thread; bitters late on; b23 it's hangs on in there, giving in to its age only in the final moments... 41.2%. nc ncf sc. The Vintage Malt Whisky Co.

**NORTH BRITISH** Lowland, 1885. Diageo & Edrington. Working.

**Berry Bros & Rudd North British 20 Years Old** cask no. 224754, dist 1996, bott 2017 **(94.5)** n23.5 t24 f23 b24 Let's say you are a blender working on a high grade 21-year-old blend and a sample of this came into your lab as you worked out the next year's batch. You would be thrilled. This gives everything you'd want as it is far from neutral and a few casks of those would bolster your honey profile to sort out any oak from elsewhere which have gone a bit dry and gung ho early on. Exemplary. 54.8%. nc ncf sc.

⬧ **Gordon & MacPhail Connoisseurs Choice North British Aged 28 Years** first fill sherry puncheon, cask no. 73847, dist 23 Oct 90, bott 29 Nov 18 **(82.5)** n21 t21.5 f21 b19 Huge grape, under which the distillery and grain vanishes entirely. Simply too one-dimensional. Delicious as in part it may be, you might as well get a bottle of sherry. 61%. sc. 181 bottles.

**The Sovereign North British 21 Years Old** refill hogshead, cask no. 14409, dist Oct 96, bott Nov 17 **(87)** n22.5 t22 f21 b21.5 A workmanlike grain keeping true to its age and type so far as a blender is concerned, the sharp clarity of the vanilla-tinged icing sugar more than useful. Likewise, the both lush yet underlyingly firm body would be of great use, especially with the marshmallow sweetness. The slight bitterness on the fade can be compensated for in a blend, though harder when a singleton like this. 54.8%. nc ncf sc. 219 bottles.

⬧ **Whisky Krüger North British 26 Years Old 1991** bott 2017 **(88)** n22 a faint spice fizz. But its ultra-friendly vanilla all the way; t23 juicy, sugar coated corn; f21 oily vanilla; b22 despite the sugars a curiously flat grain, but sweet in all the right places. 48.6%. sc.

**NORTH OF SCOTLAND** Lowland, 1957. North of Scotland Distilling Co. Silent.

**The Pearls of Scotland North of Scotland 1971** dist Dec 71, bott Apr 15 **(95.5)** n25 t23.5 f23 b24 What a beautifully elegant old lady...and one with virtually no wrinkles... 43.6%

**PORT DUNDAS** Lowland, 1811. Diageo. Demolished.

**Port Dundas 52 Year Old** refill American oak hogsheads db **(96)** n24.5 t24 f23.5 b24 Note to all other grain whisky bottlers: bourbon casks every time to show the distillery in its true colours: NEVER sherry casks...! 44.6%. 725 bottles. Diageo Special Releases 2017.

⬧ **The Cooper's Choice Port Dundas 1999 18 Years Old** Marsala finish **(87)** n21.5 t22.5 f21 b22 Pleasant enough, especially on delivery with the big grape and delicate spice interplay. But otherwise I don't get it. Grain whisky isn't full-bodied enough to react with wine casks and offer any serious complexity. And this is a lost distillery here being overwhelmed so its unique character is lost. That said, if you are looking simply for delicious, muscular spiced fruit, here's your dram! 53%. nc ncf sc.

**Old Particular Port Dundas 12 Years Old** refill barrel, cask no. 11340, dist Jun 04, bott Sept 16 **(84.5)** n22 t22 f20 b20.5 Grain ordinaire. Plenty of sugary if one dimensional flavour on delivery but the finish is a bit clumsy and bitter. 48.4%. nc ncf sc. 247 bottles.

**Old Particular Port Dundas 12 Years Old** refill barrel, cask no. 11758, dist Jul 04, bott Jun 17 **(91)** n22.5 t23 f22.5 b23 When you wanted your blend to sparkle a little bit, this was the kind of grain you'd look out for. What an enormous loss this is to the industry... 48.4%. nc ncf sc.

**Old Particular Port Dundas 28 Years Old** refill hogshead, cask no. 11526, dist Oct 88, bott Nov 16 **(92.5)** n23.5 t23 f22.5 b23.5 Port Dundas' uniquely rich yet delicate style is in full spate here. 51.8%. nc ncf sc. 205 bottles.

**The Sovereign Port Dundas 27 Years Old** refill hogshead, cask no. 14451, dist Feb 90, bott Nov 17 **(91.5)** n23 Fox's Party Rings biscuits; t23.5 light corn oils can't distract from the German caramelised biscuit; f22 most of the oils have burned off to leave roasty bourbon creams; b23 simply takes the biscuit. 51.5%. nc ncf sc. 258 bottles.

**The Sovereign Port Dundas 28 Years Old** refill hogshead, cask no. 13046, dist Oct 88, bott Nov 16 **(94.5)** n24.5 t24 f22.5 b23.5 Another lost distillery showing magnificently and why blended whisky is not going to improve anytime soon... 55.1%. nc ncf sc. 253 bottles.

**That Boutique-y Whisky Company Port Dundas 25 Year Old** batch 1 **(95)** n24 t24 f23 b24.5 A little bit special... 48.2%. 115 bottles.

**World of Orchids Port Dundas 24 Year Old** bourbon cask, dist 1989 **(92)** n22 t24 f23 b23 Don't expect great complexity...just a whole lot of technically faultless deliciousness. 56.1%.

# STRATHCLYDE Lowland, 1927. Pernod Ricard. Working.

**Glasgow Gardens Festival 30th Anniversary Strathclyde 30 Year Old 1988** cask no. 62125, dist 9 Jun 88, bott 10 Jun 18 (87) n22 t23 f20.5 b21.5 I think I remember Hunter Laing bringing out a 30-year-old Strathclyde last year which surprised me with its gentle good manners. This is probably much closer to what I was expecting, with the rough edges of the distillery at that time clearly on display here, despite a flurry of superb golden syrup notes on delivery. 54.3%. sc. Exclusive to The Whisky Barrel. 138 bottles.

**Old Particular Strathclyde 11 Years Old** sherry butt, cask no. 11952, dist Nov 05, bott Jul 17 (91) n22 t23.5 f22 b23.5 Not just a sherry butt! But a clean, 100% untainted, entirely sulphur-free sherry butt! Fabulous! 55.5%. nc ncf sc. 638 bottles.

**Old Particular Strathclyde 25 Years Old** refill barrel, cask no. 11335, dist Aug 90, bott Sept 16 (87) n21.5 t22 f21.5 b22 A tangy beast with a metallic feel that subdues the sweetness which had gathered after delivery. Plenty of nip and bite, which is fun, but refuses to settle. 51.5%. nc ncf sc. 116 bottles.

**Old Particular Strathclyde 26 Years Old** refill barrel, cask no. 11600, dist Aug 90, bott Mar 17 (94) n23 an oscillating aroma: higher and lower notes arrive from all directions, making for both complexity and confusion. Both green apple and liquorice make telling contributions; t24 a stark, salivating, corn-fuelled, starchy delivery, then a second stage of intense muscovado sugars before the vanillas arrive; f23.5 busy and a little bitter, as though a metallic element is in short supply; b23.5 offers that peculiar complexity you get from old rums made on stills with perhaps slightly below average degrees of copper in the system. Uncanny. 55.5%. nc ncf sc. 174 bottles.

**The Sovereign Strathclyde 26 Years Old** refill barrel, cask no. 13045, dist Aug 90, bott Nov 16 (77) n19 t21 f18 b19 The pugnacious, lightly off-key nose offers fair warning of the Brillo pad delivery which scratches some unforgiving sugars onto the palate. The finish, though, suffers from a mixture of poor original distillate and a cask without the means to compensate. 54.5%. nc ncf sc. 241 bottles.

**The Sovereign Strathclyde 28 Years Old** refill barrel, cask no. 15804, dist Aug 90, bott Feb 19 (90) n22.5 distinctly Canadian style; t23 sweet vanilla bordering on custard, spoonfuls of demerara sugar...; f22 superb spice grumble; b22.5 looks like Strathclyde were still going through a corn mash at this time, so soft, sweet and oily is this. Very un-Strathclyde for the era in its untroubled shifting through the gears. 51.1%. nc ncf sc. 198 bottles.

**The Sovereign Strathclyde 30 Years Old** refill hogshead, cask no. 14448, dist Sept 87, bott Nov 17 (90) n22 t22 f23.5 b22.5 It is as though the grain has fallen asleep after 30 years and finally wakes up late in the day. 50.7%. nc ncf sc. 175 bottles.

**That Boutique-y Whisky Company Strathclyde 30 Year Old** batch 1 (87.5) n22 t22.5 f21 b22 A grain that gives you a right punch in the throat on delivery. The sugars are profound but without structure and of very limited complexity. 53.1%. 228 bottles.

# UNSPECIFIED SINGLE GRAIN

**Borders** finished in Oloroso sherry casks (66) n15 t18 f15 b18. Finished being the operative word. Has no-one been listening regarding the total mess sherry butts are in. I wonder why I bother sometimes. Jeez... 51.7%. nc ncf. R&B Distillers.

**Haig Club** toasted oak casks (89) n21.5 t23 f22.5 b22 When I first saw this, I wasn't quite sure whether to laugh or cry. Because 25 years ago bottles of single grain whisky were the unique domain of the flat cap brigade, the miners and other working class in the Kirkcaldy area of Scotland. Their grain, Cameron Brig, would be drunk with a splash, mixed with Coke or ginger, even occasionally with Irn Bru, or straight and unmolested as a chaser to the ubiquitous kegged heavy, McEwan's lager or a bottle of Sweetheart stout. When I suggested to the hierarchy at United Distillers, the forerunners of Diageo, that in their finer grains they had a product which could conquer the world, the looks I got ranged from sympathy for my lack of understanding in matters whisky to downright concern about my mental well being. I had suggested the exquisite Cambus, now lost to us like so many other grain distilleries in those passing years, should be brought out as a high class singleton. It was pointed out to me that single grain was, always had been and always will be, the preferred choice of the less sophisticated; those not wishing to pay too much for their dram. Fast forward a quarter of a century and here sits a gorgeously expensive bottle in a deep cobalt blue normally associated with Ballantine's and a very classy, heavyweight stopper. In it is a grain which, if the advertising is to be believed, is the preferred choice not of the back street bar room idlers carefully counting their pennies but of its major ambassador David Beckham: it is the drop to be savoured by the moneyed, jet-set sophisticates. My, oh my. Let's not call this hype. Let's just say it has taken some genius exec in a suit half a lifetime – and probably most of his or hers - to come around to my way of thinking and convince those in the offices on the floor above to go for it. Wonder if I qualify for 10 percent of profit for suggesting it all those years back...or, preferably, five percent of their advertising budget. Meanwhile, I look forward to watching David pouring this into some of his Clynelish and Talisker. After all, no-one can Blend it like Beckham... *40%. WB15/408*

**Haig Club Clubman (87.5)** n22 t22 f21.5 b22 A yieldingly soft and easy-as-you-like and at times juicy grain with a pleasant degree of light acacia honey to make friendlier still. *40%.*

❖ **Haig Club Clubman** bourbon casks, bott code: L90860U002 **(87.5)** n21 t22.5 f21.5 b22 Once you get past the caramel on both nose and finish it is easy to be drawn into enjoying this sweet grain which seems to glisten with acacia honey influence. *40%.*

**Svenska Eldvatten Grain 1964** ex-bourbon barrel, dist Dec 72, bott Mar 16 **(95)** n23.5 t24 f23.5 b24 I remember a couple of years back someone publicly poured scorn on me for saying blends now are vastly different to yesteryear because of the grain. Well, look at the way corn has shaped this baby: far closer to Canadian or even bourbon (or US Corn Whiskey to be more precise) than today's Scotch because of the extraordinary effect of the maize... *52.1%. sc.*

**Whisky-Fässle Lowland Single Grain 52 Year Old** barrel, dist 1964, bott 2016 **(90.5)** n23 huge caramel...with a little squashed sultana for company; t23 soft and sensuous as a great grain should be. Salivating, too, after the initial caramel and vanilla surge has quietened. Some very serious chocolate through the middle section; f21.5 the caramel continues, then takes a slightly fruitier pose – before constricting slightly; b23 although from a barrel, the mystery fruitiness is there in all its strengths and weaknesses... *47.7%.*

❖ **The Whisky Works Glaswegian 29 Year Old Single Grain (92)** n23.5 t23.5 f22 b23 Not often you get ginger on the nose of a grain whisky, but this one obliges. Signs of a mis-spent youth here, as this shows all the classic signs of a roughhouse whisky when young, a bit of the Gorbals, and though still shewing the odd scar or two, now has a real touch of polished old school, debonair recalcitrance about it. *54.2%. nc ncf. 1,642 bottles.*

**WoodWinters The Five Distinguished and Rare Aged 39 Years (93)** n22.5 t24 f23 b23.5 A grain of marvellous pedigree and integrity, at least equal to the vast majority of single malts whiskies you will find...*51%. sc. 330 bottles.*

# Vatted Grain

**Angus Dundee Distillers Blended Grain 50 Year Old (91.5)** n23 as old and creaking as a soon to retire Chelsea centre-half. Has given great service, but definitely a few cracks where there had been none a few years before. That said, the very light eucalyptus and heather honey work together charmingly; t23.5 as silky as an Antonio Conte title winning side. Soaks up layers of tannins and counter attacks quickly with thrusting vanilla and ulmo honey; f22 good spice helps deflect from the tiring oak; b23 just champion...! *40.1%.*

**Compass Box Hedonism** first fill American oak cask, bott 20 Feb 13 **(84)** n22 t22 f19 b20. Just too fat, too sweet and too bitter at the finale to work to great effect. Some decent oak on both nose and delivery, though. *43%. nc ncf. Compass Box Whisky Company.*

**Compass Box Hedonism Maximus (93.5)** n25 t22.5 f23 b23. Bourbon Maximus... *46%*

**Compass Box Hedonism The Muse** bott Feb 18 **(89)** n23 t23 f21 b22 A fruit fly landing in a whisky while it is waiting to be tasted is always a good sign: these things know where to find sweetness. *53.3%. nc ncf.*

**Compass Box Hedonism Quindecimus (88.5)** n22.5 t22 f22 b22 Sweet and refreshingly ordinary grain. Well made and unspectacularly delicious. *46%*

**The Cooper's Choice Golden Grain 51 Year Old** dist 1964, bott 2016 **(87.5)** n22 t23.5 f20 b22 A lovely vatted grain with as many spoonfuls of honey as you like. Sadly, some tired oak radiates some significant bitterness at the death. *51%. nc ncf sc. The Vintage Malt Whisky Co.*

**Count Cristo** bott code: L7117HA8 **(89)** n22.5 t22.5 f22 b22 "Learning does not make one learned: there are those who have knowledge and those who have understanding. The first requires memory and the second philosophy." This is a whisky worth trying to understand. *40%.*

**The Sovereign Blended Grain 28 Years Old** bourbon barrel, cask no. 13327, dist Dec 64, bott Mar 17 **(96)** n24.5 t24 f23.5 b24 May be completely wrong, but a theory. There is a dryness here which suggests big age, maybe so big that the strength of a barrel fell below 40%abv... so had to be added to another to restore it back to whisky again. As I say: just a theory. But it'd fit the structure of this beautifully fragile old grain perfectly. *47.9%. nc ncf sc. 221 bottles.*

**William Grant & Sons Rare Cask Reserves 25 Years Old Blended Grain Scotch Whisky (92.5)** n23 t23.5 f23 b23. A really interesting one, this. In the old days, blenders always spent as much time vatting the grains together as they did the malts, for if they did not work well as a unit it was unlikely harmony would be found in their blend. A long time ago I was taught to, whenever possible, use a soft grain to counter a firmer one, and vice versa. Today, there are far fewer blends to choose from, though 25 years ago the choice was wider. So interesting to see that this grain is soft-dominated with very little backbone at all. Delicious. But screams for some backbone. *47%. Exclusive to The Whisky Shop.*

# Scottish Blends

**I**f any whisky is suffering an identity crisis just now, it must be the good old Scottish blend.

Once the staple, the absolute mainstay, of the Scotch whisky industry it has seen its market share increasingly buried under the inexorable, incoming tide that is single malt. But worse, the present-day blender has his hands tied in a way no previous generation of blenders has had before.

Now stocks must be monitored with a third eye, one that can judge the demand on their single malt casks and at increasingly varied ages. Worse, the blender cannot now, as was once the case, create blends with subtly shifting textures - the result of carefully using different types of grain. So many grain distilleries have closed in the last quarter of a century that now most blends seem remarkably similar to others. And there is, of course, the problem of sherry butts which has been fully documented over the years in the Whisky Bible.

For Jim Murray's Whisky Bible 2018 I tasted or re-tasted 128 blends in total, a quite significant number. And there is no doubt that the lack of choice of grain for blenders is beginning to pose a problem for the industry. What was particularly noticeable was the number of blends which now lack a crisp backbone and have softened their stance, making them chewy and pliable on the palate but often lacking the crispness which can maximise the complexity of the malts on display. By the time you add in the caramel, the results can sometimes be just a little too cloying.

Naturally, it was the bigger blenders - those possessing by far the largest stocks - who best escaped this narrowing down of style among the younger blends in particular, as the always impressive Ballantine's Finest displayed its usual structured enormity with aplomb to once more pick up an award.

It is fascinating, and to the purist heart-warming, that after a short succession of either very old or very young blends being named as the Whisky Bible's Scottish Blend of the Year, once more it is the incomparable Ballantine's 17, whose default mode of understated and intricate complexity of the most delicate kind - which has so far remained unaltered - that again breasted the tape ahead of the others. Curiously, though, it is now exactly 17 years since the Dumbarton distillery, the main provider of its sublime grain, closed down. Will we soon be seeing the effect of this?

| Jim Murray's Whisky Bible Scottish Blend of the Year Winners | |
|---|---|
| 2004 | William Grant's 21 Year Old |
| 2005 | William Grant's 21 Year Old |
| 2006 | William Lawson Aged 18 Years |
| 2007 | Old Parr Superior 18 Years Old |
| 2008 | Old Parr Superior 18 Years Old |
| 2009 | The Last Drop |
| 2010 | Ballantine's 17 Years Old |
| 2011 | Ballantine's 17 Years Old |
| 2012 | Ballantine's 17 Years Old |
| 2013 | Ballantine's 17 Years Old |
| 2014 | Ballantine's 17 Years Old |
| 2015 | The Last Drop 1965 |
| 2016 | The Last Drop 50 Years Old |
| 2017 | The Last Drop 1971 |
| 2018 | Compass Box The Double Single |
| 2019 | Ballantine's 17 Years Old |
| 2020 | Ballantine's 17 Years Old |

## Scottish Blends

**100 Pipers (74) n18.5 t18 f19 b18.5.** An improved blend, even with a touch of spice to the finish. I get the feeling the grains are a bit less aggressive which they for so long were. I'd let you know for sure, if only I could get through the caramel. *40%. Chivas.*

**100 Pipers** bott code LKVK2677 2016/07/01 **(74) n18 t19 f19 b18** These 100 Pipers deserve an award. How can they have played for so many years and still be so off key and out of tune? It is an art form, I swear. I feel like giving the blend a special gong for so many years of consistent awfulness. *40%. Chivas Brothers Ltd.*

**The Antiquary** bott code L 02 08 16 **(86) n20 t22 f22 b21** Appears to be going along the present day trend of spongy, super soft grain which doesn't always do the best of favours to the obviously high quality malt in here. Pleasantly sweet and chewy with an attractive base note. *40%. Tomatin Distillery.*

**Antiquary 12 Years Old (92) n23.5 t23.5 f22 b23** A staggering about turn for a blend which, for a very long time, has flown the Speyside flag. *40%. Iomatin Distillery.*

**The Antiquary Aged 12 Years** bott code L 17 12 15 **(87.5) n21.5 t22 f22 b22** The smoke I so well remember from previous bottlings appears to have dispersed. Instead we have an ultra-lush blend dependent on molasses and spice to punch through the major toffee. *40%. Tomatin Distillery.*

**Antiquary 21 Years Old (93) n23.5 t23.5 f23 b23** A huge blend, scoring a magnificent 93 points. But I have tasted better, and another sample, direct from the blending lab, came with even greater complexity and less apparent caramel. A top-notch blend of rare distinction. *43%*

**The Antiquary Aged 21 Years** bott code 2016/02/29 LK30215 **(92.5) n23** some very confident weight on the nose here: gentle, though slightly earthy, smoke mingles with the orange blossom honey; **t23.5** excellent delivery: caramel and dates hold the fort until an oily smokiness turns up. Never less than succulent; **f23** a beautiful lime note is the perfect match for the gently smoked mocha and spice; a very slight tang at the death; **b23** if you are not sure what I mean by a beautifully paced whisky, try this and find out. *43%. Tomatin Distillery.*

**The Antiquary Aged 35 Years** bott code L 24 08 15 **(96.5) n24 t24 f24 b24.5** Enjoy some of the grains involved in this beauty: their type and ability to add to the complexity is, tragically, a dying breed: the hardest whisky I have found so far to spit out...and I'm on dram number 530...! Antiquary's late, great blender, Jim Milne, would shed a tear of joy for this creation of unreconstructed beauty and brilliance, as this was just out of his school of elegance. *46%. Tomatin Distillery.*

**Ballaglass Blended Scotch Whisky (85) n21 t22 f21 b21.** Perfectly enjoyable, chewy – but clean – blend full of toffee and fudge. Very good weight and impressive, oily body. *40%.*

**Ballantine's Aged 12 Years (84.5) n22.5 t22 f19 b21.** Attractive but odd fellow, this, with a touch of juniper to the nose and furry bitter marmalade on the finish. But some excellent barley-cocoa moments, too. *43%. Chivas.*

**Ballantine's 12 Years Old (87) n21 t22 f21 b23.** The kind of old-fashioned, mildly moody blend Colonel Farquharson-Smythe (retired) might have recognised when relaxing at the 19th hole back in the early '50s. Too good for a squirt of soda, mind. *40%. Chivas Bros.*

**Ballantine's 17 Years Old (97.5) n24.5 t24 f24 b25** Now only slightly less weighty than of old. After a change of style it has comfortably reverted back to its sophisticated, mildly erotic old self. One of the most beautiful, complex and stunningly structured whiskies ever created. Truly the epitome of great Scotch. *43%.*

**Ballantine's Aged 21 Years (94) n23.5 t24 f23.5 b24** Even though the strength has been reduced, presumably to eke out rare stocks, the beauty of this blend hasn't. *40%*

**Ballantine's Aged 30 Years (95.5) n24.5 t24 f23 b24** A fascinating malt, slightly underpowered perhaps, which I have had to put to one side and keep coming back to see what it will say and do next... *40%.*

**Ballantine's Aged 30 Years** bott code LKRK1934 2016/05/16 **(96) n24.5 t24 f22.5 b24** Practically a replay of the bottle I tasted last year, right down to that very late, barely perceptible furriness. Simply one of the world's most sensual drams... *40%. Chivas Brothers Ltd.*

◈ **Ballantine's Barrel Smooth** finished in double charred barrels, bott code: 2018/11/08 **(87.5) n22 t22 f21.5 b22** A cream toffee-rich blend concentrating on molasses and caramel. A real super-soft member of the Ballantine's family, but possessing only a fraction of the age-statement bottlings' complexity. *40%.*

**Ballantine's Finest (96) n24 t24 f23.5 b24.5** As a standard blend this is coming through as a major work of art. Each time I taste this the weight has gone up a notch or two more and the sweetness has increased to balance out with the drier grain elements. Take a mouthful of this and experience the work of a blender very much at the top of his game. *40%. Chivas Bros.*

**Ballantine's Finest** bott code LKEK4068 2016/10/04 **(96) n23.5 t24 f24 b24.5** The consistency and enormity of this blend fair staggers me. It is often my go to blend when travelling the world as I pretty much know what I'll get, within its normal parameters. This bottling has a little extra sweetness on the smoke but exceeds expectation on the finish with a slightly more clever use of the spices and Demerara sugars as they merge with the peat. Just such a big and satisfying experience. 40%. *Chivas Brothers Ltd*

**Ballantine's Hard Fired** (86.5) n22 t22 f21 b21.5. Despite the smoky and toasty elements to this, you're left waiting for it to take off....or even go somewhere. Perhaps just a little too soft, friendly and grain indulgent. Decent, enjoyable blend, of course, but a little out of the Ballantine's usual circle of high class friends. 40%

**Ballantine's Limited release no. A27380** (96) n24 t24.5 f23.5 b24 Each Limited release has a slightly different stance and this one holds its posture with more debonair, lighter-on-foot poise. The vague furry note of recent bottlings is missing here or, rather, is of the least consequence. The fruit, also, is more of a sheen than a statement more room for the malt and vanilla to play and the spices to impart age. It may be soft on both nose and palate – especially the delivery – as the grains have obviously been vatted to create minimum traction, but it is a blend of quiet substance. Another Ballantine's brand this year hitting the 96 or more mark. Astonishing, absolutely astonishing...more a case of Ballantine's Unlimited... 40%. *Chivas Brothers Ltd.*

**Ballantine's Master's** (82) n21 t22 f19 b20. Excellent lively grain and chewy malt, but the always suspect, grain-drizzled finish has become even more nondescript in recent bottlings. 40%

**Ballantine's Master's** bott code LKAK1001 2016/03/09 (85) n21 t22 f21 b21 The label promises a "fresh take" on this blend. And I admit, it is far more agreeable than before with a little coconut oil and apple helping to give it a lift and the sugars herded into attractive use. But still far too dependent on caramel input, which may round the whisky but flattens it all rather too well. 40%. *Chivas Brothers Ltd.*

**Ballantine's Rare Limited** (89.5) n23.5 t22.5 f21.5 b22 A heavier, more mouth watering blend than the "Bluebottle" version. 43%. *ncf. Chivas.*

**Bell's Original** (91) n23 t22.5 f22.5 b23 Your whisky sleuth came across the new version for the first time in the bar of a London theatre back in December 2009 during the interval of "The 39 Steps". To say I was impressed and pleasantly surprised is putting it mildly. And with the whisky, too, which is a massive improvement on the relatively stagnant 8-year-old especially with the subtle extra smoky weight. If the blender asks me: "Did I get it right, Sir?" then the answer has to be a resounding "yes". 40%

**Bells 8 Years Old** (85) n21.5 t22.5 f20 b21. Some mixed messages here: on one hand it is telling me that it has been faithful to some of the old Bells distilleries – hence a slight dirty note, especially on the finish. On the other, there are some sublime specks of complexity and weight. Quite literally the rough and the smooth. 40%. *Diageo.*

**Black & White** (91) n22 t23 f22.5 b23.5 This one hasn't gone to the dogs: quite the opposite. I always go a bit misty-eyed when I taste something this traditional: the crisp grains work to maximum effect in reflecting the malts. A classic of its type. 40%. *Diageo.*

**Black Bottle** (74.5) n18 t20.5 f17 b18. Barely a shadow of its once masterful, great self. 40%.

**Black Bottle** bott code 2038310 L3 16165 (94.5) n23.5 t23.5 f23.5 b24 Not the byword for macho complexity it was 15 years ago but after a lull in its fortunes it is back to something that can rightfully boast excellence. Brilliant. 40%.

**Black Bottle 10 Years Old** (89) n22 t23 f22 b23 A stupendous blend of weight and poise, but possessing little of the all-round steaming, rampaging sexuality of the younger version... but like the younger version showing a degree less peat: here perhaps even two. Not, I hope, the start of a new trend under the new owners. 40%

**Black Dog 12 Years Old** (92) n21 t23 f24 b24. Offering genuine sophistication and élan. This minor classic will probably require two or three glass-fulls before you take the bait... 42.8%

**Black Grouse** (94) n23 t24 f23 b24. A superb return to a peaty blend for Edrington for the first time since they sold Black Bottle. Not entirely different from that brand, either, from the Highland Distillers days with the smokiness being superbly couched by sweet malts. 40%

**The Black Grouse Alpha Edition** (72.5) n17 t19.5 f17 b18. Dreadfully sulphured. 40%

**Black Hound** (83) n21 t21.5 f21 b20.5 Here's to Max! Max grain in this but no complaints here as the relatively limited caramel doesn't spoil the enjoyment of what feels like (though obviously isn't) a single distillery output. Crisp at first, then succulent, chewy cream toffee. 40%. *Quality Spirits International.*

⬦ **Black Scott 3 Years Old** bott code: 3L08460154 (85.5) n20.5 t22 f21.5 b21.5 Pretty standard, though not unattractive fare. The nose is a bit of a struggle but relaxes on delivery and even entertains with a spicy blitz. 40%. *Toorank Productions BV.*

**Black Stripe** (77) n19 t20 f19 b19 Untidy without character. 40%. *Quality Spirits International.*

**Blend No. 888** (86.5) n20 t21.5 f23 b22. A good old-fashioned, rip-roaring, nippy blend with a fudge-honey style many of a certain age will fondly remember from the 60s and 70s. Love it! 40%. *The House of MacDuff.*

**Blend No. 888** bott code L15/8185 (84.5) n21 t22 f20.5 b21 Light, breezy and sweet, this is grain dominant and makes no effort to be otherwise. Soft, untaxing and pleasant. 40%. *House of MacDuff.*

**Boxes Blend (90)** n22.5 t23.5 f21 b23. A box which gets plenty of ticks. *40.9%. ncf.*

**Buchanan's De Luxe 12 Years Old (82)** n18 t21 f22 b21. The nose shows more than just a single fault and the character simply refuses to get out of second gear. Certainly pleasant, and some of the chocolate notes towards the end are gorgeous. But just not the normal brilliant show-stopper! *40%. Diageo.*

**Buchanan's Master** bott code: L7313CE001 **(94.5)** n24 t23.5 f23 b24 Some 40-odd years ago I was in love with Buchanans: it was one of the truly sophisticated blends from which I learned so much and this pays homage to the legacy. On the down side the grains are nowhere near so complex and the vague furry bitterness at the end tells its own tale. But I doff my Panama to blender Keith Law in genuine respect: works like this don't just happen and this is a blended Scotch worthy of the name. *40%.*

**Cadenhead's Putachieside Aged 12 Years (91)** n23 no shortage of citrus and vanilla: fresh, and the flaky, puff-pastry topping is fitting; t23 the sugars and oils make an early assault. A little bitterness from the oak creeps in; f22 malty-lemon sawdust; b23 not tasted for a while and delighted to re-discover this understated little gem. Also, has to be one of the best labels of any scotch going... *40% WB15/357*

**Campbeltown Loch (94)** n23 t24 f23.5 b23.5 Over 30 years ago, this blend was one of my preferred drams at home. Not seen it for a while, so disappeared from The Bible. Found again and though it has changed a little in structure, its overall excellence takes me back to when I was a young man. *40% WB15/355*

**Campbeltown Loch Aged 15 Years (88)** n22.5 t22.5 f21 b22 Well weighted with the age in no hurry to arrive. *40%. Springbank Distillers.*

**Cambeltown Loch 21 Years Old** db **(83)** n21 t23 f19 b20 Neither the nose or finish are much to write home about, the latter being a little tangy and bitter. But the delivery is rich and comforting: like a Digestive biscuit dunked in coffee. A seemingly decent malt content and a bit of toffee before the furry finale. *46%. WB15/102*

**Castle Rock (81)** n20 t20.5 f20 b20.5. Clean and juicy entertainment. *40%*

**Catto's Aged 25 Years (85.5)** n22 t22.5 f19.5 b21.5. A hugely enjoyable yet immensely frustrating dram. The higher fruit and spice notes are a delight, but it all appears to be played out in a padded cell of cream caramel. One assumes the natural oak caramels have gone into overdrive. Had they not, we would have had a supreme blend scoring well into the 90s. Elsewhere the increased furriness on the finale has not improved matters. *40%*

**Catto's Aged 25 Years** bott code RV9499 **(94.5)** n23 the accent, as one might hope, is on varying degrees of honey: here ulmo and orange blossom have joint star billing in this very soft and friendly performance; t24 excellent grains are at the vanguard of a glorious charm offensive: maple syrup, Lubek marzipan and barley sugar dissolves slowly into the vanillas; f23 even as the sugars fade enough light spices rises to meet the demands of the oak; b24.5 a far better experience than the last time I officially tasted a Catto's 25 seven or eight years ago. Both malts and grains are of the charming style once associated with Catto's Rare : so jaw-droppingly elegant... *40%. International Beverage Holdings Ltd.*

**Catto's Deluxe 12 Years Old (79.5)** n20 t21.5 f18 b20. Refreshing and spicy in part, but still a note in there which doesn't quite work. *40%. Inverhouse Distillers.*

**Catto's Deluxe 12 Years Old** bott code L 18 03 16 **(86.5)** n21.5 t22 f21.5 b21.5 A safe, sweet and sumptuous blend which places major emphasis on the molasses. Won't win any beauty contests but there is a weighty earthiness, also. *40%. International Beverage Holdings Ltd.*

**Catto's Rare Old Scottish (92)** n23.5 t23.5 f22 b23 Currently one of my regular blends to drink at home. Astonishingly old-fashioned with a perfect accent on clean Speyside and crisp grain. In the last year or so it has taken on a sublime sparkle on the nose and palate. An absolutely masterful whisky which both refreshes and relaxes. *40%. James Catto & Co.*

**Catto's Rare Old Scottish** bott code L 25 01 16 **(83)** n20.5 t21 f20.5 b21 Once fresh as dew on morning grass, this has changed in recent years with a different grain profile which no longer magnifies the malt. Adopted a rougher, more toffeed approach from its once clean cut personality: not even a close approximation of the minor classic it once was. *40%. International Beverage Holdings Ltd.*

**Chequers Deluxe (78.5)** n19.5 t20 f19 b20. Charm, elegance, sophistication...not a single sign of any of them. Still if you want a bit of rough and tumble, just the job. *40%. Diageo.*

**The Chivas 18 Ultimate Cask Collection First Fill American Oak (95.5)** n24 t23.5 f24 b24 Immeasurably superior to any Chivas 18 I have tasted before. A true whisky lover's whisky... *48%. ncf.*

**Chivas Regal Aged 12 Years (83.5)** n20.5 t22.5 f20 b20.5. Chewy fruit toffee. Silky grain mouth-feel with a toasty, oaky presence. *40%. Chivas.*

**Chivas Regal Aged 12 Years** bott code 2017/01/31 LPAL 0162 **(93)** n23 t23.5 f22.5 b24 Last year I was in a British Airways Business Lounge somewhere in the world and spotted at the bar two different Chivas Regal 12s: the labels had differing designs. I asked for a glass of each and tried them side by side. The first one, from the older label, was the pleasant but forgettable blend I expected and knew so well. The newer version wasn't: had it not been time to get my flight I would have ordered a second glass of it....and I can't remember the last time I did that. What I have here is something very much like that surprise Chivas I discovered. This is, unquestionably, the best Chivas 12 I've encountered for a very long time (and I'm talking at least 20 years): pretty impressive use of the understated smoke, especially on the nose, which works well with that date and walnut toffee. I really could enjoy a second glass of this, though still a very different, delicate animal to the one I grew up with in the mid-70s. Actually, I just have had a second glass of this: delicious....! 40%. Chivas Brothers Ltd.

⬙ **Chivas Regal Aged 15 Years** finished in Grande Champagne Cognac casks, bott code: 2018/07/19 **(89) n23** superb, scampering nose with gentle fruit and spice fizzing around the caramel facade; **t22.5** very sweet delivery, even slightly gristy, super soft with a liquorice and toffee follow through; **f22** toasty fudge; **b22.5** can't quite escape the over-zealous caramel. But there is an undoubted charm to this and extra clever use of the sweeter elements to good effect. Probably one of the softest and most moreish whiskies launched in the last year or so. 40%.

**Chivas Regal Aged 18 Years (73.5) n17.5 t20 f17.5 b18.5.** The nose is dulled by a whiff of sulphur and confirmation that all is not well comes with the disagreeably dry, bitter finish. Early on in the delivery some apples and spices show promise but it is an unequal battle against the caramel and off notes. 40%

**Chivas Regal Aged 18 Years** bott code LKRL0346 2017/01/30 **(86) n22 t22 f21 b21** A great improvement on the last bottling I encountered with a pleasing chewiness and understated spiciness. But this remains far too dependent on a big caramel surge for both taste and structure. 40%. Chivas Brothers Ltd.

**Chivas Regal 25 Years Old (95) n23 t23.5 f24 b24.5.** Unadulterated class where the grain-malt balance is exemplary and the deft intertwangling of well-mannered oak and elegant barley leaves you demanding another glass. Brilliant! 40%

**Chivas Regal Aged 25 Years** bott code 2017/03/01 LPML0373 **(95.5) n24.5 t24.5 f22.5 b24** This is quite brilliant whisky. Maybe just one sherry butt away from what would almost certainly have been among the top three whiskies of the year... 40%. Chivas Brothers Ltd.

**Chivas Regal Extra (86) n20 t24 f20.5 b21.5.** Chivas, but seemingly from the Whyte and MacKay school of thick, impenetrable blends. The nose may have the odd undesirable element and the finish reflects those same trace failings. But if chewy date and walnuts in a sea of creamy toffee is your thing, then this malt is for you. This, though, does show genuine complexity, so I have to admit to adoring the lush delivery and early middle section: the mouth-feel is truly magnificent. Good spice, too. Flawed genius comes to mind. 40%

**Chivas Regal The Chivas Brother's Blend Aged 12 Years** bott code 2016/04/12 LPEK0613 **(81.5) n21 t21.5 f19 b20** Oh, brother! Fabulous texture but a furry finish... 40%. Chivas Brothers Ltd.

**Chivas Regal Mizunara** bott code: LPBM0253 2018/02/06 **(89.5) n22.5 t23 f22 b22** For years the Japanese copied everything the Scotch whisky industry did, not quite realising – or perhaps willing to believe – that many of their indigenous whiskies were of world class standard deserving respect and discovery in their own right. Now the Scots have, for the first time I'm aware of, openly copied the Japanese– and celebrated the fact. The Japanese oak used within the marrying process does appear to have given an extra impetus and depth to this blend. Definitely offers an extra dimension to what you'd expect from a Chivas. 40%.

**Clan Campbell (86.5) n21.5 t22.5 f21 b21.5.** I'll wager that if I could taste this whisky before the colouring is added it would be scoring into the 90s. Not a single off note; a sublime early array of Speysidey freshness but dulls at the end. 40%. Chivas.

**Clan Campbell** bott code LR3 1047 13/09/05 **(89) n21.5** attractive sweet young grain, but a little Speyside grassiness grows on top; **t23** succulent delivery: a mouth-watering mix of light icing sugars, something vaguely gristier and a wonderful clean grain velvetiness. The mid ground is soft, slightly chalky with developing butterscotch; **f22** a gentle spiciness breezes in; **b22.5** amazing what happens when you reduce the colouring Last time I tasted this I could barely find the whisky for all the toffee. Now it positively shines in the glass. Love it! 40%. Chivas Brothers Ltd.

**Clan Campbell** rum barrel finish, bott code: 2018/04/04 **(90.5) n22** a full steam ahead blend, allowing a little spice nip to gee up the sturdier fudge and molasses; **t23.5** thick on delivery, this a chewer of the first order. Again, the toffee plays a big part but as the middle beckons the notes become more stretched and complex; some tannins enter the fray and the oils mount; the spices act more in keeping with rum than a blended scotch; **f22** drier and toastier yet still with an attractive viscous depth; **b23** this blend is all about impact and staying power. All kinds of rum and caramel incursions, but a really lovely broadside on the palate. 40%.

**Clan Campbell Dark** rum barrel finish, bott code 2017/03/29 LPHL 0570 **(89.5) n22 t23 f22 b22.5** Putting my rum blender's hat on here, can't think which barrels they used to get this degree of colour and sweetness. Still, I'm not arguing; it's a really lovely, accommodating dram. *40%. Chivas Brothers Ltd.*

**Clan Gold 3 Year Old (95)** n23.5 t24 f23.5 b24. A blend-drinkers blend which will also slay the hearts of Speyside single malt lovers. For me, this is love at first sip... *40%*

**Clan Gold Blended 15 Years Old (91)** n21.5 t23 f23.5 b23 An unusual blend for the 21st century, which steadfastly refuses to blast you away with over the top flavour and/or aroma profiles and instead depends on subtlety and poise despite the obvious richness of flavour. The grains make an impact but only by creating the frame in which the more complex notes can be admired. *40%*

**Clan Gold Blended 18 Years Old (94.5)** n23 t24 f23.5 b24. Almost the ultimate prepradial whisky with its at once robust yet delicate working over of the taste buds by the carefully muzzled juiciness of the malt. This is the real deal: a truly classy act which at first appears to wallow in a sea of simplicity but then bursts out into something very much more complex and alluring. About as clean and charming an 18-year-old blend as you are likely to find. *40%*

**Clan Gold 18 Years of Age** bott code L6X 7616 0611 **(95)** n24 t24 f23 b24 Nothing like as juicy and cleverly fruity as it once was, yet marriage between malt and grain seldom comes more happy than this... *40%. Quality Spirits International.*

**Clan Gold Finest** bott code L10Z 6253 1902 **(83)** n20 t21 f21 b21 Sweet, silky, soft and caramel heavy. Decent late spice. *40%. Quality Spirits International.*

**Clan MacGregor (92)** n22 t24 f23 b23 Just gets better and better. Now a true classic and getting up there with Grant's. *43%*

**Clan Murray** bott code L9X 7694 1411 **(86)** n20 t22.5 f21.5 b22 For the avoidance of doubt: no, this not my blend. No, I am not the blender. No, I do not get a royalty from sales. If I could have had a tenner for each time I've had to answer that over the last decade or so I could have bought my own island somewhere, or Millwall FC... Anyway, back to the whisky. Far better nose than it has shown in the past and the delivery has an eye-watering bite, the finish a roguish spice. Rough-ish but very ready... *40%. The BenRiach Distillery Co. Ltd.*

**Clansman (80.5)** n20.5 t21 f19 b20. Sweet, grainy and soft. *40%. Loch Lomond.*

**Clansman** bott code L3/170/15 **(84)** n21 t22 f20 b21 More to it than of old, though still very soft, the dark sugars and spice have a very pleasant input. *40%. Loch Lomond Group.*

**The Claymore (85)** n19 t22 f22 b22. These days you are run through by spices. The blend is pure Paterson in style with guts etc, which is not something you always like to associate with a Claymore; some delightful muscovado sugar at the death. Get the nose sorted and a very decent and complex whisky is there to be had. *40%. Whyte & Mackay Distillers Ltd.*

⟨⟩ **Cliff Allen** bott 20 07 18, bott code: L1524 015503 **(87)** n21.5 t22 f21.5 b22 Though grain heavy, there is a pleasing sweetness to accompany the enveloping softness. Attractive spice prickle, too, as well as decent balance. *40%. BBC Spirits.*

**Compass Box Delilah's Limited Release Small Batch** American oak **(92.5)** n23 t23.5 f23 b23 blends rarely come more honeyed, or even sweeter, than this with every last sugary element seemingly extracted from the oak. My only sorrow for this whisky, given its American theme, was that it wasn't bottled as a 101 (ie 50.5% abv) instead of the rather underpowered 80 proof – because you have the feeling this would have become pretty three dimensional and leapt from the glass. And then down your throat with serious effect. *40%. nc ncf. WB15/171*

**Compass Box Delilah's XXV** American oak & sherry casks **(82)** n20.5 t22.5 f18 b21 A blend with an astonishing degree of natural caramels in play, giving the whole piece a soft, chewy feel with both sugars and spices coming off at a tangent. Sadly, the sherry input is distracting on the nose and distinctly tangy and furry towards the end. *46%. nc ncf.*

**Compass Box The Double Single** bott Mar 17 **(97)** n24.5 t25 f23.5 b24 By no means the first time I have encountered a single malt and grain in the same bottle. But I am hard pressed to remember one that was even close to being this wonderful...This is Compass Box's finest moment... *46%. nc ncf. 5,838 bottles.*

**Compass Box Great King St. Artist's Blend (93)** n24 t23 f22.5 b23.5. The nose of this uncoloured and non-chill filtered whisky is not dissimilar to some better known blends before they have colouring added to do its worst. A beautiful young thing this blend: nubile, naked and dangerously come hither. Compass Box's founder John Glaser has done some memorable work in recent years, though one has always had the feeling that he has still been learning his trade, sometimes forcing the issue a little too enthusiastically. Here, there is absolutely no doubting that he has come of age as a blender. *43%. nc ncf.*

**Compass Box Great King Street Experimental Batch #00-V4** bott Sept 13 **(93)** n22.5 t24 f23 b23.5. A blend combining astonishing vibrancy with oaky Russian roulette. Not a dram to do things by halves... *43%. 3,439 bottles.*

**Compass Box Great King Street Experimental Batch #TR-06** bott Sept 13 **(92)** n22 t23.5; f23 b23.5 I think this one's been rumbled... *43%.*

**Compass Box Great King Street Glasgow Blend (88.5) n22 t23.5 f21 b22** Just the odd note seems out of place here and there: delicious but not the usual Compass Box precision. 43%

**Compass Box The Circus** bott Mar 16 **(93) n23** roll up, roll up and nose a fascinating juxtapositioning of the Fisherman's Friend-style smokiness with a sharp citric malt/grain mix...; **t23.5** eye-wateringly tart start: a strange mix of undercooked and overcooked jam tarts, with a smoked liquorice middle; **f23** remains, thick, dark and brooding: no high wires here – these are all base notes; **b23.5** Scotland's very own Clown Royal... 49%. nc ncf. 2,490 bottles.

**Compass Box This Is Not A Luxury Whisky** bott Aug 15 **(81) n20 t21.5 f19.5 b20.** Correct. 53.1%. nc ncf. 4,992 bottles.

**Consulate (87) n21.5 t22 f22 b21.5** I assume this weighty and pleasant dram was designed to accompany Passport (whose chewiness it now resembles) in the drinks cabinet. I suggest, if buying them, use Visa. 40%. Quality Spirits International.

**Crawford's (83.5) n19 t21 f22 b21.5.** A lovely spice display helps overcome the caramel. 40%.

**Cutty Black (83) n20 t23 f19 b21.** Both nose and finish are dwarfed and flung into the realms of ordinariness by the magnificently substantial delivery. Whilst there is a taint to the nose, its richness augers well for what is to follow; and you won't be disappointed. At times it behaves like a Highland Park with a toffeed spine, such is the richness and depth of the honey and dates and complexity of the grain-vanilla background. But those warning notes on the nose are there for good reason and the finish tells you why. Would not be surprised to see this score into the 90s on a different bottling day. 40%. Edrington

**Cutty Sark (78) n19 t21 f19 b19.** Crisp and juicy. But a nipping furriness, too. 40%

**Cutty Sark** bott code L60355 L7 **(84.5) n21 t22 f20 b21.5** To some extent an improvement on a couple of years back when this blend was vanishing in character. But could still do with some urgent extra restorative work. For as long I can remember the grain on this was crisp and brought the sharpest, juiciest notes imaginable from the Speyside malts: indeed, that was its trademark character. Now, like so many standard blends, it is bubble gum soft and spreads the sugars evenly with the malts fighting to be heard. Only very mild sulphur tones to the crippling ones I had previously found. But it really does need to re-work the grain...if it can find it. 40%. .

**Cutty Sark Aged 12 Years (92) n22 t24 f23 b23** At last! Cutty 12 at full sail...and blended whisky rarely looks any more beautiful! 40%. Edrington.

**Cutty Sark Aged 15 Years (82) n19 t22 f20 b21.** Attempts to take the honey route. But seriously dulled by toffee and the odd sulphured cask. 40%. Edrington.

**Cutty Sark Aged 18 Years (88) n22 t22 f22 b22** Lost the subtle fruitiness which worked so well. Easy-going and attractive. 43%

**Cutty Sark Aged 25 Years (91) n21 t23.5 f22.5 b23** Magnificent, though not quite flawless, this whisky is as elegant and effortlessly powerful as the ship after which the brand was named... 45.7%. Berry Bros & Rudd.

**Cutty Sark Prohibition Edition** American oak, bott code L0401W L4 11/18 **(91) n21.5 t25 f20 b24.5** Probably the best label and presentation of any whisky in the world this year: sheer class. On the back label they use the word authentic. Which is a very interesting concept. Except authentic whisky sent to the USA back in the 1920s wouldn't have that annoying and debilitating rumble of sulphur, detectable on both nose and finish. And I suspect the malt content would have been higher – and the grain used showing far more of a corn-oily character. That all said, I doubt the blender of the day would have achieved better delivery or balance: indeed, this delivery has to be one of the highlights of the whisky year. You will not be surprised to discover my resolve cracked, and I swallowed a full mouthful of this special blend. And, gee: it was swell, bud... 50%. Edrington.

**Cutty Sark Storm (81.5) n18 t23.5 f19.5 b20.5.** When the wind is set fair, which is mainly on delivery and for the first six or seven flavour waves which follow, we really do have an astonishingly beautiful blend, seemingly high in malt content and really putting the accent on ulmo honey and marzipan: a breath-taking combination. This is assisted by a gorgeous weight to the silky body and a light raspberry jam moment to the late arriving Ecuadorian cocoa. All magnificent. However, as Cutty sadly tends to, sails into sulphurous seas. 40%. Edrington.

**Demijohn Finest Blended Scotch Whisky (88) n21 t22 f23 b22** OK, now that's spooky. You really don't expect tasting notes written ten years ago to exactly fit the bill today. But that is exactly what happens here: well maybe not quite exactly. Ten years ago I wrote of the "wonderful firmness of the grain" where today, like 90% of all blends, it is much more yielding and soft than before. Thankfully, it hasn't detracted from the enjoyment. 40%.

**Dew of Ben Nevis Blue Label (82) n19 t22 f20 b21.** The odd off-key note is handsomely outnumbered by deliciously complex mocha and demerara tones. Ditch the caramel and you'd have a sizzler! 40%. Ben Nevis Distillery. Replacement for Dew of Ben Nevis Millennium Blend.

**Dew of Ben Nevis Special Reserve (85) n19 t21 f23 b22.** A much juicier blend than of old, still sporting some bruising and rough patches. But that kind of makes this all the more attractive, with the caramel mixing with some fuller malts to provide a date and nuts effect which makes for a grand finale. *40%. Ben Nevis Distillery*

**Dew of Ben Nevis Supreme Selection (77) n18 t20 f20 b19.** Some lovely raspberry jam Swiss roll moments here. But the grain could be friendlier, especially on the nose. *40%*

⬦ **Dewar's Aged 12 Years The Ancestor** bott code: L17338ZA80109:20 **(87) n21.5 t22 f21.5 b22** A welcoming blend, relying mainly on softer grains which suck you in and caress you. A little orange peel and tart tannin helps give the blend vibrancy, but there is always a slight murkiness hanging around, too, which becomes more apparent at the death. *40%*.

⬦ **Dewar's Aged 15 Years The Monarch** bott code: L18340ZA800 1326 **(81) n21 t21.5 f18 b20.5** Sweet and chewy in part, but the fuzzy finish abdicates. *40%*.

⬦ **Dewar's Aged 18 Years The Vintage** bott code: L19030ZA8051642 **(96.5) n24** a gentle fruitiness centres around both unripe and over-ripe greengages, which offer both a sharpness and sweeter friendliness. Spices are close to the surface but refuse to break; tannins provide the anchor; **t24.5** sublime grain at work here. That is the key to the blend, finding one that can both absorb and reflect the malt at work...and this it does here almost to perfection; the key to the sweetness is its refined and relaxed balancing act with the much drier oak. The most charming heather honey pulls this off, and still has room for the sweeter fruity moments; **f23.5** a long, sophisticated finish lacking now the earlier glossy oils, but instead concentrating on the vanillas and spiced butterscotch; **b24.5** this is how an 18-year-old blend should be: complex, noble and both keeping you on the edge of your seat as you wonder next what will happen, and falling back into its furthest recesses so you can drift away on its beauty... A blend that upholds the very finest traditions of the great Dewar's name. *40%*.

⬦ **Dewar's Aged 25 Years The Signature** bott code: L18081ZA8011034 **(96) n24** high grade marzipan caresses and teases the nose, while the grains exude a softness which on excavation reveals a much firmer side; a lovely candy floss sweetness completes the extraordinary aroma; **t24** that super-soft grain on the nose turns up first and simply melts away out of existence. The residue is a gently malty spiciness which gathers in tannins by the second. The harder, secondary grain now forms the spine on which all this hangs; **f24** long, lightly spiced and back to the marzipan as the circle is completed; **b24** a 25-year-old blend truly worthy of that mantle. Always an honour to experience a whisky that has been very cleverly sculpted, not haphazardly slung together: a blender's blend. I doff my Panama to the blender. *40%*.

⬦ **Dewar's Double Double Aged 21 Years Blended Scotch Whisky** finished in oloroso sherry casks, bott code: L19106ZA500 **(88) n23.5** top notch layering. Perhaps the understated saltiness, just by its quiet authority, sticks out here if you can spot it. Then there is the heather honey and the floral notes, too: dank autumn woodlands after a shower, and here the vaguest hint of peat appears. A light orange blossom honey note sweetens and lifts; **t23.5** against all the odds, this offers a light delivery but busy and chewy, too; **f18.5** perhaps a little caramel leaks in and dulls the spices and vanillas slightly. But then, annoyingly, the sulphur... **b22.5** another blender's blend. Or would have been 30 years ago. But doesn't seem to quite take into account the Russian roulette decision to add extra oloroso into the mix – Russian roulette with only one empty chamber that is... *46%*.

⬦ **Dewar's Double Double Aged 27 Years Blended Scotch Whisky** finished in Palo Cortado sherry casks, bott code: L19106ZA501 **(96.5) n24** if I didn't have a book to write I could nose this all day: the peat, seemingly stand alone, shifts gear to weave brilliantly amid the crisper grain tones: sublime...and very, very cleverly done; **t24** fabulous delivery with the grain upholding that brittle sharpness displayed on the nose. But then gives way slowly to let in both the now smoke and voluptuous peat; the fruit offers a secondary fruitiness to the Speyside/Highland malts which present a grassy, honey freshness; **f24** although long, although the best part of three decades old, somehow the malty juiciness lasts right to the very death. The peat, also, revels in its two-towned complexity until the very final flavour rays finally set...; **b24.5** a blend not scared to embrace its peaty side. And sherry butts free from sulphur. A double miracle at work. And one of the best new blends I have tasted for a year or two. Superb. *46%*.

⬦ **Dewar's Double Double Aged 32 Years Blended Scotch Whisky** finished in PX sherry casks, bott code: L19107ZA501 **(86.5) n21.5 t24 f20.5 b20.5** I clocked the PX influence before I was aware it was officially finished in that cask type. After the staggeringly beautiful and vivid 27-year-old, this is very much a case of following the Lord Mayor's show. Yes, the sherry influence is pristine and untainted by sulphur, and the spices do a grand job. But to put a 30 year old blend into PX is like restoring an Old Master with a nine inch brush dipped into a gloss finish. Lovely in places (the astonishing delivery shews just how much sublime complexity was originally around)...but could have been so much more... *46%*.

⬦ **Dewar's White Label** bott code: L18241ZA204 2203 **(82) n20 t21 f20 b21** A great improvement on the last White Label I tasted (though nowhere near my great love of the 1970s!) but some murky grain still apparent. Definite layering and structure here, though. *40%*.

**Dhoon Glen** (86) n21 t22 f21.5 b21.5 Full of big flavours, broad grainy strokes and copious amounts of dark sugars including chocolate fudge and now a little extra spice, too. Goes dhoon a treat... 40%. *Lombard Scotch Whisky Ltd.*

**Dimple 12 Years Old** (86.5) n22 t22 f21.5 b21. Lots of sultana; the spice adds aggression. *40%.*

**Dimple 15 Years Old** (87.5) n20 t21 f24 b22.5. Only on the late middle and finish does this particular flower unfurl and to magnificently complex effect. The texture of the grains in particular delight while the strands of barley entwine. A type of treat for the more technically minded of the serious blend drinkers among you. 40%. *Diageo.*

**The Famous Grouse** (89) n22 t23 f21.5 b22.5 It almost seems that Grouse is, by degrees, moving from its traditional position of a light blend to something much closer to Grant's as a middle-weighted dram. Again the colouring has been raised a fraction and now the body and depth have been adjusted to follow suit. Have to say that this is one very complex whisky these days: I had spotted slight changes when drinking it socially, but this was the first time I had a chance to sit down and professionally analyse what was happening in the glass. A fascinating and tasty bird, indeed. 40%. *Edrington Group.*

**The Famous Grouse** bott code L4812TL1 25/08 (88.5) n22.5 t23 f21 b22 Changed its stance a few years back from light blend to a middle-weighted one and has worked hard to keep that position with thoughtful use of the phenols. Unlike many other brands it has not gone colouring mad and the little toffee apparent does nothing to spoil the narrative and complexity: I doff my hat. 40%.

**The Famous Grouse Gold Reserve** (90) n23.5 t23 f21.5 b22 Great to know the value of the Gold Reserve is going up...as should the strength of this blend. The old-fashioned 40% just ain't enough carats. 40%. *Edrington Group.*

**The Famous Grouse Married Strength** (82.5) n19 t22 f20 b21.5. The nose is nutty and toffeed. But despite the delightful, silky sweetness and gentle Speyside-style maltiness which forms the main markers for this soft blend, the nose, like the finish, also shows a little bitter furriness has, sadly, entered into the mix. Not a patch on the standard Grouse of a decade ago. 45.9% WB16/019

**The Famous Grouse Mellow Gold** sherry & bourbon casks (85) n20 t23.5 f20 b21.5. While the nose and finish tell us a little too much about the state of the sherry butts used, there is no harm tuning into the delivery and follow though which are, unquestionably, beautiful. The texture is silk normally found on the most expensive lingerie, and as sexy as who you might find inside it; while the honey is a fabulous mix of ulmo and orange blossom. 40%

**The Famous Grouse Smoky Black** (87) n22 t22 f21 b22. Black Grouse by any other name. Flawed in the usual tangy, furry Grouse fashion. But have to say there is a certain roughness and randomness about the sugars that I find very appealing. A smoky style that Bowmore lovers might enjoy. A genuinely beautiful, smoky, ugly, black duckling. Sorry, I mean Grouse. 40%

**Firean** bottling no. 005, bottling line. 003, bott code. L17066 (91.5) n23 t23.5 f22 b23 Does the heart good encounter to encounter a blend so happy to embrace its smokier self. Deliciously impressive. 40%. *Burlington Drinks.*

**Fort Glen The Blender's Reserve Aged 12 Years** (88.5) n21.5 t23 f21.5 b22.5 An entirely enjoyable blend which is clean and boasting decent complexity and weight. 40%

**Fort Glen The Distiller's Reserve** (78) n18 t22 f20 b19. Juicy, salivating delivery as it storms the ramparts. Draws down the portcullis elsewhere. 40%. *The Fort Glen Whisky Company.*

**Fraser MacDonald** (85) n21 t21.5 f21 b21.5. Some fudge towards the middle and end but the journey there is an enjoyable one. 40%. *Loch Lomond Distillers.*

**Gairloch** (79) n19 t20 f20 b20. For those who like their butterscotch at 40% abv. 40%

**Gleann Mór Blended Whisky 18 Year Old** (87) n21.5 t23 f20.5 b22. A few passages in this are outstanding, especially when the delicate honey appears to collide with the softest smoke. A slight bitterness does jar somewhat, though the softness of the grain is quite seriously seductive 43.9%

**Gleann Mór 40 Year Old Blend** (94) n23 t23.5 f23.5 b24 Some 52-year-old Carsebridge makes up about a fifth of this blend, but I suspect the big oak comes from one of the malts. A supreme old whisky which cherishes its age. 44.6%.

**Glenalba Aged 22 Years Sherry Cask Finish** batch no. JS/322, lot no. 0745C, dist 1993 (90) n22 t23.5 f23.5 b21 A pristine sherry effect. No off notes whatsoever. If there is a downside, it is the fact that the sherry evens out the complexity of the blend. I mean, surely...that has to be the purpose of a blend: complexity and balance, right....? That said, for the experience alone...all rather lovely and deserving of further exploration...! 40%

**Glenalba Aged 25 Years Sherry Cask Finish** batch no. SE/425, lot no. 0274J, dist 1990 (89) n22 t23.5 f22.5 b21.5 A lovely whisky, though again the unreconstructed sherry effect does few favours to the overall layering and balance. Maybe the vaguest hint of something with the 'S' word, though very low key... 40%

**Glenalba Aged 34 Years Sherry Cask Finish** batch no. JM/012, lot no. 0862B, dist 1981 **(95.5)** n24 t24 f23.5 b24 A beautifully dry, sophisticated blend. Benefits from the use of what is about as good a sherry butt as I have encountered: not even the hint of a hint of an off-note. Where the 22 and 25 year editions are rather overcome by the magnitude of the grape, this one has enough in reserve to take the sherry in its stride and use it to excellent effect. Truly superb Scotch. 40%

**Glen Brynth (70.5)** n18 t19 f16 b17.5. Bitter and awkward. 43%

**Glenbrynth Premium Three Year Old (82)** n19 t21 f21 b21 An enormously improved, salivating, toasty blend making full use of the rich muscovado sugars on display. Good late spice, too. 43%. OTI Africa.

**Glenbrynth 8 Year Old (88)** n21.5 t22 f22.5 b22. An impressive blend which improves second by second on the palate. 40%. OTI Africa.

**Glenbrynth Pearl 30 Year Old Limited Edition (90.5)** n22.5 t23.5 f21.5 b23 Attractive, beautifully weighted, no off notes...though perhaps quietened by toffee. Still a treat of a blend. 43%. OTI Africa.

**Glenbrynth Pearl 30 Year Old** bott code L8V 7410 28/11/11 **(88)** n22.5 t22.5 f21 b22 A genuinely strange blend. Not sure how this whisky was mapped out in the creator's mind. A hit and miss hotchpotch but when it is good, it is very good.. 43%. OTI Africa.

**The Glengarry** bott code L3/301/15 **(80)** n19 t21 f20 b20 A brand that would once make me wince has upped its game beyond recognition. Even has the nerve to now possess an attractively salivating as well as silky disposition. 40%. Loch Lomond Group.

**Glen Lyon (85)** n19 t22.5 f22 b21.5. Works a lot better than the nose suggests: seriously chewy with a rabid spice attack and lots of juices. For those who have just retired as dynamite testers. Unpretentious fun. 43%. Diageo.

**Glen Talloch Choice Rare & Old (85.5)** n20.5 t22.5 f21 b21.5. A very pleasing sharpness to the delivery reveals the barley in all its Speyside-style finery, The grain itself is soothing, especially when the caramel notes kick in. 40%. ncf.

**Glen Talloch Gold Aged 12 Years (85)** n21 t22 f21 b21. Impressive grain at work insuring a deft, velvety caress to the palate. Mainly caramel speaking, despite the age, though there is an attractive spice buzz towards the thin-ish finish. 40%

**Glen Talloch Peated (77)** n18 t20 f20 b19 The awful tobacco nose needs some serious work on it. The taste is overly sweet, mushy and shapeless, like far too many blends these days. Requires a complete refit. 40%. Boomsma Distillery.

**Glory Leading Aged 32 Years (88.5)** n22.5 t22.5 f21.5 b22 At times a little heavy handed and out of sync. But the overall experience is one of stunningly spiced enjoyment. 43%

**Glory Leading Blended Scotch Whisky 30 Years Old** American oak casks **(93)** n22.5 t23 f23.5 b24 a big, clever, satisfying blend which just gets better and better... though not too sure about the Crystal Palace style eagle on the label. Even so, love it! 43%

**Golden Piper (86.5)** n22 t21 f22 b21.5. A firm, clean blend with a steady flush through of diverse sugars. The grain does all the steering and therefore complexity is limited. But the overall freshness is a delight. 43%. Whisky Shack.

**Goldfield** bott code: L17 02796 CB1 **(86)** n21 t21.5 f21.5 b22 These days I am minded to give an extra mark to any blend that is not carrying a sulphur trace from the grain receptacles. So an extra mark here, for sure, for this fat and full-flavoured blend which, despite its unashamed cream toffee roundness, enjoys enough spice to punch through for bite, as well as some late hickory. 40%.

**The Gordon Highlanders (86)** n21 t22 f21 b22. Lush and juicy, there is a distinctive Speysidey feel to this one with the grains doing their best to accentuate the developing spice. Plenty of feel good factor here. 40%. William Grant & Sons.

**Grand Macnish (79)** n19 t21 f19 b20. Welcome back to an old friend...but the years have caught up with it. Still on the feral side, but has exchanged its robust good looks for an unwashed and unkempt appearance on the palate. Will do a great job to bring some life back to you, though. 43%. MacDuff International Ltd.

**Grand Macnish** bott code L16/8404 **(85.5)** n21.5 t22 f21 b21 Never a blend for the lily-livered this brand has always been a byword for a whisky with big character. It can still claim that, except now we have a much more absorbing grain at play which undermines the blend's former maltiness. 40%. MacDuff International Ltd.

**Grand Macnish 12 Years Old (86)** n21 t22 f21 b21.5. A grander Grand Macnich than of old with the wonderful feather pillow delivery maintained and a greater harmonisation of the malt, especially those which contain a honey-copper sheen. 40%. MacDuff.

**Grand Macnish Black Edition** charred Bourbon casks, bott code L15 8863 **(94.5)** n24 t23.5 f23 b24 A blended whisky classic. 40%. MacDuff International Ltd.

**Grant's Aged 12 Years** bott code: L6X 6682 1305 **(96)** n24 t24 f23.5 b24.5 There is no doubting that their 12-year-old has improved dramatically in recent years. Doubtless better grain than their standard blend, but also a slightly braver use of phenols has paid handsome dividends. Sits proudly alongside Johnny Walker Black as one of the world's must have 12-year-old blends. For me, the perfect daily dram. *40%.*

**Grant's Cask Editions No. 1 Ale Cask Finish** bott code: L1X 7354 1809 **(91) n22.5** attractive Demerara firmness and even a malty swirl; the green, youthful freshness charms; **t23** juicy delivery and firmer than the Family Reserve with much more sharpness and clarity; big sugars build; **f22.5** a pleasing spiced mocha fade; **b23** a much cleaner, more precise blend than when this was first launched, with less noticeable beer character: impressive. *40%.*

**Grant's Cask Editions No. 2 Sherry Cask Finish** bott code: L3Z 7760 0211 **(84.5) n21.5 t22 f20 b21** A lovely fresh, fruity and salivating edge to this even boasting an early honeyed sheen. Complexity has been sacrificed for effect, however. *40%.*

**Grant's The Family Reserve** bott code: L3A 8017 1711 **(85) n21 t22 f21 b21** What was once the very finest, most complex nose in the entire Scotch whisky lexicon is now, on this evidence, a mushy shadow of its former self. Where once there was a judicious mix of softer and firmer grain to ensure the malts could make the most eloquent of speeches, now there is just a spongy sweetness which shouts loud enough to silence the poetry. If you like your blend fat, sweet, chewy, softer than quicksand and boasting a bitter, vaguely off-key finale here you go. But for those of us who once revered Grant's as the greatest of all standard blends, a whisky whose artistry once gilt-framed the very finest Scotland had to offer, this will not be a glass of cheer. I cannot blame the blender: he can work only with what he has available. And today, after a succession of nonsensical grain distillery closures (nonsensical to anyone who understands whisky, but not the soul-less bean counters who haven't the first clue) the choice in his lab is limited. It would be like blaming the manager of Bradford City for being a third tier football club because they won the FA Cup in 1910. Times change. And not, sadly, always for the better... *40%.*

**Grant's Signature** bott code: L1Z 7468 1609 **(79) n19 t22 f18 b20** Smudged. *40%.*

**The Great Macaulay (86.5) n22 t21.5 f21.5 b21.5** The character is one mainly of trudging, attractive caramel bolstered by busy, warming spice. The nose shows some degree of complexity. By no means unpleasant. *40%. Quality Spirits International.*

**Green Plaid 12 Years Old (89) n22 t23 f22 b22** Beautifully constructed; juicy. *40%.*

**Guneagal Aged 12 Years (85.5) n21 t22.5 f20.5 b21.5.** The salty, sweaty armpit nose gives way to an even saltier delivery, helped along by sweet glycerine and a boiled candy fruity sweetness. The finish is a little roughhouse by comparison. *40%. William Grant & Sons.*

**Haddington House (81) n20 t21 f20 b20** Good grief! This has changed since I last tasted it over a decade ago. Gone is its light, bright juicy character and in its place a singularly sweet, cloying blend due, I suspect, to a very different grain input. *40%. Quality Spirits International.*

**Haig Gold Label (88) n21 t23 f22 b22** What had before been pretty standard stuff has upped the complexity by an impressive distance. *40%. Diageo.*

◈ **The Half Century Blend** batch no. 4 **(95) n24 t24 f23 b24** A rich malt making an absolute nonsense of its age statement. A fruitcake theme then moves into far maltier territory, but it is the sheer beauty of the lush mouth feel which blows you away. Dark summer cherries and chocolate Maltesers melt into the other while light spices offer a third dimension. The is even a Farley's Rusk moment, though totally in keeping with the narrative... Oh, and look out for the flawless, teasingly understated seem of ulmo honey, too. Stunning. For its age: breathtaking. *45.6%. The Blended Whisky Company.*

**Hankey Bannister (84.5) n20.5 t22 f21 b21.** Lots of early life and even a malt kick early on. Toffee later. *40%. Inverhouse Distillers.*

**Hankey Bannister 12 Years Old (86.5) n22 t21.5 f21 b22.** A much improved blend with a nose and early delivery which makes full play of the blending company's Speyside malts. Plenty of toffee on the finish. *40%. Inverhouse Distillers.*

**Hankey Bannister 21 Years Old (95) n23.5** a fruity ensemble, clean, vibrant and loath to show its age **t24** as juicy as the nose suggests, except for the odd rumble of distant smoke; a firm, barley-sugar hardness as the grains keep control; **f23.5** the arrival of the oak adds further weight and for the first time begins to behave like a 21-y-o; long, now with decent spice and with some crusty dryness at the very death; **b24** with top dressing like this and some obviously complex secondary malts, too, how can it fail? *43%.*

**Hankey Bannister 25 Years Old (91) n22.5 t24 f21.5 b23** Follows on in style and quality to 21-year-old. Gorgeous. *40%.*

**Hankey Bannister 40 Years Old (89) n22 t23 f22 b22.** This blend has been put together to mark the 250th anniversary of the forging of the business relations between Messrs. Hankey and Bannister. And although the oak creaks like a ship of its day, there is enough verve and viscosity to ensure a rather delicious toast to the gentlemen. Love it! *44%. Inverhouse.*

**Hankey Bannister 40 Year Old (94) n23.5 t23.5 f23 b24.** Pure quality. The attention to detail is sublime. *44.3%. Inverhouse Distillers.*

**Hankey Bannister Heritage Blend (92)** n23 despite the evidence of sherry the spiced chocolate fudge keeps you spellbound; **t24** at moments like this, one's taste buds are purely in love. They are being caressed, serenaded and kisses by the most glorious of old grains, encrusted with a Speyside-syle maltiness which makes you purr with pleasure; **f22** the weakness on the nose returns, though sparingly. Outstanding late Malteser candy style confirms a very decent malt depth; **b23** just so soft and sensual...46%. Inverhouse Distillers.

**Harveys Lewes Blend Eight Year Old** batch 4 **(93)** n23.5 t23 f23 b23.5 First tasted this in the front parlour of legendary Harvey's brewer Miles Jenner's home just after Christmas. It tasted quite different from their previous bottlings – and quite superb. Nosed and tasted now several months on in the cold analytical light of a tasting room...helped along with that deft addition of subtle peat, it still does. Superb! 40%

**Hazelwood 18 Year Old (88)** n23.5 top-notch dispersal of subtle notes: walnut cream cake with a pinch of vanilla. The malt is low key but distinctly Speyside-style in its clarity, despite the odd wisp of something a little heavier; **t22.5** creamy-textured. Soft ulmo honey gives way to the thickening vanilla and toffee; **f20.5** bitters slightly at the turned-up ending; **b22** until the final furry moments, a genuine little, understated, charmer. 40%. William Grant & Sons.

**Hazelwood 21 Year Old (74)** n19 t20 f17 b18. Some decent acacia honey tries to battle against the bitter imbalance. 40%. William Grant & Sons.

**Hazelwood 25 Year Old (89.5)** n22 full on fruit underscored by the muscular tannins: simple, but satisfying; **t23** wonderful delivery: a momentous mix of muscovado and maple syrup but with the toasty tannins offering an even more roasty depth; **f22** a slight, non-spiced buzz to the finish. But that roastiness – akin to burnt fudge – gives much to chew over; **b22.5** distinctly chunky. 40%. William Grant & Sons.

**High Commissioner (88.5)** n22.5 t22.5 f20.5 b22.5 Now I admit I had a hand in cleaning this brand up a couple of years back, giving it a good polish and much needed balance complexity. But I don't remember leaving it in quite this good a shape. Just a bitter semi-off note on the finish, otherwise this guy would have been in the 90s. What a great fun, three-course dram this is... 40%. Loch Lomond Distillers.

**High Commissioner** bott code L2/305/16 **(87.5)** n21.5 t22.5 f21.5 b22 Boasts an unusually well balanced disposition for a young blend, not at all cowered into being a one trick caramelled pony. Instead, we are treated to a fulsome array of huskier and duskier notes, especially the molasses mixing with a hint of phenol. Delicious. 40%. Loch Lomond Group.

⟨⟩ **High Commissioner Aged 7 Years Lightly Peated** bott code: 22 06 2018 **(89)** n22.5 soft, clean, and yet under the surface there is a lot of busy-ness going on and delicate extra smoky weight not normally associated with HC; **t22** the grain gives it the texture of the softest of beards. A little caramel with a buzzing, spicy smokiness yet always salivating; **f22** sweetens with spiced butterscotch; **b22.5** a seemingly simple malt with a lot of complexity if you want to find it. 40%.

**Highland Baron (85.5)** n21 t22 f21 b21.5. A very clean, sweet and competent young blend showing admirable weight and depth. 40%. Loch Lomond Distillers.

**Highland Baron (88.5)** n22 trace smoke works beautifully with the sweet and lithe grain; **t22.5** outstanding mouth feel: chewy and sweet but always within the realms of balance and god taste. A little chocolate and honey arrives with that hint of smoke; **f22** silky, lightly spiced, vaguely smoked, molassed mocha; **b22** has seriously upped the smoke and honey ratio in recent years. Deserves its Baronetcy. 40%. Lombard Scotch Whisky Ltd.

**Highland Bird (77)** n19 t19 f19 b20. I've had a few of these over the years, I admit. But I can't remember one quite as rough and ready as this... 40%. Quality Spirits International.

**Highland Bird** bott code L9Z 6253 2302 **(83.5)** n21 t21 f20.5 b21 I've had a few of these over the years, I can tell you. Glasses of this whisky, as well. As for the blend, this is by far and away the cleanest, enjoyable and most well-balanced yet: a dram on the up. 40%. QSI.

⟨⟩ **Highland Black Special Reserve Aged 8 Years** bott code: L9A 7064 2906 **(86)** n21.5 t22 f21 b21.5 Soft, silky, distinctly friendly and unerringly sweet, But definitely a touch too heavy on the toffee. 40%. Produced for Aldi.

**Highland Harvest Organic Scotch Whisky (76)** n18 t21 f19 b18. A very interesting blend. Great try, but a little bit of a lost opportunity here as I don't think the balance is quite right. But at least I now know what organic caramel tastes like... 40%

**Highland Mist (88.5)** n20.5 t23 f22.5 b22.5 Fabulously fun whisky bursting from the bottle with character and mischief. Had to admit, broke all my own rules and just had to have a glass of this after doing the notes... 40%. Loch Lomond Distillers.

**Highland Piper (79)** n20 t20 f19 b20. Good quaffing blend – if sweet - of sticky toffee and dates. Some gin on the nose – and finish. 40%

**Highland Pride (86)** n21 t22 f21.5 b21.5. A beefy, weighty thick dram with plenty to chew on. The developing sweetness is a joy. 40%. Whyte & Mackay Distillers Ltd.

**Highland Queen Blended Scotch Whisky** (86.5) n22 t21 f21.5 b22. Lots of grains at play here. But what grains?! Clean and crisp with a superb bite which balances the softening mouth feel attractively. Old fashioned and delicious. *40%*

**Highland Queen** bott code L12 356 (87) n22.5 t22.5 f20.5 b21.5 If the caramels on this could be reduced slightly what a brilliant blend we'd have on our hands here. As it is, the nose is a hotbed of complex intrigue with earthier and lighter honeyed notes combining sublimely while the delivery allows the sugars, vanillas and spices room to make their cases. Bar the spices, just all dies off a little too soon. *40%. Tullibardine Ltd.*

**Highland Queen Aged 8 Years** bott code L15 071 (89.5) n23 beautifully rich and rounded in its time-honoured way, though less fruit now (though some boiled apples remain) and more honeyed; t22.5 gloriously succulent with its chewability going off the scale; muscovado sugars and spices force the agenda in the mid ground; f21.5 despite a caramel onslaught the spices win by a distance; b22.5 a classy blend showing great character and entertainment value. *40%. Tullibardine Ltd.*

**Highland Queen Aged 12 Years Blended Scotch Whisky** (87) n22 t22 f21 b22. A polite, slightly more sophisticated version of the 8-year-old...but without the passion and drama! *40%*

**Highland Queen Aged 12 Years** bott code L15 071 (90) n23 delicious gooseberry tart with an earthy, tannin undertone; t22.5 golden syrup majors on delivery, then a slow spreading of a vaguely phenolic but distinctly spicy vanilla theme; f22 caramel and spice: simple but wonderfully effective; b22.5 a much weightier blend than it used to be, displaying excellent pace of flavour development on the palate. Decent stuff! *40%. Tullibardine Ltd.*

**Highland Queen Sherry Cask Finish** bott code L16 201 (81.5) n19 t22 f19 b21.5 The sherry isn't exactly free from sin, and the grape easily overpowers the nuances of the blend itself. So, attractive to a degree, but... *40%. Tullibardine Ltd.*

**Highland Queen 1561** bott code L16/80 28.01.16 (94) n23.5 t23.5 f23 b24. As it happens, I have a home where on a living room wall is an old oil painting of Fotheringhay, where the life of Mary Queen of Scots, the Highland Queen, ended on an executioners' block in 1561. Indeed, the house is quite close by and sits near the River Nene which passes through Fotheringhay. The village itself is quiet, particularly fragrant during Spring and Summer and with an unmistakable feel of history and elegance. Not at all unlike this excellent and most distinguished blend. *40%. Tullibardine Ltd.*

**Highland Queen 1561 30 Years Old** bott code LF13017261 261 (88.5) n23.5 the trick of an ancient blend is that you want it to show its age as a Victorian beauty might show her ankle: in a subtle, teasing and arousing way... The nose has pulled it off brilliantly, even if there is a hint of the dreaded S word to be caught on the fruit...; t23.5 perfect weight and sugary sheen to the delivery; the caramels and fruits are just about neck and neck in influence; the muscovado sugars are bright and crunchy; f19.5 becomes just a little too furry and tangy...; b22 shame about the finish. Until then we had one of the sweetest yet gentle blends of the year. *40%. Tullibardine Ltd.*

**Highland Reserve** (80) n19 t21.5 f19.5 b20 See tasting notes for 43% below. *40%. Quality Spirits International.*

**Highland Reserve** bott code B154 (80) n19 t21.5 f19.5 b20 An easy quaffing, silky and profoundly grained, toffee-enriched blend. *43%. Quality Spirits International.*

**Highland Warriors** (82) n20 t21 f20.5 b20.5 This warrior must be wanting to raid a few grain stores... *40%. Quality Spirits International.*

**The Highland Way** (82.5) n20 t21 f21 b20.5 Grainy, with a big sweet toffee middle which makes for a slightly juicy dram of a class barely distinguishable from so many other standard blends. *40%. Quality Spirits International.*

**The Highland Way** bott code B445 (83.5) n20 t21.5 f21 b21 More Milky Way than Highland Way... Very similar to the 40% version, except some extra milk chocolate at the finish. *43%. Quality Spirits International.*

⟐ **HM The King** (89.5) n23 pretty grain dominant. But at least you can nose the constituent parts without colouring clouding the issue. Busy with a light oaky-vanilla involvement; t22 sugars arrive early, almost with a dissolving icing sugar feel to create a delightfully fresh and mouth-watering feel; f22 busy light spice plays with the cheerful vanilla; b22.5 so majestic to find a blend these days not swamped by artificial colouring. Royalty, indeed! *40%. Branded Spirits USA.*

**Islay Mist Aged 8 Years Amontillado Napoleon Cask Finish** bott code L16/8826 (76) n19 t20 f18 b19 For those of you not carrying the sulphur recognition gene, I suspect this will be a delight. For those of us that do, well sorry: but not tonight, Napoleon. And this sulphur is a bit of a carry on, MacDuff... *43%. MacDuff International Ltd.*

**Islay Mist Aged 8 Years Manzanilla La Gitana Cask Finish** bott code L15/8293 (85) n21.5 t22 f20 b21.5 Lots of phenolic cough sweet properties but the fruit and smoke form a tight, enclosed union with little room for scope. The finish is rather too bitter. *40%.*

**Islay Mist Aged 12 Years** bott code L16/8089 **(86)** n22.5 t22 f20.5 b21 Slightly on the disappointing side by Islay Mist's high standards. The nose, with its smoked toffee apple, promises a playful complexity. But an overdose of dull caramel snuffs out any chance of that. *40%. MacDuff International Ltd.*

**Islay Mist Aged 17 Years** bott code L15/8826 **(96)** n24 t24 f23.5 b24.5 A truly brilliant blend that should have no water added and be spared as much time as you can afford. *40%. MacDuff International Ltd.*

**Islay Mist Deluxe** bott code L16/8283 **(87)** n22 t22 f21.5 b21.5 A charmingly brazen blend, offering young peat to you with far less reserve than it once did. More an Islay Fog than Mist... *40%. MacDuff International Ltd.*

**Islay Mist Peated Reserve** bott code L15 9:67 **(92.5)** n23.5 t23 f22.5 b23.5 The accent is on subtlety and balance: a very classy piece of whisky engineering. *40%. MacDuff International Ltd.*

**Isle of Skye 8 Years Old (94)** n23 t24 f23.5 b23.5. Where once peat ruled and with its grain ally formed a smoky iron fist, now honey and subtlety reigns. A change of character and pace which may disappoint gung-ho peat freaks but will intrigue and delight those looking for a more sophisticated dram. *40%. Ian Macleod.*

**Isle of Skye 21 years Old (91)** n21 t23.5 f23 b23.5 What an absolute charmer! The malt content appears pretty high, but the overall balance is wonderful. *40%. Ian Macleod.*

**Isle of Skye 50 Years Old (82.5)** n21.5 t21 f20 b20. Drier incarnation than the 50% version. But still the age has yet to be balanced out, towards the end in particular. Early on some distinguished moments involving something vaguely smoked and a sweetened spice. *41.6%*

**The Jacobite (78.5)** n18 t18.5 f22 b20. Neither the nose nor delivery are of the cleanest style. But comes into its own towards the finish when the thick soup of a whisky thins to allow an attractive degree of complexity. Not for those with catholic tastes. *40%. Booker.*

**James Alexander (85.5)** n21 t21.5 f21.5 b21.5. Some lovely spices link the grassier Speysiders to the earthier elements. *40%. Quality Spirits International.*

**James Buchanan's Special Reserve Aged 18 Years** bott code: L7237CE001 **(89)** n22.5 t24 f20.5 b22 A blend I have known and admired a very long time. Since indeed, my beard was black and I carried not an extra ounce of weight. And I am still, I admit, very much in love with, though she has betrayed me with a Spanish interloper... *40%.*

**James King (81)** n20 t19.5 f21 b20.5 A slightly more well balanced and equally weighted blend than it once was with better use of spice and cocoa. *43%. Quality Spirits International.*

**James King Aged 5 Years (84)** n19.5 t21 f21.5 b21.5 While the nose never quite gets going, things are quite different on the palate. And if you find a more agreeable chocolate fudge blend this year, please let me know. *43%. Quality Spirits International.*

**James King Aged 8 Years (86)** n21 t21 f22 b22 A far better constructed blend than of old, with the grains far more able to deal with the demands of the caramel. Fresh and salivating early on, despite the lushness, one can even fancy spotting the odd malt note before the spiced fudge takes command. *43%. Quality Spirits International.*

**James King 12 Years Old (81)** n19 t23 f19 b20. Caramel dulls the nose and finish. But for some time a quite beautiful blend soars about the taste buds offering exemplary complexity and weight. *40%. Quality Spirits International.*

**James King Aged 17 Years** bott code B289 **(84.5)** n21 t22 f20.5 b21 The malt has a far grander say than the 40% version, chipping in with an elementary Speyside note on both nose and delivery. It doesn't take long for the fudge-rich grain to take command, though. Easy, un-taxing whisky. *43%. Quality Spirits International.*

**J&B Jet (79.5)** n19 t20 f20.5 b20. Never quite gets off the ground due to carrying too heavy a load. Unrecognisable to its pomp in the old J&B days: this one is far too weighty and never properly finds either balance or thrust. *40%. Diageo.*

**J&B Reserve Aged 15 Years (78)** n23 t19 f18 b18. What a crying shame. The sophisticated and demure nose is just so wonderfully seductive but what follows is an open-eyed, passionless embrace. Coarsely grain-dominant and unbalanced, this is frustrating beyond words and not worthy to be mentioned in the same breath as the old, original J&B 15 which, by vivid contrast, was a malty, salivating fruit-fest and minor classic. *40%. Diageo.*

**J&B Rare (88.5)** n21.5 t22.5 f22 b22.5 I have been drinking a lot of J&B from a previous time of late, due to the death of their former blender Jim Milne. I think he would have been pretty taken aback by the youthful zip offered here: whether it is down to a decrease in age or the use of slightly more tired casks – or both – is hard to say. *40%. Diageo.*

**Johnnie Walker Black Label 12 Years Old (95.5)** n23.5 pretty sharp grain: hard and buffeting the nose; a buffer of yielding smoke, apple pie and delicate spice cushions the encounter; **t24.5** if there is a silkier delivery on the market today, I have not seen it: this is sublime stuff with the grains singing the sweetest hymns as they go down, taking with them a near perfection of weighty smoke lightened by brilliantly balanced barley which leans towards both soft apple and crème brûlée; **f23.5** those reassuringly rigid grains re-emerge and with them the most juicy Speyside malts imaginable; the lovely sheen to the finish underlines the good age of the whiskies used; **b24** here it is: one of the world's most masterful whiskies back in all its complex glory. A bottle like this is like being visited by an old lover. It just warms the heart and excites. 40%. Diageo.

**Johnnie Walker Aged 18 Years** bott code: L7276DN001 **(92) n23** the earthy phenols have the biggest say, though admirably reserved, before delicate diced apple and relaxed spices offer a counter weight; **t23.5** the palate is plunged into a morass of super-soft grain, light sugars filtering into the growing fruit; only towards the mid- point does the smoke, so evident on the nose, make its mark, working rather beautifully with the understated tannins; **f22** a slight trace of a fruity furriness; **b23.5** "the Pursuit of the Ultimate 18 year old Blend," says the label under the striding man. Well, they haven't reached their goal yet as, for all its deliciousness, this falls short of true Johnnie Walker brilliance thanks to an overly soft grain usage, when it was crying out for a variation which included a firmer, ramrod straight grain for extra mouth feel complexity, and give something for the malts to bounce off. That said, the extra but by no means over enthusiastic use of phenols ensures impressive depth to a genuinely lovely whisky. 40%.

◈ **Johnnie Walker Black Label Triple Cask Edition** bott code: L8327CB009 **(92.5) n23** not frightened to beat its grainy chest. The honey-rich strains of the malt take their time to arrive; **t23.5** just adore that delivery. While the malt struggled for a foothold in the nose, no such problems on presentation. The grains which follow are as soft as any in the Johnnie Walker range and hold back the spices until late into the development; **f22.5** ultra-light. The gain holds out to the end, the malt just a sub plot; **b23.5** strange this should be in under the Black Label banner as it lacks the associated weight and delicate smokiness. Still silky and seductive, but much more naked grain on show. 40%.

**Johnnie Walker Blenders' Batch Bourbon Cask & Rye Finish** bott code L7219CA002 00034598 **(89.5) n21.5 t23 f22.5 b22.5** Great to see someone have the good sense to try to make the most of rye. If they can tame the caramels the results will be better still. 40%. Diageo.

**Johnnie Walker Blender's Batch Espresso Roast** bott code: L7233IH007 **(86.5) n21 t23 f21 b21.5** Well, that was different! Can't really big up the nose or finish as it is just too tangy and furry. But the delivery – probably the softest and most well-rounded of any JW I have ever encountered - really does magic up some fabulously intense mocha notes – especially when the varying coffee and chocolate tones criss-cross or merge. The spices don't do any harm, either! 43.2%.

**Johnnie Walker Blender's Batch Red Wine Cask Blend** bott code: L7179CD002 **(91.5) n22.5** highly attractive weave of firm oak and earthy, jammy notes; very sharp, borderline aggressive in the arched intensity; **t23.5** a brittle sharpness to the muscovado sugars leads to an excellent juiciness in which both malt and fruit lay an even hand; Jammy Dodger biscuit, or even strawberry Swiss Roll with no shortage of cream; **f22** almost an old-fashioned cream sherry feel to this finish; the vaguest of furry finishes but no damage done; **b23.5** an absolutely unique fingerprint to this member of the Walker family: none has such a fruity yet creamy profile. 40%.

**Johnnie Walker Blue Label (88) n21 t24 f21 b22** What a frustrating blend! Just so close to brilliance but the nose and finish are slightly out of kilter. Worth the experience of the mouth arrival alone. 43%. Diageo.

**Johnnie Walker Blue Label The Casks Edition (97) n24.5 t24.5 f23.5 b24.5.** This is a triumph of scotch whisky blending. With not as much as a hint of a single off note to be traced from the tip of the nose to tail, this shameless exhibition of complexity and brilliance is the star turn in the Diageo portfolio right now. Indeed, it is the type of blend that every person who genuinely adores whisky must experience for the good of their soul....if only once in their life. 55.8%.

◈ **Johnnie Walker Blue Label Ghost & Rare** bott code: L8277DN006 **(96) n24** some fabulous age on this, the oak thinks about strutting ahead of the rest, but a fragile smokiness has just enough energy to keep it in line. Tingling hints of spice match the boiled gooseberry and delicate exotic fruit; **t24** salivating on delivery, which is a bit of a shock when you see how much big oak backs it up. The exotic fruit school of ye olde Speysiders comes into full view, with light molasses and smoke tp ensure there is a little rough to go with the smooth; **f23.5** medium length, lightly malted and still gently to the end; **b24.5** there is nothing new about using dead distilleries within a blend. However, finding them in one as good as this is a pretty rare occurrence. This just creaks of old whiskies all over the show. And what a marvellous show this is...for me, far more entertaining than the standard Blue Label thanks to less sherry influence, allowing the whiskies themselves to show their talents fully. 43.8%.

**Johnnie Walker Double Black (94.5) n23 t23.5 f24 b24.** Double tops! Rolling along the taste buds like distant thunder, this is a welcome and impressive addition to the Johnnie Walker stable. Perhaps not as complete and rounded as the original Johnnie Walker Black... but, then, what is? 40%.

**Johnnie Walker Explorers' Club Collection The Gold Route** (89) n23.5 t24 f19.5 b22. Much of this blend is truly the stuff of golden dreams. Like its Explorer's Club stable mate, some attention has to be paid to the disappointing finish. Worth sending out an expedition, though, just for the beautiful nose and delivery... 40%. Diageo.

**Johnnie Walker Explorer's Club Collection 'The Royal Route'** (93) n24.5 t24 f21.5 b23 A fabulous journey, travelling first Class most of the way. But to have discovered more, could have been bottled at 46% for a much more panoramic view of the great whiskies on show. 40%. Diageo

**Johnnie Walker Explorers' Club Collection The Spice Road** (84.5) n22 t23.5 f18 b21. Sublime delivery of exceptionally intense juiciness: in fact, probably the juiciest blend released this year. But the bitter, fuzzy finish reveals certain casks haven't helped. 40%.

**Johnnie Walker Gold Label Reserve** (91.5) n23 t24 f22 b23. Moments of true star quality here, but the finish could do with a polish. 40%. Diageo.

**Johnnie Walker King George V** db (88) n23 t22 f21 b22 One assumes that King George V is no relation to George IV. This has genuine style and breeding, if a tad too much caramel. 43%

**Johnnie Walker Platinum Label Aged 18 Years** (88) n22 t23 f21 b22. This blend might sound like some kind of Airmiles card. Which wouldn't be too inappropriate, though this is more Business than First... 40%. Diageo.

**Johnnie Walker Red Label** (87.5) n22 t22 f21.5 b22. The ongoing move through the scales quality-wise appears to suggest we have a work still in progress here. This sample has skimped on the smoke, though not quality. Yet a few months back when I was in the BA Business Lounge at Heathrow's new Terminal Five, I nearly keeled from almost being overcome by peat in the earthiest JW Red I had tasted in decades. I found another bottle and I'm still not sure which represents the real Striding Man. 40%. Diageo.

**Johnnie Walker Select Casks Aged 10 Years Rye Cask Finish** (90) n22.5 t23 f21.5 b23 With the use of first fill bourbon casks and ex-rye barrels for finishing, hardly surprising this is the JW with the most Kentuckian feel of them all. Yet it's even more Canadian, still. 46% (92 proof).

**Johnnie Walker X.R Aged 21 Years** (94) n23.5 t24 f23 b23.5. How weird: I nosed this blind before seeing what the brand was. My first thought was: "mmm, same structure of Crown Royal XR. Canadian??? No, there's smoke!" Then looked at what was before me and spotted it was its sister whisky from the Johnnie Walker stable. A coincidence? I don't think so... 40%.

**Kenmore Special Reserve Aged 5 Years** butt code L07285 (75) n18 t20 f19 b18. Recovers to a degree from the poor nose. For those who prefer their Scotch big-flavoured and gawky. 40%

**King Charles** (82) n21 t21 f20 b20 From the salty, sweaty armpit nose (which I know some people absolutely love in a whisky!) to the OTT sugar attack before the bitter finish, this isn't quite one for the purists. Hard to imagine a grain any more soft and enveloping. 40%. QSI.

**King Glenorsen** (81) n20 t21 f20 b20. Pleasant and easy drinking enough. But the young grains dominate completely. Designed, I think, to be neutralised by ice. 40%

**King Robert II** (77) n19 t19 f20 b19. A bustier, more bruising batch than the last 40 per cent version. Handles the OTT caramel much better. Agreeably weighty slugging whisky. 43%.

**Label 5 Aged 12 Years** bott code L515467C (90) n23 a lively nose, full of kumquat, raspberry cream Swiss Roll and deft smoke; clean for a blend these days and with the precision of an Exocet; t22.5 the vanillas wallow in the icing sugar for a while before the vanillas at last appear; f22 just a little tang, but still soft and sweet; the smoke arrives, thin and apologetically at the very end, though the late spice is much bolder; b22.5 one of the easiest drams you'll find this year with just enough complexity to lift it into the higher echelons. 40%. La Martiniquaise

**Label 5 Extra Rare Aged 18 Years** bott code L5301576 (87.5) n21.5 t22.5 f22 b21.5 You have to say this is pleasant. But from an 18-year-old blend you should be saying so much more. Salivating and at times fresh and juicy, other than the late spice little gets the pulses racing in the vanilla and sugar morass. A tad too much toffee, alas. 40%. La Martiniquaise.

**Label 5 Classic Black** bott code L403055D (87) n22 t22 f21 b22 A malt famed for its indifferent nose now boasts an aroma boasting complexity, layering and spice. The mix of spice and muscovado sugars elsewhere is no less appealing, though the mouth feel is a little too fat and yielding. But what an improvement! 40%. La Martiniquaise.

**Label 5 Gold Heritage** (92) n22.5 t23.5 f22 b24 A very classy blend very skilfully constructed. A stunningly lovely texture, one of the very best I have encountered for a while, and no shortage of complexity ensures this is a rather special blend. I'll even forgive the dulling by caramel and light milkiness from the tired bourbon barrel. The overall excellence outweighs the odd blemish. 40%

**Label 5 Premium Black** bott code: L720856A (84.5) n21 t22 f20.5 b21 An, at first, luscious, then later on ultra-firm blend with the accent decidedly on the grain and caramels. 40%.

**Lang's Supreme Aged 5 Years** (93.5) n23.5 t23.5 f23 b23.5. Every time I taste this the shape and structure has altered slightly. Here there is a fraction more smoke, installing a deeper confidence all round. This is blended whisky as it should be: Supreme in its ability to create shape and harmony. 40%. Ian Macleod Distillers Ltd.

**The Last Drop 1965** American Standard Barrel **(96.5)** n24 t24.5 f23.5 b24.5 Almost impossible to imagine a blended whisky to be better balanced than this. If there is a cleverer use of honey or less intrusive oak in any blended whisky bottled in the last year, I have yet to taste it. An award winner if ever I tasted one. Magnificent doesn't quite cover it... 48.6%. *Morrison Bowmore. The Last Drop Distillers Ltd.*

**The Last Drop 1971 Blended Scotch Whisky 45 Years Old (97)** n24.5 t24 f24 b24.5 Even though I now know many of the people involved in the Last Drop, I am still not entirely sure how they keep doing it. Just how do they continue to unearth whiskies which are truly staggering; absolute marvels of their type? This one is astonishing because the grain used is just about faultless. And the peating levels can be found around about the perfect mark on the dial. Like an old Ballantine's which has sat and waited in a cask over four decades to be discovered and tell its wonderful, spellbinding and never-ending tale. Just mesmerically beautiful. *47%.*

**The Last Drop 50 Year Old** Sherry Wood **(97)** n24 t24.5 f24 b24.5 You'd expect, after half a century in the cask, that this would be a quiet dram, just enjoying its final years with its feet up and arms behind its head. Instead we have a fairly aggressive blend determined to drive the abundant fruitiness it still possesses to the very hilt. It is backed up all the way by a surprising degree of warming, busy spice. There is a hell of a lot of life in this beautiful ol' dog... *51.2%*

⬧ **The Last Drop 56 Year Old Blended Scotch Whisky (96.5)** n24.5 so amazingly sexy: a naturally perfumed sweetness mixes with the most rounded mix of corn oil, muscovado sugar and soft vanilla. But the secret ingredient is the salty aroma, almost identical to that of your partner's sweat after making love: a truly erotic experience...; **t24.5** the mouth is caressed by that very same softness to the grain that first seduced you on the nose. Sweeter now: bruyere honey adds the most elegant touch to the silky vanillas; so salivating... **f23.5** spices arrive a little tamely but just as the sweetness is fading and a drier vanilla tone is being created; **b24** just one of those whiskies there is not enough time in the day for. One to share with your partner..when the lights are low and you are on your own... *47%.*

**Lauder's (74)** n18 t21 f17 b18. Well, it's consistent: you can say that for it! As usual, fabulous delivery, but as for the rest...oh dear. *40%. MacDuff International Ltd.*

**Lauder's** bott code L 08 10 14 4 BB **(78.5)** n19 t20 f19.5 b20 For those who like whisky with their cream toffee. Decent spice fizz, though. *40%. MacDuff International Ltd.*

**Lauder's Aged 15 Years** bott code L16/8189 **(93)** n23 hints of grape and sharper pear drop sink into a soft, grainy morass; **t23.5** beautifully salivating delivery: thick, with structured fruit rather than the overbearing grape I was expecting; the mid-ground celebrates a wonderfully marriage between over-ripe pear and light spice; molasses and toasty fudge; **f22.5** date, walnut, more fudge and molasses then, finally, a spiced butterscotch fade...; **b24** not the big fat sherry influence of a decade ago...thank heavens...!! This is a gorgeous blend for dark, stormy nights. Well, any night really... *40%. MacDuff International Ltd.*

**Lauder's Oloroso Cask** bott code L 25 01 16 4 BB **(86.5)** n21.5 t24 f19 b22 A magnificent blend for those unable to nose or taste sulphur. For those who can, a nearly whisky as this is borderline brilliant. Yes, both nose and finish especially have their weakness, but the narrative of the delivery, not to mention the brilliance of the mouth feel and overall weight and pace of the dram is sublime. Before the sulphur hits we are treated to a truly glorious Jaffa cake mix of controlled fruity sweetness as good as any blend I have tasted this year. *40%. MacDuff International Ltd.*

**Lauder's Ruby Cask** bott code L 21 05 15 4 BB **(94)** n23 excellent spice prickle and oak layering; the clean fruit gives everything a polish; **t24** mmmm! That is one outstanding mouth feel on the delivery: there is a sheen to the sharp Port-generated fruit plus a generous – though not too generous – sprinkling of muscovado sugar; a little ulmo honey thickens the middle. The trade-off between the crisp, crunchy fruit and sugars and the softer grains is sublime; **f23** the spices are on slow burn but when they arrive they complement the oak perfectly; **b24** a sophisticated little gem. *40%. MacDuff International Ltd.*

**Lauder's Queen Mary** bott code L 04 11 14 4 BB **(86.5)** n22.5 t21.5 f21 b21.5 The sweet oily aroma of Angel Cake and even some roast chestnut: the nose is certainly highly attractive. This almost translates through the body of blend when the caramel allows, the grains showing an oily strain and a slightly malty kick here and there. *40%. MacDuff International Ltd.*

**The Loch Fyne (89.5)** n22 t23 f21.5 b23. This is an adorable old-style blend....a bit of a throwback. But no ruinous sherry notes...just clean and delicious. Well, mainly... *40%*

**Loch Lomond Blended Scotch (89)** n22 t22.5 f22 b22.5 A fabulously improved blend: clean and precise and though malt is seemingly at a premium, a fine interplay. *40%*

**Loch Lomond Reserve** db **(86.5)** n21.5 t22 f21.5 b21.5. A spongy, sweet, chewy, pleasant blend which is more of a take as you find statement than a layering of flavour. 40%

**Loch Lomond Signature** bott code L3/306/15 **(86)** n22 t21.5 f21 b21.5 Not quite the malty force it can be, though the sugar almonds are a treat. Succulent and gently spiced though the caramel has just a little too much force towards the end. *40%. Loch Lomond Group.*

**Lochranza (83.5) n21 t21.5 f21 b20.** Pleasant, clean, but, thanks to the caramel, goes easy on the complexity. 40%. Isle of Arran.

**Lombard Gold Label (88) n22 t22 f22 b22** after evaluating this I read the tasting notes on the back of the label and for about the first time this year thought: "actually, the bottlers have the description pretty spot on. So tasted it again, this time while reading the notes and found myself agreeing with every word: a first. Then I discovered why: they are my tasting notes from the 2007 Whisky Bible, though neither my name nor book have been credited... A gold label, indeed... 40%. .

**Long John Special Reserve** bott code: 2017/08/10 **(87.5) n21.5 t22.5 f21.5 b22** An honest, non-fussy blend which makes a point of stacking the bigger flavours up front so it hits the ground running. The grains and toffee shape all aspects, other than this rich delivery where the malt offers both weight and a lighter, salivating quality also; an even a gentle thread of honey. The type of blend that an offer for a refill will be seldom refused. 40%.

**Lord Elcho (83.5) n20 t22 f21 b20.5** Such a vast improvement on the last bottling I encountered: this has lush grain at the front, middle and rear that entertains throughout, if a little one dimensionally. A little bit of a tweak and could be a high class blend. 40%. Wemyss Malts.

**Lord Elcho Aged 15 Years (89.5) n23.5 t22.5 f21.5 b22** Three or four years ago this was a 15-year-old version of the Lord Elcho standard blend today. So, small mercies, this has moved on somewhat and now offers up a genuinely charming and complex nose and delivery. One is therefore surprised to be disappointed by the denouement, taking into account the blend's history. Some more clever and attentive work on the middle and finish would have moved this into seriously high quality blend territory. But so much to enjoy as it is. 40%. Wemyss Malts.

**Lord Scot (77.5) n18.5 t20 f19.5 b19.5.** A touch cloying but the mocha fudge ensures a friendly enough ride. 40%. Loch Lomond Distillers.

**Lord Scot (86.5) n20 t22 f22.5 b22.** A gorgeously lush honey and liquorice middle. 43%

**The Lost Distilleries** batch 2 **(94) n22.5 t24 f23.5 b24.** Whoever lost it better find it again: this is how you dream every whisky should be. 53.2%.

**The Lost Distilleries Blend** Batch 6 **(91) n23.5 t23 f22 b22.5** The Lost Malt as well: completely grain dominant – but wonderfully lush and tasty. 49.3%

**The Lost Distilleries Blend** batch 9 **(91) n23** simplistic, gentle schmoozing of light citrus tones with more upfront vanilla; the grain has the bigger say; **t23.5** big sugar blast on delivery – eyewateringly intense. Soft mocha and maltesers amble through the middle; **f22.5** recedes back to a simple vanilla tale, though there is a little tang, too; **b23** the distilleries may be lost to us, but on the palate they are especially at home. 52.1%. 476 bottles.

**Mac Na Mara (83) n20 t22.5 f20 b20.5.** Absolutely brimming with salty, fruity character. But just a little more toffee and furriness than it needs. Enjoyable, though. 40%

**Mac Na Mara** bott code L 25 08 14 2 07 48 BB **(84) n21.5 t22 f19.5 b21** As usual, a glass of tricks as the flavours come tumbling at you from every direction. Few blends come saltier and the dry vanilla forges a fascinating balance with the rampant caramel. A fraction furry at the death. 40%. Pràban na Linne Ltd.

**Mac Na Mara Rum Finish (93) n22 t24 f23 b24** High quality blending, and the usage of the rum appears to have retained the old Mac Na Mara style. 40%. Praban na Linne.

**Mac Na Mara Rum Cask Finish** bott code L 23 05 16 3 BB **(86) n22.5 t22 f21 b21.5** Lost a degree of the sugary crispness normally associated with this brand and after the initial rum embrace resorts far too quickly to a caramel-rich game-plan. 40%. ncf. Pràban na Linne Ltd.

⬧ **Mac's Reserve** bott code: L9C 7908 0711 **(84) n21 t21.5 f21 b20.5** Perfectly acceptable, easy going soft and sweet whisky. But if they really want to pay tribute to cooper Jimmy Mackie, the Mac in question, then they should drop the toffee and let the oak do the talking. 40%. Charter Brands.

**MacArthur's** bott code L16/L31 R16/5192 IB 1735 **(87.5) n21.5 t22 f21.5 b22.5** Not quite the tricky and cleverly smoked blend of a few years back. But still a weightier chap than a decade ago, not least because of the softer grain type. The malts do come through with just enough meaning to make for a well-balanced and thoroughly enjoyable offering. 40%. International Beverage Holdings Ltd.

**MacQueens (89) n21.5 t22.5 f22.5 b22.5.** I am long enough in the tooth now to remember blends like this found in quiet country hotels in the furthest-flung reaches of the Highlands beyond a generation ago. A wonderfully old-fashioned, traditional one might say, blend of a type that is getting harder and harder to find. 40%. Quality Spirits International.

**MacQueens of Scotland Aged 3 Years (86) n20.5 t22 f21.5 b22** Rare to find a blend revealing its age at 3 years, though of course many are that.... and a day. Enjoyable, with attractive weight and even an ulmo honey note to partner the spices which, combined, makes it distinctively a cut above for its type. 40%. Quality Spirits International.

**MacQueens of Scotland Aged 8 Years (78.5) n18 t21.5 f19 b20** A little furry and off key. 40%. Quality Spirits International.

**MacQueens of Scotland Aged 12 Years (89.5) n23** certain exotic fruit notes suggest a usage of malts older than 12. Lots of marzipan and vanilla abound as well as a light kumquat note; **t22.5** silky delivery with a slow procession of drier vanillas bolstered by muscovado sugars and spice; the spices grow in confidence and effect; **f21.5** soft, though the caramel has too great a say; **b22.5** some outstanding malts have gone into this charming blend. 40%. QSI.

**Master of Malt Blended 10 Years Old 1st Edition (84.5) n21.5 t22.5 f20 b20.5.** A pleasant enough, though hardly complex, blend benefitting from the lovely malty, then silky pick-up from delivery and a brief juicy barley sharpness. But unsettled elsewhere due, mainly, to using the wrong fit of grain: too firm when a little give was needed. 47.5%. ncf. WB15/353

**Master of Malt 30 Year Old Blended Scotch Whisky (86) n21.5 t23 f20 b21.5** Typical of Master of Malt blends it is the delivery which hits fever pitch in which myriad juicy notes make a mockery of the great age. Sadly, on this occasion both the nose and finish are undone by some ungainly oak interference and, latterly quite a tang. 47.5%.

**Master of Malt 40 Year Old Blended Scotch Whisky** batch 1 **(93.5) n24 t23.5 f22.5 b23.5** Some outstanding oak at play here. For a blend the grains and malts appear a little isolated from the other, but the overall effect is still wonderful. 47.5%.

**Master of Malt 50 Year Old Blended Scotch Whisky (92.5) n24 t23.5 f22 b23** Hard to keep all the casks of over 50 years in line. But so much else is sublime. 47.5%.

**Master Of Malt St Isidore (84) n21 t22 f20 b21.** Sweet, lightly smoked but really struggles to put together a coherent story. Something, somewhere, is not quite right. 41.4%

**Matisse 12 Years Old (90.5) n23 t23 f22 b22.5** Moved up yet another notch as this brand continues its development. Much more clean-malt oriented with a Speyside-style to the fore. Majestic and charming. 40%. Matisse Spirits Co Ltd

**Matisse 21 Years Old (86) n23 t22 f20 b21.** Begins breathtakingly on the nose, with a full array of exotic fruit showing the older bourbon casks up to max effect. Nothing wrong with the early delivery, which offers a touch of honeycomb on the grain. But the caramel effect on the finish stops everything in its tracks. Soft and alluring, all the same. 40%

**Matisse Old (85.5) n20 t23 f21 b21.5.** Appears to improve each time I come across it. The nose is a bit on the grimy side and the finish disappears under a sea of caramel. But the delivery works deliciously, with a chewy weight which highlights the sweeter malts. 40%

**Matisse Royal (81) n19 t22 f20 b20.** Pleasant, if a little clumsy. Extra caramel appears to have scuppered the spice. 40%. Matisse Spirits Co Ltd.

**McArthurs (89.5) n22 t22.5 f22 b23** One of the most improved blends on the market. The clever use of the peat is exceptional. 40%. Inverhouse Distillers.

❖ **McKendrick's 3 Years Old (71) n18 t20 f16 b17** "Supple, Strong and Silky" boasts the label. Unsubtle, standard 40% abv and silky says the whisky. Cloying to a degree and with a little sulphur off note late on, presumably from the ex-sherry grain casks. Not Asda's finest. 46%. Asda

**Monarch of the Glen (81) n20 t20 f20 b20** A youthful grainfest wallowing in its fat and sweet personality. 40%. Quality Spirits International.

**Monarch of the Glen Aged 8 Years (82.5) n19 t20.5 f21.5 b21.5** The initially harsh grain takes time to settle but eventually finds a decent fudge and spiced mocha theme. 40%. QSI.

**Monarch of the Glen Aged 12 Years (88.5) n22** a lovely fudge note goes well with the mocha; **t22.5** has kept its glorious silk texture, though the fruits have vanished. Demerara sugar and chocolate hazelnut; **f22** long, soft, slow raising of spice and vanilla; **b22** I always enjoyed this for its unusual fruity nature. Well, the fruit has gone and been replaced by chocolate. A fair swap: it's still delicious! 40%. Quality Spirits International.

**Montrose (74.5) n18 t20 f18 b18.5.** A battling performance but bitter defeat in the end. 40%.

**Muirhead's Blue Seal** bott code L15 138 780 21 **(84.5) n21.5 t21 f21 b21** A clean, uncluttered and attractive blend with heavy emphasis on grain and no shortage of caramel and spice. A distinct wisp of malt can be located from time to time. 40%. Tullibardine Ltd.

**The Naked Grouse (76.5) n19 t21 f17.5 b19.** Sweet. But reveals too many ugly sulphur tattoos. 40%.

**Nation of Scots (92.5) n23** the most adroit use of smoke coupled with a vague saltiness – think Arbroath Smokies – sits comfortably with the chalky vanilla and sneezable black pepper; **t23** mouth-filling without being overly cloying or too soft. The smoke guarantees weight and backbone while a light, gristy sweetness ensures another level at work entirely; **f23** back to those spices now; smoke, vanilla and caramel make for a luxurious and satisfying fade; **b23.5** apparently, this is a blend designed to unite Scots around the world. Well, I'm not Scottish but it's won me over. If only more blends could be as deliciously embracing as this. 52%. Annandale Distillery.

**Northern Scot (68) n16 t18 f17 b17.** Heading South bigtime. 40%. Bruce and Co. for Tesco.

**Oishii Wisukii Aged 36 Years (96) n24.5 t23.5 f24 b24** Normally, I'd suggest popping into the Highlander for a pint of beer. But if they happen to have any of this stuff there...break his bloody arm off: it's magnificent! 46.2%. The Highlander Inn, Craigellachie.

**Old Masters G (93)** n24 t23 f23 b23 A high quality blend with enough clarity and complexity to suggest they have not stinted on the malt. The nose, in particular, is sublime. Thankfully they have gone easy on the colouring here, as it is so delicate it could have ruined the artistry. *40%. Lombard Scotch Whisky Ltd.*

**Old McDonald (83.5)** n20 t22 f20.5 b21. Attractively tart and bracing where it needs to be with lovely grain bite. Lots of toffee, though. *43.%. The Last Drop Distillers. For India.*

**Old Parr 12 Years Old (91.5)** n21.5 t23.5 f23 b23.5 Perhaps on about the fourth of fifth mouthful, the penny drops that this is not just exceptionally good whisky: it is blending Parr excellence... *40%. Diageo.*

**Old Parr Aged 15 Years (84)** n19 t22 f21 b22. Absolutely massive sherry input here. Some of it is of the highest order. The nose, reveals, however, that some isn't... *43%*

**Old Parr Classic 18 Years Old (84.5)** n21 t21.5 f21 b21. A real jumbled, mixed bag with fruit and barley falling over each other and the grains offering little sympathy. Enough to enjoy, but with Old Parr, one expects a little more... *46%. Diageo.*

**Old Parr Superior 18 Years Old** batch no. L5171 **(97)** n25 t25 f23 b24. Year in, year out, this blend just gets better and better. This bottling struck me as a possible Whisky of the Year, but perhaps only an outsider. Familiarity, though, bred anything but contempt and over the passing months I have tried to get to the bottom of this truly great whisky. Blended whisky has long needed a champion. This grand old man looks just the chap. This is a worthy, if unexpected (even to me), Jim Murray' Whisky Bible 2007 World Whisky of the Year. *43%.*

**Old Smuggler (85.5)** n21 t22 f21 b21.5. A much sharper act than its Allied days with a new honeyed-maple syrup thread which is rather delightful. Could still do with toning down the caramel, though, to brighten the picture further. *40%. Campari, France.*

**Old St. Andrews Clubhouse** batch no. L2519 G2362 **(89)** n22 t22.5 f22 b22.5 Very neat and tidy – and eminently quaffable. 40%.

**Old St. Andrews Clubhouse** batch no. L2997 G2716 **(87.5)** n21.5 t22 f22 b22 Just a little extra grain bite to this one means the usual juiciness is down, though the slow spice build is pretty sexy. Lots of coffee-toffee tones to chew over. 40%.

**Passport (83)** n22 t19 f21 b21. It looks as though Chivas have decided to take the blend away from its original sophisticated, Business Class J&B/Cutty Sark, style for good now, as they have continued this decently quaffable but steerage quality blend with its big caramel kick and chewy, rather than lithe, body. *40%. Chivas.*

**Passport** bott code LKBL0720 2017/02/24 **(81.5)** n20 t21 f20 b20.5 Still can't get used to the brash golden colour of the whisky that shines back at me. This was once the Passport to whisky sophistication: pale and glistening on the palate rather than from the bottle with its cut glass, precision flavour-profile – First Class in every way. Now it is fat, flat, chewy, and fudged in every sense of the word. *40%. Chivas Brothers Ltd.*

**Parkers (78)** n17 t22 f20 b19. The nose has regressed, disappearing into ever more caramel, yet the mouth-watering lushness on the palate remains and the finish now holds greater complexity and interest. *40%. Angus Dundee.*

◈ **Pure Scot** bott code: L 08 02 17 **(87)** n21.5 t22.5 f21.5 b22 The grain is both yielding and profound while the malt notes mostly are lost in a toffee swirl. Mid to late arrives spices, but complexity is at a premium and the structure perhaps a little too soft. That said, a little acacia honey goes a long way and the overall experience is very satisfying indeed, especially with the sugars always slightly ahead of the game. *40%. Bladnoch Distillery.*

◈ **Pure Scot Virgin Oak 43** virgin oak cask finish, bott code: L18/89.7 **(93)** n23 a procession of orange and tannin tones give an almost bourbony feel. Liquorice and spice abounds for this singular blend aroma; **t23.5** the voluptuous softness of the grain is not compounded by further caramel interferences. Instead, a satisfying juiciness takes hold, some of it provoked by a squeeze of tangerine, with even the odd shard or barley cutting into the piece; **f23** beautiful oils re-ignite the earlier citrus theme; **b23.5** a sensational little blend worth finding. Not particularly complex as to regards malt and grain layering, but the integration of the tannins for a blend is a rare joy. *43%. Bladnoch Distillery.*

**Queen Margot (85.5)** n21.5 t22 f21 b21. A clean, silky-textured, sweet and caramel-rich blend of disarming simplicity. *40%*

**Queen Margot (86)** n21 t22 f21.5 b21.5. A lovely blend which makes no effort to skimp on a spicy depth. Plenty of cocoa from the grain late on but no shortage of good whiskies put to work. *40%. Wallace and Young for Lidl.*

**Queen Margot Aged 5 Years (89)** n22 t22.5 f22 b22.5 A very attractive blend with a most agreeable level of chewability. The chocolate orange which bolsters the yielding grain appears to suggest some good, clean sherry influence along the way. *40%*

**Queen Margot Aged 8 Years (85)** n21 t22 f21 b21. Pleasant, untaxing, with a hint of oaky vanilla after the sugary crescendo. *40%*

**Reliance PL (76) n18 t20 f19 b19**. Some of the old spiciness evident. But has flattened out noticeably. *43%. Diageo*.

**Robert Burns (85) n20 t22.5 f21 b21.5**. Skeletal and juicy: very little fat and gets to the mouthwatering point pretty quickly. Genuine fun. *40%. Isle of Arran*.

**The Royal & Ancient (80.5) n20 t21.5 f19 b20**. Has thinned out dramatically in the last year or so. Now clean, untaxing, briefly mouth-watering and radiating young grain throughout. *40%*

**Royal Park (87.5) n22 t22 f22 b21.5** A significantly improved blend which though still showing toffee appears to have cut down the amount, to the advantage of the busy vanilla, Demerara sugar and increased spices. Wholly enjoyable. Incidentally, the label helpfully informs us: "Distilled and Matured in Oak Casks." Who needs stills, eh...? *40%. Quality Spirits International*.

**Royal Salute 21 Years Old (92.5) n23 t23.5 f23 b23.5** If you are looking for the velvety character of yore, forget it. This one comes with some real character and is much the better for it. The grain, in particular, excels. *40%. Chivas*.

**Royal Salute 21 Years Old** bott code LKSK2858 2016/07/13 **(96) n24 t23.5 f24 b24.5** Elegant, sensual and the epitome of great blending. What else would you expect...? *40%. Chivas Brothers*.

◈ **Royal Salute 21 Year Old The Lost Blend (95.5) n24** sensuous oak. It may be 21, but some of the tannins here appear to be something a lot older. Some of the notes contain a dim fruitiness, others a lazy muscovado. But amid the age and sawdust comes, as it must in all great blends, a degree of fresher, contrasting sharpness, too, revealing that the malt element is still alive and kicking; elsewhere a delicate smokiness holds a constant position; **t24** quite superb! Those creeping malt and peat notes show first on delivery, tucked in comfortably with the muscovado. This begins to thicken into molasses as the tannins make their point; **f23.5** a delightful light phenol and tannin fade; **b24** Lost Blend...? Panic over, chaps: discovered it in my Whisky Bible tasting lab....!! And well worth finding, too.... *40%. Chivas Brothers*.

**Royal Salute 21 Years Old The Polo Collection** bott code 2017/04/25 LPNL0722 **(95) n23.5 t23.5 f24 b24** A significantly different RS21 to the last standard bottling I came across, this being much meatier – which is rather apt seeing that horses are involved. Mixes suave sophistication with a certain ruggedness: not unlike polo, I suppose. Not a dram to chukka away under any circumstances... *40%. Chivas Brothers Ltd*.

◈ **Royal Salute 21 Year Old Polo Collection 3 (92) n23** more of a nod towards Speyside than a previous Polo Collection, with a deft toffee apple depth; **t23.5** salivating and mildly warming. The caramels do have a lot of influence, but the secondary spice buzzing is fascinating; **f22.5** low key: dependent on soft oaky vanilla, caramels and just the lightest malt fade; **b23** as soft as a velvet polo jumper... *46.5%*.

◈ **Royal Salute 25 Year Old The Signature Blend (93) n24** certainly makes no bones about the diced, over-ripe apple which appears to be the theme. The tannins lurk, but are not well hidden. Malts come into play as does the vaguest smokiness, which sweetens the oak slightly; **t23.5** on delivery it is the grains which have their hands on the tiller, offering both a soft and firm platform on which the light liquorice oaks and mocha-tinted malts can perform; **f22.5** remains on the grainy side with a very light finale; **b23** a curious blend which both underlines its age, yet with the lightness of touch, then proceeds to hide it, too. *40%*.

**Royal Salute 32 Years Old Union of the Crowns** bott code 2017/01/17 LPNL0102 **(96.5) n24 t24.5 f24 b24** I trust Nicola Sturgeon has given The Union of Crowns, this truly outstanding and worthy Scotch blend to celebrate the joining the kingdoms of England, Scotland and Ireland, her seal of approval and she will help promote it fervently as a great Scottish export... *40%. Chivas Brothers Ltd*.

**Royal Salute 38 Years Old Stone of Destiny** bott code 2016/12/20 LPNK2479 **(93.5) n24 t23.5 f22.5 b23.5** Knowing the blender and having a pretty educated guess at the range of stocks he would have to work from, I tried to picture in my mind's eye how this whisky would nose and taste even before I opened the bottle. In particular, I tried to pre-guess the mouth feel, a character vital especially in older blends but often overlooked by those who eventually taste it, though it actually plays a significant role without the drinker realising it. Well, both the nose and mouth feel were just as I had imagined, though some aspects of the finish were slightly different. An engrossing and elegant dram. *40%. Chivas Brothers Ltd*.

**Royal Salute 62 Gun Salute (95.5) n24.5 t24 f23 b24** How do you get a bunch of varying whiskies in style, but each obviously growing a grey beard and probably cantankerous to boot, to settle in and harmonise with the others? A kind of Old People's Home for whisky, if you like. Well, here's how...*43%. Chivas*.

**Royal Salute The Diamond Tribute (91) n23.5 t23 f21.5 b23**. Ironic that a diamond is probably the hardest natural creation, yet this whisky is one of man's softest... *40%. Chivas*.

**Royal Salute The Eternal Reserve (89.5) n23 t23.5 f21 b22** One of those strange whiskies where so much happens on the nose and delivery, but much less when we head to the finish *40%*

**Royal Silk Reserve (93) n22 t24 f24 b23** I named this the best newcomer of 2001 and it hasn't let me down. A session blend for any time of the day, this just proves that you don't need piles of peat to create a blend of genuine stature. A must have. 40%

**Royal Silk Reserve Aged 5 Years (92.5) n23 t23 f23 b23.5** I was lucky enough to be the first person outside the tasting lab to sample this whisky when it was launched at the turn of this century. It was quite wonderful then, it still is so today though the grains aren't quite as brittle and translucent as they were back then. Still, I admire beyond words the fact that the current blenders have eschewed the craze for obscuration by ladelling in the colouring as though lives depended on it. What we can nose and taste here in this heart-gladdeningly light (both in colour and personality) blend is whisky. As an aside, very unusual for a blend to hide its age away on the back label. 40%.

**Royal Warrior (86) n21 t22 f21.5 b21.5.** An entirely pleasant grain-rich, young, old fashioned blend which masters the prevalent sugars well when they appear to be getting out of hand. Extremely clean and beautifully rounded. 40%

**Sandy Mac (76) n18 t20 f19 b19.** Basic, decent blend that's chunky and raw. 40%. *Diageo.*

**Scots Earl (76.5) n18 t20 f19 b19.5.** Its name is Earl. And it must have upset someone in a previous life. Always thrived on its engaging disharmony. But just a tad too syrupy now. 40%.

**Scottish Collie (78) n18 t20 f20 b20** I thought I heard you saying it was a pity: pity I never had any good whiskies. But you're wrong. I have. Thousands of them. Thousands of them. And all drams.... 40%. *Quality Spirits International.*

**Scottish Collie (80) n20 t21 f19 b20** A greatly improved bend with a far more vivacious delivery full of surprising juiciness and attractively controlled sweetness. Not as much toffee influence as had once been the case, so the spices cancels out the harsh finish. 43%. *QSI.*

**Scottish Leader Aged 12 Years** bott code P037533 L3 09.18 16082 **(89.5) n22 t23 f22 b22.5** A vast improvement on the last Leader 12 I encountered, this really finding a relaxed yet intriguing style. 40%.

**Scottish Leader Original** bott code P03 555 L 08.35 16342 **(83) n19 t22 f21 b21** Had this been the "original" Scottish leader I tasted 20 or so years ago we'd have a lighter coloured, less caramel heavy, more malt sparkling whisky. As it is, overcomes a cramped nose to offer some excellent complexity on delivery. 40%.

**Scottish Leader Signature** bott code P038914 L316256 **(90.5) n22 t23.5 f22 b23** Thoroughly enjoyable and beautifully constructed blend in which thought has clearly gone into both weight, texture and flavour profiling: not a given for blends these days. The nose and delivery are waxy with a vague honey richness; the delivery uses that honey to full effect by offering a growing firmness and then busy interplay between light oak, spices and weightier malts. Had they gone a little easier on the dumbing-down toffee, this might have bagged an award. 40%.

**Scottish Leader Supreme** bott code P039255 I 3 14.21 16278 **(77) n18.5 t20 f19 b19.5** Sticky, sweet and overly simple. 40%.

**Scottish Piper (80) n20 t20 f20 b20.** A light, mildly- raw, sweet blend with lovely late vanilla intonation. 40%

**Scottish Piper** bott code L17033 **(82) n20 t20 f21.5 b20.5** Continues its traditional toffee drone, though with a spicier finale than before. 40%. *Burlington Drinks.*

**Scottish Prince (83.5) n21 t22 f20 b20.5.** Muscular, but agreeably juicy 40%

**Sia Blended Scotch Whisky (87) n21 t22.5 f21.5 b22.** Rare to find a blend that's so up front with its smoke. Doesn't scrimp on the salivation stakes or sheer chewiness, either. 43% .

◇ **Sir Edward's Aged 12 Years** bott 18-09-2018, bott code: L826170-00150 **(87.5) n22 t22 f21.5 b22** Worth having around the house for the charming 1930's's-style label alone. They make big play of the brand having been around since 1891 – the year of my maternal grandmother's birth! – and even have 1891 included in the mould of the bottle. But an unnecessary over-reliance of caramel takes the score down. There is enough evidence on the early clarity and texture of the grain that this blend could hold its own and entertain thoroughly in its natural state. Rather lovely spices counter the sweetness impressively. Simple, but genuinely enjoyable whisky. 40%. *Bardinet.*

**Sir Lawrence** bott code: L17 03274 CB2 **(87) n21 t22.5 f21.5 b22** An impressively clean blend having been matured in better quality oak. This allows you to enjoy the full-throttle delivery without fear of any tangy, off-note sub plots. The caramels do get a little too enthusiastic towards the end but before then the grain and Demerara sugars dig in for a delicious degree of mocha. 40%.

**Something Special (85) n21.5 t22 f20.5 b21.** Mollycoddled by toffee, any murderous tendencies seem to have been fudged away, leaving just the odd moment of attractive complexity. You suspect there is a hit man in there somewhere trying to get out. 40%. *Chivas.*

**Something Special** bott code LPFK 1116 2016/06/30 **(90) n22** lifted dramatically by a gentle citrus note adding to the cream toffee: a very clean but soft nose...; **t22.5** gorgeously lush without going down the cloyingly sweet route so many blends do, this enjoys a deliciously spiced honey middle and even the odd shaft of malt clearly bursting through; f23 the light tannins arrive with some toffee, but still that honey and spice continues; b22.5 one of the few blends that has actually improved in recent years. Always been an attractive, interesting if non-spectacular blend which I have enjoyed when meeting it at various bars with friends around the world. Now there is personality enough to punch through the toffee and leave you wanting more. 40%. Chivas Brothers Ltd.

**Something Special Legacy (92) n23 t22.5 f23 b23.5** Good, solid blender is David Boyd. And here he has married substance with subtlety. Lovely stuff. 40%

**Something Special Premium Aged 15 Years (89) n22 t23 f21 b23** Fabulous malt thread and some curious raisin/sultana fruitiness, too. A blend-lover's blend. 40%.

**Stag Hunter (79) n19 t20 f20 b20** Hard to get past the gin-type nose. Not sure if this is a bottling hall issue, or if we have a blend that celebrates a botanical-style personality. 40%. Burlington Drinks.

**Stag's Head Blended Scotch Whisky (85.5) n21.5 t21.5 f21 b21.5.** A thick, hefty nose and body, lush grain and lashings of caramel. Pleasant, sweet, nutty standard stuff. 40% (80 proof)

**Stewart's Old Blended (93) n22.5 t24 f23 b23.5.** Really lovely whisky for those who like to close their eyes, contemplate and have a damned good chew. 40%

**Storm (94) n23 t23.5 f24 b23.5.** A little gem of a blend that will take you by storm. 43%.

**Talisman 5 Years Old (85.5) n22 t22 f20.5 b21.** Unquestionably an earthier, weightier version of what was once a Speyside romp. Soft peats also add extra sweetness. 40%

**Teacher's Aged 25 Years** batch 1 **(96.5) n24 t24.5 f23.5 b24.5** Only 1300 bottles means they will be hard pushed to create this exact style again. Worth a go, chaps: considering this is India bound, it is the Karma Sutra of blended scotch. 46%. Beam Inc. 1300 bottles. India & Far East Travel Retail exclusive.

**Teacher's Highland Cream (90) n23 t23 f22 b22** Not yet back to its best but a massive improvement on the 2005 bottlings. Harder grains to accentuate the malt will bring it closer to the classic of old. 40%

**Teacher's Origin (92) n23 t23 f23 b23** Almost brings a tear to the eye to taste a Scotch blend that really is a blend. With a better grain input (Dumbarton, say),this perhaps would have been one of the contenders of World Whisky of the Year. Superb! 40%

**Teacher's Origin (88.5) n22 t23.5 f21 b22** A fascinating blend among the softest on the market today. That is aided and abetted by the exceptionally high malt content, 65%, which makes this something of an inverted blend, as that, for most established brands, is the average grain content. What appears to be a high level of caramel also makes for a rounding of the edges, as well as evidence of sherry butts. The bad news is that this has resulted in a duller finish than perhaps might have been intended, which is even more pronounced given the impressive speech made on delivery. Lovely whisky, yes. But something, I feel, of a work in progress. Bringing the caramel down by the percentage points of the malt would be a very positive start... 42.8%. ncf.

**Té Bheag** bott code L 06 12 16 3 **(83) n19 t22 f21 b21** Reverted to its mucky nose of yore but though caramel has the loudest voice it has retained its brilliant spice bite. 40%. ncf.

**Tesco Special Reserve Minimum 3 Years Old** bott code L6335 16/04171 **(83.5) n19 t22 f21.5 b21** Improved of late. Now unashamedly in the date and walnut school of blends, where before it had only dabbled; thick, uncompromisingly sweet and cloying but with enough spice and salivation to make for pleasant and characterful bit of fun. 40%.

**That Boutique-y Whisky Company Blended Whisky No. 1 50 Year Old (96) n23.5 t25 f23.5 b24** Some of the moments encountered in this blend are the exact reason why no spirit on this planet comes close to whisky at its very finest. 46.6%. 2,000 bottles.

**That Boutique-y Whisky Company Blended Whisky No. 2 18 Year Old (86.5) n20 t22.5 f22 b22** The caramels from the oak are quite startling. The off-key nose is best ignored but lovers of fruity fudge will have a field day. 46.7%. 2,104 bottles.

**That Boutique-y Whisky Company Blended Whisky No. 3 23 Year Old (91) n21 t23.5 f23 b23.5** From the stuttering start on the nose this turns into rich, well-layered blend with no age scars whatsoever. 48.2%. 463 bottles.

**The Tweeddale Blend Aged 10 Years (89.5) n22 t23.5 f21.5 b22.5** The first bottling of this blend since World War 2, it has been well worth waiting for. 46%. ncf. 50% malt. Stonedean.

**The Tweeddale Blended Scotch Whisky Aged 14 Years** batch 5 **(92) n22.5 t23.5 f23 b23** I was salivating just at the prospect of this one, as I remember what a fresh article Batch 4 was. Well, this is even sharper in some places...yet curiously far more laid back and docile in others. 46%. nc ncf.

**Tweeddale 28 Year Old Evolution (89) n22.5 t23 f21 b22.5** A blend seemingly teeming in malt and helped greatly by the natural cask strength. A blended Scotch single malt lovers will miss at their peril. 52%. R & B Distillers.

**Ushers Green Stripe (85) n19 t22.5 f21.5 b22.** Upped a notch or two in all-round quality. The juicy theme and clever weight is highly impressive and enjoyable. *43% Diageo.*

**VAT 69 (84.5) n20 t22 f21 b21.5.** Has thickened up ln style: weightier, more macho, much more to say and a long way off that old lightweight. A little cleaning up wouldn't go amiss. *40%*

**Walton Royal Blend Deluxe Reserve (91.5) n22.5 t23 f23 b23** It's amazing what a dose of good quality peaty whisky can do to a blend. Certainly ensures it stands out as a deliciously chewy — and smoky — experience.*43%*

**White Horse (90.5) n22 t23 f22.5 b23** A malt which has subtly changed shape. Not just the smoke which gives it weight, but you get the feeling that some of Diageo's less delicate malts have been sent in to pack a punch. As long as they are kept in line, as is the case here — just — we can all enjoy a very big blend. *40%. Diageo.*

**White Horse Aged 12 Years (86) n21 t23 f21 b21.** Enjoyable, complex if not always entirely harmonious. For instance, the apples and grapes on the nose appear on a limb from the grain and caramel and nothing like the thoroughbred of old. Lighter, more flaccid and caramel dominated. *40%. Diageo.*

**White Walker** bott code. L8282KS002 **(80) n19 t22.5 f19 b20.5** Pouring from the top. As you might expect, there is no nose when frozen, other than the vaguely discernible, ultra clean tip of the grain. The big surprise is that there is a decent degree of flavour on delivery — again the grains at work and carrying a presentable amount of Demerara sweetness and here's the real shock...a very thick, chewable, oily body. So, early on, much more character than I expected. But the finish is as non-specific as I had feared and trails off with a certain bitterness. OK, that was it unshaken, and pouring from the top:

Now shaken: **(85.5) n19.5 t22 f22 b22** By shaking before pouring. You lose some of the early richness of the body. But there is a degree of oak on the aroma and the delivery and the sugars now last the pace, spreading more evenly over the scattered oils. There are now even spices at work late on in this much better-balance dram. *41.7%. Both tasted direct from the freezer (directly after two days at sub-zero temperatures) as instructed on the bottle.*

Tasted Murray Method: bott code: L8282KS002 **(90) n22** very good grain: clean with an attractive bitter-sweet edge; **t23** like on the nose, it is the grain which dominates. But a mix of icing sugar and ulmo honey, dried slightly by vanilla, makes for a charmingly delicate experience; **f22.5** at last some spices arrives, dancing every bit as nimbly as the sweeter elements earlier. Some late caramel and barley sugar at the death; **b22.5** a surprisingly agile and entertaining blend. Untaxing, clean, pleasantly sweet and just so easy to enjoy. *41.7%.*

**Whyte & Mackay Aged 13 Years (89.5) n22** attractive, tangy spiced kumquat; caramel....; **t23.5** a toffee fruit bar with muscovado sugars lightening the load; still big and mouth-filling and even juicy; a little liquorice links with the date and walnut signature; **f22** toffee and butterscotch, though with a late furry fade; **b22** like the standard Whyte and Mackay...but thirteen years old and a little lighter... *40%.*

**Whyte & Mackay Triple Matured** bott code 16/04120 L6329 **(86.5) n21 t23.5 f20.5 b21.5** The kind of blend you can not only stand your spoon up in but your knife - table or carving - and fork — table or pitch - as well. The nose suggests something furry is in the offing which, sadly, the finale confirms. But the delivery really is such wonderful fun! Thick with intense toffee, which shapes both its flavour and mouth feel, and concentrated date and walnut cake. Roasty yet sweet thanks to the molasses this is about the chewiest blend on the market today. *40%.*

**William Lawson's Finest (85) n18.5 t22.5 f22 b22.** Not only has the label become more colourful, but so, too, has the whisky. However that has not interfered with the joyous old-fashioned grainy bite. A complex and busy blend from the old charm school. *40%*

**William Lawson's Scottish Gold Aged 12 Years (89) n22 t23 f22 b22.** For years Lawson's 12 was the best example of the combined wizardry of clean grain, unpeated barley and good bourbon cask that you could find anywhere in the world: a last-request dram before the firing squad. Today it is still excellent, but just another sherried blend. What's that saying about if it's not being broke...? *40%*

**Windsor 12 Years Old (81) n20 t21 f20 b20.** Thick, walloped-on blend that you can stand a spoon in. Hard at times to get past the caramel. *40%. Diageo.*

**Windsor Aged 17 Years Super Premium (89) n23 t22 f22 b22.** Still on the safe side for all its charm and quality. An extra dose of complexity would lift this onto another level. *40%*

**Windsor 21 Years Old (90) n20 t23 f24 b23.** Recovers fabulously from the broken nose and envelopes the palate with a silky-sweet style unique to the Windsor scotch brand. Excellent. *40%. Diageo.*

**Ye Monks (86) n20 t23 f21.5 b21.5.** Just hope they are praying for less caramel to maximize the complexity. Still, a decent spicy chew and outstanding bite which is great fun and worth finding when in South America. *40%. Diageo.*

# Irish Whiskey

**O**f all the whiskies in the world, it is Irish which probably causes most confusion amongst both established whisk(e)y lovers and the novices.

Ask anyone to define what is unique to Irish whiskey - apart from it being made in Ireland and the water likewise coming from that isle - and the answer, if the audiences around the world at my tastings are anything to go by, are in this order: i) it is triple distilled; ii) it is never, ever, made using peat; iii) they exclusively use sherry casks; iv) it comes from the oldest distillery in the world; v) it is made from a mixture of malted and unmalted barley.

Only one of these answers is true: the fifth. This is usually the final answer extracted from the audience when the last hand raised sticks to his or her guns after the previous four responses have been shot down.

And it is this type of whiskey, known as Irish Pot Still, which has again - indeed, for the ninth consecutive year - been named as Irish Whiskey of the Year. In 2016 it was the Midleton Dair Ghaelach, in 2014 and 2013 it was the Redbreast 12-years-old and in 2012 Power's John's Lane. Last year it was, just like 2017 and previously in 2015, the Redbreast 21-years-old. And this year....? Redbreast 12 Cask Strength once more! Considering that 25 years ago Irish Distillers had decided to end the bottling of Pure Pot Still, not bad. Just shows what a little campaigning can do.... Remarkable as it may seem, after the best part of a century of contraction within the industry, much of it as painful as it was brutal, there were only four distilleries operating on the entire island of Ireland in the autumn of 2011. Now there are over 20. The question is: how many are planning to make a Pot Still to challenge Midleton's...?

## Jim Murray's Whisky Bible Irish Whiskey of the Year Winners

|  | Irish Whiskey | Irish Pot Still Whiskey | Irish Single Malt | Irish Blend | Irish Single Cask |
|---|---|---|---|---|---|
| 2004 | Jameson | N/A | N/A | N/A | N/A |
| 2005 | Jameson | N/A | N/A | N/A | N/A |
| 2006 | Bushmills 21 | N/A | N/A | N/A | N/A |
| 2007 | Redbreast 15 | N/A | N/A | N/A | N/A |
| 2008 | Tyrconnel 10 | N/A | N/A | N/A | N/A |
| 2009 | Jameson 07 | N/A | N/A | N/A | N/A |
| 2010 | Redbreast 12 | N/A | N/A | N/A | N/A |
| 2011 | Sainsbury's Dun Leire 8 | N/A | N/A | N/A | N/A |
| 2012 | Powers John's Lane | N/A | Sainsbury's Dun Leire 8 | N/A | Jameson 2007 Vintage |
| 2013 | Redbreast 12 Year Old | Redbreast 12 C.Strength | Bushmills Aged 21 | Jameson | Tyrconnell 11 Year Old |
| 2014 | Redbreast 12 C.Strength | Redbreast 12 C.Strength | Bushmills Aged 21 | Jameson | N/A |
| 2015 | Redbreast Aged 21 | Redbreast Aged 21 | Bushmills Aged 21 | Jameson | N/A |
| 2016 | Midleton Dair Ghaelach | Midleton Dair Ghaelach | SMWS 118.3 Cooley 1991 | Powers Gold Label | N/A |
| 2017 | Redbreast Aged 21 | Redbreast Aged 21 | Bushmills Aged 21 | Jameson | Teeling S C 2004 |
| 2018 | Redbreast Aged 21 | Redbreast Aged 21 | Bushmills Aged 16 | Bushmills Black Bush | Dunville'sVR First Edition |
| 2019 | Redbreast 12 C.Strength | Redbreast 12 C.Strength | Bushmills Aged 12 | Bushmills Black Bush | Irishman Aged 17 |
| 2020 | Redbreast 12 C.Strength | Redbreast 12 C.Strength | Bushmills Aged 21 | Jameson | Kinahan's 11 Year Old |

# Pure Pot Still
## MIDLETON (old distillery)

**Midleton 25 Years Old Pot Still** db **(92) n24 t24 f21 b23.** A really enormous whiskey that is in the truest classic Irish style. The un-malted barley really does make the tastebuds hum and the oak has added fabulous depth. Interesting when tasted against an American rye – the closeness of the character is there to be experienced, but also the differences. A subtle mature whiskey of unquestionable quality. Superb. 43%

## MIDLETON (new distillery) County Cork.

**Green Spot** db **(94.5) n23.5 t24 f23.5 b23.5.** This honeyed state has remained a few years, and its sharpness has now been regained. Complex throughout. Unquestionably one of the world's greatest branded whiskies. 40%. *Irish Distillers for Mitchell & Son, Dublin.*

**Green Spot** bott code L622831252 db **(95) n23.5 t23.5 f24 b24** A slightly different weight, pace and sugar emphasis to this bottling. But remains a true classic. 40%.

**Green Spot Château Léoville Barton** finished in Bordeaux Wine Casks db **(83.5) n21.5 t22.5 f19 b20.5**. Have a kind of proprietarily, fatherly feel about Green Spot, as it was an unknown whiskey outside Ireland until revealed to the world 21 years ago in my Irish Whiskey Almanac. And fitting this is finished in Ch. Leoville Barton as I have a fair bit of that from the 70s and 80s in my cellar – and the creators of Green Spot was Dublin's oldest wine shop. However, after all that, have to say that this is a disappointment. There are warning signs on the nose and confirmation on the finish that the wine barrel did not escape the dastardly sulphur treatment. Which means it is dull where it should be bright, though the delivery does reach out for complexity and there are some excellent light cocoa moments. But the sulphur wins. 46%

**Green Spot Château Léoville Barton** finished in Bordeaux wine casks, bott code L622331248 db **(79) n20 t22 f18 b19** I'd so desperately like to see this work. But, once again, far too tight and bitter for its own good. The damaging sulphur note is worthy of neither the great Green Spot or Leoville Barton names... 46%.

**Green Spot Chateau Montelena** Zinfandel wine cask finished, bott code: L719331280 db **(88) n23 t23.5 f19.5 b22** There is something fitting that Green Spot, an Irish Pot Still whiskey brand created many generations back by Dublin's Premier wine merchants, should find itself creating new ground...in a wine cask. Any European whisk(e)ys matured in American wine casks are thin on the ground. That they should be Chateau Montelena from Napa Valley makes this all the more remarkable. Does it work? Well, yes and no. The unique style of Irish Pot Still is lost somewhat under a welter of fruity blows and the fuzzy, imprecise finish is definitely off key. But there is no denying that it is a whiskey which does possess the odd magic moment. 46%.

**Master Distiller's Selection Single Pot** db (94) n23.5 t23.5 f23 b24 At the sweeter end of the Pot Still spectrum. The use of fruit as a background noise, rather than a lead, is a masterstroke. 46%. 500 bottles. ncf

**Method and Madness Single Pot Irish Whiskey** bourbon barrels, finished in Virgin Hungarian oak (94) n23 t23.5 f23.5 b24 Now there was a nose! One that took me back almost 25 years to when I was visiting the Czech whisky distilleries soon after the fall of the communist regime. That whisky was matured in local oak, offering a near identical aroma to this Irish. 46%.

**Method and Madness Single Pot Still Irish Whiskey** sherry & American barrels, finished in French chestnut casks db (88) n22 t23 f21 b22.5 Ah...memories of the late 1970s or perhaps very early '80s. Walking in the lonely autumnal forests surrounding the tiny French village of Evecquemont, taking my girlfriend's family's soppy Alsatian for long walks, during which I would hoover up wild sweet chestnuts by the score. Never then figured it playing a part in whisky, especially Irish. Not sure it is the perfect marriage, but certainly adds to the whiskey lexicon. 46%.

**Midleton Barry Crockett Legacy** db (94) n23.5 t24.5 f22.5 b23.5. Another fabulous Pot Still, very unusual for its clever use of the varied ages of the oak to form strata of intensity. One very sophisticated whiskey. 46%. ncf

**Midleton Barry Crockett Legacy** American bourbon barrels, bott code L623631258 db (95) n23.5 t24 f23.5 b24 Thank God for my dear old friend Barry Crockett. One of the top three most knowledgeable whiskey/whisky people I have known in my lifetime, you can at least be relieved that his name is synonymous with a truly great spirit. Fittingly, his whiskey is free of sherry butts, so I can just sit back and enjoy and not be on tenterhooks waiting for the first signs of a disastrous sulphur note to take hold. Indeed, the only thing that takes hold of you here is the Pot Still's stunning beauty... 46%. ncf

**Midleton Dair Ghaelach** db (97) n23.5 t25 f24 b24.5 For heaven's sake. This is just too ridiculously beautiful...and so unmistakably Irish for all the virgin oak. Truly world class. 58.1%

**Midleton Dair Ghaelach Bluebell Forest Castle Blunden Estate** finished in virgin native Irish oak hogsheads, batch no. 1, tree number 1, bott code: L628033271 db (90.5) n22.5 t23.5 f22 b23 The vibrant pungency is matched equally by the grand dollops of natural caramel. 55.3%.

**Midleton Dair Ghaelach Grinsell's Wood Ballaghtobin Estate** American bourbon barrels, finished in Irish oak hogsheads, batch no. 1, tree no. 7, bott code L504031020 db (97.5) n24 t25 f24 b24.5 What we have here, if I'm not very much mistaken, is a potential World Whisky of the Year. Rarely these days am I given an entirely new flavour profile to chew on. Not only do I have that, but I am struggling to find any faults at all. Ireland is not known for its mountains: well, it certainly has one now. 57.9%. ncf

**Paddy Centenary Edition** db (93) n22 t23.5 f24 b23.5. This 7-year-old Pure Pot Still whiskey really is a throwback. All Paddy's original whiskey from this era would have been from the old Midleton distillery which sits, in aspic, beside the one opened in 1975. Even with the likelihood of oats being in the mash in those days, still can't believe the original would have been quite as sweet on the palate – and soul – as this. 43%

**Powers Aged 12 Years John's Lane Release** db (96.5) n24 t25 f23.5 b24 This is a style of Irish Pot Still I have rarely seen outside the blending lab. I had many times thought of trying to find some of this and bottling it myself. No need now. I think I have just tasted Irish Whiskey of the Year, and certainly one of the top five world whiskies of the year. 46%

**Powers Aged 12 Years John's Lane Release** bott code L623731261 (96) n23.5 t24.5 f23 b24.5 A slightly different slant on the toffee and fudge – and now has a degree of rye-recipe bourbon about it - but firmly remains the go to Pot Still of quite staggering beauty. 46%. ncf.

**Powers Signature Release** bott code L433231240 (87.5) n21 t23 f21.5 b22 A much lazier version of this excellent Pot Still than I have become used to. Far too much fudge at play here, undermining the layering and complexity. Sexy and chewy for sure and a must for those into dried dates. But the usual Pot Still character is a little masked and the usual slightly off key sherry butt turns up at the very last moment. 46%. ncf.

**Powers Three Swallow Release** bott code L617031171 (83.5) n21 t21 f21.5 b20 Pleasant. No off notes. But vanishes into a sea of toffee. The fact it is pure Pot Still, apparently, is actually impossible to determine, In the last six months I have seen three swallows: a barn swallow, a Pacific and a Wire-tailed. Wherever I saw them in the world, India, The Philippines, my back garden, they all swooped and darted in joyous abandon. This Three Swallow by Powers has, by vivid contrast, had its wings clipped. 40%. ncf

**Redbreast Aged 12 Years** bott code L634031413 db (88.5) n22.5 t23 f21 b22 By far the flattest Redbreast I have tasted since...well, ever. Far too much reliance on obviously first-fill sherry, which had flattened out and virtually buried the unique personality of the Pot Still itself. Enjoyable, for sure. Beautiful, even, in its own way. But it should be so much better than this... 40%.

**Redbreast Aged 12 Years Cask Strength** batch B1/11 db (96) n24.5 t24.5 f23 b24 This is Irish pot still on steroids. And sporting an Irish brogue as thick as my great great grandfather John Murray's. To think, had I not included Redbreast in Jim Murray's Irish Whiskey Almanac back in 1994, after it had already been unceremoniously scrapped and discontinued, while championing the then entirely unknown Irish Pot Still cause this brand would no longer have been with us. If I get run over by a bus tomorrow, at least I have that as a tick when St Peter is totting up the plusses and minuses... And with the cask strength, he might even give me two... 57.7%. ncf. Irish Distillers.

**Redbreast Aged 12 Years Cask Strength** batch no. B1/17 db (97) n24 t24.5 f24 b24.5 A potential World Whisky of the Year 2019: the first in over a 1,000 tasted so far whiskies I could say that about. It really is that good...! 58.2%.

◆ **Redbreast Aged 12 Years Cask Strength** batch no. B1/18 db (96) n24.5 the quintessential Irish nose! The Pot Still forming a rock-hard, beautifully-carved pillar, sharp and biting, but a pillar holding aloft the rich, thicker fruit notes. I used to nose (and champion) this form of unique beauty 30 years ago...I am nosing something almost identical today...; t24.5 fat and lush, thanks to the casks which deliver fruit at its grapiest and honey at its waxiest. But of course it is that granite-like pot still which sets it all off, with the grainy sharpness a mesmerising contrast to both grape and bruyere honey; f23 long, distinguished, spicy... but just a little nagging note from one of the sherry butts; b24 probably one very slightly sulphured cask from World Whisky of the Year. Both nose and delivery is blarney-free Irish perfection. Worth hunting this bottle down for something truly special... 56.2%. ncf.

**Redbreast 15 Years Old** db (94) n23 t24 f23 b24. For years I have been pleading for Irish Distillers to launch a pot still at 46%, natural colour and unchillfiltered. Well, I've got two out of three wishes. And what we have here is a truly great Irish whiskey and my pulse races in the certain knowledge it can get better still... 46%. ncf. France.

**Redbreast Aged 15 Years** bott code L624931266 db (84) n21 t22 f20 b21 When you have this much sherry influence on a whiskey, it is likely that one day you will fall foul of the odd furry butt, as is the case here. 46%. ncf.

**Redbreast Aged 21 Years** db (96) n24 t25 f23 b24 I have tasted no shortage of 21-year-old pot still before in my career, but that was some time back when the whiskey in question was usually from the original Jameson distillery in Dublin, or Power's. I also managed to get my hands on some old stuff from the original Midleton as well as Tullamore Dew and few others. That old spirit had been made at a time when those distilleries were in the process of being closed down and the quality was nothing like it once was. This, I admit, is the first I can remember from Midleton's rebuilt distillery and it knocks the spots off the Jameson and Power's. Those did not have the balance or the insouciance so far as the honey involvement was concerned or the all-round world-class star quality which positively radiates from the glass. Hopefully this gentle giant amongst the world's truly great whiskies and near blue print for the perfect pot still Irish is here to stay. Only for the next bottling absolutely no need for the pointless caramel and the damaging sherry, both which contribute in tarnishing the dazzling sheen. There are times when less is so significantly more. 46%. ncf. WB15/417

**Redbreast Aged 21 Years** bott code L612731109 db (97) n24.5 t24 f24 b24.5 The mercifully restrained fruit and absolute total 100% absence of sulphur allows the Pot Still to display its not inconsiderable beauty unmolested and to the fullest extent. One of the world's most beautiful and iconic whisk(e)ys without doubt. The fact that so many facets of this whiskey are allowed to say their piece, yet never over-run their time and that the tenets are equally divided makes this one of the truly great whiskeys of the year. 46%. ncf.

**Redbreast Aged 32 Years Dream Cask** db (96.5) n24 t24.5 f23.5 b24 A fabulous pot still very comfortable in its ancient clothes. Marvellous! 46.5%.

**Redbreast All Sherry Single Cask** db (73.5) n17 t23.5 f15 b18. I mean: seriously guys....??? A single cask pure pot still whiskey and you bottle one with sulphur fingerprints all over it? I don't have the number of what cask this is from, so I hope yours will have come from clean sherry. If you have, you are in for a treat, because the sheer brilliance and magnitude of this whiskey was able to blot out the sulphur for a good seven or eight seconds as it reached heights of near perfection. A bowl of raspberries now and a 20 minute break to help cleanse my palate and relieve my tongue which is still seriously furred up. So frustrating, as I could see a clean butt of this getting Single Cask Whisky of the Year ... 59.9%. sc.

**Redbreast Mano a Lámh** db (85) n22.5 t22.5 f19 b21 Curious that on an all sherry butt bottling, the most enjoyable flavour profile is a spiced chocolate one which begins about four or five beats after the original big, soppy, lush delivery. No prizes for guessing why the score goes down towards the finish. By the way: love the robin on the label – a kind of weird cross between an immature and adult robin with the face of a white wagtail thrown in. Like the whiskey type: unique! *46%. ncf.*

**Redbreast Lustau Edition** sherry finish, bott code L622131242 db **(89.5) n22.5 t23.5 f22 b21.5** I somehow would have thought that, considering recent younger bottlings, going to the trouble of making a special sherry finish for a Redbreast is on a par with giving a gift of a barrel of sand to the Tuaregs... This bottling is attractive enough, with the fruit at its best on delivery when the whiskey goes through a spectacularly delicious phase. But this soon wears out, leaving a bitterness and slightly lopsided feel, especially at the death, as the balance struggles to be maintained. For those of you I know who refuse to touch anything sherry, this is entirely sulphur free I'm delighted to report. *46%. ncf.*

⟨⟩ **Redbreast Single Pot Still All Sherry Single Cask** cask no. 10351, dist 1 Feb 02, bott code: L816433192 db **(89) n24 t23.5 f20.5 b21.5** In whisky – and whiskey – very often more can equal less, and so we have here. The nose: wow...just so beautiful, especially with the biting spice and tannin on the fruit. And the delivery: very good, again with a massive fruitcake kick. But two problems: the huge sherry influence means the Irish flag is lost under a Spanish one. And then, of course, there is the sulphur influence undermining the finish... *58.7%. 570 bottles. Bottled Exclusively for Sonny Molloy's.*

⟨⟩ **Red Spot Aged 15 Years** bourbon, sherry & marsala casks, bott code: L829131516 db **(83) n21 t22 f19 b21** Oh, what I'd give for the days when you could taste the actual magic of the Pot Still itself, such as in the original Green Spot, rather than some lumbering fruit casks, and slightly sulphured ones at that. *46%. ncf.*

**Yellow Spot Aged 12 Years** bourbon, sherry and Malaga casks db **(88.5) n23.5 t22.5 f20 b22.5.** If anything, just a shade too many wine casks used which somewhat drowns out the unique IP character. Reminds me of when Barry Walsh was working on the triple maturation theme of the Bushmills 16, probably about 15 years ago. Not until the very last days did all the components click. Just before then, it went through a phase like this (though obviously with malt, not IPS). Knowing current blender Billy Leighton as I do, I can see this whiskey improving in future batches as lessons are learned. Not that there isn't already much to enjoy... *46%.*

**Yellow Spot Aged 12 Years** bourbon barrels, sherry butts & Malaga casks, bott code L622431250 db **(87) n22 t22 f21 b22** My previous comments stand for this, too. Except here we have a persistent bitterness towards the finish which reveals a weakness with one of the butts. An exceptionally bitty whiskey that does have its moments of soaring high, especially when the varying citrus note correlate. *46%. ncf.*

## OLD COMBER County Down.
**Old Comber 30 Years Old Pure Pot Still (88) n23 t24 f20 b21.** A classic example of a whiskey spending a few Summers too many in wood: increasing age doesn't equal excellence. That said, always very drinkable and early on positively sparkles with a stunning mouthfeel. Out of respect for the old I have made the markings for taste cover the first seven or eight seconds... *40%*

# Single Malt
## COOLEY County Louth.
**Connemara** bott code L9042 db **(88) n23 t22.5 f20.5 b22.** One of the softest smoked whiskies in the world which, though quite lovely, gives the impression it can't make its mind up about what it wants to be. *40%*

**Connemara Aged 8 Years** db **(85) n22.5 t21.5 f20 b21.** Another Connemara lacking teeth. The peat charms, especially on the nose, but the complexity needs working on. *46%*

**Connemara Aged 12 Years** bott code L9024 db **(85.5) n23 t21.5 f20 b21.** The nose, with its beautiful orange, fruity lilt, puts the shy smoke in the shade. *40%*

**Connemara Cask Strength** bott code L9041 db **(90) n21.5 t23 f22 b22.5.** A juicy negative of the standard bottling: does its talking on the palate rather than nose. Maybe an absence of caramel notes might have something to do with that. *57.9%*

**Connemara Distillers Edition** db **(86) n22 t22.5 f20 b21.5.** When I give whisk(e)y tastings around the world, I love to include Connemara. Firstly, people don't expect peated Irish. Secondly, their smoked whisky stock is eclectic and you never quite know what is going to come out of the bottle. This is a particularly tight, sharp style. No prisoners survived... *43%*

**Inish Turk Beg Maiden Voyage** db **(91.5) n22 t23.5 f22.5 b22.5** Brooding and quite delicious. *44%*

**Tullamore Dew Single Malt 10 Years Old** db **(91.5) n23 t23 f22.5 b23.** The best whiskey I have ever encountered with a Tullamore label. Furtively complex and daringly delicate. If only they could find a way to minimise the toffee... *40%. William Grant & Sons.*

**The Tyrconnell Aged 10 Years Madeira Finish** bott code L8136 db **(91) n23 t23 f22 b23.** Not quite the award-winning effort of a few years back, as those lilting high notes which so complemented the baser fruit tones haven't turned up here. But remains in the top echelon and still much here to delight the palate. *46%*

**The Tyrconnell Single Cask 11 Year Old** db **(95.5) n23.5 t25 f23 b24.** Well, if there weren't enough reasons to go to Dublin, you now have this... *46%. sc. Celtic Whiskey Shop Exclusive.*

**Clonmel Peated Aged 8 Years (86) n22 t23 f20 b21.** Take the toffee away and you would have one hell of an Irish. Claims to be "Pure Pot Still". It isn't (in Irish terms): it's malt. *40%*

**Craoi na Mona Irish Malt Whiskey (68) n16 t18 f17 b17.** I'm afraid my Gaelic is slipping these days: I assume Craoi na Mona means "Feinty, badly made smoky malt"... (that's the end of my tasting for the day...) *40%*

**Glendalough Single Malt Irish Whiskey Aged 7 Years** bourbon casks **(79) n18 t22 f20 b19.** Disappointing on so many levels. Malt at Cooley at 7-year-old, should, if the casks are picked assiduously, be vibrant and brimming with barley and vitality. That only happens for the odd moment or two on delivery. The nose reveals some pretty poor barrels at work while two much toffee flattens the experience. Love the spice, though. *46%. ncf.*

**Glendalough Single Malt Irish Whiskey Aged 13 Years** bourbon casks **(90) n22.5 t23 f21.5 b23** A rather beautiful whiskey, spilling over with spices. A few tired casks evident, though. *46%. ncf.*

**Glen Dimplex (88) n23 t22 f21 b22.** Overall, clean and classically Cooley. *40%*

**Magilligan Cooley Pure Pot Still Single Malt (91) n22 t22 f24 b23.** A touch of honey for good measure ...or maybe not..!! *43%. Ian MacLeod Distillers.*

**Magilligan Irish Whiskey Peated Malt 8 Years Old (89) n21 t23 f22 b23.** Such a different animal from the docile creature that formally passed as Magilligan peated. Quite lovely...and very classy. *43%. Ian Macleod Distillers.*

**Merry's Single Malt (83) n20 t22 f20 b21.** Ultra-clean barley rich nose is found on the early palate. The finish is flat, though. *40%*

**Shannahan's (92) n23 t22 f24 b23.** Cooley natural and unplugged: quite adorable. *40%*

**Slieve Foy Single Malt Aged 8 Years** bott code L9108 **(88) n23 t22.5 f21 b21.5.** Never deviates from its delicate touch. *40%. Cooley for Marks & Spencer.*

**Tullamore Dew Aged 10 Years Four Cask Finish** bourbon, oloroso, port, madeira **(89) n24 t23 f19.5 b22.5** Just a sherry butt or two away from complete brilliance. *40% (80 proof)*

**Tyrconnell 16 Year Old Single Malt (92) n22.5 t24 f22.5 b23** If anyone on here is old enough to remember Zoom lollies – and miss them as much as I after a gap of nearly half a century – then here's your chance to wallow down Memory Lane. So different. And so delicious! *46%*

**Vom Fass Cooley Irish Single Malt 8 Years Old (88) n22 t22.5 f21.5 b22.** A very decent, if undemonstrative, example of the distillery at an age which well suits. *40%*

**The Wild Geese Single Malt (85.5) n21.5 t21 f22 b21.** Just ignore the Wild Goose chase the labels send you on and enjoy the malt, with all its failings, for what it is (and this is pretty enjoyable in an agreeably rough and ready manner, though not exactly the stuff of Irish whiskey purists): which in this case for all its malt, toffee and delicate smoke, also appears to have more than a slight touch of feints - so maybe they were right all along...!!! *43%. Cooley for Avalon.*

**The Whisky Barrel Irish Single Malt 13 Year Old** sherry hogshead, cask no. 200501, dist 2003 **(82.5) n19 t21.5 f21 b21** Good grief....!!! This is my 1,151st whisk(e)y for the 2018 Bible... and I can safely say I have not encountered anything like this before...and very few in the near 20,000 samples for all the previous editions. It seems as though there is a strange unification or pact between some kind of skewed smoke and a sherry note the like of which I cannot even begin to describe. This is a gargoyle of a malt, strangely beautiful in its very ugliness. *52.7%. sc. 180 bottles.*

# DINGLE County Kerry.

⬥ **Dingle Single Malt Whisky** batch no. 3 db **(87) n21 t22 f22 b22** Young, much closer in personality to new make than seasoned whiskey. In fact, reminds me of the blending lab when I'd come across a barely three-year-old Dailuaine, a Scottish Speysider which, at this juncture of its development, is its closest flavour-type relative. Lovely, though, if you an looking for a taste of unspoiled, gently oiled maltiness – and a piece of Irish whiskey history. Clean and beautifully made. *46.5%. ncf. 13,000 bottles.*

⬥ **Dingle Single Malt Whisky** batch no. 4 db **(84) n20 t22 f21 b21** I always prefer to discover that a distillery makes gin because I have been there or been briefed about it. Not through sampling their whiskey. And I'm afraid there is juniper quite strongly on the nose here and few other odd flavours hitting the palate. Despite the mega dry finish, lots of malt on show and seemingly otherwise well made. *46.5%. ncf. 2,000 bottles.*

# MIDLETON County Cork.

**Method and Madness Single Malt Irish Whiskey** bourbon barrels, finished in French Limousin oak casks db **(92) n22 t23.5 f23 b23.5** A very different Irish which is quietly uncompromising and seriously tasty... 46%.

# OLD KILBEGGAN County Westmeath.

**The Spirit of Kilbeggan 1 Month (90.5) n22 t23 f23 b22.5.** Wow!! They are really getting to grips with the apparatus. Full bodied and lush small still feel to this but radiating complexity, depth, barley and cocoa in equal measures. The development of the oils really does give this excellent length. Impressed! 65.5%

**The Spirit of Kilbeggan 1 Year (85) n20.5 t21 f22 b21.5.** A veritable Bambi of a spirit: a typical one year old malt which, as hard as it tries, just can't locate its centre of gravity. Even so, the richness is impressive and some highly sugared chocolate mousse near the end is a treat. 62.7%

**The Spirit of Kilbeggan 2 Years (84) n20 t21 f22 b21.** A tad raw and a little thin. There is some decent balance between oak and malt, but the overall feeling is that the still has not yet been quite mastered. 60.3%

# OLD BUSHMILLS County Antrim.

**Bushmills Aged 10 Years** matured in two woods db **(92.5) n23 t23 f23 b23.5.** Absolutely superb whiskey showing great balance and the usual Antrim 19th century pace with its flavour development. The odd bottle of this I have come across over the last couple of years has been spoiled by the sherry involvement. But, this, as is usually the case, is absolutely spot on. 40%

⬩⬩⬩ **Bushmills Aged 12 Years Single Malt Aged in Three Woods** oloroso sherry & bourbon casks, Marsala cask finished, bott code: L9102IB 001 db **(89.5) n23.5** there is a huge tannin spice to this one. The sugars hang off it like grapes from a vine; **t23** a gorgeous delivery: lush and chewy from the very first nanosecond, the malt momentarily shrugs off its fruity cloak to come through loud, proud and very clearly; excellent spices hit the midpoint and mingle superbly with the muscovado sugars; **f21** a little too bitter and clumsy; slightly tart; **b22** slightly lumpy in style, but there are some beautiful moments in there. 40%. Exclusive to Taiwan.

**Bushmills Distillery Reserve Aged 12 Years** bott code: L7331IC002 db **(95.5) n24 t24 f23.5 b24** A sublime use of faultless sherry casks. Bushmills at the very height of its form and complexity. Truly outstanding. 40%.

**Bushmills Select Casks Aged 12 Years** married with Caribbean rum cask db **(95) n23 t24 f24 b24** One of the most complex Bushmills in living memory, and probably since it was established in 1784. 40%

**Bushmills Aged 16 Years** db **(71) n18 t21 f15 b17.** In my days as a consultant Irish whiskey blender, going through the Bushmills warehouses I found only one or two sulphur-treated butts. Alas, there are many more than that at play here. 40%

**Bushmills Aged 21 Years** db **(95.5) n24.5 t24 f23.5 b24** An Irish journey as beautiful as the dramatic landscape which borders the distillery. Magnificent. 40%

⬩⬩⬩ **Bushmills Distillery Exclusive Acacia Wood** dist 2008, bott no. L8211 IB 01S db **(83.5) n21 t24 f18 b20.5** Not the first time I have ever tasted whiskey rounded off in acacia by a long stretch, though maybe the first after spending time – it appears – in sherry. The result for me just doesn't gel. For a start, I find the slightly imbalanced aroma a lot of hard work in getting used to, though as your nose acclimatises you can eventually pick out some half attractive buttery notes. And the finish isn't quite where it should be, with a fair bit of fuzziness at the finish. The delivery, though, is both intriguing and delicious, the acacia – as is its want – issuing a whole batch of sugar and honey notes not normally present in whisky and never in Irish whiskey; ironically acacia honey isn't among them! Though undone by the pretty poor finish, this still represents one of the most curious and fascinating bottlings in the world over the last year. Just needs some serious tidying up before, hopefully, the next batch as the potential is great. 47%. ncf.

**Bushmills Sherry Cask Reserve Single Malt Whiskey** first-fill Oloroso sherry butts db **(80) n20.5 t22 f18 b19.5.** Although I am always 100% impartial, I would be lying if I didn't say I wanted this whiskey to be not just a high scorer, but a potential Bible world champion. Because in my tasting room stands a fine and very large - oil portrait of the Bushmills Distillery, and it is a place I have enjoyed special moments at - and love the people there dearly. And, also, in a few moments Northern Ireland's miracle-making football team are about to take on Wales in the last 16 of the Euros. But, sadly, the news, from here at least, is not good. Among the sherry butts selected has been one - and I am sure it is only one - that has been lightly sulphur treated. It means that the fruit, rather than taking off and going into complexity overdrive, crumples slightly as the vague bitterness and tightness spreads around the palate. There are some lovely fruit moments, so there are. But Bushmills should be so much better than this. As an Irish whiskey blender of old, I have been lucky enough to work with Bushmills sherry butts in pristine condition...and they can be among the best whiskeys you'll ever find on this planet. Sadly this is not fully representative. I just hope the boys in green rise to greater heights than this bottling and don't fall to an own goal like the one scored here.... 40%

**Bushmills Single Malt The Steamship Collection #3 Bourbon Cask** db **(95)** n24.5 t23.5 f23 b24 This steamship is sailing in calm seas of complexity...Take your time over this one: it is deceptively brilliant. 40%.

**Acla Special Selection No. 5 County of Antrim 24 Years Old** sherrywood, dist 1991, bott 2016 **(91.5)** n23.5 t24 f21 b23 Some brief moments of this malt defy belief for their beauty. 478%. sc. 158 bottles.

**Acla Special Selection No. 6 County of Antrim 24 Years Old** bourbon barrel, cask no. 1073, dist 1991, bott 2016 **(96)** n23 t24.5 f24 b24.5 Truly an Antrim classic. Would love to see more of this in the actual Bushmills portfolio: well done Acla for showing the way. In other words: stopping mucking around with mixing casks types and stick at some of the breathtaking bourbon barrels on your doorstep! This is indubitably world class. 44.7%. sc. 176 bottles.

**Knappogue Castle Aged 12 Years** bourbon cask matured **(90)** n23.5 t23 f21 b22.5. The massive toffee influence deflects from the huge character elsewhere which springs a few surprises. 40%. Castle Brands Group.

◈ **The Whisky Cask Company Bushmills Capall 26 Years Old** 1st fill bourbon barrel, cask no, 8391, dist 16 Oct 91, bott 26 Mar 18 **(94.5)** n22.5 just about gripping on to life. The oak is full bodied and blood orangey, and another Antrim summer may well have been one too many. But a little sweet cedar and the most delicate ginger saves the day; t24 well...I didn't expect that...!!! My word...! What a delivery: absolutely top drawer with the malt in the most concentrated form possible, but with tree rings where you can just about count the years. The resulting balance defies credibility...; f24 mocha with quite a bit of butterscotch cream to sweeten things. Only late on do the tannins remember to pitch in with some spice...; b24 had the nose been as sensational as the experience on the palate some kind of award for this whisky would have been a certainty. Magnificent. 50.5%. sc. 175 bottles.

◈ **The Whisky Cask Company Bushmills Madra 26 Years Old** 1st fill bourbon barrel, cask no, 8386, dist 16 Oct 91, bott 26 Mar 18 **(94)** n23 exotic fruit notes more commonly associated with pensioner Speysiders; t24 yep, and there they are on delivery. the oakiness dominates, but those gorgeous lychee and chocolate tones make for a magnificent combination; f23 light ulmo honey trails from the chocolate, but a slight tangy residue late on; b24 a little nudge to Bushmills to make the most of their older casks, methinks. 49.4%. sc. 156 bottles.

# WEST CORK DISTILLERS County Cork.
**West Cork Irish Whiskey Bog Oak Charred Cask Matured** db **(88.5)** n23 t22 f21.5 b22 A little known fact: I own a 100 to 125 year-old portable Irish pot still made entirely of copper with brass handles, once owned by a Victorian or Edwardian illicit distiller. Which would explain as to why it was found in an Irish bog over 20 years ago and has been in my possession ever since. Anyway, it is extremely unlikely it ever produced a spirit which ended up quite so heavy in natural caramels... 43%. West Cork Distillers Limited.

**West Cork Irish Whiskey Glengarriff Peat Charred Cask Matured** db **(90.5)** n23 t22.5 f22 b23 Well, Ireland is on the way to Kentucky from here... 43%. West Cork Distillers Limited.

**Brean Tra Cask Strength Irish Whiskey (91)** n22.5 t23 f22 b22.5 Doesn't bother too much about complexity; this is all about sheer intensity of flavour. Wow! 60%. West Cork Distillers Limited.

**Brean Tra Single Malt Irish Whiskey** db **(86.5)** n21 t22 f21.5 b22 A very safe Irish. Distinctly oily and choc-a-bloc with intense if monosyllabic malt. The tannins take time to arrive but become moderately punchy. 40%. West Cork Distillers Limited.

**Dundalgan 10 Year Old Single Malt Irish Whiskey** db **(88.5)** n22.5 t22 f22 b22 Enjoyable, though the complexity levels appear to be limited slightly by the oils from the still which fill in the gaps between the peaks and troughs. 40%. West Cork Distillers Limited.

**Mizen Head Cask Strength Single Malt Irish Whiskey** Bodega sherry casks db **(90.5)** n22.5 t23.5 f22 b22.5 Well done chaps! Until the very death, barely a sulphur atom in sight! But such is the power of this distillery's love of caramel character, it even overtakes the fruit... which takes some doing! 60%. West Cork Distillers Limited.

# UNSPECIFIED SINGLE MALTS
**Acla Special Selection No. 2 Somewhere in Ireland 24 Years Old** barrel, cask no. 10705, dist 1991, bott 2016 **(95)** n23 t24 f24 b24 A malt coming to the end of its life, but plucked from the warehouse while its greatness remains intact and unimpacted. 47.4%. sc. 212 bottles.

**Acla Special Selection No. 3 North of Ireland 27 Years Old** barrel, cask no. 16264, dist 1989, bott 2016 **(91.5)** n24 t23.5 f21.5 b22.5 This is the malt that has put "Old" into Old

Bushmills. Very rarely does the distillery's whiskey get anywhere near this kind of age. This has withstood the test of time with remarkable fortitude and pride. *43.4%. sc. 163 bottles.*

**Clontarf Single Malt (90.5) n23 t23 f22 b22.5.** Beautiful in its simplicity, this has eschewed complexity for delicious minimalism; *40%. Clontarf Irish Whiskey Co.*

**Connemara Original Peated Single Malt** db **(81.5) n21 t21.5 f19 b20.**A bit of a while since the first thing I got off the nose and last thing on the finish was caramel. Not the Connemara I witnessed being launched in a blaze of defiant glory those decades back. This rather meek, pleasant, safe, lightly smoked version appears to have been sanitised. Today's Connemara it may sadly be. Original Connemara it is most certainly NOT...! *40%*

**Dublin in the Rare Ould Times Single Malt Irish Whiskey Aged 10 Years** bourbon barrel **(81.5) n21 t21 f19 b20.5.** It was a rare old time when they made single malt whiskey like this in Dublin, for they hardly ever did. The city was the centre of Pot Still Irish and though single malt was not unknown there, it was a scarce order at the bar. When it did come along, it is hard to believe it would have been this kind of age. And, indeed, this malt would have been happier had it been a couple of years younger: the bourbon barrel at work here has allowed little malty punch to get through, while the toffee middle and finish is disappointingly dull. *40%. Bottled by Glendalough Distillery for Pete St John.*

**The Dublin Liberties Copper Alley 10 Year Old (88.5) n23 t22 f21.5 b22** About an easy drinking a malt as you'll find with no shortage of sugars. The caramels are a bit ham-fisted, though. *46%. ncf.*

**The Dublin Liberties Copper Alley 10 Year Old Single Malt** sherry cask finish, bott no. L16 280 W3 **(94.5) n23** superb spotted dog pudding. And, after the Murray Method, slightly warm, very intense spotted dog pudding...; **t24** one of the best Irish deliveries this year: rich grape jelly but not so intense as to prohibit the rise of the tannins. Some wonderful spices burrow into the depths; **f23.5** sherry trifle...; **b24** well done, chaps! You have picked yourself a first class sulphur-free cask! What a rare treat that is this year! *46%.*

**The Dubliner 10 Year Old Single Malt** bourbon casks, bott no. L17390-179 **(89) n22** drying grass on a day before-mowed lawn; **t23** malty, custard cream biscuit sweetness; juicy with a polite spice in the mid-ground leading to a brief burst of acacia honey; **f21.5** dries exuberantly, but a lovely coppery tang, too; **b22.5** 'the real taste of Dublin" warbles the label in time-honoured Blarney tradition. Of course, the true, historic taste of Dublin is Irish Pot Still, that beguiling mix of malted and unmalted barley. But, in the meantime, this juicy little number will do no harm. *42%.*

**Dunville's VR Aged 12 Years Single Malt** finished in ex-Pedro Ximénez sherry casks **(87) n23 t22.5 f20 b21.5** The success story here is on the nose: despite its Spanish inquisition, there is a profound Kentucky note leading the way, a sharp almost rye-like note with its fruity crispness. The delivery also has its moments, the riot of dates and molasses in particular. The rest of the tale, much of it bitterly told, doesn't go quite so well, alas. *46%. ncf.*

**Dunville's VR Aged 17 Years Single Malt** Port Mourant Estate rum cask finish, cask no. 195 **(91.5) n22.5 t22.5 f23 b22.5** Putting my blending hat on (which is the same one as I wear when writing the Whisky Bible) Port Mourant – known by us rum blenders as PM – trumps PX every day of the week when it comes to maturation. PM is a bit special in the rum world: it is a Guyanan rum that you add for its depth and powering coffee flavour: indeed, if you work in a rum warehouse in Guyana you can locate where the PMs are situated just by the change in aroma. This comes about by the fact that caramel is already into the cask before the rum spirit is added to it for maturation. It is a style symbolic with British Naval Rum. So where PX can be saccharine sweet and occasionally turn a whisky into something bland and uninteresting, PM is brilliant for lengthening out the finish, especially with rich mocha notes. Here, there are some sharp features it has to contend with from the first cask and a little extra time in PM might have ensured an extra softness to the finale. *57.1%. ncf sc.*

**Egan's Single Malt Fortitude** Pedro Ximénez casks bott code: L18 003 264 **(79) n19 t22 f19 b19** Bitter and off-key. *42% (92 proof). ncf.*

**Egan's Single Malt 10 Aged Years** bott code: US001 244 **(90) n22.5 t23.5 f22 b22.5** Rich, rounded and puts the "more" into this Tullamore-based bottler...*47% (94 proof). ncf.*

**The Exclusive Malts Irish 14 Year Old** refill sherry hogshead, cask no. 200503, dist 15 Dec 03, bott Jun 18 **(86.5) n22 t22 f21 b21.5** A bewildering coming together of two irremovable forces: the peat, presumably from Cooley distillery, and a superb, faultless sherry butt. But although this cask is faultless – a rare beast in the sherry world - this has been bottled before the phenols and fruits have been able to reach a compromise. So, fun whiskey. And there is much to be said about the peat and boiled candy fruitiness. But they are too individual and each out of sync with the other. Some great moments, though! *50.5%. sc. The Whisky Barrel. 264 bottles.*

**Glendalough 13 Year Old Irish Single Malt Mizunara Finish (96) n23.5 t24 f24 b24.5** Different and adorable. *56%.*

⟞ **Glendalough Single Malt Irish Whiskey Aged 17 Years** American oak bourbon cask, Japanese Mizunara cask finish **(89.5) n21.5** the unique, tell-tale oaky sharpness of Japanese oak is there. But, oddly, so is a little juniper...; **t23** excellent delivery – and very different. Most first flavour waves are a build-up of the same thing, before changing course. Here each of the original three flavour waves gives you a very different oakiness, with varying types of tannin, accompanying sugars and toastiness. Spellbinding...; **f22** dries quite profoundly but a light oiliness carries the heather honey a long way. Lots of vanilla see it out...; **b23** quite a cerebral whiskey, and one with a unique fingerprint. But could have done without the juniper. 46%. ncf.

**Glendalough 24 Year Old Irish Single Malt Port Finish (89.5) n22.5 t23.5 f21 b22.5** If there were any cracks to this old whiskey, then the vivid Port certainly shored them up. 53%.

**Glendalough 24 Year Old Irish Single Malt Sherry Finish (94.5) n24 t24 f22.5 b24** A sherry cask with only the odd, but forgiveable, atom of renegade sulphur. Lovely people of Glendalough: allow me to shake your hands and kiss your foreheads... a very old fashioned (and now horrendously and tragically rare) style indeed: more like a lifetime top quality sherry held, rather than finished. 53%.

⟞ **Glendalough Single Malt Irish Whiskey Aged 25 Years Tree #2 Jack's Wood** American white oak bourbon cask, Spanish oloroso cask & virgin Irish oak finish **(95) n23.5** one of those beautifully huge noses which never seems to lose control: the fruit is thick but perfectly proportioned with the striking oak. And it is light enough for a little vanilla and barley to poke its way through the treacle and plum pudding; **t24** a two-toned attack with a wonderful underlying firmness holding together the more lush fruitiness. As on the nose, molasses slip into the fray quite early on but there are other lightly sweetening agents at work, not least the heather honey which allows both the fruit and oak to reveal their more toasty sides without any ill effects. Slowly the spices begin to rise; **f23.5** long with the oak making no secret of its quarter century of work, but the controlled, pastel fruits keeping everything fresh; **b24** no discernible problems from the oloroso, other than the very faintest long-distance buzz. Which means this is one hell of a malt. 46%. ncf.

**Hyde No.1 President's Cask Aged 10 Years Single Malt** sherry cask finish **(85.5) n23 t22 f20 b20.5** Pleased to report the sherry butt(s) used here offer no sulphur, so a clean malt with an outstanding fruity aroma. But it does quite literally fall flat because after the initial juicy, malty entry things go a bit quiet – especially towards the middle and finish where a dull vaguely fruity but big toffee note clings like a limpet. A wasted opportunity, one feels. 46%. ncf.

⟞ **Hyde No. 7 President's Cask Bodega** sherry casks, bott code: 20518 **(69) n15 t19 f18 b17** Riddled with sulphur. The Germans will love it! 46%. ncf.

**The Irishman Single Malt** bottle no. E2496 **(83) n20 t21 f21 b21.** Highly pleasant malt but the coffee and toffee on the finish underline a caramel-style whiskey which may, potentially, offer so much more. 40%. Hot Irishman Ltd.

**The Irishman Aged 12 Years** first fill bourbon barrels, bott 2017 **(92) n23.5 t23 f22.5 b23** Old Bushmills like you have never quite seen her before in bottle. Works a treat. 43%. ncf. 6,000 bottles.

**The Irishman 12 Years Old Florio Marsala Cask Finish** cask no. 2257 **(90) n22 t23 f22.5 b22.5** A clean, unsullied cask but the grape allows the malt little room for manoeuvre. Very pleasurable though, and definitely a whisky rather than a wine.; 46%. ncf sc. 320 bottles.

**The Irishman Single Malt 17 Year Old** 1st fill Oloroso sherry casks **(94) n23 t24 f23.5 b23.5** The sherry is far too dominant for this to be a well-balanced whiskey: it is all about effect. But this is a rare, as near as damn-it sulphur-free sherry influence and that ups the value and enjoyment of this malt greatly. 56%. ncf sc.

**The Irishman Aged 17 Years** sherry cask, cask no. 6925, dist 2000 **(95.5) n24.5 t24 f23 b24** Just a year or two after this was distilled, I was crawling around the warehouses of Old Bushmills doing some blending and sampling amazingly fine, completely un-sulphured or as near as damn it un-sulphured, sherry butts – better than any I had found in Scotland in the previous several years. This style of sherry has all the hallmarks of the Bushmills butts of that time. There is trace sulphur (so this is a as near-as damn-it butt), but unless you know exactly what you are looking for it is in such small amounts it is unlikely to be detected or trouble you. This may not be from Bushmills, but if not then someone has made a good job of hiding some gems from me. If anyone can locate half a dozen of those entirely un-sulphured butts I located, then there is an Irish Whisky of the Year (at least!) in your hands... 56%. ncf sc. 600 bottles.

⟞ **The Irishman Aged 17 Years** sherry cask, cask no. 28657 **(94.5) n24** just massive sherry influence: spiced and juicy, this is like a plum sponge-cake still warm and nibbling at the nose...wow! **t24** we are still in plum sponge-cake territory, but now a mix of maple syrup and ulmo honey has been poured on top. About halfway in the first tangible signs of tannin start making themselves heard as a mix of spices and deeper toasty notes add ballast; **f22.5** vanilla but still a hint of grape jelly. Dulls slightly as the you know what arrives in tiny amounts; **b23.5** it's the hoping that kills you. After 20-odd years of tasting sherry casks ruined in Jerez, you view every whisky from sherry butt, be it a full term maturation or partial, with suspicion. You hope...but sadly, that hope is terminated by grim disappointment. Here, though, we have a happy experience. Is it 100% perfect sherry butt? No. Does it damage the whiskey? Not really. This is a full-on sherry influenced Irish celebrating the grape with style. The finale shews the slightest of weaknesses, but in light of what is out there it is forgiveable (well, not quite forgiveable enough for it not to be robbed of an award in the Whisky Bible!) and forgettable. *56%. ncf sc. 600 bottles.*

◈◈ **J. J. Corry The Flintlock No. 1 16 Year Old Single Malt** Autumn 2018, cask nos. 11191, 11221 & 11233 **(95.5) n23.5** an essay in beautiful grist....; **t24** such a dazzling, uncomplicated exhibition of barley. Biscuity, gristy, intense...just stunning... **f24** light spices hover around. As does a thin layer of bruyere honey and molasses; **b24** should Ireland ever hold a Maltfest, then this should be on the altar of worship... *46%. 650 bottles.*

**Jack Ryan Single Malt Irish Whisky Aged 12 Years** bourbon cask **(92.5) n23.5 t23 f22.5 b23.5** Deft, very clean malt whisky where decent bourbon wood adds all kinds of beautifully paced complexity. Not even a hint of an off note. Impressive. *46%*

◈◈ **Kinahan's Heritage 10 Year Old Single Malt (93) n23** a beautiful mix of sturdy malt and diced green apple; **t23.5** excellent firmness to the malt. Intense enough to spread in multiple directions, but the two main threads and a concentrated barley core plus a secondary juicy sub plot which mixes with tannins and spices for a warming, but restrained salivating experience; **f23** excellent tannins kicking up a cocoa dustiness, though that barley is like a dog with a bone; **b23.5** a beautifully constructed whiskey where, very rare for a single malt these days, you can actually taste the malt itself... A treat of a whiskey. *46%.*

◈◈ **Kinahan's Special Release Project 11 Year Old** Armagnac finish, cask no. 48 **(95.5) n23** delicate and intricately structured, the brittle fruit tones put a pleasant seal on underlying barley; **t24.5** a much softer mouth feel than you would ever expect from the nose. Then this is backed up by a dynamic eruption of ultra-intense malt, with restrained barley sugar offering the cleverly dispersed sweetness. Al the time the malt is trying to keep the lid on the warming spice, then as the complexity develops further, the oak gets into the act with a bewildering layering of oak of varied intensity; **f23.5** almost improbably there is a late oil surge, helping to soften the oak and spread the remaining barley around. You are half expecting chocolate to arrive at some point and, indeed, a light cocoa residue begins to form, though always playing second fiddle to the barley; **b24.5** this isn't good whiskey. Or even very good whiskey. It is truly great Irish whiskey. *58.9%.*

◈◈ **Liquid Treasures 10th Anniversary Irish Malt 29 Year Old** ex-rum barrel, dist 1989, bott 2019 **(94) n23.5** probably the rum barrel but at this age it could, equally, be the spirit itself; a mixture of both, perhaps: without question a degree of rum-like esters at play; the floral tones fascinate; **t23.5** a fabulous bite on delivery. Just a light smattering lime blossom honey to soften the sweetness; **f23** a little extra bite now as the odd tannin nips, but gentle maple syrup sooths; **b24** Irish whiskies of this antiquity are as rare as leprechaun's teeth. This one is gold filled. *56.5%. sc. 127 bottles.*

◈◈ **Liquid Treasures Summer Dram 2018 Irish Malt Over 26 Years Old** ex-bourbon barrel, dist 1992, bott 2018 **(90.5) n23.5 t23 f21.5 b22.5** the oak has taken control, here but in an entirely benign manner, bringing the barley into play here, dishing out spices there, standing back and allowing the ulmo and heather honeys to do their things at other times. Complex and beautifully paced, just shewing a degree of weariness at the finale. But don't we all... *48.3%. sc.*

**The Quiet Man 8 Year Old** bourbon cask, Oloroso sherry finish **(84.5) n23.5 t21.5 f19 b20.5** Pretty decent, though still slightly sulphured sherry butt been at play here. It is the nose which takes the plaudits, with its audacious lassoing of the bigger bourbon notes, fully-fledged tannins an' all, and then tying them to the orange blossom honey of the wine cask. The marriage on the nose is nowhere near matched on the bitty, untidy palate. *46%. ncf sc. 950 bottles.*

**The Quiet Man 8 Year Old Single Malt Irish Whiskey** bourbon casks **(89) n22 t23 f21.5 b22.5** Had the finish not dulled quite so quickly this would have scored a lot higher. Nothing less than pleasant throughout. *40%*

**The Quiet Man 8 Year Old** bourbon cask, bott code L18080088 **(88.5) n23 t23 f20.5 b22** Forget the finale: salute, quietly, the nose and delivery! *46%. ncf sc. 385 bottles.*

**The Quiet Man 12 Year Old** Kentucky bourbon casks **(93) n23 t23.5 f23 b23.5** Odd, isn't it? The owner of this brand named this whisky The Quiet Man in memory of his father, John Mulgrew, who was known by that epithet. Yet, coincidentally, it was Maurice Walsh, the grandfather of one of the greatest Irish whiskey blenders of all time, Barry Walsh, who wrote the novel The Quiet Man from which the film was made. I feel another movie coming on: The Silence of the Drams. But sssshhhh: don't tell anyone... *46%. ncf.*

**The Quiet Man 12 Year Old Sherry Finished** bourbon casks, finished in oloroso sherry casks, bott code: L17304295 db **(73) n18.5 t20 f16.6 b18** Ah. Sadly, the sulphur isn't quite as quiet as one might hope. *46%. ncf.*

⬦ **Sansibar Irish Single Malt 1989 Japonism** bott 2018 **(94.5) n23** glorious oak involvement from the off, but all the better for refusing to over dominate and allowing malt to mount with just the right degree of intensity; **t23.5** wow! Just so elegantly dry. Normally you get a sweet delivery...or sometimes if over-aged one that is too dry and aggressive. But this falls charmingly between the two, so the age is immediately apparent, but the integrity of the malt is never questioned. An exotic fruity note further underlines the great age here, with a little lychee hinted at before the oaks regather for the last push; **f24** a light crème brûlée with a milk chocolate accompaniment; **b24** what a joy of an Irish whiskey! Shews its age at every turn, but does so with grace and proves a lovely tune can be played on an old violin... *43.7%. Joint bottling with Shinanoya.*

⬦ **Sansibar Irish Whiskey 1992** bott 2018 **(89.5) n23 t23 f21.5 b22.5** A honey-drenched Irish concentrating both on nose and delivery on the buttery heather-honey at the heart of its character. The finish is a little on the hot and thin side, but this forgiveable when the vanilla and honey work so beautifully together elsewhere. *49.7%.*

**The Sexton Single Malt** batch no. L71861F001 **(91) n23 t23.5 f22 b22.5** Unmistakably malt from The Old Bushmills Distillery, and seemingly from sherry cask, also, as that distillery probably enjoys an above average number unsullied by sulphur. *40% (80 proof).*

⬦ **Teeling Whiskey Aged 30 Years Single Malt** white burgundy finish **(94.5) n23.5** just abounds in heather honey and measured oak: not overcomplicated but what it does, it does gorgeously: I could nose this all day! **t24** unripened gooseberry anyone....??? Wow, this is sharp enough to cut yourself on.... Fabulously so. Slightly eye-watering, and improbably juicy for a malt so old, there is a green pastel candy feel to this, then several waves of rich, almost biscuity malt...and a layer of more light honey; **f23** back to milk chocolate malt biscuits. The fruit is now an echo, and we are now treated to a final vaguely Brazil nut fade... **b24** a beautifully clean, faultless wine cask makes a huge difference to a whisky...as is evidenced here. The fruit has a curiously unripe chardonnay-type sharpness and vividness to it. What fun! *46%. ncf.*

**Teeling Whiskey Brabazon Bottling Single Malt Series 01** sherry casks, bott Feb 18, bott code: L18 001 059 **(67) n16 t19 f15 b17** I'll let you guess what kind of sherry cask this is... *49.5%. ncf.*

**Teeling Whiskey Brabazon Bottling Single Malt Series 02** port casks, bott Aug 17, bott code: L17 002 244 **(95) n23.5 t24 f23.5 b24** An exemplary Port cask offering: such a beautiful whiskey experience. *49.5%. ncf.*

**Teeling Whiskey Single Malt Aged 24 Years** Sauterne & bourbon casks, bott Aug 16 **(95.5) n24 t24.5 f23 b24** Well done, Jack Teeling: you caught me off guard there! Done me up like a kipper - literally. Wasn't expecting a smoky malt of this great antiquity (by Irish standards) and its marriage to a Sauterne influence makes it a complete one-off. Love to be sent the wrong way sometimes. Has all the craggy charm of an Irish character actor. *46%. ncf.*

**Teeling Whiskey Single Malt Aged 26 Years** rum cask, cask no. 16231, bott 21 Feb 17 **(96) n24 t24 f24 b24** Scratching my head, but this is probably the oldest Irish whiskey I have ever tasted from a distillery still working. All others of this antiquity – and beyond – have come from those which had closed many years before. Yes, the oldest – and one of the best... *57.9%. ncf sc.*

**Teeling Whiskey Single Malt Vol III Revival Aged 14 Years** bourbon casks, finished in Pineau des Charentes barrels **(76.5) n20.5 t21 f17 b18** 'Tis a risky business, this cask finishing. Especially in French fortified wine, as well as sherry... *46%. nc ncf.*

**Teeling Whiskey Single Malt Vol IV Revival Aged 14 Years** finished in ex-muscat barrels **(95) n23.5 t23.5 f24 b24** ...Though this muscat appears to be bang on the money... indeed, this is a stunner! *46%. nc ncf.*

**Teeling Whiskey Single Malt Vol V Revival Aged 12 Years** cognac & brandy casks, bott code: L18 001 088 **(90.5) n23.5 t23.5 f21 b22.5** Sharper than a newly whetted knife. *46%. nc ncf.*

⬦ **Tullamore D.E.W. Single Malt Aged 14 Years** four cask finish: bourbon, oloroso sherry, port & Madeira, bott code: L3 5009TD 08/01/2018 **(76) n23.5 t20 f15.5 b17** Vividly reminds me of the early 1990s when I was regularly in the tasting lab of my dear old friend the late, great Barry Walsh, going through his most recent efforts to try and perfect the balance on his embryonic Bushmills 16. This works wonderfully on the nose but is immediately fragmented on delivery, a problem Barry had to battle with for a good many months, in fact the best part of a year, before things clicked into place. But, also, in those days with a malt of that age there was no such thing as a sulphur problem, either, which there is here and wrecks the finish entirely. *41.3%. William Grant & Sons.*

⬦ **Tullamore D.E.W. Single Malt Aged 18 Years** finished for up to six months in bourbon, oloroso sherry, port & Madeira casks, bott code: L3 5089TD 11/04/2018 **(88) n23** a little bite to this, the tannins boasting a certain edge and out-manoeuvring the pithy, citrus peel fruitiness; **t22.5** gorgeously rotund delivery, soft and moulding to the palate. The fruit is refined and restrained, so the age can shew its oaky badge of honour; **f20.5** I'd love to report a clean bill of health on the finish, but unable to. But the sulphur here is light and not remotely close to the 14-year-old's intensity; **b22** drop the oloroso and this malt could really take off. *41.3%. Less than 2,500 bottles. William Grant & Sons.*

**The Whistler Aged 7 Years Natural Cask Strength Oloroso Finished** batch no. 02-0360 **(91.5) n22.5 t23.5 f22 b23.5** If you are going to round your malt off using a sherry butt probably dripping in wine when it was filled, your best option is to make the tenancy in the second cask short and then bottle at cask strength. They may not have done the former, but certainly the latter action has helped no-end, as confirmed when tasted alongside Blue Note (below). Infinitely better structure and the spices here make a big difference. Very attractive whiskey, indeed. And helped no end by a clean, sulphur-free sherry butt of the old school. I doff my Panama in finding such (mainly) unsullied sherry butts. *59%. nc ncf.*

**The Whistler Aged 7 Years The Blue Note Oloroso Finished (87) n22 t22 f21.5 b21.5** The great news: no sulphur! A clean sherry butt, which is a shock in itself. The less good news: the malt was a little too young and lacking in body to really be able to be much more than a vehicle for the grape. Enjoyable, rich sultana with attractive spice. But lacking in whisky-ish structure and complexity: just too much like a straight sweet sherry! *46%. nc ncf.*

**The Whistler Aged 10 Years How The Years Whistle By Oloroso Finished (92.5) n23 t23.5 f22.5 b23.5** A fabulously clean sherry butt which is much more at home with a broader-spectrumed malt... *46%. nc ncf.*

**Writers' Tears Red Head Oloroso** sherry casks **(82.5) n21 t23 f18.5 b20** Always a dangerous game to play with sherry butts and this writer's tears are reserved for the light furry sulphur tones which, as will always be the case, stifle the enjoyment of the rich fruity delivery. *46%. ncf.*

# Single Grain
## COOLEY County Louth.
**Greenore 6 Year Old** bott code L9015 db **(89) n23.5 t22.5 f21 b22.** Very enjoyable whiskey. But two points: cut the caramel and really see the baby sing. And secondly, as a "Small Batch" bottling, how about putting a batch number on the label...? *40%. Cooley.*

**Greenore 8 Year Old** bott code L8190 db **(86.5) n20 t22 f23 b21.5.** The vague hint of butyric on the nose is more than amply compensated by the gradual build up to something rather larger on the palate than you might have expected (and don't be surprised if the two events are linked). The corn oil is almost a meal in itself and the degree of accompanying sugar and corn flour is a treat. *40%. Cooley.*

**Greenore 15 Years Old** bott code L8044 db **(90) n23 t22.5 f22 b22.5.** The advent of the Kilbeggan 15 reminded us that there must be some grain of that age around, and here to prove it is a superb bottling of the stuff which, weirdly, is a lot better than the blend. Beautiful. *43%*

**Greenore 18 Years Old** db **(91) n22.5 t22.5f23 b23.** This continuous still at Cooley should be marked by the State as an Irish national treasure. One of the most complex grains you'll ever find, even when heading into uncharted territory like this one. *46%. ncf. 4000 bottles.*

**Hyde 1916 No.3 Áras Cask Aged 6 Years Single Grain** bott Feb 16 **(87) n22 t23 f20.5 b21.5** Cooley grain probably ranks as the best being made right now, with the loss of Dumbarton and Port Dundas in Scotland. Sadly, as deliciously rich as this is, far too much toffee on the finish rather detracts from its normal excellence. Highly enjoyable, but the flag flies nowhere near full mast. By the way: the 1916 on the label doesn't represent year of distillation or bottling. Or is there to celebrate the year of my dad's birth. No, it is something a little more political than that. *46%. ncf. 5,000 bottles.*

## MIDLETON County Cork.
**Method and Madness Single Grain Irish Whiskey** bourbon barrels, finished in virgin Spanish oak casks db **(89.5) n22 t22.5 f22 b23** If you've never tasted a sweet Spanish virgin before, here's your chance... *46%.*

## WEST CORK DISTILLERS County Cork.
**Skibbereen Eagle Single Grain Irish Whiskey** Bodega sherry casks db **(88.5) n21.5 t23 f22 b22** As frictionless as the post Brexit border between Britain and Ireland shall be... *43%. West Cork Distillers Limited.*

## UNSPECIFIED SINGLE GRAIN
**Egan's Vintage Grain 10 Aged Years** bourbon casks, casked 2009, bott 2017, bott code: US001 244 **(92.5) n23 t23.5 f22.5 b23.5** Such a beautiful whiskey. Don't be put off by the fact

this is grain: this is exceptionally high grade Irish. Very much of the Cooley style, who happen to make the best grain whisky in the British Isles. *46% (92 proof). ncf.*

**Glendalough 3 Year Old Irish Single Grain** sherry & Madeira butts db **(91) n22 t23.5 f22.5 b23** A much richer and more confident grain than their first, sherry-finished version. Excellent. *43%.*

**Glendalough Double Barrel Irish Whiskey** first aged in American bourbon casks, then Spanish oloroso casks **(88.5) n22.5 t23 f21 b22** A very pleasant malt but rather vague and at times a little dull. *42%*

⬧ **Glendalough Single Cask Irish Whiskey Calvados XO Cask Finish** cask no. 3/12 CX18 **(90) n22** exceptionally light. All the hallmarks of a grain, with its ethereal, wispy softness, with just the most fragile fruitiness involved; **t22.5** silky soft and no malt to note. So, a grain I would have thought by the oiliness attractively stretching across the palate like an eldest son may spread himself across the settee.... Some pretty sweet interludes, sometimes a muscovado sugar kick, others a more oaky-vanilla imprint; **f22.5** only very late on can you really directly pick out the Calvados influence, though always a subtle one; good oils still; **b23** from its nose and mouth feel, presumably a grain whisky. If so, why don't they celebrate the fact? *42%. ncf sc. 366 bottles.*

⬧ **Glendalough Single Cask Irish Whiskey Grand Cru Burgundy Cask Finish** cask no. 1/BY19 **(87.5) n22.5 t24 f20 b22** Strikes me more of a grain than a malt whisky this, not least because of the gorgeous velvety mouth feel. The honeys on delivery are sublime: predominantly ulmo honey but a little acacia slipping in, too. There is a light fruitiness getting on the act. But the finish is undone slightly by the furry tang of a naughty wine cask. A real shame, for otherwise this would have been one hell of a score... *42%. ncf sc. 366 bottles.*

**Hyde No. 5 Áras Cask 1860 Single Grain** burgundy cask finished, bott Jul 16 **(86) n21 t22.5 f21 b21.5** When I first heard about this bottling I was intrigued: one of the softest yet most charismatic grain whiskies in the world rounded off in pinot noir grape casks. Would the grape add an intriguing flintiness to the proceedings, or be of a type to soften it further? Sadly, it was the latter. Yes, sulphur free and clean (itself a minor miracle) and with plenty of chewy fruit caramels and even a little spice. But the peaks have been levelled and what is left is a pleasant, easy drinking, sweet but mainly featureless malt. *46%. ncf. 5,000 bottles.*

**Teeling Whiskey Single Grain** wine casks, bott Mar 17, bott code: L17 004 075 **(94) n23 t24 f23 b24** What a beautiful grain whisky this is. Thankfully the wine casks don't interrupt the already spellbinding narrative. *46%. ncf.*

# Blends

**Barr an Uisce Wicklow Rare Blended Irish Whiskey** bourbon barrel, sherry cask finish **(87.5) n22.5 t22 f21 b22.** Busy whiskey with a creamy nose and sugar-gorged middle. However, the finish turns a tad bitter. *43%. ncf.*

**Bushmills 12 Years Old Distillery Reserve** db **(86) n22.5 t22.5 f20 b21.** This version has gone straight for the ultra lush feel. For those who want to take home some 40% abv fruit fudge from the distillery. *40%*

**Bushmills 1608 400th Anniversary (83) n21 t21.5 f20 b20.5.** Thin-bodied, hard as nails and sports a peculiarly Canadian feel. *46%. Diageo.*

**Bushmills 1608** db **(87) n22 t23 f20 b22.** A blend which, through accident, evolution or design, has moved a long way in style from when first launched. More accent on fruit though, predictably, the casks aren't quite what they once were. Ignoring the furriness on the finish, there is much to enjoy on the grape-must nose and how the fruit bounces off the rigid grain on delivery. *46%*

**Bushmills Black Bush (91) n23 t23 f21.5 b23.5.** This famous old blend may be under new management and even blender. But still the high quality, top-notch complexity rolls around the glass and your palate. As beautiful as ever. *40%*

**Bushmills Black Bush** bott code L6140IB001 **(95) n23.5 t24 f23.5 b24** Of all the famous old blends in the British Isles, this has probably bucked the trend by being an improvement on its already excellent self. The warehouses of Bushmills distillery boast the highest quantity of quality, unsulphured sherry butts I have encountered in the last 20 years, and this is borne out by a blend which has significantly upped the wine influence in the recipe but has not paid a price for it, as has been the usual case in Scotland. Indeed, it has actually benefitted. This is a belter, even by its normal own high standards. Truly classic and should be far easier to find than is normally the case today. *40%.*

**Bushmills Original (80) n19 t21 f20 b20.** Remains one of the hardest whiskeys on the circuit with the Midleton grain at its most unflinching. There is a sweeter, faintly maltier edge to this now while the toffee and biscuits qualities remain. *40%*

**Bushmills Red Bush** bourbon casks, bott code: L7161IB001 db **(92) n22 t23.5 f23 b23.5** A beautifully balanced and erudite blended Irish fully deserving of discovery. And after the preponderance of wine-finished Irish from elsewhere, it was great to taste one that hadn't already set my nerves jangling in fear of what was to come. A worthy and beautiful addition to the Bushmills range. I always knew I'd be a little bit partial to a Red Bush. *40%.*

**Cassidy's Distiller's Reserve** bott code L8067 **(84.5) n21.5 t22 f20 b21.** Some salivating malt on flavour-exploding delivery, but all else tame and gentle. *40%. Cooley.*

⟜ **Clonakilty Port Cask Finish** batch no. 0012 **(90) n22** ridiculously soft and dream-like. Even the grape barely seems capable of lifting more than the odd atom or two to make an impact; **t23** the brand's rock-hard style retains its place. But now a light fruitiness wraps it in cotton wool; even so, the first three or four flavour waves, assisted by peppers, are profound; **f22** gentle spices dance on the tiny fruit stage; **b23** a whiskey where you're between a rock and a soft, fruity place... *43.6%. ncf. 1,000 bottles. Cask Finish Series.*

⟜ **Clonakilty Single Batch** batch no. 003/2018 **(86) n21 t22 f21.5 b21.5** Clean and salivating, this is a hard as nails, simplistic Irish dependent on toffee as its principal flavour profile. *43.6%. ncf. 3,000 bottles.*

⟜ **The Dead Rabbit Aged 5 Years** virgin American oak finished, bott no. L18001-011 **(93) n23** quite superb tannin: the oak exudes red liquorice and a thin muscovado sugar and maple syrup blend. Impressive...; **t23.5** a stunning mouth feel: seemingly clean but just bursting with a pleasingly oily spiced vanilla, butterscotch and salivating tannins, all punctuated with an intriguing a shadow of bourbon; **f23** the dark sugars still have a toasty feel even as the sun sets on this whiskey; **b23.5** the rabbit is dead: long live Dead Rabbit...! Oh, Murray Method to take this from a decent to a truly excellent Irish, by the way. *44%.*

**The Dublin Liberties Oak Devil** bott no. L17 048 W3 **(94) n23.5 t23.5 f23 b24** The Cooley grain at work here is of superstar status. So beautifully balanced and the word "lush" hardly does it justice... *46%.*

**The Dubliner Bourbon Cask Aged** batch no. 001, bott no. L0187F252 **(87.5) n21.5 t22.5 f21.5 b22** A soft, clean attractive blend which peaks on delivery with a lilting juiciness which works brilliantly with the grain which is as yielding as a feathered silk pillow. Vague spices plot a course towards the bitter lemon finish. *40%.*

⟜ **The Dubliner Master Distiller's Reserve** bourbon casks, bott no. L17718-320 **(91) n23.5** well blow me...salt! More than that, tidal rock pools...; **t23** crisp, juicy and lightly bathed in lime blossom honey; **f22** the saltiness returns with the vanilla; **b22.5** refreshing and tender. A bit of an understated treat. *42%.*

**Dundalgan Charred Cask Irish Whiskey** db **(87) n21.5 t22 f22 b21.5** This is an interesting one: you have a spirit that produces a fair chunk of oil. You then char a cask, which produces caramel. The only result possible is a thick whiskey on both nose and palate with limited scope to develop. So although the end product is the antonym of complexity, the flavours and mouth feel are attractive and satisfying, especially if you are into malt and toffee. There are even some very late spices to stir things up a bit. *40%. West Cork Distillers Limited.*

**Dundalgan Irish Whiskey** db **(84) n21 t21 f21 b21.5** Pleasant, inoffensive, toffee-dominant and bland. *40%. West Cork Distillers Limited.*

**Dunville's Three Crowns (80) n19 t22 f19 b20** Three casks and Three Crowns. So three cheers for the return of one of the great names in Irish whiskey! Somewhere in my warehouse I have a few original bottles of this stuff I picked up in Ireland over the years and at auction. None I opened tasted quite like this. Have to say that, despite the rich-lip-smacking delivery, certain aspects of the tangy nose and finish don't quite gel and are a little off key. The coronation remains on hold... *43.5%.*

**Dunville's Three Crowns Peated (94.5) n23 t24 f23.5 b24** Even people purporting not to like peaty whisk(e)y will have a problem finding fault with this. This is a rare treat of an Irish. *43.5%.*

**Feckin Irish Whiskey (81) n20 t21 f20 b20.** Tastes just about exactly the feckin same as the Feckin Strangford Gold... *40%. The Feckin Drinks Co.*

**Flannigans Blended Irish Whiskey (87.5) n21.5 t22.5 f21.5 b22** About as mouth-watering and easy going a blended Irish as you'll hope to find. Excellent sugars and velvety body ensure the most pleasant, if simple, of rides. Even a little spice peps up the flagging finish. *40%. Quality Spirits International.*

**Great Oaks Cask Strength Irish Whiskey** db **(90.5) n22 t23 f22.5 b23** A joyful whisky brimming with personality. *60%. West Cork Distillers Limited.*

**Great Oaks Irish Whiskey** db **(87) n22 t22 f21.5 b21.5** Easy going, full of its signature caramel chewy sweetness. Pleasant and non-threatening. *46%. West Cork Distillers Limited.*

**Great Oaks New Frontiers Irish Whiskey** db **(94) n23.5 t24 f23 b23.5** Very high class and inventive Irish. West Cork have seriously raised their game here and have entered a new quality dimension. *59%. West Cork Distillers Limited.*

**Hyde No. 6 President's Reserve 1938 Commemorative Edition** sherry cask finish, bott May 17 **(77) n18 t22 f18 b19** Lush grape for sure. But the very last thing I'd commemorate anything in would be a sherry cask: unless you want sulphur to give you a good Hyding.... *46%. ncf. 5,000 bottles.*

**The Irishman Cask Strength 2016** 1st fill bourbon casks **(90) n21.5 t23 f22.5 b23** Doesn't try to overload the taste buds with too many flavour profiles: this one is all about shape, intensity and effect. *54%. ncf. 1,800 bottles.*

**The Irishman Founder's Reserve Caribbean Cask Finish** rum cask, cask no. 9657 **(93) n23** a pleasing amalgam of vanilla, light marzipan and crisp, crunchy Demerara sugars. Satisfyingly firm and malty in part; **t23.5** the kind of delivery which makes you purr...sharp and eye-watering barley in a setting of heather honey and butterscotch mixed. Hang on... there is a firm feel to this amid the honey, a backbone... Has this got Irish Pot Still...? Well, the label, confirms it has! Brilliant...! **f23** the sugars on the nose had been quiet through the thrust of this whiskey. They return now for a toasty finale; **b23.5** this brings to an end a run of tasting six consecutive Irish whiskies, each tainted by sulphur. This, naturally, has not an atom of sulphur as, sensibly, no sherry cask was used anywhere in the maturation (three hearty cheers!). Frankly, I don't know whether to drink it, or kiss it.... *46%. ncf sc. 318 bottles.*

**The Irishman Founder's Reserve Florio Marsala Cask Finish** cask no. 2/86 **(82.5) n21 t23.5 f17.5 b20** A nipping, acidic, biting nose: borderline aggressive. But, momentarily, all is forgiven! The fruit is as lush as any delivery in the world this year, helped along by a thin maple syrup sweetness and balancing vanillas. Shame, then, about the very late sulphur tang. Whoever put the sulphur candle in this cask wants shooting: this would otherwise have been real stunner. *46%. ncf sc. 204 bottles.*

**The Irishman Superior Irish Whiskey** bott code L6299L059 **(93) n23 t23 f23 b24.** What a quite wonderful blend: not of the norm for those that have recently come onto the market and there is much more of the Irish Distillers about this than most. Forget about the smoke promised in the tasting notes on the label...it gives you everything else but. And that is one hell of a lot!! *40%. Hot Irishman Ltd.*

**J. J. Corry The Battalion** finished in tequila & Mezcal casks, batch no. 1, Spring 2019, bott code: L7256L1375 **(91.5) n22** more than a little Mexican bite to this, but is impressively restrained, even allowing a light malt note to occasionally surface; **t23.5** one of the silkiest Irish whiskeys for a while. There appears to be gloss to the grain, while elsewhere oily spices capture the roof of the mouth; the baser notes are earthy and sub-phenolic; **f23** such a succulent, oily, spiced chocolate and toffee fade; **b23** my Mexican hat off to the blender here, who appears to have worked exceptionally hard to ensure there was no dominance by any single party. And succeeded. *41%. 700 bottles.*

**J. J. Corry The Gael** batch no. 1, Summer 2017, bott code: L7256L1375 **(86.5) n22 t22.5 f20.5 b21.5** An essentially bone-crushingly dry blend with a fair bit of fizz and nip here and there. Plenty of pith on both nose and delivery and soars from the prosaic to the poetic around about four flavour waves in when the malt and tannin finally combine in brief harmony. The finish, however, takes you over pretty rough terrain. Certainly the label raised a smile with the claim that this was a "Classic Irish" because I can't remember too many blends over the last four decades which included 26-year-old malt. *46%. 7000 bottles.*

**Jameson (95) n24.5 24 f22.5 b24** I thought I had detected in bottlings I had found around the world a very slight reduction in the Pot Still character that defines this truly classic whiskey. So I sat down with a fresh bottle in more controlled conditions...and was blown away as usual. The sharpness of the PS is vivid and unique; the supporting grain of the required crispness. Fear not: this very special whiskey remains in stunning, truly wondrous form. *40%*

**Jameson** bott code L701012030 **(87) n22 t22.5 f21 b21.5** Now, isn't that the way it always happens! Having tasted crisp, characterful true-to-form Jamesons around the globe for the last year or so, the one I get here for a re-taste is the "other" version. Suddenly the sexiest Irish on the market has become a dullard. Where it should be soaring with Pot Still it is laden with toffee. And a little sulphur nagging on the finish doesn't help, either. Does tick the other boxes, though. But hardly representative. *40%.*

**Jameson 18 Years Old** bott code L629231345 **(91) n22 t23 f23 b23** Definitely a change in direction from the last Jameson 18 I analysed. Much more grain focussed and paying less heed to the oak. *40%.*

**Jameson Black Barrel** bott code L700431433 **(93) n23 t23.5 f23 b23.5** An improved, more sugar-laden and spicy whiskey. *40%.*

**Jameson The Blender's Dog (92) n23 t23.5 f22 b23.5** A clever blend, as this is just as much about mouth feel as it is flavour construction. You have made this dog do some entertaining tricks, Billy Leighton, my dear old friend... *43%. ncf. The Whisky Makers Series.*

**Jameson The Blender's Dog** bott code L608231059 **(91.5) n22.5 t23 f23 b23** A very slight variance on the previous sample (above) with the grain whiskey a little more dominant here despite the softer mouth feel. All the usual tricks and intrigues though a little less orange blossom honey a tad more maple syrup, which helps lengthen the finale. *43%.*

**Jameson Bold (92) n24 t23.5 f21.5 b23** Delicious stuff. But not to be confused with the excellent Indian malt, Bold, from Paul John, which is a lot Bolder than this... That said, a blender's blend with the nose making one purr with delight and appreciation. *40%. The Deconstructed Series.*

**Jameson Bold bott code L617431172 (93) n24 t23.5 f22.5 b23** Absolutely spot on with the tasting notes above. Only changes are slightly more fudge through the centre ground and a degree less bitterness on the finish, though still there. Crucially, however, the honey has a bigger late say. *40%. The Deconstructed Series.*

**Jameson Bow Street 18 Years Old** batch no. 1/2018, bott code: L804431050 **(88.5) n22.5 t23.5 f20 b22.5** Few whiskies have such a wide flavour register between tooth-decayingly sweet and puckeringly dry. *55.3%. ncf.*

**Jameson Caskmates (91.5) n23.5 t23 f22 b23** Some serious elements of Jameson Gold involved in this, especially the acacia honey thread. Delightful. *40%*

**Jameson Caskmates IPA Edition bott code** L735315273 **(70.5) n18 t18.5 f17 b17** And you want to ruin the taste of a fine whiskey by adding the bitter taste of hops because...? Why exactly? Am I missing something here...? *40%. ncf.*

**Jameson Caskmates Stout Edition bott code** L629315085 **(93) n22 t23.5 f24 b23.5** A very different experience to the Teeling equivalent. Here, the beer is far less prevalent on nose and taste, but makes a significant, highly positive, contribution to the mouth feel. A super lush experience. *40%.*

**Jameson The Cooper's Croze (95) n24 t23.5 f23.5 b24** This is one of the most softly spoken great orations on Irish whiskey in recent years. An understated masterpiece. *43%. ncf. The Whisky Makers Series.*

**Jameson The Cooper's Croze bott code** L608231057 **(94.5) n23.5 t24 f22.5 b24** Huh! Near enough same final score as last time, though a gentle change in emphasis and shape means the scoring itself was slightly different. Remains the most astonishingly lush and richly-flavoured of whiskeys, except on this bottling there is a bigger toffee surge, especially towards the finish and a gentle bitter tail off which has cost a half mark. Just remember: whatever anyone ever tells you, no two bottlings are identical: it is impossible. *43%. The Whiskey Makers Series.*

**Jameson Crested (90) n23 t24 f20.5 b22.5** When first introduced back in the early 1960s as Jameson's first-ever bottled whiskey, this was known as Crested 10. Now probably ditched the number so not to confuse with age. *40%*

**Jameson Crested bott code** L635731441 **(91) n23 t23.5 f22 b22.5** That's curious. A slight upping of the caramels here has slightly reduced the overall complexity, and the depth of the fruit. However, the bitter, off-key finish from my last sample is missing here making, when all is said and done, a slightly more satisfying all round experience. Swings and roundabouts... *40%.*

**Jameson The Distiller's Safe (95) n23.5 t24 f23.5 b24** Not sure if head distiller Brian Nation is any relation to former comedy scriptwriter Terry Nation, creator of The Daleks. Either way, this is Dalektable stuff and as beautifully timed as the funniest skits ever written. *43%. ncf. The Whisky Makers Series.*

**Jameson The Distiller's Safe bott code** L60331023 **(93) n24 t24 f22 b23** This brand's safe, too...at least for another bottling! As near as damn it a re-run of the last bottle I tasted, though here the butteryness kicks in sooner and there is a vague bitterness on the now chocolate-flaked finale. Still a stunner. *43%. The Whiskey Makers Series.*

**Jameson Gold Reserve (88) n22 t23 f20 b22.** Enjoyable, but so very different: an absolute re-working with all the lighter, more definitively sweeter elements shaved mercilessly while the thicker oak is on a roll. Some distance from the masterpiece it once was. *40%*

**Jameson Lively (84.5) n21 t21.5 f21 b21.** The belligerent grain of Midleton appears to be coming at you at full throttle and from all direction. The nose appears to be all grain, though a little toffee apple does creep in. The delivery is uncompromising: as hard as nails. *40%. The Deconstructed Series.*

**Jameson Lively bott code** L617431174 **(85.5) n21 t22 f21.5 b21** Well you have to applaud them for keeping to the script. A couple of thumbs up from the last bottling: the impact appears to have been softened very slightly (though, sadly, via toffee) and spices at the finish do no harm at all. *40%. The Deconstructed Series.*

**Jameson Round bott code** L625831239 **(93.5) n22.5 t24 f23.5 b23.5** Just such a sensual whiskey... *40%. The Deconstructed Series.*

**Jameson Signature bott code** L617531177 **(93) n24 t23.5 f22.5 b23** No longer Signature Reserve, though every bit as good. This, though, like some other Jamesons of late appears to have an extra dose of caramel. Bring the colouring down and whiskey – and the scores here - will really fly! *40%.*

**Jameson Signature Reserve (93) n23.5 t23.5 f22.5 b23.5.** Be assured that Signature, with its clever structuring of delicate and inter-weaving flavours, says far more about the blender, Billy Leighton, than it does John Jameson. *40%. Irish Distillers.*

**Kellan** American oak cask **(84) n21 t22 f20 b21.** Safe whisky which is clean, sweet and showing many toffeed attributes. Decent spices, too. *40% (80 Proof). Cooley.*

**Kilbeggan** bott code L7091 db **(86) n21 t22 f21.5 b21.5.** A much more confident blend by comparison with that faltering one of the last few years. Here, the malts make a significant drive towards increasing the overall complexity and gentle citrus style. *40%. Cooley.*

**Kilbeggan 15 Years Old** bott code L7048 db **(85.5) n21.5 t22 f21 b21.** My word! 15 years, eh? How time flies! And on the subject of flying, surely I have winged my way back to Canada and am tasting a native blend. No, this is Irish albeit in sweet, deliciously rounded form. However, one cannot help feeling that the dark arts have been performed, as in an injection of caramel, which, as well as giving that Canadian feel has also probably shaved off some of the more complex notes to middle and finish. Even so, a sweet, silky experience. *40%. Cooley.*

**Kilbeggan 18 Year Old** db **(89) n23 t21.5 f22.5 b22.** Although the impressive bottle lavishly claims "From the World's Oldest Distillery" I think one can take this as so much Blarney. It certainly had my researcher going, who lined this up for me under the Old Kilbeggan distillery, a forgivable mistake and one I think he will not be alone in making. This, so it appears on the palate, is a blend. From the quite excellent Cooley distillery, and it could be that whiskey used in this matured at Kilbeggan... which is another thing entirely. As for the whiskey: apart from some heavy handedness on the toffee, it really is quite a beautiful and delicate thing. *40%*

**Kilgeary** bott code L8063 **(79) n20 t20 f19 b20.** There has always, and still proudly is, something strange about this blend. Cold tea on the nose and a bitter bite to the finish, sandwiches a brief flirtation with something sweet. *40%. Cooley.*

⟫ **Kinahan's Heritage Small Batch Blend (87.5) n22 t23 f21 b21.5** All aboard for the plush delivery, a gorgeous mix of briefly intense malt but overwhelmingly soft, sweet and embracing grain. The weak link is the tart and rough-edged finale, undermined further by a slight bitter note. But earlier there is plenty of fun to be had with the vanilla and spices. *46%.*

⟫ **Kinahan's KASC Project B. 001** hybrid cask (Portuguese, American, French, Hungarian & chestnut) **(86) n20 t22 f22 b22** Well, that is different. The wood has the biggest say here, especially on the nose where the spirit is left bullied, quivering and unnoticed in some inaccessible corner. While the flavour profile is very pleasant, it certainly didn't ring true and when I later spotted the chestnut inclusion, the sensations immediately made sense. Intriguing, though. *43%.*

**Locke's** bott code L8056 **(85.5) n21 t22 f21.5 b21.** Now, there you go!! Since I last really got round to analysing this one it has grown from a half-hearted kind of a waif to something altogether more gutsy and muscular. Sweeter, too, as the malts and grains combine harmoniously. A clean and pleasant experience with some decent malt fingerprints. *40%.*

**Michael Collins A Blend (77) n19 t20 f19 b19.** Michael Collins was known as the "big fellow". This pleasant, impressively spiced dram, might have enjoyed the same epithet had it not surrendered to and then been strangled by caramel on the finish. *40% (80 proof). Cooley.*

**Midleton Distillery Reserve (85) n22 t22 f20 b21.** A whiskey which, for all its muscovado sweetness offers some memorable barley moments. *40%. Irish Distillers Midleton Distillery only. Changes character slightly with each new vatting. This one is some departure.*

**Midleton Very Rare 30th Anniversary Pearl Edition** db **(91) n23.5 t24 f21 b22.5** The nose and delivery will go down in Irish whiskey folklore... *53.1%*

**Midleton Very Rare 1984 (70) n19 t18 f17 b16.** Disappointing with little backbone or balance. *40%. Irish Distillers.*

**Midleton Very Rare 1985 (77) n20 t20 f18 b19.** Medium-bodied and oily, this is a big improvement on the initial vintage. *40%. Irish Distillers.*

**Midleton Very Rare 1986 (79) n21 t20 f18 b20.** A very malty Midleton richer in character than previous vintages. *40%. Irish Distillers.*

**Midleton Very Rare 1987 (77) n20 t19 f19 b19.** Quite oaky at first until a late surge of excellent pot still. *40%. Irish Distillers.*

**Midleton Very Rare 1988 (86) n23 t21 f21 b21.** A landmark MVR as it is the first vintage to celebrate the Irish pot-still style. *40%. Irish Distillers.*

**Midleton Very Rare 1989 (87) n22 t22 f22 b21.** A real mouthful but has lost balance to achieve the effect. *40%. Irish Distillers.*

**Midleton Very Rare 1990 (93) n23 t23 f24 b23.** Astounding whiskey: one of the vintages every true Irish whiskey lover should hunt for. *40%. Irish Distillers.*

**Midleton Very Rare 1991 (76) n19 t20 f19 b18.** After the Lord Mayor's Show, relatively dull and uninspiring. *40%. Irish Distillers.*

**Midleton Very Rare 1992 (84) n20 t20 f23 b21.** Superb finish with outstanding use of feisty grain. *40%. Irish Distillers.*

**Midleton Very Rare 1993 (88) n21 t22 f23 b22.** Big, brash and beautiful – the perfect way to celebrate the 10th-ever bottling of MVR. *40%. Irish Distillers.*

**Midleton Very Rare 1994 (87) n22 t22 f21 b22.** Another different style of MVR, one of amazing lushness. *40%. Irish Distillers.*

**Midleton Very Rare 1995 (90) n23 t24 b21 b22.** They don't come much bigger than this. Prepare a knife and fork to battle through this one. Fabulous. *40%. Irish Distillers.*

**Midleton Very Rare 1996 (82) n21 t22 f19 b20.** The grains lead a soft course, hardened by subtle pot still. Just missing a beat on the finish, though. *40%. Irish Distillers.*

**Midleton Very Rare 1997 (83) n22 t21 f19 b21.** The piercing pot still fruitiness of the nose is met by a countering grain of rare softness on the palate. Just dies on the finish when you want it to make a little speech. Very drinkable. *40%. Irish Distillers.*

**Midleton Very Rare 1999 (89) n21 t23 f22 b23.** One of the maltiest Midletons of all time: a superb blend. *40%. Irish Distillers.*

**Midleton Very Rare 2000 (85) n22 t21 f21 b21.** An extraordinary departure even by Midleton's eclectic standards. The pot still is like a distant church spire in an hypnotic Fen landscape. *40%. Irish Distillers.*

**Midleton Very Rare 2001 (79) n21 t20 f18 b20.** Extremely light but the finish is slightly on the bitter side. *40%. Irish Distillers.*

**Midleton Very Rare 2002 (79) n20 t22 f18 b19.** The nose is rather subdued and the finish is likewise toffee-quiet and shy. There are some fabulous middle moments, some of flashing genius, when the pot still and grain combine for a spicy kick, but the finish really is lacklustre and disappointing. *40%. Irish Distillers.*

**Midleton Very Rare 2003 (84) n22 t22 f19 b21.** Beautifully fruity on both nose and palate (even some orange blossom on aroma). But the delicious spicy richness that is in mid launch on the tastebuds is cut short by caramel on the middle and finish. A crying shame, but the best Midleton for a year or two. *40%. Irish Distillers.*

**Midleton Very Rare 2004 (82) n21 t21 f19 b21.** Yet again caramel is the dominant feature, though some quite wonderful citrus and spice escape the toffeed blitz. *40%.*

**Midleton Very Rare 2005 (92) n23 t24 f22 b23.** OK, you can take this one only as a rough translation. The sample I have worked from here is from the Irish Distillers blending lab, reduced to 40% in mine but without caramel added. And, as Midleton Very Rares always are at this stage, it's an absolute treat. Never has such a great blend suffered so in the hands of colouring and here the chirpiness of the pot still and élan of the honey (very Jameson Gold Label in part) show just what could be on offer given half the chance. Has wonderful natural colour and surely it is a matter of time before we see this great whiskey in its natural state. *40%*

**Midleton Very Rare 2006 (92) n22 t24 f23 b23.** As raw as a Dublin rough-house and for once not overly swamped with caramel. An uncut diamond. *40%*

**Midleton Very Rare 2007 (83) n20 t22 f20 b21.** Annoyingly buffeted from nose to finish by powering caramel. Some sweeter wisps do escape but the aroma suggests Canadian and insufficient Pot Still gets through to make this a Midleton of distinction. *40%. Irish Distillers*

**Midleton Very Rare 2008 (88.5) n22 t23 f21.5 b22.** A dense bottling which offers considerably more than the 2007 Vintage. Attractive, very drinkable and without the caramel it might really have hit the heights. *40%. Irish Distillers.*

**Midleton Very Rare 2009 (95) n24 t24 f23 b24.** I've been waiting a few years for one like this to come along. One of the most complex, cleanest and least caramel-spoiled bottlings for a good few years and one which makes the pot still character its centre piece. A genuine celebration of all things Midleton and Barry Crockett's excellence as a distiller in particular. *40%. .*

**Midleton Very Rare 2010 (84) n21 t22 f20 b21.** A case of after the Lord Mayor's Show. Chewy and some decent sugars. But hard to make out detail through the fog of caramel. *40%.*

**Midleton Very Rare 2011 (81.5) n22.5 t20 f19 b20** Another disappointing version where the colour of its personality has been compromised for the sake of the colour in the bottle. A dullard of a whiskey, especially after the promising nose. *40%. Irish Distillers.*

**Midleton Very Rare Irish Whisky 2012 db (89.5) n22 t23 f22 b22.5.** Much more like it! After a couple of dud vintages, here we have a bottling worthy of its great name & heritage. *40%.*

**Midleton Very Rare Irish Whisky 2014 db (78.5) n20.5 t22 f17 b19.** Must say how odd it looks to see Brian Nation's signature scrawled across the label and not Barry Crockett's. Also, I was a bit worried by this one when I saw the depth of orange hue to this whiskey. Sadly, my fears were pretty well founded. Toffee creaks from every corner making for a mainly flat encounter with what should be an uplifting Irish. Some lift at about the midway point when something, probably pot still, throws off the shackles of its jailer and emerges briefly with spice. But all rather too little, especially in the face of a dull, disappointingly flawed, fuzzy finale. Midleton Very Rare should be, as the name implies, a lot, lot better than this safe but flabby, personality bypassed offering. The most frustrating aspect of this is that twice I have tasted MVR in lab form just prior to bottling. And both were quite stunning whiskeys. That was until the colouring was added in the bottling hall. *40%. WB15/416*

**Midleton Very Rare 2016 (87.5) n22 t22.5 f21.5 b21.5** The grain, not exactly the most yielding, has the clearest mandate to show its uncompromising personality A huge caramel presence softens the impact and leads to a big show of coffee towards the finish. But between these two OTT beasts the Pot Still is lost completely soon after its initial delicious impact on delivery. *40%.*

**Midleton Very Rare 2017 (90.5) n22 t23.5 f22 b23** Slightly less toffee than there has been, but still a fraction too much. But superb complexity levels nonetheless and one of the most attractively sweet MVRs for a little while. *40%.*

◈ **Midleton Very Rare 2018** bott code: L826431444 **(88.5) n22.5** happy to take a gentle, quietly spoken route; a little polished leather gives a slight air of grandeur; **t23** untaxing, grain-heavy and simplistic with a distinctive toffee raisin chewability...with quite a lot of raisin...; **f21** more toffee but just a little bitter at the death; **b22** all about understatement. But like many an Irish at the moment, just weakens towards the finish. *40%.*

**Mizen Head Original Irish Whiskey** Bodega sherry casks db **(87.5) n21.5 t22.5 f21.5 b22** Maybe this was a bit unlucky, in that I have just come from tasting Glenfarclas sherry casks of the 1980s to this. No damaging sulphur (though a little forms late on the finale), so some Brownie points there. But the lack of body to the spirit and shortage of complexity on the grape, beyond a delicious cinnamon spice, doesn't help the cause. Enjoyable, but thinner than you might expect or desire. *40%. West Cork Distillers Limited.*

◈ **Natterjack Irish Whiskey Blend No. 1** virgin American oak finish, bott code: L19/001 044 **(92) n22** a curious, heady aroma with a much lighter, almost grainy, subplot. Oak-spiced and with limited sweetness; **t23.5** ah! Now we get some honey, an immediately on arrival. A delicate blend of ulmo and acacia honeys sit prettily with the tannins. Really wonderful mouthfeel and balance; **f23** brilliant, soft spices at work; the tannins bitter very slight at the death; **b23.5** a delicious whiskey and looking forward to seeing Blend No 2. But I find the label confusing: a "mash bill or malted barley and corn". Does this mean that is the distillation from a mash recipe of malt and corn? Hence the mash bill comment. Or, as I don't think they actually distilled this themselves, a blend of malt and corn whiskey? Which means that it isn't a mash bill of corn and barley. Far too vague for the consumer. Very enjoyable, nonetheless. *40%. Gortinore Distillers & Co.*

**Paddy (74) n18.5 t20 f17.5 b18.** Cleaned its act up a little. And a touch of attractive citrus on the nose and delivery. But where does that cloying sweetness come from? As bland as an Irish peat bog but, sadly, nothing like so potentially tasty. *40%. Irish Distillers.*

**Powers (91) n23 t24 f22 b22.** Is it any coincidence that in this bottling the influence of the caramel has been significantly reduced and the whiskey is getting back to its old, brilliant self? I think not. Classic stuff. *40%. Irish Distillers.*

**Powers Gold Label (87) n22 t22 f21 b22.** The solid pot still, the very DNA of what made Powers, well, Powers is vanishing in front of our very noses. Yes, still some pot still around, but nothing like so pronounced in the way that made this, for decades, a truly one-off Irish and one of the world greats. Still delightful and with many charms but the rock hard pot still effect is sadly missed. What is going on here? *40%. Irish Distillers.*

**Powers Gold Label (96) n23 t24.5 f24 b24.5** A slightly different breed. This is not all about minute difference in strength...this is also about weight distribution and flavour pace. It is a subtly different blend...and all the better for it...Make no mistake: this is a truly classic Irish. *43.2%*

**The Quiet Man Traditional Irish Whiskey** bourbon casks **(88.5) n22 t22 f22.5 b22** A gentle and genteel whiskey without an unfriendly voice. And with it I toast the memory of John Mulgrew. *40%*

**Roe & Co** bourbon casks, bott code: L7173NB001 006084 **(89.5) n22** caramel laden, but a lovely mix of delicate citrus, salt and spice offers balance and intrigue; **t23** lush, sweet grain heads off in a heather-honey direction. The grains are improbably chewy; **f22.5** the spices return, as does the fudge. Light muscovado sugars add an extra edge; **b22** a joyful Irish blend, easy drinking and basking in some outrageously good grain. But the caramel levels could do with coming down slightly for greater complexity. *45%. ncf.*

◈ **Slane Irish Whiskey Triple Casked** bott code: L34638 **(86.5) n22 t22.5 f20.5 b21.5** Soft and supine, this whisky is all about softness and mouth feel: that feeling of a soothing friend by your side. Could do with a bit more personality on the flavour front so the simple sugars don't over dominate as they have a tendency to do here. Excellent spices slowly grow at the finish to offset the furry bitterness of, presumably, a sherry butt or two at work here. Pleasant and promising whiskey. *40%.*

⬦⬦⬦ **Teeling Whiskey Barleywine Small Batch** Barleywine finish, bott Sept 18, bott code: L18 016 270 **(84.5) n21 t21.5 f21 b21** Well, that's a new flavour profile after all these decades in the business! Am I big fan? Well, not really. Love the cream soda texture, I admit. And the suffused sweetness But there is a lurking semi-bitterness which seems to tighten everything about it. I'm sure there are those out there, though, that will worship it. Just not me. 46%. ncf.

⬦⬦⬦ **Teeling Whiskey Plantation Rum Small Batch** Plantation Rum finish, bott Dec 18, bott code: L18 025 336 **(88) n22** tight, as some rums can be, with the sugars forming a firm embrace; **t23** kicks off beautifully, sugars akimbo, there even appearing to be a degree of graininess to sit comfortably with the Lubeck marzipan; **f21** a slightly too enthusiastically bitter here; **b22** works really well until the untidy finish. 46%. ncf.

**Teeling Small Batch Irish Whiskey (87.5) n21 t23 f21.5 b22** Pleasant enough, and again showing high class grain. But a sharper liquorice/phenol note is out of kilter here and disrupts the natural flow of things, especially on the finish. 46%. ncf.

**Teeling Whiskey Small Batch** rum casks, bott Feb 17 **(89) n22 t23 f22 b22** You have to be a little wary with rum casks as they can easily over-ride complexity, as is the case here. This, then, is all about effect and for that it can't be faulted. 46%. ncf.

**Teeling Whiskey Small Batch** rum casks, bott Jan 18, bott code: L18 001 031 **(83.5) n21 t22.5 f19 b21** Some rum matured whisky works rather well. Others, like this bitter-sweet, monosyllabic offering, sadly I don't. 46%. ncf

⬦⬦⬦ **Teeling Whiskey Small Batch** rum casks, bott Apr 19, bott code: L19 014 093 **(86) n21.5 t22.5 f21 b21** A whiskey I just can't like as much as I'd like to. Certainly the delivery ticks all the boxes and offers an innate light treacle sweetness, just as one might hope. But there is an intruding bitterness – almost like hop – which interrupts the nose and finish and spoils the party a bit. Odd. 46%. ncf.

**Teeling Whiskey Stout Cask Small Batch** 200 Fathoms Imperial Stout finish, bott Mar 17 **(92.5) n22.5 t23.5 f23 b23.5** Whiskey and chaser in one go... The extra roastiness imparts a distinctive extra weight which works exceptionally well. 46%. ncf.

**Teeling Whiskey Stout Cask Small Batch** 200 Fathoms Imperial Stout finish, bott Jan 18, bott code: L18 001 018 **(94) n23.5 t23.5 f23 b24** A rare example of a beer finished whiskey not ruined by hops. An absolute beauty of its type. 46%. ncf.

⬦⬦⬦ **Teeling Whiskey Trois Rivieres Small Batch** rhum agricole finish, bott Jul 18, bott code: L18 001 186 **(91) n22.5** soft butterscotch; molten sugar on porridge...; **t23** a pleasing delivery: much softer than what is normally expected from a rum cask. The spices are delightfully well dispersed, so never too warming and complement the thin acacia honey and vanilla base; **f22.5** pleasingly warming...; **b23** the most even and relaxed of the three Teeling rum expressions. What it lacks in complexity it makes up for with simple charm. 46%. ncf.

⬦⬦⬦ **Tullamore D.E.W.** bott code: L1 5297TD 30/11/2018 **(81.5) n21.5 t21 f19 b20** When you are using a grain as hard as this you have to be careful of the caramel as it amplifies its effects. Lots of toffee followed by a dull buzz. Still a very dull Irish. 40%. William Grant & Sons.

⬦⬦⬦ **Tullamore D.E.W. Aged 12 Years** bourbon & oloroso sherry casks, bott code: L3 5294TD 22/11/2018 **(91.5) n23** complex, clean and superbly weighted. A lovely citrus note further freshens proceedings; **t23** the firm grain acts as the perfect skeleton on which the sherry builds the flesh. Chewy and increasingly well spiced but always fresh; **f22** long, spiced vanilla; has a shade too much toffee at the death; **b23.5** when a whiskey is this good, you wonder what the other two Tullamore blends are all about. 40%. William Grant & Sons.

⬦⬦⬦ **Tullamore D.E.W. Caribbean Rum Cask Finish** bott code: L1 5184TD 23/07/2018 **(80) n21 t20 f20 b19** Sweet, soft and a dullard of the very first order. Far more effect from the caramel than the rum casks. There may have been exotic fruit in the tasting lab. But it vanished once it entered the bottling hall. So massively disappointing. 43%. William Grant & Sons.

**Uisce Beatha Real Irish Whiskey** ex-Bourbon cask **(81) n21 t20.5 f19.5 b20**. The label blurb claims this is soft and subtle. That is, about as soft and subtle as if distilled from granite. Hard as nails with dominant grains; takes no prisoners at the death. 40%

**Walker & Scott Irish Whiskey (85) n21 t22 f21 b21.** Oddly, sharper grain has helped give this some extra edge through the toffee. A very decent blend. 40%

**West Cork Black Cask Char #5** Level bott code: L17297 db **(89) n22** huge amounts of natural caramel spill out, aided by a muscly viscosity. The barley plods quietly; **t23** the fattest blend of all time, surely. Enough oil to fill a refinery, though for a blend the malt content appears massive as barley and vanilla combine enormously...; **f22** more oil...; **b22** good grief! This must be one of the most oil-rich, heavy duty blends I have encountered in my near 30 year whisky career. Either way little grain, or it is a grain distilled to a relatively low strength. Either way...good grief! 40%. West Cork Distillers Limited.

**West Cork Bourbon Cask** db **(87.5) n22 t22.5 f21 b22** No-one does caramel like West Cork, and even in their blend – in which their own grain has attractively thinned their hefty malt, it comes through loud and clear. Indeed, had I not known the distillery, I would have marked this down as a Canadian or a young, unfulfilled bourbon. Wonderfully soft and proffers some seriously lovely moments. 40%. West Cork Distillers Limited.

**West Cork Cask Strength** bott code: L17293 db **(87) n21 t23.5 f20.5 b22** Just love the power of this malt on the delivery, relentlessly, mercilessly driving home the barley, a little ulmo honey and vanilla offering a controlled sweetness. Neither the nose or finish work so well, but worth finding just for that beautiful launch. 62%. West Cork Distillers Limited.

◈ **The Whistler Oloroso Sherry Cask Finish** bott code: L19/34018 141 **(83.5) n20 t22 f20 b21.5** Too much sulphur on the sherry kicks it out of tune. A shame, as some outstanding heather honey and raisin notes deserved better. 43%. nc ncf.

**The Wild Geese Classic Blend (80.5) n20 t21 f19.5 b19** Easy going, pretty neutral and conservative. If you are looking for zip, zest and charisma you've picked the wrong goose (see below). 40%. Cooley for Avalon.

◈ **The Wild Geese Classic Blend Irish Whiskey Untamed (90) n22.5** such an uplifting note of acacia honey; **t23** oily and chewy delivery that honey arrives on schedule and is well chaperoned by buzzing spice and multi-layered vanillas; **f22** a gorgeous texture even at the death, where the spices are now mixing with light cocoa; **b22.5** appears to shew high grain content, but when that grain happens to be excellent then there are no moans from me. 43%.

◈ **The Wild Geese Fourth Centennial Untamed (87) n21.5 t22.5 f21.5 b21.5** A very firm malt, brittle almost, which crashes onto the palate in slightly ungainly style. Only in the third to sixth flavour waves does it hit some kind of rhythmic harmony, a searingly salivating experience. But the roughhouse grain makes for an uncompromising finish with bite and a little attitude, which would be brilliant but for an off-key fade. 43%.

**The Wild Geese Rare Irish (89.5) n22 t23 f22 b22.5** Just love this. The Cooley grain is working sublimely and dovetails with the malt in the same effortless way wild geese fly in perfect formation. A treat. 43%. Cooley for Avalon.

**Writers Tears (93) n23.5 t24 f22 b23.5** Now that really was different. The first mix of pure Pot Still and single malt I have knowingly come across in a commercial bottling, but only because I wasn't aware of the make up of last year's Irishman Blend. The malt, like the Pot Still, is, I understand from proprietor Bernard Walsh, from Midleton, but the two styles mixed shows a remarkably similar character to when I carried out an identical experiment with pure pot still and Bushmills the best part of a decade ago. A success and hopefully not a one off. 40%. Writers Tears Whiskey Co.

◈ **Writers' Tears Copper Pot Florio Marsala Cask Finish** Marsala hogshead, cask no. 3150 **(84.5) n22.5 t22 f20 b20** Starts brilliantly, promising so much... but then falls away dramatically at the end...And how ironic and fitting is that? I decided to taste Irish whiskeys today as it looked very likely that Ireland would beat England at Lords in their very first Test Match against them, and here was a chance to toast their historic victory. And, after skittling England out for an embarrassing 85 on the opening, incredible morning an extraordinary victory looked on the horizon. But while tasting this, Ireland themselves were blasted off the pitch and comprehensively routed, when they were all out for just 38 – the seventh lowest score in Test history Irish writers' tears, indeed. 45%. ncf sc. 336 bottles.

◈ **Writers' Tears Double Oak** American oak barrels from Kentucky & French oak Cognac casks, bott code: L9106L2273 **(89.5) n23.5** pineapple cube candy gives a distinct opening sharpness to the nose with a distinct toffee apple back up; lively, delightfully crisp but you get the feeling it is slightly subdued by caramel; **t23** firm, fruity, lots of vanilla. The Pot Still bristles on delivery, becoming sharper by the second; **f21** slightly bitter and dull-ish; burnt; **b22** does really well until the last leg. 45%.

**Writers' Tears Vintage Cask 2016** ex-bourbon barrels, bott Sept 2016 **(89) n22 t23 f22 b22** A pleasant, but mildly muted version of Irishman Cask Strength 2016, though here the spices arrive later. 2016. 53%. ncf. 2,640 bottles.

# Poitín

◈ **Mad March Hare Irish Poitín** bott code: L16 001 021 **(86) n20 t22.5 f21.5 b22** Full flavoured, oily and sweet there is plenty of icing sugar here to help make for an easy experience: perhaps too easy for a poitin! The nose suggests a bit more copper might not go amiss, though. And, seeing as it's poitin, why not go for a full strength version while you are at it.. 40%.

**Spirit of Dublin Irish Poitín** batch. 02 db **(88.5) n22 t23 f21.5 b22** A whole lot cleaner than some – if not all - of the Irish poitin I've tasted from jam jars, lemonade bottles and recycled bottles of Power's over the last 40 years or so. Has the obvious "new make" aroma of unmatured malt, except perhaps a little less discernible copper. Peaks with a big gristy sugar surge about four or five flavour beats after the delivery, but thins a little quickly thereafter. 52.5%.

# Japanese Whisky

**H**ow fitting that in the age when the sun never sets on where whisky is produced it is from the land of the Rising Sun that the finest can now be found.

Recently Japan, for the first time ever, won Jim Murray's World Whisky of the Year with its insanely deep and satisfying Yamazaki Sherry Cask(s) 2013, a result which caused predictable consternation among more than a few. And a degree of surprise in Japan itself. The industry followed that up by commanding 5th spot with a very different but truly majestic specimen of a malt showing a style unique to Japan. How impressive.

It reminded me of when, some 20 years ago, I took my old mate Michael Jackson and a smattering of non-friends on a tour of the Yoichi distillery on Hokkaido, pointing out to them that here was a place where a malt could be made to mount a serious challenge to the best being made anywhere in the world. While there, a local journalist asked me what Japanese distillers could learn from Scotland. I caused a bit of a sharp intake of breath – and a pathetically gutless but entirely characteristic denial of association by some whisky periodical executive or other who had a clear idea which side his bread was buttered – when I said it was the other way round: it was more what the Scots could learn from the Japanese.

The reason for that comment was simple: the extraordinary attention to detail and tradition that was paid by Japanese distillers, those at Yoichi in particular, and the touching refusal to cut costs and corners. It meant that it was the most expensive whisky in the world per unit of alcohol to produce. But the quality was astonishingly high – and that would, surely, eventually reap its rewards as the world learned to embrace malt whisky made away from the Highlands and islands of Scotland which, then, was still to happen. Ironically, it was the Japanese distillers' habit to ape most things Scottish – the reason why there is a near century-old whisky distilling heritage there in the first place - that has meant that Yoichi, or the magnificent Hakushu, has yet to pick up the Bible's World Whisky of the Year award I expected for them. Because, sadly, there have been too many bottlings over the last decade tainted by sherry butts brought from Spain after having been sulphur treated. So I was also pleasantly surprised when I first nosed – then nosed again in near disbelief – then tasted the Yamazaki 2013 sherry offering. There was not even the vaguest hint that a single one of the casks used in the bottling had been anywhere near a sulphur candle. The result: something as close to single malt perfection as you will have found in a good many years. A single malt which no Scotch can at the moment get anywhere near and, oddly, takes me back to the Macallans of 30 years ago.

A Japanese custom of refusing to trade with their rivals has not helped expand their export market. Therefore a Japanese whisky, if not made completely from home-distilled spirit, will instead contain a percentage of Scotch rather than whisky from fellow Japanese distillers. This, ultimately, is doing the industry no favours at all. The practice is partly down to the traditional work ethics of company loyalty an inherent, and these days false, belief, that Scotch whisky is automatically better than Japanese. Back in the late 1990s I planted the first seeds in trying to get rival distillers to discuss with each other the possibility of exchanging whiskies to ensure that their distilleries worked economically. So it can only be hoped

White Oak ▲  Yamazaki ▲  Chita

Togouchi ▲  ●Osaka

●Fukuoka

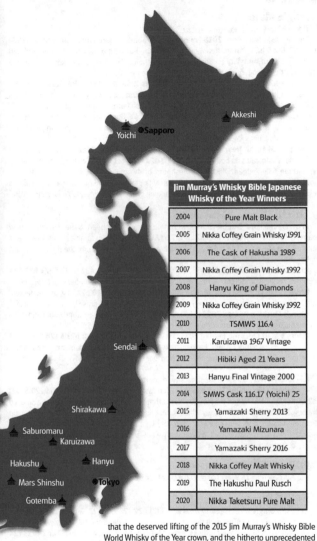

| Jim Murray's Whisky Bible Japanese Whisky of the Year Winners | |
|---|---|
| 2004 | Pure Malt Black |
| 2005 | Nikka Coffey Grain Whisky 1991 |
| 2006 | The Cask of Hakusha 1989 |
| 2007 | Nikka Coffey Grain Whisky 1992 |
| 2008 | Hanyu King of Diamonds |
| 2009 | Nikka Coffey Grain Whisky 1992 |
| 2010 | TSMWS 116.4 |
| 2011 | Karuizawa 1967 Vintage |
| 2012 | Hibiki Aged 21 Years |
| 2013 | Hanyu Final Vintage 2000 |
| 2014 | SMWS Cask 116.17 (Yoichi) 25 |
| 2015 | Yamazaki Sherry 2013 |
| 2016 | Yamazaki Mizunara |
| 2017 | Yamazaki Sherry 2016 |
| 2018 | Nikka Coffey Malt Whisky |
| 2019 | The Hakushu Paul Rusch |
| 2020 | Nikka Taketsuru Pure Malt |

that the deserved lifting of the 2015 Jim Murray's Whisky Bible World Whisky of the Year crown, and the hitherto unprecedented international press it received has helped put the spotlight back on the great whiskies coming from the east. Because unless you live in Japan, you are likely to see only a fraction of the fabulous whisky produced there. The Scotch Malt Whisky Society should have a special medal struck as they have helped in recent years with some memorable bottlings from Japan, single cask snapshots of the greatness that is still to be be fully explored and mapped.

Yet Jim Murray's Whisky Bible has provided a double-edged sword for the Japanese whisky industry. The amazing news for them was their World Whisky of the Year award precipitaed sales worth billions of yen. And, consequently, a near exhaustion of stocks. The Hibiki 17 and Hakushu 12 have now vanished as brands altogether. But it means that, at long last and deservedly, whisky drinkers around the globe finally recognise that Japanese single malt can be second to no other. Their probem is how to satisfy the thirst for Japanese whisky and knowledge on what it has to offer: at the moment they cannot. But Forsyths, the Speyside-based Scottish still manufacturers, are working overtime to supply more distilling equipment for the Land of the Rising Sun. And rapidly setting whisky stocks.

## Single Malts

### AKKESHI 2016. Kenten Co., Ltd.

**The Akkeshi New Born 2018 Foundations 1** bourbon barrel, bott Jan 2018 db **(88.5)** n22 t22 f22.5 b22 Young, clean, nutty and malty but with a very fragmented and thin body. This spirit's fragility means it will absorb the oak's influence quicker than most, a point worth bearing in mind in not too many years hence. 60%.

⬧ **The Akkeshi New Born 2018 Foundations 2 Single Malt Spirit Peated** bourbon barrel, bott Jun 2018 db **(94)** n23.5 t23.5 f23 b24 A fizzing, bucking bronco of a peated malt with spices zapping the taste buds with glee. The finish from this thoroughbred, is especially delightful as some chocolate joins forces with the smoke. Bodes incredibly well for the future. I can't wait to visit this distillery in the next year or two: if this is an average example of their output, exciting times lay ahead. 58%.

⬧ **The Akkeshi New Born 2019 Foundations 3 Single Malt Spirit Non-Peated** Hokkaido-Mizunara cask, bott Jan 2019 db **(93)** n23 t23.5 f23 b23.5 Can't wait for this beauty to become fully-fledged whisky. The freshness of the maturing new make is particularly evident on the finish. But until then the delicately tart tannin of the Mizunara cask works its usual wonders and combines with the outstanding grist with commendable elegance. 55%.

### CHICHIBU 2004. Venture Whisky.

**ePower Chichibu Double Barrel** Mizunara heads hogshead & hard charred new barrels, dist 2012, bott 2015 **(88)** n21.5 t23.5 f21 b22 Were it not for the spices, the sugars might have proved a little too much. Though not always hitting quite the right notes, this is big, profound malt. 61.1%

**Ichiro's Malt Chichibu Chibidaru** dist 2010, bott 2014 db **(92)** n22.5 t23.5 f23 b23 This distillery certainly understands the meaning of "intense"... 53.5%. Number One Drinks Co.

**Ichiro's Malt Chichibu Floor Malted 2009 (85.5)** n22 t22.5 f20 b21. Big, pre-pubescent malt and barley statement, but barely in unison. Bitterness on the finish is unchecked. 50.5%.

**Ichiro's Chichibu Peated 2009 (91.5)** n23 t23.5 f22 b23. You can stand your chopsticks up in this one...works so beautifully in so many departments. 50.5%

**Ichiro's Malt Chichibu Peated 2015** dist 2010, bott 2015 db **(95)** n23.5 t24 f23.5 b24 Had I tasted this blind, I would have mistaken it for an Islay. Quite sublimely made malt. As astonishing as it is beautiful... 62.5.%. Number One Drinks Company.

### EIGASHIMA 1919. Eigashima Shuzo co. ltd.

⬧ **Dekanta Eigashima The Kikou** Port Ellen cask, cask no. 11055, dist 2011, bott 2018 **(92)** n22.5 t23 f23.5 b23 Forget the Port Ellen cask. That is just a red herring – or, rather, a smoked herring. This is all about the barley which is thick and intense, the extra depth coming late on from the tannins and, very belatedly, from very light peat. Beyond that, the phenols barely register – which is just as well, as you don't want anything to take away from the dense purity of the malt itself. 58.4%. sc.

### FUJI GOTEMBA 1973. Kirin Distillers.

**The Fuji Gotemba 15 Years Old** db **(92)** n21 t23 f24 b24. Quality malt of great poise. 43%. Kirin.

### HAKUSHU 1973. Suntory.

**Hakushu Single Malt Aged 12 Years** db **(91)** n22 t23 f23 b23. An even more lightly-peated version of the 40%, with the distillery's fabulous depth on full show. 43.3%

**The Hakushu Single Malt Whisky Aged 15 Years Cask Strength** db **(95)** n24 t23 f24 b24. Last time round I lamented the disappointing nose. This time perhaps only a degree of over eagerness from the oak has robbed this as a serious Whisky of the Year contender. No matter how you look at it, though, brilliant!! 56%

**The Hakushu Single Malt Whisky Aged 25 Years** db **(93)** n23 t24 f23 b23. A malt which is impossible not to be blown away by. 43%

**The Hakushu Single Malt Whisky Sherry Cask** bott 2014 db **(96.5)** n24.5 t24 f24 b24 Theoretically, this should have been World Whisky of the Year. After all, Yamazaki – a distillery I regard as very slightly eclipsed in quality by Hakushu – won it last year using, like this, strictly unsulphured sherry butts. This is magnificent. One of these whiskies of the year, for sure. However, the intensity of the grape has just strayed over that invisible line by a few molecules between being a vital cog and a shade too dominant. It is the finest of lines between genius and exceptional brilliance.48%. ncf.

**The Hakushu Paul Rusch 120th Anniversary of Birth** bourbon barrel, bott code LX7CJV db **(96)** n24 t24.5 f23.5 b24 There is a tipping point where a barrel has just gone over the edge, like one might at the Niagara Falls: there is no turning back and the ending is catastrophic. There is the odd moment here where you pick up a note where you realise it has moved close to that point, then myriad flavours come to the rescue to show this whisky is still very much alive and well and, like an old cowboy, basking in its great age and sun-burned charisma. Brilliant. *58%*.

**Suntory Pure Malt Hakushu Aged 20 Years** db **(94) n23 t24 f23 b24.** A hard-to-find malt, but find it you must. Yet another huge nail in the coffin of those who purport Japanese whisky to be automatically inferior to Scotch. *56%*

## HANYU 1941. Toa Shuzo Co. Ltd.

**Ichiro's Malt Aged 20 Years (95.5) n24 t24 f23.5 b24.** No this finish; no that finish. Just the distillery allowed to speak in its very own voice. And nothing more eloquent has been heard from it this year. Please, all those owning casks of Hanyu: for heaven's sake take note... *57.5%*.

**Ichiro's Malt Aged 23 Years (92.5) n23 t23.5 f23 b23.** A fabulous malt you take your time over. *58%*

## KARUIZAWA 1955. Mercian.

**Karuizawa Pure Malt Aged 17 Years** db **(90) n20 t24 f23 b23.** Brilliant whisky beautifully made and majestically matured. Neither sweetness nor dryness dominates, always the mark of a quality dram. *40%*

**The Spirit Of Asama** sherry cask **(75) n18 t20 f18 b19.** Lots of sultanas. Sweet. Pleasant in part. But it isn't just Scotland suffering from poor sherry butts. *55%*.

## KURAYOSHI DISTILLERY 2015. Matsui Shuzo.

◈ **The Matsui Mizunara Cask** bott code: 4 18.338 **(95) n24** there is a fragility to this aroma almost unmatched in the whisky world: the malt is sharp and brittle, the sweetness limited to no more than a hint of marzipan. The oak is another matter altogether: uniquely deft but with just a sharper degree of tannin than from bourbon cask, though without any forcefulness whatsoever...; **t24** the grist and light Demerara sugars melt in slow motion, the barley always apparent, a squeeze of citrus always refreshing. The oak is the embodiment of politeness, waiting for the barley to have its says before moving in like some kind of wooden Japanese crutch to hold the structure together; **f23** the modest oils present means the finish hangs on for a little while the oak still having the last word, but with not a hint of bitterness or bravado...; **b24** if you want to see why Japanese oak can give the indigenous whisky industry a leg up on their rivals, then it might be worth tracking this down. The flavour profile is really one, to this extent, that you see only in Japan and seems to give an extra sharpness to their malt; as though the colours on the nose and palate are pastel shaded and not just water. A quite beautiful whisky, as elegant and delicate as a demure Japanese girlfriend in a flowing silk kimono. *48%. nc ncf. BBC Spirits.*

◈ **The Matsui The Peated** bott code: 4 18.338 **(87.5) n22.5 t23 f20 b22** Pleasant, though the downside is that the smoke rather detracts from the distillery's idiosyncratic charm. That said, the peat has a structure all its own, a little industrial and oily while the delivery involves some high definition grist. Its Achilles heel is the bitter-ish finale which can be predicted from the nose. *48%. nc ncf. BBC Spirits.*

◈ **The Matsui Sakura Cask** bott code: 4 18.348 **(92.5) n23** hefty, toasty tannin ensures this is a nose to be noticed, perhaps with light lavender joining the barley; **t23.5** full on sugars here, mainly of a maple syrup bent and teaming with spices; **f23** finally settles into clean, malty mode with a dry, chalky finale; **b23** matured in the wood of the cherry tree, this does impart a spicier than normal intensity, which in itself closes out the barley. Just drips with personality, however. *48%. nc ncf. BBC Spirits.*

## KIRIN 1969. Kirin Group.

**Kirin 18 Years Old** db **(86.5) n22 t22 f21.5 b21.** Unquestionably over-aged. Even so, still puts up a decent show with juicy citrus trying to add a lighter touch to the uncompromising, ultra dense oak. As entertaining as it is challenging. *43%. Suntory.*

## MIYAGIKYO 1969. Nikka.

**Nikka Coffey Malt Whisky** db **(96) n23.5 t25 f23.5 b24** Not quite the genius of the 12-year-old. But still one of the most tactile and sensual whiskies on the world whisky stage today. *45%*.

**Nikka Whisky Single Coffey Malt 12 Years** db **(97) n23.5 t25 f24 b24.5.** The Scotch Whisky Association would say that this is not single malt whisky because it is made in a Coffey still. When they can get their members to make whisky this stunning on a regular basis via their own pots and casks, then perhaps they should pipe up as their argument might then have a single atom of weight. *55%*

Nikka Whisky Single Malt Miyagikyo db **(91.5) n22** vanilla blancmange; **t23** excellent early malt thrust on delivery, then thickens and allows in all kinds of fudgy sugars; **f22.5** light spice, tannin and fudge; **b23** thick, clumsy but deliciously malty. *45%*.

## SENDAI 1969. Nikka.

Scotch Malt Whisky Society Cask 124.4 Aged 17 Years 1st fill butt, dist 22 Aug 96 **(94) n24 t24 f23 b23** If there is a complaint to be made, it is that, at times, one might forget that this is a whisky at all, resembling instead a glass of highest quality oloroso.*60%. sc.*

## SHINSHU MARS 1985. Hombo Shuzo Ltd

ePower Komagatake American Puncheon, dist Mar 13, bott Sept 16 **(96) n23.5 t24 f24 b24.5** Just fabulous for Japan's most malty whisky to be able to show its most intense and unique form without it being wrecked by awful sherry butts. What a malty treat this is! You could not ask for more. Well, actually you could...another glass, that is... *56.9%.*

## WHITE OAK DISTILLERY 1984. Eigashima Shuzo.

White Oak Akashi Single Malt Whisky Aged 8 Years bott 2007 db **(74.5) n18.5 t19.5 f17.5 b19.** Always fascinating to find a malt from one of the smaller distilleries in a country. And I look forward to tracking this one down and visiting, something I have yet to do. There is certainly something distinctly small still about his one, with butyric and feintiness causing damage to nose and finish. For all the early malty presence on delivery, some of the off notes are a little on the uncomfortable side. *40%*

## YAMAZAKI 1923. Suntory.

The Yamazaki Single Malt Whisky Aged 12 Years bott 2011 db **(90) n23 t22 f22.5 b22.5.** A complex and satisfying malt. *43%*

The Yamazaki Single Malt Aged 18 Years db **(96) n23 t24.5 f24 b24.5** for its strength, probably one of the best whiskies in the world. And one of the most brilliantly and sexily balanced, too... All told,one glass is equal to about 45 minutes of sulphur-free satisfaction... *43%*

Suntory Pure Malt Yamazaki 25 Years Old db **(91) n23 t23 f22 b23.** Being matured in Japan, the 25 years doesn't have quite the same value as Scotland. So perhaps in some ways this can lay claim to be one of the most enormously aged, oak-laden whiskies that has somehow kept its grace and star quality. *43%*

The Yamazaki Single Malt Whisky Mizunara Japanese oak cask, bott 2014 db **(97) n25 t24 f23.5 b24.5** No other malt offers this flavour profile. And as there are now very few Japanese oak casks still in the industry it is a malt worthy of as long a time as you can afford it. A very special whisky of very high quality. *48%*

The Yamazaki Single Malt Whisky Sherry Cask bott 2013 db **(97.5) n24.5 t24.5 f24 b24.5** One of the first sherry casks I have seen from Japan not in any way, shape or form touched by sulphur for a very long time. It is as if the oloroso cask was still half filled with the stuff when they filled with Yamakazi spirit. If anyone wants to find out roughly what the first Macallan 10-year-old I had in 1975 tasted like, then grab a bottle of this... *48%. ncf. WB15/180*

Yamazaki Single Malt Sherry Cask 2016 Edition db **(96.5) n24.5 t24 f24 b24** A work of art. The oils, though, are markedly younger in style than the imperious 2013 edition. *48%*

The Yamazaki Single Malt Whisky db **(86) n22 t22 f21 b21**. A tame, malty affair which, after the initial barley burst on delivery, plays safety first. *43%*

## YOICHI 1934. Nikka.

Nikka Whisky Single Malt Yoichi db **(91) n24 t24 f21 b22** This bottling may have a borderline flaw, also – even I am struggling to be sure. But what I know for a fact is that of all the single malts worldwide I have tasted for this Bible 2018, this was the first to make me yelp and then stretch with pleasure, glass in hand raised as I rode the ecstasy. Yes, there is the most minor blemish on the very end of the finale, and for that it will not be contending for World Whisky of the Year. But, it was a very close run thing... *45%.*

Yoichi Key Malt Aged 12 Years "Peaty & Salty" db **(95) n23 t25 f23 b24.** Of all the peated whiskies of the world, only Ardbeg can stand shoulder to shoulder with Yoichi when it comes to sheer complexity. Here is an astonishing example of why I rate Yoichi in the best five whiskies in the world. Forget the odd sulphur-tarnished bottling. Get Yoichi in its natural state with perfect balance between oak and malt and it delivers something approaching perfection. And this is just such a bottling. *55%. Nikka.*

Yoichi 15 Years Old batch 06I08B db **(91.5) n22 t23.5 f23 b23.** For an early moment or two possibly one of the most salivating whiskies you'll get your kisser around this year. Wonderfully entertaining yet you still suspect that this is another Yoichi reduced in effect somewhat by either caramel and/or sherry. When it hits its stride, though, becomes a really busy whisky that gets tastebuds in a right lather. But I'm being picky as I know that this is one of the world's top five distilleries and am aware as anyone on this planet of its extraordinary capabilities. Great fun; great whisky – could be better still, but so much better than its siblings... 45%

**Yoichi 20 Years Old** db **(95) n23 t23 f25 b24.** I don't know how much they charge for this stuff but either alone or with mates get some for one hell of an experience. What makes it all the more remarkable is that there is a slight sulphury note on the nose: once you taste the stuff that becomes of little consequence. 52%. Nikka.

# Vatted Malts

**All Malt (86) n22 t21 f21 b22.** The best example by a mile of an almost unique style of vatted whisky: both malt and "grain" are distilled from entirely malted barley, identical to Kasauli malt whisky in India. Stupendous grace and balance. 40%. Nikka.

**All Malt "Pure & Rich" (89) n22 t24 f21 b22.** Not unlike some bottlings of Highland Park with its emphasis on honey. If they could tone down the caramel it'd really be up there. 40%. Nikka.

**Hokuto Pure Malt Aged 12 Years (86) n20 t22 f22 b22.** An oaky threat never materialises: excellent mixing. 40%. Suntory

**Ichiro's Malt Mizunara Wood Reserve (76) n19 t21 f18 b19.** I have my Reservations about the Wood, too... 46%. Venture Whisky Ltd.

◇◇ **Kamiki Blended Malt Whisky** finished in Japanese cedar casks, batch no. 002, bott Mar 2018 **(90.5) n22** cedary....!!! **t23** a mix of gristy sugars and cake mix out of the bowl; salivating and sharp; **f22.5** it must have been a chocolate cake...; **b23** another new experience for me after 30 years of doing this job. I have, in the past, had oak casks which have offered a cedar aroma...but never cedar itself! A sedate whisky but with a definite twist... 48%. ncf.

◇◇ **Kamiki Blended Malt Whisky Intense Wood** finished in Japanese cedar casks, bott May 2019 **(91) n21.5** very cedary....!!! **t23.5** far more chocolate prevalent straight from delivery with a treacle tart middle; **f23** quite dry as the tannins bite, but the molasses keep things on an even keel; **b23** while the nose is just too cedary – it is like walking into a furniture factory – the extra sugars work wonders on the whisky itself. The texture is rather dreamy, too. 48%. ncf.

**Mars Maltage Pure Malt 8 Years Old (84) n20 t21 f21 b22.** A very level, intense, clean malt with no peaks or troughs, just a steady variance in the degree of sweetness and oak input. Impossible not to have a second glass of this. 43%. Mars.

**Nikka Malt 100 The Anniversary Aged 12 Years (73) n18 t19 f18 b18.** The depressing and deadly fingerprint of sulphur is all over this. Shame, as the spices excel. 40%

**Nikka Pure Malt Aged 12 Years** batch 10I24C db **(84) n21.5 t21 f20 b21.5** The nose may be molassed, sticky treacle pudding, but it spices up on the palate. The dull buzz on the finish also tells a tale. 40%

**Nikka Pure Malt Aged 21 Years** batch 08I18D db **(89) n23 t22.5 f21.5 b22.** By far the best of the set. 43%

**Nikka Pure Malt Aged 17 Years** batch 08I30B db **(83) n21 t21 f20 b21.** A very similar shape to the 12-years-old, but older - obviously. Certainly the sherry butts have a big say and don't always do great favours to the high quality spirit. 43%

◇◇ **Nikka Taketsuru Pure Malt** bott no. 6/22H10 1540 **(95.5) n23.5** rare complexity and balance on a nose: there is a spice buzz here that is barely perceptible, as is the gentle layer of kumquat. The vanilla is slightly more robust, almost giving a distant ice cream aroma, on which a dab of chocolate sauce hangs; **t24** forget the flavours for a moment...just take in that mouth feel. That is...perfection. The barley actually possesses its own depth and space away from the intricate oak tones, the playful spice, the teasing sweet ginger...; **f24** how can a whisky stay this complex for so long? How many different cocoa and mocha notes can there possibly be....? **b24** classy. 43%.

**Pure Malt Black** batch 06F54B **(92) n24 t24 f21 b23.** Not the finish of old, but everything else is present and correct for a cracker! 43%. Nikka.

**Pure Malt Red** batch 06F54C **(84) n21 t22 f20 b21.** Oak is the pathfinder here, but the oily vanilla-clad barley is light and mouth-watering. 43%. Nikka.

**Pure Malt White** batch 06J26 **(91) n22 t23 f22 b24.** A sweet malt, but one with such deft use of peat and oak that one never really notices. Real class. 43%. Nikka.

**Pure Malt White** batch 10F46C **(90) n23 t23 f22 b22.** There is a peculiarly Japanese feel to this delicately peated delight. 43%

**Suntory Pure Malt Whisky Kiyosato Field Ballet 25th Anniversary (88) n23.5 t22.5 f20 b22** So frustrating: a whisky destined for greatness is side-tracked by some off-kilter casks. 48%

**Super Nikka Vatted Pure Malt (76) n20 t19 f19 b18.** Decent and chewy but something doesn't quite click with this one. 55.5%. Nikka.

**Taketsuru Pure Malt 12 Years Old (80) n19 t22 f19 b20.** For its age, heavier than a sumo wrestler. But perhaps a little more agile over the tastebuds. Lovely silkiness impresses, but lots of toffee. 40%. *Nikka.*

**Taketsuru Pure Malt 17 Years Old (89) n21 t22 f23 b23** Not a whisky for the squeamish. This is big stuff – about as big as it gets without peat or rye. No bar shelf or whisky club should be without one. 43%. *Nikka.*

**Taketsuru Pure Malt 21 Years Old (88) n22 t21 f22 b23.** A much more civilised and gracious offering than the 17 year old: there is certainly nothing linear about the character development from Taketsuru 12 to 21 inclusive. Serious whisky for the serious whisky drinker. 43%. *Nikka.*

**Zen (84) n19 t22 f22 b21.** Sweet, gristy malt; light and clean. 40%. *Suntory.*

# Japanese Single Grain
## CHITA 1972. Suntory.

**Suntory Single Grain Chita Distillery** db **(92.5) n23.5 t23 f22.5 b23** Now that's more like it! Far more down the track of the Chita I have tasted through the years than the SMWS bottling. Then again, this is the brand new official distillery version, so perhaps no surprises there... 43%. *Available only in Nagoya Prefecture, Japan.*

**The Chita Single Grain** bott code L1610R db **(91.5) n23 t23 f22.5 b23** Spot on Corn Whiskey-type grain: could almost be a blueprint. Simple, but deliciously soft and effective. 43%.

## KUMESEN

⬥ **Meiyo Single Grain Whisky Aged 17 Years** bourbon cask, dist 2001, bott 2018 **(94.5) n23.5** for a moment you think the oak has gone in too hard and over-dominated. Slowly, though, a deft sweetness – not least orange blossom honey – emerges as the oak fog clears; **t23.5** and it proudly stays on the citrus theme a tangerine note warbles gently, the slightly buttery softness of the oak and growing spices its accompaniment; **f23.5** warmer now thanks to that tannin, and chocolate makes the perfect match to the earlier orangey notes; **b24** a Japanese Jaffa Cake... 42%. *Aiko Importers, Inc.*

## MIYAGIKYO 1969. Nikka.

**Nikka Coffey Grain Whisky** db **(94.5) n23.5 t24 f23 b24** Whisky, from any part of the globe, does not come more soft or silky than this... 45%

# Blends

**25th Anniversary Kiyosato Field Ballet Ichiro's Malt & Grain Japanese Blended Whisky (90.5) n22.5 t23.5 f21.5 b23** If spice is the variety of life, then this whisky certainly adds variety. 49%. 359 bottles.

**Black Nikka Aged 8 Years (82) n20 t21 f21 b20.** Beautifully bourbony, especially on the nose. Lush, silky and great fun. Love it! 40%. *Nikka.*

**The Blend of Nikka (90) n21 t23 f22 b24.** An adorable blend that makes you sit up and take notice of every enormous mouthful. Classy, complex, charismatic and brilliantly balanced. 45%

**Evermore (90) n22 t23 f22 b23.** Top-grade, well-aged blended whisky with fabulous depth and complexity that never loses its sweet edge despite the oak. 40%. *Kirin.*

**Ginko (78.5) n20.5 t20 f19 b19.** Soft – probably too soft as it could do with some shape and attitude to shrug off the caramel. 46%. *Number One Drinks Company.*

**Hibiki (82) n20 t19 f23 b20.** The grains here are fresh, forceful and merciless, the malts bouncing off them meekly. Lovely cocoa finale. A blend that brings a tear to the eye. Hard stuff – perfect after a hard day! Love it! 43%. *Suntory.*

**Hibiki Japanese Harmony** bott code LG7F04 db **(93) n23 t23 f23.5 b23.5** Immaculately spiced and as complex a bag of tricks on the palate as you're likely to find.43%.

**Hibiki Japanese Harmony Master's Select** bott code LN6CKK db **(89) n22.5** a kind of spiced-up grain whisky with a little under-ripe banana and golden syrup; **t22.5** again golden syrup on delivery, though pepped up with black peppers. The grain forms a soft spine while the vanillas mount up; **f22** an unassuming procession of caramels; **b22** as silky as a kimono, the grains dominate on this blend 43%.

**Hibiki Aged 30 Years (88) n21 t22 f22 b23.** Still remains a very different animal from most other whiskies you might find: the smoke may have vanished somewhat but the sweet oakiness continues to draw its own unique map. 43%

**Hokuto (86) n22 t24 f19 b21.** A bemusing blend. At its peak, this is quite superb, cleverly blended whisky. The finish, though, suggests a big caramel input. If the caramel is natural, it should be tempered. If it is added for colouring purposes, then I don't see the point of having the whisky non-chillfiltered in the first place. 50.5%. *ncf. Suntory.*

**Imperial (81)** n20 t22 f19 b20. Flinty, hard grain softened by malt and vanilla but toffee dulled. 43%. *Suntory.*

**Kakubin (92)** n23 t23 f22 b24. Absolutely brilliant blend of stunningly refreshing and complex character. One of the most improved brands in the world. 40%. *Suntory.*

**Kakubin Kuro 43° (89)** n22 t23 f22 b22. Big, chewy whisky with ample evidence of old age but such is the intrusion of caramel it's hard to be entirely sure. 43%. *Suntory.*

**Kakubin New (90)** n21 t24 f21 b24. Seriously divine blending: a refreshing dram of the top order. 40%.

**Kirin Whisky Tarujuku 50° (93)** n22.5 t24 f23 b23.5. A blend not afraid to make a statement and does so boldly. A sheer joy. 50%. *Kirin Distillery Co Ltd.*

**Master's Blend Aged 10 Years (87)** n21 t23 f22 b21. Chewy, big and satisfying. 40%.

**Nikka Master Blend Blended Whisky 12 Years Old 70th Anniversary (94)** n24 t23 f24 b23. An awesome blend swimming in top quality sherry. Perhaps a fraction too much sweetness on the arrival, but I am nit-picking A blend for those who like their whiskies to have something to say. And this one just won't shut up. 58%. *Nikka.*

◈ **Nikka Days** bott no. 6222H261103 **(89) n22.5** clean, supremely soft, with a thin veneer of lime blossom honey; **t22** a supine delivery, with no lead taken either by grain or oak. Melts-in-the-mouth, leaving a shortbread-like residue; **f22** just the most delicate traces of oak; **b22.5** unquestionably the softest, least aggressive whisky I have tasted for the 2020 Whisky Bible. 40%.

**Nikka Whisky From The Barrel** db **(91)** n22.5 t23 f22.5 b23 I have been drinking this for a very long time – and still can't remember a bottle that's ever let me down. 51.4%.

**Nikka Whisky Tsuru Aged 17 Years (94)** n23 t24 f23 b24. Unmistakably Tsuru in character, very much in line, profile-wise, with the original bottling and if the caramel was cut this could challenge as a world whisky of the year. 43%

**Robert Brown (91)** n22.5 t23 f22.5 b23. Just love these clean but full-flavoured blends: a real touch of quality here. 43%. *Kirin Brewery Company Ltd.*

**Royal 12 Years Old (91)** n23 t23 f22 b23. A splendidly blended whisky with complexity being the main theme. Beautiful stuff that appears recently to have, with the exception of the nose, traded smoke for grape. 43%

**Royal Aged 15 Years (95)** n25 t24 f22 b24. Unquestionably one of the great blends of the world that can be improved only by a reduction of toffee input. Sensual blending that every true whisky lover must experience: a kind of Japanese Old Parr 18. 43%

◈ **Sensei Whisky (86)** n22 t22 f20.5 b21.5 Quite a heavy whisky with big accent on the caramel. The finish is just a shade too bitter for its own good. 40%. *Aiko Importers, Inc.*

**Shirokaku (79)** n19 t21 f20 b19. Some over-zealous toffee puts a cap on complexity. Good spices, though. 40%. *Suntory.*

**Special Reserve 10 Years Old (94)** n23 t24 f23 b24. A beguiling whisky of near faultless complexity. Blending at its peak. 43%. *Suntory.*

**Special Reserve Aged 12 Years (89)** n21 t24 f21 b23. A tactile, voluptuous malt that wraps itself like a sated lover around the tastebuds, though the complexity is compromised very slightly by bigger caramel than the 10-y-o. 40%. *Suntory.*

**Suntory Old (87)** n21 t24 f20 b22. A delicate and comfortable blend that just appeals to have over-simplified itself on the finale. Delicious, but could be much better than this. 40%

**Super Nikka (93)** n23 t23 f23 b24. A very, very fine blend which makes no apology whatsoever for the peaty complexity of Yoichi malt. Now, with less caramel, it's pretty classy stuff. However, Nikka being Nikka you might find the occasional bottling that is entirely devoid of peat, more honeyed and lighter in style (21-22-23-23 Total 89 – no less a quality turn, obviously). Either way, an absolutely brilliant day-to-day, anytime, any place dram. One of the true 24-carat, super nova commonplace blends not just in Japan, but in the world. 43%. *Nikka.*

**Super Nikka Rare Old** batch 02I18D **(90.5)** n22 t23 f22.5 b23. Beautiful whisky which just sings a lilting malty refrain. Strange, though, to find it peatless. 43%. *Nikka.*

**Torys (76)** n18 t19 f20 b19. Lots of toffee in the middle and at the end of this one. The grain used is top class and chewy. 37%. *Suntory.*

**Torys Whisky Square (80)** n19 t20 f21 b20. At first glance a very similar blend to Torys, but very close scrutiny reveals slightly more "new loaf" nose and a better, spicier and less toffeed finale. 37%.

**White (80)** n19 t21 f20 b20. Boring nose but explodes on the palate for a fresh, mouth-watering classic blend bite. 40%. *Suntory.*

◈ **Yamato Japanese Whisky (87.5)** n21.5 t22 f22 b22. Attractive complexity despite the thin body on this. The sweet, light mocha notes are very attractive 40%. nc. *Aiko Importers, Inc.*

**Za (79)** n19 t21 f19 b20. Some lively boisterous grain offers a suet-pudding chewiness. A little bitter on the finish. 40%. *Suntory.*

# English & Welsh Whisky

**W**hen, exactly, do you decide that a new whisky region is born? Is it like the planets forming after the Big Bang, cosmic dust gathering together to form a solid, recognisable whole?

That is the question I have had to ask myself for a long time and, since the Whisky Bible began 15 years ago, look for an answer that is beyond the hypothetical. At last I have come to a conclusion: it is, surely, when a country or region produces sufficient whisky of high enough consistency and character that its contribution to the lexicon of the world's greatest whiskies cannot be ignored. Or should that whisky be lost for any reason its effects would be greatly felt. There is no denying that this is now the case in the varied and often glorious lands to be found south of the Scottish Border.

When in 2003, on the cusp of world whisky's very own Big Bang, I sat down and tasted the whiskies for the inaugural 2004 edition of Jim Murray's Whisky Bible, Ireland boasted just three distilleries, four if you included Cooley's grain plant. Today, England and Wales provide us with three distilleries producing exceptionally high class whiskies: Penderyn, St George's and The Cotswolds. The latter is still very much in its infancy, but the quality is already beyond doubt. Penderyn and St. George's have won numerous awards in the Whisky Bible and are remarkable for the consistency and excellence of their maturing spirit.

These three distilleries are not micro distilleries. They are set up to make whisky on an industrial scale and have forged markets all over the world. On their skirt tails comes The Lakes in the beautiful Lake District while dotted around the region comes a plethora of other distilleries of varying shapes and sizes, not least the Spirit of Yorkshire Distillery in the North Yorkshire Wolds and whose maturing spirit seems as graceful as its emblem, the gannet.

Over the last years I have been busy actively encouraging the larger English and Welsh distillers to create their own Whisky Association, especially as Britain leaves the EU during 2019. Why not? They are now their own region: they demand respect as their very own entity.

# ENGLAND
## ADNAMS Southwold, Suffolk. 2010. Working.

⬩ **Adnams Rye Malt Whisky** French oak casks, bott code: L17269 db (**90.5**) n22.5 the desired rigidity to the rye is there, though not the crispness of sugar. Instead tannins intervene and help give a swarthy feel as a light molasses sweetness grows; t23.5 what a superb delivery. A very light tobacco notes accompanies the hugely intense rye note and, as on the nose, both tannins and darker sugars form a partnership; f21.5 a little oily and tangy, mainly from the cut; b23 almost an immeasurable improvement on this distillery's early offerings. This has some serious charisma and amplifies the home-grown rye rather beautifully. 47%. ncf.

⬩ **Adnams Single Malt Whisky** French oak casks, bott code: L18039 db (**85.5**) n22 t22 f20; b21.5 Technically not quite the ticket. But there is no faulting the big malt. 40%.

⬩ **Adnams Triple Malt Whisky** American oak casks, bott code: L18103 db (**91**) n22.5 porridge and golden syrup; t23.5 oh my word..! So sweet: the golden syrup is now transforming into oaty porridge, with a tiny amount of heather honey stirred in. Excellent oaky spices, too; oily, multi-layered and lip-smacking; f22 long, beautifully spiced with a dab of marmalade to join the porridge; the spices rumble on into the far distance; b23 considering malted barley, wheat and oats have all gone into the mash, there is hardly any surprise that the nose and flavour profile is starchy and busy. Indeed, the oats have the biggest say here (a little bit of oat can go a long way in whisky!) in both aroma and on the palate; and the added sweetness from the cask gives a distinctive porridge-like feel to the delivery. But the cut is a tad wide, so the oils are a bit on the tangy side. Even so, a stylised and stylish whisky well worth experiencing, not least for that fabulous porridge delivery. A whisky to start the day with... 47%. ncf.

# BIMBER DISTILLERY London. 2015. Working.

⬩ **Bimber Single Malt Test Batch Sample** ex-bourbon cask, cask no. 15, bott 22 May 19 db (**94.5**) n23.5 t23.5 f23 b24 This cask has come on a storm with eye-watering clarity to the caramel-malt mix. The tannins have really set their stall out but superb muscovado sugars and light red liquorice softens the impact. How can this not be called a whisky....?!?!?! 57.9%. sc.

⬩ **Bimber Single Malt Test Batch Sample** ex-sherry cask, cask no. 38, bott 22 May 19 db (**94.5**) n23 t24 f23.5 b24 Well done, Bimber! You've only gone and found yourself an absolutely flawless ex-sherry butt with not a single of atom of sulphur to be found: possibly the cleanest I have tasted this year. The mixture of ripe plummy fruit and nuttiness is a wonder to behold, as is the clarity of the grape on the palate which allows the barley to filter through at the very death. If they have set out to astound and impress, then they have succeeded. Give this another ten years for the oak to integrate and...oh, my word...! 57.8%. sc.

⬩ **Bimber Single Malt Test Batch Sample** ex-sherry quarter cask, cask no. 26, bott 22 May 19 db (**87.5**) n22 t23 f21.5 b21 Lush and sticky, the thick grape hangs over this like a 6 foot 5 inch centre half over a 5 foot 6 inch forward. Ungainly and with little meaningful balance, this malt has a little way before it settles down. Have to say, though, that some of the grape is pretty delicious! 58.1%. sc.

⬩ **Bimber Single Malt Test Batch Sample** New Make Peated batch no. 140 db (**93.5**) n24 t23.5 f22.5 b23.5 Excellently clean new make with top notch cut points. The peat is non-aggressive and sits comfortably with the juicier malt tones. Interestingly, with the stills having been used more now, the amount of copper influence is slightly less in evidence than in earlier new make samples, leading to a slightly thinner finale. 60%. sc.

⬩ **Bimber Single Malt Test Batch Sample** re-charred cask, bott 3 Jun 19 db (**95**) n23.5 t24 f23.5 b24 When I taste samples like these, it is hard not to get excited about what is to come in forthcoming years. To get something this beautiful and then stick it into a PX cask or suchlike would be something akin to industrial sabotage. Brilliantly distilled, the spirit is a perfect foil for the myriad dark sugars extracted from the oak. Malty, too. 55.6%. sc.

⬩ **Bimber Single Malt Test Batch Sample** virgin cask, cask no. 7, bott 22 May 19 db (**94**) n24 t23.5 f23 b23.5 What a stunning natural caramel-lashed young Canadian this is. Hang on: with that heather honey and light liquorice mix with spice a bourbon, surely...no, wait a minute.... 57.7%. sc.

**Bimber Single Malt Test Batch Sample 22 Months Old** ex-bourbon cask, cask no. 8 db (**91.5**) n22.5 t23 f22.5 b23.5 With still another 14 months to go before this can be called whisky, this is already taking on impressive proportions....and is whisky in everything other than legal definition. The caramels extracted from the oak have had a highly attractive softening effect on both nose and palate. The sugars pose beautifully with the rich malt while the spices do much to reduce the youthfulness in perception. Beautifully distilled and matured, this is a gorgeous malt spirit experience. 63%. sc.

**Bimber Single Malt Test Batch Sample 22 Months Old** ex-port cask, cask no. 39 db (**80**) n21 t21 f19 b19 So much better than the last sample Port Cask offering from Bimber.

However, there is very limited balance to this and the bitterness, as though from sour grape skin, goes largely unanswered. *63%. sc.*

**Bimber Single Malt Test Batch Sample 22 Months Old** ex-sherry cask, cask no.31 db **(88) n20 t24 f22 b22** A great example of a malt still finding its feet and balance because at times, and on the nose especially, the grape does lurch about out of control. But this is a clean butt free from sulphurous negativity and when the grain and the grape do match up the result is some eye-watering beauty of quite staggering proportions: indeed, the delivery is one of almost carnal bliss. Elements of the late fruit chocolate finish isn't shoddy, either. *62.5%. sc.*

**Bimber Single Malt Test Batch Sample 22 Months Old** virgin oak cask, cask no.7 db **(95) n23.5 t23.5 f24 b24** For a single malt spirit of this age, it is probably impossible to ask for more. The nose makes no apology for its strong tannin accent, a little hickory combining with the caramels to massage the sugars into the broader oak. While to taste there are no rough edges at all, cleanly distilled yet mouth-filling with a thick Malteser richness, the malt combining with the milk chocolate. The oils round of the experience, softening things further... if that seemed possible. A Five Star wow! *62%. sc.*

**Bimber Single Malt Test Batch Sample 22 Months Old** Signature Cask bourbon, sherry & virgin oak casks, batch no.1 db **(85.5) n21 t22.5 f20.5 b21.5** With the lighter strength seems make the oils fragment resulting in a slightly disharmonised nose followed by a distinctly bitter and off- key finish. The delivery, though, possesses a fair degree of charm which just before the bitterness arrives is at its zenith thanks to a superb malt and sultana crescendo. *46%.*

**Bimber Single Malt Test Batch Sample 22 Months Old Signature Cask** bourbon, sherry & virgin oak casks, batch no.1 db **(89) n22.5 t23 f21 b22.5** The fruit has been outmuscled at every turn by the bountiful cream toffee. Youthful it may be, but those bourbon and virgin oak casks have been dug deep into to extract such pleasing sugars which sit with the intense malt superbly, though the slight late bitterness does create a moment of late discord. *62.5%.*

**Bimber Single Malt New-Make Test Batch Sample** batch no. 25, bott 17 Nov 16 db **(95.5) n24 t24 f23.5 b24** Quite possibly the best new make from a fledging distillery I have ever encountered: off the top of my head I cannot recall its master. Gorgeously rich despite being entirely feints-free with an astonishing castor sugar melt on the tail of the ultra-intense grist. Stylish and simply brilliant. *63%.*

# COPPER RIVET DISTILLERY Chatham, Kent. 2016. Working.

**Son of a Gun Cask Finished English Grain Spirit** db **(82.5) n20 t22 f19.5 b21** Nothing wrong with whoever is running the stills, as the body and pace of this grain spirit is impressive – especially on delivery. However, the curious feature is that despite the name of the distillery, this feels as though not enough copper has come into contact with the spirit, leaving a slightly tangy finish. At the time of writing this, I'd not yet been to the distillery, but looking forward to seeing how this was created. *474%.*

❖ **Son of a Gun Cask Finished English Grain Spirit** batch. 02 db **(87) n22 t22 f21 b22** A much sweeter cove than their first bottling. Richer and more intense, too. Still the odd hint of copper starvation but well made and a juicier, fatter all round experience. *474%.*

# COTSWOLDS DISTILLERY Shipton-on-Stour, Warwickshire. 2014. Working.

**Cotswolds Single Malt Whisky 3 Years Old** STR cask, cask no. 236 db **(94) n23.5 t23.5 f23.5 b24** If you require proof that brilliance can be achieved even when a whisky is only just legally old enough to be called whisky, then here you go. For its age, the depth to this malt is truly stunning. *62%. nc ncf sc. Bottled for That Boutique-y Whisky Company.*

**Cotswolds Single Malt Whisky 3 Years & 3 Months** bott 4 Apr 18 db **(91) n23 t23 f22 b23** Who would have thought, a quarter of a century ago, when I gave my first of many whisky tasting at Fortnum and Mason, the pantry of Piccadilly would one day have their very own label (and beautifully distilled and matured) English single malt whisky for sale. St James's may still look the same, but the whisky world has moved on beyond recognition. *46%. nc ncf sc. Bottled for Fortnum & Mason.*

**Cotswolds Single Malt Whisky 3 Years & 6 Months** bourbon 1st fill cask, cask no. 82 db **(92.5) n23 t23.5 f23 b23** About as oily as Cotswolds malt gets, ensuring the barley is spread not just to all distant corners of the palate, but stays there for a long time, also. *60.5%. nc ncf sc.*

**Cotswolds Single Malt Whisky Inaugural Release** first fill barrels, batch no. 01/2017 db **(95) n23.5 t24 f23.5 b24** Just before I officially tasted this, my 1,000th new whisky for the Jim Murray Whisky Bible 2018, (I had initially and unofficially tasted it when I spoke at the distillery's opening ceremony last Spring) I turned my telescope to the sky to see with excellent clarity the banded giant Jupiter with four moons in almost perfect alignment (one to the left, three to the right); then swung my scope slightly to the south east and there was Saturn, its rings as clear and breathtaking as I had ever witnessed, at an angle of ten past eight. In an hour or so,

Mars will rise and shine as brightly as it has done in 17 years and will not do again until the 2036 Whisky Bible. The portents were good for this malt, hopefully the distillery. And until this universally beautiful whisky, I was not remotely let down. *46%. nc ncf. 4,000 bottles.*

❖ **Cotswolds Single Malt Whisky Founder's Choice Batch No. 01/2018** STR American red wine casks db **(94.5) n23.5** two pieces of toast: one with an ulmo and heather honey blend, the other with plum jam...; **t24** amazing! Just bloody amazing! The sugars are up and primed ensuring gristy barley ramps up the juiciness to the max, which on another, deeper level, a boiled candy fruitiness ships away with a brittle clarity; **f23** darkens up on the palate as the tannins congregate for a toasty, spicy finale; **b24** this should not be happening..! How can so much flavour be extracted so evenly in so little time? Really hard to imagine better results from this kind of cask. Just purring with personality. *60.9%. nc ncf.*

❖ **Cotswolds Single Malt Whisky Founder's Choice Batch No. 02/2018** STR American red wine casks db **(92.5) n22.5** a much duller nose than 01/18 with the emphasis on the tannins; **t23.5** wow...! After such a quiet nose, the delivery strikes like a bolt from the blue, with astonishing crunchy, muscovado sugars crashing into the taste buds and Exocet spices also hitting their target; **f23** calmer now, reverting to a maple syrup and barley finale; the tannins gather late very much in this brand's style...; **b23.5** the dreamy nose lulls you into a false sense of security... *60.9%. nc ncf.*

❖ **Cotswolds Single Malt Whisky Founder's Choice Batch No. 01/2019** STR American red wine casks db **(89) n22** pretty pungent oak softened by grape jelly; **t23** the usual triumph of big salivating fruit and barley clinging limpet like to an oak frame; **f22** just a little too aggressively oaked and bitter late on; **b22** not quite the usual symphony of fruit and spice, but the delivery is faultless. *60.3%. nc ncf.*

❖ **Cotswolds Single Malt Whisky Founder's Choice Batch No. 02/2019** STR American red wine casks db **(93) n23** natural caramels gel beautifully with the full on sultanas: a real spotted dog pudding; **t23.5** bristling barley and fruit from the kick off, and pin-prick spices add to the entertainment; **f23** slightly custardy with some peppery plums thrown in for good measure; **b23.5** a slightly different angle from this line of bottling, with the busy spices making a huge difference to the mouth feel. You can never get bored by a whisky like this. *60.4%. nc ncf.*

**Cotswolds Single Malt Whisky 2014 Odyssey Barley Batch No. 02/2017** first fill oak barrels db **(95) n23.5 t24 f23.5 b24** Only two bottlings into The Cotswolds' doubtless long history and you think: "yep, this is going to be one very substantial, high class and important distillery". With less than 2,000 bottles of this improbably precocious masterpiece produced, this will be one of the most collectable whiskies for years to come. *46%. nc ncf. 1,920 bottles.*

**Cotswolds Single Malt Whisky 2014 Odyssey Barley Batch No. 03/2017** first fill oak barrels db **(88.5) n22.5 t22.5 f21 b22.5** Plays down its usual sweetness. *46%. nc ncf. 6,800 bottles.*

**Cotswolds Single Malt Whisky 2014 Odyssey Barley Batch No. 04/2017** first fill oak barrels db **(94) n23 t23.5 f23.5 b24** A return to form and its more expansive, complex and sweet framework. What a treat of a dram! *46%. nc ncf. 10,800 bottles.*

**Cotswolds Single Malt Whisky 2014 Odyssey Barley Batch No. 01/2018** first fill barrels db **(93) n23 t23.5 f23 b23.5** Whisky of this age matured in the British Isles has no right to be this beautifully rounded. *46%. nc ncf. 7,150 bottles.*

**Cotswolds Single Malt Whisky 2014 Odyssey Barley Batch No. 02/2018** first fill barrels db **(88) n23 t22 f21 b22** An enjoyable malt, though not quite up to the distillery's hitherto very high standards. The exact storyline to this malt has you scratching your head. *46%. nc ncf. 8,600 bottles.*

**Cotswolds Single Malt Whisky 2014 Odyssey Barley Batch No. 03/2018** first fill barrels db **(95) n23.5 t24 f23.5 b24** The Cotswolds is an understatedly beautiful place: it has just become more beautiful still... *46%. nc ncf. 8,550 bottles.*

**Cotswolds Single Malt Whisky 2014 Odyssey Barley Batch No. 04/2018** first fill barrels db **(92.5) n23 t24 f22.5 b23** A delicious, confident whisky not frightened of letting the oak play a leading role. *46%. nc ncf. 7,050 bottles.*

❖ **Cotswolds Single Malt Whisky 2014 Odyssey Barley Batch No. 05/2018** first fill barrels db **(90.5) n22.5** just a little lazy with the light caramels eclipsing most else; **t23** the sugars cross the line first here, a light lemon blossom honey note ensuring the barley shines; **f22** the tannins steam in with a degree of arrogance; **b23** the secret of this distillery is first class distillate being put into excellent casks. Appears to be the case again here, as it is hard to find fault technically. Not sure there is perfect harmonisation personality wise, but this distillery is now setting very high standards for itself. *46%. nc ncf.*

❖ **Cotswolds Single Malt Whisky 2014 Odyssey Barley Batch No. 06/2018** first fill barrels db **(92.5) n23** the balance between the biscuity barley and leathery tannins may basic. But it works a treat...; **t23** big caramels. Even bigger barley; **f23** salivating to the very end – how does it do that...? A little toasty but the warming embers of spice seem to up the light heather honey tones, too; **b23.5** a malt that is very happy in its own skin. *46%. nc ncf.*

◇◇ **Cotswolds Single Malt Whisky 2014 Odyssey Barley Batch No. 07/2018** first fill barrels db (**95**) **n23** such a delightful interplay between the butterscotch and ulmo honey...; **t24.5** just about perfect weight on the palate as the soft but essential oils bring together fabulously intense barley, a mix of ulmo honey and maple syrup and a softening caramel and vanilla middle, all punctuated by butterfly spices and sharpened by a squeeze of lemon: just bloody wow...!!!; **f23.5** buttery barley and delicate tannins; **b24** pure English bliss... 46%. nc ncf.

◇◇ **Cotswolds Single Malt Whisky 2014 Odyssey Barley Batch No. 09/2018** first fill barrels db (**92**) **n22.5** toffee; **t23** cream toffee; **f23** sticky toffee **b23.5** Cotswolds finest chewy toffee...! 46%. nc ncf.

◇◇ **Cotswolds Single Malt Whisky 2014 Odyssey Barley Batch No. 10/2018** first fill barrels db (**93**) **n23** there is a slight vegetable note to this one. Usually a bad sign, but somehow it chimes with another surprising visitor: the very lightest phenol. A little blood orange just lightens things; **t23.5** sharp barley dives in headfirst. The citrus notes include light kumquat moment; **f23** clean with a citrus tang to the buttery malt; **b23.5** slightly different. But works a treat. 46%. nc ncf.

◇◇ **Cotswolds Single Malt Whisky 2014 Odyssey Barley Batch No. 11/2018** first fill barrels db (**92**) **n22.5** bright grassy barley with a slight caramel border; **t23** again, a pretty straightforward duo sang between the barley and caramel. But it is pitch perfect; **f23** rare for so many unblemished sugars to make it through to the very death. The mix between spice and fudge is charming; **b23.5** this is becoming a remarkably consistent whisky. And very high class, too. 46%. nc ncf.

◇◇ **Cotswolds Single Malt Whisky 2014 Odyssey Barley Batch No. 12/2018** first fill barrels db (**86**) **n21.5 t22 f21 b21.5** Spoke a little too soon. An enjoyable malt from the shape of the buttery barley. But the oak here has a slightly bitter twist, the problem being detectable on the nose, too. 46%. nc ncf.

◇◇ **Cotswolds Single Malt Whisky 2015 Odyssey Barley Batch No. 01/2019** first fill barrels db (**89**) **n21.5** a slight overplaying of the oaky hand; **t23** much more like it! A thin sheen on lime blossom honey gives the barley a delicious lustre; **f22** the tannins turn up late and in force. An unusually dry finish despite a late gristy fly past; **b22.5** just struggles slightly to find its way here and there. But the overall theme is delightful. 46%. nc ncf.

◇◇ **Cotswolds Single Malt Whisky 2015 Odyssey Barley Batch No. 02/2019** first fill barrels db (**93**) **n22.5** biscuit barrel of Nice and Lemon Puffs; **t23.5** heart-meltingly soft delivery. The barley and oak-sponsored caramels seem to be about equally proportioned; **f23** fabulous gristy fade, again aided by a citrusy tartness; the spices are in perfect proportion; **b24** the vital sugars missing from the last couple of bottlings have been re-found and celebrated. 46%. nc ncf.

◇◇ **Cotswolds Single Malt Whisky World Whisky Forum 2018** first fill ex bourbon cask, cask no. 82, bott Jun 18 db (**96.5**) **n24** a five pipe nose: the barley is represented in at least two different guises: an underlying fresh cut hay and a crushed in the fingers Malteser; the muscovado sugars give a slightly fruity image while the nutty oak is relaxed, in warm butterscotch tart mode as well as lightly polished leather; a hint of pepper...; **t24** serious spices had been missing from the nose, other than that echo of pepper. But they are first up here as the palate is sent into shock by the early peppery onslaught. Slowly the sugars regroup, led first by the full- on grist. Then buttery barley lends a more oily feel to the structure, softening the spices impact along the way; **f24** long. The fade concentrates mainly on the intricacy of the barley, then the more molassed feel of the tannin; **b24.5** the perfect whisky for the world to see. World class...! 60.5%. nc ncf sc. 250 bottles.

**Cotswolds Test Batch Series New Make** batch no. 01/2017, bott 13 Oct 17 db (**94.5**) **n23 t24 f23.5 b24** A Test Batch Special. As English as a game of cricket, old chap, and as barley-rich as a mid-June sun-drenched Cotswold field... 63.5%. nc ncf.

**Cotswolds Test Batch Series Peated Cask Aged 25 Months** cask no. 221, bott 13 Oct 17 db (**91.5**) **n22.5 t22.5 f22 b22.5** By no means the finished article. Yet even at this tender age the marriage between the phenols, the barley and the oak is taking on a shape which is a bit of a turn on. The smoke is more meaningful than many such similar cask maturation phenolic whiskies, but still allows a delightful citrus note to wander through the entire piece. Lovely gristy sugars ensures a light touch throughout, though a hefty tannin and love heart combination gives a brief pulse. 62.4%. nc ncf sc.

◇◇ **Fortnum & Mason English Single Malt** cask no. 532, bott Mar 19 db (**94**) **n24** absolutely no faulting the wonderfully balanced intertwangling between ripe, toasty cinnamon-scented oak, genteel marmalade and light, grassy barley: a kind of breakfast whisky aroma...! **t23.5** with a nose like that, there had to be a salivating malt explosion on the cards...and it duly obliges; **f23** the tannins mount up for a dry-ish spiced and toasty finale, but always shadowed by balancing castor sugars...; **b23.5** so delicate...yet so big, too...! 46%. nc ncf sc.

◈ **Fortnum & Mason English Single Malt** cask no. 503, bott Jan 19 db (**90.5**) n22.5 some serious toasted tannins here...; t23.5 aaahhh! The most gorgeous eruption of barley first kisses, then coats the palate, those tannins on the nose represented early on by rapid fire spice; f22.5 surprisingly long, the tannins still pulsing, almost tapping out a bourbon-style beat now; b22.5 although it is obvious there is no great age to this malt, the pounding waves of tannin and the quiet elegance to the malt would have you thinking otherwise. 46%. nc ncf sc.

◈ **Fortnum & Mason English Single Malt** cask no. 527, bott Mar 19 db (**92.5**) n23 a far more evenly balanced and paced nose than Fortnum's other English malt, the lightness here emphasised with the most delicate squeeze of lemon to compliment the barley; t23.5 stunningly clean delivery with the barley taking the lead role and tiller with a delicate citrus subplot. The oak, so forthright in their other bottling, is much happier making a background noise, including a very light spice note; f23 long and buttery; b23 for a whisky of no great age, the degree of balance is both startling and wonderful. A real English treat awaits you in St. James'... 46%. nc ncf sc.

◈ **The Boutique-y Whisky Company Cotswolds Single Malt English Whisky Aged 3 Years** batch no. 1 (**92.5**) n23 the tannins are radiating all kinds of crystalised sugars, but a healthy maltiness is still apparent; t23.5 those sugars melt in the mouth upon impact. Soft caramel notes drift in to soften further before the roasted tannins begin the gather intensity; f23 a lovely spice, tannin and molasses mix gives the finale a dark, deliciously oppressive feel after the much lighter delivery; b23 a beautifully distilled malt which makes brilliant use of the oak's generous sugars. 50.4%. 1,783 bottles.

# EAST LONDON LIQUOR COMPANY

◈ **East London Liquor Company Whisky London Rye** new French oak, ex-bourbon & PX finish db (**88.5**) n22.5 a head-spinning concoction of ginger and tight, semi-impenetrable sugars. Gin-reminiscent and pleasant enough, but one of the densest aromas I have encountered this year – and this is whisky number 869..; t22.5 the nose forewarns you that you are in for something pretty huge, and it was no lie. Just now and again there is a gin-like quality to this and the dryness at times takes some believing. But there is also a highly attractive chalky subplot which appears to carry zesty lemon peel and then a treacle note to counter; f21.5 tangy, a little spicy, bitter-ish and tight; b22 a bewildering first bottling from this new distillery. As gingery as ginger liqueur, as dry as a gin, as confusing as a rye whisky matured in French, American and Spanish oak, one of which carried PX. It is almost impossible to say under all that what the actual spirit itself is like, though pleased to report not a single off note on both nose and finish. I really do hope they also bottle some whisky which gives us a chance to savour the grain. And remember that, in whisky, a little less can give you so much more. 46.8%. 269 bottles. Inaugural release.

# HEALEY'S CORNISH CYDER FARM Penhallow. 1986. Working.

**Hicks & Healey Cornish Whiskey 2004 Cask #32** dist 13 Feb 04, bott Feb 12 db (**96**) n24 t24.5 f23.5 b24. I picked this one up absent-mindedly, nosed...and was carried to Cornwall. I knew what it was without even opening my eyes. Unmistakable. And just so stunningly beautiful... 60.2%. ncf.

# LAKES DISTILLERY Cockermouth, Cumbria. 2014. Working.

**The Lakes Malt Spirit** db (**90**) n23 t22 f22.5 b22.5. I have chosen this as the 999th new "whisky" for the 2017 Jim Murray's Whisky Bible as a tribute to my dear old friend Harold Currie who was recently lost to us. Harold was behind the building of the Isle of Arran Distillery and a close bond, based mainly on mutual respect and fondness for the simple things in life – like St Mirren and football in general - formed between us. Both his sons played a part in getting this distillery off the ground, so though not yet a whisky, it is a special moment for me to taste their new-ish make. With the very first sip I ever have of this ground-breaking malt, I shall toast a very special old fiend: Harold Currie.... A lovely developing malt with a very puritanical cut ensuring the citrus has a big part to play. Massively promising as this is clean and characterful. But, my dear old friends, you have to bottle this stuff at something closer to cask strength: you have broken up the oils so we cannot quite see its full potential. 40%

# SPIRIT OF YORKSHIRE DISTILLERY

◈ **Spirit of Yorkshire Maturing Malt Distillery Projects 001** db (**92**) n23 t23.5 f22.5 b23.5 A debut bottling from this outstanding new distillery and, if anything, the casks are maturing ahead of schedule. Though not legally a whisky yet, the caramel involvement from the casks is as rich as it is profound. The stunning, buttery delivery really does make maximum use of both the hugely intense barley and spice-rammed oak. The result is a spirit simultaneously soothing and warming. The most stylish treat out of Yorkshire since Geoff Boycott was in his pomp... 46%. nc ncf. 2,000 bottles.

◈ **Spirit of Yorkshire Maturing Malt Distillery Projects 002** db **(89.5)** n22.5 t23 f22.5 **b22** A thinner model this time with the structure of the barley easily distinguishable. A little bit in a neither here nor there mode, but the impact of the barley sugar and butter is rather charming. *46%. nc ncf. 2,000 bottles.*

◈ **Spirit of Yorkshire Maturing Malt Distillery Projects 003** db **(95)** n23.5 t24 f23.5 **b24** Just ridiculously beautiful. The mouthfeel is as rich, oily and rounded as they could possibly have prayed for. If anyone remembers Fox's Butter Crinkle biscuits (another brilliant Yorkshire export, this time from Batley) with affection, then they will be making a beeline for this glorious bottling. Again, the malt appears to be on steroids and has no problems coping with the teeming natural caramels from the oak. The sugars are politely muted, the bruyere honey happy to live in the shadow of the buttery barley. This distillery uses the gannet as its emblem, my favourite sea bird as it happens. And this bottling seems to match its elegance with its feather-light touch. Magnificent. *46%. nc ncf. 2,000 bottles.*

◈ **Spirit of Yorkshire Maturing Malt Distillery Projects 004** db **(88)** n23 t22.5 f21.5 **b22** Some seriously punchy tannins here. Project 04 has bite bordering on attitude, but not quite the all-round balance to allow the malt to have an even say, as has been the case with the majority of their previous bottlings. Still loads to enjoy, especially considering this is still, in these tender years, non-whisky. But by the time it grows up, some of the rougher edges should be rounded and harmony where there is currently a slight, underdeveloped discord. *46%. nc ncf. 2,000 bottles.*

## ST. GEORGE'S Rowdham, Norfolk. 2006. Working.

**The English Whisky Co. Original** bourbon cask db **(89)** n22.5 t22.5 f22 **b22** when I first tasted this an odd thing happened. For a moment I thought I was tasting an old Scottish blend still in lab form and pre-bottled from over 25 years ago. I certainly didn't recognise it as Norfolk's finest. Pleasant, hugely enjoyable and friendly. But by EWC standards, pretty basic, too. *43%.*

**The English Whisky Co. Original** batch no.003 18, bourbon casks db **(94.5)** n24 t23.5 f23 **b24** Annoyingly, I appear to have missed out on batch 2, but I remember the original version of this – batch 1 – was a little undercooked. What you have here, I delighted to report, is the Full English....thoroughly recommend for breakfast. *43%. ncf.*

**The English Whisky Co. PX Sherry Cask Matured** db **(85.5)** n22 t22 f20.5 **b21** While their Unpeated Peated Bourbon cask is the distillery's most honeyed ever whisky, this is their most sugared. There is a difference and it's all about balance and complexity,neither of which are up to this distillery's normal high standards here... *46%. ncf.*

**The English Whisky Co. Small Batch Release Rum Cask Matured** batch no.01/2018, dist Apr 13, bott Feb 18 db **(91.5)** n23 t23 f22.5 **b23** A classic rum-matured style with a crisp, sugary outer shell and softer malt-rich middle. *46%. ncf.*

**The English Whisky Co. Single Cask Peated Triple Distilled** cask no. B1/154, dist Aug 10 db **(93)** n23.5 t23 f23.5 **b23** Almost as aggressive a peated malt as their "Smokey" bottling is relaxed. *57.4%. ncf sc.*

**The English Whisky Co. Single Cask Portuguese Cabernet Sauvignon** cask no. B1/832, dist Jun 07 db **(77)** n19 t20 f19 **b19** The closest thing to an English Whisky Liqueur. Excessively sweet, and off key on the finish, also. Hopefully a one off. *56.8%. ncf sc.*

**The English Whisky Co. Single Cask Unpeated Bourbon Cask** cask no. B1/593, dist May 08 db **(95)** n23.5 t24 f23.5 **b24** The most honeyed whisky ever produced by this distillery. An English single malt classic. *58.1%. ncf sc.*

◈ **The English Single Malt Whisky Double Cask** bourbon & oloroso sherry casks, batch no. 04/2018, dist Aug 11, bott Oct 18, nbc db **(89)** n22.5 a distinct cream sherry softness; t23 silky and supine, a malt which just curls up and allows the grape to do with it what it wishes; f21.5 a soupcon of sulphur; b22 a spineless, simpering malt. But in part delicious! *46%. 2,943 bottles.*

◈ **The English Single Malt Whisky Original** bourbon casks, batch no. 001 19, nbc db **(90.5)** n22.5 such a relaxed marriage between the barley and oak; some gentle caramels and spices combine with Opal Fruits candy to ensure a quiet complexity; t23 sensual delivery: just as on the nose caramels and barley work in tandem to ensure a soft, lilting personality; f22 long, dry and unusually, and possibly because of a delicate saltiness, salivating so late in the day; b23 the idea was to taste the remaining of my Australian and English whiskies during the semi-final of the cricket World Cup, as the two countries did battle. But I have had to bring the English tasting forward slightly as Surrey opener Jason Roy has made short work of the Australian bowlers. So this whisky is dedicated to another Surrey opener, John Edrich, my boyhood hero who played not just for England, but Norfolk as well...the home of this distillery. And as for this whisky: as gentle and as easy to put away as a Mitchell Starc bouncer.... *43%. ncf.*

**The English Whisky Co. Smokey** bourbon cask db **(93.5)** n23 t23 f23.5 **b24** They could have also written "smoky bacon cask".... *43%.*

**The English Single Malt Whisky Smokey** bourbon casks, batch no. L001 16 db **(90.5) n23** smoky; **t23** oily and smoky; **f22** smoky and bittering; **b22.5** smoky. 43%. nc ncf.

**English Single Malt Whisky Smokey The Original** bourbon casks, batch no. L002 16 db **(91) n22.5 t23.5 f22 b23** Very much a simplified version over the previous Original thanks to a significant upping on the oak-drained sugars... 43%. nc ncf.

**The English Whisky Co. Smokey** batch no.002 18, bourbon casks db **(94) n24 t23.5 f22.5 b24** This has to be one of the most relaxed peaty whiskies on the planet: the way it gets its smokiness across borders on the indolent. But, my word, it is so lovely... 43%. ncf.

⟫ **The English Single Malt Whisky Smokey** bourbon casks, batch no. 001 19, nbc db **(92) n23.5** so charmingly delicate, the minty peat introvert but comforting; **t23.5** super-soft malt with an all-embracing delicate chocolate and smoke cover; **f22** perhaps a little too dry on the vanillas: the thinning to 43% has stripped a little too many of the oils, perhaps; **b23** one of those, warm sultry malts, where the peat acts as a pillow and blanket you can snuggle into. 43%. ncf.

⟫ **The English Single Malt Whisky Smokey Oak** bourbon cask, batch no. 05/2018, dist Feb 11, bott Oct 18, nbc db **(95) n24** sweet as a nut...and nutty as a sweet. And clear as a bell. Excellent light grist and first-class peaty layering: significant, but never thuggish or arrogant: the kind of sexy peaty whisky aroma that often appeals to those who think they don't like it.... **t23.5** the layering of ulmo honey is staggering; the varied shapes of peat is more staggering still; notice the cool menthol at play...; **f23.5** flinty, Demerara sugars and almost a sugar candy quality to the phenols...; **b24** where this differs from, say, an Islay is that they, almost invariably, have a softness to them which gives the smoke a billowing quality. This, by contrast, is stark and firm, so the peat has to impress by stealth and subtlety. Which it does, quite brilliantly... 46%. 1,347 bottles.

⟫ **The English Single Malt Whisky Triple Distilled** batch no. 01/2019, dist Jun 11, bott Jun 19 db **(96) n24** a superb intertwangling of dulcet acacia honey and ultra-bright barley; **t24** it may not be a virgin cask, but this is like a virgin whisky: clean, sweet and entirely unsullied. The clarity of the grist, citrus-sprinkled barley and perfect oak tones is beyond belief; **f23.5** the oils now blossom and fatten or, rather, fill in, with the barley and oak on equal sweet terms. The spices are almost too well choreographed and goody-goody to be true....; **b24.5** malt whisky of this super-delicate type are rarely found better than this. 46%. 1,462 bottles.

⟫ **The English Single Malt Whisky Virgin Oak** batch no. 01/2019, dist Jul 13, bott Mar 19, nbc db **(95) n23.5** though the oak is never far from the surface, some delightful heather honey and Lubeck marzipan combine with the barley for a beautiful seduction; **t24** now it is the turn of the honey to lead the way and the tannins to follow on behind. The silky texture makes the buttery barley last the pace, while the cream caramels and ulmo honey glide around, slowly losing intensity; **f23.5** superb spices and now a buttery sheen to the butterscotch; dries towards a chalky vanilla fade; **b24** for those who like some whisky in their honey... This was my 500th whisky for the 2020 Bible, and it certainly lived up to the billing... Sublime. 46%. 2,689 bottles.

**The Norfolk Single Grain Farmers** American oak, batch no. 01/2016, bott 1 Nov 16 db **(91) n23 t24 f21.5 b22.5** I know that St George's outstanding distiller, David Fitt, has a partiality to this particular multi-grain (yes, multi-grain: not single grain, as seven different grain types are in the recipe...don't ask!) creation. I can see why, as it is a grand departure from his norm. It is engaging and intriguing, but falls very slightly towards the end as the harmonisation between grain and oak hasn't quite peaked... 45%. nc ncf sc. 1,998 bottles.

**The Norfolk Farmers Single Grain Whisky** batch no. 02/2018, bourbon cask, bott 28 Feb 18 db **(96.5) n23.5 t24.5 f24 b24.5** Some people might be a little confused by the labelling of this whisky, and you have my sympathy. It is called a "single grain whisky" which kind of suggests that only one grain type has been used. Well, no, there are four: in no particular order, rye, wheat, oats and several styles of malted barley. In fact, all the grains are malted, but they didn't want to call it a "Malt Whisky" in case people automatically assumed it was a single malt like Scotch, made from 100% barley. While the "single" term reflects it is from just the one distillery, St George's in Norfolk. Complicated? Well, not half as complex as this truly beautiful and gloriously idiosyncratic malt whisky. 45%. ncf sc. 392 bottles.

**The Norfolk Single Grain Malt 'N' Rye** American oak, batch no. 01/2017, bott 23 Jan 17 db **(88) n22** hefty and oily, the usual sharp fruity rye note is silenced by both barley and vanilla; **t22.5** chewy, salivating and increasingly firm in texture as it progresses. Big oils, a light buzz of spice and ever-increasing butterscotch through the middle; **f21.5** a little sharp, though oily; **b22** a strange beast, absolutely bursting with flavour yet never quite finds the rhythm it seeks. 45%. nc ncf sc. 1,962 bottles.

**The Norfolk Single Grain Parched** db **(96.5) n24.5 t24 f23.5 b24.5** A classic Irish "mod pot" style Irish pot still whiskey...from Norfolk! Nosed this when it was just a few months old...and it has moved on magnificently; indeed, beyond hope and expectation. Only the cat's bowler on the label and a green bottle seems to give the faintest hint towards anything Irish... For the record, by far the best Pot Still I have ever encountered made outside Ireland's shores... 45%. nc ncf sc.

◈ **The Boutique-y Whisky Company English Whisky Company Single Malt English Whisky Aged 8 Years** batch no. 2 **(93.5) n23.5** some prickle to this peat; a jolt of anthracite acidity, too; **t23.5** distinguished and soft on delivery, the phenols power through with a fabulous sharpness which seems to underline the dark sugars; the mid-ground is gristy with a light butterscotch mildness; **f23** long with excellent oils retaining both the smoke and minty-chocolatey fade; **b23.5** very much in the Islay style, it still has a certain St. George's quality and personality to it. Just too easy to enjoy... *52.3%. 845 bottles.*

# THE OXFORD ARTISAN DISTILLERY

◈ **TOAD Oxford Pure Rye Spirit** batch. 2 db **(87.5) n21 t23 f21.5 b22** Not a bad start, though I'm sure they'll get their cuts cleaner as the making of whisky becomes second nature to them. For the best results sit the glass in some warm water for a few minutes and then allow to cool a bit (a kind of Murray Method on steroids). This removes the heavier feints and leaves a delightfully honeyed spirit rammed full of flavour and where the rye kicks off full salivation. A distillery to watch. *40%. 458 bottles.*

# WALES
## DA MHILE DISTILLERY Glynhynod Farm, Llandysul. 2012. Working.

◈ **Dà Mhile Single Grain Welsh Whisky** db **(72) n18 t20 f16 b18** I have known John Savage-Onstwedder, whom I like to think of as a friend, for the best part of 30 years and am a massive fan of his pioneering organic whisky work. And his previous whiskies have been quite superb. Things have gone wrong here, though, having been hit by a double whammy. Firstly, there is juniper all over the nose, which made me assume, correctly it transpired, that John is now involved in gin. The juniper, by the way, is annoyingly detectable on the palate, also. And secondly, he has matured this whisky in a sulphur-treated sherry cask, leading to a disastrous finish. Two pitfalls to be avoided at all costs next time round. *46%. nc ncf sc. 180 bottles. Third Edition.*

## PENDERYN Penderyn, Aberdare. 2004. Working.

**Penderyn Celt** bott code 71172 db **(91) n22.5 t23 f22.5 b23** If a whisky got any more laid back and lighter it'd be carrying out levitation... *41%. ncf.*

**Penderyn Celt** bott code 72773 db **(92.5) n23 t23 f23.5 b23** Sssshhh! Don't drink this malt too loudly...you'll never hear what it's saying... *41%. ncf.*

**Penderyn Celt** bott code 73491 db **(94) n23.5 t23.5 f23 b24** An impossibly attractive whisky which just seems to understate everything – emphatically. *41%. ncf.*

**Penderyn Celt** bott code 80735 db **(88.5) n22 t22.5 f22 b22** A little flat this one: Wales without the hills and valleys. *41%. ncf.*

◈ **Penderyn Celt** bott code 82144 db **(95) n23.5** a quiet smokiness, but nothing understated here, either. A charming minty chocolate acts as a perfect foil for the delicate phenols; **t24** salivating gristy barley makes an early entrance but the real surprise is the oils which run through the body, giving unusual scope and depth for a Celt; the mid-point Demerara sugars are by now crisp and friable, contrasting beautifully with the oils; **f23.5** long, enigmatic and returning an extra charge of peat smoke for good measure; **b24** I have tasted some superb Penderyn Celts over the years. But this one is in a Welsh League of its own... *41%. ncf.*

◈ **Penderyn Celt** bott code 82146 db **(93) n23** the shyer phenols result in a drier, more fragmented aroma, though some citrus does wander in; **t23.5** sweet, malty delivery with a much weightier follow through of peat than the nose suggests: real sucker punch whisky! The sugars really are clean and salivating, though the vanilla latches on quickly; **f23** excellent spices combine with the remaining light smoke and melting sugars to put the whisky on cruise control; **b23.5** a toned down, less inclusive version of the 82144. But still the complexity, pace and balance of the whisky is exemplary. *41%. ncf.*

◈ **Penderyn Celt** bott code 82822 db **(94) n23** thin gruel so far as the peat is concerned, especially compared to 82144, but the light smattering of lime blossom honey on the vanilla sponge cakes certainly makes up for it; **t23.5** an unusually fragile delivery for a Celt, the maltiness being delicate but still building up magnificently in intensity; a kind of cross between Malted Milk biscuit and apologetic smoke; the muscovado sugars are superb, though; **f23.5** long with just the lightest of oils. The vanillas are relaxed, leading to a light mocha moment or two. The smoke at last rounds up sufficiently to add weight and even a little spice; **b24** a very different Celt: this is the quiet one, frowning upon intensity. But it is entirely impossible not to be seduced by its subtlety. *41%. ncf.*

◈ **Penderyn Dylan Sherrywood** bott code 90602 db **(87) n21.5 t23 f21 b21.5** Years and years and years ago, when I was a boy when there were wolves in Wales, and birds the colour of red-flannel petticoats whisked past the harp-shaped hills....when we rode the daft and happy hills bareback, it snowed and it snowed; and in Spain silly men did not put sulphur in innocent barrels... 41%. ncf. *Icons of Wales No. 3.*

**Penderyn Faraday** bott code 82321 db (86) n21.5 t22 f21 b21.5 A hefty, sticky Penderyn offering little of its usual charm and complexity. Decent spices lift it from its toffee and raisin slumber. Pleasant and not unappealing, but the lamp has gone dim... 46%. ncf. *Travel Retail Exclusive.*

**Penderyn Icons of Wales No 5/50 Bryn Terfel** bourbon casks db (96.5) n24 t24.5 f23.5 b24.5 Having seen Bryn Terfel perform live – many years ago now, I admit – I can vouch for this man's power on stage; his rare, uncanny ability to resonate with the soul. See Bryn and you get your full tenor's worth... So, this must be his alto-ego, for this is the most delicate malt ever bottled by Penderyn: ethereal, closer to the angelic voices in the closing movement of Faure's Requiem than Bryn's bass-baritone. To get that you would have needed to have added a lot of peat – and we would have ended up with Bryn Turfel....and that would never do... 41%. ncf.

**Penderyn Legend** bott code 77618 db (92.5) n23 dried apricots on a red currant and marmalade base; t23 chewy delivery with, initially, massive malt then a slow unveiling of delicate fruits – essence of apricot leading the way, f23 sexy spices jazz up the light fruits; b23.5 by no means the most taxing Penderyn. But what it does, it does just right... 41%. ncf.

**Penderyn Legend** bott code 72965 db (95.5) n23.5 t24 f23.5 ...b24.5 Not sure whiskies under 46% abv are meant to be quite this complex, rich and satisfying. A truly brilliant whisky, underlining Penderyn's world class credentials. 41%. ncf.

**Penderyn Legend** bott code 80593 db (93.5) n23.5 t23 f23 b24 A luscious malt which offers greater oils than most 41% whiskies and, mysteriously from somewhere, the lightest hint of phenol more associated with their Celt bottlings. Works here, though! 41%. ncf.

**Penderyn Legend** bott code 83045 db (95.5) n23.5 fluttering hints of fruits land and take off from your nose...; t24.5 so clean, so soft, so fruity, so subtle...so why aren't I swallowing this...? f23.5 a stream of delicate malt notes gather to try and make something big and profound...but fails. The sugars, caressing every taste bud, never quite gang up meaningfully; the vanillas form and shape but always stay in the background; b24 just like having your palate kissed by a whisky nymph... This incredible, extraordinarily beautiful whisky is the undisputed master of understatement. 41%. ncf.

**Penderyn Legend** bott code 83048 db (93) n23 a little weightier and more oak oriented than its sister batch 83045; t23.5 almost obscenely soft on delivery with a real malt depth. But the spices, so understated last time out, are here in force and make a fizzing impact; f23 a glorious malt and oak marriage, helped by a light layer of ulmo honey; the spices quietly sizzle on...; b23.5 a beautiful malt where the oak has a fair bit to say. 41%. ncf.

**Penderyn Madeira Finish** bott code 73196 db (92.5) n23 t23 f23 b23.5 And so a rocket-shaped bottle for the whisky that really has taken off around the world...how apt! 46%. ncf.

**Penderyn Madeira Finish** bott code 803912 db (91) n22 t22.5 f23.5 b23 Very elegant, indeed. 46%. ncf.

**Penderyn Madeira Finish** bott code 81036 db (94) n23.5 t23.5 f24 b23 That extra dose of oak has gone a very long way. Not perhaps how I'd like to see every Penderyn, but the extra cocoa injection makes for a delightful detour. This is the biggest Madeira Finish Penderyn ever bottled, and make no mistake. 46%. ncf.

**Penderyn Madeira Finish** bott code 81927 db (94) n23.5 how can you not just adore that alliance between the natural caramels, understated fruits and light spices...? Ridiculously yummy...!!! t23.5 full salivation levels as the malt goes on the full attack; again the natural caramels drift languidly across the palate, a little light fruit lapping on a malty shore; f23 one of the maltiest Penderyn finishes yet; b24 the understatement speaks volumes: just beautiful! 46%. ncf.

**Penderyn Madeira Finish** bott code 82418 db (91) n23 thin malt and even thinner fruit. Which leaves it to the delicate tannins to take gentle control; quite grassy at times; t23 beautiful mouth feel with just the right amount of oils to ensure depth and length, but light enough to allow the delicate heather honey through; f22.5 slightly drier and spicier than normal; b22.5 a slightly austere version of this classic. 46%. ncf.

**Penderyn Madeira Finish** bott code 82893 db (91.5) n23 the lightest breeze of smoke on the wind here; and so delicate is this aroma it doesn't take much to get noticed; t23.5 brilliantly complex delivery, that light smokiness giving an extra degree of weight alongside the oaky caramel. The light boiled sweet fruitiness skips around the palate; f22 a light spice buzz and a major degree of vanilla; b23 a delicate malt, anchored beautifully by the guesting smoke. 46%. ncf.

**Penderyn Madeira Finish** bott code 83115 db (91) n22.5 much more old school Penderyn with a chalky dryness scratching the nose; t23.5 lush, mouth-filling and grape heavy, this makes a huge impact on delivery. Light ulmo honey tapers down into lemon drizzle cake; f22 partially dry and chalky, a charming cocoa development fits in well; b23 much more of the PMF style of a couple years back. Only slightly better balanced. 46%. ncf.

꙰ **Penderyn Madeira Finish** bott code 83213 db **(94) n23** just a hint of bourbon on this one with a little red liquorice to be found, the malt teases, the fruit is but an echo; the spices a smattering; **t24** melt-in-the-mouth honey embraces the natural caramels with affection; **f23** one of the longer and sweeter versions of PMF, with a glorious boiled fruit candy mixing with minty chocolate; **b24** outside Scotland, hard to think of a more consistent malt whisky in the market place than this at the moment. Yet another treat. *46%. ncf.*

꙰ **Penderyn Myth** bott code 82262 db **(94.5) n23.5** just such an addictive verve to this, the malt enjoying a lovely citrus twist as well as a glorious malty swoosh; **t24** the malt arrives, unconcealed, in waves one to five to make this such an attractive delivery. The barley flickers at various intensities as the vanillas start to make ground; **f23** such an elegant fade of biscuit barley, vanilla and citrus: simple, perhaps, but wonderfully effective; **b24** any cleaner and you could wash your face in it. One of the maltiest Penderyns I've ever encountered. What is Welsh for Wow!? *41%. ncf.*

꙰ **Penderyn Myth** bott code 82986 db **(88) n22.5** unusually acerbic on the nose, the fruit taking off its gloves and giving you what for...; **t23.5** the kind of crunchy sweetness teeth have been known to be broken on: like munching on muscovado sugar, with fruit juices slowly filtering in; **f20** just a little bit of a tang to the spice and sweetness; **b22** it's a Myth, Jim. But not as we know it. *41%. ncf.*

꙰ **Penderyn Peated** bott code 82141 db **(94.5) n23** though called "Peated" I have encountered weightier smoke on the nose of Celt. But where this is different, is that the phenols cling tightly to the malty sweetness, neither bossing not ever letting go; **t24** this is a stunning delivery. The peat arrives briskly and for a moment brusquely, but soon softens its stance as the malts chip in beautifully along with the almost over polite vanillas from the oak; at times a little exotic fruit deliciously slaloms in and out of the picture; **f23.5** amazingly delicate finale with the smoke a little more proud now, especially as the minty chocolate and spices perk up; **b24** the smoke covers this malt like a satin negligee over the contours of your favourite body... *46%. ncf.*

꙰ **Penderyn Peated Single Cask** cask no. P277 db **(95) n23.5** shewing Penderyn's almost uniquely mint chocolate edge to their delicate peat very confidently; **t24** the delivery eschews any kind of a big phenol opening and instead concentrates on the dissolving sweetness of the malt itself. The smoke arrives in its own good time behind the prominent spices; **f23.5** long and a little more serious now: the leading sugars have been dispensed with, leaving a tide mark of slightly acidic tannins, a fraction sooty in nature and spices now much more alligned to oak; **b24** how can you not love a whisky this delicate? A gorgeous, faultless experience. *50%. ncf sc. Bottled for Topwhisky, Belgium.*

**Penderyn Portwood** bott code 80471 db **(79) n21.5 t22.5 f17 b19** One of the more understated Port matured malts on the market with an almost Chardonnay feel to it. Sadly, the sulphury finish confirms all is not what it should be. *46%. ncf.*

꙰ **Penderyn Portwood** bott code 80472 db **(93.5) n23.5** unusually dry for a Port cask, the fruit in grape must mode; the tannin adds another vanilla-led dryness, too; **t23** quite a sharp and shapely delivery; remains eye-watering, even as the light mocha begins to present itself; **f23.5** softer now, a little muscovado sugar mixing in with the praline; **b23.5** a very different, non-conforming type Port cask influence but brimming with personality. *46%. ncf.*

**Penderyn Rich Oak** bott Nov 17 db **(94.5) n23.5 t24 f23 b24** The famous Penderyn style seemingly on steroids. Any richer and it'll be buying Swansea City FC... *50%. ncf. 1,349 bottles.*

꙰ **Penderyn Rich Oak** bott code 82504 db **(94) n23** a real toasty edge to this, with the roasted tannins and caramels making for a thick set and enticing aroma; **t23.5** huge though controlled tannin from the very first giant flavour wave, backed by some excellent oils on which hangs the molasses and heather honey mix; a light muscovado sugar note offers a slightly fruity edge; **f23.5** barley sugar and slightly overcooked fudge. And those late spices? Perfection, or what...? **b24** Jack Daniels was of Welsh decent. The layered tannins here, not entirely dissimilar to some Kentucky and Tennessee whiskey, would make him feel very much at home. Superb. *46%. ncf.*

꙰ **Penderyn Royal Welsh Whisky** bott code 90532 db **(86) n22 t23 f20 b21** One of the softest deliveries of the Penderyn range, briefly enjoying a salivating grape and grain combination which for several excellent moments hit wonderful fruit and chocolate heights. But the finish is untidy and the furry buzz reveals a rogue cask in the mix. The delivery, though, is something a little special. *43%. ncf. Icons of Wales No. 6.*

꙰ **Penderyn Sherrywood** bott code 82111 db **(94) n23** faultless moist fruit cake; **t23.5** beautiful, languid mouth feel with luxuriant raisins meeting spiced up muscovado sugars and molasses; **f24** a fabulous fade, complex, wonderfully weighted and simple cannot resist going down the sherry trifle route; **b23.5** quite simple, but goes out of its way to do the simple things very well – and deliciously - indeed... *46%. ncf.*

꙰ **Penderyn Sherrywood** bott code 90113 db **(86) n22.5 t22 f20.5 b21** The nose is interesting enough, but otherwise this lies flat on the palate and steadfastly refuses to sparkle. A disappointing dullard by Penderyn's high standards. *46%. ncf.*

**Penderyn Single Cask Ex-Bordeaux Grand Cru** cask no. GC1, dist Mar 11, bott Jan 19 db (**96**) **n24** a tight, wine cork nose, pungent and heavy with arrogant grape; and like a great Bordeaux, only with time and oxidisation, does it settle into something of beauty; **t24.5** no other whisky on the planet has a delivery to match this: not only is the fruit compact and intense, but the fire to the spice offers a blue flame. A smattering of malt makes its way through for a brief, sweet interlude, then it is back to the crushing grape, an wine note of staggering intensity; **f23.5** he fruit lets up sufficiently for a chocolate fruit and but finale, with the oak making a late layered foray; **b24** you could argue there is no balance here, such is the dominance of the fruit. However, the Murray Method helps here massively, because the barley manages vital break through, which not only thins the grape but balances against the spice. Anything less than half an hour with a glass of this whisky will be doing it - and yourself - a serious dis-service... 60.2%. ncf sc. Bottled for Schlumberger.

**Penderyn Single Cask Ex-Madeira Cask** cask no. M75-32, dist Nov 13, bott Aug 18 db (**96.5**) **n24** the levels of complexity on the grape is almost nose blowing, as well as mind blowing, for there is a spiciness so intrinsic and ticklish I have twice sneezed while analysing this. Remarkable...! **t24** sublime weight on the fruit-dripping delivery. As on the nose, there is not a move without spicy counter move, though somehow the grape is sinuous enough to allow through both barley and vanilla from the oak; the sugars are just about perfect, starting as a firm molasses, then moving out towards an oilier heather honey...with spice, of course...; **f24** long, drawn out...but for not one moment even thinking of resting on its laurels and forever revisiting the fruit and sugars, now taking a slightly drier, toastier, duskier look at them...while the spices, now spattered with orange blossom honey, rumble on and on...and on; **b24.5** the best whisky I have tasted so far this year. If this isn't some kind of award winner, then the standard of the world's whiskies has risen sharply this year.... 59.2%. ncf sc. Bottled for Schlumberger.

**Penderyn Single Cask Ex-Tawny Port Cask** cask no. PT302, dist Dec 13, bott Nov 18 db (**82**) **n20.5 t22 f19 b20.5** Sings only briefly on delivery. But very tight and dry elsewhere. 48%. ncf sc. Whisky.de exclusive.

**Penderyn Single Cask Portwood** cask no. PT255 db (**94**) **n23.5 t23.5 f23 b24** The most ruby to claret-hued whisky I have ever encountered in bottled form: it like a Ch. Margaux. Only a whisky for after a fine meal, not during... 58.9%. ncf sc.

**Penderyn Single Cask Rich Madeira Cask** cask no. M334 db (**95**) **n23.5** a moody aroma: plums and dates but heavily seasoned with oak: not a single shaft of lightness to be sniffed; **t24** as the nose warns, this is a massively intense malt, again the fruit dripping in its uncompromising opaqueness, now with serial killer spices attacking the palate like a crazed knifeman at a motel guest in a shower...; **f23.5** the sugars are all around muscovado – no surprise there – and molasses. The fruit is like raisins added to a slightly overcooked treacle tart..., **b24** rich....? You're not joking...!!! 59.1%. ncf sc. Bottled for Charles Hofer SA, Switzerland.

**Penderyn Single Cask Rich Madeira** cask no. M729 db (**95.5**) **n23.5 t24.5 f23.5 b24** When they say "Rich Madeira" they really aren't joking. Huge. And very, very rich. 58.8%. ncf sc. Bottled for Charles Hofer SA, Switzerland.

**Penderyn Single Cask Tawny Portwood** cask no. PT261/1 db (**96**) **n23.5 t24.5 f24 b24** Just ridiculously good! And mind-bogglingly complex. 59.7%. ncf sc. Bottled for Bresser & Trimmer BV, The Netherlands.

**Penderyn Single Cask Vintage 2006 Ex-Bourbon Cask** cask no. 3/2006, bott Apr 18 db (**95**) **n23.5** anyone who has been to Brazil – or has/had a Brazilian partner – will immediately recognise the unique aroma of their local biscuits. The oak and barley combine here for the biggest South American Welsh experience outside Argentina...; **t24** huge! A delivery which should just be big at best even considering the strength, but this is truly massive. This is a tsunami of malt hitting the palate, but bringing with it the most sublime mix of orange blossom honey and oak-aching spice. The mid-ground sees all kinds of dark sugars at play, and tannins biting back; **f23.5** long, much drier now and the spices working in a lower key. A little praline on overdone toast finishes this beauty off with aplomb; **b24** hauntingly beautiful whisky. Not a single note out of place... 59.7%. ncf sc. Bottled for Schlumberger.

**Feingeist Ex-Moscatel Finish Single Cask Single Malt Welsh Whisky 2013** dist Nov 13 bott Apr 19 (**94**) **n24** the exceptionally fine cask has allowed the grape to come through at varying levels of intensity and even degrees of sweetness. From a dry, chalky dried grape skin element to a bruyerre honey and busy spice combination, there is even a degree of Guyanan rum to this one. Brain-scratchingly complex...; **t23.5** though the alcohol powers through, the lushness of grape acts as a shock absorber. And, as on the nose, the fruit filters through in complex and varied form. The tannins also have a say, offering a slightly bourbon-style hickory to complement the heather honey notes. But that grape softens and assuages all...except for the ever-growing spice; **f23** returns to a drier form, though those spices take their time to calm down...; **b23.5** a glorious whisky perfectly suited to its high strength. Charismatic, complex and bold. 60.9%. 90 bottles.

# Australian Whisky

It is not surprising that Australia, cast adrift it seems from the rest of the world until Captain James Cook thrust his triangulation apparatus at it some 240 years ago, has many indigenous species. The result of biodiversity having to get on with it alone, often bravely and against the odds.

From the kangaroo to the koala, the wombat to the platypus, the kookaburra to the bearded Lark. Now it is the bearded Lark (Billius Distillus) in its native Tasmanian habitat, a small creature found mainly flying around darkened buildings in the vicinity of Hobart, that has had the greatest impact on Australian whisky, and without whom there would be no new chapter given only to that singular scion of the world's malt distillation family.

Bill Lark is a one man force majeure who took a country out of a starch-knickered Victorian reactionism, so far as distilling was concerned, into one that now proudly boasts over 25 distilleries either operating or in the process of being built. And a standard achieved by many so far that is way above the norm.

We must go back to 1992, seemingly recent in the grand scheme of whisky matters but a year before many of the people I met attending a recent Shanghai whisky festival were actually born. It was the year I gave up my work as a national newspaper journalist to become the world's first full-time whisky writer. And was the year Bill Lark began taking on the Australian government to change a law that forbade private distilling in Australia. Having got sympathetic politicians on board – always a wise move – he found his battle shorter and less bloody than expected and it was not long before he and his wife Lyn were hard at work distilling an unhopped mash made at the local – and historic – Cascade brewery. Soon their daughter, Kristy, was on board showing exceptional skill as a distiller. And next a family affair became a national one, as, inspired by the Larks, small distilleries began rising around the country. First Dave Baker, whose Bakery Hill malt scooped the Whisky Bible 2020's Southern Hemisphere Whisky of the Year, across the Tasman Straight in Melbourne and then onwards along and up the coast. A new whisky nation was born. And is growing prodigiously. Now I have given Australia its own section in Jim Murray's Whisky Bible, perhaps not before time. It is a form of award well merited, because Australian malt has constantly proved to be something worth finding: often as bold and brave as Bill Lark's vision. And, like the great man and dear friend himself, you always feel better for its company.

Hellyers Road

Fanny's Bay

Launceston
Launceston Distillery
Adams Distillery

Cradle Mountain

**TASMANIA**

Nant Distillery

Belgrove Distillery
Old Kempton Distillery
Shene Estate & Distillery

Spring Bay

Nonesuch

Hobart

Killara

**Hobart**
Devil's Distillery
Lark Distillery
Old Hobart
Sullivans Cove

# AUSTRALIA
## ADAMS DISTILLERY Perth, Tasmania. 2012. Working.

⟨⟩ **Adams Distillery Tasmanian Single Malt Whisky Cask Strength** 50l American oak port cask, cask no. AD 0016 db **(84.5) n21 t22 f20.5 b21** Doesn't work in the same way as their peat finish bottling. The distillate itself seems less well made, resulting in some uncomfortable moments both on nose and finish. No faulting the cask, though, which throws a clean, rich, spicy, grapey beacon to bring you home. 55.5%. sc. 65 bottles.

⟨⟩ **Adams Distillery Tasmanian Single Malt Whisky First Release** sherry cask, peat finish, cask no. 005, 012 & 013 db **(90.5) n23.5** what a nose! The peat is sharp, acidic and proud – even a touch of anthracite in those phenols. The juicy grape appears content to allow the peat to be the star of the show; **t22** the tables are turned on delivery with a massive sultana kick on delivery The smoke is less of a support act here than the fruit had been on the aroma. It takes a while for the phenols to pick their way through the over ripe dates, and then turns up as a slight spiciness; **f22.5** the oak doubles up with the smoke to get those spices rumbling...; **b22.5** apart from an over indulgence of sweet fruit on delivery, this whisky ticks just about every box. 52.5%. 324 bottles.

## ADELAIDE HILLS DISTILLERY Nairne, South Australia. 2014. Working.

**Native Grain Project Wattleseed & Malt** db **(88) n22 t21.5 f22.5 b22** Well, for a start, this isn't whisky. However, how can wattleseed not deserve its place in my Whisky Bible when its Latin name is acacia murrayana? This confirms it a member of the acacia tree or shrub family, rather than a grain....thus rendering anything distilled from it a non-whisky. Also, it is from the stunningly beautiful Adelaide Hills, one of my favourite parts of Australia. So far as nose and taste goes, sampled blind it is no different from some of the American whiskeys smoked over native woods and certainly pokes out a spiciness not to be sniffed at...or, rather, to be. Dry with precise background sugars plus a decent cocoa finish. An enjoyable whisky cousin. 46.2%.

## ANIMUS DISTILLERY Kyneton, Victoria. 2012. Working.

⟨⟩ **Animus Distillery Alpha Whisky** db **(90.5) n23** a huge statement of intent by the tannin and spiced plums; **t23.5** the lushness of the top heavy treacle and tannin covers over the otherwise thin body; **f22** fades in its own time, a real treacle pudding effect lingering on; **b22.5** impressively forceful and confident it is helped by the clean, unsullied spirit. 54.5%.

# BAKERY HILL North Bayswater, Victoria. 1999. Working.

◈ **Bakery Hill Classic Malt Single Malt Whisky** db **(88)** n22 sharp barley and softer toffee; **t22** brief barley salivation moment, then a blanket of attractive cream toffee; **f22** dries and half-heartedly spices up, but the toffee remains; **b22** a straight as a die malt which makes little attempt to veer away from its cream toffee theme. *46%. ncf.*

◈ **Bakery Hill Classic Malt Cask Strength Single Malt Whisky** db **(94)** n23 just adore the way this malt understates its presence, yet somehow causes a quiet stir on the nose by ramping up the intensity of the malt to maximum levels...; **t23.5** you just knew this was going to be a super-salivater...and, my word, it is! The malt practically fizzes on the palate like barley sherbet; **f23.5** the barley, a little citrus tinted now, keeps its shape as the most delicate oaky marzipan enters the fray; **b24** because of the lack of oils present on Baker Hill malt, it can suffer slightly when reduced. Here the whisky, oils and all, is intact we get the malt in full glory. "Classic Malt" says the label. You hear no quibbles from me... *60.5%. ncf.*

◈ **Bakery Hill Double Wood Single Malt Whisky** db **(90)** n22 a kind of sultana infused malt loaf; **t23** usual house mouth-watering style. Except this has far more body than the standard BH, coinciding with the growth of gentle plumy tone and dry, chalky spice; **f22.5** long and still a little fat, but the malt now restored into pole position, though the spices are nibbling with sharpened teeth; **b23** a busy, attractive and quite full bodied Bakery Hill. *46%. ncf.*

◈ **Bakery Hill Peated Malt Single Malt Whisky** db **(87.5)** n21.5 t22.5 f21.5 b22 A bit on the young and slightly wobbly side, not quite having the overall balance so monumentally displayed by the cask strength version. *46%. ncf.*

◈ **Bakery Hill Peated Malt Cask Strength Single Malt Whisky** db **(95.5)** n24 the secret here is the understated phenols which proves how in whisky less can often offer more. Because the imprint of the smoke is light, there is no trampling on the sublime mix of delicate oaky vanilla and even softer citrus. Also underlines just how beautifully made the original spirit was: classic stuff... **t24** bright, salivating barley is at its most gristy and charming, the smoke wandering in almost as an afterthought and slowly building depth; **f23** medium length despite the smoke with the last traces of gristy sugars fading to be replaced by a more austere vanilla theme; **b24** doing the Australian whiskies today (well, some of them) as England and the Aussies are battling it out in the semi-final of the cricket World Cup. Duty over pleasure means I am here tasting instead of at Edgbaston. And it is so wonderful to find David Baker's malt still very much up in smoke, a bit like Australia who have slipped to 175-7 – which doubtless means the Aussies will win.... A malt as glorious as England's bowling... *60%. ncf.*

◈ **Bakery Hill Sovereign Smoke Defiantly Peated Single Malt Whisky** db **(91.5)** n22.5 though the weight is thin, the smoke moves over the scene like a blanket of cloud; **t23** oh...that is such a gorgeous delivery: the sugars are warm and rich, a blend of grist and acacia honey. The smoke enters gracefully and carefully does nothing to disturb the mouth-watering maltiness; **f23** long, with the oak chipping in with cream toffee, and still the smoke hangs in there languidly, trying not to be noticed; **b23** a beautiful diffusion of light honey and smoke. *50%. sc.*

# BELGROVE DISTILLERY Kempton, Tasmania. 2010. Working.

**Belgrove Distillery Peated Rye Whisky** bott 17 Apr 18 db **(96.5)** n24.5 t24 f24 b24 My two favourite whisky styles combining in a way that, before, I have ever only achieved in a lab. A truly great whisky: unquestionably stupendous. *60%.*

**Belgrove Distillery Rye Whisky** aged in ex-Heartwood "Release the Beast" barrel PB 020, bott 27 Apr 18 db **(95.5)** n24 t24 f23.5 b24 A whisky of mind-blowing complexity from what is emerging as one of the world's great distilleries. *65.4%.*

◈ **Belgrove Distillery Rye Whisky 100% Rye** barrel no. PB074, bott 11 Apr 19 db **(88.5)** n22 honeyed but with a curious hoppy/tobacco back note...; **t22.5** a slick delivery, pleasantly oiled but, like on the nose, there is a note I don't normally associate with this distillery giving the honey a hard time. That said, the early heather honey and grain mix is startlingly beautiful; **f22** incredibly dry, the emphasis on the vanilla, not the rye; **b22** a very different type of Belgrove rye. Actually, tasted blind I'd never have recognised it. *62.4%. ncf sc.*

◈ **Belgrove Distillery Rye Whisky 100% Rye** bott 19 Jul 18 db **(87.5)** n21.5 t22 f22 b22 Just like Barrel PB074, this has a slightly hoppy accent to it as opposed to their normal intense rye. Love the scattered muscovado sugars and the late milk chocolate, though. *46.5%. ncf.*

**Belgrove Distillery Rye Whisky 100% Rye** Shiraz casks, bott 10 Nov 17 db **(95)** n23.5 t24 f23.5 b24 A very rare case of where certain, lusty elements are at almost full throttle yet somehow all is kept in formation. Brilliant. *60%. ncf.*

◈ **Belgrove Distillery Rye Whisky 100% Rye** Shiraz cask, bott 11 Apr 19 db **(93)** n22.5 boiled black cherry candy, black peppers and all with a light sponge cake sweetness; **t24** an adorable full on delivery. The grain and grape are on full volume, stunningly clean and backed by an intense molasses toasty sweetness; **f23** quickly climbs back down to a soft vanilla fade; **b23.5** Belgrove back to its bristling self. Full set of cutlery required for this three-course rye. *62.5%. ncf sc.*

◈ **Belgrove Distillery Rye Whisky Wholly Shit Sheep Dung Smoke** bott 26 Sept 18 db **(94.5) n23.5** these sheep have been eating hickory; **t23.5** superb mouth feel with gorgeous oils on the grain, then a secondary, sharper, crisper degree of sweetness; the phenols are delicate but still add extra depth; that light hickory note is never far away; **f23.5** long with a mix of Manuka honey and creamy Victory V cough sweets; **b24** a whisky coming to a baa near you... and much better than the shit I have to endure from some sulphured ex-wine casks. Yesterday I tasted whisky matured in lychee liqueur casks and plum liqueur casks; earlier today a (sulphur-treated) pomegranate wine cask. I did wonder what the hell would be next....I should have known... *57.8%.*

**Belgrove Distillery Single Malt Peated Whisky** bott 25 Jul 17 db **(92) n23 t23 f22.5 b23.5** An interesting difference between this and the peated rye is the apparent lack of age: maybe the rye can cover a more youthful spirit with its boisterous, juicy personality, whereas the light barley can't. Or, maybe, this is a just a bit younger... *50.5%.*

# BLACK GATE DISTILLERY Mendooran NSW. 2012. Working.

**Black Gate Single Malt Whisky** first fill 100% litre Port cask, cask no. BG022 db **(92) n22.5 t23.5 f23 b23** Port casks are certainly all the rage in Australia at the moment, some working better for certain distilleries over others. This is a success story. *50%. sc.*

# CORRA LINN DISTILLERY Relbia, Tasmania. 2015. Working.

◈ **Corra Linn Distillery Single Malt Whisky** barrel no. CLD22, dist 20 Aug 16, bott Mar 19 db **(89) n22** the most Christmas puddings nose I have ever encountered; **t22.5** I am expecting someone to set fire to this, and then find a silver thruppeny bit inside...that Christmas pudding theme continues – and how! With over-ripe plums mixed in with the molasses; **f22** a pleasant spice tingle. Just lacking the double clotted cream...; **b22.5** the nose tells you that this is distilled Christmas pudding: it cannot be anything else. However you look at it an extraordinary and massively flavoured malt. *52.5%. sc. 70 bottles.*

# DEVIANT DISTILLERY Sandy Bay, Tasmania. Working.

**Deviant Distillery Anthology 10 Single Malt Spirit** Pinot Noir F.O. cask db **(88.5) n22** subtle smoke, sweet and with a minty hue disguises a lack of copper on the spirit; **t22.5** thin delivery at first, then that really outstanding peat works its magic, bringing into play gristy sugars; **f22** sugar and vanilla see us comfortably home, despite some nagging from the still; **b22** a high class bit of eating going on there. *47.5%.*

◈ **Deviant Distillery Anthology 15 Single Malt Spirit** heavily peated px sherry cask db **(89.5) n21 t23 f22.5 b23** Can't say I go a bundle on the nose at this juncture of the spirit's development. But it is certainly fights back on the palate as – and I do not say this either often or lightly – by the PX and smoke appear to complement each other, being superbly weighted and almost attuned to the other. A real surprise treat *47.6%.*

◈ **Deviant Distillery Anthology 16 Single Malt Spirit** Pinot Noir F.O. cask, finished in a coffee cask db **(91.5) n22.5 t23 f23 b23** For those of you looking for a spirit to wake you up first thing in the morning, here it is. You can even dip biscuits in it. Actually, the coffee isn't quite as profound as you might think...but it is there and its subtlety makes it all the more attractive. *43.7%.*

◈ **Deviant Distillery Tri Malt New Make Spirit** db **(93.5) n23 t23.5 f24 b23.5** That, in well over 40 years of visiting distilleries and tasting the juice from their stills, is the sweetest new make I have ever encountered. It is, by any yardstick, extraordinary! *55%.*

# DEVIL'S DISTILLERY Hobart, Tasmania. 2015. Working.

◈ **Hobart Whisky Tasmanian Dark Mofo 2019 Winter Feast Exclusive** ex-bourbon cask, rum maple finish, bott 25 Apr 19 db **(82.5) n20 t22 f20.5 b20** Not sure what to say about this. Far more a liqueur than a whisky in character with the maple dominating the aroma to the cost of all else and the muscular sugars, though attractive, decidedly OTT. *59.1%.*

**Hobart Whisky Tasmanian Single Malt First Release** American oak ex-bourbon cask, bott Aug 18 db **(94) n23.5 t23.5 f23 b24** It always does the soul good when I can report the success of a distillery's bottling of their very first whisky. And for Devil's Distillery, that's exactly what I can do as this, as they might say in that little corner of the planet, is a beaut! Oddly enough, the distillery's very weakness has become, in part, its strength. The lack of evident copper (confirmed on the very last moments of the finish) contributes to a delightful and easily overlooked complexity – a phenomenon we saw with another antipodean whisky two decades ago - Willowbank in New Zealand – and with many rums from around the globe. Their trick, though, has been to distil cleanly and use outstanding American oak. And the Tasmanian sun... A treat of a dram, I must say. *51%.*

⟨⟩ **Hobart Whisky Tasmanian Single Malt Batch 18-002** American oak ex-port cask, bott 16 Nov 18 db **(91)** n23 a sturdy nose with juicy dates and plums mixed with a little molasses; **t22.5** a pretty nose, untamed delivery. So much fruity character, but there is a slight problem in getting the varying factions to work together; **f23** settles down now and maximises the last strains of fruity intensity to balance out against the oaky spice and cocoa; **b22.5** wow! So much packed into one whisky! Takes time to decide which route it wishes to take, but the random journey is fascinating. *53.9%. 216 bottles.*

⟨⟩ **Hobart Whisky Tasmanian Single Malt Batch 19-001** ex-lightly smoked American whisk(e)y cask, bott 8 Feb 19 db **(89.5)** n22.5 cream toffee and green Lapsang Souchong tea...; **t22.5** sticky toffee pudding; a slightly minty middle; **f21.5** back, starkly, to the green tea again..oh, and toffee...! **b23** when they say lightly smoked, they ain't joking. The toffee was a much easier spot... *50.3%. 328 bottles.*

⟨⟩ **Hobart Whisky Tasmanian Single Malt Batch 19-002** ex-bourbon cask, pinot noir finish, bott 25 Apr 19 db **(94)** n23 the only Hobart I can find displaying a crispness to the nose, the fruit brittle and sugar crusted; the tannins have a big say, too; **t24** huge, beautifully manicured and choreographed delivery, the oak really making itself heard in the toastiest manner possible. Yet the muscovado sugars and Manuka honey are on hand to keep control... and balance; **f23.5** raspberry jam on slightly overcooked toast; a little butterscotch as it simmers down; **b23.5** like being hit by the waves of a tropical storm, one flavour smashing into you after another. Just brilliant...! *57.5%.*

⟨⟩ **Hobart Whisky Tasmanian Single Malt Batch 19-003** ex-bourbon cask, French oak port cask finish, bott 25 Apr 19 db **(93.5)** n23 a complex array of oak notes beef up further the big fruit; **t23.5** stunningly luxurious mouth feel: chewy cream toffee with slightly overcooked raisins; **f23.5** back to the big, complex oak, as on the nose. Massively toasty, but the cream toffee come burnt fudge softens the impact; **b23.5** more beautifully intense than a harem... *46.4%.*

⟨⟩ **Hobart Whisky Tasmanian Single Malt Batch 19-004** ex-bourbon cask, bott 25 Apr 19 db **(93)** n23 the distillery's wonderful salted butter house style come to the fore...with plenty of toffee for good measure; **t23.5** fabulous delivery. So much intense malt further sweetened by intense natural cream toffee; the tannins kick hard.. but not too hard...; **f23** much drier finale as the toast gets a little charred; but still that buttery toffee lurks around the edges; **b23.5** how the Devil do they make their bourbon matured malt so buttery...? *55.5%.*

**Tasmanian Moonshine Company Tasmanian Malt Barrel Aged New Make** db **(87)** n21.5 t21.5 f22 b22 The distillery's distinctive shortage of metal within the spirit is apparent on the nose and delivery. But the spirit itself has been well tended to with good cuts and now an excellent oak involvement ensuring a very tasty degree of natural caramels at play. The malt, also, plays a big part. All topped off with decent and busy spice. Attractive. *43%.*

**Tasmanian Moonshine Company Tasmanian Malt Barrel Aged New Make** port cask db **(91.5)** n23 t23 f22.5 b23 Big almost jammy fruit. But that is only half of it: a huge injection of hefty tannin has ensured backbone to the plummy muscle. And as for the spices....? Wow! A huge dose of flavours: this youngster isn't mucking about! *50%.*

# FANNYS BAY DISTILLERY Lulworth, Tasmania. 2014. Working.

⟨⟩ **Fannys Bay Tasmanian Single Malt** bourbon cask, barrel no. 39, bott 2 Oct 18 db **(94.5)** n23 malty and salty; **t24** quite a young one this, but beautifully busy with just the right amount of oils; mouth-watering and juicy; that saltiness helps moisten the drier tannins; the delicious intensity of the barley itself is orgasmic; **f23.5** lots of dark chocolate with the vanillas and throbbing malt taking you to a long, pulsating finish; **b24** no Port. No sherry. Just the wonderful opportunity to taste naked Fannys. This malt, like the island, shapes up perfectly. *64%. sc.*

**Fannys Bay Tasmanian Single Malt** Port cask, barrel no. 9 db **(93)** n23 t23.5 f23 b23.5 There is no fannying around with this big boy... *59%. sc.*

⟨⟩ **Fannys Bay Tasmanian Single Malt** port cask, barrel no. 42, bott 15 Dec 18 db **(89)** n22 a huge mix of tannin and peppery fruit skin; **t22.5** eye-wateringly tight deliver. The sharpness of the fruit is endorsed by the waves of dry tannin pounding in behind; **f22.5** softer fruit and chocolate; **b22** an enjoyable whisky, but with only a fraction of the complexity evident in the bourbon cask. The Port cask doesn't exactly overwhelm, but peppers and tannins apart, seems loth to allow other elements to come into play. Still very enjoyable but distinctly in your face *62%. sc.*

**Fannys Bay Tasmanian Single Malt** sherry cask, barrel no. 8 db **(90)** n22.5 t23 f22 b22.5 Now that's much more like it... *60%. sc.*

⟨⟩ **Fannys Bay Tasmanian Single Malt** sherry cask, barrel no. 35, bott 2 Oct 18 db **(89.5)** n22.5 an agreeable mix of soft fruit and slightly nutty caramel; **t23** surprisingly busy and salivating delivery with a sublime underpinning of muscovado sugars and spice; even the malt goes on a walkabout; **f21.5** just a shade bitter; **b22.5** the finale apart, this is a lightly fruited joy. 63.7%. sc.

## FLEURIEU DISTILLERY Goolwa, South Australia. 2004. Working.

**Fleurieu Distillery Atlantic Crossing** ex-Seppeltsfield Port barrels db **(91)** n22.5 t23 f22.5 **b23** That's better: much better spirit as a starting point, ensuring a more even taste profile. Excellent complexity and weight. 52%. 800 bottles.

**Fleurieu Distillery Bogart & Bacall** Aus "Apera" sherry barrels db **(90.5)** n22.5 t23 f22.5 **b22.5** Great name for a whisky; though having seen every single film Bogart and Bacall ever made together (several times) I think I would have reserved it for a traditional rye matured in virgin oak. Though I suspect this heavily peated number might allude to the fog of cigarette smoke in which the pair were often enshrouded. Anyways, you know how to taste, don't you? You just put your lips together...and suck. 61.2%. 270 bottles.

**Fleurieu Distillery River's End** ex-Seppeltsfield Port barrels db **(83.5)** n21 t21.5 f20 b21 The Port does the business early on, but even some robust grape has problems dealing with some average make. 53%. 200 bottles.

**Fleurieu Distillery The Rubicon** ex-Seppeltsfield Port barrels db **(89)** n22.5 t22.5 f22 **b22** A muscular whisky with some big flavour egos at work. When they gel, there are some magical moments. 55%. 500 bottles.

## HEARTWOOD DISTILLERS North Hobart, Tasmania. Working.

**Heartwood 3of/3** cask no. LD 643, vatted Jan 14, bott Jan 17 **(94)** n24 t23.5 f23 b23.5 Seemingly distilled by Zeus...this comes across as significantly older than Bill Lark's jokes... which until now hadn't seemed possible. 67.5%. sc. 125 bottles.

**Heartwood @#$% · &\*** 2nd fill Port cask, 2 x 1st fill sherry finish, cask no. TD0124, filled Aug 06, bott May 17 **(96)** n23.5 &%%\*+A!$ · &%$% \*\* · $+A fruit; **t24** fruit \* · $( (££A · $& %!\* · \*; **f24** $%&A)_ · spices · · A(£++\* ·; **b24.5** just f\*£%ing &%A\*)+$ 62.5%. sc. 337 bottles.

## HELLYERS ROAD Havenview, Tasmania. 1999. Working.

◇ **Hellyers Road Aged 8 Years Pinot Noir Finish** db (86.5) n22 t22 f21 b21.5 It may sound a little strange, but the Pinot Noir cask was a little too much for the whisky itself, refusing to let the malt have a meaningful presence. The result was an attractive but lop-sided feel. 61.6%. Master Series.

**Hellyers Road Henry's Legacy Wey River** American oak casks, Pinot Noir finish db **(88.5)** n22.5 t23 f21 b22 Wey River...? Thought for a moment we had our first whisky from my native county of Surrey...! Mouth-watering and entirely presentable single malt enlivened and enriched by an exceptionally healthy wine cask which has imparted just the right degree of sharpness and weight. Good spices, also. 60.8%.

**Hellyers Road Single Malt Whisky 12 Year Old Original** db (84.5) n19 t22 f21.5 b22. Forget the nose and get stuck into the massive malt. 46.2%.

**Hellyers Road Single Malt Whisky Henry's Legacy 'The Gorge'** db (83) n21.5 t21 f20 **b20.5.** Eye-wateringly sharp in places, its best bits hang on a vaguely smoky, molasses-sweetened coffee note. 46.2%.

**Hellyers Road Single Malt Whisky Original** db (84) n20.5 t22 f20.5 b21. Bolstered on last year's bottling thanks to a profound malt surge on delivery. Citrus fruity in part, but both nose and the tingle at the finish demands more copper. 46.2%.

◇ **Hellyers Road Original Aged 15 Years** db (92.5) n23.5 nectarines at full ripeness; t23.5 beautifully clean delivery: a gorgeous combination of grassy malt and muscovado sugars; shimmering oils plus a little salt; f22.5 some very good oak in play giving us a confident, praline-laden send-off; **b23** almost, literally, a peach of a whisky from Hellyers... the most deft whisky ever from this distillery. 46.2%.

◇ **Hellyers Road Original Aged 16 Years** db (90.5) n22 hang on chaps: this nose is warning that this malt might go gangbusters...; **t23** holy cow...!!! Yes, it most certainly does. All prisoners are dead and it is the malt and orange blossom honey which marches on triumphant, flame throwers at the ready...; **f22.5**...and as if nothing has happened, the chocolates are offered round..; **b23** put on your tin hats for this one – there is shrapnel everywhere... Carnage...and it's delicious..! 66.8%. Master Series.

◇ **Hellyers Road Peated** db **(91)** n22.5 that seems like pretty high octane phenols. But the usual Hellyers punctuation keeps you sniffing with a quizzical look; **t23.5** stunningly rich delivery with just about perfect weight and oiliness; soft heather honey makes for a superb mid point; **f22** the honey sticks around – literally – and now we go into smoky milk chocolate mode; **b23** Hellyers offers a unique character in its own right. Put some pretty full-on peat into the mix and you are left with one of the most idiosyncratic whiskies in the world. And a sheer, if at times perplexing, delight...! 46.2%.

**Hellyers Road Slightly Peated Aged 10 Years** db **(91.5) n23 t23 f22.5 b23** Hellyers Road has come of age in every sense: the lack of copper in their system that held them back for so long has now been mostly overcome by a mix of peat and extremely high quality oak. This is a quietly spoken little beaut. Congratulations all round: it has been a long journey... 46.2%.

 **Hellyers Road Peated Aged 14 Years** db **(87.5) n22 t23.5 f21 b21** Despite the enormity of the peat, the sheer chutzpa of the strength and sweetness for a brief few moments have you at a point of near ecstasy, the technical gremlins are still there and make themselves heard at the finish. But, my word! What a ride!!! 63%. Master Series.

**Hellyers Road Single Malt Whisky Port Matured** db **(88) n22.5 t23 f20.5 b22** Without question the direction this distillery should take. Some wonderful moments. 46.2%.

**Hellyers Road Single Malt Whisky Port Matured** db **(89.5) n23 t23 f21 b22.5** An absolutely top dog wine cask has done a splendid job on this malt. Impressive. And, what's more, Australia haven't lost a wicket – and even scored 28 runs - in all the time it took me to taste this... 48.9%

**Hellyers Road Single Malt Whisky Saint Valentine's Peak** db **(85.5) n22.5 t22 f20 b21** Regular readers of Jim Murray's Whisky Bible know that I traditionally taste the Australian whisky during the First Test of an Ashes series, if one is being played – which seems like every six months in recent years. So it is fitting I tasted St Valentine's on the day of a massacre – the Aussies are currently 128-6 in their second innings, still needing almost 300 more runs to win. This malt has done a lot better than Clarke's sorry mob. Still pretty rough towards the finish, the gorgeous fruit effect on the nose works well into the delivery. At least the last embers show some coffee cake attractiveness. Now, I'd better hurry up with the remaining Aussie whiskies before Broad and Co bring the game to an early close on just the 4th day...60.1%

## KILLARA Kingston, Tasmania. 2016. Working.

 **Killara Distillery KD01 Cask Strength** ex-port barrel db **(94) n24** incredibly salty, phenomenally rich, cleverly spiced, playfully fruity....and mesmerically enticing...; **t24** I think that scores as just about the perfect delivery. The Port part is faultlessly clean and lush, flinging rich fruit at you from all angles, the oaky back up is just severe enough to remind you this isn't all about the barrel; a superb spiced chocolate midpoint; **f22.5** a long moan of chocolate and raisin; **b23.5** now, that is impressive! And that's what I call a whisky! 64.5%. 1st Release.

 **Killara Distillery KD02** ex-port barrel db **(94.5) n23** a musky depth to this; plum and dates with a superb black pepper background; **t24** maple syrup and plums mix for a salivating and serene start. Almost immediately waves of toasty tannins arrive as do the serious spices; **f23.5** mmmm... that is one long finish. The house cocoa-rich finale sits delightfully with the butterscotch and ulmo honey tannin; **b24** a very chewable and entertaining malt just dripping with flavour. 50%.

 **Killara Distillery KD03** ex-sherry barrel db **(90.5) n23** moist fruit cake but with a drier vanilla thread acting almost like a muffler; **t23** a sumptuous, oily mouth feel does no harm on either favour intensity or length But always feels it is operating within itself with a soft toffee raisin chorus; **f22** the vanillas are back calling the shots; **b22.5** a genteel and understated whisky. 46%.

## LARK DISTILLERY Hobart, Tasmania. 1992. Working.

 **Lark Single Malt Whisky Cask Strength** db **(94) n23** weighty with plenty of natural caramels to complement the malt; **t24** there can't be a taste bud that isn't left unmolested and by the mix of industrial strength heather honey and malt. Muscular, oily, fabulously spiced and molten muscovado sugars; **f23.5** at last the vanillas get a foot hold, as do far crisper Demerara sugars; **b23.5** sweet, profound and with jaw-aching chewability. 58%.

 **Lark Single Malt Whisky Classic Cask** db **(89) n22** weighty with plenty of natural caramels to complement the malt; **t23** rich, chewy with something of a toffee apple juiciness; **f21.5** oily; slightly bitters out; **b22.5** another slightly more full-bodied version. 43%.

 **Lark Single Malt Whisky Distillers Selection Heavily Peated Port Cask** cask no. LD1016 db **(87) n21.5 t22.5 f21 b22** A massive soup of a malt. Not quite as heavily peated as some I have experienced from Lark, and the wide cut gives a degree of oiliness which helps the lush fruit and lighter smoke meld together. Seriously big stuff but not quite so technically on the ball as usual. 46%. sc. 89 bottles.

 **Lark Single Malt Whisky Rum Finish** db **(89.5) n22** quite unusual: intense oily malt, with a peppery, cooked crab spiciness all kept within a thin sugary lid; **t23.5** spectacularly huge, with a fruity peppery attack from the first moment. The malt then explodes onto the scene with stunning dash, again with a sugary accompaniment; **f22** again the big oils make themselves heard; **b22.5** and again a slightly wide cut – but, again, so much personality and flavour! 55%.

**The Beagle Tasmanian Vatted Malt Whisky** batch no. 2, bott Aug 14 db **(95) n23 t24 t23.5 b24.5** Another ridiculously fine whisky from Australia. 68.3%. 160 bottles.

⟡ **Heartwood** @#$%· &*4 bourbon PX finish, cask nos. LD 813 & LD 823, bott 18 Oct 18 (89.5) **n23** dripping in a lush dates; **t23** oily and thick, and not just from the powering PX; **f21** well spiced up but tangy; **b22.5** this @*$%· &*4 differs from their @#$%'&* because of the @%&$· 6 and everyone knows I think *@· %%8!!!! of PX casks....55.4%. 181 bottles.

⟡ **Heartwood Night Thief** sherry cask, cask nos. LD 654 & LD 775, bott Apr 18 (95.5) **n24** faultless fruit...as clean as it comes. And so well defined, the smoke does not appear immediately...your nose has to acclimatise. But when you finally spot it and notice how well its wraps itself around the grape, its drier tones nestling into the sweeter sherry...; then up the volume and wow factor by applying the Murray Method...; a lovely astringent nibble on the nose...; **t24** huge. Just bloody huge. Faultless sherry. Breathtakingly muscular peat, yet in total harmony...just try and imagine it. Or, better still try it...! The mid-ground is just brimming with muscovado sugars and the smokiest plum jam imaginable. Oh, and fizzing spice...; **f24** there is a minty coolness to the proceedings now, but the grape and peat lean against each other, offering harmonious support, **b24** though distilled at the other end of the planet, and nearly 40 years on, this bottling took me back to the very early 1980s, when I tasted a sample of Lagavulin while sitting in the distillery manager's office, the dark liquid before me having been extracted from a rare fresh sherry butt - not the normal way of maturing that great whisky in those long ago days. These days, from painful experience, not a great fan of wine and peat together. This, though is on another level: the way it should be... 64.3%. 299 bottles.

**Heartwood Shade of Night Single Malt** sherry cask, cask no. LD 653, filled Sept 10, bott Mar 18 (96) **n24 t24 f24 b24** Another enormous whisky of great beauty and from Bill Lark. Think I'll be sending Bill a bill for the extraordinary likeness of me on the label... though when you look at the exact strength, no doubt he'll be telling me to go to the (Tasmanian) devil... 66.6%. sc. 280 bottles.

⟡ **Heartwood Shot in the Dark** Australian muscat cask, cask nos. LD 961, dist Nov 13, bott Mar 19 (95) **n23.5** x-certificate heaviness with the grapes on best behaviour yet still pretty enormous with an underlying smoke not only gives further depth and weight but fills in all the gaps; **t24** a four pipe delivery as you spend an age trying to chew your way to the bottom of this monster. The delivery itself is sweet enough, toasty molasses at the fore, but there is liquorice, spice...and then a swamp of over-ripe plums to navigate...gosh! **f23.5** hope you have time to spare as this whisky doesn't go away easily. The fruit and spices hang around; a hickory-led phenol note ensures gravitas, while an overcooked treacle tart does the rest... **b24** for a shot in the dark, this hit bullseye. Anyway, after tasting that I need to lie down. I'm exhausted... 58.9%. sc. 334 bottles.

# LAUNCESTON DISTILLERY Western Junction, Tasmania. 2013. Working.

⟡ **Launceston Distillery Tasmanian Single Malt Whisky** batch no. H17-05, ex-Tawny French oak port casks db (93) **n22.5** busy and intriguing. A slight lemon drop sharpness to the fruit helps break up the weight of the oak; **t23** the kind of delivery that makes you inwardly sigh with pleasure! Really lush grape and just the right degree of bruyerre honey to allow the oak a meaningful say; **f23.5** resounding waves of liquorice and muscovado sugars that lap long and contentedly against the light spices and chalky tannins; **b24** a big whisky quite wonderfully controlled. 46%. 668 bottles.

⟡ **Launceston Distillery Tasmanian Single Malt Whisky** batch no. H17-06, Apera French oak Australian sherry casks db (86) **n21.5 t22 f21 b21.5** French oak can be tight, dry and notoriously hard to handle in fast maturation. Here it seems to have taken just a bit too much of a tight grip of proceedings, resulting in just a little a shade too much puckering, despite the chunky fruit. 46%. 512 bottles.

⟡ **Launceston Distillery Tasmanian Single Malt Whisky** batch no. H17-07, bourbon casks db (92.5) **n22.5** gristy malt and shortcake biscuit; **t23.5** a velvety delivery of malt at its most refined, cream toffee, hickory and a thin stratum of ulmo honey; **f23** the vanillas complement the spices beautifully; **b23.5** seemingly quiet on the palate, but complex and very classy. 46%. 392 bottles.

⟡ **Launceston Distillery Tasmanian Single Malt Whisky Cask Strength** batch no. H17-08, bourbon casks db (94) **n23** concentrated barley puffs out its chest with pride, as well it has to. For high quality tannin is breathing down its back; **t24** that is beautiful: really beautiful! The delivery is helped by having maximum intact oils present, which give a lustre to the ulmo honey and intense barley grist which makes the delivery memorable for all the right reasons. Spices also arrive quickly, so the tannins, like on the nose, are not far behind; **f23** bit oaky fade but with excellent molasses to balance things; **b24** have to say, chaps: this is jolly good...! 62%. 225 bottles.

⟡ **Launceston Distillery Tasmanian Single Malt Whisky Cask Strength** batch no. H17-09, Tawny casks db (91) **n22.5** throbbing, pulsing tannin; **t23.5** the fruit, entirely overshadowed but the oak on the nose, is up first and running on delivery. A complex display of green apples, black cherry and kiwi fruit all combine with a mix of spice and intense mocha for the brilliant middle; **f22** calms, but dries as the oak re-stakes its claim; **b22.5** compared to their other Tawny cask offering, this has allowed the tannins to go a little too wild, thus messing with the delicate harmony. Still some whisky, mind! *63%. 200 bottles.*

## LIMEBURNERS Albany, Western Australia. 2014. Working.

**Limeburners Single Malt Whisky Darkest Winter** ex-bourbon American oak cask, barrel no. M348 db **(96.5) n24 t24.5 f24 b24** Whatever you do, DON'T add water: you'll absolutely wreck the intricate oils which set this whisky apart and makes this fabulous malt tick, as well as ensuring a rougher ride. *65.1%. ncf sc.*

**Limeburners Single Malt Whisky Directors Cut** Australian port cask finish, barrel no. M230 db **(95) n23.5 t24 f23.5 b24** A little bit of Western Australian magic with not a single tang, off-note or any sense of disproportion. Magnificent! *59.5%. ncf sc. 202 bottles.*

## NANT DISTILLERY Bothwell, Tasmania. 2008. Working.

⬦ **Nant Distillery Single Malt Whisky Port Cask** cask no. 793 db **(94) n23.5** dry Brazilian biscuit buttressed by bruyerre and lime blossom honey; a light smattering of barley, too; **t24** silky-soft delivery with a ridiculously charming degree of ulmo honey and barley; a light fruitiness drifts in almost as an afterthought; **f22.5** just a little bitterness creeps into the vanilla ice cream with lemon topping; **b24** beautifully made and matured. The strength means a dreamy, super-soft malt has been created; at a fuller strength the finish would have had some extra sugars to see it through. Beautiful, nonetheless.. *43%. sc.*

⬦ **Nant Distillery Single Malt Whisky White Oak Cask** cask no. 951 db **(94.5) n23** dry. Big oak signature with ginger and allspice ramping up the oaky credentials; **t24.5** a soft malt and Lubeck marzipan delivery boasts labyrinthine layering. The barley is still friable and salivating while the background tannins pulse with red liquorice, kirsch and heather honey: truly superb...; **f23** the small forest of tannin evident in the later stages underscores a slight oaky imbalance but there is enough charm and charisma in the malt and vanilla-rich bank for no damage to be done; **b24** some of the passages in this malt as good as any Australian malt you are likely to taste. Just brilliantly distilled. *43%. sc.*

## NEW WORLD WHISKY DISTILLERY Melbourne, Victoria. 20070. Working.

⬦ **Starward Nova Single Malt Australian Whisky** red wine barrels, bott code: L1 19053 db **(87) n22 t22 f21.5 b21.5** Clean, thin and winey. But some superb spices do offer a narrative. *41%.*

⬦ **Starward Two Fold Double Grain Australian Whisky** Australian red wine barrels, bott code: 181130-A db **(84.5) n21.5 t22 f20.5 b20.5** When wine casks have this much impact on a whisky, it really has to be bottled at full strength to maintain its integrity. At this low strength the oils have been compromised and we are left with a little too much of a grape juice effect. Pleasant, for sure. But needs more structure and complexity. *40%.*

## NONESUCH DISTILLERY Hobart, Tasmania. 2007. Working.

⬦ **Nonesuch Tasmanian Single Malt** ex-bourbon barrel, cask no. 3 db **(87) n22 t22 f21 b22** As a child I grew up about a mile, as the parakeet flies, from Nonsuch Park in Surrey, a place which always held an air of mystery for me. So, intrigued to discovery its near namesake whisky from down under. This is quite a perfumed article with the toasty oak holding a tight hold over the caramel. Enjoyable, but needs to relax a little. *46.9%. sc.*

## OLD HOBART DISTILLERY Hobart, Tasmania. 2007. Working.

⬦ **Overeem Single Malt Whisky Port Cask** cask no. OHD-178 db **(94.5) n23.5** the Port virtually bounces off the barley giving a glorious lucidity to the grape; **t24** eye-wateringly bright on delivery: crisp and angular fruits combine with busy spice to make for one of Australia's most mouth-watering deliveries; **f23** a little liquorice blends with the fruit and barley; excellent vanilla and spice fade; **b24** one of those rare malts where a lot happens, but does so organically and with every shift in the gears getting the taste buds revving. *60%. sc.*

## OLD KEMPTON DISTILLERY Redlands, Tasmania. 2013. Working.

⬦ **Old Kempton Distillery Single Malt** French oak cask, cask no. FC01 db **(88) n22.5 t22 f21.5 b22** Easy going, fruity but curiously lacking body and depth. Good spice and rumbling tannin, though. *46%.*

⬦ **Old Kempton Distillery Single Malt** Pinot Noir cask, cask no. RD032 db **(85.5) n21.5 t22 f21 b21** This is the other side of the wine cask coin, when the fruit takes over with a little too much gusto and results in a juicy but rather flat experience. The peppery spices offer most of the limited entertainment. 46%. sc.

⇜ **Old Kempton Distillery Single Malt** Tokay cask, cask no. RD023 db **(91)** n22.5 t23 f22.5 **b23** So many Tokay casks through the years have been wasted in the whisky world through being sulphur treated. No such worry here as the fruit gets a free hand to weave its intense, almost citrusy, magic on this malt. Just love the creaminess to this whisky and the busy, prattling spices which prevent things becoming a little too comfortable. A very satisfying experience. 46%. sc.

**Redlands Distillery Single Malt** bourbon cask, cask no. RD114 #8 db **(96)** n24 t24 f23.5 **b24.5** That rarest of whiskies out of Australia: a malt whisky matured exclusively in ex-bourbon cask with no wine cask interference. Who would have thought of such a novel way of maturing beautiful whisky? Just wish it would happen more often. Don't suppose that such an outrageous maturation method will catch on, though... 64%. sc.

**Tasmania Independent Bottlers Redlands Release Single Malt 2** Port cask, cask no. TIB RD 009, bott Feb 18 **(78)** n19 t19.5 f20.5 b19 A little while since I last tasted Redlands. I certainly don't remember the feints which play such a prominent role on both the nose and delivery. The Port cask does its best to heal the wounds. The worst of the feints disappear with a little continuous warming. 49.6%. sc.

**Tasmania Independent Bottlers Redlands Single Malt Release 3** Muscat cask, cask no. TIB RD 002, bott Feb 18 **(90.5)** n22.5 t22.5 f22.5 b23 At times thick enough to stand a spoon in. Unconventional, yet the results are beautiful. 49.1%. sc.

⇜ **Tasmania Independent Bottlers Old Kempton Redlands Release 4** port cask, cask no. TIB RD 0013, bott Jun 18 **(92)** n22.5 a light cocoa note: a bit like a chocolate liqueur freshly bitten into; t23 sharp, lively and crisp, the fruit is offered a third dimension by some ranting spices; a kind of apple, grape and melon salad maximises the juiciness; f23 just love the ways the spices lightly pulse while the fruit becomes even more crystaline...; b23.5 never quite gets into its stride until a bit of the Murray Method magic is applied – then becomes a very different, and delicious, proposition... 47.7%. sc.

⇜ **Tasmania Independent Bottlers Old Kempton Redlands Release 5** muscat cask, cask no. TIB RD 0014, bott Aug 18 **(87.5)** n21 t23.5 f21.5 b21.5 The fruit on this is big enough to form a small but very sweet planet. However, there are a few feints nibbling away in the background just making inroads into the balance and overall structure. 48%. sc.

⇜ **Tasmania Independent Bottlers Old Kempton Redlands Release 8** muscat cask, cask no. TIB RD 0012, bott Nov 18 **(89.5)** n22.5 heavy duty fruit with spices to match; t23 good grief...! The tongue has to battle through the rich textured fruit, with the grape providing more weight than the tannins! f22 dries out until the spices bite; b22.5 very enjoyable though not quite as sweet as I remember their singular muscat bottling from last year. But still a three courser... 46.8%. sc.

# SHENE ESTATE DISTILLERY Pontville, Tasmania. 2014. Working.
⇜ **Mackey Tasmanian Single Malt** Apera sherry French oak cask db **(90.5)** n22.5 fond memories of 1970s Sherry Trifles...; t23 a glorious delivery: the fruit has a oiliness all its own on which muscovado sugars, mocha and spices hang: superb! f22.5 a light barley and vanilla development as a little controlled bitterness creeps in; b22.5 lush! 49%. Shene Release 3.

⇜ **Mackey Tasmanian Single Malt** Tawny port French oak cask db **(81)** n21.5 t22 f18.5 b19 Still a shoot on sight policy from this distillery, which at times seems to combine astonishing oak influence with less than perfect distillate. The nose, for instance, offers a little tobacco on toast and golden syrup before the mouth-engulfing delivery, the sugars and fruit closely knitted. But the finish is a disappointment as bitterness and the tobacco return. 49%. Shene Release 2.

# SOUTHERN COAST DISTILLERS Adelaide, South Australia. 2014. Closed.
⇜ **Southern Coast Single Malt Batch 007** db **(94.5)** n24 t23 f23.5 b24 This has to be the most rum oriented whisky on the planet. I thought their previous bottlings had to be slightly freakish: nothing could be that Guyana-Demerara style on purpose. But here we go again, with its massive esters. Stunning bruyere honey on both nose and delivery and light red liquorice for back up. But then those unmistakable rum notes strike, metallic almost. Superb. 46%. ncf.

# SPRING BAY DISTILLERY Spring Beach, Tasmania. 2015. Working.
⇜ **Spring Bay Tasmanian Single Malt Whisky Bourbon Cask** cask no. 34, dist 2016 db **(90.5)** n22.5 the tannins are winning the arm wrestle here: light barley and lime blossom honey offer a deft citrusy touch; t23 engaging clean barley with a lovely juicy thread; f22 the oak and spice arrive in good time and without fuss; b23 a slight step up from their last bourbon cask, if I remember it correctly, the sugars more even and confident. An elegant malt 46%. sc.

⬧ **Spring Bay The Rheban Cask Strength Tasmanian Single Malt Whisky Port Cask** cask no. 37, dist 2016 db **(94) n23.5** think a fruit cake where someone has gone nuts with the plums...; **t23.5** the clarity to the grape could almost make you weep with joy! Muscovado sugars and molasses in there big time, then we are back to rich plum puddings. Just...wow! **f23** long, with the oak getting a word in edgeways, offering a little spice now it is here; **b24** a plum whisky...in every sense... *58%. sc.*

⬧ **Spring Bay Tasmanian Single Malt Whisky Sherry Cask** cask no. 47, dist 2016 db **(87.5) n22 t22 f22 b21.5** Nothing particularly wrong with this. No off notes. Decent fruit in all the right places. Just.. well... dull! *46%. sc.*

# SULLIVANS COVE DISTILLERY Cambridge, Tasmania. 1995. Working.

**Sullivans Cove American Oak** 200 litre American oak bourbon cask, barrel no. HH0502, dist 29 Sept 00, bott 09 Jun 17 db **(88.5) n22.5 t22.5 f21 b22.5** Tasting this directly after watching France beat Australia 2-1 in the World Cup. Ironic Sullivan's Cove uses a convict's badge as their motif, as the Aussies were clearly robbed! VAR used to get make an initially correct decision wrong. The defender touched the ball, so no penalty. Football needs intrusive technology like whisky needs sulphur. Anyway, don't need technology to tell me this is a highly enjoyable if slightly over-oiled dram. *46%. sc.*

⬧ **Sullivans Cove American Oak** 200 litre American oak barrel, cask no. TD0144, filled 22 Sept 06, bott 14 Dec 18 db **(82) n20.5 t21.5 f19 b21** Didn't get the cuts quite right on this one. Bitter in part but some lovely toffee thread, too. *47.5%. sc.*

**Sullivans Cove American Oak Cask Strength** 200 litre American oak bourbon cask, barrel no. TD0126, dist 11 Aug 06, bott 07 Nov 17 db **(93.5) n23.5 t24 f23 b23.5** Hard to believe that this whisky and that of cask TD0172 are in any way related...sheesh! This is the real Tasmania Distillery standing up...! *69.1%. sc.*

**Sullivans Cove Double Cask** batch no. DC095, dist 29 May 08, bott 06 Oct 17 db **(78) n19 t21 f19 b19** The casks and spirit only make for an unhappy combination. *49.6%. ncf.*

⬧ **Sullivans Cove Double Cask** batch no. DC098, youngest barrel filled 12 Dec 07, youngest barrel decanted 24 Jan 18 db **(86.5) n21 t22 f21 b21.5** A silky, initially sweet malt, but limited development and complexity with the two casks seemingly cancelling each other out a little. *45%.*

**Sullivans Cove French Oak** 300 litre French oak Tawny Port cask, barrel no. HH0516, dist 12 Dec 00, bott 14 Apr 17 db **(87) n22.5 t23 f20.5 b21** An unfortunate late furry bitterness undoes some great work by the fruity muscovado sugars and firm oak. *47.5%. sc.*

**Sullivans Cove French Oak** 300 litre French oak Tawny Port cask, barrel no. TD0312, dist 22 Aug 08, bott 01 May 17 db **(93) n23 t23.5 f23 b23.5** Few can handle French oak better than Sullivan's Cove: these bottlings are always one of my highlights of the year! *47.5%. sc.*

⬧ **Sullivans Cove Double Cask** 300 litre French oak barrel, cask no. TD0269, filled 17 Apr 08, bott 1 Nov 18 db **(94.5) n23.5** abounds with kumquats and bursting gooseberries; **t24** one of the deliveries of the year – an even better one than the one by Archer that removed Finch in the World Cup semi-final being played now. Not just the most taste bud jabbing fruit known to mankind, but a voluptuous, slightly creamy mouthfeel that makes your mouth feel it is being kissed and caressed while prodded into full blown salivation; the paradox is delicious, and even more so as a little muscovado sugar leaks into the mix; **f23** much drier and borderline bitter as we hit the pomace; **b24** ooh, la la....! *47.5%. sc.*

⬧ **Sullivans Cove Special Cask** 200 litre ex-Muscat French oak barrel, cask no. TD0228, filled 29 Dec 07, bott 26 Sept 18 db **(92) n23.5** I could nose this all day: not a flaw to the grape, not a tremble in its song. Both intense yet fluty and flighty – very unusual indeed; **t23.5** fabulous...just fabulous! The malt bursts through despite the juicy prologue of the grape; **f22** dries with surprising haste; late arriving tannin-rich spice; **b23** some of the fruitier moments on this you want to revisit time and time again. Lovely stuff! *50%. sc.*

# TIMBOON RAILWAY SHED DISTILLERY Timboon, Victoria. 2007. Working.

**Timboon Single Malt Whisky Christie's Cut** dist 14 Apr 14, bott 01 Mar 18 db **(95) n24 t24 f23 b24** A way better version than the last Christie's Cut I sampled, the balance and all round oomph coming up trumps big time. *60%.*

**Timboon Single Malt Whisky Governor's Reserve** dist 2 May 14, bott 22 Jan 18 db **(71) n18 t19 f17 b17** Most un-Timboonish. The intense citrus on the nose is way too severe and is completely off road from the moment it touches the palate. Every bit as awful as their Christie's Cut is delicious. *48.8%.*

# TIN SHED DISTILLING COMPANY Adelaide, South Australia. 2013. Working.

**Iniquity Gold Label Single Malt Batch 003** db **(92) n23 t23 t22.5 b23.5** The Australians appear to have buttoned that amazing Total Grape Effect, right down to the pips: no other country produces anything even close. So if you like that mega grape effect (and, yes: entirely sulphur free!) then here's another uncompromising belter for you. *60%. ncf.*

⬧ **Iniquity Gold Label Single Malt Batch 004** db **(95)** n23 a stirringly dry crushed pips and all fruitiness adds both a flourish and depth to the heather honey, as well as delightful layering; **t24.5** fabulous delivery: the nose is turned up to full volume, except really it is the honey-sugar mix – a magnificent marriage between heather honey and golden syrup – is in total harmony with the spectacular noble rot grape and oaky vanilla; **f23.5** light spices add a slight bristle to gentle easing of the intense honey; a little marzipan and tannin; **b24** unquestionably Gold is the gold standard of Tin Shed's output. And I have never experienced anything so 24 carat from them than this honey monster... *60%. ncf.*

**Iniquity Single Malt Batch 008** db **(82)** n20 t21 f20.5 b20.5 When the heavy nougat out performs the fruit, then you know they didn't quite have the cuts on the still right. *46%. ncf.*

**Iniquity Single Malt Batch 009** db **(87)** n21.5 t22 f21.5 b22 Much more like it! Just enough oils off the still to really give weight and length. The mid-point offers an intriguing and delicious chocolate fruit cake. *46%. ncf.*

**Iniquity Single Malt Batch 010** db **(88)** n21.5 t22.5 f21.5 b22.5 Hard to know whether to drink it, chew it or name an astronomer after it... A malt of substance. *46%. ncf.*

**Iniquity Single Malt Batch 011** db **(90.5)** n22 t23 f22.5 b23 A beautifully distilled whisky bursting from the bottle with character. *46%. ncf.*

⬧ **Iniquity Single Malt Batch 012** db **(86)** n21.5 t23 f20 b21.5 No faulting the taste profile or intensity of flavour on delivery. Rich with ulmo honey and marzipan, and no little malt. But the feints are too loud on both nose and finish. *46%. ncf.*

⬧ **Iniquity Single Malt Batch 013** db **(84.5)** n20.5 t22 f21.5 b20.5 The drying tobacco leaf on the nose suggests an overenthusiastic cut. And while it struggles for balance throughout, the odd decent honey note springs up in Tin Shed fashion to offer the odd attractive warble. *46%. ncf.*

⬧ **Iniquity Single Malt Batch 014** db **(92.5)** n22.5 marzipan and lemon jelly; **t23.5** a gorgeous ulmo honey delivery, impeccably backed up by malt concentrate; **f23** lovely oak-enriched spice, mocha and malt; **b23.5** voluminous and voluptuous. Complex, too. *46%. ncf.*

⬧ **Iniquity Single Malt Batch 015** db **(84)** n20.5 t21 f21.5 b21 Wow! The feints have returned with a vengeance. A little delightful chocolate nougat cheers up the otherwise uncomfortable malt. *46%. ncf.*

# WHIPPER SNAPPER DISTILLERY Perth, Western Australia. 2012. Working

⬧ **Project Q Quinoa Whiskey** batch no. 1, ex-Upshot barrels db **(79.5)** n19 t22 f19 b19 Is this a whisky? Or whiskey, as they prefer? To be called such you much be distilled from grain. This, it appears, is distilled from seeds, which I suppose from a biological perspective is the same thing. But there are seeds, such as oranges, tomatoes – humans even – that you really cannot distil from. So perhaps it has to be cereal grain that produces whisky. And this is from a plant. A messy conundrum. But let's give this the benefit of the doubt and analyse it anyway: well, there is little to attract you to the soapy nose (unless you are big into quinoa) but there is much more on offer on delivery, which starts patchily but then hits its stride with some wonderful golden syrup notes. But then the finish is pure quinoa...I think. And that doesn't appear to be a good thing. Well, not on this evidence... *46.5%. sc.*

⬧ **Upshot Australian Whiskey Single Barrel** barrel no. 56 db **(90.5)** n22.5 a gentle , unassuming mix of demerara sugars and vanilla, **t23** again, it's all about the sugars: a light heather honey lead, followed by a red and black liquorice depth; **f22** a little thin. Big vanilla, but a slight bitterness, too; **b23** a well-made, delightful whiskey but suffering from the lack of oils which is so well exploited by their game-changing, landmark 64% bottling. *43%. sc.*

⬧ **Upshot Australian Whiskey Cask Strength Single Barrel** batch no. 1 db **(94.5)** n23.5 the most Kentuckian of noses with a magnificent depth to the Manuka honey and tannin...; oh, and the quality of the distillate....just stunning! **t24** that is sensational! The honey promised on the nose comes through though distilled by bees. New Zealand Manuka and Corsican Bruyere meet head on and in concentrated form is thickened further by lashings of liquorice; **f23** delightfully tart, the tannins are at their roastiest with hickory and mocha aplenty. But not for a moment is there even the hint of a hint of hint of bitterness...which is pretty remarkable; **b24** it has long been the tradition of the Whisky Bible to taste Australian whisky – or whiskey – on the first morning of an Ashes series. And here I am doing this again with the Aussies at 35-3. An interesting series with barely a batting side between the two teams, I won't be taking that early devastation of the Baggy Greens' top order to mean anything just yet. But I will say that if Australia need to discover how to put together something big and meaningful, with a fabulous start and carrying on from there, they could do worse than study this beaut. Western Australia now, by the way, appears to be in Kentucky... *64%. sc.*

# European Whisky

The debate about what it means to be European was one that seemingly never ended. That was until June 23rd 2016 when the people of Britain firmly decided that it should and they weren't. By contrast, the discussion on how to define the character of a European whisky is only just beginning.

And as more and more distilleries open throughout mainland Europe, Scandinavia, even Israel the styles are becoming wider and wider. Those of the British Isles have even grown large enough to warrant their own chapter in the Whisky Bible, though their awards will be linked in with Europe for now.

Small distillers in mainland Europe, especially those in the Alpine area, share common ground with their US counterparts in often coming late into whisky. Their first love, interest and spirit had been with fruit brandies. It seemed that if something grew in a tree or had a stone when you bit into it, you could be pretty confident that someone in Austria or California was making a clear, eye-watering spirit from it somewhere.

So perhaps it is not surprising that the whiskies which each year seem now to get the highest and most consistent marks are those built purely with whisky in mind. Mackmyra in Sweden. Penderyn in Wales. The aged whiskies representing Gold Cock in the Czech Republic came from state-built distilleries when the land was still Czechoslovakia. The most impressive whisky I have encountered in mainland Europe this year has come from Denmark. Thy, with their Whisky No 9, scooped European Whisky of the Year (Multiple Casks) pipping fellow Danes Stauning, whose rye was just a half point behind. The overall European Award went to Penderyn's Madeira Single Cask.

There is a pattern now: every year I taste certain whiskies and I know there will be a professionalism to their consistency. They tend to be from distilleries which have invested heavily in both their stills, usually (though not always) moving away from the German type which is harder to control, and their casks. Langatun of Switzerland, Belgium Owl, Kornog of France, Domaine Mavela of Corsica, Sweden's Mackmyra, Stauning of Denmark and certain others have set the bar.... and just keep increasing the height.

| European Whisky of the Year Winners | | |
|---|---|---|
| | **European Whisky Multiple Casks** | **European Whisky Single Cask** |
| 2004 | **Waldviester Hafer Whisky 2000** | N/A |
| 2005 | **Hessicher Whisky** | N/A |
| 2006 | **Swissky Exklusiv Abfullung** | N/A |
| 2007 | **Mackmyra Preludium 03 Svensk** | N/A |
| 2008 | **Mackmyra Privus 03 Svensk** | N/A |
| 2009 | **Old Buck 2nd Release (Finland)** | N/A |
| 2010 | Santis Malt Highlander Dreifaltaigheit | **Penderyn Port Wood Single Cask** |
| 2011 | **Mackmyra Brukswhisky** | The Belgian Owl Aged 44 Months |
| 2012 | Mackmyra Moment "Urberg" | **Penderyn Bourbon Matured SC** |
| 2013 | **Penderyn Portwood Swansea** | Hicks & Healey 2004 |
| 2014 | **Mackmyra "Glod" (Glow)** | Santis Malt Swiss Highlander |
| 2015 | **English Whisky Co. Chapter 14 N.P** | The Belgian Owl '64 Months' |
| 2016 | English Whisky Co. Chapter 16 | **Kornog Chwee'hved 14 BC** |
| 2017 | **English Whisky Co. Chapter 14** | Langatun 6YO Pinot Noir Cask |
| 2018 | Penderyn Bryn Terfel | **The Norfolk Parched** |
| 2019 | Nestville Master Blender 8YO | **The Norfolk Farmers** |
| 2020 | Thy Whisky No. 9 Bøg Single Malt | **Penderyn Single Cask no. M75-32** |

# AUSTRIA
## ACHENSEE'R EDELBRENNEREI FRANZ KOSTENZER Maurach. Working.
**Whisky Alpin Grain Whisky Hafer** 3 Years Old bott code L1/2013 db (86) n21 t22.5 f21.5 b21. A distinctly bitter-sweet affair. Good body and molasses kick. *40%*

## ALPEN WHISKY DISTILLERIE Frastanz. Working.
⟡ **Alpenwhisky Single Malt Whisky** first fill Pedro Ximenez cask, dist Jan 14, bott 21 Jan 19 db (84.5) n20 t22 f21 b21.5 It's 7:30am and I am facing my first PX whisky of the day: be strong, Jim. Be strong. You are a pro: you can do this....Right...done it. And what can I say? Technically, a slightly better whisky than their Port cask offering. Is it more enjoyable? No. In fact, that is the problem with PX. It takes any whisky on the planet, smothers it in its one size fits all fruity, sugary overcoat and suddenly the identity and shape of the distillery is lost. No sulphur. No off notes. And just no personality. *45.5%.*

⟡ **Alpenwhisky Single Malt Whisky** refill port cask, dist Oct 15, bott 10 Nov 18 db (87.5) n19.5 t24 f22 b22 This distillery should get a degree in producing monumentally huge whisky. And when it comes in at this strength, perhaps a doctorate for good measure. As usual, their whisky tends towards the feinty side. And that means something that starts out as big suddenly becomes truly massive. Yet, despite its faults, how can you not just love that mental intensity to the barley? In fact, if there is a bigger malt kick from any whisky on the planet this year, then I haven't seen it. Naturally, the finish is a delicious chocolate nougat, the Port being a bit of a bystander here, adding only a chirruping cherry sweetness. Flawed, but fabulously fulsome. *67%.*

## BRENNEREI GUGLHOF Hallein. Working.
**Tauern Rogg Single Malt Whisky** Sauternes cask no. 93, dist 2011 db (88.5) n21 t23 f22 b22.5 Soft, sweet and satisfying. *42%. sc.*

## BRENNEREI ROSSETTI Kolsassberg. Working.
**Rossetti Young & Fine Pure Single Malt** bott code L582 db (89.5) n22 t23 f22 b22.5 I remember well the previous Rossetti I tasted: a bit of a gaunt, pasty lad: youthful and undernourished. The boy has grown. Perhaps a slight buzz on the finish, but an altogether burlier and more rounded character altogether. *43.5%*

## BROGER PRIVATBRENNEREI Klaus. Working.
⟡ **Broger 25 Jahre Brennerei 10 Jahre Whisky Jubiläums Edition** bott code: LJU-11 db (82.5) n21.5 t22 f19 b20 This distillery hits the heights when bottling their smokier output. This doesn't carry phenols, but has plenty of nougat to chew on, instead. Sadly, there appears to be a sherry influence here as well which is not entirely sulphur free. *46%.*

**Broger Burn Out Single Malt Whisky** bott code L BO-12 db (95) n23.5 t24 f23.5 b24 When I saw I was faced with six new samples of Broger, I strapped myself in. I remember from old, that this is a distillery of extremes, with wildly varying quality. So I went for this one first – taking the bull by the horns. Closed my eyes...took a mouthful...and lived! Actually, the label should be one of billowing smoke, as you want as little flame as possible when smoking malt. And perhaps one, also, of sugar cane. Because the Demerara on this is highly impressive. A very pleasant surprise. Oh, and didn't I mention it? This is a mini masterpiece... *42%*

**Broger Medium Smoked Single Malt Whisky** bott code L MS-09 db (94) n23.5t23.5 f23 b24 There is no doubt that this distillery knows exactly how to make smoky whisky...because this is a very different, more subtle, style to their peated efforts. *42%*

## DACHSTEIN DESTILLERIE Radstadt. Working
**Mandlberggut Rock Whisky Single Malt 5 Years** bott code LWh13 db (86) n20 t22 f22 b22 From the nougat school of German whisky, enjoying a slow but marked light honey development. No quicker to make itself felt is the malt, but finally does – and in tandem with toasty oak – quite impressively. *40.8%.*

⟡ **Mandlberggut Rock Whisky 5 Years** bott code LWh13/4 db (87.5) n22 t22 f21.5 b22 Another very much in the house style with a big toffee-nougat statement, though this possesses extra Manuka honey to up the sweetness. The malt has a profound say, too. Attractive whisky. *41.5%*

## DESTILLERIE FARTHOFER Öhling. Working.
⟡ **Farthofer Bio-Brauweizen Hermann 2015 Single Grain Whisky** feld: Kickingerfeld, reifung: mostellofass, jahr: 2015, bott code: LbWw2115 db (84.5) n20.5 t22 f21 b21 Not exactly the most subtle whisky you'll encounter. The oils from the wide cut combine with the grain to give this a soupy effect, though the late minty chocolate notes to relieve the intensity. *40%. nc ncf sc. 202 bottles.*

◇ **Farthofer Nackthafer 2015 Single Grain Whisky Fassstärke** feld: Birdwiese Acker, reifung: weinbrandfass, jahr: 2015, bott code: LWNH2015 db **(88) n21.5** thin, half-hearted aroma. A bit untidy and unsure of its footing, though there is a semi-appealing sweetness; **t22.5** much better on delivery where the oiliness of the grain makes for a sweet and chewy experience; buttery at times or a milk porridge with molten maple syrup; **f22** much more simplistic vanilla; **b22** it's 9am and I am getting my oats.... *45.7%. nc ncf sc. 866 bottles.*

◇ **Farthofer Schlägler Roggen 2014 Single Grain Whisky** feld: Obere Erlgrube, reifung: weinbrandfass, jahr: 2014, bott code: LWSR2014 db **(83.5) n20 t21.5 f21 b21** For a rye, the grain is a little too non-specific and instead we have a slightly oily wide cut to contend with. *40%. nc ncf sc. 498 bottles.*

# DESTILLERIE GEORG HIEBL Haag. Working.
**George Hiebl Mais Whisky 2004** db **(93) n23 t23.5 f23 b23.5.** More bourbon in character than some American bourbons I know...!! Beautifully matured, brilliantly matured and European whisky of the very highest order, Ye..haahhhh!! *43%*

# DESTILLERIE ROGNER Rappottenstein. Working.
**Rogner Waldviertel Whisky 3/3** db **(86.5) n20 t22 f22.5 b22.** A beautiful display of crisp sugars and come-back-for more grainy juiciness. Lovable stuff, for all its glitches. *41.7%. ncf.*

# DESTILLERIE WEIDENAUER Kottes. Working
**Waldviertler Dinkelwhisky** bott code L10 db **(90) n22 t23 f22 b23** A cleaner (though not perfect) distillation by comparison to the last dinkelwhisky I tasted from here, though the build-up of chocolate mousse is something to behold... one for the taste buds...! *42%.*

**Waldviertler Dinkel Whisky 2/3 Dinkelwalz Süßweinfass** finish, bott code L08 db **(90.5) n22 t23 f22.5 b23** Has to be tasted using the Murray Method to make sense of this! Deceptively complex. *48.6%.*

**Waldviertler Einkorn-Whisky 100% Bio-Urweizen** bott code L09 db **(88) n22 t22.5 f21.5 b22** An unusually light and citrussy offering from this distillery: wonder if it was the yeast at play here. *42%.*

**Waldviertler Haferwhisky Classic** bott code L10 db **(94) n23.5 t23.5 f23 b24** Truly classic oak whisky from the very man who created it. Always one of the treats of the year when Weidenaur's Haferwhisky turns up on my tasting room table.. *42%.*

**Waldviertler Haferwhisky Classic** bott code L11 db **(91) n22.5 t23 f22.5 b23** As ever, a pleasure to get my oats. *42%.*

**Waldviertler Hafer-Whisky Single Malt Dunkel** bott code L10 db **(87) n21 t22 f22 b22** Just a slight technical faltering on the nose, but the sugars move in quickly compensate; the chocolate on the finish is superb. *42%.*

**Waldviertler Hafer Whisky Unit 2/3 Hafermalz** bott code L10 db **(92.5) n22.5 t23.5 f23 b23.5** Like a sensuous massage in oaty oils.... *42%.*

**Waldviertler Intensiv Getorfter Hafermalzwhisky** bott code L09 db **(88.5) n20 t22 f24 b22.5** I don't think I've experienced a peated malted oat whisky before, so how wonderful for my whisky experiences to be stretched even after all these years. Forget the nose and delivery, which take some getting used to: from the midpoint onwards we are in some kind of oaty Eden.... *42%.*

# DESTILLERIE WEUTZ St. Nikolai im Sausal. Working.
**Franziska** bott code. L070206/02 db **(93) n23.5 t23 f23.5 b23.** The 5% elderflower means this is 100% not whisky. But a fascinating and eye-opening way to create a spirit very much in the young Kentucky rye style, especially in the nose. They certainly can do delicious... For the record, the scoring for enjoyment alone: *48%.*

# DISTILLERY ZWEIGER Mooskirchen. Working.
**Zweiger Smoked Prisoner** bott code SH/L0601/17 db **(89) n22 t22 f22.5 b22.5** Probably not the whisky of choice for officials of the European Court of Human Rights. *44%.*

# EDELBRENNEREI FRANZ KOSTENZER Maurach, Working.
**Whisky Alpin Single Malt Double Wood 11 Years Old** bott code L1/2005 db **(88) n22 t22.5 f21 b22.5** One thing that cannot be levelled against this distillery is that it has no idea how to conjure up malt personalities previously unknown to the whisky world. It has done so again... *40%.*

**Whisky Alpin Single Malt Peaty 5 Years Old** bott code L1/2013 db **(89) n22 t22.5 f22 b22.5** One of the most brutally peaty whiskies I have ever encountered. The phenols hammer the palate into merciless submission, using the same force of will that tames the oily distillate. Kind of brilliant, in a truly terrifying kind of way. Outside me I hear the sound of distant thunder. Well, I think it's the thunder: it could well be this whisky... *46%.*

**Whisky Alpin Single Malt Roggen Amarone Cask Finish 7 Years Old** bott code L1/2010 db **(85) n19 t22 f21.5 b21.5** Though some of this distillery's other work is – like this - technically unsound, I enjoy it because of the sheer entertainment value provided and the sensation of exploring unknown worlds. The one-dimensional quality of the grape, though offering moments of true deliciousness, reduces that last element without entirely seeing off the excesses of the overly generous cut. *46%.*

**Whisky Alpin Single Malt Sherry Cask Finish 9 Years Old** bott code L2/2008 db **(84) n18.5 t22 f21.5 b22** Enjoy the grape: this is an excellent sherry cask at work and at its zenith akin to a sultana fest. The usual feinty gremlins elsewhere. *40%.*

**Whisky Alpin Single Malt Smoky 6 Years Old** bott code L2/2011 db **(87.5) n21.5 t22.5 f21.5 b22** The distillery's distinctive nougat rich style is in full voice here. But hats off to the sturdiness of the peat which impresses in the way it is able to gather up the balm of the ulmo honey for a charming mid session. The heavier oils fur up the finish slightly. *42%.*

**Whisky Alpin Single Malt Tiroler Whisky** organic Obernberger black oats, bott code L1/2014 db **(80) n22 t21.5 f17.5 b19** Not sure last time I encountered a nose and finish singing off such different hymn sheets. An eye-wateringly bitter finale after a green, refreshing and promising aroma and sweet start on the palate. *42%.*

## LAVA BRÄU Feldbach. Working.

**Mehr Leben Brisky Single Malt Eiche** dist 2013, bott code H 02|13 db **(87) n22 t22.5 f21.5 b22** "Brisky". Thought this was the first whisky made in Britain after the people had decided to get the hell out of Europe. But apparently not... A very well made malt with some serious loganberry on the nose – not exactly the most usual of aromas. But eventually disappears under its own weight of caramel on the palate. *40.8%.*

## LEBE & GENIESSE Lagenrohr. Working

◇ **Bodding Lokn Blended Malt Nr. 3** French oak, refilled oloroso & Pedro Ximenez casks, flaschennr. 100, dist 2012 db **(90) n21.5** a very slight feint note, but more than compensated for by the depth of the nuttiness; **t23** a rich cream sherry feel to this with sparring spices light molasses; **f22.5** long fade, thanks to both the extra oils and creamy fruit; **b23** these chaps do believe in giving their fans lots of flavour... *45%. ncf.*

◇ **Bodding Lokn Double Cask PX Master** American white oak & Pedro Ximenez sherry casks, fassnr. 11/18, flaschennr. 48, dist 2012, bott Jan 19 db **(92) n22.5** a real Christmas pudding feel to this, complete with nuts; **t23** chewy, lush but the spices actually out-perform the maple syrup sweetness; **f23** a light liquorice, almost bourbony, feel to the oak as, with the spices, it tames the grape; **b23.5** this unlocks at least a couple of the secrets of an enjoyable PX whisky: firstly the spirit has to have bristle and character enough to punch through the enveloping grape. And, secondly, the PX cask must be entirely free of sulphur, which this is. So, a rare treat! *55%. ncf.*

**Bodding Lokn Golden Wheat Single Malt Lagerung Double Cask** fass nr. 1120 & 111, gebrannt 2008 db **(91.5) n22.5 t23 f23 b23** Though perhaps a little too sweet for some, this is truly one of a kind. Almost too beautiful and demure to drink... *45%. ncf.*

◇ **Bodding Lokn Single Cask Classic** American white oak cask, fassnr. 17, flaschennr. 70, dist 2013 db **(94) n23.5** nutty; shaved coconut, toffee and nose-nipping toasty tannin; **t24** superb oils immediately coat the mouth and both soften and exploit the malty impact; spiced praline makes way for some very juicy, crisp barley; the tannins are roasty and omnipotent; **f23** the chocolate tannins milk the oils for a long range finale; the spices rumble on; **b23.5** a delicious, beautifully made malt bursting with personality, vitality...and chocolate! *43%. ncf sc.*

**Bodding Lokn Single Malt Blended Malt Nr. 2** refilled bourbon & sherry casks, dist 2011, bott 2018 db **(94) n23 t23.5 f23.5 b24** Confusingly, the label describes itself as both a single malt and a blended malt. I presume they mean it is from a single distillery but from more than one barley or perhaps cask type...though I could be wrong. Whatever it is, there is no doubting its high quality. *43%. ncf.*

**Bodding Lokn Single Malt Double Cask** American white oak & a 50 Litre Oloroso sherry cask, dist 2010, bott 2018 db **(88) n22 t22.5 f21.5 b22** A generous cut gives the big grape something to work on. *49.5%. ncf.*

**Bodding Lokn Single Malt Double Cask Classic** French Limousine oak & American white oak casks, dist 2012, bott 2018 db **(92) n22.5 t23.5 f22.5 b23.5** The limousine takes you on a very pretty journey... *43%. ncf.*

## MARILLENHOF DESTILLERIE KAUSL Mühldorf. Working.

**Wachauer Whisky Single Pure H** bott code L:1WH db **(88.5) n21.5 t22.5 f22 b22** Attractive but a real odd fish. *40%.*

**Wachauer Whisky Malt Royal** bott code L:1malt db **(87.5) n22 t22 f21.5 b22** The slightly wide cut on this certainly has a kick on delivery and finish. But the extra oils ensure a comfortable ride for the most part, as does the big cream toffee presence. *40%.*

**Wachauer Whisky Malt Royal** bott code L:1mR db **(92) n23 t23.5 f22.5 b23** Even a little bitterness at the death cannot undermine the brilliant character of this malt. And those who love oat or oak-style whisky...just dig in...!!! *40%.*

◈ **Wachauer Whisky M43 Double Oak** bott code L:WD01 db **(80.5) n21 t21.5 f19 b19** This is the 1,137th whisky I have tasted for the 2020 Bible, but none of the previous 1,136 have given me quite the shock this has done. I cannot say exactly what kind of oak this has been in, other than to admit that I would not be surprised if one was a vat of cough syrup. Well, it certainly made me cough... There appears to be a huge, bitter, tannin kick, as well as sweet cherry juice. But you just can't get away from the cough mixture. A whisky to be taken three times a day after meals... *43%.*

◈ **Wachauer Whisky M48 Triple Cask** bott code L:WTC1 db **(77) n19 t20 f19 b19** I have in the past greatly enjoyed whisky from this distillery. But the three offerings that have come my way this year have left me scratching my head. This begins life far closer to being a liqueur than a whisky. And though a light ginger note on the mid-point distracts you from the bizarre goings on of before, it isn't close to being enough to save it. *48%.*

◈ **Wachauer Whisky Multicorn** bott code L:13WE db **(87.5) n21 t23 f21.5 b22** You get the distinct feeling that oats lay at the heart here as the mid-point give you a delightful, sticky porridge, complete with dollop of honey. But both the nose and finish are a little untidy from the barrels, the latter heading out towards a bitter tannin kick. *40%.*

## MARKUS WIESER GMBH Woesendorf in der Wachau. Working.

**Wieser Wahouua Single Malt WIESky Pinot Noir** bott code L1015 db **(87) n21 t22 f22 b22.** A curious malt. Always soft, always polite and at times positively charming. But the fruit never makes much of a stand while the toffee has no such reservations. *40%. nc.*

## MICHELEHOF Vorarlberg. Working.

**Micheles Single Malt 6 Years Old** 100% barley, dist 2008, bott code L8121 db **(78.5) n19 t21 f19 b19.5.** An oily, nutty affair which struggles hard to get over the effect of the wide cut. A few attractive salivating fudgy moments at about the halfway point. *43%*

## PETER AFFENZELLER Alberndorf in der Riedmark. Working.

**Peter Affenzeller Single Malt Whisky 7 Years Old** dist 2008, bott code: L-0841201 db **(95.5) n23.5 t24.5 f23.5 b24** I defy any malt whisky lover, wherever you are in the world, not to entirely fall head over heels for this stunning whisky. *42%*

## PFANNER Vorarlberg. Working.

**Pfanner Single Malt** dist 2009, bott code L 212 db **(74) n19 t20 f16.5 b18.5.** Nutty and some hefty feints late on puts a Pfanner in the works... *43%*

**Pfanner Single Malt Single Barrel 2011** first fill sherry oak cask, cask no. 5, dist 16 Jun 11, bott 09 Oct 17 db **(93.5) n23 t23.5 f23 b23.5** Delightful whisky benefitting from an entirely clean sherry cask. *56.2%. sc. 412 bottles.*

**Pfanner Single Malt Smokey Whisky** bott code L217 db **(87.5) n21.5 t22 f22 b22** I'd love to know what they used to smoke the malt with. Rather than peat, it reminds me of some of the weird and wonderful aromas concocted over flame in distilleries in America's west coast. An engulfing, rounded mouth feel where the sugars are maybe just a little too enthusiastic. Not a bad shout for someone with a sweet tooth, though. *43%.*

## REISETBAUER Axberg, Thening. Working.

**Reisetbauer 7 Year Old Distillers Choice Single Malt Whisky** Chardonnay & Trockenbeerenauslese casks, bott code. 180120 db **(89) n22.5 t22.5 f22 b22** I suppose the grape style used with the chardonnay, TBA, is Austria's answer to Spain's PX or maybe Slovakian Tokay – and, having tasted quite a few over the years, you can really stand your spoon up in the darker ones. It was inevitable, then, that they would end up maturing whisky at one point. I think there is no secret of the fact that I am no great fan of PX in relation to whisky, as the intense sweetness has a tendency to kill subtlety and complexity. Because of this, this is a whisky that takes a lot longer than normal for all the nuances to filter through. A hard work whisky.. *43%.*

**Reisetbauer 12 Year Old Single Malt Whisky** Chardonnay & Trockenbeerenauslese casks, bott code. 180120 db **(80) n19 t20.5 f20 b20** Despite the cask yet, hard to get away from the feinty nose revealing a weakness in the distillate. No amount of patience sees the TBA improve matters. *48%. 1,253 bottles.*

**Reisetbauer 15 Year Old Single Cask Single Malt Whisky** dist 2001 db **(86.5) n20 t21.5 f23 b22** From the earliest days of this distillery, the technical flaws of the distillate are obvious. However, the malt has reacted favourably with some high class oak. The result is a whisky that grows in confidence as it goes along, like the girl who thought she was too plain to go to the ball, only to find she was as pretty as many. Late on the mix of chocolate nougat and treacle tart is rather compelling and worthy of drinking from a glass shoe.... 48%. sc. 500 bottles.

## STBG BRAUEREI SCHLOSS STARKENBERG Tarrenz. Working.

**STGB Tiroler Single Malt Whisky Aged 3 Years** db **(94.5) n23.5 t23.5 f23.5 b24** A charmingly relaxed single malt which has been beautifully crafted. You cannot really ask for more from a three-year-old single malt. 40%

## WHISKY-DESTILLERIE J. HAIDER Roggenreith. Working.

**J H. 12 Years Single Malt Single Cask** bott code L SM 05 SL db **(94) n23 t23.5 f23.5 b24** Not quite in the same Super League as their unforgettable 13-year-old but this is a huge, uncompromising but always classy Austrian, again making the most of their generous cut. 46%. ncf sc.

**J.H. 13 Years Old Single Malt** bott code L SM 03 FS db **(96) n24 t23.5 f24 b24.5** One of the beauties of feints in whisky, is that the longer the spirit hangs around the more chance there is that they'll be burnt off. And I suspect this has happened here because this astonishing malt, doubtless from a cask they have matured for one of their longest periods, has little interference from the dark side of distilling. Its colossal malt, this distillation of genius, is honeyed uplands all the way... 69%. ncf sc.

◈ **J.H. Dark Rye Malt Fassfinish Ex-Laphroaig** 100% roggenmalz dunkel geröstet, 9 jahre gelagert &1 jahr fassfinish, bott code L2R08LP db **(86.5) n20 t22.5 f22 b22** I have been tasting the whisky from this excellent distillery for some 20 years or so and I know their style pretty well. Or thought I did! This is not just a departure from their consistently attractive whiskies, but here represents a flavour profile I have never before encountered in my career.... anywhere! The one weak spot is the nose, a butyric hit and out of kilter. But the flavour profile is, I can vouch on my life, entirely unique. The mix of rye and significant peat is something I have before encountered elsewhere. But take into account the distillery's own intense style off the still and you are entering previously uncharted territory. Despite the modest score by their standards, I do rather love this, not least because it even provides a minty effect which appears to chill the lips! Get past the nose and this is pure fun. 46%. ncf sc. 314 bottles.

**J.H. Dark Single Malt Peated Single Cask 7 Jahre** bott code L SMP 10 BRM db **(93) n23.5 t23 f23.5 b23** Not sure if they have bothered about the malt: it just seems like peat-smoked peat turf. No, not really! But it takes a while to acclimatise to phenols this toasty, this intense. What's the Austrian for bloody hell!...? 46%. ncf sc.

**J.H. Original Rye 12 Jahre** bott code L3S05 db **(91) n22.5 t23 f22.5 b23** Deploy the Murray method for best results by far. 46%. ncf sc.

**J.H. Rare Selection Rye Malt 6 Jahre Fassfinish Likörwein Porteweinmethode** bott code L 1R 11 db **(92) n23 t23 f22.5 b23.5** J.H. whisky without nougat is akin to the World Cup being without one of Germany, Brazil or Spain in the semi-finals. Oh, hang on a minute... 46%. ncf sc.

**J.H. Rare Selection Rye Malt TBA Chardonnay 4 Jahre** bott code L RM 13 MÜ db **(86.5) n19 t22 f23.5 b22** Takes an age to find its niche. Unless you are willing to leave the glass open in a hot environment for an hour, the nose, sadly, doesn't work – the oils and grape make everything claustrophobic, while at least the dense delivery does allow the rye to plant its flag. The finish, though, is sublime with a rich chocolate nougat intensity aided by a two-tone fruit from the grain and grape. 46%. ncf sc.

**J.H. Rare Selection Single Malt TBA Chardonnay 4 Jahre** bott code L SM 13 MÜ db **(87) n22 t22 f21.5 b21.5** An enjoyable whisky but never seems to get the shackles off the rye. 46%. ncf sc.

## DESTILLERIE WEIDENAUER Kottes. Working.

**Waldviertler Hafer-Malz** (2007 Gold Medaille label on neck) db **(91) n22 t22.5 f23 b23.5**. One of those whiskies that just gets better the longer it stays on the palate. Also, a master class in achieving near perfection in the degree of sweetness generated. 42%

## BELGIUM
### THE BELGIAN OWL Grâce-Hollogne. Working.

◈ **Belgian Owl Single Malt 36 Months** bott code: LF036858 db **(90.5) n22** a pleasing malt and citrus mix; **t23** light, young, fresh but the intertwangling of barley sugar and thin golden syrup is a joy; **f22.5** lovely strands of caramel and vanilla, with a light spice accompaniment; **b23** young it may be, but already rather beautifully formed. 46%. nc ncf.

◈ **Belgian Owl Single Malt 44 Months Glen Els Firkin Sherry Cask Finish** bourbon cask & sherry finish, cask no. 872 db **(88)** n22 old fashioned cream sherry on a bed of lively barley; t22.5 lush textured with a dryness to the grape skin; loads of custard and caramels f21.5 dry, a kind of strange sherry trifle but without the sugars; b22 a subdued Belgian Owl which has had its wings clipped by the introduction of a sherry cask. *46%. Bottled for Kirsch Whisky.*

**Belgian Owl Single Malt 11.5 Years Old** first fill bourbon cask, cask no. 4275920 db **(90.5)** n23 t23.5 f22 b22 An owl which takes no prisoners... *71.4%. nc ncf sc.*

**Belgian Owl Single Malt 12 Years Old** first fill bourbon cask, cask no. 4275897 db **(93.5)** n23.5 t23.5 f23 b23.5 An owl that hangs on to its sugars like some others owls hang on to their mice... *71.9%. nc ncf sc.*

**Belgian Owl Single Malt 12.5 Years Old** first fill bourbon cask, cask no. 4275928 db **(95)** n23.5 t24 f23.5 b24 A surprisingly wise and gentle old owl considering its alcoholic strength after the passing of a dozen years... *72.5%. nc ncf sc.*

**Belgian Owl Single Malt 42 Months** first fill bourbon barrel, cask no. 1523509 db **(94.5)** n23.5 t24 f23 b24 Slightly less proactive oak involvement means not just a bigger say for the malt but great alcohol bite. Both gentle and big whisky at one and the same moment. *73.7%. nc ncf sc.*

**Belgian Owl Single Malt «By Jove» Collection No. 1 48 Months** first fill bourbon cask db **(88)** n21.5 t22.5 f22 b22 May this malt be a tribute to British comedy legend and proud Englishman Ken Dodd, who was lost to us during the writing of this book. By Jove, missus, what a fine day to say to that Guy Verhofstadt fellow: if you want More Europe stick a bottle of this where the sun doesn't shine and then try whistling Ode to Joy! By Jove yes, Mr Verhofstadt. What a fine day to keep pouring this excellent whisky into your diddy pal Jean-Claude Juncker's glass and see what comes first: proper Brexit or the word "when". By Jove, missus! That hair. Have you seen that Mr Verhofstadt's hair? Well, at least something's straight about him. By Jove! Tatty bye! Yes tatty bye, Mr Verhofstadt! See you at my dentist's. If we let you back in the country. Tatty bye! *46%. nc ncf.*

**Belgian Owl Single Malt Distillery Intense 42 Months** first fill bourbon cask, cask no. 6033600, edition 2017-02 db **(86.5)** n22 t22 f 21 b21.5 The nose sticks vehemently to the cream toffee theme but the palate unmasks this as a warm and relatively aggressive bottling. Younger in style to some with a vague new make lightness to measure against the wall of natural caramels. The late bitterness points an accusatory finger at the cask.*72.5%. nc ncf sc.*

◈ **Belgian Owl Single Malt Distillery Intense 42 Months** first fill bourbon cask, cask no. 1538181, edition 2019-02 db **(93)** n22.5 t23.5 f22.5 b23.5 Never quite manages to get out of its nappy as the youth of this malt dominates from first sniff to last flavour wave. That said, the glorious, ultra-delicate lime blossom honey note lifts this way above the normal, especially in the way it combines with the cleanest barley imaginable. Such a ridiculous amount of flavour despite the new makey undertones. A bit of a paradox, this one. And a delicious one. *72.6%. nc ncf sc.*

**Belgian Owl Single Malt Distillery Passion 39 Months** first fill bourbon cask, cask no. 1519105, edition 2017-01 db **(88)** n22 t23 f23.5 b21.5 It is as if the whisky has yet to work out exactly where to put the extra tannin: flavoursome, but disjointed. *46%. nc ncf. sc*

◈ **Belgian Owl Single Malt Distillery Passion 42 Months** first fill bourbon cask, cask no. 6220001, edition 2019-01 db **(91)** n22.5 t23 f23 b22.5 Despite the use of first fill bourbon cask as lot of the malt's youth is on display here, on the nose especially. But very few mainland European whiskies match BO for mouth feel, and the house toffee and barley style works wonders. *46%. nc ncf sc.*

**Belgian Owl Single Malt Intense 40 Months** first fill bourbon cask, cask no. 5558589, edition 2018-02 db **(92)** n23 t23.5 f22.5 b23 One of Belgium Owl's famous plaque dissolvers, though also a celebration of all things malt and caramel. *72.6%. nc ncf sc.*

◈ **Belgian Owl Single Malt Intense 40 Months** first fill bourbon cask, cask no. 1538194, edition 2019-06 db **(92.5)** n22.5 t24 f23 b23 Obvious there is no great age to this, but if you find a more salivating, concentrated barley delivery anywhere in the world this year, you will have done well! Stunning clarity to this malt which for best results, by the way, requires the Murray Method (body temperature, no water added despite the strength) and take this glorious malt full on. The rewards sparkle... *72.6%. nc ncf sc.*

◈ **Belgian Owl Single Malt Intense 40 Months** first fill bourbon cask, cask no. 1538452, edition 2019-08 db **(89.5)** n22 t23 f22 b22.5 The tannins have a fractionally bigger say here. Which results in slightly subdued barley but much more cream toffee. Still a beauty, though. *72.7%. nc ncf sc.*

**Belgian Owl Single Malt Intense 41 Months** first fill bourbon cask, cask no. 6033608, edition 2017-04 db **(96)** n24 t24 f24 b24 Truly world class whisky: amazing from a dram so young. Magnificently made, magnificently matured. Simple as that. *72.4%. nc ncf sc.*

**Belgian Owl Single Malt Intense 42 Months** first fill bourbon cask, cask no. 1519134, edition 2018-07 db **(94.5)** n23.5 t23.5 f23.5 b24 What a delightfully consistent distillery this is. *72.6%. nc ncf sc.*

**Belgian Owl Single Malt Intense 42 Months** first fill bourbon cask, cask no. 5560227, edition 2017-06 db **(88) n23 t22 f21.5 b21.5** Sometimes the casks at Belgian Owl appear to be emptied at a point when the growing pains can still be felt. *73%. nc ncf sc.*

**Belgian Owl Single Malt Intense 42 Months** first fill bourbon cask, cask no. 5698086, edition 2018-08 db **(92.5) n23 t23.5 f23 b23** A substantial and complex malt of greatly conflicting personality. *72.4%. nc ncf sc.*

**Belgian Owl Single Malt Intense 42 Months** first fill bourbon cask, cask no. 6033554, edition 2018-04 db **(93.5) n24 t23 f23 b23** Another delightful malt from one of Europe's great distilleries. *72.4%. nc ncf sc.*

**Belgian Owl Single Malt Intense 42 Months** first fill bourbon cask, cask no. 1538169, edition 2019-04 db **(93.5) n23 t23.5 f23.5 b23.5** Does exactly what it says on the tin. Everything – the toffee and barley especially are on steroids – and though youth is evident, this brings out a fabulous degree of mouth-watering qualities. Just beautifully made and matured. *72.4%. nc ncf sc.*

**Belgian Owl Single Malt Passion 39 Months** first fill bourbon cask, cask no. 5673151, edition 2017-03 db **(93) n23.5 t23.5 f22.5 b23.5** The kind of whisky of which a glassful can send you to sleep – before you've drunk it! It is that laid back... *46%. nc ncf sc.*

**Belgian Owl Single Malt Passion 40 Months** first fill bourbon cask, cask no. 1538449, edition 2019-07 db **(91.5) n22.5 t23 f22.5 b23** Another beautifully consistent cask quietly emphasising the charming, lush toffee notes and languid barley undertones. *46%. nc ncf sc.*

**Belgian Owl Single Malt Passion 40 Months** first fill bourbon cask, cask no. 5643556, edition 2017-05 db **(92.5) n23 t23 f23 b23.5** Probably one of the most relaxing and easy going single malts you'll find this year. *46%. nc ncf sc.*

**Belgian Owl Single Malt Passion 40 Months** first fill bourbon cask, cask no. 5698143, edition 2018-01 db **(91) n22.5 t22.5 f23 b23** Pretends to be a little toffee dominant...but look carefully and much more going on besides. *46%. nc ncf sc.*

**Belgian Owl Single Malt Passion 42 Months** first fill bourbon cask, cask no. 1538178, edition 2019-05 db **(84) n21 t22 f20.5 b20.5** Tasting Belgian Owl is each year one of my highlights of writing the Whisky Bible. Very rarely do they come up with a malt which is off beam. But here is one, alas, despite its usual malty charm. Too many tangy notes as the barley and tannins refuse to unite. Bottled at the wrong time, I suspect. *46%. nc ncf sc.*

**Belgian Owl Single Malt Passion 42 Months** first fill bourbon cask, cask no. 1519110, edition 2018-09 db **(91) n22.5 t23 f22.5 b23** Such a sweet natured owl. *46%. nc ncf sc.*

**Belgian Owl Single Malt Passion 42 Months** first fill bourbon cask, cask no. 5558604, edition 2018-06 db **(87) n21.5 t22 f21.5 b22** As youthful as the England team that lost to Belgium in the World Cup (twice, sob...!). The occasional flash of inspirational brilliance, especially early in the second half. But the first touch lets it down a little too often. A little raw at the end. *46%. nc ncf sc.*

**Belgian Owl Single Malt Passion 42 Months** first fill bourbon cask, cask no. 5665829, edition 2018-05 db **(94) n23 t23.5 f23.5 b24** A really graceful owl. *46%. nc ncf sc.*

**Belgian Owl Single Malt Passion 42 Months** first fill bourbon cask, cask no. 6219123, edition 2019-03 db **(88) n21.5 t23 f21.5 b22** A delicious new make and natural caramel mix. The muscular and juicy barley on delivery raises the game. *46%. nc ncf sc.*

**Belgian Owl Single Malt Passion 47 Months** first fill bourbon cask, cask no. 5660299, edition 2018-03 db **(94) n23 t23 f24 b24** Heading now towards 400 whiskies for this year's Bible and the entire day spent tasting the whiskies of the Belgian Owl has been by far the most enjoyable yet. This really is a very special distillery. *46%. nc ncf sc.*

**Belgian Owl Single Malt The Private Angels 60 Months** first fill bourbon cask, cask no. 037/200 db **(87) n23 t22 f21 b21** Doesn't quite live up to the expectation after such a great nose which is fresh and much more on the fruity side with diced apple where there is normally toffee. On the palate, though, too much bitterness builds. *46%. nc ncf sc.*

**Belgian Owl Single Malt The Private Angels 60 Months** first fill bourbon cask, cask no. 038/200 db **(94) n23** even at this strength, the malt comes through with an angel-like touch; **t24** clean, salivating barley on delivery, then the most stunning structure of interweaving citrus and malt of fascinatingly varied intensity; the mid-ground is a wonderful mix of light heather honey and butterscotch; **f23.5** a gorgeous mocha fade; **b23.5** angelic. *72.5%. nc ncf sc.*

**Belgian Owl Single Malt The Private Angels 60 Months** first fill bourbon cask, cask no. 039/200 db **(87.5) n23 t22.5 f20.5 b21.5** A curious pattern here emerging of the Private Angels, just shewing a little bitterness and imbalance when they are reduced from cask strength to 46%. Almost certainly this is due to the breaking up of the oils carrying the sweeter elements which counter the oaky action. At a later age more sugars from the oak may negate this. Fascinating to watch a whisky evolving. *46%. nc ncf sc.*

**Belgian Owl Single Malt The Private Angels 60 Months** first fill bourbon cask, cask no. 041/200 db **(91.5) n23.5** a lovely Malteser candy mix of malt and milk chocolate; polished mix of ulmo honey and demerara sugar; **t23** exemplary sweet, gristy barley surrounded by a pillow of custardy vanilla; **f22** the intensity of the malt stretches through to the dying embers; **b23** much better with a cask shewing no negative impact and allowing the concentrated malt an uninterrupted say; *46%. nc ncf sc.*

⟫ **Belgian Owl Single Malt The Private Angels 60 Months** first fill bourbon cask, cask no. 042/200 db **(96.5) n24** faultless: the famed distillery barley overture, but here with a few extra flutes where there is normally cello; **t24.5** just magnificent! Almost eye-watering in the barley intensity, but impossible not to taste this without a smile: the barley-ulmo honey and butterscotch trio sing without a single false note and in total harmony; **f24** the fabulous oils carry the intense faultless barley to the very end, though the fade and the letting in of the vanillas is classic; **b24** elegant, charming, charismatic, witty and a triumph: something everyone would want in their home and eagerly to spend time with. In other words, Belgium whisky's total antidote to Guy Verhofstadt. *72.6%. nc ncf sc.*

⟫ **Belgian Owl Single Malt The Private Angels 60 Months** first fill bourbon cask, cask no. 043/200 db **(93.5) n23.5** not just the house toffee, but chocolate wafer, too; **t23.5** the usual stunning house style mouth feel: lush, perfectly oiled and weighted with some spices pricking the comfort zones of the cream toffee, ulmo honey and barley; **f22.5** some drier oaky tones: not a BO standard! **b23** this malt is developing with rare panache. *46%. nc ncf sc.*

⟫ **Belgian Owl Single Malt The Private Angels 60 Months** first fill bourbon cask, cask no. 044/200 db **(88.5) n23** barley and lemon drizzle cake; **t22** a trademark juicy barley delivery before a toff-rich follow through; **f21.5** dries and bitters a little; **b22** wobbles a bit late on, but no denying the early quality. *46%. nc ncf sc.*

**Belgian Owl Spirit Drink Unaged** bott code. Ld 000101 db **(92) n22 t23.5 f23 b23.5** I'm presuming this new make malt spirit is from the old Caperdonich stills as there is an ethereal quality to this that used to found in the days when they operated in Speyside. Whoever is handling them now is probably doing a better job than in its Scotch days as every nuance of the delicate malt appears to have been squeezed out. Exceptionally pleasing, with just the right degree of gristy sweetness. *46%. nc ncf.*

⟫ **Belgian Owl Single Malt Origine Unaged Spirit Drink** bott code: LE000107 db **(92)** **t23 f23 b23** As tasting notes above, except creamier and more barley intense. *46%. nc ncf.*

## BROUWERIJ PIRLOT Zandhoven, Working.
**Kempich Vuur Single Malt Aged 3 Years** Laphroaig quarter casks, cask no. L5, bott 24 Jan 17 db **(91) n22 t23 f23 b23** Well, those quarter casks weren't wasted! What a joy of a malt! *46%. sc.*

## DESTILLERIE RADERMACHER Raeren. Working.
**Lambertus Single Grain Aged 10 Years** db **(44) n12 t12 f10 b10.** This is whisky...? Really???!!!!???? Well, that's what it says on the label, and this is a distillery I haven't got round to seeing in action (nor am I now very likely to be invited...). Let's check the label again... Ten years old...blah, blah. Single grain... blah, blah. But, frankly, this tastes like a liqueur rather than a whisky: the fruit flavours do not seem even remotely naturally evolved: synthetic is being kind. But apparently, this is whisky: I have re-checked the label. No mention of additives, so it must be. I am stunned. *40%*

## IF GOULDYS FILLIERS DISTILLERY Deinze. Working.
**Goldly's Belgian Double Still Whisky Aged 10 Years** db **(88) n21.5 t23 f21.5 b22.** Having actually discovered this whisky before the distillers – I'll explain one day...!! – I know this could be a lot better. The caramel does great damage to the finish in particular, which should dazzle with its complexity. Even so, a lovely, high-class whisky which should be comfortably in the 90s but falls short. *40%*

**Goldys Distillers Range 14 Years Old Belgian Single Grain Whisky** Madeira cask finish, bott code: L16240900 db **(90.5) n22.5 t23 f22.5 b22.5** A big whisky, but one without muscle or threat. The Madeira cask is a little too rich to allow this whisky to move up into the next level of excellence: in whisky less is often more... *43%.*

**Sunken Still 4 Years Old Belgian Single Rye Whisky** bourbon barrels, bott code: L16450900 db **(85.5) n21 t22 f21.5 b21** There is no escaping that a degree of Genève character has leaked into this rye, affecting both nose and taste. Whether it was from the filters in the bottling hall, or some other reason I can't say. Lots of positive, busy flavours at play but the incursion of the local spirit is just a little too distracting. *45%.*

## STOKERIJ DE MOLENBERG Willebroek, Working.
**Golden Carolus Single Malt** first fill bourbon cask, Het Anker cask finish db **(88) n22 t22.5 f21.5 b22** Cream toffee, anyone? *46%. nc ncf.*

Stokerij De Molenberg 4th Anniversary Muscad'or 2017 db (82.5) n20 t22 f20 b20.5 A haphazard whisky (lots of Hazards in Belgium...) revealing a slight distilling flaw on the nose which the outrageous grape does its best to conceal. But the palate is accosted by some maniacal fruit before the wide cut is re-exposed on the finish. 46%.

# CORSICA
## DOMAINE MAVELA Aléria. Working.

**P & M Red Oak Corsican Single Malt Whisky** bott code L1783 db (91.5) n22.5 t23.5 f22.5 b23 A wonderfully understated, complex malt, despite the voluptuousness of the fruit. 42%. nc ncf. 567 bottles.

**P & M Signature Corsican Single Malt Whisky** bott code L1684 db (89.5) n21.5 t23 f22 b23 A very charming malt which at its peak sings like a Corsican Finch. 42%. nc ncf. 6,600 bottles.

**P & M Tourbé Corsican Single Malt Whisky** bott code L1682 db (92) n22.5 t23 f23 b23.5 A beautifully paced, gentle malt which always carries a threat on the peaty wind. 42%. nc ncf. 1,700 bottles.

❖ **P & M Aged 13 Years Corsican Single Malt Whisky** bott code L2984 db (95.5) n23.5 gorgeous tannin that makes its mark but never over steps it. Toasty, but also with that distinctive beautiful mark of Jamaican Blue Mountain coffee...and Corsica has nothing if not mountains....; t24 how does it do that...? How does it get all those dark sugars, all those full-on tannins, all those creamy cocoa notes...and then end up with a malt so gentle you could almost shed a tear of delight; f24 more intense with the tannins now, deeper with the molasses, roastier with the cocoa...but the style stays true...; b24 enough oak to make a Corsican nuthatch sing with happiness. This has swallowed up the years with ease and maximised complexity. World class whisky. 42%. nc ncf. 217 bottles.

# CZECH REPUBLIC
## Single Malt
## RUDOLF JELÍNEK DISTILLERY Vizovice. Working.

**Gold Cock Single Malt Whisky 8 Years Old** Czech oak barrels db (93) n23 t23.5 f23 b23.5 A delightful whisky making full use of the wheat content to ramp up the oils and spices while the sugars missing on the 8-year-old appear to have found their way here... 49.2%. nc ncf.

**Gold Cock Single Malt Whisky 2008 Virgin Oak** Czech oak barrels, dist Feb 08, bott Mar 17 db (96) n24 t24 f24 b24 Not often you get gold cocks and virgins mentioned in the same sentence in a drinks guide. Or anywhere else, come to that. Equally few rampant cocks can crow so loudly; no virgin give so passionately. A consummate whisky consummated... 61.5%. nc ncf sc. 270 bottles.

## STOCK PLZEN - BOZKOV S.R.O. Plzen. Working

**Hammer Head 1989** db (88.5) n22 t22.5 f22 b22. Don't bother looking for complexity: this is one of Europe's maltiest drams...if not the maltiest... 40.7%

## Blends

**Gold Cock Aged 3 Years "Red Feathers"** bott 22/06/09 (86) n22 t21 f21.5 b21.5. Sensual and soft, this is melt-in-the-mouth whisky with a big nod towards the sweet caramels. 40%.

**Granette Premium** (82) n21 t22 f19 b20. Lighter than the spark of any girl that you will meet in the Czech Republic. Big toffee thrust. 40%

**Printer's Aged 6 Years** (86.5) n21.5 t22.5 f21 b21.5. Blended whisky is something often done rather well in the Czech Republic and this brand has managed to maintain its clean, malty integrity and style. Dangerously quaffable. 40%

# DENMARK
## BRAENDERIET LIMFJORDEN Øster Assels. Working.

**Lindorm Danish Single Malt Whisky 1st Edition** db (90) n22 a breakfast cereal maltiness to this one −with some marmalade on toast sitting nearby...; t22.5 super-salivating, again with a delicate interplay between malt and citrus; f22.5 extra complexity as the oak gives the malty mix a light chocolate stir; some lovely late spices, too; b23 this distillery appears to have created its very own understated and elegant style. Most enjoyable. 46%. ncf. 899 bottles.

## BRAUNSTEIN DISTILLERY Køge. Working.

**Braunstein Danish Single Malt Cask Edition no. 2** db (94) n23.5 t23.5 f23 b24 Seriously high quality distillate that has been faithfully supported by good grade oak. Complex, satisfying, and for its obviously tender years, truly excellent malt. A welcome addition to the Scandinavian − and world! − whisky lexicon.62.4%

# FARY LOCHAN DESTILLERI Give. Working.

**Fary Lochan Forår** db **(90) n22 t23 f22.5 b22.5** Denmark's most delicate whisky...by a distance. Youthful but quite lovely. 47%.

**Fary Lochan G25 Summer** cask no. 2011-15, dist 26 Nov 11, bott 4 Sept 17 db **(90.5) n22.5** the spices are sublime: complex, beautifully weighted tannins fly around the nose; **t23** those spices pile in on delivery. Delicious treacle tart to chew on; the weight and pace of the flavour development is spot on; **f22** long, thanks to excellently controlled oils; toasty in all the right places; **b23** a moody, brooding whisky balancing out the sugars and muscular tannins delightfully. 50%. 74 bottles. sc.

**Fary Lochan Rum Edition** ex- bourbon barrels, casks no. 2012-15 & 2012-16, dist 18 Oct 12, bott 6 Nov 17 db **(85.5) n21t22 f21 b21.5** Not entirely sure I understand the narrative of this whisky. Impressed by the odd honeyed high point. But there is an innate bitterness which runs through all sections, a wideness to the cut which offers extra oils and a general all round confusion. 64.7%. 639 bottles.

**Fary Lochan Summer** batch no. 2, ex-bourbon barrels, cask nos. 2013-05, 2013-09, 2013-10 & 2013-11, bott 13 Feb 18 db **(84.5) n21 t21.5 f21 b21** Plenty of brown sugars to stir into the background coffee. But a degree of bitterness betrays a weakness in the cut. 46%. 1,715 bottles.

# MOSGAARD DISTILLERY Oure. Working.

**Mosgaard New Make Spirit Organic** db **(94.5) n23.5 t24 f23 b24** Outstanding new make malt. Truly exemplary, bursting with the cleanest and most intense grist you could hope for. What a fine piece of distilling this is. Put this on the market and none will mature long enough ever to reach whisky...! 68%.

**Mosgaard Peated New Make Spirit Organic** 25 ppm db **(92.5) n23 t24 f22.5 b23.5** More superb new make from Mosgaard. There is a sharp interaction between the copper and phenols which offers a slight edge to this, a phenomenon which will probably pass within 18 months. But enjoy it while you can...! 66.8%.

**Mosgaard Peated Young Malt** batch no. 18-02, production date. 060218, 25 ppm, bourbon barrels db **(90) n22 t22.5 f22.5 b23** The phenols come across as about half the stated dose while the oak has whipped up quite a storm. As curious as it is enjoyable. And rather beautifully made. 48%.

**Mosgaard Port Young Malt** batch no. 18-03, production date. 200318 db **(84) n21 t22 f21 b20** A big whisky, but the flavour profiles are far from relaxed. The tannins are gargantuan and feel a little forced, thus knocking the fruit out of kilter. Plenty of big enjoyable flavours and spice. But balance is at a premium. 41%.

◈ **Mosgaard Organic Single Malt Whisky** oloroso cask, batch no. 1, bott 25 Mar 19 db **(88) n22** a lot of saltiness amid the diced apple and grape; **t22** silky delivery with the grape in control and allowing in a little spice for punctuation; **f22** silky even to the death, though the drier vanillas bring the salt back into play; **b22** about as steady as any whisky goes... 46.4%. 212 bottles.

◈ **Mosgaard Organic Single Malt Whisky** Pedro Ximenez cask, batch no. 1, bott 22 Mar 19 db **(86.5) n22 t22.5 f21 b21** No off notes: perfectly good butts at work here. The trouble, as can so often be the case, the PX does too much and obliterates the rest of the whisky, so only the intensely sweet grape shows. Good spice and a decent fruitcake quality. But ironic that an organic whisky is not allowed to develop organically... 46.3%. 300 bottles.

**Mosgaard Young Malt** Pedro Ximenez cask finish, batch no. 18-01, production date. 170118, 25 ppm db **(86.5) n21 t22 f22.5 b21** A very pretty whisky with plenty of fruit and nut. Technically well made. And also filled into a decent and not overly-sweet PX. However, has been bottled at a point where both the young spirit and the oak influence are at times a little at cross purposes, perhaps not helped by lazy, slightly incoherent peat. That said, the chocolate towards the finale is sublime. 41%.

# NYBORG DESTILLERI Nyborg. Working.

◈ **Nyborg Destilleri Ardor Isle of Fionia** batch no. 117 db **(92.5) n23** youthful, clean and gristy, the sugars luxuriate in their delicate citrus tones; **t23** sweet and mouth-watering on delivery, this could easily be mistaken for a Speysider as the grain is imbued with the light vanillas of a high quality, previously used cask. Admirably simple, yet what it does is done with panache; **f23** really classy fade: again gristy, but a little mocha and spice moves in just as it is meant to; **b23.5** as sweet and well controlled as Sweden's vital World Cup victory over Switzerland today. Technically, a right little beauty... 46.8%.

◈ **Nyborg Destilleri Ardor Isle of Fiona** batch no. 165 db **(89) n22.5 t23 f21.5 b22** Keeping up their clean, malty style but this has slightly more active fruit at play here, including over-ripe greengages. Slightly more bitter than normal at the death, also. 46%. nc ncf.

◈◈ **Nyborg Destilleri Danish Oak Isle of Fiona** batch no. 167 db **(93)** n23 t23.5 f23 b23.5 Denmark is by far and away the least forested of all Scandinavian countries. So finding an oak tree to make a barrel from must have been a major achievement in itself. It was well worth the effort, because this is a stunner and the impact of the tannin is the least assertive of any European oak I have encountered outside of Spain. The balance of the nose is spot on with lazy harmony between grain and light toasty tannin with a little orange blossom honey as the buffer. The grist is on overdrive on the palate, the oak providing a slightly salty back up. With its Jaffa Cake sub-strata, there is mMuch to celebrate here. *46%. nc ncf.*

## SMALL BATCH DISTILLERS Holstebro. Working

**Small Batch Distillers Peat by Peat 3rd Edition** American white oak virgin barrels, db **(89)** n22.5 t23 f21 b22.5 It is probably this whisky's foibles that make this so attractive. *60%.*

**Small Batch Distillers Peated Mystery 2nd Edition** French virgin oak barrels db **(88)** n21.5 t23 f21 b22.5 Again, drops a few points for a few technical weaknesses, on the nose and finish especially. But the over-all picture is very pretty. *56%.*

**Small Batch Distillers Peated Rye** db **(90)** n23 t22 f22.5 b22.5 Playing around my lab over the years I have experimented with amalgamating the intense aroma and flavour of rye with the depth of a smoky malt. I had come up with some interesting concoctions but none, to my memory, quite matched the unique shape of this remarkable whisky, especially on the nose. Memorable...and very beautiful. *58%.*

**Small Batch Distillers RugBy** db **(91.5)** n22.5 t23.5 f22.5 b23 A profound rye which, if cleaned up a bit would represent the grain with a touch of classicism. *58%.*

**Small Batch Distillers RugBy Extend** French virgin oak barrels db **(86.5)** n21.5 t23.5 f21 b20.5 No denying the impact of the rye, or its high class crisp fruitiness, which can be fully enjoyed on the astonishing delivery and for a short while beyond. But a combination of the wide cut off the still and the unforgiving tannin means the balance of the whisky is lost far too early and easily. *60%.*

## STAUNING WHISKEY Skjern. Working.

**Stauning Heather** dist 2013/14, bott Sept 17 db **(87.5)** n22 t22 f22 b21.5 When I was a teenage trainee reporter my first girlfriend was called Heather – and she was every bit as sweet as the delivery on this malt. However, a wisp of a thing, she was nothing like so stodgy nor so inelegant. Intense and chewy (this whisky, not Heather) there are some beautiful moments to savour (both the Stauning and Heather) but ultimately let down by a feinty bitterness (again, the whisky, not Heather). And kisses quite beautifully (Heather, not the Stauning). *48.7%.*

**Stauning Kaos** dist 2013/14, bott Apr 17 db **(90.5)** n23.5 t22.5 f22 b22.5 Youthful and orderly to me... *473%.*

◈◈ **Stauning Kaos** dist 2014/15, bott Jun 18 db **(85)** n21.5 t21.5 f21 b21 A real surprise here: a mild feintiness detectable on the nose and visible on the palate from delivery to finish. That said, the acacia honey and malt thread running through this doesn't compensate entirely, but concentrate on that alone and you have a very rich and full-flavoured and lightly phenolic whisky. *46.8%.*

◈◈ **Stauning Kaos** dist 2014/15, bott Sept 18 db **(90)** n22 an imperfect nose, though the genteel phenols help in the repairs. Very young...; t23 the wide cut of the spirit ensures that this is off the scale from a chewability perspective. The lightest smoke is mixed into the marzipan and golden syrup; f22 dries with a surprising degree of sootiness; late feints; b23 one of those whiskies where its technical failings end up adding to the overall enormity and enjoyment of the experience. *471%.*

◈◈ **Stauning Peat** virgin cask, dist 2014, bott Jan 19 db **(95.5)** n23.5 peated bourbon... Of the two camps the tannins larges it over the smoke...; t24.5 a real head-on smash on delivery with not a scintilla of harmony to be found in the first two or three flavour waves. Quite quickly a compromise is reached, mainly involved the rich muscovado sugars which tone down the excesses of the tannin and bring the peat in to the fold. By the mid-point, the combination of smoke, tannin and sugars are as near as perfect as you are likely to find...but a bit of a battle to get there..; f23.5 the faultless spirit – entirely free of any kind of feint - has settled down now to a butterscotch-based finale with the peat providing a delightful anchor, both in weight and with the vaguely spicy sootiness drawing out any lingering sweetness; b24 a virgin that smokes...you have to have at least one vice in your life, I suppose. *52.1%.*

**Stauning Peated 7th Edition** dist 2012, bott May 18 db **(91)** n23 t23 f22 b23 Understated peat at work here: indeed, when I last visited Stauning, it was still a working farm and the earthiness of the animals there had a more rugged phenolic quality than this sexy, gentle teaser. *48.4%.*

◈◈ **Stauning Peat Festival 2018** cask no. 64, dist 2012, bott Aug 18 db **(95)** n23.5 a fabulous mix of mostly peat and sharp, acidic bite of anthracite combine for a pugnacious nose. Very youthful still, but the freshness appears to add to the experience; **t24** top quality delivery! There is a rare crispness to the phenols, hard edged and cutting through the palate with the ultra-salivating barley sugars; a fabulous blend of high propane phenol, Manuka honey and molasses make for an astonishing follow through; **f23.5** dries to allow some semblance of oak into the mix, a light vanilla streak dousing the sweetness; **b24** the last Stauning Peated malt I encountered was a muted affair, the smoke charming rather than barnstorming. Quite the opposite here with a big, memorable statement by the phenols. And though an obviously young whisky, this is so beautifully made you cannot help but fall completely in love. A Danish Saga which turns into a classic. 47.1%. sc.

⬩ **Stauning Rye** dist 2015, bott Nov 18 db **(89) n22** a wide cut plus chiselled rye...; **t23** the muscular grain takes on a distinctly honeyed hue; salivating molten Demerara sugars; **f21.5** just a little heavy on the feints; **b22.5** the handsome bad boy of the family... 50%.

⬩ **Stauning Rye** dist 2016, bott Mar 19 db **(96) n24** a rye freak's rye. There is nothing like the intensity of beautifully malted rye...and it doesn't come more intense than this.... **t24.5** rye to the power of rye....multiplied by bruyeree honey. Plus peppers. Also bracketed by a light salty, vanilla and butterscotch number....; **f23.5** toasted honeycomb with the most dazzling pieces **b24** don't know about Stauning... Stunning, more like...! 50%.

⬩ **Stauning Rye Cask Strength** dist 2015/16, bott Feb 19 db **(92.5) n22.5** malted rye has an aroma so far removed from anything else in the whisky world, it is just too easy to sit here and nose in pure wonderment! But once you go into professional mode, you soon spot a slight generosity on the cut which ups the oiliness even further and increases the weight significantly; you also spot some sublime lime blossom honey to add to the intense rye; **t23.5** massive! Imagine ulmo and heather honey combining with rye on steroids. There you just about have it...; **f23** anyone who knows Crunchie chocolate bars will recognise this...; **b23.5** even with the odd imperfection from the distillation, this is still an incredible whisky to experience, just pounding with insane degree of rye intensity. 58.7%.

⬩ **Stauning Rye The Master Distiller** cask no. 33, dist 2011, bott Aug 18 db **(95.5) n24** an essay of complexity: not just prickly, two-dimensional rye but eucalyptus too. Some lovely hickory Victory V cough sweet; **t24** a huge delivery, juicy beyond words, again with the cough sweet hickory on the nose not just marking its mark but being the guiding hand which is followed by honey embossed rye. Red liquorice and molasses leak in to add to the complexity, then a wonderful countering, drier, tannin note ramps up the peppers; **f23.5** ridiculously long and complex with a waxy feel to the vibrant grain. Still salivating even now...; **b24** this would not be out of place in the shelves of very high end Kentucky rye.... 51%. sc.

⬩ **Stauning Røg** dist 2014, bott Oct 18 db **(92.5) n22** sharp, acidic and nipping. The peat takes on a distinctly angular personality...; **t24** fantastically busy, with a real brittleness to both the sugars and phenols. The honey, you would expect, would have some heathery utterances, seeing as that plant was used in the smoking process. However, much more bruyere in style – and texture - with accompanying molasses; **f23** remains firm and with virtually no give until the last. A touch bitter as the sugars recede; **b23.5** I always love discovering new whisky styles, and this definitely falls into that category. Brilliantly inventive on the palate. 49.6%.

**Stauning Traditional** rum cask finish, dist 2014, bott Nov 17 db **(80) n21 t20 f19 b20** When I did some of the first experimentation with rum cask maturation some 20 years ago, one of the first things I noticed, very early on, was the danger of the sugars closing down development and conversation within the whisky. This tight and limited expression is a good example of what I mean. 48.2%.

**Stauning Web Kaos** dist 2013/14, bott Apr 17 db **(95) n24 t23.5 f23.5 b24** It seems wonderfully perverse to mark a whisky which is supposedly chaotic so highly for its balance. But rather than Kaos, perhaps this should be regarded as a controlled explosion...! One of the best whiskies I have ever experienced from Stauning: an absolute classic by any standards. 49.9%.

**Stauning Young Rye** dist 2014, bott Oct 17 db **(93.5) n23.5 t23.5 f23 b23.5** The mark of a very good distillery is that they learn from their mistakes. They had noted and acknowledged that their earlier cuts with the rye was too wide. The result is this: a true rye whisky, as clean and clear as a penny whisky and just as penetrating. 51.1%.

**Stauning Young Rye** dist 2014, bott Feb 18 db **(92) n23.5 t23.5 f22 b23** Does what it says on the tin: a substantial young rye! 43.3%.

**Stauning Young Rye** rum cask finish, dist 2014, bott Jan 18 db **(87.5) n23 t22.5 f20 b22** Some magnificent clipped honey tones really does bring out the more fragile and fruity elements of the rye. Annoyingly let down by a poor finish which leaves the bitterness unchecked. 46.5%.

## THY WHISKY Snedsted. Working.

⬩ **Thy Whisky No. 7 Bøg Single Malt** ex-Olorosso fad, dist Aug 14, tappet Sept 17 db **(90.5) n22** fruit buns with a little butter; **t23** voluptuous delivery: the grape is in full flow, mixing muscovado sugars and manuka honey. Oak and barley jut through the morass to ensure some serious salivation; **f22.5** toastier tannin and a little fruit chocolate; **b23** a gorgeous late night whisky. *52.1%. nc ncf. 677 bottles.*

◈ **Thy Whisky No. 8 Fjordboen Single Malt** ex-Olorosso fad, cask nos. 46 & 74, dist Mar 15, tappet May 18 db **(93.5) n23** almost a PX sugar intensity to this: the rich fruit dominates, but with a kind hand; **t23.5** there we go again: early strains of PX, until it is rowed back and a more must-style grapiness emerges; the spices offer just the right weight and pace; **f23** plum pudding with a little Manuka honey an no little spice; **b24** sherry lovers will be on their knees worshipping this bottling. A truly faultless butt at work, fresh and very accessible on the palate. *51.6%. nc ncf. 569 bottles.*

◈ **Thy Whisky No. 9 Bøg Single Malt** ex-Olorosso fad, cask nos. 42, 43 & 44, dist Dec 14, tappet Jan 19 db **(96.5) n24** like my old farmhouse fireplace in Melton Mowbray back in the early 1980s, when I was cleaning it out: sooty, dry...and hauntingly beautiful...; **t24** extraordinary subtlety to this: varying spiced strata amid the chocolate raisins. The delivery starts dry and builds, minor wave after another into something sweeter and alluring; **f24** lighter spices now but it is the layering of the grape which is spellbinding...what a finish! **b24.5** one of the most complete, complex and compelling whiskies I have tasted this year. A Danish masterpiece... *50.8%. nc ncf. 741 bottles.*

◈ **Thy Whisky Spelt-Rye** virgin oak and ex-sherry fad, dist Mar-April 17, tappet Sept 18 db **(87.5) n21.5 t22.5 f21.5 b22** A punchy, hard-nosed whisky with lots of angular aromas and flavours. Only on delivery when the golden syrup and spelt link arm in arm does it really sit comfortably. But always salivating and sharp and the late, eye-watering tannins adds to the big personality. *46.3%. nc ncf. 644 bottles.*

## TROLDEN DISTILLERY Kolding. Working.
**Trolden Nimbus The Kolding Single Malt Nimbus** cask no. 4 db **(89) n22 t22.5 f22 b22.5** Happy memories of many a tasting I conducted at Kolding back in the day. Before even there was a Whisky Bible! None of those bottles we tasted as Denmark slowly woke up to whisky was anything like this idiosyncratic little beauty, though. *46%. nc ncf sc.*

◈ **Trolden Nimbus The Kolding Single Malt Nimbus** cask no. 5 db **(93) n23** the oak is dynamic in this, really belting out toasty tannins for all it is worth. The malt offers sweetness enough to keep it honest, but this was bottled in the nick of time...; **t23** soft and beautifully oiled on delivery, but still light enough for there to be all kinds of intricate malt notes to double up with the lightest heather honey; **f23.5** the oak resurfaces, now with a gorgeous praline presence, and with the spices a whole lot louder; **b23.5** it has been many years since I was in Kolding giving a Jim Murray whisky tasting. Indeed, so long ago, there wasn't even any Danish whisky in existence, let alone allowing the locals to savour something as delightful as this. An excellent single malt to toast many pleasant memories. *46%. nc ncf sc.*

# FINLAND
## THE HELSINKI DISTILLING COMPANY Helsinki. Working.
**Helsinki Whiskey 100% Rye Malt Release #2** new French oak casks db **(80) n19 t21.5 f20.5 b19** A wide cut on the distillate is accentuated by the oak's inability to compromise. But there is a massive onrushing of icing sugars and golden syrup which for a moment or two takes the pressure off the taste buds. The rye, however, is lost without trace...; *45%.*

**Helsinki Whiskey Rye Malt Release #3** small new French oak casks db **(82.5) n21 t20 f21.5 b20** Probably ideal for drinking nude in a sauna while being flagellated with birch. Like this, it will be enjoyable and painful at the same time. I just hope whoever does the whipping shows more mercy than the French oak... *47.5%. 350 bottles.*

**Helsinki Whiskey Rye Malt Release #4** new American oak casks db **(78.5) n20.5 t20 f19 b19** Not what I was expecting, or looking forward to. Earlier "test" bottlings of maturing spirit using American oak had been positive. This, surprisingly, takes the same route as the French casks with over aggressive tannins. The oils don't help, either. Having tasted their recent new make, which was good, a different wood profile is now a matter of urgency. *47.5%.*

## KYRÖ DISTILLERY COMPANY Isokyrö. Working.
**Rye Whisky #1** bott 10 Aug 17 db **(83.5) n19 t21.5 f21.5 b21.5** No doubting the grain: the rye turns up big and loud, especially at the crescendo on about the fourth flavour wave. But too much oil at work here dulls the sparkle. Recovers beautifully late on with some chocolate milkshake. *47.8%.*

## PANIMORAVINTOLA KOULU Turku. Working.
**Sgoil Sherry Cask** db **(90) n23 t23.5 f21.5 b22.5** Sherry...and clean as a whistle! A sulphur-free dram from Finland. *59%. sc. 80 bottles.*

### TEERENPELI Tahti. Working.

◇ **Teerenpeli 7 Year Old** sherry casks db (87.5) n21.5 t22.5 f21.5 b22 Despite the sherry cask influence, it is the tannin which conquers. Hefty, dry and spicy, there is a unusual fatness to this whisky for them. *50.7%.*

**Teerenpeli 10 Year Old Single Malt** bourbon & sherry casks db (80) n20 t21 f19 b20. Very hard to see what an average sherry butt can add to a malt as good as Teerenpeli's. And, sad to say, this is very average sherry wood, indeed...*43%*

**Teerenpeli Islay Cask** db (95) n24 t24 f23 b24 They have pulled this one off brilliantly. The cleanness of the spirit means there is a glorious impression of a lightly, and delightfully peated malt. Really, after so many years nothing this wonderful distillery does should surprise me. *61.7%*

◇ **Teerenpeli Juhlaviski 13 Year Old** bott Mar 19 db (95) n24 a real stone fruit dryness to this, despite the biting spice and accompanying molasses; t24 usual Teerenpeli take off on delivery, by which I mean a rocket blasting through the taste buds... a mix of concentrated date and prunes, then back to a hoarse dryness; f23.5 at last the malt surfaces, then goes into manic overdrive; b23.5 I have no idea how they do this. But nothing about this distillery is by half measures, Everything you find is at mega intensity. Amazing. *58.5%.*

**Teerenpeli Peated New Make** db (94.5) n24 t23.5 f23 b24 Finland's finest now in fabulous phenols and.... fantastic! *63.5%.*

**Teerenpeli Savu** db (85.5) n21 t22.5 f21 b21 Unusual to find a Teerenpeli at such a relatively weak strength, and it does little to help this whisky. The oils have fractured, resulting in a dry, chalky offering which struggles to find a rhythm or purpose. Pleasant in part and some intriguing phenol tones. But Finns aren't as they should be. *43%.*

# FRANCE
## Single Malt
### DISTILLERIE ARTISANALE LEHMANN Obernai. Working.

**Elsass Whisky Single Malt Whisky Alsacien Premium** db (86) n20.5 t21.5 f22 b22. This is about as close as you'll get to an abstract single malt. The early discordant notes of the distillate are thrown against the canvas of the malt, and then fruit is randomly hurled at it, making a juicy, then spicy, splash. The overall picture when you stand back is not at all bad. But getting there is a bit messy. *50%. ncf.*

### DISTILLERIE BERTRAND Uberach. Working.

**Uberach** db (77) n21 t19 f18 b19. Big, bitter, booming. Gives impression something's happening between smoke and grape... whatever it is, there are no prisoners taken. *42.2%*

### DISTILLERIE CASTAN Villeneuve-sur-Vère. Working.

**Vilanova Berbie** db (80) n20 t21 f19 b20 For what it boasts in intensity it lacks in grace and elegance. Uncomfortable on both nose and finish thanks to less than impressive oak, it just has too much of everything. Some will doubtless find the concentrated prunes and molasses very much to their liking. *44%. ncf.*

**Vilanova New Spirit Single Malt Classic** db (90.5) n23 t23 f22.5 b22 A well-made, light bodied and clean new made showing distinct signs of gristy barley and, surprisingly, vanilla. *45.1%. ncf.*

**Vilanova New Spirit Single Malt Terrocita** db (91.5) n23.5 t23 f22 b23 The peat adds both weight and sweetness to this lean white dog. Plenty of gristy chewiness; the toasty smoked molasses lingers. *45.1%. ncf.*

**Vilanova Terrocita** db (91.5) n23 t23.5 f22 b23 Have to admit that this is a nose and flavour profile I have never quite encountered before. What a shame it wasn't at about 55% abv, I think we might have been heading off the planet from terra firma to terro cita... *43%. ncf.*

### DISTILLERIE DE MONSIEUR BALTHAZAR Hérisson. Working.

**Hedgehog Straight Whisky Bourbonnais** bott code. L2.16 db (85.5) n20 t22.5 f21.5 b21.5. You'd expect this to be a prickly little beast. Yet it is anything but: it celebrates the oils and honeys generated by the ample cut to the full and with only a minimum degree of spice. Eye-watering at its height, an unmistakable rye tartness maximises the flavour profile and dominates deliciously to the end. Get that cut a little tighter and what a magnificent whisky we would have here. *45%. ncf.*

### DISTILLERIE DE LAGUIOLE Laguiole. Working.

◇ **Espirit De Twelve Malt Spirit** lot no. 9.5, port cask db (90) n22 t23 f22 b23 Clean and glimmering with sparkling malt, this spirit shews an unusual early feel for the complexities of absorbing fruit into the system. At this age has every right to be disjointed and out of sorts, but this is anything but! *52.5%. sc.*

⟨⟩ **Espirit De Twelve Malt Spirit** lot no. 10, pedro ximenez & port casks db **(74)** n17 t19 f18 b18 The complete opposite in quality to their Port Cask spirit. Boiled vegetable nose, off key, bitter on the palate. Grim. *48%.*

# DOMAINE DES HAUTES GLACES Saint-John-d'Hérans. Working.

**Domaine des Hautes Glaces Flavis Single Cask Organic Whisky** db **(84.5)** n21 t20 f22.5 b21. Well, you can't say it doesn't have personality. Actually, the maltiness, which improves as it goes along, does hit impressive proportions. And the gathering cocoa also shows the oak plays an important part. But one or two verses of this are well out of tune. *46%. sc.*

**Domaine des Hautes Glaces Moissons Single Malt Organic Whisky** db **(86.5)** n20.5 t22 f22 b22. Warming this to body temperature is vital as, when cool, it is not the most attractive proposition and scores badly. But when it is opened by body heat, the most delicate phenols show a subtlety and weight which were not before apparent, as do the tannins which reveal a more generous and inclusive element. The sugars are decidedly of an oaky bent with a dark toastiness which melt towards the tannins. *42%*

# DISTILLERIE DES MENHIRS Bretagne. Working.

**Eddu Gold** db **(93)** n22 t23 f24 b24. Rarely do whiskies turn up in the glass so rich in character to the point of idiosyncrasy. Some purists will recoil from the more assertive elements. I simply rejoice. This is so proud to be different. And exceptionally good, to boot!! *43%*

**Eddu Grey Rock** db **(87.5)** n21.5 t22 f22 b22. A docile whisky reliant on friendly muscovado sugars which match the vanilla-oak very attractively. *40%*

**Eddu Grey Rock Affinage Porto** db **(83)** n19 t21 f22 b21 Tasting whisky from this distillery is like taking part in a lucky dip: no idea if you'll pick a winner or the booby prize. This has the uncontrollable nose of a dud, but the fruit helps it pick up on the palate to an acceptable level. Good late spices, too. *40%.*

**Eddu Grey Rock Brocéliande** db **(86.5)** n22 t22.5 f20.5 b21.5. Dense whisky which enjoys an enjoyable molassed fruitcake theme. A bit thin and wonky towards the finish. *40%*

**Eddu Silver Broceliande** db **(92.5)** n23 t23 f23 b23.5 Pure silk. A beautiful and engaging experience. *40%.*

**Eddu Silver The Original** db **(92.5)** n23 t23 f23.5 b23 J'adore! *40%.*

# DISTILLERIE DU PÉRIGOLD Sarlat. Working.

**Lascaw Aged 12 Years Blended Malt Whisky** bott 2-12-15 db **(87)** n21 t22 f22 b22. A very pleasant blend, very much of a Scotch style. Super soft, safe though sometimes juicy, this is perhaps held back by a constant caramel theme which tames the expected high points. *40%*

# DISTILLERIE GILBERT HOLL Ribeauvillé. Working.

**Lac'Holl 8 Year Old Single Malt Whisky** db **(69)** n19 t20 f14 b16 If memory serves, this is the youngest Lac'Hol I have tasted. But without doubt it is the most singular and disappointing. The profile of their whisky is usually far from conventional but attractive; this one is utterly bizarre and ugly. The peculiar scenting on the Swedish aquavit-style nose, which appears to include coconut sunscreen and orange liqueur, is matched only by the finish which reminds me, late on, of Milk of Magnesia. This has not been a good tasting day: it just got a whole lot worse... *42%.*

**Lac'Holl Vieil Or 10 Years Old Single Malt Whisky** db **(92.5)** n22.5 t23.5 f23 b23.5 A malt which gives one's taste buds a real working over. Superb balance. *42%*

**Lac'Holl Junior 13 Years Old Single Malt Whisky** db **(89)** n22 t22.5 f22 b22.5 Wow!! Bursts from the glass with so much charisma and charm. Perhaps not technically the finest of all time, but such fun! Delicious!! *43%*

**Lac'Holl 15 Years Old Single Malt Whisky** db **(90.5)** n23.5 t22.5 f22 b22.5 Such a rare display of barley and gristy sugars. Very impressive malt. And fabulously refreshing. *42%*

# DISTILLERIE GLANN AR MOR Larmor-Pleubian. Working.

**Glann Ar Mor 2018** db **(94.5)** n23.5 t23.5 f23.5 b24 There is always something alluring and sexy about effortless elegance...what a classy act. *46%.*

⟨⟩ **Glann Ar Mor 2019** bourbon barrels db **(89.5)** n22 t23 f21.5 b22.5 This brand is usually one of the highlights of my European whisky tasting year. However, this bottling has come up a little short compared to previous years having jettisoned some of its honeyed sweetness for a much thicker, more buxom malt. Still enjoyable, the usual fudge remains in situ, even employing an extra square of chocolate. But there is also a slight bitterness which has knocked the malt out of kilter. Doubtless next year it will be back to its brilliant best. *46%.*

**Glenn ar Mor Maris Otter Barley 2017** bourbon barrels db (**94.5**) **n23 t24 f23.5 b24** She was only the brewer's daughter, as she sat by the mill. Maris Otter was in the mash tun, but she was 'otter still... The kind of malt that moves you to poetry.. *46%. nc ncf.*

**Glann Ar Mor Maris Otter Barley** batch. Autumn 2017 db (**95**) **n23.5 t24 f23.5 b24** This is a cleaner version their other Maris Otter bottling with less oil. Every nuance involves subtlety. Simply great whisky as technically excellent as Pavard's sweetly struck volley against Argentina this afternoon... *46%.*

**Kornog Côteaux du Layon** db (**87.5**) **n22 t22 f22 b21.5** I am rapidly coming to the conclusion that this is a distillery that benefits from bourbon cask above all else. Nothing unattractive about the peppery grape. But it does fill in the many of the natural contours as the malt develops, the so instead of complexity we have a constant (though very attractive) toffee-fruit note. Maybe this distillery has now become so well established as one of the finest, if not the finest, on mainland Europe, I have become hyper critical. Such is the price of excellence. *52.8%. sc.*

**Kornog En E Bezh 10 Year Old** bourbon barrel db (**95.5**) **n23 t24.5 f24 b24** Probably the first Kornog I have encountered with oak taking top billing. The tannins are profound, yet controlled on the nose. The delivery, though, takes some matching: yes, the oak is big and bustles slightly, but the malt – seemingly supercharged with deft spice and tinned maple syrup, hits heights perhaps never before reached in the history of French whisky: it is just a molecule or so away from perfect...The much drier finish soaks up the oak and the almost house cocoa style, aided by the lightest oils to further the distance. This is, by any definition or stretch of the imagination, remarkable whisky and among the best I have tasted this year... *58.9%. sc.*

**Kornog Hanter-Kant 11 Year Old** bourbon barrel db (**89**) **n22.5 t23.5 f21 b22** Not sure the quality of the spirit 11 years ago was quite up to the standards of later years. The oak certainly makes a decent contribution here, but after the malty middle things become just a little too confused. The nose is the outlet for complexity and the delivery for drama, especially with the light chocolate and maple syrup intensity. Lovely whisky, but hard to make head or tail of... *50%. sc.*

**Kornog Pedro Ximenez Finish** bourbon barrel db (**90.5**) **n22.5 t23 f22 b23** This is a top draw PX cask. And, although there is peat, thankfully it is delicate enough not to make for yet another PX-Peat bore where each twain cancels the other out. So just a playful phenol thread followed by some supersonic grape, a little maple syrup lurking about here and there. Simple complexities, so to speak. But pleasantly effective. *46%.*

**Kornog PX Finish 2016** bourbon barrel & PX butt db (**87**) **n21.5 t22 f22 b21.5** Some people will adore this whisky, I know. But, for me, getting a PX cask with a vaguely smoky malt to gel is one of the hardest tricks in the book. Often, as this malt does, it can come across as a little disjointed and aggressive. There is no denying there are some delightfully succulent and attractive phrases, the delivery the pick of the lot. But, despite the idiosyncratic type of wine cask, this is a little too thin and angular for its own good. Enjoyable...but with caveats. *58.1%. nc ncf.*

**Kornog Roc'h Hir 2017** bourbon barrels db (**87**) **n21 t21.5 f23 b21.5** Spoke a little too soon about Roc'h Hir's feinty days being over. Distinct tobacco on the nose – perfectly acceptable if you smoke, I suppose – and a bit of an oily mishmash on the delivery and follow up. On the subject of mash, there is no escaping the gristiness, nor the chocolate mint finale. *46%. nc ncf.*

**Kornog Roc'h Hir 2018** db (**88.5**) **n22 t22.5 f22 b22** very straightforward malt, eschewing a path of twists and turns for a pleasant simplicity. *46%.*

**Kornog Roc'h Hir 2019** bourbon barrels db (**94**) **n23.5 t24 f23 b23.5** Had to check the label twice. Normally one of their more feinty offerings, this has been turned on its head by not only being beautifully made with excess oils kept to a minimum but with a deft smokiness to offer layering and a better sort of weight altogether. The delivery, though, is Glann Ar Mor at the very top of its game, the richness of the gristy barley rocketing off the scales. *46%.*

**Kornog Saint Erwan 2017** first fill bourbon barrel db (**96**) **n24 t24 f23.5 b24.5** If you don't succeed first time, try and try again.... Previous editions of this lightly smoked rendition of Kornog has been found just short of the mark: pleasant but not quite there. Eureka! They've cracked it: this is truly beautiful. Big time... *50%. nc ncf sc. 277 bottles.*

**Kornog Saint Erwan 2018** bourbon barrel db (**95.5**) **n23.5** seaweeds **t24 f23.5 b24.5** A malt which has gone from merely coastal in previous years to tidal. You would swear that some of the English Channel, seaweed and all, has been used to reduce this whisky while the peat used to give this such a proud richness must have been cut just yards from where waves crash against shore. Less a glass of whisky than a sojourn, with your taste buds being explored and, in turn, every aspect of the malt's integrity being re-examined back. How do you explain the tenderness of the citrus, the truffle quality of the cocoa, the myriad layering and the delicate entrance of the bruyere honey..? There are no words. Just the experience. *50%. sc.*

**Kornog Saint Erwan 2019** bourbon barrel db (**92.5**) **n23 t24 f22 b23.5** Tries incredibly hard to capture the genius of the 2018 bottling, but falls a little short. Even so, this is still Premier League malt, though here lighter with greater salivation levels and far more intensity to the barley at the coast of its coastal feel – a kind of coastal erosion, if you like. The peat on the nose is lost slightly in the natural caramels, while there is also a slight bittering out late on. *50%. sc.*

**Kornog Saint Ivy 2017** bourbon barrel db (94.5) n23.5 t23.5 f23.5 b24 Beautifully made and matured: satisfying in every respect. Back in November I celebrated my 60th birthday in London's magnificent Ivy Restaurant: this malt should be a fixture there. I, for one, would have savoured a glass to mark my special day... *59.9%. nc ncf sc. 259 bottles.*

⬥ **Kornog Saint Ivy 2018** bourbon barrel db (92.5) n23.5 t23.5 f22 b23.5 Don't remember the last St Ivy having this understated smoky thread running through it! Puts it into the same herd at the St Erwan bottlings, though the emphasis here appears to be on a lovely diced pear and citrus theme. Naturally we are talking massive juiciness here, that smoke constantly rumbling below for balance. Another lovely whisky from this excellent distillery. *59.7%. sc.*

⬥ **Kornog Saint Ivy 2019** bourbon barrel db (95) n23 t24 f24 b24 A much sharper vintage than the 2018 with passion fruit replacing the citrus. Less phenols, though still enough – and some of them are slightly anthracitish - to contribute to both weight and complexity. But the mint chocolate on the finish is what sets this apart. When the 2018 version struggles slightly with some bitterness, this enters an entirely different dimension, with the cocoa and Manuka and ulmo honey mix making this not just the best finale from this distillery, but among the top three of any malt I have tasted so far this year. Fabulous. *58.2%. sc.*

**Kornog Sauternes Cask 2016** db (88.5) n22 t23 f21.5 b22 The excellence of the cask patches up some unhappy oils. *46%. nc ncf sc.*

**Kornog Sauternes Cask 2018** db (88) n21.5 t22 f22 b22.5 Eye-wateringly intense. *46%.*

⬥ **Kornog Sauternes Cask 2019** db (81) n20 t22 f19 b20 Usually Sauternes casks offer the best returns to whisky of all the wine casks. Unless they are sulphur treated. And that would explain the overall dullness to this peaty malt and the highly unimpressive finish. *46%. sc.*

**Kornog Sherry Oloroso Finish** db (92) n23 t23 f22.5 b23.5 How heart-warming to find not only a clean oloroso butt at work, but the smoke and fruit entirely harmonised. *46%.*

⬥ **Teir Gwech** bourbon barrel db (88.5) n22 t23 f21.5 b22 A serious, simplistic blast of sweet, citrussy barley. A little too bitter on the finish, though. *46%.*

# DISTILLERIE GRALLET-DUPIC Rozelieures. Working.

**G.Rozelieures Whisky De Lorraine Single Malt Whisky** bott code: L446 db (87) n21.5 t22.5 f21 b22. Exceptionally nutty. The blossoming of the sugars on delivery is always attractive, as are the complex nougat/caramel/cocoa tones. Though the feints are always a threat, the genteel pace and softness of the malt makes it well worth a look. *40%*

**G.Rozelieures Whisky De Lorraine Single Malt Whisky Fumé Collection** bott code: L415 db (91.5) n23 t24 f22 b22.5 But for a lingering offnote, this would have scored very highly indeed. A vague smokiness gives this a lovely weight. *46%*

**G.Rozelieures Whisky De Lorraine Single Malt Whisky Rare Collection** bott code: L446 db (88.5) n19.5 t23.5 f22.5 b23 One of the sweetest and most lush malts this year, but always delicious. *40%*

**G.Rozelieures Whisky De Lorraine Single Malt Whisky Tourbé Collection** bott code: L416 db (92) n22 t23.5 f23 b23.5 There is a feinty flaw to this, and even perhaps a slight lack of copper in the system; but the overall picture is a very pretty one. *46%*

# DISTILLERIE GUILLON Louvois. Working.

**Guillon No. 1 Single Malt** de la montagne de Reims db (87) n22 t21 f22 b22. Right. I'm impressed. Not exactly faultless, but enough life here really to keep the tastebuds on full alert; By and large well made and truly enjoyable. Well done, Les Chaps! *46%*

# DISTILLERIE HEPP VUM MODERTAL Uberach. Working.

**Authentic Whisky D'Alsace Whisky Single Malt Doble Fût No. 6** db (82.5) n19 t22.5 f20 b21 Well, that was different! The nose is vaguely on the soapy side and the dry finish conjures up a late burn. The delivery, though, does have a brief spasm of enjoyably intense barley at its heart, and a little cocoa to follow through. *42%. ncf.*

**Authentic Whisky D'Alsace Whisky Single Malt Doble Fût No. 7** db (87) n21 t23 f21 b22 A much more complete malt than their No.6. The nose is a tad austere and, again, the finale requires a fire extinguisher as the degree of burn increases. But there is no doubting the beauty and integrity of the delivery, a kind of malt and chocolate bonbon, even with a Milky Way element. My word it's hot, though. *40%. ncf.*

**Authentic Whisky D'Alsace Whisky Single Malt Pinot Noir & Pinot Gris** db (85) n21.5 t22.5 f20 b21 The unspoiled grape offers a magnificent salivating juiciness. But even barrels as excellent as these cannot completely cover the flame-throwing traits of the original spirit. *47%. ncf. 640 bottles.*

**Authentic Whisky D'Alsace Whisky Single Malt Russian Imperial Stout #01** db (76) n19 t22 f16 b19 I adore malt whisky. And my cellars are never without a case of Harvey's Russian Imperial Stout. But would I drink the two together? Never! The nose, though sweet, is undone by hop and there is not enough cover on the attractive, viscous malt to see off the incendiary tendencies of the spirit. 43%. ncf.

**Authentic Whisky D'Alsace Whisky Single Malt Squaring the Circle** Pinot Noir & Pinot Gris casks db (86.5) n22 t23 f20 b21.5 Hot as Hades. But at least the nose and the delivery does offer us an all to brief vision of Pinot perfection... 48.6%. ncf. 890 bottles.

**Authentic Whisky D'Alsace Whisky Single Malt Timeless Intemporel** db (81) n20 t21.5 f19 b20.5 Something a little beery about this. The late burn is as unforgiving as usual but the maltiness does have a little extra sweetness to counter the flames. 47%. ncf.

# DISTILLERIE J.ET M. LEHMANN Obernai. Working.

**Elsass Single Malt Whisky Gold Aged 7 Years** Bordeaux Blanc finition db (90) n23 t22.5 f22 b22.5 Deceptive and delicious. 40%.

**Elsass Single Malt Whisky Origine Aged 7 Years** Bordeaux Blanc barrel db (90.5) n23 t23 f22 b22.5 A picture of understated elegance. 40%.

**Elsass Single Malt Whisky Premium Aged 8 Years** Sauternes barrel db (94.5) n23 t24 f23.5 b24 There is no finer wine cask in which to mature whisky than a clean Sauternes one. This does nothing to undermine my argument. Truly superb. 50%.

# DISTILLERIE MEYER Hohwarth. Working.

**Meyer's Le Whisky Alsacien Blend Superieur** bott code: L1808595 db (87.5) n21.5 t22.5 f21.5 b22 Some feints kick in early here but recovers for a date and walnut chewiness on the delivery in particular. Not quite as well constructed as their last blend but at least here we see a fine example of extra oils being put to good use. And the malt making its mark deliciously and with gusto. 40%.

**Meyer's Le Whisky Alsacien Blend Superieur Affinage En Fut De Sauternes Finition Pinot Noir** bott code: L179895 db (91.5) n23 t23 f22.5 b23 Now, I may just have mentioned that I have a Meyer's Parrot called Percy. Percy likes raspberries and cherries. And he also likes grapes. As well as grains. I'd better not tell him I've tasted this whisky today or there might just be one very upset bird. This is mine...all mine...! 40%.

◇ **Meyer's Le Whisky Alsacien Pur Malt No. 0395 Affinage En Fut Sauternes Finition En Fut De Bourgogne** bott code: L1830656 67430 db (90.5) n22.5 just little feint, but the spices attached to the oozing fruit are nimble and fascinating; t23 only a top Sauternes cask is able to stoke up this degree of thick, controlled sweetness, a mix of golden syrup and ulmo honey. The tannins intervene with a nonchalance bordering on the arrogant; f22 just a little bitter as the feints reform; good spices, though; b23 a beautiful malt from Meyer's. Not quite technically as fine as last year's but still a treat. 40%.

◇ **Meyer's Le Whisky Alsacien Pur Malt No. 3632** bott code: L1834296 67430A db (86) n22 t22 f20.5 b21.5 Percy, my Meyer's Parrot, wasn't too happy with the last bottling I showed him last year, and he's still turning his beak up at this one. The feints are just a little too problematical, though a mixture of Murray Method and keeping the glass in warm water for a few minutes does help dispel the worst of them to allow some heather-honey-tinged malt to flourish. 40%.

**Meyer's Le Whisky Alsacien Pur Malt No. 06857** bott code: L173469667430 db (84) n20.5 t21.5 f21 b21 Now, I won't be offering this one to Percy my Meyer's Parrot. He would have been mightily impressed with the gristy sweetness of their last pure malt I encountered. But this has a feinty edge which limits the scope of the sugars and overall development. Pleasant, oily of course, but lost its chirpiness. 40%.

**Meyer's Le Whisky Alsacien Pur Malt 12 Ans** db (92.5) n23 t23.5 f23 b23 An astonishing role reversal: usually it the older whiskies of the microdistilleries which are weaker as the distiller has yet to learn to master his stills. Yet this is as clean as a whistle, unlike their younger malt. A wonderfully precise and nutty experience. Percy....!!! Daddy's got a treat for you...! 53%.

◇ **Meyer's Le Whisky Artisanal Blend Superieur** bott code: L1905595 67430A db (93) n23 complex, almost playful with its dry grape skin and crushed pips; soft peppery tones compliment wonderfully; t23.5 salivating malt then a plethora of even juicier fruit injections; the oak has much to say here, not least with the spices; f23 a dry, elegant finish allowing the complexity of the delivery to play out with minimum fuss but maximum spice; b23.5 a feint-free, beautifully clean Meyer's showing great understanding between the relative weights of fruit and oak. Impressive. 40%.

◇ **Meyer's Le Whisky Artisanal Blend Superieur Affinage En Fut Sauternes Finition Pinot Noir** bott code: L1833895 67430 db (86) n21 t23 f20.5 b21.5 While the nose and finish may be less than perfect and the balance is somewhat... errr, unbalanced, there is absolutely no denying the brilliance of the delivery and the following half dozen flavour shock waves. There are a few moments of fruity genius in there. *40%*.

## DISTILLERIE WARENGHEM Lannion. Working.

**Armorik** db (**91**) n23 t22 f23 b23. I admit it; I blanched, when I first nosed this, so vivid was the memory of the last bottling. This, though ,was the most pleasant of surprises. Fabulous stuff: one of the most improved malts in the world. *40%*

**Armorik Millésime Matured for 10 Years** cask no. 3261 db (**92**) n22.5 t23 f23 b23. Never quite know what you are going to get from these messieurs. Didn't expect this bottle of delights, I must say. The sweetness is a bit OTT at one point, but just copes. *56.1%. sc.*

**Armorik Sherry Finish** db (**92**) n22.5 t23.5 f23 b23.5. The first sherry finish today which has not had a sulphur problem...and I'm in my eighth working hour...! Bravo guys! If their Classic was a note on sophistication, then this was an essay. *40%*

## KAERILIS Le Palais. Working.

**Kaerilis l'Aube du Grand Dérangement 15 Ans** db (**83.5**) n20 t22.5 f20 b21. Misfires when the revs are up, but purrs for moment on two on delivery as the sugar and barley kicks in to delicious effect. An enigmatic fruitiness enriches. *57%. nc ncf sc.*

## WAMBRECHIES DISTILLERY Wambrechies. Working.

**Wambrechies Single Malt Aged 8 Years** db (**83**) n20 t21 f21 b21. There's that aroma again, just like the 3-y-o. Except how it kind of takes me back 30 years to when I hitchhiked across the Sahara. Some of the food I ate with the local families in Morocco and Algeria was among the best I have ever tasted. And here is an aroma I recognize from that time, though I can't say specifically what it is (tomatoes, maybe?). Attractive and unique to whisky, that's for sure. I rather like this malt. There is nothing quite comparable to it. One I need to investigate a whole lot more. *40%*

## UNSPECIFIED

**Brenne French Single Malt Whisky Estate Cask** finished in Cognac barrels, batch no.001, bott 2017 (**80.5**) n19 t21.5 f19.5 b20.5 In over 25 years of professionally tasting whisky, I cannot recall a single sample that has this profile. Firstly, had I tasted blind I would not have recognised this as a single malt. The nose has an almost synthetic quality, candy floss and pear drops. The body is thin, though not unpleasant when the sugars settle, and the vanilla makes its mark. Once you are over the peculiar nose, there is nothing to fear...or be particularly excited about, either. *40%*.

**Brenne Ten French Single Malt Whisky Aged 10 Years** bott 2016 (**85.5**) n21 t22.5 f21 b21 I'd love to know what kind of warehouse this whisky has spent the last ten years maturing in: the most dominant trait is fruit. Indeed, the malt is lost entirely, as though it has lived exclusively in the environment of cider brandy and Armagnac, to the extent that it has changed character into the content of its brother casks. Have to enjoy the mega-fruity delivery, though it doesn't possess an atom of whisky character; and quite a bite, too. *48%*.

◆ **Maison Benjamin Kuentz Aux Particules Vimes Single Malt Whisky** (**91**) n23 t22.5 f22.5 b23 Anyone who tasted Glen Scotia during the 1980s may remember their odd slightly peated version. This has an almost identical fingerprint, except this is slightly better constructed on the palate and with none of the saltiness of the Campbeltowner. Repays the Murray Method *46%. nc ncf.*

◆ **Maison Benjamin Kuentz (D'un) Verre Printanier Single Malt Whisky** (**91**) n22.5 t23 f22.5 b23 A delicately smoked and beautifully distilled whisky which revels in its light, malty character despite the phenols. Even lightens things further with a gentle twist of lime. A well-known style of malt, impressively achieved. *46%. nc ncf.*

◆ **Maison Benjamin Kuentz Fin de Partie Single Malt Whisky** (**84**) n21 t22 f20.5 b20.5 Very simplistic malt with not quite enough personality to go it alone without much in the way of oak back up. *46%. nc ncf.*

◆ **Maison Benjamin Kuentz Le Guip Single Malt Whisky** (**92**) n22.5 t24 f22.5 b23 This is an impressive bunch of whiskies and cask strength does their malty demeanour no harm whatsoever. Light, in the house style, with a salivating gristy barley note that makes it worth finding a bottle of this alone. The most beautifully intact maltiness of any whisky I have tasted for some while. *55%. nc ncf.*

## Blends

**Moon Harbour Pier 1 Sauternes cask finish** (**86.5**) n20 t22.5 f22 b22. A sticky toffee, chewy number with a beautiful flavour spike as the apricot on the Sauternes kicks in and lingers. Shame about the nose, though, which cannot disguise far from peerless malt. *45.8%. ncf.*

## Vatted Malts

◆ **Bellevoye Bleu Whisky Triple Malt Finition Grain Fin** bott code: A18184A **(87.5)** n21.5 t22 f22 b22 Goes pretty hefty on the tobacco note on both nose and delivery. But the wide cut delivers impressively on the chocolate nougat and even, surprisingly, a degree of chewy date alongside the malt. *40%*.

◆ **Bellevoye Blanc Whisky Triple Malt Finition Sauternes** bott code: A18199A **(82.5)** n20 t21.5 f21 b20 I am tasting in the near dark here for maximum sensory effect – and this one nearly knocked me off my chair. Certainly one of the strangest malts I have tasted this year with the most vividly citrusy nose on a Sauternes finish I have ever encountered – almost like washing up liquid. To say this whisky has a clean nose would be an understatement... Malty on the palate, but never quite feels right.*40%*.

◆ **Bellevoye Rouge Whisky Triple Malt Finition Grand Cru** bott code: A18200A **(83)** n21.5 t22 f19.5 b20 Despite the Grand Cru, there Smoke Blue as a tobacco element makes an undesired contribution. The fruit is sweet and intense, though. The finish a bit of a mess. *43%*.

◆ **Bellevoye Noir Whisky Triple Malt Édition Tourbée** bott code: A18232A **(87)** n22.5 t22 f21 b21.5 There is a certain primitive quality to the peatiness which, for all its simplistic naïvety, packs no end of charm. Lots of toffee kicks in, reducing the complexity somewhat. But that peat, flighty on the nose and warming on the palate, has a distinctly more-ish quality. *43%*.

# GERMANY
## ALTE HAUSBRENNEREI A. WECKLEIN Arnstein. Working.
**Wecklain A.53 Frankonian Single Malt** barrels 4, 3 & 9, bott code LN 1004-17 db **(89)** n22 t22.5 f22 b22.5 An amiable, sweet malt. *50%. 560 bottles.*

**Wecklain A.54 Rushburn Frankonian Single Malt** barrels 8 & 19, bott code LN 1005-17 db **(90)** n23.5 t23 f21.5 b23 A very different, highly evocative whisky. *43%. 650 bottles.*

## BAULAND BRENNEREI ALT ENDERLE ROSENBURG. WORKING.
**Alt Enderle Neccarus 8 Years Old Single Malt Whisky** db **(90.5)** n22 t23 f23 b22.5 A gently complex, delightful malt. Had it been scotch, I would have thought it was a coastal dram. Odd...! *43%*

**Alt Enderle Neccarus 12 Years Old Single Malt Whisky** db **(94)** n23.5 t23.5 f23 b24 Technically, among the best malt I have ever encountered from Germany. *43%*

**Alt Enderle Neccarus 15 Years Old Port Fass Single Malt Whisky** db **(92.5)** n23 t23.5 f23 b23 A chocolate mousse is on the loose. *51%*

**Alt Enderle Neccarus 15 Years Old Sherry Fass Single Malt Whisky** db **(86.5)** n21 t22 f21.5 b22. Clean sherry. But, after the mouth-watering delivery, relatively sweet and simple with just not enough gear changes. Pleasant, if not up to the standard of the other Neccarus. *49%*

## BIRGITTA RUST PIEKFEINE BRÄNDE Bremen. Working.
**Van Loon 5 Year Old Single Malt Whisky** batch 2012 db **(85)** n21.5 t22 f20 b21.5 Usually, a little extra strength will greatly enhance a complex whisky - if given time in the glass. The exception is when the cut is already a little too wide, resulting in a lumpy, ultimately bitter effort. Where this does benefit is in the richness of the fruit and the light mocha effect. *55%*.

## BRENNEREI BERGHOF RABEL Owen-Teck. Working.
**Whisky Stube Spirit of the Cask OWEN Albdinkel** Jamaika rum fass finish, destillert am 01/2012, abgefüllt am 11/2017 **(90)** n21.5 t23 f22.5 b23 The spirit is not exactly faultless. But a stupendous rum cask has generated a treasure chest of untold honeyed riches. *46%*.

## BRENNEREI DANNENMANN Owen. Working.
**Danne's Single Malt Schwäbischer Whisky Vom Bellerhof** dist 09, cask strength, bott code L 0017 db **(87)** n20 t23 f22 b22. A huge whisky which kicks a lot harder than its 55% abv. Works a lot better than its sister 43% bottling, making the most of the golden syrup and grist mix, and the spiced cocoa fade. Pretty enjoyable. *54.9%*

## BRENNEREI FELLER Dietenheim-Regglisweiler. Working
**Augustus Dinkel Port Single Grain** port cask finish, bott code los 903 db **(89)** n21.5 t22.5 f23 b22 The odd Feller whisky I have tasted of late has been found guilty of going easy on the character front. No such charge can be levelled at this peculiar feller...enjoy the ride! *46%*.

**Augustus Single Grain** port cask finish, bott code los 1001 db **(85.5)** n21 t22 f21 b21.5 I seem to remember their last Port pipe being slightly on the faulty side. No such problem this time, but the grain and spirit make hard work of gelling. Peculiarly angular on both nose and delivery there is a spirit note which doesn't quite ring true. A real mixed bag. *58.8%*.

⟨⟩ **Augutus Single Grain Emmer Urkorn** bott code los 1001 db **(85.5)** n23 t21.5 f20 b21 A fabulous nose with its fair share of kumquats, but this never registers on the palate and is unbalanced and bitter, showing an orange peel tartness. *46%. nc ncf.*

**Valerie Rye Malt** bott code los 901 db **(88.5)** n22 t22.5 f22 b22 Highly attractive but you seriously implore the grain to take firmer control. *46%.*

**Valerie Rye Malt** bott code los 901 db **(91.5)** n22.5 t23.5 f22.5 b23 The extra strength and oils offer a sharper edge to the rye and greater overall depth and length. *59.9%.*

**Valerie Single Malt** bott code los 113 db **(87.5)** n22 t22 f21.5 b22 A sweet, silky and malty dram guilty perhaps of resting on its laurels and allowing the ever-intensifying caramels to have far too great a say. *40%.*

⟨⟩ **Valerie Single Malt** French Pineau cask finish, bott code los 113 db **(88.5)** n22 a heavy, tight nose of dried dates and muscovado sugars; **t22.5** lush delivery, the thickness of flavour even more intense than the nose. Outline dark sugars, the gaps filled with molasses and plum pudding; **f22** a little chocolate but still no relaxing; **b22** the kind of malt that wears you out... *46%. nc ncf.*

⟨⟩ **Valerie Single Malt** sherry cask, bott code los 115 db **(92.5)** n23.5 delightful boiled fruit candy, diced apple and fresh barley. Who could ask for more...? **t23.5** a salivating delivery with melt-in-the-mouth muscovado sugars and barley in happy tandem with the toffee apple; **f22.5** a little spice and cocoa; **b23** first things first: no off notes – yep, a faultlessly clean sherry cask. And this surprisingly light and delicate whisky certainly takes full advantage! *46%. nc ncf.*

⟨⟩ **Valerie Single Malt** French Pineau cask finish, bott code los 113 db **(94)** n23.5 charming greengages and dank, juicy dates; **t24** stupendous delivery: faultless distillate and cask combine to offer a complex weave between barley and raisin concentrate. So many layers...it is almost bewildering...; **f23** big chocolate; **b23.5** big difference between this and the 46% version with the oils stretching the sugars further and helping to balance out the fruit intensity. Lush, in every sense of the word... *60.3%. nc ncf.*

⟨⟩ **New Make Barley Malt** dest 15 Mar 19 db **(94.5)** n23.5 t24 f23 b24 Borderline incredible that a malt new make of this ultra-high strength can be with so much barley-packed flavour. But this really is the strength on the bottle – 1/2 proof brilliance! Have a cigar with this at your peril... *86.1%.*

⟨⟩ **New Make Barley Malt Peated** bourbon cask, dest 20 Feb 18 db **(95.5)** n23.5 exceptionally dry: sooty and deep phenols; **t24** a brilliant composition of two exact opposites: dry as dust phenols an super sweet sugars and grist. The result is a delightfully sweet malt with a firm, peaty spine. Not Islay style with a salty, sea-swept edge: dry phenol. And very, very effective with its uncompromising intensity; **f23.5** a light hickory moment before moving into full-blown chocolate and smoke mode. So, so long...; **b24.5** a truly unique take on the peaty malt whisky genre. I can see this building a cult status. Wow! *65.2%.*

## BRENNEREI FRANK RODER Aalen - Wasseralfingen. Working.

**Frank's Suebisch Cask Strength 2008** db **(91)** n22 t23 f23 b23. Frank has really got the hang of how to make the most of his still...a little stunner! And his cleanest yet *57%*

## BRENNEREI HENRICH Küftel, Hoccia. Working.

**Gilors Port Cask** sherry, bott code L13033, dist 2010, bott 2013 db **(86)** n20 t22 f22.5 b21.5. Thoroughly enjoyable and full of depth and no little fruit and spice. But the wide cut, apparent in the sherry version, is not tamed in quite the same effortless way. *44%. sc.*

⟨⟩ **Gilors Single Malt Whisky Peated** bourbon fass, destilliert Nov 12, abgefüllt Mar 18, bott code: L 18021 db **(88)** n21.5 peatiness in shape and proportions of Dali-esque weirdness; **t22.5** you expect big peat...you get gentle smoke over even gentler peat and demerara sugar; **f22** a light spice but the gorgeous butterscotch wins the day; **b22** a malt full of surprises: after a pretty scary start on the nose, it goes on a charm offensive. *42%. 336 bottles.*

⟨⟩ **Gilors Single Malt Whisky Portwein Fass** destilliert Nov 15, abgefüllt Nov 18, bott code: L 18069 db **(87.5)** n21 t23 f21.5 b21.5 Suffers a little from the strength of the bottling: the oils have been broken up and a few cracks appear later on. At cask strength this would have held together much better and made the most of the delightful Fry's Turkish Delight delivery. *40%. 511 bottles.*

⟨⟩ **Gilors Single Malt Whisky Portwein Finish** Islay & portwein fass, destilliert Jul 13, abgefüllt Oct 18, bott code: L 18068 db **(87)** n21.5 t22.5 f21.5 b21.5 It's a bumpy old road for the journey this whisky takes you on: rarely does the peat and fruit appear to be on the same wavelength once they have untangled after the excellent delivery. Juicy and not short of character, either. Enjoyable in its rough and ready way. *45%. 276 bottles.*

⟨⟩ **Gilors Single Malt Whisky PX Sherry Finish** Islay & px sherry fass, destilliert Feb 14, abgefüllt Mar 19, bott code: L 19001 db **(87)** n20 t23.5 f21.5 b22 Gilors seem to be cornering the market in thick set, leaden-weighted soupy whisky. Throw the distillery's generous cut into this particular mix and you really do end up with a jaw-aching single malt. Have to admit I adore the delivery once it gets into its stride and the molasses come into play. *45%. 522 bottles.*

⬦ **Gilors Single Malt Whisky Sherry Fass** destilliert Feb 16, abgefüllt Mar 19, bott code: L 19002 db **(86.5)** n22.5 t21.5 f21.5 b21 A distinctly impressive nose to wow any and all sherry whisky lovers. But flattens out once on the palate. *40%. 654 bottles.*

# BRENNEREI HÖHLER Aarbergen, Kettenbach. Working.

**Whesskey Hessischer Barley-Whisky** bott code GW 01-15 db **(84)** n19 t22 f21.5 b21.5. Follows a similar path to the corn whisky, except this has a dried grass/hay edge and never quite reaches those same heights of chocolatey deliciousness. *44%*

**Whesskey Hessischer Blend-Whisky** bott code BW 01-15 db **(90.5)** n23 t22 f23 b22.5 A typical Hohler slightly flawed stunner. *44%*

**Whesskey Hessischer Corn-Whisky** bott code MW 01-15 db **(87.5)** n20.5 t23 f22 b22. Though the nose leaves you in no doubt about the feints at work, the beauty of the chocolate wafer and Nutella is there to be savoured. *44%*

**Whesskey Hessischer Rye-Malt-Whisky** bott code MW 01-15 db **(84.5)** n19 t22 f21.5 b22. After the usual less than impressive nose, this is an earthy beast which grows on you. Hefty hardly touches it: the chunky sugars aids the clanking rye no end. *44%*

**Whesskey Hessischer Single Malt Whisky** bott code CA 01-15 db **(81)** n18.5 t21 f21 b20.5. Despite the fact it has all kinds of flavour permutations, it is hard to get beyond the butyric. *44%*

**Whesskey Hessischer Whisky au Dinkel** bott code DW 01-14 db **(86)** n21 t21.5 f22 b21.5. Brimming with character, the oils ensure the flavours keep building to the sweet end. Gristy at times, then more spicy as the oils accumulate. Plenty of burnt fudge as it progresses. *40%*

# BRENNEREI MACK, Gütenbach. Working

**Kilpen Single Malt Malt Whisky Single Barrel** bott code L14092108 **(88)** n21.5 the vague heaviness of the still is perfectly countered by toffee and dates; t22.5 gorgeous spice and barley mix. The sugars are half Demerara and half molasses; f22 more creamy toffee, but beautifully spiced up; b22 attractively distilled and delightfully matured whisky. *40%*

# BRENNEREI ZIEGLER Freudenberg, North Württemberg. Working.

**Aureum 1865 5 Year Old** db **(87)** n21.5 t22 f21.5 b22. A tad feinty and nutty, but the huge barley makes this entertaining and sweet in all the right places. *43%*

**Aureum 1865 2008 Cask Strength** db **(84.5)** n21 t21.5 f21 b21. A massive whisky, in no little part due to the very wide cut back in 2008. The usual nougat, hazelnut and cocoa gang up in the thick oils. *53.9%*

**Aureum 1865** Château Lafite Rothschild casks, dist 2008, bott 2015 db **(85)** n20.5 t23 f20 b21.5. Tight, hard, grapey, beautifully sweet on delivery but with some furriness. *47%*

**Aureum 1865 Grave Digger 6 Year Old** db **(88)** n22 t22.5 f22 b22 This grave digger goes deep. *43%*

# DESTILLERIE ARMIN JOBST E.K. Hammelburg. Working.

**Single Malt Whisky 4 Jahre Holzfass** bott code: L SM Whisky 12 db **(82)** n19 t21 f21 b21 Incredibly sweet malt, as though the grist has been distilled into intense barley sugar candy. The spirit suffers from a generous cut, though the feinty nose proves a bark worse than its bite. *43%.*

**Single Malt Whisky 5 Jahre Holzfass** bott code: L SM Whisky 16 db **(80.5)** n18 t20 f21.5 b21 Big feints means it takes a while before the rich malt is able to settle things down. By comparison a lovely finish, but the nose and start leave something to be desired. *43%.*

**Whisky 5 Jahre Holzfass Sherry Cask** bott code: L 5 WhisSher 01:11 db **(85)** n20 t22 f22 b21 This distillery appears to specialise in remarkable whiskies that are loud, brash wrong in so many ways yet strangely compelling and attractive. A clean sherry cask does all in its power to inject an intense fruitiness, and succeeds. The spices are insane and the base spirit is obviously eccentric. The result is a whisky you want on technical grounds to dislike but can't help being dangerously attracted to. *46%.*

**Whisky 6 Jahre Holzfass Madeira Cask** bott code: L 6 WhisMad 06:10 db **(82.5)** n18.5 t22.5 f20 b21.5 Jolly well done and take a bow that Madeira cask. The grain itself offers little that is positive but the soft golden syrup and grape carries a distinct charm. *46%.*

**Whisky 6 Jahre Holzfass Moscatel Cask** bott code: L 6 WhisMos 06:10 db **(85)** n19.5 t22 f21.5 b22 We know what to come to expect by now: a nose a few pfennigs short of a Deutschemark, the entire currency of the whisky propped up by an outstanding cask. It is all about the grape here, which is clean and succulent, the oils and oak giving a kind of chocolate and jam Swiss roll combo. *46%.*

**Whisky 9 Jahre Barrique Barrel Strength** bott code: L 9 Whisky 17 db **(85.5)** n19 t23 f22 b21.5 Another poor nose. But the delivery is like receiving a cherry pie bang in the kisser. Technically a bit of a miss, but for sheer chutzpah, a resounding hit. Outrageous fruity juiciness on delivery that has to be experienced to be believed, and spices are pretty bold, too. And there really is a degree of chocolate cherry tart to this... 48.7%.

# DESTILLERIE HERMANN MÜHLHÄUSER Oberwälden. Working.

**Mühlhäuser Schwäbischer Whisky aus Korn** db **(90)** n22.5 t23 f22 b22.5. So different! If you are into this, it'll be pastoral perfection. 40%

# DESTILLERIE & BRENNEREI MICHAEL HABBEL Sprockhövel. Working

**Hillock 4 1/2-12** bott code L4512 db **(88.5)** n23.5 t22 f21 b22 On the nose I thought: wow! They've come up with a peatiness as close to an Islay style as I've ever seen in mainland Europe – watch out Scotland! Later I discovered that the whisky had been matured in ex-Islay casks. Either way, all rather lovely. 45%

◈ **Hillock 8 Year Old Single Malt Whisky** 82 monate in ex bourbon fässern, 14 monate zum finish in ex Recioto fässern, bott code: L-2118 db **(87)** n22 t22 f21.5 b21.5 A soft, friendly malt determined not to upset any apple carts, but in so doing rather lays too supinely at the feet of the dominant toffee. Malt and spices apparent and, overall, quite pleasant in the German style. 45.3%.

# DESTILLERIE RALF HAUER Bad Dürkheim. Working.

**Saillt Mór Peated Torf Single Malt Whisky** ex bourbon fass, fass-nr. 43, jahrgang 2013, gefüllt am 11/17 db **(92)** n22 t23.5 f23 b23.5 At the best of times this distillery thinks it is planted in the Highlands of Scotland producing, as it does, one of the most Scottish of mainland European whiskies. It appears now to have removed itself to Islay – though it doesn't appear to have picked up the inherent saltiness on the way. Even so, another malty treat from Ralf Hauer – this time peated. Very. 59.8%. sc.

◈ **Saillt Mór Single Cask Malt Whisky** oloroso sherry cask, fass-nr. 44, jahrgang 3/14, gefüllt am 11/18 db **(81.5)** n21 t22 f19 b19.5 Fails to work on too many levels. Never manages to find a sensible balance between the grape and what appears to be a phenolic-style malt while the finish is bitter and off-key. 60.9%. sc.

◈ **Saillt Mór Single Cask Malt Whisky** ruby port cask, fass-nr. 7, jahrgang 1/13, gefüllt am 11/18 db **(95)** n23.5 if you want to know what salty port and malt noses like, have a sniff of this...; t23.5 mouth-filling from the start and immediately eye-watering as the saline depth to the under-ripe fruit becomes apparent. The tannins and malt join forces to produce and lovely heather honey and butterscotch middle; f24 all the more boisterous edges are blunted as light cocoa and molasses form a late and very long creamy duet; b24 such a blissful yet incredibly complex malt. Just rattles the glass with its personality. 57.6%. sc.

◈ **Spirit of the Cask Saillt Mór Single Cask Malt Whisky** pfälzer eiche Jamaika rum, dest Mar 14, gefüllt am Apr 19 db **(92)** n22.5 t23 f23 b23.5 A more than attractive offering, the rum cask acting like a security guard allowing little to pass outside its strict confines. A soft toffee and coffee note is the main theme, helped along with a light saltiness and even a vague hint of bourbon. But the light sugary exoskeleton ensures it keeps its shape throughout. Lovely. 45%. sc

# DESTILLERIE RIEGER & HOFMEISTER Fellbach. Working.

**Rieger & Hofmeister Schwäbischer Malt & Grain Whisky** bott code LWMG06062016 db **(89.5)** n21.5 t22.5 f23 b22.5 Anyone who loves Milky Way chocolate will be a sucker for this 42%.

**Rieger & Hofmeister Schwäbischer No. 4** sherryfass finished, bott code LWSF281117 db **(83.5)** n21 t21.5 f20.5 b21 A wider cut than usual results in extra oils which make it hard work for the fruity notes to knit together as they might. 42%.

**Rieger & Hofmeister Schwäbischer Rye Roggenmalz-Whisky** bott code LWR281117 db **(95)** n23.5 t24 f23.5 b24 A deliciously macho rye of the highest order. 42%.

**Rieger & Hofmeister Schwäbischer Single Malt Whisky** bott code LWSM26082015 db **(85)** n21.5 t21 f21.5 b21 The malt hangs together well, improving in its stature as the intensity increases. Some mocha notes amid the late bitterness. 40%.

# DESTILLERIE THOMAS SIPPEL Weisenheim am Berg. Working.

**Palatinatus Single Malt Whisky American Oak Peated 6 Years Old** db **(92.5)** n22.5 t23.5 f23 b23.5 A sure fire winner amongst peat lovers. Simplistic, maybe. But wonderfully effective and beautifully made. 45%. 218 bottles.

**Palatinatus Single Malt Whisky Bordeaux Single Cask 5 Years Old** db **(81.5) n21.5 t21 f19.5 b20.5** Oddly enough, the wine cask may be sulphur-free, but not so sure about the original distillate. When the fruit shines, all is well. *578%. sc.*

**Palatinatus Single Malt Whisky German Oak Single Cask 2013** db **(85.5) n20.5 t22.5 f20.5 b22** Still a little cabbage water on the nose but the oak appears to already be ramping up the sugars. From the first moment that distinctive melt-in the mouth icing sugar bursts through, followed up by a more measured, gristier charm; long strands of vanilla and barley sugar; bitters out towards the end. Even so, thrilled that Thomas Sippel is still using German oak which I can now see does impart a unique sweetness to maturing malt. *45%. sc.*

**Palatinatus Single Malt Whisky Port Single Cask 2013** db **(81) n19 t21 f21 b20** You know all that effortless beauty and harmonisation displayed by their stunning, peated whisky. Well, this hasn't got it. The cut from the still was too wide and the big grape's attempt to find a balance with it has become like an Argentine football striker: a little messy. *45%. sc.*

# EDELBRÄENDE-SENFT Salem-Rickenbach. Working.

**Senft Whisky** bott code L-SW44, dist 2013, bott 2017 db **(88) n22 t22 f22 b22** Boasts the usual Senft foibles, but light years ahead of their previous bottling. *42%. nc.*

◇ **Senft Whisky** dist 2013, bott 2018, bott code: L-SW47 db **(86.5) n20.5 t22 f22 b22** Perfect example where the wide cut on the still takes on one hand – in this case the nose in particular– but gives on another. For this is one big chewy toffee and nougat beast. *42%. nc.*

**Senft Whisky Edition 78** dist 2013, bott 2017, bott code: L-WE178 db **(85) n19 t22.5 f21.5 b21.5** Absolutely true to the Senft house style, especially on the nose. Plenty of nougat knocking around but that wide cut has also grabbed some oils which beef up the sugars almost towards a meaty molasses. A very good chewing whisky. *47%. nc.*

◇ **Senft Whisky Edition 79** dist 2013, bott 2018, bott code: L-WE179 db **(87.5) n21 t22.5 f22 b22** Although, technically, the nougat style speaks volumes, there is no getting away from the fact that mix of intense toffee and chocolate to accompany it is highly attractive. A kind of distilled Milky Way candy. *47%. nc.*

# EDELBRENNEREI BISCHOF Wartmannsroth. Working.

**Stark & Eigenwillig Rebell Der Whisky Single Grain Chestnut Barrel Finish** db **(93) n23 t23 f23.5 b23.5** I didn't need to be told chestnut maturation was involved here: just one sniff tells you all you need to know. *44%*

# EDELBRENNEREI DIRKER Mömbris. Working.

**Dirker Blended Whisky Aged 3 Years** bott code L L 15 db **(87.5) n21 t22.5 f22 b22.** Beautifully soft and viscous with a highly attractive fruit and nut theme. Even some rather excellent spices late on to keep the show going. Impressed. *45%*

**Dirker Whisky Aged 3 Years** bourbon cask, bott code L E 15 db **(81.5) n18 t22 f20.5 b21.** After the boiled sprouts, unfriendly nose, recovers quickly and nimbly on the palate. The burst of sugars and gristy oils attractively repairs some of the damage. *53%*

**Dirker Whisky Aged 4 Years** Sassicaia cask, bott code L A 16 db **(80.5) n18.5 t22.5 f19 b20.5.** A deeply frustrating whisky. This is one exceptionally beautiful cask at work here and - in the mid ground - offers all kinds of toffee apple and muscovado-sweetened mocha. Sadly, the initial spirit wasn't up to the barrel's standard. This really needs some cleaning up. *53%*

# EIFEL DESTILLATE Koblenz. Working.

**Eifel Whisky Duo Malt & Peat 2018** ex-Bordeaux American oak barrique, dest 2012, bott 2018 db **(89) n22 t23 f22 b22** Rarely subtle. But always delicious. *50%.*

◇ **Eifel Whisky Editions Serie 746.9 German Single Malt Whisky 10 Jahre Alt** 5 jahre refill bourbon fass & wein barrique, 5 jahre Amontillado sherry barrique, bott 2019 db **(84) n21 t21.5 f20.5 b21** A soft, toffee-rich composition. But the degree of feints visible shews how far this distillery has improved technically over the last decade. *46%. nc ncf sc. 640 Flaschen.*

◇ **Eifel Whisky Editions Serie 746.9 German Single Peated Malt Whisky 7 Jahre Alt** 5 jahre refill bourbon fass & wein barrique, 2 jahre 2 x 150l first fill Moscatel sherry, bott 2019 db **(93) n23.5** stupendous smoke: almost vertical in its stance against the fruit, which tries to gain a foothold but takes only one step forward for every three tried...; **t23.5** at last the fruit has an entry. Soft-textured and alluring it is happy to embrace the phenols, which in turn tone down their act and welcome in the chocolate fruit liqueur mid-ground; **f22.5** just bitters very slightly on the oak; **b23.5** when they say peated, they mean peated! This is a whisky which after this number of years and the make-up of malt and cask could easily have gone very wrong. It went very right... *46%. nc ncf sc. 858 Flaschen.*

**Eifel Roggen Whisky Regional Serie Ahrtaler** first fill Pinot Noir Barrique db **(94) n23** the rye has plays a surprisingly big part here, despite the richness of the grape; **t24** the best delivery of the day! Sweet ultra-ripe grape and maple syrup part for a moment for the grain to have its firm, clean say. The mid ground is the rye reasserting its presence...superb! **f23.5** fruit chocolate; **b23.5** Eifel have found a number of ways for their rye whisky to appear in some fascinating and delicious situations. 46%.

⬦ **Eifel Whisky Regional Serie Hohes Venn Quartett** first fill Bordeaux barrique 3 jahre & first fill Eifel rum cask 2 jahre db **(87.5) n21.5 t24 f20.5 b21.5** You never crack the art of blending completely until you fully understand that by adding something, you are taking away something else. This whisky is enjoyable, but is simply doing too much. The delivery, it must be said, a kind of smoky chocolate rum truffle, is to die for: one of the best deliveries anywhere this year; but it is too fleeting. Elsewhere the whisky lurches about unconvincingly, especially towards the long but uncomfortable finish. 46%. nc ncf.

⬦ **Eifel Whisky Roggen Whisky Eilay** 4 jahre first fill sherry barrique, 2 jahre first fill Laphroaig barrel, bott 2019 db **(87) n22 t22 f21 b22** An interesting whisky where the fruit appearance to make a smoother ride of some turbulence elsewhere. A curious, husky, phenolic note and some oaky strangeness at the death. It is never not keeping you guessing... 46%. nc ncf sc. 540 Flaschen.

⬦ **Eifel Whisky Einzelfass Single Rye 2019** ex Bordeaux American oak barrique 3 jahre, first fill Malaga cask 3 jahre, dest 2013, bott 2019 db **(88) n22** fruit pastels but little sign of the grain; **t23** lush delivery: a mix of prune and greengage juice with toasted raisins thrown in for good measure. Warming and fizzing on the palate with the rye getting a slow purchase – too slow, perhaps; **f21** disjointed...; **b22** have to say that as a whisky per se it is enjoyable, but as a rye it is disappointing. Don't see the point of having grains with so much character drowned out by huge fruit. 50%.nc ncf sc.

⬦ **Eifel Whisky Einzelfass Triple Malt 2019** refurbished French oak barrique light toast 3 jahre, first fill port cask 4 jahre, dest 2012, bott 2019 db **(89) n23** an intriguing, conflicting nose: salty coffee and walnut cake, with strands of lemon blossom honey and bourbon-style liquorice; **t22** huge vanilla and natural caramel surge; **f22** close to being a little too toasty...; big spicy chocolate; **b22** the oak puts a tremendous strain on the balance of this malt. But just about gets away with it. In the end proves to be quite a character. 50% nc ncf sc.

⬦ **Eifel Whisky Signatur Serie Smoky Blend** 4 Jahre finish im PX sherry fass db **(88) n22 t23 f21 b22** Another fat whisky from this distillery where the delivery is a thing of beauty but elsewhere is growls around like a malcontent. Can't help enjoying it, though. Having said that, apart from some spices, not sure what happened to the smoke... 50%. nc ncf.

**Eifel Whisky Signature Serie Single Rye** ex-Rotwein cask db **(86) n21.5 t22 f21 b21.5** A little disappointing as the rye doesn't sparkle as usual, save for the odd moment about third or flavour fourth wave in. The fruit is enormous, but a shade too loose. 50%.

**Eifel Weizenmalz Whisky Regional Serie Moseltaler** first fill Weisswein Barrique db **(87) n20.5 t23 f21.5 b22** Though the off-key nose promises little, the delivery and follow through are a pleasant surprise. Indeed, the very first notes offer a satisfying and beautifully balanced intensity, allowing the grape and spice full freedom. The finish reveals an expected patchiness. 46%.

## ELCH WHISKY Gräfenberg. Working.

⬦ **Elch Torf vom Dorf** losnr.: 19/05 db **(95) n23.5** one of the most polite and elegant noses in European whisky: an exhibition of how to offer a distinct peatiness, but do so so it neither overwhelms or threatens to. Perhaps the odd nougat molecule, but this is soon lost in the demilitarised zone between the phenols and fruity muscovado sugars; **t24** the type of malt which, despite its abv and peatiness does not remotely attack the palate but instead arrives with a volley of soft kisses, each one delivery smoke or salivating barley or the crunchiest, friendliest Demerara sugars or lively spices; the mid-ground is now more like a smoky sponge cake, all vanilla and muscovado sugars; **f23.5** long with a lovely interplay between spices and phenols. The oak offers a butterscotch thread, beautifully interwoven and layered; **b24** when you get a whisky that combines a fascinating narrative with clever and subtle understatement yet fortified by occasional boldness, it is hard not to be won over and seduced. Fantastic. 51%.

## FEINDESTILLERIE BÜCHNER Langenbogen. Working

**Büchner Single Malt** db **(89) n22.5** superb malt: clean and alive with gristy sugars. Refreshing and sexy; **t22** light oils, but never enough to discourage the barley from showing to full effect; **f22.5** those oils confirm the wider cut, but celebrate their extra body with a malty, spicy display of defiance; **b22** a wonderfully characterful and enjoyable malt. 43%

## FINCH WHISKYDESTILLERIE Nellingen, Alb-Donau. Working.

**Finch Schwäbischer Hochland Whisky Barrel Proof** bott code LA0006 db **(92)** n23 t23 f22.5 b23.5 I think Finch have cracked it. Previous bottlings had been a 42% abv, allowing the oils to shatter and the narrative of the whisky to become disjointed when the water was added for reduction. This whisky is far happier at full strength...and now so am I... 54%.

**Finch Schwäbischer Hochland Whisky One Decade** bott code L18026 db **(87.5)** n21 t23 f21.5 b22 A slight weakness to the distillate – evident on both nose and finish - is royally compensated for by the lush sugars and chewable oils which act more than just sticking plaster. Big and fun! 51%. sc. 372 bottles.

**Finch Single Malt Kronberger Genuss-Messe 2017 4 Years & 353 Days** sherry cask db **(94.5)** n23.5 t23.5 f23.5 b24 A clean sherry butt to be applauded and an overall experience to be savoured. 58%. sc. 81 bottles. Bottled for Taste-ination.

## GUTSBRENNEREI JOH. B. GEUTING Bocholt. Working.

**J.B.G Münsterländer Single Grain Whisky Aged 7 Years** oloroso casks, cask nos. 9,10 & 29, dist 12 Nov 11, bott 20 Feb 18 db **(89.5)** n22 t23 f22 b22.5 Probably the best distillation I have seen from this distillery with the cuts being more on the mark, while the oloroso butts are clean and drip enticingly with grape. 42%. 1,036 bottles.

**J.B.G Münsterländer Single Malt** American white oak, cask nos. 148, 149, 150 & 151, dist 12 Mar 13, bott 27 Apr 17 db **(87.5)** n22 t22 f21.5 b22 By the time they had got round to distilling malt for this, it is obvious that they had learned to control their cuts a bit better. So not so much nougat and chewy oils here. A lighter malt altogether with the barley far more vocal though the dry, spiced finale does offer something for the nougat fans to grip on to. 43%. 1,319 bottles.

## HAMMERSCHMIEDE Zorge. Working.

**The Alrik Harz Mountain Single Malt The Handfilled** triple cask, bott 7 May 18, bott no.1827 db **(91)** n22 one of the most fruity yet salty aromas I have encountered for a while: deliciously different; t23 again, this screams the sea: light saline compounds work beautifully with a mix of heather honey and intense malt; really impressive oaky-vanilla tones, also...; f22.5 salty milk chocolate with a malty twist; b23.5 mountains...? Germany...? This is one of the most coastal–style whiskies I have tasted in weeks...! Very different. But never less than delightful. 53%. nc ncf sc. 145 bottles.

**The Glen Els Château d'Yquem Sauternes Casks Aged 5 Years** dist 2012, bott 2017, bott code. 1795 db **(69)** n16 t19 f17 b17 A d'Yquem mass required: this has been murdered by sulphur. 56%. nc ncf. 384 bottles.

**The Glen Els Claret Aged 5 Years** cask 439, dist 15 Apr 13, bott 17 Apr 18, bott code. 1871 db **(95.5)** n24.5 t23.5 f23.5 b24 Heartily recommended by me to my many old friends at Burnley Football Club. One of the most complex and beautiful European whiskies this year. 57.7%. nc ncf sc. 258 bottles.

**The Glen Els Edition Boudoir** db **(92.5)** n23 t23.5 f23 b23 If you find anything spicier in the sack than this, good luck to you... 51.73%. 695 bottles.

**The Glen Els The Handfilled Sherry Firkin Ltd Release** cask no. 872, bott 5 Apr 18, bott code. 1807 db **(91)** n23 t23 f22; b23 Big, clean and fruity and very big, but makes only limited efforts on the complexity front. 53.2%. nc ncf sc. 62 bottles.

**The Glen Els The Journey Distiller's Cut** bott code. 1807 db **(73)** n18 t19.5 f17 b18.5 Glen Els has done the European whisky project proud this year with some malts of exquisite beauty. A poor cask at work here means, sadly, this isn't one of them... 57.7%. nc ncf. 1,000 bottles. 2018 Edition.

**The Glen Els PX Sherry Casks Aged 10 Years** bott code. 1708 db **(94)** n22.5 t24 f23.5 b24 Anyone who regularly reads the Whisky Bible is well acquainted with my views on PX casks: a lot more trouble than they are worth. Have to say, though, that this little (or perhaps I should say big) charmer dramatically bucks the trend: this must have been one hell of an unsullied PX butt..; 49.6%. nc ncf. 750 bottles.

**The Glen Els Tokaji Casks Aged 5 Years** dist 2012, bott 2017, bott code. 1798 db **(76)** n19 t20 f18 b19 Before tasting this, I think I could count the number of successful Tokaji-matured whiskies from around the world on one hand. Sadly, I still can. Incredibly tight, the sugars and salt – and something else besides - bite hard. 55.5%. nc ncf. 472 bottles.

## HAUSBRAUEREI ALTSTADTHOF Nürnberg. Working.

**Ayrer's Bourbon Barrel Aged Organic Single Malt** db **(87)** n22.5 t22.5 f21 b21. A slightly wide cut here has undone some supreme work by the casks. And at 51% abv, close to a Kentucky 101, has just the right mouth feel for the light liquorice and ulmo honey on display. But when so little metal is apparent in the spirit, those cuts have to be as clean as a whistle. 51%

**Ayrer's PX Sherry Cask Finished Organic Single Malt** dist 2009 db **(90) n22 t22.5 f23 b22.5** Always brave to use PX, as the intensity of the sugars can sometimes put the malt into the tightest of straight-jackets. However, this is fine, sulphur-free butt and is eventually relaxed enough for the malt to share equal billing once it finds its rhythm. *56%*

**Ayrer's Red Organic Single Malt** db **(86) n21.5 t22 f21 b21.5.** Quite dry and niggardly in places, a degree of chalkiness on the nose and delivery slightly undoing the sugars as they attempt to soar. Pleasant enough, but never quite gets into stride. *43%*

**Ayrer's Red Organic Single Malt** db **(90.5) n22.5 t22.5 f22.5 b23** An impressive malt, probably benefitting from the full strength, as the unbroken oils play a leading role in length and balance. *58%*

**Ayrer's White Organic Single Malt** db **(86) n21.5 t22 f21 b21.5.** An attractive enough new make with good cut points, particularly hitting the heights with a big sugar surge in the mid-ground. But in this naked form, reveals a slight shortage of copper in the system. *46%*

## HINRICUS NOYTE´S-BRAUHAUS AM LOHBERG Wismar. Working.

**Baltach Wismarian Single Malt Whisky** db **(83) n20.5 t21 f20.5 b21.** Needs a defter touch on the still to ensure those hefty oils don't get through. Some decent redeeming honey, though. Fascinating light curry on the nose! *43%*

## KAUZEN-BRÄU Ochsenfurt. Working.

**Old Owl Feinster Fränkischer Single Malt Whisky** dest 08/2013, abgef 11/2017 **(87.5) n22 t22.5 f21 b22** The barley is attractive and intense; enormous caramels coat the palate, a little spiced molasses offering an alternative, darker sweetness. A little oily late on (unlike a previous bottling of theirs I tasted), this is an attractive, untaxing single malt. *46%*.

## KINZIGBRENNEREI MARTIN BROSAMER Biberach. Working.

**Kinzigtäler Whisky Single Malt Smoke** db **(88.5) n21.5 t22.5 f22 b22.5** The phenols have much to say. *42%*

## KLEINBRENNEREI FITZKE Herbolzheim-Broggingen. Working.

◈ **Derrina Einkorn Schwarzwälder Single Grain Whisky** bott code L 11213 db **(93) n22.5 t24 f23 b23.5** Totally uncompromising in its stature, this kicks and bites like a cask strength bottling. The flavour profile explodes off the charts with a mocha and toffee delivery and follow through which is unique in its style and signature. The mouth feel is also better than could be hoped for, the light, creamy oils filling in all cracks on the whisky and palate. What a joy to experience! *43%*.

◈ **Derrina Gerstenmalz Torfrauch "Stark" Schwarzwälder Single Malt Whisky** bott code L 13112 db **(91) n23 t23 f22.5 b22.5** If memory serves, the last peated malt I had from these fellows was a gentle, understated affair. Well, not this time: absolutely no ambiguity about this whisky at all! The peat appears to be carved from stone on the nose, so rock hard and uncompromising is it. But the delivery is every bit as gentle: the malt forms a sweet oily pouch into which the phenols are cradled. A lovely malt handsomely displaying this distillery's idiosyncratic style. *43%*.

◈ **Derrina Grünkern Schwarzwälder Single Grain Whisky** bott code L 11013 db **(88) n21.5 t22.5 f22 b22** A typical Derrina full bloodied whisky bursting at the seams with flavour. Oily, chewy grain has a great ally in the heather honey. *43%*.

◈ **Derrina Hafer Schwarzwälder Single Malt Whisky** bott code L 6212 db **(91) n22 t23.5 f22.5 b23** I started today's tasting with an oat whisky and now, nearly ten hours on, I taste my 25th and final whisky of the day with another one. This is far the superior of the two, more cleanly distilled and the grain far more prominent in its rich and sweet character. The blend of ulmo honey and mocha is irresistible. *43%*.

◈ **Derrina Karamell-Malz Gerste Schwarzwälder Single Malt Whisky** bott code L 13412 db **(87.5) n21.5 t22 f22 b22** One from the Central European School of Heavyweight Nougat and Toffee Whisky. You could stand a spoon up in this sweetie! *43%*.

◈ **Derrina Karamell-Malz Roggen Schwarzwälder Single Malt Whisky** bott code L 13512 db **(77) n19 t20 f19 b19** Lots of flavour. Just not necessarily all the ones I'd expect or want to see on a rye whisky... *43%*.

◈ **Derrina Karamell-Malz Weizen Schwarzwälder Single Malt Whisky** bott code L 13313 db **(89) n22 t22.5 f22 b22.5** Cream toffee and nuts: you are as likely to find this flavour combination in a Christmas tin of chocolates as you are on a whisky. Love it! *43%*.

◈ **Derrina Khourasan Ur-Weizen Schwarzwälder Single Grain Whisky** bott code L 13811 db **(93.5) n23 t23.5 f23.5 b23.5** When I think Derrina, I think their wheat whisky. This is their best style and they have hit the heights again with a whisky technically superior to anything else they offer. Clean and with the oils coming less from the still and more from the grain itself. The accompaniment of heather honey and delicate spice ticks every wheat whisky box. Would love to see this at cask strength. 43%.

## KORNBRENNEREI J.J. KEMPER Olpe. Working.

⟡ **Spirit of the Cask Roggen Whisky** Amerikanische weisseiche fass, dest Jun 15, gefüllt am Nov 18 db **(89) n22** a bit off key with the cut, but acacia honey storms in to make amends; biscuity; **t23.5** and that gorgeous honey makes a point of getting in early: the delivery is like a throat lozenge, but the matching spices ensure a pleasant burn; **f22** big vanilla and oils from the cut; **b22** maybe not quite technically perfect, but you can't be too harsh on a whisky offering this much honey... 58.9%. sc.

## KYMSEE WHISKY Grabenstätt. Working.

⟡ **Kymsee Der Chiemsee-Whisky Single Malt 3 Years Old Sherry Cask Finish** db **(88) n22** outwardly some superb fruit. But some trouble down the line, too; **t23** succulent, chewy, sweet and attractive: very much in the sherry trifle style of whiskies; **f21.5** bitters out a shade; **b21.5** has its faults (though not sulphur!), but the delivery is a superb mouthful. 42%.

**Kymsee Der Chiemsee-Whisky Single Malt** fass nr. 12, dest Dec 14 db **(87) n22 t22 f21.5 b21.5** As usual, an attractive and competent malt from Kymsee. The barley and oak support each other deliciously early on but the increasing dryness does reveal an overall lack of sugars. 42%.

⟡ **Kymsee Der Chiemsee-Whisky Single Malt Cask Strength** db **(87) n20.5 t23 f21.5 b22** Cask strength sweet nougat! 62.5%.

⟡ **Kymsee Der Chiemsee-Whisky Single Malt Garrison Quarter Cask** db **(92) n23** clean toffee apple and a few major barley announcements; a semi-bourbon style oakiness lurks at every corner; **t23.5** the influence of the oak kicks in immediately. Helpful oils soften the impact while heather honey, spice and a cunningly dry, cotton wool vanilla oakiness keeps everything in check; **f22.5** returns to a more malt-rich theme; **b23** charismatic distillate makes the most of a very good cask. 42%.

**Kymsee Der Chiemsee-Whisky Single Malt Quarter Cask Finish** fass nr. 2, dest Dec 13 db **(82.5) n19 t21 f21.5 b21** Malty and nutty. But perhaps not Kymsee's finest-ever distillate. 42%.

**Kymsee Der Chiemsee-Whisky Single Malt Sherry Cask Finish** fass nr. 2, dest Dec 14 db **(91) n22.5 t23 f22.5 b23** Well balanced, elegant and satisfying. 42%.

## MARDER EDELBRÄNDE Albbruck-Unteralpfen. Working.

**Marder Single Malt 3 Years Old** bott 2017, bott code L 2017 MARDER db **(88) n22 t23 f21.5 b21.5** Pleasant, though the vague bitter thread does knock the sugars out of true slightly. 43%.

**Marder Single Malt Black Forest Reserve Cask No. 90 Single Malt 5 Years Old** db **(91) n22.5 t23 f22.5 b23** This malty monster sits prettily on the palate. 54.6%. 369 bottles.

## MÄRKISCHE SPEZIALITÄTEN BRENNEREI Hagen. Working.

**DeCavo Single Malt Höhlenwhisky** fassbelegung 2/2014, fass-nr L 22 db **(82) n20 t21.5 f21 b20.5** Malty but the bitterish sub plot is never far from the surface. 42%.

**DeCavo Single Malt Höhlenwhisky** fassbelegung 3/2014, fass-nr L 14 db **(89.5) n22.5 t23 f21.5 b22.5** Sugars on so many levels and at different intensities. Impressive! 59.7%.

## NORDPFALZ BRENNEREI Höning. Working.

**Taranis Pfälzer Single Malt Whisky 3.5 Years Old** chestnut cask finish, dist Sept 13 db **(92.5) n22.5 t23.5 f23 b23.5** Very different and strikingly attractive in its own right. 51.4%. 480 bottles.

⟡ **Taranis Pfälzer Single Malt Whisky 5 Years Old** Sauternes cask, dist Winter 12 db **(87) n21 t22 f22 b22** Just a little extra feinty nougat evident on the nose and has no second thoughts about presenting itself on the palate also. Curiously thick and lightly fruited for a Sauternes cask, offering toffee aplenty. 49.5%. sc. 166 bottles.

## NUMBER NINE SPIRITUOSENMANUFAKTUR
Leinefelde-Worbis, Working.

**The Nine Springs Single Malt Whisky Age 3 Years** batch no. 5 db **(86.5) n19 t23 f22 b21.5** An attractive whisky, though the nose isn't entirely happy. Exceptionally sweet delivery with some serious maple syrup moments. Some red and black liquorice which underlines the bourbon-style which by the time it is in full flow late on, makes up a lot of the ground lost by the off- key nose and delivery. One careful cut away from being a classic. 45%. nc ncf.

**The Nine Springs Single Malt Whisky Cask Pineau Des Charentes** cask no. 119 db **(87.5) n20 t23.5 f22 b22** The wine gives a charming polish to this malt −once on the palate. The grape is too light to make a telling difference to the off-key nose. But the spices fizz and marmalade covers the buttered toast rather beautifully. 57.9%. nc ncf sc.

**The Nine Springs Single Malt Whisky Peated Breeze Edition** Muscatel wine cask db **(95)** n23 t24 f24 b24 This is how fruit and peat can work together - just exploding with flavour. Beautiful! 49%. nc ncf.

## SAUERLÄNDER EDELBRENNEREI Ruthen-Kallenhardt. Working.

**Thousand Mountains Mc Raven Single Malt Whisky** cask no. L1003 03.2012 db **(74.5)** n16 t21 f18.5 b19. A massively wide cut means this is a gluepot of a whisky. Best ignore the nose and concentrate on the delivery which has its magnificently sugared moments. But, as is to be expected, an oily, untamed beast. 46.2%.

⊲⊳ **Thousand Mountains McRaven Single Malt** cask no. L 1028 05.2015 db **(85)** n20 t22 f21.5 b21.5 From the somewhat Feinty School of German whisky, it gets over a faltering start on the nose to recover with a volley of maple syrup on the palate...and a slow deliverance of barley. Ignore the nose and enjoy the flawed but tasty follow up. 46.2%. nc ncf sc.

## SCHLENKERLA Bamberg, Working.

**Schlenkerla** db **(79.5)** n21 t18.5 f21 b19. Very much more like German lebkuchen biscuit/cake than whisky. Soft, vaguely phenolic, gingery and friendly – and the finish is surprisingly lovely, especially after the chaotic and confusing opening. A challenging whisky to say the least. 40%

## SCHRAML - DIE STEINWALD - BRENNEREI E.K. Erbendorf. Working.

⊲⊳ **Stonewood 1818 Bavarian Single Grain Whisky 10 Jahre Alt** bott code: L4118 db **(90.5)** n22 vaguely feinty, but the barley is so rich and well weighted, it is easy to overlook the trespasses; t23 it's all about the malt and nothing but the malt; juicy, grassy barley; f22.5 spiced barley sugar candy; b23 a delightful, simplistic malt for its years which wrings out every last atom of barley. 45%.

⊲⊳ **Stonewood Drà Bavarian Single Malt Whisky 3 Jahre Alt** bott code: L1119 db **(93)** n23 chocolate and cherry; t24 brilliantly weighted barley helped along by robust oils. Then comes something rather special: an ulmo honey and maple syrup blend which somehow intensifies the barley and even gets the taste buds salivating. The spices are building to a point where they can no longer be contained; f22.5 a little feint refluxes back onto the palate, but the vanillas and soft, mocha more than make amends; b23.5 in some ways quite simple; but simply beautiful... 43%.

⊲⊳ **Stonewood Smokey Monk Bavarian Single Malt Whisky 3 Jahre Alt** bott code: L10118 db **(88)** n22 well, it's definitely smoky, but nutty too perhaps from a slightly wide-ish cut; t22 the oils seem to give a buttery texture to the milk chocolate smoke; f21.5 dry with a little vanilla invading the cocoa powder; light feints, too; b22.5 one of those rare whiskies which tick the wrong boxes for technical achievement, but all the rights ones for overall enjoyment. 40%.

⊲⊳ **Stonewood Woaz Bavarian Single Wheat Whisky 5 Jahre Alt** bott code: L1219 db **(87)** n21.5 t22 f21.5 b22 Unmistakably wheat whisky: almost like cutting into a newly baked brown loaf and breathing in the moist fumes. But this is a slightly imperfect distillation with the prickle and oils of the wider than desired cut a distraction. Even so, the grain coupled with the light maple syrup has more than its fair share of attractions. 43%.

## SEVERIN SIMON Alzenau-Michelbach, Aschaffenburg. Working.

**Simon's Bavarian Pure Pott Still** db **(86)** n21 t22 f21 b22. Always great to renew acquaintances with this idiosyncratic malt. I remember lots of pine last time out. Here the pine is remarkable for its almost lack of interest in this whisky after the nose. Which means this is a better bottling, with the malt – man marked by crisp sugars – having a much louder say than normal. Some soft, creamy toffee and nougat at play. But the spices and barley are most enjoyable. 40%

## SLYRS Schliersee-Neuhaus. Working.

**Slyrs Bavarian Single Malt Sherry Edition No. 1** finished in Oloroso, lot no. L00354, bott 2013 **(86)** n20 t22 f22 b22. Anyone out there who loves cream toffee and spice? This malt has your name on it. 46%

**That Boutique-y Whisky Company Slyrs 3 Year Old (94.5)** n24 beautifully clean, thumping, in-your-face barley; the light citrus background adds even more clarity; t23.5 good grief! I'm not sure I have ever seen Slyrs in more malt-dominating mode; a background of grist and lemon drops enlivens the palate further; f23.5 the vanillas rise slightly, but it is all about the fading malt; b23.5 from the ultra-intense school of whisky. A malt-lover's dream and the most Scottish style dram they have yet produced. 52.5%. 691 bottles.

# SPERBERS DESTILLERIE Rentweinsdorf. Working.

**Sperbers Destillerie Malt Whisky Anno 2010** los-nr. 40 db **(86.5) n21.5 t22 f21.5 b21.5.** One gets the distinct feeling this was distilled to a pretty high strength before being put into cask. Hard to spot the malt, but plenty of tannins from the oak. Still, quite delicious! 59%

# SPREEWÄLD BRENNEREI Schlepzig. Working.

**Spreewälder Sloupisti Single Malt Whisky** dist Oct 11, bott Mar 16 db **(94) n23 t23.5 f24 b23.5** Absolutely my best whisky of the day! And with its portrayal of a stork in a bow tie and top hat, probably the best label of the year! My kind of whisky; my kind of distillery...!! 68.5%

# SPREEWOOD DISTILLERS GMBH Schlepzig. Working.

⬦ **Stork Club 100% Rye New Make** bott 26 Mar 19 db **(90) n22 t24 f22 b22** Surprisingly tight and quiet on both nose and finish. But the delivery is another matter entirely with explosive grain followed by exemplary new make chocolate mousse follow through. 72.01%. ncf.

⬦ **Stork Club 100% Rye Still Young Aged 2 Years** heavily toasted virgin American oak casks, bott 26 Mar 19 db **(94.5) n23.5** fabulous aroma: no feints whatsoever. The excellent cut allows the rye maximum voltage; **t24** exemplary mouth-watering quality. Again, the high quality spirit plays a huge part here, first allowing the rye full freedom, then the acacia and bruyere honey blend a fabulously open stage to display their considerable charms; **f23** the tannins make their mark, drying things considerably and upping the toastiness. But still the honey and rye work in tandem, but with a little late spiced cocoa; **b24** still young...but grey hairs already, and all in the most distinguished places... 59.87%. ncf.

⬦ **Stork Club 100% Rye Still Young Aged 2 Years** medium toasted virgin German Napoleon oak casks, bott 26 Mar 19 db **(91.5) n23** muscular tannin with some teasing dark sugars providing excellent balance; **t23** exceptionally effervescent, even for its young age: the rye is crispy and sharp, the tannins come at you with a wooden club; **f22.5** overcooked chocolate cake and late molasses; **b23** on this evidence the Germans should have an annual celebration of local whisky matured in native wood: Oaktoberfest.... 59.7%. ncf.

**Stork Club Single Cask Whiskey 1207 Days** ex Bordeaux cask, cask no. 173, bott 13-11-17 db **(82.5) n20 t21.5 f20 b21** A tight, eye-watering whisky which steadfastly refuses to open beyond the gripping sugars and the restricting fruit. A little late coffee does it no harm at all, especially as the weakness of the cask become more evident. 55%. ncf sc. 860 bottles.

**Stork Club Single Malt Whiskey** ex-bourbon, ex-sherry & ex-Weißwein casks, lot no. 008543 L002 db **(88.5) n22.5 t22.5 f21 b22.5** Not a faultless sherry butt. But one that offers more ticks than crosses. 47%. ncf.

**Stork Club Straight Rye Whiskey** ex-bourbon & ex-Weißwein casks, batch no.2, lot no. 001030 5317 db **(92) n23 t23.5 f22 b23.5** Despite the spelling of whiskey, not to be confused with the American definition of a Straight Rye: the Weisswein cask sees to that! And I doubt if it is virgin American oak in play, either. That said, no faulting the overall composition of a rather lovely rye whisky – straight or otherwise 55%. ncf.

# ST. KILIAN DISTILLERS GMBH Rüdenau. Working.

⬦ **St. Kilian Turf Dog Cask Strength** los no. 180409 db **(95) n24 t23.5 f23.5 b24** Technically superb. Clean as a whistle while the peat has a politeness and decorum which suggests finesse and elegance in later life. As for the 63.5% abv – rarely come across a new make as soft and less fractious. Now let's just hope they find casks good enough to match the spirit: easier said than done. 63.5%.

**The Spirit of St. Kilian Single Malt Batch No. 2 15 Months Old** American standard barrels, dist 2016, los-no 180222 db **(94.5) n23 t23.5 f24 b24** Another astonishing example of deliciously complex maturing mate make which suggests this distillery has what it takes to become one of the finest on mainland Europe. The secret is the integrity of the spirit – beautifully cut with little or no feints to be found. Next, they have sourced great oak. Put the two together – and you get this: a proudly and unambiguously malty young number full of barley passion and luxuriating in an oak-fed chocolate fest. Brilliant. 46%.

**The Spirit of St. Kilian Single Malt Batch No. 3 8 Months Old** 30 Liter Jamaica rum casks, dist 2017, los-no 180312 db **(94) n23.5 t22.5 f24 b24** Seriously: who needs a spirit to travel three years in a cask to be called whisky when at eight months something beautiful and dynamic is fit for savouring? The esters on shew remind me of a mix between Long Pond and Hampden, starting boringly and with a hint of honey on the nose, quietening on delivery, but then that stunning mix of esters and malt taking off for a late middle and finish that will blow you away. Glorious! 44.5%. 832 bottles.

⟫ **The Spirit of St. Kilian Batch No. 4 16 Months Old** Islay, Texas & Kentucky casks, dist 2016 db **(91) n22.5 t23 f22.5 b23** The serenity of the spirit is there for all to see: one of the softest touches to any distillery on mainland Europe, which allows the most gentle wisp of smoke to add more of a backbone than might otherwise be expected. Playful tannins help beef up the sugars and, wonderfully, the barley itself is always fully detectable. 45%. 3,000 bottles.

⟫ **The Spirit of St. Kilian Batch No. 5 27 Months Old** Amarone casks from Valpolicella, dist Apr 16 db **(95) n23 t 24 f23.5 b24.5** Although I adore the wine from the Valpolicella region – indeed, the region itself, I have seldom encountered whisky which has been able to harness the brilliance of the grape. The fact that sulphur gets into the mix somewhere is probably the main reason. Well, no problem with that here. And while this is not officially a whisky, the ease with which the power of the fruit is combined with outstanding oak input and then rounded off by the unmistakable and unique barley-gorged gentleness of the spirit itself makes this a special experience. Can't wait until this is officially a whisky: if they can keep this balance (much easier said than done) I can see an award or two heading this distillery's way. 50%. 4,900 bottles.

⟫ **The Spirit of St. Kilian Batch No. 6 21 Months Old** France, Texas & Kentucky casks, dist 2016 db **(86.5) n21.5 t22 f22 b21.5** No mistaking the St. Kilian style of a malt spirit: softer than a baby's bum. Just not quite so sure here of the flavour profile created. Beyond the sleepy phenols the other factors seem to cancel each other out, though a few spices do begin to emerge to shake things up a little. 44.9%. 5,200 bottles.

⟫ **The Spirit of St. Kilian Batch No. 7 22 Months Old** bourbon, sherry & virgin oak casks, dist 2016/17 db **(77.5) n19 t22.5 f17 b19** While the delivery is stunningly textured with a near perfect degree of sweetness, the sulphur present does little for either the nose or finish. 44%. 4,600 bottles.

# STEINHAUSER 1. BODENSEE-WHISKY-DESTILLERIE Kressbronn. Working.
**Brigantia 3 Years Old** bott L-12/12 db **(79) n19 t21 f19 b20** Huge malt statement, as is the distillery style. But it appears someone decided to try and extract as much spirit as possible, because the cut seems to be a little too wide for comfort here: the oils are unforgiving. 43%

# WEINGUT MÖßLEIN Kolitzheim. Working.
**M Mößlein Fränkischer Single Malt Whisky 5 Jahre** fass nr. 5, bott code. L730-1-15 db **(85) n21 t22 f21 b21.** More comfortable with the single malt than with the grain, though better cut point selection has helped. Even so, the oils are still big on this while the light liquorice works well with the buzzing spices. 41%. sc.

# WHISKY-DESTILLERIE DREXLER Arrach. Working.
**Bayerwold Pure Rye Malt Whisky** dest Aug 13, abge Sept 17 db **(83) n19.5 t22.5 f20 b21** The feints steer much of the course for this sweet rye but when the grain itself is heard loud and clear there are moments rye lovers will cherish. Just could do with them lasting a bit longer... 42%. 215 bottles.

**Bayerwold Single Malt Whisky** dest Aug 13, abge Sept 17 db **(86) n19 t22.5 f22.5 b22** Right out of the Drexler school of ultra-intense whiskies. The feintiness is a bit too much on the nose, but I doff my Panama to the way they have orchestrated the delicious chocolate nougat delivery and finish without the feints ever becoming too cloying - a rare feat. 42%. 356 bottles.

**Drexler Arrach No 1 Aged 10 Years Bayerwold Single Cask Malt Whisky** sherryfass, fass nr. H44, dest Sept 07, abge Oct 17 db **(88.5) n22 t22 f22 b22.5** As soft a whisky as it comes. A little bit of the cough syrup about his early on, but on the third of fourth mouthful the quiet richness of this malt does begin to win your heart over. Decidedly idiosyncratic. 46%. sc.

# WHISKY-DESTILLERIE GRUEL Owen/Teck. Working.
**Tecker Single Malt Whisky Port Cask Matured** db **(82.5) n19 t21.5 f21 b21.** A toffee-raisin whisky with a big degree of burnt sugar. 43%. ncf.

**Tecker Single Grain Whisky Aged 5 Years** db **(84) n21.5 t22 f20 b20.5.** Somewhere in the five years between the ten and this five-year-old, someone appears to have made the cut a little wider. 40%. ncf.

**Tecker Single Grain Whisky Aged 10 Years** Chardonnay casks db **(93) n23.5 t23 f23 b23.5** Now, that is all rather beautiful... 53.2%. ncf.

# WHISKY DESTILLERIE LIEBL Bad Kötzting. Working.
⟫ **Coillmór Single Malt Whisky Bavaria x Toscana II Caberlot Rotwein Cask Finish** cask no. 687, destilliert 08 Jun 10, abgefüllt 13 Feb 19 db **(80.5) n18.5 t23 f19 b20** A fantastic cask which radiates high quality grape from the moment it hits the palate. But even that struggles against the feints from the distillate. 46%. sc. 364 bottles.

⬦ **Coillmór Single Malt Whisky Bayerische Weihnacht 2018 Edition** rum cask, cask no. 268, destilliert 07 Sept 11, abgefüllt 18 Oct 18 db **(87.5) n21 t23 f21.5 b22** Salty and almost seaworthy. The salt forms an interesting combination with the sweeter rum notes. Fantastically chewy and fulsome delivery, though! *46%. sc. 414 bottles.*

⬦ **Coillmór Single Malt Whisky Bourbon Single Cask 8.5 Jahre** cask no. 209, destilliert 30 May 10, abgefüllt Jan 19 db **(77) n18 t21 f19 b19** Custard sweet and malty in part. But the spirit is off key. *46%. sc. 650 bottles.*

⬦ **Coillmór Single Malt Whisky Sherry Quarter Cask 12 Jahre** destilliert März 2006, abgefüllt 19 Dec 18 db **(90.5) n22.5** proud, unsullied dates and figs; lovely cocoa back story; **t23** rich-textured, the delivery strikes home with a delicious salty fruitiness; **f22** salted chocolate on the finale; **b23** just about unrecognisable from the three other Coillmór whiskies I tasted this year as the feints don't impact detrimentally. Loads to enjoy here. *44%. sc. 464 bottles.*

# WHISKY DESTILLERIE BLAUE MAUS Eggolsheim. Working.

**Blaue Maus New Make** los nr. 516, destilliert May 16 db **(96) n23.5 t24 f24.5 b24** No chance of smelling a rat with this young mouse. Worth investing in a bottle of this so you can see the indescribably complex and stunningly beautiful skeleton on which their whiskies hang. And this really is complex indeed, not unlike the metal composition of the old Lammerlaw, New Zealand, new make in its day, which has to be its closest relative in style. The amount of chocolate on this is almost obscene. Easily one of the best new makes on the market in the world. *872%.*

⬦ **Blaue Maus Single Cask Malt Whisky** German oak cask, fass/los nr. 1, destilliert May 10 db **(89.5) n22** a friendly, buttery nougat; **t22.5** well-weighted and chewy – yes, with a bit of nougat and toffee – but the oak is also making important noises. A light molasses for balance; **f22.5** a lovely milk chocolate and marzipan mix; **b22.5** a very quiet mouse with a penchant for nougat. *40%. sc.*

**Blaue Maus Single Cask Malt Whisky 14 Years Old** German oak casks, fass/los nr. 1, destilliert Apr 04, abgefüllt Jun 18 db **(83) n20 t22 f20 b21** Feinty at first and then an outbreak of slightly bizarre spice. The sticking plaster honey is superb! *45.7%. sc.*

**Blaue Maus Single Cask Malt Whisky 30 Years Old** German oak casks, fass/los nr. 1, destilliert May 88, abgefüllt Jun 18 db **(89) n22 t23.5 f21.5 b22.5** Not quite as memorable as some of the older Blaue Maus whiskies of the past, the spices curtailing development early. But the sweetness to this is beautifully controlled and elegant. *40.4%. sc.*

⬦ **Blaue Maus Single Cask Malt Whisky Fassstärke** German oak cask, fass/los nr. 2, destilliert Feb 05 db **(85) n20.5 t22.5 f21 b21** One of the feinty Blaue Maus efforts, with the usual mix of drying spices and richer honey tones. *45.2%. sc.*

**Grüner Hund Single Cask Malt Whisky 16 Years Old** German oak casks, fass/los nr. 1, destilliert Feb 02, abgefüllt Jun 18 db **(92.5) n23 t23.5 f22.5 b23.5** There are a lot of Germans in Kentucky (or at least people from German descent) and there is a lot of Kentucky in this German. Beautifully bourbony in style. *49.5%. sc.*

⬦ **Grüner Hund Single Cask Malt Whisky Fassstärke** German oak casks, fass/los nr. 1, destilliert Oct 05 db **(91) n22.5** salty heather honey and oak; **t23** mouth-filling delivery: fat with the oils carrying both honey and chocolate in equals proportions; **f22.5** more milky chocolate and a little Turkish delight; **b23** usually expect a little bourbon theme, but this one is toned down. *46.7%. sc.*

⬦ **Grüner Hund Single Cask Malt Whisky Fassstärke** German oak casks, fass/los nr. 1, destilliert Apr 04 db **(88.5) n21** a dry, peculiarly floral, spicy aroma; **t22.5** a peculiar toasted honeycomb theme; **f22.5** peculiarly spicy; **b22.5** peculiar. *42.1%. sc.*

**Jubiläums Abfüllung 2018 Single Cask Malt Whisky 16 Years Old** German oak cass, fass/los nr. 1, destilliert May 02, abgefüllt Jun 18 db **(87) n21.5 t22.5 f21 b22** One of the most feinty offerings from this distillery for a while. But in typical style recovers with a big honeyed volley of malt. The finish is slightly bitty, though. *40%. sc.*

⬦ **Jubiläums Abfüllung 2018 Single Cask Malt Whisky 16 Years Old** German oak casks, fass/los nr. 1, destilliert Feb 02 db **(89.5) n22** feinty for sure. But a little heather honey amid the nougat; **t22** fat and sweet delivery with the malt erupting on arrival. The oak dries in roasty fashion, giving extra weight and chewability; **f23** still that oil persists, but now does a magnificent job of broadcasting the milk chocolate and burnt raisin; **b22.5** any oilier and they would be able to sell the drilling rights. That apart, a wonderfully relaxed German whisky. *40%. sc.*

⬦ **Mary Read Single Cask Malt Whisky** German oak cask, fass/los nr. 3, destilliert May 08 db **(89.5) n22** bourbon-leaning tannins and mixed spices dampened by marzipan; **t22** a busy spicy buzz bonding with maple syrup; **f22.5** surprisingly juicy and malty late on; **b22.5** despite the jagged spices, the sugars do a superb job. *40%. sc.*

**Mary Read Single Cask Malt Whisky 20 Years Old** German oak cass, fass/los nr. 1, destilliert Apr 98, abgefüllt Jun 18 db **(86) n21.5 t23 f20.5 b21.5** When the nose offers you something of an Indian Balti curry in style you know you are in strange territory. Uniquely Blaue Mauss with spices, presumably from the German oak, which send you into places where no other European whisky has gone before. 46.8%. sc.

◇◇ **Old Fahr Single Cask Malt Whisky** German oak cask, fass/los nr. 5, destilliert May 09 db **(89)** **n22.5** lovely mix of golden syrup, spice and oak; **t22.5** deft malt; even defter muscovado sugars; **f22** just drifts away on the breeze; **b22.5** delicate and delightful. 40%. sc.

◇◇ **Schwarzer Pirat Single Cask Malt Whisky** German oak cask, fass/los nr. 1, destilliert Mar 00 db **(90)** **n22** not technically perfect, but a big tannin and spice kick; **t22.5** oily and forceful on delivery. Takes time for a rhythm to be created but, finally, and at about the mid-point, the barley breaks cover and the tannins go into hickory overdrive; **t23** so much creamy chocolate; **b22.5** imagine Kentucky bourbon chocolate.. 51.2%. sc.

◇◇ **Schwarzer Pirat Single Cask Malt Whisky** German oak cask, fass/los nr. 4, destilliert Jun 10 db **(90.5)** **n22.5** a lovely blend of pineapple and citrus...and even malt; **t23** salivating and fresh. The citrus lurks; the malt stands at the front of stage, chest puffed out; **f22** soft vanilla and spice **b23** a relaxed, even, high class malt. 40%. sc.

◇◇ **Seute Deern Single Cask Malt Whisky** German oak cask, fass/los nr. 1, destilliert Mar 10 db **(90.5)** **n22** all about delicate notes, this: light muscovado sugars give a vaguely fruity edge to the malt; a little butterscotch, too; **t23** the spices are complex, light and buzzy. Milk chocolate notes appear earlier than usual, linking with a soft nougat to create Milky Way candy; **f22.5** just more of the same as the fade is carried by the oils; **b23** for once, it is a shame that I live and work nearly five miles from the nearest shop: I could do with a Milky Way bar right now... 40%. sc.

**Spinnaker Single Cask Malt Whisky 20 Years Old** German oak cass, fass/los nr. 1, destilliert May 98, abgefüllt Jun 18 db **(89.5)** **n21.5 t23 f22.5 b22.5** A sublime cask makes the most of a wide cut on the stills. 40%. sc.

◇◇ **Sylter Ellenbrogen Single Cask Malt Whisky** German oak cask, fass/los nr. 2, destilliert Feb 07 db **(86.5)** **n22 t22 f21 b21.5** Changed tack from the last time I tasted this, now taking an extra dry course, at one point to near eye-watering effect. 40%. sc.

◇◇ **Spinnaker Single Cask Malt Whisky Fassstärke** German oak cask, fass/los nr. 1, destilliert Apr 12 db **(81.5)** **n19 t21.5 f20 b21** Just too aggressively spicy and dry in key places to find a good equilibrium. A touch of butyric on the nose, also. 43.5%. sc.

## UNSPECIFIED

◇◇ **Trader Sylter Single Malt Whisky** PX cask, cask no. 15, dest Sept 14, bott Nov 17 **(92)** **n23 t23.5 f22.5 b23** When people talk about Cream Sherry, this is what they sometimes have in mind. This is as glutinous as whisky gets and it is impossible not to love the concentrated sultana and spice blend. The personality of the malt, however, is lost without trace... 56.5%. sc.

◇◇ **Trader Sylter Single Malt Whisky** PX cask, cask no. 20, dest Dec 14, bott May 18 **(89)** **n22 t22.5 f22 b22.5** Syrupy fruitiness from the cask makes for what at first seems like a one-dimensional experience. But spices erupt in the right places, and a little outbreak of caramel, too, to give needed shape. 56.5%. sc.

◇◇ **Trader Sylter Single Malt Whisky** Ardmore PX cask, cask no. 36, dest Oct 14, bott Nov 18 **(89.5)** **n22.5 t23.5 f21.5 b22** If was hoped that the Ardmore would infuse some magical light phenols into the character, then they were being slightly too optimistic. Any peat there may have been has been crushed out of existence by the marauding grape. But no faulting the lush fruit effect, which has a real Christmas pudding feel to it. 56.5%. sc.

◇◇ **Trader Sylter Single Malt Whisky** PX cask, cask no. 1018, dest Dec 14, bott Nov 18 **(90.5)** **n22.5 t23 f22 b23** A much better PX cask here with the malt actually getting some air-time despite thickness of the grape. Superb heather honey in the mix. 56.5%. sc.

## Blends

**Kahlgrund Whisky Blend (86.5)** **n21.5 t22 f21 b22.** A well balanced, impressively weighted whisky full of enjoyable sugars. But definitely from the nougat school of German distilling. 46%

## German Vatted Malt

**Germania 2016 Malt Whisky (73)** **n18 t19 f18 b18** Off key and target. 40%.

## ISRAEL
## THE MILK & HONEY DISTILLERY

**The Milk & Honey Distillery Single Malt Whisky** db **(91.5)** **n23 t23 f22 b23.5** Some years back I made a film about whisky in Israel – and they weren't then even making their own malt! So a reason to return. For this is a beautiful country...now with a beautiful whisky. Well done people of Milk and Honey with this charming malt: you have set yourself a high standard. Mazel Tov. And Lechaim! 46%. nc ncf sc. 391 bottles.

## ITALY
### L. PSENNER GMBH Tramin an der Weinstrasse. Working.

◇ **Erético Italian Single Malt Whisky** aged in grappa & sherry casks, bott code: L.19003 db **(91)** n22 rounded but still forceful nose with some dry, grape must moments; t23 the fat lady is singing from quite early on…The oils and overall buxomness of the malt fair takes the breath away. Becomes increasingly nutty, then as the oak make their mark, moves more towards a French-style praline middle; f23 the praline persists but that grape must returns for another go…; b23 the grappa cask influence is much stronger than I imagined could have been possible. Gives this whisky a unique signature…and one in italics, of course… 43%.

### PUNI WHISKY DISTILLERY Glurns, Bozen. Working.

◇ **PUNI Alba Italian Single Malt** batch no. 3, Marsala & Islay casks db **(95)** n23.5 considering it is only the casks having a say, the Islay comes across with far more muscle than, say, a Penderyn, and even puts the grape in the shade. Overall, though, the effect is stunning…; t24 magnificently juicy from the first moment. The malt at first arrives crystal clear and unblemished, but successive flavour waves intensifies first the polished fruit and then rumbling smoke; by the mid-point both cocoa and spice are fully established; f23.5 long, elegant and with more of the same, ending with some extra vanilla-oaky tones; b24 they are getting rather good at this whisky lark, these Italians. The Marsala and Islay fit as elegantly as an Armani suit… 43%. nc ncf.

◇ **PUNI Gold 5 Year Old Italian Single Malt** ex-bourbon barrels db **(92.5)** n23 just love the way the acacia honey dovetails with the faultless barley; t23.5 the palate is brushed by a genteel icing sugar and lightly spiced vanilla: such elegance! f22.5 biscuity now just a little bitterness to add to the big vanilla; b23.5 an understated honey fest. 43%. nc ncf.

**PUNI Nero Italian Single Malt** bott code LE/2017, Pinot Nero casks db **(88.5)** n23.5 t22 f21.5 b21.5 It is to my shame and chagrin that, even after they forged a magnificently complex 95 pointer the last time I tasted them, I still have not been able to sculpt my diary in a way that has made a visit to their distillery possible: there are simply too many distilleries in the world!! This bottling, for all its intermittent charm, doesn't come close to the clever use of marsala and phenols which made their last expression so extraordinary. But the grape on show here does at times revel in a certain élan… 46%. nc ncf. 3,000 bottles. Limited Edition 2017.

◇ **PUNI Vina 5 Year Old Italian Single Malt** Marsala casks db **(94)** n23.5 seriously sexy intertwangling between muscovado sugar, light pepper and salted butter on fresh toast; a touch of French toast about this…; t24 pounding, salivating plum juices delicate enough to give the malt a fair hearing; the mid-ground luxuriates in the juicy concoction of boiled fruit candy and balancing spices; f23 back now to slightly burnt toast; b23.5 amazing what happens when you put very decent malt spirit into excellent, untainted casks. Bravo!! 43%. nc ncf.

## LATVIA
### LATVIJAS BALZAMS Riga. Working.

**L B Lavijas Belzams** db **(83)** n20 t22 f20 b21. Soft and yielding on the palate, this is said to be made from Latvian rye, though of all the world's rye whiskies this really does have to be the softest and least fruity. I'll be astonished if there isn't a fair degree of thinning grain in there, too. 40%

## LIECHTENSTEIN
### TELSER DISTILLERY Triesen. Closed.

◇ **Telser Liechtenstein Annual Release No. 1 Double Grain** triple cask db **(92)** n22.5 t24 f22 b23.5 Just incredible mouth feel to this. And to add to the joy, the sugar profile is just about unique, the lion's share of the flavour profile dedicated to a beautifully lush malt concentrate. Liquid ulmo honey fills in the gaps. Something very different and simply brilliant. 44.6%. sc. 130 bottles.

◇ **Telser Liechtenstein Annual Release No. 2** rum & bourbon cask db **(84.5)** n20 t22 f21 b21.5 Slightly bitter and unbalanced. By this distillery's normally high standards, they have fired a blanc… 46%. sc. 150 bottles.

◇ **Telser Liechtenstein Jubilee 300 Release** sherry cask db **(86.5)** n23 t22.5 f20 b21 Fat, oily, chewy and nutty. A mainly decent sherry cask (a little sulphur at the death) at play but overwhelming: a bit like a size 44 overcoat on an eight-year-old boy… 44.4%. sc. 66 bottles.

## LUXEMBOURG
### DISTILLERIE DIEDENACKER Niederdonven. Working.

**Diedenacker Number One Aged 5 Years Rye & Malt 2012** db **(85.5)** n21.5 t22 f21 b21 With flavour this complex, it is too easy to misfire slightly. The extra feints wipe out much of the complexity. 42%.

# THE NETHERLANDS
## ZUIDAM BAARLE Nassau. Working.

⟐ **Millstone Dutch Single Malt Whisky Aged 10 Years American Oak** bott code: 0378ZU db **(92.5) n24** the best nose I have yet encountered from this distillery. There is a teasing fruity thread woven into the fabric of bruyere honey-sweetened barley, ranging from lemon drops to Chinese gooseberries. Wonderful! **t23** soft and silky textured, the barley and heather honey arrives first followed by a little grizzled oak and spice; **f22.5** a little honeycomb and milk chocolate; **b23** bang on the money with the honey and the malt. Love it!! *43%*.

⟐ **Millstone Dutch Single Malt Whisky Aged 10 Years French Oak** bott code: 2927 ZU db **(88.5) n22** a little nougat on the caramels and barley; **t22** a lovely metallic lilt to this: sharp delivery with a soft malty follow through; **f22.5** light golden syrup, spice, very even barley and at last a gentle toasty flourish; **b22** a surprise malt. French oak normally belts out a bit more bite and tannic pungency. Here it seems to be happy to go with the malty flow. *40%*.

⟐ **Millstone Dutch Single Malt Whisky Aged 12 Years Sherry Cask** nbc db **(86) n22 t21.5 f21 b21.5** A clean sherry butt, but there are buts. There is a tang from the spirit itself which gives a slight feinty buzz. Characterful, but there is a dark side. *46%*.

⟐ **Millstone 1999 Dutch Single Malt Whisky Single Pedro Ximénez Cask** nbc db **(91.5) n23** prune juice and molasses; **t23** spiced prune juice and molasses; **f23** prune juice, molasses and vanilla **b22.5** I cannot say I am any kind of fan of whisky matured in PX. But here I have thought: if you can't beat 'em... The grape dominates entirely and it is, as a drinking experience, entirely enjoyable as this must have been an absolutely top quality PX cask – and one free of sulphur (a rarity back in 1999). The malt, of course, long ago waved the white flag... *46%. ncf sc. Special #2.*

⟐ **Millstone 2010 Dutch Single Malt Whisky Double Sherry Cask Oloroso & PX** nbc db **(88) n22.5** hefty grape: only some half-hearted spice makes any meaningful penetration; **t22** the PX is in total command here: rich muscovado sugars hit the palate, followed by a more basic fruitiness; **f21.5** slightly uneven bitterness; **b22** like most PX involved whiskies, don't bother looking too hard for complexity. *46%. Special #16.*

⟐ **Millstone Dutch Single Malt Whisky Oloroso Sherry** bott code: 0328ZU db **(81) n19 t23 f18 b21** Make no mistake: this is a fabulous, faultless sherry butt at work here. And the delivery offers grapey bliss. But, sadly, the underlying structure of the spirit itself throws up a few question marks. *46%*.

⟐ **Millstone Dutch Single Malt Whisky Peated Double Maturation** American oak, Moscatel cask finish, dist 2013, nbc db **(89) n22** a little mint on the lightly smoked nose; **t22.5** charming degree of spiced molasses and muscovado sugars; **f22** some slight roughage on the biting finale; late blood orange and mocha; **b22.5** an oily and deceptively full bodied whisky. Full entertainment value here. *46%. Special #14.*

⟐ **Millstone Dutch Single Malt Whisky Peated Pedro Ximenez** bott code: 0659ZU db **(89.5) n22.5** clunking heavyweight acidic peat battles it out with sopping grape; **t22** the delivery will have you blinking a bit as World War Three is staged on your taste buds. Eventually the peat calms sufficiently for it to offer a soothing undertone; **f22.5** some agreeable spice interrupts the peat-grape dominance; **b22.5** one of the combinations which most consistently fails around the world is peat and PX, one seemingly always cancelling out the other. Here, though, it somehow works and though complexity and elegance are at a premium, it is not short on personality. *46%*.

⟐ **Millstone Dutch Single Rye 92 Rye Whisky** 100% new American oak casks, nbc db **(94) n23.5** beautifully bright rye. Clean and with the perfect brittleness desired; light liquorice accompaniment; **t23.5** the mix of stunning rye and acacia honey is truly irresistible; **f23** the rye moves into a more Demerara sugar mode, though with superb spices and even a slightly fruity trifle and custard fade; **b24** everything I was hoping from their 100 Rye, but never got. A European mainland classic! And less of a Millstone: more of a milestone... *46%*.

⟐ **Millstone Dutch Single Rye 100 Rye Whisky** 100% new American oak casks, bott code: 0338ZU db **(77) n19 t19 f20 b19** As the world's first, longest serving and still most full bloodied advocate of rye whisky, had to say I was looking forward to this one - the grain having been ground in a Dutch windmill, no less. However, I have problems getting past a Geneve-style nose and delivery which, as much as I like, just isn't talking "rye whisky" to me. Good cocoa on the finale, though. *50%*.

# SLOVAKIA
## NESTVILLE DISTILLERY Hniezdne. Working.

**Nestville Master Blender 8 Years Old Whisky** barrel nos. 509208, 509825, 509859 & 509872, dist 20 May 09, bott 19 Sept 17 db **(95.5) n23.5 t24 f24 b24** This is as slick and sublime as they come. Stupendous layering and rare to find a European malt so well structured and balanced. *46%. 1,386 bottles.*

**Nestville Master Blender 9 Years Old Whisky** barrel nos. 504894, 504895, 504896 & 517380, dist 2009, bott 20 Jun 18 db **(93)** n23 t23.5 f23 b23.5 My initial thoughts on tasting this was an extraordinary marriage between malt and bourbon styles. So it came as no surprise to learn that the grains involved in this clever vatting of barrels include both wheat and corn. You need to listen carefully to this whisky, as its subtlety means much can too easily go unheard, as some of what it says is shyly and gently spoken. And such is its unique style, in foreign tongue. The never-to-be-forgotten beauty and elegance, however, comes in the translation.... 46%. 1,475 bottles.

**Nestville Single Malt 2013 Single Barrel** cask no. 509707, bott 20 Jun 18 db **(92)** n23 t23.5 f22.5 b23 Curious: while much of the music was loud, this whisky bottled to celebrate the event, was anything but... 43%. 427 bottles. sc. For Nestville Open Fest 2018

**Nestville Cast Strength Single Barrel 2011** cask no. 502011, bott 20 Jun 18 db **(94)** n23 t24 f23 b24 Another beautiful cask from the only distillery I know on the planet which has an active white stork's nest in the middle of its operation. The young storks appear to thrive on the angel's share, while the distillery appears to thrive on outstanding wood management. 63.9%. 227 bottles. sc. For Nestville Open Fest 2018.

# SPAIN

**DYC Aged 8 Years (90)** n22 t23 f22.5 b22.5. I really am a sucker for clean, cleverly constructed blends like this. Just so enjoyable! 40%

**DYC Selected Blended Whisky (85.5)** n21.5 t22 f21 b21. One of the cleanest and perhaps creamiest whiskies in Europe. Some gooseberry, like the malt, occasionally drifts in, ramping up the flavour profile which is anything but taxing. 40%

**DYC Single Malt Whisky Aged 10 Years (91)** n22 t23 f23 b23 Far more complex than it first seems. Like Segovia, where the distillery is based, worth exploring...40%

## DESTILERÍAS LIBER Granada. Working.

◈ **Whisky Puro Malta de Granada** bott code: LOTE WM 08/001 db **(86.5)** n22 t22 f21 b21.5 A rock hard malt with a titanium backbone. The flavours all tend towards the slightly bitter, toasty side, other than the softer malts which briefly star on delivery. Takes time to get used to the style, but worth the effort. 40%.

# SWEDEN
## GUTE DESTILLERI Havdhem. Working.

**Gute Single Malt Whisky** db **(95.5)** n24.5 t24 f23 b24 This is really quite weird. Back in the late 1970s and early 1980s, I used to comb old village stores looking for 1960s bottlings by Gordon and MacPhail single malts of Speyside and Highland whiskies as they were distilled just after the Second World War and early 1950s. Then, those whiskies had a little more smoke than was being used in the later 1950s. This malt has just hurled me back nearly 40 years. A malt very much in tune with a lost style in Scotland from some 60 years ago: I am stunned...!! 40%

## HIGH COAST DISTILLERY Bjärtrå. Working.

◈ **High Coast Distillery Archipelago Baltic Sea 2019** bott Dec 2018 db **(95)** n24 a beautiful coastal, earthy, sea spray-spattered aroma: as though the barrel has been matured inside a cave that floods with the tide; t23 salty but the deliver is an almost perfect marriage of treacle tart and phenols giving enormous body, but light enough for the tannins to buzz through; the mid-ground becomes a mix of Manuka and heather honey; f23 much drier, with a toasty tannin vibe; b24 nautical...but nice! A deep whisky...and deeply impressive. 54.5%. nc ncf. 1,000 bottles.

◈ **High Coast Distillery Dálvve The Signature Malt** bourbon casks, batch no. 8 db **(88)** n22.5 a frisson of peat stirs up the more staid citrus and vanilla; t22.5 sweet delivery with gristy malt at the fore and a lovely smoke back up; the mid ground is a little rough, though; f21.5 a hint of oily feint but the lightly spiced vanillas are impressive; b21.5 the gentle smoke and light vanilla tones compensate for a jerky base spirit; 46%. nc ncf.

◈ **High Coast Distillery Dálvve Sherry Influence** sherry & bourbon casks db **(87)** n21.5 t22.5 f21.5 b21.5 Sometimes you can a little too much going on and here is a case of the fruit and smoke never quite getting it together. Perhaps not helped by the distillate, either. Smoke, juicy fruit and chocolate to be found. But it's all a muddle. 48%. nc ncf.

◈ **High Coast Distillery Quercus III Petraea** unpeated, bourbon casks, 9 month virgin oak finish, bott Oct 18 db **(89)** n22.5 some powerful tannins leave you in no doubt about the virgin oak finish; t23 so salivating on delivery...and so sweet! Usually you can find a descriptor for the sugars, but not here. All appears to be derived from first the grist and then the oak itself, giving a thin yet intense feel; f21 the more bitter aspects of the oak return; a little balance is lost; b22.5 a remarkable whisky which appears to have driven every last sugar atom out of the grist and cask. 50.8%. nc ncf.

◈ **High Coast Distillery Small Batch No. 09** oloroso sherry casks, bott Dec 18 db **(94.5)** **n23.5** a flawless sherry butt at the top of its game: a real old fashioned fruit cake, smothered in sultanas and nuts...; **t24** classically dry on delivery, then a slow unfolding of muscovado sugars and molasses; increasing mouth-watering, always rich but never for a single moment unctuous; **f23** a little behind the scenes untidiness, but smoothed over by the lush grape; **b24** there are many great reasons to visit Taiwan. Here's another one... *56%. nc ncf. 1,200 bottles. Exclusive to Taiwan.*

◈ **High Coast Distillery Visitor Center Cask** batch no. 5 db **(95.5)** **n24** pretty close to perfect harmony between delicate smoke and marzipan-sweetened oak; **t24** technically the best spirit I have ever tasted from this distillery: no flaws whatsoever, and there can't be because they would show through the most delicate vanilla and icing sugar. The smoke growls quietly; **f23.5** no faults on the peated barley sugar finale, either; **b24** that's their best use of bourbon casks yet. Superb. There are many great reasons to visit Sweden. Here's another one...Hang on a minute, I'm on my way... *50%. nc ncf.*

## MACKMYRA Gästrikland. Working.

◈ **Mack by Mackmyra** bott code:080012 db **(84.5)** **n21 t21.5 f21 b21** Have to admit: did a double take when I nosed this one. For the first time in a very long while I came across an independent distiller lacing their nose with added caramel, the dry dustiness coupled with the total lack of expected malt sharpness or charm giving the game away. The bland pleasantness on delivery and failure of development confirmed it. Not sure what the Swedish is for "in God's name, why ?" I'll have to find out. *40%.*

◈ **Mackmyra Brukswhisky** art nr. MB-003 db **(95.5)** **n24** take your time on this nose: just look at the way the fragile barley and lime-squeezed tannin are lifted by a delicate mix of salt and pepper to tickle and tantalise your nose and make seductive promises for the palate...; **t24** perhaps, of all the world's whiskies, only Mackmyra can produce this kind of clarity on delivery: perfect gristiness, thin lime blossom honey and the busiest of light spices; **f23.5** now the barrels come into play with a soft kiss of marzipan...before the barley returns to be spotted with the clarity of a starfish in a rock pool; **b24** like many of Mackmyra's whiskies, your senses have to be on full alert to enjoy it to its fullest...and as the whisky deserves. This is another Swedish tease, a whisky at the end of a fingertip and searching for all your secret nerve endings... *41.4%.*

◈ **Mackmyra Moment Efva** oloroso and birch sap wine casks, warehouse: Bodås Mine, art. nr. MM-028 db **(82)** **n22 t21 f19.5 b20** A very dull whisky strangling Mackmyra's famous flair at birth. And certainly at the deathy, also! *4,111 bottles.*

◈ **Mackmyra Moment Fjällmark** Swedish cloudberry wine casks, fatlagrad: Bodås Gruva, art. nr. MM-026 db **(90)** **n22** presumably a malt, as barley appears to be on shew here. But has to be on full volume to get through a fascinating, almost indecipherable fruitiness; **t22.5** a uniquely thick and musky-flavoured whisky: fruity but with an unusual depth to match the sharpness; **f22.5** superb length and body. Busy, slightly bitter tannins balance beautifully with the spiced fruit and light heather honey; **b23** having spent quite a lot of time in Sweden, I can vouch they have a lot of clouds in that country, so a cloudberry wine is truly apt. A delightful flavour profile, and one unmatched by any other whisky in the world. *42%. 4,411 bottles.*

◈ **Mackmyra Moment Prestige** fatlagrad: Bodås Gruva, art. nr. MM-025 db **(95)** **n23.5** an astonishing crispness to the plummy fruit. The sugars are almost of a rye style, with a Demerara crunchiness that seems carved from granite; **t24** not the hint of a note out of place or off course: the delivery is as formal and strict as the aroma. The flavours are again fruit dominated, but so regimented and disciplined that it is hard to tell if it is plum or grape must in the ascendancy. No doubting the growing spices, though; **f23.5** a delightfully charming throb of spice sits well with the ever growing vanilla and light coffee tones; **b24** this could equally have been called "Precise" because every single aroma and movement in this whisky appears to have been orchestrated and choreographed to the last detail... *46.1%. 4,111 bottles.*

◈ **Mackmyra Gruvguld** art. nr. MC-010 db **(93.5)** **n23** a lovely mix of lighter caramel wafer and quite a punchy oak kick, shewing a semi-Kentucky leathery note; **t24** adore the softness of the mouthfeel; the otherwise naked malt drapes over the taste buds dressed only in light oaky-caramel and spice; **f23** those spices just keep on their rhythmic strumming; some mocha and praline begins to develop late on; dulls as the toffee takes hold; **b23.5** some whiskies possess a serious and delicious chewability. And this is one of them... *46.1%.*

◈ **Mackmyra Vinterglöd** art. nr. MC-011 db **(84)** **n21.5 t22 f20 b20.5** I couldn't quite put my finger on why this was jarring with me a little, despite the spice kick. Then, on spotting the back of the bottle "aromatic profile: mulled wine" I suddenly realised exactly why I was marking it down. The degree of spice, like mulled wine, seemed forced and aggressive rather than a natural, organic progression from the oak maturation. Curious. *46.1%.*

◈ **Mackmyra Skördetid** art. nr. MC-009 db **(93)** n23 green banana, remote Demerara sugars and vanilla ice cream with a lime source; **t23.5** perhaps Europe's cleanest delivery of the year: amazing distillation here which rips out any oils and instead bestows the job of carrying the flavours to the light tannins. The muscovado sugars and ultra-light spice make happy companions; a little light greengage suffices for fruit; **f23** very cool menthol and spice softens towards a milk chocolate fade; **b23.5** a whisky impossible not to love. 46.1%.

◈ **Mackmyra Svensk Ek** art. nr. ME-002 db **(95)** n24 now there's a novel nose: something here I have never nosed before...think I need to look at that label... Right, well the oak offers sappy sugars and nipping spice is uniquely equal measure: perfect balance right on the nose; **t23.5** wow...!! Those sugars apparent on the nose need no second invitation. They gush forth like waters from a spring on delivery, a unique blend of ulmo honey, marzipan, grist and muscovado sugars, sweetening and soothing the palate before giving way to a playful spice and the darkest of liquorice; **f23.5** long and increasingly toasty with the sugars now more of a molasses bent; the spices are increasingly more peppery and belligerent, but never is the balance lost even when the drier vanillas arrive; **b24** Mackmyra has branched out into whisky matured from oak grown in the south of Sweden. Before I tasted this I was rooting for them. Soon I twigged that this is an avenue they must continue along. Brilliant! 46.1%.

◈ **Mackmyra Svensk Rök** art. nr. MR-001 db **(95.5)** n23.5 at first you might think the smoke is quite full on. But then you realise the company it keeps, it is part of a tapestry; for there are subtle oaky vanillins at play here, as well as diced fresh apple and elegant understated spices...; **t23.5** a plethora of mixed sugars, which not for a moment had been overtly evident on the nose, mingle together from the first moment on delivery. There is a little icing sugar to thin out the muscovado, but then this is strengthened by light heather honey. All the while the smoke is rising, but no more than the lightest liquorice from the oak; **f24.5** and now it all comes together. The sugars have merged into a slightly dull maple syrup, the oak has evened out and joined the grain for a creamy vanilla and the smoke has taken on a slightly spicier persona, though uniting with the very late mocha sublimely: brilliant! **b24** forget about the peat: the secret to this whisky is its subtlety, something not normally associated with smoky whiskies. It is a whisky so constructed that its many parts take time to gather, a segment at a time, until eventually, at the very finish, the whole picture is revealed. Fascinating, and quite brilliant. Now this is real blending... 46.1%.

◈ **Mackmyra Svensk Rök/Amerikansk Ek** db **(90)** n22 delicate and perhaps a little shy with he caramel dominating over the lighter phenols which become a little lost; **t23** mouth-filling and sweet, spices erupt with a surprising degree of force before setting into a pleasant pulse; the tannins a shade over aggressive perhaps; **f22.5** a big toasted toffee fudge fade; **b22.5** a huge amount of natural toffee from the barrel slightly quietens the party. 46.1%.

◈ **Mackmyra 10 Ten Years Single Malt** art. nr. MC-008 db **(89)** n22.5 in my tastings, I sometimes make a joke about people writing they find wild strawberries on the nose of this or that whisky. Guess what: wild strawberries. Only a fragmentary aroma, but dovetails pleasantly with the even malt and light spice; **t23** sexy delivery with a satisfying sharpness to the sugars and busy buzz to the oak; a little toffee butterscotch and light chocolate enters the mid ground; **f21.5** just a little dull and even slightly bitter; **b22** taking into account the use of the number on this bottling, not sure if I should be tasting this to Ravel's Balero... 46.1%.

◈ **Motörhead Whisky** new American oak, batch VIII db **(91)** n23 crunching tannins clatter into the nose, packing their spicy, toasty molecules tightly. Some heather honey also makes it into the mix to offer welcome balance; **t23** you almost find yourself picking twigs from your palate, so oaky is this. But, just as on the nose, honey notes, now accompanied by full on liquorice, makes sense of it all; **f22** a tad too much caramel, though the spices still ping; **b23** as someone who prefers balance and harmony in their music, be it (preferably) classical or Pink Floyd or Gryphon, I have to admit that Motörhead are anathema to me. So I feared the worst for this whisky. I shouldn't have: as raucous as the oak may be, it plays rather well. 40%.

## SMÖGEN WHISKY Hunnebostrand. Working.

◈ **Smögen Aged 5 Years Single Malt Sherry Quaters** db **(85)** n22.5 t22 f21 b20 You can have too much of a god thing. And here the oak is relentless and way over the top. Far too much tannin, though there is a fleeting moment early on when the oak and smoke hold hands. 61%. nc ncf sc.

**Smögen Single Malt Barrique 7 Years Old** db **(87)** n22 t22 f21.5 b21.5 Pretty straightforward fare, big on the juicy grape but low on subtlety and development. Lots of toffee and raisin, but a shade too bitter at the death. 60.3%.

**Smögen Svensk Single Malt Single Cask 18** dist 2012 db **(96)** n24 t24.5 f23 5hb21 On this evidence, previous Smogen whiskies I had tasted had criminally underperformed. This is not only a superstar single malt, but probably the sharpest rise in quality at a distillery I have ever witnessed. Very well done! If you have never been seduced by a beautiful Swede by now, you will after experiencing this. It should carry an X-certificate... *61.3%. sc.*

⟨⟩ **Smögen Svensk Single Malt Single Cask 7 Year Old Rum Finish** cask no. 56/2011, dist 26 Nov 11, bott Jan 19 db **(94.5) n23.5 t24 f23.5 b23.5** You would be hard pressed to pick this out in an identity parade alongside a gang of Islay of a similar age. Truly bursting at the seams with gristy, malty smokiness, the rum cask having a negligible effect on the overall picture. A peat-lover's multiple orgasm. *62.4%. nc ncf sc.*

# SPIRIT OF HVEN DISTILLERY Sankt Ibb. Working.

⟨⟩ **Spirit of Hven Hvenus Rye Whisky** bott code: 66R297 05736 db **(92.5) n23.5** the grain is allowed to display its crisp fruity, mildly spicy charms with only minimum distraction from the vanilla-rich oak; **t23.5** fabulously precise grain, though unusual in the way it radiates differing degrees of intensity against the natural caramels; **f22.5** creamy vanilla fade; **b23** well, Having cracked the art of making great single malt whisky, they have now gone after rye. And pretty much nailed that, too... *45.6%.*

**Spirit of Hven Seven Stars No. 5 Alioth Single Malt** db **(94.5) n23.5 t24 f23.5 b23.5** Another Russian roulette European distillery where you have no idea of the quality you are about to face. This, though, is Hven. *45%.*

**Spirit of Hven Seven Stars No. 6:1 Mizar Single Malt Whisky** db **(94.5) n23.5 t24 f23.5 b23.5** Doesn't this distillery know how to make very ordinary whisky....? An exhibition of complexity....again! *45%.*

⟨⟩ **Spirit of Hven Seven Stars No. 7 Alkaid Single Malt Whisky** bott code: 74S015 00655 db **(94.5) n23.5** such varied weight and intricate layering of the peat.... This is just too sexy...; **t24** honey on delivery, then a light peat and tannin take turns for the attention; **f23** long, quietly warbles its smoky song to the death; **b24** just what more can you say about this exceptional distiller?. Even when they offer a peated version of their malt, they simply refuse to settle for very good. This is excellent... *45%.*

# SWITZERLAND
## BRENNEREI STADELMANN Altbüron. Working.

**Dorfbachwasser Single Malt 10 Years Old** Moschtfass Eiche cask, dist Sept 05, bott Mar 16 db **(90.5) n22.5 t23 f22 b23** This distillery really does know how to distil! Another above-average example of the art. *40%. ncf. Bottled for the Whisky Club Melchnau.*

**Luzerner Hinterlander Single Malt Whiskey Old Nr. 7** Jack Daniel's cask db **(92) n22.5 t24 f22.5 b23** A beautifully distilled, clean, highly complex and busy malt. *45%.*

⟨⟩ **Buechibärger Whisky Single Malt Fassstärke 10 Jahre** herstellungsjahr 2008, fass 33 db **(92) n22.5** a mix of dried prunes and dates mixed with grape must. The malt hangs around limply; **t23.5** fulsome on delivery, slightly malty – and juicy - at first, then a huge flavour wave. The third and fourth waves are best though as the slightly jammy marzipan, sweetened further by ulmo honey....wow! **f22.5** retains the chocolate marzipan persona to the increasingly oaky end; **b23.5** a big whisky which carries its weight and muscle with great dignity. *55%. sc.*

# BRENNEREI-ZENTRUM BAUERNHO Zug. Working.

⟨⟩ **Swissky** db **(91) n23 t23 f22 b23.** While retaining a distinct character, this is the cleanest, most refreshing malt yet to come from mainland Europe. Hats off to Edi Bieri for this work of art. Moving stuff. *42%*

# DESTILLERIE EGNACH Egnach. Silent.

**Thursky** db **(93) n24 t23.5 f22.5 b23.** Such a beautifully even whisky! I am such a sucker for that clean fruity-spice style. Brilliant! *40%*

# DISTILLERIE ETTER Zug. Working.

**Johnett Whisky Aged 7 Years** dist May 10, bott Aug 17 db **(93) n22.5 t23.5 f23.5 b23.5** Yet another sublime whisky from Switzerland. It's not just cuckoo clocks, you know... *44%. ncf.*

⟨⟩ **Johnett Swiss Single Malt Single Cask Whisky No. 50** 2 years Pinot Noir barrel, Merlot finish, dist May 10, bott Sept 18 db **(89.5) n23** if you find a cleaner, fruitier aroma among all Europe's whiskies this year, please let me know...; plenty of dried dates, too; **t23** too soft for words on delivery. Despite the big grape influence the salivating barley still comes through; **f21** just a little untidy and tangy; **b22.5** a real belt and braces job with the fruit! *50.3%. ncf sc. 389 bottles.*

⟨⟩ **Johnett Swiss Single Malt Single Cask Whisky No. 74** bourbon barrel, Islay whisky barrel finish, dist May 10, bott Sept 16 db **(91.5) n23** how about that for Islay influence? Faultless and surprisingly complex phenols totally in tune with the malt; **t23** fat barley with a gently phenolic lilt. Lots of chewing – and minty chocolate for the mid-gound; **f22.5** the mint chocolate lingers with a little spice; **b23** that was some Islay cask they found: the smoke travelled a long way and with purpose. *58.7%. ncf sc. 256 bottles.*

# DESTILLERIE MACARDO Strohwilen. Working.

**Macardo 10th Anniversary Single Malt** db **(87) n19.5 t24 f21.5 b22** Were it not for the feinty, off-kilter nose, this would have scored so much higher – and would have deserved to. The complexity of the malt deserves a round of applause alone: the delivery is the stuff of dreams. The maltster-style intensity comes complete with cocoa plus light spices. The finish, though, confirms the weakness of the nose. Even so, the 10th anniversary is marked with some stupendous whisky moments. *42%. 999 bottles.*

**Macardo Bourbon** dist 2010, bott code 6020 db **(84.5) n20.5 t21.5 f21.5 b21** You can see where this is coming from – and where it is trying to go. But it gets stuck, literally, with bubble gum clogging up the works – on both delivery and finish. A little too sticky and indistinct. *42%.*

**Macardo Single Malt** dist 2010, bott code 7002 db **(92.5) n22.5 t23.5 f22.5 b23.5** An honest and attractive, beautifully distilled, single malt squeezing out every last barley note. *42%.*

# EDELBRENNEREI BRUNSCHWILER Oberuzwil. Working.

**B3 Fürsterländer Single Malt Whisky** Los Nr. 2015 db **(88.5) n22 t22 f22 b22.5** Does a great job of elevating the malt to prominence and keeping it there. Understatedly lovely. *40%*

# HIGHGLEN WHISKY DISTILLERY Santa Maria Val Müstair. Working.

**HighGlen Raetia Secunda Single Malt Swiss Whisky** db **(93) n23.5 t24 f22 b23.5** Magnificent whisky of Alpine beauty. *64.1%. 30 bottles.*

**HighGlen Raetia Terza Single Malt Swiss Whisky** db **(88) n22 t23 f21 b22** Another mainly sweet malt, but this time barley-based and less oak oriented. *58.5%. 64 bottles.*

# HUMBEL DISTILLERY Stetten Aargau. Working.

**OURBEER Aged 36 Months Single Malt Whisky Tokaj Finish** dist 2002 db **(88.5) n22 t22 f22.5 b22** A friend of mine who lives just a few villages from me was one of the people who successfully got Tokaj wine back on the map and he was a little surprised when I told him that for the whisky lover that has been something of a mixed blessing: most Tokay-finished or matured casks have been wrecked beyond redemption by sulphur. Thankfully, not this offering. Though, like its distant cousin, PX, the improbable intensity of the sugars do restrict the overall development of the malt. *50%*

# KOBELT Marbach, St. Gallen. Working.

**Glen Rhine Whiskey** db **(88) n21 t22.5 f21.5 b22.** Try and pick your way through this one...can't think of another whisky in the world with that kind of fingerprint. *40%.*

# LANGATUN DISTILLERY Langenthal, Kanton Bern. Working.

◇ **Langatun 10 Year Old Single Malt Chardonnay** cask, cask no. 4, dist 2008, bott 2018 db **(95.5) n24 t24 f23.5 b24** One of those great moments where, 12 hours into my tasting day, I pick up a sample that is gently warmed and prepared, nose it, taste it and instantly recognise it as the best whisky of the day so far. Only afterwards I see it is Langatun which, for sheer consistency, can now be labelled as truly world class. Is it the mouth feel? The intensity? The diaspora of sugars: Chilean ulmo honey here, Corsican bruyere honey there, a cube of muscovado tucked away there?...while the malt astonishes in its intensity and a slight fruitiness is nothing but an adornment. *49.12%. sc.*

**Langatun Cardeira Cask Finish Single Malt** dist 25 Oct 10, bott 2 May 17, bott code L 0291 db **(95.5) n23.5 t25 f23 b24** Trust Langatun to come up with something very different, indeed. The effect of this less than common Portuguese wine dovetails with rare precision with the malt. The first ten seconds of the delivery is as delicious as any whisky on the planet this year. *61.4%. nc. 100 bottles.*

**Langantun Hell Fire** cask nr. 666, sherry cask, dist Sept 10, Bott Okt 16 db **(93) n22 t24 f23.5 b23.5** Use the Murray method of tasting and it becomes a mere pussycat (OK, one with a few sharp claws) – even with no water added. I was going to make this the 666th whisky tasted for the 2018 Bible...but I forgot. So it is the 1,111th. Oh, hell...!!!! *81%. 444 bottles.*

**Langatun Jacob's Dream Single Malt Whisky** pinot noir cask, cask no. 97, dist 23 Mar 09, bott 15 Jun 15 db **(92.5) n23.5 t24 f22 b23** Quite astonishing how this malt has the presence to comfortably fit into the shoes of such big wine casks.

◇ **Langatun Nero D'Avola Cask Finish Single Malt** cask no. 87, dist Feb 14, bott Feb 19 db **(89.5) n22** very, very different! A dusky, fruity nose of almost opaque intensity; **t23** good grief...! One of the most explosive and startling deliveries of the year, with this Sicilian grape giving the taste buds an offer they can't refuse. Not sure I have ever encountered a grape quite so intense and concentrated, and quite soon a thick tannin note follows up for a double thump...; **f22** quite a tart finale and bitter, too; **b22.5** a new flavour profile to be added to the world's whiskies. Unusually for Langatun, it's all about effect rather than complexity. *62.9%. nc sc.* 100 bottles.

**Langatun Old Bear Single Malt** bott code L 0116 db **(88) n21.5 t22.5 f22 b22** Langatun whisky is such a force of nature, it doesn't seem natural to taste it much below natural strength, let alone at 40%. *40%*

**Langatun Old Deer Single Malt** bott code L 0116 db **(87.5) n21.5 t22.5 f21.5 b22.** This is one of the great distilleries of Europe, make no mistake. But here the cut strays just onto the wide side of things, though it is still brimming with hay and marmalade notes. The sugars are of the heather-honey variety. But those feints, a rarity - a collectors' item - for Langatun, just stifle the overall complexity. *40%*

**Langatun Old Deer Cask Strength Single Malt** bott code L 0116 db **(95.5) n24 t24 f23.5 b24** Now that is what I was expecting...not the character of the 40% bottling. This is, quite simply, brilliant. *62.1%*

⟨ **Langatun Old Woodpecker** chardonnay cask, cask no. 167 db **(94.5) n23.5** seemingly a tight nose where the grape is intense, slightly enclosed. But opens up sufficiently for the brighter malt element to shine, if only briefly; **t23.5** much sweeter and more open on delivery, some light ulmo working hand-in-glove with the grape; **f23.5** gorgeous vanillas and light spices do little to dampen the enthusiasm of the grape and honey which lingers long; **b24** a superb malt which handsomely repays patient opening up. *46%. sc.*

⟨ **Langatun Old Woodpecker Organic Single Malt** white wine cask, batch no. 03/19, dist 2011, bott 2019 db **(96) n24.5** pretty much the near perfect wine cask nose: the fruit arrives in a variety of guises, sometimes sharp and business-like, occasionally sweet and relaxed. But always clean and light enough for the malt to get a decent say; **t24** you almost feel like punching the air, so brilliant is the wine influence. Rather than white wine, it feels closer to a cream sherry and, like on the nose, there is dichotomy between the sharpness and sweetness. Elsewhere vanilla wafers and barley add to the mix, as does the ulmo honey...but the juiciness is all about the young barley...as it should be; **f23.5** light spices and vanilla. But aren't those creamy sultanas lovely...; **b24** creamy and dreamy, not sure if the sweeter notes could be more beautifully in tune... Sheer woodpeckery bliss... and something to bang on about... *46%. nc.*

**Langatun Quinta do Zambujeiro Cask Matured** dist 17 Dec 11, bott 12 Oct 17 db **(90.5) n22.5 t23.5 f22 b22.5** A curious stop-start malt which when it manages to hit top gear genuinely purrs along the palate. *49.12%.*

⟨ **Langatun Ruchè Cask Finish Single Malt** cask no. 383, batch no. 1, dist 14 Mar 13, bott 23 Nov 18 db **(86.5) n22 t22 f21 b21.5** Another big fruity Langatun. But this one is just a little too tart and bitter, especially on the finish. *62.8%. nc sc.* 344 bottles.

**Langatun Sherry Cask Finish** Oloroso cask, cask no. 319, dist 12 Dec 11, bott 14 Aug 17 db **(95.5) n24 t24 f23.5 b24** If anyone tells you there has been nothing wrong with the sherry butts which have blighted Scottish whisky for the last 20 years, they should find a bottle of this. It is the closest thing to a time machine I know: a former member of the Gentleman's Club to which I belong, Mr H. G. Wells, would have approved with gusto. What a privilege to experience a whisky like this. *49.12%. sc.*

**Langatun White House Single Malt** db **(88) n22.5 t22.5 f21 b22** Trumps many other European whiskies, but not quite up to many of its predecessors... *45%.*

# SEVEN SEALS DISTILLERY AG Schweiz, working.

⟨ **Seven Seals Peated Double Wood Finish** db **(94.5) n23.5 t23.5 f23.5 b24** A beautiful malt where they have got their sums right here in adding up just the required amounts of phenols, dark sugars and oak. Even the oil for body and weight is spot on. Doubtless on the sweet side, but the spice and tannin really do put the anchors on in spectacular style. Superb! *58.7%.*

⟨ **Seven Seals Single Malt Peated Port Wood Finish** db **(85.5) n21.5 t22.5 f20.5 b21** The nose is one of good old British Black Country pork scratchings – or maybe in this case Port scratching...A malt that's about as subtle as a punch in the kisser and as rough and ready as a bare knuckle fighter. But there is a certain basic enjoyment to the fruit cake sugars on display. Technically, though, not quite at the races. *58.7%.*

⟨ **Seven Seals Single Malt Port Wood Finish** db **(87) n21 t22.5 f21.5 b22** A lush frenzy of fruit. A little cloying, but the spices are a treat. *58.7%.*

⟨ **Seven Seals Single Malt Whisky Sherry Wood Finish** db **(88) n21.5 t23 f21.5 b22** Big on the grape and even bigger on the spice and maple syrup. A bit of an untidy mishmash. But when it is good, it is very good. *58.7%.*

# Deciphered and Distilled. The Bible's European Guide to Whisky Labels

| English | German | French |
|---|---|---|
| Malt | Malz | Malt |
| Grain | Getreide | céréales |
| Wheat | Weizen | blé |
| Barley | Gerste | orge |
| Rye | Roggen | seigle |
| Spelt | Dinkel | épeautre |
| Corn | Mais | maïs |
| Oat | Hafer | avoine |
| Peated | getorft | tourbé |
| Smoked | geraucht | fumé |
| Organic | biologisch | biologique |
| Cask | Fass | fût |
| Matured in/Aged in | gereift in | vieilli en |
| Finish | Nachreifung | déverdissage |
| Double Maturation | Zweitreifung | deuxième maturation |
| Oak | Eiche | chêne |
| Toasted | wärmebehandelt | grillé |
| Charred | ausgeflammt, verkohlt | carbonisé |
| Years | Jahre | ans |
| Months | Monate | mois |
| Days | Tage | journées |
| Chill Filtration | Kühlfiltration | filtration à froid |
| Non Chill Filtered | nicht kühlgefiltert | non filtré à froid |
| No Colouring | nicht gefärbt | non coloré |
| Cask Strength | Fassstärke | brut du fût |
| Single Cask | Einzelfass | single cask |
| Cask No. | Fass-Nummer | numéro du fût |
| Batch | Charge | Lot/charge |
| Distillation Date | Destillations-Datum | date de distillation |
| Bottling Date | Abfüll-Datum | date de mise en bouteille |
| Alcohol by Volume/abv | Volumenprozente/% vol. | teneur en alcool/abv |
| Proof (American) | amerikanische Einheit für % vol. | unité américaine |

| Danish | Dutch | Swedish |
|---|---|---|
| Malt | Gerst | Malt |
| Korn | graan | säd |
| hvede | tarwe | vete |
| byg | gerst | korn |
| rug | rogge | råg |
| spelt | spelt | speltvete |
| majs | mais | majs |
| havre | haver | havre |
| tørv | geturfd | torvrökt |
| røget | gerookt | rökt |
| organisk | biologisch/organisch | ekologisk |
| fad | vat | fat |
| modning i | gerijpt in | mognad på/lagrad på |
| finish | narijping/finish | slutlagrat |
| dobbelt modning | dubbele rijping | dubbellagrat |
| egetræ | eik | ek |
| ristet | getoast | rostad |
| forkullet | gebrand | kolad |
| år | jaren | år |
| måned | maanden | månader |
| dage | dagen | dagar |
| kold filtrering | koude-filtratie | kylfiltrering |
| ikke kold filtreret | niet koud gefilterd | ej kylfiltrerad |
| ikke farvet | niet bijgekleurd | inga färgämnen |
| fadstyrke | vatsterkte | fatstyrka |
| enkelt fad | enkel vat | enkelfat |
| fad nr. | vat nummer | fatnummer |
| parti/batch | serie/batch | batch |
| destillations dato | distillatie datum | destilleringsdatum |
| aftapnings dato | bottel datum | buteljeringsdatum |
| volumenprocent | alcoholpercentage/% vol | volymprocent/% vol. |
| Proof | amerikaanse aanduiding voor % vol | Amerikanska proof |

# World Whiskies

I have long said that whisky can be made just about anywhere in the world; that it is not writ large in stone that it is the inalienable right for just Scotland, Ireland, Kentucky and Canada to have it all to themselves. And so, it seems, it is increasingly being proved. Perhaps only sandy deserts and fields of ironstone can prevent its make physically and Islam culturally, though even that has not been a barrier to malt whisky being distilled in both Pakistan and Turkey. Whilst not even the world's highest mountains or jungle can prevent the spread of barley and copper pot.

Outside of North America and Europe, whisky's traditional nesting sites, you can head in any direction and find it being made. Australia, in particular, has gained a deserved reputation for magnificent malt though, like its finest wines, it can be hard to locate outside its own country. Indeed, Australian whiskies are of such high quality and relatively abundant that it has, like England and Wales now been rewarded with its own section in the Whisky Bible, though Australian whisky will still be found in the World Whisky awards section. World class whisky can be found in other surprisingly lush and tropical climes with Taiwan leading the way thanks to the wonderful Kavalan distillery, no stranger to the Whisky Bible awards.

Japan has long represented Asia with distinction and whisky-making there is in such an advanced state and at a high standard Jim Murray's Whisky Bible has given it its own section - and World Whisky of the Year for 2015! But while neighbouring South Korea has ended its malt distilling venture, further east, and at a very unlikely altitude, Nepal has forged a small industry to team up, geographically, with fellow malt distillers India and Pakistan. The main malt whisky from this region making inroads in world markets is India's Amrut single malt, though Paul John is also now beginning to forge a deserved following of fans. 'Inroads' is hardly doing Amrut justice. Full-bloodied trailblazing, more like. So good now is their whisky they were, with their fantastically complex brand, Fusion, deservedly awarded Jim Murray's Whisky Bible 2010 Third Finest Whisky in the World. That represented a watershed not just for the distillery, but Indian whisky as a whole and in a broader sense the entire world whisky movement: it proved beyond doubt that excellent distilling and maturation wherever you are on this planet will be recognised and rewarded.

## Jim Murray's Whisky Bible World Whiskies of the Year Winners

|  | Asian Whisky | Southern Hemisphere Whisky |
|---|---|---|
| 2010 | **Amrut Fusion** | N/A |
| 2011 | **Amrut Intermediate Sherry Matured** | N/A |
| 2012 | Amrut Two Continents 2nd Edition | **Kavalan Solist Fino Single Cask** |
| 2013 | N/A | **Sullivan's Cove Single Cask HH0509** |
| 2014 | Kavalan Podium Single Malt | **Timboon Single Malt Whisky** |
| 2015 | Kavalan Single Malt Whisky | **NZ Willowbank 1988 25 years Old** |
| 2016 | **Amrut Greedy Angels 46%** | Heartwood Port 71.3% |
| 2017 | **Kavalan Solist Moscatel** | Heartwood Any Port in a Storm |
| 2018 | Paul John Kanya | **Limeburner's Dark Winter** |
| 2019 | Amrut Greedy Angels 8 Years Old | **Belgrove Peated Rye** |
| 2020 | **Nantou Distillery Omar Bourbon Cask** | Bakery Hill Peated Malt |

# ARGENTINA
## Blends
**Breeders Choice (84) n21 t22 f21 b20.** A sweet blend using Scottish malt and, at the helm, an unusually lush Argentinian grain. *40%*

# BRAZIL
## HEUBLEIN DISTILLERY
**Durfee Hall Malt Whisky** db **(81) n18 t22 f20 b21.** Superbly made whisky; the intensity of the malt is beautifully layered without ever becoming too sweet. Very light bodied and immaculately clean. Good whisky by any standards. *43%*

## UNION DISTILLERY
**Barrilete** db **(72) n18 t19 f18 b17.** Nothing particularly wrong with it technically; it just lacks vitality. Thin but extremely malt intense. *39.1%*

# BHUTAN
**K5 Premium Spirit Himalayan Whisky** bott 2013 **(88) n22 t23 f21 b22** Absolutely nothing wrong with the Bhutan grain but more judicious cask selection (i.e remove the odd one or two sub-standard Scotch barrels) and this really could be an irresistible little charmer. As a first attempt, really impressive. This whisky is a mix of Scotch malt and grain made in Bhutan. So it was fitting that seeing as parts of that mysterious, land-locked mountainous country rises to some 23,000 feet, I was just slightly above that height when I first learned of the whisky. While on board a flight to Asia I witnessed the brand's manager trying to talk an airline into carrying it. He then assured me I'd love it. Actually, clean that malt up a bit and I really could! *40%*

# INDIA
## AMRUT DISTILLERY
**Amrut Double Cask** batch no. 3, ex-bourbon & port pipe casks, Scottish peated barley, cask nos. 3189 & 2715, dist Mar/May 12, bott Jun 17 db **(94.5) n23.5 t23.5. f23.5 b24** A deeply complex, satisfying and high quality Indian whisky. *46%. 1,050 bottles.*

**Amrut Greedy Angels 8 Years Old** batch no. 2, unpeated Indian barley & Scottish peated barley, bott Jun 17 db **(96) n23 t24.5 f24 b24.5** Had the nose just been as in tune as the unforgettable sequence of favours and counter-flavours on the palate, we would have had a contender for World Whisky of the Year... *50%.*

◇ **Amrut Greedy Angels 10 Years Old Chairman's Reserve** ex bourbon cask, batch no. 01, bott 25 Jun 19 db **(94.5) n23** it could be said that Indian whisky is getting a style of its own, because when I picked up to nose this I thought I had picked up the Paul John by mistake. I hadn't! Rich and coppery with a hint of butterscotch; **t24** so much honey on delivery! Lip-smacking as the acacia honey works overtime alongside the intense barley. The oak weaves in and out with integrity and charm; **f23.5** long, warming and dries back towards vanilla and the butterscotch found on the nose. Again, just a little coppery sharpness at the death; **b24** high quality whisky. And a must find for honey lovers... *55%. 900 bottles.*

◇ **Amrut Greedy Angels Peated Sherry Finish Chairman's Reserve 10 Years Old** batch no. 01, bott Feb 19 db **(94) n23.5** thick fruit. Reminiscent of a sherry trifle with a dribble of Ardbeg...(and trust me, I've had it....!!!); **t24** just huge on delivery. The grape sparkles in the same way the whisky does in the glass. The spices are controlled. The more intense fruits boast a weightier dried date alongside muscovado sugars; **f23** long: very long! But a duller finish here, becoming a little sooty at the finale; **b23.5** a faultless sherry cask at work here: the rarest of the rare! So powerful the peat at times has problems making itself heard and has to content itself as being the backing group. Elegant, intense and very high quality. *60%. 324 bottles.*

**Amrut Kadhambam** batch no. 10, bott Jun 17 db **(89.5) n22 t23 f22 b22.5** Almost as though the rum, sherry and brandy casks, rather than adding complexity, have neutralised each other somewhat: in blending more can often lead to less A pleasant malt, all the same. *50%.*

◇ **Amrut Kadhambham 2019 Release** bott 20 Jun 19 db **(93) n23** this is hefty stuff here. The malt is almost soup-like. A little salty nibble to the tannin and hint of light marmalade in there, too; **t23** amiable and pliable: so chewy as the malt gathers in intensity to very attractive levels; a slight vaguely fruity tartness though the middle ensures there is no chance of cloying; **f23** a gorgeous spice buzz to match the very dry, almost chalky vanillas; **b23.5** a beautifully rich Amrut; a much heavier, maltier style than normal. *50%. 7,200 bottles.*

**Amrut Naarangi** batch no. 3, bott Jun 17 db **(90) n21 t23 f23.5 b22.5** The whisky with peel appeal... *50%.*

**Amrut 100 Peated Single Malt** ex-bourbon/virgin oak barrels db **(92) n23 t23 f23.5 b22.5.** Ironically, though one of the older whiskies to come from this distillery, the nose shows a little bit of youth. A quite different style from Amrut's other peated offerings and it was obviously intended. Further proof that this distillery has grown not only in stature but confidence. And with very good reason. 57.1%. nc ncf.

🦚 **Amrut Peated Port Pipe Single Cask** batch no. 01, bott 12 Feb 19 db **(95.5) n24** an unusual thickness to the peat...the smoke almost oozing from the glass...; **t24.5** and no less mouth-filling on delivery! Actually, this has to be one of the best mouth feels of the year, the smoke buzzing through slightly and carried on a lightly fruity but mainly honeyed platform: stunning...; **f23** dries...and dries...and dries.... A little bitterness kicks in from the oak, but that warm spice background heather honey; **b24** very often a well peated malt and wine cask don't work particularly well together, one element cancelling out the other. This, it must be recorded, works a treat. It is so good, in fact, I raise this glass to the memory of Amrut's founding father, whisky visionary Neelakanta Rao Jagdale...and friend. 48%. nc ncf. The Vault Biennale Edition

**Amrut Spectrum 004** batch no. 1, ex-oloroso, new French oak, new American oak & ex-PX sherry casks, bott Apr 17 db **(81) n20 t23 f19 b19** I admit I feared the worst when I saw the make-up of this malt: using such casks is like jumping around in a minefield. Even had all the barrels been top notch, to create something that would make sense and balance out would either be the most enormous luck or some of the greatest blending ever known in whisky history. But there are flaws to the casks which you may well pick up on both nose and finish. And though elsewhere, especially on delivery, there are a few moments of balmy, insanely intense beauty, they are fleeting. Maybe, though, enduring a day of stormy seas and lightning is worth the dazzling beauty of the brief rainbow. 50%.

# JOHN DISTILLERIES

**Paul John Brilliance** db **(94.5) n23.5 t24 f23.5 b23.5** Yet another astonishing malt from India. 46%

**Paul John Chairman's Reserve** db **(89) n22 t23 f22 b22** I cannot say I am much of a fan of the mixing of PX and peat. Sometimes it works, usually it doesn't: often it is a case of two heavyweight fighters landing punches simultaneously, each knocking the other out. Well, both contestants hit the deck here but, thankfully, got up again briefly for a becalmed finish. Oh, and the really good news: 100% sulphur free...! 59.7%. ncf.

🔸 **Paul John Christmas Edition** batch no. 02, mfg. date 16-nov-18 db **(95.5) n24** the label tells you "a hint of peat". It lies. There is more than a hint of phenols here, giving the aroma the overall impression of a smoky Christmas pudding and accompanying dates...; **t24** the mouth feel is just as much a star of the show here as the actual taste. Though having said that, the slow build-up of caramel to accompany the mixed fruit and molasses is truly wonderful. Rich, with a fabulously measured honey sweetness; **f23.5** more vanilla and caramel mix, the smoke intertwangling with the persistent honey; **b24** question: when is a big whisky not a big whisky? Answer: when it is as well balanced as this... 46%. ncf.

🔸 **Paul John Classic Select Cask** db **(94.5) n23** rich and tingly, there is copper and distinct saltiness to add to the mix of malt and powerful vanilla. At once delicate yet intense...; **t24** PJ does this so well: a huge delivery of concentrated malt and natural caramel. The sweetness is of spot on intensity, the light molasses meeting the copper and spice head on; **f23.5** just more natural caramels, now beautifully warmed by the spices; **b24** one of those whiskies which just overflows with flavour. Delicious! 55.2%. nc ncf.

**Paul John Edited** db **(96.5) n24.5 t24.5 f23.5 b24** A new Indian classic: a sublime malt from the subcontinent. To be more precise: a world classic! Think of Ardmore at its most alluring: one of Scotland's finest and most complex single malts, yet somehow possessing a saltiness and depth more befitting Islay. Then stir in a small degree of ulmo honey and bourbon-style hickory and liquorice. Plus subtle chocolate mint. And there you have it...the smoke drifting around stirring up spicy tales of the east. A world class whisky to be talked about with reverence without doubt... 52.9%

**Paul John Exceptional** db **(95) n23 t24 f24 b24** The sheer élan of the controlled intensity is something to behold: Indian malt at its maltiest and most charmingly expressed. 47%. ncf.

**Paul John Kanya** db **(96) n23.5 t24 f24 b24.5** When a distillery can find honey at the very end of the its flavour range and profile, you know they have cracked it. Superb! 50%. ncf.

🔸 **Paul John Nirvana Unpeated Single Malt** batch no. 01, mfg. date 12-nov-18 db **(94) n24** hints of Kentucky, fortified with a kumquat and honeycomb theme; **t23.5** Indian silk. Mesmerically soft and alluring, gentle ulmo honey and vanilla forming a graceful partnership in which barley slowly builds its stake; **f23** light spices and a slightly waxy honey thread. The sugars remain constant, despite a bitter-ish subplot; **b23.5** while writing these notes a wasp decided to fly into my tasting glass, fall into the whisky called Nirvana...and die. Ironic, or what? But wasps have a sweet tooth, so tells you all you need to know. That and the fact it climbed back in three times before it finally succumbed... 40%. ncf.

**Paul John Olorosso Sherry Cask Finish** db **(94.5)** n23.5 t23.5 f23.5 b24 Oh, for the rare joy of a sulphur-free malt. And as complex a one as this, to boot. 57.4%. ncf.

**Paul John Peated Single Malt** db **(89)** n23 t22 f21.5 b22.5. A delicately peaty guy which gangs up on you slowly. The smoke-infused layering of sugars is the star turn, though. 55.5%

**Paul John PX** db **(90.5)** n22.5 t23.5 f21.5 b23 The plan was to write these tasting notes while England were playing India during the first Test match in Birmingham. England, as usual, collapsed after previously having their foot on India's throat and potentially all out for a very low score...but then blew it. So with India now favourites to win, thought I'd better get these tasted today, rather than tomorrow, while there is still a Test match. For the cricket: why do England have only one Surrey player, Sam Curran? And not surprisingly the only one to show any resistance. And as for the whisky: enjoyable with a truly brilliant delivery. But not showing the true subtlety and colours of PJ's excellent malt. 48%. ncf.

**Paul John Single Malt-Classic (Un Peated)** db **(95)** n23.5 t24 f23.5 b24 Further evidence that Indian whisky is on the rise. Just so charming...and irresistible. 55.2%

**Paul John Select Cask Peated (96)** n24 t24 f24 b24 A peated malt whisky which will make a few people sit up and take even further notice of Indian whisky. World class... 46%

⬦ **Paul John Tula 100%** virgin American oak casks db **(96)** n23.5 find yourself half an hour and pick your way through this: beeswax, orange blossom honey in league with vanilla pods, red liquorice...and dovetailing in and out of this is malt, still. Just so soft and though oak plays a big role not one that is allowed to dominate in any way; t24.5 one of the best whiskies, one of the best of the year from anywhere in the world. Spitting this was not easy by any means, trust me! The varying degrees of honey are borderline mind-blowing. Indeed, anyone for a penchant for Crunchie honeycomb chocolate bars will think something has just happened and they're in heaven. To be more precise, this is more like the Crunchies which were slightly more roasted and dark, so the intensity is at near off the scale. Imagine Molasses and heather honey mixed together for the toastiest effect. The spices rumble politely but not wishing to disturb the near perfection that in unravelling on your palate; amazingly, amid all this, comes some salivating moments, also...; f23.5 long, very long, with the distillery signature light coppery mark being made, but now a greater waxiness to the honey. The vanillas arrive late to the party but now the barley becomes more visual, too...; b24.5 think of an artist with a beautiful mind and spirit, painting, sculpting, restoring, creating...all these things have happened here as this is a work of art as much as a bottle of whisky. 58%. ncf.

**Cadenhead's Paul John 5 Years Old** dist 2012 **(94.5)** n23 t24 f23.5 b24 Typical of the outstanding Cadenhead brand to celebrate for their 175th anniversary an Indian whisky that many others in their sector of the market would prefer to rubbish. As ever, Cadenhead's have called it right for this is a superb single malt. 57.4%. 175th Anniversary bottling

# PONDA DISTILLERY

**Stillman's Dram Single Malt Whisky Limited Edition** bourbon cask no. 11186-90 **(94)** n23 t23 f24 b24. Well, I thought I had tasted it all with the Amrut cask strength. And then this arrived at my lab...!! I predicted many years back that India would dish out some top grade malt before too long. But I'd be stretching the truth if I said I thought it would ever be this good... 42.8%. McDowell & Co Ltd, India.

# RAMPUR DISTILLERY

⬦ **Rampur Indian Single Malt Whisky Sherry PX Finish** American oak barrels, finished in Spanish sherry PX butts db **(86)** n22 t22.5 f20 b21.5 A real shame this. It is obvious that the underlying malt is very attractive. But the PX has intervened to slightly flatten and dull and then leave a sulphurous deposit on the finish. Indian distilleries have to learn, like some in Scotland and Ireland refuse to, that using Spanish oak can be a very dangerous game. 45%. ncf.

**Rampur Vintage Select Indian Single Malt Whisky** batch no. 383, bott Jun 16 db **(89)** n22.5 t23 f21 b22.5 Although I first went to this distillery over 20 years ago, it is the first time I have ever tasted it in my own lab back here in the UK. In those days, it was 100% designated for blended whisky: I argued it should be a single malt. On this evidence, you can see why... 43%. ncf.

## Blends

**Signature (81.5)** n22.5 t22 f17.5 b19.5. Excellent, rich nose & delivery helped along with a healthy display of peat reek. But more attention has to be paid to the brutally thin finish. 42.8%

# NEW ZEALAND
# THE NEW ZEALAND WHISKY COMPANY

**High Wheeler 3070 Singlewood Aged New Zealand Whisky (88.5)** n23 t22.5 f21 b22 This is 30% grain (which has a very different, much thinner feel to the grain found in Scotland, for instance) and 70% malt. As soft and friendly as you like. 43%.

## THE SOUTHERN DISTILLING CO LTD

**The MacKenzie Blended Malt Whiskey (85) n20 t22 f21 b22.** A vaguely spicier, chalkier, mildly less honeyed version of Coaster. Quite banana-laden nose. *40%*

## THOMSON WILLOWBANK

**Thomson Single Malt 21 Years Old (84) n21 t22.5 f20.5 b20.** Bit of a bimbo whisky: looks pretty and outwardly attractive but has picked up very little in its 21 years... *46%. sc.*

## WILSON DISTILLERY

**Cadenhead's World Whiskies Lammerlaw Aged 10 Years** bourbon, bott 07 **(91.5) n22 t23.5 f23 b23.** Stunning bottlings like this can only leave one mourning the loss of this distillery. *48.9%*

## SOUTH AFRICA
## JAMES SEDGWICK DISTILLERY

◈ **Bain's Capetown Mountain Single Grain Whisky** bott code: 1869721 L5 18260 db **(87.5) n22 t22 f21.5 b22** Even though the strength of Capetown Mountain has been reduced slightly, it offers a marginally better whisky than of old with far better balance and far greater presence to ensure a more satisfying finale. Its weakness, still, is simplicity though the nip of the spice has been enhanced and fares well against the rich cream toffee. *40%.*

### Blends

**Knights (83) n20.5 t21 f20 b20.5.** While the Harrier has crashed, the Knights is now full of promise. Also shows the odd bitter touch but a better all-round richer body not only absorbs the impacts but radiates some malty charm. *43%. South African/Scotch Whisky.*

**Knights Aged 3 Years (87) n22 t22 f22 b22.** This now appears to be 100% South African whisky if I understand the label correctly: "Distilled Matured and Bottled in South Africa." A vast improvement on when it was Scotch malt and South African grain. Bursting with attitude and vitality. When next in South Africa, this will be my daily dram for sure. Love it. *43%.*

**Three Ships Bourbon Cask Finish (90) n22 t23 f22.5 b22.5.** A soft, even whisky which enjoys its finest moments on delivery. Clean with a pressing, toasty oakiness to the sweeter malt elements. Always a delight. *43%*

**Three Ships Premium Select Aged 5 Years (93) n23 t23.5 f23 b23.5.** What a fabulous whisky. The blender has shown a rare degree of craft to make so little smoke do so much. Bravo! *43%. James Sedgwick Distillery.*

**Three Ships Select (81) n19 t21 f20 b21.** Busy and sweet. But I get the feeling that whatever South African malt may be found in Knights does a better job than its Scotch counterpart here. *43%. James Sedgwick Distillery.*

## TAIWAN
## KAVALAN DISTILLERY

◈ **Kavalan Single Malt Whisky 10th Anniversary Bordeaux Margaux Wine Cask Matured** bott code: 2018.12.26 db **(95) n23.5** complex interplay between confident dry notes and an almost sour fruit kick. Always hefty, the grape coming across like a day-old used Bordeaux cork; **t24** succulent with early emphasis on the heather honey. Then come the deeper grape tones. But the spices are withheld by none of this and glow warmly; **f23.5** still impressively intense. The sharp rhubarb and custard theme offers up some sweetness with the ulmo honey, but there are the brooding tannins and sombre grape skin which guarantees depth and complexity; **b24** a very quiet, understated complexity and confidence that just exudes class. Much more here than originally meets the eye...and nose. *57.8%. nc ncf sc.*

◈ **Kavalan Single Malt Whisky 10th Anniversary Bordeaux Pauillac Wine Cask Matured** bott code: 2018.12.26 db **(90.5) n23** grape and green plums carved into granite; **t22.5** for the first three or four flavour waves there is even less yield than on the nose; finally a little French bruyere honey and oil lightens the load; **f22** spicy and a tad tight; **b22.5** the fruit appears to have armoured plating. This is one very, very firm and grave Monsieur. *57.8%. nc ncf sc.*

◈ **Kavalan Distillery Reserve Single Cask Strength Rum Cask** cask no. M111104056A, bott code: 2018.01.04 db **(90.5) n22.5** you get the feeling the cut here was a little more generous than normal, allowing in some extra oils to soften the firmer sugars muscovado included, which encourages the delicate fruits; the salty light nougat is also somewhat intriguing; **t23** chewy as a toffee bar, with corresponding caramel. There is also an interesting oily buzz which impacts on the mouth — and finally a surge of lovely malt; salivating and helped along by a dose of light lime blossom honey; **f22** much duller as the oils congregate, but the spice buzz is persistent; **b23** on the nose it seems innocuous enough, but turns into being a huge whisky. *59.4%. sc. 401 bottles.*

⬧ **Kavalan Single Malt Whisky ex-Bourbon Oak** bott code: 2018.06.27 db **(93.5) n23** the slightest exotic fruit hangs from every edge of the caramel-rich malt; **t23** these must be first-fill bourbon casks at work, because the tannins arrive ahead of the sweeter barley. This makes for an attractively tart start to proceedings and a real fizz to the chewiness; **f23.5** not often the finale is the best bit of a whisky, but it is here. The early game is a bit of a battle; this is much more relaxed and better balanced with the knotty oak now calmed into equal depth and input as the heather honey and spices; **b24** something for everyone with a malt with early attitude but reveals some class late on, too. *46%.*

⬧ **Kavalan Single Malt Whisky Kavalan Classic** bott code: 2018.06.26 db **(88.5) n22.5** they have upped the kumquats; malty, too...; **t22.5** soft and malty, but at every turn some fruit sneaks into the proceedings; **f22** fades slowly with a light vanilla, caramel and barley wave farewell; **b22** a malt which is actually at its best when barely warmed. A little less expansive than of old. *40%.*

⬧ **Kavalan Single Malt Whisky Kavalan Distillery Select** bott code: 2018.07.17 db **(87.5) n22 t22 f22 b21.5** Must have been distilled on the silk road. As this is exceptionally soft but much simplified from the Distillery Selects of old. Very good spice fruity spice. *40%.*

⬧ **Kavalan Single Malt Whisky Port Cask Finish Concertmaster** bott code: 2018.06.30 db **(92.5) n23** for fruit candy connoisseurs...; **t23** another from the silky school of Kavalan whisky. Zero jagged edges or conflicts as the malt and polite fruit join together without a visible join...; **f23** relatively long with a mix of chocolate and raisin and mocha, though vanilla has the final say, **b23.5** Kavalan at this strength always seems a little underpowered, as if the woodwind haven't turned up for a Bruckner concert. But the elegant restraint of this whisky should certainly be admired. *40%.*

⬧ **Kavalan Single Malt Whisky Podium** bott code: 2018.04.20 db **(88) n22** lively spices graze on the abundant fruit; **t23** spot on delivery with juicy stone fruits and spices at high volumes. But the later waves are nowhere near so convincing in their integrity; **f21** strangely tangy and out of sync, though this appears to be the spirit rather than the cask; **b22** a very fat malt but not quite shewing the usual Kavalan character. *46%.*

⬧ **Kavalan Single Malt Whisky Sherry Oak** bott code: 2018.06.27 db **(87.5) n22.5 t22 f21.5 b21.5** The nose leaves little doubt about the keen sherry influence but beyond the delivery the malt has surprisingly little to say. Pleasant, but hardly stirs your blood or makes you gird your loins *46%.*

⬧ **Kavalan Solist Single Cask Strength Amontillado Sherry Cask** cask no. AM100623009B, bott code: 2017.07.27 db **(95.5) n23.5** astonishing layering. Even more astonishing is that the malt becomes visible from time to time, slipping between the grape layers that shine, then fade, then shine again in their juicy intensity; **t24.5** just too good! So intense and confident on delivery, the fruit still has elegance enough to allow through the tannins, spice and barley in complex strata. By the mid-point we have moved into a gentle rum and raisin chocolate theme; **f23.5** such complexity! There have been whispers of honey, but now we go into heather honey mode which embraces both the oaky vanilla and the spiced dates; **b24** another absolutely flawless sherry cask from Kavalan: at the moment they are easily in the top three distilleries for wine casks to die for. *57.1%. nc ncf sc. 501 bottles.*

⬧ **Kavalan Solist Single Cask Strength Manzanilla Sherry Cask** cask no. MA100716026A, bott code: 2018.01.27 db **(96) n24.5** now this just reeks of Kavalan: absolutely their style with the juiciest fruit cake on display with black cherry, molasses, diced macadamia nuts and vanilla. Sublime and quite faultless...; **t24.5** wonderfully balanced delivery: medium roast Blue Mountain Jamaican coffee rounds off the salivating, juicy yet crisp muscovado sugars; a little ginger and warmer spices buzz in brilliantly; **f23** the lightness of the vanilla is stark against the earlier riches, yet still so charming; **b24** tie yourself into a chair for this one, otherwise you will just float away in a state of sheer Kavalanian bliss... *57.8%. nc ncf sc. 467 bottles.*

⬧ **Kavalan Solist Single Cask Strength Moscatel Sherry Cask** cask no. MO110321014A, bott code: 2017.03.14 db **(84.5) n20 t22 f21 b21.5** Fruity for sure. But the oily, disconcerting tang is usually the result of a wide cut, not the barrel. *56.3%. nc ncf sc. 518 bottles.*

⬧ **Kavalan Solist Single Cask Strength Pedro Ximenez Sherry Cask** cask no. PX100630027A, bott code: 2018.03.12 db **(89) n22** liquorice and stewed plums; **t23.5** ah, now this is where it comes alive after the flattish nose. Concentrated – or do I mean concentrated? - everything on delivery: molasses, liquorice, dates, raisins and maple syrup; **f21.5** just a shade light and underwhelming as the molasses and vanillas fail to gel; **b22** sticky and full-bodied. *56.3%. nc ncf sc. 480 bottles.*

⬧ **Kavalan Solist ex-Bourbon Cask** cask no. B101214030A, bott code: 2018.06.13 db **(94) n23.5** brilliant complexity: the oak is weaving patterns here of varying degrees of weight and honey richness, but the barley is a glistening constant; **t23.5** how subtle can those bourbon notes get? Almost as though there is a hint of rye to this, with a firm fruitiness and crystal clear Demerara finesse, coupled with a light hickory, piano (to accompany the spices forte; **f23** lovely light oils allow the Demerara and liquorice to fade with barely detectab adroitness; **b24** a beautifully relaxed malt which shows the distillery off in a golden glow. Such class! 56.3%. nc ncf sc. 169 bottles.

◇ **Kavalan Solist Fino Sherry Cask** cask no. FI00714038A, bott code: 2018.07.26 db **(94.5) n23** mainly dry, especially the grape skin; some blistering spices and just a light sub plot of muscovado sugar; **t24** wow! That spice steps way beyond blistering for an immediate eye-watering attack; the sweetness is far more easily discernible here than on the nose, with soft ulmo honey melting into the brilliant mix of vanilla and toasted raisin; **f23.5** long, with a few oils forming but that honey and grape note refusing to die, as does the pulsing spice...; **b24** an essay in subtlety and understatement despite the apparent bigness. 57.1%. nc ncf sc. 489 bottles.

◇ **Kavalan Solist Oloroso Sherry Cask** cask no. S090102047, bott code: 2018.02.03 db **(87) n22.5 t21.5 f22 b21** Nearly three decades ago I was criticising these kind of sherry butts, then, unlike now, found exclusively in Scotland, as they were simply too heavy and cumbersome for the malt they had conjoined: rather than integrate, it had conquered. The opaque colour of the malt – almost blackcurrant juice in its darkness – offers a fair warning. The nose is attractive, especially if you happen to love oloroso sherry. But that is the problem: the whisky has vanished with barely a trace beneath it. Nonetheless, enjoyable for sure with all the spices present and correct. 57.1%. nc ncf sc. 470 bottles.

◇ **Kavalan Solist Port Cask** cask no. 0090619059A, bott code: 2018.08.10 db **(95) n23.5** earthy, dry and even a touch phenolic, it looks as though the tannin has decided that the fruit won't have it all its own way; **t24** the mouth feel of a whisky rarely comes as rich and thick as this without being even remotely cloying. Spices erupt from the first moment, but the sheer juiciness of the pulpy fruit deserves a standing ovation; **f23.5** long with increasing degrees of chocolate to go with the fruit and nut; **b24** very much in the Kavalan house style of rich and substantially spiced - but never hot - single malt. Superb whisky from a faultless cask. 59.4%. nc ncf sc. 183 bottles.

◇ **Kavalan Vinho Barrique Cask** cask no. W120614024, bott code: 2018.02.21 db **(94.5) n24** stunning mix of greengage and ginger....wow! **t23.5** lush and fabulously faultless barrique: spices arrive at the van with thin Manuka and heather honey lightening the plum pudding; **f23** butterscotch and kirsch; **b24** Kavalan has that very rare talent for brilliance without apparent effort... 54.8%. nc ncf sc. 205 bottles.

◇ **King Car Whisky Conductor Single Malt** bott code: 2018.03.26 db **(89) n22.5** soft vanilla and golden syrup; an earthier, semi-phenolic note too of dank English bluebell woods; **t22.5** a striking, single layered sweetness of delivery, one of heather honey, a single torch of brightness in pretty heavy and dark delivery; **f22** another shewing a spiced nougat, very weighty finale; **b22** hefty malt with a rare but disarming honey thread. 46%.

## NANTOU DISTILLERY

◇ **Nantou Distillery Omar Cask Strength Aged 8 Years III Bourbon Cask** cask no. 11090102, dist May 09, bott 1 Mar 18 db **(90.5) n23.5** superb structure to the nose, a gentle blood orange note to the refined sugary tannin. Remarkably light and nimble for its age; **t23** early oils then a big mix of heather honey and intense barley; **f21.5** just a little extra oil gives this a much fatter finish than any other from this distillery and stretches the vanillas; **b22.5** charming and full bodied, you can see how the house style has changed slightly since this was distilled eight years ago 52.8%. sc. 150 bottles.

◇ **Nantou Distillery Omar Cask Strength Bourbon Cask** cask no. 11100221, dist Sept 10, bott 8 Jun 16 db **(93) n23** the barley lives in the spotlight intensifying by the moment; there is almost a perfumed element to the delicate tannins which, like the malt, steadily builds in intensity; **t23.5** the delivery gives an immediate half-heated gristiness. But what follows, on flavour waves four and five, fair takes the breath away as the malt goes nuclear, to eye-watering and fabulously tart effect; the after shockwaves are of a biscuity barley and spice combination; **f23** the barley fade remains intense and very unusual; **b23.5** a delightfully idiosyncratic style of intense maltiness gives this whisky a unique and dangerously drinkable disposition. Wow! 58%. sc. 206 bottles.

◇ **Nantou Distillery Omar Cask Strength Bourbon Cask** cask no. 11140804, dist May 14, bott 25 May 17 db **(96.5) n24** if every nose was this amazing I'd never get the book completed: smoky, but with as much subtlety as there is phenol. A light mint and chocolate note, too. But it is the layering which blows you away...; **t24.5** the nose insists on brilliance. And brilliance is, indeed, achieved on delivery. The softness almost defies belief – and I'm not sure I have ever encountered so many layers to a peated malt. In between the phenols lie equally numerous layers of delicate liquorice and mocha, or sometimes praline, while strands of Manuka honey and grist keep the sweetness levels up to a controlled intensity; **f23.5** long, with no lessening the chocolate, and though the oak has upped its game it dries rather than dominates; **b24.5**

...autifully distilled; beautifully matured. Simply stunning! One of the single casks of the year, ...ot least for its unique and almost exhaustingly delicious style. *56%. sc. 248 bottles.*

 **Nantou Distillery Omar Cask Strength Lychee Liqueur Barrel Finished** bott 28 Sept 17 db **(94)** n23 a lightly toasted tannin comes through before lemon blossom honey softens alluringly; **t23.5** superb delivery where the barley celebrates a rare intensity by fully embracing the rich tannins; the mid-ground offers up a distinctive chocolate quality, which hangs around; **f23.5** plenty more chocolate, though now with a lightly salted edge; **b24** this whisky astounds me as much as it delights me! Curiously, lychee is a flavour sometimes picked up in well-aged Speyside-style light single malts. However, this is the first time I have ever encountered a malt matured in a lychee barrel. And it offers nothing like the cloying sweetness of say, PX. Thank god! A charming, classy malt. Oh, and the first whisky ever to include the stunning black-naped oriole (for those wondering what it is) on its label! *55%. 887 bottles.*

 **Nantou Distillery Omar Cask Strength Plum Liqueur Barrel Finished** bott 28 Sept 17 db **(93)** n23 spice prickle with a difference: a sharp, under-ripe greengage edge to this, too; **t23.5** a controlled explosion on the palate. A kind of a malt sandwich with a distinct fruity sharpness on delivery, like the nose with a under-ripe greenness, then powering gristy malt...followed by a reversion to lightly spiced prunes; **f23** muscovado sugars and vanilla-rich tannins bristle at each other at the death; a lovely fade of treacle and prunes, then tannins keeping a curb on the sweetness...; **b23.5** another new flavour profile kindly brought to me by Nantou Distillery. And another that is absolutely impossible not to like. *53%. 795 bottles.*

 **Nantou Distillery Omar Cask Strength Sherry Cask** cask no. 21130120, dist Jun 13, bott 1 Mar 18 db **(87.5)** n22 t22.5 f22 b21 A good clean sherry cask — entirely sulphur free — but the balance between the oak and grape isn't quite there yet as the fruit is far too pugnacious. Still, the spiced-up delivery is a delight and the intensity of grape something to grapple with. *59%. sc. 246 bottles.*

 **Nantou Distillery Omar Single Malt Whisky PX Solera Sherry Cask** cask no. 22160006, dist Jun 08, bott Nov 18 db **(84)** n22 t22 f20 b20 First things thirst. No sulphur: hurrah! The not such great news: the single malt whisky which was filled into this PX cask has vanished without trace. It will probably take archaeologists and sonar equipment to find. And this is the problem with PX, it is so all-consuming that if you are not careful you're left with massive grape. But not a single hint of an outline of the whisky itself. *52.1%. sc. 251 bottles.*

 **Nantou Distillery Omar Cask Strength Black Queen Wine Barrel Finished** bott 29 Sept 17 db **(91)** n23 a gentle, creamy fruitiness envelopes the whole. Just a playful hint of spice, but also a light barley and tannin note, too; **t23.5** beautifully controlled molasses and an early spice kick generate just the right degree of bite for the black cherry and raisin fruit to generate maximum juiciness; **f22** long, with the dusky tannins giving extra, drying weight to the cherry...; **b23** the sheer red-ness of this whisky means that you stare at it in near disbelief for a while before you even get round to tasting it. But when you do, you are well rewarded. Another very different whisky — and delicious, too! *56%. 863 bottles.*

# URUGUAY
**Dunbar Anejo 5 Anos (85.5)** n20 t22.5 f21.5 b21.5. A clean, mouth-wateringly attractive mix where the grain nips playfully and the Speyside malts are on best salivating behaviour. Decently blended and boasting a fine spice prickle, too. *40%*

# MISCELLANEOUS
 **Sir John Moore Blended Whisky** bott code: L-1805 **(71)** n17 t19 f17 b18 It is as though their Galacian water source comes directly from the Pump Room at Bath. Or, more likely, it's the sherry butts at play. *40%. Sansutex Alimentacion. Scotch blended with Galacian water.*

 **Sir John Moore Blended Whisky Malta** bott code: L-1812 **(73)** n18 t20 f17 b18 Riddled with sulphur. Ironic when you think about it.... *40%. Sansutex Alimentacion. Scotch blended with Galacian water*

 **Sir John Moore Blended Whisky Malta 10 Años** bott code: L-1814 **(87.5)** n21.5 t22.5 f21.5 b22 Well, after the last two bottlings I was fearing the worst. But no sulphur here and instead we have an amazingly salty malt, especially on the nose, which offers up a sweet and juicy light fruitiness on the palate. The finish, like the nose, has a certain peculiarity, but when hitting the heights the sugar-tannin combination works attractively. *40%. Sansutex Alimentacion. Scotch blended with Galacian water.*

# CROSS-COUNTRY VATTED WHISKIES
**Golfer's Shot Barrel Aged Whisky** blend of Indian malts & Scotch **(84)** n21 t22 f20 b...
An immaculately preened whisky with a lovely initial softness replaced by ever-increas...
spice. Its main handicap is the big toffee kick and a sometimes skewed flavour reg...

consistent with flavour additives. If additives are being used, then there is no need: the basics are good enough, If not, my apologies. *42.8%. Alcobrew Distilleries India Pvt. Ltd.*

⟡ **The Lakes Distillery The One Fine Blended Whisky** port cask finished, bott code: L 30 04 19 (**93**) **n23** clean, almost crystalline, there is a little fruity candyfloss at work here; **t23.5** melt-in-the-mouth (candyfloss gain?). The spices really have a big prickle to them, which stands out stark against the clarity of both the malt and grain. And on the subject of the malt, it takes its time, but just before the midpoint it begins to make itself heard loud and clear; **f23** soft oaky vanillas with a fruit pastel both in its shading and controlled sweetness; **b23.5** someone should build a grain distillery in England so we can have English blended whisky. This refuses to bow in quality to many a Scotch blend. *46.6%. nc ncf. The Lakes single malt blended with Scotch grain and malts.*

⟡ **Lucifer's Gold** bott code: L8257 (**85.5**) **n22 t22 f20.5 b21** A thin but pleasant blend which starts at a gallop on the palate but soon flags and bitters out slightly. Still, a delightful mouth feel early on and the odd kick and sparkle for entertainment. *40%. A blend of bourbon and three year old grain Scotch whisky. Charter Brands.*

⟡ **Mister Sam Tribute Whiskey** bott code: L19011331914E db (**94.5**) **n24** insane amounts of torched oak here with liquorice and molasses coming at you from every angle...; **t23.5** insane amounts of torched oak here, with liquorice and molasses coming at you from every angle....; **f23.5** insane amounts liquorice and molasses here with torched oak coming at you from every angle; **b24** big, brash...absolutely love it! What a fantastic tribute to the great whiskies of North America. I was going to say this is without parallel...but then I remembered the 49th one...*66.9% (133.8 Proof). A blend of American and Canadian whiskey.*

**The One British Blended Whisky** (**84.5**) **n22 t21.5 f20 b21.** Although it doesn't say so on the bottle, I understand this is made from a blend of malts from England, Ireland, Scotland and Wales. It says "blend" which implies the use of grain, though this is probably not so...another example of the confusion caused by the brainless and arrogant change of terminology from "vatted" to denote a blend of malts insisted upon by the Scotch Whisky Association. Not yet checked, but would have thought that as not Scotch, they still would have been entitled to call it a vatting. The mind boggles over what they will do with this whisky if Scotland votes for independence in a few weeks' time. Doubtless the SWA will make some kind of noise... Anyway, back to the action. The label does claim this is a whisky of "intriguing complexity". If true, the term will have to be redefined. The nose, sure enough, does offer just enough smoky and citrus twists and turns to wonder what will happen next. But the delivery on the palate is a disappointment, with any complexity desired submerged under a welter of dull caramels. Just too flat and soft for its own good: back to the drawing board....and possibly without Scotch... *40% WB15/406*

⟡ **The One British Blended Whisky Sherry Expression** finished in Spanish sherry casks, bott code: L 01 10 18 (**94**) **n22.5** bit of a Euro whisky here, as the sherry seems to wish to dominate the proceedings of the British interests; **t23.5** ah, soft and yielding. Initially shews a degree of British pluck but then slowly accedes control to the sherry. Blended by Theresa May to a Philip Hammond recipe, perhaps; **f24** finishes beautifully. The control of May and Hammond has been kicked out and the malts are now in full voice. Rich, confident, a tad spicy and with a can do attitude and the sherry now vanquished this augers well for the British malts; **b24** can't be any backstop agreement here as things are working really well between the UK, Ireland and mainland Europe with its sherry influence. Shewing all the elegance and refinement of a Jacob Rees-Mogg this, surely, should be known as the Boris Blend... *46.6%. nc ncf. 5,500 bottles.*

**Steel Bonnets** bott code: L 13 06 18 (**83**) **n19 t23 f20 b21** This would have been so much better had, presumably, sherry butts not been involved... The nose is a classic case of smoke and fruit neutralising the other, leaving a tangy note to rule. Such a contrast to the big and boisterous palate: nothing like the white-flag-ishness of the nose. A serious tannin-induced spice prickle kicks in from the very first moment and keeps its foot on the throat of the roast fudge and raisin delivery; light wisps of smoke mingle with mocha at the mid-point. The furriness on the finale underscores where things have gone slightly awry. *46.6%. ncf. The Lakes Distillery. Blend of English & Scottish Malts.*

**White & Blue** blend of Indian malts & Scotch (**68**) **n17 t18 f16 b17** OK, certain this one is riddled with flavour additives – my tongue is buzzing. Good people of Alcobrew: the world has moved on and Indian malt deserves better respect. A decent blend can be created just from the whisky itself – I'll come and show you! If I'm wrong and this is all natural, I apologise unreservedly. But I don't think I am. *42.8%. Alcobrew Distilleries India Pvt. Ltd.*

# Slàinte

his is the point where I say a Boeing 747 ego-sized thank you to all those who have
helped me write the Whisky Bible, showing my appreciation to the many who have
chipped in with their time, help and kindnesses, small and large, one way or another.

Also, of course, my usual thanks to my team of Vincent Flint-Hill, Peter Mayne, James
Murray, and, of course, the glue that holds us all together: our very own and very special
Jane Garnett, especially for all the amazing work she did tomorrow. As well as my support
team of Paul and Denise Egerton, Linda Mayne, David Hartley and Julie Barrie, my personal
encyclopedia. Also, Charlie Jones and Kelly May for their outstanding assistance in Kentucky.
As always, a huge hug to Heiko Thieme. Thanks, also, to those below who have provided
assistance and samples for the 2013 Bible onwards, as well as those who assisted in the
previous decade. Finally, a thank you and fond and sad farewell to Mr Tiel (frontispiece), a
beautiful cockatiel who noisily added charm, colour and fun to my tasting days after
mysteriously moving into the trees and fields surrounding my English home. Tragically, just
as this book was being completed, and before I could rescue him, he fell prey to a tawny owl.

Mitch Abate; Andrew Abela; Hayley Adams; Emma Alessandrini; Mary Allison; Mike Almy; Ally Alpine;
Nicole Anastasi; Tommy Andersen; Wayne Anderson; Gareth andrews; Kristina Anerfält-Jansson; Clint
Anesbury; Jane & Martin Armstrong; Hannah Arnold; Teemu Artukka; Scott & Sam Ashforth; Paul Aston;
Kevin Atchinson; Ryan Baird; Andrew Baker; David Baker; Emma Ball; Duncan Baldwin; Clare Banner;
Keith Barnes; Lauren Barrett; Hans Baumberger; Stefan Baumgart; Steve Beam; Lauren Beck; Stefan
Beck; Jan Beckers; Kirsteen Beeston; Sarah Belizaire-Butler; Becky Bell; Annie Bellis; Sigurd Belsnes;
Franz Benner; Alexander Berger; Akash Beri; John Bernasconi; Barry Bernstein; Stuart Bertia; Jodi Best;
Marilena Bidaine; Peter Bignell; Menno Bijmolt; Lee Bilsky; Sonat Birknecker Hart; Franziska Bishof; Rich
Blair; Olivier Blanc; Mike Blaum; Elisabeth Blum; René Bobrink; Andreas Boessow; Anna Boger; Arthur
H. Boggs, III; Amy & Steve Bohner; Hans Bol; Mark Boley; Yvonne Bonner; Keith Bonnington; Etienne
Bouillon; Borat, Birgit Bornemeier; Phil Brandon; Caroline Brel; Stephen Bremner; Rebecca Brennan;
Franz Brenner; Cam Brett; Stephanie Bridge; Chris Brown; James Brown; Sara Browne; Chris Bryne; Ralf
Brzeske; Michael Brzozowski; Alexander Buchholz; Ryan Burchett; Amy Burgess; Nicola Cameron;
Andrew Campbell Walls; Euan Campbell; Nathan Campbell; Kimla Carsten; Lauren Casey-Haiko; Bert
Cason; Stuart Cassells; Jim Caudill; Danilo Cembrero; Lisa Chandler; Thomas Chen; Yuseff Cherney; Ashok
Chokalingam; Julia Christian; Morten Christensen; Michelle Clark; Claire Clark; Nick Clark; Anne-Marie
Clarke; Joseph Clarkson; Fredi Clerc; Dr Martin Collis; Shelagh Considine; Peter Cooney; Mathew & Julie
Cooper; Christina Conte; Gabriel Corcoran; Lynn Cross; Lauren Crothers; Rosie Cunningham; Brian Cox;
Jason Craig; David Croll; Molly Cullen; Nathan Currie; Larry Currier; Benjamin Curtis; Danni Cutten; Dave
Cuttino; Larry Currier; Mike DaRe; Alan Davis; Bryan Davis; Stephen Davies; Alasdair Day; Dick & Marti;
Scott Dickson; Martin Diekmann; Sharton Deane; Dixon Dedman; Conor Dempsey; Paul Dempsey;
Lauren Devine; Marie-Luise Dietich; Rob Dietrich; Hugo Diez; Arno Josef Dirker; Caroline Docherty; Oscar
Dodd; Korrie Dodge; Angela D'Orazin; Georgia Donmall; Jean Donnay; Kellie Du; Quinzil Du Plessis; Tim
Duckett; Camille Duhr-Merges; Mariette Duhr-Merger; Gemma Duncan; Shane Dunning; Christophe
Dupic; Jens Drewitz; Reinhard Drexler; Jochen Druffel; Michael D'souza; Kollie Du; Jonas Ebensperger;
Lenny Eckstein; Ray Edwards; Winston Edwards; Bernd Ehbrecht; Carsten Ehrlich; Ben Ellefsen; Rebecca
Elliott-Smith; Lucie Ellis; Thimo Elz; Maximilian Engel; Camilla Ericsson; Beanie Espey; James Espey; Brad
Estabrooke; Patrick Evans; Jennifer Eveleigh; Selim Evin; Thomas Ewers; Charlotte Falconer; Lauren
Fallert; Bruce Farquhar; David Faverot; Joanna Fearnside; Angus Ferguson; Walter Fitzke; Roland Feller;
Andrea Ferrari; Bobby Finan; Brigette Fine; Holly Forbes; Holly Forbes; Jean-Arnaud Frantzen; Sascha Frozza;
Barry Gallagher; Hans-Gerhard Fink; Sarah Fisher; David Fitt; Walter Fitzke; Kent Fleischman; Eric Flynn;
Mara Flynn; Martyn Flynn; Holly Forbes; Carole Frugier; Danny Gandert; Arno Gänsmantel; Patrick Garcia;
Dan Garrison; Ralph Gemmel; Stefanie Geuting; Carole Gibson; Jonathan Gibson; Daniel Giraldo; John
Glaser; John Glass; Emily Glynn; Emma Golds; Rodney Goodchild; Chloe Gordon; Jonathon Gordan;
Tomer Goren; Bob Gorton; Lawrence Graham; Kelly Greenawalt; Hannah Gregory; Andrew Grey; George
Grindlay; Rebecca Groom; Jason Grossmiller; Jan Groth; Viele Grube; Immanuel Gruel; Barbara Grundler;
Katia Guidolin; Stefanie Geuting Josh Hafer; Jasmin Haider; Jamie Hakim; Georgina Hall; Georges
Hannimann; Denis Hanns; Claire Harris; Scott E Harris; Alistair Hart; Andrew Hart; Donald Hart; Stuart
Harvey; Ralf Hauer; Elizabeth Haw; Steve Hawley; Ailsa Hayes; Ross Hendry; Lianne Herbruck; Thomas
Herbruck; Nils C. Herrmann; Bastian Heuser; Jennifer Higgins; Jason Himstedt; Brian Hinson; Roland
Hinterreiter; Paul Hletko; Eva Hoffman; Marcus Hofmeister; Tom Holder; Julie Holl Rebsomen; Genise
Hollingworth; Arlette Holmes; Bernhard Höning; Jason Horn; Mike Howlings; Emma Hurley; Alex
Huskingson; Thomas B. Ide; Jill Inglis; Rachel Showalter Inman; Victoria Irvine; Hannah Irwin; Kai Ivalo;
Emma Jackson; Caroline James; Richard Jansson; Amelia James; Ulrich Jakob; Andrew Jarrell; Don
Jennings; Big John; Pascal Jobst; Michael John; Celine Johns; Eamonn Jones; Robert Joule; Aista

383

Jukneviciute; Emiko Kaji; Jeff Kanof; Raphael Käser; Alfred Kausl; Christina Kavanaugh; Serena Kaye; Colin Keegan; Joy Kelso; James Kiernan; Kai Kilpinen; Jessica Kirby; Daniel Kissling; Sara Klingberg; Martina Krainer; Franz Kostenzer; Pavlos Koumparos; Matt Kozuba; Martina Krainer; Larry Krass; Armin Krister; Karen Kushner; Sophie Lambert-Russell; Ryan Lang; Oliver Lange; Jürgen Laskowski; Sebastian Lauinger; Alan Laws; Darren Leitch; Christelle Le Lay; Danguole Lekaviciute; Cédric Leprette; Eiling Lim; Bryan Lin; Lars Lindberger; Mark T Litter; Tom Lix; Steven Ljubicic; Kelly Locker; Vincent Löhn; Richard Lombard; Alistair Longwell; Dorene Lorenz; Claire Lormier; Sarah Ludington; Valentin Lutikov; Urs Lüthy; C. Mark McDavid; James Macdonald; Jane Macduff; Jenna Macfarlane; Myriam Mackenzie; Julia Mackillop; Bethan Mackenzie; Damian & Madeleine Mackey; John Maclellan; Rosalyn MacLeod; Derek Mair; Dennis Malcolm; Jari Mämmi; Sarah Manning; Stefan Marder; Ole Mark; Amaury Markey; Gene Marra; Tim Marwood; Jennifer Masson; Gregor Mathieson; Leanne Matthews; Josh Mayr; Roxane Mazeaude; Stephen R McCarthy; Mark McDavid; Christy McFarlane; Angela Mcilrath; Catherine McKay; Mark McLaughlin; Jonny McMillan; Douglas McIvor; Heinz Meistermann; Sarah Messenger; Uwe Meuren; Raphael Meuwly; Herman C. Mihalich; Joanna Miller; Maggie Miller; Gary Mills; Tatsuya Minagawa; Clare Minnock; Ashish Misra; Euan Mitchell; Jacqueline Mitchell; Paul Mitchell; Jeroen Moernaut; Stephan Mohr; Henk Mol; Kim Møller-Elshøj; Nick Morgan; Celine Moran; Katy Moore; Maggie Morri; Elyse Morris; Michael Morris; Brendan J. Moylan; Miroslav Motyčka; Fabien Mueller; Raphael Meuwly; Dennis Mulder; Mike Müller; Tarita Mullings; Tom-Roderick Muthert; Michael Myers; Simone Nagel; Arthur Nägele; Andrew Nelstrop; Sandra Neuner; Stuart Nickerson; Alex Nicol; Jane Nicol; Jennifer Nicol; Jens Nielsen; Thorsten Niesner; Sharon Nijkerk; Zack Nobinger; Soren Norgaard; Julia Noumey; Michael Nychyk; Nathan Nye; Tom O'Connor; Sinead Ofrighil; Richard Oldfield; Linny Oliphant; Jonas Östberg; Casey Overeem; Serdar Pala; Ted Pappas; Lauri Pappinen; Allison Parc; Jason Parker; Richard Parker; Katie Partridge; Sanjay Paul; Pascal Penderak; Percy; Nadège Perrot; Jörg Pfeiffer; Alexandra Piciu; Amy Preske; Phil Prichard; Rupert Ponsonby; Andreas Poulsen; George Quiney; Rachel Quinn; George Racz; Robert Ransom; Nidal Ramini; Sarah Rawlingson; Julie Holl Rebsomen; Michael Reckhard; Guy Rehorst; Michel Reick; Bärbel & Lutz Reifferscheid; Marco Reiner; Drexler Reinhard; Carrie Revell; Frederic Revol; Kay Riddoch; Massimo Righi; Nicol von Rijbroek; Karen Ripley; Patrick Roberts; James Robertson; Dr. Torsten Römer; Mark Rosendal Steiniche; Casey Ross; Anton Rossetti; Fabio Rossi; David Roussier; Ronnie Routledge; Stephane Rouveyrol; Matthias Rosinski; Ken Rose; Miriam Rune; Michal Rusiňák; Jim Rutledge; Caroline Rylance; Simi Sagoo; Paloma Salmeron Planells; Kiran Samra; Jasmine Sangria; Carla Santoni; Colette Savage; John Savage-Onstwedder; Kirsty Saville; Manuela Savona; Ian Schmidt; Fred Heinz Schober; Karl Schoen; Lorien Schramm; Becky Schultz; Birgitta Schulze van Loon; John Scott; Chris Seale; Mick & Tammy Secor; Tad Seestedt; Tanya Seibold; Marina Sepp; Paul Shand; Steven Shand; Mike Sharples; Lorien Schramm; Rubyna Sheikh; Caley Shoemaker; Lauren Shayne Mayer; Jamie Siefken; Peter Siegenthaler; Fred Siggins; Sam Simmons; Alastair Sinclair; Thomas Sippel; Sukhinder Singh; Thomas Sippel; Thomas Smidt-Kjaerby; Aidan Smith; Barbara Smith; Beccy Smith; Gigha Smith; Phil Smith; Marianna Smyth; Gunter Sommer; Orlin Sorensen; Oliver Späth; Cat Spencer; Colin Spoelma; Alexander Springensguth; Tom Stacey; Jolanda Stadelmann; Silvia Steck; Guido Stohler Jeremy Adam Spiegel; Jolanda Stadelmann; Silvia Steck; Marlene Steiner; Vicky Stevens; Karen Stewart; Jakob Stjernholm; Katy Stollery; Greg Storm; Jarret Stuart; Jason Stubbs; Nicki Sturzaker; Peter Summer; Michael Svendsen; Henning Svoldgaard; Tom Swift; Cameron Syme; Daniel Szor; Solene Tailland; Shoko Takagi; Cheryl Targos; Chip Tate; Marko Tayburn; Elizabeth Teape; Emily Tedder; Marcel Telser; Celine Tetu; Kevyn Termet; Sarah Thacker; Johanne Theveney; Ryan Thompson; Laura Thomson; Kelly Tighe; Brian Toft; Jarrett Tomal; Cole Tomberlain; Katy Took; Hamish Torrie; Louise Towers; Hope Trawick; Matthias Trum; Anne Ulrich; Jessie Unrah; Jens Unterweger; Richard Urquhart; Stuart Urquhart; CJ Van Dijk; Rifino Valentine; Zvi A. Vapni; Lisandru Venturini; Rhea Vernon; Adam Vincent; Mariah Veis; Aurelien Villefranche; Lorraine Waddell; Josh Walker; Grace Waller; Emma Ware; Katharina Warter; Patrick Wecklein; Oswald Weidenauer; Micheal Wells; Katrin Werner; Arne Wesche; Zoe Wesseon; Anna Wilson; Georgia Wilson; Nick White; Peter White; Robert Whitehead; Lucy Whitehall; Stephanie Whitworth; Daniel Widmer; Markus Wieser; Julien Williems; George Wills; James Wills; Rinaldo Willy; Georgia Wilson; Ken Winchester; Arthur Winning; Ellie Winters; Lee Wood; Stephen Worrall; Kate Wright; Frank Wu; Tom Wyss; Junko Yaguchi; Laura Young; Kiyoyuki Yoshimura; Bettina Zannier; Jörg Zahorodnyj; Ruslan Zamoskovny; Ulrich Jakob Zeni; Rama Zuniga; Ernst Zweiger. And, as ever, in warm memory of Mike Smith.